WYOMING HANDBOOK

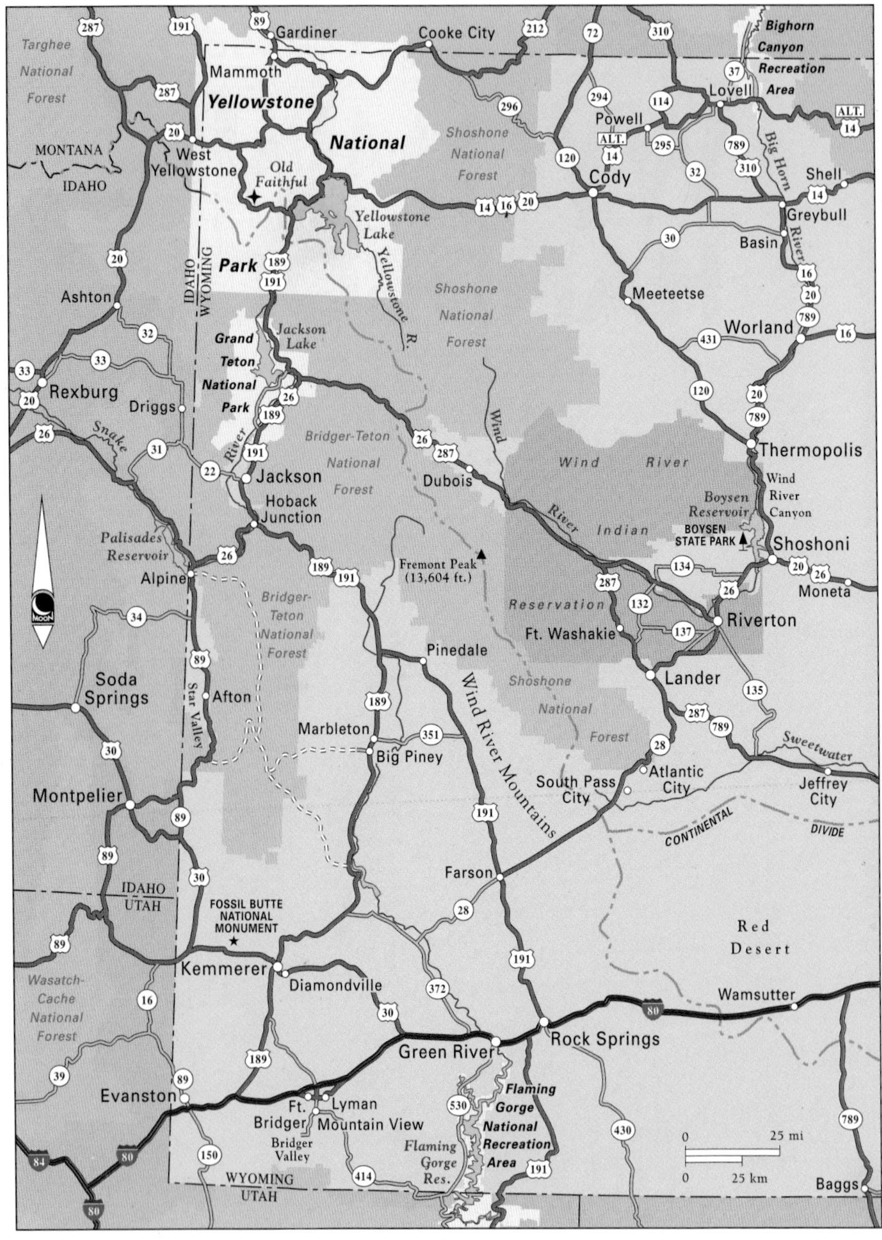
Gardiner
Cooke City
Mammoth
Yellowstone
National
Park
Old Faithful
Yellowstone Lake
West Yellowstone
MONTANA
IDAHO
Targhee National Forest
Shoshone National Forest
Bighorn Canyon Recreation Area
Lovell
Powell
Cody
Shell
Greybull
Basin
Big Horn River
Meeteetse
Worland
Thermopolis
Wind River Canyon
Boysen Reservoir
BOYSEN STATE PARK
Shoshoni
Moneta
Riverton
Wind River Indian Reservation
Ft. Washakie
Lander
Ashton
Rexburg
Driggs
Grand Teton National Park
Jackson Lake
Yellowstone R.
IDAHO
WYOMING
Snake River
Jackson
Hoback Junction
Bridger-Teton National Forest
Dubois
Wind River
Palisades Reservoir
Alpine
Fremont Peak (13,604 ft.)
Pinedale
Wind River Mountains
Soda Springs
Afton
Star Valley
Marbleton
Big Piney
Atlantic City
South Pass City
Sweetwater
Jeffrey City
CONTINENTAL DIVIDE
Montpelier
Farson
IDAHO
UTAH
FOSSIL BUTTE NATIONAL MONUMENT
Kemmerer
Diamondville
Red Desert
Wamsutter
Wasatch-Cache National Forest
Rock Springs
Green River
Evanston
Ft. Bridger
Lyman
Mountain View
Bridger Valley
Flaming Gorge National Recreation Area
Flaming Gorge Res.
WYOMING
UTAH
Baggs
0 25 mi
0 25 km
MOON

MAP SYMBOLS

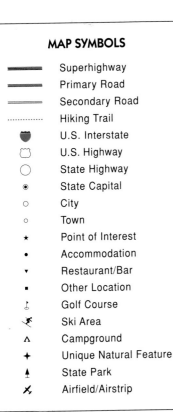

- Superhighway
- Primary Road
- Secondary Road
- Hiking Trail
- U.S. Interstate
- U.S. Highway
- State Highway
- State Capital
- City
- Town
- Point of Interest
- Accommodation
- Restaurant/Bar
- Other Location
- Golf Course
- Ski Area
- Campground
- Unique Natural Feature
- State Park
- Airfield/Airstrip

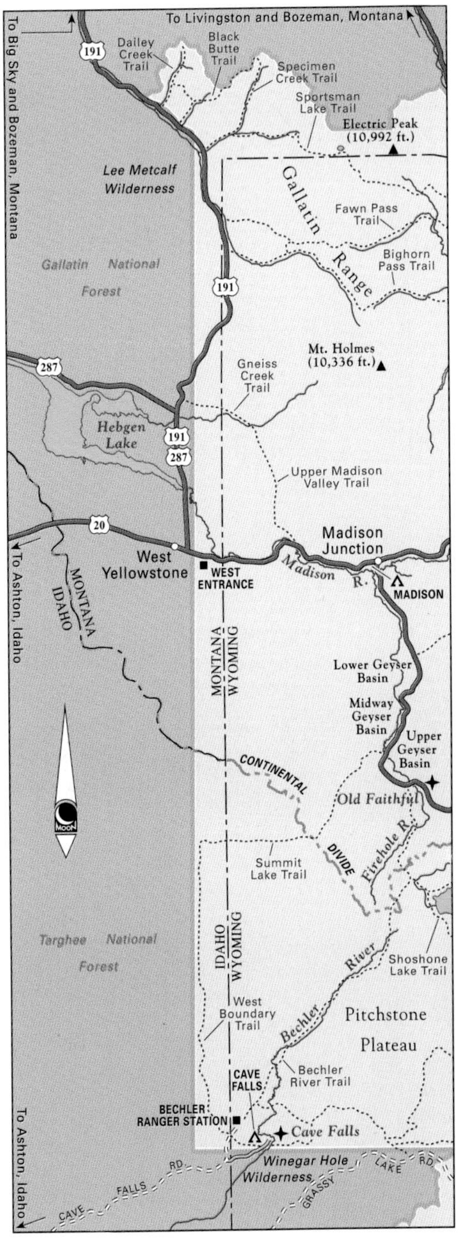

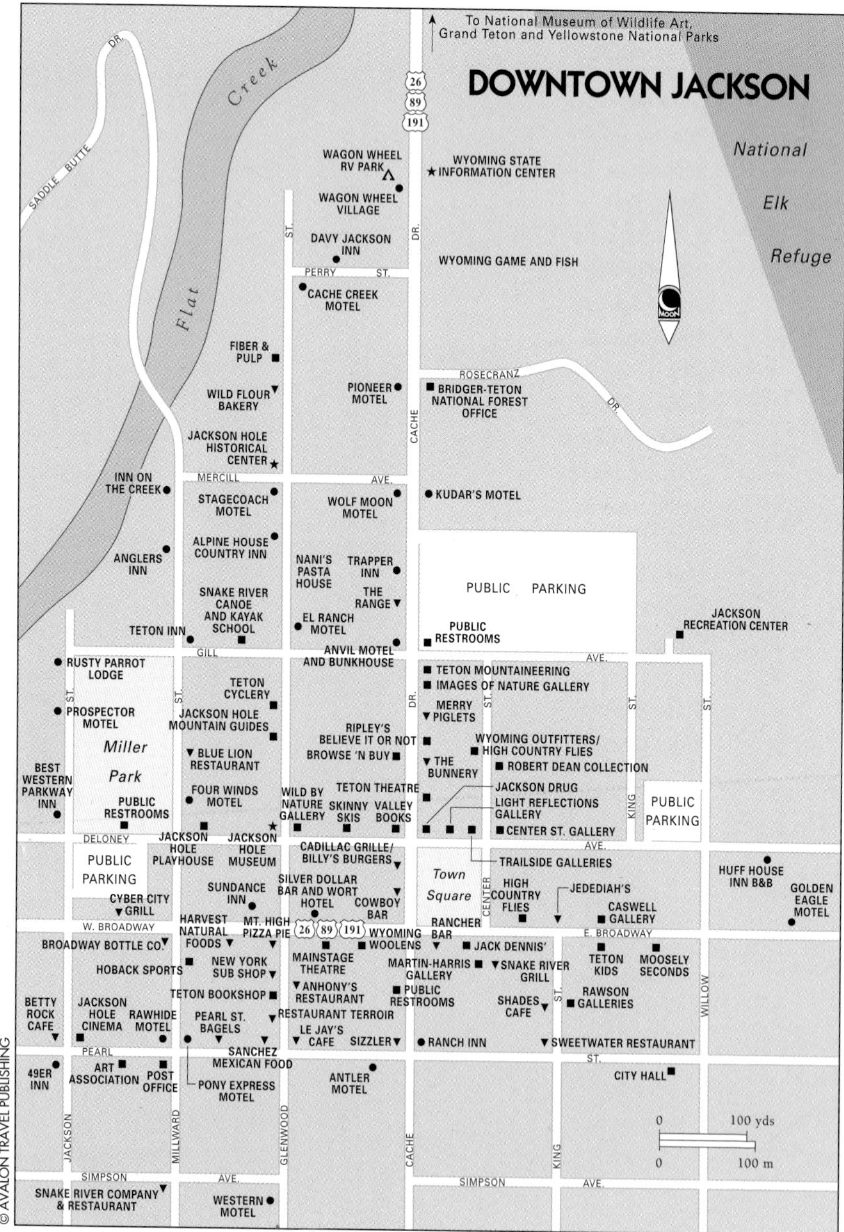
DOWNTOWN JACKSON
To National Museum of Wildlife Art, Grand Teton and Yellowstone National Parks
National Elk Refuge
Flat Creek
SADDLE BUTTE DR.
WAGON WHEEL RV PARK
WYOMING STATE INFORMATION CENTER
WAGON WHEEL VILLAGE
DAVY JACKSON INN
WYOMING GAME AND FISH
PERRY ST.
CACHE CREEK MOTEL
FIBER & PULP
PIONEER MOTEL
BRIDGER-TETON NATIONAL FOREST OFFICE
ROSECRANZ DR.
WILD FLOUR BAKERY
JACKSON HOLE HISTORICAL CENTER
CACHE DR.
INN ON THE CREEK
MERCILL AVE.
STAGECOACH MOTEL
WOLF MOON MOTEL
KUDAR'S MOTEL
ALPINE HOUSE COUNTRY INN
ANGLERS INN
NANI'S PASTA HOUSE
TRAPPER INN
PUBLIC PARKING
SNAKE RIVER CANOE AND KAYAK SCHOOL
THE RANGE
EL RANCH MOTEL
TETON INN
PUBLIC RESTROOMS
JACKSON RECREATION CENTER
ANVIL MOTEL AND BUNKHOUSE
GILL AVE.
RUSTY PARROT LODGE
TETON MOUNTAINEERING
IMAGES OF NATURE GALLERY
TETON CYCLERY
PROSPECTOR MOTEL
JACKSON HOLE MOUNTAIN GUIDES
MERRY PIGLETS
RIPLEY'S BELIEVE IT OR NOT
WYOMING OUTFITTERS/ HIGH COUNTRY FLIES
Miller Park
BLUE LION RESTAURANT
BROWSE 'N BUY
THE BUNNERY
ROBERT DEAN COLLECTION
BEST WESTERN PARKWAY INN
FOUR WINDS MOTEL
TETON THEATRE
JACKSON DRUG
LIGHT REFLECTIONS GALLERY
PUBLIC RESTROOMS
WILD BY NATURE GALLERY
SKINNY SKIS
VALLEY BOOKS
CENTER ST. GALLERY
PUBLIC PARKING
DELONEY AVE.
JACKSON HOLE PLAYHOUSE
JACKSON HOLE MUSEUM
CADILLAC GRILLE/ BILLY'S BURGERS
TRAILSIDE GALLERIES
PUBLIC PARKING
Town Square
HUFF HOUSE INN B&B
SUNDANCE INN
SILVER DOLLAR BAR AND WORT HOTEL
HIGH COUNTRY FLIES
JEDEDIAH'S
GOLDEN EAGLE MOTEL
CYBER CITY GRILL
COWBOY BAR
CASWELL GALLERY
W. BROADWAY
HARVEST NATURAL FOODS
MT. HIGH PIZZA PIE
26 89 191
WYOMING WOOLENS
RANCHER BAR
E. BROADWAY
BROADWAY BOTTLE CO.
JACK DENNIS'
TETON KIDS
MOOSELY SECONDS
NEW YORK SUB SHOP
MAINSTAGE THEATRE
MARTIN-HARRIS GALLERY
SNAKE RIVER GRILL
HOBACK SPORTS
ANHONY'S RESTAURANT
PUBLIC RESTROOMS
RAWSON GALLERIES
TETON BOOKSHOP
SHADES CAFE
BETTY ROCK CAFE
JACKSON HOLE CINEMA
RAWHIDE MOTEL
PEARL ST. BAGELS
RESTAURANT TERROIR
LE JAY'S CAFE
SIZZLER
RANCH INN
SWEETWATER RESTAURANT
PEARL ST.
SANCHEZ MEXICAN FOOD
49ER INN
ART ASSOCIATION
POST OFFICE
PONY EXPRESS MOTEL
ANTLER MOTEL
CITY HALL
JACKSON
MILLWARD
GLENWOOD
CACHE
KING
WILLOW
CENTER
0 100 yds
0 100 m
SIMPSON AVE.
SNAKE RIVER COMPANY & RESTAURANT
WESTERN MOTEL
© AVALON TRAVEL PUBLISHING

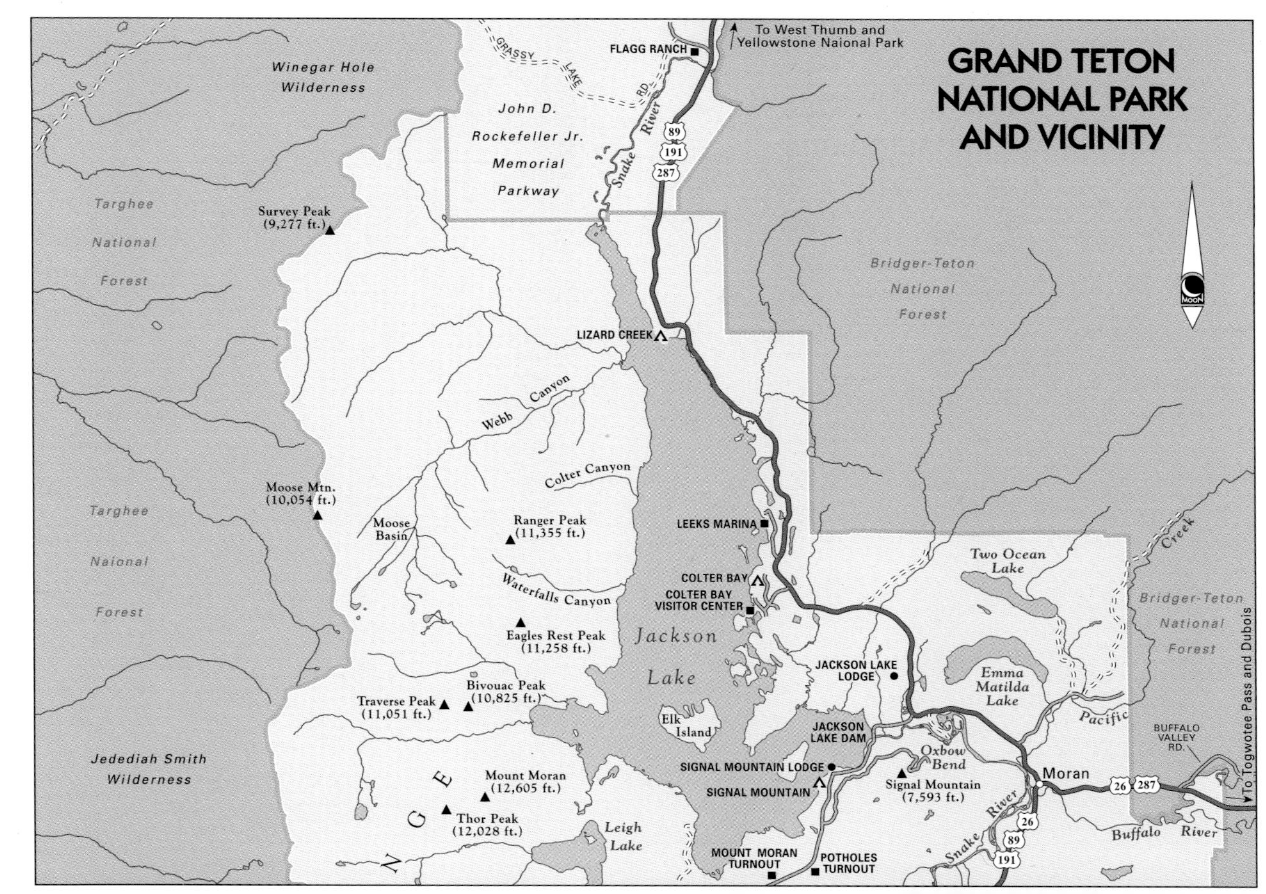
GRAND TETON NATIONAL PARK AND VICINITY
To West Thumb and Yellowstone Naional Park
FLAGG RANCH
GRASSY LAKE RD.
Winegar Hole Wilderness
John D. Rockefeller Jr. Memorial Parkway
Snake River
89
191
287
Targhee National Forest
Survey Peak (9,277 ft.)
Bridger-Teton National Forest
MOON
LIZARD CREEK
Webb Canyon
Colter Canyon
Moose Mtn. (10,054 ft.)
Targhee Naional Forest
Moose Basin
Ranger Peak (11,355 ft.)
LEEKS MARINA
Waterfalls Canyon
COLTER BAY
COLTER BAY VISITOR CENTER
Two Ocean Lake
Creek
Bridger-Teton National Forest
Eagles Rest Peak (11,258 ft.)
Jackson Lake
JACKSON LAKE LODGE
Emma Matilda Lake
Traverse Peak (11,051 ft.)
Bivouac Peak (10,825 ft.)
Elk Island
JACKSON LAKE DAM
Pacific
BUFFALO VALLEY RD.
Jedediah Smith Wilderness
SIGNAL MOUNTAIN LODGE
Oxbow Bend
Moran
Mount Moran (12,605 ft.)
SIGNAL MOUNTAIN
Signal Mountain (7,593 ft.)
26
287
To Togwotee Pass and Dubois
Thor Peak (12,028 ft.)
Leigh Lake
Snake River
26
89
191
Buffalo River
N G E
MOUNT MORAN TURNOUT
POTHOLES TURNOUT

LARAMIE

To Rawlins
To Rock River and Medicine Bow
To Airport and Centennial
To Woods Landing
To Fort Sanders Site
To Fort Collins and Denver, CO
To Cheyenne

West Laramie
SUPER 8 MOTEL
EXIT 310
RIVERSIDE
ECONO LODGE
LARAMIE KOA
McCUE ST.
BANNER RD.
CURTIS ST.
ALBERTSON'S
N-H TRAILER RANCH
REYNOLDS ST.
HANCOCK ST.
SHIELD ST.
HIGH SCHOOL (POOL)
18TH ST.
19TH ST.
30TH ST.
GAS LITE MOTEL
Labonte Park
CANBY
GIBBON
GATEWAY PLAZA
K MART
RANGER MOTEL
LEWIS ST.
TRAVEL INN
CLARK ST.
River
Laramie
WYOMING TERRITORIAL PRISON & OLD WEST PARK
FOSTERS COUNTRY CORNER MOTEL
EXIT 311
SNOWY RANGE RD.
FOREST SERVICE OFFICE
SNOWY RANGE TRAILER PARK
CAMELOT MOTEL
SEE DOWNTOWN DETAIL
BUD'S BAR
CEDAR ST.
1ST ST.
GRAND AVE.
3RD ST.
PARK AVE.
POST OFFICE
LARAMIE PLAINS MUSEUM
CITY HALL
PRAIRIE BREEZE B&B
ALBANY COUNTY LIBRARY
LARAMIE PLAINS CIVIC CENTER
GEOLOGICAL MUSEUM
AGRICULTURAL BUILDING
SEE UW DETAIL
SOFTBALL COMPLEX
NATIONAL GUARD ARMORY
ARMORY RD.
JACOBY GOLF COURSE
AMERICAN HERITAGE CENTER/ART MUSEUM
ARENA-AUDITORIUM
LAW SCHOOL
STUDENT APARTMENTS
MEMORIAL STADIUM
HOSPITAL
UNIVERSITY INN
COWBOY COFFEE
THE LIBRARY RESTAURANT & BREWING CO.
22ND ST.
24TH ST.
26TH ST.
5TH
7TH
8TH
9TH
11TH
15TH
17TH ST.
CHAMBER OF COMMERCE
RUSSELL ST.
SUNSET INN
SPRING CREEK DR.
FIRST INN GOLD
VISITOR CENTER (CABOOSE)
CAFE OLÉ
EXIT 313
MOTEL 6
HOLIDAY INN
SKYLINE RD.
ALBANY COUNTY FAIRGROUNDS
FORT SANDERS RD.
SOLDIER SPRINGS RD.
UNIVERSITY OF WYOMING
GRAND AVE.
0 0.5 mi
0 0.5 km

DOWNTOWN LARAMIE

FREMONT ST.
1ST ST.
2ND ST.
3RD ST.
4TH ST.
UNIVERSITY AVE.
GRAND AVE.
CUSTER ST.
TRAVELODGE DOWNTOWN MOTEL
THE FRONT GALLERY
COWBOY SALOON
WHOLE EARTH GRAINERY
PERSONALLY RECOMMENDED BOOKS
ST. MATTHEW'S CATHEDRAL
BUCKHORN BAR
JEFFREY'S BISTRO
THE OVERLAND
EL CONQUISTADOR
PEDAL HOUSE
BRIGHT SIDE GALLERY
EARTH, WIND, AND FIRE GALLERY
GRAND AVE. PIZZA
COAL CREEK COFFEE
ROCKY MTN. SPORTS
HOME BAKERY
THE RANCHER
CROSS-COUNTRY CONNECTION
WYOMING CHILDREN'S NATURE CENTER AND MUSEUM
FIRESIDE

BIOLOGICAL SCIENCES/PLANETARIUM
HALF ACRE GYM
AVEN NELSON BUILDING
CONSERVATORY
WYOMING UNION
OLD MAIN
ANTHROPOLOGY MUSEUM
COE LIBRARY
IVINSON AVE.
UNIVERSITY OF WYOMING VISITOR CENTER
COOPER MANSION
PRESIDENT'S RESIDENCE
9TH ST.
15TH ST.
GRAND AVE.

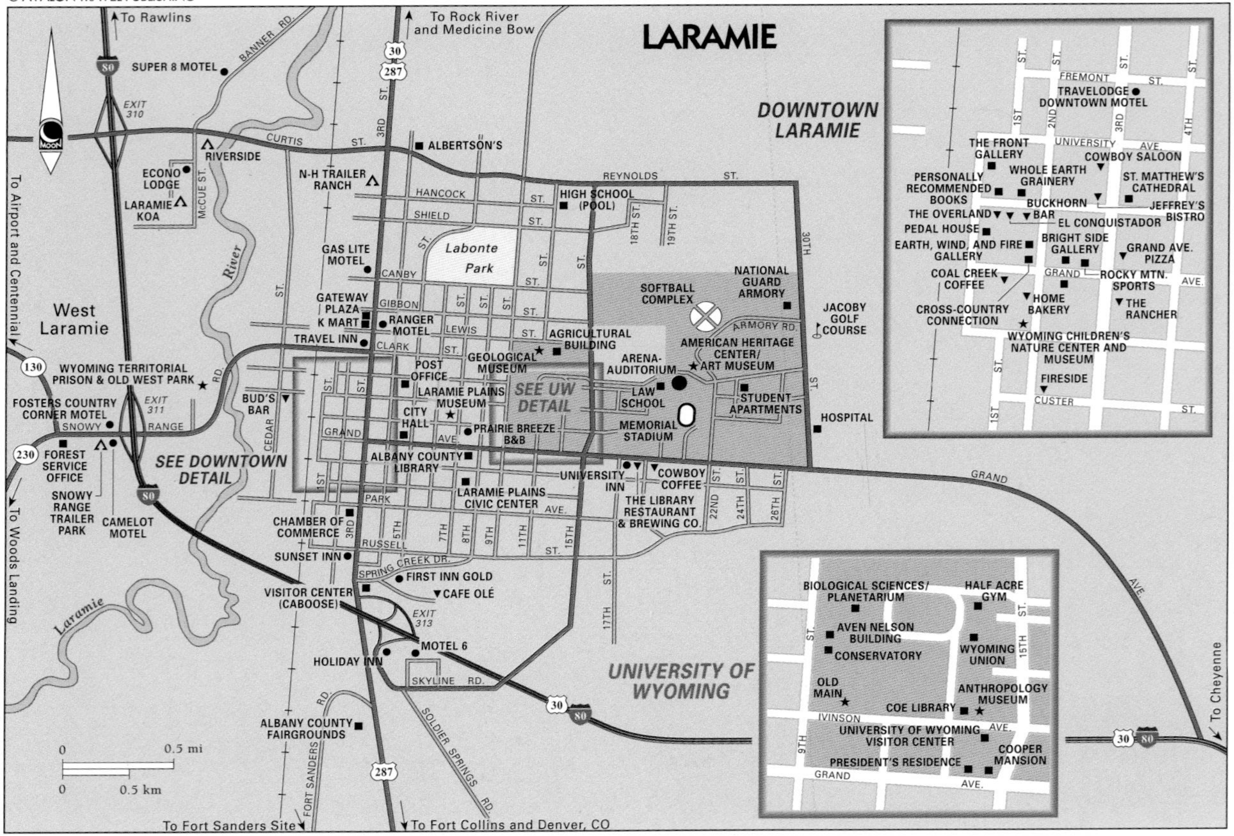

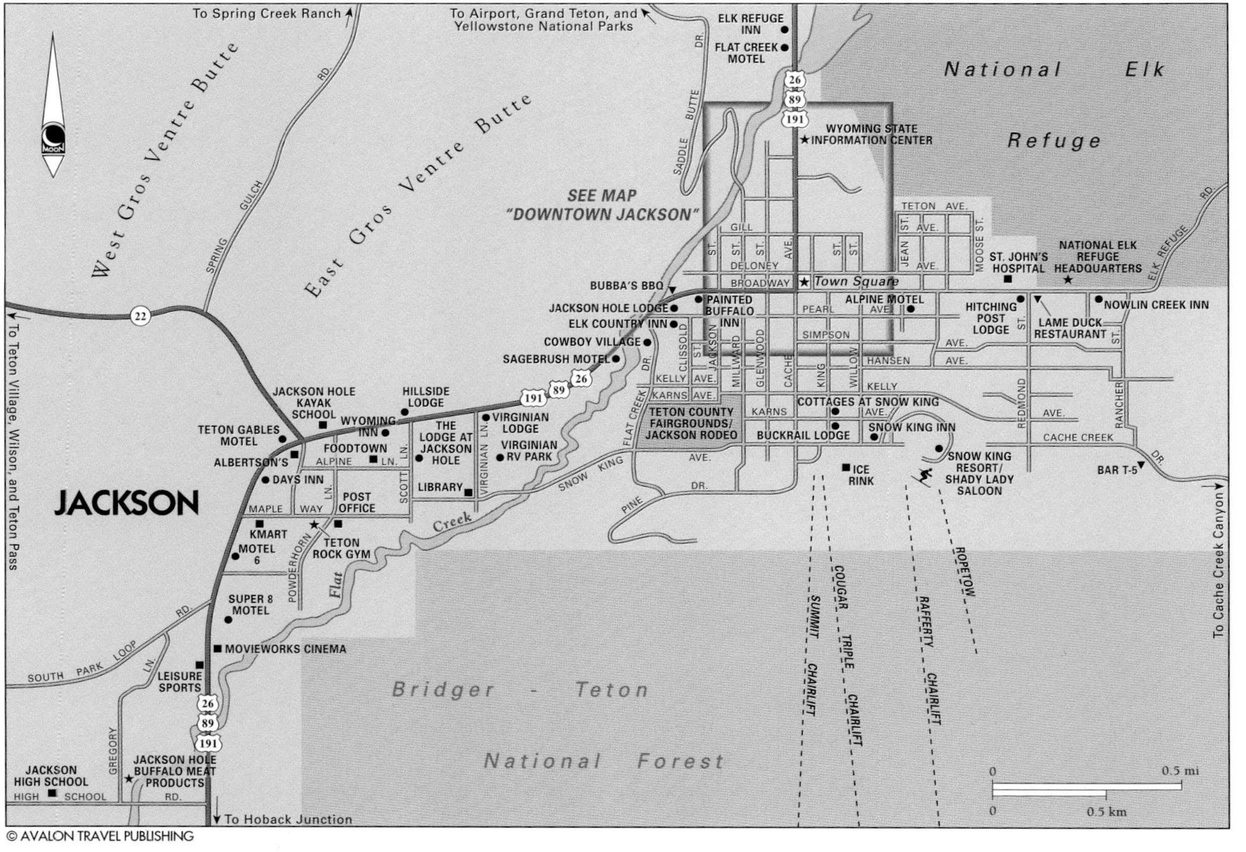
JACKSON
National Elk Refuge
Bridger - Teton National Forest
East Gros Ventre Butte
West Gros Ventre Butte
SEE MAP "DOWNTOWN JACKSON"
Town Square
To Airport, Grand Teton, and Yellowstone National Parks
To Spring Creek Ranch
To Teton Village, Wilson, and Teton Pass
To Hoback Junction
To Cache Creek Canyon
WYOMING STATE INFORMATION CENTER
NATIONAL ELK REFUGE HEADQUARTERS
ST. JOHN'S HOSPITAL
NOWLIN CREEK INN
LAME DUCK RESTAURANT
HITCHING POST LODGE
ALPINE MOTEL
COTTAGES AT SNOW KING
SNOW KING INN
SNOW KING RESORT/ SHADY LADY SALOON
BUCKRAIL LODGE
ICE RINK
BAR T-5
ROPETOW
RAFFERTY CHAIRLIFT
COUGAR TRIPLE CHAIRLIFT
SUMMIT CHAIRLIFT
ELK REFUGE INN
FLAT CREEK MOTEL
PAINTED BUFFALO INN
TETON COUNTY FAIRGROUNDS/ JACKSON RODEO
BUBBA'S BBQ
JACKSON HOLE LODGE
ELK COUNTRY INN
COWBOY VILLAGE
SAGEBRUSH MOTEL
VIRGINIAN LODGE
VIRGINIAN RV PARK
HILLSIDE LODGE
THE LODGE AT JACKSON HOLE
LIBRARY
WYOMING INN
FOODTOWN
POST OFFICE
TETON ROCK GYM
JACKSON HOLE KAYAK SCHOOL
DAYS INN
KMART
MOTEL 6
SUPER 8 MOTEL
MOVIEWORKS CINEMA
TETON GABLES MOTEL
ALBERTSON'S
LEISURE SPORTS
JACKSON HOLE BUFFALO MEAT PRODUCTS
JACKSON HIGH SCHOOL
Flat Creek
0.5 mi
0.5 km
© AVALON TRAVEL PUBLISHING

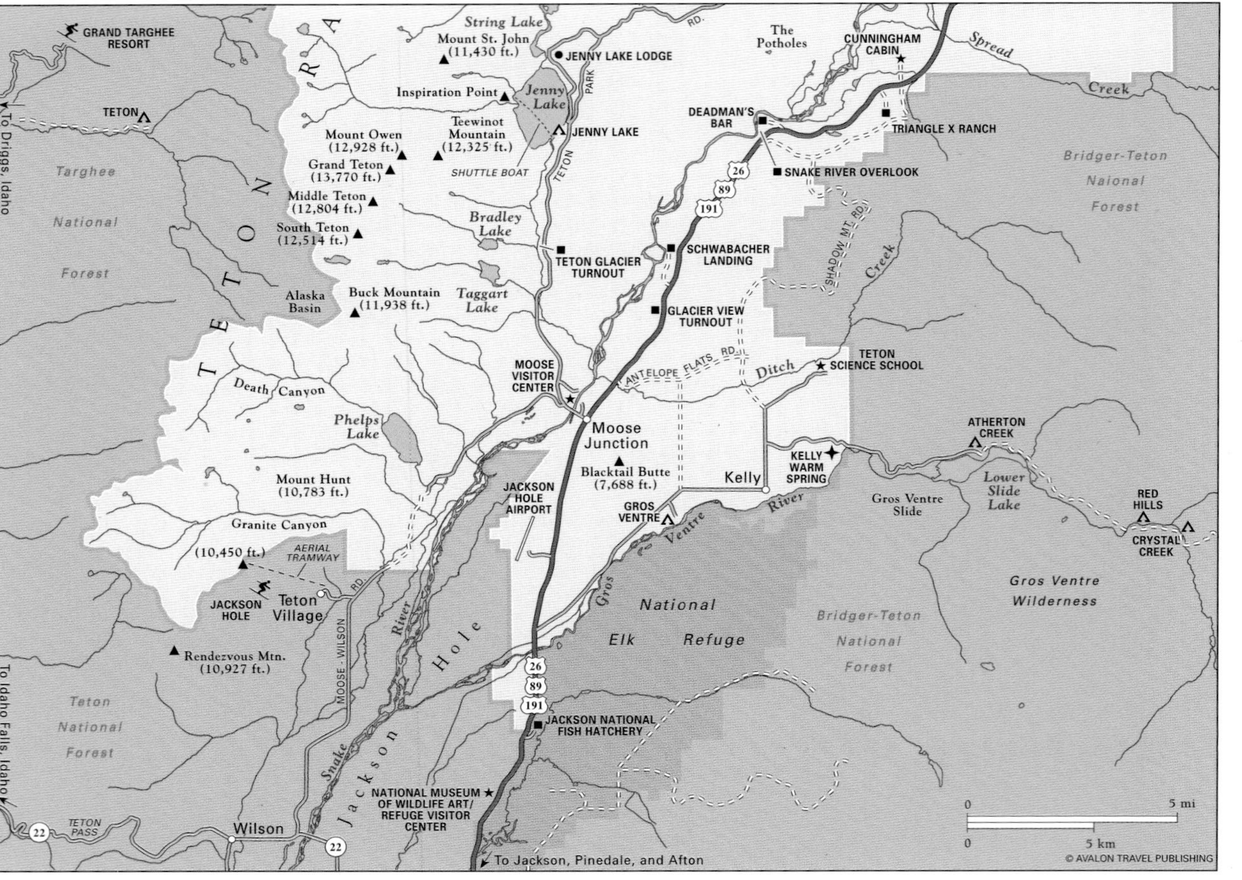
GRAND TARGHEE RESORT
TETON
To Driggs, Idaho
Targhee National Forest
String Lake
Mount St. John (11,430 ft.)
JENNY LAKE LODGE
Inspiration Point
Jenny Lake
JENNY LAKE
TETON PARK RD.
Teewinot Mountain (12,325 ft.)
SHUTTLE BOAT
Mount Owen (12,928 ft.)
Grand Teton (13,770 ft.)
Middle Teton (12,804 ft.)
South Teton (12,514 ft.)
Alaska Basin
Buck Mountain (11,938 ft.)
Bradley Lake
Taggart Lake
Death Canyon
Phelps Lake
Mount Hunt (10,783 ft.)
Granite Canyon
(10,450 ft.)
AERIAL TRAMWAY
JACKSON HOLE
Teton Village
Rendezvous Mtn. (10,927 ft.)
Teton National Forest
To Idaho Falls, Idaho
TETON PASS
22
Wilson
22
MOOSE - WILSON RD.
Snake River
Jackson Hole
NATIONAL MUSEUM OF WILDLIFE ART/ REFUGE VISITOR CENTER
To Jackson, Pinedale, and Afton
The Potholes
CUNNINGHAM CABIN
DEADMAN'S BAR
TRIANGLE X RANCH
SNAKE RIVER OVERLOOK
26
89
191
SCHWABACHER LANDING
TETON GLACIER TURNOUT
GLACIER VIEW TURNOUT
MOOSE VISITOR CENTER
ANTELOPE FLATS RD.
Ditch
TETON SCIENCE SCHOOL
Moose Junction
Blacktail Butte (7,688 ft.)
JACKSON HOLE AIRPORT
GROS VENTRE
Kelly
KELLY WARM SPRING
Gros Ventre River
National Elk Refuge
JACKSON NATIONAL FISH HATCHERY
Spread Creek
Bridger-Teton Naional Forest
SHADOW MT. RD.
Creek
ATHERTON CREEK
Gros Ventre Slide
Lower Slide Lake
RED HILLS
CRYSTAL CREEK
Gros Ventre Wilderness
Bridger-Teton National Forest
0 5 mi
0 5 km
© AVALON TRAVEL PUBLISHING

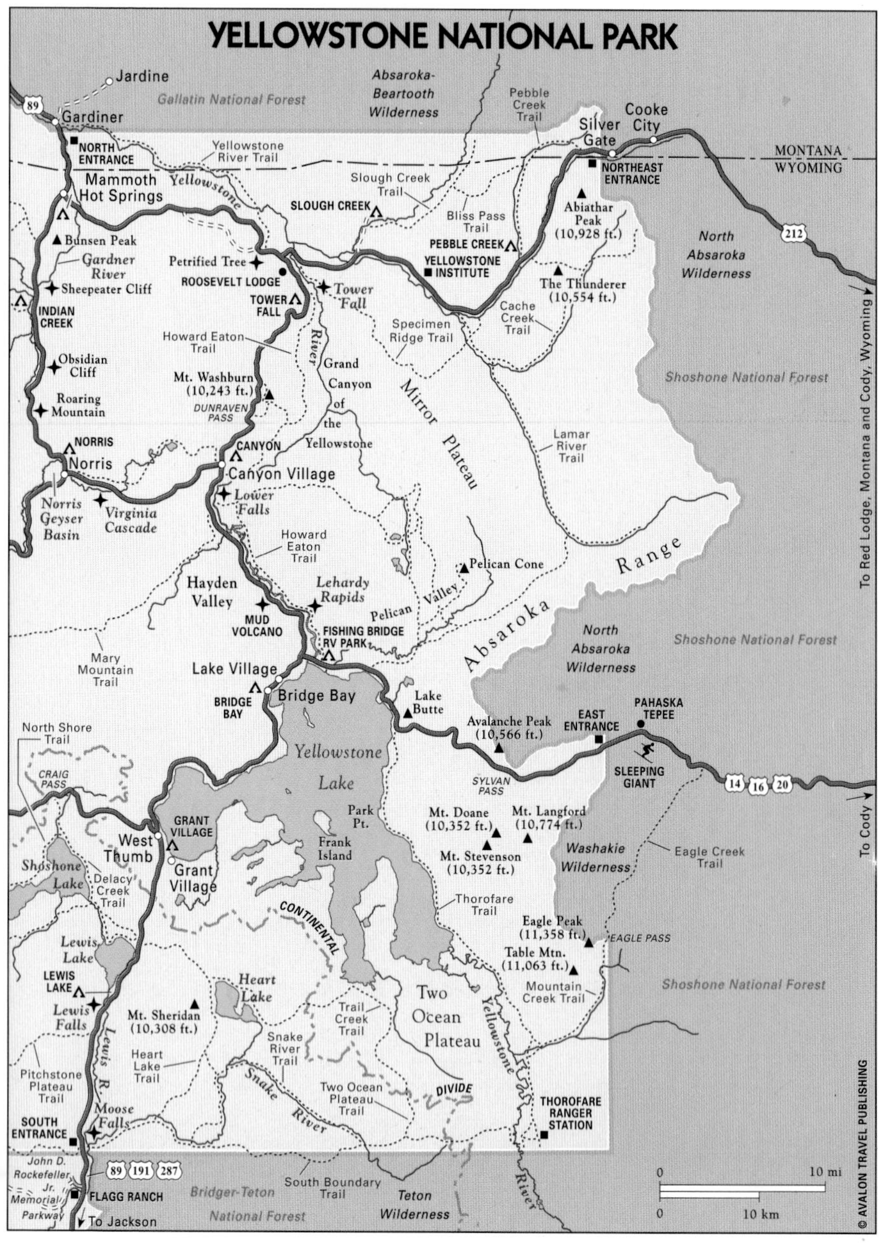
YELLOWSTONE NATIONAL PARK
Jardine
Gardiner
Gallatin National Forest
Absaroka-Beartooth Wilderness
Pebble Creek Trail
Cooke City
Silver Gate
MONTANA
WYOMING
NORTH ENTRANCE
Yellowstone River Trail
Mammoth Hot Springs
Yellowstone
Slough Creek Trail
SLOUGH CREEK
Bliss Pass Trail
NORTHEAST ENTRANCE
Abiathar Peak (10,928 ft.)
North Absaroka Wilderness
Bunsen Peak
Gardner River
Sheepeater Cliff
Petrified Tree
ROOSEVELT LODGE
PEBBLE CREEK
YELLOWSTONE INSTITUTE
The Thunderer (10,554 ft.)
TOWER FALL
Tower Fall
INDIAN CREEK
Cache Creek Trail
Specimen Ridge Trail
Howard Eaton Trail
River
Obsidian Cliff
Grand Canyon of the Yellowstone
Mt. Washburn (10,243 ft.)
DUNRAVEN PASS
Roaring Mountain
Mirror Plateau
Shoshone National Forest
To Red Lodge, Montana and Cody, Wyoming
NORRIS
Norris
CANYON
Canyon Village
Lamar River Trail
Lower Falls
Norris Geyser Basin
Virginia Cascade
Howard Eaton Trail
Pelican Cone
Range
Hayden Valley
Lehardy Rapids
Pelican Valley
MUD VOLCANO
FISHING BRIDGE RV PARK
Absaroka
North Absaroka Wilderness
Shoshone National Forest
Mary Mountain Trail
Lake Village
BRIDGE BAY
Bridge Bay
Lake Butte
Avalanche Peak (10,566 ft.)
EAST ENTRANCE
PAHASKA TEPEE
North Shore Trail
CRAIG PASS
Yellowstone Lake
SYLVAN PASS
SLEEPING GIANT
14
16
20
Park Pt.
GRANT VILLAGE
Mt. Doane (10,352 ft.)
Mt. Langford (10,774 ft.)
West Thumb
Frank Island
Mt. Stevenson (10,352 ft.)
Washakie Wilderness
Eagle Creek Trail
To Cody
Shoshone Lake
Grant Village
Delacy Creek Trail
Thorofare Trail
CONTINENTAL
Eagle Peak (11,358 ft.)
EAGLE PASS
Lewis Lake
Table Mtn. (11,063 ft.)
LEWIS LAKE
Heart Lake
Two Ocean Plateau
Mountain Creek Trail
Shoshone National Forest
Lewis Falls
Mt. Sheridan (10,308 ft.)
Trail Creek Trail
Snake River Trail
Lewis R.
Yellowstone
Heart Lake Trail
Pitchstone Plateau Trail
Two Ocean Plateau Trail
DIVIDE
Snake River
Moose Falls
SOUTH ENTRANCE
THOROFARE RANGER STATION
John D. Rockefeller, Jr. Memorial Parkway
89
191
287
South Boundary Trail
Bridger-Teton National Forest
Teton Wilderness
River
FLAGG RANCH
To Jackson
0
10 mi
0
10 km
212
© AVALON TRAVEL PUBLISHING

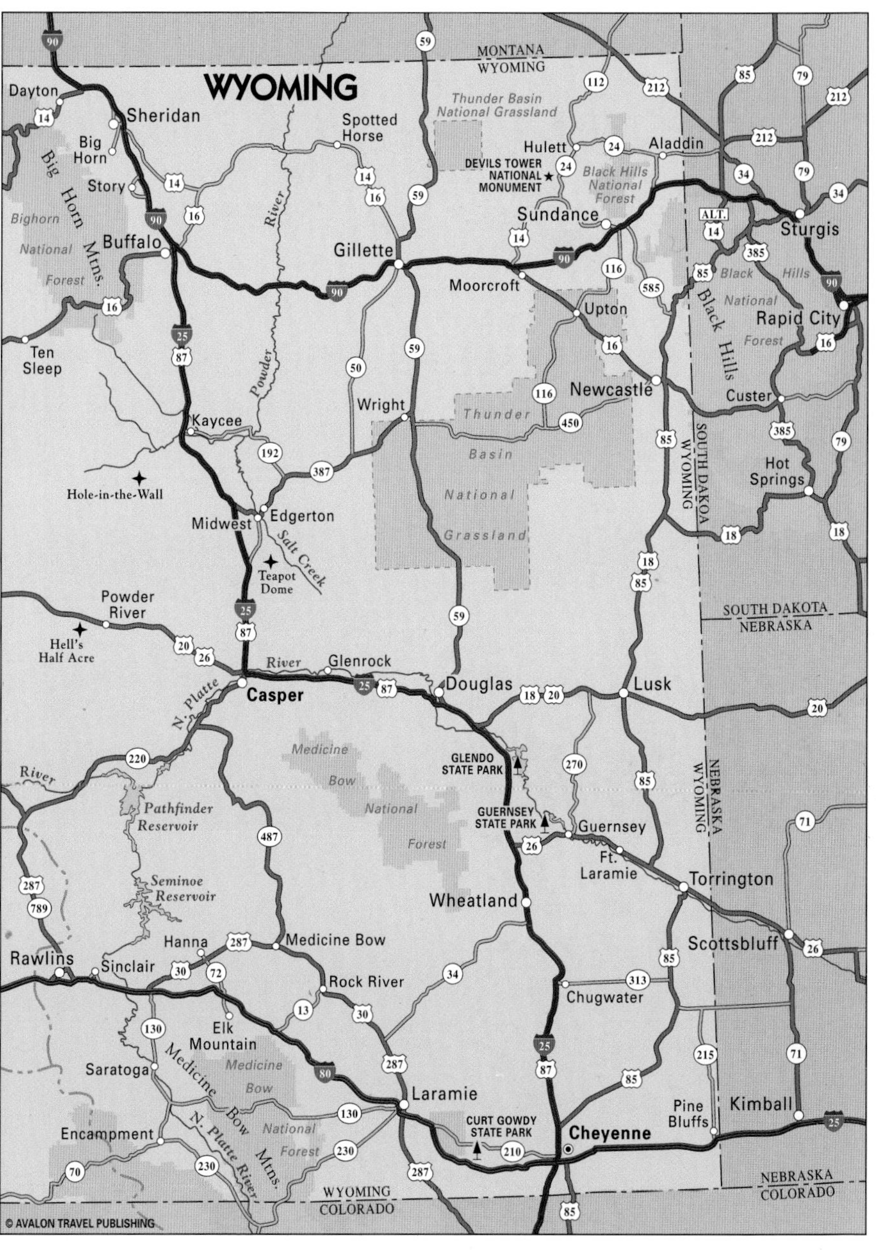
WYOMING
MONTANA
WYOMING
Dayton
Sheridan
Big Horn
Story
Big Horn Mtns.
Bighorn National Forest
Buffalo
Ten Sleep
Spotted Horse
Thunder Basin National Grassland
Hulett
Aladdin
DEVILS TOWER NATIONAL MONUMENT
Black Hills National Forest
Sundance
Sturgis
Gillette
Moorcroft
Upton
Black Hills National Forest
Rapid City
Newcastle
Custer
Wright
Thunder Basin National Grassland
Hot Springs
SOUTH DAKOA
WYOMING
Kaycee
Hole-in-the-Wall
Midwest
Edgerton
Salt Creek
Teapot Dome
Powder River
Powder River
Hell's Half Acre
SOUTH DAKOTA
NEBRASKA
River
Glenrock
Casper
N. Platte River
Douglas
Lusk
Medicine Bow National Forest
GLENDO STATE PARK
GUERNSEY STATE PARK
Guernsey
Ft. Laramie
Torrington
NEBRASKA
WYOMING
Pathfinder Reservoir
Seminoe Reservoir
Wheatland
Scottsbluff
Hanna
Medicine Bow
Rawlins
Sinclair
Rock River
Chugwater
Elk Mountain
Saratoga
Medicine Bow Mtns.
Medicine Bow National Forest
N. Platte River
Laramie
CURT GOWDY STATE PARK
Cheyenne
Pine Bluffs
Kimball
Encampment
WYOMING
COLORADO
NEBRASKA
COLORADO
ALT.
© AVALON TRAVEL PUBLISHING

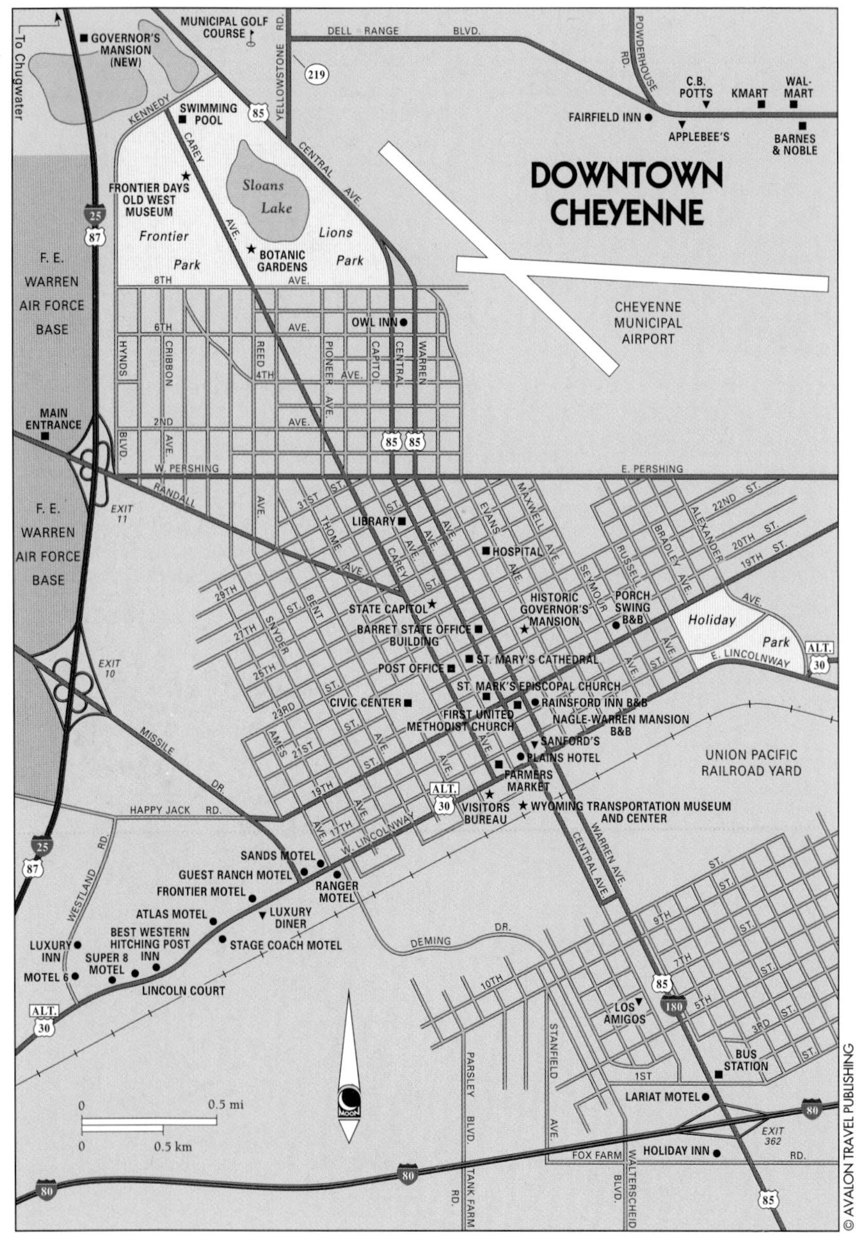
DOWNTOWN CHEYENNE
To Chugwater
GOVERNOR'S MANSION (NEW)
MUNICIPAL GOLF COURSE
DELL RANGE BLVD.
POWDERHOUSE RD.
YELLOWSTONE RD.
C.B. POTTS
KMART
WAL-MART
FAIRFIELD INN
APPLEBEE'S
BARNES & NOBLE
KENNEDY
SWIMMING POOL
CAREY AVE.
CENTRAL AVE.
Sloans Lake
FRONTIER DAYS OLD WEST MUSEUM
Frontier Park
Lions Park
BOTANIC GARDENS
8TH AVE.
F. E. WARREN AIR FORCE BASE
6TH AVE.
OWL INN
CHEYENNE MUNICIPAL AIRPORT
HYNDS BLVD.
CRIBBON AVE.
REED AVE.
4TH AVE.
PIONEER AVE.
CAPITOL
CENTRAL
WARREN
MAIN ENTRANCE
2ND AVE.
W. PERSHING
E. PERSHING
RANDALL
EXIT 11
31ST ST.
LIBRARY
THOME AVE.
EVANS AVE.
MAXWELL AVE.
HOSPITAL
22ND ST.
20TH ST.
19TH ST.
ALEXANDER
BRADLEY AVE.
RUSSELL AVE.
SEYMOUR AVE.
29TH ST.
BENT
STATE CAPITOL
HISTORIC GOVERNOR'S MANSION
PORCH SWING B&B
Holiday Park
E. LINCOLNWAY
27TH
SNYDER
BARRET STATE OFFICE BUILDING
EXIT 10
25TH
POST OFFICE
ST. MARY'S CATHEDRAL
ST. MARK'S EPISCOPAL CHURCH
CIVIC CENTER
23RD ST.
RAINSFORD INN B&B
FIRST UNITED METHODIST CHURCH
NAGLE-WARREN MANSION B&B
MISSILE DR.
AMES
21ST
SANFORD'S
PLAINS HOTEL
UNION PACIFIC RAILROAD YARD
19TH
FARMERS MARKET
HAPPY JACK RD.
17TH
VISITORS BUREAU
WYOMING TRANSPORTATION MUSEUM AND CENTER
W. LINCOLNWAY
WESTLAND RD.
SANDS MOTEL
GUEST RANCH MOTEL
RANGER MOTEL
FRONTIER MOTEL
ATLAS MOTEL
LUXURY DINER
BEST WESTERN HITCHING POST INN
STAGE COACH MOTEL
LUXURY INN
SUPER 8 MOTEL
MOTEL 6
LINCOLN COURT
DEMING DR.
10TH
9TH
7TH
5TH
3RD ST.
LOS AMIGOS
BUS STATION
1ST
LARIAT MOTEL
PARSLEY BLVD.
STANFIELD AVE.
TANK FARM RD.
FOX FARM RD.
WALTERSCHEID BLVD.
HOLIDAY INN
EXIT 362
0 0.5 mi
0 0.5 km
MOON
© AVALON TRAVEL PUBLISHING

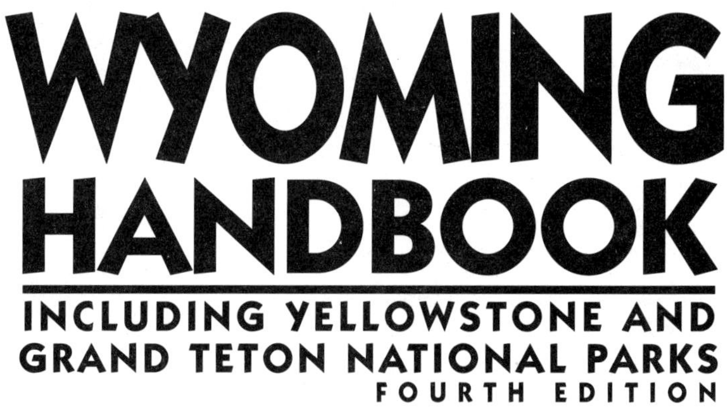

INCLUDING YELLOWSTONE AND GRAND TETON NATIONAL PARKS

FOURTH EDITION

DON PITCHER

WYOMING HANDBOOK
FOURTH EDITION

Published by
Avalon Travel Publishing, Inc.
5855 Beaudry St.
Emeryville, CA 94608, USA

Please send all comments, corrections, additions, amendments, and critiques to:
WYOMING HANDBOOK
AVALON TRAVEL PUBLISHING, INC.
MOON TRAVEL HANDBOOKS
5855 BEAUDRY ST.
EMERYVILLE, CA 94608, USA
e-mail: travel@moon.com
www.moon.com

Printing History
1st edition—1991
4th edition—May 2000
5 4 3 2 1 0

ISBN: 1-56691-204-0
ISSN: 1091-3386

Editors: Karen Gaynor Bleske, Don Root
Production & Design: Stephanie Bird
Cartography: Brian Bardwell, Bob Race, Chris Folks, Mike Morgenfeld
Index: Sondra Nation

Front cover photo: tepee at Fort Bridger, Wyoming, by Don Pitcher © 2000

All photos by Don Pitcher unless otherwise noted.
All illustrations by Bob Race unless otherwise noted.

Distributed in the United States and Canada by Publishers Group West

Printed in U.S.A.

God bless Wyoming and keep it wild.
—last entry in the diary of a girl
who died in the Tetons

CONTENTS

SPECIAL TOPICS

MEDICINE BOW COUNTRY . . . . 117~167

SPECIAL TOPICS

SOUTHWEST WYOMING . . . . 168~218

SPECIAL TOPICS

SPECIAL TOPICS

SPECIAL TOPICS

SPECIAL TOPICS

MAPS

COLOR SUPPLEMENT

INTRODUCTION

ON THE ROAD

SOUTHEAST WYOMING

MEDICINE BOW COUNTRY

SOUTHWEST WYOMING

CENTRAL WYOMING

WIND RIVER MOUNTAINS COUNTRY

JACKSON HOLE AND THE TETONS

MAP SYMBOLS

Superhighway	State Capital	State Park
Primary Road	City	Campground
Secondary Road	Town	Ski Area
Unpaved Road	Point of Interest	Golf Course
U.S. Interstate	Accommodation	Unique Natural Feature
U.S. Highway	Restaurant/Bar	Airfield/Airstrip
State Highway	Other Location	Trail

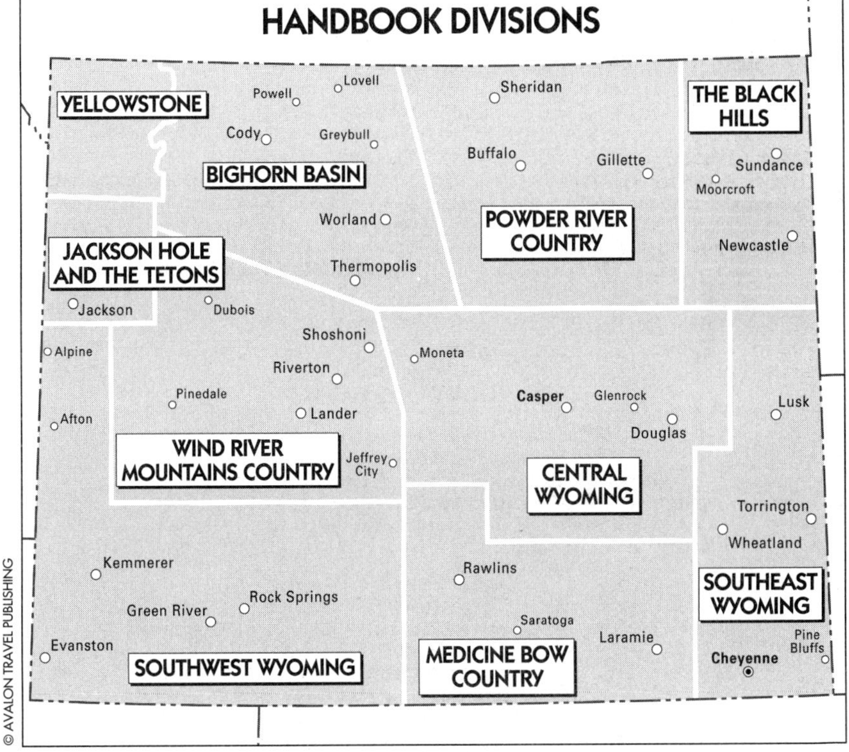

HANDBOOK DIVISIONS
YELLOWSTONE
BIGHORN BASIN
POWDER RIVER COUNTRY
THE BLACK HILLS
JACKSON HOLE AND THE TETONS
WIND RIVER MOUNTAINS COUNTRY
CENTRAL WYOMING
SOUTHEAST WYOMING
SOUTHWEST WYOMING
MEDICINE BOW COUNTRY
Powell
Lovell
Cody
Greybull
Sheridan
Buffalo
Gillette
Sundance
Moorcroft
Worland
Newcastle
Thermopolis
Jackson
Dubois
Shoshoni
Alpine
Moneta
Riverton
Pinedale
Casper
Glenrock
Lusk
Afton
Lander
Douglas
Jeffrey City
Torrington
Wheatland
Kemmerer
Rawlins
Rock Springs
Green River
Saratoga
Laramie
Pine Bluffs
Evanston
Cheyenne

ABBREVIATIONS

B&B—bed and breakfast
BLM—Bureau of Land Management
CCC—Civilian Conservation Corps
CG—campground (used on maps only)
d—double occupancy
F—Fahrenheit
4WD—four-wheel drive
I—interstate highway
km—kilometer
mph—miles per hour
RV—recreational vehicle
s—single occupancy

TELL US ABOUT YOUR TRIP

This book, like all travel guides, *is* out of date. The nature of the publishing business means that words in print were always written at some earlier time, and much can change in the two years between editions. Wyoming is not a static place; prices rise, businesses fail, restaurants change hands, and new places wait to be discovered. And sometimes I simply miss interesting sights entirely, or don't give them the coverage that they deserve. This fourth edition of *Wyoming Handbook* contains extensive revisions and additions—a number of which were suggested by readers of the third edition.

If you find any notable omissions, take offense at what is said, discover a new (or old) place worthy of mention, find inaccurate maps, or just want to rant and rave about this book, I'd be happy to hear from you. Although I try to respond to all letters and messages, you may need to wait awhile for a response since I'm often on the road. To reach me via the Internet, put "Wyoming Handbook" in the subject heading and send e-mail messages to me at: travel@moon.com. Send your snail-mail observations to:

Don Pitcher
Moon Travel Handbooks
c/o Avalon Travel Publishing
5855 Beaudry Street
Emeryville, California 94608

You may also want to visit www.donpitcher.com to send e-mail directly or to learn about my various books, photographic ventures, and other projects. The site contains links to a number of useful travel websites for Wyoming and other destinations.

ACCOMMODATIONS RATINGS

In addition to including specific prices, all accommodations in this book are further rated by price category for comparison with other Moon Travel Handbooks. Categories are based on double-occupancy, high-season rates; the categories are:

Budget: under $35
Inexpensive: $35-60
Moderate: $60-85
Expensive: $85-110
Premium: $110-150
Luxury: $150 and up

ACKNOWLEDGMENTS

When I began this book back in the horse-and-buggy days four editions ago, it was a relatively concise guide to Wyoming. Over the years my understanding of Wyoming has grown, tourism has become increasingly important, and the book has evolved into a more comprehensive source for travelers. This new edition incorporates Internet references wherever possible and adds depth to many lodging descriptions. It also, of course, contains a plethora of updated information on the wonderful state of Wyoming.

Many people helped me in creating this edition. I especially appreciate those who offered insights gleaned from a life's experience in their hometowns: the chamber of commerce volunteers and employees who endured a barrage of questions, the readers who wrote or e-mailed me with comments, the B&B owners who filled me with details of little-known local attractions, the government officials who offered tips on the most scenic backcountry trails, and the countless others whose advice landed in this guidebook.

Very special thanks are due the following people for their help in the researching of this edition: Michelle Aldrich, Vicki Arundale, Dave Baker, Wyndi Ballard, Susie Barnett-Bushong, Twila Barnette, Ruth Benson, Dave Black, Marlyn Black, Megan Bogle, Ruth Bookout, Donna Boyd, Rosanna Bremer, Kathleen Chase, Gay Collar, Karen Connelly, JoAnn Davis, Toddi Darlington, Eugene Debs Downer Jr., Sam Eliopoulos, Sharon Earhart, Todd Ennenga, Patty Ewing, Marcia Fagnant, Nadine Gross, Dave Hanks, Harvey Harger, Myrna Hay, Kathy Hiatt, Barbara Hill, Carrie-Lyn Hoffman, Ann Holman, Betty Hunt, Jennie Hutchinson, Marie and Toby Johnson, Jan Jones, Cristie Lee, Loretta Long, Jan Lynch, John Mack, Pam Malone, Donna Martin, Leanne McClain, Riley Mitchell, Mark Madia, David McGinnis, Jay McLaurin, Sue Murphy, Dorothy Neckels, Jeanne M. Newton, Jim and Jacquie Osterfoss, Jane Pennell, Carole Perkins, Joan Peterson, Teri Picerno, Mary Priquet, Dan Ringle, Marcia J. Rose-Ritchie, Julie Rotondo, Eileen Richmond, Darren Rudloff, Nancy Rumney, Angela Safranek, Rolinda Sample, Rob Schmitzer, Skip Shoutis, Irene Spillane, Jim Staebler, Kim Stahr, Norma Strand, Joel Strong, Susan Taylor, Lisa Thorson, Tim Thorson, Neville Tuft, Mitzi Voss, Harold Whitefoot, Hank Williams, Kim Wimmler, and Mike Yauck. Kudos to everyone!

Four people deserve a special medal of honor for their over-the-top assistance during my work on this book. Jesse O'Connor is the man travelers often encounter when they arrive at the visitor center in Jackson and is *the* font of all knowledge for the Jackson Hole-Grand Teton-Yellowstone area. But don't challenge him to race up Snow King; you'll lose. Claudia Wade of the Cody Country Chamber of Commerce was extraordinarily helpful once again, and her rich understanding of the Bighorn Basin proved invaluable. Also deserving a special commendation is Rick Hoeninghausen of Amfac Parks & Resorts who provided last-minute assistance and helpful information within Yellowstone National Park. Freelance editor Beth Kaeding did a thorough reading of the Yellowstone chapter of this book, and her care prevented a quite a few errors from creeping into the final version of this book.

This book was produced by the staff at Avalon Travel Publishing, who saw it through the long process from computer screens to the bookstore. Thanks especially to my long-suffering editor Karen Bleske, designer Stephanie Bird, illustrations guru Bob Race, and mapmakers Bob Race, Brian Bardwell, Chris Folks, Mike Morgenfeld, and Rob Warner for their hard work.

A very special thank you is reserved for my wife, Karen Shemet, and daughter, Aziza Bali, both of whom supported me through the sometimes-trying experience of researching and writing this new edition. It's amazing the miracles that a child's smile and hug can perform!

INTRODUCTION

It's kind of funny how you get used to the country. When I go to town, the noises keep me awake. The coal trains, the sirens going down the road, even if they are a long ways away. People get used to that. We've had people come out here who couldn't sleep because it was so quiet. No noise to lull them to sleep or whatever. My nearest neighbor is five miles away. It takes all kinds of people to make the world go around. If everybody in the world wanted to be a rancher, I probably wouldn't, because there wouldn't be anyplace to live.

—Ed Swartz, quoted in
Steve Gardiner's
Rumblings From Razor City

The expansively rugged land called Wyoming resonates with the spirit of the American West. For anyone who has spent time in Wyoming, the state evokes vivid images: cattle standing in the lee of snow fences, children riding horses along dusty dirt roads, weather-beaten ranches lit by the slanting light of late afternoon, oil-covered roustabouts struggling with the furious machinery of a drilling rig, the sounds of drumming and singing at a powwow, and cow towns where the area code is larger than the population. Here is the original "Wild West," the real-life inspiration for countless Western novels, movies, and songs.

A frontier spirit pervades both Wyoming's landscape and its people, mixing the past and present so completely that it sometimes seems as though around the next bend you might see Chief Washakie's braves circling a massive herd of bison, or Butch Cassidy and the Sundance Kid shooting it out with lawmen, or a party of fur trappers setting out for the mountains. Officially known as "The Equality State" because it was the first to allow women to vote, Wyoming actually revels in another title, "The Cowboy State." License plates carry the state emblem: a cowboy, hat in hand, atop a furiously bucking bronco. A cowboy hat and boots are acceptable dress anywhere, and the unpolished individuality embodied in the cowboy remains the state's heritage, even for those whose only connection is country-and-western music.

The earliest Anglo explorers described Wyoming in less than flattering terms. The image that stuck was the "Great American Desert," a place where the native peoples flourished along with buffalo, antelope, jackrabbits, and rattlesnakes, but where homesteaders and ranchers struggled to survive. Hundreds of thousands of travelers pushed across Wyoming's basins and mountain ranges in the 19th century, bound for greener pastures and gold. Very few considered staying in such an unforgiving environment. Even today, the vast majority of those who enter Wyoming are en route to someplace else.

Seeing Wyoming

Although Wyoming is divided by three major interstate highways, the best way to see the state is from the smaller asphalt and gravel roads where the pace slows and tumbleweeds pile against fences. From the freeways, the landscape is just a blur, but along the back roads this same land becomes a thing of raw-edged, surreal beauty. Old ranches hunker in the valleys, herds of deer and antelope glance up warily at passing cars, oddly colored rock pinnacles crown the hills, and winding streams become glowing silver ribbons of light. The sense of stillness is broken only by the wind, the singing of birds, and the buzz of insects. Writer Gretel Ehrlich in *The Solace of Open Spaces* describes it best:

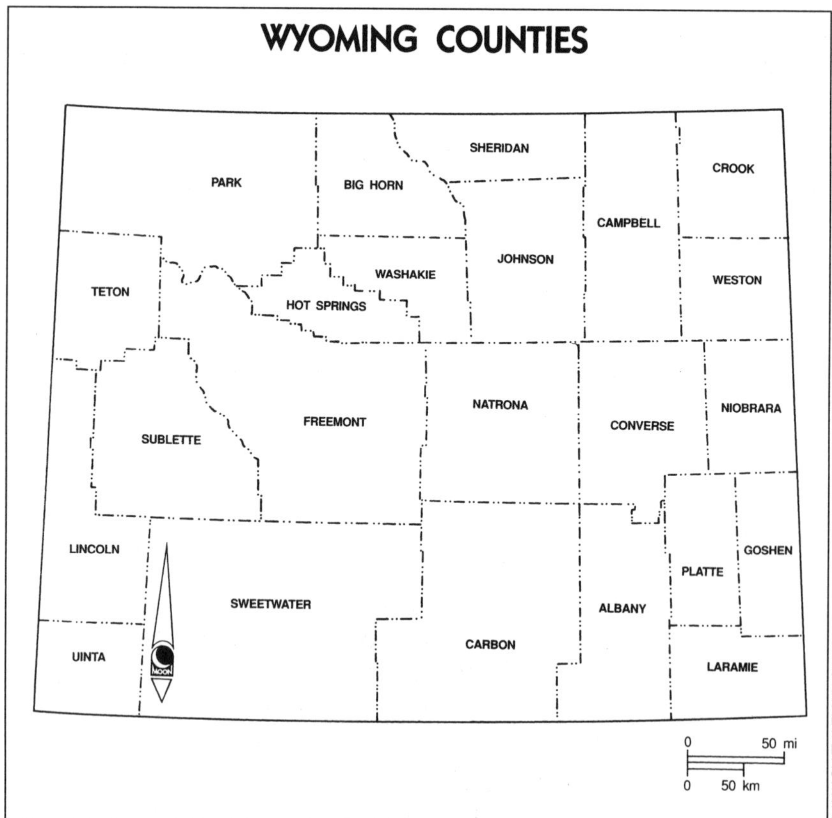

To live and work in this kind of open country, with its hundred-mile views, is to lose the distinction between background and foreground. When I asked an older ranch hand to describe Wyoming's openness, he said, "It's all a bunch of nothing—wind and rattlesnakes—and so much of it you can't tell where you're going or where you've been and it don't make much difference.

On the back roads you'll find folks lifting a hand to wave as you pass. Small-town cafes serve down-home food, friendly motel owners greet tired travelers, and the pace of living slows measurably. You can almost feel the stress of city life dissipating. People leave their homes, cars, and bikes unlocked; they load up clothes in the laundromat and come back later to move them to the dryer. They pull in at the drive-up liquor store for a six-pack and a to-go cup. Unlike big cities, where waiting in lines becomes a way of life, the bank, grocery store, and post office queues are short or nonexistent. Try on a cowboy hat and boots, take a look around the local museum, or stop in for a beer at a country bar and joke with the locals. In a short while you'll gain an appreciation for Wyoming and the down-to-earth people who live here.

The Sky

In the vast open spaces of Wyoming, the sky takes on its own importance, sometimes making the land seem like an afterthought. The land changes slowly with the seasons—first a carpet of winter white, then the mud and first luminescent green buds of spring growth, followed by the verdant summer flowers, and finally the brilliance of fall cottonwood trees along a dry creekbed. But the sky follows the beat of another drummer, changing moment by moment throughout each day. cotton ball clouds float overhead, sending moving shadows across the landscape and coloring the sun's light. Storm clouds build on a summer afternoon, and in the distance a lightning bolt leaps to earth. Perhaps the most memorable times are the lingering sunsets, when colors seem to bounce back and forth across the sky, finally exiting as a fringe of color on the western horizon. At night, coyotes howl the same way they have for millennia, and an enormous panorama of stars arches above, undimmed by discordant city lights.

THE LAND

Covering nearly 98,000 square miles, Wyoming is America's ninth-largest state. The states of Connecticut, Delaware, Hawaii, Maryland, Massachusetts, New Hampshire, New Jersey, Rhode Island, Vermont, and West Virginia would all fit within Wyoming's borders with room to spare. With just 482,800 inhabitants in 1999—the smallest population of any state—Wyoming remains a remarkably undeveloped and unsettled place. Cattle outnumber people by nearly three to one. The population density averages fewer than five people per square mile, and in some counties there is nearly a square mile of land for each person. With an average elevation of 6,700 feet (and a range of 3,125 to 13,804 feet), Wyoming is the third-highest state in the nation. Only Alaska and Colorado are higher.

GEOGRAPHY

On the map, Wyoming is simply a gigantic trapezoidal chunk of earth. Its straight-line border (375 miles from east to west and 276 miles north to south) is an arbitrary human creation that encompasses a surprising diversity of country. The Continental Divide wanders diagonally across the state's mountains from the northwest corner to south-central Wyoming, forming the barrier that separates waters flowing into the Atlantic

Mt. Moran is an unmistakable landmark in Grand Teton National Park.

and Pacific Oceans. More than 71% of Wyoming's lakes, rivers, and streams drain into tributaries of the Missouri River, eventually reaching the Atlantic Ocean; most of the rest flow into tributaries of the Colorado and Columbia Rivers and thence to the Pacific Ocean. Small portions drop into the Great Basin (Salt Lake) or the Great Divide Basin (between Rock Springs and Rawlins), where the water evaporates or percolates into the ground

Wyoming's mountains generally trend northwest to southeast, but this gross overall pattern is broken up by smaller ranges. Northwest Wyoming is dominated by a complex melange of mountains: the Absaroka, Teton, Gros Ventre, Wyoming, and Wind River Ranges. North-central Wyoming is divided by the Big Horn Mountains, while the Laramie Range and the Medicine Bow Mountains dominate the south-central region. The far northeast corner holds the Black Hills. In among these ranges, the land spreads out in broad basins, including Bighorn Basin and Powder River Basin in the north, Wind River Basin in the west-central region, and the Green River, Red Desert, and Washakie basins in the southwest. The eastern portion of Wyoming drops gently into the Great Plains.

CLIMATE

Wyoming's climate mirrors its diverse geography, ranging from arid deserts to cool mountain forests. The mountain ranges act as barriers to eastward-moving weather systems. Moist air is forced upward by the mountains, releasing rain or snow along the western slopes. By the time the clouds reach the east side, much of the water has been wrung out, creating a "rain shadow." Because of this, midwinter finds Togwotee Pass smothered under many feet of snow while Dubois, in the lee of the Absaroka Range, may have only a dusting on the ground.

Visitors to Wyoming discover weather typical of the West's high plains and mountains: hot, dry summers punctuated by fierce thunderstorms, and cold winters with a fair amount of snow. Conditions vary greatly throughout the state, however, with cooler summers and heavy winter snows in the mountains.

Extremes

Wyoming has a reputation for extreme conditions. Wintertime blizzards periodically lash the land, and strong winds pile the snow into huge drifts. Summertime thunderstorms—particularly in the mountains—can be an almost daily occurrence. Southeast Wyoming has an average of nine hailstorms a year—it's the hail capital of North America. Temperatures have been recorded from -66° F (Yellowstone National Park) to 114° F (the town of Basin). Precipitation shows a similar variation—high mountain ranges of northwest Wyoming see as much as 60 inches (mostly snow) a year, while parched desert areas in Bighorn Basin and Great Divide Basin receive only six.

Wyoming is well known for its wind. Through much of the state, the wind never seems to stop blowing, averaging more than 16 miles an hour along the eastern border. Buffalo Bill Cody, a man who symbolizes the West in the American conscience, once defended Wyoming when a friend complained of the wind: "You know where those winds come from? Well, this country up here is so close to paradise you can feel the breezes from heaven. That wind comes from the angels' wings. When they flap their wings the wind comes right down this valley."

Basin Weather

In the expansive basins that cover much of Wyoming, typical midsummer daytime temperatures are in the 80s and 90s, with nights dropping into the 50s and 60s. Low relative humidity makes the heat easier to take. The wettest months are April and May, with lots of sun in the summer. Afternoon thunderheads often build up, temporarily blocking the sun, but generally dropping more lightning than rain. Fall can be a most pleasant time of year, with shirt-sleeve days and cool evenings.

When winter arrives in November and December, it can do so with a vengeance, pushing the mercury well below zero. Snowfall is not great, totaling 15 to 60 inches over the winter months, but when combined with winds pushing 50 mph, it can look like a lot more. In places, snow fences extend for many miles beside the highways, attempting to blunt the blowing snow. Ground blizzards sometimes halt traffic along I-

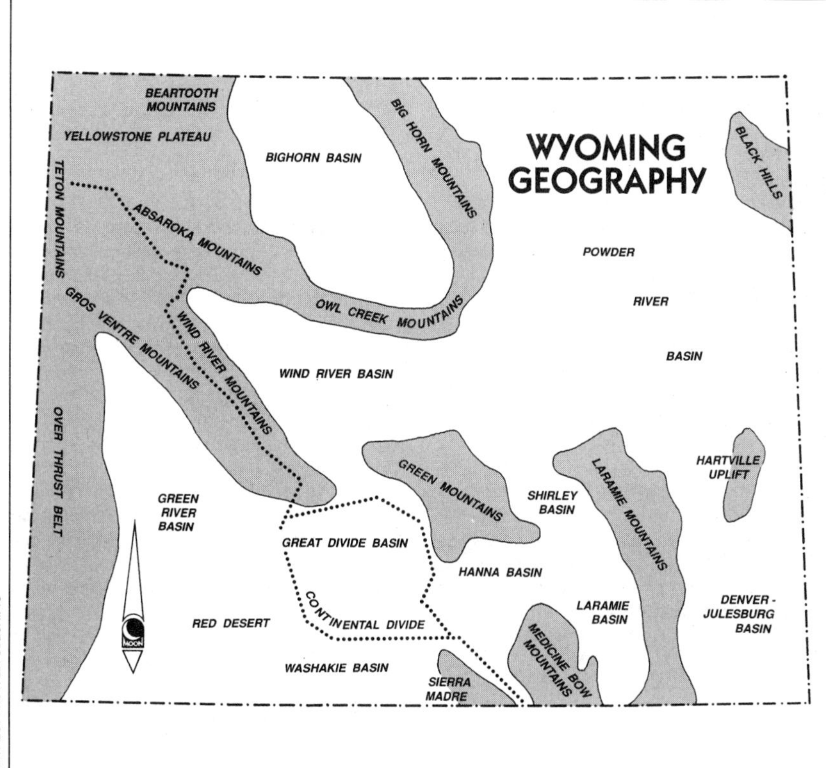

TROPICAL WYOMING

Sometimes I wish that Wyoming had more vegetation and less catarrh, more bloom and summer and fragrance and less Christmas and New Year's through the summer. I like the clear, bracing air of 7,500 feet above the civilized world, but I get weary of putting on and taking off my buffalo overcoat for meals all through dog days. I yearn for a land where a man can take off his ulster and overshoes while he delivers a Fourth of July oration, without flying into the face of Providence and dying of pneumonia. . . . As I write these lines I look out across the wide sweep of brownish gray plains dotted here and there with ranches and defunct buffalo craniums, and I see shutting down over the sides of the abrupt mountains, and meeting the foothills, a white mist which melts into the gray sky. It is a snow storm in the mountains.

I saw this with wonder and admiration for the first two or three million times. When it became a matter of daily occurrence as a wonder or curiosity, it was below mediocrity. Last July a snow storm gathered one afternoon and fell among the foothills and whitened the whole line to within four or five miles of town, and it certainly was a peculiar freak of nature, but it convinced me that whatever enterprises I might launch into here I would not try to raise oranges and figs until the isothermal lines should meet with a change of heart.

—19TH-CENTURY HUMORIST
BILL NYE

80 for days at a time. Locals joke that it only snows a couple of inches in December and then the snow blows back and forth across the state the rest of the winter until it is finally worn out. Actually, winters are not all so bleak, and temperatures occasionally rise into the 50s. You can expect sun 60% of the time. Chinooks—warm downslope winds—are common in the winters along the eastern slopes of the mountains, particularly around Sheridan, Dubois, and Cody.

Mountain Weather

Many of the favorite sites in Wyoming—including Yellowstone and Grand Teton National Parks—lie primarily above 7,000 feet. Here, the weather is considerably cooler than in the basins. Summertime temperatures rarely top 80° F, while nights often dip into the 40s. Snow is possible at any time of the year. April and May are generally the wettest months. Spring comes late in the mountains, and high passes are often blocked by drifts until mid-July. Summer thunderstorms are common, especially in the northwest mountains, where they gather over the high peaks most afternoons. Mid-September brings fall conditions as mountain temperatures often drop 20-30 degrees below summer readings, quickly turning the aspen leaves a brilliant orange and sending most folks scurrying for warmer climes.

High-country winters are often severely cold and snowy, with temperatures below zero for days at a time. Snow depths often exceed six feet in the higher mountains. Grand Targhee Ski Resort receives some 42 feet of snow over a typical winter! Fortunately, the relative humidity is quite low, making the temperatures easier to tolerate and creating fluffy powder snow conditions. One surprising winter feature is the presence of temperature inversions in intermountain valleys such as Big Piney and Jackson Hole. These often occur on cold, clear nights when the cold air sinks into the valley floors. Skiers who leave the lodge bundled in down parkas and polypro are often surprised to find temperatures 30 degrees warmer at the top of the mountain.

LIGHTNING SAFETY

Lightning is a significant hazard for travelers on foot or horseback in Wyoming, particularly in the high mountains such as the Tetons, Wind River Range, Snowy Range, or the Big Horns. Three people were killed by lightning strikes in 1998 and 1999 in the Snowy Range west of Laramie, and others are struck almost every year around the state. Perhaps the most famous incident came in the 1990s when acclaimed writer Gretel Ehrlich was struck while riding a horse on her ranch at the foot of the Big Horns. Her long and excruciating recovery is detailed in *A Match to the Heart* (New York: Pantheon Books).

Creating a Thunderhead

Thunderstorms are created by a combination of convective forces, moisture, and unstable air. On sunny days as the ground warms, heat begins to rise convectively. When the air above is unstable (much cooler at higher altitudes than closer to the ground), the warm air rises rapidly. As it rises, the air cools enough that tiny droplets of moisture precipitate out, forming clouds that may grow into thunderheads if there is enough moisture and atmospheric instability. The rapid development of thunderheads generates enormous amounts of energy that is released as lighting, wind, hail, and rain. During a lightning strike, an electrical charge reaches toward the ground and is met by an opposite charge rising from the earth. They connect in a brilliant flash of light, heat, and noise as 35,000 amperes of charge are released.

Protecting Yourself

Nearly 100 people die each year from lightning strikes in the United States, and hundreds of others are injured. Statistically speaking, golfers are the most likely to get zapped because they are often in open areas carrying metal golf clubs when a storm rolls in. Others at risk include softball and soccer players, mountain climbers, horseback riders, swimmers, and hikers.

Several factors are important in protecting yourself from lighting. One defense is to pay attention to building storms, even distant ones, and especially those that build quickly. Mountain thunderstorms—created when winds push air masses upslope against a mountain range—are five times more likely than storms over adjacent valleys. The color of thunderheads is another factor to watch; black bases means that they contain significant amounts of moisture and may create a more violent thunderstorm.

The most dangerous times are—surprisingly—before a thunderstorm comes directly overhead. Strikes can hit up to five miles in front of a fast moving thunderstorm. In 1999, a Boy Scout was struck in the Tetons while watching a distant thunderstorm; overhead it was mostly blue sky! To determine your distance from an approaching storm, count the number of seconds between a lightning strike and the subsequent thunderclap, and divide by five to get the approximate distance in miles. If thunder arrives within five seconds, the storm is dangerously close, just a mile away.

If you see a storm approaching, get off ridgetops and other high places, move out of open fields, away from single trees or other tall objects, and out of the water. Lightning follows the path of least resistance, and that usually means taller objects or those containing metal. Safer places are inside a car or house, or in a stand of even-sized trees. If those options aren't possible, lie down and stay as low as possible—preferably in a *dry* ditch (stay away from wet areas). If you're caught on an open ridge, sit on an insulated pad or a backpack. Metallic objects attract lightning, so stay away from fenceposts, golf clubs, climbing gear, or metal objects in your backpack. Don't stand in a group of people. If you're indoors when a storm hits, move away from windows, doors, appliances, pipes, and telephones.

Lightning strikes are sometimes preceded by a tingling sensation and your hair may stand on end. If this happens, immediately crouch down (but don't lie down or put your hands on the ground) and cover your ears. If someone near you is struck by lightning, get immediate help, and be ready to perform CPR. For additional lightning safety information, contact the **Lightning Protection Institute,** tel. (800) 488-6864, www.lightning.org.

FLORA AND FAUNA

VEGETATION

Wyoming's topography and climate are reflected in its vegetation, with dense forests in the mountains and dry grasses and shrubs at lower elevations. The vegetation can be classified into six broad categories (see map): mixed-grass prairie, sagebrush steppe, desert shrubland, evergreen forest, deciduous forest, and alpine tundra. Mixed-grass prairies dominate the eastern third of Wyoming and contain such species as grama grass, wheatgrass, junegrass, bluegrass, and sage. The western two-thirds of Wyoming contains vast areas of sagebrush steppe, a threadbare carpet of big sagebrush, wheatgrass, needle-and-thread grass, grama grass, tumbleweed, and other plants. This is the country most folks associate with Wyoming—sagebrush extending to the horizon. (An old

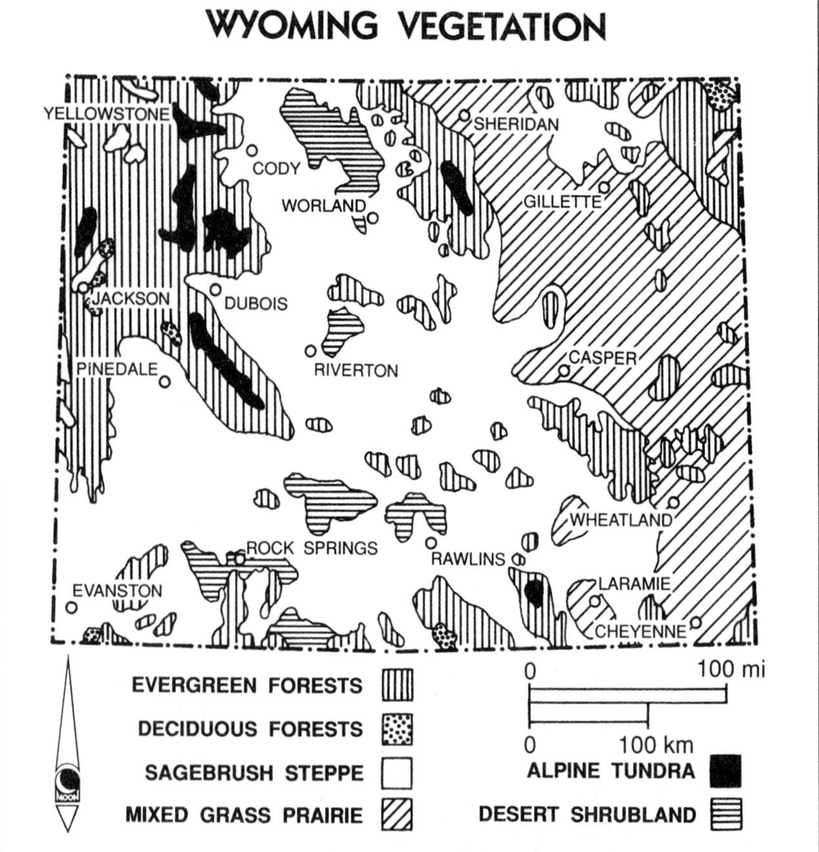

SAGEBRUSH

Sagebrush is Wyoming's ubiquitous common denominator, a sweetly pungent bush found from the lowest deserts to 10,000-foot mountains. More sage grows here than anyplace else in North America. The volatile oils make it a last choice for cattle and act as a natural herbicide, preventing competition from other plants. Ranchers consider the plant less than worthless, but native animals such as sage grouse, antelope, and mule deer depend upon sage for survival. You won't even find sage grouse where sage doesn't grow.

The terms sagebrush and sage are generally used interchangeably in the West. Note, however, that the spice on your kitchen shelf is not the same as the Wyoming plant *(Artemesia),* and any attempt to cook with sagebrush is likely to leave you gagging. Sage has been in the West for some 25 million years and is well adapted to the poor soils and arid conditions of the desert. Sage survives by using its network of shallow roots to draw moisture from the ground as it percolates down. Wyoming actually has at least seven different species of sage. Some of these exist only on very specific sites: black sagebrush grows on windy ridges between 5,000 and 8,000 feet, where the soil is shallow and stony; alkali sagebrush grows in impermeable soils that are highly alkaline. The predominant species across much of Wyoming is big sagebrush, a bush that grows to three feet in height and often covers extensive areas.

cowboy saying goes, "I reckon the Lord done put tumbleweeds here to show which way the wind was a-blowin'.")

Wyoming also contains desert areas, notably the Red Desert and a large part of Bighorn Basin. Dominant plants in the desert shrublands include greasewood, saltbush, shadscale, and various kinds of sagebrush. At higher elevations, where more moisture falls, the land is covered with evergreen forests. Ponderosa pines dominate forested parts of eastern Wyoming, while lodgepole pine, Douglas-fir, Engelmann spruce, and subalpine fir exist in mountains to the west. A few areas also have pinyon pine and juniper trees. Deciduous forests are scattered in small patches around Wyoming consisting of cottonwoods along riverbottoms, aspens in the middle elevations, and bur oak in the Black Hills. Treeline in much of Wyoming is around 9,500 feet. Above this, one finds alpine tundra, where the dominant plants are low-growing herbs, grasses, and forbs.

WILDLIFE

When the first mountain men and explorers wandered into the vast land that became Wyoming, they found an incredible abundance of wildlife: herds of bison stretching to the horizon, antelope, elk, and deer grazing on the broad plains, and grizzly bears, wolves, coyotes, cottontails, and jackrabbits. Although wolves were poisoned to extinction, and only a few hundred bison and grizzlies remain, other animals fared better. Today, the two most common large mammals are mule deer and pronghorn antelope, both of which are found across much of the state. The sagebrush lands also provide cover for sage grouse, a large chickenlike bird (the males perform an elaborate X-rated mating display). In the mountains, one often hears the early-summer drumming of ruffed grouse. Rarest of Wyoming's animals is the endangered black-footed ferret (see the special topic Black-footed Ferrets in the Medicine Bow Country chapter for more on these).

Watchable Wildlife

Wyoming's undeveloped character makes it a mecca for those who enjoy watching wild animals. Yellowstone National Park is a favorite place to look for bison, elk, coyotes, moose, mule deer, bighorn sheep, river otters, and trumpeter swans. Both black and grizzly bears also live here, though they're less commonly seen. Another popular place is the National Elk Refuge in Jackson Hole, the winter home for a herd of more than 10,000 elk. Excellent places to see bighorn sheep are the Whiskey Basin Habitat Area, near Dubois, and the Bighorn National Recreation Area. Wyoming has around 3,500 wild horses; watch for them at Bighorn National Recreation Area or in the Red Desert. Mountain goats live in the Beartooth Mountains along Wyoming's border with Montana. The high mountains of the Tetons and the Wind River Range have such animals as pikas and yellow-bellied marmots, while the sagebrush country abounds with deer, antelope, coyotes, jackrabbits, cottontails, and prairie dogs. Certainly the most distinctive Wyoming critter is the jackalope (see the special topic in the Central Wyoming chapter).

The Wyoming Game and Fish Department publishes *Wyoming Wildlife,* an attractive monthly publication available for just $10 a year. To subscribe, call (307) 777-4600 or (800) 710-8345. Call (800) 548-9453 for a catalog of other wildlife-related products and publications, including videos, T-shirts, caps, mugs, books, posters, and cards. Find Game and Fish on the web at www.gf.state.wy.us.

Rattlesnakes

Everyone's least favorite reptile is the prairie rattlesnake, a heavy-bodied venomous creature with a telltale rattle. Prairie rattlesnakes often reach nearly a yard in length (the longest was 57 inches!) and are found in the plains and foothills of eastern and central Wyoming, generally below 7,000 feet. They're especially common around rock piles and in prairie dog towns. You *won't* find them in mountain country over 7,200 feet, in the Laramie area, in Yellowstone and Grand Teton National Parks, or in the southwestern desert country (with the exception of the lower Green River Valley area). Prairie rattlers feed primarily on ground squirrels, rabbits, chipmunks, prairie dogs, and other small rodents, but can also kill birds and lizards. They reproduce every other year, and large groups of rattlesnakes gather in dens to spend the winter months in a dormant state.

Prairie rattlesnakes usually offer a warning of their presence—hence the name—but not all the time. At times aggressive, their size and appearance will certainly send your blood pressure up, but the venom is actually less toxic than that of other rattlers and is usually only one-eighth the amount needed to kill a human. Because of this, snakebite fatalities are rare in Wyoming.

A smaller snake, the midget faded rattlesnake, is found in southern Wyoming within the lower Green River Valley around the cities of Green River and Rock Springs, and in Flaming Gorge National Recreation Area. They frequent rocky outcrops and, though smaller, are 10 to 30 times more poisonous than prairie rattlesnakes. Fortunately, midget faded rattlesnakes are quite timid and pose little threat to humans. They will coil and strike, but only if cornered.

The best defense against rattlers is to always use care when walking in their country and to keep your distance if you spot one. Be especially careful when clambering over rock piles or walking through dense grasses and sage. Shake out sleeping bags, boots, and bedding, and wear tall leather boots rather than sneakers.

If someone is bitten by a rattlesnake, immobilize the area of the bite and immediately get him or her to a hospital or medical facility. If the bite is on an arm or leg, keep it below the level of the heart. Time is of the essence. Other treatments are possible for emergency situations when there is no chance of getting to a doctor in time, but the potential for harm is great if you don't know what you are doing. Take a good first-aid class to learn how to handle these situations, or talk with your doctor about where to get and how to use suction pumps. Your best bet is always preventing a bite in the first place. For more on rattlers and other crawly things, see *Amphibians and Reptiles of Wyoming,* by George T. Baxter and Michael D. Stone (Cheyenne: Wyoming Game and Fish Department).

Pronghorn Antelope

One of the most commonly seen Wyoming animals is the antelope (biologists prefer the name

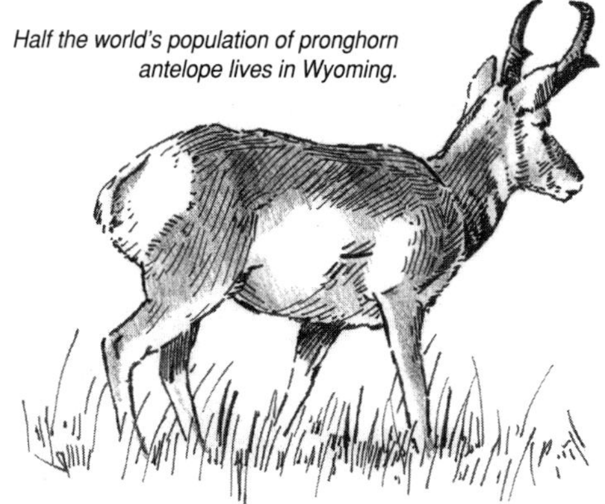
Half the world's population of pronghorn antelope lives in Wyoming.

"pronghorn"). More than 400,000 live here, constituting half the world's pronghorn population. Antelope survive on grasses, forbs, and sagebrush—perhaps Wyoming's most abundant plant. They are built for speed: oversized lungs and windpipes give them the ability to run for miles at 30 mph and to accelerate to twice that for short bursts. Despite this speed, pronghorn have an innate inquisitiveness that makes them relatively easy to hunt, an attribute that nearly drove them to extinction by market hunting early in this century. Strictly enforced laws and careful management have brought antelope populations back.

Deer

Wyoming has almost as many deer as people. You can see two species along the state's roads: white-tailed deer—common in the Black Hills—and the larger mule deer, found across the state. Be especially careful when driving after dusk during the fall breeding season, since the hormone-crazed bucks tend to leap out in front of cars. Nearly everyone who has lived in Wyoming has hit a deer under these circumstances. Slow down at night, especially in areas posted with Deer Crossing signs.

Elk

A majestic member of the deer family, elk (many biologists prefer the term "wapiti") are a favorite with both tourists and hunters. Elk inhabit much of Wyoming, with the largest herds along the western mountains. More than 30,000 elk graze in Yellowstone National Park alone. With bulls averaging 700 pounds and cows averaging 500 pounds, they are some of the largest antlered animals in the Americas.

Elk spend summers high in the mountains, feeding in alpine meadows and along forest edges. Mature bulls graze alone, but the cows and calves—generally born in late May and early June—group in large herds for protection. When the fall rutting season arrives, bulls attempt to herd the cows and calves around, mating with cows when they come into estrus and defending their harems from other bulls. During this time of year the bugling of bull elk is a common sound in the mountains, a challenge to any bull within earshot. When a competitor appears, a dominance display often follows—complete with bugling, stomping, and thrashing of the ground—to show who is the baddest bull around. In a fight, bulls lock their massive antlers and try to push and twist until one finally gives in and retreats. These battles help ensure that the healthiest bulls produce the most offspring. Ironically, other bulls often wait in the wings for battles over harems to occur, then rush in to mate with the cows while the larger bulls are sparring. (When the cat's away. . . .) The snows of late fall push elk to lower-elevation winter ranges, notably at the National Elk Refuge in Jackson Hole. When spring comes, the bulls drop their antlers and immediately begin to grow new ones. The elk head back into the high country, following the melting snowline.

Elk and bison both can be infected with brucellosis, a bacterium causing spontaneous abortions. Brucellosis is transmitted to other animals by contact with the dead fetus or birthing material, and can cause undulant fever in humans. Though the evidence is circumstantial at best for this, ranchers worry that brucellosis can spread from elk and bison to cattle, particularly around elk feeding grounds in western Wyoming. To lessen the incidence of brucellosis, state employees now routinely vaccinate elk at the feeding grounds, shooting them in the hindquarters with vaccine-loaded pellets.

BISON

The bison is the definitive frontier animal and Wyoming's state mammal—its outline graces the state flag. Weighing up to 2,000 pounds, these are the largest land mammals in the New World. Bison commonly live 12-15 years. The calves weigh 30 to 40 pounds at birth and within minutes are standing and able to nurse. Two races of bison exist: the plains bison, primarily east of the Rockies, and the mountain bison (sometimes called wood bison) in the higher elevations. Technically, these huge, hairy beasts are bison—the only true buffalo are the water buffalo of Southeast Asia—but the name buffalo is commonly used.

With their massive heads, huge shoulder humps, heavy coats of fur, and small posteriors, buffalo are some of the strangest animals in North America. They look so front-heavy as to seem unstable, ready to topple forward onto their snouts at any time. Despite this impression, buffalo are remarkably well adapted to life on the plains. A bison will use its strong sense of smell to find grass buried in a deep snowdrift and then sweep the snow away with a sideways motion of its head. The animals are also surprisingly fleet-footed, as careless Yellowstone photographers have discovered. In addition, the buffalo is one very tough critter. In 1907, a buffalo was pitted against four of the meanest Mexican bulls at a Juarez, Mexico, bullring. After knocking heads several times with the buffalo, the bulls fled and were saved only when bullfighters opened the chute gates to let them escape.

"Blackening the Plains"

When Europeans first reached the New World, they found massive herds of bison in the Appalachians and even more as they headed west. Daniel Boone hunted them in North Carolina in the 1750s; Pennsylvanians shot hundreds of buffalo that were invading their winter stores of hay. By 1820, settlers had nearly driven the buffalo to extinction in the east. But there were far more living to the west. As explorers, mountain men, and the first tentative settlers reached the "Great American Desert," they were awestruck by the numbers. Travelers told of slowly moving masses of buffalo blackening the plains and watched in astonishment as the herds stopped at rivers and nearly drank them dry. A fair estimate of the original population of buffalo in North America is 60 million. Even in the middle 1860s, travelers through Wyoming's Wind River Valley reported seeing 10,000 bison at one time. A pioneer Kansas settler named William D. Street recalled a trip in which a herd roared past his camp for an entire night. The next morning, he climbed a nearby butte and saw buffalo covering the plains below. According to Street:

> *The herd was not less than 20 miles in width—we never saw the other side—at least 60 miles in length, maybe much longer; two counties of buffaloes! There might have been 100,000, or 1,000,000, or 100,000,000. I don't know. In the cowboy days in western Kansas we saw 7,000 head of cattle in one roundup. After gazing at them a few moments our thoughts turned to that buffalo herd. For a comparison, imagine a large pail of water; take from it or add to it a drop, and there you have it. Seven thousand head of cattle was not a drop in the bucket as compared with that herd of buffalo.*

Indians and Buffalo

The Plains Indians depended heavily upon the buffalo for food and—like the proverbial hot dog, which "contains everything but the moo"—they used every part of the animal. Hooves were carved into spoons, skins became buffalo robes and covers for boats and tepees, rawhide was used for drumheads, calf skins became storage sacks, hair was turned into earrings, and horns were formed into cups and arrow points. Everything that remained—including the muzzle, penis, eyes, and cartilage—was boiled down to use as glue for arrowheads. Their dried testicles and scrotum were used for rattles, and the ubiquitous buffalo chips became a cooking fuel on the treeless prairies.

Hunting techniques varied depending upon the terrain. When possible, the Indians drove herds of bison into arroyos with no exits, over cliffs, or into deep sand or snow, making them easier to kill. The arrival of Spanish horses in the 16th century made it far easier to hunt bison. In a surround, mounted hunters attacked from at least two sides, creating chaos in the herd and allowing buffalo to be shot with arrows or guns.

When whites first spread across the plains, they found the bison a plentiful food source, but also viewed the massive herds as a hindrance to agriculture and cattle raising. But these were not the only reasons whites wanted to destroy the buffalo. Killing off the bison would starve the Indians into submission and force them to take a more "civilized" way of life. General Philip Sheridan, commenting in support of white buffalo hunters, said

> *Instead of stopping the [white] hunters they ought to give them a hearty, unanimous vote of thanks, and appropriate a sufficient sum of money to strike and present to each one a medal of bronze, with a dead buffalo on one side and a discouraged Indian on the other. They are destroying the Indian's commissary, and it is a well-known fact that an army losing its base of supplies is placed at a great disadvantage. Send them powder and lead, if you will; for the sake of a lasting peace, let them kill, skin and sell until the buffaloes are exterminated.*

This reckless slaughter did indeed endanger the Indians, but it also had an unwanted side effect: the Indians went on the warpath. The loss of their primary food source helped convince many Indians that their own extinction was next. The warriors who massacred Custer and his men at Little Big Horn had watched their people pushed to the brink of starvation by the destruction of the buffalo.

A hunter finishes off a wounded animal.

The Slaughter

Two factors propelled the slaughter to new heights in the 1870s: new railroads across the plains, and a sudden international demand for buffalo robes and hides. Buffalo meat proved to be a readily available food source for railway construction workers, and hunters such as "Buffalo Bill" Cody provided a steady supply, generally taking just the hindquarters and hump and leaving the rest on the plains. Hundreds of thousands were killed. Once the railroads were completed in 1869, a new "sport" appeared—shooting buffalo from the moving railcars and leaving them to rot on the prairie. Wealthy gentry from the East Coast and Europe also discovered the joys of killing. One Irish nobleman had an entourage of 40 servants, with an entire wagon just for firearms; he killed 2,000 buffalo in a three-year carnage.

Conservationists tried to halt the buffalo slaughter through legislation in 1874, but President Grant's corrupt Secretary of the Interior, Columbus Delano, said, "I would not seriously regret the total disappearance of the buffalo from our western prairies, in its effect upon the Indians. I would regard it rather as a means of hastening their sense of dependence upon the products of the soil and their own labors." The legislation was pocket-vetoed by Grant.

In 1872, thousands of hide hunters spread through Kansas, Nebraska, and Colorado in search of buffalo. Over the next three years, they brought in more than three million buffalo hides, with Indians killing another 400,000 bison for meat and robes. Good hide hunters could bring down 25 to 100 buffalo in a typical day, keeping five skinners busy from sunup to sundown. One hunter, Jim White, killed at least 16,000 buffalo in his career. Only the hides, cured hams, and buffalo tongues (which could be salted and shipped in barrels) were saved. When Gen. Grenville M. Dodge toured Kansas in the fall of 1873, he noted that "the air was foul with a sickening stench, and the vast plain, which only a short twelvemonth before teemed with animal life, was a dead, solitary, putrid desert." Buffalo carcasses dotted the plains in such numbers that in later years bone pickers would collect massive piles of bones for knife handles, combs, and buttons or to be ground up for sugar refining, fertilizer, or glue.

When the buffalo of the central states approached extinction, hunters turned their attention elsewhere, reaching Wyoming, Montana, and the Dakotas in 1880. In 1882, more than 200,000 hides were taken, and another 40,000 the following year. By 1884, only 300 hides were shipped. The slaughter was nearly over; only a few private herds and scattered individual bison remained. The Indians who had once depended so heavily on buffalo for all the necessities of life were reduced to eating muskrats, gophers, and even grass. Some killed their horses, others stole settlers' cattle, and the rest had to beg the government for food. In only a couple of years, an entire culture had been devastated.

But the slaughter ruined the lives not just of the buffalo or the Indians; hide hunters often spiked buffalo carcasses with strychnine, returning later to skin the wolves that had come to feed on the meat. Coyotes, kit foxes, badgers, vultures, eagles, ravens, and anything else that ate the meat were also killed. With both the buffalo and the "vermin" out of the way, Wyoming and the West were safe for domestic sheep and cattle.

Protection

The first federal legislation protecting buffalo (only in Yellowstone National Park, however) did not pass until 1894. The following year, only 800 buffalo remained in all of North America, a little over one-thousandth of one percent of their original numbers. Despite this dismal picture, the population has rebounded dramatically; today an estimated 65,000 bison roam across America. In Wyoming, small populations can be seen in Hot Springs State Park and Grand Teton National Park, while one of the few large wild populations remains in Yellowstone National Park.

A strong demand for buffalo meat has led some Wyoming ranchers to raise bison. It's a highly specialized ranching endeavor, since the animals can flatten most fences and standard roundup techniques don't work. Durham Buffalo Ranch near Wright has one of the largest private buffalo herds in the country: 3,500 head. Ranchers have discovered that bison are more efficient grazers than cattle, making it possible to produce more meat per acre, and they are less susceptible to disease. Perhaps someday the vast herds of bison may return to Wyoming's rangelands in the form of bison ranches.

HISTORY

Although Wyoming is a young state—only reaching the century mark in 1990—it seems to have more history per square inch than just about any other place in America. This history is a mixture of Indians and cowboys, settlers and outlaws, schemers and dreamers, railroad magnates and cattle barons, and plain folks clinging to plots of marginal farmland despite unbelievable odds. Wyoming's 19th-century frontier is a recurring theme in America's imagination, as revealed in countless books, songs, and movies. This rich treasure trove from the past is stored not just in the little-changed landscape, where the ruts from wagon trains are still visible and emigrant names remain carved in rocky buttes, but also in the cattle drives and rodeos and the weather-etched faces of sheepherders and cowboys working the range. It is hard to imagine a place with a richer past.

NATIVE AMERICANS

Humans have been in Wyoming for perhaps 25,000 years. The Plains Indians—comprising 27 different tribes—were found from the Mississippi River to the Rockies, and from Texas to central Canada. The lives of these people revolved around the buffalo; they followed the vast herds, migrating where the buffalo led. Because of this nomadic lifestyle, everything they had was pared to the minimum. Pottery, so common in the southwestern deserts, was replaced by woven baskets on the plains. The tepee, an easily portable lodge, offered protection from the elements, and clothing was warm yet not burdensome.

Days of Glory

Although many people view the Plains Indians as existing in a state of balance with their environment, there is ample evidence that things were changing even before whites first pushed their way onto the plains. The arrival of horses and guns in the 17th and 18th centuries created a time of plenty that has rarely been known among nomadic hunting tribes. Horses made it easier to follow and hunt the huge bison herds, and tribes that had been at least partially farmers turned entirely to hunting. Native populations grew rapidly with the abundance of food. The warrior also gained importance with the changing culture as raiding parties stole horses and attacked other tribes. Villages grew larger as families gathered for mutual protection from their enemies.

The turmoil that resulted led to a constantly changing situation in Wyoming during the 19th century, as the tribes each strove for control. It was this turbulent society that greeted the first Euro-American explorers. Whites were accustomed to well-defined land ownership, with definite boundaries within which one lived; here the territories were in a state of flux, with tribes claiming overlapping areas.

During the 1700s, Indians from the Great Lakes and Canadian plains had moved into what would become Wyoming. By the 1850s, the Sioux were in Powder River Basin, the Crow in Bighorn Basin, and the Cheyenne and Arapaho south of the North Platte River. The Shoshone and the Bannock—originally from the Great Basin—had moved into the Green River and Wind River valleys, while their relatives, the Utes, held the Sierra Madre and desert land to the west. Communication between these diverse tribes was possible in a sophisticated sign language.

Treaties

During the first half of the 19th century, American explorers, fur trappers, traders, and settlers began to push across Wyoming. As emigration westward increased in the 1840s, so did conflicts with Indians. Whites complained of random attacks and stolen horses. Indians complained of trampled grass, polluted water, and wasteful killing of bison. To deal with these problems, a great council was called at Fort Laramie in 1851, attracting 10,000 Indians from many different tribes. Indian agent Thomas Fitzpatrick was eager to gain permission for settlers to use the Oregon Trail across Indian lands in Wyoming. In exchange for gifts from the federal government in the form of annuities, the tribes agreed to stay within specified boundaries and to

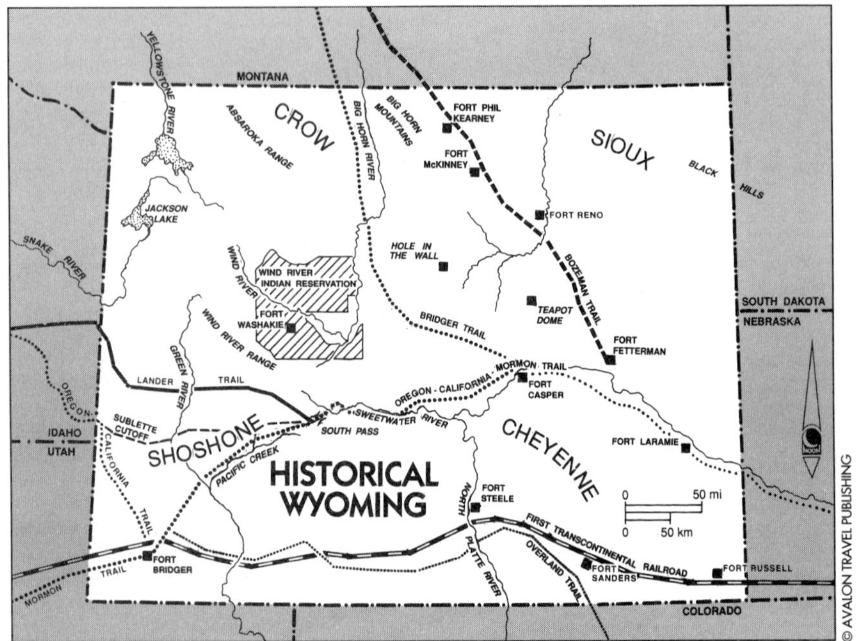

punish those who violated the accord or attacked white emigrants.

Father Pierre DeSmet drew up the boundaries, with allowances for hunting outside the "home" regions. The unstated long-term goal of the treaty was to transform the Indians from hunters into farmers. By developing a paternalistic system of dependency on the government, combined with educational programs and settlement, the Indians would—in theory—become like the whites. Violence erupted almost immediately among the tribes and between them and the Anglo emigrants. Soon, whites would be more concerned over how to dispossess the Indians of their land than how to get through it safely.

In 1861, the Fort Wise Treaty abrogated much of the Treaty of 1851, forcing the Arapaho and Cheyenne onto a desolate reservation at Sand Creek, Colorado, to get them away from the suddenly valuable land to the north. The treaty was signed by some leaders, but only after the starving individuals saw that they would not receive their annuities without affixing their Xs.

The Battle Begins

Colorado's Sand Creek Massacre of 1865 proved a turning point in the history of Indian-white relations. A small band of Arapaho attacked a family farm, brutally murdering the family. When the mutilated bodies were put on display in Denver, public outrage pushed Col. John M. Chivington—formerly a Methodist minister—to lead one of the most vicious and unwarranted attacks ever perpetrated by the army. Two hundred Cheyenne and Arapaho died in the daybreak attack on Chief Black Kettle's peaceful village.

The Indians—not just the Cheyenne and Arapaho, but also the Sioux—quickly retaliated by striking throughout Colorado and Wyoming, killing some 75 settlers around the Rock Creek Station (northwest of present-day Laramie) and destroying stage stations all along the Oregon Trail. Over the next several years, hundreds died on both sides. The main focus of Indian attacks was the Bozeman Trail through the lush Powder River country of the Sioux. The army responded with an alternating series of military campaigns and peace overtures as the national mood flip-flopped between war and accommodation.

A major cause of these conflicts was the hysteria that gold created. Each new gold rush—California in 1849, Colorado in 1859, Montana in 1864, and finally the Black Hills in 1874—led to new incursions onto Indian lands. When whites found Indians standing in the way of development, they attempted to renegotiate the treaties or, failing that, to find some excuse to set them aside. Once gold had been found, the end of Indian culture was almost a given. Senator John Sherman noted: "If the whole army of the United States stood in the way, the wave of emigration would pass over it to seek the valley where gold was to be found."

Other factors also played critical roles in the destruction of the Indian way of life on the plains. Perhaps the most crucial was the loss of their primary food source, the buffalo. But many tribes were devastated as well by diseases brought by contact with Europeans, especially smallpox, cholera, whooping cough, and venereal diseases.

AMERICAN HERITAGE CENTER, LARAMIE, WY

The Sioux warrior Red Cloud proved a formidable military leader during the Plains Indian wars.

Cultural Mistrust

Many whites viewed the Indians with deep distrust. Writer James Chisholm reflected a typical frontier attitude, calling them "useless, strutting, ridiculous, pompous humbugs—lying, faithless, stealing, begging, cruel, hungry, howling vagabonds—cowardly, treacherous red devils." In 1869, Gen. Philip Sheridan took matters even further by declaring, "The only good Indian is a dead Indian."

The Indians themselves were not entirely innocent. Attacks on wagon trains were frequent, and many of the trappers, stagecoach drivers, and ranchers who settled in Wyoming were murdered and their bodies mutilated by the Sioux, Cheyenne, or Arapaho. Scalping—a practice introduced by white traders—became commonplace. Whites complained that the federal government was arming and feeding the Indians at the same time it was leading military campaigns against them.

Evicting the Indians

More than a thousand engagements were fought between Indians and whites in the late 19th century, killing at least 2,500 whites and twice as many Indians. On the plains, most of the battles involved the Sioux, Cheyenne, Arapaho, Kiowa, and Comanche tribes. The Shoshone under Chief Washakie always remained peaceful. The final drama came in the 1870s, beginning with the discovery of gold in the Black Hills of Dakota Territory. A flood of miners overwhelmed attempts by the government to keep them out of Sioux territory, and negotiations to purchase the land bogged down when Red Cloud demanded a $600 million payment.

In 1876, General Sheridan led a three-pronged invasion to forcibly evict the Sioux from the Powder River region. He hadn't counted on two problems: the large numbers of Indians ready to do battle, and the rashness of junior officer Col. George A. Custer. At Little Big Horn on June 25, 1876, all 225 of Custer's men were wiped out by a combined force of Indians led by Crazy Horse, Sitting Bull, and others. This massive Indian victory quickly became the rallying cry for whites anxious to "solve" the Indian problem by forcing them onto reservations. Within five years, the last of the tribes had given up the fight. The uprising that led to the infamous Wounded Knee Massacre of 1890 was a last dying gasp in the attempt to regain land that had once all belonged to Native Americans.

Those who had lived in this land for centuries had been evicted by new peoples from another world. Chief Washakie of the Shoshones described the painfulness of this change (quoted in *Chief Washakie,* by Mae Urbanek):

> *The white man, who possesses this whole vast country from sea to sea, who roams over it at pleasure, and lives where he likes, cannot know the cramp we feel in this little spot, with the undying remembrance of the fact, which you know as well as we, that every foot of what you proudly call America, not very long ago belonged to the red man. The Great Spirit gave it to us. There was room enough for all his many tribes, and all were happy in their freedom. But the white man had, in ways we know not of, superior tools and terrible weapons, better for war than bows and arrows; and there seemed no end to the hordes of men that followed them from other lands beyond the sea. And so, at last, our fathers were steadily driven out, or killed, and we, their sons, but sorry remnants of tribes once mighty, are cornered in little spots of the earth all ours of right—cornered like guilty prisoners, and watched by men with guns, who are more than anxious to kill us off.*

TRAPPERS AND EXPLORERS

The first Europeans to explore Wyoming were in a party of Frenchmen led by François and Louis-Joseph Verendrye, who crossed northern Wyoming in 1743. During the winter of 1807-08, John Colter—a trapper and former guide for the Lewis and Clark Expedition—explored northwestern Wyoming in an attempt to develop the fur trade with Crow Indians. Colter was soon followed by other trappers in search of beavers. It was a hazardous business, with the constant threat of Indian attacks and the many natural hazards such as angry grizzlies, disease, and injuries. Help was hundreds of miles away. The era of the mountain-man lasted only until 1840, when demand for the furs plummeted, but the trappers' knowledge of the terrain proved invaluable. Many became guides for civilian and military expeditions, wealthy hunters, and government explorations of the West. The mountain passes they found (or, more likely, had been shown by Indians) provided a route for the exodus westward in the 1850s.

THE OREGON TRAIL

> *When God made man,*
> *He seemed to think it best*
> *To make him in the East*
> *And let him travel West.*
>
> —*FROM AN OREGON TRAIL PIONEER'S DIARY*

To 19th-century emigrants the Oregon Trail represented perhaps the best example of "Manifest Destiny"—the idea of an American nation reaching from the Atlantic to the Pacific. The Oregon Trail is actually a general term used to describe a whole series of wagon roads that headed west from Missouri. At different times, and over various paths, this route encompassed the Oregon Trail (to both Oregon and Washington), the California Trail (to the gold fields), the Mormon Trail (to Salt Lake City), and the short-lived Pony Express route. To emigrants it was not a trail but always "The Road."

Wyoming contains the least-changed and longest stretch (487 miles) of the Oregon Trail. From eastern Wyoming, the trail—actually a series of braided paths spreading across the river valleys—followed the North Platte and Sweetwater Rivers upstream to the Continental Divide at South Pass. Travelers chose this route because of abundant forage for stock, good water, and a gentle grade over the divide. As the only route that met all three criteria, the Oregon Trail became a national thoroughfare to the Promised Land of the West.

"Oregon Country" was not simply the area that would become the state of Oregon, but the entire region west of South Pass. Thus, the hills just beyond the Continental Divide in Wyoming became the "Oregon Buttes," and emigrants wrote of entering Oregon as they crossed the pass: "Today we entered Oregon. . . . We nooned beyond at a small spring and drank the waters of the Pacific!" (The vast land collectively called Oregon actually belonged to the British, but this legal nicety was quickly pushed aside by the influx of Americans.) West of South Pass, the route divided at the "Parting of the Ways." California- and Utah-bound travelers turned south to Fort Bridger, while those en route to Oregon and Washington headed due west on the Sublette or Lander Cutoffs.

Origins

Americans emigrated west for a number of reasons: to escape a severe economic depression in the East and falling crop prices, to get out of the crowded and polluted cities, to find religious freedom in Utah, to search for gold in the mountains of California, or simply to join in a great adventure in a new and undiscovered land. (More than a few also headed west to get away from debts or the law.) The first whites to cross the Continental Divide on what would become the Oregon Trail were a party of fur trappers known as the Astorians. They rode horses over South Pass in 1812, but it was not until a decade later that trappers really moved deeply into this country. The first freight wagons rolled over the pass in 1830, en route to a mountain-man rendezvous on the Green River. By the early 1840s, emigration westward was getting easier and more inviting. Fort Laramie, in eastern Wyoming, and Fort Bridger, in southwestern Wyoming, provided valuable way stations where travelers could rest up, repair their wagons, trade worn-out stock for fresh animals, and purchase food, whiskey, and supplies.

The turning point in the history of the Oregon Trail came in 1843, when the Applegate Wagon Train left Independence, Missouri, with 875 people, 120 wagons, and 5,000 head of livestock. It was the largest wagon train ever assembled. Under the leadership of Marcus Whitman (later killed in an Indian attack near present-day Walla Walla, Washington) and guided by mountain man Bill Sublette, the party made it all the way to the Columbia and Willamette Rivers by September. It had taken six long months to travel the 2,000 miles, but they had shown that the route was feasible. The gates of history had been cracked open, and they could never be closed again. Soon, the trickle westward turned into a flood tide.

Rolling West

Most travelers tried to depart Independence or St. Joseph, Missouri, in the spring, leaving as soon as the grass would support their stock. Typically, each evening found the emigrant just 15 miles farther down the trail, and it generally took five or six months to travel from Missouri to California or Oregon. They had to be over the mountains before the first snows of winter struck, and those who erred—such as the infamous Donner Party of 1846—paid a high price.

Emigrants were forced to travel as light as possible to lessen the burden on oxen. Some traders grew rich on the castoffs from overburdened wagon trains, while others profited by operating toll bridges and ferries across the North Platte and Green Rivers. (Toll at the Green River crossing was sometimes an amazing $16 per wagon!) Guidebooks—there were several; this was a big business even in the 19th century—described the crossings and camping places and suggested provisions for the 2,000-mile journey. A wagon, harness, and eight oxen cost travelers around $400.

Because of the scarcity of wood, Oregon Trail travelers used dry grass, sagebrush, or buffalo chips for fuel. Meals were simple but hearty, often consisting of a few staples plus whatever game might be found along the trail. Today, when you drive across the state it is easy to see how trying an experience this must have been for the emigrants—gale-force winds, dust, and lightning combine with the parched ground, the deceptively long distances, and the lack of shade. Wyoming can be a harsh and unforgiving land; it is not a place to wander into unprepared. The words of a 17-year-old emigrant, Eliza Ann McAuley, are typical of the Oregon Trail experience in Wyoming. On July 4, 1852, she wrote:

Four miles brought us to the forks of the Salt Lake and California roads. We took the Sublett cut-off, leaving Salt Lake to the south. Made eighteen miles today and camped on Big Sandy. Had to drive the cattle about six miles toward the hills for grass. It had been so windy and dusty today that some times we could scarcely see the length of the team, and it blows so tonight that we cannot set the tent or get any supper, so we take a cold bite and go to bed in the wagons. The wagons are anchored by driving stakes in the ground and fastening the wagon wheels to them with ox chains. . . .

Perhaps a tenth of the people who set out on the Oregon Trail never made it to their destination, and fellow travelers noted in their diaries the disturbing presence of graves—sometimes every 80 yards. Many died from diseases such as cholera, or from accidents and drownings; others were killed by early winter storms and Indian attacks. Few of the graves are marked.

At the peak of migration in 1850—when California gold fever had struck America—some 55,000 men, women, and children pressed their way across the plains and mountains. One of the lesser-known facts was the two-way nature of the route; in 1851 vast numbers of disillusioned miners headed back east the same way they had come the previous years. The route was also heavily used in both directions by Mormon emigrants to Utah, many of whom returned east for supplies or to guide family members left behind. In addition, stagecoach and freighting operations, along with a limited mail service, were established by 1852, operating in both directions.

It is easy to imagine the impact these wagons had with their thousands of cattle, horses, and mules. The grass quickly became overgrazed under this onslaught, and the already-scarce water badly polluted around popular campsites. Late-summer travelers were forced to range far and wide for better conditions, creating even more paths. The Indians who had lived here were shocked by the magnitude of the migration and began to realize not just what the whites were doing to their buffalo, but also how overwhelmed the native peoples would be by the newcomers. (The entire Plains Indian population probably numbered 40,000 individuals at its peak, and disease and war greatly reduced these numbers.) Indian attacks on Oregon Trail travelers were quite rare, and only 350 emigrants are known to have been killed by Indians. The biggest battles between Indians and Anglos came in 1865, more than a dozen years after the peak of westward travel on the Oregon Trail.

Finale

By 1870, perhaps 350,000 people had traveled across Wyoming by wagon train, stagecoach, horseback, and foot. It was the greatest peacetime migration in history. For most of them, this country seemed a worthless stretch of sagebrush and a barrier to the green lands farther west. It took the railroad to change this. Completion of the transcontinental railroad in 1869 turned the Oregon Trail into an anachronism. Suddenly one could cross the nation in relative comfort and in days instead of months. The trail continued to be used by freighters and some pioneers even as late as the turn of the 20th century, but the vast majority of travelers turned to rail travel. An era had ended.

The Trail Today

It has been well over 150 years since the first wagon train traveled along the Oregon Trail, but the mystique of the "great migration" continues to draw people from around the world. Much of the trail cuts across publicly owned land, and the tracks are readily visible in many places even after a century and a half. Explorers still discover artifacts strewn along the way. Visitors to Wyoming will enjoy delving into this rich past at such places as Fort Laramie, Oregon Trail Ruts, Register Cliff, Fort Caspar, Independence Rock, Devil's Gate, South Pass, Names Hill, and Fort Bridger. Hundreds of other lesser sights line the route, from the remains of old trading posts to countless emigrant graves. Portions of the Oregon Trail are described in greater detail in the Southeast, Central, Wind River Mountains, and Southwest chapters of this book. See Outdoor Recreation later in this chapter for descriptions of companies that lead Oregon Trail wagon-train treks.

THE PONY EXPRESS

On April 3, 1860, a lone rider galloped westward from the town of St. Joseph, Missouri. Nearly 2,000 miles away, another rider left the booming city of San Francisco, heading east. One of the most celebrated passages in American history had begun. Although it only lasted 18 months and was a financial disaster, the Pony Express caught the national imagination, proved that rapid mail service was possible even in the winter, and helped keep California in the Union.

The Pony Express was the brainchild of William H. Russell, one of the great wheelers and dealers of the late 19th century and director of the Central Overland California & Pike's Peak Express Company. Russell, along with partners Alexander Majors and William Bradford Waddell, managed the largest freighting company in the West, a business that at one time owned 50,000 oxen for its 3,500 wagons and employed 4,000 workers.

In 1855, the firm of Russell, Majors, & Waddell secured a monopoly to supply all U.S. government military posts west of the Missouri River. Because of Mormon raids on the supply wagons and the failure of the War Department to pay the company for its services, it was soon in financial trouble. To escape, the company needed the contract for mail service between California and St. Louis, a route then held by the Butterfield Overland Mail Company. Butterfield's route took mail along a circuitous 25-day trek through Texas and Arizona into southern California. With the nation slipping rapidly toward the Civil War—and Texas on the side of the South—there were fears that mail service would be halted and that California might join the Confederacy.

PONY EXPRESSIONS

We had had a consuming desire from the beginning, to see a pony-rider, but somehow or other all that passed us and all that met us managed to streak by in the night, and so we heard only a whiz and a hail, and the swift phantom of the desert was gone before we could get our heads out of the windows. But now we were expecting one along every moment, and would see him in broad daylight. Presently the driver exclaims: "HERE HE COMES!"

Every neck is stretched further, and every eye strained wider. Away across the endless dead level of the prairie a black speck appears against the sky, and it is plain that it moves. Well, I should think so! In a second or two it becomes a horse and rider, rising and falling, rising and falling—sweeping toward us nearer and nearer—growing more and more distinct, more and more sharply defined—nearer and still nearer, and the flutter of the hoofs comes faintly to the ear—another instant a whoop and a hurrah from our upper deck, a wave of the rider's hand, but no reply, and man and horse burst past our excited faces, and go winging away like a belated fragment of a storm!

So sudden is it all, and so like a flash of unreal fancy, that for the flake of white foam left quivering and perishing on a mail-sack after the vision had flashed by and disappeared, we might have doubted whether we had seen any actual horse and man at all, maybe.

—Mark Twain in *Roughing It*

Express Mail

In 1859, the postmaster general signed a contract with Russell, Majors, & Waddell to operate coaches and horses along the central route to California. The Pony Express was born as a flamboyant symbol of the superiority of this route. Experienced young horsemen, some as young as 14 and none weighing more than 120 pounds, would ride the finest horses at a full gallop, carrying telegrams and mail through some of the most desolate land on earth. The trip was to take just 10 days.

Each horse had four mail pouches sewn into a leather *mochilla,* which could be easily transferred between horses. (At $7.50 per half ounce, Pony Express mail was primarily urgent messages and newspapers.) Riders changed horses at relay stations—crude huts with station keepers and stock tenders—every 10 to 15 miles, continuing on for 75-100 miles before passing the precious package to another rider. After a short break, the rider would speed back to his home station with mail headed in the opposite direction. The whole operation required a military precision to keep the 119 relay and home stations stocked, make sure the horses were in good condition, and guard against attack. For their work, riders received $120 per month (including room and board).

The Demise

The threat of Indian hostilities became real when Nevada Piutes, angry after decades of abuse and the theft of their land, began attacking white settlements, killing 16 of the men working at the relay stations, taking 150 horses, and burning seven stations. A full-scale war was avoided, but it took more than a month to get the Express back into operation, at a cost of $75,000. Already a money loser, this helped ensure the collapse of the Pony Express. But it was not just money that brought down the Pony Express. Completion of the first continental telegraph line on October 24, 1861, also contributed; its mission replaced by a much more rapid means of communication, the Pony Express ended just two days later. Riders had delivered 34,753 pieces of mail, losing only one *mochilla* (both horse and rider were killed) in 616 cross-country runs.

The Final Chapter

The story of the Central Overland California & Pike's Peak Express Company does not end here. By late 1860, a year before the Pony Express ceased operations, Russell, Majors, &

Waddell's firm already teetered on the verge of bankruptcy (its employees nicknamed it "Clean Out of Cash and Poor Pay"). To stave this off, William Russell met with a clerk in the U.S. Dept. of the Interior and received $150,000 in bonds belonging to the Indian Trust Fund. Russell collected more than $870,000 in illegal government funds before being caught.

The whole house of cards came tumbling down when partner Alexander Majors declared bankruptcy and Russell's partner in crime, Godard Bailey, confessed. Russell spent Christmas of 1860 in prison, but he somehow managed to escape prosecution and he never repaid the money. With the start of the Civil War, Congress had greater concerns. In 1861, a joint agreement moved all western mail delivery to the central route, combining the forces of Butterfield's Overland Mail Company with the remnants of the Russell, Majors, & Waddell firm to avoid travel through the Confederate states. Later, Ben Holladay bought up the bankrupt firm and transformed it into the Overland Stage Line. Both Russell and Waddell died poor men. Years later, one of the Pony Express riders, "Buffalo Bill" Cody, found Alexander Majors living in a tiny Denver shack. In a gesture typical of him, Cody put Majors on a cash retainer for the rest of his life.

THE OVERLAND TRAIL

Lesser known and shorter lived than the Oregon Trail, the Overland Trail was established by Ben Holladay, owner of the Overland Stage Company. Although the Oregon Trail had served for many years as the primary route west, by the 1860s a need was developing for a new path. Increasing Indian attacks made the Oregon Trail dangerous, and the rapidly growing mining town of Denver was too far away. After Holladay was given the contract to deliver mail to the West, he quickly rerouted travel along a trail originally scouted by Jim Bridger.

The new route proved 60 miles shorter than the Oregon Trail, but it passed directly through the difficult desert country of western Wyoming rather than along the relatively lush North Platte and Sweetwater Rivers. Holladay established stage stations for changing teams every 10-15 miles, and built home stations where travelers could stop for meals or lodging every 50 miles.

WYOMING STATE MUSEUM

railroad building on the Great Plains, from Harpers Weekly, *1875*

Conditions at these relay stations were primitive at best; one traveler described southwestern Wyoming's Sand Springs station as "roofless and chairless, filthy and squalid, with a smoky fire in one corner, and a table in the center of an impure floor, the walls open to every wind and the interior full of dust." But the stations were better than sitting outside in the blazing hot sun or the bitter winter winds.

The stages covered 100-125 miles in a 24-hour period but were extraordinarily expensive for the time: $500 from Atchison, Kansas, to San Francisco. Still, emigrants began using the new route instead of the Oregon Trail; in a single year (1864), some 17,584 men, women, and children used the Overland Trail, along with 50,000 head of livestock and 4,264 wagons.

Although the new route remained relatively free from attacks for several years, the 1865 Sand Creek Massacre sent Indians on the warpath throughout the plains. Stage stations were destroyed, stagecoaches were attacked, and many died on both sides. The attacks continued sporadically for the next two years. With completion of the transcontinental railroad in 1869, the Overland Stage rapidly faded in importance, and stagecoach service ended. The old Overland Trail continued to be used by wagons until the turn of the 20th century.

CONNECTING THE COASTS

More than any other event, the completion of the transcontinental railroad led to the settlement and development of Wyoming. Most of its major towns and cities originated along the railroad lines. Not only did the railroad bring Wyoming within a couple of days of either coast, but it also led to the opening of coal mines to fuel the engines, hastened development of the logging industry (for railroad ties and mine props), and made it easy to ship cattle to market. Settlers could order most anything—Sears Roebuck even shipped prefabricated houses that filled two boxcars. It was no coincidence that Wyoming became a territory just as the railroad was being pushed across its southern border. An enduring impact from the railroad is a checkerboard pattern of public and private land ownership along the Union Pacific's route across Wyoming.

Surveying the Route

The Union Pacific's route was planned by Gen. Grenville M. Dodge, a veteran of battles with the Sioux in the Powder River country. The traditional Oregon Trail route ran too close to Sioux country, was too far from the gold-mining city of Denver, and didn't have the rich coal deposits of southwestern Wyoming. The course Dodge chose headed almost straight across southern Wyoming, climbing the Laramie Mountains west of Cheyenne, then cutting through the Laramie Plains and the Red Desert before winding across the mountains of eastern Utah.

Despite Dodge's efforts to avoid direct confrontation with the Indians, and the government's diversionary tactic of building the Bozeman Trail through the Powder River country, the Arapaho did not take kindly to the presence of railroad surveying and construction parties in their traditional hunting grounds. They pulled up survey stakes, stole horses, and killed surveyors and loggers, forcing Dodge to request military escorts. Three forts (Russell, Sanders, and Steele) were built in Wyoming to house these troops.

Working on the Railroad

To span the continent, the Union Pacific headed west from Omaha, while the Central Pacific worked east from Sacramento. By July 1867 tracklayers had reached the main division point, which would become Cheyenne, and headed on west to found Laramie, Rawlins, Green River, and Evanston. Most of the Central Pacific's workers were Chinese contract laborers, while those on the Union Pacific were a mixture of Americans and emigrants, especially Irishmen. Great competition grew between the two groups, and a record was set as the tracklayers worked across the searing heat of Wyoming's Red Desert: the men laid seven and a half miles of track in a single day. Laborers were paid an extraordinary $2.50 an hour, but the work was equally dangerous; some estimate that the transcontinental railroad was built at the cost of 10 men's lives per mile of track! Many were buried right in the roadbed. The tracklayers finally pushed their way into Utah and met workers of the Central Pacific at Promontory Point on May 10, 1869.

The railroad brought with it a gang of men who seemed to thrive on corruption, thievery, prostitution, gambling, drunkenness, and murder. As construction moved westward, temporary towns sprang up along the way; many were gone as soon as the tracks were out of sight. The entire procession of construction workers and hangers-on quickly became known as Hell-on-Wheels.

Worst of the temporary frontier towns was Benton, a few miles east of present-day Rawlins. Those who passed through called it "nearer a repetition of Sodom and Gomorrah than any other place in America" and a "congregation of scum and wickedness . . . by day disgusting, by night dangerous." There was no grass, little water, and the alkali dust stood eight inches deep. Murders were a nightly affair at the 25 saloons and five dance halls. The big attraction was gambling, with hundreds of men crowding the big tent each evening, paying for whiskey, dance-hall girls, or roulette wheels. Before the short-lived settlement could disappear in the alkali dust—just three months after its founding—more than 100 men lay buried in boot hill.

Newspaper reporter James Chisholm described these men in less than appealing terms:

> *I often speculate on what will finally become of all that rolling scum which the locomotive seems to blow onward as it presses westward. Will they get blown clean off the continent at last into the Pacific Ocean? One is gradually surrounded by the same faces in each successive town, the same gamblers, the same musicians playing the same old tunes to the same old dance, the same females getting always a little more dilapidated. As the excitement dies out of one town, and the railroad leaves it behind in a kind of exhausted repose, these old familiar faces die out to reappear in a new state of existence.*

A rolling newspaper press tagged along with the flotsam and jetsam across Wyoming, printing the weekly *Frontier Index* in each new camp. Its editor, Legh Freeman, angered the primarily northern-born workers by constantly showing his support for the Confederacy; he once labeled Gen. Ulysses Grant "the whiskey bloated, squaw ravishing adulterer, nigger worshipping mogul rejoicing over his election to the presidency." In Bear River City (long gone but near present-day Evanston), Freeman made the mistake of suggesting that several accused murderers then in jail should meet up with Judge Lynch. After a gang of vigilantes followed his suggestion by throwing a necktie party for the three, other ruffians destroyed the *Frontier Index* office and chased its editor out of town.

STATEHOOD

Because of its difficult climate, a paucity of good agricultural lands, and the lack of major deposits of gold, Wyoming was one of the last states to be settled. At various times, portions of Wyoming were parts of Indian country, Mexico, Louisiana, Missouri, Texas, Nebraska, Dakota, Idaho, Oregon, and Utah. In 1868, the Wyoming Territory was carved out of the Dakota Territory, a move primarily intended to keep the Democratic voters building the Union Pacific Railroad from overwhelming the Republican power base in distant Yankton. The folks out west were equally happy

the state capitol in Cheyenne

BILL NYE ON WOMEN'S SUFFRAGE

There have been many reasons given, first and last, why women should not vote, but I desire to say, in the full light of a ripe experience, that some of them are fallacious. I refer more particularly to the argument that it will degrade women to go to the polls and vote like a little man. While I am not and have never been a howler for female suffrage, I must admit that it is much more of a success than prohibition and speculative science. . . . In Wyoming, where female suffrage has raged for years, you meet quiet, courteous and gallant gentlemen, and fair, quiet, sensible women at the polls, where there isn't a loud or profane word, and where it is an infinitely more proper place to send a young lady unescorted than to the post office in any city in the Union. . . . All these things look hopeful. We can't tell what the Territory would have been without female suffrage, but when they begin to hang men by law instead of by moonlight, the future begins to brighten up. When you have to get up in the night to hang a man every little while and don't get any per diem for it, you feel as though you were a good way from home.

—19TH-CENTURY HUMORIST
BILL NYE

to gain independence from such a tenuous governmental link. It was not until May 19, 1869, that an organized government was established in the new territory. The first census of Wyoming, in 1870, found just 9,000 people (Indians were not counted).

The word "Wyoming" comes from the Leni Lanape Indians of Pennsylvania; their word "mecheweami-ing" meant "at the Great Plains." The term was first applied to the land that would become Wyoming in 1865, when Ohio's J.M. Ashley introduced a bill to form a "temporary government for the territory of Wyoming." Newspaper editor Legh Freeman has been credited with popularizing the name and having it inserted in the bill that created the Wyoming Territory in 1868.

A triumvirate of politicians—Francis E. Warren, John B. Kendrick, and Joseph M. Carey—governed Wyoming for much of its first half century. Carey, a Republican turned Democrat, was a founder of both the powerful Wyoming Stock Growers Association and the Cheyenne Club. He was a strong proponent of Wyoming statehood and introduced the enabling legislation in the U.S. House. During the debate, he claimed a Wyoming population of something over 110,000 people, an exaggeration that helped sway enough House votes to pass the measure. (The next year, the U.S. census found just 62,555 people in Wyoming.) The act was signed into law by Pres. Benjamin Harrison on July 10, 1890, making Wyoming the 44th state. Interestingly, this was the same year that the director of the U.S. Census Bureau declared that the "frontier of settlement" was no more.

The Equality State

Wyoming's first territorial legislature passed an act granting women the right to vote. The measure was signed into law by Gov. J.A. Campbell on Dec. 10, 1869, making this the first government in the world to grant women the right to vote. (Technically, Wyoming was not the first state to allow women suffrage; New Jersey widows already had limited voting rights.) The name "Equality State" comes from this bold step. It would be another 50 years before the 19th Amendment was finally passed, giving all women in America the right to vote. Not everyone looked upon women's suffrage as such a good step. In 1871, Democrats in the second territorial legislature repealed the measure, then came within one vote of overriding Governor Campbell's veto.

When the territory of Wyoming was seeking admission to the Union in 1890, the issue of giving women the right to vote—a measure included in Wyoming's new constitution—became a hotly contested topic. Alabama's Sen. John T. Morgan led the fight against admitting the new state, with the argument that the other half of the population would be polluted by politicians (such as himself?): "It is the immoral influences of the ballot upon women that I deprecate and would avoid. I do not want to see her drawn in contact with the rude things of this world where the delicacy of her senses and sensitivities would be constantly wounded by the attrition with bad and desperate and foul politicians and men."

Wyoming's status as the home of equal rights took another big step in 1925 after the death of Gov. William B. Ross. His wife, Nellie Tayloe Ross, was nominated to replace him and won the special election on a sympathy vote. She made no effort to get elected, noting, "I shall not make a campaign. My candidacy is in the hands of my friends. I shall not leave the house." She served ably as the nation's first woman governor and achieved considerable national attention. Despite a good record, Ross lost her bid for re-election, primarily because she was a Democrat in a heavily Republican state. In 1933, President Roosevelt appointed her as director of the U.S. Mint, a title she held for the next 20 years. She died in 1967 at the age of 101.

CATTLE COUNTRY

Hardly had the thunder of the Sioux ponies, along the Powder, the thunder of the cavalry died down, when over the southern horizon came a new army. An army of tossing horns, white in the sun; of lithe young men lolling in their saddles; riding at point, on the flanks, on the drag. The Cowboy was coming to Wyoming.

—STRUTHERS BURT IN
POWDER RIVER LET 'ER BUCK

Opening the Range

Once the bison herds had been devastated and the Indians evicted, cattlemen found what seemed like a Garden of Eden in Wyoming: land, grass, and water were essentially free for the taking. The cattle industry began innocently enough. In December 1863, Tom Alsop was returning to Omaha with a train of 50 wagons when a snowstorm pinned them down near present-day Cheyenne. Alsop abandoned the oxen and wagons on the plains and led his men safely home on horseback. The following spring, they rode back to recover the freight and were startled to discover that the cattle they had left to die of exposure had not only survived the winter but were thriving. The discovery soon attracted droves of ranchers.

The first cattle drive through Wyoming came in 1866, when a Montana merchant named Nelson Story decided that what the Virginia City miners needed was fresh beef. Heading south to Kansas with $10,000 sewn in the lining of his clothes, he filled a wagon with supplies, bought 3,000 Texas longhorns, hired 27 cowboys, gave them the finest Remington breech-loading rifles, and headed north for the gold fields. At Fort Kearny (see Sheridan Vicinity in the Powder River Country chapter for more on this notorious fort), Colonel Carrington forbade them from continuing north through Sioux country since they did not have the required 40 armed guards. (Some feel that Carrington actually hoped to requisition the cattle for his men; most of the army's had already been stolen.) In response, an angry Story thumbed his nose at the government, heading north under cover of darkness. Discovering his departure, Carrington was forced to cave in, sending 15 soldiers along to bring Story's force up to the legal minimum. Although one man died, the rest of the men and cattle made it to Virginia City on December 9. Nelson Story had gained himself a place in history.

Millions of cattle headed into or through Wyoming in the 1870s and 1880s. Ranching looked like a can't-lose business; dump a couple thousand head of cows and calves on the range in spring and return a year later to round them up for market. What could be simpler? Investors from Omaha, New York, England, Scotland, and France quickly took note of the potential fortunes to be made.

By 1883, English and Scottish investors had poured some £6 million into Wyoming cattle and had turned Cheyenne into a country club for the European gentry. Some were more gullible than others; stories are still told of an Englishman who watched as the cattle he was buying were driven by to be counted, not noticing that the same cattle had come around the hill a couple of times before. The use of "book counts" also inflated the value of the herds; frequently, nobody

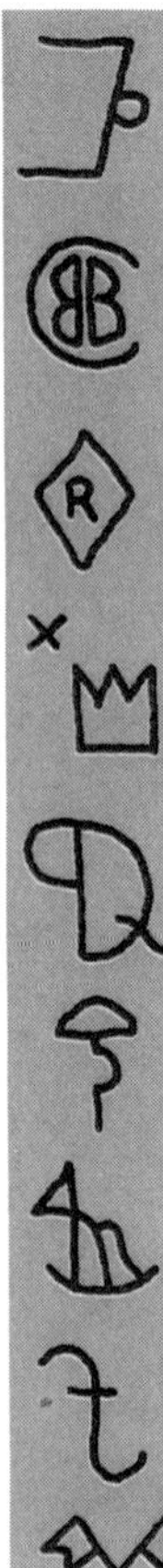

BRANDS

Branding dates back to the Egyptian pharaohs, who branded not only their cattle, camels, and donkeys, but even their slaves. Slave branding was also practiced in America. The American tradition of cattle branding comes down from the Spanish conquistadors and their vaqueros but was adapted for use on the spacious western plains. Because there were no fences, cattle belonging to various ranchers became intermixed, leading to inevitable questions of ownership, which brands helped answer.

Brands appear almost anywhere on an animal, and a given ranch may have a half dozen or more for its cattle, sheep, and horses. An individual animal often has several different brands or marks. To make them easier to identify on the hoof, cattle are frequently distinctively marked by cutting a notch in the ear, slicing the skin that hangs under the cow's throat (the dewlap), or hacking a flap of hide (a wattle) so that it hangs loose from the neck.

In Wyoming, having a brand is something of a status symbol, and the Wyoming Brand Book lists more than 27,000 currently in use (one for every 17 residents!). Not everyone who has a brand has stock; some are simply used for mailbox decorations on suburban ranchettes. The more complex ones aren't likely to appear on any cows since they become illegible as the scar heals. Brands that are hard to alter or of historic significance may sell for more than $5,000. Coming up with a design for a new brand can be a problem, since the state looks askance on brands that resemble others in the same area or that might be easily altered by rustlers (they still exist). One 19th-century rancher, fed up with having his brand suggestions rejected, wrote the brand department, demanding, "Send me a brand P.D.Q." They complied by giving him the brand PDQ. Reading brands is an art gained by years of experience. They are read from left to right, top to bottom, and outside to inside.

Branding usually takes place in the spring, before cattle and calves are driven into the higher pastures or set loose on the plains. A branding iron is heated to a dull red in a fire and then pressed against the calf as it is held down. Freeze branding is also often used. Most male calves are castrated at the same time.

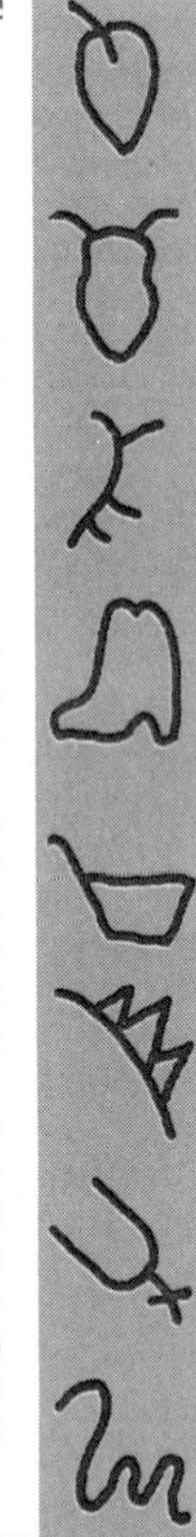

bothered to make sure that numbers in the books equaled cattle on the range. The aristocrats were regarded with a mixture of humor and disdain by the hardened cowboys whose every other utterance was a swear word. One British lord rode up to a cowboy in his buggy, asking, "My good man, could you tell me where your master is?" The cowboy glowered back, spat out his tobacco, and said, "The son-of-a-bitch ain't been born yet!"

During the early years of ranching in Wyoming, cattle were allowed to roam at will and were not sorted out until the annual roundups. Sounds fine in theory, but in practice a few flaws showed up, notably the problem of mavericks. The term maverick refers to an unbranded calf or cow of questionable ownership, or, as writer Struthers Burt put it, "A calf whose mamma has died and whose father has run off with another lady cow." Unbranded calves were generally divvied up among the ranchers on the basis of which herd they were with, but when herds became mixed together, conflicts were inevitable. In addition, multiple roundups meant that the first cowboys on the scene could pretty much decide for themselves which calves were theirs. Some even went so far as to slit the tongues of calves so they could no longer suckle and would not follow their mothers, thus becoming instant mavericks.

Cattle Barons and Rustlers

To curb the temptations for such "sooners," the powerful Wyoming Stock Growers Association—an organization dominated by the wealthiest of the cattlemen—gained the authority to dictate when roundups could be held. The organization dominated the political landscape of Wyoming for many years; by the 1880s, a third of the state legislature belonged to the association. The 1882 Maverick Bill gave the association control over all cattle roundups in the territory, with proceeds from the sales of mavericks going into the association's coffers. It could blacklist cowboys as "rustlers" on the basis of hearsay, and cattle shipped without the association's permission risked being impounded by inspectors in Chicago or Omaha. Even worse, ranchers suspected of rustling (which seemed to include anyone except members) were sometimes ambushed and murdered by enforcers, the most notorious of whom was Tom Horn. Whole regions of Wyoming were terrorized by the practice of dry-gulching, in which suspected rustlers would be shot from behind and left in an out-of-the-way gulch.

Meanwhile, the big cattlemen—commonly called cattle barons—also ran into trouble, especially in the Powder River country. The fierce winter of 1886-87 devastated their herds; some lost all their cattle, while others had just 20-30% of the numbers from the previous year. Big ranching outfits also found themselves hemmed in by homesteading settlers who fenced the land. Fences created a hazard, since cattle often moved with the winter winds until they hit the fences and then piled up there to die.

The big cattlemen accused these "nesters" not only of fencing the land, but also of taking stray cattle for themselves. Using a "long rope" and a "running iron," they could easily alter the brands and soon have their own herd. The cattle barons decided to put an end to this thievery once and for all with the infamous Johnson County War of 1892, but the campaign proved a complete fiasco. Two men died on each side in pitched battles between the "barons" and the "rustlers." Although the invaders managed to escape prosecution, the small nesters and rustlers had won the day. From that time on, the range would increasingly be fenced in.

SHEEP

History

Cattle arrived in most parts of Wyoming a decade or so before the first sheep munched their way across the grazing lands, but by 1902 the rangeland was crowded with close to six million sheep. Cattlemen considered the public land their own—by right of previous use—although legally it was all open range owned by the government. As competition increased, cattlemen declared "dead lines," across which no sheep would be allowed. Conflicts quickly erupted, and the single herder and his dogs proved no match for a gang of cattlemen on horseback. Herders were murdered throughout the state, and the violence escalated into the infamous Ten Sleep Raid of 1909 (see the special topic in the Bighorn Basin chapter), in which three sheepmen were brutally murdered. After this, things quieted down as the land became increasingly settled and government policies divided up the areas. Some cattlemen even turned to raising sheep, but animosity still remains between sheepmen and cattlemen in some areas.

Times have not always been easy for herders. Alfred Mokler in *History of Natrona County* describes one horrific night:

> *During a severe storm the latter part of March 1895, Noel R. Gascho was with a band of sheep on the open range. The band became unmanageable and drifted with*

the storm. Gascho went with the sheep, which was the only thing to do. The snow came down in blinding sheets, the cold wind swept over the bleak prairie and hundreds of the sheep were frozen. Gascho said it seemed as though the blood in his veins and the marrow in his bones were frozen. He became numb and sleepy and to keep awake he would stick his legs with a knife blade. About midnight he caught one of the sheep, cut its throat and drank the blood. Then he set fire to the wool on the dead sheep and the greasy wool burned readily. Before daylight, he had burned six sheep after he had cut their throats and drank of their blood. This was all that saved his life.

Sheepherding

Over the years, the number of sheep in Wyoming has steadily dropped; today there are around 660,000 at any given time. Sheep are generally moved up into the mountains each spring to graze in the high meadows and then brought back down in the fall. A long drive along country roads is a sight straight out of the history books. Sheep are sheared in spring, generally just before lambing season. By fall the lambs are big enough to send to market, and the ewes are bred.

A good number of the first sheepherders in Wyoming were from Europe's Basque region. Many preferred to take sheep instead of a salary and so gradually gained flocks of their own. The frugal ones eventually became ranch owners in their own right. The herding business has not changed much over the years, however, and herders still spend weeks at a time alone, seeing nobody but the camp mover when he arrives to help move the outfit to new feeding grounds. Today many herders are Mexican immigrants, although some Basque and American herders are still around. The herder's life is a simple and quiet one, with plenty of time for reflection. It takes someone with the right temperament to be a sheepherder.

The sheepherder's wagon—an early version of the RV—was invented by James Candlish, a Rawlins blacksmith, and later improved and marketed by Casper's Schulte Hardware Company. The design proved an efficient one, and herders still use the old wagons, though rubber tires have replaced wagon wheels and the roof is now tin instead of canvas. The layout is simple: a Dutch door opens into a small space filled with a bed at the back with drawers underneath and shelves above. A small woodstove near the entrance is used for both heating and cooking. Almost every Wyoming museum seems to have one tucked away in a corner, but many more are still in use on the lonely high plains.

ENERGY BOOM AND BUST

Wyoming's economy is heavily linked to the energy industry, with coal, oil, and gas all major employers. The state's first oil well was drilled in 1884, and by 1908—the year of the first oil boom—production approached 18,000 barrels per year. Production continued to climb over the decades, reaching a peak in 1970, when more than 155 million barrels were pumped. Since then, production has declined as older fields have become exhausted and low prices discourage further exploration. By 1998, production had fallen to 55 million barrels. The drop in oil production has been offset somewhat by dramatic increases in two other energy sources: natural gas and coal. Coal production has skyrocketed in the last decade, and natural gas is an increasing focus, particularly in the Powder River Basin where coalbed methane production is increasingly important.

In the 1970s and '80s, Wyoming rode an economic bucking bronco as oil prices shot up and then suddenly dove, throwing this energy-rich state out of the saddle. The Arab oil embargo of 1973 and subsequent price increases turned Wyoming upside down. Oil-patch towns—particularly Casper, Rock Springs, Evanston, and Green River—became madhouses of pickup trucks, heavily muscled oil workers, honky-tonk bars, strip joints, fast-food outlets, and trailer courts. Drugs, crime, prostitution, and gambling rippled across the state. The population of Rock Springs doubled in two years. In the heady rush of new workers and high-paying oil jobs, many towns embarked on ambitious construction projects such as schools and housing developments, while trailer parks sprouted up across the countryside. (Wyoming still holds top honors as the state with the highest percentage of mobile homes.)

This economic bubble collapsed with the sudden halving of oil prices in 1982, and Wyoming's population actually *dropped* by almost three percent during the 1980s. The hard-hit Douglas area lost 20% of its population between 1985 and 1990. The bust left many towns struggling to survive as unemployment skyrocketed, the state government was forced into consolidation mode, and local residents were saddled with a bloated set of facilities.

The inevitable booms and busts associated with the energy and mining industries will affect Wyoming for the foreseeable future, but growing numbers of tourism and service-sector jobs will help cushion the blows next time around. The money may not approach that of the $24-per-hour coal mining jobs, but at least a sales position at Wal-Mart pays the bills.

ECONOMY AND GOVERNMENT

Throughout the 1990s, Wyoming seemed in something of a holding pattern, with virtually no growth at a time when the national economy was expanding rapidly. The state population is growing slightly as more people are born than die, but more people are still moving out of than into Wyoming. This isn't to say that all is gloom and doom. In the Powder River Basin the economy is doing very well due to increasing coal mining and methane gas production, and tourism in edge-of-the-mountain towns such as Jackson is pushing economic growth at a breakneck speed.

Who Owns Wyoming?

Wyoming's economy is affected not only by private developments but also by the government. The federal government owns almost 47% of the land, while the state government holds another 10%—leaving 43% in private hands. The largest public land agency—the Bureau of Land Management (BLM)—owns nearly 18 million acres in Wyoming, but most of this exists in a checkerboard of small parcels with limited public access. The BLM manages only a few patches of wilderness scattered around Wyoming. The U.S. Forest Service has 8.7 million acres within nine national forests which cover the state's largest mountain ranges, and the National Park Service has another 2.3 million acres in five national parks, monuments, and recreation areas. Warren Air Force Base—the most important ICBM base in North America—is in Cheyenne and represents the state's only major military installation. The military also owns land in other parts of Wyoming today, notably the Camp Guernsey training area north of Wheatland and a Naval Petroleum Reserve at Teapot Dome.

Partly because of all this federal involvement, Wyoming residents are on the receiving end of generous federal monies; the state is second only to Alaska in per-capita federal aid. Interestingly, both states are also rich in oil and gas, have most of their land in federal ownership, are small in population, and suffered similar economic doldrums through the 1990s. You'll meet quite a few former Alaskans in Wyoming, and an equal number of former Wyomingites in Alaska. Coincidence?

WORKING FOR A LIVING

Oil and Gas

Wyoming's economy putters along on a mix of oil and gas extraction, coal and trona mining, cattle and sheep ranching, and tourism. Oil production—mainly in the Powder River and Bighorn Basins—has long been the most important, but it is increasingly being eclipsed by coal mining and natural gas production. Despite the decrease, some 1,000 Wyoming fields annually produce 55 million barrels of oil (sixth in the nation) and 800 million cubic feet of natural gas (sixth in the nation).

Coal

A quarter of the nation's coal reserves lie beneath Wyoming, and it is easily the largest coal-producing state, far outstripping (pun intended) runners-up West Virginia and Kentucky. Nearly all the over 300 million tons extracted each year comes from enormous open-pit mines, primarily in the Powder River Basin. With perhaps a *trillion* tons of coal still below the surface,

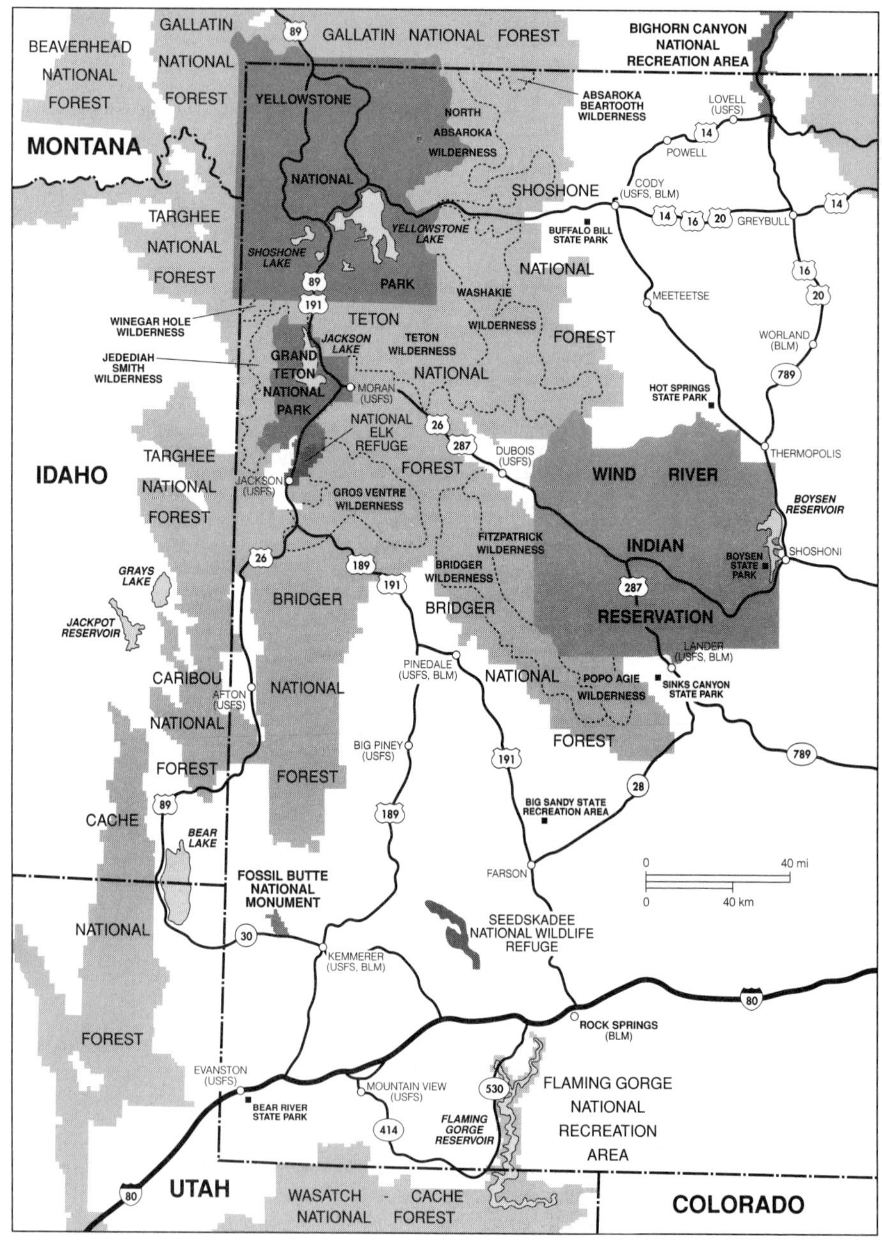

GALLATIN NATIONAL FOREST
BEAVERHEAD NATIONAL FOREST
GALLATIN NATIONAL FOREST
BIGHORN CANYON NATIONAL RECREATION AREA
MONTANA
YELLOWSTONE NATIONAL PARK
NORTH ABSAROKA WILDERNESS
ABSAROKA BEARTOOTH WILDERNESS
LOVELL (USFS)
POWELL
CODY (USFS, BLM)
SHOSHONE NATIONAL FOREST
GREYBULL
BUFFALO BILL STATE PARK
YELLOWSTONE LAKE
SHOSHONE LAKE
TARGHEE NATIONAL FOREST
WASHAKIE WILDERNESS
MEETEETSE
WORLAND (BLM)
WINEGAR HOLE WILDERNESS
JEDEDIAH SMITH WILDERNESS
JACKSON LAKE
GRAND TETON NATIONAL PARK
TETON WILDERNESS
TETON NATIONAL FOREST
MORAN (USFS)
HOT SPRINGS STATE PARK
NATIONAL ELK REFUGE
DUBOIS (USFS)
THERMOPOLIS
IDAHO
TARGHEE NATIONAL FOREST
JACKSON (USFS)
GROS VENTRE WILDERNESS
WIND RIVER INDIAN RESERVATION
BOYSEN RESERVOIR
FITZPATRICK WILDERNESS
BOYSEN STATE PARK
SHOSHONI
GRAYS LAKE
BRIDGER WILDERNESS
JACKPOT RESERVOIR
BRIDGER NATIONAL FOREST
LANDER (USFS, BLM)
PINEDALE (USFS, BLM)
CARIBOU NATIONAL FOREST
AFTON (USFS)
POPO AGIE WILDERNESS
SINKS CANYON STATE PARK
BIG PINEY (USFS)
BIG SANDY STATE RECREATION AREA
CACHE NATIONAL FOREST
BEAR LAKE
FOSSIL BUTTE NATIONAL MONUMENT
FARSON
0 40 mi
0 40 km
SEEDSKADEE NATIONAL WILDLIFE REFUGE
KEMMERER (USFS, BLM)
ROCK SPRINGS (BLM)
EVANSTON (USFS)
MOUNTAIN VIEW (USFS)
FLAMING GORGE NATIONAL RECREATION AREA
BEAR RIVER STATE PARK
FLAMING GORGE RESERVOIR
UTAH
WASATCH - CACHE NATIONAL FOREST
COLORADO
89 14 16 20 191 26 287 189 789 28 30 80 530 414

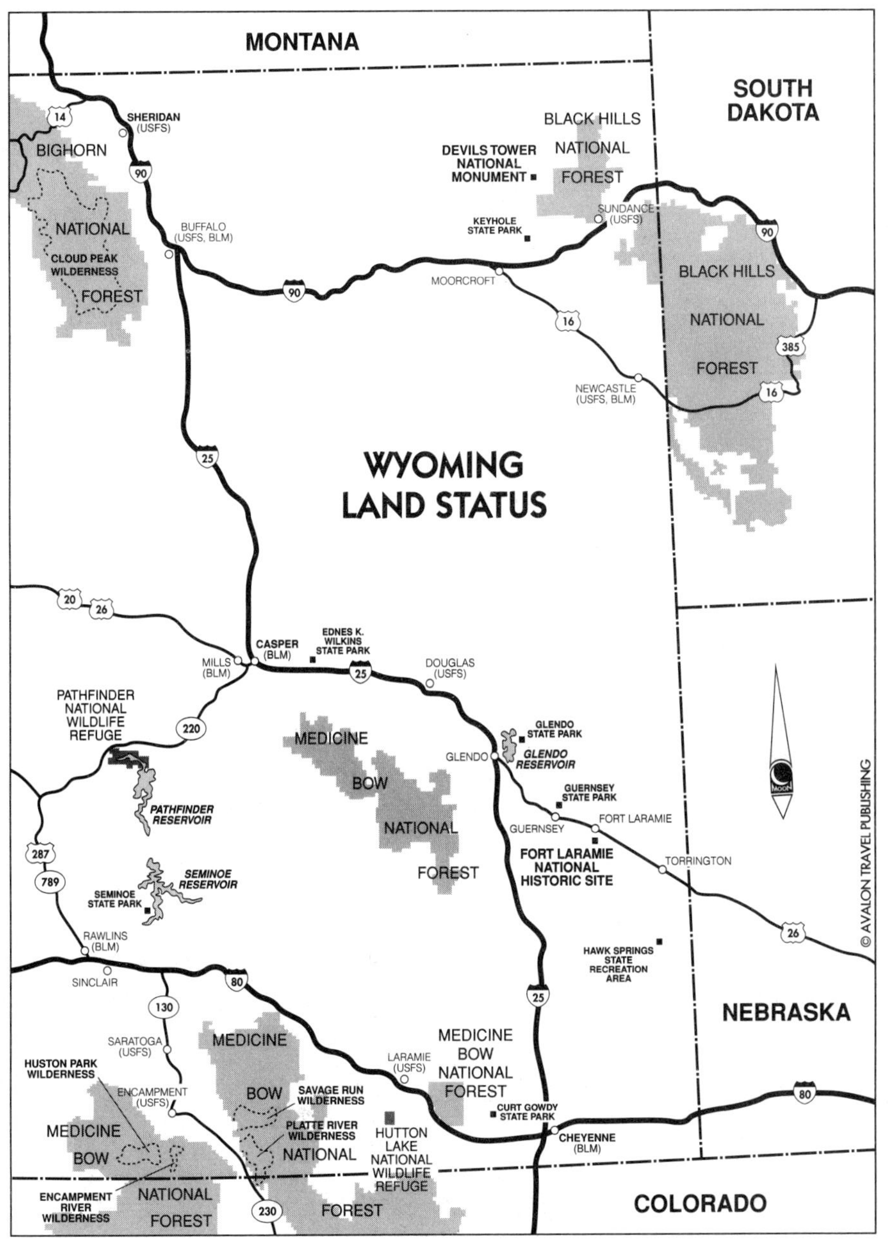
WYOMING
LAND STATUS
MONTANA
SOUTH DAKOTA
NEBRASKA
COLORADO
SHERIDAN (USFS)
BIGHORN NATIONAL FOREST
CLOUD PEAK WILDERNESS
BUFFALO (USFS, BLM)
BLACK HILLS NATIONAL FOREST
DEVILS TOWER NATIONAL MONUMENT
KEYHOLE STATE PARK
SUNDANCE (USFS)
MOORCROFT
NEWCASTLE (USFS, BLM)
CASPER (BLM)
MILLS (BLM)
EDNES K. WILKINS STATE PARK
DOUGLAS (USFS)
PATHFINDER NATIONAL WILDLIFE REFUGE
PATHFINDER RESERVOIR
SEMINOE RESERVOIR
SEMINOE STATE PARK
MEDICINE BOW NATIONAL FOREST
GLENDO STATE PARK
GLENDO
GLENDO RESERVOIR
GUERNSEY STATE PARK
GUERNSEY
FORT LARAMIE
FORT LARAMIE NATIONAL HISTORIC SITE
TORRINGTON
HAWK SPRINGS STATE RECREATION AREA
RAWLINS (BLM)
SINCLAIR
SARATOGA (USFS)
HUSTON PARK WILDERNESS
ENCAMPMENT (USFS)
ENCAMPMENT RIVER WILDERNESS
SAVAGE RUN WILDERNESS
PLATTE RIVER WILDERNESS
LARAMIE (USFS)
HUTTON LAKE NATIONAL WILDLIFE REFUGE
CURT GOWDY STATE PARK
CHEYENNE (BLM)
14
90
16
385
20
26
25
220
287
789
130
80
230
MOON
© AVALON TRAVEL PUBLISHING

WYOMING LINGO

Absaroka—Alternatively pronounced "ab-SOR-ka" or "ab-SOR-aka," the word means "People of the Large-beaked Bird" (hence the name of the Crow Indians, who lived here). The Absaroka Mountains lie east of Yellowstone National Park.

Arapaho—The word is often spelled Arapahoe. An Indian tribe of Algonquin stock originally living on the Canadian plains, the Northern Arapaho now reside on the Wind River Reservation. The name comes from a Crow Indian term meaning "Tattooed People." They call themselves simply "Our People."

bentonite—A special kind of clay that originates from volcanic ash, bentonite absorbs large amounts of water, increasing in volume by 30%. Bentonite is used in oil drilling, to line ponds, and even in candy bars. Wyoming is the nation's largest producer of this mineral.

booshway—the boss at a mountain-man rendezvous.

buck-and-rail fence—Consisting of X-shaped supports and connecting poles, this is the classic fence of Jackson Hole, where the soils proved too rocky for ranchers to dig postholes. The abundant lodgepole pines made fine fences. Today, buck-and-rail fences are built more for beauty than function, and they are becoming less and less common in an era of metal fence posts.

calcutta—the auctioning off of various rodeo teams or contestants; it's a popular way to wager on rodeo events. Rules vary.

cattle baron—a cattle owner with extensive holdings; primarily used during the heyday of the giant cattle spreads in the 1880s.

cattle guard—Although immediately obvious to most Westerners, cattle guards are virtually unknown on the East Coast. These wide metal grates are used where fence lines and roads meet; cattle and horses won't cross them but vehicles can do so easily.

chaps—pronounced "shaps"'; protective leather leg coverings, useful when riding horses through brush.

chiselers—ground squirrels, also called "ground cougars." The lemmings of Wyoming, they seem to delight in waiting till the last minute and then dashing toward car wheels. Lots of them get nailed on dirt roads all across the state.

coup—pronounced "coo"; a Plains Indian word that signified an act of great skill and daring, such as striking an enemy in the midst of a battle or performing some other deed of valor. "Counting coups" was similar to gaining today's military medals of honor. Those with many coups wore warbonnets with many feathers.

coyotes—Fans of these ubiquitous critters call them "ky-O-tees," while those who regard them as "varmints" tend to pronounce the word "KY-oats."

creek—Everyone knows what it is, but old-timers in Wyoming pronounce the word "crik."

dead line—a line established by turn-of-the-20th-century cattlemen who feared competition from sheep. Those herders who brought sheep across the imaginary line risked death and the destruction of their flocks.

dogger—a rodeo term used for steer wrestlers; it originated from Will Pickett, an early wrestler who threw steers to the ground by biting their lips in the manner of a bulldog. The name stuck, even though the lip-biting part didn't.

dogie—a motherless calf. A famous old cowboy poem begins:

As I walked out one morning for pleasure,
I spied a cowpuncher all riding alone;
His hat was throwed back and his spurs was a-jingling,
As he approached me a-singin' this song,

Whoopee ti yi yo, git along, little dogies,
It's your misfortune, and none of my own.
Whoopee ti yi yo, git along, little dogies,
For you know Wyoming will be your new home. . .

dog-trot—a type of log cabin common on old Wyoming ranches. Two cabins were connected by a breezeway, making a favorite place for dogs to hang out on hot summer days. This cabin style actually originated in the southern Appalachians.

dude—This is a term that has changed in meaning over the years. Writer Nathaniel Burt called the dude "any fancy-pants young man who wore a boutonniere and parted his hair in the middle." Later, the term came to mean a wealthy easterner vacationing on a western ranch, in contradistinction to "tourists," who were viewed as an inferior species. Today, Wyoming's many dude ranches are more proletarian. The wealthy elite generally prefer the term "guest ranches," which are really luxury resorts with a few horses thrown in.

emigrants—The dictionary defines emigrants as people who leave one place to settle elsewhere, in contrast to immigrants, who come into a new place. Guess it all depends on your perspective, but for some reason folks heading west on the Oregon Trail were almost always called emigrants, not immigrants.

hazer—a rodeo term used in steer wrestling. It refers to a cowboy who rides beside the steer to keep it in position for the dogger.

hog ranch—an establishment of ill repute where booze, gambling, and loose women were the primary attractions. The most famous were located near military forts in Wyoming, notably Fort Fetterman and Fort Laramie. The name is generally attributed to the appearance of the women, but may also refer to the tiny, squalid rooms where they plied their trade. Author David Lavender called them places offering "the poorest whiskey and women in the west."

hooey—a tie used in calf-roping events at rodeos. Three of the calf's feet are wrapped with a piggin' string and completed with a half hitch.

jackalope—an antlered jackrabbit found most commonly in the vicinity of Douglas, Wyoming, but proliferating throughout the West.

maverick—an unbranded cow or calf of questionable ownership. The term originated from Samuel Maverick, owner of a two-million-acre Texas ranch in the 1840s. Because many of his cattle were never branded, cowboys coming across unbranded cattle on the open range would joke that they were Maverick's. Eventually the term was applied to all unbranded cattle.

piggin' string—a short piece of rope used to tie a hooey around the feet of a roped calf or steer at a rodeo.

rendezvous—French for "appointed place of meeting." Between 1825 and 1840 the annual rendezvous was the big shindig for Rocky Mountain trappers, Indians, and traders. Modern-day versions try to re-create this trading and partying atmosphere.

runnin' iron—an improvised branding iron used by cattle rustlers.

rustler—a cattle thief or someone accused of taking cattle from the cattle barons; during the Johnson County War the term actually became a badge of honor in parts of Wyoming. "Packing a long rope" became the common term applied to folks who rustled.

sage hen—another name for the sage grouse, a common bird across Wyoming. This was also cowboy slang for women.

scoria—a red rock commonly used on Powder River Basin roads. It was formed when coal beds caught fire and burned underground, baking adjacent shale and sandstone to create a bright red slag. The red comes from iron oxide. Clinker is another term commonly used for scoria.

Shoshone—an Indian tribe on Wyoming's Wind River Reservation. The word is also frequently spelled Shoshoni, and it's generally pronounced with a long *e* at the end.

Sioux—The word was derived from a derogatory term meaning "enemy" or "snake" and used by the Chippewa Indians to describe the Indians who lived just to their west. The Sioux actually called themselves Dakota, meaning "alliance of friends."

trona—a mineral (sodium sesquicarbonate) used in glass, detergents, baking soda, and other products. It's mined in huge underground mines west of Green River.

varmint—any animal you don't like; especially used for prairie dogs, ground squirrels, and coyotes.

wapiti—pronounced WOP-a-tee. The Indian word for elk, it is occasionally used by biologists who consider it a more precise term.

Wyoming is one of the largest energy storehouses anywhere on the planet. Eight of the nation's 10 largest coal mines are in Wyoming, and the low-sulfur coal produced is shipped by train to utility companies in 29 different states.

Other Minerals

Vast deposits of trona (used primarily in glass and chemicals such as baking soda) occur in southwestern Wyoming, where mines produce 90% of the nation's supply. The state is also a major supplier of bentonite, helium, and sulfur. Uranium was once an important industry—a third of America's reserves lie in Wyoming—but since Three Mile Island, production has dropped to almost nothing.

Tourism

Well over four million people come to enjoy Wyoming's abundant recreational opportunities each year, and tourism contributes more than $1.3 billion annually to the economy. It is particularly important in northwestern Wyoming, where Yellowstone and Grand Teton National Parks and other attractions are creating a booming Jackson Hole economy (and astronomical land valuations). Smaller levels of growth are taking place in other near-the-mountain towns such as Cody, Sheridan, Buffalo, Laramie, Pinedale, Dubois, Lander, and Saratoga.

Agriculture

The state's most obvious industry, and the one that encompasses 90% of its land base, is agriculture. Surprisingly, however, grazing and farming employ less than six percent of the population. Wyoming is third in the nation in terms of sheep and lamb production and has 1.5 million cattle and calves. But it takes 30 acres to support a single cow (versus one acre per cow in parts of Nebraska!), which is why the average Wyoming farm is 3,761 acres—eight times the national average. Only four percent of the state is cultivated; primary crops are sugar beets, barley, alfalfa hay, wheat, oats, and dry beans. These are mainly grown within Bighorn Basin and Wind River Basin, and along Wyoming's eastern plains.

Other Economic Mainstays

The state has no truly large manufacturing plants, though every town has its own specialty. The services sector of the economy—from flipping burgers to running copy machines—is the unheralded source of real growth in Wyoming, though the wages are nothing to brag about.

For detailed Wyoming economic information, check the web at http://eadiv.state.wy.us.

POLITICS

During the campaign in those days there were always a great many "doubtful voters," and it sometimes required several quarts of liquor and an unlimited number of cigars to convince them.
—Alfred J. Mokler, describing the 1898 election campaign for Frank W. Mondell, running for U.S. Senate (he won)

Unlike in many states, where apathy reigns, Wyomingites take their right to vote seriously, with turnout during presidential election years sometimes topping 80% of registered voters. Wyoming has 64 elected state representatives (who serve two-year terms) and 30 state senators (elected for four-year terms). The elected statewide officials—governor, secretary of state, auditor, treasurer, and superintendent of public instruction—all stand for office every four years.

Republicans have controlled both houses of the legislature almost since statehood; Wyoming's congressional delegation has long been entirely Republican, and in 1994, for the first time in nearly two decades, Wyoming voted in a Republican governor, creating what is essentially a one-party government. Sierra Clubbers and other liberals might want to keep a low profile in most parts of Wyoming.

State Symbols

The Great Seal of the State of Wyoming is filled with symbolism. The two dates commemorate establishment of the territorial government (1869) and statehood (1890). The Roman numerals (XLIV) represent Wyoming as the 44th state to be admitted to the Union; the male figures represent the livestock and mining industries, while the central female figure stands for political equality. In early versions the woman was unclothed, but legislators quickly sensed the problems inherent in nudity on Wyoming's official emblem and rejected the design. After a swath of cloth made everything acceptable, the symbol was finally adopted by the state legislature in 1893. The state flag includes both this symbol and the outline of a bison.

Wyoming's best-known symbol is its bucking horse, a figure that has appeared on state license plates since 1936. The silhouette was created by artist Allen True of Denver and was reputedly inspired by the rodeo cowboy Albert "Stub" Farlow. The bucking horse insignia had been used earlier by Wyoming soldiers during WW I.

Despite jokes to the contrary, Wyoming's state tree is *not* the telephone pole! Wyoming has all kinds of other official designations: state flower (Indian paintbrush), bird (meadowlark), tree (plains cottonwood), stone (jade), mammal (bison), fossil (a fish called *knightia*), fish (cutthroat trout), and even a state dinosaur *(Triceratops).* The state nickname seems to suffer from a split personality, being both "Equality State" and "Cowboy State." (To be honest, this really isn't a contest; I'll be the first to tell you that in the hearts and minds of all true Wyomingites, it's the COWBOY STATE.)

DOVER PUBLICATIONS, INC.

ON THE ROAD

OUTDOOR RECREATION

Wyoming is famous for its great outdoors, with horizon-to-horizon vistas and an extraordinary variety of activities. The biggest attractions are Yellowstone and Grand Teton National Parks, but other National Park Service, U.S. Forest Service, Bureau of Land Management, and state park lands offer an array of adventures, from whitewater rafting to horseback riding to skiing.

Note that many popular Forest Service sites in Wyoming and elsewhere now charge a $2-3 fee for day-use access. Eighty percent of this money goes back to the maintenance of the area where it is collected, so you can at least be assured that it isn't being wasted on the salaries of Wyoming's congressional delegation.

FISHING AND HUNTING

Outstanding fishing opportunities abound throughout Wyoming, and a number of places—mostly in the Yellowstone area—have attained recognition as some of the finest in America. Cutthroat, brown, rainbow, brook, and lake trout are favorites of many anglers, but the state's waters also contain mountain whitefish, kokanee, grayling, channel catfish, smallmouth bass, largemouth bass, and others.

The Wyoming Game and Fish Dept. produces an excellent free *Wyoming Fishing Guide,* with descriptions of the various river drainages, what fish you can catch in each, state record fish, and basic information on techniques, access, and maps.

Fishing and Hunting Licenses

Nonresident fishing permits cost $6 for one day or $70 for a season. Resident fishing licenses are $20 for the year. Nonresident youths (ages 14-19) pay $20 for the year ($8 for resident youths). With the exception of the one-day rate, all these prices include a mandatory $5 conservation stamp. Kids under 14 don't need a license if they're with an adult who has a valid fishing license. Purchase permits at most sporting-goods stores or from Game and Fish offices. Note that the Wind River Indian Reservation and Yellowstone National Park have their own regulations and permits; see appropriate sections of this book for details. Report fishing violations and illegal fish stocking by calling (800) 442-4331.

For detailed fishing and hunting information, contact the Wyoming Game and Fish Department at 5400 Bishop Blvd., Cheyenne, WY 82006, tel. (307) 777-4601 or (800) 842-1934. Find the department on the web at www.gf.state.wy.us.

Wyoming game laws are enforced with a vengeance, so out-of-state hunters must be sure they know and obey the regulations thoroughly. Access to private land is often available only for a fee, and trespassers are subject to stringent prosecution. For guided hunts, contact the Wyoming Outfitters and Guides Association, tel. (307) 527-7453, www.wyoga.org.

ON THE SNOW

Downhill Skiing and Snowboarding

Alpine skiing and snowboarding enthusiasts will be pleased to find developed facilities at 11 different Wyoming locations. The finest and largest are in the Jackson area: Jackson Hole, Grand Targhee, and Snow King. Other midsize ski areas include Snowy Range (west of Laramie), Hogadon (near Casper), Sleeping Giant (west of Cody), Big Horn (east of Ten Sleep), and Antelope Butte (east of Greybull). More limited facilities can be found at Pine Creek (east of Cokeville), **White Pine** (near Pinedale), and Snowshoe Hollow (near Afton). See the appropriate chapters for descriptions of each of these. During the winter months you can call the Wyoming Division of Tourism at (800) 225-5996 for the statewide ski report, or visit its website, www.wyomingtourism.org.

Cross-country Skiing

Skinny-skiers have an overwhelming choice of places to ski in Wyoming. The only developed Nordic areas are around Jackson Hole, but all of the mountain ranges fill with deep snow and provide inexhaustible opportunities for discovery. See the special topic Safety in Avalanche Country for precautions to take while cross-country skiing in the backcountry.

Groomed ski trails are maintained in mountain country all across the state, with notable cross-country ski areas near the following towns: Afton, Buffalo, Casper, Cody, Douglas, Dubois, Encampment, Evanston, Jackson, Lander, Laramie, Pinedale, Saratoga, Sheridan, South Pass, Sundance, and Ten Sleep. In addition, Yellowstone and Grand Teton National Parks have world-class skiing, though the trails are not groomed. See specific chapters for details on all these cross-country skiing places.

Snowmobiling

Wyoming has one of the most extensive snowmobile trail systems in America, covering more than 2,000 miles. The most popular snowmobile areas lie on national forest lands in the mountains of northwestern Wyoming, in the Medicine Bow Mountains, the Wind River Range, the Big Horn Mountains, and the Laramie Range. Best known is the 365-mile **Continental Divide Snowmobile Trail,** stretching from Lander around the Wind River Mountains and then north through Grand Teton National Park (this section is quite controversial) to Yellowstone.

Snowmobile trail maps and registration information are available from local visitor centers, or call (307) 777-6560 for the nearest place to purchase permits. For trail conditions around the state, call (307) 777-7777 or (800) 225-5996 and ask for the snowmobile hotline. Snowmobile rentals are available in most mountain towns; see appropriate sections of this book for specifics. Find more detailed snowmobile info and other snowmobile links on the web at http://commerce.state.wy.us/sphs/snow.

RIDING INTO HISTORY

A number of businesses attempt to re-create the days of the great westward migration with wagon trips along the historic Oregon Trail and in other historic areas. The trips are all-inclusive, with horses, meals, tents, and other gear provided; you'll need to bring a sleeping bag. They are typically limited to small groups, with a maximum of 12 or so on horseback trips. Wagon trains are larger—as were the original wagon trains—and may have up to 30 people.

A unique way to discover the Old West is the not-for-profit **Outlaw Trail Ride** in mid-August. This six-day, 100-mile trip follows the Outlaw

Trail from the Hole-in-the-Wall country of Butch Cassidy and the "Wild Bunch" to Thermopolis. You'll need to bring your own horse, bedroll, and gear, but meals are provided for a fee. There's a limit of 100 riders. Call (800) 443-6235 for details.

Based in Casper, **Historic Trails West,** tel. (307) 266-4868 or (800) 327-4052, www.historictrailswest.com, leads a wide range of Conestoga wagon and horseback rides—from four hours to five days long—along the Oregon Trail. A two-day wagon ride costs $175 per person ($195 if you ride a horse); five-day treks are $895 per person ($995 on horseback). These trips are about as authentic as you can get.

Based in Lander, **Great Divide Tours,** tel. (307) 332-3123 or (800) 458-1915, www.rmisp.com/greatdivide, provides a wide range of horseback and wagon trips, including Oregon Trail rides, cattle drives in the Big Horns, outlaw trail rides (Hole-in-the-Wall), pony-express trail rides, and horse drives. Five- to seven-day treks cost $1,050-1,495 per person.

Also in Lander is **Rocky Mountain Horseback Adventures,** tel. (307) 332-8535 or (800) 408-9149, with a similar array of offerings including cattle drives, pack trips, and horseback trips along the Oregon Trail and to Hole-in-the-Wall. One-week adventures range from $995 to $1,495 per person.

BEST OF WYOMING

It isn't just the spectacular places in Wyoming—Yellowstone, the Tetons, Devils Tower—that make it wonderful. It's also the absence of such spectacles, the lack of "sights," the lack of people, the lack of civilization. This is a land of rutted dirt roads and a sky that envelops it all. The following places offer a cross section of Wyoming's delights. This highly selective list features just a few of the many places worth exploring; this book is filled with hundreds of others.

The "Biggies" Everyone Should See

Big Horn Mountains
Bighorn Canyon National Recreation Area
Buffalo Bill Historical Center
Devils Tower National Monument
Fort Laramie
Grand Teton National Park
Hot Springs State Park
Jackson Hole
National Museum of Wildlife Art
Snowy Range
Wind River Mountains
Yellowstone National Park

Lesser-known Attractions Well Worth a Look

Ayres Natural Bridge
Black Hills
Casper Mountain
Castle Gardens
Flaming Gorge National Recreation Area
Fort Bridger
Fossil Butte National Monument
Frontier Prison
Guernsey State Park
Hells Half Acre
Independence Rock
Killpecker Dunes
Little Snake River Museum
Medicine Lodge State Park
Medicine Wheel
Mormon Handcart Visitor Center
Oregon Trail ruts
Sacagawea Cemetery
St. Stephens Mission
Sierra Madre Range
Snake River Canyon
South Pass City
Sunlight Basin
Trail Town
Vedauwoo Rocks
Wyoming Territorial Prison & Old West Park

Interesting Offbeat Attractions

Accidental Oil Company, Newcastle
CallAir Museum, Afton
Charcoal kilns, Piedmont
Crimson Dawn Museum, Casper Mountain
Eagle Bronze Foundry, Lander
Easter Island statue, Rock Springs
Elk antler arch, Afton
Elk antler arches, Jackson
J.C. Penney house, Kemmerer
Jackalope statue, Douglas

Western Encounters, tel. (307) 332-5434 or (800) 572-1230, www.horseriders.com, leads one-week horseback trips across various parts of Wyoming, including the Oregon Trail, Butch Cassidy's Hole-in-the-Wall country, and the Great Divide Basin, and also offers a cattle drive in the Big Horn Mountains. Trips cost $1,475 to $1,755 per person.

Overnight wagon-train rides in Jackson Hole (which isn't even close to the Oregon Trail) are offered by **Wagons West,** tel. (307) 886-9693 or (800) 447-4711, and **Double H Bar,** tel. (307) 344-6101 or (888) 734-6101. The latter charges $745 for a three-night package. Wagons West is a bit cheaper at $595 for four days (bring your sleeping bag), and it also offers one-night and five-night packages.

GETTING INTO THE WILDERNESS

To get a real feel for Wyoming, you need to abandon your car, get away from the towns, and head out into the vast undeveloped public lands. Wyoming's most popular backcountry areas are in the Wind River, Medicine Bow, and Big Horn Mountains, along with the entire northwest corner of the state, including Yellowstone and Grand Teton National Parks. The Yellowstone region contains one of the largest nearly natural ecosys-

Joss house, Evanston
Little America
Midwest-area pumpjacks
Mother Featherlegs monument, Lusk area
Star Valley Cheese factory, Thayne
Torrington Livestock Auction
Windfarm, Arlington
World's "Oldest" Building, Como Bluff
Wright-area coal mines

Great Country Roads
Bitter Creek Rd. between Smoot and Fairview
Grays Loop Rd. (gravel) east of Afton
Little Sandy Rd. (partly gravel) between Farson and Boulder
Red Gulch Scenic Byway between Shell and Hyattville
Sinks Canyon Rd. (partly gravel) between Lander and Atlantic City
Pass Creek Rd. (gravel) between Elk Mountain and State Hwy. 130
State Hwy. 24 between Devils Tower and Aladdin
State Hwy. 70 between Encampment and Baggs
State Hwy. 89 between Cokeville and Alpine
State Hwy. 211 between Chumwater and Cheyenne
State Hwy. 215 between Pine Bluffs and LaGrange
State Hwy. 230 between Laramie and Encampment
State Hwy. 296 through Sunlight Basin
State Hwy. 414 between Mountain View and Manila
State Hwy. 487 through Shirley Basin
US Hwys. 14 and 14A over the Big Horn Mountains
US Hwy. 14-16 between Ucross and Gillette
US Hwy. 14-16-20 between Cody and Yellowstone
US Hwy. 16 between Worland and Buffalo
US Hwy. 18-85 between Newcastle and Lusk
US Hwy. 212 between Cooke City and Red Lodge
US Hwy. 287 between Fort Washakie and Dubois
US Hwy. 26-287 between Dubois and Moran Junction

Fascinating Small Towns
Aladdin
Atlantic City
Buffalo
Dayton
Dubois
Elk Mountain
Encampment
Esterbrook
Fort Washakie
Jay Em
Kelly
Medicine Bow
Meeteetse
Saratoga
Sundance
Superior
Ten Sleep
Wilson

tems and some of the most remote country in the Lower 48.

Many campers prefer to use horses for longer trips, but backpacking is very popular on the shorter trails, especially in the Wind River Mountains and in the national parks. Backcountry permits are required only within Yellowstone and Grand Teton. It is, however, a good idea to check in at a local Forest Service ranger station to get a copy of the regulations since each place is different in such specifics as how far your tent must be from lakes and trails and whether wood fires are allowed. Be sure to take insect repellent along on any summertime trip since mosquitoes, deerflies, and horseflies can be quite thick, especially in July and early August.

A number of hiking trails, mostly two- or three-day hikes, are described for each of Wyoming's best-known backcountry areas. For more detailed hiking information on Yellowstone, Grand Teton, the Big Horns, or the Wind Rivers, see the Booklist at the end of this book. An overall guide is *The Hiker's Guide to Wyoming,* by Bill Hunger (Falcon Press, Helena, Montana). The National Park Service and the U.S. Forest Service can also provide specific trail information.

Horses

For many people, the highlight of a Wyoming vacation is the chance to ride horseback into wild country. Although a few folks bring their own steeds, most visitors leave the driving to an expert local outfitter instead. (If you've ever worked around horses in the backcountry, you'll understand why.) Horse packing is an entirely different experience from backpacking. The trade requires years of experience in learning how to properly load horses and mules with panniers, which types of knots to use for different loads, how to keep the packstrings under control, which horses to picket and which to hobble, and how to awaken when the horses decide to head down the trail on hobbles at three in the morning. Add to this a knowledge of bear safety, an ability to keep guests entertained with campfire tales and ribald jokes, a complete vocabulary of horse-cussing terms, and a thorough knowledge of tobacco chewing, and you're still only about 10% of the way to becoming a packer.

Dozens of outfitters are scattered across Wyoming, but you'll find concentrations in the Jackson Hole, Pinedale, Cody, Dubois, Sheridan, and Saratoga areas. For a listing of permitted outfitters in a given region, contact local Forest Service offices. The **Wyoming Outfitters and Guides Association,** tel. (307) 527-7453, maintains a statewide listing; find it on the web at www.wyoga.org.

Although horses are far more common, **llamas** are increasingly being seen in some backcountry areas. Although you can't ride them, they are easier to control than horses and do not cause as much damage to trails and backcountry meadows. Llamas are perfect for folks who want to hike while letting a pack llama carry most of the weight. Contact local Forest Service offices for permitted llama packers.

Trail Etiquette

Because horses are so commonly used in Wyoming, hikers should follow a few rules of courtesy. Horses and mules are not the brightest critters on this planet, and can spook at the most inane thing, even a bush blowing in the breeze or a brightly colored hat. Hikers meeting a pack string should move several feet off the trail and not speak loudly or make any sudden moves. If you've ever seen what happens when just one mule in a string decides to act up, you'll appreci-

> *We did not think of the great open plains, the beautiful rolling hills, the winding streams with tangled growth as wild. Only to the white man was nature a wilderness, and only to him was the land infested with wild animals and savage people. To us it was tame. Earth was bountiful, and we were surrounded with the blessings of the Great Mystery. Not until the hairy man from the east came, and with his brutal frenzy, heaped injustices upon us and the families we loved, was it wild to us. When the very animals of the forest began fleeing from his approach; then it was that for us, the 'wild west' began.*
>
> —Sioux Chief Standing Bear

ate the chaos that can result from sudden noises or movements. Anyone hiking with a dog should keep it well away from the stock and not let it bark. Last of all, never walk close behind a horse, unless you don't mind spending time in a hospital. Their kick is *definitely* worse than their bite.

Backcountry Ethics

Wyoming's wilderness areas represent places to escape the crowds, enjoy the beauty and peace of the countryside, and develop an understanding of nature. Unfortunately, as more and more people head into backcountry areas, these benefits are becoming endangered. To keep wild places wild, always practice "leave no trace" hiking and camping. This means using existing campsites and fire rings, locating your campsite well away from trails and streams, staying on designated trails, not cutting switchbacks, burning only dead and down wood, extinguishing all fires, washing dishes 200 feet from lakes and creeks, digging "catholes" at least 200 feet from lakes or streams, and hanging all food well above the reach of bears. Your tent site should be 100 yards from the food storage and cooking areas to reduce the likelihood of bear problems. Wood fires are not allowed in many areas, so be sure to bring along a portable gas stove. And, of course, haul your garbage out with you. Burning cans and tinfoil in the fire lessens their weight (and the odors that attract bears), but be sure to pick them out of the fire pit before you depart. And make sure that fire is completely out.

For a detailed brochure on minimizing your impact and treating the land with respect, call (800) 332-4100. Get the same info on the web at www.lnt.org. (Trivial note: the "leave no trace" (LNT) concept was spearheaded by a Lander-based organization, the National Outdoors Leadership School.)

Range Etiquette

Wyoming's land ownership pattern includes many areas where private and public lands are intermingled in a complex checkerboard. This creates all sorts of problems for management of and access to public lands, and for private owners. The conflict is most apparent in grazing country, where many ranchers jealously guard their land from trespassers for any reason. There are places where access to public lands is blocked by private landowners who have had problems in the past. A gate left open by a careless visitor, or sheep sent running by a barking dog can quickly sour even the most generous rancher. Many of them are living a marginal existence already, so every little problem becomes magnified, especially if created by a city slicker—or even worse, a city slicker with California license plates and a "Save the Planet" bumper sticker.

Private boundaries are not always marked by "No Trespassing" signs, so it's a good idea to use a detailed and up-to-date map (such as those sold at BLM offices throughout the state) to be sure you are walking on public land. This is a particularly big issue during the fall hunting season, when many ranchers require a hefty "trespass fee" for access. If you *do* hunt despite warning signs, don't expect any help from the state, since Game and Fish officers are very supportive of private-property rights. Also note that you need to get permission from the landowner—public or private—before collecting anything, including fossils. And since we're talking ethical issues, here's some more advice: never ask a rancher how many cattle he has; it's like asking someone how much money he earns.

BACKCOUNTRY SAFETY

Beaver Fever

Although Wyoming's lakes and streams may appear clean, you could be risking a debilitating sickness by drinking the water without treating it first. The protozoan *Giardia lamblia* is found throughout the state, spread by both humans and animals (including beaver). The disease is curable with drugs, but it's always best to carry safe drinking water on any trip, or to boil any water taken from creeks or lakes. Bringing water to a full boil is sufficient to kill Giardia and other harmful organisms. Another option is to use water filters available from backpacking stores. Note, however, that these may not filter out other organisms such as *Campylobactor jejuni,* bacteria that are just 0.2 microns in size. Chlorine and iodine are not always reliable, taste foul, and can be unhealthy.

Hypothermia

Anyone who has spent much time in the outdoors will discover the dangers of exposure to

BEAR COUNTRY

Bears seem to bring out conflicting emotions in people. The first is an almost gut reaction of fear and trepidation: What if the bear attacks me? But then comes that other urge: What will my friends say when they see these *great* bear photos? Both of these reactions can lead to a multitude of problems in bear country. "Bearanoia" is a justifiable fear but can easily be taken to such an extreme that one avoids going outdoors at all for fear of meeting a bear. The "I want to get close-up shots of that bear and her cubs" attitude can lead to a bear attack. The middle ground incorporates a knowledge of and respect for bears with a sense of caution that keeps you alert for danger without letting fear rule your wilderness travels. Nothing is ever completely safe in this world, but with care you can avoid most of the common pitfalls that lead to bear encounters.

Brown and Black Bears

Old-timers joke that bears are easy to differentiate: a black bear climbs up the tree after you, while a grizzly snaps the tree off at the base. Black bears live in forested areas throughout Wyoming, but grizzlies exist mainly in the northwest corner of the state, primarily within and around Yellowstone National Park. Both grizzlies and black bears pose potential threats to backcountry travelers, although you are considerably more likely to be involved in a car accident while driving to a wilderness area than to be attacked by a bear once you arrive.

Grizzlies once ranged across the entire Northern Hemisphere, from Europe across what is now Russia and through the western half of North America. When whites arrived, there were perhaps 50,000-100,000 grizzlies in what would become the Lower 48 states. Unfortunately, as white settlers arrived, they came to view these massive and powerful creatures (average adult males weigh 500 pounds) as a threat to themselves and their stock. The scientific name, *Ursus arctos horribilis,* says much about human attitudes toward grizzlies. Grizzlies still have healthy populations in Alaska and western Canada, but elsewhere they were shot, trapped, and poisoned nearly to the brink of extinction. In the Lower 48 states grizzlies survive in only a few of the most remote parts of Montana, Wyoming, Idaho, and Washington. By 1975, when the Fish & Wildlife Service listed them as threatened, fewer than 1,000 grizzlies survived south of Canada. Since that time the population appears to have recovered somewhat and includes approximately 300-600 grizzlies in Wyoming's Greater Yellowstone Ecosystem.

Avoiding Bear Hugs

Surprise bear encounters are rare but frightening experiences. There were just 22 bear-caused injuries in Yellowstone National Park between 1980 and 1997—one injury for every 2.1 million visitors. Avoid unexpected encounters with bears by letting them know you're there. Most bears hear or smell you long before you realize their presence, and hightail it away. Surprising a bear—especially a sow with cubs—is the last thing you want to do in the backcountry. Before heading out, check at a local ranger station to see whether there have been recent bear encounters. If you discover an animal carcass, be extremely alert since a bear may be nearby and may attack anything that appears to threaten its food. Get away from such areas. Do not hike at night or dusk, when bears can be especially active. Safety is also in numbers: the more of you hiking together, the more likely a bear is to sense you and stay away.

Make noise in areas of dense cover or when coming around blind spots on trails. If you're unable to see everything around you for at least 50 yards, warn any hidden animals by talking, singing, clapping your hands, tapping a cup, or rattling a can of pebbles. Some people tie bells to their packs for this purpose, while others regard this as an annoyance to fellow hikers. In general, bells are probably of little value since the sound does not carry far, and they might actually serve to attract bears. If bears can't hear you coming, don't be shy—make a lot of noise! It might seem a bit foolish, but yelling may prevent an encounter of the furry kind. Unfortunately, it will probably scare off other animals, so you're not likely to see many critters, and other hikers may not appreciate the noise. Personally, I reserve yelling "Hey Bear!" for situations where I'm walking in brushy bear country with low visibility and I have to compete with other noises such as a nearby creek. I wouldn't recommend doing so while walking the paved path around Old Faithful Geyser; you might get carried off in a straitjacket.

Hunters and photographers are the main recipients of bear hugs. Never under any circumstances approach a bear, even if it appears to be asleep. Move away if you see bear cubs, especially if one comes toward you—mom is almost always close by. Dogs create dangerous situations by barking and exciting bears—leave yours at home (dogs are not allowed in the backcountry in national parks). And, of course, never leave food around for bears. Not only is this illegal, but it also trains the bears to associate people with free food. Fed bears become garbage bears, and that almost inevitably means that the bear gets killed. Remem-

(continued on next page)

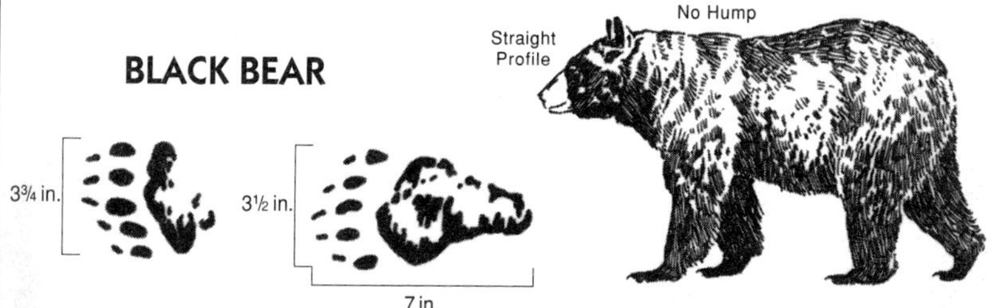

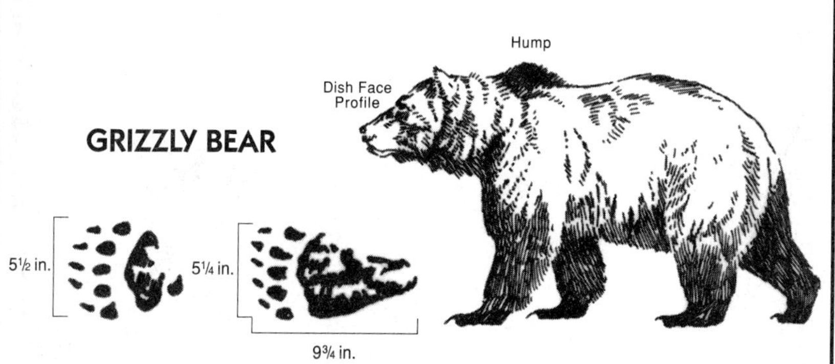

Note: Color can't be used for identification.

BEAR COUNTRY

(continued)

ber, bears are dangerous wild animals. This is *their* country, not a zoo. By going in you accept the risk—and thrill—of meeting a bear.

At the Campsite

Before camping, take a look around the area to see if there are recent bear tracks or scat and to make sure you're not on a game trail. Bears are attracted to odors of all sorts, including food, horse feed, soap, toothpaste, perfume, and deodorants. Your cooking, eating, and food storage area should be at least 50 yards away from your tent. Keep your campsite clean and avoid such smelly items as tuna, ham, sausage, and bacon; freeze-dried food is light and relatively odorless (though also relatively tasteless). Store food away from your sleeping area in airtight containers or several layers of plastic bags, and be sure to hang all food and other items that bears may smell at least 12 feet off the ground and four feet from tree trunks. Bring 50 feet of rope for this purpose. Tie two cups or pots to it so you will hear if it's moved. Some Forest Service and Park Service wilderness areas provide food storage poles at campsites. In the Teton and Bridger Wilderness Areas you can also rent bear-resistant backpacker food tubes or horse panniers from Forest Service offices. Camping stores in Jackson, Cody, and elsewhere sell similar containers.

Good news: researchers have reported no evidence that either sexual activity or menstrual odors precipitate bear attacks, despite reports to the contrary. The Park Service does recommend several common-sense precautions, including that menstruating women use tampons instead of pads and store soiled tampons in double ziplock bags above the reach of bears.

Encounters of the Furry Kind

If you do happen to suddenly encounter a bear and it sees you, try to stay calm and not make any sudden moves. Do not run, since you could not possibly outrun a bear; they can exceed 40 mph for short distances. Bear researchers now suggest that quickly climbing a tree is also not a wise way to escape bears and may actually incite an attack. Instead, make your-

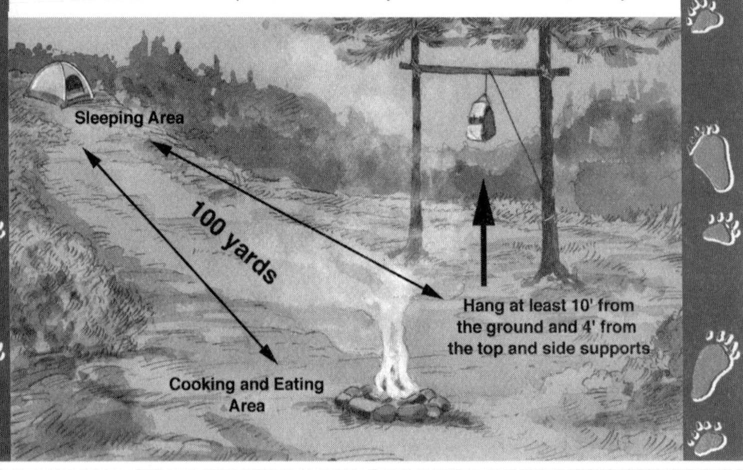

self visible by moving into the open so the bear will (hopefully) identify you as a human and not something to eat. Do not stare directly at a bear. Sometimes dropping an item such as a hat or jacket will distract the bear, and talking calmly (easier said than done) also seems to have some value in convincing bears that you're a human. If the bear sniffs the air or stands on its hind legs it is probably trying to identify you. When it does, it will usually run away. If a bear woofs and postures, don't imitate it—this is a challenge. Keep retreating. Most bear charges are also bluffs; the bear will often stop short and amble off.

If a **grizzly bear** actually attacks, hold your ground and freeze. It may well be a bluff charge, with the bear halting at the last second. If the bear does not stop its attack, curl up face-down on the ground in a fetal position with your hands wrapped behind your neck and your elbows tucked over your face. Your backpack may help protect you somewhat. Remain still even if you are attacked, since sudden movements may incite further attacks. It takes an enormous amount of courage to do this, but often a bear will only sniff or nip you and leave. The injury you might sustain would be far less than if you tried to resist. After the attack, prevent further attacks by staying down on the ground till the grizzly has left the area.

Bear authorities now recommend not dropping to the ground if you are attacked by a **black bear,** as they tend to be more aggressive in such situations and are more likely to prey on humans. If a black bear attacks, fight back with whatever weapons are at hand; large rocks and branches can be surprisingly effective deterrents, as can yelling and shouting. (This, of course, assumes you can tell black bears from brown bears. If you can't, have someone who knows—such as a park ranger—explain the differences before you head into the backcountry.)

In the rare event of a night attack in your tent, defend yourself very aggressively. Do not play dead under such circumstances, since the bear probably views you as prey; it may give up if you make it a fight. Before you go to bed, try to plan escape routes should you be attacked in the night, and be sure to have a flashlight and pepper spray handy. Keeping your sleeping bag partly unzipped also allows the chance to escape should a bear attempt to drag you away. If someone is attacked in a tent near you, yelling and throwing rocks or sticks may drive the bear away.

Protecting Yourself

Recently, cayenne pepper sprays (sold in camping goods stores) have sometimes proven useful in fending off bear attacks. Note, however, that these "bear mace" sprays are only effective at close range. This is particularly true in open country where winds quickly disperse the mist or may blow it back in your own face. Another problem with bear mace is that you cannot carry it aboard commercial jets due to the obvious dangers should a canister explode. If you do carry a pepper spray, make sure it is readily available by carrying it in a holster on your belt or across your chest. Also be sure to test-fire it to see how the spray carries. Though they *are* better than nothing, pepper sprays are not a cure-all or a replacement for caution in bear country. It's far better to avoid bear confrontations in the first place. A few clueless individuals have sprayed themselves with the pepper spray thinking it would work like mosquito repellent. Needless to say, this isn't of much help, and there is some evidence it might even attract bears looking for a spicy meal!

A fine source for detailed bear safety information on the web is the Yellowstone Grizzly Foundation's site: http://home.wyoming.com/~ygf. Two good bear safety books are *Bear Attacks: Their Causes and Avoidance* by Stephen Herrero (New York, NY: Lyons Press) and *Bear Aware: Hiking and Camping in Bear Country* by Bill Schneider (Helena, MT: Falcon Publishing Company).

cold, wet, and windy conditions. Even at temperatures well above freezing, hypothermia—the reduction of the body's inner core temperature—can prove fatal.

In the early stages, hypothermia causes uncontrollable shivering, followed by a loss of coordination, slurred speech, and then a rapid descent into unconsciousness and death. Always travel prepared for sudden changes in the weather. Wear clothing that insulates well and that holds its heat when wet. Wool and polypro are far better than cotton, and clothes should be worn in layers to provide better trapping of heat and a chance to adjust to conditions more easily. Always carry a wool hat, since your head loses more heat than any other part of the body. Bring a waterproof shell to cut the wind. Put on rain gear *before* it starts raining; head back or set up camp when the weather starts to look threatening; eat candy bars, keep active, or snuggle with a friend in a down bag to generate warmth.

If someone in your party begins to show signs of hypothermia, don't take any chances, even if the person denies needing help. Get the victim out of the wind, strip off his clothes, and put him in a dry sleeping bag on an insulating pad. Skin-to-skin contact is the best way to warm a hypothermic person, and that means you'll also need to strip and climb in the sleeping bag. If you weren't friends before, this should heat up the relationship! Do not give the victim alcohol or hot drinks, and do not try to warm the person too quickly since it could lead to heart failure. Once the victim has recovered, get medical help as soon as possible. Actually, you're far better off keeping close tabs on everyone in the group and seeking shelter *before* exhaustion and hypothermia set in.

Frostbite

Frostbite is a less serious but quite painful problem for the cold-weather hiker. It is caused by direct exposure to the cold or by heat loss due to wet socks and boots. Frostbitten areas will look white or gray, and they'll feel hard on the surface and softer underneath. The best way to warm the area is with other skin; put your hand under your arm, your feet on your friend's belly. Don't rub the affected area with snow or warm it near a fire. In cases of severe frostbite, in which the skin is white, quite hard, and numb, immerse the frozen area in water warmed to 99° to 104° until it's thawed. Avoid refreezing the frostbitten area. If you're a long way from medical assistance and the frostbite is extensive, it is better to keep the area frozen and get out of the woods for help; thawing is very painful, and it would be impossible to walk on a thawed foot.

Other Safety Tips

Dealing with bears is discussed in the Bear Country special topic within this chapter. The most important part of enjoying—and surviving—the backcountry is to be prepared. Know where you're going; get maps, camping information, and weather and trail conditions from a ranger before setting out. Don't hike alone. Two are better than one, and three are better than two; if one gets hurt, one person can stay with the injured party and one can go for help. Bring more than enough food so hunger won't cause you to continue when weather conditions say stop. Tell someone where you're going and when you'll be back.

Always carry the **10 essentials:** map, compass, water bottle, first-aid kit, flashlight, matches (or lighter) and fire starter, knife, extra clothing (a full set, in case you fall in a stream) including rain gear, extra food, and sunglasses—especially if you're hiking on snow.

Check your ego at the trailhead; stop for the night when the weather gets bad, even if it's 2 p.m., or head back. And don't press on when you're exhausted—tired hikers are sloppy hikers, and even a small injury can be disastrous in the woods.

ACCOMMODATIONS AND FOOD

LODGING CHOICES

Lodging in Wyoming covers the complete spectrum, from the very finest of luxury accommodations where a king would feel pampered, all the way down to flophouses so tawdry that even the roaches think twice. In general, visitors will find motel prices considerably lower than what they might pay in other parts of America. This is especially true in the smaller towns and places where the economy is weak. During the summer, rates at the mom-and-pop motels that line the streets of every Wyoming town start around $27 for one person and $32 for two people. Tack on another $5-10 for slightly fancier places with the AAA sign out front. Come wintertime, rates may drop 25% or more. In general, visitors will be very pleased with Wyoming motels. The low rates reflect a less-expensive economy, not shoddy conditions. Don't be scared off by a price that seems far too low by New York or Paris standards!

The exception to these low rates is the northwest corner of the state—notably Cody and most egregiously Jackson. During peak summer or winter season in Jackson Hole, you should expect to pay $80-100 for a decent room; even fairly basic rooms with older furnishings fetch $60 a night! Also beware that rates for Cheyenne motel and hotel rooms skyrocket during Cheyenne Frontier Days (late July). Motel prices have a way of changing even in a given day. The law of supply and demand holds, and many owners raise prices as the evening progresses and the rooms start to fill up, when a convention comes to town, and on weekends.

For a complete listing of motels, hotels, bed and breakfasts, dude ranches, and camping places in Wyoming, request a copy of the free ***Wyoming Accommodations Directory*** from the Wyoming Division of Tourism and State Marketing, I-25 at College Dr., Cheyenne, WY 82002, tel. (307) 777-7777 or (800) 225-5996, www.wyomingtourism.org. The booklet lists lodging and campgrounds in every part of the state.

Throughout this book I have typically listed only two prices for most lodging places: single, or s (one person), and double, or d (two people). Prices listed are the midsummer rates—which are generally the highest of the year. These prices do not include state and local taxes, which can sometimes be substantial. These prices are not set in concrete and will certainly head up over time. If a convention is in town or the motel is nearly full, they may rise; if the economy is marginal or if it's the off-season at a seasonal area, you may pay considerably less. Always ask to see the room before deciding to stay at one of the less-expensive motels—places that I consider more than adequate may be beneath your standards.

If in doubt about where to stay, you may want to choose one that gets the American Automobile Association seal of approval. The annual ***AAA TourBook*** for Idaho, Montana, and Wyoming (free to AAA members) is a helpful guide to the better hotels and motels, offering current prices and accurate ratings. Members often get discounts on lodging rates.

Hotels

Most of the historic hotels that once offered lodging for weary Wyoming travelers have either fallen to the wrecking ball or have been turned into residence flophouses. Only a few of these gems have been restored to their glory; they include Cheyenne's Plains Hotel, Cody's Irma Hotel,

ACCOMMODATIONS RATINGS

In addition to including specific prices, all accommodations in this book are further rated by price category for comparison with other Moon Travel Handbooks. Categories are based on double-occupancy, high-season rates; the categories are:

Budget: under $35
Inexpensive: $35-60
Moderate: $60-85
Expensive: $85-110
Premium: $110-150
Luxury: $150 and up

Jackson's Wort Hotel, and Saratoga's Wolf Hotel. Other interesting historic hotels that may or may not be up to your standards include Medicine Bow's Virginian Hotel and the Elk Mountain Hotel in the town of Elk Mountain. Yellowstone National Park offers some of the finest old-time luxury accommodations anywhere in America: Old Faithful Inn, Lake Hotel, and Mammoth Hot Springs Hotel. Of these, Old Faithful Inn is in a category all its own, and is perhaps the grandest hotel in any American national park. Don't miss this one!

Motels

The various motel chains—Best Western, Days Inn, Holiday Inn, La Quinta, Motel 6, and Super 8—all operate motels across the state, primarily in the larger towns. These cinder block monuments to the bigger-is-better school of lodging stand on the edges of towns, their towering signs glaring eyesores (but visible at 75 mph from the freeway). Each chain publishes a directory listing all its locations and rates; you can pick up a copy at the chain's location nearest your home. And all the major chains are now on the web. See the special topic National Motel Chains for a list of toll-free phone numbers and websites.

If you're staying with the pricier chains, always be sure to ask about the sometimes substantial discounts such as AAA-member rates, senior discounts, corporate or government rates, business travel fares, military rates, or other special deals. Try not to take the first rate quoted at these places, especially if you're calling their 800 number; these "rack rates" are what they

MOTEL CHAINS IN WYOMING

In Wyoming as in most of America, many motels are now part of big national or international chains. These lodging options are typically created in a cookie-cutter fashion and lack any sense of place or history. Their styling might best be characterized as utilitarian, which translates as a rectangular box, covered entryway, and towering sign out front to pull folks off the freeway. They tend to be staffed by people who are simply there because it's a job. The chains do, however, provide well-kept and dependably clean rooms, along with toll-free phone numbers and Internet reservations. Many also offer such amenities as continental breakfasts, weight rooms, swimming pools, and jacuzzis. Several of the larger chains with motels in Wyoming are listed below.

America's best-known budget chain, **Motel 6** (tel. 800-466-8356, www.motel6.com), is now owned by the French conglomerate, Accor (www.accor.com). Motel 6 rooms are standard, but the chain's newer motels have gotten considerably more stylish, with prices to match.

Cendant Corporation (www.cendant.com) owns several midrange motel chains that include quite a few Wyoming lodging places: **Days Inn** (tel. 800-325-2525, www.daysinn.com), **Howard Johnson** (tel. 800-446-4656, www.hojo.com), **Ramada** (tel. 800-272-6232, www.ramada.com), **Super 8** (tel. 800-800-8000, www.super8.com), and **Travelodge** (tel. 800-578-7878, www.travelodge.com).

Choice Hotels International (www.choicehotels.com) operates the following midpriced chains in Wyoming: **Clarion Inn** (tel. 800-252-7466, www.clarioninn.com), **Comfort Inn** (tel. 800-228-5150, www.comfortinn.com), **Econo Lodge** (tel. 800-553-2666, www.econolodge.com), **Rodeway** (tel. 800-228-2000, www.rodeway.com), **Sleep Inn** (tel. 800-753-3746, www.sleepinn.com), and **Quality Inn** (tel. 800-228-5151, www.qualityinn.com).

Best Western (tel. 800-528-1234, www.bestwestern.com) has many lodging places scattered across the state. These tend to vary greatly in age and design but are typically some of the nicest places in town.

Holiday Inn (tel. 800-465-4329, www.holiday-inn.com) typically offer some of the most expensive lodging options in Wyoming towns, but they typically include such features as indoor pools and atriums.

Other chains with motels in Wyoming include **Fairfield Inn by Marriott** (tel. 800-228-2800, www.fairfieldinn.com) in Cheyenne; **Hampton Inn** (tel. 800-426-7866, www.hampton-inn.com) in Casper; Hilton Inn (tel. 800-445-8667, www.hilton.com) in Casper; **Kelly Inns** (tel. 800-635-3559, www.kellyinns.com) in Casper and Cody; **La Quinta Inn** (tel. 800-531-5900, www.laquinta.com) in Cheyenne; **Red Lion** (tel. 800-733-5466, www.redlion.com) in Jackson; and **Shilo Inns** (tel. 800-222-2244, www.shiloinns.com) in Casper.

charge if they can get away with it. Ask if they have any promotional rates. You may also get better prices sometimes by bargaining with clerks who are more likely to be able to dicker over price than the 800 number operators who work out of their room in a Texas prison. Of course, if it's a big convention or festival weekend, you may have no choice. Note that the "free continental breakfast" claimed at some motels can be pretty meager, often just a pile of doughnuts and a pot of rotgut coffee.

Every town in Wyoming has its locally owned small motels, often run by an elderly woman with a yip-dog slightly larger than a small shrew (but twice as feisty). These motels vary widely in quality and price but tend to offer the best rates and friendliest service. Actually, many of Wyoming's cheapest motels are owned by immigrants from India or other Asian countries. In some towns (Rawlins is the most egregious), native-born owners play on racist fears with big signs proclaiming "American Owned." In my experience, immigrant-owned places are equal—and sometimes better—than those who wave the American flag in an attempt to suggest otherwise. And today, many of the AAA-approved Comfort Inns, Best Westerns, Super 8s, and other reputable chain motels are owned by people born in India or Pakistan. If you have any doubts about a budget place, take a look at a room and then decide, but don't avoid a place just because the owner's last name is Patel or Khan!

If you don't smoke and can't stand the stench of tobacco in motel rooms, be sure to ask about nonsmoking rooms; many motels (and nearly all the newer ones) have them. Older motel units may also suffer from the permanent smell of tobacco smoke. Also, take a look around the motel to see if the railroad or a busy highway lies next door. If so, try to get a room on the opposite side of the motel, or prepare to put in earplugs. Another thing to watch for is the checkout time; at some places it's as early as 10 a.m.

Bed and Breakfasts

Bed and breakfasts are a relatively recent addition to Wyoming's lodging picture but more are appearing each year. These range from remote places where the accommodations are not unlike those at a guest ranch, to historic Victorian homes in the center of town. Some of the best are found in Big Horn, Buffalo, Cheyenne, Cody, Douglas, Dubois, Jackson Hole, Lander, Laramie, Rawlins, Saratoga, and Wheatland. Get a detailed brochure listing many of the state's B&Bs by writing to **Wyoming Homestay & Outdoor Adventures (WHOA),** 1031 Steinle Rd., Douglas, WY 82633. Head to their website (www.wyomingbnb--ranchrec.com) for descriptions of member B&Bs. Two other good websites providing details on Wyoming B&Bs are Cruising America (www.cruising-america.com/wy/bb.html) and Bed & Breakfast Inns Online (www.bbonline.com/wy).

A few of Wyoming's B&Bs don't allow kids and almost none allow pets or smoking inside. Most guest rooms have private baths, and if they don't, one is probably just a few steps away. Bed and breakfasts, favorites of 30- and 40-something professional couples, are a fine way to get acquainted with a new area—a good choice if you're traveling alone, since you'll have opportunities to meet fellow travelers in the library, over tea, and at breakfast. Note, however, that often the single person rate differs little if at all from the price for couples.

One problem with B&Bs is that they sometimes get a bit too homey and lack the privacy afforded by motels. I've been in some where the owner sits by your table in the morning, feeling it his duty to hold a conversation. This may be fine sometimes, especially if you want to learn more about the local area, but it's not so great if you're looking for a romantic place or you just want to read the newspaper in peace. In some places the intense personal attention and strict rules (no hard-soled shoes, no noise after 10 p.m., and so on) get a bit much, making you feel less a guest than an intruder. In others, hosts serve breakfast at precisely 8 a.m. and guests who sleep in miss out. Other B&Bs are more flexible, and some even offer separate cottages or suites for honeymooners seeking privacy.

Dude Ranches

An old and respected Western tradition is the dude ranch, which began as a sideline to the business of raising cattle. Friends from back east would remember old Jake out there in wild Wyoming, where the buffalo roam and the antelope play, and would decide it was time for a visit. So off they would head, living in the rancher's outbuildings and joining in the chores.

The "dudes," as they became known, soon told their friends, and Jake found his ranch inundated. After a couple of years of this the next step was obvious: get those eastern scoundrels to fork over some cash for the privilege of visiting. Pretty soon the dude ranching business was born. At its peak in the 1920s, dude ranching spread through much of Wyoming and the West. Dude ranching saved many cattle ranches from extinction by providing a second source of income and simultaneously brought these magnificent lands to the attention of people who had the money to prevent their development (most notably John D. Rockefeller Jr. in Grand Teton National Park).

At the older ranches, generations of families have returned year after year for a relaxing and rejuvenating vacation in the "Wild West." Many dude ranches now call themselves guest ranches, a term that reflects both the suspicious way people view the word "dude" and the changing nature of the business. Most city folks today lack the desire or skill to actually saddle up their own horses, much less push cattle between pastures. As a result, guest/dude ranches tend to emphasize grand scenery, horseback riding—the centerpiece of nearly every ranch—campfires, hiking, fishing, hearty meals, chuck wagon cookouts, sing-alongs, and evenings around the fireplace. Some folks even camp overnight out there in the fearful wilderness, where the coyotes howl and the mice chew into your stash of potato chips. A few ranches still offer the chance to join in on such activities as cattle drives, branding, pregnancy testing, shot-giving, calving, and roundups. For some folks it's a great chance to learn about the real West; others view it as paying good money (sometimes a lot of good money!) to work as a cowhand.

Wyoming has literally dozens of dude ranches and ranch resorts offering accommodations ranging from spartan to so sumptuous that they bear absolutely no resemblance to ranch life. Not all dude ranches are created equal—some are slick and modern with tennis courts and hot tubs while others are funky and old-fashioned with delightful rough edges. The smaller ones offer more personalized service, but in larger ones you're more likely to find someone your own age (particularly important if there are teens in your entourage). Dudes normally sleep in log cabins. Conditions inside can vary widely, but don't expect TVs or phones in the rooms. The cabins are usually near a central lodge where meals are served family-style. Many also have large libraries, along with outdoor games such as volleyball and horseshoes. Fishing and photography are other big attractions.

Dude ranch rates generally cost around $2,000 for two people per week, with lower rates for kids and surcharges for those staying by themselves. The price includes all meals, lodging, and horseback rides, but you'll usually pay more for features such as airport shuttles, rafting trips, guided fishing, beer and wine, or backcountry pack trips, not to mention local taxes and tips. The fanciest resort, Lost Creek Ranch in Jackson Hole, will set you back over $5,000 for two people per week! Many guest ranches offer discounted rates in early June and late September, and for repeat guests. A few also have special adults-only weeks. Most require that you stay a week, or at least three nights, though a few places offer overnight accommodations. To really get into the comfortably slow pace of ranch life, try to set aside at least a week.

Ask plenty of questions before you visit, such as what activities are available, what to bring in the way of clothing, what sort of meals to expect (vegetarians may have a hard time on some ranches), whether there are additional charges, whether they accept credit cards (many don't), what the living accommodations are like, and how many other guests will likely be there at the same time—some house up to 125, others fewer than a dozen. Upon request, the better ranches will provide lists of references from previous clients. Note that it is considered proper to tip the ranch hands, kitchen help, and others who work hard to keep the ranch running; the standard total is 15% of your bill. For many of them, this is a way to fund their college education (or buy a winter in Belize).

An outstanding source for detailed information about guest ranches in Wyoming (and elsewhere) is ***Kilgore's Ranch Vacations,*** by Eugene Kilgore (Santa Fe: John Muir Publications). Find Kilgore on the web at www.ranchweb.com.

The **Dude Ranchers' Association** was formed in 1926 and includes only the most established and authentic dude ranches in the nation. Call (970) 223-8440 for a listing of member ranches throughout the West, or visit the organization's website, www.duderanch.org, for links to more than two dozen Wyoming ranches. Another useful website is www.guestranches.com/usa/wy, where you'll find links to 30 Wyoming dude ranches. Also helpful is a Montana travel agency called **Off the Beaten Path,** tel. (800) 445-2995, www.offthebeatenpath.com. The agency specializes in arranging ranch vacations, and it also sets up other Wyoming trips for independent travelers. Many dude ranches now have their own websites, and most of these include photos of their operations to give you an idea of the setting and accommodations.

CAMPING

Wyoming has hundreds of public campsites scattered across the state, primarily on Forest Service, BLM, and Park Service lands, and in state parks. Most of these have potable running water, garbage pick-up, and outhouses but no showers. The fee is generally around $9-12 per night (some are free), and most are open from early June to mid-September. After that, many of the campgrounds remain open (unless inaccessible due to snow) at no charge, but do not have garbage pick-up or running water. There is a 14-day limit on camping at any site, so don't plan on moving in permanently. It's generally legal to camp for free on undeveloped Forest Service or BLM land throughout the state, but check with local offices for any restrictions.

Many Forest Service campgrounds are now on a reservation system; for an extra service charge of $8.65 you can reserve a site up to a year in advance. Call (877) 444-6777 for details, or visit the web at www.reserveusa.com. Budget cutbacks have forced the Forest Service and Park Service to contract out the management of many campgrounds. The effect is not especially noticeable to most visitors, but many of these places charge a higher fee.

Every town of any size contains at least one private RV park and so-called campground. Most of these are little more than vacant lots with sewer and electrical hookups, showers, and toilet facilities. These private campgrounds generally charge $2-4 for showers if you're not camping there. A better deal in many towns is to use the shower in the local public swimming pool, where you get a free swim thrown in for the entrance charge.

FOOD AND DRINK

Wyoming is not a state known for its haute cuisine. This is cattle country, the land of the free and the home on the range, where juicy steaks and the finest prime rib can be found in every Podunk town in the state. (The two best steak houses may well be in the don't-blink-or-you'll-miss-it town of Hudson.) If you don't like that, try chicken-fried steak, the house specialty at every truck stop and greasy spoon in Wyoming. Wash it down with a beer and then sit back for a big hunk of apple pie. For breakfast, it's pretty much

Chugwater's old-fashioned soda fountain is a favorite stop for both locals and travelers.

standard all-American fare accompanied by a dark brew that folks in these parts call coffee. Real cowboy coffee, made only over an open smoky fire and not available within 20 miles of any town, is a potent medicine, not advised for children or the weak-kneed. Check local outfitters for a "café au grounds" prescription. Of course, nearly all of the larger Wyoming towns now also have at least one restaurant or drive-through outlet selling lattes and mochas.

Unfortunately, in Wyoming—as in the rest of the nation—the real dining-out kings are McDonald's, Wendy's, Domino's, Dairy Queen, and all the other fast-food outlets that are turning regional differences into a bland mediocrity of frozen burgers and whipped-shortening "milk shakes." For Mexican fare, many locals head to the appropriately named Taco John's, a Wyoming chain that is—unfortunately—now being unleashed on other parts of the West. (A recent specialty was Taco John's meat-and-potato burrito!) No wonder the residents of Wyoming are becoming increasingly obese.

Actually, Wyoming food is not quite as uniformly bland as might be imagined, and travelers will discover several innovative and surprisingly reasonable restaurants in Laramie, Jackson, Cody, Lander, and Sheridan; authentic Chinese food in Cheyenne and Casper; and relatively authentic Mexican restaurants scattered around the state. The most creative (and pricey) food can probably be found in the tourist town of Jackson and the college town of Laramie. One more note about Wyoming restaurants: they can be quite smoky. In many towns there are no regulations mandating no-smoking sections so if you don't enjoy a dose of cigarette smoke with your food you may just be out of luck.

Typical Wyoming breakfasts cost $3-6, with lunches running $4-7. Dinner prices show a greater range, from simple $5 burgers to complete steak, prime rib, chicken, or seafood dinners for $7-15.

On the Town

No man, woman, or child should let a day pass without drinking a good glass of beer. Beer is an article of food and nourishing as bread if it is pure and free from adulteration.

—1892 AD FOR THE GREEN RIVER BREWERY

In many Wyoming towns, drinking and carousing hold as much interest as eating, especially on Friday and Saturday nights. Every burg of any size has its resident country-and-western band, and saloon dance floors fill with duded-up cowboys and cowgirls out for a night on the town. Many of these bands also play Eagles-style rock tunes for variety. The larger cities and tourist towns have several nightclubs, some with disc jockeys, others with basic rock and roll fare. Don't expect a steep cover charge to get in the door—most places are free.

In the last few years breweries and brewpubs have begun to spread across Wyoming. Otto Brothers Brewery in Jackson Hole was the first, but at last count nine different places had opened in Jackson, Laramie, Lander, Pinedale, Saratoga, Sheridan, Gillette, and Cheyenne.

Astronomical eclipses are of infrequent occurrence, but there is an eclipse taking place on Eddy Street daily and nightly. It is Professor McDaniel's Museum, which eclipses every other place of amusement in Cheyenne. The more money you invest with the Professor the greater equivalent you receive. Call upon him, imbibe one of those Tom and Jerrys, etc., and if not satisfied we pronounce you incorrigible. "Ye Gods!" What nectar the Professor concocts in those little china mugs. Better than the dew on a damsel's lips. Speaking of damsels just step into the museum and you'll see 'em large as life, besides 1,001 other sciences, embracing every known subject. It is an awe-inspiring view.

—AD FOR MCDANIEL'S THEATER AND MUSEUM IN THE 1860S, QUOTED IN *THE MAGIC CITY OF THE PLAINS: CHEYENNE 1867-1967*

EVENTS AND ACTIVITIES

During the summer months, every town in Wyoming has its own main event, generally centered on a morning parade, an afternoon rodeo, and an evening of country music and dancing. Rodeos are the definitive Wyoming activity, reflecting an enduring nostalgia for cattle and cowboys. Nightly summertime rodeos can be found in Cody and twice-weekly in Jackson. Informal roping events go on all summer long around the state; ask locally for times. See Rodeo Today, below, for more details.

Laramie's weeklong **Jubilee Days** starts on the Fourth of July and celebrates Wyoming's statehood with rodeos, parades, the biggest fireworks show in Wyoming, live music, barbecues, a pancake breakfast, a carnival, art exhibits, and other activities. Call (307) 745-7339 or (800) 9445-5303 for rodeo tickets.

Wyoming's most famous event is **Cheyenne Frontier Days,** a 10-day bash that fills every hotel for a hundred miles and makes Cheyenne streets look like a miniature Los Angeles. It starts the last full week of July each year. The centerpiece of Frontier Days is, of course, the rodeo, which attracts the nation's finest riders, but there are also parades, pancake feeds, art exhibits, and much more. Don't miss this one! The **Cody Stampede** (early July) is another very popular rodeo, parade, and all-round chance to party. The **PRCA Rodeo Finals**—Wyoming's largest indoor rodeo—comes to Casper each October.

Tastes of History

The **Gift of the Waters Pageant** arrives in Thermopolis in early August. It celebrates Chief Washakie's gift of this wonderful hot spring to the federal government to be used by all people. ***The Legend of Rawhide,*** an outdoor play held each July since 1947, has a cast that seems to include half the town of Lusk. The story is loosely based on the 1849 killing of a Sioux girl by a white gold-seeker and the Indians' retaliatory skinning-alive of the protagonist, hence the name.

For a more sanguine view of life in the early days, visit one of the many mountain-man rendezvous held around the state. The biggest and best are the **Fort Bridger Rendezvous,** held each Labor Day, and Pinedale's **Green River Rendezvous** in July. Also of note are those in Lander (early June), Riverton (early July), and Jackson (mid-July). A good time is had by all in an authentic and picturesque setting. (See below for more on rendezvous.)

Wyoming's largest powwows are the **Plains Indian Powwow** in Cody each June, Fort Washakie's **Eastern Shoshone Powwow and Rodeo** in early July, and the **Labor Day Powwow** in Arapahoe.

Other Events

Cutter races—essentially wild chariot races on a quarter mile of ice—take place in Afton throughout the winter and in Jackson each February.

Wyoming's biggest winter event is the **International Rocky Mountain Stage Stop Sled Dog Race,** the largest sled dog race in the Lower 48. It begins in Jackson in late January and lasts for 12 days, taking mushers on a race across western Wyoming with stops in a different town each night.

Hundreds of people flood the tiny settlement of Encampment for the **Woodchopper's Jamboree** in late June. Another big attraction is the **Wyoming State Fair,** held in Douglas during mid-August. County fairs take place in each of Wyoming's 23 counties during the summer. Casper's biggest event is the **Central Wyoming Fair and Rodeo** in early August.

Jackson Hole has a number of popular events through the year including the highly acclaimed **Grand Teton Music Festival** in July and the **Fall Arts Festival,** which attracts entries from all over the world. Jackson's annual **Elk Antler Auction** in late May attracts aphrodisiac (!) buyers from all over the globe. For something completely different, head to Chugwater in late June for the **Chugwater Chili Cook-off.** Bring along a bottle of Maalox.

All of these events—and many more—are described in greater detail in appropriate sections of this book. For a complete calendar of Wyoming events, contact the Wyoming Division of Tourism and State Marketing, I-25 at College Dr., Cheyenne, WY 82002, tel. (307) 777-7777 or (800) 225-5996, www.wyomingtourism.org.

MODERN-DAY RENDEZVOUS

In recent years, mountain-man rendezvous have become major summertime attractions in Wyoming. These unusual events attract both tourists and locals to gawk at guys in buckskin pants or breechcloths and women in tanned leather skirts. Unlike the original rendezvous, you won't see many Indians at these get-togethers. The participants are a mixture of Joe Blow Businessman who likes a little diversion, Wendy Waitress who dreams of simpler times, and a lot of folks who find this a great way to live a fantasy life in a semilegitimate way. More long hair, beards, braless women, and barefoot kids than you've seen in three decades.

Although the rendezvous offer escapism for both participants and tourists, they also provide a real taste of a far simpler era. Spend an evening at a rendezvous—especially the Fort Bridger Rendezvous on Memorial Day weekend—and you'll soon be in the market for your own buckskins. Lanterns glow inside tepees, musicians play guitars and sing classic songs, and friends sit on folding chairs inside a wall tent, telling jokes and playing cards. True, they didn't have port-a-potties at the original rendezvous, but the sense of history rings true. Participants bake bread over fires, race horses bareback, fire muzzle-loaders, and mug for tourists' clicking cameras. You'll find lots of beef jerky, Indian tacos, and fry bread for sale. This isn't a good place for the animal-rights crowd, since many of the trade items at the modern rendezvous (as at the original ones) come from wild animals. Many of the people who attend rendezvous have something to offer: old beads, leather clothing, tomahawks, knives, moccasins, woven crafts, tanned hides, and lots of fox, coyote, rabbit, ermine, and other furs.

Events at rendezvous include black-powder shooting contests, storytelling, fiddle music, dancing, hide-tanning demonstrations, tomahawk and knife throwing, and footraces for the kids. In the evening, when all the gawkers head back to their air-conditioned motel rooms, the rendezvous really come to life with big campfires, more storytelling, carousing, drinking, and a raucous good time for all. But woe to the visitor who shows up after dark in modern-day civilian clothes!

RODEO

Sometimes I think life is just a rodeo,
The trick is to ride and make it to the bell . . .
—John Fogerty

It may come as a revelation to many, but rodeo—in Wyoming, always pronounced "ROE-dee-oh"—is one of the most popular sports in Amer-

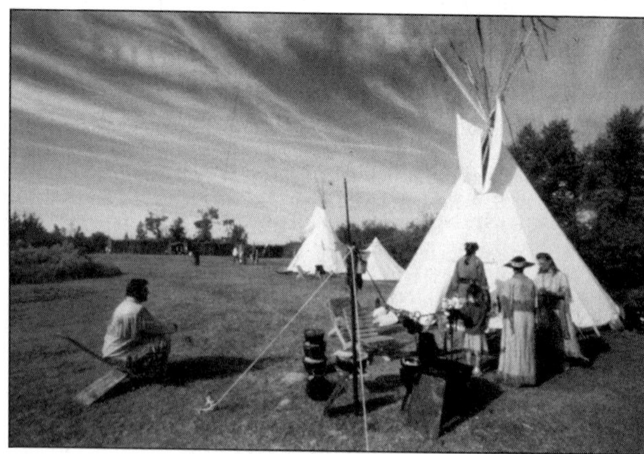

Held on Labor Day weekend, the Fort Bridger Rendezvous is Wyoming's largest.

ica; more people watch professional rodeos than attend NFL football games! In Wyoming, where even the license plate is graced with a cowboy astride a bucking bronc, it's no surprise that rodeo is king. Every small town in the state has a rodeo of some sort during the summer, and the larger cities have world-class rodeos that attract hundreds of riders and ropers from the Professional Rodeo Cowboys Association (PRCA).

History

Although rodeo seems to have a few drops of the Spanish bullfight in its blood, and while many of the words—rodeo, bronco, lariat, arena, and honda—have Spanish origins, rodeo's true genesis was in the days of cowboys and cattle in the Wild West. Gradually, groups of cowboys got together to show off their riding and roping skills and to compete with neighboring outfits. Everyone argues over the official origin of rodeo, but credit is generally given to a bucking and roping competition between the Mill Iron and Hash Knife outfits who met near Deer Trail, Colorado, in 1869.

As the West began to be fenced in, the cowboy events moved into the nearby towns as organized "buckin' shows." Buffalo Bill Cody probably had more to do with popularizing the sport than any other person. For many years his Wild West Show traveled the world, providing a spectacle that included several of the events in present-day rodeos. Lander lays claim to the oldest rodeo in Wyoming; begun in 1893, the Lander Pioneer Days rodeo still comes around each July. By far the most famous Wyoming rodeo, the "Daddy of 'em All," is the Cheyenne Frontier Days, one of the top four rodeos in the world. A good source for rodeo information on the web is www.prorodeohome.com.

Rodeo Today

Over the years, rodeo has become more professional and less connected to the true cowboy. Many participants today come from cities and have never spent time herding cattle or working on a ranch; a few of the best came from Harlem and the Bronx. Of course, many other cowboys still come from more traditional farming and ranching backgrounds, though they may work part-time at the local grocery store to fund their travels on the rodeo circuit. When they get enough money, they attend a weeklong rodeo school to pick up pointers from past champions.

Those who make it to the top do so the hard way. Grand Nationals winners are decided on the basis of rodeo earnings, which means that cowboys must compete almost continuously, flying from one rodeo to another and staying in cheap motels or living out of their RVs. Semipros and amateurs compete in the hundreds of smaller rodeos that dot Wyoming and the West, hoping to make it to the professional level. Most don't even come close, losing their stiff entry fees to more experienced competitors and taking home only bruises or broken bones.

The major rodeo events generally fall into two categories: riding and roping. Riding events include saddle bronc riding, bareback bronc riding, and bull riding; roping events include steer wrestling, calf roping, and steer roping. Women's barrel racing, clown bullfighting, and chuck wagon races complete the roundup. In most of the events, luck has much to do with who wins. Much of the scoring is based on the difficulty of the ride; consequently, the toughest broncs or bulls are favorites because they mean higher scores. Times for ropers depend upon the speed and behavior of the calf or steer they're trying to tackle.

Many rodeo riders are young, skinny-as-a-rail types, but ropers tend to be bulkier and older. The two groups don't mix much and generally have disparaging words to say about the "skinny cowboys on their rocking horses" or "those fat bulldoggers with no style and no skill." But behind this bluster lies respect—and even more for competitors in a cowboy's own events. Hang around the chutes awhile and you'll discover a surprising generosity among fellow riders and ropers as they warn what to expect from a given bronc, help cinch down the straps, and joke over the new shiner from the horseshoe firmly planted in the bareback rider's face. They party together late into the night, looking for the rodeo queens and girls who like the smell of horse sweat. Small-time winners often spread the loot back among the losers, buying drinks and renting a motel room where everyone can sneak in for a night's rest. In *Rodeo! The Suicide Sport,* writer Fred Schnell tells a story that seems to epitomize rodeo life:

Once, when rodeo announcer Mel Lambert explained to the audience that a champion who had just made a good ride neither drank nor smoked and was a college athlete, Jim Shoulders, who has won 16 world titles, turned to a friend behind the chutes and said disgustedly, "Isn't that the worst crap you've ever heard? What the hell is rodeo coming to?"

One thing newcomers soon notice about rodeo cowboys is the clothes they wear—long-sleeve shirts, cowboy hats, Wrangler jeans (never Levi's—the seam is in the wrong place for riding), and cowboy boots. As writer Mary S. Robertson noted, "In no other sport but rodeo do the players and the spectators dress alike." Interestingly, the PRCA actually has a rule requiring long-sleeve shirts and cowboy hats; apparently at one time too many riders and ropers were wearing baseball caps and T-shirts, so the more traditional attire was made mandatory. And, of course, there is one additional piece of attire worn by rodeo cowboys: the plate-sized silver and gold belt buckles. Top winners get these as awards for surviving a season of abuse; others buy them for flash and dash.

The Suicide Sport

A title occasionally used for rodeo is "the suicide sport." It is, unfortunately, all too true, especially for bull riders. Accidents are very common and rodeos always have an EMT ready to tend to the inevitable smashed legs, kicked-in ribs, and broken collarbones. Many cowboys are crippled for life and at least several die each year in the sport, including two at Cheyenne Frontier Days in the 1980s. I recall watching a man in a wheelchair behind the bull chutes at a Jackson rodeo as he encouraged the riders; he had been paralyzed two years earlier in a bull-riding accident at that same rodeo. Even the nation's top riders and ropers can be killed; Lane Frost, a champion bull rider, died at Cheyenne Frontier Days in 1989. Most dangerous of all are the bull rides, but just watching a "dogger" leaping off his horse onto the horns of a speeding steer can give the crowd pause. Rodeos are criticized by animal-rights activists as unnecessarily cruel to animals—steers occasionally die from broken necks and broncs sometimes injure themselves (and their riders) by trying to jump out of the chutes—but the cowboys really do all they can to prevent injury to the animals they ride or rope. And rodeo announcers always point out that the animals spend very little time in the arena; nearly all their time is in the pasture.

Steer Wrestling

Steer wrestling, or bulldogging, involves leaping from a quarter horse onto the back of a 700-pound Mexican steer running at 25 miles an hour, grabbing his horns, and wrestling him to the ground. If you think that sounds easy, try it some time! Steer wrestling originated in 1903, when Bill Pickett, a black Texas cowboy (many early cowboys were black), jumped on the back of an ornery steer, grabbed its horns, bent over its head and bit the steer's lower lip like an attacking bulldog. Soon he was repeating the stunt for the 101 Ranch Wild West Show. Others copied this feat, and though the lip-biting part has long since disappeared, the name bulldogging has stuck.

Steer wrestling is a complex endeavor involving two men: a dogger and a hazer. When the steer hurtles into the arena, the two spur their horses in quick pursuit, with the hazer trying to force the steer to run straight ahead while the dogger gets into position to leap onto the steer's horns and wrestle him to the ground with his feet and head facing the same direction. Since they are competing with other doggers on time, every second counts. Good doggers can get a steer down in less than seven seconds.

Calf Roping

Calf roping originated in the Old West when ropers would pull down a calf and quickly tie it up for branding. Today, this is the most competitive of all rodeo events, and there is often big money for the winners. Calf ropers chase a 300-pound calf on their expertly trained horses, rope it, and then quickly throw it on its side. The piggin' string is wrapped around three ankles and secured with a half hitch ("hooey"), and then the calf is allowed to try to break free. If it can't within six seconds, the time stands and an untie man rides in to free the calf. Time is of the essence in calf roping, and a roper's horse is his most valuable asset. The best horses are in high demand and are often rented to other riders for a cut of any winnings.

Steer Roping

The most controversial of all rodeo contests is steer roping, an event banned from most rodeos because it is so hard on the animals. Cheyenne Frontier Days is one place where you can still see it. The procedure is essentially the same as calf roping, but with a much larger animal. When the 700-pound steer is jerked back by the rope and then thrown down with a thud, you can almost feel the impact. Fortunately, injuries to the tough old steers are uncommon.

Saddle Bronc Riding

When you say the word "rodeo," many people immediately think of saddle bronc riding. The oldest of all rodeo sports, it originated in cowboys' attempts to train wild horses. Rodeo saddle bronc riding is more complex than this, however; it requires a special "association" saddle and dulled spurs, and is played by very precise rules. It is a judged event, with points taken away for not being in the correct position or in control. The bronc is saddled up in the chute (a fenced-in enclosure along the edge of the arena) and the rider climbs on, grabbing a thick hemp rope in one hand and sinking his boots into the stirrups. When the gate opens the bronc goes wild, trying to throw the rider off. The smooth back-and-forth motion of a good saddle bronc rider makes it appear that he is atop a rocking chair. Rides only last eight seconds (leading to lots of ribald cowboy jokes); when the horn sounds, a pick-up man rides alongside the bronc and the rider slides onto the other horse.

Bareback Bronc Riding

Bareback riding is a relatively recent sport, having arrived on the scene in the 1920s. The rules are similar to those for saddle bronc riding but the cowboy rides with a minimum of equipment—no stirrups and no reins. A small leather rigging held on by a leather strap around the horse is topped with a suitcaselike handle. A second wool-lined strap goes around the flank of the horse to act as an irritant so that he bucks more. The cowboy holds on with one hand and bounces back and forth in a rocking motion, an effort akin to trying to juggle bowling pins while surfing a big wave. Eight seconds later it's over and a pick-up man comes in to rescue the rider—if he hasn't been thrown to the ground.

Bull Riding and Rodeo Clowns

Bull riding is in a class of danger all its own. Unlike broncs, which just want that man off their back, bulls want to get even. When a bull rider is thrown off (and this is most of the time, even with the best riders), the bull immediately goes on the attack, trying to gore or trample him. Many bull riders are seriously injured and some die when hit by this 2,000 pounds of brute force. There are no saddles in bull riding, just a piece of thick rope wrapped around the bull's chest, the free end wrapped tightly around the rider's hand. A cowbell hangs at the bottom of this contraption to annoy the bull even more. When the chute opens, all hell breaks loose as the bull does everything it possibly can to throw his rider off—spinning, kicking, jumping, and running against the fence.

If the rider hangs on for the required eight seconds (style isn't very important), the next battle begins—getting out of the way of one very angry bull. Here the rodeo clowns come in. Dressed in bright red-and-white shirts and baggy pants, they look like human Raggedy Andy dolls. In reality they are moving targets. Clowns use every trick in the book—climbing into padded barrels that the bulls butt against, weaving across the arena, mocking the bulls with matador capes, and simply running for their lives to reach the fence ahead of the bull. Frequently, two clowns work in tandem to create confusion, one acting as the barrel man and the other as a roving target. The rodeo clown also plays another role, that of entertainer between events. A clown's stock of supplies includes rubber chickens, trick mules, pantomime jokes with the announcer, and anything else that might keep folks from getting restless.

In a few of the larger rodeos there are clown "bullfights," in which a clown is pitted against a bull in a specially constructed small arena. He taunts the bull in every possible way, running past and around him, touching him, and maybe even leaping over him—all the while trying to stay out of the way of those horns and hooves. These last only 45 seconds, but that seems like an eternity of danger. No wonder they call this the suicide sport!

Other Events

One of the funniest of all rodeo events is the **wild horse race,** a zany event that since 1897 has ended each day at Cheyenne Frontier Days.

Twelve teams of three cowboys try to rope, saddle, and then race a collection of the wildest horses imaginable. If they manage to get on the broncs, their next problem is convincing the horses to run around the half-mile track in the right direction. It seems the definition of bedlam, with horses breaking loose and starting off in opposite directions, crashing into mounted riders and other horses. For sheer chaos, wild horse races would even put a Democratic Convention to shame!

Another crowd favorite at Frontier Days is the **chuck wagon race,** a Canadian invention with mostly Canadian teams. It is a confusing, fast-paced, chaotic, noisy, and dusty sport that involves four wagons, each pulled by four horses. Each team also has two "outriders," boys on horseback. At the sound of the starting gun, an outrider throws a 50-pound "cookstove" into the back of the chuck wagon and climbs back on his horse to chase the wagons. Then everyone takes off on a tight figure-eight course around several barrels and onto the half-mile circular track. The outriders ride in pursuit; they must cross the finish line near their chuck wagons. Needless to say, with four wagons pulled by 16 horses running at a full gallop and another eight horses running alongside, the race is both exciting and very dangerous. When the wagons come around the last corner, the spectators in the stands are all on their feet, yelling and cheering.

Barrel racing—the only female-dominated event—is found at nearly every rodeo and consists of a triangular course around three barrels arranged a hundred feet apart. The event requires riding a fast horse in a set pattern around these barrels, trying not to knock any over. The fastest time wins.

Some rodeos also have what is called a **calf scramble**—featuring dozens of children from the stands chasing a calf to get a ribbon off its tail—and a **colt race,** in which young colts are let loose in a race toward their mares. Both are real crowd pleasers.

INFORMATION AND SERVICES

INFORMATION SOURCES

Chamber of commerce information centers are described for each town in this book. Large **state information centers** are located near Cheyenne, Evanston, Jackson, Laramie, Pine Bluffs, Sheridan, and Sundance. The telephone area code for all of Wyoming is 307.

For a helpful overall guide to Wyoming, along with a listing of events, chamber of commerce offices, and lodging and camping places, request a copy of the free ***Wyoming Vacation Directory*** from the Wyoming Division of Tourism and State Marketing, tel. (307) 777-7777 or (800) 225-5996, www.wyomingtourism.org. Summer and winter versions are available. They also have free **state maps,** or pick them up at any local visitor center.

A great way to check the pulse of Wyoming is to read the letters to the editor in the ***Casper Star-Tribune,*** the state's largest paper. They fill several pages every day and are sometimes quite amusing. Find them on the web at www.trib.com.

On the Web

Internet addresses are listed in the text for local chamber of commerce offices and many businesses. The Internet changes rapidly, and by the time you read this a multitude of new sites will exist for Wyoming businesses and organizations. Most local libraries have computers with Internet access, and if you have a free e-mail service such as hotmail or excite, you can check in from almost anywhere. In addition, Wyoming's larger towns generally have Internet cafes or businesses with computer terminals for rent by the hour. Find a listing of Wyoming libraries and links to their homepages at www-wsl.state.wy.us.

The official Wyoming state homepage is www.state.wy.us, and the state's tourism homepage is www.wyomingtourism.org. Here are a few other useful websites to start your search for Wyoming information:

www.wyominggold.com
http://home.wyoming.com/wyolinks
www.wyomingvisitor.com
www.wyomingnetwork.com

On the Radio

If you like country-and-western music, you'll love traveling through Wyoming, where the radio dial is packed with country stations playing mournful songs about leaving small towns for greener pastures, hard times, loose women, and truck-driving men. My favorite has to be the one that begins: "You're the first thing that I thought of/when I thought I'd drink you off my mind." Pretty much says it all.

Wyoming Public Radio is based in Laramie, with repeaters throughout the state providing in-depth morning and evening news from National Public Radio, the BBC, the Canadian Broadcast Corporation, Wyoming news reports, and the "World Cafe" for eclectic music. It's a vast improvement over the Rush Limbaugh broadsides, Top 40 hit stations, and recycled rock pabulum found elsewhere on the radio dial. In northern Wyoming's Bighorn and Powder River Basins, you'll find National Public Radio coming to you via Montana's "Yellowstone Radio" instead.

Museums

For a listing of more than 225 museums and galleries, contact the Wyoming Arts Council, tel. (307) 777-7742. The state's finest large museum—Cody's Buffalo Bill Historical Center—should not be missed, but a visit to the smaller and lesser-known museums is also well worth your time. Some of the best museums and historical sites are found in Buffalo, Casper, Cheyenne, Douglas, Fort Bridger, Fort Laramie, Grand Teton National Park,

WYOMING TRIVIA

Size: 62,664,960 acres or 97,914 square miles (ninth-largest state)
Lowest Point: 3,125 feet, where Belle Fourche River leaves Wyoming
Highest point: 13,804 feet, Gannett Peak in the Wind River Mountains
Number of people in 1970: 332,416
in 1980: 469,557 (+41.3%)
in 1990: 453,588 (-3.4%)
estimate for 2000: 485,590 (+7.1%)
Number of people per square mile: 4.96
Overall crime rate in 1997: 48th in the nation
Abortion rate in 1992: 50th in the nation
Racial mix in the 1990 census:
White: 94.2%
Hispanic: 5.7%
Native American: 2.1%
Black: 0.8%
Asian or Pacific Islander: 0.6%
Other races: 2.3%
Number of cattle in 1998: 1,560,000
Number of sheep in 1900: 3.3 million; in 1999: 660,000
Number of antelope: 400,000
Percentage of people in Wyoming with four or more years of college: 21
Median age of Wyoming residents: 35
Average age of a Wyoming farmer in 1975: 40; in 1997: 54
Marriage rate: ninth highest in the U.S.
Divorce rate: second highest in the U.S.
Number of eligible voters who actually vote: second highest in the U.S.
One-time Wells Fargo agent in Cheyenne and later restaurant critic who had a cake mix named for him in 1949: Duncan Hines
Former president who once worked as a Yellowstone park ranger: Gerald Ford
Consumer activist who once worked in Yellowstone: Ralph Nader
1960s' pop singer who once owned a Cody nightclub: Glen Campbell
Retail-chain founder who named his original Kemmerer shop the Golden Rule Store: J.C. Penney
1976 world champion bareback rider and country musician from Kaycee: Chris LeDoux
Best-known Wyoming attorney: Jerry Spence
Best-known Wyoming resident: Harrison Ford
Number of Democratic governors: 10
Number of Republican governors: 12
Number of years that Democrats controlled both houses of the Wyoming state legislature between 1890 and 2000: 4; controlled by Republicans: 106
Last time a majority of Wyomingites voted for a Democratic presidential candidate: 1964 (Johnson)
World's largest piece of jade: a 3,366-pound nephrite jade boulder found near Lander in the 1940s
National rank in terms of:
coal production: first
trona production: first
bentonite production: first
mobile homes: first (on a per capita basis)
average size of farms: first (3,761 acres)
wool production: second
per-capita federal aid: second
sheep and lambs: third
natural gas production: sixth
oil production: sixth
per-capita alcohol consumption: eighth
sugar beets: seventh
dry beans: ninth
spring wheat: 10th
cattle and calves: 22nd
population: 50th
average value of farmland in 1997: 49th ($222/acre)
Estimated Wyoming coal resources: one trillion tons
Years Wyoming's coal would last if it supplied all the world's coal: 200
Price for a ton of Wyoming coal in 1999: $5.41
Price for a six-pack of Sierra Nevada Ale in 1999: $6.79 (a bit more expensive, but it tastes a lot better)
Size of Sweetwater County, Wyoming: 10,495 square miles
Size of Rhode Island, Delaware, and Connecticut combined: 7,859 square miles
Number of Wyoming farms in 1920: 15,800; in 1999: 9,100
Percentage of water behind North Platte River dams in Wyoming used to irrigate Wyoming fields: 20%; used for Nebraska fields: 80%

Number of acres submerged by the Pathfinder dam: 22,000
Number of acres irrigated in Wyoming by the Pathfinder dam: 4,000
Number of "Peacekeeper" MX missiles in the Cheyenne area: 50
Number in the rest of the nation: 0
Nation's first national park: Yellowstone
Nation's first national monument: Devils Tower
Nation's first national forest: Yellowstone Timber Reserve (now Shoshone National Forest)
Nation's first polo field: north of Sheridan
"Oldest" building on earth: cabin built from dinosaur bones at Como Bluff
Oldest military building in Wyoming: Fort Laramie's "Old Bedlam"
First business west of the Missouri River: a fur trading post called Fort William (it later became Fort Laramie)
First American Legion post in the nation: in Van Tassell, Wyoming
Current population of Van Tassell: 8
First county public library system: Laramie County (Cheyenne) in 1886
First state to grant women full citizenship: Wyoming (in 1868, while still a territory)
First woman governor in America: Wyoming governor Nellie Tayloe Ross (1925)
First football game played under artificial lights in the nation: in Midwest, Wyoming (1925)
First female voter in the nation: Louisa Gardner Swain ("Grandma Swain"), who voted in Laramie on Sept. 6, 1870
World's first female jurors: in Laramie in 1870
World's first female prison chaplain: Mrs. May Slosson at the Laramie Penitentiary in 1899
World's first female fire lookout: Lorraine Lindaley, stationed at Medicine Bow Peak Lookout (west of Laramie) in 1921

Jackson, Lusk, Pinedale, South Pass City, and Thermopolis. See appropriate chapters for specific details.

FEDERAL AND STATE OFFICES

The U.S. government owns more than 30 million acres within Wyoming, primarily in national forests, national parks, and BLM lands. In addition, the State of Wyoming owns another 3.8 million acres, including more than 118,000 acres of state park lands.

National Park Service

The National Park Service manages 2.3 million acres in Wyoming, including:

Grand Teton National Park, tel. (307) 739-3399, www.nps.gov/grte
Yellowstone National Park, tel. (307) 344-7381, www.nps.gov/yell
Bighorn Canyon National Recreation Area, tel. (307) 548-2251, www.nps.gov/bica
Devils Tower National Monument, tel. (307) 467-5283, www.nps.gov/deto
Fossil Butte National Monument, tel. (307) 877-4455, www.nps.gov/fobu
Fort Laramie National Historic Site, tel. (307) 837-2221, www.nps.gov/fola

Forest Service

The U.S. Forest Service manages 8.7 million acres in Wyoming and has ranger district offices in Afton, Big Piney, Buffalo, Cody, Douglas, Dubois, Encampment, Evanston, Greybull, Jackson, Kemmerer, Lander, Laramie, Lovell, Moran, Mountain View, Newcastle, Pinedale, Saratoga, Sheridan, Sundance, and Worland. Find links to the Wyoming offices at www.fs.fed.us/recreation/states/wy.shtml. The following national forests cover portions of the state:

Bighorn National Forest, Sheridan, tel. (307) 672-0751, www.fs.fed.us/r2/bighorn
Black Hills National Forest, Sundance, tel. (307) 283-1361, www.fs.fed.us/r2/blackhills
Bridger-Teton National Forest, Jackson, tel. (307) 739-5500, www.fs.fed.us/btnf
Flaming Gorge National Recreation Area (Ashley National Forest), Manila, Utah, tel. (435) 784-3445, www.fs.fed.us/r4/ashley
Medicine Bow-Routt National Forest, Laramie, tel. (307) 745-2300, www.fs.fed.us/r2/mbr

Shoshone National Forest, Cody, tel. (307) 527-6241, www.fs.fed.us/r2/shoshone

Targhee National Forest, St. Anthony, ID, tel. (208) 624-3151, www.fs.fed.us/tnf

Wasatch-Cache National Forest, Evanston, tel. (307) 789-3194, www.fs.fed.us/wcnf

Bureau of Land Management

Although not well known by the general public, the Bureau of Land Management (BLM) is one of the biggest landholders in America. In Wyoming the agency manages nearly 18 million acres. The **Wyoming State BLM Office** is in Cheyenne, tel. (307) 775-6256, www.wy.blm.gov. Local BLM offices are found in Buffalo, Casper, Cheyenne, Cody, Kemmerer, Lander, Newcastle, Pinedale, Rawlins, Rock Springs, and Worland.

State Parks

Wyoming's Department of State Parks and Cultural Resources maintains 26 parks, historic sites, recreation areas, and archaeological sites scattered across the state. Most of these charge day-use fees, or you can purchase an annual day-use pass for $40 ($25 for Wyoming residents). For details, contact the **Department of State Parks and Cultural Resources,** Barrett Building, 2301 Central, Cheyenne, WY 82002, tel. (307) 777-6303, or find them on the web at http://commerce.state.wy.us.

State parks and recreation areas in Wyoming include the following (see appropriate parts of this book for details): **Bear River State Park,** near Evanston; **Big Sandy State Recreation Area,** near Farson; **Boysen State Park,** near Shoshoni; **Buffalo Bill State Park,** near Cody; **Curt Gowdy State Park,** between Cheyenne and Laramie; **Edness K. Wilkins State Park,** near Casper; **Glendo State Park,** near Glendo; **Guernsey State Park,** near Guernsey; **Hawk Springs State Recreation Area,** south of Torrington; **Hot Springs State Park,** near Thermopolis; **Keyhole State Park,** near Moorcroft; **Seminoe State Park,** north of Sinclair; and **Sinks Canyon State Park,** near Lander.

SERVICES

Money and Banking

Travelers checks (in U.S. dollars) are accepted without charge in most stores and businesses around Wyoming. It's not a good idea to travel with travelers checks in non-U.S. currency; they are only accepted at certain banks and are a time-consuming hassle. If you do arrive with pounds, yen, or Deutsche marks, several banks in Jackson, along with the park hotels inside Yellowstone, will exchange foreign currency for greenbacks.

When traveling in Wyoming, I pay for expenses by credit card whenever possible, but also keep an automated teller machine (ATM) card and a small stash of travelers checks as a backup. You'll find ATMs in all the larger towns and increasingly they're also available in even the most remote Wyoming settlements. In this book, I've mentioned ATM locations in the smaller towns, but new ones are added all the time. Note that nearly all Wyoming ATMs now tack on a charge—usually $1.50-2 per transaction—to your own bank's fees, making this an expensive way to get cash. If the bank imposes such a charge it will be posted on the machine. It has become increasingly difficult to avoid these fees, but a few places don't charge. Your best bet are ATMs at credit unions. Another way to avoid the charge is to make a purchase at a grocery store that takes ATM cards and simply ask to get cash back over the amount. For an up-to-date listing of Cirrus system ATMs, call (800) 424-7787 or visit the website: www.mastercard.com/atm. For the Plus system, call (800) 843-7587 or point your browser to www.visa.com/atms.

The major credit cards—especially Visa and MasterCard—are accepted almost everywhere, even in many grocery stores. This is probably the easiest way to travel—especially if you can get airline mileage credit at the same time. The miles can quickly add up if you make all your purchases this way, but so can your credit card bill!

Post Offices

Post offices generally open between 7 a.m. and 9 a.m. and close between 5 p.m. and 6 p.m.; only a few are open on Saturday. After hours, the outer doors usually remain open so you can go in to buy stamps from the machines. Some drug or card stores also operate postal substations where you can buy stamps or mail packages within the U.S. (you'll have to go to a real post office for mailing to foreign addresses or for other special services). Many grocery store checkout counters also sell books of stamps with no markup.

HEALTH AND SAFETY

See earlier in this chapter for advice on rattlesnakes, and see the special topic Bear Country for precautions on travel in bear country. Safety in lightning storms is also dealt with in a special topic.

A common annoyance for Wyoming travelers will likely be insects, especially the mosquitoes and blackflies. These are most prevalent in early summer in the mountains; by late August mosquito populations thin considerably. Use insect repellents containing DEET to help keep them away.

Ticks

Ticks can be a real bother in parts of Wyoming, particularly lower-elevation brushy and grassy areas in the spring and early summer. They drop onto unsuspecting humans and other animals to suck blood, and can spread several potentially devastating diseases, including Rocky Mountain spotted fever, ehrlichiosis, and Lyme disease. All of these have been reported in low numbers throughout Wyoming.

Avoid ticks by tucking pant legs into boots and shirts into pants, using insect repellents containing DEET, and carefully inspecting your clothes while outside. Light-colored clothing and broad hats may also help. Check your body while hiking and immediately after the trip. If possible, remove ticks before they become embedded in your skin. If one does become attached, use tweezers to remove the tick, making sure to get the head. Apply a triple antibiotic ointment such as Neosporin to the area, and monitor the bite area for two weeks.

Lyme disease typically shows up as a large red spot with a lighter bulls-eye center, and it often causes muscle aches, fatigue, headache, and fever. Get medical help immediately if you show these symptoms after a tick bite. Fortunately, the disease can usually be treated with antibiotics. If untreated, it can cause a facial nerve palsy, memory loss, arthritis, heart damage, and other problems. A relatively effective vaccine has been developed for Lyme disease, but it requires a one-year regimen of doses and is quite expensive; check with your doctor for specifics. In Wyoming, where the disease is relatively uncommon, the vaccine is probably not warranted, and it may give a false sense of security since ticks can still spread other—and more dangerous—diseases. There are no vaccinations available against either Rocky Mountain spotted fever or ehrlichiosis, both of which sometimes kill people. The best action is to prevent tick bites in the first place. For more on tick-borne diseases, see the Johns Hopkins Institute website at www.intelihealth.com.

TRANSPORTATION

Public transportation is limited in Wyoming. Amtrak no longer offers train service through the state, and air service is limited to a handful of hubs. Fortunately, the state has reasonably good bus service, though even this is minimal in some parts of the state. A few Wyoming towns and cities have local bus services, including Jackson, Cheyenne, and the Wind River Basin.

BY AIR

Commercial airline service to Wyoming is provided to the towns of Casper, Cheyenne, Cody, Gillette, Jackson, Laramie, Riverton, Rock Springs, Sheridan, and Worland. Three major airlines serve the state—United, Delta, and American—but all connections are via Denver or Salt Lake, even if you want to fly from one part of Wyoming to another. Deregulation at work!

BY CAR

Given the expanse and small population of Wyoming, it's no surprise that the automobile—the pickup truck in rural areas—is the primary means of transportation. Thousands of miles of paved and gravel roads cut across the state. Dan Lewis's *8,000 Miles of Dirt: A Backroad Travel Guide to Wyoming* (Casper: Hawks Book Co.) has descriptions of interesting back roads, but I don't find it especially readable. Free Wyoming maps

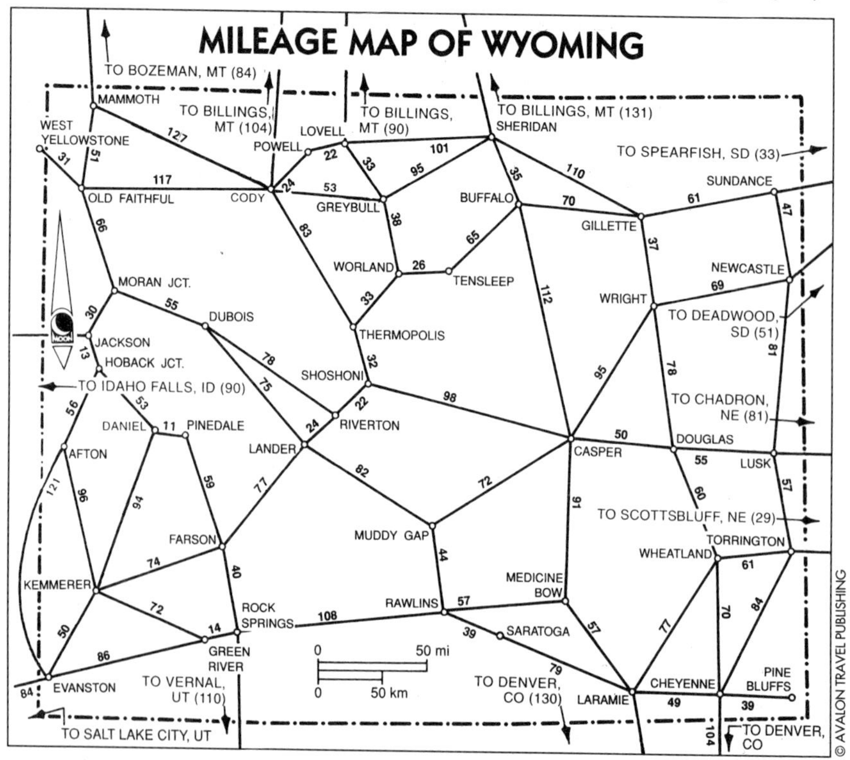

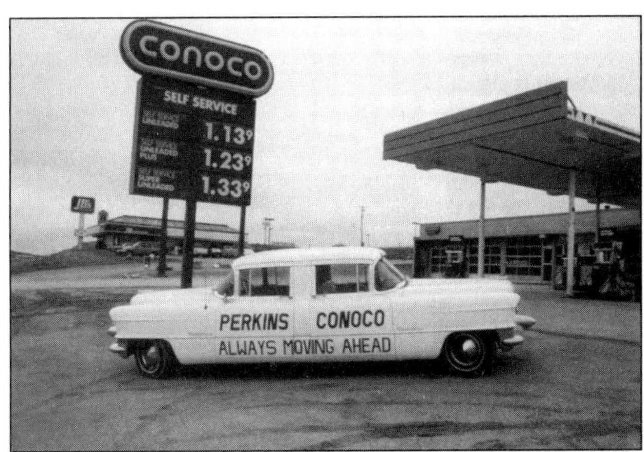

the perfect solution for those drivers who have trouble backing up

can be found at visitor centers across the state, but map aficionados should be certain to purchase ***Wyoming Atlas & Gazetteer*** (Freeport, Maine: DeLorme Mapping), which has detailed topographic maps of Wyoming. It is indispensable for travelers who are heading off main routes. National forest maps are also very helpful for mountain driving in many parts of Wyoming; buy them at local Forest Service offices.

Wyoming drivers seldom slow down when meeting other vehicles, so flying gravel is a frequent problem on unpaved roads. It's even a problem on paved roads, so make sure your insurance pays for windshield repairs!

Wyoming official speed limits are 65 mph on most paved state highways (once you get away from the towns) and 75 mph on the interstate highways. Drive at those speeds and you'll find yourself constantly passed by cars going well over the limit. But look out when driving through small towns throughout Wyoming; the cops vigorously enforce local speed limits. When darkness falls on the main interstate highways (I-80, I-15, and I-90), the trucks come out in force, like bats emerging from caves. It can be a bit intimidating if you're driving a compact.

Car Rentals

You can rent cars in all the larger towns, and those with airports generally have Hertz, Avis, and other national chains. See individual city descriptions in this book for local rental companies. You'll find 4WD sport utility vehicles available in many locations, including Jackson Hole, but you will pay dearly for the privilege.

I've generally found the best car rental rates in the larger cities where there's more competition. You'll pay considerably more in a resort town such as Jackson. If you plan to rent a car for an extended period, it's probably worth your while to check travel websites such as www.travelocity.com to see which company offers the best rates. Note, however, that these quotes do not include taxes, which can be substantial, especially if you rent at the Denver or Salt Lake City airports. Even once you've made a reservation it pays to call around again when you arrive at the airport. On a recent visit I saved hundreds of dollars by getting a last-minute quote for a one-month rental. Cool tip: if you're visiting in the summer, try to get a light-colored car; the dark ones can get incredibly hot in the blazing sun!

Winter Travel

During the winter months, Wyoming travelers need to take special precautions. Snow tires are a necessity, but you should also have on hand a number of emergency supplies including tire chains, a shovel and bag of sand in case you get stuck, a first-aid kit, booster cables, signal flares, a flashlight, lighter and candle, transistor radio, nonperishable foods (granola bars, canned nuts, or dried fruit), a jug of water, an ice scraper, winter clothes, blankets, and a sleeping bag. The most valuable tool may well be a **cell phone** to call for help—assuming you're in an area with reception. If you become stranded in a blizzard, stay in your car. You're more likely to be found, and the vehicle provides shelter from the weather. Run the engine and heater sparingly, occasionally opening a downwind window for ventilation. Don't run the engine if the tailpipe is blocked by snow—you may risk carbon monoxide poisoning. For up-to-date road and travel conditions in Wyoming, call (307) 772-0824 or (888) 996-7623, or log onto the web at http://wydotweb.state.wy.us.

BIKES

Because of Wyoming's small population, cyclists will find uncrowded roads to ride in many parts of the state. The long distances between towns, windy conditions, and frequent summer thunderstorms add to the adventure/danger. The Wyoming Department of Transportation publishes a very useful map—on waterproof paper—showing the amount of traffic on each paved road, the width of paved shoulders, and profiles of the steeper road grades. Anyone touring on a bike will find this map immensely valuable. Get a copy by calling the Bicycle Coordinator at (307) 777-4719.

Many thousands of miles of gravel and dirt roads provide excellent places to explore on mountain bikes; check at local bike shops for nearby routes. Get the BLM 1:100,000-scale area maps (available at most BLM offices for $4) before heading out. They show land ownership, contour lines, and all roads. On Forest Service lands, purchase equally detailed maps from local district offices. Mountain bikes can be rented in most of the larger Wyoming towns.

LONG-DISTANCE BUSES

Greyhound, tel. (800) 231-2222, www.greyhound.com, covers the southern end of Wyoming along the I-80 corridor, stopping in Evanston, Lyman, Fort Bridger, Rock Springs, Wamsutter, Rawlins, Laramie, and Cheyenne, and connecting onward to other cities throughout the country.

Based in Wyoming, **Powder River/Coach USA,** tel. (800) 442-3682, focuses on the northern and eastern parts of the state. Powder River has daily service to Basin, Buffalo, Casper, Cheyenne, Cody, Deaver, Douglas, Gillette, Greybull, Lovell, Moorcroft, Powell, Riverton, Sheridan, Shoshone, Sundance, Thermopolis, Torrington, Wheatland, and Worland. They also serve Colorado (Boulder, Denver, and Ft. Collins), Montana (Billings, Bridger, Hardin, and Laurel), and South Dakota (Rapid City, Spearfish, and Sturgis).

Jackson Hole Express, tel. (307) 733-1719 or (800) 652-9510, www.jacksonholebus.com, provides daily bus or van connections between Salt Lake City or Idaho Falls and the resort town of Jackson, and **Community and Rural Transportation** (CART), tel. (208) 354-2240 or (800) 657-7439, www.cyberhighway.net/ ~cartbus, also has daily bus service running between Idaho Falls and Jackson. Another option is the nonprofit **Wind River Transportation Authority,** tel. (800) 439-7118, with on-demand service. Travelers can call for a pickup in Jackson, Salt Lake City, Dubois, Pinedale, Rock Springs, and other places.

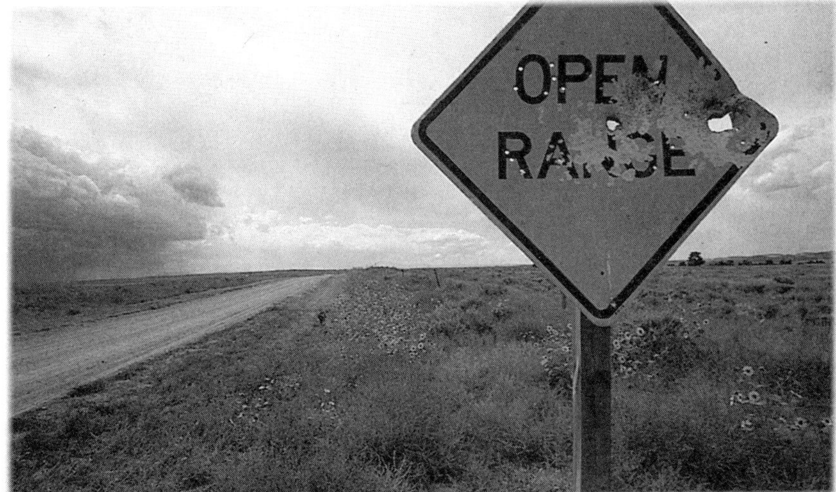

SOUTHEAST WYOMING

Southeast Wyoming is farming and ranching country, part of the vast prairie region that drapes America's heartland. In many ways, it is indistinguishable from western Nebraska or eastern Colorado—one long continuum of grass, grain, and grazing. Folks drive big American cars and Ford pickups. Instead of the saddleries and oil companies elsewhere in Wyoming, you'll find farm-equipment dealers and more feed caps than cowboy hats (they hold down better in the wind that seems to never stop blowing).

Buffalo roamed through southeast Wyoming for thousands of years, hunted by nomadic tribes of Plains Indians. Now sheep and cattle follow the same trails, and farmers grow wheat where Cheyenne Indian villages once stood. Alternating bands of wheat and fallow land give some areas a candy-striped appearance, while in others the expansive prairie extends in all directions. Old windmills, white farmhouses, hip-roofed barns, rusting retired farm machinery, and tall silos mark the old homesteads that became permanent farmsteads. The gravel roads cut straight across this gently rolling land with sudden right-angled jags around old homestead boundaries. Drive out on these roads and the pace slows to country speed and meadowlarks call from the fence posts. Folks raise a hand to wave as you pass and stop to chat on the crest of a hill. Tune in the radio and you're likely to hear country music, farm market reports, and Paul Harvey commentaries. This is Wyoming's most important agricultural region.

SIGHTSEEING HIGHLIGHTS FOR SOUTHEAST WYOMING

- State Capitol, Frontier Days Old West Museum, Wyoming State Museum, and Nelson Museum of the West in Cheyenne
- Register Cliff and Oregon Trail ruts near Guernsey
- Fort Laramie National Historic Site
- Torrington Livestock Market
- Stagecoach Museum in Lusk
- Popular events: Chugwater Chili Cook-off in Chugwater (June), Frontier Days in Cheyenne (July), and *Legend of Rawhide* in Lusk (July)

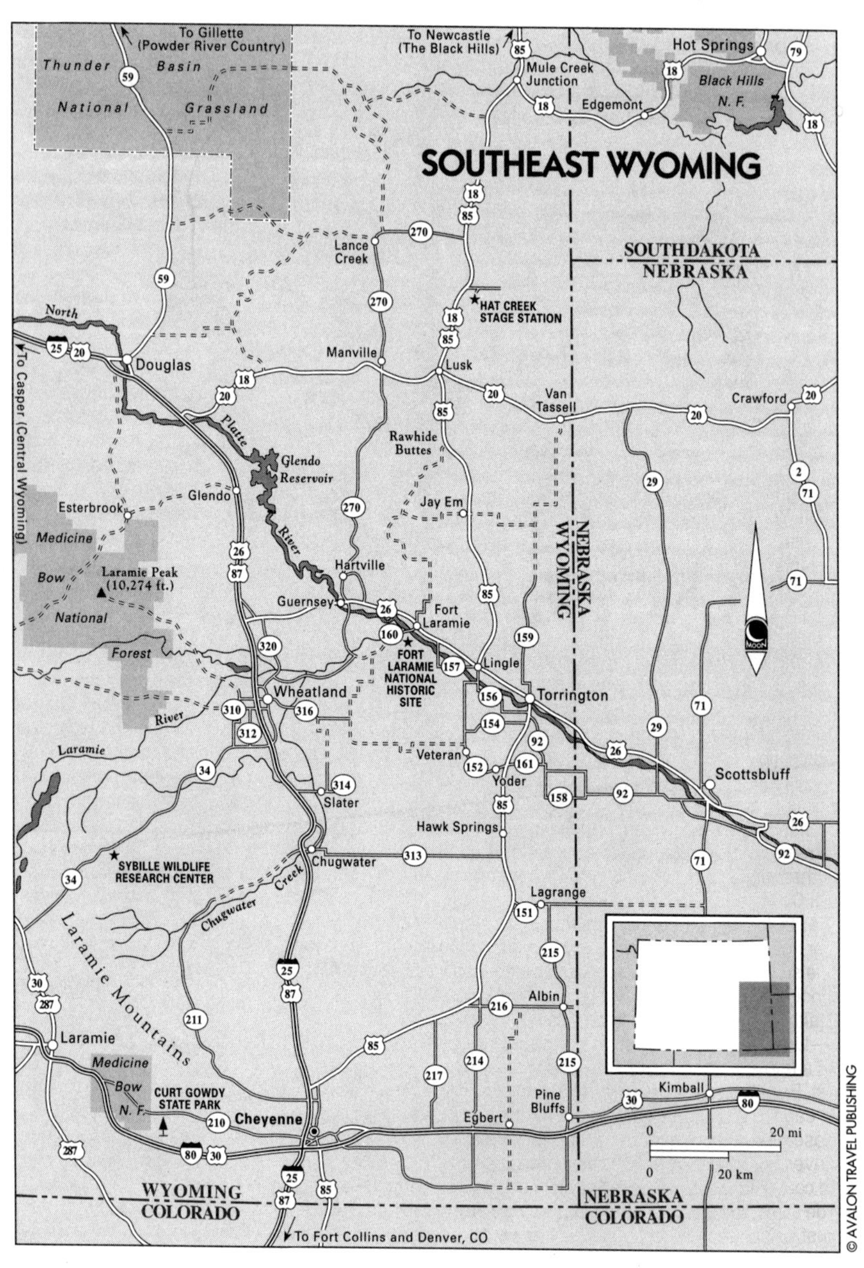
SOUTHEAST WYOMING
To Gillette (Powder River Country)
Thunder Basin National Grassland
To Newcastle (The Black Hills)
Mule Creek Junction
Hot Springs
Black Hills N. F.
Edgemont
Lance Creek
SOUTH DAKOTA
NEBRASKA
HAT CREEK STAGE STATION
North Platte River
Douglas
To Casper (Central Wyoming)
Manville
Lusk
Van Tassell
Crawford
Rawhide Buttes
Glendo Reservoir
Glendo
Esterbrook
Jay Em
Medicine Bow National Forest
Laramie Peak (10,274 ft.)
Hartville
Guernsey
Fort Laramie
FORT LARAMIE NATIONAL HISTORIC SITE
Lingle
Torrington
Wheatland
Laramie River
Veteran
Yoder
Scottsbluff
Slater
Hawk Springs
Chugwater
Chugwater Creek
SYBILLE WILDLIFE RESEARCH CENTER
Lagrange
Laramie Mountains
Albin
Laramie
Medicine Bow N. F.
CURT GOWDY STATE PARK
Cheyenne
Egbert
Pine Bluffs
Kimball
WYOMING
COLORADO
NEBRASKA
COLORADO
To Fort Collins and Denver, CO
0 20 mi
0 20 km
© AVALON TRAVEL PUBLISHING

The capital city, Cheyenne, dominates the economy of southeast Wyoming, one of only two real cities in the state (the other is Casper). The other major settlements—Wheatland, Torrington, and Lusk—are small agricultural focal points and governmental centers for their respective counties.

Southeast Wyoming experiences typical high-plains weather. It is hot and windy in the summer, cold and windy in the winter. The wind—averaging over 13 mph—is a given; this is great country for kites, but not much fun when the gales of winter slice through like a knife. Partly because of this wind, however, Cheyenne has some of the cleanest air in the nation. Explore the back roads and you'll find busy cattle ranches, abandoned mining towns, remnants of many historic trails, archaeological sites, dinosaur bones, and old sod homesteads. Hiking through the gently undulating plains is a delightful experience for vast expanses of this land remain almost unchanged from the time when bison roamed the great grasslands of the West.

CHEYENNE

As you drive west toward Cheyenne (pop. 58,000), the Colorado Rockies loom on the southwestern horizon like whitecaps in a sea of barely rolling plains, snow fences, stunted grass, and the highway slashing toward the boundary of sight. You catch quick glimpses of the great mountain ranges that ramble across Wyoming—like tantalizing flashes in a burlesque show. Gradually they grow larger, and finally you know that the Great Plains will soon be left behind. It's easy to imagine how this must have looked to the railroad passengers who passed this way in the 1860s, watching the mountains loom on the horizon as they rolled into Wyoming. Suddenly you're shaken into the present by the highway sign "Cheyenne Next 4 Exits." Suburban homes crowd over the gentle hillsides, and the state capitol gleams in the setting sun. You have arrived at Wyoming's political and transportation fulcrum.

The city of Cheyenne hunkers down in the southeastern corner of Wyoming, just 10 miles from Colorado and 40 miles from Nebraska. Its wide, tree-draped urban streets and graceful older homes form a gridwork through downtown, while suburbia spreads its tentacles into the surrounding prairie. Cheyenne is remarkably similar to (although smaller than) another state capital—Lincoln, Nebraska. For many visitors, it offers a taste of the West without leaving the Midwest. Folks in Casper or Cody view Cheyenne as the capital of eastern Wyoming and as a city whose ties are really closer to the markets of Denver or Omaha than to the sagebrush, oil, and coal of Wyoming. People in Cheyenne brush aside these criticisms. They know everyone else is just jealous.

As the state capital, the largest city, home to a strategic military base, a center for various governmental agencies, and a major transportation hub, Cheyenne is a big fish in the small pond called Wyoming. The city has one of the most stable and prosperous economies in the state. Its largest employer (nearly 5,000 people) is giant Francis E. Warren Air Force Base, but several thousand other folks work for the federal, state, and local government agencies around town. Railroad tracks of the Union Pacific and Burlington Northern Railroads head to the four points of the compass, and Cheyenne is right at the junction of two of the primary transportation routes across the Plains and the Rockies: I-25 and I-80. Some 800 folks work for Union Pacific, with hundreds more employed in light industry, communications, and shipping firms. Head out Dell Range Boulevard on the north side of town and you'll run into mile after mile of new developments, with national chains of all stripes moving in: Red Lobster, Burger King, Sam's Club, Kmart, Barnes & Noble, Target, Taco Bell, Applebee's, Chili's, and more. The homogenization of America continues, even in Wyoming.

HISTORY

Like so many other Wyoming cities, Cheyenne is a creation of the railroad. It is the oldest of Wyoming's railroad towns, established as the Union Pacific raced westward in 1867. When Gen. Grenville M. Dodge was planning the new railroad's route, he decided to establish a major rail terminal in the plains just before the long climb over the Laramie Mountains. He named the new settlement Cheyenne, for the Indians who lived in this country. The word is from the Sioux Indian term "Shey an nah," meaning "People of a Strange Tongue." (Some have suggested a less complimentary origin for the word, the French term *chienne,* meaning "bitch.") While Dodge was there, Indians attacked a Mormon grading crew, killing two men. The graveyard was started before the first building was up. By November of that year the new town of Cheyenne had swollen to 4,000 people, earning the nickname "Magic City of the Plains." It was easily the largest town in Wyoming and has remained that way for much of the state's history.

At first, Cheyenne consisted of the usual hell-on-wheels railroad settlement of tents and hastily erected buildings. Railroad workers and army men from nearby Fort D.A. Russell turned the town into a rip-roaring place—every second building was a saloon and burlesque shows were the rage. At center stage stood a 36- by 100-foot tent housing Headquarters Saloon. Reporter James Chisholm noted:

> *The wildest roughs from all parts of the country are congregated here, as one may see by glancing into the numerous dance houses and gambling halls—men who carry on the trade of robbery openly, and would not scruple to kill a man for ten dollars.*

Settling Down

Within a decade, however, Cheyenne had settled into a more urbane stage. The railroad provided access to the East, not only allowing cattle to be shipped but also keeping the town abreast of the latest fashions and furnishings and bringing news of world events. With the discovery of gold in the Black Hills, Cheyenne became the primary shipping center for supplies to the Black Hills and gold bullion from the smelters.

By the 1880s, Cheyenne had grown to a cosmopolitan small city of 14,000 people and was declared the wealthiest city per capita in the world. It was one of the first cities in the West to have electric lights—a power plant charged batteries during the day and then delivered them by wagon in time for the evening's use. In 1882, the elaborate Cheyenne Opera House opened with great fanfare. With seating for up to 1,000 people, luxurious furnishings, and a huge 52-light gas chandelier overhead, it was regarded as the equal of any in New York and attracted such performers as Lily Langtry, Sarah Bernhardt, P.T. Barnum, Buffalo Bill Cody, and the Royal Opera Company.

Despite its edge-of-the-state location, Cheyenne was the logical place for Wyoming's territorial capital. The railroad was here, as were Fort D.A. Russell and most of the wealthy cattlemen. In 1869, the first territorial governor, John A. Campbell, made it the temporary capital, with the legislature meeting in rented quarters. Five years later it almost lost that title to Laramie

FRANCIS E. WARREN

One of Wyoming's best-known politicians was Francis E. Warren (1844-1929). A lifelong Republican, Warren served as both a territorial and state governor before being elected to the U.S. Senate in 1890. One of the millionaire cattle barons, his ranch once held more than 100,000 sheep. This land later got him in trouble when he was charged with fencing public land for his own gain, but his friendship with Pres. Theodore Roosevelt helped keep him out of prison. While territorial governor in the 1880s, Warren ardently agitated for statehood. His 37 years in the U.S. Senate made him one of its most powerful members, and newspapers labeled him the "Boss of Wyoming." Upon his death, Fort D.A. Russell was renamed in his honor.

WYOMING STATE MUSEUM

in a rump session of the legislature, but after completion of the capitol building in 1888 it became obvious that the governmental seat would remain in Cheyenne.

Rule of the Cattle Barons

Destruction of the once-vast herds of bison and the widespread slaughter of Indians who had lived in Wyoming suddenly opened up nearly all the territory to cattle grazing. At the time, Laramie County extended all the way to the border with Montana, so it was logical that Cheyenne became the focal point for hundreds of cattlemen who rushed in to make a killing on the booming cattle market. The most famous of these was Alexander Swan, founder of a spread so large that it required a special book to keep track of all its cattle brands. Other part-time residents included members of English nobility such as Moreton Frewen (nephew of Sir Winston Churchill) and Sir Oliver H. Wallop, seventh earl of Portsmouth.

Fort D.A. Russell

In 1862, President Lincoln approved creation of a military fort to guard the then-proposed transcontinental railroad against Indian attacks. When the railroad finally arrived—five years later—the army established a fort near the new town of Cheyenne. Both the town and fort were officially established on the same day. Originally named for a Civil War general—David A. Russell—the new fort grew into America's largest cavalry outpost. Troops from the base were sent out to protect railroad survey and construction parties and later served as guards along the route. The **Cheyenne Depot,** commonly called Camp Carlin, was established adjacent to the fort, providing vital equipment for a dozen army posts scattered throughout the Indian frontier. It was abandoned in 1890.

With the Indians' forced relocation to reservations, the role of Fort D.A. Russell changed and it became a training center and strategic garrison for the Rockies. New brick barracks and officers' quarters were completed in 1885, and the dusty parade ground was planted with grass and trees. Wyoming senator Francis E. Warren had long "brought home the bacon" by gaining political plums for his constituents and one of the biggest was continued support for the fort in Cheyenne. After his death in 1929, the fort was renamed **Francis E. Warren Air Force Base.** The base served as a training center and POW camp in WW II and was transferred to the newly created Air Force in 1947.

The fort's current role began in 1958, when the arrival of Atlas missiles made Warren the nation's first nuclear-missile base. The event was greeted with glee by Cheyenne's then mayor, Worth Story, who exclaimed, "Cheyenne is proud to be the nation's number one target for enemy missiles." Today, the city enjoys a similar privilege as the only place in the nation where the 10-warhead "Peacekeeper" MX nuclear missiles are based. Cheyenne even has a Missile Drive. Warren Air Force Base houses 150 Minuteman III missiles—now rendered unlaunchable in the post-Cold War era—plus all 50 "Peacekeeper" MX missiles in existence, giving it 40% of the nation's intercontinental ballistic missiles (ICBMs) and making it one of the most important ICBM centers in America. The missiles are dispersed over a 150-mile radius in Wyoming, Colorado, and western Nebraska, creating an attractive bull's-eye target centered on Cheyenne. Missile silos are manned by two crew members working some 60 feet underground on 24-hour shifts. Each of these "capsules" controls 10 missiles in surrounding areas. The missiles are launched by steam (!) for the first 150 feet before the missile itself ignites, an event one hopes never occurs.

SIGHTS

For a fine introduction to Cheyenne, take one of the **trolley tours** that depart from the old depot at 16th and Capitol daily between mid-May and mid-September. These two-hour tours cost $8 ($4 for kids) and include a stop at the Frontier Days Old West Museum. Get tickets at the visitors bureau, 309 W. Lincolnway, tel. (307) 778-3133 or (800) 426-5009.

State Capitol

Capitol Avenue—one of the primary streets in Cheyenne—seems to symbolize the city's history. State government buildings line the street and at the ends are the two main reasons for Cheyenne's existence: the old Union Pacific depot to the south and the State Capitol to the

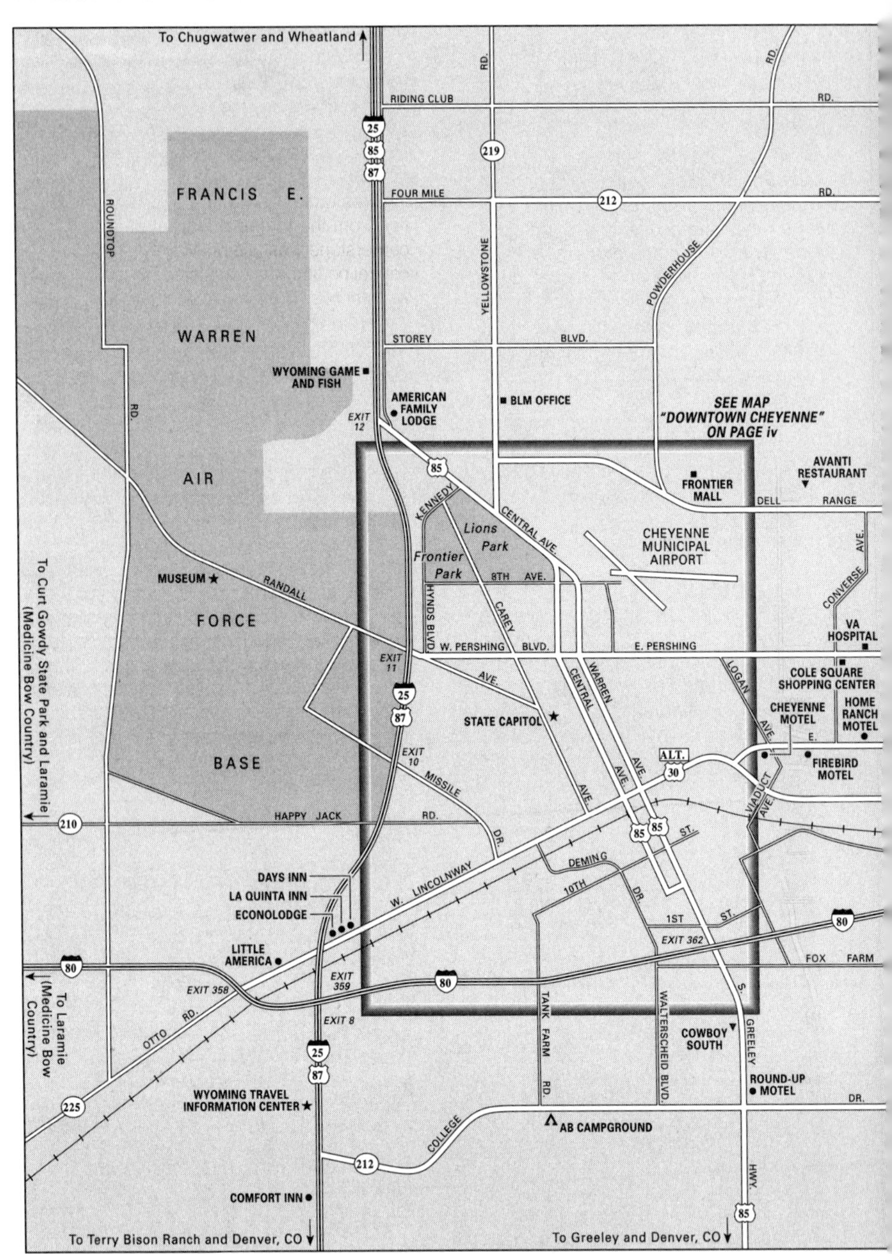

To Chugwatwer and Wheatland
RIDING CLUB RD.
FOUR MILE RD.
YELLOWSTONE RD.
ROUNDTOP RD.
POWDERHOUSE RD.
FRANCIS E. WARREN AIR FORCE BASE
STOREY BLVD.
WYOMING GAME AND FISH
AMERICAN FAMILY LODGE
BLM OFFICE
EXIT 12
SEE MAP "DOWNTOWN CHEYENNE" ON PAGE iv
AVANTI RESTAURANT
FRONTIER MALL
DELL RANGE
KENNEDY
Lions Park
Frontier Park
CENTRAL AVE
CHEYENNE MUNICIPAL AIRPORT
8TH AVE.
CONVERSE AVE.
MUSEUM
RANDALL AVE.
HYNDS BLVD
CAREY
VA HOSPITAL
W. PERSHING BLVD.
E. PERSHING
EXIT 11
LOGAN AVE.
COLE SQUARE SHOPPING CENTER
CENTRAL AVE.
WARREN AVE.
CHEYENNE MOTEL
HOME RANCH MOTEL
STATE CAPITOL
EXIT 10
MISSILE DR.
FIREBIRD MOTEL
VIADUCT AVE.
To Curt Gowdy State Park and Laramie (Medicine Bow Country)
HAPPY JACK RD.
ST.
DEMING DR.
W. LINCOLNWAY
10TH
DAYS INN
LA QUINTA INN
ECONOLODGE
1ST ST.
EXIT 362
LITTLE AMERICA
FOX FARM
EXIT 358
EXIT 359
To Laramie (Medicine Bow Country)
OTTO RD.
EXIT 8
TANK FARM RD.
WALTERSCHEID BLVD.
S. GREELEY HWY.
COWBOY SOUTH
ROUND-UP MOTEL
DR.
WYOMING TRAVEL INFORMATION CENTER
AB CAMPGROUND
COLLEGE
COMFORT INN
To Terry Bison Ranch and Denver, CO
To Greeley and Denver, CO

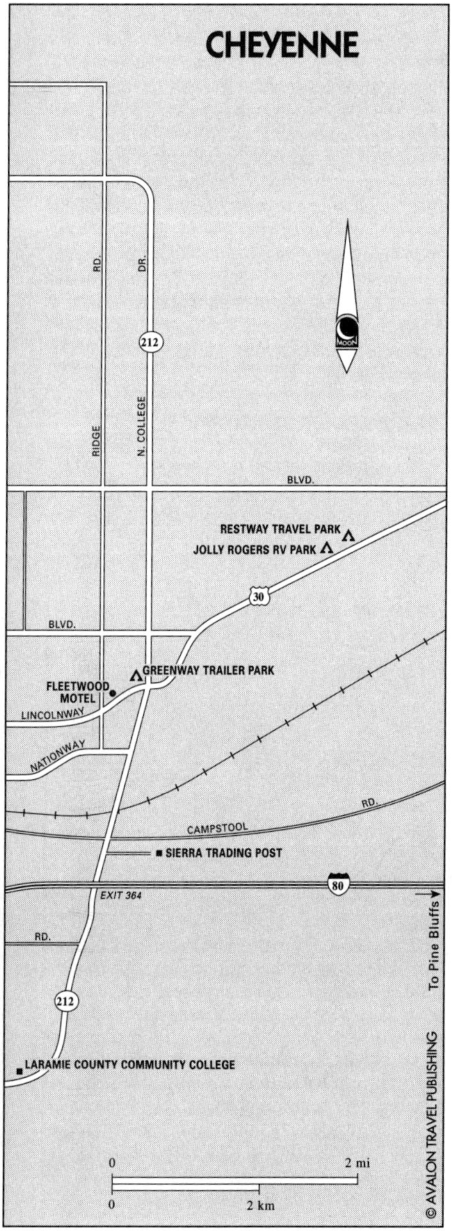

north. The Capitol building is open Mon.-Fri. 8 a.m.-5 p.m. and free guided tours are available throughout the year. Call (307) 777-7220 for more info or group reservations.

Wyoming's capitol falls in the tradition of ostentatious political structures and is modeled after the Capitol in Washington, D.C. The initial building was authorized with a $150,000 appropriation from the territorial legislature in 1886. The cornerstone was laid on May 18, 1887, and the central portion was completed the following year, with the two wings added later. When completed in 1917, the building measured its present 300-foot length. The 146-foot-tall dome has been regilded four times, most recently in 1986. (Don't bother trying to climb up to steal any; the entire dome is covered with less than an ounce of gold.)

CHEYENNE AREA CLIMATE

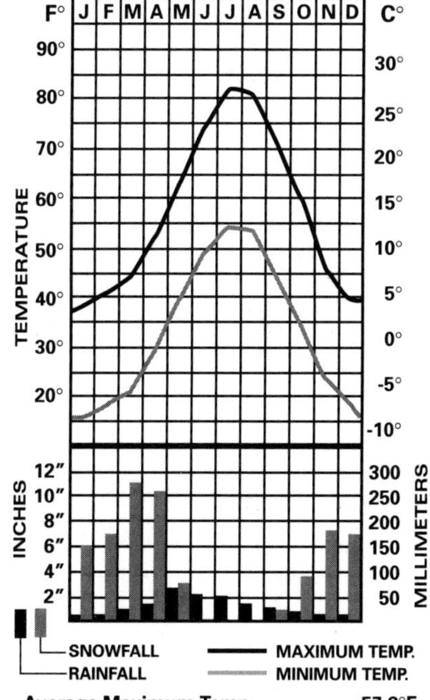

Average Maximum Temp.	**57.8°F**
Average Minimum Temp.	**33.1°F**
Annual Rainfall	**15.29″**
Annual Snowfall	**56.1″**

The capitol's central rotunda has a checkered marble floor with cherry wood staircases leading to the second story. Directly overhead is a beautiful blue stained-glass window imported from England. Interesting historical photographs line the second-floor walls. The senate chambers are in the west wing; the house meets in the east wing. You can view the legislature from the third-floor balconies when it is in session. Inside the legislative chambers are four Western murals painted by Allen T. True—designer of Wyoming's bucking-bronco symbol—along with others by Joseph Henry Sharp and Bill Gollings. Look upward in each chamber to see the large Tiffany stained-glass ceilings with the state seal.

From the outside, the capitol dome seems strangely tall; rumor has it that architects once voted it the nation's ugliest state capitol—although Alaska's would give it a run for this dubious honor. Out front stands a bronze statue of **Esther Hobart Morris,** the person credited (incorrectly) with making Wyoming the first state to grant women voting rights. Directly behind the capitol building is the much newer **Herschler Building,** named for the only Wyoming governor to serve three terms, Ed Herschler. It has an attractive interior atrium and houses a cafeteria and various state offices. In between the two buildings is an 18-foot-tall bronze statue by Edward Fraughton, *Spirit of Wyoming,* a bucking horse and rider that seem almost suspended in space. It is perhaps fitting that the two nicknames of Wyoming—"the Equality State" and "the Cowboy State"—are symbolized by statues on either side of the State Capitol. Wander around the flower-garnished grounds and you'll discover a monument to the Spanish-American War, a bronze bison statue, and a replica of the Liberty Bell.

Historic Governors' Mansion

The old governors' mansion, 300 E. 21st St., tel. (307) 777-7878, is open year-round Tues.-Sat. 9 a.m.-5 p.m. There is no admission charge. A 10-minute video provides information about the

CHEYENNE AND BLACK HILLS STAGE

With the 1874 discovery of gold in the Black Hills, a stampede of miners headed north in search of riches. A fierce competition quickly developed between Cheyenne, Wyoming, and Sidney, Nebraska, to be the jumping-off point for miners. With support for road construction from the Wyoming Territorial Legislature, a 300-mile stage route was soon laid out, and the first coach headed north on Feb. 3, 1876. The Cheyenne and Black Hills Stage, Mail and Express Line had begun.

The line ran almost straight north from Cheyenne to the vicinity of present-day Lusk before veering into Dakota Territory and ending at Deadwood. Drivers made the trip in three days and three nights, with station stops every 15 miles that usually lasted less than three minutes—just long enough to change horses. It was a strenuous and tiring journey through Sioux Indian territory, over treacherous river crossings, and past hideouts of notorious road agents. On the long trip south from the mines, special armored coaches carried gold bullion in steel strongboxes, protected by four to six armed guards. Often they held up to $100,000 in gold dust and nuggets and sometimes as much as $350,000! Outlaws—including Frank and Jesse James and Big Nose George Parrot's gang—targeted these coaches, riding off with both the gold and the horses. One of the most infamous attack sites was near the Robber's Roost Stage Station, along the Cheyenne River north of Lusk. Here the stages were frequently attacked, sometimes every day.

The "Deadwood Coaches," such as the one used by Buffalo Bill in his Wild West Show, were actually the famed Concord coaches built by Abbott and Downing of Concord, New Hampshire. They could jam nine passengers inside (first and second class) for $15-20 a head and an equal number on top (third class) at $10 apiece. Riders on top sometimes had to get off and push the stage up hills. (Despite the attention given to stagecoaches, much of the traffic along the goldfields route was in freight wagons pulled by long strings of oxen.) Upon completion of the Chicago and Northwestern Railroad to Rapid City, traffic on the Cheyenne to Deadwood stage dropped, and the last coach ran on Feb. 19, 1887. In just 11 years, the stage line had carved out a big piece of history, and its closing marked the end of one of the most romantic chapters in the history of the West.

house and its inhabitants, including the nation's first woman governor, Nellie Tayloe Ross; she lived here from 1925 to 1927. The home is furnished with pieces from several periods. The two-and-a-half-story brick building was completed in 1905 at a cost of $33,000. It's in the Georgian style, with four Corinthian columns out front.

The current governors' mansion—completed in 1976—sits near the intersection of Central Ave. and I-25. Tours of the new mansion are offered only for groups; call (307) 777-7398 for appointments.

Wyoming State Museum

Inside the Barrett Building at 24th and Central, the Wyoming State Museum features a mix of continuing and changing exhibits. Permanent displays showcase coal mining, wildlife, dinosaurs, and Indian artifacts. Visitors will also find a 3-D model of the state (showing historic sites), the impressive silver service set from the decommissioned battleship USS *Wyoming,* and a fun hands-on history room for kids. Be sure to stop by the museum gift shop for high-quality regional items. The museum is open Tues.-Sat. 9 a.m.-4:30 p.m.; admission is free. Call (307) 777-7022 for additional information, or visit the museum's website: http://commerce.state.wy.us/cr/wsm.

Frontier Days Old West Museum

Right next to the rodeo grounds in Frontier Park, this is one of the nicest museums in Wyoming. It's open Mon.-Fri. 9 a.m.-5 p.m. and Sat.-Sun. 10 a.m.-5 p.m. year-round (daily 8 a.m.-8 p.m. during Frontier Days); admission is $4 for adults, free for kids under 13. Call (307) 778-7290 or (800) 778-7290 for details. The museum's focus is on Western heritage, with changing historical and art exhibits, Indian artifacts, early clothing, old films, Frontier Days displays—including a bronc-riding saddle that you can try out—and a special "Hole in the Wall" hands-on kids room. The museum is best known for its extraordinary collection of horse-drawn transportation of all types. More than 40 carriages—including many that appear in the annual Frontier Days parade—are displayed. The stars are a Cheyenne-to-Deadwood stage, a prairie schooner, sleighs, a buckboard (the name came from the lack of springs on the axles), and, of course, a surrey with a fringe on top. Be sure to check out the luxurious landau—sort of an early convertible. The gift shop sells various Frontier Days souvenirs and historical books. Out front is a sculpture of champion bull rider Lane Frost, who was killed during a 1989 ride at Frontier Days. A big **Western Art Show and Sale** takes place at the museum during Frontier Days.

Nelson Museum of the West

This surprising private museum is right in the heart of downtown Cheyenne at 1714 Carey Ave., tel. (307) 635-7670. The collection was acquired by Robert L. Nelson, a retired lawyer, big-game hunter, and owner of Manitou Gallery (across the street). It reflects his tastes, with an

one exhibit in the large collection of horse-drawn transportation at the Frontier Days Old West Museum

odd mix of Old West artifacts and memorabilia, along with big-game trophies from around the globe. You'll find a silver and gold saddle valued at $300,000 in the same room as an African lion. Despite its idiosyncrasies, the museum is well worth the price of admission, particularly if you're interested in century-old Indian and cowboy items. The museum covers three floors, so be sure to see it all, including the collection of Western movie posters, furnishings from the homes of Wyoming cattle barons, a painted buffalo robe, Mexican sombreros, cowgirl clothing, and even gruesome photos of dead outlaws. Students of the West will also want to spend time in the museum's research library.

It's open Mon.-Sat. 8 a.m.-5 p.m. June-Aug., and Mon.-Fri. 8 a.m.-noon and 1-5 p.m. the rest of the year. Admission costs $3 for adults or $5 for couples, and $2 for seniors; kids under 13 are free.

Botanic Gardens

One of Cheyenne's lesser-known gems is the fine Botanic Gardens in Lions Park, tel. (307) 637-6458. Building hours are Mon.-Fri. 8 a.m.-4:30 p.m., and Sat.-Sun. 11 a.m.-3:30 p.m.; no charge. Troubled kids, handicapped people, and seniors grow flowers and vegetables here. Visitors find this a pleasant place to relax, especially during the winter, when the warmth and the showy flowers are a welcome break. Inside the passively solar-heated greenhouse (look for the black metal drums filled with water) are three sections containing everything from vegetables to cacti. The central portion is home to tall banana plants, tropical flowers, and a pond filled with goldfish and turtles. The angel's trumpet, with its beautiful orange flowers, is the centerpiece. Upstairs is a small library containing gardening magazines and books. Outside are pleasant picnic tables and a gazebo set among the flower beds and shade trees. The grounds are popular for weddings.

F.E. Warren Air Force Base

For something different, try a visit to Wyoming's primary military base. The entrance to Warren Air Force Base is flanked by four missiles, but the buildings are surprisingly quaint—two- and three-story redbrick structures set back from the tree-lined streets. Some 220 of these immaculate structures are on the National Register of Historic Places! Expansive green lawns give it a country-club feeling. This is essentially a self-supporting city, with child-care facilities, schools, stores, a veterinary clinic, and that old neighborhood standby, nuclear warheads. The only aircraft kept here most of the time are UH-60 Blackhawk helicopters, but during Frontier Days jets take off constantly from the airport, screaming overhead in sharp climbs that elicit gasps from the crowd.

The small **Warren ICBM & Heritage Museum,** tel. (307) 773-2980, is open to the public Mon.-Fri. 8 a.m.-4 p.m., but you'll need to stop at the main gate for permission to enter. No charge. The museum actually consists of two buildings. One has a few artifacts such as sabers, uniforms, and other military memorabilia; more interesting is the annex, which houses missiles exhibits. These include photos of the early Atlas rockets and Minuteman I missiles, a model of the MX missiles the Air Force euphemistically calls "Peacekeepers," and old launch-control equipment. A staff member here will tell you how the missiles are fired and where they are located—more or less. Grave gazers may want to visit the base cemetery, where soldiers and others have been interred since 1867. An interesting pamphlet available at the museum tells the stories of some who lie here, including German POWs who died here during WW II. Detailed three-hour **Tours** of F.E. Warren Air Force Base are offered on the first and third Friday of each month, but call ahead for reservations, tel. (307) 773-3381. Tours are also given during Frontier Days.

Cattle Baron's Row

Cheyenne has quite a number of interesting Victorian buildings. Stop by the visitors bureau for a free brochure that leads you on an informative tour of historic downtown. **Guided historical walking tours** ($7) depart from the visitor center every Saturday at 9 a.m., June-August. Call (307) 634-2021 for details. Of particular note are the Victorian homes along 17th St., "Cattle Baron's Row."

The **Whipple House,** 300 E. 17th St., is a wonderful Victorian built in 1883 by Ithamar C. Whipple, a wealthy merchant, cattleman, mayor, and state legislator. The home was later occupied by attorney and one-time Wyoming Territorial Supreme Court Justice John W. Lacey, who defended both the notorious outlaw Tom

Horn and the equally infamous oilman Harry Sinclair. The building is on the National Register of Historic Places and is now occupied by Botticelli Ristorante Italiano.

Right across the street is the **Nagle-Warren Mansion,** another grand place from the same era. Built by businessman Erasmus Nagle in 1888, it later belonged to Francis E. Warren, who served as governor and U.S. senator. Warren's friend Pres. Theodore Roosevelt slept here several times. Nagle built his home at the same time as the state capitol was being constructed, and he used stones that the capitol masons had rejected. Unfortunately, the masons were proven correct. The stones deteriorated when exposed to the weather and had to be covered with stucco. Today, the Nagle-Warren Mansion is a four-star bed and breakfast (see Accommodations below) that has been lovingly restored inside and out.

For a taste of gentility, attend the mansion's **English High Tea,** served in Victorian style every Friday and Saturday 3:15-4 p.m. The cost is $8. These usually fill up, so be sure to make reservations; tel. (307) 637-3333 or (800) 811-2610. Guests are treated to tea, scones, cookies, tea sandwiches, tartlets, and other sweets served in the elegant parlor.

CHEYENNE CLUB

One of the most unusual organizations in frontier Wyoming was the Cheyenne Club, first established in 1880 as an exclusive English-style country club. With membership limited to 200, it included only the wealthiest of the cattlemen, men who quickly became known as cattle barons. Many came from aristocratic social backgrounds, and the club included graduates of the finest universities on the East Coast and Europe. Some were millionaires who summered in Cheyenne and then sailed back to Europe for luxurious winters. With the growing prosperity of the cattle business, the Cheyenne Club claimed the finest French-Canadian chef and steward in the country and was said to be the first club in America to have electricity. Dinner dress was always formal. Despite strict rules on behavior (no card cheating, pipe smoking, or profanity), one member did manage to shoot a hole through a painting of a cow and bull—he claimed it to be an abomination against purebred cattle. Upstairs were elaborate apartments for members and guests, while the lavishly furnished downstairs included a spacious dining room, billiard room, reading room, card room, lounge, and wraparound porch. With the sudden bust that followed the harsh winter of 1886-87, the cattle barons were brought abruptly back to reality. Many went out of business, and the club quickly followed. The historic Cheyenne Club was razed in 1936.

Cathedrals

Cheyenne has several of Wyoming's most ostentatious and interesting churches. **St. Mark's Episcopal Church,** 1908 Central Ave., tel. (307) 634-7709, is the oldest, begun in 1886 but not completed until 1893. The exterior is of red lava stones with traditional stained-glass windows, including one by Tiffany. This was the home church for many transplanted British and Scottish cattle barons, so it is fitting that the funeral for gunman Tom Horn—who worked for some of them—was held here in 1903.

Two other impressive churches are **St. Mary's Catholic Cathedral,** 2107 Capitol Ave., tel. (307) 635-9261, built in 1907 of native sandstone in the Gothic Revival style, and the **First United Methodist Church,** 18th and Central Aves., tel. (307) 632-1410, completed in 1894 and also made from sandstone. The previous Methodist church, on the same site, was where marshal, gunman, and gambler Wild Bill Hickok married a circus performer, Agnes Lake Thatcher, in 1876. The officiating clergyman wrote in the registry, "Don't think they meant it." Five months later, Wild Bill was shot in the back in a Deadwood saloon. Agnes Thatcher is *not* the woman buried next to Hickok in the Deadwood cemetery; instead it's Calamity Jane.

Railroad Paraphernalia

The railroad business reached its peak in the 1940s, when Cheyenne had the finest equipment and service anywhere in America. The railroad is still an important part of the city's economy, with freight trains rumbling through day and night. Drop by the gorgeous old **Union Pacific Railroad depot** at the south end of Capitol Ave. to see one of the finest remaining depots in the West. Built of red and gray sandstone in 1886, the structure was at one time the largest building in the territory and the most elaborate depot between Omaha and San Francisco. (The depot was a reward to Governor Francis E. Warren for restoring order after the 1885 massacre of Chinese workers at the Union Pacific's vital Rock Springs coal mines.) It occupies an entire block, with clock tower and Romanesque arched openings adding a touch of class. The depot underwent a major renovation in the 1990s and is now officially called the **Wyoming Transportation Museum and Learning Center,** tel. (307) 637-3376. Currently the building is primarily used for gatherings of various kinds, but a museum of transportation (hence the name) is scheduled to open here around 2004. In the meantime, the historic structure is open Mon.-Sat. 9 a.m.-4 p.m. in the summer, and Mon.-Fri. 10 a.m.-4 p.m. the rest of the year. Behind the depot is an enormous Union Pacific roundhouse built in 1931 and still used to maintain locomotives. It is not open to the public.

Holliday Park, along E. 17th St., has a **Big Boy locomotive,** one of only 25 ever made and one of the largest steam locomotives ever built. It was used to haul freight over the mountain tracks between Cheyenne and Ogden, Utah. A couple of blocks east of here is a boxcar from the **French Merci Train,** given as a thank-you for food Americans gave the French after WW II.

Wyoming Hereford Ranch

In 1883, cattle barons Alexander and Thomas Swan, backed by European investors, formed the Wyoming Hereford Association, placing 400 purebred Hereford bulls and cows on a ranch near Cheyenne. This was the first real attempt to bring quality cattle to the state and was at one time the world's largest herd of thoroughbred cattle. Gradually other ranches followed this lead and the rangy longhorns of Texas were replaced by the more manageable Herefords—now the dominant breed in Wyoming. The 60,000-acre Wyoming Hereford Ranch has survived for more than a hundred years and contains many historic structures in immaculate condition. This is the oldest continuously registered livestock operation in the nation. A small visitor center shows off awards and old photos. Out front you'll find monuments to prize bulls Prince Domino and Lerch, who sired many of the prize whiteface Herefords in America today. Prince Domino's memorial reads, "He lived and died and won a lasting name." How touching. You can wander around the showcase ranch and explore the red barns and other buildings. Wyoming Hereford Ranch is five miles east of Cheyenne; take Campstool Rd. (exit 367) off I-80. Call (307) 634-1905 for free tours. Since 1980, the ranch has been owned by a local surgeon, Dr. Sloan Hales, who lives in the enormous Tudor mansion just up the hill.

Other Sights

The **Wyoming Department of Game and Fish,** 5400 Bishop Blvd., tel. (307) 777-4554, has a small museum/visitor center with wildlife dioramas, wildlife photographs, and an aquarium containing native trout. It's open Mon.-Fri. 8 a.m.-5 p.m. and Sat.-Sun. 9 a.m.-5 p.m. in summer, and Mon.-Fri. 8 a.m.-5 p.m. the remainder of the year. No charge.

For details on points to the south, see *Colorado Handbook,* by Stephen Metzger (Moon Travel Handbooks, www.moon.com).

ACCOMMODATIONS

Cheyenne has more than two dozen different lodging places. Generally finding a room is not difficult, but when Frontier Days comes to town, motels and campgrounds book up six months in advance, and the rates often double or even triple; some places that cost $28 d in the winter months are $130 d during Frontier Days! Obviously the quality doesn't suddenly improve so drastically. Elsewhere this would be called price gouging, but the motels somehow get away with it. Even towns as far away as Torrington are affected by Frontier Days, so be sure to plan well ahead for accommodations during the rodeo.

Motels and Hotels

A handful of Cheyenne motels and hotels are described below, and you'll find the rest in the appendix of this book under Additional Cheyenne Motels. Be certain to take a look around before paying for a room at Cheyenne's cheaper motels, and also check the location. Motels near the railroad—and this includes nearly all the less-expensive places—may suffer from noise as freight trains rumble past at all hours. Bring earplugs or look for a room away from the tracks.

Inexpensive: Cheyenne is fortunate to have one of Wyoming's few surviving historic lodging places, the five-story **Plains Hotel,** tel. (307) 638-3311. Built in 1911 for a then-astounding $250,000, this 140-room hotel was the political center of Cheyenne for decades, with politicians repairing to the bar to broker issues over beers and stogies. The grand lobby has a central chandelier, and a marble stairway leads to the mezzanine. Note the tile mosaic of Chief Little Shield in the sidewalk along Central Avenue. Standard rooms in the hotel are $35 s or $43 d, and they also have a four-person suite with a full jacuzzi available on weekends for $100 ($80 on weekdays). Saunas are accessible to all guests, and a restaurant is on the premises.

A good economy place is **Fleetwood Motel,** 3800 E. Lincolnway, tel. (307) 638-8908 or (800) 634-7763, where the clean and quiet rooms are $35 s or $43-46 d. An outdoor pool is on the premises. Also recommended is **Luxury Inn,** 1805 Westland Rd., tel. (307) 638-2550, a friendly motel with rooms for $35 s or $39 d ($129 s or d during Frontier Days!), including a continental breakfast. Its off-season rates are an even better bet.

Expensive: One of the nicest (and largest) local places is the **Best Western Hitching Post Inn,** 1700 W. Lincolnway, tel. (307) 638-3301 or (800) 221-0125, www.hitchingpostinn.com. The newly remodeled rooms follow a Western motif, and featured attractions include indoor and outdoor pools, a jacuzzi, saunas, a large fitness center, and airport shuttle, along with two fine restaurants, a coffeehouse, and two lounges. Motel rooms go for $79-95 s or $85-105 d ($179 s or d during Frontier Days).

Another large and upscale place is **Little America Hotel,** 2800 W. Lincolnway, tel. (307) 775-8400 or (800) 445-6945. The hotel is set on 80 acres of beautifully landscaped grounds, and offers a quiet location, Olympic-size outdoor pool, exercise facility, airport shuttle, and nine-hole golf course. The spacious rooms go for $75-89 s or $85-99 d.

Inexpensive-Moderate. Also of interest is **Terry Bison Ranch,** tel. (307) 634-4171, located eight miles south of Cheyenne along I-25, just on the Wyoming side of the state line. This 27,500-acre ranch has bunkhouse rooms for $38 d and rustic cabins with kitchenettes for $79 (these sleep four). All room contain private baths.

Bed and Breakfasts

With the exception of Jackson, the Cheyenne area has more B&Bs—eight in all—than any other Wyoming city.

Occupying a grand old home built in 1888 and listed on the National Register of Historic Places, the **Nagle Warren Mansion B&B,** 222 E. 17th St., tel. (307) 637-3333 or (800) 811-2610, provides updated Victorian lodging near the center of Cheyenne. Owners Jim and Jacquie Osterfoss have transformed the old mansion into Cheyenne's premier lodging option. Amenities include luxurious rooms with period furnishings and original artwork, a gazebo housing the jacuzzi, and an exercise room. Massage is available ($40/hour), along with special honeymoon packages. The gourmet breakfast menu changes every day. The B&B contains 11 guest rooms ($105 s or d) in the house, along with a suite ($135 s or d) in the carriage house. All rooms have private baths, and children are accepted. A formal English High Tea ($8) is served in the parlor on Friday and Saturday afternoons. This is one of only a few AAA-rated four-diamond B&Bs in the nation. For details, visit the mansion on the web at www.naglewarrenmansion.com. The mansion itself is described above in Sights. Expensive-Premium.

Another classic downtown place, just a block away, is **Rainsford Inn B&B,** 219 E. 18th St., tel. (307) 638-2337. This elegant 1903 home in the heart of Cheyenne has six antique-furnished guest rooms (private or shared baths), ceiling fans, and jacuzzi tubs. Room rates are $67-85 s or d, including a full breakfast. Rainsford Inn is on the National Register of Historic Places. Well-behaved children only. Moderate.

Also right downtown, **Porch Swing B&B,** 712 E. 20th St., tel. (307) 778-7182, is an attractive cottage built in 1907. Inside are two small rooms with shared bath ($49 s or d) and a larger room with private bath ($59 s or d). The back porch, surrounded by flower and herb gardens, is perfect for a summer evening. Guest rooms contain antiques, and a full breakfast is served by the helpful hosts. Find them on the web at www.cruising-america.com/porch.html. Inexpensive.

For more Victorian-era lodging, stay at **Avenue Rose B&B,** 100 E. 27th St., tel. (307) 632-0274. Built in 1906, this home is close to downtown and furnished with a mix of antiques and modern pieces. The owner is a masseuse, so massage and aromatherapy are available here, and the flower and herb gardens create a calming ambience. Two guest rooms share a bath, and children are welcome. Rates are $65 s or d, including a full breakfast. Moderate.

On the north side of town, **Storyteller Pueblo B&B,** 5201 Ogden Rd., tel. (307) 634-7036, is a contemporary home with Native American art, country antiques, fireplaces, and four guest rooms with shared or private baths. It's in a quiet neighborhood and run by dynamic owners. Room rates are $50 s or d, including a full breakfast. Children accepted. Inexpensive.

The friendly **Howdy Pardner B&B,** tel. (307) 634-6493, www.cruising-america.com/howdy, is out in the country five miles north of Cheyenne—call ahead for directions. The hilltop ranch-style home offers three guest rooms (all with private bath), a fireplace, and great views of the rolling plains. Each morning, the owners produce a gourmet country breakfast. Rates are $65 s or $85-95 d, and kids are welcome. For an authentically Wyoming experience, sleep inside the antique sheepherder wagon for $75 d (bath in the house). Moderate-Expensive.

Adventurer's Country B&B, tel. (307) 632-4087, is a modern ranch home in the countryside 15 miles east of Cheyenne. Guests share the grounds with a variety of farm critters, including horses, chickens, geese, turkeys, ducks, cats, and dogs. The five guest rooms ($45-75 s or d) and a three-room suite ($135 s or d) are arranged around a central courtyard. A four-course breakfast and evening dessert are served. Kids, pets, and horses are welcome. In addition to the B&B, the owners also run High Mountain Horseback Adventures from a base camp in the Snowy Range, described in the Medicine Bow chapter. Get more info on the B&B and horseback trips at www.bbonline.com/wy/adventurers. Inexpensive-Premium.

Double M&N, 773 Latigo Loop, tel. (307) 778-7021, has four guest rooms with shared baths in a trilevel home. Rates are $45 s or d, including a full breakfast. Kids okay. This is also perhaps Wyoming's only B&B where smoking is allowed inside. Inexpensive.

Halfway between Cheyenne and Laramie on Happy Jack Rd. (State Hwy. 210) lie three excellent B&Bs: A. Drummond's Ranch B&B, tel. (307) 634-6042; Bit-O-Wyo B&B, tel. (307) 638-8340; and Windy Hills Guest House, tel. (307) 632-6423. They are described later in this chapter in the Curt Gowdy State Park section.

Campgrounds

Cheyenne's closest public campgrounds are 26 miles west on State Hwy. 210 in **Curt Gowdy State Park,** tel. (307) 632-7946; $9 for nonresidents, $4 for residents. Campgrounds can also be found within the scenic Pole Mountain area of Medicine Bow-Routt National Forest, 30 miles west on I-80; $10. Showers are available at the swimming pool in Lions Park, or from many of the private RV parks listed below. Note that RV and camping rates are higher during Frontier Days; reserve well ahead to be sure of a space at that time.

AB Campground, 1503 W. College Dr., tel. (307) 634-7035, charges $13 for tents and $20 for RVs; open March-October.

Fifteen miles east of town, **Cheyenne KOA,** 8800 Archer Frontage Rd. (I-80 exit 377), tel. (307) 638-8840 or (800) 562-1507, charges $27 for RVs, $20 for tents, and $35 d for basic cabins. Amenities include an outdoor pool, mini-golf, and horseshoes. Open April-October.

Greenway Trailer Park, on the east edge of Cheyenne at 3829 Greenway St., tel. (307) 634-6696, has RV hookups for $14; open year-round.

On the south side of Cheyenne, **Hide a Way RV Park,** 218 S. Greeley Hwy., tel. (307) 637-7114, charges $14 for both tents and RVs; open year-round.

If you have an RV and don't mind the lack of bathrooms, you may want to stay at **Hyland Park RV Campground,** 2415 Missile Dr., tel. (307) 634-0517; $14 for full hookups. No tents. Open May-September.

Jolly Rogers RV Park, 6102 E. Hwy. 30, tel. (307) 634-8457 or (800) 458-7779, provides east-side tent sites for $8, RV hookups for $12; open mid-April through September.

Open year-round, **Restway Travel Park,** 4212 Whitney Rd., tel. (307) 634-3811 or (800) 443-2751, is one of the nicest RV parks in the area, with an outdoor pool, horseback rides, chuck wagon dinners, mini-golf, volleyball, and horseshoes. Tent sites are $13; RV hookups cost $16.

Terry Bison Ranch, eight miles south of Cheyenne on I-25 (exit 2), tel. (307) 634-4171, is a favorite of families, with rodeos, bison tours, trout fishing, horseback and pony rides, and chuck wagon dinners. Tent spaces are $11; RV hookups cost $20. Cabins and bunkhouse rooms are also available. Open year-round.

A half dozen miles from downtown Cheyenne is **T-Joe's RV Park,** at I-80 exit 370, tel. (307) 635-8750. Open year-round, it has tent spaces for $13 and RV hookups for $20.

Fifteen miles east of Cheyenne at exit 377, **WYO Campground,** tel. (307) 547-2244, has RV sites close to I-80. Rates are $15-22 for RVs, $13-19 for tents; open May-October.

FOOD

The city of Cheyenne offers a surprisingly diverse choice of eateries. In addition to all the places listed below, the city is jammed with all the usual fast-food chains, particularly along East Lincolnway.

Breakfast and Lunch

One of the real treats in Cheyenne is **Lexie's,** 216 E. 17th St., tel. (307) 638-8712, a quaint and classy downtown place with great breakfasts. At noon, Lexie's gets crowded with local office workers savoring burgers (best in town), quesadillas, chicken piccata, BLT sandwiches, or other house specialties. Return in the evening for a romantic dinner. But get there early: Lexie's closes Monday at 3 p.m., Tues.-Thurs. at 8 p.m., and Fri.-Sat. at 9 p.m. They're closed all day Sunday.

The Egg & I, 2300 Carey Ave., tel. (307) 632-5577, specializes in—surprise—eggs, with "egg-ceptional" omelets, fritatas, and other dishes. The atmosphere is bright and friendly, and classical tunes spill from the speakers. They also make commendable croissant sandwiches, soups, and salads for lunch. Early birds will appreciate the 6 a.m. weekday openings.

The **A & B Cafe,** 2102 E. Lincolnway, tel. (307) 632-0343, and **Driftwood Cafe,** 200 E. 18th St., tel. (307) 634-5304, are also good for breakfast. The enormous **Little America** coffee shop, 2800 W. Lincolnway, tel. (307) 634-2771, is open 24 hours a day and offers better-than-average truck-stop fare. Little America also has a Sunday buffet brunch and weekday lunch buffet. Another place with a popular Sunday brunch is **Terry Bison Ranch,** eight miles south of Cheyenne off I-25, tel. (307) 634-4171.

For a taste of the East Coast, try a Philly steak sandwich or pierogi from **Little Philly,** 1121 W. Lincolnway, tel. (307) 632-6824. A downtown lunch and dinner favorite of many locals is **Albany Restaurant,** 1506 Capitol Ave., tel. (307) 638-3507.

The cheapest meal in Cheyenne can be found at the state government cafeteria in the **Herschler Building,** directly behind the capitol. A filling lunch will set you back less than $5. Sit in the spacious atrium on rainy days, or head outside to brown-bag it with government workers when the sun pops out. Open Mon.-Fri. 6 a.m.-4 p.m., with limited service after 1:30 p.m.

Espresso

In addition to caffeine jolts, **Java Joint,** downtown at 1171 Carey Ave., tel. (307) 638-7332, has tasty light lunches: sandwiches, salads, and soups. **Wild Wicks Coffee,** 1439 Stillwater Ave., tel. (307) 638-9313, features more gourmet coffees, along with muffins and pastries. Barnes & Noble Books, 1851 Dell Range Blvd., tel. (307) 632-3000, houses the only **Starbucks** coffeehouse in Wyoming.

Mexican Food

Several places in Cheyenne make very good south-of-the-border food. **La Costa,** 317 E. Lincolnway, tel. (307) 638-7372, has perhaps the best Mexican meals, with all the favorites, including fajitas, chile rellenos, and chalupas. Housed in Cheyenne Plaza Mall, **The Armadillo,** 3617 E. Lincolnway, tel. (307) 778-0822, has been in business for 30 years, with locally famous margaritas. Also popular is **Estevan's Cafe,** 1820 Ridge Rd., tel. (307) 632-6828.

Asian Restaurants

Wyoming is definitely not known for its Asian food, but Cheyenne does offer two surprisingly authentic Chinese restaurants worth a visit: **Twin Dragon Restaurant,** 1809 Carey Ave., tel. (307) 637-6622, and **San Dong Chinese Restaurant,** 801 W. Pershing Blvd., tel. (307) 634-6613. Twin Dragon's lunchtime buffet is an outstanding deal, and the dinner menu includes such specialties as sesame crispy beef and moo shu pork. Keep your orders small since the portions are huge. **Dynasty Cafe,** 1809 Carey Ave., tel. (307) 632-4888, has a big menu of reasonably priced Chinese and Vietnamese dishes and vegetarian specialties, along with a lunchtime buffet.

Pizza and Italian Restaurants

L'Osteria Mondello Italian Cucina & Pizzeria, 1507 Stillwater Ave., tel. (307) 778-6068, is *the* place for authentic Southern Italian meals in Cheyenne. If you're looking for atmosphere, **Botticelli Ristorante Italiano,** tel. (307) 634-9700, is hard to beat. The restaurant is housed in the Whipple Mansion at 300 E. 17th St. (see Cattle Baron's Row above) and serves all the Italian and pizza standards.

The food isn't anything special, but stuff yourself into obesity at **Avanti Restaurant,** 4620 Grandview Ave. (between Wal-Mart and Office Max!), tel. (307) 634-3422, where the Italian-American evening buffet is $8.25.

Pete's Pizza, 1801 Warren Ave., tel. (307) 632-2267, makes decent pizzas but is better known for its Italian sub sandwiches. For pizza, most folks in Cheyenne seem to prefer **Pizza Hut,** 2215 E. Lincolnway, tel. (307) 635-4151.

Dinner

A popular Cheyenne eatery is **Applebee's,** 1401 Dell Range Blvd., tel. (307) 638-3434. Although it's part of a chain, the grilled specialties, crunchy munchies, and decadent desserts earn long waits most evenings.

Poor Richard's, 2233 E. Lincolnway, tel. (307) 635-5114, has Cheyenne's only Saturday brunch. The seafood and prime rib are excellent and reasonably priced, and the salad bar is one of the biggest around. Enjoy a drink at the fireside lounge. Another favorite steak place is **Cowboy South,** 312 S. Greeley Hwy., tel. (307) 637-3800. For prime rib, fly up to **Cloud 9 Restaurant** at the airport terminal (300 E. 8th Ave.), tel. (307) 635-1525.

Housed inside the Best Western Hitching Post Inn at 1700 W. Lincolnway are three fine eateries, including a locals' favorite, **Cheyenne Cattle Company,** tel. (307) 633-3301. The specialty here—not surprisingly—is steak, but the menu also offers a variety of other meals. Entrées are in the $13-24 range. A patio menu has lighter entrées. Also at the Hitching Post is **Carriage Court,** tel. (307) 638-3301, *the* place to go for fresh fish or oysters, steaks, prime rib, and pasta. The wine list is one of the best in town.

In business since 1935, **Owl Inn,** 3919 Central Ave., tel. (307) 638-8578, remains a busy family dining establishment, well known for its giant cinnamon rolls. The menu covers the spectrum from herb-roasted chicken to chili rellenos. Unfortunately, the cooking is not especially memorable.

Get away from downtown for a pleasant evening at **Little Bear Inn,** five miles north on I-25, tel. (307) 634-3684, where steak, frog legs, shrimp, rainbow trout, and scallops fill the menu. Entrées are a bit overpriced ($13-17) given the rather pedestrian quality, but the location is relaxing.

Pubs

Sanford's Grub & Pub, 115 E. 17th St., tel. (307) 634-3381, is Cheyenne's *happening* place, with a young crowd and live music on weekends. Part of a small chain—others are in Sheridan, Gillette, and Casper, along with Spearfish, South Dakota—Sanford's exudes frat-house chic. Every square millimeter is packed with old photos, sports memorabilia, lawn-sale junk, and TV screens. The chaos ups the volume, though the 55 beers on draught probably help. Sanford's menu is big enough to satisfy almost anyone and includes shrimp jambalaya, barbecued chicken wings, and mushroom monster burgers. On weekend evenings, you should get there early or be prepared for a lengthy wait.

C. & B. Potts Bighorn Brewery, 1650 Dell Range Blvd., tel. (307) 632-8636, is another hopping pub/sports bar with a brewery on the premises and an eclectic menu that rambles through pasta, burgers, Tex-Mex food, salads, New York-style pizzas, nachos, and buffalo wings. The big-screen TV is great for sports fans.

Grocers

The **Cheyenne Farmers Market** is held Saturdays 8 a.m.-1 p.m. during August and September in the big parking lot at 16th and Carey. This is the best place to get fresh fruits and vegetables. Cheyenne has several of the regional grocery chains, including Smith's, Albertson's, and Safeway. The largest store in town—with a deli, seafood counter, bakery, and the best produce selection—is the **Safeway,** tel. (307) 632-5171, in the Cole Square Shopping Center at 19th and Converse. Get Asian specialties from **International Groceries,** 1609 W. Lincolnway, tel. (307) 634-4888.

You'll find a big selection of beer and wine at **Town & Country Supermarket Liquors,** 614 S. Greeley Hwy., tel. (307) 632-8735, or downtown at **Albany Liquormart,** 1506 Capitol Ave., tel. (307) 632-8735.

Bakeries

Mary's Bake Shoppe, 206 W. 16th St., tel. (307) 635-6279, is a little place with delicious breads, muffins, cookies, coffee cakes, pastries, and hand-dipped chocolates. Get fresh bagels and coffee at **Mort's Bagels,** 1815 Carey Ave., tel. (307) 637-5400. Best pies in town? Try **Pie Lady Bakery & Cafe,** 3705 A E. Lincolnway, tel. (307) 637-8838.

ENTERTAINMENT

During June and July, visitors gather at Lincolnway and Carey Sts. to watch the **Cheyenne Gunslingers** put on a Hollywood-style shoot-'em-up. Hope I don't give anything away, but the good guys invariably win. It's pretty tacky, and bears absolutely no relation to Cheyenne's history. The "gunfights" take place at 6 p.m. on weekdays and at "high noon" on Saturdays (more frequently during Frontier Days). Also here at "Gunslinger Square" is a replica of the gallows used to hang Tom Horn (no mock hangings, alas) and a "Sody Saloon." A *sody saloon?* What would a real cowboy say?

During July and August, tourists fill the historic Atlas Theatre (built in 1887) at 211 W. 16th St. to watch comic Western melodramas by the **Little Theatre Players.** The experience includes plenty of audience participation, and popcorn, pizza, and beer are for sale. Call (307) 638-6543 or 635-0199 for tickets. For something more highbrow, attend Sept.-May performances of the **Cheyenne Symphony Orchestra,** tel. (307) 778-8561.

Nightlife

Cheyenne is a hopping town when it comes to nightlife—especially during Frontier Days, when every country-and-western band this side of the Mississippi finds a place to play. **Cowboy South,** 312 S. Greeley Hwy., tel. (307) 637-3800, is the biggest and best country-music bar in Cheyenne. They also have happy hour specials on weeknights. Other places that often have live music include **Hitching Post Inn Lounge,** 1700 W. Lincolnway, tel. (307) 638-3301; **Mingles,** 1318 Stillwater, (307) 632-9966; and **Little Bear Inn,** three miles north of Cheyenne, tel. (307) 634-3684. If you're looking for tunes without the booze, **Java Joint,** 1171 Carey Ave., tel. (307) 638-7332, has folk music on weekends.

Cheyenne Club, 1617 Capitol Ave., tel. (307) 635-7777, is a favorite of the Air Force crowd. The big dance floor fills as the DJ spins Top 40 dance tunes nightly. **C. & B. Potts Bighorn Brewery,** 1650 Dell Range Blvd., tel. (307) 632-8636, has DJ tunes Thurs.-Sat. nights and sports on the big-screen TV other evenings.

Lamp Lounge, 101 W. 6th, tel. (307) 635-7557, is a locals' bar with five tables for pool sharks. For something more risqué, head 10 miles south of town to the Wyoming-Colorado border, where **The Clown's Den,** tel. (307) 635-0765, is a "gentleman's club" featuring topless performers. Back on the tamer side, you'll find live piano music in the **Western Gold Lounge** at Little America, 2800 W. Lincolnway, tel. (307) 775-8400.

Movies

Local film houses are **Frontier Six Theatres,** tel. (307) 634-9499 in the Frontier Mall at 1400 Dell Range Blvd.; **Cole Square 3,** tel. (307) 635-2923 at 19th and Converse; and **Lincoln Movie Palace,** tel. (307) 637-7469, 1615 Central Street. The last of these is a classic place that opened in 1926 and today offers discount flicks.

FRONTIER DAYS

Cheyenne Frontier Days—the "Daddy of 'em All"—is Wyoming's largest and most famous annual event, with entertainment covering the spectrum from professional rodeos to parades and free pancake breakfasts. Festivities begin the last full week of July and continue for 10 action-packed days. There's something for everyone at this memorable event—in existence for more than a century—but the rodeo is the main attraction for upward of 300,000 visitors from all 50 states and many other nations. The largest number commute in from Denver, while others jam the campgrounds and motels for a hundred miles in all directions.

History

There are several versions of the origin of Cheyenne Frontier Days, the most plausible being that it was inspired when a Union Pacific employee, F.W. Angier, watched a group of cowboys from the Swan Land and Cattle Company trying to load an ornery horse into a railroad car. The spectacle sparked his imagination and when he suggested the idea of a Wild West buckin' and ropin' contest, others quickly jumped on the bandwagon. Just one month later (September 1897), the first Cheyenne Frontier Days celebration began. It was a rip-roaring success, with 15,000 people in attendance. In addition to various cowboy contests, Frontier Days included several events that you won't see today—a staged battle between Sioux Indians and the U.S. Cavalry, Pony Express demonstrations, and a mock stage holdup and hanging by vigilantes. Obviously, the production had been influenced by Buffalo Bill's Wild West Show, which was then touring Europe. Most amusing of all was the dog and hare event, where a rabbit was released to be chased by dogs. Unfortunately, the dogs in the race were quickly joined by many more from the stands so no winner was declared, although the loser was obvious. Cheyenne Frontier Days has grown over the years to a 10-day celebration (two weekends) and is regarded as one of the top four rodeos in the world (the others being California's Salinas Rodeo, Canada's Calgary Stampede, and Oregon's Pendleton Round-Up). Local enthusiasts call it the world's largest outdoor rodeo.

Activities

Frontier Days centers on the daily rodeos, with the nation's top rodeo cowboys showing their stuff. The rodeo has all the standard contests: bareback bronc riding, saddle bronc riding, Brahma bull riding, steer roping, calf roping, and steer wrestling. Other events include exciting and dangerous chuck wagon races, chaotic and amusing wild horse races, and a real crowd pleaser, the colt race (where young colts race toward their mares). With a purse of more than $400,000, the largest regular-season payoff in rodeo, Frontier Days attracts more than 1,000 contestants so many of the timed events must begin at 7 each morning!

Frontier Park is the center for a range of other activities during Frontier Days, including daily performances by the **Wind River Indian Dancers** and a **tepee village** on the south end of the parking lot. Each evening brings **musical performances** by the top stars in country music (along with some rock acts). A large and well-run **carnival** provides stomach-churning rides, sugar and grease in all forms (cotton candy, candy

Bob "Bull Dancer" Romer, a long-time rodeo clown

apples, ice cream, corn dogs, burgers, ad nauseam), plus thousands of stuffed animal prizes, stretched-out Coke bottles, velvet paintings, and other necessities. Other entertainment includes comedians, balloon "sculptors," magicians, square dances, a chili cook-off, and a costume contest. After all this debauchery, try attending the **cowboy church services** held nightly at 7 p.m. on the rodeo grounds.

Also in Frontier Park is the Cheyenne Frontier Days Old West Museum (described above), where the annual **Cheyenne Frontier Days Western Art Show and Sale** offers the chance to view or purchase works from more than 50 different Western artists.

Not everything happens in Frontier Park. On Monday, Wednesday, and Friday mornings during Frontier Days, a free **pancake feed** stuffs close to 10,000 folks. The feeding frenzy runs 7-9 a.m. Check out the cement mixer used (in theory at least) to stir up 3,600 pounds of pancake batter and the Boy Scouts trying to catch the furiously flying flapjacks. Visitors sit on bales of hay and are treated to performances by Native American dancers and musicians of all stripes. For many children, the four **parades** (held at 9:30 a.m. on both Saturdays, Tuesday, and Thursday) are a special treat featuring the largest collection of horse-drawn vehicles in the nation. You'll see everything from popcorn wagons to hearses.

The first weekend of Frontier Days is also the time for **Fort D.A. Russell Days** at F.E. Warren Air Force Base. Events include a living history camp, mountain-man rendezvous, black powder shoot, tours of the base, and a hair-raising air show starring the **U.S. Air Force Thunderbirds.** Ride the shuttle bus to the base from Frontier Mall.

Specifics

For information on Frontier Days, including a schedule of events, call (307) 778-7222 or (800) 227-6336. The event website is www.cfdrodeo.com. Some of the night shows sell out well ahead of time so advance reservations are advised. Rodeo tickets cost $11-18, while tickets to concerts are $14-24. The best deal is a combination ticket ($26) for both the rodeo and concert. Tickets are available from the ticket office south of the main grandstand or by calling the 800 number. Entrance to the midway is $2 for adults, but persons holding tickets to Frontier Days events are admitted free. Parking costs $5 per vehicle in the huge lot along Carey and 8th Avenues. (Note, however, that overnight camping is not allowed here.) Because of the large number of participants in the calf-roping, steer-roping, and steer-wrestling contests, preliminary events are held each morning 7-10 a.m., with no entrance fee charged. The main rodeo events start promptly at 1:30 p.m. and last three hours. Information wagons are in various locations around the park.

OTHER EVENTS

In addition to Frontier Days, Cheyenne plays host to a number of popular events. The Cheyenne Gunslingers and Atlas Theater melodramas are described under Entertainment above.

Night Rodeos take place Tuesday and Saturday evenings June-Aug. at Terry Bison Ranch, eight miles south of Cheyenne off I-25, tel. (307) 634-4171. The cost is $6 for adults and $3 for kids under 11. The ranch also features wagon tours, horseback and pony rides, chuck wagon dinners (Thurs.-Sat. nights), trout fishing, and even a wine cellar with locally made fruit wines.

In mid-June, the **Wyoming Brewer's Festival** attracts microbrewers and beer lovers from Wyoming and Colorado for a chance to sample the best local brews. Beer tasting is held at the Wyoming Transportation Museum, tel. (307) 637-3376. For a rather different take on beer, drive 40 miles south to Fort Collins, Colorado, where the enormous Anheuser-Busch Brewery has daily tours in the summer; call (970) 490-4691 for details.

Super Day in late June brings rides, games, a carnival, arts and crafts, and entertainment to Lions Park. Another popular event is the **Laramie County Fair,** held the first full week in August at the fairgrounds. It has all the usual county-fair activities, including art and craft contests, rodeos, exhibits, and 4-H competitions. Regional **horse shows** take place all summer at Laramie Community College; call (307) 778-1291 for upcoming shows.

The **Cheyenne Western Film Festival** in mid-September provides a chance to view classic Old West flicks and to meet minor Hollywood celebrities from the days of yore. Other events include discussions on Western films and a gunslinger's "shoot-out."

The year winds down with a **Christmas Parade, Craft Show, and Concert** in late November. The nighttime parade includes more than 100 lighted horse-drawn wagons, cars, tractors, and floats, plus a visit from St. Nick. Call (307) 638-0151 for more info.

RECREATION

Horseback and pony rides, chuck wagon dinners, trout fishing, rodeos, and wagon tours are available at **Terry Bison Ranch,** eight miles south of town along I-25, tel. (307) 634-4171.

The **Cheyenne Greenway** consists of 10 miles of paved walking and biking trails that cross the city. The trails are perfect for a romantic stroll or a morning run. One section follows Crow Creek, and the other parallels Dry Creek. Pick up a map brochure of the trails from the Convention & Visitors Bureau downtown.

Swim or play on the water slide at Lions Park's **indoor municipal pool,** tel. (307) 637-6455, or the **outdoor swimming pool** at 7th St. and House Ave., tel. (307) 637-6457. **Sloans Lake,** in Lions Park, is a summertime swimming hole and has paddleboat rentals. The park also has a botanic garden (described above), an 18-hole **municipal golf course** (tel. 307-637-6418), picnic areas, playgrounds, ponds that turn into skating rinks in the winter, and several bison. Cheyenne is also home to three other public golf courses: **Little America Golf Course,** tel. (307) 775-8400; **Prairie View,** tel. (307) 637-6420; and the 18-hole **Warren Air Force Base Golf Course,** tel. (307) 775-3556.

SHOPPING

Cheyenne is an automobile town, so most folks shop at the big malls scattered around the edges of the city. **Frontier Mall,** 1400 Dell Range Blvd., is one of the state's largest, with more than 75 stores. Also impressive is **Cole Square Shopping Center** at 19th and Converse. Wal-Mart, Sam's Club, Target, and Kmart add to the town's shop-'til-you-plop allure.

Western Wear

Downtown Cheyenne is home to one of the largest Western clothing stores in the state: **Wrangler** (owned by Corral West), 1518 Capitol Ave., tel. (307) 634-3048. This is a great place to pick up a cowboy hat or boots. Another place for quality Western wear and other gear is **Snubbing Post,** 1802 Dell Range Blvd., tel. (307) 638-6421. **Sierra Trading Post,** tel. (307) 775-8050, has a factory outlet store at the Campstool exit off I-80, a few miles east of Cheyenne.

Outdoor Gear

Out in Frontier Mall, **Gart Sports,** 1400 Dell Range Blvd., tel. (307) 632-0712, is a large sporting-goods shop. Get used outdoor gear from **Play it Again Sports,** in the Cole Shopping Center at 19th and Converse, tel. (307) 637-4030. **Marv's Place Pawn Shop,** 223 W. Lincolnway, tel. (307) 632-7887, is run by a decidedly unique owner. His ads brag of offering the "worst free coffee in town." Give it a taste. For cheap clothes, stop by the large **Salvation Army Thrift Store** at 1401 E. Lincolnway, tel. (307) 632-1507.

Galleries

Cheyenne has quite a few art galleries. The **Wyoming Arts Council Gallery,** 2320 Capitol Ave., tel. (307) 777-7742, features changing exhibits throughout the year. **Cheyenne Artist Guild,** tel. (307) 632-2263, is the state's oldest art guild (since 1949) and has a nonprofit gallery at 1010 E. 16th St. in Holliday Park. One of the best private collections can be found at **Manitou Gallery,** 1715 Carey Ave., tel. (307) 635-0019.

Books

Cheyenne has several of the largest bookstores in Wyoming. **City News,** at 18th and Carey Sts., tel. (307) 638-8671, has a big selection of Wyoming titles. **Waldenbooks** in Frontier Mall, tel. (307) 634-7099, is another good-sized shop. The largest bookshop in Cheyenne—in all of Wyoming, in fact—is **Barnes & Noble Books,** 1851 Dell Range Blvd., tel. (307) 632-3000. The store has frequent book talks, signings, and poetry nights. For used books, head to **Book Rack,** 3583 E. Lincolnway, tel. (307) 632-2014. **Abundance,** 1809 Warren Ave., tel. (307) 632-8237, will fill New Agers' needs for crystals and metaphysical titles.

INFORMATION

You'll find the **Cheyenne Convention & Visitors Bureau** at 309 W. Lincolnway, tel. (307) 778-3133 or (800) 426-5009, or on the web at www.cheyenne.org. The bricks-and-mortar version is open Mon.-Fri. 8 a.m.-5 p.m., Saturday 10 a.m.-4 p.m., and Sunday noon-4 p.m., from Memorial Day to Labor Day (daily 8 a.m.-6 p.m. during Frontier Days), and Mon.-Fri. 8 a.m.-5 p.m. the rest of the year.

The state also maintains a spacious **Wyoming Travel Information Center** at the College Dr. off-ramp (exit 7) along I-25, tel. (307) 777-7777 or (800) 225-5996. It's so windy at this exposed site that the garbage cans are all set inside concrete pipes to keep them from blowing away! The center is open daily 8 a.m.-5 p.m. all year except Thanksgiving, Christmas, and New Year's.

SERVICES

You'll find **ATMs** all over Cheyenne, including in most banks. Nearly all of these will hit you with a surcharge. Two that don't are run by First Education FCU; find them at 1400 E. College Dr. and 300 Cole Shopping Center.

Laundromats include **Duds 'n Suds,** 1802 Dell Range Blvd., tel. (307) 632-4873; **Sparkling Brites,** 912 E. Lincolnway, tel. (307) 635-6881; **Easy Way Laundry,** 900 W. 16th St., tel. (307) 638-2177; **Lady Saver Self Service Laundry,** 117 W. 5th St., tel. (307) 632-2292; and **Tip Top Laundry,** 1900 E. 21st St., tel. (307) 638-9938.

Other practicalities include the expansive **Laramie County Public Library** at 2800 Central Ave., tel. (307) 634-3561, and the main **post office** at 4800 Converse Ave., tel. (307) 772-6580. The statewide **Bureau of Land Management Office** is north of town at 5353 Yellowstone Rd., tel. (307) 775-6256.

Laramie County Community College, 1400 E. College Dr., tel. (307) 778-5222, offers both day and night classes for some 3,500 students. Founded in 1968, the school focuses primarily on technical fields, although there are two-year degrees in everything from accounting to wildlife conservation. The 271-acre campus has 18 buildings, most built in the ugly concrete-box style common to the early 1970s.

TRANSPORTATION

Bus

Cheyenne Transit Program, tel. (307) 637-6253, provides minibus service around Cheyenne for $1. Buses run Mon.-Fri. and connect various parts of the city.

The bus depot is at 222 Deming Dr. on the southeast end of town. **Greyhound,** tel. (307) 634-7744 or (800) 231-2222, www.greyhound.com, provides connections east and west along I-80. **Powder River/Coach USA,** tel. (307) 635-1327 or (800) 442-3682, has daily bus service from Cheyenne to towns in northern and central Wyoming, continuing north all the way to Billings or Rapid City and south to Denver.

Air Travel

Cheyenne Airport is just south of Dell Range Blvd., with the entrance at the east end of 8th Avenue. **United Express/Great Lakes Aviation,** tel. (800) 241-6522, has daily flights to Denver. **Armadillo Express,** 416 E. Lincolnway, tel. (307) 634-1123, provides daily van service to Denver International Airport for $28 one-way.

Cars and Taxis

At the Cheyenne airport you can rent cars from **Advantage,** tel. (307) 778-2889 or (800) 777-5500; **Avis,** tel. (307) 632-9371 or (800) 831-2847; **Dollar,** tel. (307) 632-2422 or (800) 800-4000; **Enterprise,** tel. (307) 632-1907 or (800) 325-8007; and **Hertz,** tel. (307) 634-2131 or (800) 654-3131. **Affordable Rent A Car,** 701 E. Lincolnway, tel. (307) 634-5666 or (800) 711-1564, has used cars for lower rates. The local Chevy and Honda dealer also rents cars, calling itself **Price King Rent-a-Car,** 1919 Westland, tel. (307) 638-0688.

There are five Cheyenne taxi companies: **A-A Taxi,** tel. (307) 634-6020; **A-1 Veterans Cab,** tel. (307) 634-4444; **Checker Cab,** tel. (307) 635-5555; **T.L.C. Taxi Limousine Company,** tel. (307) 634-8294; and **Yellow Cab,** tel. (307) 633-3333.

CURT GOWDY STATE PARK

The 1,645-acre Curt Gowdy State Park is 26 miles west of Cheyenne along State Hwy. 210 (Happy Jack Rd.), the scenic "back way" to Laramie. The road rises slowly through the grasslands west of Cheyenne. At Curt Gowdy, the Granite Reservoir and Crystal Reservoir offer recreation for anglers, boaters, snowmobilers, and cross-country skiers. The small lakes, constructed between 1904 and 1910, are parts of Cheyenne's water supply—no swimming. An elaborate Rube Goldberg scheme completed in 1964 now carries 12 million gallons of water from the west and across the Continental Divide, the Sierra Madre, the Snowy Range, and the Laramie Range to get it to thirsty Cheyenne.

In 1971, the two lakes at the eastern end were set aside as a state park and named for Wyoming native **Curt Gowdy.** Born in the town of Green River in 1919, Gowdy was a basketball player on the University of Wyoming's national championship team in 1943 and the long-time voice of the New York Yankees and Boston Red Sox. He later served as host of television's *The American Sportsman* for two decades and as a broadcaster of professional sporting events of all types including the World Series, the Olympics, and NFL games. Day-use of the park is $5 for non-Wyoming vehicles or $2 for cars with Wyoming plates. No entrance fees are collected in the winter months. Camping at any one of five campgrounds costs $9 for nonresidents or $4 for Wyoming residents. There's pleasant hiking in the surrounding pine-covered countryside, but by late summer the lakes tend to get severely drawn down. There are some interesting granitic formations to explore and climb. Also in the park is the historic **Hynds Lodge,** a stone structure completed in 1923 and available for families and groups to rent in the summer. For details, call park headquarters at (307) 632-7946. An **ice fishing derby** takes place in mid-February at the park.

Lodging

The open country surrounding Curt Gowdy State Park boasts three bed and breakfasts well worth the drive from either Cheyenne or Laramie. An outstanding lodging option is **A. Drummond's Ranch Bed and Breakfast,** 399 Happy Jack Rd., tel. (307) 634-6042, just a mile and a half away from the park and offering vistas of the Vedauwoo Rocks. Set on 120 acres, this is a fine place to splurge. The New England-style home includes four guest rooms, one of which contains a fireplace, steam sauna, and private jacuzzi. A second room also has its own jacuzzi. Guests will meet the menagerie of pets: llamas, goats, chicken, and sheep, plus a horse, cat, dog, and goose. The Drummonds can serve lunch and dinner (extra fee), and they have an indoor arena for folks who bring their own horses. They will also set up adventure packages to suit your interests—mountain-biking, skiing, hiking, camping, or hiking with a llama. Guest rooms have private or shared baths and cost $65-175 s or d. A delicious full breakfast is served, and kids are welcome. The website is www.cruising-america.com/drummond.html. Moderate-Luxury.

A mile west of the Drummond's home is **Windy Hills Guest House,** 393 Happy Jack Rd., tel. (307) 632-6423 or (877) 946-3944, a modern home with a deck overlooking Granite Lake and the nearby mountains. Seven guest rooms are available: two suites in the main house with private entrances; a log home with three guest rooms, a kitchen, hot tub, and jacuzzi tub; and a two-bedroom guest house with a kitchen, fireplace, and jacuzzi tub. All rooms contain private baths. Mountain bikes are available and a full breakfast is served. Rates are $75-165 s or d. Find it on the Internet at www.windyhillswyo.com. Kids welcome. Moderate-Luxury.

Another impressive place is **Bit-O-Wyo,** 470 Happy Jack Rd., tel. (307) 638-8340, a three-story 4,800-square-foot log home with picture windows overlooking Table Mountain. Inside you'll find an indoor jacuzzi and six guest rooms with shared or private baths. On Friday and Saturday nights the family puts on memorable dinner shows with Western entertainment. Lodging is available on a nightly basis for $65 s or d including a full breakfast, or you can opt for a traditional dude ranch stay: $600 for two people for three nights or $1,500 for two people per week, including lodging, meals, horseback rides, and other activities. Guests get the chance to move cattle, explore the backcountry, and enjoy trout fishing, overnight camping, and chuck wagon cookouts. The ranch is open Memorial Day to Labor Day, with B&B accommodations continuing till mid-October, and has space for up to 12 guests. For more info, look on the web at www.bitowyo.com. Moderate-Luxury.

PINE BLUFFS

Pine Bluffs (pop. 1,100) is a small agricultural and transportation center on Wyoming's eastern border. The local economy seems to be spiraling downwards, leaving a downtown that is virtually abandoned. But people continue to live in graceful homes beneath spreading shade trees. The surrounding area feels like western Nebraska, with ponderosa pines atop the long ridge just south of town. Wheat fields and irrigated potato fields surround Pine Bluffs, and the countryside is filled with silos, farm equipment, and rifle-racked pickup trucks, while the airwaves feature market reports and hog futures. The spuds head to a potato-chip factory here; look for Rocky Mountain brand—the crunchiest chips anywhere—in Wyoming stores.

Sights

The most interesting sight in Pine Bluffs is the ongoing **archaeological excavation** near a major Native American occupation site that dates back 8,000 years. Indians pitched their tepees atop the pine-covered bluffs here and headed down to the fertile valley below to hunt game and collect berries. Their tepee rings are still visible. Each summer, University of Wyoming students under the direction of Pine Bluffs native Dr. Charles Reher arrive to slowly dig through the soil in search of a buried treasure trove of prehistory. The staff will be happy to answer your questions. The covered site, open Memorial Day to Labor Day, is a 10-minute walk from the tourist information center at the rest area on the south side of I-80. Also here are a number of painted tepee replicas; pick up the brochure describing the various designs. Call (307) 766-5136 for tour information.

Several **nature trails** with interpretive signs depart from the rest area and loop to the top of the bluff. You can also access the hills by car by following Beech St. south under the freeway and turning right on the dirt road at the crest of the hill. This is an excellent place to watch sunrises and sunsets or to enjoy a picnic lunch amid the pines.

Pine Bluff's oddest sight is the five-story-tall **Our Lady of Peace Shrine**—the largest statue of the Virgin Mary in the United States. Find her in all her concrete glory overlooking I-80 just off Hwy. 30.

Pine Bluffs lies right along the great **Texas Trail;** at its peak in 1871, more than 600,000 cattle were trailed north from Texas past this point. The town became not just a watering place for the stock, but also a vital shipping point. For several years, more cattle were shipped from the railroad station at Pine Bluffs than anywhere else in the world. A monument to the Texas Trail stands in the adjacent park.

The free **Texas Trail Museum** at 3rd and Market Sts., tel. (307) 245-9347, houses a Conestoga wagon, old photos, and a small collection of homesteading and ranching items. It's open Mon.-Fri. 9 a.m.-5 p.m., Sunday1-4 p.m. May-Sept.; by appointment (stop by the town hall) at other times. Next to the museum are a caboose and several historic buildings—a one-room schoolhouse, an old church, and a railroad boardinghouse.

The **University of Wyoming High Plains Archaeology Field Lab and Visitor Center** (try saying that one fast) is at 2nd and Elm, tel. (307) 766-2208, and is open daily during the summer. Inside are interesting archaeological displays and artifacts. Call for details.

Lodging and Camping

Gator's Travelyn Motel, 515 W. 7th, tel. (307) 245-3226, has comfortable rooms for $34 s or $40-48 d (Inexpensive); while **Sunset Motel,** 315 W. 3rd, tel. (307) 245-3591, offers a few small, somewhat run-down rooms for $21-34 s or d (Budget). Motel rates may be much higher during Cheyenne Frontier Days.

Pine Bluff RV Campground, tel. (307) 245-3665 or (800) 294-4968, is a half mile east of town, and has tent spaces with no shade but lots of wind for $10. RV sites are $18. Showers cost an exorbitant $5 for noncampers; open March-October.

Food

Restaurant options are pretty slim in Pine Bluffs. Best bet is **Uncle Fred's Place,** 701 Parsons, tel. (307) 245-3443, where you'll find family meals and a salad bar. Locals also eat at the **Wild Horse Restaurant** in the Total station, 600 Parsons, tel. (307) 245-9365, but it's a cigarette smoker's heaven and a nonsmoker's hell—open 24 hours for your breathing enjoyment. The Total station also has an **ATM.**

Subway, tel. (307) 245-3405, is housed in the Ampride gas station/mini-mart on Parsons Street. Get groceries at **Texas Trail Market,** 3rd and Elm, tel. (307) 245-3302. This is a cooperatively run store, as is the auto-repair shop and the local grain elevator. Socialism in a rock-ribbed Republican state!

Events and Entertainment

Texas Trail Days comes in late July or early August with rodeos, barbecues, a parade, melodrama, and dancing.

The **Pine Bluffs Friday Night Rodeo** takes place June-Aug. at the rodeo grounds, with barrel racing, bareback riding, team roping, saddle bronc riding, and bull riding. Call (307) 632-3626 for specifics. You're also likely to see local cowboys and cowgirls practicing roping here on several afternoons a week in the summer.

The primary hangout in Pine Bluffs is the local bowling alley, **Pine Bowl,** at 3rd and Pine, tel. (307) 245-3622.

Other Practicalities

There's no chamber of commerce in town, but the state-run **Tourist Information Center** at the I-80 rest area, tel. (307) 245-3695, has both local and statewide info; open from late May to September. The **library** is at 108 E. 2nd, tel. (307) 245-3646, and Pine Bluffs has a free outdoor **swimming pool** (open summers only) at 200 E. 8th, tel. (307) 245-3783.

No bus service exists to Pine Bluffs; the nearest Greyhound stops are in Cheyenne and Kimball, Nebraska.

North from Pine Bluffs

For a delightful break from busy I-80, drive north of Pine Bluffs along State Hwy. 215 through the wheat and grasslands on the Wyoming/Nebraska border. The high plains landscape has a smattering of ponderosa pines capping the rocky bluffs, a handful of ranches, and to-the-horizon vistas. The road rolls past **Albin** (pop. 80) 18 miles north of Pine Bluffs, where an old sod house is the local claim to fame. **Albin Days** is held each July; call (307) 547-2206 for details. The nothing farm village of **LaGrange** (pop. 150) is approximately 25 miles northwest of Albin. Just to the north is 66 Mountain, so called because it supposedly has the number hidden in its profile. **Bear Mountain Station,** tel. (307) 834-2294, provides RV hookups for $10. Open Memorial Day to Labor Day. Stop in LaGrange each August for the **Mini Fair & Rodeo.**

CHUGWATER

Chugwater (pop. 200) was once headquarters for the giant Swan Land and Cattle Company, the greatest of Wyoming's cattle spreads during the 1880s. The town itself was founded in 1913 on land sold by the Swan Company. "Chugwater" has to have one of the strangest origins of any town name in America, coming from the Indian practice of driving buffalo over cliffs into the creek. The "chug" sound they made as they hit the water led Mandan Indians to call it "Water at the Place Where the Buffalo Chug." The prominent flat-topped mesa over which the bison were driven rises just north of town. When the railroad was built here thousands of buffalo bones were discovered at the base of these cliffs.

Sights

Chugwater is perhaps best known for **Chugwater Chili,** sold in stores throughout the Rockies or by mail order. Get a free taste at 210 1st St., tel. (307) 422-3345 or (800) 972-4454. The **Chugwater Chili Cook-off** is held the third Saturday in June and attracts dozens of chefs and hundreds of fire-breathing chili-eaters. Other events include a rodeo and country music. Call (307) 422-3493 or (307) 422-3201 for details on the cook-off.

Chugwater's small and free **museum** occupies an old bank building. It contains an impressive collection of brands, aging farm machinery, and various homestead-era items, along with a turn-of-the-20th-century caboose out front. Open Sat.-Sun. 1-4 p.m.; if it's closed, stop across the street at the **Chugwater Soda Fountain,** tel. (307) 422-3222, for access. In addition to great malts, the old-fashioned soda fountain also sells T-shirts, gifts, a few groceries, and liquor.

For an extraordinarily scenic drive, take State Hwy. 211 from Chugwater to Cheyenne. The road is a mix of gravel and pavement and takes longer than I-25 but is virtually free of traffic. The road passes through a Wyoming landscape of grass and sage-carpeted hills, tree-lined creeks, magnificent old ranches, and herds of deer and antelope. Stop to listen to the meadowlarks on a spring day or to watch the clouds roiling overhead in this peaceful place.

Practicalities

On a historic 75,000-acre cattle ranch 15 miles west of Chugwater, **Diamond Guest Ranch,** tel. (307) 422-3564 or (800) 932-4222, is popular with families and retirees. The ranch began in 1884 and was for many years a breeding center for Clydesdale and Morgan horses. It has been a guest ranch since 1968, but retains many of the original buildings. Outdoor recreation opportunities include horseback rides, fishing, hiking, hayrides, mountain-biking, and an outdoor swimming pool. Also here are a restaurant (open for dinner) and a bar. Campsites cost $14 for tents or $18 for RVs. Cabins (perfect for families) run $50-70 d, and guest rooms are $55 s or d. Open mid-May to mid-October. The Internet address is www.diamondgr.com. Inexpensive.

Back in town, **Super 8 Motel,** 100 Buffalo Dr., tel. (307) 422-3248 or (800) 800-8000, has a small outdoor pool and rooms for $55 s or $59 d. It's considerably better than most Super 8 Motels. Inexpensive.

The building also houses a restaurant serving burgers, sandwiches, chicken, pasta, pork chops, and more. Lunches and dinners are also served inside a rough-hewn restaurant called **The Steak-Out,** 417 1st St., tel. (307) 422-3251. **Pitzer's RV Park,** tel. (307) 422-3421, has RV hookups for $10; open year-round.

The state has a rest area just south of Chugwater on I-25.

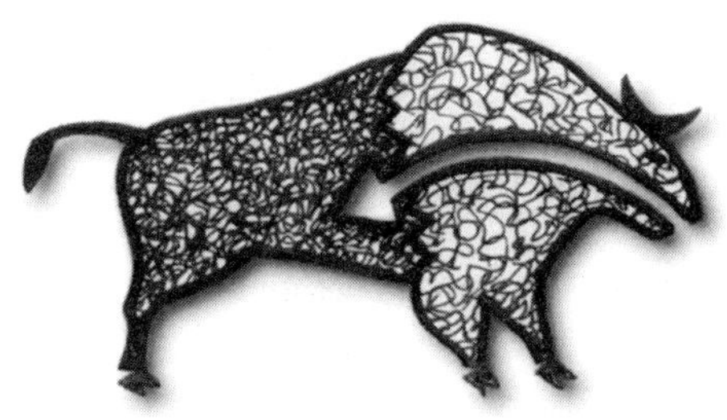

WHEATLAND

Wheatland (pop. 3,500) is a friendly middle-America town with a shady downtown and farming country in all directions. Despite the name, wheat is not the primary crop grown here; sugar beets, dry beans, and barley are. The largest local employer is Laramie River Station, a 1,650-megawatt coal-fired power plant five miles north of town. It supplies electricity to a grid that feeds an eight-state area. Another substantial employer is a local marble quarry that mines dolomite in the Laramie Mountains and crushes it for use in everything from aquarium gravel to cattle feed. Don't let on that I told you, but Wheatland also has Minuteman III nuclear missiles out in the country near the power plant. Perhaps for this reason, the town boasts one of the highest number of churches per capita anywhere—23 different houses of worship crowd the town.

History

An early settler in this part of Wyoming called it "a desolate looking place, nothing but sagebrush, cactus, rocks, mudhole, rattlesnakes, and coyotes." It took water to change all this. Wheatland is a creation of the Wyoming Development Company, founded in 1883 by a number of individuals, including Senators Joseph M. Carey and Francis E. Warren. In one of the few successful applications of the famous Carey Act in Wyoming, the company built a dam on Big Laramie River and canals to carry the water to some 50,000 acres where homesteaders formed the Wheatland Colony. Today it remains the largest privately owned irrigation system in the nation. In 1905 the town of Wheatland was incorporated (the name won out over Wheatdale and Wheatridge) and became the hub of activity for the region—and later the Platte County seat. During the late 1970s and early '80s, Wheatland followed the boom pattern common to other Wyoming towns: nearby oil and gas exploration and construction of the giant power plant attracted thousands to town. When things went bust, Wheatland was pulled down, but it has recovered somewhat. Downtown may not be bustling, but it's clean and attractive. Agriculture, that old standby, has increased in importance. Wyoming Premium Farms runs a gigantic hog farm a dozen miles north of Wheatland that produces 100,000 pigs annually. Hold your nose!

Sights

The free **Laramie Peak Museum** on 16th and Elliot Sts. is open Mon.-Fri. 1-5 p.m. mid-May to mid-September (till 8 p.m. on Tuesday, Thursday, and Friday in midsummer), or by appointment at other times; tel. (307) 322-2322. It houses a variety of homestead-era flotsam and jetsam ranging from turn-of-the-20th-century tricycles to a stuffed vulture. A saddle and cowboy hat here have burn marks from when lightning struck a local cowboy (he lived). The marble-columned **Platte County Court House** at 9th and Walnut is easily the most imposing structure in Wheatland. It was built in 1911.

Call (307) 322-9601 for free weekday tours of the huge **Laramie River Station** power plant just north of town.

For a delightful all-day loop drive, head west from Wheatland out **Palmer Canyon Road** through the farm fields and open plains, past the old stone buildings of Muleshoe Ranch, and high into the cool Laramie Range. The first 10 miles are paved. Once in the hills, the dirt road (avoid after rains or in the spring) winds through a rocky ponderosa pine-covered landscape that comes alive with springtime flowers. You can return to Wheatland the same way, or do a big loop by turning north onto Cottonwood Park Rd. and then east again on Fletcher Park Road. Check with the visitor's center for the specific route, or look over Forest Service or topo maps.

Approximately 30 miles southwest of Wheatland on State Hwy. 34 is the Wyoming Department of Game and Fish **Sybille Wildlife Research Center** (Sybille is pronounced "suh-BEEL"). The facility houses elk, mule and white-tailed deer, bighorn sheep, and black-footed ferrets. The separate black-footed ferret facility is operated by the U.S. Fish & Wildlife Service. The visitor center, tel. (307) 322-2784, is open daily 8:30 a.m.-4:30 p.m. June to mid-September (closed the rest of the year) and includes exhibits and videos on the endangered black-footed ferret. To lessen the impact and potential health threats from introduced diseases, tours of the research facility are not available, but TV monitors show activity in the ferret facility, where around 200 of these cute black-masked furries live. A couple of live ferrets may be actually in the visitor center itself. Behind the visitor center is an observation deck and short nature trail along Sybille Creek. Find out more about ferrets on the Internet at www.blackfootedferret.org.

Accommodations

Several places provide lodging in Wheatland. Expect to pay higher rates during Frontier Days, even though it is an hour's drive to Cheyenne. Lodging is listed below by price, with the least expensive places first. Add a five percent tax to these rates.

Budget-Inexpensive: The friendly **Wyoming Motel,** 1101 9th St., tel. (307) 322-5383 or (800) 839-5383, has older but clean furnishings, along with in-room fridges and a barbecue. Rates are $24 s or $31-37 d. **Parkway Motel,** 1257 South Rd., tel. (307) 322-3080, has standard rooms for $30 s or $34-36 d.

Inexpensive: Motel West Winds, 1756 South St., tel. (307) 322-2705, charges $35 s or $40-45 d. **Motel 6,** 95 16th St., tel. (307) 322-1800 or (800) 466-8356, www.motel6.com, is a fairly new motel, with predictable rooms for $40 s or $46 d.

Vimbo's Motel, 203 16th St., tel. (307) 322-3842 or (800) 577-3842, features large and well-maintained rooms for $43 s or $45 d.

Blackbird Inn Bed & Breakfast, 1101 11th St., tel. (307) 322-4540, is a lovingly restored 1910 Victorian home with a wraparound front porch that makes a fine place to sit on a summer evening. Inside are four guest rooms with shared baths and a two-room suite with a private bath. The home is furnished in antiques. Rates are $45 s or d, including a full breakfast. Kids are welcome.

Inexpensive-Moderate: Best Western Torchlite Motor Inn, 1809 N. 16th St., tel. (307) 322-4070 or (800) 662-3968, charges $51-56 s or $56-61 d and has an outdoor pool and jacuzzi.

SWAN LAND AND CATTLE COMPANY

The most famous of all Wyoming ranching operations was the Swan Land and Cattle Company, Ltd., founded in 1883 by Alexander and Thomas Swan with enormous financial backing from Scottish investors—£600,000 the first year and an additional £1.6 million over the next three years. At its peak in the mid-1880s, the company's holdings reached from its headquarters along Chugwater Creek westward for 120 miles to the North Platte River near Rawlins. More than 110,000 cattle ranged across this vast expanse. The company bought 550,000 acres of Union Pacific Railroad land (and therefore controlled the checkerboard of public land in alternating sections) and purchased government land along major creeks in the area. By doing this, it controlled access to water in this semiarid country, thus keeping others from settling on surrounding public lands. All told, the Swan Land and Cattle Company had its tentacles over nearly a million acres covering more than 30 different ranches. The company had dozens of different brands, but locals knew it as the "Two Bar." Cowboys loved the company because it always provided good working conditions and wages ($20 a month to start) and the best grub around.

In the mid-1880s, though, things began to turn sour and by 1886 the Scottish investors accused Alexander Swan of fraud and misrepresentation; the 110,000 cattle shown on the books did not all exist on the hoof. A lawsuit eventually led to Swan's firing. Even more devastating was the severe winter of 1886-87, which killed off thousands of the firm's cows and calves, pushing the company to the brink of bankruptcy. Amazingly, the reorganized company managed to survive for more than 50 years, though it began raising sheep instead of cattle after 1903. It was quite prosperous during WW I, when wool prices soared, but its fortunes gradually declined with the economy. By 1950, the vast operation had been entirely liquidated. Some folks claim that Steamboat, a wild bronc from the old Two Bar Ranch, was the inspiration for the bucking horse symbol found on Wyoming license plates. Many of the historic ranch's buildings are still intact, and the complex has been designated a National Historic Landmark.

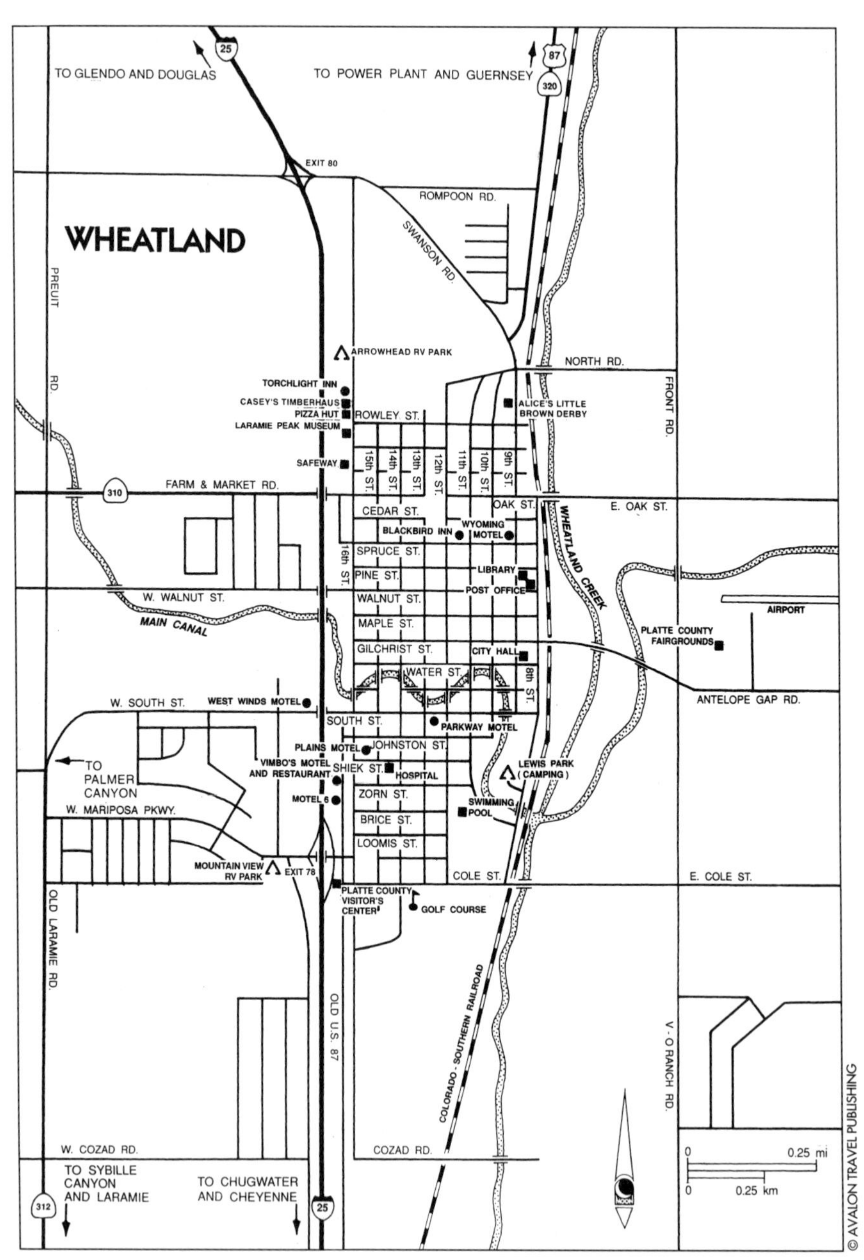

WHEATLAND
TO GLENDO AND DOUGLAS
TO POWER PLANT AND GUERNSEY
25
87
320
EXIT 80
ROMPOON RD.
SWANSON RD.
PREUIT RD.
ARROWHEAD RV PARK
TORCHLIGHT INN
CASEY'S TIMBERHAUS
PIZZA HUT
LARAMIE PEAK MUSEUM
ROWLEY ST.
ALICE'S LITTLE BROWN DERBY
NORTH RD.
FRONT RD.
SAFEWAY
15th ST.
14th ST.
13th ST.
12th ST.
11th ST.
10th ST.
9th ST.
310
FARM & MARKET RD.
OAK ST.
E. OAK ST.
CEDAR ST.
BLACKBIRD INN
WYOMING MOTEL
WHEATLAND CREEK
16th ST.
SPRUCE ST.
PINE ST.
LIBRARY
POST OFFICE
W. WALNUT ST.
WALNUT ST.
MAIN CANAL
MAPLE ST.
AIRPORT
PLATTE COUNTY FAIRGROUNDS
GILCHRIST ST.
CITY HALL
WATER ST.
8th ST.
W. SOUTH ST.
WEST WINDS MOTEL
ANTELOPE GAP RD.
SOUTH ST.
PARKWAY MOTEL
PLAINS MOTEL
JOHNSTON ST.
TO PALMER CANYON
VIMBO'S MOTEL AND RESTAURANT
SHIEK ST.
HOSPITAL
LEWIS PARK (CAMPING)
MOTEL 6
ZORN ST.
W. MARIPOSA PKWY.
SWIMMING POOL
BRICE ST.
LOOMIS ST.
MOUNTAIN VIEW RV PARK
EXIT 78
COLE ST.
E. COLE ST.
PLATTE COUNTY VISITOR'S CENTER
GOLF COURSE
OLD LARAMIE RD.
OLD U.S. 87
COLORADO - SOUTHERN RAILROAD
V - O RANCH RD.
W. COZAD RD.
COZAD RD.
0 0.25 mi
0 0.25 km
TO SYBILLE CANYON AND LARAMIE
312
TO CHUGWATER AND CHEYENNE
25

Camping

You can camp for free beneath the cottonwoods at 40-acre **Lewis Park** right in town; tel. (307) 322-2962. This quiet spot is a perfect place to relax. Showers and RV hookups are available; three night maximum stay.

Camping is also free at **Grayrocks Reservoir,** northeast of Wheatland beyond the power plant. No RV hookups, but coin-operated showers are available. The nearby Cottonwood Canteen, tel. (307) 322-2242, sells a few groceries, beer, gas, and bait. Open summers only. In addition, free campsites can be found along Wheatland Reservoir and Rock Lake a few miles southwest of town, as well as on Forest Service land in the Laramie Mountains west of Wheatland.

RVers may prefer to park at **Mountain View RV Park,** tel. (307) 322-4858, 77 20th St. (just west of exit 78). Rates are $14; open May-September. On the north end of town, **Arrowhead RV Park,** 2005 N. 16th St., tel. (307) 322-3467, has RV hookups for $10 and tent sites for $5. Open all year.

Twenty-eight miles west of Wheatland, **Blue Grass Ranch & Cattle Co.,** tel. (307) 322-4406, has catch-and-release fishing and secluded camping, but no electricity, running water, or toilets. And for this you pay $75 a day! Open May-September.

Food

Marie's Goodie Shop, 719 9th St., tel. (307) 322-5321, makes good sandwiches for lunch—including cabbage burgers—and serves hot coffee and pastries for a quick breakfast. Directly across the street, **Mom's Kitchen,** tel. (307) 322-5912, is a hole-in-the-wall eatery with burgers big enough to feed two. Pseudo-Mexican food comes to you—in all its microwaved glory—courtesy of the Korean chefs at **El Gringo's,** 705 10th St., tel. (307) 322-4402.

Vimbo's Family Restaurant, 203 16th St., tel. (307) 322-3725, is a longtime star on the local scene, with dependable homemade food, a big menu, and friendly waitresses. The breakfast buffet ($6) is especially popular, as is the Friday night seafood buffet ($11). Recommended.

Housed in an attractive log building, **Casey's Timberhaus Family Restaurant,** 1803 16th St., tel. (307) 322-4932, is another bring-out-the-gang restaurant, with a so-so salad bar and standard American burgers and steak. Breakfasts are a better bet.

Terra Grano Pizza, 1557 South St., tel. (307) 322-4888, is a friendly little place with from-scratch bagels, sandwiches, big salads, homemade soups, espresso, pizzas, and calzones. They even make a tasty "breakfast pizza" with scrambled eggs.

Pizza Hut, 1801 N. 16th St., tel. (307) 322-4001, is the only place open late most nights. Other chains in Wheatland include Subway and Burger King.

Wheatland's surprise is **Alice's Little Brown Derby,** 1707 9th St., tel. (307) 322-4257. Occupying a 1950s-era trailer house, it has great food, reasonable prices, and huge portions. They always offer lunch specials, and the burgers and chicken-fried steak are famous. For something different, try the Friday night prime rib specials, but get there early or it may be gone. Even the Burlington Northern freight train stops so the crew can come over for dinner!

Groceries are available at the homey **Huffer's Food Pride,** 702 10th St., tel. (307) 322-3343, or the larger **Safeway,** 16th and Oak Sts., tel. (307) 322-4530.

Recreation

There is a fine outdoor **swimming pool** (tel. 307-322-9254) in Lewis Park, open in the summer. The nine-hole **Wheatland Golf Course** is at 1253 Cole, tel. (307) 322-3675. **Cinema West,** 609 10th St., tel. (307) 322-9032, is the local movie house.

Seven miles south of Wheatland, the century-old **Grant Ranch,** tel. (307) 322-2923, offers guided horseback tours and three-day cattle drives in the summer.

Events

Wheatland has a big fireworks show at the fairgrounds on the **Fourth of July.** The **Summer Fun Fest and Antique Tractor Pull** takes place in June with live music, dancing, food and craft booths, and a tractor pull in Lewis Park. The **Platte County Fair and Rodeo** comes to town in early August and offers a street breakfast, barbecue, parade, rodeo, entertainment, and all the usual fun of a country fair. Most enjoyable of all is the pig wrestling. Call (307) 322-2322 for details.

Information and Services

The always helpful **Platte County Visitor's Center,** tel. (307) 322-2322, www.plattechamber.com, is next to I-25 exit 78. Hours are Mon.-Fri. 8 a.m.-6 p.m. and Sat.-Sun. 10 a.m.-2 p.m. Memorial Day to Labor Day, and Mon.-Fri. 8 a.m.-5 p.m. the rest of the year.

Other practicalities include the **Platte County Library** at 904 9th St., tel. (307) 322-2689, and the **post office** at 852 Walnut St., tel. (307) 332-3287. Get fast cash from **ATMs** in local banks, gas stations, and markets. Wash clothes at **Sunrise Laundry,** on 8th and Maple, or at **North 16th St. Laundromat,** next to Torchlight Inn on 16th Street.

Transportation

Powder River/Coach USA, tel. (307) 322-2725 or (800) 442-3682, has daily bus service from Wheatland to towns in northern and central Wyoming, continuing north to Billings or Rapid City and south to Cheyenne or Denver. Buses stop at the North 16th St. Laundromat.

Rent cars from **Laramie Peak Motors,** tel. (307) 322-2355 or (800) 564-2355.

GUERNSEY AND VICINITY

Guernsey (pop. 1,200) is a scenic railroad and ranching town along the once mighty North Platte River. The river is now just a trickle in late summer, thanks to all the upstream dams. The town is named for Charles A. Guernsey, a prominent local rancher and legislator who came here in the late 19th century. The town is right in the heart of Oregon Trail country, with Fort Laramie just 11 miles east and numerous 19th-century historical markers. The Wyoming Army National Guard maintains Camp Guernsey, a large troop training facility just north of town. Watch your speed here; local cops strictly enforce the 30 mph limit!

Emigrant Trail Sights

The Oregon Trail ran just on the other side of the North Platte River from Guernsey. One mile south of town are some of the deepest **Oregon Trail ruts** anywhere along the historic route. Informative plaques describe the site, and a short trail leads uphill to four-foot-deep gouges cut into the soft sandstone. The paths of bullwhackers are visible alongside. The old wagon trail is easy to follow in both directions, and the surrounding landscape has probably changed little since the last wagon train rolled past. Perhaps better than any historic photos or written descriptions, these deep ruts serve as permanent reminders of the great westward migration. Not far away is a white obelisk marking the grave of Lucindy Rollins, one of the thousands who died on the hard road west.

The hundred-foot-tall **Register Cliff** is four miles south of Guernsey. Here the soft limestone made a perfect place for passing emigrants to carve their names, and thousands took the time to do so. The oldest—dating to the 1850s—are now behind a chain-link fence to keep folks from defacing them further. Hundreds of swallows nest on the cliff here. North of Guernsey, ruts of the historic Mormon Trail are visible along **Emigrant**

The ruts near Guernsey are some of the deepest anywhere along the Oregon Trail.

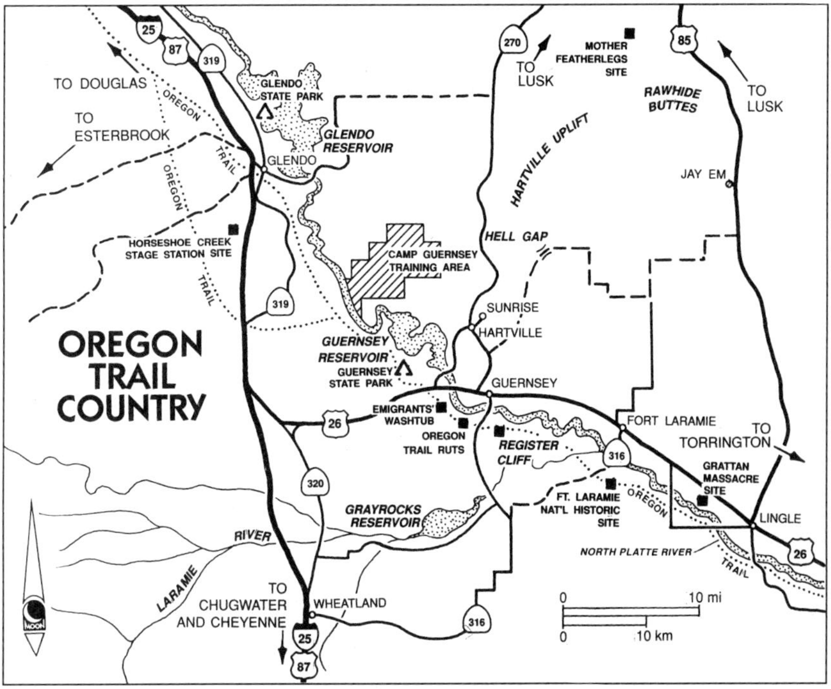

Hill, where Mormon pioneers struggled to hoist their wagons up the steep slope.

Another important nearby site was **Emigrants' Washtub,** a warm springs where weary travelers stopped to bathe and wash clothes. The springs are an enjoyable place to relax even today and are a two-mile walk along a dry creekbed. Access is a bit tricky since you pass through private land along the way and need to watch out for old shells left behind from National Guard training exercises. Get access information from the visitor center.

Lodging and Camping

No bunkhouse accommodations are to be had at the **Bunkhouse Motel,** tel. (307) 836-2356, but nice motel rooms are $47-49 s or d. Down the street, **Sagebrush Motel,** tel. (307) 836-2331, charges $32 s or $37 d. All the rooms have fridges, and some also contain microwaves. Both Inexpensive.

You'll find pleasant riverside campsites near the Oregon Trail ruts at the town-managed **Larson Park,** tel. (307) 836-2255. Camping is $5 for tents or $9 for RVs, including showers. Those who aren't camping here can use the showers for $2. Open April to mid-October.

Food

Riverview Restaurant, tel. (307) 836-2191, has specials most nights, including roast prime rib Saturday evenings. Big portions, too. **Burrito Brothers Mexican Food** offers decent Mexican food, and **Trail Inn,** tel. (307) 836-2573, is the place to go for steaks and a Sunday buffet.

Guernsey Lunch Box on the east side of town has standard American fare in a fast-food setting: burgers, chicken-fried steak, pizzas, corn dogs, sandwiches, and a salad bar. The pizzas are actually quite tasty. Get groceries at **B&F Super Foods.**

Other Practicalities

Guernsey's small **visitor center/museum** at S.W. Wyoming and W. Sunrise Sts. opens during the summer months. It's right in front of the town **swimming pool,** which is also open seasonally. The small **Guernsey library** is open Mon.-Saturday.

Get fast cash from the **ATM** inside the Phillips 66 station. The nine-hole **Trail Ruts Golf Course** provides a place to putt around, or you can bowl a few lines at **Oregon Trail Lanes.** Guernsey's airport is surprisingly large and well equipped, not because of any commercial service—there isn't any—but because of the nearby National Guard training facilities.

Each Fourth of July, the **Old Timer's Rodeo** comes to Guernsey, and offers all the standard small-town fun: a parade, a rodeo, a barbecue, a street dance, and fireworks. **Labor Day** brings a demolition derby and an arts-and-crafts fair.

HARTVILLE AREA

Six miles north of Guernsey on State Hwy. 270 is the picturesque old mining community of Hartville (pop. 80). Established in 1884, it is the **oldest incorporated town in Wyoming.** It was named for Col. Verling Hart, an officer at nearby Fort Laramie and owner of a copper mine here. The Hartville Uplift—as it is known by geologists—is one of the most mineral-rich regions in Wyoming. Indians used its iron as pigment to make war paint. During the 1870s, prospectors found gold, silver, copper, onyx, and iron ore in these scenic pine- and juniper-dotted hills. Copper brought the first miners, but by 1887 it had been mostly mined out and they turned to iron ore. Hartville arose as a shopping, gambling, boozing, and whoring center for the miners; many of the historic stone and false-front buildings still stand.

Of note is **Miners Bar**—the state's oldest drinking establishment. The cherry wood back bar was made in Germany in 1864 and shipped to Fort Laramie before landing in Hartville in 1881. The bar is only open in the summer and has a horseshoe pit next door. Also in Hartville is an old stone jail.

The mining ghost town of **Sunrise** (closed to the public) is just a mile east of Hartville. An extraordinarily rich body of iron ore was discovered here in 1887, and a dozen years later the Colorado Fuel and Iron Corp. established an open-pit iron mine, a mine that would eventually reach 650 feet in depth, the largest glory hole in the world. It closed in 1984 and reclamation work has restored the gaping hole to a more natural contour. When the mine first opened, the company hired some 750 predominantly Italian and Greek emigrants to dig the ore, which was shipped to a smelter in Pueblo, Colorado. To house the workers, the well-planned company town of Sunrise sprang up. The mine was closed in 1980 due to a lessened demand for ore, and its brick buildings now stand abandoned. It is a fascinating place to explore but isn't open to the public. You may be able to get access by asking locally for permission. Sunrise claims a minuscule footnote to history: *Ripley's Believe It or Not!* noted that the town had the longest string of car garages in the world. They are still standing, but it is doubtful that just six garages would merit such a rating today.

The Hartville area is part of the so-called **Spanish Diggings,** an extensive archaeological site that covers hundreds of square miles. Early settlers believed this to be the site of a Spanish gold mine—hence the name—but it is now known to have been used instead by Native Americans gathering flint for arrowheads. They mined quartzite, jasper, moss agate, and chalcedony here for perhaps 10,000 years. Stone flakes and countless old pits up to 15 feet deep and 50 feet across abound in this region. The material mined was carried all the way to the Missouri River. You'll find hundreds of tepee rings and rock chips here. One of the most important aboriginal places in Wyoming is in this area—an 11,000-year-old paleo-Indian site called **Hell Gap.**

The road north from Hartville (State Hwy. 270) leads over pine-carpeted hills and then descends through rolling grassland with a backdrop of rocky buttes and antelope grazing beside old windmills. There are dramatic views of Laramie Peak from the hilltops. At **Manville** (pop. 130) the road meets U.S. 18/20, which leads to Lusk. There's not much in Manville other than a few old buildings including one of the smallest post offices in Wyoming, a water tower, a school, and a gas station/cafe/bar.

GUERNSEY STATE PARK

Two state parks are found along the North Platte River in eastern Wyoming. Seven miles long and covering 6,538 acres, Guernsey is the smaller of the two but is far more interesting than its sister, Glendo State Park. The south entrance to Guernsey State Park is a mile northwest of Guernsey, and the road connects through to the Hartville area. The park surrounds Guernsey Reservoir, which is backed up behind a 105-foot-tall, 560-foot-long earthen dam completed in 1927. Originally, the dam stored 74,000 acre-feet of water, but half that capacity has been lost due to siltation. To reduce this problem, authorities now drain the reservoir each summer after the Fourth of July—killing off many of the fish and sometimes creating havoc with boaters, since it can take place with almost no warning. Don't bother bringing your fishing pole. It generally fills up again by Labor Day weekend.

Guernsey is surrounded by scenic grass-and-sage-covered hills topped with juniper and pine. The drive from Hartville through the park is a surprise after the open sage-and-grass country north of here. Pink-walled sandstone cliffs suddenly appear as the narrow, winding road (not for RVs) enters the canyon, hugs the cliffs as it passes the lake, and then climbs into the pines. There is a pleasant sandy beach five miles west along the southern shore and there are 19 different **campgrounds,** each costing $9 for nonresidents or $4 for Wyoming residents year-round. The water is quite warm, making this a popular swimming hole.

Day-use at Guernsey State Park costs $5 for nonresident vehicles or $2 for folks with Wyoming plates, but fees generally aren't collected after mid-September. Call (307) 836-2334 for more information.

Other than the scenery, the main attractions in Guernsey State Park are the wonderful stone structures built by the Civilian Conservation Corps during the 1930s—some of the best examples of CCC craftsmanship in existence. **Guernsey State Park Museum**—built in 1936—is the finest of all, with an arched stone entrance facing impressive Laramie Peak 35 miles to the west. Inside are enormous hand-hewn timbers, wrought-iron light fixtures, and flagstone floors. This place was built to last! The free museum, tel. (307) 836-2900, is open daily 10 a.m.-6 p.m. Memorial Day to Labor Day, closed the rest of the year, and houses 14 displays created by the CCC to illustrate the geology and human use of the surrounding country. Take a look at the historical slide show.

Other park structures built of native materials include roads, overlooks, rock walls, culverts, bridges, and picnic shelters. Most impressive is a massive sandstone picnic shelter known as "The Castle," which faces the reservoir and Laramie Peak. Take the side road up to **Brimmer Point Overlook** for outstanding sunset vistas. Not far away is the "million dollar privy," so named because it took so much time and money to build. Guernsey State Park also contains eight miles of hiking trails and a short nature trail near the museum. Pick up a trail guide inside.

GLENDO STATE PARK

Twenty-five miles east of Douglas and 32 miles north of Wheatland, 10,000-acre Glendo State Park surrounds Glendo Reservoir. A 167-foot-high earthen dam backs up water for 14 miles and generates some 24,000 kilowatts of electricity. This is one of the largest reservoirs on the North Platte River, and it has almost 80 miles of shoreline. Note, however, that drought years sometimes reduce the reservoir to little more than a puddle. The surrounding country is treeless and windy but the towering 10,272-foot summit of Laramie Peak dominates the skyline to the west. The surprisingly warm water at Sandy Beach makes this a play area for families from surrounding towns. Other attractions are the Red Cliffs, where cliff divers agonize over the long drop, and Muddy Bay, where anglers look for walleye (there are some lunkers here), perch, or trout. You can explore dozens of small coves by boat or float down the river below the dam. The wind can really blow, making for good windsurfing conditions but also creating hazards for folks who go out in small boats.

Practicalities

There are seven state park campgrounds ($9 for nonresidents, $4 for Wyoming residents; open year-round) on the eastern end of Glendo Reservoir. Get permits from park headquarters, tel. (307) 735-4433, near the dam. Day-use costs $5 for nonresident vehicles or $2 for Wyoming vehicles.

Town of Glendo

The desolate town of Glendo (pop. 200) is just two miles from Glendo State Park, near the site of the old **Horseshoe Creek Stage Station.** Built by Mormons in the 1850s, this station was later burned by them to keep it out of government hands. A small **Glendo Historical Museum** next to the town office is open Mon.-Fri. 8 a.m.-noon and 1-4 p.m. and displays early settlers' gear, dinosaur bones, and rocks.

Lodging (in mobile homes) is available at **Howard's Motel,** 106 A St., tel. (307) 735-4252, for $20 s or $27 d. Budget. The store here has an ATM. **Lakeview Motel & Trailer Court,** tel. (307) 735-4461, is just north of town overlooking the lake, with RV hookups for $12 and tent sites for $10. Simple cottages are also available.

Hall's Glendo Marina, near the dam, tel. (307) 735-4216, has rustic motel accommodations overlooking the lake for $48-58 s or d. Inexpensive. Also here are a restaurant and small grocery store, plus RV sites with hookups ($15). Hall's rents fishing boats, pontoon boats, jet skis, and other equipment for water play, and is open April-September.

Rooster's Old Western Saloon, tel. (307) 735-4451, serves the best dinners around, with steak, prime rib, fresh walleye, and Indian fry bread on the menu. The restaurant is open Thurs.-Sat. evenings only. Meals are also available at **Corner Cafe,** tel. (307) 735-4476.

Cribbage players take note: Diamond A's Lounge and Grill, tel. (307) 735-4265, hosts the **Platte Valley Cribbage Tournament** the last weekend of February. It's said to be the oldest consecutive tournament in the United States. **Glendo Days** arrives in mid-June, featuring a hot-air-balloon rally, craft fair, games, a flea market, food booths, and a street dance. Probably the strangest event is "chicken-poop poker." You probably don't want to know the rules. Call (307) 735-4265 for details on Glendo Days. The **Glendo Marina Walleye Tournament,** tel. (307) 735-4216, comes around in early June, and a fireworks display takes place on the Fourth of July.

FORT LARAMIE NATIONAL HISTORIC SITE

One of the most important historic sites in all Wyoming is old Fort Laramie, located three miles south of the town of the same name. The fort played a variety of roles as the West was developed: Indian trading post, emigrant way station, and military center. Fort Laramie stood at the crossroads of history. The budding territory's first school and post office opened here, and nearly every famous citizen of the frontier era—from Jim Bridger to Mark Twain—stopped in. Today Fort Laramie is one of the most popular stopping points for visitors who want a taste of the rich history of this region.

HISTORY

In 1834, trader William Sublette halted along the banks of the Laramie River near its confluence with the North Platte. With him were 35 mountain men, their pack animals weighted down with trade items for the annual rendezvous along the Green River. Sublette had a bold plan to build a permanent trading post here, one that would make it easier to bring supplies west and beaver furs and buffalo robes back east, a place where Indians and whites could parley and profit. He left behind a dozen men to begin work on what would become Fort William (named after its founder) and hurried west to the rendezvous. The men threw up a cottonwood stockade with blockhouses on the corners and a tunnel to the outer gate for trading with the Indians.

The post changed hands a couple of times in the next two years. Changing its name to Fort Lucien, it became an important trade center for Pierre Chouteau's American Fur Company. By 1841, competition from another trading post—built just a mile away—forced the company to start again. This time they spent $10,000 building a whitewashed adobe fort near the already rotting old one. Fort John-on-the-Laramie was the official name given to the second fort, but this was quickly shortened to Fort Laramie.

During the next eight years, Fort Laramie emerged as a strategic center trade with the Indians; more than 10,000 buffalo robes were purchased each year. (Traders generally paid the

Old Bedlam, the oldest building at Fort Laramie National Historic Site

equivalent of $1 per robe in the form of gunpowder, hatchets, tobacco, coffee, sugar, blankets, and, of course, liquor. The robes were sold in St. Louis for $4 each.) But its time as a trading post gradually gave way to a new role for the fort.

The Army Takes Over

Fort Laramie stood right along the main trail to Oregon and California. It was one-third of the way from Missouri to the Columbia River mouth and provided a much-anticipated break before the long, desolate trek over the Continental Divide. In 1843, nearly a thousand people passed the fort. The numbers increased each year, reaching a crescendo after gold was discovered in California in 1849. Soon thereafter, more than 50,000 emigrants were trudging into Fort Laramie each summer. They stopped to repair wheels at the carpentry and blacksmith shops, purchase food and whiskey at the store, or trade tired stock for fresh oxen and horses. The latter was the best deal for traders at the fort; all they had to do was put the oxen and horses they had gotten in trade (generally a two-for-one deal) out to pasture for a couple of weeks and then trade them as fresh stock to subsequent emigrants.

This great migration westward had its negative consequences. Indians complained that buffalo were being shot and forced away from their traditional migration routes and that the thousands of stock brought by the emigrants were destroying the grass. The inevitable conflicts began as young warriors halted wagon trains, demanding "tolls" in the form of tobacco, coffee, or sugar. Quickly, this escalated into attacks against the emigrants, and a great hue and cry went up for protection from the "savages." Thus it was that Congress gave Fort Laramie the new role of military garrison mandated to protect the Oregon Trail.

In 1849, the army purchased Fort Laramie for $4,000, establishing the first military post in what would become Wyoming. Some 180 men—both cavalrymen and infantrymen—were assigned to the post. A rapid expansion program was begun; the old adobe fort served as temporary quarters while more elaborate facilities were built. The army's Fort Laramie did not fit the Hollywood stereotype of a frontier fort—it had no log perimeter or blockhouses. The fort was instead laid out around a central parade ground, with clapboard and "lime grout" concrete buildings forming a loose perimeter. In case of attack, the army was prepared to retreat to a single, heavily fortified building. Despite this general lack of protection and the fact that Indians once brazenly drove off the fort's horses, the fort was never attacked by Indians, and most soldiers never engaged in battle with the Indians.

Fort Laramie was essentially a male bastion, though a few officers' wives were present. The only exceptions were laundresses, hired generally on the basis of their physical appearance: the less attractive the better, so as to not appeal to the soldiers' prurient interests. A small group of Indians, derisively termed "Laramie Loafers," soon attached themselves to the fort, camping nearby and providing scouts, interpreters, errand boys, and paramours. Fort Laramie was not a pleasant place. The food was deplorable, discipline so strict that even the smallest infraction could land a man in the brig, and sanitary conditions were so bad that by 1880 it was getting hard to find a place to dig latrines that had not already been contaminated. The infrequent paydays turned into drunken brawls. No wonder so many men deserted their post and slipped off for the promising goldfields of California! The inevitable "hog ranches" also grew up near the fort and offered an escape from the day-to-day monotony of the soldiers' lives. In 1877, Lt. John G. Bourke described the "ranches" as

> *tenanted by as hardened and depraved a set of witches as could be found on the face of the globe. Each of these establishments was equipped with a rum-mill of the worst kind and each contained from three to half a dozen Cyprians, virgins whose lamps were always burning brightly in expectance of the coming of the bridegroom, and who lured to destruction the soldiers of the garrison. In all my experience I have never seen a lower, more beastly set of people of both sexes.*

For the next four decades, Fort Laramie served as the nerve center for this part of the plains, providing troops and cavalry to retaliate against Indian attacks and serving as a meeting place for treaty arrangements when the political wind shifted toward negotiation instead of confrontation. The first of these treaties came in 1851, under the forceful leadership of Indian agent Thomas Fitzpatrick, a former mountain man. More than 10,000 Indians attended, representing the Sioux, Cheyenne, Arapaho, Shoshone, Crow, Gros Ventre, and Assiniboin tribes. The treaty consisted essentially of annual bribes (annuities) to be given to the Indians to compensate them for their losses to whites. The various tribes would be assigned to distinct territories but could hunt in other areas. After signing the treaty, a mountain of presents awaited—the first of the $50,000 in annuities for each of the next 50 years. Shortly thereafter, the federal government reneged on the promise, increasing the annual amount to $70,000 per year but cutting the time to just 10 years. Peace lasted but a short while.

Grattan Massacre

One of the few Indian-white conflicts to occur in the vicinity of Fort Laramie took place in 1854. It began innocently enough when a Mormon emigrant's lame cow wandered off and was butchered by a hungry Miniconjou Indian waiting for the government to dispense annuities. A hotheaded young lieutenant, John Grattan, was sent out to bring in the Indian. Unfortunately, Grattan's interpreter was drunk and began immediately shouting insults at the Sioux in whose village the man was camped. Grattan himself was anxious for a fight, hoping to gain a piece of fame, so when

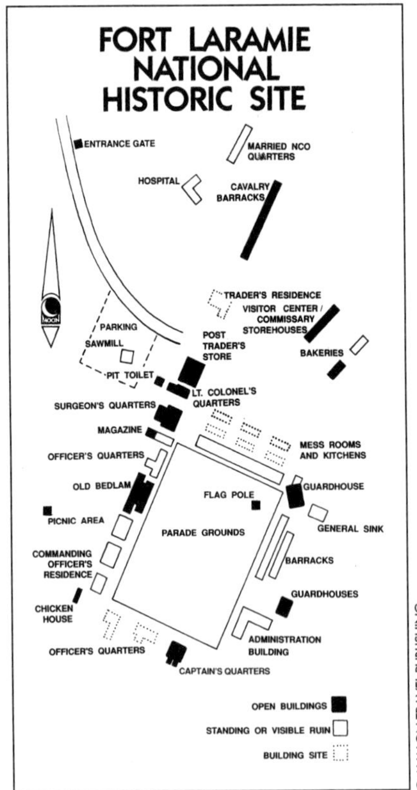

the Sioux refused to give up the man—offering instead to pay for the cow with two horses—Grattan would have nothing of it. His soldiers opened fire and were themselves immediately attacked by a vastly superior force of Sioux. All 29 soldiers died in the massacre that followed, and Fort Laramie stood in danger of being destroyed. But the Indians instead raided local storehouses for the promised annuities and headed out. The army used the Grattan Massacre as proof that the Indians could not be trusted. In reality, the entire incident was an instance of utter stupidity on the part of the army.

More Trouble

One of the least distinguished post commanders at Fort Laramie was the hard-drinking and ill-tempered Col. Thomas Moonlight. In 1865, he publicly hanged two Sioux subchiefs who had brought in two white women captives for reward. Their bodies were left dangling in chains for several days, an act that brought condemnation from the Eastern press. In retaliation, the Sioux killed several soldiers and then managed to drive off most of the horses from Colonel Moonlight's cavalry. A sullen Moonlight led his almost horseless cavalry in the 120-mile hike back to the fort. Though shortly thereafter stripped of his command, Moonlight later served as the politically appointed territorial governor of Wyoming.

With the decline in importance of the Oregon Trail, Fort Laramie became a staging area for military expeditions against the Indians. In the Treaty of 1868, signed at the fort, the Sioux were guaranteed the Powder River country "as long as the grass shall grow and the buffalo shall roam." But the discovery of gold in the Black Hills abruptly changed the picture, and whites now wanted the land itself, not just a road through it. They eventually got it, but not before the massacre of Custer and his men at Little Big Horn in 1876. After this, with the Indians tucked away on reservations, most of the hostilities died down and the fort lost its strategic importance. The railroad had long since supplanted the Oregon Trail as the primary route west, and for the decade of the 1880s Fort Laramie served as a way station along the Cheyenne-to-Deadwood stage road. During this time the fort grew more genteel with the planting of trees and completion of numerous substantial homes.

The Army Departs

By 1889, it was clear that Fort Laramie had outlived its usefulness and it was ordered closed. The following year, the 35,000 acres of military land were opened to homesteaders and the buildings auctioned off. Because of the scarcity of wood in the area, many were stripped and hauled away to become cabins or other structures. Others remained on the site and were used as homes, businesses, or barns. For the next half century the historic fort slowly deteriorated, but in 1937 the state of Wyoming purchased the site and donated it to the federal government. The following year it was declared a national monument, to be managed by the National Park Service. A lengthy and difficult restoration process managed to stabilize the ruins and restore a dozen of the historic structures, but it was not until 1964 that the fort was restored to something approaching the conditions in the 1880s.

FORT LARAMIE TODAY

Each year nearly 90,000 visitors come to historic Fort Laramie for a rewarding traipse back in time. The clear, tree-lined Laramie River still flows close by, and the spacious parade ground engenders a feeling of this fort's importance, while the bleak, windswept setting speaks of its hardships.

Visiting the Fort

Buildings and grounds of the 830-acre Fort Laramie National Historic Site are open yearround 8 a.m. to sunset. Entrance costs $2 for adults, no charge for kids under 16 or seniors with Golden Age passes. There's no camping at the site but there is a pleasant picnic area. For a good orientation to Fort Laramie, head to the old commissary building, now the **visitor center/park headquarters,** tel. (307) 837-2221. Inside are excellent displays and historic photos, including a scale model of the fort, an 1876 Gatling gun, and many photos. Ask about interpretive talks and tours and the dramatic firings of historic weapons. The center is open daily 8 a.m.-7 p.m. mid-May through mid-September and daily 8 a.m.-4:30 p.m. the rest of the year. Excellent videos about the fort and the Old West are shown at scheduled times during the summer and by request the rest of the year. The shop here sells what may be the most complete collection of historic books on the frontier anywhere in Wyoming. It also rents out CD audio tours and sells such authentic items as lye soap, brass cavalry spurs, military insignias, and hardtack. The **Fort Laramie Historical Association,** tel. (307) 837-2662 or (800) 321-5456, manages the bookshop and also produces a big publication describing several hundred Western history books available by mail-order. Find Fort Laramie on the web at www.nps.gov/fola.

If you're in the area in early July, be sure to drop by Fort Laramie for an **Old-Fashioned Fourth of July Celebration** with old-time music, locals in period clothing, games, and dancing. In late August comes a **Military Encampment Weekend** with special moonlight programs.

Historical Buildings

By the time it was abandoned in 1890, Fort Laramie was approaching the size of a small town; 60 buildings of all types were scattered around the grounds. The remains of 21 of these are still visible—some simply lime-grout concrete ruins maintained in a state of arrested decay. A dozen have been completely restored and refurbished with authentic period pieces behind Plexiglas doors. The Park Service has an informative *Historic Buildings Guide* available at the visitor center. Several of the buildings are particularly noteworthy: the cavalry barracks, Old Bedlam, the bakery, and the guardhouse.

Most of the men who soldiered out of Fort Laramie lived under crowded conditions with little privacy. Sometimes this meant living in tents for long periods. The **cavalry barracks** on your left as you enter the fort were an improvement, but quarters were still tight. Walk up to the restored second floor to find row upon row of cots where an entire company of 60 men slept. Then try to imagine all the snoring and the smelly feet after being out on duty for weeks at a time! Baths were taken, in theory, every Saturday night in a half barrel.

The **post trader's store** just right of the entrance provided a break from the army's monotonous food and supplies. Built in 1849, it served not only the military but also the thousands of civilians who poured west along the Oregon Trail and the Indians who traded for various items. The store owner provided everything from essential food supplies to fresh oxen for weary emigrants. He also sold alcohol and benefited from the tons of excess belongings that many overburdened travelers cast aside to lighten their loads.

The officers enjoyed far better living conditions than the cavalry and infantry, including access to a pleasant officers' club and a hired cook. The 1884 **lieutenant colonel's quarters** has been restored to the era when Lt. Col. Andrew Burt and his family lived here (1887-88). Inside you'll see a number of the family's original furnishings. Next door is the **post surgeon's quarters,** completed in 1875. The surgeon had a highly respected rank in the fort and was accorded the responsibility of gathering weather data as well as scientific specimens. The surgeon dealt primarily with such problems as kicks by horses, injuries from brawls, frost-bitten fingers and toes, and venereal diseases. War wounds were far less common but when they did occur many could not be adequately treated and the men often died.

The oldest and most prominent building at Fort Laramie is **Old Bedlam,** an attractive clapboard structure that dominates the west end of the parade grounds. Built in 1849, it was the center of life at the fort. Old Bedlam served a variety of purposes when the military was here; initially the post headquarters, it later became a hotel of sorts for bachelor officers and housing for married officers and their families. The name apparently comes from the bedlam that existed with so many folks jammed together—particularly after payday, when parties raged. Old Bedlam is now refurbished to represent two different periods. Upstairs are displays representing the living quarters of Lt. Colonel William O. Collins, while the bachelor officers' quarters are downstairs.

Behind the attractive **Captain's Quarters** on the south end of the parade ground is a model of adobe-walled Fort John, which stood on this spot in 1841. The "bat house" near here was recently built in an attempt to keep bats from roosting in the Captain's Quarters. A footpath leads to the Laramie River. The old stone **guardhouse** on the east side of the fort could house up to 40 prisoners, ranging from soldiers who had violated minor conduct rules to those charged with murder. The basement jail had no furniture, toilet, or light, and no heat even in the dead of winter. Stop by the historic **bakery**—one of four built here at different times—for a taste of bread. One loaf of bread, along with greasy salt pork, beans, rice, and rotgut coffee, was the typical daily allotment for soldiers. Fresh vegetables were often unavailable for months at a time, and scurvy was a constant threat. In the field, the rations were even worse, generally consisting of salt pork, beans, and wormy hardtack.

One of the less-visited sights in the area is **Old Bedlam ruts,** two miles northwest of Fort Laramie. A gravel road leads to the location; get a map from park headquarters. The ruts (marked by posts) climb up into the gentle hills west of the old fort, offering a marvelous panorama of a landscape that has not changed much in the last century. From here, it's easy to imagine emigrants looking back on the fort, their last touch with civilization for hundreds of miles. Laramie Peak is prominent to the west. Nearby is the grave of Mary Homsley, one of the thousands who died along the difficult trek west. The ruts can be traced all the way to Guernsey, where they grow even deeper. A similar series of ruts extends eastward from the fort. If you're heading to Wheatland from the fort, try the "back way" via Grayrocks Reservoir—the source of cooling water for the Laramie River Power Plant. The road is rough for the first eight miles or so, but it is paved beyond that and offers an enjoyable taste of the rugged countryside around the reservoir. Signs point the way to Wheatland.

THE TOWN OF FORT LARAMIE

The town of Fort Laramie (pop. 220) lies three miles north of the historic fort and across the North Platte River. Wyoming's oldest post office is here, dating back to the 1880s when the army was occupying the nearby fort. A mile south of town is an **iron bridge** built in 1875. Though long superseded by a concrete span just upriver and not much to look at, the bridge bears historical importance. Funded by a $15,000 congressional appropriation, the bridge ensured the establishment of the Cheyenne-Deadwood Stage and Express through here. It remained the major route north for many years thereafter. Note how much longer the old bridge is than the new one. Upstream dams have blocked the river flow, making it barely a third of the original width. A highway monument east of town along U.S. 26 notes the site of the Grattan Massacre (described above).

Accommodations and Camping

Fort Laramie Motel, tel. (307) 837-3063, provides basic accommodations for $25 s or $30-40 d, along with kitchenettes for $35 d. Open mid-May through October. Budget-Inexpensive.

Pitch tents for free at the **Fort Laramie town park** just across the railroad tracks on the south side of town; no showers. **Chuckwagon Campground,** tel. (307) 837-2828, is open mid-April to mid-October, and charges $9 for tents or $12 for RVs. **Bennett Court Campground,** tel. (307) 837-2270, charges $9 for RVs, $7 for tents. **Pony Soldier RV Park,** tel. (307) 837-3078, five miles east of Fort Laramie and five miles west of Lingle, is open April-Oct. with tent spaces for $10, RV sites for $15.

Carnahan Ranch, a half mile south of Fort Laramie Historic Site, tel. (307) 837-2917 or (800) 837-6730, offers both tent sites ($15) and RV sites with hookups ($20); open mid-April to mid-October. Teepees are $25-35. Campers get use of the communal kitchen, and the opportunity to explore this peaceful 2,400-acre ranch overlooking the fort.

Other Practicalities

A couple of places serve rather pathetic meals in Fort Laramie; personally, I'd go hungry till I reached a town with a better choice! If you can't wait, you could try **Outfitter Restaurant,** at Chuckwagon Campground on the west end of town, tel. (307) 837-2570, which serve three meals a day.

A small log-cabin **visitor center** on the main street is staffed daily May to mid-October. Drop by **Fort Laramie Frontier Trading Post,** tel. (307) 837-2021, for quality leather crafts, Indian beadwork, and other locally made crafts.

TORRINGTON

Torrington (pop. 5,800) is a quiet farming and retirement town just eight miles from the Nebraska border. It's the seat of Wyoming's most important agricultural county—Goshen, alias "The Land of Goshen"—and lots of sugar beets, alfalfa, oats, dry beans, corn, and hay are grown here. The tree-lined North Platte River drifts lazily through town.

Torrington's economy is relatively stable; the biggest local employer, a Holly Sugar factory, is on the edge of town and many productive farms are scattered in the surrounding countryside. Two long waterways—Fort Laramie Canal and the Interstate Canal—provide irrigation water to much of this farmland. Trains filled with coal from Campbell and Weston Counties constantly rumble through toward the south and east, a stench from the sugar refinery hangs in the air each fall, and the livestock auction is the big weekly event. A walk along Main Street is a trek

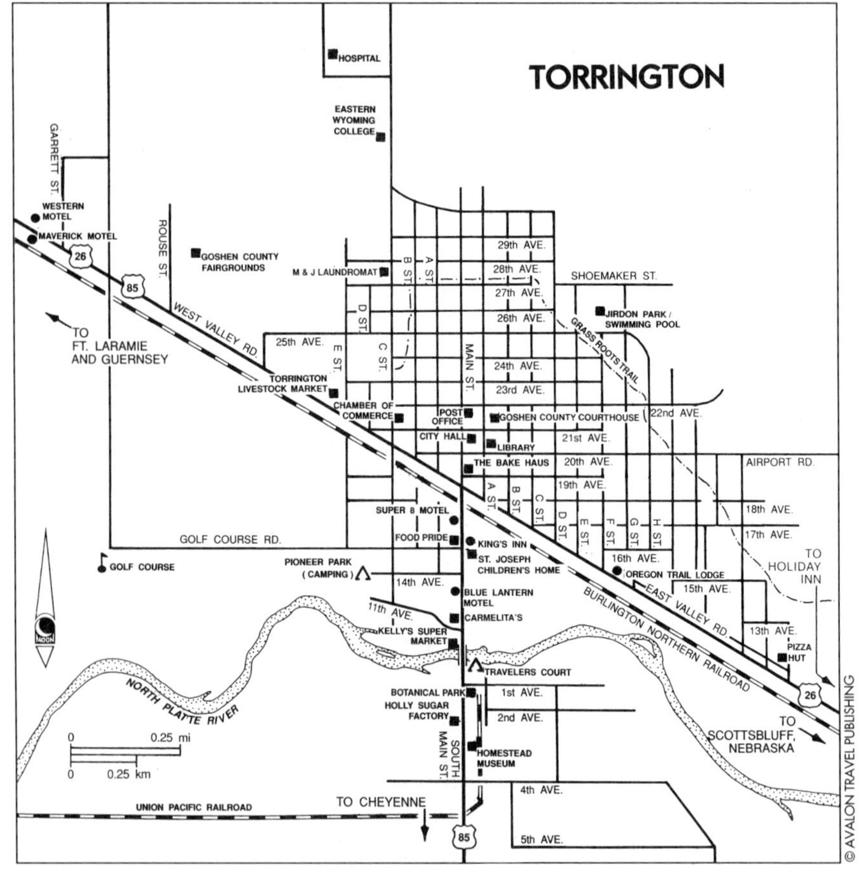

through the American heartland; if the cars were older, Torrington could model for a *Saturday Evening Post* cover from the '50s. In recent years the agricultural economy has sputtered a bit, but retirees and wealthy refugees from the Colorado Front Range are moving into the area.

History

Although several hundred thousand emigrants passed through Goshen County on their way to Oregon, California, or Utah, none bothered to stop. The area was not settled until cattlemen came in the 1880s, followed by homesteaders around the turn of the 20th century including many from Russia and Germany. Many of the "soddies" and wooden shacks these emigrants built still stand in the fields throughout the county. Named for Torrington, Connecticut, the town was incorporated in 1907 as a ranching and farming center. Completion of the Interstate Canal in 1915 and the Fort Laramie Canal in 1924 brought North Platte River water, making it possible to grow a wide variety of crops. The Burlington Railroad arrived from the east in 1900, but it was not until 1926 that the Union Pacific built a line connecting Torrington with Pine Bluffs to the south. That year proved a pivotal one, for it brought a new train depot and the Holly Sugar plant. The town has grown slowly over the years and except for a brief flirtation with oil and gas in the 1970s has remained true to its farming and ranching roots.

Homestead Museum

Located right at the crossroads of the Oregon Trail, the Cheyenne-to-Deadwood stage route, the Mormon Trail, and the Texas Cattle Trail, the Homestead Museum seems to sit atop history. It is housed in the 1926 brick-and-masonry Union Pacific depot just south of town. The last train stopped at the depot in 1964. The museum, tel. (307) 532-5612, is open Mon.-Sat. 10 a.m.-4:30 p.m. and Sunday 1-4 p.m. during the summer and Mon.-Fri. 10 a.m.-4:30 p.m. in winter. Although it contains a substantial paleo-Indian collection, the museum focuses on the thousands of turn-of-the-20th-century homesteaders who flocked to eastern Wyoming. The Yoder Ranch collection (artifacts from 1881 on) is particularly noteworthy. Other displays include items from the 4A Ranch and the Bordeau Trading Post near Fort Laramie, a homemade baseball bat from 1920, and a marvelous collection of historic black-and-white photos. Sit down and spend some time looking through these pictures; they will quickly transport you back to a simple era when pioneers scratched out a hardscrabble life on the mixed-grass prairie in wooden or sod shacks. The KKK robe displayed in the museum comes from the 1920s, when a vehemently racist and anti-Catholic spirit dominated much of rural America. Outside are an old homestead cabin, a windmill, and a caboose housing historic railroad photos and memorabilia.

TODD CLARK

Other Sights

Over 120,000 cattle are raised in Goshen County each year—more than in any other Wyoming county—so it is logical that Torrington should also be at the center of the state's livestock trade. Each year nearly a quarter of a million cattle are marketed at the **Torrington Livestock Market,** on U.S. 26 at W. E St., tel. (307) 532-3333. Auctions take place every Friday beginning at 10 a.m. and lasting into the early afternoon, with additional load lot auctions on Wednesday in the fall. All of these auctions are open to the public and are quite interesting, but don't raise your hand or you might just purchase a bull.

Two miles west of town is the University of Wyoming's **College of Agriculture Research and Extension Center,** also open to the public. Tours of nearby cattle ranches are available through the **Goshen Cattlewomen.** Advance arrangements are necessary; call (307) 532-4346.

For a nice walk, saunter along the paved **Grassroots Trail,** built atop an old irrigation canal that slices across the northern edge of town. A small **Botanical Park** occupies the corner of 1st Ave. and S. Main St. with paths and plants. South of Torrington a sign marks the **Cold Springs Campground** used by travelers on the Oregon Trail and later the site of a stage station and a pony express stop. A few miles east of town is a memorial marker to the party of Astorians who camped nearby in the winter of 1812.

STARVING TO DEATH ON A GOVERNMENT CLAIM

My name is Frank Taylor, a bachelor I am,
I'm keeping old batch on an elegant plan,
You'll find me out West in the county of Lane
A-starving to death on a Government claim.

Hurrah for Lane County, the land of the free,
The home of the bedbug, grasshopper and flea,
I'll sing of its praises and boast of its fame
A-starving to death on a Government claim.

My clothes they are ragged, my language is rough,
My bread is case-hardened and solid and tough,
But I have a good time and live at my ease
On common sop-sorghum and old bacon grease.

How happy am I when I crawl into bed,
With rattlesnakes rattling just under my head,
And the gay little bedbug, so cheerful and bright,
He keeps me a-going two-thirds of the night.

How happy am I on my Government claim,
I've nothing to lose and I've nothing to gain,
I've nothing to eat and I've nothing to wear,
And nothing from nothing is honest and fair.

Oh, come to Lane County, there's room for you all,
Where the wind never stops and the rains never fall,
Oh, join in the chorus and sing of her fame,
A-starving to death on a Government claim.

Oh, don't be downhearted, you poor hungry men,
We're all just as free as the pigs in the pen,
Just stick to your homestead and fight with your fleas,
And pray to your Maker to send some more breeze.

Now all you poor sinners, I hope you will stay
And chaw on your hardtack till you're toothless and grey,
But as for myself I don't aim to remain
And slave like a dog on no Government claim.

Farewell to Lane County, the pride of the West
I'm going back East to the girl I love best,
I'll stop in Missouri and get me a wife,
And live on corn doggers the rest of my life.

—ANONYMOUS

Eastern Wyoming College, 3200 W. C St., tel. (307) 532-8200, is one of the oldest junior colleges in the state, first established in 1948 as an extension of the University of Wyoming but now independent. The hilltop campus has 1,200 full- and part-time students studying in nearly 60 vocational and academic fields.

Accommodations

Note that noisy freight trains roll through Torrington at all hours of the night, so you may want to choose a place as far as possible from the tracks. Accommodations are arranged below from least to most expensive. Add an eight percent tax to these rates.

Budget-Inexpensive: Oregon Trail Lodge, 710 E. Valley Rd., tel. (307) 532-2101, provides lodging for $22-38 s or $24-40 d. The cheaper units are quite basic, but all rooms include fridges. Also on the low-price end is **Blue Lantern Motel,** 1402 S. Main St., tel. (307) 532-8999, where a handful of older units are $25 s or $35 d; some with microwaves and fridges. Very friendly owners.

Maverick Motel, 1.5 miles west of town on US 26/85, tel. (307) 532-4064, charges $36 s or $40 d; kitchenettes run $50 for four people. Also on the west side and just across the street is the well-maintained **Western Motel,** tel. (307) 532-2104, where rooms are $34-40 s or $40-46 d, including fridges and microwaves.

King's Inn, 1555 S. Main St., tel. (307) 532-4011, includes a jacuzzi and boot-shaped indoor pool, but the furnishings and carpets are much-abused. Rooms cost $45-50 s or $50-55 d.

Super 8 Motel, 1548 S. Main St., tel. (307) 532-7118 or (800) 800-8000, has lodging for $46 s or $52 d, including an indoor pool, jacuzzi, and an exercise room.

Inexpensive-Expensive. On the east side of town, **Holiday Inn Express,** tel. (307) 532-7600 or (800) 465-4329, is Torrington's newest and nicest place to stay, with a breakfast bar, indoor pool, jacuzzi, and fitness center. Rates are $57 s or d in standard rooms. Suites include jacuzzi tubs, microwaves, and fridges for $78-110 d.

Camping

Camp for free in **Pioneer Park** along the North Platte River on the edge of town. It's open year-round and has electrical hookups, but during the winter you'll need to get water elsewhere. Additional sites are also available year-round at the **Goshen County Fairgrounds,** tel. (307) 532-2525. RV sites with hookups cost $8, tent sites $5. Open year-round. In town—but not recommended because of rundown facilities—is **Travelers Court,** 750 S. Main, tel. (307) 532-5517, with riverside tent sites and RV sites with hookups.

Food

For reasonable breakfasts (starting under $2) and fresh baked goods, head to **The Bake Haus,** 1915 Main St., tel. (307) 532-2982. Lots of locals hang out here in the morning, and the Friday and Saturday night prime rib is another favorite. **Chuckwagon Cafe,** 2113 N. Main St., tel. (307) 532-2888, serves breakfast all day long and has great all-American stuff-yourself meals. The fare includes inexpensive burgers, steaks, Rocky Mountain oysters, a salad bar, and homemade pies. The Sunday all-you-can-eat buffets are especially popular. **Java Jar,** 1940 N. Main, tel. (307) 532-8541, has espresso coffees, soup served in bread bowls, and sandwiches.

Deacons Restaurant, 1558 S. Main St., tel. (307) 532-4766, opens Mon.-Sat. at 5 a.m. for dependable meals. Offerings include a substantial salad bar and homemade pies. Be sure to stop by **Cabbage Patch Cuisine,** out the west end of town, tel. (307) 534-2203, where the menu mixes American and Old European fare. It's a good place for barbecued beef or cabbage burgers (popular in this part of Wyoming).

Peking Garden, 2126 N. Main St., tel. (307) 532-8883, serves up surprisingly good and authentic Chinese food, and **Carmelita's,** 1250 S. Main, tel. (307) 532-8622, has Mexican meals and margaritas. **Buck's Pizza,** 300 W. Valley Rd., tel. (307) 534-4616, has decent pizza.

Geno's, in the King's Inn at 1555 S. Main St., tel. (307) 532-2702, presents a romantic setting for gourmet dinners featuring the likes of chateaubriand, Alaskan king crab, and pork tenderloin (entrées $10-29). For lunch, try the soup and make-your-own-sandwich buffet. An adjacent lounge has happy hours on weekdays.

For reasonably priced steaks and seafood in an attractive setting, head to **Little Moon Lake Supper Club,** tel. (307) 532-5750, on the state line eight miles east on U.S. 26.

Get groceries from **Kelly's Super Market** on S. Main, tel. (307) 532-3113, or **Food Pride Grocery Store,** 1542 S. Main, tel. (307) 532-3401.

Recreation

Torrington has a summertime outdoor **swimming pool** (tel. 307-532-7798) in Jirdon Park. Kids will love the 180-foot water slide. There is also an 18-hole municipal **golf course,** tel. (307) 532-2418, outside of town. Bowl at **Ten Pin Tropics** out the east side of Torrington, tel. (307) 532-2187.

Entertainment and Events

Watch movies at **Wyoming Theatre,** 126 E. 20th Ave., tel. (307) 532-2226. Two local places have live country music on some weekends: **Bronco Bar,** 1924 Main St., tel. (307) 532-8660, and **Tote-Away Bar,** 1934 1/2 W. A St., tel. 532-5506. Many locals also head over to the **Stateline Oasis,** tel. (307) 532-4990, next to the Nebraska line, for the chance to watch the strippers Tues.-Sat. nights. The Oasis typically has live bands on Saturday nights.

The biggest annual event in Torrington is the **Goshen County Fair,** held the second full week in August and presenting everything from a parade to pig wrestling. It's a good place to check out all the 4-H hogs and sheep on display. The indoor arena here is Wyoming's largest. Call (307) 532-2525 for details.

Information and Services

The **Goshen County Chamber of Commerce** office, 350 W. 21st Ave., tel. (307) 532-3879 or (800) 577-3555, is open Mon.-Fri. 8 a.m.-5 p.m. Find local details on the web at www.town-of-torrington.com.

Other practicalities include the **public library** at 2001 E. A St., tel. (307) 532-3411, which sells a few used books, and the **post office** at 2145 Main St., tel. (307) 532-2213. Wash clothes at **M&J Laundromat,** 27th Ave and W. C St., tel. (307) 532-9993.

Powder River/Coach USA, tel. (800) 442-3682, has daily bus service from Torrington to towns in northern and central Wyoming, continuing north to Billings or Rapid City and south to Cheyenne or Denver. **Denver Coach,** tel. (308) 632-8400 or (800) 658-3125, provides transportation to Denver International Airport. Rent cars from **Big Sky Ford,** 510 W. Valley Rd., tel. (307) 532-2114 or (888) 532-2114.

TORRINGTON AREA

South of Torrington

The town symbol for Torrington is the ring-necked pheasant—a fitting logo in this farming country. **Downar Bird Farm,** 17 miles south on U.S. 85, tel. (307) 532-3449, raises some 11,000 pheasants each year. It is run by the Wyoming Game and Fish Department, which releases the birds each fall for area hunters. This is basically a release-and-shoot operation, since the birds are let go in unfamiliar territory just in time for hunting season. The farm is an interesting place to visit and boasts 27 different pheasant breeds. Incidentally, although the ring-necked pheasant is abundant throughout the Midwest, it is a native of China.

The minuscule town of **Veteran** (pop. 20)—basically a post office and general store located 15 miles southwest of Torrington—was established by Iowa veterans of WW I. A prisoner-of-war camp was established here in WW II. The surrounding landscape is a mixture of grass, wheat, sage, and rocky buttes, with cattle grazing the land and vultures circling above.

Hawk Springs State Recreation Area lies 27 miles south of Torrington off U.S. 85. Call (307) 836-2334 for details. The small park contains campsites ($9 for nonresidents, or $4 for Wyoming residents), picnic tables, and a boat ramp along Hawk Springs Reservoir. Fishing is good for walleye, largemouth bass, yellow perch, black crappie, and channel catfish. Boaters will discover a blue heron rookery on the south end of the reservoir. Park entrance costs $3 for nonresident vehicles or $2 for Wyoming residents. Not far away is the town of **Hawk Springs** (pop. 100), home to the **Longbranch Saloon & Steakhouse,** tel. (307) 532-4266, open for three meals a day.

Lingle

Ten miles northwest of Torrington is the prosperous farming crossroads called Lingle (pop. 490). Trains laden with coal roll through almost continuously. The town has two good places to eat but no lodging places. **Lira's,** tel. (307) 837-2826, offers authentic Mexican food that attracts folks from miles around. Also here is **Stagecoach Cafe,** tel. (307) 837-2614, with Saturday night prime rib specials. Lingle's **Harvest Festival** takes place the third weekend of August. An **outdoor pool** is open in the summer months.

Camping is available five miles west of Lingle at **Pony Soldier RV Park,** tel. (307) 837-3078. Rates are $10 for tents or $15 for RVs; open mid-April to mid-October. Adjacent to the RV park is the small but surprisingly informative **Western History Center,** tel. (307) 837-3052, where you'll find a number of displays, including mammoth bones and Indian artifacts. The center is open Mon.-Sat. 8 a.m.-5 p.m. Anthropologist George Zeimens—who manages this private museum—also leads tours to historic and archaeological sites in Wyoming.

Jay Em

North of Lingle on U.S. 85, the irrigated pastures and green fields give way to endless prairies. This is a land of sandy hillocks carpeted with short grasses, similar to the sandhill country of western Nebraska which lies just a dozen miles eastward. Halfway between Lingle and Lusk, the road passes the near-ghost town of Jay Em (pop. 15), named for the cattle brand of rancher Jim Moore. Just to the north lies his old Jay Em Ranch. A few people still live in the old wooden houses of Jay Em, and the post office becomes a meeting place each morning, but the town is otherwise deserted. It's a peaceful spot to stop and walk along narrow Rawhide Creek among the cottonwood trees and tall grass. The town is a National Historic District and the rustic old buildings are a photographer's treat. Tours are available by reservation; call (307) 735-4364 or (307) 322-2839. Continuing north to Lusk, the country again opens into grassland, windmills, cattle, a few tree-topped hills, and small rocky buttes.

LUSK

Lusk (pop. 1,600) is the seat of Wyoming's least-populated county. Just 3,200 people live in rural Niobrara County—an average of almost 524 acres per person! It's remote grassland country here with long, straight highways heading out in the compass directions. The oil industry that was once so prominent has faded considerably in recent years, but ranching provides a relatively stable, albeit limited, economic base. The town itself has a quiet, Midwestern feel, with tree-lined streets and attractive older homes. Lusk's main claim to fame is the *Legend of Rawhide,* a July extravaganza.

History

The first settlers in this part of Wyoming were miners in search of copper, silver, and gold. They built a small settlement around the Silver Cliff Mine but moved a mile east when the Fremont, Elkhorn, and Missouri Valley Railroad arrived in 1886. Lusk was named for Frank Lusk, a local rancher who donated land for the new townsite. In 1917, oil was discovered along Lance Creek 20 miles north of here and almost overnight Lusk became a boomtown, reaching more than 10,000 residents during the peak years of oil production. Pipelines were built to the 200 producing wells and a refinery was added in Lusk. By the 1940s, Lance Creek had become Wyoming's largest oil field. More recently, oil production has declined and the old standby of ranching has regained prominence. In 1984, the town succeeded in getting a women's correctional center built; this is now the second-largest employer in the county (after the local school district).

Lusk has seen its share of lust over the years. The Yellow Hotel brothel occupied a place of local importance until the late 1970s; rumor has it that the madam, Del Burke, was allowed to keep it open because she owned most of Lusk's water bonds! **Mother Featherlegs**—so named because she often rode horseback with her red pantaloons blowing in the wind—was a well-known 19th-century madam who was murdered in 1879, apparently for money. Some claim that a fortune in gold she had buried nearby still waits to be claimed. A granite marker southwest of Lusk notes the site of her old place of entertainment along the Cheyenne-Black Hills Stage Line; it's said to be the nation's only historical marker commemorating a prostitute. Get here by heading two miles west of town on U.S. 18 and then turning south at the rest area for another 11 miles. In 1990, Lusk locals swept into a Deadwood saloon and recovered her famous pantaloons, stolen from the historic site in 1964. Today, you'll find them on display at the town museum.

Sights

Lusk has one of the better historic collections in the state at the aptly named **Stagecoach Museum,** 342 S. Main St., tel. (307) 334-2950 or (800) 223-5875. The hours change through the year; in July and August the museum is open Tues.-Sat. 1-8 p.m. and Sunday 2-8 p.m. In May, June, September, and October it's open Mon.-Fri. 1-4 p.m. Call (307) 334-2372 for access at other times. Admission is $2 for adults, free for kids under 12. Climb up the stairs to find the reason for its name—an old coach built in 1863 by Abbott & Downing of Concord, New Hampshire. Used for many years on the famed Cheyenne and Black Hills Stage and Express Line, the stagecoach is

When my earthly trail is ended
And my final bacon curled
And the last great roundup's finished
At the Home Ranch of the world
I don't want no harps nor halos,
Robes nor other dressed up things—
Let me ride the starry ranges
On a pinto hawse with wings!

Just a-ridin, a-ridin'—
Nothing I'd like half so well
As a-roundin' up the sinners
That have wandered out of hell,
And a-ridin'

—CHARLES BADGER CLARK, JR.

one of only two in existence; its sister resides in the Smithsonian Institution. The museum also houses a treasure chest broken open during the Canyon Springs Stage robbery of 1879; it contained gold bullion from the Black Hills destined for Cheyenne. Here, too besides the standard fare—an old buggy, a sulky, a dray wagon, covered wagons, and various Indian artifacts and arrowheads—you'll find such intriguing odds and ends as a 1950s' iron lung, a two-headed calf, an antique bedpan collection and suppository machine, more than 300 salt and pepper shakers, photos of Niobrara County's many one-room schoolhouses, and a 31-star 1876 U.S. flag. Try not to snicker at the kitschy collection of dolls dressed up as the wives of various presidents (including Barbara Bush as a busty Barbie doll). Out back is an old one-room log schoolhouse built in 1886. And, oh yes, the famous Mother Featherlegs pantaloons are next to the museum director's desk, where she can make sure they aren't stolen again by folks from Deadwood.

The city park at 14th and Linn contains a **homestead cabin** built in the 1880s and originally located at Running Water Stage Station. Another site of minor historical interest is on the east side of town along the railroad tracks. Here you'll find a **redwood water tank** built in 1886 to supply water for steam engines of the Chicago and Northwestern Railroad. It is one of only six still standing in the nation.

Accommodations

Lusk has a number of comfortable motels for reasonable rates, but prices may be higher during the *Legend of Rawhide*. Lodgings are arranged below by price, with the least expensive first. Add an eight percent tax to these rates.

Hospitality House Motor Hotel, 201 S. Main, tel. (307) 334-2120, has rather plain accommodations, some with king size beds, in upstairs rooms for $24-32 s or d. No phones in the rooms. Budget.

Townhouse Motel, 565 S. Main, tel. (307) 334-2376, has a range of rooms for $26-48 s or $32-48 d. **Rawhide Motel,** 805 S. Main, tel. (307) 334-2440, charges $28 s or $36-38 d. Both Inexpensive.

At **Trail Motel,** 305 W. 8th, tel. (307) 334-2530 or (800) 333-5875, rooms cost $52 s or d, and the grounds contain an outdoor pool. Inexpensive.

Best Western Pioneer Court, 731 S. Main, tel. (307) 334-2640 or (800) 542-9936, has an outdoor pool and rooms for $56-67 s or d. Inexpensive-Moderate.

Covered Wagon Motel, 730 S. Main, tel. (307) 334-2836 or (800) 341-8000, is the nicest local motel, with an indoor pool, jacuzzi, sauna, and exercise room. Rooms cost $60 s or $73 d. Moderate.

Also of interest is **Mill Iron 7 Ranch,** a working cattle ranch in the badlands 25 miles east of Lusk along the Wyoming/Nebraska border. There's no pretense here; guests stay in wall tents and eat with the ranchers. Call (308) 668-2148 for details.

Camping

BJ's Campground, 902 S. Maple St., tel. (307) 334-2314, has unshaded RV sites for $16; open May to mid-October. **Prairie View Campground,** two miles west of Lusk on U.S. 18/20, tel. (307) 334-3174, isn't particularly attractive either, but does offer RV hookups and tent sites for $14.

Food

You'll find the best breakfasts in town, along with burgers, homemade pies, and shakes, at **The Diner,** 234 S. Main, tel. (307) 334-3606. **Fireside Inn,** 904 S. Main, tel. (307) 334-3477, serves family-style meals. The Sunday brunch is a bargain, and the soup and salad bar offers an inexpensive way to pig out. **El Jarro Restaurant,** 625 S. Main St., tel. (307) 334-5004, is the local Mexican eatery. Get pizzas at **The Pizza Place,** 218 S. Main, tel. (307) 334-3000, and quick lunches at **Subway,** 601 S. Main Street.

Outpost, on the south end of town, tel. (307) 334-3085, serves meals 24 hours a day, and the most expensive entrée here barely tops $10.

Get groceries from **Decker's Food Center,** 405 S. Main. St., tel. (307) 334-3810.

Recreation and Entertainment

Swim at the **Lusk Plunge** on the north side of the tracks during the summer. The **Lusk Municipal Golf Course,** tel. (307) 334-9916, has one of the better nine-hole golf courses in the state. Bowl at **Rawhide Lanes,** 326 S. Main St., tel. (307) 334-0159, or catch live country-and-western music at the **Cowboy Bar,** 904 S. Main St., tel. (307) 334-3634.

Information and Services

The **Lusk Visitor Center** is housed in the museum at 342 S. Main St.; open Mon.-Fri. 10 a.m.-5 p.m. Call (307) 334-2950 or (800) 223-5875 for more information, or visit its website: luskwyoming.com.

The local **library** is at 425 S. Main, tel. (307) 334-3490, and the **post office** is at 116 W. 3rd St., tel. (307) 334-3700. There are no laundromats in town. Get fast cash from the **ATMs** in local gas stations.

True Hatters, 214 S. Main St., tel. (307) 334-2746, is an old-time shop (in business since 1908) with custom-made boots, hats, and saddles.

The **Lusk Roundup PRCA Rodeo** takes place in late May, and the **Niobrara County Fair** comes to town the first week of August, but the featured event is the *Legend of Rawhide.*

LEGEND OF RAWHIDE

In 1946, the people of Lusk were looking for an event to attract visitors—something, say, along the lines of Cheyenne Frontier Days, only different. A local doctor, Walter Reckling, faintly remembered a tale that had been passed down for generations—the legend of Rawhide Buttes. It was one of the enduring yarns of the Old West, one with a thousand variations, claimed by half a dozen states. In the story, an emigrant wagon train headed west to the California goldfields carrying a young man who boasted that he would shoot the first Indian he saw. He killed an innocent Indian girl—a princess, of course—and her tribe retaliated by attacking the wagon train and forcing the young man to surrender. He was skinned alive in revenge. Nobody has ever been able to substantiate the tale, but then again, nobody has proved it *didn't* happen, either.

Dr. Reckling managed to stir up considerable interest for the idea in Lusk and then found a local college student, Eva Lou Bonsell, who was studying theater in Colorado. She wrote a play to be pantomimed as a narrator described the scenes, and the *Legend of Rawhide* was off and running. The first production gained a measure of realism by being staged in the midst of a thunderstorm. The crowd of 10,000 loved it. The *Legend of Rawhide* made the covers of *Life* and *Look* magazines at various times and ran from 1946 to 1966. It was revived again in 1986. Today, the annual production is still a decidedly local affair, with a cast of 200 folks from the surrounding area. The spectacle has evolved over the years with the addition of 13 "soiled doves," Father DeSmet, Jim Bridger, some 15 wagons, and several dozen Indians on ponies. The skinning alive of bad guy Clyde Pickett is the gory climax. It's also quite a trick, but I won't give away the secret.

The *Legend of Rawhide* is put on the second weekend in July every year and begins at 8 p.m. on Friday and Saturday nights. Other activities include a parade, art show, square dancing, country music, pancake breakfasts, and a barbecue. For more information, call (307) 334-2950 or (800) 223-5875. The *Legend of Rawhide* attracts upwards of 3,000 visitors, so be sure to book motel rooms far ahead of your visit.

Whether or not the story is true, the **Rawhide Buttes** actually do exist; they are 10 miles south of Lusk. Some stories give a less interesting origin of the name Rawhide Buttes, claiming they were the site where raw buffalo hides were prepared for shipment east. A highway marker notes the Cheyenne and Deadwood Stage station that once stood here. Two miles west of Lusk on U.S. 18/20 is a historical marker along the Cheyenne-Deadwood Trail. The ruts are still visible for a ways here, and George Lathrop, one of the best-known stage drivers, is buried nearby.

HEADING NORTH

U.S. Hwy. 18/85 points due north from Lusk toward Newcastle, passing through mile after mile of rolling and windy grassland with scattered rocky buttes—a few wearing top hats of ponderosa pines. For the first dozen miles the road parallels the historic Cheyenne-Deadwood Stage Route. Bottomland creeks curl through with cottonwoods and willows on both sides. This is gorgeous big-sky country; the land seems almost an afterthought. It's about as remote a place as you'll find, with just a few ranches, windmills, and cattle for company.

Some 13 miles north of Lusk a sign marks the old **Fort Hat Creek Stage Station,** mistakenly built (in 1876) along Sage Creek, Wyoming, instead of Hat Creek, Nebraska! It's easy to see how the country could start to blend together here. The old stage station, on private land but right next to the road, is two miles east of here on a paved road and then one mile southwest on a gravel road. It is an impressive two-story log structure built in 1887 to replace the original buildings, which had burned. The small fort garrisoned 40 soldiers who would ride out to protect the Cheyenne-Deadwood Stage from attack. Hat Creek was typical of stage stations along the route. One writer of the time, Leander P. Richardson, noted: "At any of these places a traveler can purchase almost anything, from a glass of whiskey to a four-horse team, but the former article is usually the staple of demand."

Tiny **Lance Creek** (pop. 180) lies in the middle of Niobrara County and is surrounded by the Lance Creek oil fields. An oil boom peaked here during WW II; more recently production has declined and the community now ekes out a minimal survival. The Lance Creek area is the site of discoveries of horned dinosaurs (Ceratopsians) and other fossils. Beginning in the 1880s, scientists found an incredible number of fossil plants, dinosaurs, and ancient mammals, including at least 75 different species of vertebrates, many of which were previously unknown. There are no signs or facilities to mark the location.

Halfway between Lusk and Newcastle is **Mule Creek Junction** (no services since the gas station/motel burned in 1999), where you'll find a state rest area. A couple of miles north of this, U.S. 85 crosses Cheyenne River near the site of the aptly named **Robber's Roost Stage Station.** Here outlaws sometimes attacked the Cheyenne-Deadwood Stage when it slowed to cross the river. In an 1878 robbery attempt an outlaw was killed here by the shotgun messengers, but his partners managed to escape with the mail sacks.

DOVER PUBLICATIONS, INC.

MEDICINE BOW COUNTRY

West from Cheyenne, I-80 climbs a long, gentle ramp into the Laramie Mountains, reaches the highest point on its 3,000-mile trek across America, and then abruptly begins a steep descent onto the spacious Laramie Plains. A distinctly frontier feeling envelops this land: mountains rim the valley, and as you continue west the grass intermixes with more and more sagebrush. You are entering the real West of mountains, sage, and sky.

Medicine Bow Country consists of Albany County—with Laramie and the Laramie Plains at its center and the Laramie and Medicine Bow Mountains on either side—and Carbon County, where Rawlins is the main town and the Sierra Madre mountains dominate the southern horizon. The name "Medicine Bow" has a convoluted origin. The mountains in southern Wyoming were considered a sacred place, and each year Indians gathered nearby to celebrate powwows and build bows from the cedar wood. The Indian term for "medicine" means something spiritually powerful—symbolized by the mountains, the cedar that made fine bows, and the annual powwows. Whites combined the various tribal activities into "Medicine Bow" and applied the name to a river, a mountain range, a national forest, and a town.

The land is remarkably diverse in terms of both topography and vegetation. Laramie Basin contains the highest short-grass prairie in the world, some 7,200 feet above sea level. Three mountain ranges cross through this region: the Laramie Mountains, the Medicine Bow Mountains (also called the Snowy Range), and the Sierra Madre. Mountain slopes are covered with lodgepole pine, Engelmann spruce, and subalpine fir, while alpine meadows, tundra, and rock dominate the highest elevations. To the north and west of these mountain ranges, the country is a dry landscape of sage and desert.

History

For many centuries this land was filled with buffalo, elk, and deer, providing a rich home for wandering tribes of Indians. By the time whites arrived in large numbers, the area was claimed and fought over by many tribes including Oglala

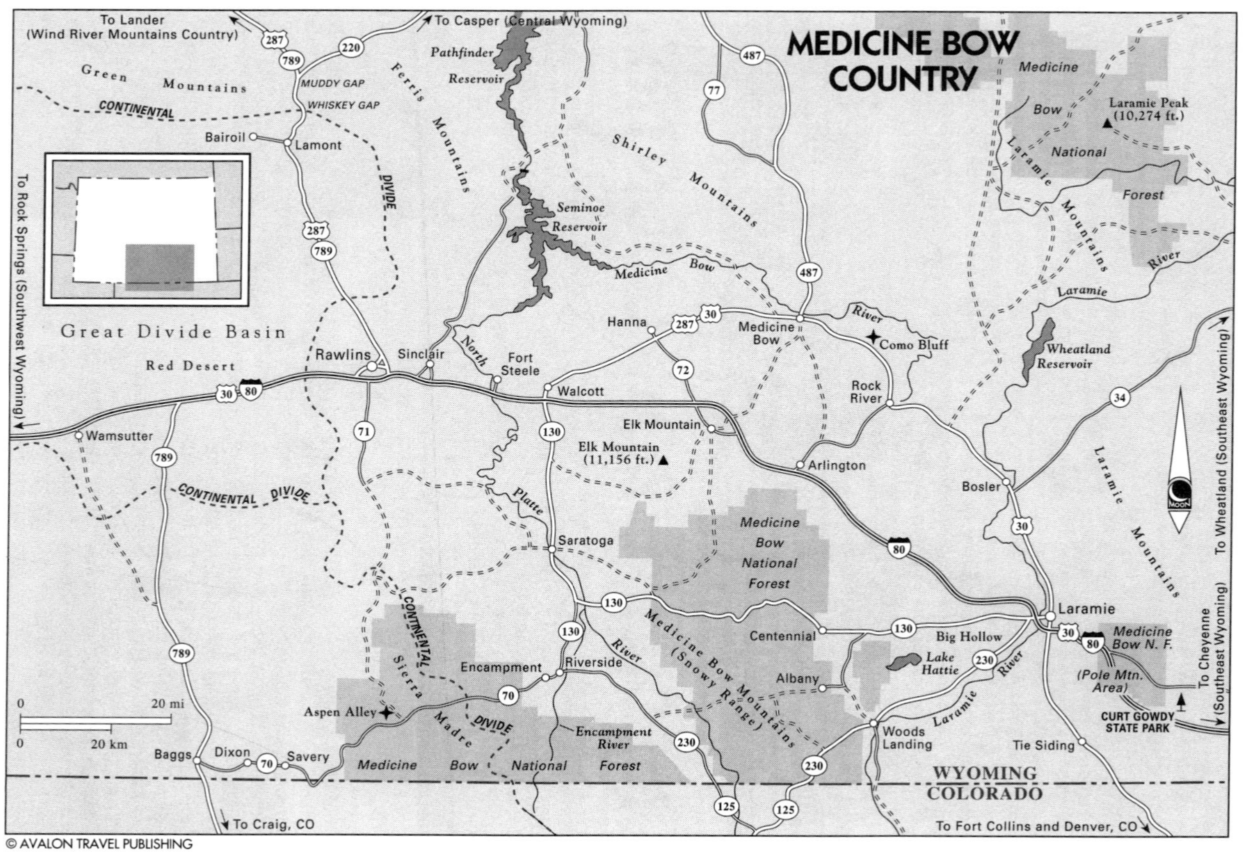
MEDICINE BOW COUNTRY
To Lander (Wind River Mountains Country)
To Casper (Central Wyoming)
To Rock Springs (Southwest Wyoming)
To Wheatland (Southeast Wyoming)
To Cheyenne (Southeast Wyoming)
To Fort Collins and Denver, CO
To Craig, CO
Green Mountains
CONTINENTAL DIVIDE
MUDDY GAP
WHISKEY GAP
Bairoil
Lamont
Ferris Mountains
Pathfinder Reservoir
Seminoe Reservoir
Shirley Mountains
Medicine Bow River
Medicine Bow National Forest
Laramie Peak (10,274 ft.)
Laramie Mountains
Laramie River
Wheatland Reservoir
Great Divide Basin
Red Desert
Rawlins
Sinclair
North Platte
Fort Steele
Walcott
Hanna
Medicine Bow
Como Bluff
Rock River
Elk Mountain
Elk Mountain (11,156 ft.)
Arlington
Bosler
Wamsutter
Saratoga
Centennial
Big Hollow
Lake Hattie
Laramie
Medicine Bow N. F. (Pole Mtn. Area)
CURT GOWDY STATE PARK
Medicine Bow Mountains (Snowy Range)
Albany
Encampment
Riverside
Encampment River
Sierra Madre
Aspen Alley
Baggs
Dixon
Savery
Woods Landing
Tie Siding
WYOMING
COLORADO
0
20 mi
0
20 km

SIGHTSEEING HIGHLIGHTS FOR MEDICINE BOW COUNTRY

University of Wyoming Geological Museum, American Heritage Center, Ivinson Mansion, and Wyoming Territorial Park in Laramie

Vedauwoo Rocks

Sugarloaf Recreation Area in the Snowy Range

Hobo Pool (hot springs) in Saratoga

Grand Encampment Museum in Encampment

Frontier Prison and Carbon County Museum in Rawlins

Popular events: Woodchopper's Jamboree in Encampment (June), Jubilee Days in Laramie (July), University of Wyoming football games in Laramie (fall)

Sioux, Northern Arapaho, Eastern Shoshone, Northern Cheyenne, and White River Utes. Although mountain men long trapped in this part of Wyoming, it remained off the beaten path for many years, with emigrants preferring the Oregon Trail through the central part of the state. This began to change in 1862, when the Overland Trail opened across southern Wyoming. Ben Holladay's stage traversed the route, as did many thousands of emigrants who found it shorter and generally safer from Indian attack. As with the rest of southern Wyoming, the coming of the Union Pacific Railroad transformed this from a place to get through into a place to live. The railroad provided the region's lifeblood for many years. Later, Laramie gained the University of Wyoming and Rawlins the state penitentiary.

Economy

The economy of the Medicine Bow region is much like that of the rest of Wyoming—heavily dependent upon grazing and energy. More than 170,000 cattle and 75,000 sheep graze this land of sage and grass, mines near Hanna produce large amounts of low-sulfur coal, and wells in Carbon County pump natural gas. Other important pieces of the regional economy are the University of Wyoming, in Laramie, and tourism—particularly in the Snowy Range and Upper North Platte River Valley. Transportation has long been a vital factor in the region. Ben Holladay's stage and the Union Pacific Railroad were followed on this route eventually by I-80, the primary artery across America for truckers and travelers. The remote stretch of I-80 between Laramie and Elk Mountain is still called the "Snow Chi Minh Trail," a joking reference to the ceaseless blowing snow that sometimes shuts down traffic for days at a time during the winter. Gale-force winds have even been known to blow semis over!

LARAMIE

The countryside around Laramie (pop. 27,000) differs little from that in much of Wyoming—arid plains abruptly broken by rugged mountain ranges—but the town itself offers a real change of pace. True, Laramie does have rodeos, restaurants with names like the Cavalryman, and great country-and-western tunes at the ever-popular Cowboy Saloon, but it also seems to violate one's expectations of a Wyoming town. It's the kind of place where bumper stickers demand "Free Leonard Peltier" while others jokingly suggest that we should "Reunite Gondwanaland." This has to be the only place in the Wyoming where the Chuckwagon Restaurant features espresso! Take a stroll along downtown's Ivinson Ave. and you'll discover a shop selling fancy chocolates, an upscale children's store, art galleries, flower shops, cafes, bookstores, and even an organic foods store complete with post-hippie decor. Nearby are vegetarian restaurants, bars that attract reggae and blues bands, and galleries filled with handcrafted items from all over the planet. With the addition of the American Heritage Center and Wyoming Territorial Prison & Old West Park, Laramie has been drawing an increasing number of visitors.

Laramie is one of my favorite cities in Wyoming, a place that has a sense of intelligence without being stultified, where culture mixes with fun and games. Tourist brochures call Laramie "Gem City of the Plains." It has the laid-back college-town feel of Chico, California, or Fort Collins, Colorado. The students add a playful, literary atmosphere—bikes on the streets, rock concerts, heady conversations over beers, and theatrical productions. Laramie has both crowded fast-food outlets and sophisticated restaurants offering more substantial fare. It's probably the only place in the state (other than Jackson) where a restaurant would dare carry wine descriptions on its menu: "A complex, medium-bodied wine with black cherry and wild berry flavors, balanced by toasty-oak nuances. . . ."

The Union Pacific Railroad splits Laramie into two distinct parts. The campus, stately older homes, and nearly the entire city lie on the east side; less pretentious quarters lie on "the other side of the tracks." Long freight trains roll through every few minutes at all hours of the day and night piled high with double-deck containerized freight boxes destined for Chicago, Denver, or Los Angeles.

Located close to the Medicine Bow Mountains (hiking and skiing), Vedauwoo Rocks (rock climbing), Lake Hattie (windsurfing), and the Colorado Rockies (Coors beer), Laramie is a

Students cross Prexy's Pasture, where the first university president once grazed his livestock.

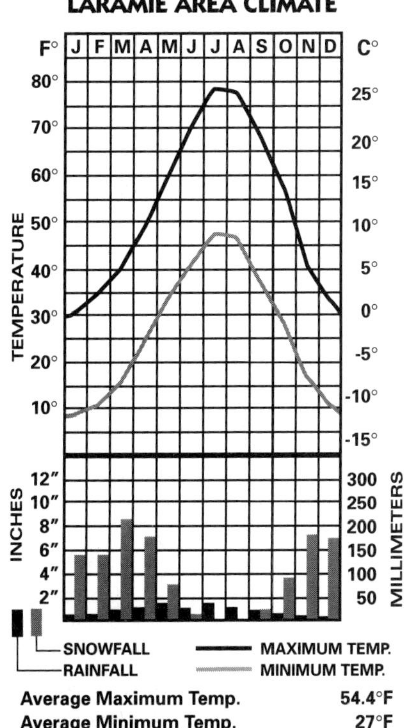

Average Maximum Temp.	**54.4°F**
Average Minimum Temp.	**27°F**
Annual Rainfall	**10.87″**
Annual Snowfall	**48.8″**

haven for those who love the outdoors. The only problem is the midwinter wind, which makes life in this part of the state difficult. Temperatures may be relatively mild—in the low 20s—but add in a 30-mph wind and it feels like 20 below zero. Bitter gale-force winds can howl through for days on end in this open country.

HISTORY

The city of Laramie (and several other places in eastern Wyoming) has the name of a French-Canadian trapper who was killed by Indians in the mountains now also named in his honor. Nearly everything about the man is open to question. Jacques LaRamee (or was it Joseph De la Ramie?) was killed in 1820 (or 1821) by Arapahoes (or another tribe), who stuffed his body under the ice in a beaver pond (or left his corpse in his cabin). Be that as it may, he attained a far more lasting legacy through his death than through anything he did while alive.

Fort Sanders

The first permanent settlement in the Laramie area was Fort Sanders, originally known as Fort John Buford, built in 1866. Located approximately two miles south of present-day Laramie, it served to protect emigrants and stagecoaches along the Overland Trail and, later, Union Pacific Railroad construction workers. At its peak, Fort Sanders housed nearly 600 soldiers. As with other posts on the frontier, desertions were rampant; 41 men went AWOL in a single month, taking with them whatever supplies they could grab. As the threat of Indian attacks lessened over the years, so did the value of Fort Sanders. It was abandoned in 1882, and very little remains.

The Union Pacific Arrives

Laramie City (as it was first called) was named and established by Gen. Grenville Dodge, the man in charge of planning the Union Pacific's route westward. The location was chosen because of a major spring that still produces millions of gallons of water, and because ties could be cut in the mountains to the west and brought down the Laramie River. The proximity of Fort Sanders also influenced the location. By the time the first train rolled into Laramie City on May 10, 1868, many "sooners" had already set up business in tents. The first passengers were met with 23 saloons, one hotel, and no churches. Within three months, Laramie had 5,000 people.

Many of the earliest to arrive were the usual end-of-the-track types: hoodlums, gamblers, prostitutes, and others out to make a fast buck. When the tracks headed on westward, the riffraff stayed behind, kept busy by the soldiers. Within a short time, a saloon owner named Asa Moore gained the support of various gambling houses, brothels, and other bars to create a rump town government with himself as mayor. The man they appointed town marshal had recently left Cheyenne after being acquitted on a murder charge, and his assistant was caught stealing mules. Laramie quickly became one of the wildest towns on the frontier, with murders occurring almost daily. Men who were arrested often faced trial in a back room of Asa Moore's saloon, where his men robbed and then killed them, burying their bodies out on the plains. Stories tell of up to 10 men disappearing in a single night.

Seeing that the law was in the hands of criminals, the more respectable citizens decided to put an end to the mayhem. More than 500 men joined a vigilante committee that swept into the saloons, brothels, dance halls, and casinos on the night of October 18, 1868. Three men died in gun battles (including a musician and a vigilante) and dozens of others were wounded. Another three were hanged by vigilantes, including the mayor, Asa Moore. The next day, outlaw Big Steve Young met the same fate, and more than a hundred crooks were piled into railroad cars and sent west. These actions calmed things down rather quickly, and thereafter Laramie City became something of a model town. It is perhaps fitting that four years later Laramie would be awarded the territorial prison.

For many years the main reason for the existence of Laramie was the presence of the railroad and the operations it established, including a roundhouse, an iron foundry, a tie-treating plant, machine shops, and a mill for reprocessing old rails. Gold discoveries in the Snowy Range to the west helped Laramie's economy grow, but the railroad remained the largest employer in Laramie until the 1950s, when it was supplanted by the university.

Women's Suffrage

Laramie was the site of two of the most notable events in the history of women's rights. On Sept. 6, 1870, Louisa Gardner ("Grandma") Swain became the first woman in the nation to vote in an open and public election. A few months before this, a judge in Laramie established the world's first jury with women members. (Reporters noted that the female jurors hid behind heavy veils and held crying babies on their laps.) The women brought about a change in the jury system: breaks for boozing and gambling were ended, and smoking and chewing tobacco in the jury box were also halted. The women also proved more likely to convict men of murder than their male peers, who regarded killing humans a less serious crime than rustling cattle. A stone monument near 1st and Garfield Sts. marks the location where the first all-woman jury met.

The University

In 1886, Laramie received a gift from the state legislature that would eventually transform it from a cow town into a college town. Under the leadership of Col. Stephen W. "Father of the University" Downey, the legislature voted to establish the new University of Wyoming. It was part of a deal that carved up Wyoming: Laramie got the university, Cheyenne became the capital, Rawlins landed the prison, and Evanston got the state asylum. The bill was signed into law by Gov. Francis E. Warren in 1886, four years before Wyoming achieved statehood. The school opened the following year with a single building—now called Old Main—built at a cost of $49,000. The new program had five professors and a coed student body of 42, who paid $7.50 each to attend. Over the years, the railroad gradually diminished in importance while the university added more and more to the local economy, until it became the biggest local employer. It remains so today. Because of the university, Laramie has never really experienced the economic booms and busts common to much of Wyoming.

A 1998 crime brought unwelcome notoriety to Laramie when Matthew Shephard, a gay University of Wyoming student, was brutally beaten to death. The two murderers apparently targeted Shephard because of his homosexuality. Anyone who knows Laramie and its people will see this as a frightening anomaly, since the town has a reputation for tolerance. Find out more by visiting the Matthew Shephard Foundation online at http://matthewsplace.com.

UNIVERSITY OF WYOMING

Wyoming is the only state to have just one baccalaureate-granting institution. The University of Wyoming campus in Laramie thus gains the state's undivided financial support, much to the chagrin of the two-year colleges. The university lays claim to being the highest university campus in the nation—at 7,200 feet, it makes Denver's mile-high claim to fame look puny. Although not a major research institution, UW has respected programs in atmospheric sciences (ozone-depletion studies), coal production, aquatic toxi-

BILL NYE

Laramie lays claim to one of the most popular humorists of the 19th century, Edgar "Bill" Nye (1850-1896). Born in Maine and raised in Wisconsin, Nye arrived in Laramie in 1876 and soon began writing columns for a local newspaper. His sharp wit and wry sense of humor quickly showed through the news. Local Republicans backed him in publishing his own paper, the *Laramie Boomerang*—named for a flea-bitten gray mule that kept returning no matter how hard Nye tried to get rid of him. The paper first rolled off his "lemon-squeezer" press in 1881. When the news wasn't all that interesting, Nye would embellish it: "[I] write up things that never occurred with a masterly and graphic hand. Then, if they occur, I am grateful; if not, I bow to the inevitable and smother my chagrin."

AMERICAN HERITAGE MUSEUM

Even Nye's appointment as Laramie City postmaster (a political plum gained because of his connection with the dominant Republican party) became grist for his humor mill. He wrote the postmaster general, noting, "I look upon the appointment, myself, as a great triumph of eternal truth over error and wrong. It is one of the epoches, I may say, in the Nation's onward march toward political purity and perfection. I do not know when I have noticed any stride in the affairs of state, which so thoroughly impressed me with its wisdom. . . ." Nye only kept the position for a year.

In 1883, an attack of spinal meningitis forced him to leave high-elevation Laramie for a lower climate. By the time he departed, Nye's newspaper was in dire financial condition, but it managed to survive under new, more responsible, management. The *Boomerang* is still published today and is one of the state's few daily papers. The old livery stable where it was originally published is on the corner of 3rd and Garfield; Nye's office was on the second floor.

Bill Nye's witty *Boomerang* columns gained a national following, and by the 1890s he had become the best-paid humorist in America. Nye would eventually write 14 books of humor; *Bill Nye's History of the United States,* published in 1894, sold an incredible 500,000 copies. Unfortunately, the intense stress of life on the road helped shorten his life. Nye died of a stroke when just 45 years old.

Much of Nye's humor falls flat today, and its racial stereotypes are certainly dated, but some of the short pieces still have a delightful zing, particularly when he tweaks the noses of famous people such as Oscar Wilde (whom Nye called "Thou bilious pelican from o'er the sea") or a competing newspaper editor ("We have nothing more to say of the editor of the Sweetwater *Gazette.* Aside from the fact that he is a squint-eyed, consumptive liar, with a breath like a buzzard and a record like a convict, we don't know anything against him . . ."). None of his works are currently in print, but you'll find *Bill Nye's Western Humor* in many Wyoming libraries.

The following insightful commentary on Wyoming agriculture and "reclamation" efforts is typical of Nye's tongue-in-cheek writing:

> *I do not wish to discourage those who might wish to come to this place for the purpose of engaging in agriculture, but frankly I will state that it has its drawbacks. In the first place, the soil is quite course, and the agriculturist, before he can even begin with any prospect of success must run his farm through a stamp-mill in order to make it sufficiently mellow. This, as the reader will see, involves a large expense at the very outset. Hauling the farm to a custom mill would delay the farmer two or three hundred years in getting his crops in, thus giving the agriculturist who had a pulverized farm in Nebraska, Colorado, or Utah, a great advantage over his own, which had not yet been to the reduction works.*

cology, oil recovery technology, water management, agricultural research, and infrared astronomy. Approximately 12,000 students attend the university under the tutelage of 2,000 faculty and staff members.

The university offers a wide spectrum of degree programs—98 at the undergraduate level and 97 at the graduate. It operates on a semester system, with a summer session open to visiting students. A summertime **Elderhostel** provides classes for folks over 60, and various noncredit classes are also offered throughout the year, covering the spectrum from ballroom dancing to LSAT preparation. For a copy of the school's *General Bulletin,* call the admissions office at (307) 766-5160 or (800) 342-5996, or find it on the Internet at www.uwoy.edu.

Seeing the Campus

Begin your campus visit at the very helpful **University of Wyoming Visitor Information Center,** 1408 Ivinson Ave., tel. (307) 766-4075. It's open Mon.-Fri. 8 a.m.-5 p.m. and Saturday 9 a.m.-1 p.m. all year. The center can provide maps and complete info on the university, including lectures, films, concerts, dances, and other events open to the public. Also stop here for details on **campus tours,** offered Mon.-Fri. at 1 p.m. in the summer, and Mon.-Fri. at 11 a.m. and 2 p.m. during the school year.

Right next door to the visitor center you'll find the historic **Cooper Mansion,** built in 1920 in the Mission Pueblo style and now on the National Register of Historic Places. An **information desk,** tel. (307) 766-3160, in the Wyoming Union building is open Mon.-Sat. 6 a.m.-11 p.m., Sunday noon-9 p.m. during the school year; Mon.-Fri. 7 a.m.-5 p.m. in the summer months. Check the ride board here if you're looking for a ride or offering transportation. Also stop in the union for a listing of campus activities, stamps, cash from the ATM, or snacks. The main campus buildings center around **Prexy's Pasture,** where the school's first president grazed his personal cattle. Today Prexy's is a favorite place to relax on sunny days—and it's still legal to leave your horse here.

American Heritage Center

The American Heritage Center serves as both a research facility and exhibition space for art and historical pieces. Designed by famed architect Antoine Predock, this multilevel conical building contains expansive art galleries and thousands of manuscripts, rare books, and artifacts from Wyoming and the West. The building was designed to represent the mountains surrounding Laramie and is oriented so that one small section is lit by the sun during the summer solstice. The building gets a decidedly mixed reaction. To be honest, I found it a big disappointment. The exterior resembles (take your pick) a Darth Vader mask or a stealth jet, and the wonderful central loggia is ruined by a claustrophobic tangle of 32 concrete columns intended, the architect claimed, to resemble a forest.

Nine oil paintings by Alfred Jacob Miller hang on the walls of the loggia, including his best-known work, *The Rendezvous Near Green River—Oregon Territory,* valued at $750,000. Miller was the only artist ever to witness a mountain-man rendezvous; he documented the West during a trip in 1837. Also in the loggia are the saddles of Hollywood cowboys William Boyd ("Hopalong Cassidy") and Duncan Renaldo ("Cisco Kid"). The George Rentschler room on this level contains nine paintings by the Western artist Henry Farney. Also nearby are a room with changing exhibits, and another one containing the university's 50,000-volume rare book repository. Wander around a bit more and you will find—surprisingly—Jack Benny's old violin.

Take the elevator to the fourth-floor reading room for access to an outstanding research collection of Western books, documents, and photographs, including the papers of Buffalo Bill Cody, F.E. Warren, Jack Benny, and Irving Wallace. Other pop culture icons have collections here too, including Ozzie and Harriet Nelson, Don Knotts, and Andy Griffith. The fifth floor provides a dramatic view across Laramie to the Snowy Range and historic photos on the walls. There's no charge to walk around the center, which is open Mon.-Fri. 7:30 a.m.-4:30 p.m. and Saturday 11 a.m.-4:30 p.m. in the summer; Mon.-Fri. 8 a.m.-5 p.m. and Saturday 11 a.m.-5 p.m. during the school year. Call (307) 766-4114 for more information. The web page is www.uwyo.edu/ahc/ahcinfo.htm.

Art Museum

The excellent University Art Museum, tel. (307) 766-6622, is housed in the same building as the

American Heritage Center and encompasses nine large galleries, including an outdoor sculpture court. Exhibits change several times a year, so you aren't likely to see the same thing twice. Some of these are from the university's permanent collection of 6,000 paintings, pieces of sculpture, and other works of art. The permanent collection is mostly by 19th- and 20th-century artists, including paintings and drawings by Thomas Hart Benton, Charles M. Russell, Winslow Homer, Paul Gauguin, Andy Warhol, Thomas Moran, and Pablo Picasso. The museum puts on a variety of special programs, lectures, and other art events throughout the year and has a fine **gift shop** selling distinctive arts and crafts. The Art Museum is open Mon.-Fri. 10 a.m.-7 p.m., Saturday 10 a.m.-5 p.m., and Sunday noon-5 p.m. from mid-June to Labor Day; and Mon.-Sat. 10 a.m.-5 p.m. the rest of the year. Entrance is free.

Another place to view artwork on campus is **Gallery 234,** which exhibits student pieces. It's in the Wyoming Union building and is open Mon.-Fri. 8 a.m.-5 p.m.

Geological Museum

Established in 1887, this is Wyoming's oldest museum and one of the most interesting campus sites. A life-size bronze *Tyrannosaurus rex* greets visitors at the entrance, while dinosaur bones surround the doorway. Inside the museum you'll find fossil and mineral displays from around the state (including a selection of fluorescent minerals). An enormous woolly mammoth skull found near Rawlins is one of the most impressive fossils, but the museum's real centerpiece is a 75-foot-long skeleton of an *Apatosaurus excelsus,* better known as a brontosaurus. Excavated along Sheep Creek in Albany County, it's one of just five *Apatosaurus* skeletons on display in the whole world. Also here, you'll find a cast of the largest *Allosaurus* skeleton ever found and the largest complete freshwater fossil fish in the world. The Geological Museum is open Mon.-Fri. 8 a.m.-5 p.m. and Sat.-Sun. 10 a.m.-3 p.m. year-round; no charge. Call (307) 766-4218 for more information.

Right next door to the Geological Museum is the **Wyoming Geological Survey Building,** which sells interesting maps of all types and guides to the state's geology.

Other University Sights

The first campus building was **Old Main,** completed in 1887 and now housing the administrative offices. The prominent tower that once adorned the building was removed in 1915. Look for Wyoming's territorial seal over the west entrance. Head to the Anthropology Building to view the university's **Anthropology Museum,** representing a small portion of the department's extensive cultural collection. The museum (tel. 307-766-5136) is open Mon.-Fri. 7:30 a.m.-4:30 p.m. and focuses on the Plains Indians. A mammoth skull is here, along with a display on the Vore Site buffalo jump in northeastern Wyoming, where thousands of buffalo were trapped and killed.

On the fourth floor of the Agriculture Building is the **Entomology Museum,** housing thousands of insect specimens. Although primarily for research, it's open to the public. Also in the same building is the **Range Herbarium,** considered one of the most complete collections of grasses in the western states. It's open by request; tel. (307) 766-5263. At the **Rocky Mountain Herbarium,** on the third floor of the Aven Nelson Building, tel. (307) 766-2236, you'll find one of the nation's largest plant collections, but it's open to the general public only by prior arrangement.

The fine **Williams Botany Conservatory** fronts the Aven Nelson Building and is a warm, bright place to escape on a winter day. Inside are dozens of tropical plants, including orchids and bananas. It's open Mon.-Thurs. 10 a.m.-4 p.m., Friday 10 a.m.-3 p.m., and Saturday 10 a.m.-noon (closed Saturday in the summer). Call (307) 766-2380 for details.

WYOMING TERRITORIAL PRISON AND OLD WEST PARK

In 1869, the territorial legislature voted to construct a penitentiary at Laramie. (Wyoming prisoners had previously been housed in the Detroit House of Correction at a cost of $1.25 a week.) The imposing three-story stone building in west Laramie off Snowy Range Rd. was dedicated to "evil doers of all classes and kinds"; fittingly enough, a bottle of bourbon was deposited in the cornerstone. It remained a prison until 1902, when the inmates were transferred to

Now a historical park, Wyoming Territorial Prison once housed the outlaw Butch Cassidy.

a new facility in Rawlins. After the prisoners were moved out, the building was turned over to the university for use as an experimental livestock farm; the cells became cattle stalls and the prison broom factory a sheep barn. In the 1980s, the university farm moved to a more modern facility elsewhere and the historic prison was officially established as Wyoming Territorial Prison & Old West Park. A $5 million facelift transformed the badly deteriorated buildings into one of the largest western-heritage parks in the Rockies. Some of the stuff here gets a bit cutesified and corny—children can help recapture a "prisoner" attempting an "escape"—but the park does offer a unique and fascinating way to step into Wyoming's frontier past.

Prison

The cornerstone of the historic park is the beautifully restored prison. A wooden stockade surrounds the sandstone building and adjacent broom factory where prisoners were forced to work. Other prisoners made candles, furniture, or musical instruments, or braided leather. Pick up a self-guided tour brochure as you enter the prison, or take a guided tour. The interior has been reconstructed using the original cells and period fixtures. Excellent displays and short videos describe the prisoners' lives. The convicts who served time here—including inmate number 187, Butch Cassidy—glare down from giant photos on the walls. Each cell held two prisoners in a tiny six-by-eight-foot arched brick enclosure sealed with an iron door. Inmates slept on straw mattresses. Walk inside one of the cells to get a feeling for the claustrophobic conditions. No wonder Butch Cassidy promised to "never molest the state of Wyoming again" when he was pardoned after 18 months here!

Horse Barn

The old horse barn has been transformed into a museum and dinner theater. Downstairs is the **National U.S. Marshals Museum,** housing everything from frontier-era artifacts—including a bullet-riddled Wells Fargo cash box—to displays on the crack-cocaine busts of today. The Marshals Service is the oldest civilian law-enforcement agency in the world and was responsible for managing the Wyoming Territorial Prison. Visitors will enjoy finding John Wayne, Clint Eastwood, and Ronald Reagan in the film clips that feature Hollywood's version of Old West marshals. Here, too, you'll learn all sorts of lawman trivia and see guns belonging to Bat Masterson and Butch Cassidy. Bet you didn't know that the five-pointed star worn by U.S. Marshals was derived from a pentacle worn by 17th-century soldiers; it was supposed to make them bulletproof.

Upstairs you'll find a **dinner theater** where on summer nights a professional cast puts on a Western musical revue. It's pretty foolish, but the production and singing are first-rate, and the meal is fine. The Horse Barn Dinner Theatre runs summers only.

Frontier Town and Ranchland

Just west of the prison lies an "end-of-the-tracks town" featuring simple wood and canvas buildings that come alive with living history characters such as outlaws, marshals, and Calamity Jane—played by her great-great niece. The old warden's house contains a variety of period artisans at work. Frontier Town also houses a blacksmith (in real life the chairman of UW's language department) who creates authentic period items. Other buildings house a printing press that cranks out wanted posters, a saloon, photo studio, general store, and livery stable (but no whorehouse). The Warden's house sells antiques. Horseback rides are available, and the amphitheater provides entertainment.

The newest addition to Wyoming Territorial Prison & Old West Park is a collection of historic buildings called Ranchland. Here you can explore a homesteader's log cabin, one-room school house, a chicken house, barn, and other buildings moved to the site from surrounding ranches and furnished with period pieces. It's a good way to learn about the small ranchers and farmers who lived in Wyoming in the late 19th century.

The quarter-mile **Laramie River Interpretive Trail** follows the banks of the river near the prison, providing a place to relax and explore.

Practicalities

Wyoming Territorial Prison & Old West Park is west of town on Snowy Range Rd. and has a gift shop that sells souvenirs and books. Combination tickets include guided prison tours (offered on the hour from 10 a.m. to 5 p.m.) and entrance to the Marshals Museum and Frontier Town. These tickets cost $8 for adults, $6 for ages 6-12; free for kids under six. The prison and Marshals Museum are open daily 9 a.m.-6 p.m. from early May to early October. Frontier Town is open daily 10 a.m.-6 p.m. Memorial Day to Labor Day. Everything is typically closed Oct.-April, but call for off-season hours.

Horse Barn dinner theater performances take place Thurs.-Sat. evenings in June, and Wed.-Sat. evenings in July and August. Theater prices are $26 for adults, $17 for ages 6-12.

The entire park, including the old prison, is fully accessible to those in wheelchairs. For more information, call (307) 745-6161 or (800) 845-2287. The park's web address is www.wyoprisonpark.org. See Territorial Prison Events below for additional park activities.

MORE LARAMIE SIGHTS

Ivinson Mansion

Although its official name is the Laramie Plains Museum, this historic site is known to most folks as the Ivinson Mansion. Located at 603 Ivinson, the home is a delightful example of the Queen Anne style of Victorian architecture. The home was built in 1892 for Edward Ivinson, a millionaire merchant turned banker and politician. It's now on the National Register of Historic Places. After his death, the mansion became an Episcopal girls' school. When the school closed, locals managed to raise more than $74,000 to purchase the mansion and turn it into a museum.

The Ivinson Mansion occupies an entire city block, with a carriage house out back and attractive Victorian-style gardens. Few of the original furnishings remain but much of the interior woodwork—including a freestanding stairway built without nails or screws—is still here. The museum is furnished with antiques, including some elaborate hand-carved furniture built at the Wyoming Penitentiary in 1901, handmade toys (including a doll from the 1840s), a piano that arrived by covered wagon, and a number of Indian artifacts. More unusual are a quilt that took 60 years to complete (listed in *Ripley's Believe It or Not!*), a seven-headed shower that looks like a medieval torture device, and a square Steinway grand piano. The back carriage house contains a small visitor center, carriages, old bikes, impressive fur coats, and two wonderful antique woodstoves. Also on the grounds is a one-room log schoolhouse built in 1924.

The museum, tel. (307) 742-4448, is open Mon.-Sat. 9 a.m.-6 p.m. and Sunday 1-5 p.m. June-August. It's closed mid-December through January and open Mon.-Fri. 1-4 p.m. (or by appointment) at other times. Guided hour-long tours are given throughout the day, with the last one starting an hour before closing time; $4 for adults, $2 for students and children.

Downtown

Laramie's downtown buildings, many of them dating from the 19th century, are on the National

See Laramie map in the color map supplement.

Register of Historic Places. Along Ivinson Avenue, a major renovation turned what had been a collection of sleazy flophouses and bars into a lively, attractive, and fun section of town. Pick up **walking tour** brochures describing Laramie's historical and architectural downtown buildings from the chamber of commerce visitor center. **St. Matthew's Cathedral,** at the corner of 3rd and Ivinson, is one of Wyoming's more interesting churches. The limestone structure was built in 1868 and funded by Edward Ivinson.

Laramie has a number of small art galleries in addition to the larger ones at the university. **Earth, Wind and Fire Gallery,** 220 S. 2nd St., tel. (307) 745-0227, sells designer jewelry, Indian art, art prints, and fine pottery. Other places worth a look include **Bright Side Gallery,** 205 E. Grand Ave., tel. (307) 745-0222, with all sorts of fun and fanciful art and furniture; and **The Front,** 119 S. 1st St., a student-run gallery with alternative art. If you're around on the first Friday evening of the month, join the **gallery walk,** which features artists and authors.

The **Wyoming Children's Nature Center and Museum,** 412 S. 2nd St., tel. (307) 745-6332, is open Tues.-Thurs. 9 a.m.-5 p.m., Saturday 10 a.m.-4 p.m., plus Friday 9 a.m.-5 p.m. in the summer. This small museum contains fun hands-on exhibits for kids, including an Oregon Trail exhibit with a wagon, trading post, and gold panning. The nature center is home to salamanders, turtles, a great horned owl, and a crawl-through "beaver lodge." Admission costs $2 for adults, $3 for kids; free for children under three.

On the grounds of the **Laramie Plains Civic Center** at 710 Garfield, you'll find **East Side School.** Built in 1878, this is the oldest stone schoolhouse in Wyoming. Inside the civic center theater are six murals painted in the early 1930s by noted artist Florence E. Ware.

Farther Afield

A granite monument to **Fort Sanders** stands two miles south of town along U.S. 287. Most of the fort site lies under an avalanche of residential and commercial development—the highway bisects the old parade grounds—but parts of the old stone guardhouse and the powder house still stand. One of Fort Sanders' wooden buildings was moved to LaBonte Park, at 9th and Canby Sts. in Laramie, where it is used as a recreation center.

Hutton Lake National Wildlife Refuge lies six miles south of Laramie on State Hwy. 230, then three miles south on County Rd. 37. It is a quiet, peaceful place to look for ducks, shorebirds, and migratory birds.

ACCOMMODATIONS

Space is generally not a problem at Laramie's motels, though you should reserve well ahead during graduation week (mid-May), Jubilee Days (Fourth of July), Cheyenne Frontier Days (mid-July), and on football weekends in the fall. The old rule of supply and demand holds, so rates also rise considerably over those listed below at these times. An eight percent tax is added to motel rooms.

Long-term housing can be difficult to find in Laramie; if you're moving here, check with Golden Key Realty, 310 University Ave., tel. (307) 742-8131, for apartments.

Easiest on the Wallet

The places listed below provide Laramie lodging at a reasonable price and are arranged from least to most expensive. (See also Sunset Inn—in the higher-end section following—which also offers some budget rooms.)

Inexpensive: For unpretentious accommodations, check out **Ranger Motel,** 453 N. 3rd St., tel. (307) 742-6677, where the furnishings are old but clean. Some rooms have fridges and microwaves, and weekly rates are available. Rates are $34 s or $38-46 d.

Motel 6, 621 Plaza Lane, tel. (307) 742-2307 or (800) 466-8356, has a small outdoor pool and standard rooms for $34 s or $40 d.

Travel Inn, 262 N. 3rd St., tel. (307) 745-4853 or (800) 227-5430, charges $36-42 s or $36-49 d and has an outdoor pool and continental breakfast.

Super 8 Motel, 1987 Banner Rd., tel. (307) 745-8901 or (800) 800-8000, offers rates of $40 s or $48 d. Similar prices ($42 s or $48 d) are available at **Motel 8,** 501 Boswell Dr., tel. (307) 745-4856 or (888) 745-4800. It also has kitchenettes for the same price.

Travelodge Downtown Motel, 165 N. 3rd St., tel. (307) 742-6671 or (800) 942-6671, www.vcn.com/~travelodge, charges $46 s or $51 d.

University Inn, 1720 Grand Ave., tel. (307) 721-8855 or (800) 869-9466, has accommodations for $49-59 s or d, with microwaves and fridges in the rooms.

Inexpensive-Moderate: For very nice accommodations, stay at **Best Western Gas Lite Motel,** 960 N. 3rd, tel. (307) 742-6616 or (800) 942-6610, where amenities include continental breakfast and an indoor pool with a retractable roof. Rates are $42-66 s or $43-79 d.

Camelot Motel, 523 Adams, tel. (307) 721-8860, charges $45 s or $55-75 d.

Higher-end Motels

The following places start around $50 a night, and include the nicer properties in town. They're arranged from least to most expensive.

Inexpensive: Sunset Inn, 1104 S. 3rd St., tel. (307) 742-3741 or (800) 308-3744, has a mix of accommodations. Recently remodeled rooms cost $50 s or $56 d, and half of these contain fridges and microwaves. Older and more basic units (no phones) are a very reasonable $20 s or $25 d. A few kitchenettes are available on a weekly basis, and the motel also offers an outdoor pool and jacuzzi.

Moderate: First Inn Gold, 421 Boswell, tel. (307) 742-3721 or (800) 642-4212, offers comfortable lodging for $56 s or $68 d, including an outdoor pool, indoor jacuzzi, and light breakfast.

Comfort Inn, 3420 Grand Ave., tel. (307) 721-8856 or (800) 228-5150, has such amenities as an indoor pool, jacuzzi, fitness room, and continental breakfast. Rates are $60 s or $70-75 d.

At **Econo Lodge,** 1370 McCue St., tel. (307) 745-8900 or (800) 303-6851, rooms go for $64 s or d, including access to an indoor pool with a fun 90-foot water slide. A light breakfast is served.

Rooms cost $79 s or d at **Holiday Inn,** 2313 Soldier Springs Rd., tel. (307) 742-6611 or (800) 526-5245. Facilities include an indoor pool, jacuzzi, and continental breakfast.

Moderate-Expensive: Best Western Foster's Country Corner Motel, 1561 Jackson St., tel. (307) 742-8371 or (800) 526-5145, features an indoor pool, jacuzzi, and sundeck. Rates are $82-97 s or $84-99 d, including a full breakfast.

Bed and Breakfasts

Built in 1888 and now on the National Register of Historic Places, **Prairie Breeze B&B,** 718 Ivinson Ave., tel. (307) 745-5482, is just a block from the university campus. The Victorian house was once home to the university president and offers a gracious place to spend a night or two. The four guest rooms contain Victorian antique furnishings and private baths. Rates are $60-80 s or d, including a tasty light breakfast, and kids are accepted. Get more info on the website: www.prairiebreezebandb.com. Moderate.

For an authentic Western experience with a fourth-generation ranching family, spend a night or a week at **Two Bars Seven Ranch,** 27 miles south of Laramie near Tie Siding, tel. (307) 742-6072. The owners raise horses and beefalo on 7,000 acres of mountains and meadows along the Colorado border. Guest accommodations are available in the summer and fall for $35 s or $70 d, including a hearty breakfast. Other meals and horseback rides are extra, or you can simply relax in the outdoor jacuzzi. The homestead also houses a pool table, antique jukebox, and player piano. For more info, stop by the website: www.twobarssevenranch.com. Moderate.

Camping

The closest public campgrounds ($10) are in the scenic Pole Mountain portion of **Medicine Bow-Routt National Forest,** approximately 10 miles east of Laramie. Other public campsites are 30 miles west in the Snowy Range. Both areas are described below. **Curt Gowdy State Park,** 22 miles east of Laramie on State Hwy. 210 (Happy Jack Rd.), has campsites ($9 for nonresidents, $4 for Wyoming residents; open all year). See the Southeast Wyoming chapter for more on this park. Several tepees are available at the **Wyoming Territorial Prison,** starting at $15 for a nine-foot diameter version that sleeps four. Call (307) 745-6161 or (800) 845-2287 for details.

The local private camping options are pretty miserable, unless you enjoy treeless gravel lots. **Riverside Campground,** I-80 at Curtis, tel. (307) 721-7405, charges $13 for RVs and is open year-round. Showers for noncampers run $3. **Laramie KOA,** 1171 Baker, tel. (307) 742-6553 or (800) 562-4153, charges $15 for tents and $22 for RVs. It also has an outdoor pool and is open April-October. Simple "kamping kabins" cost $30 d. **N-H Trailer Ranch,** 1360 N. 3rd., tel. (307) 742-3158, charges $12 for RV parking with hookups (no tent spaces); open year-round. **Snowy Range Trailer Park,** 404 S. Taylor, tel. (307) 745-0297, has tent spots for $10 and RV sites with hookups for $17; open all year.

FOOD

If you like reasonable prices, creative cooking, and a wide selection (who doesn't?), you're bound to appreciate all that Laramie has to offer in the way of dining out. You'll discover some of the best food in Wyoming here, from thick, juicy steaks to nouvelle cuisine.

American

For earthy breakfasts, lunches, and dinners, visit **The Overland,** 100 Ivinson Ave., tel. (307) 721-2800, but be ready for a wait on weekend mornings. The dinner wine list here includes more than 125 choices. Get traditional steaks and seafood at **The Cavalryman Supper Club,** 4425 S. 3rd, tel. (307) 745-5551, where the beef is considered the best around. Also well liked is **The Rancher,** 309 S. 3rd, tel. (307) 742-3141. A fun and friendly feeling are featured in this favorite of famished families. Not fancy, and no fake food or flaky fodder to be found! Prime rib is the house specialty, but they also have hearty breakfasts, inexpensive lunch buffets, and Sunday brunches.

You'll find inexpensive cafeteria food, pizza, ice cream, and deli food at the **University Cafeteria,** downstairs in the Wyoming Union building on campus. **CowBelle Cookouts** are put on by local ranches several times each summer. Just $8 gets you a tour of a ranch, a barbecued beef dinner, and entertainment. Call (307) 745-3686 for reservations.

International Eats

Several places in town offer Mexican food. The best are **El Conquistador,** 110 Ivinson Ave., tel. (307) 742-2377; **Corona Village,** 421 Boswell, tel. (307) 721-0167; and **Cafe Olé,** 519 Boswell Dr., tel. (307) 742-8383. **Chelo's,** 357 University Ave., tel. (307) 745-5139, is a tiny greasy spoon that locals rave over, but I find just mediocre. Judge for yourself.

Grand Avenue Pizza, 301 Grand Ave., tel. (307) 721-2909, bakes some of the best homemade pizzas in Wyoming. Get Italian food, Wyoming-style, at **Vitale's Italian Cowboy,** 2127 E. Grand Ave., tel. (307) 755-1500. Open only for dinner.

Two places offer decent Chinese food: **The Great Wall,** 1501 S. 3rd, tel. (307) 745-7966, and **The New Mandarin,** 1254 N. 3rd, tel. (307) 742-8822. The latter serves up spicier and more authentic (but inconsistent) fare.

Eclectic

Jeffrey's Bistro, 123 Ivinson Ave., tel. (307) 742-7046, is a personal favorite. The atmosphere is relaxed and friendly, with a mix of brick, oak, and brass. On the menu are light meals, creative vegetarian specialties, and great homemade bread. Reasonable prices too; the most expensive entrée is $9. Next door is **Jeffrey's Too,** tel. (307) 742-0744, where you'll find tasty salads, sandwiches, breads, pastries, and other healthy fast food (Is this a culinary oxymoron?). The hidden patio is an enjoyable place on sunny days.

Coal Creek Coffeehouse, 110 Grand Ave., tel. (307) 745-7737, is a great spot to meet friends over espresso in an art-filled setting. On the menu are sandwiches, salads, soups, and freshly baked sweets. Use the computer terminal for Internet access ($4/hour).

Right across from campus, **The Library Restaurant and Brewing Co.,** 1622 E. Grand Ave., tel. (307) 742-0500, is a favorite of college students, with fresh-brewed beer, reasonable prices, and ample servings of food.

Bakers and Grocers

Australian bakers Allison and Kim Campbell crank out delicious homemade breads and pastries at **Home Bakery,** 304 S. 2nd, tel. (307) 742-2721. In the 1800s, this building served as the second office of Bill Nye's *Boomerang* newspaper. A bakery has been on the premises since 1901. Head to **Old Town Bagels,** 307 E. Grand Ave., tel. (307) 721-8965, for the best bagels in these parts, plus smoothies, ice cream, and espresso.

The Chocolate Cellar, 115A Ivinson Ave., tel. (307) 742-9278, sells imported chocolates. Get groceries from **Albertson's, Smith's,** and **Safeway** stores along the main route through town. **Whole Earth Grainery and Truck Store,**

111 Ivinson, tel. (307) 745-4268, is a funky and friendly grocery with all sorts of organic produce, dried foods, teas, spices, and coffees. There are not many places like this in Wyoming!

OTHER PRACTICALITIES

Entertainment

You'll find plenty of night action in this youthful town, where bumper stickers proclaim: "I go from zero to horny in 2.5 beers." Laramie's oldest saloon—dating to 1890—is the **Buckhorn Bar,** 114 Ivinson Ave., tel. (307) 742-3554. Mounted heads of all types—including a two-headed calf—adorn the walls, while students and bikers adorn the pool table and barstools. Notice the bullet hole in the mirror behind the bar—the result of a 1971 incident in which a man opened fire on the bartender (he missed). The Buckhorn is a popular place for TV sports, and when school's in session, the back room thumps to rock or blues most weekends. The bar opens early, attracting the after-school college crowd. **Fireside,** 201 Custer St., tel. (307) 721-5097, another very popular club, hosts live rock, blues, or comedy nightly. More rock, pop, or blues tunes are **Ranger Lounge,** 463 N. 3rd Ave., tel. (307) 745-9751. **Coal Creek Coffeehouse,** 110 Grand Ave., tel. (307) 745-7737, has mellower live music some weekends.

For hot country-and-western tunes, duded-up cowboys, and fresh-faced cowgirls, saunter on down to **The Cowboy Saloon,** 108 S. 2nd, tel. (307) 721-3165. It's a spacious place with a big dance floor, two bars, and several pool tables. You'll find more country tunes (and free hors d'oeuvres on weeknights) at **Mulligan's,** 1115 S. 3rd, tel. (307) 745-9954. At the popular **Mingles Sports Bar,** 3206 Grand Ave., tel. (307) 721-2005, you can sample the 21 beers on tap or shoot pool at any of the 14 tables (free pool daily 3-7 p.m.). It's especially popular for happy hour. **Bud's Bar,** 354 W. University Ave., tel. (307) 745-5236, is a favorite with university alumni. Everyone goes there before and after university football or basketball games. Students hang out at "Club UDub"—the **Beergarden** in the basement of the Wyoming Union building—which has live music during the school year. The **Sports Bar & Grill** at the Holiday Inn, 2313 Soldier Springs Rd., tel. (307) 742-6611, also has two big-screen TVs, 17 smaller ones, pool tables, and draft beer from all over the globe.

Local movie houses are the **Fox 4 Theatres,** 505 S. 20th St., tel. (307) 742-2842, and the **Wyo Theatre,** 309 S. 5th St., tel. (307) 745-4442.

Territorial Prison Events

There's an event of some sort at the Territorial Prison & Old West Park every weekend of the summer; call (307) 745-6161 or (800) 845-2287 for the complete story. Several of the larger ones include the following. The first weekend of June brings an **Antique & Classic Tractor Festival** with tractor pulls, chuck wagon cookouts, cowboy poetry, and music. Then comes **Mountain Man Rendezvous** on the fourth weekend of June, with costumed traders and trappers, black-powder shoots, and tomahawk throws. The **U.S. Marshals Day & Posse Rendezvous** takes place the third weekend of July and attracts marshals from around the country; highlights include an auction and special demonstrations by law-enforcement teams. **Vintage Baseball** games are held the third weekend of August. Players pitch underhand and don't wear mitts. Each Halloween, the Wyoming Territorial Prison opens for spooky nighttime **haunted prison tours.**

Other Events

The Laramie events hotline, tel. (307) 721-7345, provides info on upcoming activities in the area. **Summer productions** at the university include dance and music festivals and lighthearted plays; call (307) 766-4075 for details. **Band concerts** are held at the Washington Park band shell on Wednesday evenings in June and July.

Laramie Jubilee Days starts on the Fourth of July and lasts a week, bringing PRCA rodeos, parades, the biggest fireworks in Wyoming, live music, barbecues, a free pancake breakfast, street dancing, a cattle drive, carnival, melodramas, square dancing, art exhibits, and other activities to celebrate Wyoming's statehood. It's easily the biggest event in Laramie, and it attracts folks from throughout the region. Call (307) 745-7339 or (800) 445-5303 to order rodeo tickets.

The annual **Ranch Tour** includes visits to four local ranches in mid-July. Contact the chamber of commerce at (307) 745-7339 or (800)

445-5303 for specifics. The ever popular **Albany County Fair** is held the first week of August, with 4-H contests, a carnival, and a demolition derby.

Sports

The biggest attraction in Laramie comes each fall with the arrival of football season. Half the state seems to turn out to join in the festivities at War Memorial Stadium—tailgate parties, rooting sections, and rock-'em-sock-'em helmeted soldiers battling it out against other citadels of higher learning. Up to 30,000 fans crowd the stadium Saturday afternoons to cheer on the Wyoming Cowboys—better known as "the 'Pokes"—as in "Cowpokes." The football team has a mixed record over the years—a Cody rodeo announcer once joked that Nebraska and Wyoming were uniting so that Nebraska could share Yellowstone and Wyoming could have a real football team! Needless to say, the crowd did not appreciate the humor. The university also competes in a number of other sports—men's basketball is a primary draw. The athletic facilities are among the finest in the nation and include a modern 15,000-seat arena-auditorium for basketball games, concerts, and other events. For tickets, call (800) 442-8322.

Recreation and Outdoor Supplies

The public **swimming pool** is in the high school at 11th and Reynolds, tel. (307) 721-4426. (University facilities are only for students, faculty, and staff.) Shallow **Lake Hattie,** 20 miles southwest of Laramie on State Hwy. 230, is a good place to swim or to fish for kokanee or rainbow trout in the summer. **West Laramie Fly Store,** 1657 Snowy Range Rd., tel. (307) 745-5425, has fishing gear.

Horseback and wagon rides are offered by **Prairie Rides,** on Sprague Lane west of Laramie, tel. (307) 745-5095, and **Two Bars Seven Ranch,** tel. (307) 742-6072.

The University's **Jacoby Park Golf Course,** on N. 30th, tel. (307) 745-3111, is an 18-hole course open to the public. For the lilliputian version, head to **Oasis Mini-Golf,** S. 15th and Skyline Rd., tel. (307) 745-7574, which is also home to **Skyline Skate** for roller skating. **Laramie Lanes,** 1270 N. 3rd St., tel. (307) 745-3835, is the local bowling alley.

Rent skis, snowboards, snowshoes, and other winter gear from **Cross Country Connection,** 221 S. 2nd St., tel. (307) 721-2851; **Rocky Mt. Sports Outlets,** 217 E. Grand Ave., tel. (307) 742-3220; **Westgate Ski & Sports,** 1979 Snowy Range Rd., tel. (307) 742-6742 or (800) 308-6742; or **Fine Edge Ski Shop,** 1660-E N. 4th St., tel. (307) 745-4499.

Rent mountain bikes at **Pedal House,** 207 S. 1st St., tel. (307) 742-5533. The folks here are very knowledgeable about local cycling trails and also rent rollerblades and snowboards. **Rocky Mt. Sports Outlets** also rents bikes.

Purchase outdoor supplies from **Rocky Mt. Sports Outlets,** which rents and sells all sorts of used outdoor gear, including sleeping bags, tents, backpacks, stoves, bikes, rollerblades, skis, and snowshoes. Other places to pick up outdoor gear include **All Terrain Sports,** 412 E. Grand Ave., tel. (307) 721-8036, and **Cross Country Connection.**

Other Shops

Mountain Woods, 209 S. 2nd St., tel. (307) 745-3515, sells a selection of rustic and attractive handcrafted aspen and lodgepole furniture. Buy hemp garments, imported items, and hippie garb from **Terrapin,** 301 S. 2nd St., tel. (307) 745-3027.

Information

The **Laramie Chamber of Commerce,** 800 S. 3rd St., tel. (307) 745-7339 or (800) 445-5303, is open Mon.-Fri. 8 a.m.-5 p.m. Also look for the chamber visitor center in the caboose on the south end of town; open daily 9 a.m.-5 p.m. Memorial Day to Labor Day. The chamber's web address is www.laramie-tourism.org.

The University of Wyoming also has its own visitor centers; see the earlier section on the university for location and hours.

If you're heading out to the Medicine Bow Mountains, be sure to stop by the **Forest Service Supervisor's Office,** 2468 Jackson St., tel. (307) 745-2300, for maps and up-to-date trail and campground information. The office is open Mon.-Fri. 8 a.m.-5 p.m. all year, and it may also be open Saturday mornings in the summer. Find the office on the web at www.fs.fed.us/mrnf.

The 100,000-watt **Wyoming Public Radio** station KUWR (91.9 FM) is based in Laramie, with repeaters throughout Wyoming providing in-depth news and music sans commercials.

Libraries

Albany County Library is at 310 S. 8th, tel. (307) 745-3365, and its Wyoming Room has a big selection of historic books and other documents. It also provides computers with free Internet access. Much more impressive are the eight university libraries which house more than 1.1 million volumes—including the most complete collection of Wyoming books in existence—plus 150,000 maps and 13,000 periodicals. Most of these publications are in the **William Robertson Coe Library,** tel. (307) 766-5312, which also has a map room, an extensive depository of government publications, and the American Heritage Center's outstanding collection of historic books about Wyoming and the West. Also of note are the **Geology Library,** in the Geology Building, tel. (307) 766-3374; the **Science and Technology Library,** in the Science Complex, tel. (307) 766-5165; and the **Law Library,** in the College of Law, tel. (307) 766-2210.

Bookstores

Laramie is home to several excellent bookstores. The spacious **University Bookstore,** in the student union, tel. (307) 766-3264, has many regional titles and travel books. **Chickering Bookstore,** 307 S. 2nd, tel. (307) 742-8609, is a small and friendly bookshop in downtown Laramie. **Personally Recommended Books,** 105 Ivinson, tel. (307) 745-4423, is a relaxing upstairs place to look over local literary favorites while enjoying a coffee or pastry. **The Grand News Stand,** 214 E. Grand Ave., tel. (307) 742-5127, has a big magazine selection and lots of Wyoming titles. **Hastings,** 654 N. 3rd St. in Gateway Plaza, tel. (307) 745-0312, is a chain store that sells books, CDs, software, and videos.

Transportation

Laramie Airport is just west of town on State Hwy. 130. **United Express/Great Lakes Aviation,** tel. (307) 742-5296 or (800) 241-6522, has daily flights from Laramie to Denver. Two companies provide scenic flightseeing trips: **Executive Air Transport Service,** tel. (307) 742-9381, and **Backcountry Air Service,** tel. (307) 755-1755.

Rent cars at the airport from **Avis,** tel. (307) 745-7156 or (800) 331-1212; **Dollar,** tel. (307) 742-8805 or (800) 800-4000; **Enterprise,** tel. (307) 721-9876 or (800) 325-8007; **Laramie Auto Rental,** tel. (307) 742-8412 or (800) 982-5935; **N&K Rental,** tel. (307) 742-6329; or **Price King Rent-A-Car,** tel. (307) 721-8811.

Laramie Cab Service, tel. (307) 745-8294, provides local taxi service.

Greyhound buses, tel. (800) 231-2222, www.greyhound.com, stop at the Tumbleweed Express Gas Station on E. Grand at I-80. Buses operate daily in both directions along I-80.

POLE MOUNTAIN/VEDAUWOO AREA

Heading east from Laramie on I-80, the freeway climbs steadily up into the second-growth ponderosa and lodgepole pine forests of the Pole Mountain area. It's a scenic land punctuated by unusual and colorful rock formations. For many years much of the land here belonged to the military and was used as a target and maneuver area for the army's version of off-road vehicles—tanks. Amazingly, the land seems to show little sign of all this abuse today.

Ten miles east of Laramie is the Summit Rest Area, located at the highest point (8,640 feet) along I-80. A 13-foot-tall bronze bust of **Abraham**

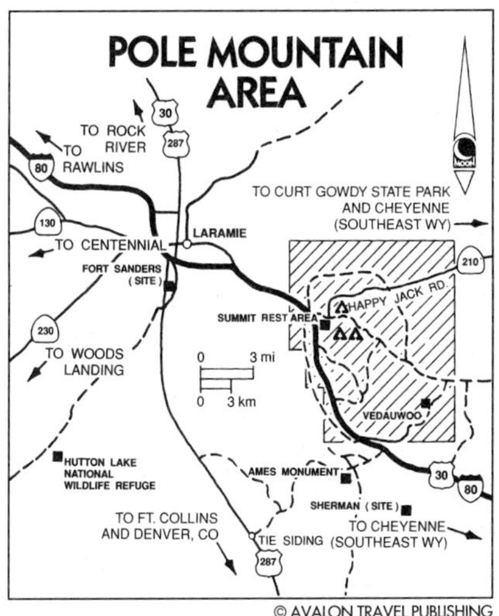

Lincoln looks over the freeway from atop a granite base. This—the largest bronze bust in the nation—was created by Robert I. Russin, former art professor at the university and Wyoming's best-known sculptor. The old road through this pass was known as the Lincoln Highway and was the first transcontinental highway. The sculpture was placed in this area in 1959, on the 150th anniversary of Lincoln's birth. It was moved to the present location when the interstate highway came through in 1968. The **visitor center** here has information on nearby areas and is open daily 9 a.m.-7 p.m. mid-May through October. Also here is a small theater showing videos.

Choose from four Forest Service campgrounds (free to $10; open May-Sept.) in the Pole Mountain/Vedauwoo area or camp for free on land away from the roads. **Headquarters Trail** extends 4.5 miles from the Summit Rest Area to Headquarters Road. During the winter, Pole Mountain's groomed trails make it a popular cross-country ski area. Many others come to play on the tubing and tobogganing hill near Happy Jack Trailhead. A $2-3 day-use fee is charged at trailheads and picnic areas in the Pole Mountain/Vedauwoo area.

East of the summit, I-80 follows a long open plateau and then drops gradually into the shortgrass prairie of southeastern Wyoming via "The Gangplank." The Colorado Rockies form a jagged southern horizon line. This crossing of the Laramie Range was discovered by Gen. Grenville Dodge in 1865. While exploring the railroad's new route, an attack by a party of Indians forced his men to flee eastward. In the process they discovered this gentle ramp to the plains of Cheyenne. Unfortunately, today the route is marked for miles by a domino-like line of billboards advertising everything from McDonald's to fireworks. It's too bad the billboards can't topple like dominoes to reveal the expansive grassland beyond!

Vedauwoo

Just five miles east of the summit you'll find the turnoff to strange rock formations known as Vedauwoo (pronounced "VEE-dah-voo"), a name meaning "earthborn" in Arapaho. In this area—considered a sacred place where young Indian men went on vision quests—oddly jumbled rocks form all sorts of shapes: mushrooms, balancing rocks, feminine curves, rounded knolls, lizards, faces, turtles, and anything you might dream up. Imagine it as a Rorschach test. Indians believed that the rocks were created by animal and human spirits. Today, Vedauwoo is considered one of Wyoming's best and most unique places for rock climbing. Climbs go from a difficulty level of 5.0 all the way up to 5.14, with many easy places to practice crack climbs. Nonclimbers come just to view the rocks, eat a picnic lunch, ride mountain bikes along the dirt roads, hike in the countryside, or scramble up for marvelous vistas of the surrounding land. Vedauwoo Glen Rd. connects with Happy Jack Rd. for a nice loop trip. There's

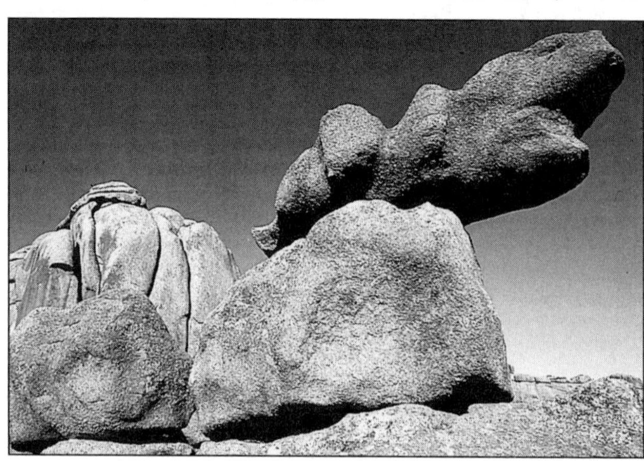

Vedauwoo rocks are a favorite destination for rock climbers.

a campground right at Vedauwoo. The Forest Service charges a $2 fee for day-use.

Pyramid Power

Head two miles south from the Vedauwoo exit to one of the strangest monuments in Wyoming: a 60-foot-tall pyramid in the middle of nowhere. The memorial commemorates Oakes and Oliver Ames, two of the most influential figures in the building of the transcontinental railroad. As a U.S. congressman, Oakes Ames gained passage of a bill that allowed the railroad to sell bonds equal to the amount loaned by the federal government—some $60 million. The company they established to handle this financing was the infamous Credit Mobilier of America. It later came to light that Oakes had bribed fellow congressmen with discounted railroad stock and greatly exaggerated construction costs for his own gain. A congressional investigation labeled Oakes "King of Frauds" and censured him. He died before he could stand trial, and the money was never recovered.

Despite this bit of infamy, nearly $65,000 was spent in 1882 to build this monument to the Ames brothers. It was originally located at the highest elevation of the transcontinental railroad route, near the town of Sherman, a place where trains halted to check their brakes before the long descent on either side. In 1902, the tracks were rerouted a couple of miles to the south, leaving the grandiose pile of rocks by itself. Nothing remains today from the Sherman townsite except a cemetery. The Ames Monument seems to bring out two conflicting emotions: dismay at the obscenity of this monstrosity and amusement at the irony that so much money was wasted on a self-aggrandizing monument soon abandoned even by the railroad the Ames brothers had helped build.

MEDICINE BOW VICINITY

Two roads head west from Laramie. Most people follow I-80 straight to Rawlins, but US 30/287 (the old Lincoln Hwy.) gets you there in about the same time and provides a strong flavor of the Old West. State Hwy. 34 heads northeast from US 30 near the dot on the map called **Bosler,** climbing over the low mountains to Wheatland 50 miles away. It's a pretty drive with little traffic and is worth a detour to visit **Sybille Wildlife Research Center,** 26 miles up the road. This is where the endangered black-footed ferrets are raised. (The center is described in the Southeast Wyoming chapter.) Two miles east of Sybille is the Johnson Creek Wildlife Habitat Management Area, a popular place for fishing. There are no trails, but hiking is easy in the open country here.

Rock River

This almost-ghost town of 180 lonely souls is home to the small **Rock River Museum,** tel. (307) 378-2386; open Tues.-Sun. 10 a.m.-3 p.m. June-August. Inside you'll find exhibits on dinosaurs, a collection of phosphorescent rocks, and local memorabilia. A statue of a triceratops stands in the town park. The town also has a bar, a motel, a general store/laundromat, a cafe, and a pretty red-doored church. **Longhorn Lodge Motel,** 362 N. 4th, tel. (307) 378-2555, charges $25 s or $30 d for log cabin units. Budget. **Dodge Creek Ranch,** tel. (307) 322-2345, is 35 miles northeast of Rock River, 40 miles southwest of Wheatland, on State Hwy. 34. This cattle ranch specializes in weeklong vacations, with backpacking trips, fishing, photography, and other activities. It does not, however, have horseback rides.

West of Rock River, the road sails through desolate treeless country, with sagebrush to the horizon and the impressive summit of Elk Mountain rising to the southwest. The Union Pacific Railroad parallels the highway most of the way, and antelope glance up at the passing trains. Anyone coming through in the winter will appreciate the miles of snow fences along the south side of the highway. Still, the snow streams over the roadway almost constantly.

COMO BLUFF

Halfway between the towns of Rock River and Medicine Bow on U.S. 30/287 is a long, low ridge known as Como Bluff. There isn't much to distinguish this from countless other buttes in the West, but paleontologists consider it one of the most important sites ever discovered, a place one author likened to Darwin's *Origin of the Species* in terms of its impact on scientific thought. This was the first large discovery of dinosaurs anywhere, and the first place *Diplodocus* dinosaurs—the largest ever found—were discovered. The mammals discovered here are prized around the world and include all but three of the 250 known Jurassic mammals found in North America. Combined, the dinosaur and mammal fossils from Como Bluff make up a major part of the collections of Yale's Peabody Museum, the Smithsonian Institution, the New York Museum of Natural History, the National Museum in Washington, D.C., and many others around the world.

History

In July of 1877, Professor Othniel Charles Marsh of Yale College received a letter from two Wyoming men calling themselves Harlow and Edwards. They told of finding

> *a large number of fossils, supposed to be those of the Megatherium, although there is no one here sufficient of a geologist to state for a certainty. We have excavated one (1) partly, and know where there is several others that we have not, as yet, done any work upon. . . . We are desirous of disposing of what fossils we have, and also, the secret of the others. We are working men and are not able to present them as a gift, and if we can sell the secret of the fossil bed, and procure work in excavating others we would like to do so. We have said nothing to anyone as yet. . . . We would be pleased to hear*

from you, as you are well known as an enthusiastic geologist, and a man of means, both of which we are desirous of finding—more especially the latter.

Marsh was in stiff competition with other paleontologists around the country, and his rival, Professor E.D. Cope from the Philadelphia Academy of Sciences, had just scooped him on a major dinosaur discovery in Colorado. The letter from "Harlow and Edwards" piqued Marsh's curiosity. An assistant sent to investigate wrote that the find was indeed substantive and suggested that Marsh immediately hire the two discoverers—actually two railroad employees, William Reed and William Carlin—to keep them from revealing the secret to others. Reed would later work for many years as a collector for the University of Wyoming and eventually as an instructor in geology and curator of the Geology Museum on the Laramie campus.

Work began almost immediately and continued right through the blizzards of winter, but despite efforts to keep the find a secret, Professor Cope soon had his own men working at Como Bluff. The rivalry almost came to blows, and Marsh's men made it a point to smash any bones left behind after their digging was complete and to backfill the quarries with rocks, even if their rivals were working below. Excavations continued until 1889, by which time most of the finest specimens had been unearthed.

Today geology and paleontology classes still visit Como Bluff, but the quarries where the bones were found are now abandoned and can't be seen from the road. Como Bluff itself is visible a little over a mile north of U.S. 30 and a sign describes the site. Travelers will want to stop to see **"the world's oldest building"** at Como Bluffs, a now-closed museum/gift shop built from dinosaur bones.

MEDICINE BOW

The little town of Medicine Bow (pop. 360) is the sort of place where headlines in the weekly *Medicine Bow Post* complain of dogs getting into garbage or barking at kids. For the most part it's a nondescript town with old boxlike houses and newer boxlike trailers. Medicine Bow is not unlike hundreds of places all over the West, but it was here that novelist Owen Wister had his legendary cowboy hero, the Virginian, face off with Trampas. Over a game of cards, Trampas calls the Virginian a "son-of-a-bitch," leading to the famous encounter in which the Virginian pulls his pistol and says, "When you call me that, smile!" It remains one of the classic lines in American folklore. *The Virginian* became the prototype for the modern Western and was later made into three movies and a TV series.

History

The town of Medicine Bow began in the 1870s as a Union Pacific pumping station along Medicine Bow River and grew into a local supply point and minor army garrison. It has always been a center for the ranchers who run thousands of head of livestock in the surrounding countryside, so it was a logical place for Wister to base his cowboy hero. During the 1930s, Medicine Bow prospered because it lay along the Lincoln Hwy. (U.S. 30) but, following completion of I-80, it lapsed into decay. The coal mines of Hanna (20 miles west) and uranium and oil explorations in Shirley Basin led to temporary energy booms, but the economy has now returned to its ranching base.

Sights

Medicine Bow's main attraction is the boxy, three-story **Virginian Hotel,** built in 1909—seven years after *The Virginian* came out. At the time, it was the largest hotel between Denver and Salt Lake City. It's still a marvelous building, so take a look around, even if you aren't planning on staying here. The Virginian's authentic old-time bar is one of the best in Wyoming. Just down the street is the modern **Diplodocus Bar** (alias "the Dip"), tel. (307) 379-2312, containing the largest jade bar in existence, cut from a 4.5-ton jade boulder discovered near Lander. Look down for the only hand-painted dance floor west of the Mississippi. While you're here for a beer, be sure to ask owner Bill Bennett to show his unusually intricate woodcarvings.

Across from the hotel is the **Medicine Bow Museum,** housed in the old wooden railroad depot (1913). Out front is a cabin built by Owen Wister—it stood in Jackson Hole until being moved here in 1976—and a petrified-wood mon-

> *Town, as they called it, pleased me the less, the longer I saw it. But until our language stretches itself and takes in a new word or closer fit, town will have to do for the name of such a place as Medicine Bow. I have seen and slept in many like it since. Scattered wide, they littered the frontier from the Columbia to the Rio Grande, from the Missouri to the Sierras. They lay stark, dotted over a planet of treeless dust, like soiled packs of cards. Each was similar to the next, as one old five-spot of cards resembles another. . . . Yet this wretched husk of squalor spent thought upon appearances; many houses in it wore a false front to seem as if they were two stories high. There they stood, rearing their pitiful masquerade amid a fringe of old tin cans, while at their very doors began a world of crystal light, a land without end, a space across which Noah and Adam might come straight from Genesis. Into that space went wandering a road, over a hill and down out of sight, and up again smaller in the distance, and down once more, and up once more, straining the eyes, and so away.*
>
> —FROM OWEN WISTER'S *THE VIRGINIAN*

ument to the novelist. The museum contains the typical things found in small-town museums—various homesteading items, a lamb warmer, a coyote scare made from sawdust and firecrackers, and old fire equipment. It's kind of like wandering through an old attic where you wonder how half the stuff was ever used. There's an old caboose on the side. The museum, tel. (307) 379-2383, is open daily 10 a.m.-5 p.m. Memorial Day through Labor Day, and Mon.-Thurs. 10 a.m.-3:30 p.m. the rest of the year.

Five miles south of Medicine Bow is the remains of a giant **wind turbine** built in 1982 for the U.S. Department of the Interior. The largest wind generator in existence, it's located in one of the windiest spots in America. Originally there were two such windmills here, each producing five million kilowatt hours of electricity a year, but the 400-foot-tall monsters proved unwieldy embarrassments and were abandoned by the government when it discovered that repairs would be prohibitively expensive. One of the $6 million turbines was blasted over with dynamite and sold for $13,000 on the scrap market in 1988. The remaining turbine is now privately owned and produced electricity until a 1994 storm destroyed the blades.

Practicalities

Rooms at the historic **Virginian Hotel,** tel. (307) 379-2377, are remarkably inexpensive, starting at just $22 s or $25 d with a bath down the hall. You should, however, check them out first, since they definitely aren't to everyone's liking and can get noisy when downstairs bar patrons shift into high gear. For $65 s or $75 d, sleep in the two-bedroom suite where Owen Wister stayed. If you miss your TV and private bath, try a room in the annex next door for $40 s or $45 d. Budget-Moderate. The downstairs restaurant provides good home cooking, or you can tip a beer in the old-time bar. A few doors away, **Trampas Lodge,** tel. (307) 379-2280, has rooms with private baths, fridges, and cable TV for $29 s or $33 d. Budget. Pitch your tent or park RVs for free at the town park. Groceries are available from **Bow Market.**

Medicine Bow Days is the annual celebration in town, held at the end of June and including rodeos, parades, a picnic, foot races, live music, and dancing. The "highlight" is the hanging of Dutch Charlie at high noon. In 1879 and 1871, respectively, Dutch Charlie and Big Nose George were lynched for the murder of two deputies. (See the special topic Big Nose George Parrot in this chapter.)

SHIRLEY BASIN

State Hwy. 487 heads north from Medicine Bow across vast and remote Shirley Basin, some of the finest cattle rangeland in Wyoming. The road is smooth with wide shoulders (perfect for bikes), and the vistas are dramatic—colorful badlands, rolling hills covered with sage and grass, and cottonwood-lined creeks. There's lots of wildlife here, too—especially antelope and deer. The basin has been home to major prairie-dog towns, and the endangered black-footed ferrets were released here in the early 1990s. Unfortunately, sylvatic plague later decimated prairie-dog populations, and the ferrets did not survive. If the prairie-dogs recover, more ferrets may be placed here.

BLACK-FOOTED FERRETS

On Sept. 25, 1981, near Meeteetse, Wyoming, a dog walked up to its master with a strange creature in his mouth. It was a black-footed ferret, a sleek, black-masked animal last seen in 1972 and feared extinct. Biologists soon discovered that a nearby prairie dog colony housed the only living population of ferrets, the world's rarest mammal. Ferrets eat prairie dogs and were once found in prairie dog colonies from Saskatchewan to Texas. The colonies were huge—one along the Cheyenne River in eastern Wyoming stretched for a hundred miles—but the prairie dogs went the way of many other animals, hunted and poisoned by settlers and their land taken over by plowed fields. Although still present in Wyoming, prairie dog colonies are now far smaller and more isolated. The population of ferrets declined with their shrinking food source.

With the discovery of ferrets living near Meeteetse, national attention focused on saving the population from extinction. A 1985 outbreak of canine distemper threatened to kill all the remaining wild ferrets, so all 18 survivors were captured and taken to the Wyoming Game and Fish Wildlife Research Unit at Sybille. After inoculations, an ambitious captive breeding program was begun. Only five of the animals actually reproduced, but the program proved so successful that the population was split up to reduce the chance that all might be killed in an accident such as a fire or in an outbreak of disease. Ferrets are now raised not only at Sybille, but also at breeding facilities in Colorado, Kentucky, Virginia, Arizona, New Mexico, and Toronto, Canada.

Reintroducing Ferrets

The captive breeding program has proven highly successful, but the ultimate goal is to reestablish at least 10 healthy ferret populations in the wild. Beginning in 1991, ferrets were released in Shirley Basin (north of the town of Medicine Bow). Unfortunately, sylvatic plague swept through the area, killing both ferrets and their prey, prairie dogs. Most other efforts at reintroduction have also been hampered by plague, but ferrets are doing well in South Dakota and Arizona, with limited success in Montana. There are plans to eventually release them in Wyoming at Thunder Basin National Grassland if the population of prairie dogs recovers from plague outbreaks and unregulated hunting.

Because of their relatively short life span (three years in the wild) and their susceptibility to diseases and predators such as owls and coyotes, ferrets will almost certainly remain endangered for decades to come. The plague, continued destruction of prairie dog colonies by "varmint hunters," and poisoning by ranchers have all made it more and more difficult to find places to release wild ferrets. The habitat is becoming increasingly fragmented into "islands" separated by areas where the prairie dogs have been killed off; only seven large and healthy black-tailed prairie dog populations still exist in all of North America! It would indeed be sad if we managed to breed black-footed ferrets in zoos, but they were unable to survive in the wild because of habitat loss.

The **Sybille Wildlife Research Center,** on State Hwy. 34 halfway between Bosler and Wheatland, tel. (307) 322-2784, is open daily 8:30 a.m.-4:30 p.m. June to mid-September (closed the rest of the year). Inside are exhibits and videos on the endangered black-footed ferret. TV monitors show activity in the adjacent ferret facility, and a couple of live ferrets may be exhibited in the visitor center itself. Behind the visitor center you'll find an observation deck and a short nature trail along Sybille Creek. Find out more about ferrets at the website: www.blackfootedferret.org.

Extensive deposits of uranium have been discovered in Shirley Basin—some of the largest and richest in the world—but low prices and an oversupply have all but halted the uranium-mining business. Ask in Medicine Bow for directions to the petrified forest. Nearly every yard in town has a piece out front.

HANNA

The town of Hanna (pop. 1,100) lies at the center of one of the state's major coal fields. There are lots of mobile homes and company housing in Hanna, but there is nothing particularly interesting about the town, unless you care to check out the miners memorials or the enormous Union Pacific snowplow. Near Hanna are two large coal mines: the Medicine Bow strip mine, 23 miles west, and the larger Cyprus Shoshone mine, five miles north. Mining has been a mainstay of the local economy since coal was discovered here in the late 1800s. Two disastrous explosions in 1903 and 1908 killed 228 miners, but the mines remained open until 1954 and were reactivated in the 1970s. Two monuments commemorate the men who died. The mining ghost town of **Carbon**—established in 1868 as the state's first coal town—once stood a few miles east of here. The coal ran out in 1902, and today only a few ruins and the graveyard remain. **Hanna Basin Museum,** tel. (307) 324-3915, has local memorabilia.

Practicalities

Golden Rule Motel, tel. (307) 325-6525, charges $24 s or $26 d, for basic prefab rooms. Friendly owners make this the de facto chamber of commerce office. Budget. **The Tucker Box,** 624 Madison, tel. (307) 325-6353, serves good breakfasts and lunches, or try **Jade Cafe,** tel. (307) 325-6355, for other meals. Hanna's fine **recreation center** houses a sauna, swimming pool, jacuzzi, and gym. Groceries are available at **The Super Market.** Other businesses include a hardware store, two liquor stores, a video shop, and a bank—but no ATM.

ARLINGTON

Approximately 30 miles west of Laramie, I-80 drivers are suddenly confronted with a strange apparition: towering **windmills** lining the crest of a long ridge. Completed in 1998, these 69 turbines crank out 41,000 kilowatt-hours of electricity, enough to power 20,000 homes. One of the windiest spots in America, this hilltop location is perfect for wind power; the wind farm here is the biggest outside California.

Below the windmills is the freeway off-ramp called Arlington, a tiny place with a surprising amount of history. Park RVs ($17) or pitch tents ($11) at **Arlington Outpost Campground,** tel. (307) 378-2350; open mid-May to mid-October.

You'll find several buildings from the **Rock Creek Stage Station** which stood along the Overland Route, including one of the oldest structures in Wyoming, a log cabin built around 1860. Also in Arlington, on private land south of the freeway, is a combination blacksmith shop/dance hall/gambling palace. In 1865, Indians attacked a wagon train near the Rock Creek Stage Station and captured two girls, Mary and Lizzie Fletcher. Mary was eventually sold to a white trader, but Lizzie remained with the Arapahoes for the rest of her life. It wasn't until 35 years later that Mary discovered her sister alive and living on the Wind River Reservation. Having grown accustomed to the Arapaho way of life and enjoying a high status in the community, Lizzie chose to stay in her home. She is buried next to her husband, Broken Horn, in the St. Stephen's Mission Cemetery.

ELK MOUNTAIN

The tiny settlement of Elk Mountain (pop. 200) stands just off I-80 halfway between Laramie and Rawlins. Although almost within sight of the freeway, the town seems a world apart. Big cottonwoods line the quiet streets, and the Medicine Bow River, home of blue-ribbon trout fishing, flows right through town. Several buildings are noteworthy: the small New England-style community church, the Elk Mountain Trading Company (with a few groceries), and an enormous log barn still in perfect condition after more than a century. Directly behind town is the rounded, snowcapped 11,156-foot summit of Elk Mountain, one of the most prominent natural landmarks anywhere along I-80. Unusual clouds frequently hang off its peak, making it a valuable site for the University of Wyoming's atmospheric research program. Ask in town for access information to the mountain; you'll need to get permission from local ranchers.

Elk Mountain Hotel, tel. (307) 348-7774, built in 1905, is an old-fashioned, slightly run-down hotel where bath-down-the-hall rooms are $30 s or $38 d. Inexpensive. The hotel also runs a bar and restaurant specializing in steaks, burgers, and seafood. **Wild Wonder Cafe,** tel. (307) 348-7478, serves three meals a day. Still standing on the east end of town next to Elk Mountain Hotel is **Garden Spot Pavilion,** a decrepit former dance hall that in the 1930s and '40s attracted the likes of Louis Armstrong, Tommy Dorsey, Glenn Miller, and Lawrence Welk. Five miles west of town, a stone monument marks the site of **Fort Halleck,** a short-lived military post built in 1862 to guard the Overland Trail. With the arrival of the transcontinental railroad, it was abandoned in 1866 and its fixtures moved east to Fort Buford (later called Fort Sanders), near present-day Laramie.

Head south from Elk Mountain on Pass Creek Rd. (Rd. 404) for a wonderful round-the-mountain drive. The gravel road curves south past Elk Mountain, then west along the willow-lined Pass Creek to a junction with State Hwy. 130, where you can continue to Saratoga. This little-traveled road offers open hills with wide vistas of the mountains and plains. While you listen to meadowlarks singing and wind rustling through the grass, you can watch—as the song says—the deer and the antelope play. Not even a line of telephone poles breaks the view, and seldom is heard a discouraging word.

MEDICINE BOW MOUNTAINS AND VICINITY

Medicine Bow-Routt National Forest is scattered over four disjunctive areas in Wyoming. The northern portion—the Laramie Mountains—is discussed in the Central Wyoming chapter; the Pole Mountain section is described under Laramie earlier in this chapter. The other two mountainous areas are west of Laramie: the Medicine Bow Mountains, locally called the Snowy Range, and the Sierra Madre. The Forest Service has controlled most of this land since 1902, although the name and boundaries have changed over the years. Mining was the big attraction in the late 1800s, but the major gold and copper deposits were quickly mined out and logging became the primary use of this mountainous country. Between 1867 and 1940, millions of railroad ties were brought out of the Laramie and Medicine Bow Mountains by tie hacks who logged almost every driveable creek they could find. The area provided ties for not only Wyoming but western Nebraska and Colorado as well. Logging for lumber is still important in the Medicine Bow-Routt National Forest but recreational use is increasing each year as more and more people discover this very scenic country. The supervisor's office for Medicine Bow National Forest is in Laramie; district offices are in Saratoga, Encampment, and Douglas. Pick up a copy of the Medicine Bow-Routt National Forest Map ($4) at any of these offices before heading out.

LARAMIE PLAINS VICINITY

Heading west from Laramie on State Hwy. 130, you pass through some of the most desolate country in Wyoming, with flat grassland stretching in all directions, interrupted by mountains to the east, south, and west. An enormous windswept bowl here—**Big Hollow**—was created by howling winds during the last ice age. The only other place like this is in Russia. Laramie Basin is also unique in having the highest short-grass prairie in the world, some 7,200 feet above sea level. Eleven miles west of Laramie, State Hwy. 130 crosses the historic **Overland Trail,** which carried emigrants, mail, and freight west between 1862 and 1868, when the railroad replaced it. The wagon ruts are still visible, with markers tracing the old route. As you approach the Medicine Bow Mountains, the highway dips down to sample the tree-lined beauty of Little Laramie Creek and then begins the long ascent to Snowy Range Pass.

Albany

State Hwy. 11 heads south along Little Laramie Creek to the foothills town of Albany, passing rolling grass and sagebrush country with pine-topped hills. Old ranches are sprinkled around this gorgeous little valley. Rustic cabins with

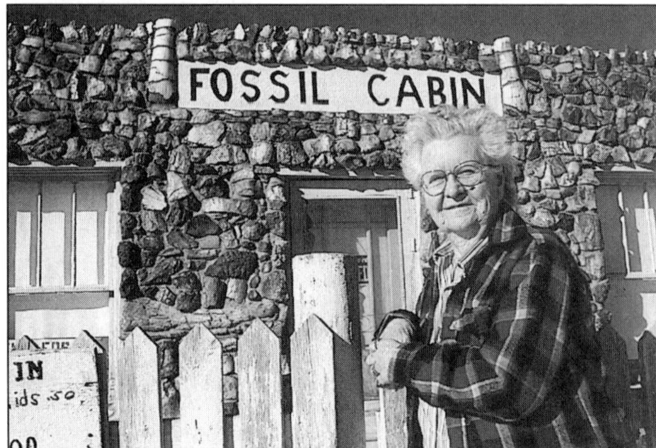

Como Bluff is home to "the world's oldest building," built from dinosaur bones.

shared bath at the **Albany Lodge,** tel. (307) 745-5782, cost $30 for up to four. They also have a four-person cabin with private bath, microwave, and fridge for $65, along with a large cabin that sleeps 12 and has a full kitchen for $150 (three-night minimum stay here). Albany Lodge is closed mid-April through May. Budget. On Saturday nights, this is a popular place with tasty $15 prime rib dinners. A dirt road continues south from Albany to Woods Landing, but blowing snows often cause its closure in the winter. Albany is a favorite base for snowmobilers.

Three miles east of Albany, **Double Mule Shoe Ranch,** tel. (307) 742-5629, has two modern cabins with kitchens and private baths. The smaller one sleeps four for $65; the largest is $95 and sleeps six people. Budget.

Centennial

Thirty-five miles west of Laramie, State Hwy. 130 widens to include the funky old mining town of Centennial (pop. 50). Situated at the foot of the Snowy Range, Centennial was founded in 1875 and gained its name the following year—the centennial of the founding of America. (James Michener claimed not to have known of the town when he wrote his novel of the same name about an early Rocky Mountain town.) Prospectors came here in search of gold. That first year the Centennial Mine produced more than $90,000 worth, but when the vein ran out only a few people stayed around. Another short boom created by infusions of cash from a Boston financier brought a fish hatchery, hotels, mining explorations, and an exclusive country club to Centennial, but the bubble burst again when the expected gold deposits failed to materialize. Eventually, Centennial became a minor ranching center. Today, it's a tourist way station with a devil-may-care mix of old log homes and house trailers.

The small **Nici Self Museum** in the 1907 railroad depot building contains exhibits on the area's mining, ranching, and logging history. It's open Sat.-Sun. 1-4 p.m. from mid-June through Labor Day, and by appointment the rest of the year (tel. 307-742-7158). Out front are a Union Pacific caboose and various aging farm implements. Check out the "police car" as you roll through town.

Inexpensive Accommodations: Old Corral Motel, tel. (307) 745-5918 or (800) 678-2024, has rooms in the lodge for $40 s or $59 d, including a full breakfast. Its restaurant, open for all three meals in summer but dinners only in winter, serves outstanding steaks in a comfortably rustic atmosphere, and it sometimes has live music on summer weekends. **Friendly Motel,** tel. (307) 742-6033, has eight motel rooms for $36 s or $43 d, and a pair of cabins for $75. The latter sleep six and have a two night minimum. Open year-round. Across the road is **Trading Post Restaurant & Lounge,** tel. (307) 721-5074, where you'll find country, blues, or rock on Saturday nights. It also has two cabins for rent year-round: $45 d, or $55 for four, including a kitchen, but no phones or TVs.

Sarah Rose Hotel, tel. (307) 742-5476 or (888) 400-9953, has two apartments available, both with full kitchens. The larger unit sleeps seven and costs $85; the smaller one sleeps four and costs $60.

Eight miles west of Centennial, **Mountain Meadow Cabins,** tel. (307) 742-6042, features eight cabins. Built in the 1950s, the cabins have been updated with private baths and kitchenettes and are open year-round; you'll need a snowmobile or skis for winter access. The smallest ones sleep two for $48, while four-person cabins are $65, and eight-person units cost $85.

Built as a bank in 1903, **Centennial Trust B&B,** tel. (307) 721-4090, contains two guest rooms furnished in a Victorian style. Rates are $40 s or d, including a continental breakfast. Open all year, and kids are welcome.

Expensive-Luxury: East of Centennial, **Vee Bar Guest Ranch,** tel. (307) 745-7036 or (800) 483-3227, www.vee-bar.com, offers luxury at the foot of the Snowy Range. Stay in comfortable old cabins or in a grand old lodge listed on the National Register of Historic Places. The emphasis is on horseback riding, but the Vee Bar also offers hayrides, cattle drives, trap shooting, archery, trout fishing, and hiking. And when the day is done, relax tired muscles in the outdoor hot tub. The 26,000-acre ranch attracts a clientele that includes celebrities and politicians. Accommodations from mid-June to early September cost $2,895 d for six nights, all-inclusive. A less expensive option is to stay for Saturday night only. The $150 d price includes breakfast; a big barbecue dinner is $25 more. During the winter, the ranch has nightly B&B accommodations for $100 s or d.

SNOWY RANGE

In between the Laramie Plains and the valley created by the upper North Platte River lie the Medicine Bow Mountains, locally called the Snowy Range. The latter is an appropriate name; it can snow here at any time of the year. Ten-foot drifts are not uncommon in the winter, and snow remains on high passes until late summer. The Snowy Range contains the **Savage Run Wilderness** (15,260 acres) and the **Platte River Wilderness** (22,749 acres), both lying along the southwestern end of the range just above the Wyoming-Colorado border. Most visitors simply enjoy the drive over the mountains and the

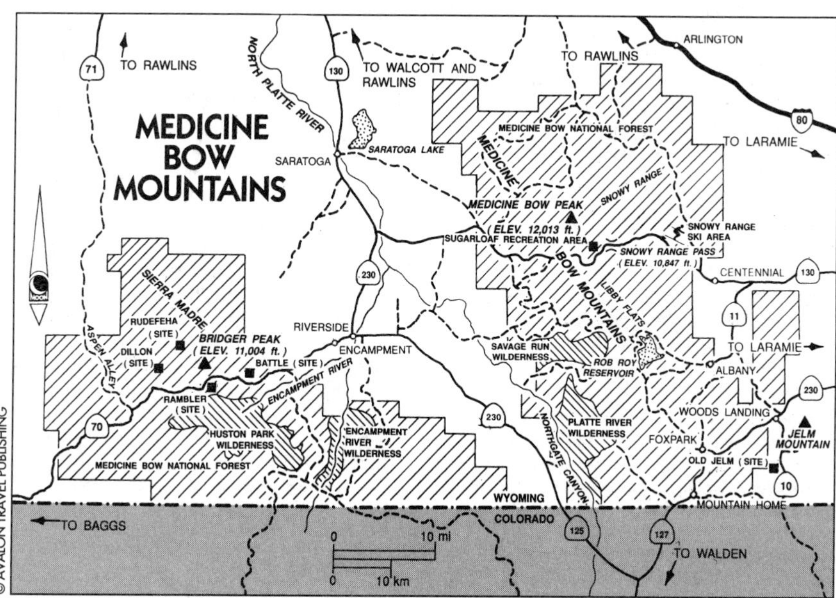

chance to camp beside an alpine lake with a backdrop of 12,000-foot mountains. Numerous short hiking trails and outstanding trout fishing make this a favorite spot for locals.

The Forest Service has detailed maps and helpful brochures at its Laramie office, 2468 Jackson St., tel. (307) 745-2300, or on the web at www.fs.fed.us/mrnf. You'll also find Forest Service information centers on both sides of the Snowy Range along State Hwy. 130. The **Centennial Visitor Center,** tel. (307) 742-6023, a mile west of Centennial, is open daily 9 a.m.-4 p.m. Memorial Day to Labor Day and Sat.-Sun. 9 a.m.-4 p.m. in the winter. **Brush Creek Visitor Center,** tel. (307) 326-5562, 20 miles east of Saratoga, is open daily 8 a.m.-5 p.m. Memorial Day through September. Saturday evening interpretive programs—including full-moon walks—are offered at both the Centennial and Brush Creek Visitor Centers during the summer. Other full-moon walks are offered Jan.-Oct. at various sites around the forest; contact the Laramie District office for details, tel. (307) 745-2300.

Over the Top

The 40-mile drive on State Hwy. 130 over the Snowy Range is one of the most dramatic in Wyoming and is designated a National Scenic Byway. The pass is closed by snow from late October to Memorial Day but remains open year-round to just beyond the Snowy Range Ski Area on the east side and 20 miles up from the west side. Higher-elevation parts of the road are very popular with snowmobilers and cross-country skiers. West of Centennial, the highway climbs sharply through lodgepole and spruce forests to beautiful Snowy Range Pass at 10,847 feet (second-highest in the state). Even taking a short hike is likely to leave you a bit out of breath unless you're acclimated to the altitude.

Be sure to stop at **Sugarloaf Recreation Area,** just east of the pass. Sharp, glacially carved spires rise above the small lakes, and islands of stunted Engelmann spruce dot the alpine country. Trails head out to nearby lakes and flower-covered alpine meadows. At the summit, a viewing platform provides panoramic vistas of Libby Flats, massive Medicine Bow Peak, and the valleys on both sides. Pull off at the Medicine Bow Peak Observation Point for a three-quarter-mile hike to the picturesque remains of an old mine. Just west of here, **Mirror Lake** and **Lake Marie** are two of the most photographed spots in Wyoming, with a spectacular backdrop of steep mountain faces reflected in the dark blue lake waters. Campgrounds and picnic areas are all along here. A wheelchair-accessible path leads along one shore of Lake Marie, and the west parking lot acts as a trailhead for the path up **Medicine Bow Peak** (see below). On the western side of the pass, the highway drops steadily down through the forest, eventually reaching the rolling sage and grass of the Upper North Platte River Valley. Stop at the Brush Creek Visitor Center for directions to **Kennaday Peak Lookout,** one of the few fire lookouts still staffed in Wyoming. It's open July to Labor Day and is accessible by high-clearance cars. No RVs.

Route 230

Another route west is State Hwy. 230. While this highway is not as dramatic as the Snowy Pass trek, it's open year-round and is still quite scenic. The road curves around the southern end of the Snowys and passes through tiny Woods Landing en route to the Colorado border. This is the only real settlement between Laramie and Encampment—a distance of 87 miles. **Woods Landing Resort** comprises most of the town, with a combination country store/gas station/cafe/bar, tel. (307) 745-9638. Park RVs for $14, or stay in their cabins for $30-35 d; the larger ones contain kitchenettes, but all use a shared bath facility. Budget. The floor of the bar was built atop 24 boxcar springs—courtesy of railroad workers—so the dance floor really starts rocking on Saturday nights when country-and-western bands play. Anglers will find excellent fishing for brown trout in the nearby Big Laramie River.

A number of old clapboard buildings from the mining ghost town of **Old Jelm** lie on private property four miles west of Woods Landing. The university's **Jelm Mountain Observatory** is up a five-mile dirt road from here. Call the university in advance (tel. 307-766-6150) for a tour of the infrared telescope facilities. The **Guest House at Jelm,** tel. (307) 742-6081, is a three-bedroom log home with kitchen, living room, bath, and front porch. Rates are $75 d; more for additional people. Open May-October. Moderate.

Located along the Big Laramie River, **Richardson's B&B,** tel. (307) 742-6012, offers country accommodations in a separate apartment that sleeps four and costs $60. This is a nice place to relax and enjoy the deer and birds. A full breakfast is served, and guests will enjoy the outdoor jacuzzi. Open April-November. Inexpensive.

Beyond Woods Landing, State Hwy. 230 dips south and passes several mountain lodges including **Wy-Colo Lodge,** tel. (307) 755-5160, just two miles north of the state line. Here, you'll find three rustic cabins with a shared bathhouse for $20 s or d. These are mainly used by hunters and hardy snowmobilers who bring their own bedding. Four-person rooms in the home are $50-70 and include private baths. Also at Wy-Colo are a bar and restaurant. The lodge is open year-round. Budget.

Snowy Mountain Adventures, tel. (307) 721-9811 or (800) 546-4098, rents out three modern cabins during the winter months. These are popular with snowmobilers and cost $65-125 per night. The largest sleeps 10 people.

South of Mountain Home, the road continues into Colorado for nine miles along Colorado Hwy. 127, then back north on Colorado Hwy. 125 for another nine miles before again crossing into Wyoming on State Hwy. 230. Much of this is open rangeland with hills on either side. Only a few abandoned cabins and fences mark the presence of humans on this vast landscape. The huge white hip-roofed barn of the Big Creek Ranch is one of the most beautiful in Wyoming. Turn around for outstanding views of the Colorado Rockies. See Stephen Metzger's *Colorado Handbook* (Moon Travel Handbooks, www.moon.com) for details on sights to the south.

Campgrounds

Twenty-eight different Forest Service campgrounds dot the Snowy Range portion of Medicine Bow-Routt National Forest. Most of these are typically open June-Oct., but the season varies depending upon snow conditions and budget constraints. A few of the campgrounds—those with no water or trash pickup—are free, but most cost $10 per night. Because of heavy use during the summer, you should arrive at the most popular sites early in the day. Five campgrounds along State Hwy. 130 over the Snowy Range—Brooklyn Lake, Libby Creek-Willow, North Fork, Ryan Park, and Sugarloaf—can be reserved ($8.65 fee) by calling (877) 444-6777. Find reservation information on the web at www.reserveusa.com. In addition to the official campgrounds, dispersed camping is permitted in most areas as long as you're off the main roads—although not along the crest of the Snowy Range. Check with the Forest Service for specifics. **Campfire talks** are given during the summer; Forest Service visitor centers have the details.

Public Cabins

The Forest Service rents out the **Bow River Ranger Station,** a cabin with two bedrooms and a kitchen, plus electricity and running water. You'll need to bring sleeping bags, dishes, and other supplies. It's 15 miles south of Elk Mountain on Forest Rd. 101, and it costs $80 per night for up to eight people, with a two-night minimum stay. Call (307) 326-5258 for reservations and more information.

Also available for rent is **Spruce Mountain Fire Lookout Tower,** seven miles west of Albany on a gravel road. No longer used for fire detection, the tower can sleep two people and is available mid-June through September for $40 per night. You'll need to bring water, sleeping bags, and other supplies; call (307) 745-2300 for reservations. See Cross-country Skiing and Snowmobiling below for details on the winter-only Forest Service cabin at Little Brooklyn Lake.

Mountain Lodges

Snowy Mountain Lodge, tel. (307) 742-7669, is just beyond the Snowy Range Ski Area, seven miles west of Centennial. Built as a University of Wyoming science camp in 1927, the lodge includes cozy accommodations. Basic older cabins (these sleep four) are $45 with shared bath. Larger cabins, some with kitchens and lofts, are $110-150, and can sleep up to eight. Snowy Mountain Lodge is especially popular with groups of wintertime cross-country skiers and snowmobilers looking for a cheap place in the mountains. In the winter you'll need to ski in or catch a snowcat ride from the lodge for the last third of mile since the road isn't plowed. The restaurant here serves three solid meals a day and has a bar. It's not a place to be pampered but a great place for folks who want to explore the nearby mountains by foot, bike, ski, or snowmobile. The

Internet address is www.snowymountainlodge.com. Inexpensive.

Another 1.5 miles uphill from Snowy Mountain Lodge is **Mountain Meadow Cabins,** tel. (307) 742-6042. The eight log cabins here start at $48 d for a one-room unit, up to $85 for a two-room cabin that sleeps eight. All units have private baths and kitchens. Open all year, but you'll need a snowmobile or skis for winter access. Inexpensive.

Another delightful place is **Brooklyn Lodge B&B,** tel. (307) 742-6916, west of Centennial in the Snowy Range at an elevation of 10,200 feet. Built in 1918 and refurbished in the 1990s, the log lodge is on the National Register of Historic Places. Inside, two guest rooms have king-size beds and share a bath. The living room contains a big stone fireplace, and the front porch overlooks a mountain meadow. There's a minimum two-night stay on most weekends and a three-night minimum on holidays and in the winter, when access is by skis or snowmobile. The room price of $125 d includes a full breakfast and fresh-baked cookies each evening. Brooklyn Lodge fills up far ahead; reserve six months in advance for summer weekends. It is also a favorite spot for summer weddings. Premium.

Historic **Medicine Bow Lodge & Guest Ranch,** tel. (307) 326-5439 or (800) 409-5439, is just inside the western national-forest boundary along State Hwy. 130. The main building opened in 1917 and is still in use. Refurbished historic log cabins are $140 d, including three home-cooked meals and access to a workout facility, hot tub, and sauna. Available for an extra charge: horseback rides, float trips, and mountain-biking in summer; cross-country skiing and snowmobile tours in winter. Open all year except November and mid-April to mid-May. Get details on the website: www.medbowlodge.com. Premium.

Historic Ryan Park, 24 miles east of Saratoga, is home to a pair of lodging places. **Brooksong B&B,** tel. (307) 326-8744, is a modern log home where two guest rooms share a bath. Rates are $49 s or $59 d, and a hearty breakfast is served. Kids are accepted. Inexpensive. **B&B Mountain Retreat,** tel. (308) 235-3881 or (307) 326-8012, has a four-bedroom log home available by the day or week. Rates are $75 d or $100 for four people. Guests will also enjoy the jacuzzi. Moderate.

Trails

The Medicine Bows are ideal for short one- to five-day hikes; get maps from Forest Service offices or visitor centers. The 4.5-mile **Medicine Bow Peak Trail** climbs 1,600 feet to the summit of this 12,013-foot mountain, highest in southern Wyoming, providing extraordinary vistas. The trail leaves from the west Lake Marie parking area and is in exposed alpine terrain most of the way. You can make a seven-mile loop by following this route to the top and then dropping down the east side to the **Lakes Trail,** which takes you past rock-rimmed Lookout Lake—keep a lookout for marmots—and on to Mirror Lake. Your starting point is just down the road. Medicine Bow Peak can also be climbed via a steeper and shorter trail (four miles roundtrip) that leaves from the Lewis Lake Trailhead. The Forest Service charges a $2 day-use fee at the Libby Lake and Lewis Lake Trailheads and picnic areas.

North Gap Lake Trail departs from the Lewis Lake parking lot in the Sugarloaf Recreation Area and follows a gentle grade past Gap Lakes, continuing on to Sheep Lake. Here, you can follow the **Sheep Lake Trail** to Brooklyn Lake, before returning to your starting point via **Lost Lake Trail.** Total distance for this delightful high-mountain loop is 15 miles. This entire area is crisscrossed with other alpine trails, some of which are not shown on topographic maps. Check with the Forest Service for details.

Platte River Trail, a 6.5-mile-long path, parallels the river through a deep and narrow canyon lined with ponderosa pines and Douglas-firs. Access is from the south via a trailhead near Sixmile Gap Campground (22 miles south of Encampment). The trail follows the west bank of the river, but by July the river can sometimes be forded, allowing hikers to continue another two miles northward to Pickaroon Campground. Check with the Forest Service for current water levels.

Savage Run Trail crosses the wilderness area of the same name. Nine miles long, it parallels Savage Run Creek, dropping 2,400 feet along the way. Access is too convoluted to describe, but it's not that hard to find if you have a Medicine Bow-Routt National Forest map.

Snowy Range Ski and Recreation Area

In the mountains 32 miles west of Laramie on State Hwy. 130, the Snowy Range Ski and

Recreation Area has four lifts and 25 different runs. Outside of Jackson Hole, this is the best place to ski in Wyoming, with a good variety of skiing conditions, uncrowded slopes, and soft powder snow. Snowy Range is open mid-November through mid-April and charges $29 for adults ($22 per half day), $15 for kids ages 6-12 and seniors ($11 per half day). Children under six are free with a paying adult. The area is open daily 9 a.m.-4 p.m., with ski and snowboard rentals and lessons, along with guided snowmobile trips. The lodge has cafeteria food, beer, and a fireplace. For more information, call (307) 745-5750 or (800) 462-7669, or go to the web at www.snowyrange.com.

Cross-country Skiing and Snowmobiling

The Forest Service maintains dozens of miles of groomed Nordic ski trails in the mountains around Snowy Range Ski Area, with a wide variety of loops and longer treks available for those willing to strike out on their own. Get avalanche and trail information on the web at www.trib.com/~mbna/index.html.

The Forest Service's **Little Brooklyn Lake Guard Station** is available for rent in the winter months. Built in 1931, this classic log building can accommodate seven people and costs $40 per night; call (307) 745-2300 for reservations.

Snowmobiling is one of the most popular winter activities in the Snowy Range, and parking lots on all sides of the range fill with vehicles on winter weekends. More than 200 miles of groomed trails follow summertime roads and are maintained by the state of Wyoming. For details on both cross-country skiing and snowmobiling, stop by Forest Service offices in Laramie or Saratoga.

River Recreation

The North Platte River forms a major focal point for visitors staying in Saratoga or Encampment. The trout fishing is excellent and the scenery grand; no wonder they call this the "Good Times Valley!" Many travelers float downriver either on their own or with guides. Whitewater enthusiasts enjoy **North Gate Canyon,** typically putting in at Routt Access (just inside Colorado) and taking out at Sixmile Campground. Check with local Forest Service offices for river access information and a list of guides.

In Saratoga, **Great Rocky Mountain Outfitters,** 216 E. Walnut, tel. (307) 326-8750 or (800) 326-5390, sells quality Orvis fly-fishing gear and can fill you in on the latest fishing and floating conditions. Rent rafts for $75-90 a day or canoes for $35. All-day fishing trips run $290 for two people; overnight camping and fishing trips and boat shuttles are also available. Great Rocky Mountain Outfitters also rents cross-country skis in the winter.

Medicine Bow Drifters, 120 E. Bridge St., tel. (307) 326-8002, has scenic float trips for $60 per person (minimum of four people), and all-day float and fishing trips costing $290 for two people. Other guides with similar services include: **Platte Valley Outfitters,** tel. (307) 326-5750; **Hack's Tackle & Outfitters,** tel. (307) 326-9823; **Wyoming Trout Company,** tel. (307) 326-3055; and **Old Baldy Club,** tel. (307) 326-5222.

As the North Platte River enters Wyoming from Colorado it drops into **North Gate Canyon,** a class III and IV stretch of whitewater with several hairy sets of rapids. Beyond Sixmile Gap, the river broadens and becomes a gentler float. If you are a whitewater enthusiast, get here early—the water level drops after June. Check with the above places for guided whitewater trips in May and June.

Horseback Trips

High Mountain Horseback Adventures, tel. (307) 632-4087, operates from a base camp in the Snowy Range. Eight-day trips cost $900 per person, including horses, guided rides (six to eight hours per day), tents, sleeping bags, and meals. Shorter trips are also available. All trips are limited to eight people max, so they fill up fast. Get more info at www.cruising-america.com/horseback.

SARATOGA

The friendly, laid-back town of Saratoga (pop. 2,000) is one of two towns in Wyoming—the other being Thermopolis—that center around hot springs. The name was borrowed from another well-known spa: Saratoga, New York. Wyoming's version of Saratoga straddles the North Platte River and putters along on a mixed economy. Louisiana Pacific Company has a large lumber mill in town, and many cattle graze

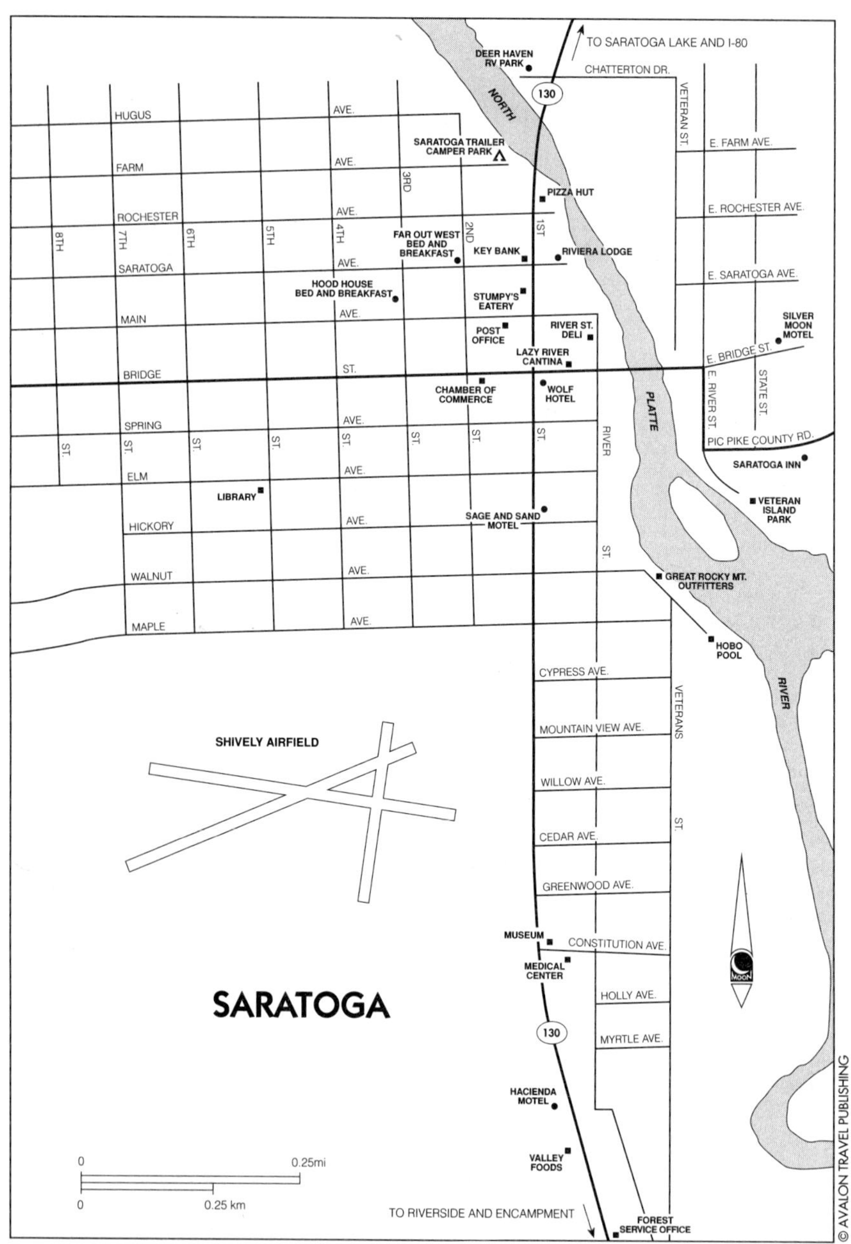
TO SARATOGA LAKE AND I-80
DEER HAVEN RV PARK
CHATTERTON DR.
130
NORTH
HUGUS AVE.
FARM AVE.
ROCHESTER AVE.
SARATOGA AVE.
MAIN AVE.
BRIDGE ST.
SPRING AVE.
ELM AVE.
HICKORY AVE.
WALNUT AVE.
MAPLE AVE.
8TH ST.
7TH ST.
6TH ST.
5TH ST.
4TH ST.
3RD ST.
2ND ST.
1ST ST.
SARATOGA TRAILER CAMPER PARK
PIZZA HUT
FAR OUT WEST BED AND BREAKFAST
KEY BANK
RIVIERA LODGE
HOOD HOUSE BED AND BREAKFAST
STUMPY'S EATERY
POST OFFICE
RIVER ST. DELI
LAZY RIVER CANTINA
CHAMBER OF COMMERCE
WOLF HOTEL
LIBRARY
SAGE AND SAND MOTEL
RIVER ST.
PLATTE
RIVER
VETERAN ST.
E. FARM AVE.
E. ROCHESTER AVE.
E. SARATOGA AVE.
SILVER MOON MOTEL
E. BRIDGE ST.
E. RIVER ST.
STATE ST.
PIC PIKE COUNTY RD.
SARATOGA INN
VETERAN ISLAND PARK
GREAT ROCKY MT. OUTFITTERS
HOBO POOL
CYPRESS AVE.
MOUNTAIN VIEW AVE.
WILLOW AVE.
CEDAR AVE.
GREENWOOD AVE.
CONSTITUTION AVE.
HOLLY AVE.
MYRTLE AVE.
VETERANS ST.
SHIVELY AIRFIELD
MUSEUM
MEDICAL CENTER
SARATOGA
130
HACIENDA MOTEL
VALLEY FOODS
FOREST SERVICE OFFICE
TO RIVERSIDE AND ENCAMPMENT
0
0.25mi
0
0.25 km
MOON
© AVALON TRAVEL PUBLISHING

in the beautiful river bottom country along the North Platte. Saratoga is also something of a bedroom community for coal miners who work in Hanna but prefer the country around here. Others commute as far as Rawlins to work.

Like many places in Wyoming, Saratoga has long depended upon various extractive industries for a livelihood and is only now discovering how attractive the land itself is. With mountains on both sides, "blue ribbon" trout fishing, river float trips, a free hot springs, a rich history, and lots of wildlife, it's certain that tourism will grow increasingly important. Each year more folks arrive and new businesses sprout up, creating concerns that Saratoga could go the way of other edge-of-the-mountains towns. The town has also become something of a retreat for executives and others in the rich-and-famous crowd who find that locals allow them a measure of privacy and anonymity. Head out to homes bordering Old Baldy Club Golf Course and you just might meet a former president, supreme court justice, or Hollywood star.

History

Indians called Saratoga Hot Springs "Place of the Magic Water"; it was a site of healing where various tribes could mingle without fear of attack. When whites arrived and first bathed here, the Indians noted that the waters boiled more violently than before, indicating an evil spirit. Thereafter most shunned the hot springs, but an 1874 smallpox epidemic forced some to return. Patients were soaked in the hot water in an attempt to boil out the disease and then dipped in the cold river water. When all the patients died, the Indians decided that whites had turned the waters from good medicine to bad medicine. The area was littered with the graves of smallpox victims. Thereafter, the Indians moved even farther from the hot springs.

In 1877, William H. Cadwell homesteaded near the springs, built a wooden bathhouse on the site, and offered hot baths, meals, and a place for travelers to stretch out for a night's sleep. People flocked here from all over the region—some even came from England to soak in the waters claimed to cure "rheumatism, eczema, paralysis, stomach trouble, kidney disease, nerves, and all forms of blood and skin disease." The copper-mining boom in the Sierra Madre brought prosperity as miners came to Saratoga to relax and freighters used it as a way station and supply center. A spur route from the Union Pacific line was built south to Saratoga in 1907 to haul ore from the mines, but when they closed shortly thereafter the town was forced to turn to other pursuits—becoming a ranching and logging center.

Sights

The main attraction in Saratoga is **Hobo Pool,** on the east end of Walnut Ave., where a sandy-bottomed outdoor pool is fed by the odorless 117-128° F water of Saratoga Hot Springs. It's open 24 hours a day and is fully accessible. No charge, no alcohol, and no naked bodies allowed. Heated changing rooms have showers. A larger swimming pool—not mineral water—is open daily in the summer. The mineral baths attract both old and young, with more adventurous types sprinting down to the adjacent North Platte River to cool off or to soak in smaller hot springs that feed directly into the river. All this hot water keeps stretches of the river open year-round, and **Odd Fellows Park** at River St. and Main Ave. is a good place to find ducks and geese at all times of the year. You can also use the luxurious spring-fed pool and hot tubs at **Saratoga Inn Resort,** 601 E. Pic Pike Rd., tel. (307) 326-5261. The cost is $8.

Saratoga's wonderful **Wolf Hotel,** tel. (307) 326-5525, 101 E. Bridge St., was built in 1893 by a German emigrant named Frederick Wolf. Today it's a National Historic Landmark. The old brick building with steeply gabled windows served for many years as a stage stop along the road to the mines of the Sierra Madre. Now restored with antique furnishings, the Wolf offers an enjoyable taste of the past.

Saratoga Museum, tel. (307) 326-5511, is housed in the old railroad depot on the south end of town. Inside are items from the region's ranching, logging, and sheepherding past, along with a hands-on archaeology exhibit. The museum is open daily 1-5 p.m. Memorial Day through Labor Day, and by appointment the rest of the year. Outside you'll find an old Union Pacific boxcar and caboose, along with a gazebo.

The **North Platte River** is one of the only rivers in the U.S. that flows predominantly north. From the Wyoming-Colorado border to the mouth of Sage Creek, 65 miles north, it is also the only "blue ribbon" trout fishery in southern Wyoming, with outstanding fishing for rainbow and brown trout. Studies have found over 4,200 catchable wild trout averaging 13-17 inches per mile in the river. See River Recreation above for details on floating and fishing the river. You can find Indian petroglyphs along the bluff above the river just north of Saratoga. Fish are raised at the **Saratoga National Fish Hatchery,** five miles north of town, tel. (307) 326-5662; open Mon.-Sat. 8 a.m.-4 p.m. Constructed in 1915, the hatchery produces fingerling cutthroat, rainbow, and brook trout for Wyoming rivers and lakes.

Accommodations

Built in 1893, the historic **Wolf Hotel,** 101 E. Bridge St., tel. (307) 326-5525, is described in Sights above. Lodging options here include a range of upstairs rooms. Basic rooms with baths down the hall are $30 s or $34 d; these are over the bar and can get noisy when it is hopping. Deluxe rooms with private baths cost $37 s or $43 d, while two-room suites are $74 for four people. Two luxury suites (including a wet bar) are also available on the third floor for $85 d. Any of these choices offer a wonderful change from standard motel rooms. Budget-Moderate.

Hacienda Motel, a half mile south of town, tel. (307) 326-5751, has rooms for $49 s or $59 d, some containing fridges and microwaves. Inexpensive.

Riviera Lodge, 303 N. 1st St., tel. (307) 326-5651, offers a riverside location with a variety of recently remodeled rooms. The smallest are $33 s or $38 d. Larger rooms cost $48 s or $56 d, and suites with two beds and a deck over the river are $90. Inexpensive-Expensive.

Sage and Sand Motel, 311 S. 1st St., tel. (307) 326-8339, charges $35 s or $39-48 d. Some rooms contain kitchenettes. Inexpensive.

Saratoga Inn Resort, 601 E. Pic Pike Rd., tel. (307) 326-5261, underwent a multimillion-dollar remodeling in the late 1990s and is easily the most luxurious lodging in town. All rooms follow a Western theme, with rustic lodgepole furniture; some rooms are quite small. The trophy room has a big central fireplace and overstuffed chairs, and the central courtyard contains a large hot-spring-fed pool and five soaking tubs, four of which are covered by tepees. The resort also features a golf course, horseback rides, massage, river trips, and other activities. Guest rooms or suites go for $69-109 s or $138-218 d. No kids under 16. Premium-Luxury.

The rooms are a bit old fashioned, but you'll find clean and cozy accommodations at **Silver Moon Motel,** 412 E. Bridge St., tel. (307) 326-5974, where rates are $37-40 s or $43-45 d. Full-kitchen units are $40 s or $45 d. The adjacent Louisiana Pacific lumber mill can get noisy at night. Inexpensive.

Great Rocky Mountain Outfitters, tel. (307) 326-8750, rents out three places in Saratoga: two houses with full kitchens for $125 d ($25 per person for additional guests); and a suite for $85 d. Expensive-Premium.

Built in 1893, the Wolf Hotel remains a focal point for the town of Saratoga.

Bed and Breakfasts

Two Saratoga B&Bs offer comfortable in-town accommodations in historic homes. Built in 1920, **Far Out West B&B,** 304 N. 2nd St., tel. (307) 326-5869, www.cruising-america.com/farout.html, contains five guest rooms, all with private baths and TVs. Some of these also feature private entries and king-size beds. Families will appreciate the spacious one-bedroom cottage with a full kitchen. There's also a children's playroom. Deer wander through the yard most summer evenings. Rates are $80 s or $95 d, including a creative home-cooked breakfast. Expensive.

A few blocks away is **Hood House B&B,** 214 N. 3rd, tel. (307) 326-8901, a simple historic home with an enclosed porch and antique furnishings. The four guest rooms contain shared baths, and a full breakfast is served. The owner does not live on the premises. Rates are $70 s, $75 d. Kids are accepted. Moderate.

Guest Ranches

Brush Creek Guest Ranch, 15 miles southeast of Saratoga, tel. (307) 327-5241 or (800) 726-2499, www.duderanch.org/brush-creek, is a wonderful 6,000-acre cattle ranch that dates back almost a century. Guests can choose to stay in the grand 6,500-square-foot main lodge or in comfortable modern cabins. The emphasis is on horseback riding, guided fly-fishing—it's an Orvis-endorsed lodge—hayrides, creekside barbecues, hiking, mountain-biking, and wintertime cross-country skiing. Guests can help move cattle between pastures or simply relax on the big front porch overlooking the flower-filled yard. Weekly rates are $2,100 for two people, all-inclusive; open year-round. Saddle tramps should ask about the annual roundup in late summer. Luxury.

Ten miles northeast of Saratoga along scenic Deer Creek, **Flying S Ranch,** tel. (307) 326-8600, is a blend of comfort and Old West charm. From mid-May through mid-September, this 1,300-acre ranch operates as a bed and breakfast, offering two spacious private cabins, each with king-size beds, private baths, and a private jacuzzi. The ranch is a great place to explore on foot, and trout fishing is not far away. Rates are $125-150 d, including a full breakfast served each morning in the main lodge. A three-night minimum stay is required. It's an adult-oriented place, so no kids under 14. Get more info by visiting the website: www.flyings.com. Premium.

A-Bar-A Ranch, tel. (307) 327-5454, also has guest ranch facilities in the Saratoga area, but it's typically full all summer with a select clientele; call for details.

Campgrounds

Saratoga Lake Campground, 1.5 miles north of town, tel. (307) 326-5629, has campsites ($7.50, or $10 with RV hookups) next to the lake. No trees or showers. It's open May-October. The closest Forest Service campground is 25 miles east, with many more campgrounds ($10) as you continue on State Hwy. 130 over Snowy Range Pass.

Saratoga Camper & RV Park, 116 W. Farm Ave., tel. (307) 326-8870, has tent spaces for $10, RV sites for $16. Showers cost $3 for non-campers. Although right in town, the riverside location has lots of shade.

Food

Get savory breakfasts (including eggs Benedict or Belgian waffles) along with espresso and homemade ice cream at **Lollypops,** on E. Bridge St., tel. (307) 326-5020. **River St. Deli,** 106 N. River St., tel. (307) 326-8683, creates memorable lunches, including everything from grilled meat loaf sandwiches to a "dude vegie" complete with grilled zucchini, green pepper, and onion. Open Tues.-Sat. for lunch, and Sun.-Mon. only for breakfast burritos.

Historic **Wolf Hotel** is especially known for its Sunday-night prime rib dinners but also makes very good burgers and other fare. The Wolf is open Mon.-Sat. for lunch and dinner (no breakfast). The bar is the local hangout and offers live country-and-western music periodically.

For gourmet meals, head to **The Baron's Restaurant,** inside Saratoga Inn at 601 E. Pic Pike Rd., tel. (307) 326-5261. The menu includes seafood, prime rib, pasta, and grilled steaks. Breakfast is especially good. A bright and open interior and substantial wine list add to the charm, but locals complain of a snooty staff and stiff prices (dinner entrées $16-22). **Silver Saddle Brewery,** also on the premises, cranks out Winkin' Willy's Wild Wheat, Cheatin' Heart Red Ale, and other homemade brews.

The **Rustic Bar,** 124 E. Bridge St., tel. (307) 326-5965, is known for its "fighting" mountain lion mounts and has live music some weekends.

For pizzas, burgers, salads, and sandwiches, you won't go wrong at **Stumpy's Eatery,** 218 N. 1st, tel. (307) 326-8132. **Lazy River Cantina,** 110 E. Bridge Ave., tel. (307) 326-8472, has inexpensive Mexican food and a bar with darts and TV sports. Service is notoriously slow.

Get groceries at **Valley Foods** on the south end of town; the deli has baked goods. Or you can hang out with the locals over at **Donut Ranch Bakery** on W. Bridge Street. The best place to find locals is the Kum & Go Market, where Saturday mornings find the high school's entire junior and senior classes parked out front. It's obviously the place to be seen.

Events

Start the year dressed in winter clothes for the **Saratoga Lake Ice Fishing Derby** each January. It's considered one of the top fishing derbies in the Lower 48. The following month brings **cutter races** and **mule races**—which offer lots of excitement as two-horse teams race down the straightaway. The three-day **Platte Valley Festival of the Arts** is held around the Fourth of July each year and features a juried art show, plus a parade, barbecue, live music, cowboy poetry, melodrama, a high-noon shoot-out, and the obligatory fireworks show. In early August the **Wyoming Microbrewery Competition** attracts brewers from around the state. At the **River Festival & Rodeo**—held the same weekend—you can join a rubber-duck race down the North Platte River, watch the amateur rodeo, or two-step to live bands playing for the street dance.

Shopping

Blackhawk Gallery, 100 N. 1st St., tel. (307) 326-5063, sells Western artwork, jewelry, and crafts. Bill Naylor of **Peg Leg Mountain Furniture,** 413 E. Bridge St., tel. (307) 326-5022, makes unique lodgepole items, from walking sticks to bunk beds. **Whitney's Saddle Shop,** inside the Saratoga Inn on E. Pic Pike Rd., tel. (307) 326-5935, has quality Western gifts and clothing. Also check out **Cedar Chest Galleries,** 106 W. Bridge St., tel. (307) 326-5815.

Information and Services

The **Saratoga Chamber of Commerce,** 115 W. Bridge St., tel. (307) 326-8855, www.trib.com/spvcc, is open Mon.-Fri. 9 a.m.-5 p.m.

The Forest Service's **Saratoga Ranger Station** faces the mountains on the south edge of town, tel. (307) 326-5258, and is open weekdays. Find the town **library** at 503 W. Elm St., tel. (307) 326-8209, and the **post office** at 105 Main Ave., tel. (307) 326-5611. Get cash from **ATMs** at Community First Bank, 302 N. 1st St., or the pretentious Rawlins National Bank at 217 N. 1st Street.

A real surprise in Saratoga is the airport, with an 8,400-foot runway. No scheduled service, but **Saratoga Aviation,** tel. (307) 326-8344, has charter flights. In the summer and fall (especially on the weekend after Labor Day), aircraft executives and other wealthy enthusiasts—alias "the conquistadors"—flock here for a rendezvous at the A-Bar-A Ranch. The tarmac is jammed with corporate jets, turning Shively Field into the third-busiest jetport in Wyoming. There's no bus service to Saratoga.

ENCAMPMENT AND RIVERSIDE

The quaint ranching and tourism town of Encampment (pop. 500) lies in the gorgeous foothills of the Sierra Madre, country once home to thousands of copper miners. Today the area abounds with ghost towns from that era. Encampment's twin settlement of Riverside (pop. 80) lies just a mile to the east. This is a very popular area with hunters, who come for deer, antelope, and elk, and with photographers, who enjoy the colorful autumn leaves, and anglers, who cast about for trout. The community is decidedly conservative: bumper stickers proclaim, "If you're out of work and hungry eat an environmentalist" and each fall finds the back roads crowded with gun-racked pickup trucks and silent, orange-capped hunters scanning the horizon for bucks. Back in town, the smoky bars fill each night with tales of the chase and chubby old men winking at the waitresses over their Budweisers.

History

Encampment takes its name from the Grand Encampment of French-Canadian trappers who rendezvoused along the Encampment River in 1838. Miners had long suspected that the Sierra Madre contained a wealth of minerals, but it was not until 1896 that the first significant gold strike was made. It was another mineral, however, that transformed the region. Encampment itself began in 1897, when British sheepherder Ed Haggerty discovered a rich vein of copper in the Sierra Madre to the west. The mine he developed was named Rudefeha, a word concocted from the letters of the various partners' names—J.M. *Ru*msey, Robert *De*al, George *Fe*rris, and Ed *Ha*ggerty. In the first three months of digging miners recovered $300,000 worth of copper ore. Haggerty took his 10% share and returned to England.

As the wealth of the discovery became known, Chicago promoter and newspaperman Willis George Emerson purchased the mine and built a 16-mile-long aerial tram to haul the ore up over the 10,600-foot Continental Divide and then down to the Boston-Wyoming Smelter at Encampment (elevation 7,200 feet). The tram consisted of 304 wooden towers with buckets supported on thick steel cables. Each bucket held 700 pounds of ore and moved at four miles an hour. The tram could carry almost 1,000 tons of ore a day and was powered by water flowing through a four-foot wooden pipeline. Thousands of men flocked to the mines, creating almost overnight the settlements of Elwood, Battle, Copperton, Dillon, Halfway House, and Rambler. A railroad was completed from the smelter to the main Union Pacific line at Walcott in 1905, and by 1908 more than 23 million pounds of copper had been produced.

The main regional settlement was Encampment, located at the foot of the mountains and numbering 1,500 rough and hardened souls at its peak. By 1900, the town featured three general stores, two lodging houses, two hotels, two restaurants, and three lumber yards, along with nine saloons and two houses of prostitution. Nearby Riverside served as a shipping center for the mines. (Originally known as Dogget, the name was changed to Riverside after folks began calling it "Dog Town.") Another 1,500 people lived in the other mining towns. The mining boom came to an abrupt halt after two disastrous fires destroyed the concentrating mill, the smelter, the boiler room, and the powerhouse. Combined with falling copper prices, it forced the company into bankruptcy. Soon, all sorts of illegal actions surfaced, including overcapitalization and fraudulent stock sales.

All but a few diehards left the area, and what had once been the town of Grand Encampment was eventually reduced to simply Encampment. Logging, first for ties and mine supports and later for lumber, became an important part of the economy, but the last mill closed in the 1990s, and many locals now commute to work in the Sinclair refinery or Hanna coal mines. Tourism is becoming increasingly important in the area, and retirees are attracted to the slow pace, moderate prices, and beautiful setting.

Sights

On the south side of Encampment at 6th and Barnett Sts., the excellent **Grand Encampment Museum** includes items from the turn-of-the-20th-century mining camps that filled the Sierra Madre. Displayed here are historic photographs, 19th-century clothing, Indian artifacts, Forest Service memorabilia, and even a folding bathtub from the 1890s. Teddy the (stuffed) dog greets visitors. Most interesting of all are the 14 historic buildings set up as a frontier town with wooden boardwalks. These include a tie-hack cabin, a bakery, a lookout tower, and a stage station. The transportation barn even houses Noah's Ark—though, alas, it's probably not the original one. Oddest of all is a two-story outhouse modeled after one used in the mining ghost town of Dillon. The lower level was used in summer, with the upper floor reserved for wintertime when the snows drifted many feet deep. The Australian term for privies—"long drop"—is especially fitting here! Also at the museum are parts of the 16-mile-long aerial tramway that brought ore from the Rudefeha mine.

This free museum is open Mon.-Sat. 10 a.m.-5 p.m. and Sunday 1-5 p.m. Memorial Day to Labor Day; and Sat.-Sun. 1-5 p.m. the rest of September. After that, you can see the museum by special appointment only; tel. (307) 327-5308. Retired locals provide informative tours in July and August, and you can even buy bars of homemade soap inside the main building. On Memorial Day weekend the museum has turn-of-the-20th-century living history demonstrations.

At the museum, pick up a copy of the local **walking tour** brochure, which ws some of the most interesting buildings in town. Be sure to also see the pretty white **Presbyterian Church** at 9th and Rankin.

A three-quarter-mile trail leads to the **Indian Bathtubs,** natural geologic formations that collect rainwater. Indian hunters used them for bathing. Get there by heading one mile west of Riverside on State Hwy. 230. Turn right onto Blackhall Rd. and follow it a mile to the trailhead.

Lodging

Although popular with visitors all year, this area is doubly so during the fall hunting season; book ahead if you're coming through at that time, and bring your bright orange clothes to keep from getting shot. In Encampment, stay at **Vacher's Bighorn Lodge,** 508 McCaffrey, tel. (307) 327-5110, where basic rooms go for $32 s or $40-45 d; kitchenettes available. Open all year. Inexpensive. The other four lodging options are all in nearby Riverside.

Lazy Acres Campground & Motel, tel. (307) 327-5968, has motel units for $25 s or $29-32 d and a basic cabin (shared bath) for $20 s or d. Open May-October. Budget.

Bear Trap Cafe & Cabins, tel. (307) 327-5277, charges $28 s or $33 d for rustic cabins or modular motel rooms; open May-November. Budget.

More Riverside rusticity can be found at **Riverside Cabins,** tel. (307) 327-5361, where most cabins include kitchenettes and private baths, but no phones or TVs. Rates start at $32 d for a two-person cabin, up to $76 for a two-bedroom unit that sleeps six and has a full kitchen. Open mid-May to October. Budget-Moderate.

Cottonwood Cabins, tel. (307) 327-5151, offers two modern cabins with full kitchens, TVs, and picnic tables. Rates are $50 d with a two-night minimum stay. Open June-October. Inexpensive.

Bed and Breakfasts

Twelve miles south of Encampment is **Platt's Rustic Mountain Lodge B&B,** tel. (307) 327-5539, www.plattoutfitting.com, an 8,000-acre ranch where a spacious log lodge offers dramatic vistas of the Sierra Madre Range. The lodge also offers horseback trail rides, fishing, pack trips, photo safaris, cross-country skiing, snowmobiling, and surprisingly, both "varmint" hunting and women's retreats! Lodging rates are $45 s or $65 d, including a full breakfast. Also here is a cozy cabin with kitchen and two bedrooms for more seclusion. It sleeps four, and costs $1,075 for five days, including fishing access to private ponds and creeks. Kids are welcome both in the main lodge and in the cabin. Moderate-Expensive.

In Encampment, **Grand & Sierra B&B,** 1016 Lomax, tel. (307) 327-5200, has its own distinctive features, including animal mounts lining the walls, a pool table, and shag carpet on the floor. This is a hunter's paradise; when I last dropped by, someone was skinning beavers in the garage. The five guest rooms have shared or private baths. Also here is a hot tub. Rates are $55-65 s or d. Kids accepted, and a full breakfast is served. Inexpensive-Moderate.

Riverside's **Old Depot B&B,** tel. (307) 327-5277, was built in 1906 and served as a train depot until 1954. Now completely remodeled, it provides three guest rooms for $80 s or d. Each has its own bath, and one features a jacuzzi tub. Guests are given a full breakfast at Beartrap Restaurant (same owners). Kids are welcome. Moderate.

Camping

The BLM's **Encampment River Campground** ($7) is three miles from town. Head west from Encampment and turn south on Rd. 353 (Hog Park Rd.). Ask locally for directions to two free BLM campgrounds: Bennett Peak and Corral Creek.

The nearest Forest Service campsite ($10; open June-Oct.) is **Bottle Creek Campground,** seven miles southwest of town on State Hwy. 70. Five more campgrounds (free to $10) lie west of here in the Sierra Madre.

Lazy Acres Campground & Motel in Riverside, tel. (307) 327-5968, has shady tent sites for $13 and RV spaces for $18. Open May-October.

Food

Eat in Encampment at **Pine Lodge Saloon,** 518 McCaffrey, tel. (307) 327-5203. Open for breakfast Fri.-Sun.; lunch and dinner Wed.-Sunday. An interesting old two-story brick building at 706 Freeman houses both **Kuntzman's Cash Store** and the **Sugar Bowl,** tel. (307) 327-5271, which has an old-fashioned soda fountain with malts, subs, soups, and banana splits. **Bear Trap Cafe** in Riverside, tel. (307) 327-5277, serves standard American food. Riverside's **town park** is a great place for picnic lunches amid tall cottonwoods, but there's no camping.

Events

On the first full week of February, the **Sierra Madre Winter Carnival** includes dogsled and snowmobile races, snow sculptures, broom ball, a casino night, a melodrama, dances, and other activities. One of the most popular events in Wyoming is the **Woodchoppers Jamboree and Rodeo** at Encampment the third full weekend of June. Begun in 1961, this is the state's largest loggers' show, with all sorts of events, including tree-felling, chainsaw log-bucking, handsawing, pole-throwing, and axe-throwing contests. Other activities include a fun amateur rodeo, a parade, a barbecue, and a melodrama featuring "dance hall girls." The town erupts with lots of drunken and rowdy behavior at night, befitting such a festival. Call (307) 326-8855 for details. In July, the **Sierra Madre Mountain Man Rendezvous** brings mountain men and women to Encampment.

Both **Pine Lodge Saloon,** 518 McCaffrey, tel. (307) 327-5203, and the **Mangy Moose** in Riverside, tel. (307) 327-5117, have live music during the jamboree.

Information and Services

Get local details at a small **information cabin** next to the rodeo grounds in Encampment; open Mon.-Fri. 9 a.m.-4:30 p.m. in the summer months. Otherwise, stop by the Grand Encampment Museum for local info. Encampment's **city hall** is in the historic Opera House, a wooden building with a bell tower that looks like a lighthouse. The **Encampment Library** is on the east end of town at 202 Rankin Ave., tel. (307) 327-5775. The Encampment **post office,** tel. (307) 327-5747, sits on the corner of 6th and McCaffrey Streets.

SIERRA MADRE

The historic Sierra Madre—a finger from the Medicine Bow Range that stretches south into Colorado—cover a small section of Wyoming. This is one of the lesser-known parts of the state. Worth a visit are the many mining ghost towns and historic mine sites, and hikers will find quite a few miles of wilderness trails. The highest mountain in the range is 11,004-foot Bridger Peak, named for mountain man Jim Bridger. Before heading out, get maps ($4) and camping and hiking information from the Forest Service's **Hayden Ranger Station,** 204 W. 9th in Encampment, tel. (307) 327-5481. Open Mon.-Fri. 7:30 a.m.-4:30 p.m. all year. Ask for the self-guided auto-tour brochure available here.

Sights

Now entirely paved, Battle Highway (State Hwy. 70) crosses the Sierra Madre from Encampment on the east to Baggs on the west, a distance of 57 miles. The smooth, wide-shouldered road (perfect for bikes) is extraordinarily scenic, especially in the fall when the aspens turn golden. Lodgepole pines are the dominant trees at higher elevations. During the winter—generally November to mid-June—State Hwy. 70 is closed at the forest boundary, though snowmobilers and skiers may continue up the road. Approximately 10 miles west of Encampment the road reaches the Continental Divide at 9,916-foot Battle Pass. This is the location of **Battle,** one of many ghost towns capping the Sierra Madre. Battle is named for an 1841 fight between Indians and whites that took place near here.

A 4WD road good for mountain bikes heads north from the east side of the pass to the Bridger Peak summit and then down the western side to the Ferris-Haggerty mine site at the ghost town of **Rudefeha,** where remains of the tramway towers are still visible. A mile to the west you'll find the remains of **Dillon,** established after the company town of Rudefeha banned saloons; the saloon owners simply moved a short distance away and started anew, and in no time at all Dillon was the largest town in the Sierra Madre. Many buildings remain here, hidden in the trees.

Two miles west of the Continental Divide on State Hwy. 70 is a turnout overlooking pretty Battle Lake and a monument to **Thomas A. Edison.** While vacationing here in 1878, Edison was pondering over what substance to use as a filament for incandescent lights. One night he threw a broken bamboo fishing pole in the fire and was intrigued by the way the frayed pieces glowed. Carbonized bamboo would make a fine nonconducting filament for his bulbs. This tale has been passed down as fact through the years, but in reality Edison didn't come up with the idea until a year later. Maybe he remembered the old fly rod at that time.

The town of **Rambler** once stood along the lake shore, with the Doane-Rambler copper mine nearby. The mine operated from 1879 to 1902, producing a half million tons of copper. Another six miles west are a few remains from the settlement of **Copperton.**

Aspen Alley

The western slopes of the Sierra Madre are carpeted with extensive stands of quaking aspen trees that came up after fires swept this region during the mining era. These reach for many miles along State Hwy. 70. A favorite of photographers is Aspen Alley, a half-mile stretch of fabulously flamboyant fall foliage. Get here by turning north onto Deep Creek Rd. (Forest Rd. 801). The colors generally peak in late September, but call the Encampment Forest Service office, tel. (307) 327-5481, for current conditions. Adventurous souls will enjoy the 50-mile drive north from Aspen Alley to Rawlins. Camping is available at the no-longer-maintained Sandstone camping area, approximately four miles up the road.

Once the gravel road emerges from the national forest, the land broadens into sage and grass before once again climbing over the Continental Divide. Stop here on a fall night and listen to the quiet. A few clouds hang on the western horizon. A few pickups churn clouds of dust up the road—en route to either hunting grounds or a bar. The night lies over the land like a blackened canvas splattered with stars. There aren't many places like this anymore.

Campgrounds

The Forest Service has six campgrounds (free to $10; open June-Oct.) in the Sierra Madre, all of which are along State Hwy. 70, the main road across the mountains. These campgrounds are not nearly as crowded as those in the Snowy Range to the east.

Built in 1934, the Forest Service's **Jack Creek Guard Station** is a one-room log cabin in the mountains northwest of Encampment. Facilities are rustic—two sets of bunk beds (bring sleeping bags), wood or propane heat, and propane lights. The cabin costs $40 per night, and sleeps four. Call (307) 326-5258 for reservations.

Huston Park Wilderness

The 30,726-acre Huston Park Wilderness straddles the Continental Divide just south of Battle Pass. It contains spruce, fir, aspen, and lodgepole forests, as well as open alpine country reaching to 10,500 feet. **Continental Divide National Scenic Trail** provides an enjoyable high-elevation trek along the crest of the mountains. The trail stretches 3,100 miles from Canada to Mexico, and 16 miles of it pass through this wilderness area. The route is marked with rock cairns and blazed trees. Trailheads are located one mile south of the Battle townsite and 2.5 miles west of Hog Park Reservoir.

The nine-mile-long **Baby Lake Trail** is an enjoyable overnight trip through high meadows and along a mountain creek. Take in excellent vistas of the Snake River Valley from the Continental Divide. The trail is accessible from State Hwy. 70 on both ends, but for the easiest hiking start from a trailhead at the end of a two-mile gravel road just south of Battle Pass. From here, the trail drops 2,600 feet in elevation to a second trailhead off Forest Rd. 811 (near Lost Creek Campground).

North Fork Encampment Trail takes you two miles up North Fork Creek to Green Mountain Falls. Get to the trailhead by driving west from Encampment to Bottle Creek Campground and then south on Forest Rd. 550 for 1.5 miles. This is one of the few waterfalls in the area (but it typically dries up after mid-June).

Encampment River Wilderness

At just 10,400 acres, Encampment River Wilderness is one of the smallest and least-visited wilderness areas in Wyoming. The centerpiece is the Encampment River, with its narrow canyon, rushing rapids, quiet pools, and fine fishing. Despite the Encampment's current wilderness status, much of this land was logged over at the turn of the 20th century to supply railroad ties and mine timbers for the Union Pacific Railroad. Old cabins and mines offer endless opportunities to explore. The well-maintained **Encampment River Trail** is a 15-mile-long path that follows this scenic river through the heart of the wilderness. Roads provide access from either end, so the trail is easier to hike if you can shuttle a second vehicle to the other end. Start from a trailhead near the BLM's Encampment River Campground, three miles south of Encampment. The trail follows the river upstream, beginning in low-elevation sage-and-grass country and gradually climbing into dense lodgepole and spruce forests. The first five miles are considerably easier hiking than higher up, where the canyon narrows and becomes more rugged. The trail ends at Hog Park, near the Colorado state line.

Another off-the-beaten-path sight near the Encampment River Wilderness is an old abandoned fire tower at **Blackhall Mountain,** approximately 15 miles south of Riverside on Forest Rd. 409. The last several miles are narrow but passable. From the top are long vistas into the mountains of Wyoming and Colorado.

Winter Recreation

During the winter months the Forest Service maintains many groomed miles of **cross-country ski trails** around the Bottle Creek Campground 5.5 miles west of Encampment and along the South Brush Creek 20 miles east of Saratoga. Call (307) 326-5258 for access details. The rustic **Green Mountain Cabin,** a popular spot for cross-country skiers, stands near the South Brush Creek and Bottle Creek Trails. Rates are $25 for up to four people. The cabin has a woodstove, firewood, and basic supplies. Call the Trading Post in Riverside at (307) 327-5720 for details. Many forest roads in the Sierra Madre are used extensively by snowmobilers, with 26 miles of groomed trails and an equal amount of ungroomed trails. Contact Forest Service offices in Encampment and Saratoga for details.

LITTLE SNAKE RIVER VALLEY

The Little Snake River Valley is one of the most isolated parts of Wyoming; it lies right along the Colorado border, with the desolate Red Desert to the west and the Sierra Madre to the east. Three little towns—Savery, Dixon (pop. 60), and Baggs (pop. 260)—spread out along the irrigated farmland that follows Savery Creek. Visitors will find a slow pace to life in the valley and a sense of history exemplified by the solid old log cabins that dot the landscape. See Stephen Metzger's *Colorado Handbook* (Moon Travel Handbooks, www.moon.com) for details on sights south of the Wyoming line.

Savery

Housed in an old grade school, Savery's **Little Snake River Museum,** tel. (307) 383-7262 or (307) 383-6388, provides a sampling of the area's rich history. The museum, open Wed.-Sun. 2-5 p.m. Memorial Day to Labor Day, contains the dugout canoe of mountain man Jim Baker, along with many other historical items. Out front is a distinctive two-story log blockhouse built by Baker; he and his wife are buried a mile west of town. Also on the museum grounds are a one-room schoolhouse from the Brown's Hill area and a grand two-story log home that is more than a century old.

The **Savery Store,** tel. (307) 383-2711, has groceries, supplies, and a campground. **Stage Stop General Store** also sells supplies. The town's **Russell Community Park** has tent and RV camping (with hookups) and a rodeo grounds where you'll see weekly roping events in the summer.

Not far from town is **Savery Creek Thoroughbred Ranch,** tel. (307) 383-7840, a riding ranch for those serious about horses. The owner spent extensive time in Europe, so the emphasis is English riding (although she will also train in Western riding). Beautiful country surrounds the ranch, which offers gracious lodging in an antique-furnished home. The three guest rooms have shared or private baths; also available for lodging are two covered wagons. The ranch only hosts six people at a time, allowing for personalized attention. Open May-September.

Dixon

Four miles west of Savery and seven miles east of Baggs, the small agricultural settlement of Dixon holds the **Little Snake River Valley Rodeo** each July. It also hosts a **Cutting Horse Contest,** where cowboys work specially trained horses to move cattle. Built in 1911, the classic **Dixon Club Bar,** tel. (307) 383-7722, is a fun place to explore; its walls are lined with old junk and antiques. Free camping is available at **Dixon Town Park** along Main St.; no hookups or showers.

Baggs

Named for rancher George Baggs and his wife Maggie, Baggs's isolated location and proximity to the state line made it a gathering place for outlaws. In 1900, following a $32,000 bank robbery in Winnemucca, Nevada, Butch Cassidy helped build a cabin here to serve as a refuge for his gang. The cabin, now called the **Gaddis-Matthews House,** still stands in the center of town. Another noteworthy building is the **Bank Bar Club,** listed on the National Historic Register. Built as a bank, it later became a bar. Find it off the main drag on North and Miles.

Stay at Drifters Inn, tel. (307) 383-2015, for $35 s or $40 d; rooms have microwaves and fridges. Inexpensive. Pitch tents or park RVs (no hookups or showers) for free at Baggs Park on Hunt Street.

FORT FRED STEELE

Fort Fred Steele—named for Civil War hero Maj. Gen. Frederick Steele—was built in 1868 as one of three Wyoming posts established to protect the transcontinental railroad from Indian attacks. Soldiers from the fort fought against the Utes in northern Colorado during their 1879 uprising against tyrannical Indian agent Nathan C. Meeker. The troops also helped reestablish peace after the 1885 anti-Chinese riots in Rock Springs.

After the fort was abandoned by the army in 1886, civilians took over the buildings and turned this into a supply base for ranchers and sheepherders. It was headquarters for the Carbon Timber Company, which controlled the enormous tie market for the Union Pacific Railroad in the Rockies and owned nearly 25,000 acres of timberland. Lodgepole pine were felled in the Medicine Bow Mountains and floated down the North Platte River during high flows each spring. At Fort Steele, they were caught by a log boom and loaded onto railway cars or used in the sawmill or box factory. The tie industry remained important well into this century—

WHY DO THE TREES ALL LEAN IN WYOMING?

He said, "The wind never blows in Wyoming."
I said, "Mister, where you from?"
It'll take the top off a big R.C.
Or peel an unripened plum!

Wherever you been, you been lied to!
I lived in Wyoming and I know.
I once seen a horse turned clean inside out
From standin' outside in a blow!

You don't have to shave in the winter
Just pick a cool, windy place
Stand there a minute, yer whiskers'll freeze
And break off next to yer face!

They claim that a boxcar in Rawlins,
A Denver and Rio Grande
Was picked up off the tracks and blowed to the east
And beat the whole train to Cheyenne.

Why they tell you of a feller in Lander
Who jumped off a bale of hay
Before he hit ground the wind picked 'im up
He came down in Casper next day!

They have to shear sheep in Worland
When they're ready, they wait for a breeze
And bunch 'em in draws where the willers are thick
Then pick the wool offa the trees!

But the windiest tale that I heard
Was about the small town of Sinclair.
It used to set on the Idaho line
Than one spring it just blew over there!

I carry this rock in my pocket
For good luck and here's one for you.
Every little bit helps in Wyoming
If you're skinny you better take two!

—Baxter Black
From *Coyote Cowboy Poetry*

300,000 ties were sent down the North Platte River in 1938 alone—but when the Union Pacific stopped using hand-hewn ties in 1940 the town of Fort Steele suffered. With the loss of its main industry and the 1939 rerouting of the Lincoln Highway, all but a few people moved away.

Fort Steele Today

Fort Steele, nine miles east of Sinclair on I-80, is now a 137-acre state park. A small visitor center in the old bridge tender's house contains many historical photos of the fort and the Carbon Timber Company. The park is open daily 9 a.m.-7 p.m. May to mid-September, but closed to entry the rest of the year. Call (307) 320-3013 for additional information. Historical plaques are scattered over the grounds, but not much remains of what had been a substantial settlement: just a couple of clapboard buildings, some sandstone foundations and chimneys, and the walls of a house once owned by Fenimore Chatterton—Wyoming's governor from 1903 to 1905. Stone walls from the military quartermaster's corral remain just west of the parade grounds, but a disastrous arson fire on New Year's Eve 1976 destroyed two enlisted men's barracks that had stood here for more than a century. Just up the hill from the fort site is a square stone ordinance magazine (1881) with an adjacent cemetery containing the graves of civilians who died in the area. Only a few headstones remain. The slow-moving North Platte River right next to the fort is a great place for picnics—but there's no camping. Despite the paucity of historical buildings, there's something rather nice about the authenticity of the site. Stop in at dusk on a summer evening and you'll hear the distant rumble of freight trains while coyotes howl from nearby hills and the North Platte River rolls quietly away from this lonely place.

SINCLAIR

Sinclair (pop. 500) is one of the more distinctive small settlements in Wyoming. In 1923, the Producers Oil and Refining Company (Parco) established a 50,000-barrel-a-day oil refinery here, built a town to house its employees, and named the settlement Parco. When the Sinclair Oil Company bought the refinery in 1934, the name changed, but ownership of all business and homes remained in corporate hands for three decades. In 1967, Sinclair finally sold the homes to renters and gave the business buildings to the town government. Today, the refinery still lights up the night sky for miles around, and hundreds of giant oil tanks stand behind the facility. Interstate 80 passes right by Sinclair and most folks don't bother to stop except to fill up at the Burns Brothers Truckstop a mile east of town. Actually, Sinclair is a pleasant little resting place and a nice spot for a shady picnic lunch.

Parco built the company town, including the large Parco Inn at the center, in Spanish-mission style with red-tile roofs and stucco walls. You'd think you were in Southern California. An elaborate fountain and a nice small park stand across from the inn, now virtually abandoned but listed on the National Register of Historic Places. A pair of Civil War-vintage cannons guard the water fountain from attack by marauding oil executives. They were brought here originally to blow holes in burning oil tanks (if the need ever arose), allowing the oil to drain into the surrounding dikes before the tanks could explode from the heat.

The **Sinclair/Parco Museum** is in the old bank building and contains a number of local items, including clamp-on ice skates from the 1920s, old photos, and the high point, a newspaper headlined "Nixon Resigns." Open Mon.-Fri. 1-4 p.m. in the summer; if it's closed stop at the town hall next door for access. The town also has a branch library and recreation center.

Of note in Sinclair is **Su Casa Cafe,** tel. (307) 328-1745, which makes genuine Mexican food. There are no motels in town, but the road north of Sinclair leads to popular Seminoe and Pathfinder Reservoirs, where camping is available. (See the chapter on Central Wyoming for more information on these recreation areas.) Sinclair is also home to the nine-hole **Sinclair Golf Course,** tel. (307) 324-3918. The Burns Brothers Truck Stop has an **ATM** and a restaurant with trucker meals.

RAWLINS

The small city of Rawlins (pop. 9,700) sits right in the middle of southern Wyoming. To the east and south lie mountain ranges and rich grazing land; to the west is the Great Divide Basin and a vast expanse of desert country. During the late 1970s and early '80s, Rawlins was a hub of development as the "Oil Patch" blossomed and energy companies pumped petrodollars into the economy. But as in so many other Wyoming towns, the inevitable bust that followed was traumatic. Layoffs affected everyone in town in one way or another, and downtown Rawlins still has quite a few empty storefronts. Not everyone packed up and left, however. Most of the people who lived here before the oil boom stayed around when the bust hit, scraping by on business brought in by freeway travelers, local ranchers, and the energy companies. Many Rawlins workers now commute 40 miles to work in the Hanna coal mines or the Sinclair refinery, while others are employed in the state penitentiary. New businesses have started to spread over the east end of Rawlins, creating the now-standard mix of fast food, discount megamarts, gas stations, and chain motels.

HISTORY

Rawlins is named for Gen. John A. Rawlins, secretary of war under President Grant. In 1867, as the railroad route was being surveyed westward, the crew of Gen. Grenville Dodge met up with soldiers under Rawlins's command. When they discovered a clear, alkali-free spring at the base of a hill, Rawlins remarked, "If anything is

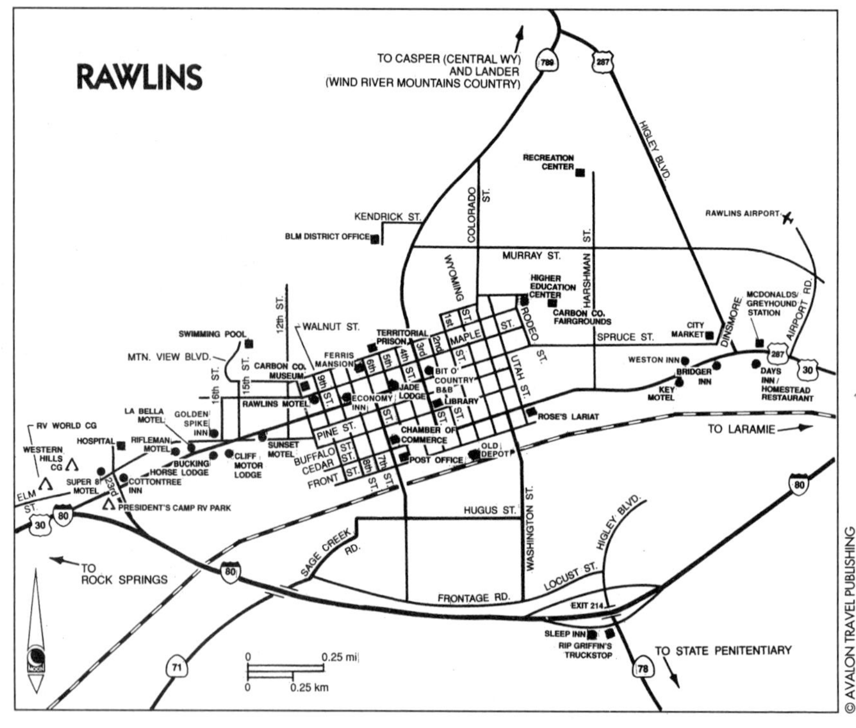

TOM HORN

The story of the murderer Tom Horn will always remain something of a mystery. Over the years, Horn worked as a stage driver, an army scout, a deputy sheriff, a Pinkerton investigator, and a detective for the Wyoming Stock Growers Association. When J.M. Carey (later Wyoming governor and senator) discovered that Tom Horn was out to murder—rather than bring in for trial—accused rustlers, he had Horn fired from the association. Other cattle barons quickly moved to hire him, however, paying $500 for each man killed. Horn is generally blamed for ambushing and assassinating two ranchers (and suspected rustlers) in the Laramie Mountains in 1895, along with two others in Brown's Park, Colorado, five years later.

BUFFALO BILL HISTORICAL SOCIETY

Wherever Horn went, a trail of dead men was left behind, but nobody was able to pin the blame on him until 1901, when a 14-year-old boy was shot in the back and killed in the Laramie Mountains. It was a case of mistaken identity, since the boy had been wearing his father's hat and clothes. The older man was later shot from ambush but survived. Horn was implicated in the boy's slaying by his trademark: a small stone placed under the victim's head.

Horn would probably have escaped even this heinous crime had he not bragged about it. (The confession would never hold up in court today; Deputy U.S. Marshal Joe LeFors had plied Horn with liquor and had a court stenographer listen through a crack in the door as he boasted of the slaying.) Horn had little money to help himself, but his well-heeled supporters spent $100,000 in his defense. They hired the finest legal counsel, John W. Lacey, who had never lost any of his 50 previous murder trials (and who, not coincidentally, also represented the Wyoming Stock Growers Association and the Union Pacific Railroad).

Despite this, Horn was adjudged guilty and sentenced to hang. Horn's supporters tried to free him with a dynamite blast, and later he did briefly escape from jail, but on Nov. 20, 1903, Horn was hanged before a large crowd at the corner of Pioneer and 19th Aves. in Cheyenne. Until the last minute, everyone expected a pardon, and many wealthy cattlemen feared what Horn might reveal about them. His last words were to his friend T. Joe Cahill: "Joe, they tell me you are married now. I hope you're doing well. Treat her right."

ever named after me, I hope it will be a spring of water." Dodge immediately decided to name this Rawlins Spring. When a division point on the Union Pacific was established here in 1868, the town was also named Rawlins Spring. Its name was later shortened to Rawlins.

In 1886, the Wyoming Legislature appropriated $100,000 for a state penitentiary in Rawlins. Two years later, construction began with enormous slabs of sandstone cut and hauled by wagon from a quarry south of town. Because of inadequate funding the new prison was not completed and occupied until December 1901, some 13 years after it was begun. By that time the town had grown, and what had been a relatively remote location was now in central Rawlins. For the next eight decades this would be Wyoming's only state prison, housing its most hardened criminals. The prison was finally abandoned in 1981, when the inmates were transferred to a new facility south of Rawlins.

FRONTIER PRISON

Rawlins's main attraction is the Frontier Prison at 5th and Walnut Sts., first opened in 1901 and in use until 1981. Actually, it was a state prison for all of its existence, but locals prefer to call it a frontier prison since construction began while Wyoming was still a territory. The imposing turret towers and stonework of the prison's exterior give it the oppressive appearance of a medieval castle. Inside, conditions for the inmates were almost as primitive—bordering on ghastly. There was no plumbing or electricity for the first 15 years, and it wasn't until 1978 that hot water was installed in one block of cells. A special dungeon house was built for uncooperative inmates, and beatings were common in the early years. Ten prisoners were hanged—one by fellow inmates—and another five were executed in the gas chamber in Rawlins, the last in 1965. The gallows were a uniquely gruesome device in which the victim actually hanged himself through an elaborate mechanism by which his weight displaced a water counterbalance, thus releasing a trapdoor and leaving him hanging by a noose. It was built to hang notorious cattle detective and murderer Tom Horn in 1903 and moved into the prison later (Horn was never in this prison). The instrument did not always work; one man had to be strangled by the "humane" guards when he didn't die fast enough. Science marches onward: Wyoming's death-row inmates now face lethal injection instead.

The old prison was the scene of several escape attempts, including one in which four death-row inmates tunneled out as far as the west wall before being caught. The dirt was secreted away in the ceiling panels where it's still visible. Two other breakouts were successful—one involved 28 men—although nearly all the escapees were caught or killed in the surrounding community. In later years the penitentiary housed 500 prisoners and employed 100 guards and other workers.

In 1987, the grade-B movie *Prison* was filmed on location here with a number of locals as extras. Parts of the movie set are still visible, and some of the prison floors are still red from the fake blood. If you missed it in the theaters, don't despair; this is one of those godawful flicks that will eventually make it to the 4 a.m. slot on some obscure cable-TV station. Or, you can buy a copy in the Frontier Prison gift shop.

The Lone Bandit

The most famous inmate to spend time here was William Carlisle, the "gentleman train robber." In three Union Pacific train robberies in Wyoming, Carlisle netted barely $1,000. He never robbed female passengers, never shot or injured anyone, and was reported to have bought gifts for children with the loot. After the third robbery, he was caught and sentenced to life in prison. Carlisle was sent to Rawlins in 1916 but escaped in a shirt crate three years later. In another train robbery Carlisle was shot and wounded but still managed to remain free for two weeks before a posse caught up with him. The last conviction landed him another life sentence, but the governor pardoned Carlisle in 1936. He walked out a changed man and eventually became a respected Laramie motel owner and author of a book about his life, *The Lone Bandit.* Carlisle died in 1964.

Practicalities

During the summer months, the prison is open daily 8:30 a.m.-5:30 p.m., with guided hourly tours at half past the hour. The prison motto: "No visitors locked inside since 1981." These excellent, hour-long tours cost $4.25 for adults, $3.75 for seniors or kids (children under six are free), and $15 for families. During the rest of the year, tours are generally offered on the half-hour between 8:30 a.m. and 5:30 p.m. daily in the summer. Winter tours are by appointment, but someone is generally here weekdays; call (307) 324-4422 for details. Ask for Mark Setright to get the most entertaining and educational tours. Be sure to bring a sweater or coat with you since the stone prison is a chilly place even in midsummer. For a scarier visit, ask about the nighttime flashlight tours offered some summer evenings ($5 per person) and on Halloween. Night tours are by reservation only and not recommended for young children.

The Smell of Sage

A portion of the old prison serves double-duty as the **Wyoming Peace Officers Museum,** with memorials, artifacts, and badges. Also here are photos and descriptions of various inmates, along with a souvenir shop selling postcards, books, and other items. One book well worth a look is *The Sweet Smell of Sagebrush.* This is a collection of stories by William Stanley Hudson, a man who served four separate sentences here for such crimes as horse stealing and passing stolen checks. It offers not only a glimpse of turn-of-the-20th-century prison life but also a fascinating account of criminal logic. The title comes from his release from prison after serving his first sentence:

> *i thought little of those things that august day as i walked out from the damp prison air into the glorious sunshine of this enchanted land. i felt only a desire to get away somewhere out of sight. after walking towards the buisness part of town a short way, i turned and went straight out of town untill i reached the high sagebrush. the smell of the sage was that day sweeter to me than a breath from a bed of rarest flowers. for an hour i was content to sit and breathe the pure mountain air and enjoy the warm sunshine.*

Hudson's fate is unknown. After release from his fourth incarceration in 1921, he disappeared. Perhaps he was a reformed man. Or perhaps he learned enough to avoid getting caught again.

OTHER SIGHTS

Carbon County Museum

Housed in an old Mormon church at 9th and Walnut Sts., the Carbon County Museum, tel. (307) 328-2740, is open Mon.-Fri. 10 a.m.-noon and 1-5 p.m. May-Sept., and Monday, Wednesday, and Saturday 1-5 p.m. the rest of the year. No charge. The museum is a mixed bag, containing Oregon Trail and Indian relics, historic photos, an Essex Motors race car from 1922, a 1920 hook-and-ladder truck, and various stage-station and Civil War artifacts. One case even contains 400-year-old Spanish artifacts discovered in a cave near Hanna. Easily the strangest object in the museum is a pair of two-tone shoes made from the skin of Big Nose George Parrot, a train robber and murderer. These were crafted by Dr. John E. Osborne, who also decided to saw open George's skull to see if the brains of desperadoes differed from those of common men. The skullcap became an ashtray now on exhibit at the Union Pacific Railroad Museum in Omaha, but the bottom of the skull is here, along with Big Nose George's death mask and a photo of the old whiskey barrel in which Osborne decided to store the body. The barrel wasn't discovered until 1950 when a construction crew found it while digging at an old Rawlins drugstore. Incidentally, this same Dr. Osborne went on to serve as Wyoming's governor from 1893 to 1895!

Looking for more criminals? Try **St. Joseph's Cemetery,** where two early train robbers are buried. Ask at the museum for the exact grave locations. Still more crooks? Try the state penitentiary, south of town; you'll meet real live ones there.

Buildings

Quite a number of interesting old sandstone buildings are scattered throughout downtown, built from stone quarried around Rawlins. Pick up a detailed walking-tour brochure of historic buildings from the chamber of commerce at 517 Cedar Street. Notable ones include the Shrine Temple at 5th and Pine (completed in 1909), the Elks Club at 4th and Buffalo (completed in 1909), and the Presbyterian church at 3rd and Cedar (built in 1882). The Union Pacific Railroad depot at 400 W. Front was built in 1901 of granite and brick and is now used as a community meeting room. One of the most attractive buildings in Rawlins is the **Ferris Mansion** at 607 W. Maple, built for the widow of an early mining pioneer, George Ferris. An old **steam locomotive** rests in Tully Park on Elm Street next to the hospital.

"Rockology"

The country around Rawlins is a geologist's and rock hound's paradise; jade; petrified wood, agate, and other minerals are here to be discovered. Of course, oil, gas, and coal are what geologists are most interested in around here. The **Rawlins Uplift** (a thrust-faulted anticline) rises immediately north of town, providing a textbook example of stratigraphy. Plenty of fish and invertebrate fossils are here, too. As a side note, the paint known as "Rawlins Red" originated from iron oxide mined just north of town. The color is still used for barns and buildings in the eastern U.S., and this was the color originally chosen by General Rawlins to paint the Brooklyn Bridge (as Secretary of War, he approved the bridge plans).

PRACTICALITIES

Accommodations

Given its relatively small size, Rawlins has a surprising number of places to stay. Partly this is a legacy of the boom era, when tight housing conditions forced many workers into motels and mobile homes; partly it's attributable to the nightly influx of tired I-80 travelers. If you plan to stay at one of the cheap motels—particularly those not listed below—take a look at the rooms first since some may not be up to your standards. Listed below are more than a dozen local motels, arranged by price. Add a seven percent tax to these rates.

Budget: Ideal Motel, 1507 W. Spruce, tel. (307) 324-3451, is an older place with clean but basic furnishings and some in-room fridges. Rates are a bargain: $20 s or $24 d. **Economy Inn,** 713 W. Spruce, tel. (307) 324-4561, has rooms (some with fridges and microwaves) for $25 s or $30 d; while **Rawlins Motel,** 905 W. Spruce, tel. (307) 324-3456, charges $25 s or $31 d.

Although most of its rooms are rented on a long-term basis, **La Bella Motel,** 1819 W. Spruce St., tel. (307) 324-2583, has a handful of nightly rooms for $25 s or $30-33 d. The rooms are large and contain fridges.

Inexpensive: Golden Spike Inn (National 9), 1617 W. Spruce, tel. (307) 328-1600 or (800) 457-7820, charges $30 s or $36-40 d. Two other economy places are **Jade Lodge,** 405 W. Spruce, tel. (307) 324-2791, where rooms cost $30 s or $35 d; and **Key Motel, 1806 E. Cedar, tel. (307) 324-2728, charging $32 s or $35 d.**

Sunset Motel, 1302 W. Spruce, tel. (307) 324-3448, has well-maintained rooms for $30 s or $35-45 d. Most have fridges and microwaves; kitchenettes are $5 extra.

The accommodations are plain at **Weston Inn,** 1801 E. Cedar, tel. (307) 324-2783, but guests have access to an outdoor pool, and prairie dogs can be seen out back. Rates are $35 s or $39-45 d. **Bridger Inn,** 1904 E. Cedar, tel. (307) 328-1401, has standard motel rooms, some with microwaves and fridges, for $35 s or $40 d.

BIG NOSE GEORGE PARROT

George Manuse, better known as Big Nose George Parrot, was a rustler from the Powder River country who joined up with Dutch Charley Burris and Frank James (of the James Gang) on an 1878 robbery attempt. The trio tried to derail a Union Pacific train by prying up a piece of track and waiting in ambush. Unfortunately for the outlaws, an alert UP employee discovered the missing rail before the train arrived, and a manhunt ensued. The posse tracked the gang into Rattlesnake Canyon and then stopped in a freshly deserted camp. As a deputy sheriff bent over to check the coals, he commented, "They're hot as hell." Immediately, a voice shouted from behind the bushes, "We'll show you how hot hell is." Two deputies were shot dead, and the three robbers escaped.

After the murders, the trio split up. Dutch Charlie was caught the following year and sent back via train to Carbon, Wyoming, for trial. But the trial never came; a group of masked men pulled him from the train and threw a noose around his neck. When Dutch Charlie was asked if he had any last words, the widow of one of the deputies yelled out, "No, the son-of-a-bitch has nothing to say!" and booted the barrel from under his feet. The newspaper noted, "the train was delayed only thirteen minutes by the operation."

In 1880, the law finally caught up with Big Nose George in Montana, and he too was hauled back to Rawlins in shackles. When the train pulled into town, 15 armed men forced the sheriff to release the prisoner to them and hauled him off to be hanged. Big Nose George managed to avoid his fate this time by reminding his would-be lynchers that "dead men tell no tales," but he confessed to and was convicted of the murders the following spring and was sentenced to hang. In an escape attempt shortly after the trial, George cracked the skull of a guard with his shackles before finally being subdued. When word of the escape attempt spread through Rawlins, a mob of masked men broke into the jail. Big Nose George was hauled out and lynched in the street, though it took two tries—the rope was too long the first time. The Rawlins jail register notes that Big Nose George Parrot "Went to join the angels via hempen cord on telegraph pole front of Fred Wolf's saloon."

Stay at **Super 8 Motel,** 2338 Wagon Circle Rd., tel. (307) 328-0630 or (800) 800-8000, for $50 s or $56 d, including access to an exercise facility.

Moderate: Days Inn, 2222 E. Cedar, tel. (307) 324-6615 or (888) 324-6615, has an outdoor pool and offers a light breakfast each morning. Rates are $55-65 s or $61-71 d.

On the south edge of town, **Sleep Inn,** 1400 Higley Blvd., tel. (307) 328-1732 or (800) 753-3746, rents modern rooms for $53-58 s or $58-63 d. Amenities include a continental breakfast, sauna, game room, and VCR rentals.

Expensive: Rawlins's premier motel is **Best Western CottonTree Inn,** at 23rd and Spruce, tel. (307) 324-2737 or (800) 662-6886, with an indoor pool, jacuzzi, and sauna, plus access to a local health club. Newly remodeled rooms (some with fridges) are $74-79 s or $84-89 d.

Bed and Breakfast

In the heart of town, **Bit O' Country B&B,** 221 W. Spruce St., tel. (307) 328-2111 or (888) 321-2111, is a friendly and comfortable place to spend a night or two. The home was built in 1903 and has been restored to its original grandeur by owners Andrew and Michelle Aldrich. The two guest rooms ($60 s or d) have private baths and are furnished with antiques. Guests will also enjoy relaxing on the enclosed front porch. A light breakfast is served, and kids are welcome. Moderate.

Campgrounds

The nearest public campground (free; open June-Oct.) is at **Teton Reservoir,** 17 miles south of Rawlins. More public facilities ($9 for nonresidents, $4 for Wyoming residents; open year-round) are in Seminoe State Park, 28 miles north of Sinclair.

You'll find four parking lot campgrounds in Rawlins. Expect to pay $12-18 for tents or $16-27 for RVs at: **Western Hills Campground,** 2500 Wagon Circle Rd., tel. (307) 324-2592 or (888) 568-3040; **Rawlins KOA,** 205 E. Hwy. 71, tel. (307) 328-2021 or (800) 562-7559; **American President's Camp RV Park,** 2346 W. Spruce St., tel. (307) 324-3315 or (800) 294-3218; or **RV World Campground,** 2401 Wagon Circle Rd., tel. (307) 328-1091 or (800) 478-9753. All four of these are great places to swelter in the simmering heat of summer as you listen to the freeway traffic. Western Hills and American President's are open all year, the others typically April-September. If you aren't camping here, you can take showers at American President's or RV World for $3.

historic Ferris Mansion, built in 1903

Food

Rawlins has a surprising number of good restaurants. Start the day at **Square Shooter's Eating House,** 311 W. Cedar, tel. (307) 324-4380, serving standard American fare amid the ambience of mounted animal heads. **Rustler Family Restaurant,** 1800 E. Cedar St., tel. (307) 324-5539, has a similar menu and serves breakfast all day. Good Navajo tacos too.

Locals rave about **Rose's Lariat,** 410 E. Cedar, tel. (307) 324-5261, an old favorite with heavy and old-fashioned Mexican meals. Only one small table; everyone else sits at the counter stools, so you'll probably end up waiting to eat. Open Tues.-Sat. 11 a.m.-7 p.m. only. For Chinese food, head to **China Panda,** 1810 E. Cedar

St., tel. (307) 324-2198; for pizza, try **Pizza Hut,** 506 Higley Blvd., tel. (307) 324-7706, where you'll find lunchtime stuff-yourself specials.

Occupying a vintage-1881 building, **The Pantry,** 221 W. Cedar St., tel. (307) 324-7860, is a fine, family-run place with reasonable prices and all-American food. Lots of grub for the buck. Another historic home at 318 5th St. is now home to **Aspen House Restaurant,** tel. (307) 324-4787. The menu includes steaks, seafood, chicken, pasta, and Asian specialties, and the Singaporean owner brings an Eastern touch to the cookery. Open for lunch and dinner only.

Cedar St. Coffee Co., 509 W. Cedar St., tel. (307) 324-5233 or (800) 484-5808, has several inside tables and serves espresso, bagels, and ice cream.

Get fast service and decent truck-stop grub at **Flying J Truckstop,** two miles west of Rawlins, tel. (307) 324-3463, or from **Rip Griffin's Truckstop,** I-80 at Higley Blvd., tel. (307) 328-2103. Groceries can be found at **City Market,** 602 Higley Blvd., tel. (307) 328-1421, which also has a deli.

Entertainment and Events

Images Lounge at Day's Inn, 2222 E. Cedar, tel. (307) 324-6615, has Top 40 DJ tunes most nights and occasional rock bands. Also try **The Keg,** 307 E. Cedar, tel. (307) 324-9826, for live music.

Cowboy poetry is becoming a big attraction throughout Wyoming. In Rawlins, poetry enthusiasts will want to take in the **Carbon County Gathering of Cowboy Poets** in late July. The event also includes a Western arts and crafts show, and country-and-western music and dancing.

The biggest local event is **Carbon County Fair and Rodeo,** held the second full week of August each year. Attractions include livestock and farm exhibits, rodeos, truck pulls, arts and crafts displays, parades, a carnival, street dance, pancake breakfast, and demolition derby. **Summerfest** takes place during the fair and includes a chili cook-off, booths, bed races, fireworks, stagecoach rides, and country music.

Recreation

The **Rawlins Family Recreation Center,** 1616 Harshman, tel. (307) 324-7529, has racquetball, basketball, and volleyball courts, a weight room, an indoor track, and other facilities. Swim at the **high school pool. Galaxy Skate Center,** 3rd and Cedar, tel. (307) 324-7850, has evening skating. Other minor-league attractions are the **Jeffrey Lanes** bowling alley, 1917 W. Spruce St., tel. (307) 328-0263, and **mini-golf** courses at RV World Campground and Western Hills Campground. The nearest regular golf course is in Sinclair, six miles east of Rawlins.

Information and Services

The **Rawlins-Carbon County Chamber of Commerce** is next to City Hall at 519 Cedar St., tel. (307) 324-4111, and is open Mon.-Fri. 8 a.m.-5 p.m. year-round. Its web address is www.trib.com/~rcccoc. For Carbon County information and publications, call (800) 228-3547 or head to the web at www.wyomingcarboncounty.com.

Carbon County Public Library is at 3rd and Buffalo, tel. (307) 328-2618, and the **post office** is at 106 5th St., tel. (307) 324-3521. The Higher Education Outreach Center, 600 E. Mahoney, tel. (307) 328-9204, has public access computers with **Internet access** for just $2 a day.

Wash clothes at **The Washboard,** 504 23rd, tel. (307) 324-2434, or **Wash & Dry Laundry,** 515 15th Street.

The **BLM district office** is at 1300 N. 3rd, tel. (307) 328-4200. **Cedar Chest Gallery,** 416 W. Cedar, tel. (307) 324-7737, is a gift shop and art gallery with a small collection of Wyoming books. The Frontier Prison also sells books on Wyoming. Find **ATMs** at several local banks, grocers, and truck stops, and even in the McDonald's.

Transportation

Community Action Transit System, tel. (307) 324-9571, provides local bus transportation Mon.-Fri. for 50 cents. **Greyhound,** tel. (307) 324-5496 or (800) 231-2222, www.greyhound.com, has bus service along I-80 in both directions but there are no direct connections between Rawlins and Casper or other cities in the northern part of Wyoming; the closest routing is via Cheyenne or Rock Springs. Greyhound buses stop at McDonald's, 2225 E. Cedar Street.

Rent cars from **Kar Kraft,** 1111 E. Daley, tel.

(307) 324-6352, or **Quality Motors,** 121 W. Cedar St., tel. (307) 324-7131.

There is no commercial air service to Rawlins.

HEADING NORTH

U.S. Hwy. 287-State Hwy. 789 points north from Rawlins into Wyoming's heartland, crossing the Continental Divide twice along the way as it dips into the Great Divide Basin and then back out again. Once inside the basin, the highway throws itself straight across this sandy land from point A to point B, with not much in between to deflect it. No need to touch the steering wheel here. Fences collect both tumbleweeds and bits of miscellaneous junk. To the northeast the tilted face of 10,037-foot Ferris Mountain rises, but your sense of distance falters in the featureless desert land where only fence lines and a few gullies halt the relentless horizontal geography. Geologists love this place: long, eroded ridges and scarps in the distance which appear so parched of water that their barren slopes could be the bleached rib cages of some prehistoric monster. Some amazing badlands formations are here as well.

Lamont and Bairoil

The diminutive settlement of Lamont lies 33 miles north of Rawlins near the Continental Divide. A paved road leads five miles west to another tiny place, Bairoil. The latter is named for Charles Bair, who discovered oil (hence the name) here in 1916. Today the surrounding area is part of BP-Amoco's Lost Soldier Oil Field, and pumpjacks sprinkle the landscape.

Bairoil lays claim to a slice of air-travel trivia. In 1989, Kevin Christopherson set a world foot-launched hang gliding record when he took off from Whiskey Peak, caught favorable wind currents, and rode them all the way into North Dakota, 287 miles away.

Get meals in Bairoil at **Lost Soldier Saloon,** tel. (307) 328-0171. Campsites and RV hookups can be found in the **Bairoil town park,** tel. (307) 324-7653. In Lamont, **Grandma's Cafe & Campground,** tel. (307) 324-9870, serves three meals a day (starting at 5 a.m.) and provides RV and tent sites.

Over Whiskey Gap

Forty miles north of Rawlins, the highway climbs through Whiskey Gap, with Green Mountain to the west and the Ferris Mountains to the east. The gap received its name in 1862 when Maj. Jack O'Farrell caught his soldiers drinking from an illegal barrel of whiskey in a trader's wagon. The whiskey was dumped on the ground, but some flowed into a spring that one soldier later called the "sweetest water he had ever tasted."

Another five miles north of Whiskey Gap is the junction of U.S. 287-State Hwy. 789 and State Hwy. 220 at **Muddy Gap,** where you can gas up. The road diverges, with one fork leading northeast to Casper, passing the Oregon Trail landmarks of Devil's Gate and Independence Rock (see Casper Vicinity in the Central Wyoming chapter) and the other heading northwest to Lander, with Split Rock and Jeffrey City along the way (see Lander Vicinity in the Wind River Mountains Country chapter for more on Jeffrey City). In either direction you will find stereotypical Wyoming vistas—sagebrush, grass, cattle, and sky. But no whiskey barrels.

SOUTHWEST WYOMING

Southwest Wyoming is the state's forbidden quarter, a place seen primarily from the windows of cars speeding along I-80. At first glance the land appears stark, barren, and worthless. In 1866, Gen. William T. Sherman wrote, "The Government will have to pay a bounty for people to like it up here." Others said people wouldn't come no matter how many incentives the government might offer. But despite the lack of trees, the broiling hot summers, and the wind-iced winters, people *have* settled here, primarily to extract the area's immense energy and mineral resources. Southwest Wyoming contains both the state's largest county (Sweetwater) and its smallest (Uinta), as well as Lincoln County, seemingly named for its L-shape. The Green River cuts across this part of Wyoming, eventually joining the Colorado River in Utah.

History

When whites first arrived in southwest Wyoming, they found the Shoshone and Ute Indians hunting buffalo and antelope in this desert country. The first mountain-man rendezvous took place here, and many of the vital emigrant routes passed through—including the Oregon, Mormon, and Overland Trails—as did the Pony Express and the transcontinental telegraph. But it was the Union Pacific Railroad that opened the land to settlement. Completion of the railroad in 1869 brought about the establishment of Rock Springs, Green River, and Evanston, and coal mines were developed in the Rock Springs, Evanston, and Kemmerer areas to fuel these trains. Men of all nationalities came to work the mines, creating a racial diversity still visible.

Just as the coal mines began to close in the 1950s, enormous trona deposits were developed in western Sweetwater County, and many miners simply switched employers. Other mines extract phosphates and coal, and the natural-gas fields of Sweetwater and Uinta Counties are the most productive in Wyoming. Southwest Wyoming has the world's biggest coal mine, biggest coke-producing plant, biggest trona mine, and biggest helium plant. Put all this together and it's obvious that despite the desert setting and small population, southwest Wyoming is in some ways the most industrialized part of the state.

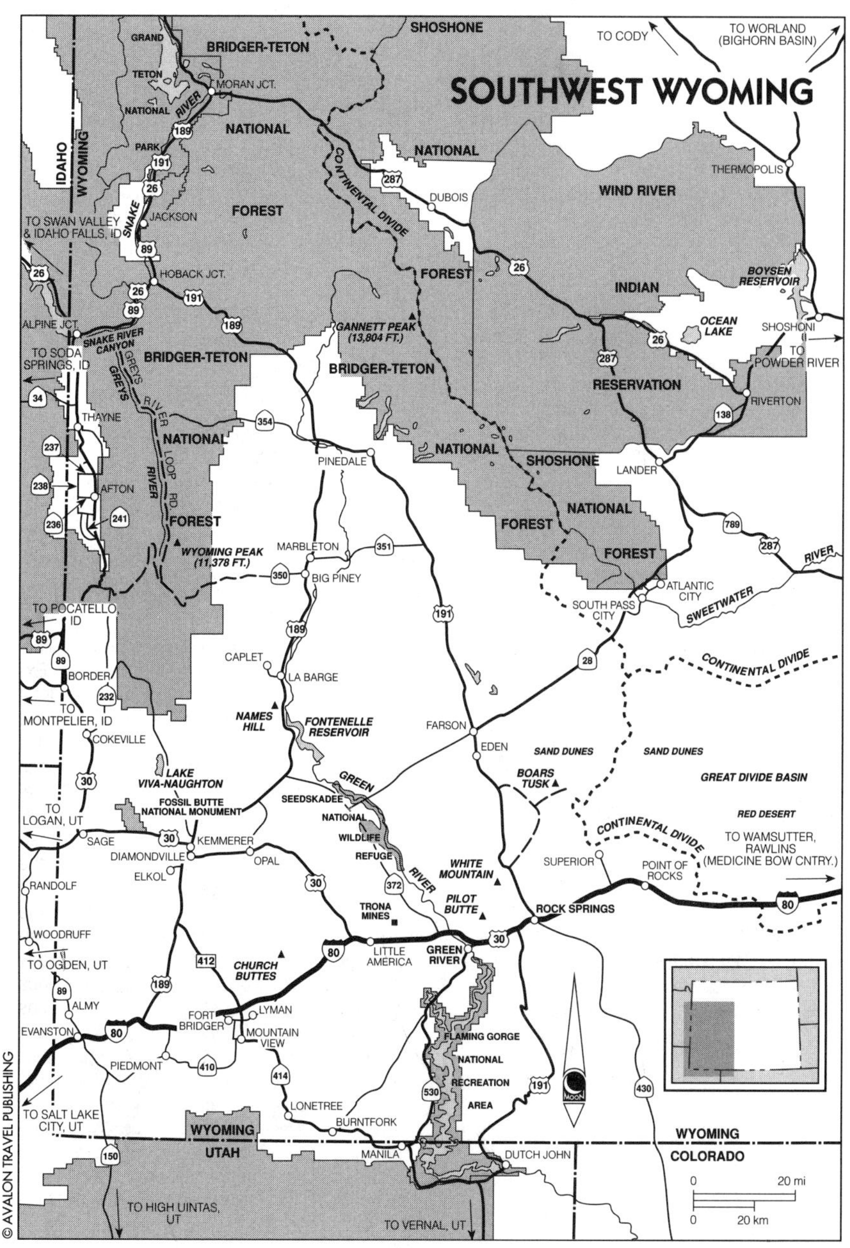
SOUTHWEST WYOMING
SHOSHONE
TO CODY
TO WORLAND (BIGHORN BASIN)
GRAND
TETON
NATIONAL
PARK
BRIDGER-TETON
MORAN JCT.
RIVER
NATIONAL
IDAHO
WYOMING
NATIONAL
THERMOPOLIS
CONTINENTAL DIVIDE
DUBOIS
WIND RIVER
FOREST
SNAKE
JACKSON
TO SWAN VALLEY & IDAHO FALLS, ID
HOBACK JCT.
FOREST
BOYSEN RESERVOIR
INDIAN
ALPINE JCT.
SNAKE RIVER CANYON
GANNETT PEAK (13,804 FT.)
OCEAN LAKE
SHOSHONI
TO SODA SPRINGS, ID
BRIDGER-TETON
GREYS
GREYS
RIVER
BRIDGER-TETON
TO POWDER RIVER
RESERVATION
RIVERTON
THAYNE
NATIONAL
LOOP RD.
RIVER
PINEDALE
NATIONAL
SHOSHONE
LANDER
AFTON
FOREST
NATIONAL
FOREST
WYOMING PEAK (11,378 FT.)
MARBLETON
FOREST
RIVER
BIG PINEY
ATLANTIC CITY
SOUTH PASS CITY
SWEETWATER
TO POCATELLO, ID
CONTINENTAL DIVIDE
CAPLET
LA BARGE
BORDER
TO MONTPELIER, ID
NAMES HILL
FONTENELLE RESERVOIR
FARSON
COKEVILLE
EDEN
SAND DUNES
SAND DUNES
LAKE VIVA-NAUGHTON
GREEN
BOARS TUSK
GREAT DIVIDE BASIN
FOSSIL BUTTE NATIONAL MONUMENT
SEEDSKADEE
TO LOGAN, UT
NATIONAL
RED DESERT
CONTINENTAL DIVIDE
SAGE
KEMMERER
WILDLIFE
TO WAMSUTTER, RAWLINS (MEDICINE BOW CNTRY.)
DIAMONDVILLE
OPAL
REFUGE
WHITE MOUNTAIN
SUPERIOR
POINT OF ROCKS
ELKOL
RIVER
RANDOLF
TRONA MINES
PILOT BUTTE
ROCK SPRINGS
WOODRUFF
LITTLE AMERICA
GREEN RIVER
TO OGDEN, UT
CHURCH BUTTES
ALMY
FORT BRIDGER
LYMAN
EVANSTON
MOUNTAIN VIEW
FLAMING GORGE
NATIONAL
PIEDMONT
RECREATION
AREA
MOON
TO SALT LAKE CITY, UT
LONETREE
BURNTFORK
WYOMING
WYOMING
UTAH
MANILA
DUTCH JOHN
COLORADO
0
20 mi
0
20 km
TO HIGH UINTAS, UT
TO VERNAL, UT

THE RED DESERT

The eastern half of Sweetwater County contains a vast treeless area known as the Red Desert, so named because of the brick-red soil that stretches in all directions. It's not a place to be trifled with. Less than nine inches of precipitation falls each year, and summertime temperatures frequently top 100° F in this forbidding, lonely place—the largest stretch of unfenced land in the Lower 48. Some of the biggest remaining herds of wild horses roam here, along with desert elk and one of the last wild herds of bison. Antelope are found throughout this country, as are a few cattle and lots of sheep. The signs of humans are few and far between: dirt roads, oil and gas wells, and a few wind-scoured buildings.

Interstate 80 is most folks' sole acquaintance with the Red Desert—two double-wide rivers of asphalt cracking open the desiccated land. There are not many sights to see unless you pull off the main road and slow down. Despite its harshness, the Red Desert has a desolate beauty that grows on you. Pick what may seem the least interesting place, where the ramp ends at a cattle crossing and the road immediately turns to gravel. When you're far enough from the interstate that you can no longer hear the trucks, get out of your car and use all your senses to grasp this place. Feel the intensity of the sun on a blistering summer day. Look at the way the thin-crusted snow lies in the lee side of the sage in winter, worn out by the incessant wind. Listen to the "scree!" cry of the red-tailed hawk. Taste a couple of the pungent sage leaves. Smell the rusty air as the first drops of a sudden shower pummel the road dust. Watch a herd of antelope bound away and then turn warily back to see who might be stopping in such a place. Or simply let the stillness of this vast land sweep over you, broken by the howl of a distant coyote. This is Wyoming without pretenses.

The Red Desert lies within **Great Divide Basin,** a 90-mile-long region where the little water that falls never makes it to either ocean. Red Lake—a salty playa—fills with water during rare rainy spells, only to have it soak into the sandy soil or evaporate in the summer sun. The Continental Divide splits south of Great Divide Basin and then rejoins on its northern margin, leaving a bowl in the middle. Highway travelers on I-80 thus cross the Continental Divide twice.

SIGHTSEEING HIGHLIGHTS FOR SOUTHWEST WYOMING

- Killpecker Dunes and White Mountain Petroglyphs in the Red Desert
- Flaming Gorge National Recreation Area
- Fort Bridger
- Fossil Butte National Monument and Kemmerer area fossil quarries
- Periodic Spring and elk-antler arch in Afton
- Greys River Loop Road
- Star Valley Cheese factory in Thayne
- Snake River Canyon
- Popular events: Red Desert Round Up in Rock Springs (July), Oyster Ridge Music Festival in Kemmerer (August), Fort Bridger Rendezvous at Fort Bridger (Labor Day), Cowboy Days in Evanston (Labor Day), and Cutter Races near Afton (winter)

Wamsutter

As you drive the 108 miles west from Rawlins to Rock Springs, the only town worth noting—and marginally so—is Wamsutter (pop. 250). Natural-gas wells sprinkle the country to west and south, and the town itself consists of a trashy collection of old trailer homes, oil field equipment, and smashed-up trucks hauled here from I-80 accidents. This is a good place to read a romance novel and pretend you're somewhere else. Butch Cassidy's Hole-in-the-Wall gang robbed a Union Pacific train near here in 1900, and freight trains still roll by every few minutes, day and night. The surrounding country is a rock hound's paradise, with petrified wood, fossils, and tortilla agate—beautiful when polished—all found on public lands in the area.

Rest your head at the pleasant **Wamsutter Inn,** tel. (307) 324-7112, where rooms with kitchenettes are $29-32 s or d. **Sagebrush Motel,**

> *Wyoming seems to be the doing of a mad architect—tumbled and twisted, ribboned with faded, deathbed colors, thrust up and pulled down as if the place had been startled out of a deep sleep and thrown into a pure light.*
>
> —GRETEL EHRLICH IN *THE SOLACE OF OPEN SPACES*

tel. (307) 328-1584, charges $24-27 s or d, but the rooms are in modular homes. Both Budget. Enjoy good home cooking at **Broadway Cafe,** tel. (307) 324-7830, or tip a beer at the **Desert Bar,** tel. (307) 324-4949.

Point of Rocks

At Point of Rocks (I-80 exit 130), 25 miles east of Rock Springs, the state has restored an **Overland Stage station** and adjacent stables built in 1862. Constructed from sandstone, the station served as a jumping-off point for a road to South Pass City during the gold-rush years. Get here by following the sign to the historical marker for the Overland Trail and then continuing another half mile over the railroad tracks and south to the stage station. It sits on a hillside overlooking the railroad and freeway. The historic stone building is well worth the brief side trip from I-80. The "town" of Point of Rocks has a gas station/restaurant/store/bar and several dozen trailer homes.

Coal is dug from the ground at two enormous strip mines not far from Point of Rocks. The Jim Bridger Mine feeds directly into the equally gargantuan Jim Bridger Power Plant, built in the early 1970s to supply power for Utah and Wyoming.

Superior

For a delightful change of pace from the onward rush of commerce, take I-80 exit 122 (20 miles east of Rock Springs). Follow this winding country road through seven miles of sage and grass to the town of Superior. Movie trivia buffs might recognize the town; parts of the 1992 film *Leaving Normal* were shot here.

Superior was once home to 3,000 people, but most moved away after the coal mines closed in 1963, leaving fewer than 300 today. The only surviving business is Canyon Bar; even the Ghost Town Bar is boarded up! Enjoy a picnic in the shady town park or just check out the many aging structures. Most interesting are the roofless remains of **Union Hall,** a trapezoidal building constructed in 1921. Interpretive signs here detail local history. Additional abandoned structures can be found at Old Superior, just up the road.

A mile north of Superior are the **Natural Corrals,** an area of small corral-like enclosures in the rocks. Caves reach into the volcanic hills and often contain ice even in midsummer. Check with the Rock Springs BLM office, tel. (307) 382-5350, for directions.

KILLPECKER DUNES AREA

North of Rock Springs, White Mountain rises like a cresting wave over the valley through which US 191 passes. Approximately 11 miles up is the turnoff to Tri-Territory Rd., providing access to the Killpecker Sand Dunes, the largest active dunes in North America. The dunes—some topping 150 feet in height—extend eastward for 55 miles in a band that averages two to three miles wide but sometimes reaches 10. The constantly shifting dunes are formed from Eden Valley dirt that blows east on the prevailing winds. Signs point the way to most of the sights in the Killpecker Dunes area. As an aside, the Tri-Territory area received its name as the point at which three major American land acquisitions met: the Louisiana Purchase, the Northwest Territories, and the Mexican Cession.

Petroglyphs and Boars Tusk

Follow gravel Tri-Territory Rd. 12 miles east from U.S. 191 and head left at the turnoff to **White Mountain Petroglyphs,** following a very rough four-mile track. Avoid this road after rains and early in the year. The road ends at a low sandstone cliff. Several hundred petroglyphs were carved into this soft rock by the Indian peoples who lived here in centuries past. Look closely to find elk, bison, horses, feather headdresses, and even a human footprint. Many petroglyphs relate to hunting. Because of the horses pictured here—horses didn't reach this region until the 16th century—it's likely that many of the petroglyphs are of relatively recent origin. The cliff provides a safe location for several large raptor

nests. Juniper and sage poke up through the remote desert landscape.

Return to the main gravel road and turn left to reach other interesting sights. Six miles to the east, the road splits. Turn right to reach the ORV area of the dunes, left to visit **Boars Tusk** and dunes where vehicles are not allowed. Follow the latter road a mile and a half to an unmarked road that leads to the base of Boars Tusk, a 400-foot-high rocky spire—a volcanic plug—that local rock climbers love. The 2.5-mile side road to Boars Tusk may be passable in a high-clearance vehicle, but I'd recommend a 4WD.

The Dunes

The dunes begin a mile and a half beyond the turnoff to Boars Tusk, 22 miles from US 191. This fascinating area is most beautiful in the early morning or at dusk, when sunlight gleams off the sand. Because it is a wilderness study area, vehicles are not allowed off the roads. Animals are surprisingly common in the Killpecker Dunes, and even a cursory examination will reveal tracks of coyotes, deer, elk, birds, and insects.

Small pools of water on the lee side of some dunes are fed by melting snow that gets covered by drifting sand in the winter. This is a great place to hike but be sure to come prepared for a desert climate: bring food and water, a compass, and a topographic map. The dirt roads are also fine for mountain-biking. See the BLM office in Rock Springs for more details on this unusual area.

ROCK SPRINGS

As an energy and transportation center, Rock Springs (pop. 23,000) is western Wyoming's largest city. It's also Wyoming's whipping boy and the focus of derisive jokes. Despite recent renovation efforts, the city still doesn't offer much beyond a place to rest up on the way to somewhere else. Pull off the freeway and you'll find the standard grouping of fast-food eateries, chain motels, gas stations, and convenience stores. The rest of Rock Springs consists of a patchwork of dead-end downtown streets, trailer parks, and split-level homes sprawling in various directions with the train tracks cutting through the middle of it all. The convoluted street system is a legacy of the coal-mining era, when paths taken by miners walking to work gradually evolved into a road network.

Like most other mining and energy towns, Rock Springs has always experienced booms and busts. Most of the underground coal mines are closed, but they still create a hazard as they settle, dropping the buildings above as they go. In

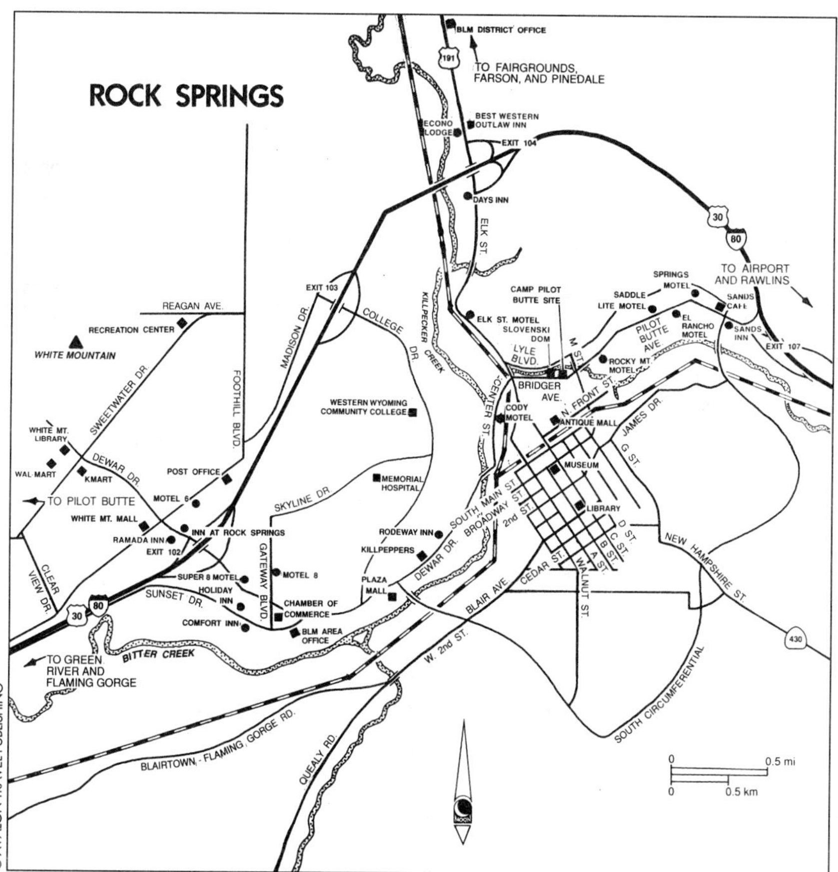

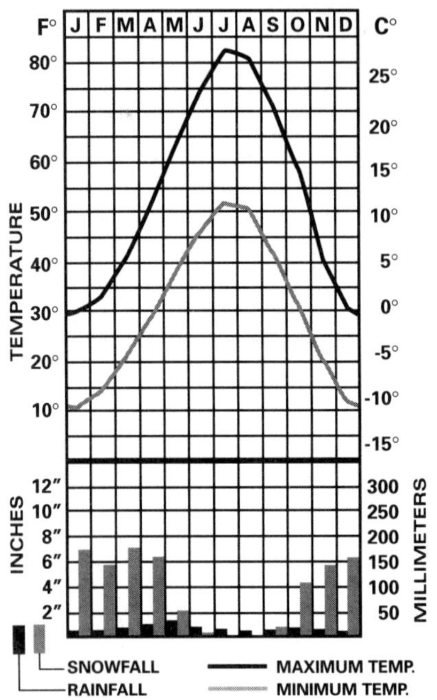

Average Maximum Temp.	**54.7°F**
Average Minimum Temp.	**30.7°F**
Annual Rainfall	**9.09″**
Annual Snowfall	**45.6″**

the last decade the citizens of Rock Springs have worked hard to clean up their image. Extensive restoration work on the historic city hall—now a museum—and along Front St. is helping transform downtown into a more likable place, and the backfilling of old coal tunnels has lessened subsidence problems. The local economy rebounded in the late 1990s with the growth of natural gas developments, but downtown Rock Springs still seems to be barely hanging on.

HISTORY

Rock Springs began as a stage station along the Overland Trail but grew because of the Union Pacific's need for coal to run its trains. The Railway Act granted the Union Pacific rights to all coal along the transcontinental route. Although nearly all of Sweetwater County is underlain with coal, in Rock Springs the coal was close to the surface and easily accessible; the mines actually ran beneath the tracks in many places. Eventually the mines spread over a mile in various directions, creating a honeycomb of tunnels under Rock Springs.

Water and Coal

Despite the fact that Rock Springs is named for flowing water, the lack of water has always been a problem. Rock Spring dried up once coal mining began, and Bitter Creek provided only muddy, bitter water. Killpecker Creek, a sometime stream that flows through Rock Springs, was named by soldiers who noted the alkaline water's rather painful biological effects when they visited the outhouse. Honest. In the early years, Rock Springs was so short on drinking water that it had to be brought by train from Green River. Baths were once-a-week events despite the coal dust that blackened everyone.

Coal mining brought workers from all over the globe; locals call it the 57-variety town, and flags of many nations decorate local streets. Many arrived from Great Britain or Ireland, but others included Chinese, Italians, Scandinavians, Austrians, Hungarians, Yugoslavians, and Czechs. It was an uneasy melting pot. They lived in company housing, riverbank dugouts, or shanties and used Bitter Creek—already notorious because of its undrinkable water—as the local cesspool and garbage dump. Rock Springs continued to expand as more mines were opened by the UP, and the Chinese Massacre of 1885 (see special topic) had only a minimal impact on production. By 1892, some 943,513 tons of coal were being hauled out by 1,500 miners.

Although various companies mined here, it was the Union Pacific Coal Co. that really owned Rock Springs and its miners. And it was the UP that was to blame for many of the problems: the filth, the poor housing, the lack of water, and the working conditions that spawned racial hatred. After Union Pacific engines switched from coal to diesel in the 1950s, the underground mines were closed and the economy began to fade. During another boom in the '70s, Rock Springs' population doubled, and by 1982 high-paying energy and construction jobs had made it the wealthiest city in the nation on a per-capita basis. With the crash in oil prices, however, many companies fled town and the economy went into a tailspin. More recently, the city has once again rebounded as coal and trona mining, a phosphate fertilizer plant, and gas and oil production bring steady jobs to Rock Springs. An open-pit mine east of Rock Springs provides coal for the enormous Jim Bridger Power Plant—the largest power plant in Wyoming—while the Black Buttes strip mine in the same area feeds power plants elsewhere in the nation. The latter may eventually spread its tentacles over 60 square miles of desert land. There are also two underground coal mines in the vicinity.

SIGHTS

Downtown

The **Rock Springs Historical Museum,** in the old city hall, 201 B St., tel. (307) 362-3138, is open in the summer Monday and Wednesday 10 a.m.-8 p.m.; Tuesday, Thursday, and Friday 10 a.m.-5 p.m.; Saturday 11 a.m.-4 p.m. The rest of the year it's open Wed.-Sat. 10 a.m.-5 p.m. Admission is free. Built in 1894, this attractive sandstone building looks more like a medieval castle than a city hall. The local memorabilia—some dating to the 1880s—spreads over two floors and includes exhibits on coal mining and the diverse mix of people who came here for work. The old city jail cells are still in the building; check out the horsehair bedding. Be sure to pick up a copy of the excellent historical downtown walking-tour brochure while here.

THE CHINESE MASSACRE

Rock Springs had the dubious honor of hosting one of the most infamous incidents in Wyoming history—the Chinese Massacre. In 1875, the Union Pacific Railroad tried to step up coal production at its Rock Springs mines, but miners refused when they found their wages simultaneously being cut. To fill the gap, the company brought in Chinese contract laborers who were willing to work for less money. The Chinese immediately became targets of harassment. The railroad hired more and more Chinese while turning whites away, and within a decade over 500 Chinese miners were in Rock Springs.

Things came to a head on Sept. 2, 1885, when the supervisor of one of the mines began assigning Chinese workers to locations where whites had previously been working. Whites attacked the Chinese, first with picks and shovels, then with rifles. The violence spread, and Chinatown—a ramshackle assemblage of shacks along what is now Ahsay Ave.—was burned to the ground. A mob of 60 men swept after the defenseless Chinese workers, robbing and then murdering them. Twenty-eight Chinese died in the melee and many more fled and may have died while trying to cross the desert. The sheriff came down from Green River to protect the whites but did nothing to stop the murders in Chinatown. No one ever faced trial for the attacks.

The riots spawned similar anti-Chinese violence and strikes all over the West and led Gov. Francis E. Warren to call for federal troops to protect the remaining Chinese workers. As a result, Camp Pilot Butte was established to serve as a buffer between the Chinese and the whites. This was the only place in America where an international treaty post was ever established. Some 250 soldiers remained here until the Spanish-American War forced the fort's abandonment in 1899.

The workers—both white and Chinese—gradually filtered back after the riots, and by December the mines had 85 whites and 457 Chinese workers. The massacre led the U.S. to pay the Chinese government $149,000 in compensation; it was used to fund Chinese student scholarships in America. In the 1920s and '30s, the Union Pacific Coal Co. finally rewarded the few remaining Chinese workers with passage back to their homeland and endowments to pay for their retirement. Only one of the men remained in Rock Springs all his life. The bones of others who died were shipped home to China.

An unusual legacy of the riots is a still-burning coal mine at Potter St. in Rock Springs. During the melee, several miners stole a large amount of Chinese tea and stored it in a mine tunnel, hoping to sell it later. When the authorities came for it, the miners set it on fire, and the burning tea ignited an adjacent coal seam. Smoke still emerges from the ground at what is now called Burning Mountain.

Old City Hall now houses the Rock Springs historical museum.

Next to the main library, the **Community Fine Arts Center,** 400 C St., tel. (307) 362-6212, is open Mon.-Sat. 10 a.m.-noon and 1-5 p.m., plus Monday, Wednesday, and Thursday evenings 6-9 p.m. Free admission. You'll find some surprising works here, including paintings by Conrad Schwiering, Hans Kleiber, Grandma Moses, and Norman Rockwell. Also here is a 1993 painting of the Chinese Massacre by Taylor Spence.

The building at 432 S. Main, now a copy center, was once a butcher shop. According to some historians, it was while working here and in other local meat shops that Robert LeRoy Parker ("Butch Cassidy") acquired his nickname "Butch." (Several other tales purport to explain how he got the name, but nobody really knows which one is true.) The walking tour details several other Cassidy hangouts, plus the beer garden where Calamity Jane "announced her appearances in town by emptying both of her six shooters and 'shouting verbal oaths well tarnished.'" A monument to Rock Springs coal miners stands next to the old train depot downtown. The second JCPenney store ever opened (it was then called Golden Rule Mercantile) was housed in the building at 531 N. Front Street.

The site of **Camp Pilot Butte** (see the special topic on the Chinese Massacre) is now occupied by the Saints Cyril and Methodius Catholic Church at 633 Bridger, a major Slovenian center in the community. (Formerly part of Yugoslavia, Slovenia became an independent nation in 1991.) Only one of the original buildings from Camp Pilot Butte remains—a soldiers' barracks now used as a parish school. Chinatown was just north of here.

Slovenski Dom, the old Slovenian community center, is just down the street from Saints Cyril and Methodius Church, at 513 Bridger Street. Built in 1913, this was the home of Slovenian-American fraternal lodges and was a center for dances, skits, raffles, and concerts. A few pieces of the original furniture are still here, including a long back bar in the basement. The building now houses **Local Color Art Gallery,** tel. (307) 382-0990, selling quality pottery, crafts, furniture, and paintings created by local artisans.

Community College

On a hilltop overlooking town, Western Wyoming Community College, 2500 College Dr., tel. (307) 382-1600, is a two-year college housed in modern brick buildings. Stop here to explore the **art gallery** (open weekdays), to enjoy a light meal in the bright and spacious atrium, or to wander past imposing displays. You'll find several full-size **dinosaurs** (okay, they are actually fiberglass casts of dino bones), including *Triceratops* and *Tyrannosaurus rex.* Also here are fish, turtle, and plant fossils and a tall pendulum. The small **Natural History Museum** (open daily 8 a.m.-7 p.m.; free) contains Indian artifacts, Wyoming minerals, and more fossils.

The most unusual campus sight sits on the lawn out front—a nine-ton replica of an **Easter Island Statue.** The statue is an exact copy of these mysterious stone carvings and was used to test theories on how they were moved across the island. Anthropology professor Charles Love showed that 25 men could drag the piece 135 feet in two minutes by putting it upright on long log rollers. The project was featured in a Nova program about Easter Island.

The community college offers a Western Studies series during the summer, with courses in prehistoric archaeology, flowering plants, backpacking, insects, nature literature, and other topics. Many of these are field classes lasting two or three weeks. Get additional class info on the web at www.wwcc.cc.wy.us.

Farther Afield

The **Reliance tipple,** five miles north of town on U.S. 191 and then two miles in on County Rd. 4-42, was used to load coal into railroad cars in the 1930s. Today the impressive structure is open for self-guided walking tours. A paved path leads to interpretive signs describing the facility.

Several miles northwest of Rock Springs is **Pilot Butte,** a prominent spire visible for miles in all directions and a milestone for emigrants along the Overland Trail. Get there via Gookin-White Rd. on the west side of town. You'll need a 4WD or a mountain bike unless you want to hoof it. A staircase leads up the rock from the east side. Another interesting rock formation stands across from Plaza Mall on Dewar Drive.

Just east of Pilot Butte is Simpson's Hollow, where Mormon guerrillas attacked a government supply train in 1857 during the short-lived "Utah War." A second train of wagons had been destroyed the previous day at the Green River as part of Brigham Young's war against the federal government. In these two incidents 74 wagons were captured and burned by the Mormons.

Wild Horses

More than 1,500 wild horses still run free in southwest Wyoming. Though they're often spotted east of Rock Springs along I-80, the best place to view them is along the west side of U.S. Hwy. 191 approximately 28 miles north of Rock Springs. Other Wyoming places to see them are near Lander, Worland, Cody, and Lovell. The BLM Rock Springs District Office is north of town on U.S. 191, tel. (307) 352-0256, and can supply info on wild horses and the Killpecker Dunes area (described above). For information on adopting a wild horse from one of the BLM's Red Desert roundups, call the Rock Springs office or visit the website: www.adoptahorse.blm.gov.

ACCOMMODATIONS AND CAMPING

Economy Motels

Rock Springs has quite a number of reasonably priced places to stay, but you should take a look inside the rooms at the cheapest motels. As you're driving into town on I-80, keep a watch for billboards proclaiming motel discount rates; sometimes you need to mention the ad to get the discount. Accommodations are arranged below from least to most expensive. Add a seven percent tax to these rates.

Budget: You'll find low rates and basic rooms at **El Rancho Motel,** 1430 9th St., tel. (307) 362-3763; $22 s or $26 d. All rooms contain fridges and microwaves. **Rocky Mountain Motel,** 1204 9th St., tel. (307) 362-3443, is another basic and older motel with microwaves and fridges in the rooms; $25 s or $35 d.

Cody Motel, 75 Center St., tel. (307) 362-6675, charges $26 s or $30 d for old fashioned rooms. Microwaves and small fridges are in all rooms, and some contain kitchenettes.

Elk St. Motel, 1100 Elk St., tel. (307) 362-3705, is a well-maintained older motel with fridges and microwaves in the rooms; rates are $28-35 s or d.

Inexpensive: Sands Inn, 1556 9th St., tel. (307) 362-3739, also has microwaves and fridges in some rooms. Approximately half of the rooms were recently remodeled. Rates are $32-38 s or $35-43 d.

Motel 8, 108 Gateway Blvd., tel. (307) 362-8200 or (888) 362-8200, has standard motel units for $34-37 s or $46 d.

Springs Motel, 1525 9th St., tel. (307) 362-6683, offers comfortable accommodations for $36 s or $36-44 d.

Rodeway Inn, 1004 Dewar Dr., tel. (307) 362-6673 or (800) 228-2000, charges $37 s or $42-54 d, including a continental breakfast.

At **Motel 6,** 2615 Commercial Way, tel. (307) 362-1850 or (800) 466-8356, rooms cost $38 s or $44 d, including access to an outdoor pool.

Higher-end Lodging

The following places offer rooms costing $50 or more per night, and are arranged from least to most expensive.

Inexpensive-Moderate: Econo Lodge, 1635 N. Elk St., tel. (307) 382-4217 or (800) 548-6621, has reasonable prices ($40-60 s or $50-70 d), plus an outdoor pool, jacuzzi, and continental breakfast.

Days Inn, 1545 Elk St., tel. (307) 362-5646 or (800) 329-7466, has an outdoor pool and in-room microwaves and fridges. Rates are $51-60 s or $56-60 d, including a light breakfast.

Amenities at **Comfort Inn,** 1670 Sunset Dr., tel. (307) 382-9490 or (800) 228-5150, include an outdoor pool, jacuzzi, exercise room, and continental breakfast; rates are $51-71 s or $51-77 d.

With 142 rooms, **Inn at Rock Springs,** 2518 Foothill Blvd., tel. (307) 362-9600 or (800) 442-9692, is the largest local lodging place. Attractions include an indoor pool, jacuzzi, and continental breakfast. Rooms cost $53 s or $59 d; some contain fridges.

Ramada Inn, 2717 Dewar Dr., tel. (307) 362-1770 or (888) 307-7890, has an outdoor pool and charges $55-60 s or $65-75 d, including a continental breakfast.

Super 8 Motel, 88 Westland Way, tel. (307) 362-3800 or (800) 800-8000, has an indoor pool and jacuzzi. Rates are $56 s or $59 d, including a continental breakfast.

Holiday Inn, 1675 Sunset Dr., tel. (307) 382-9200 or (800) 465-4329, features an indoor pool, wading pool, and jacuzzi, plus the star attraction: a rain machine. Rates are $64-75 s or d.

Moderate-Expensive: One of Rock Springs' finest lodging places, **Best Western Outlaw Inn,** 1630 Elk St., tel. (307) 362-6623 or (800) 528-1234, has an indoor pool and atrium, with rooms for $74-84 s or $81-91 d.

Camping

The nearest public camping is **Firehole Campground,** 27 miles southwest of Rock Springs in Flaming Gorge National Recreation Area. Camping costs $12; open mid-May to mid-September. Call (877) 444-6777 for reservations ($8.65 fee), or make them on the web at www.reserveusa.com. The **Rock Springs KOA Kampground,** two miles west of town on North Service Rd., tel. (307) 362-3063 or (800) 562-8699, provides great scenic vistas of the oil storage tanks—and you won't need to worry about trees blocking the sun. If you still want to stop, tent sites cost $17, RV sites $22. Simple "kamping kabins" are $32 d. Amenities include a pool and hot tub. Open April to mid-October.

FOOD

Ask people in Rock Springs where they go for meals and they're likely to say, "Green River." Interestingly, the same question posed to someone from Green River elicits the response, "Rock Springs." Something strange is going on here. Rock Springs does have one place you should not miss: **Grub's Drive In,** 415 Paulson, tel. (307) 362-6634, where the thick shakes, grease-drenched—but exceptional—fried chicken, and homemade fries are favorites of both locals and visitors. This old-time family operation features Shamrock burgers, loaded down with all the fixin's. You can almost feel your arteries clogging.

The best place for a down-home breakfast in a greasy-spoon atmosphere is **Renegade Cafe,** 1610 Elk St., tel. (307) 362-3052. **Crueljacks Restaurant,** west of Rock Springs, tel. (307) 382-9018, has a decent truck-stop menu. **The Fountain,** inside Plaza Mall, tel. (307) 382-4675, has old-fashioned soda treats and claims Wyoming's biggest candy selection.

Southwest Wyoming's only microbrewery, **Bitter Creek Brewing,** 604 Broadway St., tel. (307) 362-4782, is a downtown favorite with award-winning beers. The menu features tasty pub fare, including pasta, sandwiches, and 16 different burgers for lunch, along with pizzas, steaks, pork medallions, baby back ribs, and chicken at dinner. Dinner entrées are a reasonable $7-16, and six fresh brews are always on tap. Open brick walls, high ceilings, big front windows, and oak tables add to the charm.

Three places in town offer Chinese-American fare in quantity: **Lew's Family Restaurant,** 1506 9th St., tel. (307) 382-9894; **Wonderful House,** 1676 Sunset Dr., tel. (307) 382-5462; and **Sands Cafe and Bar,** 1549 9th St., tel. (307) 362-5633. The Sands has probably the best all-around meal deal in Rock Springs. Try **Santa Fe Trail,** 1635 Elk St., tel. (307) 362-5427, for distinctive Mexican and Native American cooking.

Rocky Mountain Noodle, 1679 Sunset Dr., tel. (307) 382-7076, has a bistro menu that includes chicken cordon bleu pasta, Italian cowboy pasta, and crawfish portofino. Prices are the same for lunch or dinner: entrées $7-12. The same chef also manages **The Greens,** at the White Mountain Golf Course, tel. (307) 362-3950. Here, his focus is on Cajun cooking, but the Greens also offers a popular Friday night prime rib and seafood buffet. Dinner entrées run a stiff $16-33.

Three very good steak-and-seafood places operate off I-80 west of town: **Log Inn Supper Club,** tel. (307) 362-7166; **Ted's Supper Club** (closed Sundays), tel. (307) 362-7323; and **White Mountain Mining Co.,** tel. (307) 382-5265. You won't go wrong at White Mountain Mining. **Fred's Breads,** 601 Broadway St., tel. (307) 362-9212, has breads, bagels, cakes, and cookies, as well as an adjacent coffee shop.

OTHER PRACTICALITIES

Entertainment

In 1903, some 40% of the businesses in Rock Springs were bars; even during Prohibition, many "soft-drink parlors" dispensed Kemmerer moonshine. To produce this booze, 100 train cars of grapes arrived in Rock Springs within a two-month period. Quite a few places still offer nightlife, though many tend toward the sleazy side—particularly those along the railroad tracks. The best places for live country-and-western music are **White Mountain Mining Co.,** west of Rock Springs, tel. (307) 382-5265, and **Saddle Lite Saloon,** 1704 Elk St., tel. (307) 362-8704. For exotic dancers, try **Mike's Astro Lounge,** 822 Pilot Butte Ave., tel. (307) 382-9876.

Local movie houses are **White Mountain Theatres,** tel. (307) 362-8633, in the White Mountain Mall, and **Reel Theatres,** at two addresses: 618 Broadway, tel. (307) 362-2101, and 591 Broadway, tel. (307) 382-9707.

Events

Start the summer with rhymes and tunes at the **Cowboy Poetry & Music Festival** on the second weekend of May at the Sweetwater Events Complex. The **Red Desert Round Up,** held the last weekend of July, is the second-largest professional rodeo in Wyoming and the primary summertime event. It also features a Saturday-morning pancake breakfast followed by a big parade.

Sweetwater County Fair takes place in early August right after the Round Up. The biggest county fair in Wyoming, this eight-day festival attracts families to 4-H auctions, a carnival, and headline entertainers. Call (307) 352-6789 for details. Auto-racing enthusiasts will find stock-car racing, motocross, and demolition derbies all summer long at **Sweetwater Speedway.** If you're in the area the second weekend of July, be sure to ask about the **Desert Balloon Extravaganza,** which includes some 30 different hot-air balloons, concerts, a crafts fair, pancake breakfasts, and a three-on-three basketball tournament. In late August, the **Great Wyoming Polka & Heritage Festival** attracts polka dotties from all over the nation.

Recreation

The impressive **Rock Springs Recreation Center,** 3900 Sweetwater Dr., tel. (307) 382-3265, has an indoor pool and gym, ice skating rink, racquetball and tennis courts, plus a weight room, sauna, and jacuzzi. Out front are unique carved-brick sculptures. Additional swimming pools are located at **Rock Springs Civic Center,** 410 N St., tel. (307) 362-6181; the **YMCA,** 1035 Jackson St., tel. (307) 352-6635; and **Western Wyoming Community College.** The championship 18-hole **White Mountain Golf Course,** tel. (307) 382-5030, lies three miles north of town.

Information and Services

The **Rock Springs Chamber of Commerce,** 1897 Dewar Dr., tel. (307) 362-3771, is open Mon.-Fri. 8 a.m.-5 p.m. year-round. If it's closed you can check the pamphlet rack in the entryway (open 24 hours).

The **BLM Rock Springs District Office,** tel. (307) 352-0256, is just north of town on U.S. 191; open weekdays. Stop here for information on the Red Desert and wild horses.

The **main library** at 400 C St., tel. (307) 362-6212, houses a fine collection of Wyoming books. **White Mountain Library** at 2935 Sweetwater Dr., tel. (307) 362-2665, is a delightful place to enjoy the view of White Mountain or stroll through a pleasant rock garden. There's a paperback book swap just inside the front door. Find the local **post office** at 2829 Commercial Way, tel. (307) 362-9792.

Wash clothes at **Imperial Laundromat,** 1669 Sunset Dr., tel. (307) 382-2774; **Launderette,** 328 Paulson, tel. (307) 362-6108; or **9th Street Laundromat,** 1215 9th St., tel. (307) 382-6092.

Shopping

For books in the White Mountain Mall visit **B. Dalton,** tel. (307) 382-4900 or **Hastings Books, Music, & Video,** tel. (307) 382-6610. You can also buy books from **Campus Bookstore,** tel. (307) 382-1600, at the community college.

Kickin Horse General Store, 7530 Foothill Blvd., tel. (307) 382-2606, sells cowboy gear of all types, from boots and saddles to Western jewelry. The downtown **Antique Mall,** 411 N. Front St., tel. (307) 362-9611, contains a big selection of antiques and collectibles.

Transportation

The Rock Springs airport is eight miles east of town and has daily service to Denver on **United Express/Great Lakes Aviation,** tel. (800) 241-6522. Rent cars at the airport from **Avis,** tel. (307) 362-5599 or (800) 831-2847; **Enterprise,** tel. (307) 362-8799 or (800) 325-8007; **Hertz,** tel. (307) 382-3262 or (800) 654-3131; or **Wayne's Car Rental,** tel. (307) 362-6970.

Greyhound Bus, 1655 Sunset Dr. (behind the Burger King), tel. (307) 362-2931 or (800) 231-2222, www.greyhound.com, has I-80 service in both directions.

Wind River Transportation Authority (WRTA), tel. (307) 856-7118 or (800) 439-7118, provides on-demand service in western and southwestern Wyoming. You can call them for rides between Salt Lake City and Rock Springs, or to other Wyoming towns, including Pinedale, Dubois, Evanston, Jackson, Lander, and Riverton.

Sweetwater Transit Authority Resources (STAR), tel. (307) 875-7827 or (307) 382-7827, provides around-town bus service.

GREEN RIVER

Green River (pop. 13,000) straddles the river of the same name and is a prosperous trona-mining and transportation town as well as the seat of Sweetwater County. Interstate 80 cuts a swath just north of town, plunging through tunnels beneath memorable badlands topography. The huge Union Pacific Railroad yard divides Green River. Run-down buildings crowd the railroad tracks, but elsewhere the town appears vibrant. Wander through the older sections to find tidy wooden frame homes, while ranch-style suburbs spread to the south. During the 1970s and '80s, Green River saw an enormous growth surge as the trona mines expanded their operations, as oil and gas explorations attracted thousands of roustabouts, and as a helium facility opened nearby. The population jumped from fewer than 5,000 in 1970 to almost 13,000 in 1980 and has held steady since then.

History

Green River was established in 1868 as workers constructed the Union Pacific Railroad across southern Wyoming. Three years later, Frederick Dellenbaugh described the town he found in less than flattering terms:

> *This place, when the railway was building, had been for a considerable time the terminus and a town of respectable proportions had grown up, but with the completion of the road through this region, the terminus moved on, and now all that was to be seen of those golden days was a group of adobe walls, roofless and forlorn. The present 'City' consisted of about thirteen houses, and some of these were of such complex construction that one hesitates whether to describe them as houses with canvas roofs, or tents with board sides.*

In May of 1869, Maj. John Wesley Powell brought fame to the town when his expedition of 10 men climbed off the train at Green River City and began a long float down the Green and Colorado Rivers. According to one observer, while in Green River awaiting orders, Powell and his men "tried to drink all the whiskey there was in town. The result was a failure, as Jake Field persisted in making it faster than we could drink it." They made it all the way through the Grand Canyon in stout wooden boats. Seven men survived; three who decided to hike out rather than face the treacherous rapids were never seen again. Powell returned to Green River in 1871 for a second voyage with a large contingent of scientists who helped map this region and later directed the U.S. Geological Survey.

Green River claims title to a minor legal footnote. In 1931, Green River passed an antipeddling ordinance that achieved national notoriety and inspired similar ordinances in many other towns and cities. The "Green River Ordinance" declared uninvited peddlers or hawkers to be a nuisance punishable by a fine of $25 and up. The Fuller Brush Company unsuccessfully fought the ordinance all the way to the U.S. Supreme Court.

Trona Mining

Wyoming leads the world in the mining of an obscure but important mineral: trona. With processing, trona—sodium sesquicarbonate—becomes soda ash and is used in glass, detergents, pulp and paper, metal refining, and baking soda. Trona is found in a few widely scattered places around the globe, but a third of the worldwide production comes from a thousand-square-mile area 25 miles west of Green River. Most trona here occurs in a 10-foot-thick bed some 1,500 feet underground. No chance of running out soon—there's enough here to supply the world for two thousand years. The mineral was deposited 50 million years ago when a saline lake developed, reaching 100 by 60 miles in size and up to 2,000 feet in depth. As the climate fluctuated, the lake periodically dried out, precipitating sodium salts. The trona deposits were first discovered in 1938, when an unsuccessful natural-gas well brought up core samples containing trona. Commercial production began in 1948.

Today, the five major trona mines are the region's largest employers, producing over 18 million tons of trona and 8 million tons of soda ash annually. The world's largest trona mine is run by FMC Corporation and has 2,000 miles of tunnels, more than all the streets of San Francisco. Its tunnels are 14 feet wide and eight feet tall, big enough to use as two-lane roads. Miners get around by driving diesel-powered jeeps or electric golf carts through the maze. Mining methods include a continuous mining machine that grinds out six tons of trona a minute; a long-wall process in which hydraulic rams hold the roof up as it is being mined and then allow the walls to collapse behind after the ore is removed; and solution mining, by which the trona is dissolved underground and pumped to the surface. Once at the surface, trona is processed and sent out on railroad tank cars or in 100-pound bags of soda ash. The production is staggering: at FMC's plant alone the mine extracts more than 900 tons an hour.

SIGHTS

Sweetwater County Historical Museum, in the county courthouse at 80 W. Flaming Gorge Way, tel. (307) 872-6435, is open Mon.-Fri. 9 a.m.-5 p.m. and Saturday 1-5 p.m. in July and August, and Mon.-Fri. 9 a.m.-5 p.m. the rest of the year. Free admission. The exhibits change each year but always include photographs from the Powell expedition, turn-of-the-20th-century home furnishings, mining and Indian exhibits, and an impressive hadrosaur footprint found in a nearby coal mine. Pick up the *Self-Guided Tour of Historic Green River* from the museum for a detailed walking tour of the town's oldest buildings. Be sure to also walk across the pedestrian overpass that crosses the sprawling **Union Pacific railroad yard.** It's a great place to take in the sounds and sights of freight trains being moved around.

The most distinctive feature of the country around Green River is **Castle Rock,** the stunning rocky pinnacle that rises above the freeway north

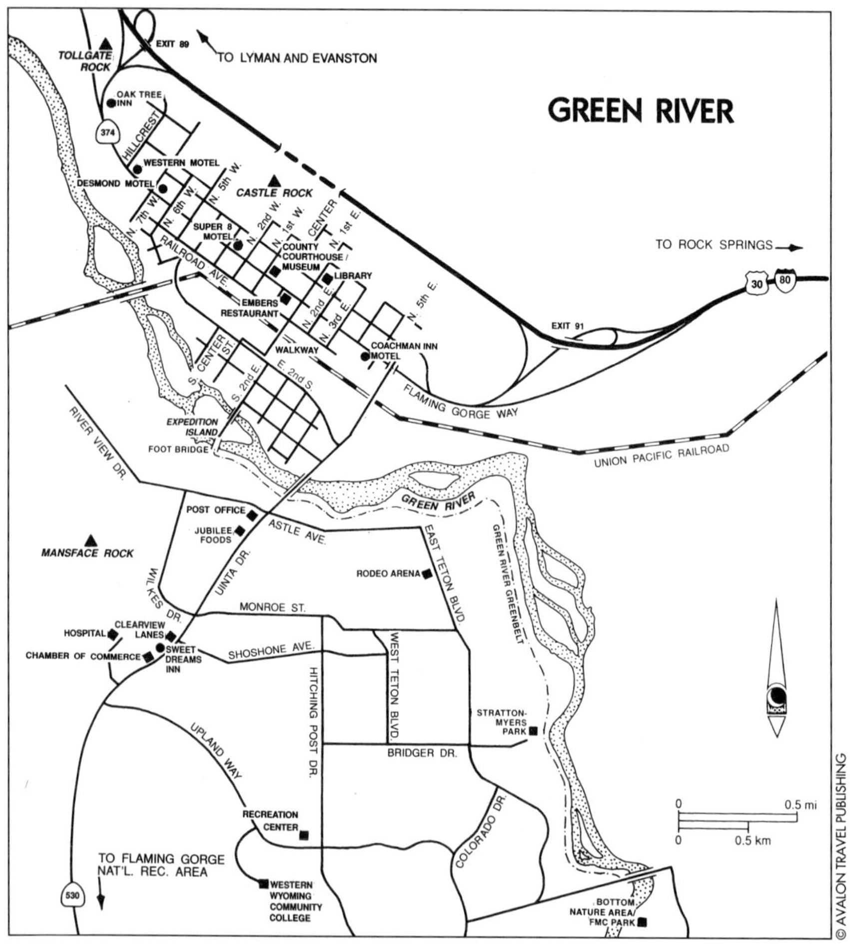

of town. Other unusual buttes are **Tollgate Rock** on the northwest end of town and **Mansface Rock** behind the post office. The visitor center has a fascinating brochure describing the stories behind these and many other buttes in the area.

Expedition Island—a National Historic Site—is where John Wesley Powell began his expeditions down the Green River. A small plaque memorializes these voyages of discovery. The **Green River Greenbelt** consists of a series of riverside trails that start at Expedition Island and continue to Scott's Bottom Nature Area on the southeast edge of town. Portions of these are paved, while others are dirt. Pick up a map from the visitor center, or just follow the easy path from the Expedition Island footbridge.

ACCOMMODATIONS AND CAMPING

Motels

Green River motels are listed below from least to most expensive. Add a seven percent tax to these rates. A few other places are available in town, but they are primarily for long-term stays and can be rather decrepit.

Budget: Western Motel, 890 W. Flaming Gorge, tel. (307) 875-2840, charges $30 s or $32-34 d. All rooms contain fridges and some also include microwaves.

Inexpensive: At **Coachman Inn Motel,** 470 E. Flaming Gorge, tel. (307) 875-3681, the rooms are $36-38 s or $42-50 d; some units contain fridges and microwaves.

Super 8 Motel, 280 W. Flaming Gorge, tel. (307) 875-9330 or (800) 800-8000, charges $41 s or $46 d, including a continental breakfast.

Oak Tree Inn, just off I-80 at exit 89 (1170 W. Flaming Gorge Way), tel. (307) 875-3500, is Green River's newest motel. It is also a base for Union Pacific Railroad workers, who occupy the three front buildings. The comfortable motel has inside corridors, along with an indoor jacuzzi and workout room. Rates are $45 s or $50 d. Out front is a gleaming 24-hour diner (fitting given all the railroad workers who stay here).

Inexpensive-Moderate: Fill your lodging, food, and entertainment needs at **Sweet Dreams Inn,** 1410 Uinta Dr., tel. (307) 875-7554, located next door to the Clearview Lanes bowling alley, Liquid Emotions Lounge (karaoke), and Other Place Restaurant. Standard motel rooms cost $50-60 s or d, while suites are $80 d.

Desmond Motel, 140 N. 7th W, tel. (307) 875-3701, also has lodging, but was for sale when this was written.

Camping

The nearest public camping is at **Buckboard Crossing Campground** ($13; open mid-May to mid-September), inside Flaming Gorge National Recreation Area and 25 miles south of Green River on State Hwy. 530. Call (877) 444-6777 for reservations ($8.65 fee), or make them on the web at www.reserveusa.com.

Tex's Travel Camp, four miles west on State Hwy. 374, tel. (307) 875-2630, is right along the river and has some shade trees. Tenters camp for $16, RVs for $22-26; showers cost $5 for noncampers. Open May-September. If you're on a bike, ask about pitching a tent next to the chamber of commerce office.

FOOD

Some of the most popular local restaurants lie on the way east; see Rock Springs above for details.

A cozy Alaska-themed restaurant, **Denali Grill & Bakery,** 375 Uinta Dr., tel. (307) 875-4654, serves three meals a day, including breakfast omelets and buttermilk pancakes. Prices are reasonable—most dinner entrées are under $10—and menu headliners include pasta, chicken, ribs, steaks, fish, and Navajo tacos. Buy fresh-baked breads at the front counter.

Sage Creek Bagels, 36 E. Flaming Gorge Way, tel. (307) 875-4877, is a local hangout. The cafe features an attractive exposed-brick interior, along with freshly baked bagels, breads, muffins, and espresso. Stop by for a lunchtime tea and sandwich. It's open at 6 a.m.-3 p.m. Mon.-Fri., and 6 a.m.-1 p.m. on Saturday.

Penny's Diner, on the west side of town at 1170 W. Flaming Gorge Way, tel. (307) 875-3500, is open 24 hours a day. Built to resemble a 1950s' diner, Penny's serves breakfasts, burgers, sandwiches, chicken, and salads, along with soda-fountain faves. The shiny silver jukebox plays your dad's tunes. Directly behind the diner are three buildings that house workers from the Union Pacific Railroad.

Ember's Family Restaurant, right downtown at 95 E. Railroad Ave., tel. (307) 875-9983, has good breakfasts, home-style cooking, and delicious prime rib.

Green River is a good place for those who like stuff-yourself buffets. Housed in an old Dairy Queen building, **R&B Meats and Deli,** 515 E. 2nd St. N, tel. (307) 875-2556, is a family place serving inexpensive all-American buffets for breakfast and lunch. The dinner specialty is, predictably, steak. Other restaurants with lunch buffets are **Pizza Hut,** 615 E. Flaming Gorge Way, tel. (307) 875-4562, and **China Gardens,** 190 N. 5th, tel. (307) 875-3259.

Don Pedro's, 520 Wilkes, tel. (307) 875-7324, has reasonably authentic Mexican food.

Get groceries and baked goods from **Jubilee Foods,** 400 Uinta Dr., tel. (307) 875-2577, or **Smith's,** 905 Bridger Dr., tel. (307) 875-6900. Both are open 5 a.m. to midnight.

OTHER PRACTICALITIES

Entertainment

Given its blue-collar base, it's no surprise that Green River has plenty of bars. You'll find half a dozen along Railroad Ave., including **The Brewery,** 50 W. Railroad Ave., tel. (307) 875-9974, housed in an amusing castle built in 1901. The building was part of Green River Brewery, Wyoming's first brewery. **Wild Horse Saloon,** 580 E. Flaming Gorge Way, tel. (307) 875-8550, has country-and-western or rock music on Friday and Saturday nights. **The Other Place Restaurant,** in the Clearview Lanes Bowling Alley at 1410 Uinta Dr., tel. (307) 875-2695, has karaoke Thurs.-Sat. nights. **Mast Lounge,** 24 E. Flaming Gorge Way, tel. (307) 875-9990, is a biker hangout with rock music, go-go dancers, and striptease artisans. Watch movies at **Star Theatres,** 699 Uinta Dr., tel. (307) 875-4702.

Events

Flaming Gorge Days, the last weekend of June, features a parade, bull-riding events, a chili cook-off, country and rock concerts, horseshoe contests, and tug-of-war. Call (307) 875-5711 for details. On the **Fourth of July** Green River has rock concerts at the softball complex, along with the obligatory fireworks show. The town's **Overland Stage Stampede Rodeo** follows a week later.

Recreation

The big **Green River Recreation Center,** 1775 Hitching Post Dr., tel. (307) 872-0511, has an Olympic-size pool, jacuzzi, sauna, steam room, gym, weight room, racquetball courts, nursery services, and even miniature golf. During the winter, rent cross-country skis here to explore the nearby Uinta Mountains. **Highland Desert Flies,** 79 N. 1st E, tel. (307) 875-2358, sells Orvis fishing gear, and **Wind River Sporting Goods,** 420 Uinta Dr., tel. (307) 875-4075, has a range of outdoor and fishing gear.

Roll black balls down the lanes at **Clearview Lanes,** 1410 Uinta Dr., tel. (307) 875-2695, or **Rancho Lanes,** 445 Uinta Dr., tel. (307) 875-4324.

Information

The **Green River Chamber of Commerce,** 1450 Uinta Dr., tel. (307) 875-5711, is open Mon.-Fri. 8 a.m.-5 p.m. and Sat-Sun. 8 a.m.-4:30 p.m. Memorial Day-Labor Day; and Mon.-Fri. 9 a.m.-5 p.m. the rest of the year. Be sure to stop here to see the large relief map of Flaming Gorge and to purchase Forest Service maps or local books. The chamber's webpage is www.grchamber.com.

Services

Sweetwater County Library is at 300 N. 1st E, tel. (307) 875-3615. Built over an old cemetery, it's said to be haunted. Librarians claim to have seen the ghosts, heard voices from empty rooms, and watched gates open on their own.

The local **post office** is at 350 Uinta Dr., tel. (307) 875-4920. Wash clothes at **Liberty's Laundry,** 1315 Bridger Dr., tel. (307) 875-8134.

Get new and used volumes—along with espresso coffees—from the friendly folks at **Book & Bean,** 55 E. Railroad Ave., tel. (307) 875-5445. There's also a small bookstore in the Green River campus of **Western Wyoming Community College** on College Way, tel. (307) 875-2278. The school sits atop a hill just south of town, providing a fine view of the surrounding badlands.

Find **ATMs** at several local banks. Greyhound no longer stops in Green River except by special request, and there are no local taxis.

GREEN RIVER VICINITY

LITTLE AMERICA

Find Little America approximately 20 miles west of Green River. From either direction along I-80, billboards announce, "Little America, only 350 [250, 150, 100 . . .] miles ahead!" And then, out in the desolate, windblown landscape, drivers suddenly come to this oasis of consumption where you can cozy up to cable TV or enjoy fresh produce trucked in from California. The repair bays can hold half a dozen tractor-trailers at once and often do. Ten bright red fuel tanks have "Little America" emblazoned on their sides, flanked by two emperor penguins, and a small town's worth of tidy brick buildings occupy the site, including a gift shop, restaurant, grocery mart, and cafe. It's as if a small suburban town had suddenly been plunked down into the middle of nowhere.

Little America had its origins in the mind of S. M. Covey, a sheepherder who spent a fearful winter near here in the 1890s. Covey resolved to build a way station for travelers, a place to escape the blizzards and wind. Many years later he saw a photo of Admiral Byrd's "Little America" in Antarctica and was inspired in 1932 to create his own Little America, adding over the years a restaurant, a motel, and dozens of gas pumps (65 at current count—OK, one is a propane tank). He died in the 1960s and the operation was bought by Earl Holding. Other Little America stations are flung across the West—Cheyenne, Sun Valley, Flagstaff, Salt Lake City, and even San Diego—but this is the real thing, and the only one that rates a name on the map.

Practicalities

Little America Motel, tel. (307) 875-2400 or (800) 634-2401, has immaculate rooms for $63-83 s or $69-89 d. Family rooms and suites are also available. Moderate-Expensive. The coffee shop is always open and good; you'll find reasonably priced meals both here and in the restaurant. The pastries and pies are favorites, and nearly everyone gets a 35-cent soft ice cream cone to go. But the real reason for Little America's existence is fuel to propel you on down the road. It's fitting that a place with such a patriotic name should be built to worship the internal-combustion engine.

Church Buttes

West of Little America, I-80 lies across colorful badlands country, passing a temple of a different kind—Church Buttes. Brigham Young and his Mormon pioneers held religious services under these churchlike spires in 1847. Take the Church Buttes exit from I-80 and head 5.5 miles north on a gravel road past a number of gas wells. The 75-foot-high buttes are at the intersection with Granger Rd. (County Rd. 233). The historic Mormon Pioneer Trail parallels Granger Rd. in this area and is marked by concrete posts.

Granger

The dinky town of Granger (pop. 130) is five miles north of Little America on US Hwy. 30, and contains the **Granger Stage Station.** The sandstone building was a stopping point on the Overland Trail, and housed such visitors as Mark Twain and Horace Greeley.

Seedskadee National Wildlife Refuge

The 22,000-acre Seedskadee National Wildlife Refuge is 37 miles northwest of the town of Green River on State Hwy. 372. The word comes from the Shoshone Seeds-kee-dee, meaning "River of the Prairie Chicken." The refuge stretches 35 miles along the Green River and contains marshes and riparian areas that provide outstanding waterfowl and wildlife habitat. It's one of the finest birding areas in the state; over 200 species have been sighted. Canada geese are common, along with sandhill cranes, coots, shorebirds, great blue herons, and a variety of ducks. Good fishing here, and canoeists and rafters will see quite a few moose, deer, and antelope along the banks. This is a relatively gentle float trip, though you will need to watch for boulders placed in the channel to improve fish habitat. Make sure unoccupied boats are tied to the shore since river levels may rise suddenly due to releases from Fontenelle Reservoir. The reservoir backs up behind a 139-foot earthen dam a few miles upstream from the refuge.

Refuge headquarters (tel. 307-875-2187) is two miles north from the intersection of State Hwys. 372 and 28. Be sure to pick up the brochure detailing the Seedskadee's surprisingly rich history.

Camping is not allowed within the refuge, but you can camp just upstream at the BLM-run **Weeping Rock, Tailrace,** and **Slate Creek** Campgrounds. Weeping Rock and Slate Creek Campgrounds are also used as access points to float the river.

FLAMING GORGE NATIONAL RECREATION AREA

Flaming Gorge National Recreation Area covers 94,308 acres of wild country, reaching 91 miles from the town of Green River into northeastern Utah. The region is named for the impressive canyon that Major John Wesley Powell described in his famous 1869 expedition down the river:

> *At a distance of from 1 to 20 miles a brilliant red gorge is seen, the red being surrounded by broad bands of mottled buff and gray at the summit of the cliffs, and curving down to the water's edge on the nearer slope of the mountain. This is where the river enters the mountain range—the head of the first canyon we are to explore, or rather, an introductory canyon to a series made by the river through the range. We name it Flaming Gorge.*

Flaming Gorge Reservoir backs up behind a 502-foot-high concrete arch dam, completed in 1964 and located 15 miles south of the Wyoming border. Each of the dam's three enormous generators produces 50,000 kilowatts of power. The reservoir also provides irrigation for Utah farmers and recreation for boaters, water-skiers, and anglers. Many osprey nest on the rocky pinnacles and cliffs around the edges, while below the dam is a river-runner's funhouse. The area attracts over two million visitors annually.

ACCESS AND SIGHTS

The landscape surrounding the Wyoming portion of Flaming Gorge is typical high-desert country, but once you cross into Utah, the road climbs into spectacularly rugged mountains covered with forests of juniper and pinyon, lodgepole, and ponderosa pine. This area was a favorite hideout of Butch Cassidy and other outlaws who operated out of nearby Brown's Hole. Flaming Gorge Reservoir is encircled by roads—total loop distance 160 miles—providing a pleasant overnight break from the grinding I-80 routine. The main roads don't come particularly close to the dramatic gorge itself except at the dam, but side roads provide access. A $2 day-use fee ($5 for 16 days) is charged within Flaming Gorge; get passes at visitor centers and Forest Service offices.

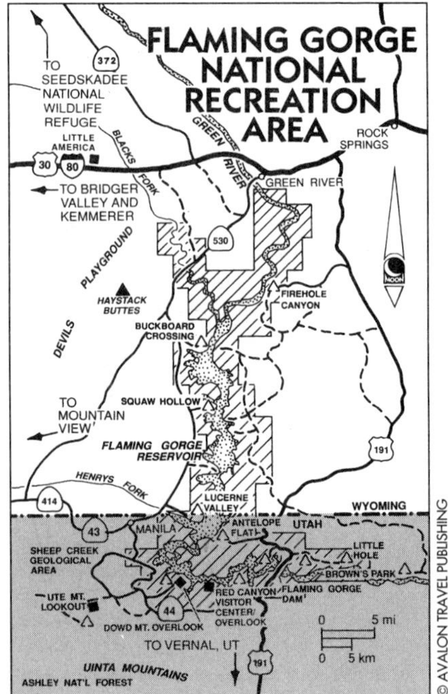

Red Canyon in Flaming Gorge National Recreation Area

One of the most interesting ways to reach Flaming Gorge is via State Hwy. 414 heading southeast from the town of Mountain View. The road climbs past colorful, eroded badlands topography—as though an enormous skeletal landscape were showing through—before emerging into wide-open spaces carpeted with grass and sage. Then the road dips down along the Henrys Fork, where cottonwoods and willows border lush green pastures. Huge piles of hay crowd the pastures. Keep your eyes open for the many historic log structures. A sign notes the location of the **Henrys Fork mountain-man rendezvous** in July of 1825, when 120 trappers and 680 Indians traded furs for supplies from the East. This was the first mountain-man rendezvous in America. Butch Cassidy and other outlaws later frequented Uncle Jack's Cabin Saloon, which stood nearby. Today, tiny **Lonetree** is the "smallest town in the world with a parking meter"—it was brought in from Denver—and **McKinnon** has a little store and a post office, but that's about it till you reach Manila, Utah. This is the real West!

Flaming Gorge National Recreation Area is administered by the U.S. Forest Service. Get information and topo maps at the Ashley National Forest offices in Manila, Utah, tel. (435) 784-3228, or Green River, Wyoming, tel. (307) 875-2871. The Manila office is open daily 8 a.m.-4:30 p.m. in the summer.

The Bureau of Reclamation and U.S. Forest Service maintain a year-round **Flaming Gorge Dam Visitor Center** atop the dam; open daily 8 a.m.-6 p.m. Memorial Day to Labor Day, and daily 9 a.m.-5 p.m. the rest of the year. **Guided dam tours** are offered daily 9 a.m.-4:30 p.m. April-Oct.; call (435) 885-3135 for specifics.

The **Red Canyon Overlook Visitor Center** is open daily 10 a.m.-4 p.m. Memorial Day to Labor Day (closed the rest of the year) and offers breathtaking canyon views. Campfire programs are given on Friday and Saturday evenings in the summer. Check at the visitor centers for a current schedule of activities.

US Hwy. 191 heads south from the Rock Springs area over the dry sage-and-juniper landscape. Take the paved turnoff to **Firehole Canyon,** where there are some interesting geological treats, including the two fingerlike projections known as North and South Chimney Rocks. Look for sheepherders tending big flocks nearby. A dirt road continues south along the canyon to the Wyoming border, or you can return to US Hwy. 191 to eventually reach the dam. Utah Hwy. 44 meets US Hwy. 191 near the dam and climbs through the scenic mountain country to the west before dropping down to the town of Manila, where it joins State Hwy. 530 heading north.

Sheep Creek Geological Area is a side loop from the southwestern end of the National Recreation Area and has all sorts of craggy rock formations. It's a good place to witness a billion years of geologic history and to watch for bighorn sheep. A road leads west from here to **Ute Mountain Fire Tower,** an old wooden lookout with grand vistas. Built in 1935 by the CCC, it is open Fri.-Mon. 9 a.m.-5 p.m. June through Labor Day.

Swett Ranch, just south of Flaming Gorge Lodge, is another historic site and a good place to see deer and elk. Open Thurs.-Mon. 10 a.m.-5 p.m. Memorial Day to Labor Day.

The Forest Service's **Flaming Gorge National Recreation Area District Office** in the town of Manila, Utah, is open Mon.-Fri. 8 a.m.-4:30 p.m. year-round; tel. (435) 784-3445. Just northeast of Manila and barely in Wyoming are a number of unusual Indian petroglyphs; ask at the Forest Service office for directions. As you continue north along the western side of Flaming Gorge along State Hwy. 530, the road passes by the **Haystack Buttes,** a series of beehive-shaped rocky mounds, followed by the barren, eroded badlands of **Devils Playground,** where sagebrush, sand, and cactus extend as far as you can see.

PRACTICALITIES

Lodges

Because of the popularity of this area, it's a good idea to reserve a week or two ahead during the summer to be assured of a motel room—or in July if you need a place on Labor Day weekend.

Four miles southwest of the dam, **Flaming Gorge Lodge,** tel. (435) 889-3773, www.fglodge.com, has motel rooms for $59 s or $65 d and one-bedroom condos with kitchens for $103 s or $109 d. Also here are a general store, cafe, and full-service restaurant. The lodge is open year-round. Moderate-Expensive.

One of the nicest places in the area is **Red Canyon Lodge,** tel. (435) 889-3759, near Red Canyon Overlook nine miles southwest of the dam. Rustic cabins with a central shower house are $35-60. For more luxurious lodging, stay in the duplex log cabins overlooking the lake. These have private baths, kitchenettes, vaulted ceilings, and covered porches; $110 for four people. Also here are horseback rides, mountain-bike rentals, boat rentals—for East Greens Lake only—a fine restaurant, and a store with limited groceries, souvenirs, and fishing tackle. Kids fish for free in a private lake on the grounds. The lodge is open daily April through late October and on weekends Jan.-March; the restaurant and store are only open in the summer. The lodge's web address is www.redcanyonlodge.com. Recommended. Inexpensive-Expensive.

Manila, Utah

The town of Manila, just three miles south of the Wyoming border on the west side of the reservoir, has several lodging places. Cheapest is **Steinaker's Motel,** tel. (435) 784-3363, where rooms are $28 s or $33 d. Stop by the Chevron station to register. Budget. **Flaming Gorge Motel and Cafe,** tel. (435) 784-3531, charges $35 s or $39 d for rooms and has a friendly eatery. Inexpensive. **Vacation Inn,** tel. (435) 784-3259 or (800) 662-4327, has condos with kitchens for $56 d or $62 for four people. The inn is very clean and nice, and it can accommodate pets, horses, and boats. Open March-October. Inexpensive.

On the west end of Manila, **Niki's Inn,** tel. (435) 784-3117, is a modern and comfortable place to stay for $42-46 s or d. Inexpensive. The restaurant here serves three meals a day and specializes in charbroiled steaks.

Get groceries and pizzas in Manila at the **Flaming Gorge Market,** tel. (435) 784-3582. For Mexican food, head to **The Mustang,** tel. (307) 874-6103, on State Hwy. 530 just across the Wyoming-Utah border; open for lunch and dinner, with live music most weekends. For more on this area and points south see *Utah Handbook,* by Bill Weir and W.C. McRae (Moon Travel Handbooks, www.moon.com).

Camping

The Forest Service maintains 25 different roadside campgrounds ($5-14) in the Flaming Gorge National Recreation Area. Showers are available at the Deer Run, Firehole, and Mustang Ridge Campgrounds. (Showers cost $2 if you aren't camping here.) Most campgrounds are on the Utah side of the border, particularly around the dam, and they typically open by mid-May and close in mid-September, though a few remain open year-round. Red Canyon Campground is a favorite, with spectacular canyon vistas. You can make reservations ($8.65 service fee) for approximately half these campgrounds; call (877) 444-6777 or visit the web at www.reserveusa.com. You can also camp for free in undeveloped parts of the Flaming Gorge National Recreation Area or in one of several boat-in camps. A **KOA Campground** in Manila, Utah, tel. (435) 784-3184 or (800) 562-3254, has tent sites for $17, RV sites for $21, and basic "kamping kabins" for $31 (these sleep four). Open mid-April to mid-October. The KOA has an array of facilities, including an outdoor pool and game room.

Hiking

Several trails are noteworthy in Flaming Gorge. **Little Hole Trail** follows the north bank of Green River from just below the dam to Little Hole, seven miles away. You may want to set up a car shuttle to save having to hike back the same way. The scenic five-mile **Canyon Rim Trail** connects Greendale Overlook with the Red Canyon Visitor Center. The trail is also accessible from the Skull Creek, Greens Lake, and Canyon Rim Campgrounds.

The steep **Dowd Mountain-Hideout Canyon Trail** drops five miles from Dowd Mountain Overlook to Hideout Boat Campground; it's open to mountain bikes. The overlook itself is four miles off the main road. A helpful brochure describing these and other trails is available from the Forest Service offices in Manila or Green River.

A cautionary note for hikers in the Flaming Gorge area: rattlesnakes are common in the desert and can be deadly. Keep your eyes and ears open at all times.

If you want to explore further, head 30 miles west of Manila to the wonderful **High Uintas Wilderness.** This area is very popular with hikers and cross-country skiers from the Evanston and Green River areas and includes Kings Peak, the highest mountain in Utah. Several access roads come in from the north, including Highway 150, a National Scenic Byway. See the Forest Service office in Evanston for details, or stop at the **Bear River Ranger Station,** tel. (435) 642-6662, located 30 miles south of Evanston and open June-October. Cabins, boat rentals, and meals are available at **Spirit Lake Lodge,** tel. (435) 880-3089; open June-October.

Mountain-biking

Excellent opportunities exist for mountain-bikers throughout the Flaming Gorge area, particularly on trails in the more rugged southern end. Pick up a brochure describing the most popular routes Forest Service offices in Manila or Green River. Rent mountain bikes from **Red Canyon Lodge,** nine miles southwest of the dam, tel. (435) 889-3759.

Fishing and Boating

Flaming Gorge Reservoir is famous for its monster fish, including a record 51-pound Mackinaw and a 33-pound world-record brown trout. In addition to these two species, anglers catch lake and rainbow trout, kokanee, and smallmouth and largemouth bass. **Flaming Gorge Fishing Derby** in mid-May is one of the biggest such events in Wyoming. Return on the **Fourth of July** for fireworks over Flaming Gorge Dam.

Three places on the reservoir rent skiffs, ski boats, fishing gear, and ski equipment: **Buckboard Marina,** tel. (307) 875-6927 or (800) 824-8155; **Cedar Springs Marina,** tel. (435) 889-3795; and **Lucerne Valley Marina,** tel. (435) 784-3483 or (888) 820-9225. Lucerne Valley also rents houseboats and jet skis. Most fishing guides operate out of Manila and Dutch John on the Utah side; see the Forest Service office in Manila for a complete listing.

Below the dam, the Green River is considered the finest fishing in Utah, with up to 20,000 trout per mile. If you have a Wyoming fishing license and plan to fish in the Utah part of Flaming Gorge—or vice versa—you'll need to purchase a special Flaming Gorge Reservoir Reciprocal Stamp for $10. Get them from the Chevron station in Manila.

River Rafting

One of the most popular summertime activities is floating the Green River below Flaming Gorge Dam. An entry station below the dam has safety information. The first several miles of the float are relatively gentle—although there are a half dozen small rapids—and can be run without a guide, but life jackets are mandatory. Float tubes are not recommended. Most folks put in just below the spillway and take out at Little Hole, seven miles downriver. Plan on three hours for the run. There's no overnight camping allowed along this stretch, but you'll find campsites below Little Hole. You can also continue on down the river to Gates of Lodore, 31 miles beyond Brown's Park. Check at the various visitor centers for details and precautions for these longer float trips. For information on lake elevation and river flow, call (800) 277-7571 or check the web at: www. uc.usbr.gov/wrg/crsp/crsp_40_fgd.txt.

Rent rafts ($50 for a six-person vessel) from **Flaming Gorge Recreation Services** in Dutch John, tel. (435) 885-3142; **Flaming Gorge Lodge,** four miles south of the dam, tel. (435) 889-3773; or **Green River Outfitters** in Dutch John, tel. (435) 885-3338. All these companies offer guided fishing trips (around $325 a day for two people) and shuttle services (from Little Hole, $45 for up to eight people). Flaming Gorge Recreation Services and Green River Outfitters also have hot showers. Note that varying releases from the dam may push the river up or down three to four feet in a matter of 15-30 minutes.

Winter Recreation

Snowplows keep the paved highway circling Flaming Gorge National Recreation Area clear throughout the winter, providing access to outstanding places for exploration. (Note, however, that the plows don't operate on weekends in Wyoming!) The Forest Service maintains **cross-country ski trails** at six areas along the Utah side of Flaming Gorge: Death Valley, Elk Park, Dowd Mountain, Canyon Rim, Lake Creek, and Swett Ranch. These vary greatly in length and difficulty; pick up a map from the Ashley National Forest offices in Manila (tel. 801-784-3228) or Green River (307-875-2871). Rent skis from **Flaming Gorge Lodge,** tel. (435) 889-3773. Snowmobiling is also very popular in the Flaming Gorge area.

Information

Get details on Flaming Gorge from the Forest Service's **Flaming Gorge National Recreation Area Ranger District Office** in Manila, Utah, tel. (435) 784-3445, www.fs.fed.us/r4/ashley. The office is open Mon.-Fri. 8 a.m.-4:30 p.m. year-round. Additional visitor centers (described above) are at Flaming Gorge Dam, Red Canyon, and in the town of Green River.

BRIDGER VALLEY

Beautiful Bridger Valley is a large splotch of green in the midst of desert country, nourished by numerous irrigation ditches channeling water from the Blacks Fork River. This was the first place in Wyoming to be farmed, having been settled by Mormons in 1853. (By the way, the various branches of the Green River—Smiths Fork, Blacks Fork, Henrys Fork, La Barge, and Hams Fork—are all named for trappers in Jedediah Smith's party of mountain men, who first spread over this country in 1824.) At the time these were considered the richest beaver-trapping waters ever discovered.

Since this is a Mormon town, July 24 has a special meaning; it was on this date in 1847 that pioneers first reached what would become Salt Lake City. Lyman's **Mormon Pioneer Days** offers a week full of activities, including a rodeo, parade, and dance. Call (307) 787-6573 for details.

Both Mountain View and Lyman are stops in early February's **Rocky Mountain Stage Stop Sled Dog Race,** an event that attracts some of the nation's best mushers with a $100,000 purse. The race begins and ends in Jackson. Call (307) 734-1163 for details, or check the website: www.wyomingstagestop.org.

LYMAN

Lyman (pop. 2,000) consists of a wide main street and not a whole lot else. Named for a Mormon leader, the town's initial settlers included many members of that religion. Lyman's pretentious town complex is the only building of note, more because of its size than for any architectural merit. Upstairs the small **Trona Mining Museum,** tel. (307) 787-6916, has exhibits on trona, how it's mined and processed, and its uses. Open Tuesday and Thursday 11 a.m.-3 p.m., Wednesday 6-8 p.m. Downstairs in the town hall is a **chamber of commerce** office, tel. (307) 787-6738; open Mon.-Thurs. 8 a.m.-1 p.m.

Stay at **Valley West Motel,** tel. (307) 787-3700 or (800) 884-7910, where comfortable rooms are $35-45 s or d. Inexpensive. **Rent-A-Flick,** tel. (307) 787-3737, has videos on one side and fast food—including thick malts and homemade pizzas—on the other. Meals are also available at **Longhorn Restaurant.** Just north of town, the **KOA Kampground,** tel. (307) 786-2762 or (800) 562-2762, has an outdoor pool. The charge is $16 for tents or $20 for RVs; open late May through September. Simple "kamping kabins" are $28 d.

Greyhound, tel. (307) 787-6192 or (800) 231-2222, www.greyhound.com, stops at Taco Time in Lyman. Wash clothes at **Valley West Laundry,** tel. (307) 786-4328. The town also has a public **swimming pool,** tel. (307) 787-6333.

MOUNTAIN VIEW

The town of Mountain View (pop. 1,200) is appropriately named; to the south, the Uintas form a rough-edged horizon. Mountain View is in the heart of farming and ranching country. There's not much to see in the town itself. You'll find good sub sandwiches, burgers, salads, and ice cream at **Pony Express,** tel. (307) 782-6782, and more quick meals at **Mt. View Drive Inn** or **Pizza Hut.** Get groceries from **Thriftway.** For entertainment . . . well, there's always the bowling alley. **Hoedown on the Smiths Fork** comes to Mountain View on Labor Day weekend with polka and country music; call (307) 782-3100 for specifics.

The closest public campground is 22 miles away along the Wyoming-Utah line. Get recreation info from the **Wasatch National Forest District Office** in Mountain View, tel. (307) 782-6555. The town also has a public **swimming pool,** tel. (307) 782-3525.

PIEDMONT

The ghost town of Piedmont is a rarely visited part of Wyoming but worth the seven-mile drive south from I-80. Take the LeRoy Rd. exit (mile 24), head west on County Rd. 128, and follow an old railroad grade south. Continue straight at the intersection and keep your eyes open for the herd of

These charcoal kilns in the ghost town of Piedmont once burned charcoal for a Utah smelter.

wild buffalo that roams this country. Established as a water and wood refueling station for the Union Pacific, Piedmont was also the scene of an 1869 incident in which 300 railroad workers blocked a train carrying UP vice president Dr. Thomas Durrant en route to ceremonies at Promontory Point. The workers demanded $200,000 (some reports put the figure at $500,000) in back pay before they finally let Durrant proceed.

Around 1869, Moses Byrne built five **charcoal kilns** near Piedmont, each 30 feet high and 30 feet across and made of stone and mortar. Wood was sealed in the ovens and slowly burned until it turned into charcoal for Utah's Pioneer smelter. Three of these massive kilns still stand, like three oversized Dolly Parton breasts emerging from the plains.

A half mile south of the kilns are a dozen buildings from the ghost town of Piedmont, abandoned when the railroad tracks were moved farther north in 1901. The last store closed in 1940. A local legend claims that Butch Cassidy buried loot from one of his bank holdups near here. Treasure hunters still search for it. The father of Calamity Jane, gunned down in a saloon, lies buried in an unmarked grave in the small Piedmont cemetery.

FORT BRIDGER

The most interesting historic site in Southwest Wyoming is Fort Bridger, located in the town of the same name. The Uinta Mountains form a majestic backdrop to the south, and the Blacks Fork River winds through. The old fort is just three miles off I-80 and provides an easy diversion from the interstate-highway blahs.

History

Fort Bridger was built in 1843 by the famed mountain man Jim Bridger and his Mexican partner, Louis Vásquez. The location—right on the Oregon and Mormon Trails—quickly made this a vital stopping point for emigrants heading west to California, Oregon, or Salt Lake City. In a letter dictated to Vásquez, Bridger remarked

> *I have established a small store with a blacksmith shop, and a supply of iron in the road of the emigrants, on Black Fork of Green River, which promises fairly. They, in coming out are generally well supplied with money, but by the time they get there, are in want of all kinds of supplies, horses, provisions, smithwork, etc. They bring ready cash from the states, and should I receive the goods ordered, will have considerable business in that way with them, and establish trade with the Indians in the neighborhood, who have a good number of beaver among them.*

The new "fort" consisted of a few crude log huts and a corral surrounded by a log stockade, while the lush riverside country provided pasturage for stock. Conflicts quickly developed between Bridger and the Mormon emigrants, who eyed his prosperous trade with envy and his good relations with the Indians as competition in their own efforts to turn them against the U.S. government. Under the pretext that Bridger was supplying weapons to Ute Indians, Brigham Young ordered Bridger arrested and sent 150 men to do the job. Bridger managed to escape, hiding in a nearby eagle nest while the men searched in vain. He finally fled with his Indian wife to Fort Laramie but lost all his merchandise, livestock, and buildings to the raiders. The Mormons then built their own base, **Fort Supply,** 12 miles south of Bridger's trading post, and established the first agricultural settlement in Wyoming. Soon Fort Supply had more than 100 log buildings surrounded by a palisade. In 1855, they purchased Fort Bridger from Vásquez—without Bridger's knowledge or consent—and added a variety of structures. When the so-called Mormon War began two years later, the Saints decided to leave nothing for the U.S. Army. They burned both forts and fled to Salt Lake City.

Jim Bridger leased his land to the army in 1858 for $600 a year. The army rebuilt the fort with room for 350 resident troops. A Pony Express station was established in 1860, followed later by an Overland Stage station. The fort was the site of the first newspaper published in Wyoming (1863) and also served as a base for Chief Washakie's band of Shoshone Indians until a treaty signed here in 1868 established the Wind River Reservation. Fort Bridger was abandoned by the military in 1890, and many of its buildings were sold at auction. Thirty years later, the state of Wyoming bought the site and has since restored or reconstructed many of the structures.

Sights

Fort Bridger, tel. (307) 782-3842, is open daily 9 a.m.-5:30 p.m. May-Sept. and Sat.-Sun. 8:30 a.m.-4:30 p.m. in April and October; closed Nov.-March. Day-use costs $2 for nonresidents, $1 for Wyoming residents; free for youths under 18. A number of buildings are open to the public during the summer, but only the museum is open the rest of the year. In June, July, and August the staff dresses in 1880s costumes and provides living-history demonstrations and historical information. Various activities take place throughout the year, including a mountain-man rendezvous (see below) and Wednesday evening historical talks in the summer. In August, take the special moonlight tour ($5), on which you'll meet characters from the past; call several months ahead to book this popular tour.

The attractive grounds are sprinkled with aspen and cottonwood trees and beautifully restored buildings. First stop is the **museum and visitor center,** housed in the enlisted-men's barracks. Inside you'll gain an excellent glimpse into the past with a model of the old fort, displays of army uniforms and weapons, Indian artifacts—including a bowl made from the hump of a buffalo—a chuck wagon, papoose board, and even a working telegraph on which to practice your Morse code. Be sure to look for Jim Bridger's old powder horn, vest, and other items, including a photo of a "young" Jim Bridger created by computerized reverse aging. Visitors can watch a slide show on the fort's history.

The **Bridger-Vásquez Trading Co.** stands in one corner of the fort; it's open the same hours as the museum May-Sept. but closed Oct.-April. This replica of Bridger's original trading post is run by Dick and Sandy Gregory, who will be happy to talk about the trapper's life or to sell trade beads, furs, Indian sweetgrass, clothing, and even bull-scrotum bags. Be sure to ask for demonstrations of the fire steels.

Just south of the museum is a rock wall built by Mormons when they controlled the fort. Other buildings include a small commissary and two guardhouses. On the east side of the fort is the antique-filled **commanding officer's quarters,** built in 1884. Aspen trees line the alleyway connecting this building with the **log officer's quarters,** built in 1858. Look inside for the section from an aspen tree carved by Buffalo Bill Cody. On the south side of the fort is a century-old ranch home—**Goodrick House**—that was moved here and furnished with antiques.

The **post sutler's complex** contains several furnished buildings including Wyoming's oldest schoolhouse (1860), the post trader's store, and five other structures. Not far away is the fenced-in grave of a local hero—Thornburgh the dog, who once saved a drowning boy and later warned the post of an Indian attack. A small human cemetery is near the commanding officer's quarters. Ongoing archaeological digs take place each July, and talks are given on Wednesday evenings. A display case in the museum houses items found in the dig, including buttons, trade beads, and other items.

Practicalities

The town of Fort Bridger contains **Wagon Wheel Motel,** tel. (307) 782-6361, where rooms are $25-45 s or $30-50 d. Budget-Inexpensive. You can park RVs here for $18, but you'll find no showers or tent spaces. A restaurant is on the premises, or get limited groceries at **Fort Bridger Cash Store,** tel. (307) 782-6744. **Jim Bridger Trading Post,** tel. (307) 782-6115, sells souvenirs, some groceries, and—if you're in the market—washing machines. **Fort Bridger RV Camp,** tel. (307) 782-3150 or (800) 578-6535, has RV hookups or tent spaces for $16. Open April-October.

Fort Bridger Rendezvous

Each Labor Day weekend the largest modern-day mountain-man rendezvous in Wyoming comes to Fort Bridger. This is one of Wyoming's most enjoyable events, so don't miss it! In addition, there's a big rodeo the same weekend in Evanston, just 30 miles to the west. During the rendezvous, tents and tepees sprawl across the fort grounds, and hundreds of costumed revelers join in the celebration. Trader's row offers 1840s-style crafts and trade items, including beads, furs, and tomahawks. Participants take part in cannon shoots, muzzle-loading contests, Indian dancing, Dutch-oven cooking, tomahawk throwing, and acoustic music. Great cooked-over-the-fire food too. Be sure to attend performances of *A Ballad of the West,* written by a great grandnephew of Jim Bridger. The rendezvous attracts 400 buckskinners, squaws, hunters, and pilgrims, along with thousands of spectators.

Other summer events at Fort Bridger include a parade, a rodeo, and a town dance on the **Fourth of July,** and **moonlight tours** of the fort grounds in August; call (307) 782-3842 for reservations.

EVANSTON

West of Fort Bridger, I-80 begins a lengthy climb into the hills, leaving the desert behind as it heads toward the Utah border. The attractive, friendly town of Evanston (pop. 13,000) lies just six miles from Utah and only 80 miles from Salt Lake City. Evanston's economy depends upon gas and oil wells, tourists, ranching, and a state hospital. On the outskirts of Evanston, fireworks stands crowd the freeway off-ramps, waiting to lure Utahans who create weekend traffic jams in pursuit of booze, bars, betting, and pornography.

Evanston is a blend of the old and new; you'll even find a New Agey vegetarian cafe next to an old-time cowboy boot and saddle shop. Given its proximity to Salt Lake City, the 2002 Winter Olympics are expected to be a boon for the local economy. Keep your eyes open for members of the famous **Jamaica Bobsleigh Team** who train here (they use the English term bobsleigh for what Americans call bobsleds). Evanston plans to build a push-start facility for bobsleds, and the town supports the Jamaican team with housing, transportation, and jobs. Order a pizza in the winter, and they just may be the ones doing the delivery!

HISTORY

As the transcontinental railroad's construction crews raced across Wyoming in 1868, the settlement of Evanston was established as the last division point before the Wasatch Range. The town received its name from the railroad's surveyor, James A. Evans. In 1886, the territorial legislature offered Uinta County representatives the choice of either a university or an insane asylum. They chose the asylum. By the following year, Evanston had 1,500 people, many of whom worked at the Union Pacific car and machine shops, at an ice plant, or on the tracks. Others logged railroad ties in the mountains or raised sheep and cattle. Rich deposits of coal were discovered four miles north of Evanston, and several mines soon opened, creating the town of **Almy.** In 1869, hundreds of Chinese miners were hired as strikebreakers at the mines, creating tensions that would later erupt into race riots and force the temporary abandonment of Evanston's Chinatown. The Almy mines became notorious for deadly methane-

JIM BRIDGER

Legendary figures fill the history of the West, but Jim Bridger ranks as the uncrowned king of the mountain men. Like many other 19th-century frontiersmen, Bridger never learned to read or write, but his deep knowledge of the mountains and Indians gained him the name "Old Gabe"—his skills were said to rival those of the angel Gabriel. Jim Bridger has 21 different Wyoming places named for him—more than any other individual.

Bridger was born in 1804 in Virginia and later moved with his family to Missouri. When both his parents died, he was sent off to apprentice with a blacksmith, but the wild country beckoned, and when William Ashley advertised for "Enterprising Young Men" to go into the Rockies to trap beaver, Bridger quickly joined up. He was on the first keelboat that headed out in 1822 and wintered that year on the Bear River of southern Idaho. When men began speculating on where the Bear River led, Bridger volunteered to find out, thus becoming the first white man to discover the Great Salt Lake. Bridger took any challenge in stride. When Ashley needed a volunteer to test the possibility of running furs down the Bighorn River, Bridger stepped forward. He nearly died taking his log raft through the wild waters of Bighorn Canyon, but the adventure added to his growing reputation.

Bridger entered the fur trading business in 1830 when he and four others bought the Rocky Mountain Fur Company from Ashley. They in turn sold the business to William Sublette five years later. Bridger continued to lead trapping parties until the last rendezvous in 1840, after which he turned his attention to the growing tide of emigrants heading west to California and Oregon. Together with partner Louis Vásquez, Bridger built a trading post (Fort Bridger) along the Blacks Fork of the Green River. He later served as a scout for the U.S. Army in the Powder River Basin, although his sage advice was often ignored.

BUFFALO BILL HISTORICAL SOCIETY

Like many other mountain men, Jim Bridger had several wives. His first was a white Mormon woman, but when Jim refused to join her religion they separated. He later married three different Indian women, none of whom spoke English. The first two died early but the last one—daughter of the great Shoshone Chief Washakie—returned to Missouri with him.

Bridger's knowledge of sign language was legendary; he once kept an audience of Sioux and Cheyenne Indians in rapt attention for over an hour as he signed a lengthy adventure. In one of his yarns, told to a naive British army captain, Bridger described how the Indians had him trapped in a canyon with his only escape up a 200-foot waterfall. When the captain insisted upon discovering how he escaped this predicament, Bridger wryly went on, "Oh bless your soul, Captain, we never did get out. The Indians killed us right there!" Partly because of such yarns, few believed Bridger's true accounts of the geysers and hot springs he had found in Yellowstone or of the stream that split along the Continental Divide, with waters flowing in both directions. Bridger died on his Missouri farm in 1881 at the age of 77.

gas explosions. At least 60 whites and uncounted Chinese miners were killed in blasts in 1881, 1886, and 1895. The mines closed in 1906, leaving many of the fires unextinguished; you can still see evidence of the smoldering fires. Many of the old mine buildings still stand at the townsite, but the town itself is long since abandoned.

The Overthrust Belt

Evanston lies at the center of the energy-rich Overthrust Belt, which extends from Canada to Mexico. This 40-mile-wide uplift was formed when two land masses smashed together, thrusting the western portion atop the eastern half and creating folds that trapped oil and gas. It was long believed to contain rich energy deposits, but hundreds of dry holes were drilled before one finally hit home. In 1976, the Yellow Creek Oil Field was discovered, producing both oil and natural gas and unleashing a boomtown atmosphere. Many more oil and gas fields have been discovered since then. Although Uinta County is Wyoming's smallest, it's the largest in terms of natural-gas production; more than a third of the state's output comes from here.

SIGHTS

Depot Square

A major renovation project in downtown Evanston has created an attractive central area with a fountain and open grassy lawns for relaxing. The focal point is the old **Evanston Depot.** Built in 1900, it was one of the finest along the line and had separate waiting rooms for men and women. A 1944 Union Pacific dining car and caboose stand outside the depot, and the nearby **Beeman-Cashin Implement Depot** is used for dances and community activities. Built around 1886 and restored a century later, this unique wooden structure has no supporting posts.

Located in the old town library (which also houses the visitor center), the **Uinta County Museum,** tel. (307) 789-2757, is open Mon.-Fri. 9 a.m.-5 p.m. year-round, plus Sat.-Sun. 10 a.m.-4 p.m. during the summer. No charge. Of interest here are various Chinese items; including opium pipes, an impressive turn-of-the-20th-century dragon, a Buddha figure, a gong, and lanterns. The museum also houses hundreds of historic photos and various Indian artifacts. While here, pick up a walking-tour brochure of Evanston that details many of the older buildings in town. Outside the museum are a number of old wagons.

Joss House

Early in this century, Evanston had a prominent Chinatown located along the north side of the tracks. Life centered around the Joss House, a Taoist temple built in 1894 and one of just three in the nation (the others were in San Francisco and New York). Thousands of pilgrims came from hundreds of miles away to worship. After the Chinese workers returned to their homeland, the building was destroyed in a suspicious 1922 fire that leveled much of Chinatown. A replica of the Joss House was completed in 1990 and furnished with historic photos, an 1874 Chinese signboard, decorative panels from the original Joss House, and other items. Also here are pottery, coins, and other artifacts found during archaeological digs at the Chinatown site. The dig continues each July; ask here for details. Be sure to see the video on Mormon Charlie and China Mary, the only Chinese who remained after 1922. The few Chinese-Americans in Evanston today moved here more recently. The Joss House, tel. (307) 789-1472, is open daily 7 a.m.-7 p.m. mid-May through September; ask at the museum for access the rest of the year.

Bear River State Park

This 300-acre park surrounds the Bear River Information Center just south of Evanston (I-80 at exit 6). The Bear River—just a creek here—flows northward, eventually draining into Great Salt Lake. At 400 miles in length, it's the largest river in the Western Hemisphere that doesn't reach the ocean.

There's no camping, but Bear River State Park has three miles of trails (one mile is paved) for hiking and biking, and it connects with the paved Bear Parkway, which extends westward for 1.5 miles along the river. The park is also home to a small herd of **bison and elk.** In the winter, eight km of groomed cross-country ski trails are maintained within the park, and a small ice rink is cleared on the ponds. Call (307) 789-6547 for park information.

ACCOMMODATIONS AND CAMPING

Motels

You'll find quite a few inexpensive places to stay in Evanston. Reserve ahead on summer weekends to be sure of having a place, and on Labor Day you'll need to reserve a month in advance. In the winter months, the town provides inexpensive lodging opportunities for skiers from Park City, Utah, just 50 miles away. Accommodations are listed below from least to most expensive. Add a seven percent tax to these rates.

Budget: Stay at the comfortable **Vagabond Motel,** 230 Bear River Dr., tel. (307) 789-2902 or (800) 789-2902, for $25 s or $30 d.

A good place to hitch your wagon for the night is **Weston Plaza (Lamplighter),** 1983 Harrison Dr., tel. (307) 789-0783 or (800) 255-9840. Rates are $30 s or $35 d, including use of an indoor pool and jacuzzi. A light breakfast is available in the morning.

Inexpensive: Economy Inn, 1724 Harrison Dr., tel. (307) 789-9610, charges $33 s or $43-46 d.

Prairie Inn, 264 Bear River Dr., tel. (307) 789-2920, is a good place with clean rooms for $35 s or $43-48 d, including a continental breakfast.

At **Motel 6,** 261 Bear River Dr., tel. (307) 789-0791 or (800) 466-8356, rooms cost $37 s or $42 d, including access to the heated outdoor pool and jacuzzi. You'll find the same prices at **Super 8 Motel,** 70 Bear River Dr., tel. (307) 789-7510 or (800) 800-8000; some rooms contain fridges.

Inexpensive-Moderate: Weston Super Budget Inn, 1936 Harrison Dr., tel. (307) 789-2810 or (800) 255-9840, has rooms for $45-66 s or $50-71 d. An outdoor pool is on the premises, and guests also have access to the jacuzzi at the Weston Plaza (across the street).

Moderate-Expensive: Days Inn, 339 Wasatch Rd., tel. (307) 789-2220 or (800) 357-2220, has lodging for $65-80 s or $70-90 d, including a jacuzzi, sauna, and continental breakfast. Kitchenettes cost $15 more, and suites are also available. Moderate-Expensive.

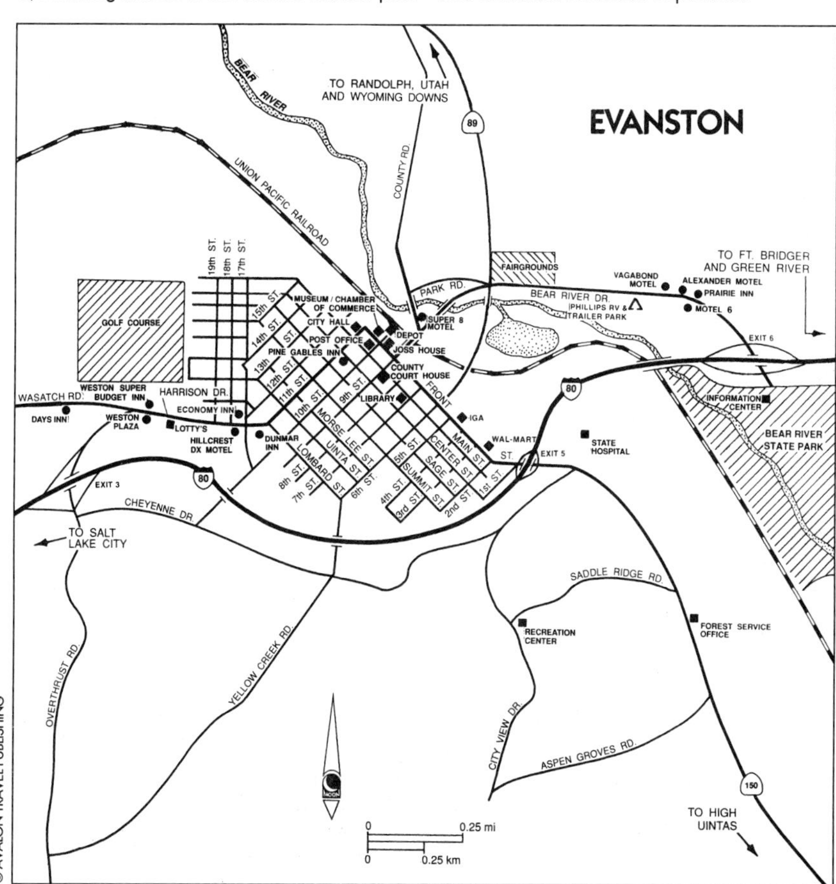

Best Western Dunmar Inn, 1019 Lombard, tel. (307) 789-3770 or (800) 654-6509, is one of the nicest places in Evanston, with an outdoor pool and exercise facility, plus a popular restaurant and lounge. Rates are $69-89 s or $79-109 d.

Motels with basic accommodations (see rooms first) include **Hillcrest DX Motel,** 1725 Harrison Dr., tel. (307) 789-1111, and **Alexander Motel,** 248 Bear River Dr., tel. (307) 789-2346.

Bed and Breakfast

Evanston's homiest spot is **Pine Gables Inn B&B,** 1049 Center St., tel. (307) 789-2069 or (800) 789-2069, built in 1883 and used as a European-style lodging place during the 1920s and '30s. The house was restored in 1981, furnished with antiques, and reopened as a delightful bed and breakfast. Four guest rooms are available, all with private baths. Rates are $45-50 s or $55-70 d, including a full breakfast. The web address is www.cruising-america.com/pinegables. Inexpensive-Moderate.

Camping

The nearest public campgrounds are in the Uinta Mountains, 30 miles to the south. **Phillips RV Trailer Park,** 225 Bear River Dr., tel. (307) 789-3805 or (800) 349-3805, charges $16 for tents or $18 for RVs. It's open April-Oct. and has shaded sites.

FOOD

Meet Evanston cops over coffee and doughnuts at **Main Street Deli,** 1025 Main St., tel. (307) 789-1599. The deli also offers breakfast bargains, along with lunchtime soup, sandwiches, and cornbread.

Main St. Artisans Cafe and Gallery, 927 Main St., tel. (307) 789-4991, is an earthy spot with pastries, salads, vegetarian and vegan sandwiches, and very good espresso. The back room contains a gallery displaying the works of local artisans. Just up the street on the corner of 10th and Main is **City Drug,** tel. (307) 789-4000, home to an old-time soda fountain.

Michael's Bar & Grill, 1011 Front St., tel. (307) 789-1088, doesn't look that inviting outside, but it's actually a fine lunch and dinner spot that fills with local business folks over the noon hour. Sandwiches, burgers, and healthy salads round out the menu.

Legal Tender Dining Room in the Dunmar Inn, 1601 Harrison Dr., tel. (307) 789-3770, is an attractive establishment with lunch specials and reasonably priced steak-house fare.

The atmosphere is rustic in the family-friendly **Last Outpost,** 205 Bear River Dr., tel. (307) 789-3322, where the buffalo burgers and steaks are the best in town. Everything is made from scratch, and Greek food is served on Tuesday nights.

Lotty's Family Restaurant, 1925 Harrison Dr., tel. (307) 789-9660, has a big salad bar and buffet with all-you-can-stuff-in prime rib Fri.-Sun. nights.

New Garden Cafe, 933 Front, tel. (307) 789-2882, offers very reasonably priced Chinese and American cooking, but you might want to peek in the kitchen before deciding whether to eat here.

Don Pedro's Family Mexican Restaurant, 909 Front St., tel. (307) 789-2944, is the place to find outstanding and authentic Mexican fare. The restaurant has proven so popular that Don Pedro has now opened restaurants in four other Wyoming and Utah towns.

Best pizza around is at **Pizza Hut,** 134 Yellow Creek Rd., tel. (307) 789-1372. Be assured that Evanston also has most of the fast-food chains, including Subway, Little Caesars, Wendy's, Arby's, Domino's, KFC, Taco John's, Burger King, and McD's. **Hamblin Park,** next to the fairgrounds on Bear River Drive, is a pleasant place to enjoy a picnic lunch beneath tall cottonwood trees. Get groceries from the **IGA Super-Center,** 524 Front St., tel. (307) 789-6788, or **Smith's,** 70 Yellow Creek Rd. N, tel. (307) 789-0532.

OTHER PRACTICALITIES

Entertainment

Evanston is jam-packed with liquor stores and lounges to quench the parched throats of Utahans who cross the border in droves. **Legal Tender Lounge** at Dunmar Inn, 1019 Lombard, tel. (307) 789-3770, has two bars—an upstairs disco and a downstairs saloon where you can dance to country-and-western bands on weekends—and draws mainly a young crowd. For rock tunes, try **Pete's Rock-N-Rye Club,** a long-time bar east of town on U.S. Hwy. 30, tel. (307) 789-2135. Or just hang out in the relaxing atmosphere of **Kate's Bar,** 936 Main, tel. (307) 789-7662.

Watch movies at **Evanston Valley Cinema,** 45 Aspen Grove Dr. E, tel. (307) 789-0522 or **Strand Theatre,** 1028 Main, tel. (307) 789-2974.

Events

Evanston is one of 12 stops in early February's **Rocky Mountain Stage Stop Sled Dog Race,** an event that attracts some of the nation's best mushers with the inducement of a $100,000 purse. The race begins and ends in Jackson. Call (307) 734-1163 for details, or check the website: www.wyomingstagestop.org.

One of the most unusual Evanston events is **Chinese New Year,** featuring a parade, fireworks, rickshaw races, and, of course, the dragon. With so few Chinese-Americans in Evanston today, many of the performers are of other ancestry. On summer weekends, **Wyoming Downs Racetrack,** 12 miles north of Evanston on State Hwy. 89, tel. (307) 789-0511 or (800) 842-8722, has horse racing with pari-mutuel betting. This is particularly popular with folks from Salt Lake, since horse racing is illegal in Utah. At the Western Super Budget Inn, race enthusiasts can also watch and wager off-track bets on races as far away as California. The **Evanston Rodeo Series** includes amateur rodeo events several times a month throughout the summer; call (307) 789-5511 for a schedule.

Mid-June brings the spicy **Evanston Chili Cook-Off,** to the fairgrounds. Ads proclaim "It's a gas!" In late June, cyclists compete in the **High Uintas Classic Bike Race,** which traverses the Uinta Mountains in a spectacular 80-mile route; cyclists must climb over a 12,000-foot pass along the way. More cycling in mid-August, when mountain-bikers compete in the **Wolverine Ridge XC Race** on trails south of town.

Evanston's **Uinta County Fair** the first week of August includes a greased-pig contest, 4-H animal judging, rodeos, carnival rides, concerts, and even pedal-power tractor pulls. The low-key **Bear River Rendezvous** takes place at Bear River State Park on the weekend before Labor Day, attracting mountain men and women who re-create the spirit of the West.

Evanston's main event is, predictably, the annual rodeo, here known as **Cowboy Days.** Labor Day weekend festivities pack all the motels in town as folks come from surrounding states to watch professional cowboys show their stuff at "the biggest little rodeo in the world." The three-day event also includes musical entertainment, dances, an arts-and-crafts fair, a parade, a pancake breakfast, a spaghetti dinner, and clowns. Labor Day is also the weekend for the very popular Fort Bridger Rendezvous, just 30 miles east at historic Fort Bridger.

Recreation

See Bear River State Park above for outdoor adventures on the edge of Evanston. The excellent **Evanston Recreation Center,** 275 Saddle Ridge Rd., tel. (307) 789-1770, includes a swimming pool, gyms, racquetball courts, a weight room, and a hot tub.

Purple Sage Golf Course, on Country Club Dr., tel. (307) 789-2383, is a nine-hole public course. **Fireside Lanes,** 2631 Hwy. 150 S, tel. (307) 789-6716, is the local bowling alley.

Cross-country skiers head to groomed trails at **Deadhorse Ski Trail,** 18 miles south of Evanston, and **Lily Lake Touring Area,** 30 miles south in the Uintas. Lily Lake also has three furnished yurts for overnight stays ($35 for up to eight people); call (307) 789-1770 for details, or see the website: www.evanstonwy.com/brora.

City Slickers of Wyoming, tel. (307) 789-3378, leads a variety of horseback and 4WD adventures, including cattle drives and historic pioneer trips.

Shopping

The old Federal Building (built in 1915), on the corner of 10th and Center Sts., is home to several shops, including an antique store, T-shirt shop, and the **Glass Cat,** tel. (307) 783-7901, where you'll find stained-glass pieces with a cat motif. Another classic structure, the Blyth & Fargo Building at 927 Main St., houses **Quilt Trappings,** tel. (307) 789-1675, a good place to find quality quilts and fabric.

Get new and used books, along with magazines and music, from **Bear River Books,** 1008 Main, tel. (307) 789-6465 or (888) 641-2665. Wash clothes at **Sunfresh Laundro,** 116 Yellow Creek Rd., tel. (307) 789-1163. **Rocky Mtn.**

Lodgepole Furniture Co., 1049 Main St., tel. (307) 789-9042 or (800) 827-9042, creates rustic and functional chairs, benches, beds, and other furnishings.

Sports World, inside the IGA at 524 Front St., tel. (307) 789-6788, sells outdoor gear, and its walls are lined with big-game mounts. Rent mountain bikes, ATVs, float tubes, pontoon boats, rollerblades, and other items from **The Bear,** 163 Bear River Dr., tel. (307) 789-1409.

Information and Services

Evanston has two places to go for information. If you're entering the state from the west, stop at **Bear River Information Center,** I-80 exit 6, tel. (307) 789-6540. The center has a wealth of statewide information, a pleasant picnic area, and short trails. It's open daily 8 a.m.-5 p.m. year-round. The info center lies within Bear River State Park (see above).

The **Evanston Chamber of Commerce,** 36 10th St., tel. (307) 783-0370 or (800) 328-9708, is housed in the county museum and provides more local info. Hours are Mon.-Fri. 9 a.m.-5 p.m. Learn more about the area at www.etown-chamber.com.

Find the **Uinta County Library** at 701 Main, tel. (307) 789-2770.

High Uinta Mountains

The **Evanston Ranger District,** 1565 Hwy. 150 S, tel. (307) 789-3194, has maps of Wasatch National Forest, but only a tiny corner of the forest comes into Wyoming. The **High Uintas Wilderness** is 30 miles south of Evanston via Mirror Lake Highway/Wyoming 150 (a National Scenic Byway). This wilderness area is very popular with hikers and cross-country skiers from the Evanston and Green River areas and includes Kings Peak, the tallest mountain in Utah. Get additional info from the **Bear River Ranger Station,** tel. (435) 642-6662, 30 miles south of Evanston inside Utah; open June-October. Recreation access fees are charged on the Wasatch: $3 per day per car, or $25 for an annual pass.

Bear River Lodge, tel. (800) 559-1121, www.bearriverlodge.com, has cabins, outdoor jacuzzis, a general store, snowmobile and ATV rentals, and gas. It's in Utah 32 miles south of Evanston. See *Utah Handbook* by Bill Weir and W.C. McRae (Moon Travel Handbooks, www.moon.com) for details on the beautiful Mirror Lake Highway.

Transportation

Greyhound, tel. (307) 789-2810 or (800) 231-2222, www.greyhound.com, runs buses both east and west on I-80 and stops at the Weston Super Budget Inn, 1936 Harrison Drive.

Wind River Transportation Authority (WRTA), tel. (307) 856-7118 or (800) 439-7118, provides on-demand service in western and southwestern Wyoming. You can call them for transportation to other Wyoming towns, including Pinedale, Dubois, Jackson, Lander, Riverton, and Rock Springs.

Rent cars from **Evanston Motor Co.,** 2000 Hwy. 30 W, tel. (307) 789-3145. **F&M Taxi,** tel. (307) 799-7306, will take you around town, and **Star West Aviation,** tel. (307) 789-2256, offers charter service from the Evanston airport.

NORTH TO KEMMERER

North of Evanston, US Hwy. 189 follows a long valley most of the way to Kemmerer. A hogback ridge hems you in to the east. Stop for a look back at the ragged snow-topped Uintas that form a southern horizon line. Near the junction with State Hwy. 412 (36 miles up) is the small **Cumberland** cemetery, enclosed within a white picket fence. Turn down State Hwy. 412 to see what's left of the ghost town of Cumberland. This was a booming coal-mining town between 1920 and 1935, with four underground mines going at once. Today all that remains are the sandstone Ziller ranch buildings—the old whorehouse and saloon—and the cemetery. The buildings are not open to the public.

KEMMERER

The twin towns of Kemmerer (pop. 3,000) and Diamondville (pop. 900) are at the center of the coal industry in southwestern Wyoming. Drive west of town and you'll even pass coal seams in the road cutbank. Kemmerer is the Lincoln County seat and is located on the Hams Fork River; Diamondville lies just a few yards south. The surrounding country is dotted with mining and energy plants of various types. P&M Coal Mine—the nation's largest strip mine—is several miles south, and a nearby Exxon plant is the world's largest manufacturer of helium and the state's largest consumer of electricity. Another major employer is the FMC coke plant, which provides metallurgical coke for a phosphorous plant in Pocatello, Idaho. It, too, is the largest such operation in the world. Natural gas, oil, and sulfur are also very important locally, as are cattle and sheep ranching. Given this setting it should come as no surprise that this is a pickup-truck town. Either that or you better drive a Mustang with growling glaspak mufflers.

HISTORY

Coal Mining

Explorer John C. Frémont first chanced upon coal here in 1843, but it wasn't until 1881 that the Union Pacific opened the first underground mine. Things really began to boom when Patrick J. Quealy and his partner Mahlon S. Kemmerer established the Kemmerer Coal Company. Hundreds of men died in mine accidents; the worst was a 1923 explosion that killed 99 miners, mostly emigrants. The operation moved aboveground in 1950, and the Kemmerer mine became the Pittsburg & Midway Coal Company, now a subsidiary of Chevron. (As of this writing, however, Chevron was attempting to sell it.) Located six miles south of Kemmerer along US Hwy. 189, P&M is America's largest (physically, but not in terms of production) open-pit coal mine, reaching 800 feet deep and producing nearly five million tons per year. Two-thirds of the coal is used at Pacific Power's adjacent Naughton Plant, which produces 710 megawatts of power. The mine—the longest continuously operating mine in Wyoming—and the power plant are the largest employers in the region. Call (307) 828-2200 for tour information.

Moonshine and Shady Ladies

During the 1920s, Kemmerer became a national center for bootlegging and a major supplier for Chicago. Kemmerer "moon" was a favorite of speakeasies, and winemakers ordered grapes by the trainload. A 1931 bust near Kemmerer found 24,000 gallons of liquor. All this ended when Prohibition was repealed in 1933.

With all the coal miners, the ratio of men to women in Kemmerer was nearly 50 to one, prime pickings for the world's oldest profession. Into these conditions stepped Madam Isabelle Burns, fresh off the train from Salt Lake City with considerable experience in the "sporting" trade. She arrived in 1896 looking for somewhere to invest the $28,500 inheritance from her husband's suicide. With $5,000 in cash she bought a dance hall with enough convenient side rooms to house 50 prostitutes. In a short while, the Green House was a roaring success, allowing Madam Isabelle to build the most elegant house then in town—still standing at 301 Ruby Street. Because of the demand for "evening wear," Kemmerer's shoe store reportedly sold more high-heeled satin slippers than any shop west of the Mississippi. A nude painting of one of the Green House ladies with her brother (and lover) is now in the Golden Nugget Bar in Las Vegas. Madam Isabelle quit the business in 1926, left town, and married a New Orleans physician. Her business went on in fresh hands.

Several deaths took place at the Green House, leading to a grand conflagration when a man whose sons had been murdered there burned one of the women to death, igniting the building in the process and leaving it a pile of ashes. After the 1926 fire, it was replaced by the Southern Hotel. A newly elected sheriff finally shut things down in 1967, despite pleas from locals that the loss of all the Utah and Idaho clients would hurt business in town. For more on this tantalizing bit of history, see Ray Essman's *Only Count the Sunny Hours* (Winona, MN: Apollo Books).

SIGHTS

James Cash Penney House

The most unusual sights in Kemmerer relate to James Cash Penney, founder of the JCPenney chain. Penney moved to Kemmerer in 1902 from Evanston to open a dry goods store in the booming mining town, and his Golden Rule Store quickly achieved a reputation for quality and honesty. By 1912 there were 34 Golden Rule stores; the following year their name was changed to JCPenney, and the rest is history. See the special topic on James Cash Penney for more on the founder of this national department store chain. The company homepage (www.jcpenney.com) has more on JCPenney history.

The James Cash Penney House is a six-room cottage where Penney and his family lived between 1903 and 1909. The house is right behind the chamber of commerce office downtown and is open summers Mon.-Sat. 9 a.m.-6 p.m. and Sunday 11 a.m.-4 p.m. The JCPenney "mother store" is also in Kemmerer, just a few doors up the street (JC Penney Dr. of course). If the home is closed, ask at the store for access. No admission charge. Guides are ready to show you around or put on a video about the company's history. One room houses family and JCPenney company memorabilia.

Museum

Kemmerer's **Fossil Country Frontier Museum,** 400 Pine Ave., tel. (307) 877-6551, is open Mon.-Fri. 9 a.m.-5 p.m. in summer and Mon.-Sat. 10 a.m.-4 p.m. the rest of the year; no admission charge. It contains a variety of art, mining, and archaeological exhibits, a walk-through

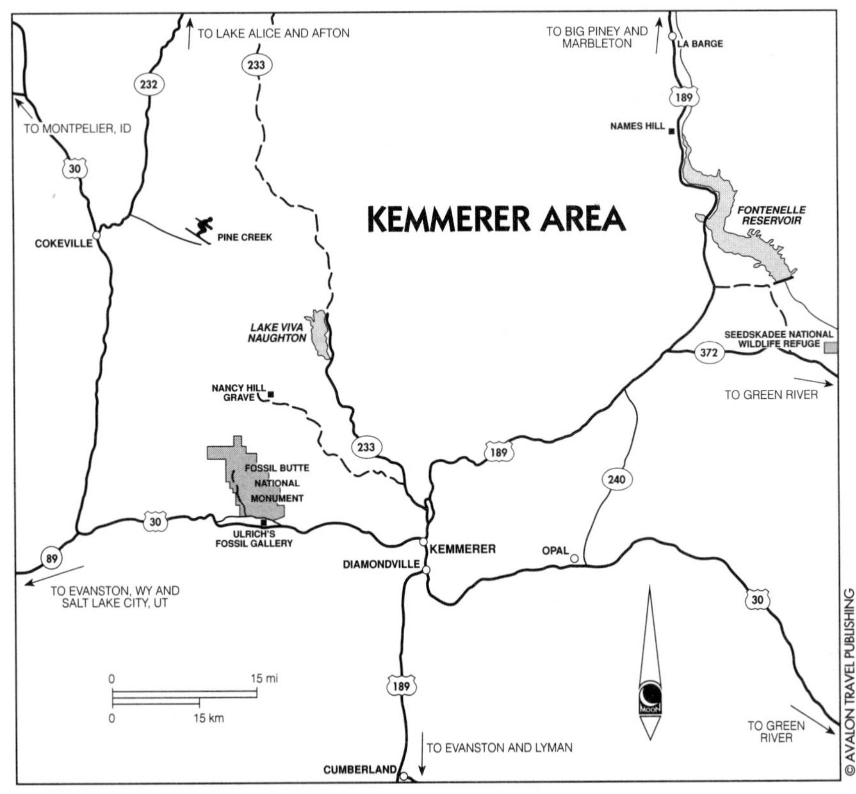

JAMES CASH PENNEY

One of America's best-known retail chains, JCPenney, had its start in Kemmerer, Wyoming, in 1902. The founder was James Cash Penney, a man whose life exemplified the proverbial rags-to-riches story. Born in 1875 to a devout Missouri family, Penney grew up in poverty. His father was a farmer and Baptist minister who, together with his mother—a Southern belle—instilled in the young man a Christian ethical base that emphasized the Golden Rule and self-reliance.

It didn't take long for Penney's resourcefulness to reveal itself. At age eight he needed new shoes and used his meager savings to buy young pigs that he later sold for a profit. After high school he took a job in a local dry goods store where he learned the trade, then he moved to Colorado to open a butcher shop. The shop failed when Penney refused to continue paying bribes (in the form of a bottle of bourbon per week) to his biggest account, a local hotel.

The Golden Rule Stores

J.C. Penney's big break came in 1898 when he began work with a small chain called the Golden Rule Stores. The owners quickly recognized the skills in this ambitious young man and offered Penney a third interest in any new stores he would open. With $500 in savings and $1,500 in borrowed money, Penney quickly seized the chance, opening a dry goods store in Kemmerer on April 14, 1902. It wasn't much, just a one-room building away from the center of town and furnished with makeshift fixtures. But Penney was shrewd enough to recognize what people wanted: fair prices that were the same no matter who walked in the store, and a cash-only operation; he was opposed to credit since it was often used by unscrupulous merchants to create a class of workers who were never able to pay off their bills. The store proved an immediate hit, and within a year he had opened another store in Rock Springs, followed by a third in Cumberland, Wyoming, in 1904.

Three years later his partners sold the entire operation to Penney, and under his guidance the company took off, quickly making him a millionaire. By the end of 1912 he was the head of a chain of 34 Golden Rule stores, and the following year the name was changed to the J.C. Penney Company. It soon became one of the fastest-growing national retail chains. By 1920, the company had 197 stores from coast to coast, and it continued to open stores through the next decade at the blistering pace of one new store every three days. By 1929, 1,400 Penney stores were scattered across the country. The bubble burst with the stock market crash of 1929, and Penney's financial empire collapsed around him. It took decades for Penney to recover the wealth he had lost so suddenly.

Later Years

Penney was a devoted family man, but his first two wives died young, the first in 1910 from pneumonia, and the second in 1924. He married a third time and remained married till his death in 1971. The loss of his wives led Penney to philanthropy and charitable projects as a way to ease his own pain by helping others. Even today, his charitable foundations continue to fund community renewal, world peace, and environmental efforts.

In later years, Penney turned his attention to farming and developed an international reputation for his champion cattle, especially the Guernseys that became the basis for another company he helped found, Foremost Dairies.

Penney remained very active far beyond when most people retire. He never forgot a name or face, and even at the age of 85 he kept up a grueling schedule of store visits, conventions, and speaking engagements. He only stopped taking the city bus to work in his 90s, and he was still coming to work within a few months of his death at the age of 95. Today the stores he founded have moved beyond the religious devotion personified in James Cash Penney, but they still bear his name and a reputation for quality merchandise. The town of Kemmerer contains both the JCPenney "mother store" and Penney's old home, now open as a small museum.

underground coal mine exhibit, and dozens of kinds of barbed wire dating from the 19th century. Freak-show enthusiasts will appreciate the lamb with one head and two bodies. The small gift shop sells inexpensive fossil fish. The museum puts on evening **campfire chats** every Thursday at 7 p.m. June-Aug. at Archie Niel Park. This is a great way to learn about the natural and cultural history of the area.

The nicely restored **Lincoln County Courthouse** at Sage and Topaz Sts. was built in 1925 and contains a fine collection of fossils. Stop by the post office at Cedar and Sapphire Sts. to view the **fossil murals** painted by WPA artists in 1938. For additional historical buildings, head to "downtown" Diamondville, where several classic structures line the old main street.

Fossil Collecting

Although it's illegal to collect fossils within Fossil Butte National Monument, several local areas permit it for a fee. These are only open in the summer months, and children generally aren't allowed since it is considered dangerous for them. The best place—its fossils are exhibited in the Smithsonian—is **Ulrich's Fossil Gallery,** tel. (307) 877-6466, located just outside the national monument, 14 miles west of Kemmerer. Out front are enormous dinosaur tracks discovered in a coal mine. Ulrich's has a nearby quarry on state land where you can dig your own fish fossils for $55 (advance reservations required). You're allowed to keep a wooden pallet full of the most common species, although the state gets any rare specimens that turn up. If you don't want to dig, you can buy beautifully prepared fossils at Ulrich's gallery.

Severns Studio, seven miles west of Kemmerer, tel. (307) 877-9402, charges $55 per day and is open Mon.-Friday. Reservations are advised, and you need to arrive before 8:30 a.m. to be transported to the dig site. Severns also sells prepared fossils in its studio.

Warfield Fossil Quarry, tel. (307) 883-2445, 12 miles south of Kemmerer on Hwy. 189, charges diggers $35 per day and has free tent and RV sites.

Tynsky's Fossil Fish Shop, next to the JCPenney store in Kemmerer, tel. (307) 877-6885, has fossil fish for sale. (The store is closed Feb.-May.) You can also dig at Tynsky's quarry, 12 miles west of town. The cost is $55 for three hours or so, and you can keep up to 10 fossils.

PRACTICALITIES

Accommodations

Antler Motel, 419 Coral St. in Kemmerer, tel. (307) 877-4461, has older units for $23-31 s or d, along with remodeled rooms for $29-35 s or d. Budget.

Fairview Inn, 501 N. Hwy. 30 in Kemmerer, tel. (307) 877-3938, offers standard rooms for $32 s or $44 d. Larger units containing microwaves and fridges are $40-50 s or d. This is the nicest motel in the area. Inexpensive.

Over in Diamondville, **Energy Inn,** tel. (307) 877-6901, rents motel rooms for $40 s or $50 d. All of these have fridges, and some also include kitchenettes. Inexpensive.

Campgrounds

Tent camping (no RVs) is available for $5 at **Kemmerer Community Camp,** on State Hwy. 233 north of Kemmerer; open Memorial Day-September. Call (307) 828-2360 for details. Public camping is also available at **Fontenelle Creek Campground** ($5; open Memorial Day-Sept.), 25 miles northeast of Kemmerer on US Hwy. 189 beside Fontenelle Reservoir. In addition, three free campgrounds are located along the Green River just below the Fontenelle dam, and dozens of free campsites border the lake.

Riverside Trailer Park, 216 Spinel St., tel. (307) 877-3416, has RV spaces for $13, but it's a shadeless gravel lot and doesn't have tent sites. Open May-October. **Foothills RV Park,** on N. Hwy. 189, tel. (307) 877-6634, has grassy RV sites with hookups for $14; open May-October. Farther away is **Lake Viva-Naughton Marina,** 15 miles north of Kemmerer, tel. (307) 877-9669, with tent spaces ($5), RV hookups ($15), and a few basic cabins.

Food

No standouts for meals in Kemmerer, but several places have solid meals for reasonable prices. Start your day at **Busy Bee Cafe,** 919 Pine Ave., tel. (307) 877-6820; open at 5:30 a.m. on weekdays, and also for lunch and dinner. Another place with good breakfasts, plus the best local burgers, is **Polar King Drive In,** 315 US Hwy. 189, tel. (307) 877-9448.

Bootlegger's Grill & Steak House, in town at 817 S. Main St., tel. (307) 828-3067, has a full menu. **Bon Rico's,** 12 miles south of town, tel. (307) 877-4503, is another favorite place to stuff yourself with steak or fish.

Lake Viva-Naughton Marina, 15 miles north of Kemmerer along the reservoir, tel. (307) 877-9669, has a pleasant setting and attracts a surprising number of Salt Lake City people with a seafood and steak menu.

Don Pedro's, 801 S. Main St., serves authentic Mexican meals.

There's a **Pizza Hut** in Diamondville, tel. (307) 877-6969, offering lunch deals and predictable pizzas. Local chain outlets include an Arby's, Arctic Circle Hamburgers, Subway, and Taco Time.

Entertainment

The **Stock Exchange Bar** downtown has a pool table and fills with locals most nights. For live music, try **Bon Rico's,** 12 miles south of town, tel. (307) 877-4503, or **Lake Viva-Naughton Marina,** 15 miles north of Kemmerer, tel. (307) 877-9669. The **Frontier Theatre** shows movies every day.

Events

Kemmerer is one of 12 stops in early February's **Rocky Mountain Stage Stop Sled Dog Race,** an event that attracts some of the nation's best mushers with a $100,000 purse. The race begins and ends in Jackson. Call (307) 734-1163 for details, or check the website: www.wyomingstagestop.org.

For four days in late July, Kemmerer celebrates **Turn of the Century Days** with a parade, chili cook-off, carnival, melodrama, shootout, and food and craft booths. The **Oyster Ridge Music Festival** is held in Kemmerer on the third weekend of August and features an outdoor barbecue, contests, and concerts from guitar, fiddle, banjo, and mandolin musicians. The star attraction is the flatpick guitar contest, but the "band scramble" is particularly fun—musicians must play together without time to rehearse. Anglers may want to join in the **Ice Fishing Derby** on the third weekend of February or the **Open Water Fishing Derby** on the last weekend of June at Lake Viva-Naughton.

Recreation

Kemmerer Recreation Center, 1776 Dell Rio Dr., tel. (307) 877-9641, has an indoor pool, weight room, jacuzzi, sauna, racquetball courts, and even a climbing wall. The outdoor pool (tel. 307-877-9641) in **Archie Neil Park** is open during the summer. Kemmerer's nine-hole golf course is north of town on Hwy. 189, tel. (307) 877-6954. Bowl at **Sage Bowling Lanes,** 918 Sage Ave., tel. (307) 877-6642.

Lions Club Park, just north of Kemmerer along scenic Hams Fork River, is a fine place for a picnic. Good fishing is the rule at **Lake Viva-Naughton,** 15 miles north of Kemmerer on State Hwy. 233; the marina, tel. (307) 877-9669, rents boats.

Information and Services

The **Kemmerer Chamber of Commerce** is housed in a log cabin in Herschler Triangle Park at the center of town, tel. (307) 877-9761 or (888) 300-3413. (Locals joke that Kemmerer is too small to have a town square, so it has a town triangle instead.) It's open summers Mon.-Sat. 9 a.m.-5 p.m., and the rest of the year Mon.-Fri. 9 a.m.-2 p.m., plus additional weekend hours in September and October. Inside are displays of fossils and historical pictures, and you can buy local books and old Wyoming license plates. The office can also provide helpful information on nearby fossil-fish quarries and details on tours of industrial plants in the area. Find the chamber on the web at www.kemmerer.org.

The **Rock & Wash**—a combination car wash and rock shop at 502 Coral, tel. (307) 877-3220—is a fun place to get petrified wood and other interesting rocks. See Fossil Collecting below for a list of places to dig for fish fossils.

Head north on Hwy. 189 to find both the Forest Service's **Kemmerer Ranger District,** tel. (307) 877-4415, and the adjacent **BLM Area office,** tel. (307) 877-3933.

The **Lincoln County Library** is at 519 Emerald St., tel. (307) 877-6961. Get crisp $20 bills from the **ATM** at Community First Bank, 801 Pine Ave. in Kemmerer, or the one at Chevron Food Mart in Diamondville.

FOSSIL BUTTE NATIONAL MONUMENT

Established in 1972, Fossil Butte is an 8,198-acre natural area managed by the National Park Service and located 14 miles west of Kemmerer. The dominant feature is an 800-foot-tall escarpment rising above the arid plains. Within this butte are millions of fossil fish, insects, snails, turtles, and plants. This is also one of the few places in the world where fossilized birds and bats have been found. The Green River Formation fossils were first collected by geologist Dr. John Evans in 1865.

Origins

Fossil Butte is not unlike countless other buttes throughout Wyoming: an exposed rocky cliff lit with the red, yellow, and buff colors representing millions of years of deposition and erosion. Despite the arid conditions today, this land once supported a subtropical climate similar to that along the Gulf Coast. During the Eocene Epoch (50 million years ago), palm trees grew along the shore of a lake, now called Fossil Lake, whose waters teemed with fish, crocodiles, turtles, stingrays, and other animals. Over a period of two million years, changing salinity levels and variations in runoff from calcium-rich streams caused calcium carbonate to precipitate out. Dead animals and plants on the deep lake bottom were covered with a blanket of fine sediment. Eventually they were fossilized, and when the lake dried up the sedimentary deposits were gradually thrust upward by geological forces.

Visitor Center

The free **Fossil Butte Visitor Center,** tel. (307) 877-4455, is open daily 8 a.m.-7 p.m. June-Aug. and daily 8 a.m.-5 p.m. the rest of the year (closed winter holidays). Find it on the web at www.nps.gov/fobu. Located 3.5 miles off US Hwy. 30 (follow the signs), the visitor center houses a fossil preparation lab, along with impressive displays on the area's geology, paleontology, and natural history. Here you can view videos on the area's geology and paleontology, and on fossil preparation. Natural-history books are sold in the gift shop.

Visitors can assist a Park Service paleontologist in collecting fossils June-Aug. weekends 10 a.m.-3 p.m. You'll hike into the quarry site and actually participate in the collection of fossils and data. Be ready to work! Evening campfire programs are offered at the picnic area periodically in the summer; check the visitor center for specific times.

Camping is not allowed at Fossil Butte, and the nearest lodging, campground, and RV parks are in Kemmerer. You can, however, camp on nearby BLM lands; see the bureau's Kemmerer office for details.

Hiking

The 2.5-mile **Historic Quarry Trail** on the south side of the monument provides access to an old fossil quarry site (600 feet up) and has various interpretive signs along the way. It is illegal to remove fossils or other items from the monument; see Fossil Collecting above for nearby areas where it is legal.

Fossil Lake Trail begins near a pleasant picnic area three miles north of the visitor center. It provides an enjoyable 1.5-mile loop hike through open sage country and a grove of aspen trees. Many varieties of flowers are blooming throughout the summer. Keep your eyes open for mule deer, coyotes, sage grouse, prairie dogs, and other animals on these paths. The visitor center has a brochure on these trails. Other than these two, you're on your own, although the open country makes hiking relatively easy. Topographic maps are sold in the visitor center. Be sure to carry water on any hike in this arid area.

Diplomystus are among the more common species found at Fossil Butte National Monument.

KEMMERER VICINITY

OREGON TRAIL SIGHTS

Ten miles north of Kemmerer on State Hwy. 233 are the still-noticeable ruts of the Oregon Trail's **Sublette Cutoff.** Named for mountain man William Sublette, who first took this route in 1826, the cutoff saved Oregon emigrants more than 50 miles of travel, but bypassed the chance to rest and resupply at Fort Bridger. Wagons traversed a rough and waterless desert before finally climbing into the cool and wooded mountains. Thirteen miles west of State Hwy. 233 along the Sublette Cutoff is the grave of a young emigrant, Nancy Hill. An 1852 letter written by her uncle describes how suddenly life could end on the treacherous journey west:

> *July the 6th. Since left off writing we have made slow progress in traveling on account of sickness and lame cattle. On last Friday & Saturday we layby on account of abe. He was very bad but is now in a fair way to get well. This day was called on to consign to the tomb one other of our company N.J. Hill. She was in good health on Sunday evening, taken unwell that knight worse in the morning & a corps at nine o'clock at knight. We had two doctors with her. They pronounced her complaining cholera but I believe it was nothing more than cholera with conjestion connecter.*

Names Hill

Oregon Trail travelers paused to carve their names into the rocks at three well-known places in Wyoming: Register Cliff, Independence Rock, and—westernmost of the three—Names Hill. The last of these is six miles south of the oil and gas town of La Barge, along the Sublette Cutoff at the hazardous Green River crossing. Over 2,000 old names are carved in the sandstone cliff—along with two Indian petroglyphs. The oldest name is dated 1827, when John Danks (probably a trapper) carved his still-visible appellation. Many others are from the 1840s and '50s. A fence surrounds one that reads, "James Bridger 1844 Trapper." Its authenticity is suspect since Bridger could neither read nor write and always signed his name with an X. But Jim Bridger *did* run a ferry at the nearby Green River crossing, so I'll give him the benefit of the doubt; perhaps a companion carved it while he watched. Please do not add your name to this historic rock face; in all too many places modern tourists have incised their inane graffiti next to names more than a century and a half old.

Fontenelle Reservoir

Fontenelle Reservoir lies just east and south of Names Hill and provides the area with irrigation water and electricity. The lake backs up behind a 139-foot earthen dam on the Green River, and it's a favorite spot for trout fishing, boating, and camping. The river below the dam makes for a relatively gentle float trip, and the trout fishing (rainbow, brown, and cutthroat) is excellent. Van Beacham's **Solitary Angler,** tel. (307) 877-9459, offers guided fly-fishing on this uncrowded stretch of the river.

La Barge

As you drive north from Names Hill, red and yellow badlands rise along the east side of the Green River while oil pumpjacks punctuate the land in all directions. Clean and comfortable lodging is available in La Barge (pop. 500) at **Wyoming Inn,** tel. (307) 386-2654, where rooms are $34-40 s or $40-46 d; the more expensive rooms are newer. Inexpensive. **Red Cliff Motel,** tel. (307) 386-9269, charges $36 s or $42 d, including fridges and microwaves. Inexpensive. **Timberline Restaurant,** tel. (307) 386-2800, serves three meals a day. The twin towns of Marbleton and Big Piney, 21 miles north of La Barge, are covered in the Wind River Mountains chapter.

COKEVILLE

Cokeville (pop. 500) lies in a long, fertile valley along the Idaho border south of Star Valley. Directly behind the town is an impressive triangular mountain, **Rocky Point.** The ranching and farming country is punctuated with small white farmhouses, but many locals commute to work at the coal mine and power plant near Kemmerer. Nearly everyone is Mormon here.

The town of Cokeville was founded in 1874 with the arrival of the Oregon Shortline Railroad and is named for the coal that was used to produce coke. By the turn of the 20th century it had become the "sheep capital of the world" and claimed more millionaires per capita than anywhere on earth. Cokeville's proximity to the state line also made it a haven for outlaws—with Utah and Idaho just six miles away, lawbreakers found it easy to leave the posse behind as they fled to a different jurisdiction.

Practicalities

Highway 30 through Cokeville is heavily traveled by trucks and cars heading north to Pocatello, Idaho, or south to I-80; because of this you'll find two gas stations and a large Flying J truck stop in town. Rooms are available at **Valley Hi Motel,** tel. (307) 279-3251, and **Hideout Motel,** tel. (307) 279-3281. The Forest Service's **Hams Fork Campground** ($5, open Memorial Day through October) is the closest public campground; it's 28 miles from Cokeville along the Smiths Fork Road. Get local specifics from the **Cokeville Visitor Center,** open in the summer months.

Pine Creek Ski Area, six miles east of Cokeville, consists of a chairlift and rope tow with a 1,200-foot vertical rise. Ski rentals and instruction are available. It's open Tuesday, Saturday, and Sunday Jan.-March. The mountains east of Cokeville also contain many miles of groomed wintertime snowmobile trails.

Lake Alice

Take an enjoyable side trip to Lake Alice, a pristine mountain lake at the end of a 1.5-mile trail in Bridger-Teton National Forest. Three-mile-long Lake Alice was created many centuries ago when a mountain slid across the valley and dammed the creek. Water from the lake flows underground for more than a mile before emerging in springs. Get here by heading northeast from Cokeville on State Hwy. 232 and bearing right at the "Y" 12 miles up where the pavement ends. The gravel road continues to the trailhead 34 miles from Cokeville, where you'll find the very nice **Hobble Creek Campground** ($5; open July-Oct.). There's good fishing both in the creek and at Lake Alice. The road into Lake Alice is generally closed by snow from October to late June. The country around here is some of the only unroaded land left in the Wyoming Range. The route to Lake Alice passes the **Kelly Guard Station,** which you can rent for $30 a night for up to five people Nov.-April. Access is by snowmobile or cross-country skis, approximately nine miles in. Call the Forest Service in Kemmerer, tel. (307) 877-4415, for specifics

Heading North

The drive north from Cokeville to Star Valley follows Salt Creek from the sage and grass lowlands into lodgepole pine-covered mountains, eventually reaching Salt River Pass at 7,610 feet. It's a taste of the majestic mountain country that fills the northwest corner of Wyoming. On the north side of the pass, the road begins a long descent into beautiful Star Valley. Lodging is available at **Canyon Inn Motel,** tel. (307) 849-0100, 24 miles north of Cokeville and just inside the Wyoming state line. Rooms go for $30 s or d; open mid-April to mid-November. Budget.

STAR VALLEY

West of the Wyoming Range, the mountains seem exhausted as they dip into a broad, fertile farming valley that stretches across the Idaho border. This is Star Valley, a place with closer ties to Idaho—in terms of geography, farming, sheep ranching, transportation, and even religion—than to Wyoming. Locals call it the "home of 5,000 people and 20,000 cattle." The valley reaches 10 miles across and 40 miles north to south; an early settler labeled it "The Star of all Valleys." Star Valley is a very pretty place; the Salt River—named for the salt deposits and saline springs along its banks—creates an oasis of greenery and the mountains make a grand backdrop. Irrigation ditches flow alongside the roads, barbed wire stretches between old lodgepole posts, and dairy cows graze in the velvet green farm fields. Spacious old ranches—built to house large Mormon families—alternate with more modern ranch-style homes. A single main road, US Hwy. 89, heads north the full length of Star Valley, with a network of side roads and scattered pinprick settlements. For details on the land just west of Star Valley, see *Idaho Handbook* by Don Root (Moon Travel Handbooks, www.moon.com).

HISTORY

The **Lander Cutoff** of the Oregon Trail angles through the southern half of Star Valley, follows the Salt River as far as the Auburn area, and then cuts northwest along Stump Creek. This 250-mile path—constructed in 1858 under the direction of Frederick W. Lander—was the first federal road built west of the Missouri River. Fur trappers had used the route for 45 years before Lander and his men, funded with a $300,000 appropriation from Congress, upgraded it for wagon travel. The Lander Cutoff saved Oregon-bound travelers more than 100 miles but also entailed climbing over a rugged 9,000-foot pass. You can see parts of the route along the south end of Greys River Rd., where concrete posts and emigrant graves mark the way.

The first white settlers came to Star Valley from Idaho in the 1880s, fleeing laws restricting the number of wives a man could have. Polygamy, while outlawed by the federal government in 1882, was winked at by Wyoming authorities for many years. They needed all the settlers they could get—especially the conservative, hardworking Mormons. When Frank W. Mondell was running for Congress in 1894, he came to Star Valley and found that the Afton mayor was a polygamist. Mondell noted,

> *We assured our friend we were not disposed to question the propriety of his family affairs and would be glad to accept his hospitality. Thereupon our party partook of a fine supper in the modest home of very pleasant and comely wife No. Three, and thereafter, leaving Miss Reel with her, the remainder of our party was comfortably housed in the larger homes of Wives One and Two.*

Polygamy has long since been outlawed, but a large brick LDS church still stands in every Podunk town in Star Valley.

AFTON

The primary settlement in Star Valley is Afton (pop. 1,700), a typical small American town and the sort of place where parents complain of kids partying with kegs and making out on back roads. Meanwhile, high-schoolers complain they've nothing to do. The local economy suffered in the early '90s as farmers struggled on fertile land in a marginal climate, but tourism began to kick in as the overflow from Jackson Hole spilled into Star Valley. Ranchettes and summer homes are sprouting in what had been farmland, and new real estate offices on the edge of town entice more folks to move in.

Aviat, Inc. manufactures a variety of small aircraft in Afton, including the Pitts Special, considered the finest aerobatics plane in existence; the Eagle homebuilt kit; and the Husky A-1, similar to the famous Super Cub. Also in Afton is a small plant that sews Wyoming Wear garments. Note: Afton phone service is in transition, and some telephone numbers listed below as 886- may change to 885- in the future.

Sights

Afton's best-known attraction is the world's largest **elk antler arch,** an 18-foot-high arch that extends over the main street. Built in 1958, it contains 3,011 antlers. At today's antler prices—they're prized as aphrodisiacs in Asia—the arch would be worth over $300,000!

The **CallAir Museum,** tel. (307) 886-9881, is housed in a hangar on the south end of Afton and honors a small aircraft manufacturing company. CallAir began in 1937 and survived until 1962. Many CallAir planes are still in use all over the world, primarily as crop dusters. Founder Reuel Call later made money in the oil business with Maverick Country Stores (still headquartered in Afton) and Flying J truck stops, and he invested $2 million to found this free museum. Inside you'll find several CallAir aircraft, historic photos, and a squadron of more than 75 model airplanes. You can watch workers restoring old planes, view educational videos, or purchase flying paraphernalia and books in the gift shop. There's even a kid-size plane for the younger set. Museum hours are daily 9 a.m.-5 p.m. Memorial Day to Labor Day. Staff may be around in the off-season; try knocking on the door. See Events below for details on the CallAir Fly-In. **Aviat,** 672 Washington, tel. (307) 886-3151, does not officially offer tours of its aircraft manufacturing facility, but you may want to drop by on weekdays between 11 a.m. and 3 p.m. just in case.

The small **Pioneer Museum,** 46 5th Ave., tel. (307) 886-3667, is open Mon.-Fri. 1-5 p.m. June-Aug., and by appointment the rest of the year. No charge. Inside are various items collected by the Daughters of the Utah Pioneers, including a loom, a spinning wheel, and other memorabilia. The enormous **Afton Tabernacle**—LDS, of course—sits at the corner of Jefferson and 3rd and serves as a community focal point. This impressive sandstone building (architects call this a Middle English design) was

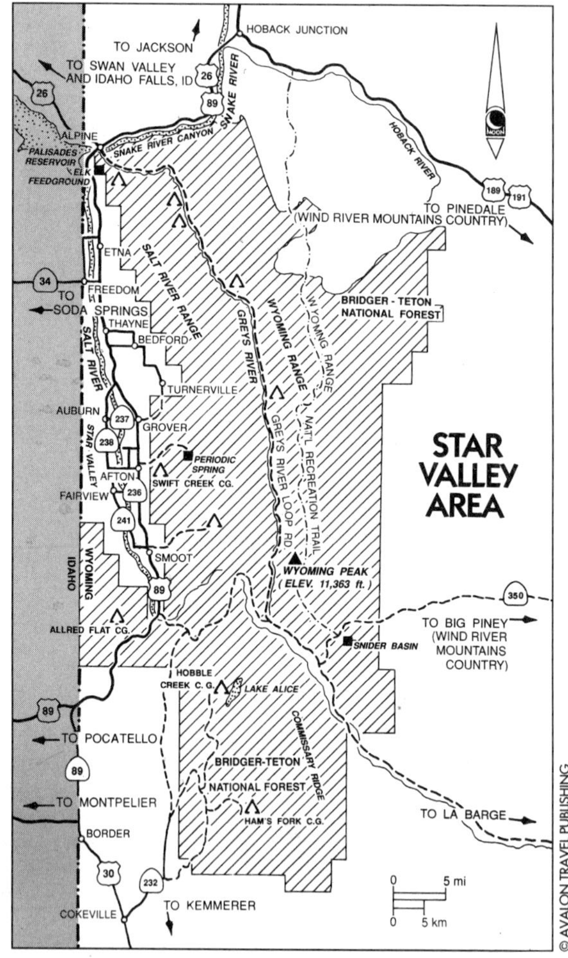

begun in 1904 and received further additions in the 1940s.

Periodic Spring

Afton's most unusual sight is Periodic Spring, located in Swift Creek Canyon east of town (take 2nd Avenue). The six-mile drive is quite a contrast to wide-open Star Valley—it parallels a pretty tree-bordered creek and steep rocky slopes. The largest of only three intermittent springs known to exist, Periodic Spring is reached via a three-quarter-mile trail. The crystalline water of this spring emerges from the base of a cliff to feed Swift Creek, the water source for Afton, and is so pure that no chlorination is needed. When the spring is operating it seems as though there were a timer and an on-off switch buried in the mountain. Icy water gushes from a gaping opening in the cliff for approximately 18 minutes, then stops for an equal period.

The Shoshones regarded this as a sacred place of healing and said that a powerful medicine man was able to turn the waters on and off by command. Today, hydrologists believe that a large underground chamber periodically fills with and then empties of water through a natural siphon in the porous limestone rock. The spring loses its intermittence in spring and flows constantly. Best time to see it in action is in late summer or early fall.

Accommodations

When you check into a room in Afton, you're likely to find two scriptures: the Bible and the Book of Mormon. Travelers should be advised that some motels in this conservative LDS valley frown upon unmarried couples and on rare occasions might even refuse to rent them a room. Your best bet is to avoid the potential for trouble by using the key words "husband" or "wife" when getting a place for the night! Afton motels are arranged below from least to most expensive. Add a seven percent tax to the rates.

Budget: On the south edge of Afton next to Trailside Store, **Trailside Motel,** 1850 S. Washington, tel. (307) 885-8204, has eight modern units for a reasonable $29 s or $34 d.

Inexpensive: Bar-H Motel, tel. (307) 885-2274, rents modern cabins, all with kitchenettes. Rates are $30 s and $35 d; two-bedroom units cost $50 d. No phones or credit cards. Right next door is **Colters Lodge,** 355 N. Washington, tel. (307) 885-9891 or (800) 446-7005, with upstairs rooms for $35 s or $40 d and suites for $60 d.

Lazy B Motel, 219 Washington, tel. (307) 885-3187, charges $40 s or $50 d, and has kitchenettes available. This is also one of the few local places that takes pets.

The **Corral Motel,** 161 Washington, tel. (307) 886-5424, is an American icon, with clean, well-maintained log and plaster cabins from the 1940s. All are no-smoking, and two contain kitchenettes ($5 extra). Rates are $35 s, $40-50 d, or $60-65 for families; open mid-April through October. Recommended.

Approximately eight miles north of Afton, **Silver Stream Lodge,** tel. (307) 883-2440, charges $42-45 s or d for cabins, $56-59 s or d for kitchenettes. No TVs or phones; open all year. Also here is a fine-dining restaurant and lounge (dinners only).

Inexpensive-Moderate: Three-quarters of a mile south of Afton, the modern **Best Western Hi Country Inn,** tel. (307) 886-3856 or (800) 528-1234, has an outdoor pool and jacuzzi. Rooms cost $48-80 s or $55-90 d. A mile south of Afton, **Mountain Inn,** tel. (307) 886-3156 or (800) 682-5356, is a spotless motel with large rooms and suites, an outdoor pool, sauna, jacuzzi, and continental breakfast. Rates are $52-67 s or d.

The Rocking P Bed & Breakfast is in Smoot (nine miles south of Afton), tel. (307) 886-0455, and has two guest rooms with private baths. A hot tub sits on the deck, and a big country breakfast is served each morning. Rates are $60 s or d. Kids and horses are welcome.

Two miles south of Afton is **The Old Mill,** 3497 Dry Creek Rd., tel. (307) 886-0520, where you'll find three modern log cabins set on five acres. All are nicely furnished with handcrafted log beds and gas fireplaces. Guests will also enjoy the jacuzzi in a glass-enclosed gazebo. Two cabins sleep four and cost $104; the third is larger and sleeps up to six for $130. Rates include a continental breakfast that is brought to your door each morning. In the winter, you can cross-country ski or snowmobile right from your cabin.

Campgrounds and Public Cabins

The Forest Service has three campgrounds ($5; open late May to mid-September) in the Star

Valley area. Closest is the attractive **Swift Creek Campground,** only a mile and a half east of Afton (take 2nd Ave.—Periodic Spring is farther up the same road). **Allred Flat Campground** is 20 miles south of Afton, right along US Hwy. 89. **Cottonwood Lake Campground** is a very nice place with lakeside sites and nearby hiking trails. It's seven miles up the Cottonwood Lake Rd., south of Smoot.

The Forest Service rents out four nearby cabins when they are not being used by field crews. These are particularly popular with snowmobilers and skiers in the winter, but running water is only available in the summer months. The cabins are **Corral Creek Guard Station, Deer Creek Guard Station, McCain Guard Station,** and **Meadow Guard Station.** Each sleeps six in bunk beds and costs $30 per night. Call (307) 886-3166 for reservations and details.

Food

Colters Lodge, 355 N. Washington, tel. (307) 886-9597, is the best place for meals in Afton—filling breakfasts, all-you-can-eat lunch and dinner buffets ($7 for dinner!), along with pasta, steaks, seafood, burgers, and chicken. The rustic Old West atmosphere and outside patio are added attractions. Recommended. Get standard American breakfasts at **Golden Spur Cafe,** 486 Washington, tel. (307) 886-9890, or the somewhat nicer **Elkhorn Restaurant,** 465 Washington, tel. (307) 886-3080. The latter also has good lunch specials and a big salad bar.

Red Baron Drive-In, 838 Washington, tel. (307) 886-3745, is the hangout for folks who want burgers and fries. **Subway** and **Taco Time** have quick meals. Try the lunchtime pizza buffets at **Gunnar's Pizza,** 845 S. Washington, tel. (307) 886-9795, or **Pizza Hut,** 228 Washington, tel. (307) 886-9794. Get south-of-the-border fare at **Melina's Mexican Restaurant,** 470 Washington, tel. (307) 883-2617.

Homestead Restaurant, just south of town on Hwy. 89, tel. (307) 886-3878, offers the area's finest prime rib, along with rich double-fudge desserts.

Get groceries from two stores on the north side of town: **Familee Thriftway,** tel. (307) 886-5550, and **Nield Foodland,** tel. (307) 886-5537. Prices are typically a bit lower here than in Jackson, so you may want to stock up before heading north.

Entertainment

For live country-and-western or rock music on Friday and Saturday nights, head to **Colters Lodge,** 355 N. Washington, tel. (307) 886-9597. Watch flicks at downtown Afton's **Ford Theatre.**

Events

Afton and nearby Box Y Ranch (in the Greys River area) are two stops in early February's **Rocky Mountain Stage Stop Sled Dog Race,** an event that attracts some of the nation's best mushers with a $100,000 purse. The race begins and ends in Jackson. Call (307) 734-1163 for details, or visit the website: www.wyomingstagestop.org.

The **CallAir Fly-In/Star Valley Aviation Days** takes place the last Friday and Saturday of June and includes a free breakfast, air show, museum tours, and aircraft fly-in. Each July the community puts on a two-day **historical pageant** at the high school football field. It typically involves a homespun tale of the Mormon pioneers who settled the valley. July kicks off with an **Independence Day** celebration that features a parade and fireworks in Afton, followed by two nights of rodeo action during the Ted Linford Memorial Rodeo. The **Lincoln County Fair** is held in Afton in late July and early August, with all the country fair favorites: musical entertainment, a carnival, a parade, rodeos, 4-H agricultural exhibits, and lots more. Rodeos are also held several other times each summer; see the visitor center for specifics. In late November, Afton's **Parade of Lights** is a small-town event with lighted floats.

Cutter races are held at race grounds a mile northwest of Afton on Saturday throughout the winter; call (800) 426-8833 for details.

Recreation

Golfers will find a pair of nine-hole courses near Afton, and Star Valley Ranch Resort in Thayne offers two 18-hole courses: **Cedar Creek Golf Course,** tel. (307) 883-2230, and **Aspen Hills Golf Course,** tel. (307) 883-2899.

During the winter, the town operates **Snowshoe Hollow Ski Area,** tel. (307) 885-9831, a small area just east of Afton. The hill has a rope tow and snack bar.

Stop by the Forest Service office for information on the many miles of groomed **cross-country ski trails** in Star Valley. Closest are trails in

Afton at Canyon View Park and a mile to the south at Valli Vu Golf Course.

The Wyoming Range to the east offer unlimited opportunities for exploration by skiers and snowmobiles, with snow till the Fourth of July some years. Greys River Rd. (see below) is an especially popular snowmobiling area. Rent snowmobiles from **M&J Enterprises** in Grover, tel. (307) 886-5299, and **Star Valley Ski-Doo** in Thayne, tel. (307) 883-2714. Call (800) 225-5996, ext. 4, for current snowmobile-trail conditions.

Shopping

If you're driving north from Afton toward Jackson be sure to fill up with gas either here or in Thayne; it won't get any cheaper. Besides gas, the best deals in town can be found at the **Wyoming Wear** factory outlet store, tel. (307) 886-3851, on the north side of Afton. The jackets, hats, socks, vests, pullovers, and other quality outdoor gear sold here are all sewn at factories in Afton and Cokeville, and their prices can't be beat: up to 75% off. **Lone Pine Sports,** at Washington and Nield String Rd., tel. (307) 886-9581, sells additional outdoor gear and rents cross-country skis in the winter.

Two Afton places sell LDS and other religious books: **Quiet Place Books,** 460 N. Washington, tel. (307) 886-5246, and the **Hastings Store,** inside Ace Hardware on the south end of town, tel. (307) 886-3048. For a real dose of Star Valley culture, check out the world map in Hastings showing where local kids have gone as Mormon missionaries.

Information and Services

Afton's tiny **visitor center** at 2nd and Washington is open Tues.-Sat. 10 a.m.-6 p.m. summers only. For more information, call (307) 886-3156 or (800) 426-8833, or visit the website: www.starvalleychamber.com.

A fountain outside the visitor center provides a taste of Afton's famous spring water; next door is a University of Wyoming Research and Extension Center. Directly across the road, the **Forest Service Greys River District Office,** tel. (307) 886-3166, dispenses local maps, natural history books, and info on recreational opportunities.

The **Star Valley Branch Library** at 261 Washington St., tel. (307) 886-3158, carries plenty of genealogy titles. You'll find the **post office** at 31 W. 4th Ave., tel. (307) 886-3625. Get fast cash from **ATMs** at First Security Bank of Wyoming, 485 N. Washington, or First National Bank, 302 Washington.

GREYS RIVER LOOP ROAD

Star Valley is bordered on the east by two parallel mountain ranges: the Salt River and the Wyoming. The Greys River flows between them. Alongside it runs an exceptionally scenic 80-mile-long gravel road used by small numbers of vacationers, hikers, anglers, and hunters. This untrammeled area makes for a great escape from the Jackson Hole mob scene in the summer. The road begins a dozen miles south of Afton and continues north all the way to Alpine. Plan to camp overnight along the way; the narrow and potholed dirt road makes for a torturous day-trip. You'll fine excellent fishing for cutthroat, rainbow, brown, and brook trout in the river, and good opportunities to see deer and moose along

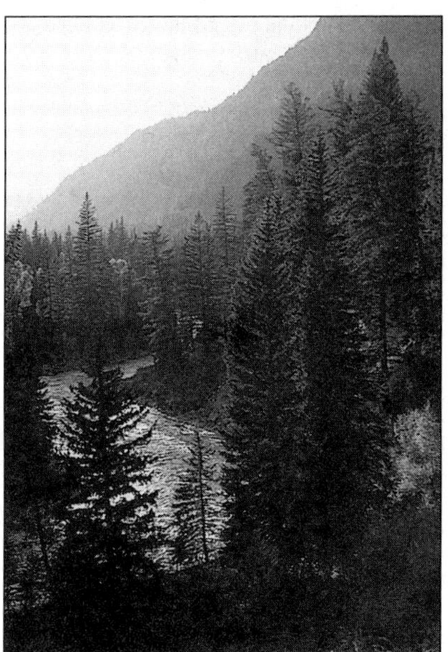

The loop road follows the beautiful Greys River for 80 miles.

the way. All this country lies within Bridger-Teton National Forest. Considerable logging takes place in the mountains, and many thousands of sheep and cattle graze the open areas, but much of the land remains wild and beautiful. It is an almost unknown part of Wyoming. If you drive north along the Greys River Rd. you'll be able to watch the Greys grow from a small creek into a river. Kayakers often paddle the lower stretches of the river; see the Forest Service for specifics.

Another fascinating drive (great for mountain bikes) is to continue east through Snider Basin to the town of Big Piney on Forest Rd. 10128. The road parallels the still-visible Lander Cutoff of the Oregon Trail for a long distance, and a number of emigrant graves are noted along the way. Keep your eyes open for elk and deer on the slopes and beaver dams in Piney Creek. The high country is lodgepole-pine forests, passing into open sage land as you descend toward Big Piney. Note that this route can be confusing (signs are often missing) and sometimes muddy, so be sure to get a Forest Service map and current conditions before heading out from Afton. The **La Barge Guard Station** is located approximately 22 miles from the Afton end of the road and is available for rent ($30 a night for up to six people) Nov.-April. Access is by snowmobile or cross-country skis. Call the Forest Service in Kemmerer for specifics, tel. (307) 877-4415.

Camping

Camping is available at five places along the Greys River Rd; nicest are the campgrounds at **Murphy Creek** and **Forest Park,** both of which cost $5 from June to September. At other times of year the campgrounds are open at no charge, but you'll need to bring in water and haul out your own garbage. Also note that the road is not plowed in the winter. You can camp off the road for free in most parts of the national forest.

Recreation

More than 450 miles of trails cut across this country, including the 70-mile-long **Wyoming Range National Recreation Trail,** which climbs through beautiful alpine meadows and over narrow, rocky ridges. Snow covers the trail until July most years.

A side road off the Greys River Rd. leads to a two-mile trail that climbs 11,363-foot **Wyoming Peak,** tallest in the range. During the winter cross-country skiers will find four groomed ski trails and snowmobilers can cruise on 100 miles of groomed routes in the area. See the Forest Service office in Afton for maps and recreation information, including a listing of permitted guides and outfitters.

Lodging

Box Y Lodge is a grand old ranch with a beautiful setting along Greys River Rd. 30 miles from Alpine. The ranch has a main lodge and eight comfortably rustic log cabins (each sleeps up to six) with propane heat and lights. Activities include fishing, horseback rides, float trips, and mountain-biking. All-inclusive summertime rates are $400 for two people per day. The ranch is also a busy wintertime resort for snowmobilers; winter rates are $190 for two people including lodging and three meals a day. The ranch hosts a maximum of 12 people in the summer, but can house twice that when the snow flies. Call (307) 654-7564 for information, but it may take several days for them to return your call due to the remote location. Box Y is one of 12 stops in early February's **Rocky Mountain Stage Stop Sled Dog Race,** call (307) 734-1163 for details. Luxury.

Greysnest Mountain Retreat Camp, tel. (307) 886-3356 or (307) 654-9900, has a rustic wall-tent camp 19 miles southeast of Alpine on Greys River Road. It offers three family-style meals a day, tent lodging, and horseback riding for $95 per adult/day, $75/day for teens, and $60/day for ages 4-12. Luxury.

THAYNE

The claim to fame of Thayne (pop. 350) is the invention in the 1920s of **cutter races.** It's said that racing began with dairymen who used sleighs to haul milk to the local creamery. To avoid having to wait in line, the dairy farmers often raced each other to get to the creamery first; this sparring eventually grew into a competition that now encompasses seven western states. (The "world finals" are held in Ogden, Utah.) In a cutter race, horses pull wheeled chariots over a snow-covered field at breakneck speeds; the world record stands at 21.64 seconds for the quarter-mile run. Star Valley cutter races now take place at race grounds north of Afton.

Attractions

If you're heading north to Jackson Hole, fill your gas tank in Thayne; prices only go up from here. Before tanking your car, fill your belly at **Star Valley Cheese,** tel. (307) 883-2510, one of the most unusual eating places in Wyoming. The restaurant—an old-fashioned shop straight out of the 1950s—serves reasonably priced buffalo burgers, homemade pies, ice cream, malts, shakes, and other fare, and sells fresh cheeses from the coolers. It's open daily all year, and it's almost always filled with locals and tourists. Some 60,000 pounds of mozzarella, provolone, and Swiss cheese are made in the plant right behind the shop. Everything here gets the Star Valley label although the plant is now a part of Western Dairymen Cooperative. Well worth a stop.

Across the highway from Star Valley Cheese is **Star Valley Gift & Rock Shop,** tel. (307) 883-2028, selling fossils, gold, jade, and crystals.

Accommodations

Cabin Creek Inn, tel. (307) 883-3262, www.cabincreekinn.com, has all new log cabins in Thayne. The six-person cabins feature lodgepole beds, homemade quilts, kitchenettes, and jetted tubs for $60. Open May-October. Moderate.

Sunset Motel tel. (307) 883-2462, is an older place with rooms for $35 s or $40 d. Inexpensive.

RV Parks

Flat Creek Cabins, tel. (307) 883-2231, has RV parking for $18 and tent sites for $12. (The cabins here are rented only on a monthly basis.)

Flat Creek RV Park, south of Thayne, tel. (307) 883-2231, charges $18 for RVs or $12 for tents. Showers cost $3. It's open year-round.

A few miles north of Thayne is **Star Valley Ranch Resort,** tel. (307) 883-2670, an obscenely elaborate place with several hundred summer homes, a restaurant, RV park, two pools, two golf courses, a sauna, bumper boats, and tennis courts.

Food

JH Ranch Cafe, tel. (307) 883-2357, has homemade breads and pastries along with daily lunch specials. **Dad's Steak House,** tel. (307) 883-2300, offers live music on weekends and the finest steaks and prime rib in the area. This is home to a small cutter-racing museum (the sport was established by "Dad" Walton). Also in Thayne is a little fruit stand with great summertime deals.

Field of Greens Pizza Pub, at the Star Valley Ranch, tel. (307) 883-4653, serves pizza and burgers, along with chicken on Friday and baby back ribs on Saturday. Open summers only.

Events

The **Little Buckaroo Rodeo** is the big summertime event for Thayne, with all sorts of fun kid events, including sheep and calf riding, pig chasing, and barrel racing. For adults, the day also brings the **Salt River Canoe Race,** where canoeists have unusual obstacles: the fire department points fire hoses at passing contestants.

OTHER STAR VALLEY TOWNS

Auburn

The town of Auburn, eight miles north and west of Afton, contains a small area of travertine terraces and hot springs on private land. The nearby countryside is filled with old log homes, cabins, and barns. A historic stone church, built in 1889, sits across from the tiny Auburn post office and is used for summertime melodramas by the **Star Valley Historical Theatre;** call (307) 885-3640 for details. Not far away is the Davis Ranch, where Butch Cassidy and his gang holed up one winter.

West of Auburn on County Rd. 134 is **Auburn Fish Hatchery,** where some 50,000 trout are raised annually. It's open daily 8 a.m.-5 p.m. The road to the hatchery parallels the Lander Cutoff of the Oregon Trail for several miles.

Bedford

The tiny farming and sheep-ranching settlement of Bedford lies near the center of Star Valley. On fall days you're likely to meet huge herds of sheep being driven down the main roads as they return from a summer in the mountains.

Freedom

Freedom (pop. 100), Star Valley's oldest settlement, straddles the Idaho-Wyoming border. The town was established by Mormons in 1879 and offered an escape from the Idaho Territory's efforts to ban polygamy. Arthur Clark named the town for his freedom to have multiple wives. Today, Freedom has a small country store just a few feet from the border where you can buy Idaho lottery tickets. **Horse Shoe Cafe** in Etna is a classic small-town eatery, filling with locals every day and deer hunters on cool fall mornings.

Freedom is famous in National Rifle Association circles for a small factory, **Freedom Arms,** tel. (307) 883-2468, which makes handguns, including the massive .454 Casull, the world's most powerful revolver—and one of the most expensive at up to $1,800 apiece. No surprise that Clint Eastwood owns one. Don't ever get on the wrong end of this deadly instrument. Visitors can watch a short video and view a gun display here.

Free camping is available three miles west of Freedom, inside Idaho, at the Forest Service's **Tincup Campground.**

Haderlie's Tincup Mountain Guest Ranch is near the Idaho-Wyoming border and surrounded by national forest land. Homesteaded in 1888, it is still a working ranch. The ranch specializes in horseback rides ($35 per half day) but also has cabin accommodations and RV parking, along with chuck wagon dinners, pack trips, and backcountry fishing. The ranch is open May-September. For details, call (307) 873-2368 or (800) 253-2368, or visit the website: www.silverstar.com/htmgr.

Etna

Etna lies near the northern end of Star Valley and has a small country store and an outsized brick LDS church that seems big enough to house the entire population of 200. In late summer, the sweet scent of new-mown hay hangs in the air. **Etna Trading Co.,** tel. (307) 883-2409, is an old-time country store.

Horse Shoe Motel, tel. (307) 883-2281, has rooms for $40-50 s or d. Open June-October only. Inexpensive.

Salt River B&B, tel. (307) 883-2453, offers cozy in-town lodging in three guest rooms ($25 s or $45 d) and a suite ($55 d). A full breakfast is served, and kids are welcome. The owner is a quilter and sells locally made quilts in the shop next-door. Lunch is served in the summer months, and dinners are available on request. Inexpensive.

ALPINE

At the intersection of US Highways 26 and 89, the crossroads settlement called Alpine (pop. 300) is an ugly place with a quickly multiplying collection of businesses—fireworks stands, real estate offices, motels, restaurants, and bars strung out in all directions. It's a sad sight, and it's all here because of the tourists en route to or from Jackson Hole. The area is called Lower Valley and borders on **Palisades Reservoir,** built at the convergence of Snake River, Greys River, and Salt River. Water enthusiasts come to the reservoir for fishing, water skiing, camping, and picnicking. A massive highway reconstruction project through the Snake River Canyon will continue to create lengthy summertime delays between Alpine and Hoback Junction. Construction work will probably not be completed before 2004.

Approximately 700 elk gather each winter at the **Elk Feedground** a mile south of Alpine on Hwy. 89. You can view the elk from the parking area here—they often approach parked cars rather closely. Best time to visit is in the mornings, when they are fed.

Get cash from the **ATM** at the Amoco station. For details on westward destinations, see *Idaho Handbook,* by Don Root (Moon Travel Handbooks, www.moon.com).

Lodging

Alpine Junction has a number of good lodging choices at considerably lower rates than Jackson, where even the Motel 6 is $70 a night! Reservations are advised during July and August, when everything fills up fast. Accommodations are listed below from least to most expensive.

On the south end of town, **Snake River Resort & RV Park,** tel. (307) 654-7340, has a half dozen older motel units that sleep four people for $35. Budget.

Twin Pines Motel, tel. (307) 654-7506, charges $35 s or $40 d and has fridges and microwaves in all rooms. Kitchenettes are also available. Inexpensive.

Three Rivers Motel, tel. (307) 654-7551, has standard rooms for $45 s or $50 d, kitchenettes for $10 extra. Inexpensive.

Just west of town on US Hwy. 26 is **Alpine Inn,** tel. (307) 654-7644. Motel rooms in the main building are $55. Separate cabins run $45, or $65 with a second bedroom and kitchenette. All rooms have two queen beds and sleep four people. The inn is set on 10 acres and has picnic tables covered by tepees. Inexpensive-Moderate.

For homey and immaculate lodging, stay at the **Nordic Inn,** tel. (307) 654-7556, where the 12 rooms are a reasonable $68-86 s or d, including use of a jacuzzi. The inn gets lots of repeat visitors, so be sure to reserve ahead for midsummer. Open late May to mid-October. Moderate-Expensive.

Alpine's biggest lodge is **Royal Resort,** tel. (307) 654-7545 or (800) 343-6755, a chalet-style hotel decorated with Austrian scenes and featuring a jacuzzi, exercise room, children's carousel, a fine restaurant, and a bar. Standard rooms cost $70 d; more spacious ones with balconies, queen or king beds, and VCRs are $85-95 d. (Travelers returning to Alpine may know the resort by its former name, Alpen Haus Hotel.) Moderate-Expensive.

You'll find very attractive rooms and cottages ($105-160 s or d) at **Best Western Flying Saddle Lodge,** tel. (307) 654-7561 or (800) 528-1234, where amenities include an outdoor pool and jacuzzi; open June-September. Expensive-Luxury.

Camping

There's plenty of public camping at nearby Forest Service campgrounds; see Snake River Canyon below or **Greys River Loop Road** above. The closest spot is **Alpine Campground** ($8; open Memorial Day to Labor Day), located two miles west of town along Hwy. 26. Call (877) 444-6777 for reservations ($8.65 charge), or make them on the web at www.reserveusa.com. The turnoff to the Forest Service's **McCoy Campground** is three miles south of Alpine on Hwy. 89, and then another five miles along Palisades Reservoir. In addition to these official campgrounds, dispersed camping spots (turnouts off the road) can be found approximately five miles up the Greys River Rd., which is just east of Alpine.

Several private places provide in-town RV and tent spaces. **Snake River Resort & RV Park,** tel. (307) 654-7340, has tent sites for $10 and RV sites for $25; open year-round. You can also park RVs ($20) at **Royal Resort,** tel. (307) 654-7545 or (800) 343-6755, open April-Oct.; showers for those not staying here are $3.50. **Twin Pines Motel,** tel. (307) 654-7506, has RV hookups ($8) and tent spaces ($5) right behind the motel; open April-October. Additional RV parking can be found at **Aspen Grove Mobile Home & RV Park,** tel. (307) 654-7559.

Food and Entertainment

Alpine is home to several cafes and restaurants offering standard American fare. **Royal Ridge Restaurant,** in the Royal Resort, tel. (307) 654-7508, has a fine-dining menu, while **Gunnar's Pizza,** tel. (307) 654-7778, creates good sub sandwiches and pizzas—including whole-wheat and deep-dish versions. They also offer outside dining in the summer. In addition to meals, **Bull Moose Saloon and Restaurant,** tel. (307) 654-7051, brings live music to Alpine on summer weekends.

The real surprise in town is **Brentoven's Restaurant,** where the chef—Brent Johnston—is not only talented in the kitchen but is also an international concert pianist. You'll find everything from fresh fruit crepes for breakfast to steak and venison for dinner. The bar has a fine wine selection, and friendly owner Mike Clinger will be happy to discuss opera or tell you about his distinctive Colonial home located behind the Nordic Inn. The restaurant and inn are open late May to mid-October. Call (307) 654-7556 for details, or find them on the web at www.starvalleywy.com/brenthoven.htm.

Recreation

Contact **Alpine Riding & Rafts** at Royal Resort, tel. (307) 654-9900, for horseback rides in the area and raft trips down the Snake River Canyon. Float trips can also be booked through **Nordic Inn,** tel. (307) 654-7556. Many similar rafting operations are run out of Jackson Hole.

Rent snowmobiles for Greys River tours from **TJ's Sports,** tel. (307) 654-7815 or (800) 544-7054, or **Alpine Adventures,** tel. (307) 654-7289 or (888) 654-7289.

Events

Alpine is one of 12 stops in early February's **Rocky Mountain Stage Stop Sled Dog Race,** an event that attracts some of the nation's best mushers with a $100,000 purse. The race begins and ends in Jackson. Call (307) 734-1163 for details, or check the website: www.wyomingstagestop.org.

Alpine Mountain Days, on the third weekend of June, is the big summer celebration, with mountain men, Indian dancing, a black-powder shoot, arts and crafts, Dutch-oven cook-off, and other activities.

SNAKE RIVER CANYON

Above Alpine, the country abruptly changes as US Hwy. 89/26 enters Snake River Canyon, paralleling it all the way to Hoback Junction 23 miles away. In places the highway hangs high over the river with only a guardrail blocking the way—and sometimes not even that. This is a delicious way to enter Jackson Hole, offering numerous pullouts where you can view the roiling, rambunctious rapids of the sinuous Snake River as it slithers through millions of years of rocky cliffs. At sunset, the river glows a silver ribbon of light. A big, powerful river, the Snake eventually feeds into the Columbia in Washington. Riverbanks are lined with ancient cottonwoods while the higher slopes show lodgepole pines.

The whitewater of Snake River Canyon is a favorite of recreationists, and during the summer you're bound to meet cars with kayaks on their roofs and vans filled with happy rafters heading back to Jackson. See the Jackson Hole section for details on the many river-running options. River access is generally via the West Table Creek and Sheep Gulch boat ramps.

Five Forest Service **campgrounds** ($12-15, open late May to early September) are scattered through the Snake River Canyon. Many fill up early in the day during midsummer, but you can make reservations ($8.65 extra) for **Station Creek Campground** by calling (877) 444-6777, or checking the web at www.reserveusa.com.

The highway through the Snake River Canyon is currently being widened in a major multiyear construction project that will probably last until 2004. Expect delays of at least 20 minutes, and the road may be closed for extended periods at night during this massive project. You may be better off avoiding the construction zone if possible, especially if you're in a hurry. For the current status, call the Wyoming Department of Transportation in Jackson, tel. (307) 733-3665. Because of this construction, some campgrounds may be temporarily closed. Check with Forest Service offices in Afton and Jackson for the latest.

CENTRAL WYOMING

The counties of Natrona and Converse enclose definitive Wyoming country: sage-and-grass-carpeted plains, desolate badlands, impressive tree-draped mountainsides, and the big, lazy North Platte River. This is grazing country; each year nearly a quarter of the sheep raised in Wyoming, and 120,000 cattle, come from these two counties. The dominant industry, however—and the one that dictates the region's economy—is oil. It means jobs for roughnecks in dozens of oil fields, but it also greases the wheels of city life, creating refinery and transportation jobs, government positions, and a wave of other effects in the local community as the wages pass on to construction workers, shop owners, and schoolteachers. Without oil, Casper—Wyoming's second-largest metropolitan area—would be little more than a cattle town crossroads on the way to Yellowstone.

The Land

Geographically, central Wyoming is quite diverse. The north portion is an open, expansive place. Driving across the long, straight highways that divide this land is like sailing a boat over an ocean of gentle rollers—the mountains are so far in the distance that they could well be islands. Golden eagles spin giant loops in the sky, and the coal black clouds of distant summertime thunderheads are pierced by brilliant slashes of lightning. The wind blows on, bending the grass as it passes in waves of motion, whirling the old windmills that pump water to sheep, cattle, and deer. This is rolling mixed-grass prairie and sagebrush country, with sharp ridges appearing suddenly, topped by narrow bands of ponderosa pine and juniper.

South of this rangeland lies the North Platte River, carving a slow curve first north, then east, and finally southeast toward Nebraska. Giant dams hold back the water for irrigation and electricity. A green stripe of riparian forests and irrigated fields borders the river. South of the Platte, the land changes again, with the Laramie Mountains rising in a rough-edged jumble of rugged canyons and pine-covered peaks. Elk stand along mountain meadows, bugling in the cool air of late fall. Pickup trucks slow as wild turkeys speed-walk across the gravel roads. Clear mountain brooks cascade down mountain slopes. West of here, central Wyoming be-

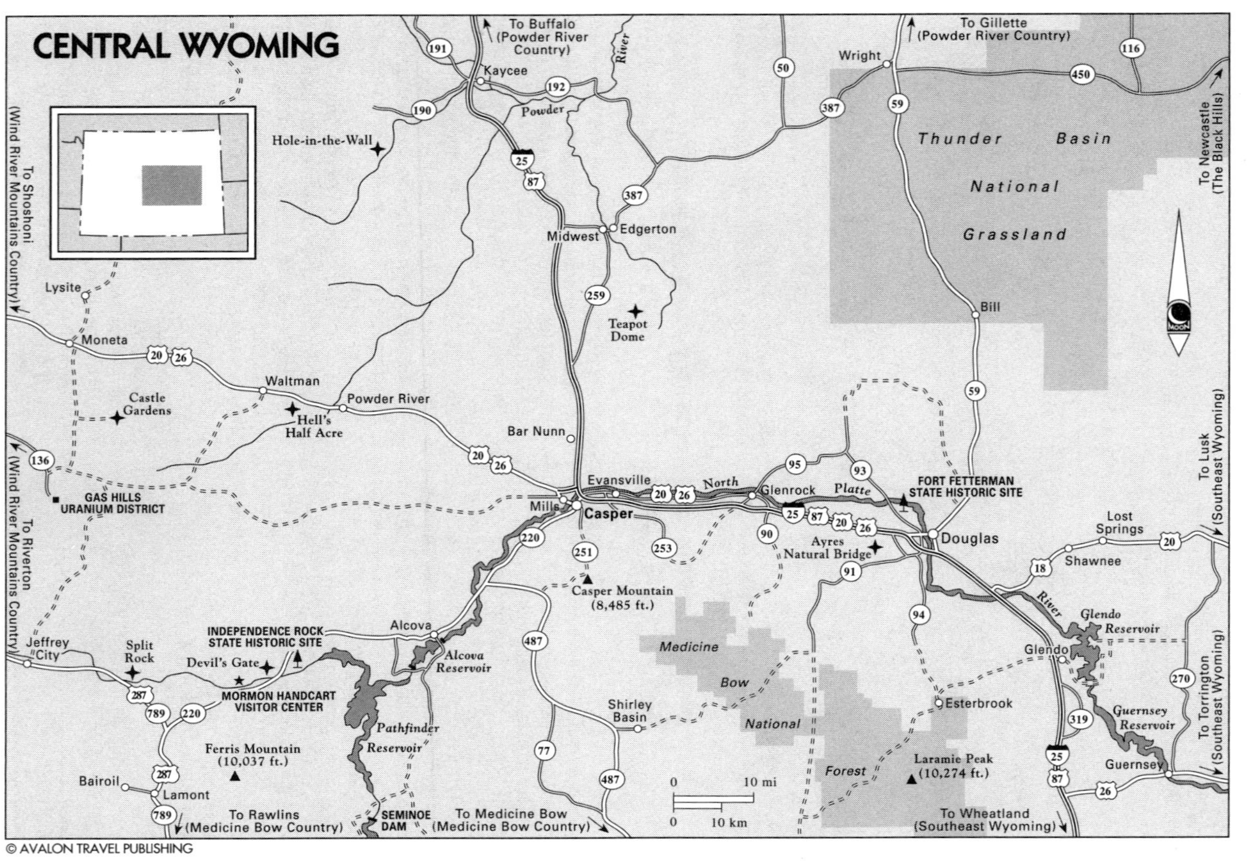
CENTRAL WYOMING
To Buffalo (Powder River Country)
To Gillette (Powder River Country)
To Newcastle (The Black Hills)
Kaycee
Powder
River
Wright
Hole-in-the-Wall
Thunder Basin National Grassland
Midwest
Edgerton
Teapot Dome
Bill
Lysite
Moneta
Waltman
Powder River
Castle Gardens
Hell's Half Acre
Bar Nunn
To Shoshoni (Wind River Mountains Country)
To Riverton (Wind River Mountains Country)
GAS HILLS URANIUM DISTRICT
Evansville
North
Glenrock
Platte
FORT FETTERMAN STATE HISTORIC SITE
Mills
Casper
Douglas
Ayres Natural Bridge
Lost Springs
Shawnee
To Lusk (Southeast Wyoming)
Casper Mountain (8,485 ft.)
River
Glendo Reservoir
Glendo
Alcova
Alcova Reservoir
INDEPENDENCE ROCK STATE HISTORIC SITE
Jeffrey City
Split Rock
Devil's Gate
MORMON HANDCART VISITOR CENTER
Medicine Bow National Forest
Shirley Basin
Esterbrook
Guernsey Reservoir
Guernsey
To Torrington (Southeast Wyoming)
Pathfinder Reservoir
Ferris Mountain (10,037 ft.)
Laramie Peak (10,274 ft.)
Bairoil
Lamont
0 10 mi
0 10 km
To Rawlins (Medicine Bow Country)
SEMINOE DAM
To Medicine Bow (Medicine Bow Country)
To Wheatland (Southeast Wyoming)
© AVALON TRAVEL PUBLISHING

comes drier and more desolate, wrinkled by the badlands of Hell's Half Acre and the barren crests of desert mountain ranges.

Casper dominates the central Wyoming economy with an oil refinery, the primary statewide newspaper, and the state's largest junior college and shopping mall. The towns of Douglas and Glenrock go their own ways, with a mixture of ranching, oil, coal, and tourism. Farther north, the tiny settlements of Midwest and Edgerton cap the vast Salt Creek Oil Field. Between these few outposts of civilization lie hundreds of square miles of sagebrush and grass, jackrabbits, and rattlers. Only the scattered roads, oil pumpjacks, windmills, and old ranch houses mark the presence of humans.

DOUGLAS

Douglas (pop. 5,500) epitomizes life in small-town America. It's the sort of place where the big summertime events are the state fair and weekly drag races, where a night on the town means joining a bowling league or doing the two-step at the LaBonte Inn, and where old-timers hang out in the historic College Inn Bar. On both ends of Douglas are more modern slices of Americana—suburban ranch-style homes cover the hills. It's a friendly, conservative town with pickup trucks, dense American food, and an unusual history.

SIGHTSEEING HIGHLIGHTS FOR CENTRAL WYOMING

- Pioneer Museum and Jackalopes in Douglas
- Fort Fetterman
- Thunder Basin National Grassland
- Laramie Peak and Esterbrook in the Laramie Mountains
- Ayres Natural Bridge Park
- Fort Caspar, Nicolaysen Art Museum, National Historic Trails Interpretive Center (opens in 2001) in Casper
- Casper Mountain
- Independence Rock, Devil's Gate, and the Mormon Handcart Visitor Center along the Oregon Trail
- Salt Creek oil field near Midwest
- Hell's Half Acre west of Powder River
- Castle Gardens near Moneta
- Popular events: Wyoming State Fair in Douglas (August), Central Wyoming Fair and Rodeo in Casper (August), PRCA Rodeo Finals in Casper (October)

HISTORY

Douglas came into existence with the arrival of the Fremont, Elkhorn, and Missouri Valley Railroad. Platted in 1886, the town was named for Stephen A. Douglas, the senator from Illinois best known for his debates with Abraham Lincoln. It quickly boomed to 1,600 people that first year, boasting three newspapers, several restaurants and hotels, two dance halls, 12 stores, and 21 saloons (easy to see where priorities lay). Once the railroad construction had moved on down the line to Casper, the population dwindled and it became a sleepy little ranching center for the next 70 years. Only the late-summer state fair brought Douglas to life each year.

World War II

One of the strangest pieces of Douglas history is its prisoner-of-war camp, built in 1943 along the North Platte River. The camp contained 180 barracks-style buildings and housed up to 3,000 prisoners of war. The camp was surrounded by an electrified fence, watchtowers, German shepherds, and army guards. One prisoner was shot by a guard and a few others escaped, but they didn't get far in this remote country—2,000 miles from the sea. Though some of the prisoners at Douglas were German Nazi and SS officers, the majority were Italians, many of whom were happy to be away from the war.

The prisoners worked in local agricultural fields harvesting potatoes and sugar beets for $4 a day, or at a variety of art projects in the camp. Most impressive was the work of several Italian artists who painted the interior of the U.S. officers' club with 15 murals of Old West scenes. After the war, the prisoners returned home, though some have returned to visit in later years. The land was sold to Converse County for $1, and the barracks were dismantled or bought by locals who moved them to other parts of town. Today the POW camp site is an open meadow on the west bank of the North Platte south of Richards Street.

Boom and Bust

Like much of Wyoming, Douglas has watched its fortunes wax and wane over the years. In the 1950s, with the Cold War at fever pitch, prospectors combed Wyoming with Geiger counters, discovering major uranium deposits just north of Douglas. Others found oil, gas, and coal. A giant coal-fired power plant opened in nearby Glenrock, and by the late '70s the region was one of the most prosperous in the state. At the peak of the oil-and-uranium orgy of the early 1980s, the town of Douglas had doubled in size to over 10,000 people. But then the bust hit, and within a couple of years the population plummeted back to where it had been. Longtime locals had mixed feelings when the balloon suddenly burst—they were happy to see the rabble leave town but were also suddenly burdened with paying for all the new schools, roads, and other facilities ordered up

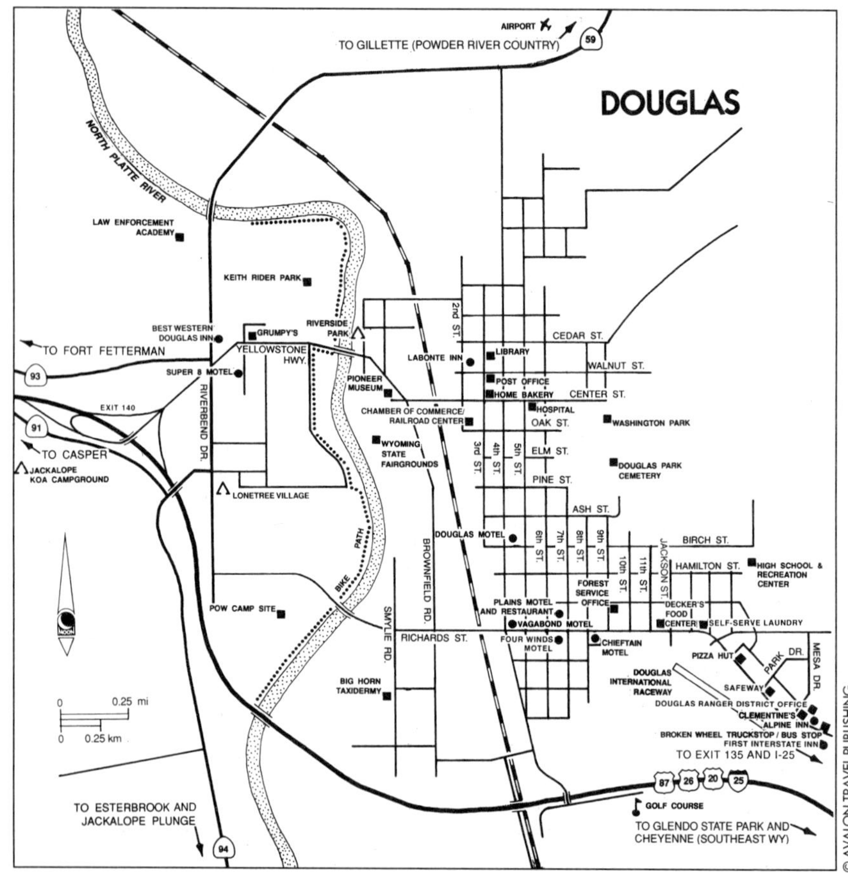

JACKALOPES

What's a jackalope? Definition: a mammal that moves by bounding, found originally in Converse County, Wyoming, but now distributed throughout the western states. It has the horns of an antelope, the body of a jackrabbit, and the stealth of both. First observed by trapper Roy Ball in 1829, the jackalope was later noted by cowboys and others after too little sleep, too many days in the saddle, and too much cheap whiskey. Nocturnal animals, jackalopes are never seen during the day. These powerful and vicious animals are reputed to attain speeds approaching 90 mph and often sing and mate during thunderstorms. The hornless does are commonly seen by tourists, while the bucks remain elusive. Westerners—particularly members of the militias—feel that the federal government is hushing up the true story of these dangerous critters to make cowboys look like liars.

Okay, I admit to liking plastic pink flamingos and tacky postcards, but jackalopes are another story. The first time you see a mounted jackalope specimen, it is mildly amusing, but with each tourist junk shop west of the Mississippi offering more jackalopes, the originality quickly fades. The town of Douglas takes credit for this harebrained idea, though its claim is a bit suspect. In the 1920s, a Douglas resident saw a jackalope mounted in a store in Buffalo, Wyoming. He described the creature to his grandson, Douglas Herrick, who was intrigued by the animal. In 1941, he attached the antlers of a deer to the head of a large jackrabbit he had shot and sold the specimen to the LaBonte Hotel. The rest, as they say, is history.

In 1960, the State of Wyoming gave the Douglas Chamber of Commerce "jackalope" as a registered trademark. Today you see jackalopes everywhere in Douglas: the town symbol contains one; an eight-foot-tall jackalope statue greets visitors at Jackalope Square; another statue has hopped atop the LaBonte Hotel; and a roadside sign warns "Watch Out For Jackalope." You can buy cans of jackalope milk in the stores, "Rabbit Punch" at a local bar, and jackalope hunting licenses at several spots around town. And, of course, the critters multiply like rabbits on the shelves of local shops.

in the heady heyday. Today, the economy of Douglas is back to its old mixture of energy and ranching, with some people commuting 60 miles each way to the busy coal mines near Wright while others work for the railroad or at two small uranium mines northwest of town. Most folks are happy to live a simpler life. Of course, the next energy boom could be just around the corner in the form of coalbed methane gas.

SIGHTS

Pioneer Museum

The people of Douglas point with pride to their large local museum, easily one of the finest in Wyoming. Located just inside the fairgrounds, the spacious and free museum, tel. (307) 358-9288, is open Mon.-Fri. 8 a.m.-5 p.m. and Saturday 1-5 p.m. (closed Sunday) June-Sept., and Mon.-Fri. 8 a.m.-5 p.m. the rest of the year.

The main room is filled with old rifles and saddles, including one that belonged to outlaw Tom Horn. Check out the special "running irons" used by rustlers to alter cattle brands. Fittingly enough, the rifle of Nate Champion—a rustler murdered in the Johnson County Wars—is also here. Above one doorway is a pole from the original transcontinental telegraph line; it's one of just six known to survive. Look around the other rooms and you'll discover the bison-fur mittens worn by Portugee Phillips on his ride to get help for Fort Kearny and an army trumpet and bullets from the Custer battlefield.

The museum also contains hundreds of historic photos, a big doll collection, clothing from the 1890s, and a back room filled with impressive Indian artifacts including baskets, pottery, Sioux and Crow war clubs, a bow from the Custer battleground, and a tepee used in the movie *Dances with Wolves*. Downstairs are several wonderful old quilts and a collection of homestead items. The stairwell features the 64-inch-waist overalls that belonged to flamboyant C.B. Irwin, one of outlaw Tom Horn's closest friends. Irwin was a stockman, railroad detective, rodeo performer, and manager of Cheyenne Frontier Days. Outside is a schoolhouse constructed in 1886.

Douglas Railroad Interpretive Center

This center consists of seven train cars parked outside the old Chicago Elk Horn Railroad depot (built in 1888 and now home to the chamber of commerce). The collection includes a steam locomotive, dining car, sleeper, baggage car, coach, cattle car, and caboose. They represent many different eras—oldest is the 1884 caboose. Volunteers give tours of the train cars Sat.-Sun. 9 a.m.-5 p.m. May-September.

More Sights

Ruts of the **Oregon Trail** are still visible nine miles south of Douglas; ask at the chamber of commerce for directions. The old **officers' club** from the Douglas POW camp is now an Odd Fellows Hall at 115 S. Riverbend Dr., tel. (307) 358-2421. Ask to take a look inside at the wall-to-wall murals painted by Italian artists who were prisoners during WW II.

One of Wyoming's oldest churches is the **Christ Episcopal Church,** built in 1896 and now on the National Register of Historic Places. The attractive white structure is at 411 Center, tel. (307) 358-5609.

The **Plains Complex,** 628 E. Richards, tel. (307) 358-4489, has several historic structures hauled in from all over this part of Wyoming. Included are the old officers' quarters from Fort Fetterman and a POW-camp building. The ice-cream parlor served at various times as a barn, a boardinghouse, and maternity center. Check out the doors on the ceiling of the ice-cream shop.

Douglas Park Cemetery, at 9th and Ash Sts., has a number of interesting old graves, including that of horse thief and later saloon-keeper "Doc" Middleton. Also here is the grave of the outlaw George W. Pike, whose exploits managed to lead to at least two appearances in court annually for 15 consecutive years. His gravestone (found near the center of the cemetery) reads:

Underneath this stone in eternal rest
Sleeps the wildest one of the wayward west
He was gambler and sport and cowboy too
And he led the pace in an outlaw crew.
He was sure on the trigger and staid
to the end
But he was never known to quit on a friend
In the relations of death all mankind is alike
But in life there was only one George W. Pike.

ACCOMMODATIONS AND CAMPING

Seven different motels are available in Douglas, along with two B&Bs and three nearby guest ranches. In July and August you should book reservations up to two months ahead—especially for the weekend drag races and state fair week. Several locals rent out rooms in their homes to visitors while the fair is going on; get a list from the chamber of commerce, tel. (307) 358-2950.

Motels

Douglas motels are listed below from least to most expensive. Add a seven percent tax to these rates.

Budget: Four Winds Motel, 615 E. Richards, tel. (307) 358-2322, charges just $28 s or $30-34 d, but when this was written, most rooms were rented out by the week. It's a bit heavy on the Christianity. You'll find more plain rooms at the **Plains Motel,** 628 E. Richards, tel. (307) 358-4484, where the rates are $30 s or $32 d. Kitchenettes available.

Inexpensive: Chieftain Motel, 815 Richards, tel. (307) 358-2673, has spacious rooms with fridges and microwaves for $36-39 s or $36-45 d.

Out on the east side of town, **Alpine Inn,** 2310 E. Richards, tel. (307) 358-4780, has well-maintained rooms for $38 s or $44 d, including use of a free washer and dryer.

Opened in 1914, the historic **LaBonte Inn,** 206 Walnut, tel. (307) 358-9856, has newly refurbished rooms with private baths for $42-51 s or d. The bar downstairs can be noisy when bands are playing (Thurs.-Sat. nights).

Stay in standard chain-motel accommodations at **Super 8 Motel,** 314 Russell Ave., tel. (307) 358-6800 or (800) 800-8000, where the rooms cost $44 s or $52 d.

On the east end of town, **First Interstate Inn,** 2349 E. Richards, tel. (307) 358-2833, has accommodations for $45 s or $50 d, some with in-room fridges.

Expensive: Best Western Douglas Inn, 1450 Riverbend Dr., tel. (307) 358-9790 or (800) 344-2113, www.chalkbuttes.com/bwdouglas, is the nicest place in Douglas. Rates are $79-89 s or $89-99 d, including a large indoor pool, jacuzzi, sauna, and weight room.

Bed and Breakfasts

More than a century old, **Carriage House B&B,** 413 Center St., tel. (307) 358-2752, was originally built as a barn, then remodeled into a home in the 1950s. It offers three guest rooms with private or shared baths. Rates are $45 s or d, including a continental breakfast. Kids are welcome. Inexpensive.

Another classic is the lovingly restored **Morton Mansion Bed & Breakfast,** 425 E. Center St., tel. (307) 358-2129. This stately 1903 Queen Anne has a wraparound porch, along with three spacious guest rooms ($75 d) and a two-bedroom suite ($100 for four people), all with private baths. A continental breakfast is served; no kids under 12. Moderate-Expensive.

Guest Ranches

Deer Forks Ranch, 24 miles south of Douglas, tel. (307) 358-2033, provides a fine chance to join in horseback riding and other activities on a 5,000-acre working cattle and sheep ranch. It's a long ways out here and the road gets muddy when it rains, but the Laramie Mountain backdrop and friendly down-home owners make this a fun place. Guests stay in two modern houses with kitchens ($45 s or $90 d without meals) and can ride horses ($35) or simply relax in the country. Accommodations are also offered at a second large ranch in the rolling grasslands 25 miles east of Bill. A two-night minimum stay is required. Expensive.

An excellent place to experience ranch life is **Cheyenne River Ranch,** 50 miles northeast of Douglas, tel. (307) 358-2380, www.ranchweb.com/cheyenne. This 8,000-acre working cattle and sheep ranch offers an old-time ranch experience. Guests can go on trail rides, feed orphan lambs, gather eggs, or simply sit back and relax in the country. All-inclusive rates are $320 per day for two people, with a minimum stay of three days. The ranch has space for a maximum of 12 guests, with lodging in two cabins and the ranch house. The season is May-September. Luxury.

Two Creek Ranch, tel. (307) 358-3467, www.chalkbuttes.com/2creekranch, is a 25,000-acre spread eight miles south of Douglas. The owners run 600 cows with their calves over this land and take on working dudes late April to October. Guests ride horseback while helping out in calving, work a 75-mile cattle drive, or assist with branding, roundups, and other ranch activities. Prices are a reasonable $100 per person per day all-inclusive, and most dudes stay five to 11 days. This is the real thing, with guests sleeping in the bunkhouse, travel trailers, or tents; no hot tubs or swimming pools here. Luxury.

Camping

Pitch tents or park RVs for free at **Riverside Park** along the North Platte River. The free showers have an amusing Western-decor bathroom covered with branded wood. Camping is limited to two nights, and the sprinklers come on at 8 a.m., so get up early! Call (307) 358-9750 or (307) 358-3311 for details.

See Douglas Vicinity below for details on Forest Service campsites in the nearby Laramie Mountains. In town, the RV crowd heads to **Jackalope KOA,** tel. (307) 358-2164 or (800) 562-2469, west of Douglas on State Hwy. 91. Rates are $16 for tents, $21 for RVs, $28 d for basic "kamping kabins"; open April-October. **Lonetree Village Mobile Home Park,** 1 Lonetree Dr., tel. (307) 358-6669, also has RV parking for $11 and tent sites for $5. During the state fair, camping is available on the fairgrounds; call (307) 358-2398 for specifics.

FOOD

With a few exceptions, restaurant food in Douglas is pretty standard Wyoming fare. For dependable meals and big portions three times a day, you won't go wrong at **LaBonte Inn,** 206 Walnut St., tel. (307) 358-9856. The restaurant specializes in skillet breakfasts, specialty hamburgers, and prime rib, but also has a fair-sized salad bar and homemade pies.

Broken Wheel Truckstop, just east of town, tel. (307) 358-4446, serves breakfast 24 hours a day. The so-so coffee shop at **Plains Complex,** 628 E. Richards, tel. (307) 358-4489, is also open 24 hours, but its old-fashioned ice-cream parlor is a better bet.

The best lunch spot in town is **Thru-the-Grapevine Coffee Co.,** 301 Center St., tel. (307) 358-4567, where you'll find homemade soup, bagels, sandwiches, salads, sweets, and espresso. For a more traditional American version of coffee culture, hang out with the locals at **Bright's Cafe,** 108 N. 3rd St., tel. (307) 358-3509. It's a good place for greasy curly fries, burgers, sandwiches, and shakes.

Hoops & Dreams, 1199 Mesa Dr., tel. (307) 358-3355, is a family restaurant filled with Douglas-area sports memorabilia. Watch sports on five TV screens while sampling the standard mix of pasta, steaks, burgers, and Mexican dishes. **La Costa,** 1213 Teton Way, tel. (307) 358-2449, has more authentic Mexican meals.

Chute's Eatery, in the Best Western, 1450 Riverbend Dr., tel. (307) 358-9790, has a soup and salad buffet and an all-you-can-eat Sunday brunch. The quality seems to vary depending upon who's cooking that day. **Pizza Hut,** 1830 Richards, tel. (307) 358-3657, also has stuff-yourself lunch specials.

For fresh-baked pastries, head downtown to **Home Bakery,** 119 N. 3rd, tel. (307) 358-9251.

Local grocery stores include **Peyton Bolln Grocery,** 100 S. 3rd St.; **Decker's Food Pride,** 1100 E. Richards, tel. (307) 358-3645; **Douglas Grocery,** 130 S. 4th St., tel. (307) 358-2250; and **Safeway,** 1900 E. Richards St., tel. (307) 358-3446.

OTHER PRACTICALITIES

Recreation

A two-mile paved path follows the west bank of the North Platte River through **Riverside Park** and is a great spot for an evening stroll or bike ride. Take along your fishing pole to try for trout, walleye, or channel catfish. If you have your own raft or canoe, the river is a fun place for leisurely float trips; pick up a map of river access points from the chamber of commerce.

The free **Douglas Recreation Center** at the high school, 1701 Hamilton, tel. (307) 358-4231, houses an indoor pool, gyms, racquetball courts, a sauna, and weight room. An excellent **outdoor swimming pool** in Washington Park is open in the summer.

An 18-hole **golf course,** tel. (307) 358-5099, is southeast of Douglas, but it has no sand traps—the fierce winter winds kept blowing them away.

Entertainment

Chutes Saloon in the Best Western Douglas Inn, 1450 Riverbend Dr., tel. (307) 358-9790, has lounge-lizard tunes, a big-screen TV, and free hors d'oeuvres on weeknights. **LaBonte Lounge,** 206 Walnut, tel. (307) 358-5210, is the place for live music Thurs.-Sat. nights. The historic **College Inn Bar,** 103 N. 2nd, tel. (307) 358-9976, is a favorite place for major-league drinking. Drop by on Wednesday nights for 50-cent draft beers. For movies, head to **Mesa Theatre,** 104 N. 3rd St., tel. (307) 358-6209.

Wyoming State Fair

In 1905, the Wyoming Legislature appropriated $10,000 for a Wyoming State Fair in Douglas. With land donated by the Chicago and Northwestern Railroad, the "Show Window of Wyoming" opened that summer, offering a variety of agricultural exhibits, horseback wrestling, Roman races, and concerts. To top it off, two cavalry soldiers added their own drama by putting on an impromptu gunfight. Later, auto polo and motorcycle-riding events were added, but the big hit was Professor Carver's High Diving Girl, who leapt with her horse off a 40-foot platform into a pool of water.

The Wyoming State Fair is held the entire third week of August each year, drawing thousands of visitors from all over the nation. The 113-acre fairgrounds is right next to town and includes a 4,300-seat grandstand, an arts-and-crafts building, a cafeteria, an arena, an open-air pavilion, livestock barns and stalls, and, of course, plenty of carnival rides, cotton candy, and stuffed-animal prizes in the midway. Keep yourself entertained at the market swine evaluation, the 4-H vegetable judging, the demolition derby, or the sheep-to-shawl contest. A free "people shuttle" (tractor-pulled wagon) takes folks around the fairgrounds. Other attractions include evening country-and-western concerts, the Miss Rodeo Wyoming contest, and a Saturday morning parade. Since this is Wyoming, the biggest events at the fair are the **PRCA rodeos** held the final three days. Call (307) 358-2398 for additional state fair information.

Other Events

Both locals and visitors enjoy the **High Plains Country Music Festival & Crafts Fair,** held in early May. Plenty of hot fiddle, guitar, and banjo players provide the entertainment; call (307) 358-9006 for specifics. **Fort Fetterman Days,** held the second weekend of June at the old fort, attracts a troop of soldiers and other period-attired folks for a festival featuring black-powder contests, old-time music, folklore, crafts, living-history demonstrations, Indian dancing, and games. Call (307) 358-2864 for details. Also in mid-June is the **Douglas Invitational Western Art Show,** which takes place at the museum; call (307) 358-9288 for details.

On the third weekend of June, **Jackalope Days** offers a free pancake breakfast, street dance and beer garden, games, arts and crafts, a motorcycle and classic car show, bed races, and live music. Call (307) 358-2398 for details.

The **Wyoming High School Rodeo Finals** take place in late June at the fairgrounds. The first weekend of August brings in a very popular **Senior Pro Rodeo.**

From May through September, the grandiosely named **Douglas International Raceway** on the southeast edge of town hosts **drag races** of all types. Located on an old airport runway, it's considered one of the top quarter-mile strips in the nation. The biggest races take place in mid-July; call (307) 234-0685 for the rundown. In early August, Douglas plays host to hundreds of motorcycle enthusiasts en route to the Sturgis Rally, with the town providing hospitality tents and other facilities.

Information

The **Douglas Area Chamber of Commerce** is inside the old train depot at 121 Brownfield Rd., tel. (307) 358-2950, www.jackalope.org. Open Mon.-Fri. 9 a.m.-5 p.m. all year. You can also pick up brochures inside on summer weekends when the railroad center is open.

The Forest Service's **Douglas Ranger District Office,** 2250 E. Richards St., tel. (307) 358-4690, www.fs.fed.us/mrnf, has maps ($4) and info on Medicine Bow-Routt National Forest and Thunder Basin National Grassland.

Services and Transportation

The **Converse County Library,** is at 300 Walnut St., tel. (307) 358-3644, and the **post office** is at 129 N. 3rd St., tel. (307) 358-3106. **ATMs** can be found in local banks and gas stations.

R-D Pharmacy & Books, 206 Center, tel. (307) 358-3266, sells a good selection of Wyoming books. Visit the **Meadowlark Gallery** at 300 S. 4th St., tel. (307) 358-3808, for local arts and crafts.

Wash your duds at **Sudsy Duds,** 1400 E. Richards St., tel. (307) 358-8022, or **Clay St. Laundry,** 2nd and Clay, tel. (307) 358-8085.

Powder River/Coach USA, tel. (800) 442-3682, has daily bus service from Douglas to towns in northern and central Wyoming, continuing north to Billings or Rapid City and south to Cheyenne or Denver. Buses stop at The Plains Motel, 628 E. Richards.

DOUGLAS VICINITY

FORT FETTERMAN

Seven miles northwest of Douglas on State Hwy. 93 is Fort Fetterman State Historic Site. The fort was named for Lt. Col. William J. Fetterman, who was killed by Indians in the Fetterman Massacre of 1866 (see the section on "Powder River Country"). Begun in 1867, this was the last fort built in the Rockies. With the signing of the Fort Laramie Treaty of 1868, Forts Casper, Reno, Phil Kearny, and C.F. Smith were all closed, leaving Fort Fetterman the only army base in northern Wyoming. The remote hilltop location afforded commanding views along the infamous Bozeman Trail in both directions, but the location proved inhospitable. A report to headquarters the first winter noted "officers and men were found under canvas exposed on a bleak plain to violent and almost constant gales and very uncomfortable."

Even after the buildings were completed the fort remained a dreaded, windswept, lonely place, and many soldiers deserted as soon as they could get to the nearest railroad. The regimen was strict, with daily parade drills and the prospect of long rides to fight Indians in the surrounding country. Soldiers called the place "Hell Hole," while the Sioux derisively labeled it "Fort Fetterman Reservation." Not far away stood the "Hog Ranch"—sin city on the plains—where gambling, drinking, and women offered a choice of ways to spend the $13 a month the calvarymen received.

Fort Fetterman served as a supply base for the army during the mid-1870s, and both General Crook and Colonel MacKenzie led expeditions from here to attack the Sioux, but the fort itself was never the scene of any conflicts. After the battles had finally died down, the fort was abandoned in 1882. Instead of immediately disappearing, however, "Fetterman City" became the center of ranching and trade in the area. For a while, at least, it was a wide-open town with enough gunfights, hangings, whoring, gambling, and drunkenness to give Fox television stations a run for the money. In his novel *The Virginian,* Owen Wister used Fetterman as the basis for his rough-and-tumble town of "Drybone."

Alferd Packer

One of the characters attracted to Fetterman was a prospector who called himself John Swartz. When a waiter was slow in bringing water at a local restaurant, he pulled a gun, saying, "Damn you, ain't you going to bring me that water?" Service quickly improved. The man turned out to be Alferd Packer, wanted for robbing, killing, and then eating his five mining partners in Colorado during the winter of 1875. (Packer called human breast meat the sweetest he'd ever eaten.) After escaping from a Colorado jail, he remained free for the next decade before finally being recognized in Fetterman City. The sheriff captured him at a nearby ranch and spent several nervous nights on the long stage ride to Rock Creek before finally turning Packer over to Colorado authorities. Although convicted of murder, Packer managed to escape from prison again; his body was found in the Rockies in 1903.

The Fort Today

After the railroad arrived in 1886, Douglas became the new center for trade, and Fetterman quickly faded from the scene. Most of the buildings were torn down or moved to Douglas; only two of the original buildings remain: an adobe ordnance warehouse and a log officers' quarters. Inside the officers' quarters is a small state-run **museum** (free) which includes historic displays on the fort, Indian battles, and Fetterman City. The buildings are open daily 9 a.m.-5 p.m. from Memorial Day to Labor Day, and by appointment only (tel. 307-358-2864) the rest of the year. The grounds are open sunrise to sunset in the summer. Entrance is $2 per person for nonresidents or $1 for Wyoming residents; no camping. The surrounding country still exudes a sense of barren loneliness, and it's easy to see how much the soldiers must have hated this windswept post. Ask the museum staff to point out the faint tracks of the "Bloody Bozeman" Trail to the south.

PRAIRIE DOGS

Prairie dogs are cat-sized rodents that live in underground communities and feed on roots and plants. Prairie dog towns sometimes cover thousands of acres with burrow holes spaced every 50 feet or so; a Texas colony was once 100 miles long and 250 miles wide! Two species are found in Wyoming: white-tailed and black-tailed. The latter occur in more than a hundred towns covering some 14,000 acres within Thunder Basin National Grassland, while white-tailed prairie dogs are found in parts of south-central and western Wyoming. Ranchers often complain of lost grazing range due to feeding and digging by the "dogs" and injuries to horses and cattle that step into the holes. Research, however, has shown that prairie dogs may actually improve grazing in some situations and that cattle seem to prefer to graze in prairie dog colonies. In addition, prairie dogs provide food for many predators and create habitat used by many other animals.

An Endangered Species?

For many decades, ranchers and the Forest Service systematically poisoned prairie dog colonies in the name of "range improvement." These practices proved devastatingly effective and helped create a fragmented population that is susceptible to inbreeding and disease. A century ago, prairie dogs occupied 700 million acres of western grasslands; today they are found on just two million acres. Sightings of the endangered black-footed ferret on Thunder Basin National Grassland helped end most of the poisoning in the 1970s, and prairie dog populations rebounded dramatically. Unfortunately, they are highly susceptible to sylvatic plague, an exotic disease that sweeps through the colonies killing thousands of animals in a short period. In addition, because prairie dogs are still considered varmints in many areas, "sport" hunters don't need a license to shoot them and aren't limited on how many they can kill.

Meanwhile, the U.S. Fish & Wildlife Service is raising a covey of once-wild ferrets at a Sybille Canyon facility, hoping to someday return them to such places as the national grassland (see the special topic on black-footed ferrets in the Southeast Wyoming chapter for more). By trying to contain the prairie dog population to small and fragmented areas, the hunters and private ranchers may well be endangering the long-term survival of the black-footed ferret, one of the world's rarest mammals. The story may well have changed dramatically by the time you read this, since black-tailed prairie dogs themselves may be declared an endangered species by the U.S. Fish & Wildlife Service. It's an astounding situation: although prairie dogs may be headed for the endangered species list, hunters are still killing them by the thousands! For more information, see the Fish & Wildlife Service's website at www.r6.fws.gov/btprairiedog.

Seeing Prairie Dogs

If you're interested in seeing prairie dogs, ask at the Douglas Forest Service office for a copy of its prairie dog town map. The largest area is along Horse Creek in the Rochelle Hills, with smaller prairie dog colonies along N. Antelope Road. Another good place to view black-tailed prairie dogs is Devils Tower National Monument; see the Black Hills chapter for details. Use caution if you're hiking around prairie dog colonies since the dogs may be infected with the plague bacteria, cause of Europe's infamous "black death" in the 1300s. Fleas carry the disease, which is potentially deadly but relatively easy to halt with antibiotics.

Fort Fetterman Days, the second weekend of July, brings military demonstrations, Indian dancing, fort tours, firing of artillery pieces, old-time music, crafts, and games. Many of the participants dress in authentic 1870s costume.

THUNDER BASIN NATIONAL GRASSLAND AND VICINITY

Thunder Basin National Grassland is an expansive blend of high rolling plateaus, steep rocky escarpments, and gentle plains. It's one of the few places in Wyoming where mountain ranges are not visible, giving the countryside a North Dakota feel. The country seems to reach forever. There's virtually no traffic on some of the main routes across the grassland, especially State Hwy. 450 between Wright and Newcastle. Most of the national grassland is covered with a mixture of western wheatgrass, blue grama grass, and big sagebrush, but some of the ridges have stands of ponderosa pine and juniper, while creek bottoms contain cottonwood trees or greasewood. Naturalists count 170 golden-eagle nests on Thunder Basin—one of the biggest concentrations in Wyoming—along with abundant populations of sandhill cranes, turkeys, antelope, mule deer, elk, and coyotes. Many bald eagles winter here. Look out for the jackalopes, too; lots of the antlerless variety get hit by cars.

Thunder Basin National Grassland covers 1.8 million acres within Powder River Basin. The land is a mix of private ranches and property belonging to the Forest Service, the BLM, and the state. The federal government owns 572,000 acres of the total. In the past, a patchwork quilt of land ownership created access and management problems for the grassland. Through a series of land trades, the grassland is now more consolidated and accessible. Get a current ownership map ($4) from the Forest Service's **Douglas Ranger District Office,** 2250 E. Richards St., tel. (307) 358-4690, www.fs.fed.us/mrnf.

History

Thunder Basin came about during the glory days of the New Deal and remains today an enclave of pseudosocialism within the rock-ribbed Republican state of Wyoming. Although ranchers had grazed sheep and cattle in the area since the mid-19th century, the arrival of homesteaders caused the land to be divided into smaller parcels. In the arid mixed-grass prairies of eastern Wyoming, it was nearly impossible for a family to survive—the rains fell too infrequently for farming, and profitable cattle or sheep operations required more than 640 acres of grazing land.

Overgrazing, soil erosion, and five consecutive drought years in the 1930s combined to force many families off the land. Counties risked bankruptcy because of lost tax revenue. The Agricultural Adjustment Administration finally began purchasing homesteads in 1934, giving money to the counties in lieu of taxes. Programs were begun to reestablish grasses to protect the soil and to develop water sources for livestock, while private land ownership was consolidated into larger, more economically manageable units.

Management

Today, local ranchers use the grassland in a cooperative grazing scheme that allows 21,000 cattle and an equal number of sheep on the federal land. Improvements such as dams, wells, and fences are cooperatively developed. In addition to livestock grazing, practically every acre of Thunder Basin has been leased for petroleum exploration. Currently, over 375 oil and gas wells pump from 58 oil fields. Vast deposits of subbituminous coal underlie almost the entire area, and there are a number of gigantic strip mines, including Black Thunder Coal Mine, the largest coal mine in the nation. Revenues from oil and coal development on the grassland top $50 million a year for the federal and state treasuries, a figure unmatched anywhere else in the Forest Service system. Bentonite—a lubricant and absorptive clay used in everything from oil-drilling muds to candy bars—is also mined on the grassland, and major uranium deposits wait for the public to forget about Three Mile Island and Chernobyl.

Recreation

A network of over 1,200 miles of gravel and dirt roads crisscrosses Thunder Basin National Grassland. No developed campgrounds or trails, but you can camp for free anywhere on the public lands. A couple of areas are popular with hunters, birdwatchers, photographers, and others looking for a chance to get out and about.

The **Rochelle Hills** area, a forested volcanic escarpment near the intersection of Converse, Campbell, and Weston Counties, is one of the prettiest parts of the national grassland. A scenic gravel road takes you on a long loop north of the tiny settlement of **Bill** (the name came from four early homesteaders, all of whom had the same first name) and then for 50 miles through the Rochelle Hills before dropping back to State Hwy. 59 eight miles south of Wright. Unfortunately, massive landslides have destroyed a section of this road, and it may be too expensive to repair.

The Upton-Osage area also contains miles of ponderosa-pine-topped hills and many small ponds that attract birds. Another fascinating area is in the northern part of the grassland in the Soda Well/Weston area (30 miles north of Gillette on State Hwy. 59). This is a fine place to camp or explore; see the Forest Service for access details throughout the grassland.

As with much of Wyoming's rangelands, you should be on guard for prairie rattlesnakes, especially around rock piles and prairie-dog towns. Also, beware of thunderstorms and the lightning that can strike in this open country—this isn't called Thunder Basin for nothing. Because of the lack of drinking-water sources, carry plenty with you in your travels.

LARAMIE MOUNTAINS

The Laramie Peak portion of Medicine Bow-Routt National Forest lies approximately 30 miles south of Douglas, cutting from northwest to southeast along the Laramie Mountains. The mountains are draped with stands of ponderosa, lodgepole, and limber pine, and Engelmann spruce and subalpine fir at higher elevations. Lower elevations are dominated by grass and sagebrush. It's pretty but rugged country, with deep valleys dividing the high granitic ridges and peaks—several exceeding 9,000 feet. Deer, elk, antelope, and wild turkeys are commonly seen in the Laramie Mountains, and rainbow, brook, and brown trout are found in the creeks.

Public and private lands intermingle here, with only a few large tracts of Forest Service property—the biggest being around Laramie Peak. This impressive mountain, clearly visible from Douglas, served as a landmark for travelers along the old Oregon Trail, who called this country the Black Hills. There is some logging around Esterbrook and Albany Peak, especially in insect-killed forests, but Laramie Peak is de facto wilderness. The Medicine Bow-Routt National Forest **Douglas Ranger District Office,** 2250 E. Richards St., tel. (307) 358-4690, www.fs.fed.us/mrnf, has maps ($4) and additional information. A $2 fee is charged for parking at Forest Service trailheads and picnic grounds throughout the Medicine Bow-Routt National Forest, including those in the Laramie Mountains. Annual passes ($10) are also available.

Esterbrook

The Esterbrook area, 32 scenic miles south of Douglas on State Hwy. 94, began as a copper-mining town in 1886 but never really had much to show for its effort. Today it provides a delightful escape from the stifling summer heat at lower elevations. Don't attempt this dirt road after heavy rains or in the spring, when it becomes virtually impassable. Continuing south from Esterbrook, the road cuts through the Laramie Mountains along beautiful Horseshoe Creek Valley, eventually depositing travelers in the town of Rock River. Along the way are numerous side roads into the mountains, including the access road to the Laramie Peak Trail (described below).

Esterbrook is famous for an **old log church,** whose rear window frames snowcapped Laramie Peak. It's a favorite place for country weddings. **Esterbrook Lodge,** tel. (307) 358-6103, is another classic log building. Stay at small and very rustic cabins for $30 d. Budget. Also here are tent sites ($10), RV sites with hookups ($15), and a restaurant known for its homemade pies. A fine Forest Service campground is close by, or you can camp at three other small campgrounds in the Laramie Mountains; see the map for access. Campgrounds cost $5 and are open mid-May to mid-October.

The Forest Service's **LaPrele Guard Station** is available for rent July to mid-October for $60 per night. Built by the Civilian Conservation Corps between 1937 and 1941, this two-bedroom log house served for many years as a ranger's home. Inside is space for six people (bring sleeping bags), plus a full kitchen and bath, stone fireplace, and battery-powered lamps. The station is approximately 40 miles south of Douglas and close to the 2.5-mile **Twin Peaks Trail.** Call (307) 358-4690 for cabin reservations and information.

The **Esterbrook Rendezvous** takes place in early August with a black powder shoot, live music, hayrides, food and craft booths, and a barbecue.

Hiking

Some of the finest hiking in central Wyoming is found along the **Laramie Peak Trail,** a five-mile (one-way) path that climbs to the top of the 10,272-foot peak. The trail begins right behind Friend Park Campground, 48 miles south of Douglas (via a rough gravel road). A $2 parking fee is charged. The first mile is relatively easy as the trail parallels Friend Creek, but after this it's a long, arduous climb. Be sure to bring ample water, food, clothing, and supplies since weather conditions can change rapidly. Afternoon thunderstorms occur on an almost-daily basis in the summer. Two miles from the start is a small cascade; water can be hard to find above this point. Periodic forest openings offer dramatic vistas as you continue up the mountain, gaining 2,800 feet along the way. On top find expansive vistas in all directions—including into

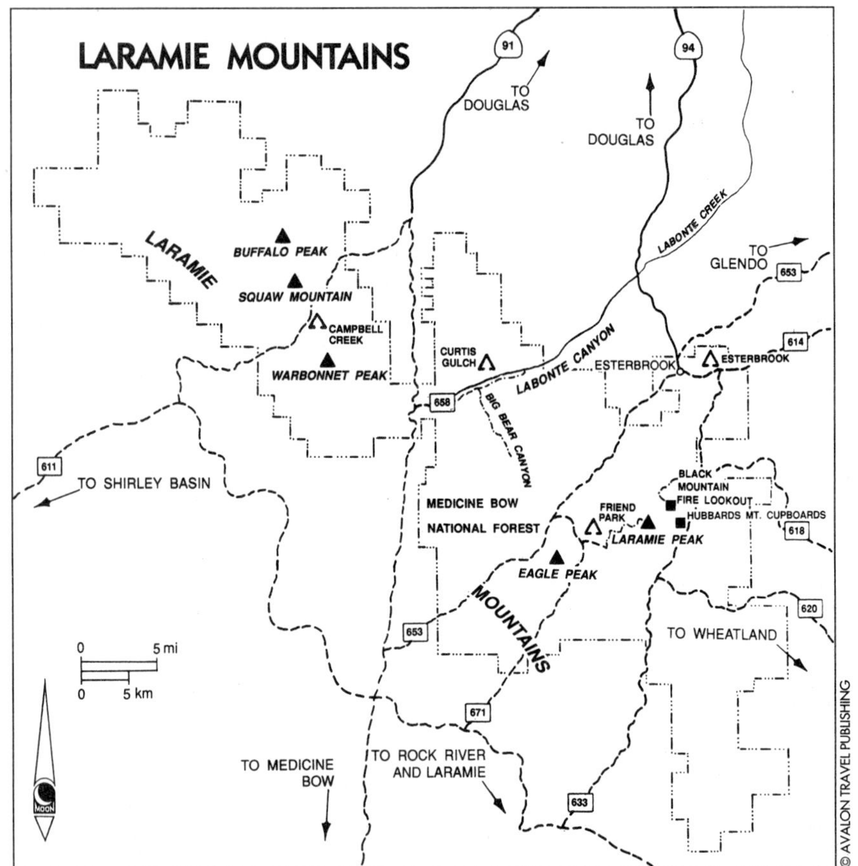

Nebraska, Colorado, and South Dakota on a clear day. Communication buildings and towers are also here. The trail is generally free of snow by late June. Plan on four to seven hours for the roundtrip hike. Note that a few ATVs also use the trail for access to communications buildings at the top. A second trailhead is a quarter mile north of Friend Park Campground, providing access to the four-mile **Friend Park Trail,** which follows Arapahoe Creek.

The two-mile-long **La Bonte Canyon Trail** offers both pleasant hiking and good fishing for brook trout. The trailhead is at Curtis Gulch Campground, 38 miles south of Douglas. The path drops along a gorgeous steep-walled canyon (keep your eyes open for bighorn sheep and elk) and ends at a big-game refuge. Along the way are meadows, forests of poplar and Douglas-fir, and flowers galore. Also near the Curtis Gulch Campground is a 4WD road/hiking trail that climbs for three miles up **Big Bear Canyon** to scenic Devils Pass.

Another good climb is up the 4WD road to **Black Mountain Lookout,** one of the last operating fire towers in the nation. You'll find great views down pristine Ashenfelder Creek. Get there by following Forest Rd. 633 south of Esterbrook Campground for six miles to the Laramie Peak Scout Camp. Turn right onto Forest Rd. 667 and park inside the Forest boundary. Hike up the 4WD road 2.5 miles to the lookout, which is staffed June-September.

The **North Laramie River Trail** starts approximately 20 miles west of Wheatland and descends for 2.5 miles into the North Laramie River Canyon, losing 1,000 feet in elevation along the way. There's good fishing for brown and rainbow trout in the river, and the remains of 15 buildings from a 1920s' resort are fun to explore. Get to the trailhead by taking the El Rancho exit from I-25 (between Glendo and Wheatland) and heading west on Fish Creek Rd. to Fletcher Park Road. Continue on past Camp Grace to the intersection of Fletcher Park and Cow Camp Rds., where signs point the route to the trailhead.

Sunset Ridge Trail is a short 1.6-mile climb to a scenic view over the plains to the east. It originates from the Esterbrook Campground and gains 400 feet along the way before looping back down the hill.

Contact the Forest Service (307-358-4690) for details on these and other trails, including a number of challenging backcountry routes near Laramie Peak.

Winter Recreation

Wintertime snow closes all roads over the Laramie Mountains, transforming the mountains into an excellent place for cross-country skiing, with many miles of scenic country and untracked snow. Over 20 miles of groomed trails surround the Esterbrook area, used primarily by snowmobilers, but also by skiers. A warming hut is also here. Pick up a map of snowmobile/ski trails from the Douglas ranger station.

AYRES NATURAL BRIDGE PARK

One of the most unusual geological formations in Wyoming lies 14 miles west of Douglas on I-25. Take exit 151 and continue five miles south to tiny, 22-acre Ayres Natural Bridge Park, where the main attraction is a 100-foot-long, 50-foot-high rock arch over LaPrele Creek. This natural arch was formed when a meander bend in LaPrele Creek gradually eroded the base of the rock face, leaving the upper part of the cliff unscathed. Eventually the weakened rock gave way, and the creek flowed through the hole that had been created at the bend. The ancient creekbed is 300 feet away from the present creek and 50 feet higher.

History

For the Indians who first lived in this country, the natural bridge was a deadly place. A young brave had been struck by lightning and killed while hunting in the canyon; thus began a legend that an evil spirit lived below the bridge, ready to grab anyone who ventured into his lair. When white settlers realized this, they used the natural bridge as a place to escape from Indian attacks, knowing they would not be pursued across the arch. Early-day mountain men lived in caves here, and Mormon settlers built cabins nearby in the 1850s. It took an expedition by Dr. Ferdinand V. Hayden, director of the U.S. Geological Survey in 1869, to bring the rock arch to national attention. He found it odd "that so great a natural curiosity should have failed to attract the attention it deserves." In

Ayres Natural Bridge spans the waters of LaPrele Creek.

1881, Alva Ayres bought the land and used the lush LaPrele Creek country as headquarters for a freighting business. The natural bridge and surrounding land were donated to Converse County in 1920 by Ayres' heirs.

Visting the Bridge

Today, Ayres Natural Bridge offers a beautiful side trip from I-25. Box elders and cottonwoods line LaPrele Creek, fluorescent green patches against the brilliant red sandstone and the rich blue sky. Along one face of the red-walled amphitheater that circles the park are carved the names of many visitors, some dating from the 1880s. This is a popular weekend picnic and swimming spot and a great place to watch birds. It was also for many years a welcome camping spot, but unfortunately, camping is now only allowed with written permission. Ayres Natural Bridge Park is open daily 8 a.m.-8 p.m. May-October. A gate blocks the road during the winter, but you can walk in the last half mile. Call caretaker Ray Morton at (307) 358-3532 for more information.

GLENROCK

The Podunk cattle-and-coal town of Glenrock (pop. 2,400) lies halfway between Casper and Douglas at the confluence of Deer Creek and the North Platte River. The town's name comes from Rock in the Glen, a large rocky outcrop just to the west. Deer Creek was a favorite camping spot along the Oregon Trail, a place to rest up, do a little fishing, and let the stock graze on the lush creekside grass. Starting in 1847, Mormon emigrants mined the coal visible along the north bank of the river; it was the first coal mined in Wyoming. The first bridge to span the North Platte was built here in 1851 but was washed out in a flood the following year. Deer Creek Station was established in 1857, operating first as a trading post and later as a relay terminal for the Overland Stage and a home station for the short-lived Pony Express. After telegraph wires replaced the Pony Express, Deer Creek became a telegraph relay station. Indians burned the station to the ground in 1866 and it was never rebuilt.

Boom and Bust

Around the turn of the 20th century, several underground coal mines opened, transforming the quiet settlement of Glenrock into a raucous mining town. They closed in 1916, just as oil was discovered west of Glenrock. Some 5,000 oil workers flooded the town, along with a raft of less-honorable professionals. Two oil refineries were built, fed by 200 Big Muddy oil wells. One refinery closed in the 1920s and the other in the '50s. More oil was found in 1949 and again in 1973, leading to temporary booms. The massive coal-fired Dave Johnston Power Plant became one of the largest local employers when it opened in 1958, and the discovery of uranium 25 miles northeast of Glenrock attracted hundreds of people to the area when several large uranium mines opened. Most of them closed in the 1980s, but the nearby Highland Uranium Project is still running.

SIGHTS

Museums

The free **Glenrock Museum,** tel. (307) 436-2514, occupies an old church building on the west side of town. Inside is a collection of local memorabilia, along with bones from a nearby buffalo jump used by prehistoric hunters. Hours are Fri.-Tues. 10 a.m.-4 p.m., summers only. In addition, find dinosaur bones—including bones from a triceratops—at the **Glenrock Paleontological Museum,** next to the high school on the east side of town. Open Mon.-Sat. 10 a.m.-4 p.m. in the summer, and Tuesday and Thursday 10 a.m.-4 p.m. the rest of the year. Call (307) 436-4727 or (800) 996-3466 for details. The museum also offers dinosaur dig trips and field schools in the summer.

Other Sights

Rock in the Glen, a half mile west of Glenrock, has the carved names of a few of the 19th-century emigrants who passed by on the way to Oregon, California, or Utah. Several **graves** from this era are scattered around Glenrock, sad reminders of the thousands who never made it. One is that of A.H. Unthank, just east of the Dave Johnston Power Plant on Tank Farm Rd., who died of cholera just a week after carving his name in Register Cliffs near present-day Guernsey. Four miles west of town is the grave of Ada Magill, a young girl who died of dysentery in 1864 as her parents headed west in a wagon train. Stones were piled on top of the grave to keep wolves from digging up her body.

Glenrock City Park has a granite monument to **Dr. Ferdinand V. Hayden,** a physician who devoted his life to exploration of the West. Hayden helped found the U.S. Geological Survey and led the famed Hayden Yellowstone Expedition of 1870. The Indians considered Hayden a bit wacky, calling him "Man-who-picks-up-stones-running." Hayden used the Deer Creek Station at present-day Glenrock as a base of operations for several of his expeditions around Wyoming, hence the monument—placed here in 1931 by his photographic partner on these trips, William H. Jackson.

A pleasant picnic and fishing spot is **Boxelder Canyon,** approximately 10 miles south of Glenrock on State Hwy. 90. Boxelder Creek is bordered by steep rocky walls.

The country around Glenrock is laced with energy projects of all types. Immediately west of town is the Big Muddy oil field, where more than 2.6 million barrels have been pumped out over the last 40 years. The giant **Dave Johnston Power Plant** is six miles east of Glenrock along the North Platte River. It's one of the largest coal-fired power plants in the Rockies, generating 810,000 kilowatts of electricity for the Pacific Northwest. A private railroad feeds the plant with coal from the Glenrock Coal strip mine 16 miles to the north.

Visit the **Central Wyoming Livestock Exchange,** just east of town, tel. (307) 436-5327, where cattle, sheep, pigs, and even a few goats are auctioned off on Monday and Saturday during the summer months. This is an enjoyable way to learn about ranching and to rub shoulders with local cowboys.

PRACTICALITIES

Accommodations

Glenrock has two motels, a B&B, and a wonderful old hotel. **All American Inn,** 500 W. Aspen, tel. (307) 436-2772, has rooms starting at \$29 s or \$39 d, some with fridges and microwaves. Inexpensive. **Hotel Higgins,** 416 W. Birch, tel. (307) 436-9212 or (800) 458-0144, is plain vanilla on the outside—pink shingles on a building built in 1916—but the inside is a pleasant surprise. The entire hotel has been lovingly furnished with antique brass beds, wardrobes, lamps, and a ticking old grandfather clock. Rooms cost \$46 s or \$60 d including a full breakfast; \$56 s or \$70 d with breakfast in a two-bedroom suite. Kids are welcome. Moderate.

Camping

Camping is free at the town's **South Recreation Complex,** three miles south of Glenrock along the river. **Deer Creek RV Park,** on the east end of town, tel. (307) 436-8121, is open mid-April through October. Tent sites cost $12, RV sites with hookups $14. Showers for non-campers are $3.

Food

The owners of the Higgins Hotel also run a gourmet restaurant here, **The Paisley Shawl,** named after the delicate old Scottish shawl—a family heirloom—in the dining room. The restaurant (open summers Tues.-Sat. only) has a regional reputation for its lunches and its prime-rib, steak, and veal dinners. The menu changes nightly and includes a fine wine selection. Unfortunately, the restaurant gets quite smoky sometimes.

Get pizza at **Classic Cafe & Pizza,** 201 S. 4th, tel. (307) 436-2244. **Fort Diablo Steak House & Saloon,** tel. (307) 436-2288, specializes in prime rib, steaks, and buffalo. Glenrock is also home to a **Subway.** Buy groceries from **Williams' Town & Country Food Center,** 218 W. Cedar, tel. (307) 436-2344.

Entertainment and Events

At least one of the local bars (**Four Aces, El Diablo, Knotty Pine,** or **Deer Creek Lounge**) will have a country-and-western band on most weekends. Knotty Pine also serves decent Mexican food and the best Bloody Marys in town. Drinkers will want to try the "Humphrey," which isn't for the fainthearted.

The big annual event is **Deer Creek Days,** a carnival with a parade, pancake breakfast, games, craft and food booths, street dancing, and lots of drinking. It takes place in either July or August.

Information and Services

Get local information and brochures inside the **Glenrock Town Hall** on the corner of 3rd and Cedar Sts., tel. (307) 436-5652; open Mon.-Thurs. 10 a.m.-2 p.m. The **Glenrock Library,** 518 S. 4th, tel. (307) 436-2573, exhibits a few dinosaur fossils found in the area.

A free indoor **swimming pool** is in the middle school at 225 Oregon Trail, tel. (307) 436-9201. The spacious **Recreation Center,** 125 Mustang Trail, tel. (307) 436-5434, contains weight rooms and basketball courts. Golfers may want to check out the nine-hole **Glenrock Golf Course,** tel. (307) 436-9294.

CASPER

Wyoming's second-largest city, Casper (pop. 50,000) is in transition from an oil-dependent economy to a more diversified base. The city sprawls across both sides of the North Platte River and is surrounded by the outlying settlements of **Evansville** (pop. 1,500), **Mills** (pop. 1,600), and **Bar Nunn** (pop. 900), with more suburbs filling the intervening land.

As "Oil Capital of the Rockies," the city has long been chained to the fortunes of oil. Casper sits at the center of several large oil fields and is home to a refinery and a large tank farm. Oil-related manufacturing and service industries crowd the city; the Casper Yellow Pages contain more than 20 different types of oil-related listings—from oil and gas exploration companies to directional drilling outfits.

With its central location, substantial population, spacious convention facilities, and ties to the state's energy and ranching industries, Casper considers itself the true heart and soul of Wyoming. The only statewide newspaper, the *Casper Star-Tribune,* is based here, along with one of the state's premier medical centers. To Casperites, arch-rival Cheyenne is just a Nebraska city that happened to sneak into Wyoming. The rest of Wyoming, however, views Casper with equal suspicion; in 1904 Casper aspired to become the state capital but failed miserably, coming in third behind Cheyenne and Lander in a statewide vote. A working-class town, Casper isn't a major tourist destination. Despite this, you'll find outstanding recreational opportunities on nearby Casper Mountain, at local reservoirs, and on the North Platte River, along with a surprising variety of cultural activities centered around the Nicolaysen Art Museum, Casper College, and the spacious Casper Events Center. The National Historic Trails Interpretive Center, scheduled to open in 2001, should become a major draw for "rut nuts" (as Oregon Trail enthusiasts are known) and other visitors.

HISTORY

The Astorians

Although Casper is identified today with oil, the city began as a way station along the Oregon Trail. Seven of John Jacob Astor's fur traders led by Robert Stuart first traveled through this area in 1812 on their return from Oregon, arriving in late October. Knowing they could not make it back to St. Louis in their emaciated condition, the explorers constructed a rock-walled cabin (the first Anglo building in Wyoming) and covered it with buffalo hides. Game proved amazingly plentiful. They returned from a hunting trip

downtown Casper

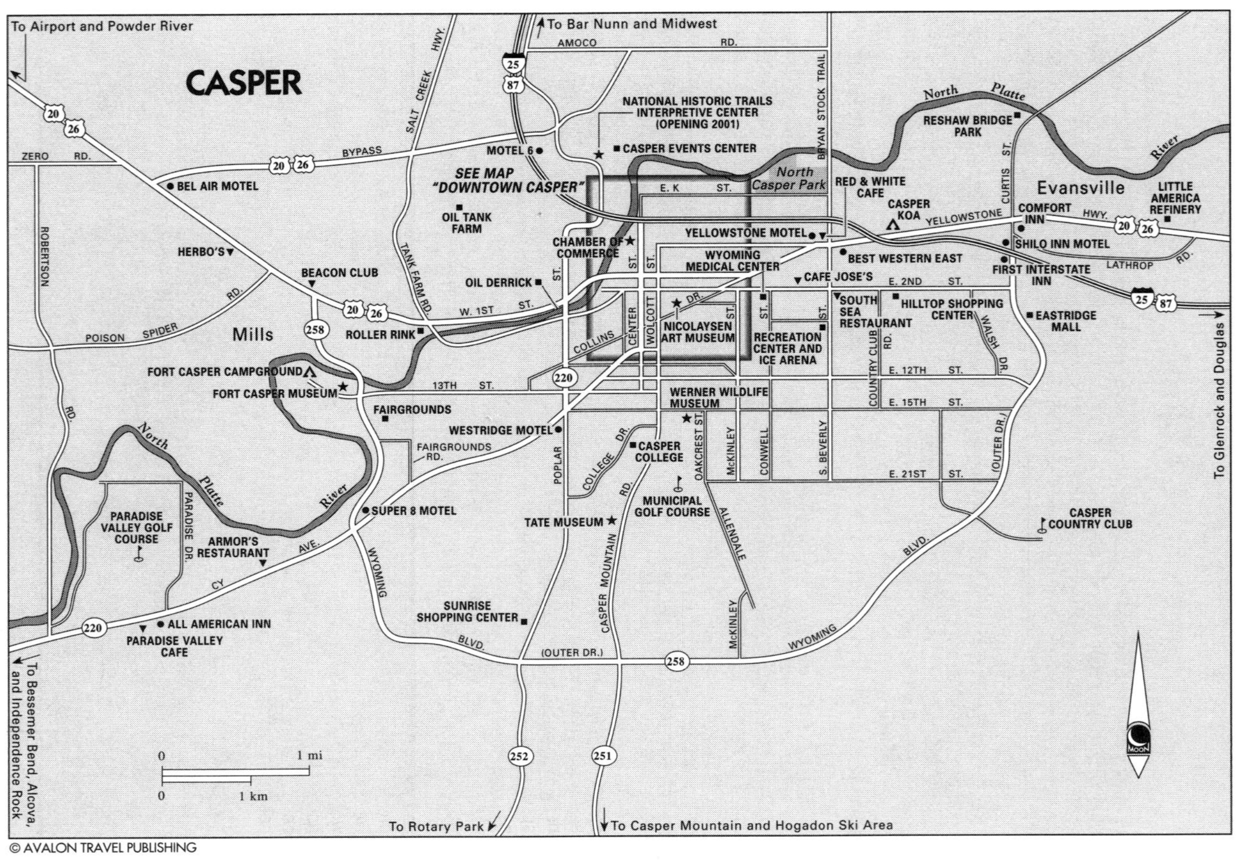
CASPER
To Airport and Powder River
To Bar Nunn and Midwest
To Glenrock and Douglas
To Rotary Park
To Casper Mountain and Hogadon Ski Area
To Bessemer Bend, Alcova, and Independence Rock
Evansville
Mills
North Platte River
North Casper Park
NATIONAL HISTORIC TRAILS INTERPRETIVE CENTER (OPENING 2001)
CASPER EVENTS CENTER
MOTEL 6
SEE MAP "DOWNTOWN CASPER"
OIL TANK FARM
BEL AIR MOTEL
HERBO'S
BEACON CLUB
OIL DERRICK
CHAMBER OF COMMERCE
ROLLER RINK
FORT CASPER CAMPGROUND
FORT CASPER MUSEUM
FAIRGROUNDS
WESTRIDGE MOTEL
SUPER 8 MOTEL
PARADISE VALLEY GOLF COURSE
ARMOR'S RESTAURANT
ALL AMERICAN INN
PARADISE VALLEY CAFE
SUNRISE SHOPPING CENTER
TATE MUSEUM
CASPER COLLEGE
MUNICIPAL GOLF COURSE
WERNER WILDLIFE MUSEUM
NICOLAYSEN ART MUSEUM
RECREATION CENTER AND ICE ARENA
WYOMING MEDICAL CENTER
YELLOWSTONE MOTEL
RED & WHITE CAFE
CASPER KOA
BEST WESTERN EAST
CAFE JOSE'S
SOUTH SEA RESTAURANT
HILLTOP SHOPPING CENTER
RESHAW BRIDGE PARK
COMFORT INN
SHILO INN MOTEL
FIRST INTERSTATE INN
LITTLE AMERICA REFINERY
EASTRIDGE MALL
CASPER COUNTRY CLUB
AMOCO RD.
SALT CREEK HWY.
ZERO RD.
BYPASS
ROBERTSON RD.
POISON SPIDER RD.
TANK FARM RD.
W. 1ST ST.
ST.
E. K ST.
BRYAN STOCK TRAIL
CENTER ST.
WOLCOTT ST.
DR.
COLLINS
13TH ST.
FAIRGROUNDS RD.
POPLAR ST.
COLLEGE DR.
CASPER MOUNTAIN RD.
OAKCREST ST.
McKINLEY
CONWELL
S. BEVERLY
ALLENDALE
COUNTRY CLUB RD.
E. 2ND ST.
E. 12TH ST.
E. 15TH ST.
E. 21ST ST.
WALSH DR.
(OUTER DR.)
CURTIS ST.
YELLOWSTONE HWY.
LATHROP RD.
PARADISE DR.
CY AVE.
WYOMING BLVD.
25
87
20
26
220
258
252
251
0
1 mi
1 km
MOON
© AVALON TRAVEL PUBLISHING

with 47 bison, 28 deer and bighorn sheep, and a bear! But five weeks later, a band of 23 Arapaho warriors appeared on their way to raid the Crow Indians farther north. Intimidated, the Astorians invited them in for a meal. They stayed for a day and a half, promising to return in two weeks. The Astorians quickly decided discretion was the better part of valor and moved to a new camp just across what is now the Nebraska border. They finally reached Missouri the following spring.

Ferries and Bridges

The route pioneered by the Astorians eventually became a virtual highway to the West. The North Platte River was one of the main barriers to this migration, with many emigrants choosing to ford near what is now Casper. In early summer, when the river ran dangerously high, people often died trying to cross. Others lost their wagon or watched as their oxen and horses were swept downriver. When Brigham Young's party of Mormon emigrants arrived here in 1847, they built a 23-foot-long raft and floated their wagons across. The Mormon ferry became Casper's first business venture, with gentiles charged $4-5 per wagon. Business boomed, and for the first two years the Mormons had a monopoly on ferry service. By 1849, however, several different ferries were competing with the Mormon ferry. Despite this, there were still delays of up to a week as California gold-rush travelers waited to cross. (This has to rate as one of Wyoming's only recorded traffic jams.)

In 1852, a French-Canadian trader named John Reshaw built a long wooden toll bridge at present-day Evansville, charging $5 in gold per wagon—less when the river was low and folks would risk fording. To stifle competition, he bought the Mormon ferry for $300 and shut it down. Edwin R. Bird, an 1854 Oregon Trail pioneer, wrote of the toll bridge in his diary:

> *Here we found a good bridge far better than some I have seen at home. There is a store & other buildings connected with it. In the store saw two Frenchmen gambling. The owner of the bridge says he took in seventeen thousand dollars last season. He charges five dollars for a team & five cents a head for loose stock.*

In 1859, another bridge was built six miles upriver by Louis Guinard to compete for the lucrative Oregon Trail traffic. Guinard's bridge must have been one of the most impressive structures along the entire 2,000-mile route. Built at a cost of $40,000, the bridge was 17 feet wide, 1,000 feet long, and supported by 28 log and rock cribs. It soon became the preferred crossing point along the North Platte; the old Reshaw bridge was torn down and the lumber used to build a fort—Platte Bridge Station—to protect the new bridge. Guinard made so much money at the toll station that he reportedly threw handfuls of gold into the river, exclaiming, "You have given me all my wealth; I now give back to you a tithe!"

Red Cloud's War

Platte Bridge Station served as a trading post for travelers, a Pony Express mail stop, and later a telegraph office. A volunteer force of up to 50 soldiers was posted to protect the telegraph and those traveling along the Oregon Trail from Indian and Mormon attacks. After a massacre of Indians at Colorado's Sand Creek in 1865, full-scale war broke out between Indians and whites. One of these battlegrounds that July was at Platte Bridge Station. Expecting a wagon train with vital supplies and ammunition, 20 men under the command of Lt. Caspar Collins left the fort to escort the expected convoy. Once across the bridge, the soldiers found themselves surrounded by Red Cloud and 3,000 of his Sioux warriors. In their flight back across the bridge, five soldiers died. Collins was killed when he stooped to rescue a fellow soldier and his horse bolted, carrying him into the onrushing warriors. Other soldiers said that when last seen, he had his reins in his teeth and was firing pistols from both hands. His body was found two days later with 24 arrows in it.

A second battle occurred that afternoon—Custard's Wagon Train Fight. When the supply wagons of Sgt. Amos Custard came within sight of the fort, the soldiers tried to warn them with cannon fire. Three men from an advance guard made it to safety within the fort, and the others quickly corralled the three wagons together. Although they put up a fierce fight, within hours Red Cloud's men had killed and mutilated the 23 defenders and burned their wagons. In honor of Caspar Collins, Platte Bridge Station was renamed Fort Caspar.

(Fort Collins, Colorado, is named for his father, William Collins.) Due to a never-corrected error by an army telegraph operator—he typed a dot instead of a dot-dash—the town that eventually grew up nearby was misspelled Casper. Two years later, when most traffic on the Oregon Trail had been rerouted south to avoid conflicts with the Indians, Fort Caspar was abandoned. Shortly thereafter, the bridge and fort were burned by the Sioux.

Lawless Days and Nights

In 1888, the Fremont, Elkhorn, and Missouri Valley Railway extended its line up the North Platte River to the site of old Fort Caspar. A tent city quickly sprang up, followed by more permanent buildings. For the next 17 years the town of Casper lay at the end of the tracks. It was an exceptionally violent place; employees of the first grocery store surrounded their beds with sacks of flour for protection from stray bullets, and Casper's first public building was a jail. Even the mayor got in on the act, murdering his business partner in an 1890 gun duel on Main Street. The jury let him go free. When the ruffians became too much to tolerate, a street trial was held and those who refused to leave town faced the prospect of being strung up in a "necktie party." Pinned to the shirt of one murderer lynched by a vigilance committee was the following note: "Process of law is a little slow, so this is the road you'll have to go. Murderers and sinners, Beware! People's Verdict."

Oil Changes Everything

In 1851 Jim Bridger, Cy Iba, Kit Carson, and Basil Cimineau Lajeunesse discovered an oil spring just west of Casper at Poison Spider Creek. The oil was mixed with flour and sold as axle grease for wagon trains. By 1889, when the first oil well was drilled near Casper, it was clear that much more oil lay beneath the ground. Land speculators and claim jumpers flocked to Wyoming, and battles quickly broke out over who had staked the first claim; the winner generally had more burly men, guns, and lawyers. Soon the massive Salt Creek oil field, 40 miles north of Casper, was producing; wagons towed by teams of up to 20 horses hauled the oil back to Casper. A small refinery was built in 1895, the first in Wyoming. It was later replaced by more modern facilities including the now-closed Standard Oil plant, at one time the largest refinery on earth, handling 25,000 barrels of oil per day. Over time, Casper became a center for oil and refining in the northern Rockies.

Boom and Bust

Casper grew into a major industrial town with the development of Salt Creek and other oil fields. So many roustabouts flooded Casper that they had to sleep in shifts in the available tents, motels, garages, basements, or shacks. Dozens of illegal gambling houses and speakeasies helped make a trip to town memorable, and more than 2,000 prostitutes pursued their own boomtimes in the Sandbar district—prostitution was blatant here until the 1950s. Oil production peaked in the 1920s, but the crash of 1929 burst this economic bubble and cut the city's population in half within five years. World War II sent oil prices and Casper's economy soaring. An army air base—home to 4,000 men—opened nearby; it's now the site of Casper's airport. In the late '50s, new technology—injecting water to force the remaining oil to wellheads—helped boost recovery dramatically at Salt Creek, and there followed another boom for Casper. The discovery of massive uranium deposits in the Pumpkin Buttes, Gas Hills, and Shirley Basin areas further fueled this growth.

The roller-coaster ride has continued in recent decades: down in the late '60s, back up in the '70s. When oil prices soared following the OPEC oil embargo in 1973, Casper experienced such an orgy of growth that planners predicted a population rivaling Denver's by the year 2000. After oil prices plummeted in the 1980s, however, these optimistic—or apocalyptic, depend-

CASPER AREA CLIMATE

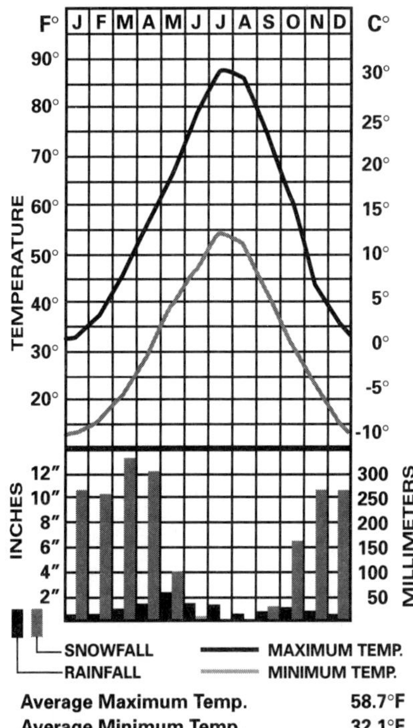

Average Maximum Temp.	**58.7°F**
Average Minimum Temp.	**32.1°F**
Annual Rainfall	**15.16"**
Annual Snowfall	**79.6"**

ing upon your point of view—predictions failed to materialize. Sales tax receipts dropped by half, many of downtown Casper's storefronts were covered with plywood, and the Amoco refinery shut down. The economy has improved dramatically in recent years as Casper has diversified its industrial base to include everything from a copper foundry to pepper-spray manufacturing. New stores have invigorated the commercial sector, and the addition of the Nicolaysen Art Museum has added an artistic focal point. Downtown is thriving, the suburbs are once again creeping over the countryside, and Eastridge Mall—Wyoming's largest shopping mall—is packed with chain stores. But you can still find a few homes for under $30,000 (along with others that top $200,000).

SIGHTS

Fort Caspar

Although the original fort had long since disappeared, in 1936 the WPA reconstructed a half dozen of Fort Caspar's log buildings. Included are a blacksmith shop, an overland stage station, a commissary storehouse, a barracks building, and a sutler's store where you can buy various Western items. Many supports from Guinard's long bridge across the North Platte are still visible as mounds of rock. Also here you'll find a replica of the Mormon ferry and a reconstruction of part of the bridge (in poor shape). During summer, guides dressed as 1860s' cavalrymen answer your questions.

A newer brick building at the fort houses an excellent small museum displaying a variety of items, including a reconstructed Mormon handcart and a W.H. Jackson painting of Platte Bridge Station. Be sure to check out the photos and story of the 14-inch-tall Pedro Mountain mummy, a find that seemed to confirm the "little people" stories told by many Indian tribes. From mid-May to mid-September the museum, tel. (307) 235-8462, is open Mon.-Sat. 8 a.m.-7 p.m., Sunday noon-7 p.m. The rest of the year, it's open Mon.-Fri. 8 a.m.-5 p.m., Sunday 1-4 p.m. No charge. The fort buildings are open only mid-May to mid-September, but you can wander around the grounds at any time of year. Over in Evansville, the **Town Hall** (open Mon.-Fri. 8 a.m.-5 p.m.) also contains a number of artifacts found along the Oregon Trail.

National Historic Trails Interpretive Center

This $10 million facility was still in the early stages as this was written, but is expected to open in 2001. The Platte River crossing at present-day Casper was a junction for most of the major routes west, including not just the Oregon/Mormon/California Trail, but also the Pony Express, Bridger, and, Bozeman Trails. This museum will introduce visitors to the Indian peoples who first lived (and still live) here, as well as the whys, wheres, and ways of 19th-century travel. Call (800) 852-1889 for the latest information and to request a pamphlet describing historic trail sites throughout the area.

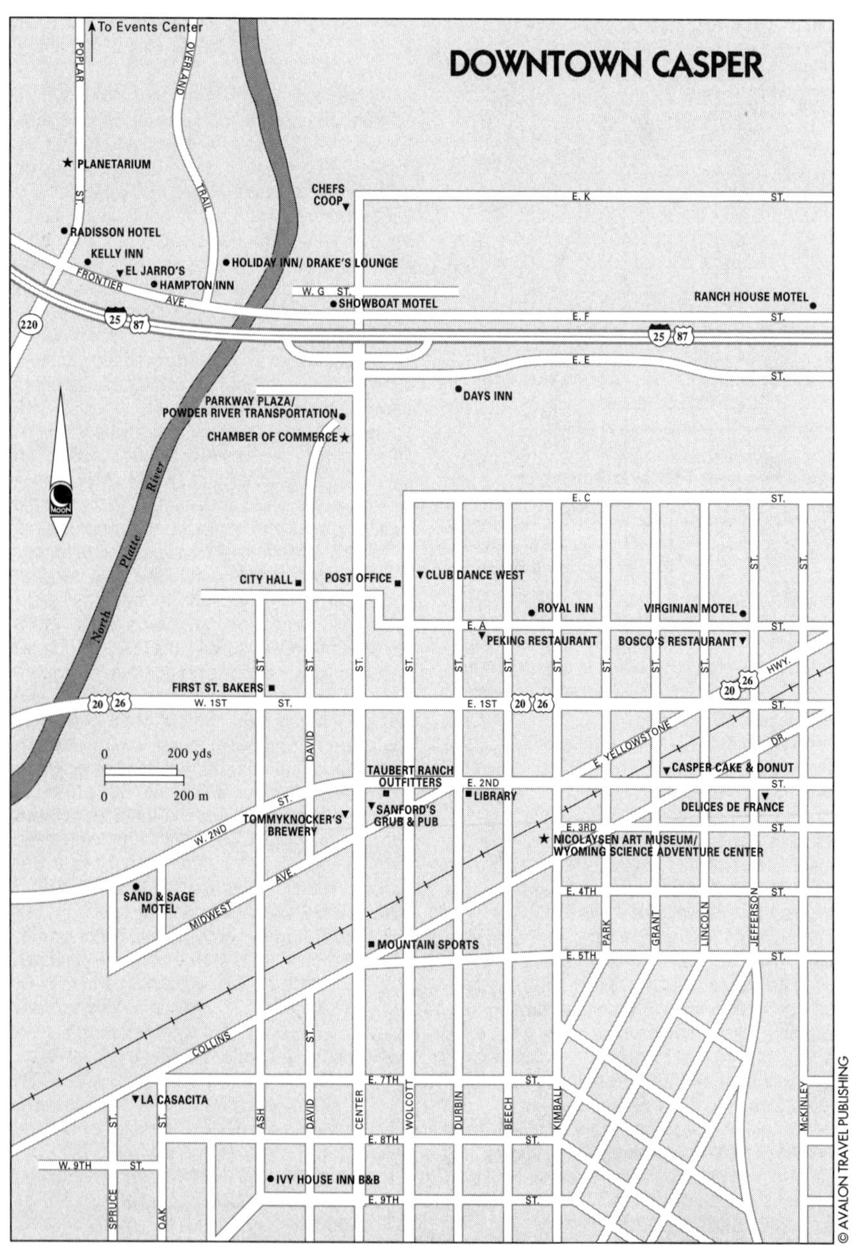
DOWNTOWN CASPER
To Events Center
PLANETARIUM
RADISSON HOTEL
KELLY INN
EL JARRO'S
HAMPTON INN
HOLIDAY INN/ DRAKE'S LOUNGE
CHEFS COOP
SHOWBOAT MOTEL
RANCH HOUSE MOTEL
DAYS INN
PARKWAY PLAZA/ POWDER RIVER TRANSPORTATION
CHAMBER OF COMMERCE
CITY HALL
POST OFFICE
CLUB DANCE WEST
ROYAL INN
VIRGINIAN MOTEL
PEKING RESTAURANT
BOSCO'S RESTAURANT
FIRST ST. BAKERS
TAUBERT RANCH OUTFITTERS
LIBRARY
CASPER CAKE & DONUT
DELICES DE FRANCE
TOMMYKNOCKER'S BREWERY
SANFORD'S GRUB & PUB
NICOLAYSEN ART MUSEUM/ WYOMING SCIENCE ADVENTURE CENTER
SAND & SAGE MOTEL
MOUNTAIN SPORTS
LA CASACITA
IVY HOUSE INN B&B
North Platte River
POPLAR ST.
OVERLAND TRAIL
FRONTIER AVE.
W. G ST.
E. K ST.
E. F ST.
E. E ST.
E. C ST.
E. A ST.
W. 1ST ST.
E. 1ST ST.
W. 2ND ST.
E. 2ND ST.
E. 3RD ST.
E. 4TH ST.
E. 5TH ST.
E. 7TH ST.
E. 8TH ST.
E. 9TH ST.
W. 9TH ST.
E. YELLOWSTONE HWY.
DR.
MIDWEST AVE.
COLLINS
SPRUCE ST.
OAK ST.
ASH ST.
DAVID ST.
CENTER ST.
WOLCOTT ST.
DURBIN ST.
BEECH ST.
KIMBALL ST.
PARK
GRANT
LINCOLN
JEFFERSON
McKINLEY
25
87
220
20
26
0 200 yds
0 200 m
MOON

Nicolaysen Art Museum

One surprising aspect of Casper is an emphasis on art and culture as exemplified by the Nicolaysen—"The Nic." Originally a power plant, this beautiful brick building houses six different galleries and is one of the finest contemporary art exhibition spaces in Wyoming. Exhibits change every few months, but you're unlikely ever to see the standard moose-in-the-meadow pieces here. The permanent collection includes some 1,900 drawings by German-American illustrator Carl Link, along with a variety of Native American paintings, pottery, and rugs. Children love the fun **Discovery Center,** where artistic activities and classes take place. The third floor houses the **Wyoming Science Adventure Center,** where you can create six-foot-wide bubbles, learn how things work, or compose a symphony. A gift shop sells books and work by local artisans. Lectures, concerts, and slide shows are offered throughout the year. The Nic is at 400 E. Collins, tel. (307) 235-5247, and is open Tues.-Sat. 10 a.m.-5 p.m. (till 8 p.m. on Thursday), Sunday noon-4 p.m.; closed Monday. Entrance costs $3 for adults, $2 for ages 2-12; free for toddlers. Everyone gets in free on Thursday evenings. The website is www.thenic.org.

More Art

One legacy from Casper's oil-boom times is an abundance of outdoor sculpture, including three pieces by Laramie sculptor Robert Russin. His energetic bronze ***Prometheus*** livens the library entrance at 307 E. 2nd St., while ***Man and Energy*** at the chamber of commerce, 500 N. Center, symbolizes Casper's ties to oil and coal. Neither is as controversial as ***The Fountainhead,*** a red and blue metal sculpture placed in front of the city hall in 1981. Its unorthodox (some say "ugly") appearance and $230,000 price tag raised a few eyebrows—and blood pressures. A statue of Caspar Collins on horseback guards the Casper Events Center, a monument to sheepherders is in front of the Wyoming Wool Growers Building at 117 Glenn Rd., and a statue of Chief Washakie stands at 1st and Walcott.

Other places to see local artwork include **West Wind Gallery,** an artists' co-op at 1040 W. 15th, tel. (307) 265-2655; **Artist's Choice,** 647 W. Yellowstone Hwy., tel. (307) 234-7000; **The Artist's Gallery** in Eastridge Mall, tel. (307) 577-1662; **Garden Creek Studio,** 3520 S. Coffman, tel. (307) 284-0388; **Ray Pebbles Gallery,** 1605 E. 2nd Ave., tel. (307) 235-8766; **Daisy Patch Galleries,** 137 S. Center St., tel. (307) 234-8882; and the student art gallery at Casper College.

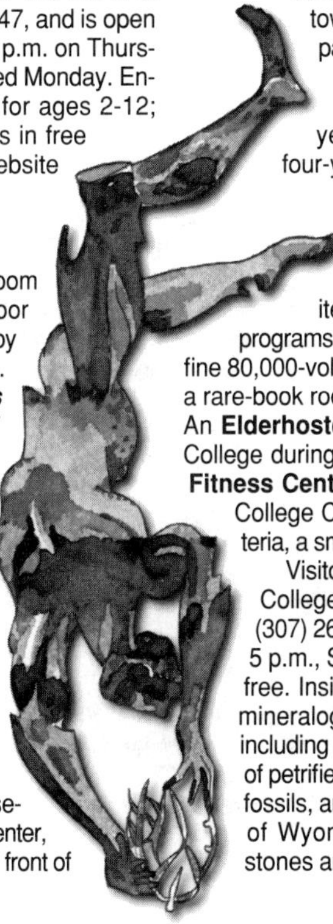

Casper College

Casper College first opened its doors in 1945 and has grown into the state's largest junior college, with over 6,000 full- and part-time students. The college's brick buildings sprawl up a long hillside. Although many students live in dorms, most commute from around town, making for traffic jams in the parking lots and along adjacent city streets.

Casperites fought for many years to turn their college into a four-year school, but the university at Laramie successfully fended off those moves until 1987. In a joint venture, the University of Wyoming now offers a limited number of bachelor's degree programs at the Casper College campus. A fine 80,000-volume **library** on campus includes a rare-book room with unusual Wyoming titles. An **Elderhostel** program operates at Casper College during the summer, and the excellent **Fitness Center** is open to the public. In the College Center building you'll find a cafeteria, a small bookstore, and other facilities.

Visitors will enjoy stops at two Casper College collections. **Tate Museum,** tel. (307) 268-2447, is open Mon.-Fri. 8 a.m.-5 p.m., Saturday 10 a.m.-3 p.m. all year; free. Inside, you'll find one of the largest mineralogical collections in the Rockies, including several meteorites, various types of petrified wood, Indian artifacts, dinosaur fossils, and probably the largest collection of Wyoming jade anywhere. Polished stones are sold at a small gift shop here.

BRIAN BARDWELL

Werner Wildlife Museum, 405 E. 15th St., tel. (307) 235-2108, is open Mon.-Sat. noon-5 p.m. from mid-May to early September, and Mon.-Fri. 2-5 p.m. the rest of the year; free. The museum houses the usual stuffed critters from Wyoming—dozens of antelope heads, deer mounts, bears, bison, and many birds—along with several African and Alaskan trophies.

Edness Kimball Wilkins State Park

Six miles east of Casper on State Hwy. 256, this 1,420-acre park is perfect for quiet picnics among the cottonwoods, birdwatching (more than 200 species have been observed), and fishing and canoeing in the North Platte River. The park began as a rock quarry but has been transformed into a delightful place to explore. No camping is allowed, but several trails—including a three-mile paved path—provide pleasant day-hikes or bike rides, and on hot summer weekends families crowd the sandy beach along the swimming pond. Oregon Trail wagon ruts are visible near the entrance to the park. Day-use costs $5 for nonresident vehicles, $2 for cars with Wyoming plates. Call (307) 577-5150 for more information.

More Sights

The **Platte River Parkway** is a five-mile paved riverside path and a fine place to walk, rollerblade, or bike. The chamber of commerce has a map of the route, or just look for it along the river. Eventually it will extend for almost 12 miles.

At the intersection of 1st and Poplar Sts. a wooden **oil derrick** stands as a monument to the city's heritage. One of Casper's minor claims to fame is having Wyoming's largest convention and performance center. At **Casper Events Center,** you might run across a mining trade show, rock concert, wrestling tournament, basketball game, graduation ceremony, cat show, or even a monster-truck pull. On a hill overlooking the city, the center is a spacious, modern building with room for over 10,000 people. Call (800) 442-2256 for upcoming events.

The **Casper Planetarium,** 904 N. Poplar, tel. (307) 577-0310, is open daily during the summer, with programs starting at 8 p.m. Admission costs $2. **Dr. Spokes Cyclery & Museum,** 240 S. Center St., tel. (307) 265-7740, is a unique bike shop with an array of classic bikes and toy pedal cars arranged around the room. Some date back nearly a century.

The Wyoming Game & Fish Dept. produces a helpful booklet of wildlife viewing in the area; pick it up at the agency's office (3030 Energy Lane, tel. 307-473-3400) or from the visitors bureau. Springtime visitors will enjoy a detour from Casper out Hat Six Rd. (State Hwy. 253) east of town, where **sage grouse** perform spectacular mating displays mid-March to mid-May. Farther out this road is a large prairie dog town.

ACCOMMODATIONS AND CAMPING

Motels

Casper motels cover the complete quality spectrum, from dumpy little holes-in-the-wall to an elaborate Radisson Hotel. In general you'll find prices in Casper to be among the least expensive in Wyoming. At the cheapest places, you'd better take a look at the rooms before plunking down any money. In addition to the places listed below, another dozen lodging places are listed under **Additional Casper Motels** in the appendix of this book. Casper motels included below are listed from least to most expensive. Add a seven percent tax to these rates.

Inexpensive: A good economy place is **Royal Inn,** right downtown at 440 E. A St., tel. (307) 234-3503 or (800) 967-6925. Standard rooms go for $28 s or $40 d, and amenities include an outdoor pool, fridges, and microwaves. Kitchenettes are $49 s or d.

For a few bucks more, stay at the predictable **Motel 6,** 1150 Wilkins Circle, tel. (307) 234-3903 or (800) 466-8356. Rates are $32 s or $38 d, including use of an outdoor pool. Other recommended places for those on a budget include **Westridge Motel,** 955 CY Ave., tel. (307) 234-8911 or (800) 356-6268, where rooms are $33-39 s or d; and **National 9 Inn Showboat,** 100 W. F St., tel. (307) 235-2711 or (800) 524-9999, where the cost is $35 s or $40-45 d, including a continental breakfast.

Moderate: You'll find spacious and clean rooms at **Best Western Casper,** 2325 E. Yellowstone, tel. (307) 234-3541 or (800) 675-4242. Rates here are $54-79 s or $57-79 d, with such amenities as a large indoor pool, continental breakfast, and exercise facilities.

Days Inn, 301 East E St., tel. (307) 234-1159 or (888) 307-0959, is a well-kept newer facility with an outdoor pool, small exercise room, and a light breakfast. There's even a popcorn machine. Rooms go for $55-60 s or $60-65 d.

The large hotel formerly known as Hilton is now a **Radisson Hotel.** Find it at I-25 and Poplar, tel. (307) 266-6000 or (800) 333-3333. Amenities here include an indoor pool, jacuzzi, and exercise facility; rates are $75 s or d.

Hampton Inn, 400 W. F St., tel. (307) 235-6668 or (800) 426-7866, is another fine place to stay. Rooms cost $70-75 s or $80-85 d, including a continental breakfast and use of a sauna and outdoor pool.

Premium: The most expensive local place is **Holiday Inn,** 300 W. F St., tel. (307) 235-2531 or (877) 576-8636. Many rooms face the central atrium, and the hotel also contains an indoor pool, jacuzzi, sauna, and fitness center. Rates are $119 s or d.

Bed and Breakfast

Only one B&B has survived in Casper. The **Ivy House Inn,** 815 S. Ash St., tel. (307) 265-0974, offers three guest bedrooms (shared bath) in a 1941 home furnished in art deco pieces. A light breakfast is served on weekdays, along with a buffet breakfast on weekends. Rates are a reasonable $35-55 s or $40-60 d, and kids are welcome. Open year-round. Inexpensive.

Camping

The nearest public camping ($5) is in the pines atop Casper Mountain, 10 miles south of Casper and 3,000 feet higher in elevation—well worth the drive. See Casper Mountain below for details.

The **Fort Caspar Campground,** tel. (307) 234-3260 or (888) 243-7709, operates year-round on the river just beyond the old fort site and has an outdoor pool. Sites run $11 for tents, $16 for RVs.

Casper KOA, 2800 E. Yellowstone, tel. (307) 237-5155 or (800) 562-3259, charges $15 for tents or $20 for RVs; open late Feb.-November. Features include an outdoor pool and jacuzzi, and buffalo barbecue dinners in the summer.

Antelope Run Campground, in Bar Nunn at 1101 W. Prairie Lane, tel. (307) 577-1664, has tent sites for $12, RV sites for $18, including access to an indoor pool and jacuzzi. Open April-October.

FOOD

Casper has a wide range of dining options that will suit almost any taste, and it shows more diversity every time you visit. All the standard fast-food greasers are here—from Taco Time to Hot Dog on a Stick—but so are a number of fine dining establishments.

Breakfast

Chef's Coop, 1040 N. Center St., tel. (307) 237-1132, makes terrific breakfasts, and it always has something special for lunch or dinner. Open at 6 a.m. daily. For a home-style, reasonably priced breakfast, visit **TK's Diner,** 5755 CY Ave., tel. (307) 266-2027. On the other end of town is the **Red and White Cafe,** 1620 E. Yellowstone, tel. (307) 234-6962, a popular greasy-spoon hangout.

Lunch

During the school year, visitors will find Casper's cheapest lunch eats at the **Casper College cafeteria.** Notable soup, sandwich, and salad places in town are **Cottage Cafe,** 116 S. Lincoln St., tel. (307) 234-1157, and **Cheese Barrel,** 544 S. Center, tel. (307) 235-5202 (which also serves good breakfasts).

For the best sub sandwiches in Casper, head to **Mountain View Sub Shop,** 239 E. 1st St., tel. (307) 237-7999. Create your own sandwiches (and pay by the pound) at the downtown **Sandwich Bar,** 124 E. 2nd St., tel. (307) 266-1527. Another downtown eatery with casual meals is **Wrap & Roll,** 208 S. Center St., tel. (307) 472-0883, which creates take-away fajita wraps, Thai wraps, and fruit smoothies.

Steak and Seafood

The best local top-carnivore eateries are **Poor Boys Steak House,** in the Parkway Plaza Hotel at 123 W. E St., tel. (307) 235-1777, and **Duke's Steak House,** in the Shilo Inn at 739 Luker Lane in Evansville, tel. (307) 237-1335. **Dorn's Fireside,** 1745 CY Ave., tel. (307) 235-6831, is another popular beef-and-seafood house. In the same vein is **Goose Egg Inn,** nine miles southwest of Casper on State Hwy. 220, tel. (307) 473-8838, where prime rib, seafood, and pan-fried chicken are house specialties. Well worth the drive.

Packed with Casperites, **Herbo's,** 4755 W. Yellowstone, tel. (307) 266-2293, is one of the local restaurants where the size of the servings wins out over the quality. **Sedar's Restaurant,** tel. (307) 234-6839, serves prime rib, cabbage rolls, lobster, and steak at Sunrise Mall, 4370 S. Poplar.

Italian and Pizza

Casper has several decent Italian restaurants. The down-home **Bosco's,** 847 E. A St., tel. (307) 265-9658, fills with the business crowd on weekday lunches, and offers such specialties as veal scallopini, eggplant parmigiana, and chicken piccata.

Botticelli Ristorante Italiano, 129 W. 2nd, tel. (307) 266-2700, is one of a small chain of Northern Italian restaurants, with decent food (including panini, pastas, and pizza) in a pleasantly romantic setting.

If you're looking for good pizza in Casper, try **Barry's Pizzaria** on the east side of Parkway Plaza Hotel, 123 W. E St., tel. (307) 237-8523, or one of the chains such as Godfather's, Little Caesars, Papa John's, or Pizza Hut.

Mexican

For Mexican food, everyone in Casper goes to **El Jarro's,** 500 W. F St., tel. (307) 577-0538. Be ready for a long wait most any evening. El Jarro's has reasonable prices, big margaritas, crispy chips, tangy salsa, and mass quantities of food. Besides, the bleached-blond hostesses and the beefy waiters (who gather around tables to sing "Happy Birthday" at least a dozen times each hour) make for lots of ogling. Be forewarned that this is Americanized Mexican food. More critical locals call El Jarro's "El Horrible's."

Get authentic Mexican fare at **La Cocina,** a bit out of the way at 522 S.W. Wyoming Blvd. in Mills, tel. (307) 266-1414. Everything is freshly made, including the hand-rolled tortillas. Also popular is **La Casacita,** 633 W. Collins, tel. (307) 234-7633, the oldest Mexican cafe in Casper. **Cafe Jose's,** 1600 E. 2nd St., tel. (307) 235-6599, has Tex-Mex fare, including chimichangas, flautas, and fajitas. Another recommended place is **Las Margaritas,** 3350 CY Ave., tel. (307) 234-4699, with nearly a dozen different margaritas and tasty crab enchiladas. Decidedly not Tex-Mex.

Chinese

A real surprise in Casper is the large number of Asian restaurants that dot the town—seven places at last count. The food has suffered a bit from Americanization, but several of these places are fairly good. **South Sea Chinese Restaurant,** 2025 E. 2nd, tel. (307) 237-4777, offers the more authentic fare—though the no-smoking section is a joke. Also good is **Peking Chinese Restaurant,** 333 E. A, tel. (307) 266-2207. **China Buffet,** 4005 CY Ave., tel. (307) 237-8911, has a big variety of Asian choices served buffet-style for lunch and dinner.

Coffee Shops

Three downtown spots offer a chance to espresso yourself. **Blue Heron Books & Espresso,** 201 E. 2nd St., tel. (307) 265-3774 or (800) 585-3774, is a pleasant downtown spot to browse books and enjoy a coffee. Across the street is **The Coffee Shamen,** 232 E. 2nd St., tel. (307) 234-1599, a New Age bookstore and coffeehouse. Poetry readings take place on Thursday evenings. **Uncle Bruno's,** upstairs inside Taubert's, 125 E. 2nd St., tel. (307) 234-2500, also has espresso and pastries.

Pubs

Tommyknocker Brewery, tel. (307) 472-7837, is right in the heart of town at 256 S. Center Street. It's a big place with half a dozen freshly brewed beers on draught, including Butthead Bock and Jack Whacker Wheat Ale. The menu features steaks, meat loaf, barbecued beef, salads, sandwiches, and crunchy appetizers.

Directly across the street is another bustling beerhouse, **Sanford's Grub & Pub,** tel. (307) 234-4555. This cluttered pub is part of a small chain; others are in Sheridan, Gillette, and Cheyenne, along with Spearfish, South Dakota. On the menu you'll find dozens of sandwiches, all the standard bar appetizers (along with some that aren't so standard such as gizzards and fried pickle spears), burgers, salads, pasta, and more.

Bakeries

First Street Bakers, 260 W. 1st St., tel. (307) 472-0255, bakes bagels, breads, and sweets, including enormous cinnamon buns. The shop also sells freshly made pasta. **Casper Cake**

and Donut, 604 E. 2nd, tel. (307) 234-1180, is another other good bakery, and has an additional shop in Eastridge Mall. For the authentic French variety, head to **Delices de France,** 845 E. 2nd St., tel. (307) 237-6614. In addition to fresh croissants, breads, and sweets, the shop offers a lunch menu of quiches, soups, and sandwiches.

Get fresh bagels at **Chesapeake Bagel Bakery & Cafe,** 2711 CY Ave., tel. (307) 237-3036.

Grocers and Produce

Casper has a number of giant grocery stores scattered across the city, including Albertson's, Buttrey, Safeway, and Smith's; all have in-store bakeries and delis. If you're looking for fresh produce, be sure to check out the **farmers market** at the fairgrounds every Saturday morning during the summer.

ENTERTAINMENT

Movies

Casper's downtown movie theaters—**Rialto Theatre,** 100 E. 2nd St., tel. (307) 237-2416; **Fox Movie Palace,** 150 W. 2nd St., tel. (307) 235-0900; and **America Theatre,** 119 S. Center, tel. (307) 235-5440—have some of the cheapest flick-viewing to be found: $3 for all shows. Other movie houses include **Beverly Cinema Twin,** 2117 E. 12th St., tel. (307) 265-6061; and **Eastridge Mall Cinema Four,** 601 S.E. Wyoming Blvd., tel. (307) 234-5831.

Barhopping

See the *Casper Star-Tribune* for the latest on local nightlife. The biggest and best-known place for live music every night of the week is the **Beacon Club,** 4100 W. Yellowstone Hwy., tel. (307) 577-1503, with country tunes and a fun, trendy crowd. Dance lessons are offered on Thursday nights. The **Avalon Club,** 260 E. Yellowstone Hwy., tel. (307) 473-7544, has Western dance bands most nights. **Club Dance West,** 225 N. Wolcott, tel. (307) 234-8811, has country music upstairs and rock or rap downstairs; open Friday and Saturday nights. Find rock bands most weekends at **Moonlight Lounge,** 2305 E. 12th, tel. (307) 234-7787, and **Tommyknockers,** 256 S. Center, tel. (307) 265-0030.

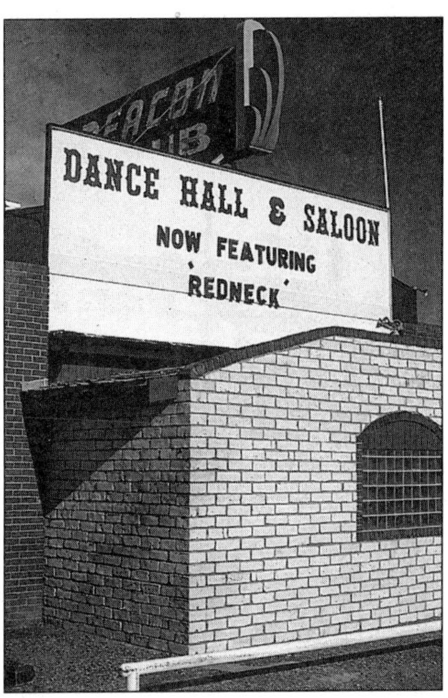

The sign says it all.

Sidelines Sports Bar, next to Anthony's Italian Restaurant in Eastridge Mall, tel. (307) 234-9444, is a sports bar with live music some nights and a young crowd. Other places to check for musical entertainment and dancing include **Dukes,** at Shilo Inn Motel, 739 Luker Lane, tel. (307) 237-1335, and **Goose Egg Inn,** 10580 Goose Egg Rd., tel. (307) 473-8838.

The Arts

The **Wyoming Symphony Orchestra,** tel. (307) 266-1478—the state's only professional orchestra—presents eight performances Sept.-May at the high school auditorium. The **Casper Municipal Band** plays free concerts on Thursday nights in the summer in Washington Park. **Stage III Community Theatre,** 4080 S. Poplar, tel. (307) 234-0946, puts on plays on weekends throughout the year. More actors on stage at Casper College's 450-seat **Gertrude Krampert Theatre,** tel. (307) 268-2500. In the summer, the theater is home to musicals and comedies. Also on campus are free recitals scheduled by the Casper College Music Dept.; call (307) 268-2606. Contact **Artcore,** tel. (307) 265-1564, for tickets to upcoming concerts, literary events, and theatrical productions in Casper.

EVENTS

Casper features a multitude of enjoyable events throughout the summer months, so there's bound to be something going on when you visit. On the second weekend of June the **Cowboy State Games** are an Olympic-style multisport festival with teams from all over the state competing in everything from archery to wrestling. A winter version of the games takes place in February. On the third weekend of June the **Mountain Man Rendezvous** brings dozens of costumed mountain men, women, and Indians to old Fort Caspar. See Crimson Dawn Museum, below, for the year's most unusual event, **Midsummer's Eve** atop Casper Mountain during the summer solstice (June 21).

Casper is home to the **College National Finals Rodeo** in mid-June. This event attracts 350 of the best young cowboys and cowgirls from all over the nation with a full range of events. Call the chamber of commerce at (800) 442-2256 for details and tickets. All summer long, you'll find stock car racing at **Casper Speedway,** 2201 East Rd., tel. (307) 472-7223.

Casperites kick up their heels at the city's biggest annual event, the **Central Wyoming Fair and Rodeo** in early- to mid-July. The various arts-and-crafts displays, farm animals, rodeos, demolition derby, and midway attract thousands of locals and visitors. Rodeo festivities include a downtown parade, all the standard rodeo events, chuck wagon races, and clown "bullfighting." Each October, the **PRCA Rodeo Finals**—Wyoming's largest indoor rodeo—comes to the Casper Events Center.

Up on Casper Mountain the **Bear Trap Summer Festival** brings jazz and blues music during mid-July. For a glimpse of the city's past, come to Fort Caspar for the **Platte Bridge Encampment** the fourth weekend of July. It includes period fashion shows, living-history demonstrations, and military drills. The **Casper Troopers Drum and Bugle Corps**—one of the finest in the nation—often performs for the encampment. The corps has been performing together since 1957; call (307) 234-7005 for a schedule of performances.

In early September, the **Downtown Arts Festival** displays arts and crafts, food, and entertainment on a blocked-off section of 2nd Street. Also in September is **Brewfest,** held on the Platte River Parkway. The Nicolaysen Art Museum has an **Arts and Crafts Festival** on the first weekend of November with more than 75 artisans exhibiting their wares. It's a good place to shop early for Christmas.

RECREATION

The fine **Casper Recreation Center,** 1801 E. 4th St., tel. (307) 235-8383, provides racquetball and volleyball courts, a weight room, gym, and game room. Next door is **Casper Ice Arena,** tel. (307) 235-8484, with skating Aug.-April. Wyoming's largest roller-skating palace, **Wagon Wheel Roller Skating,** is in Mills at 305 Vanhorn Ave., tel. (307) 265-4214.

Mountain-bikers will find many miles of roads and trails on Casper and Muddy Mountains south of town. For maps and info, contact **Backcountry Mountain Works,** 4120 S. Poplar (Sunrise Center), tel. (307) 234-5330.

The Peak, 408 N. Beverly St., tel. (307) 472-4084, has a big indoor climbing wall, with climbing shoes and harnesses available for rent. They also lead guided climbs in Fremont Canyon.

Casper is one of the nation's windiest cities; winds averaging 13 mph make this a great place for kite flying, hang-gliding, and sailboarding. Pathfinder and Alcova Reservoirs are both popular sailboarding spots.

Golfers will have fun at the 18-hole **Casper Municipal Golf Course,** 2120 Allendale Blvd., tel. (307) 234-2405.

Horse and Wagon Trips

Looking for a taste of the Old West? **Historic Trails West** leads a wide range of Conestoga wagon and horseback rides—from four hours to five days long—along the Oregon Trail. All of these include guided tours of Fort Casper and plenty of historical stories. The four-hour trips are $45 per person, including lunch; overnight rides are $85. A three-day wagon ride costs

$550 ($650 on horseback) and includes all meals and teepees; bring your own sleeping bag. Five-day rides are $895 per person, or $995 if you ride a horse. These trips are about as authentic as you can get. Get details at (307) 266-4868 or (800) 327-4052, or on the web at www.historictrailswest.com.

Happy Trails Stables, tel. (307) 234-7484, offers two-hour horseback rides along the base of Casper Mountain.

Water Recreation

If you're looking for a little water activity, check out one of Casper's half dozen **swimming pools.** Five summer-only outdoor pools, tel. (307) 235-8403, are scattered throughout the city. The Paradise Valley pool (5200 W. Iris) also has a very popular corkscrew water slide. Indoor pools can be found at Kelly Walsh High School and the YMCA, 315 E. 15th, tel. (307) 234-9187. Trivial note: Casper's high school was the first in the nation to have an indoor swimming pool, built in 1929.

The **North Platte River** flows right through the city of Casper, providing both the city's drinking water and a variety of recreational opportunities. The Platte's slow current and shallow depth—just two to four feet in most places—make for a gentle and scenic float trip with plenty of wildlife along the way: beaver, muskrats, ducks, geese, hawks, eagles, mule deer, and antelope. For a map and brochure describing public landings, camping, and parking areas along the 45-mile stretch of the Platte between Alcova Reservoir and Casper, contact the Bureau of Land Management at 1701 E. E St., tel. (307) 261-7600.

Wyoming's Choice River Runners, 513 N. Lennox, tel. (307) 234-3870, rents canoes and rafts, and provides shuttle boat service. In addition, they offer scenic half-day float trips for and guided drift fishing. Fishing is excellent for both German brown and rainbow trout; locals call the North Platte one of the West's largest and finest trout fisheries. See the chamber of commerce for a listing of other local fishing guides. Two good fishing shops are **Ugly Bug Fly Shop,** 316 W. Midwest Ave., tel. (307) 234-6905, and **Platte River Fly Shop,** 7400 Alcova Hwy. 220, tel. (307) 237-5997. See Edness Kimball Wilkins State Park above for more on-water recreation.

GETTING MALLED

Casper is Wyoming's version of shop-till-your-car-dies. Sprawling suburbia, fast food, and a half dozen park-anywhere malls combine to make Casper indistinguishable from Modesto, California, or Columbus, Ohio. This is the sort of place where even the Highland Park Community Church is housed in what looks like an old Kmart store. At Wyoming Blvd. and E. 2nd St., **Eastridge Mall** is Wyoming's largest, with 90 stores, including Bon Marché, Sears, JCPenny, and Target. If Norman Rockwell were alive today, he would be painting the high-school girls eyeing the hunks on parade and the over-60, post-heart-attack crowd doing their fast walks around the mall.

Okay, so not all of Casper's stores are in shopping malls. Downtown is the impressive **Lou Taubert Ranch Outfitters,** 125 E. 2nd St., tel. (307) 234-2500 or (800) 447-9378, a four-level department store with everything from cowboy boots (10,000 pairs in stock!) to gourmet coffee. It's a great place to try on a new cowboy hat or shop for fashionable Western wear.

Outdoor Supplies

Mountain Sports, 543 S. Center, tel. (307) 266-1136 or (800) 426-1136, sells quality outdoor gear and rents windsurfers, downhill and cross-country skis, and rollerblades. While there, take a look at the various rock-climbing maps and books. **Beaver Lodge Recreation,** 2419 Nuclear Dr., tel. (307) 234-0644, rents RVs, camping trailers, canoes, sleeping bags, tents, and other outdoor supplies. Also check out **The Peak,** 408 N. Beverly St., tel. (307) 472-4084, for rock-climbing equipment.

Bookstores

A number of places sell new books in Casper. Among them are: **B. Dalton,** in Eastridge Mall, tel. (307) 247-0793; **Waldenbooks,** also in Eastridge Mall, tel. (307) 235-2046; **Ralph's Books,** at Hilltop Shopping Center, tel. (307) 234-0308; **Blue Heron Books & Espresso,** 201 E. 2nd St., tel. (307) 265-3774 or (800) 585-3774; and **The Book Peddler** at Sunrise Shopping Center, tel. (307) 266-2021. **West-**

erner Newsstand, 245 S. Center, tel. (307) 235-1022, sells history books, paperbacks, out-of-state newspapers, and all sorts of magazines. **Book Exchange,** 323 S. Center St., tel. (307) 237-6034, offers Wyoming's largest selection of used books and is a great place to browse. More used titles—and a tea room—at the **Book Nook,** 536 E. Yellowstone Hwy., tel. (307) 237-2211.

INFORMATION AND SERVICES

The friendly **Casper Area Convention & Visitors Bureau,** 500 N. Center, tel. (307) 234-5311 or (800) 852-1889, is the place to go for tourist paraphernalia. Between Memorial Day and Labor Day it's open Mon.-Fri. 8 a.m.-6 p.m. and Sat.-Sun. 9 a.m.-6 p.m. The rest of the year, the hours are Mon.-Fri. 8 a.m.-5 p.m. The Visitors Bureau also has a detailed booklet with self-guided tours of Casper's historic buildings. Find a plethora of details on Casper on the web at www.casperwyoming.org.

The **Bureau of Land Management (BLM) Casper District Office** is at 1701 East E St., tel. (307) 261-7600. Other potentially useful Casper services include the **Natrona County Library,** 307 E. 2nd, tel. (307) 237-4935, and the **post office,** 411 N. Forest Dr., tel. (307) 266-4000. **ATMs** are in many places around Casper, including nearly all the local banks. If you're into Christian music, Casper will fill you up with two radio stations offering preaching and countrified Christian tunes.

TRANSPORTATION AND TOURS

Natrona County Airport is eight miles northwest of Casper on US Hwy. 20/26. **United Express/Great Lakes Aviation,** tel. (800) 241-6522, has commuter service to Denver, and **Delta/Sky West,** tel. (800) 221-1212, has daily service to Salt Lake City. The airport is an official Foreign Trade Zone.

Powder River Transportation, 123 W. E St. in the Parkway Plaza Hotel, room 1159, tel. (307) 266-1904 or (800) 442-3682, has daily bus service to towns in northern and central Wyoming, continuing north to Billings or Rapid City and south to Cheyenne and Denver.

Call **RC Cab,** tel. (307) 235-5203, or **Tom's Taxi,** tel. (307) 237-8178, for local taxi service.

Rent cars from **Around Town Rent-A-Car,** tel. (307) 265-5667; **Avis,** tel. (307) 237-2634 or (800) 331-1212; **Budget,** tel. (307) 266-2251 or (800) 527-0700; **Enterprise,** tel. (307) 234-8122 or (800) 325-8007; **Foss Toyota,** tel. (307) 237-3700; or **Hertz,** tel. (307) 265-1355 or (800) 654-3131. You'll find the cheapest rates inside the Royal Inn at **Aries Car Rentals,** 440 E. A St., tel. (307) 234-3503 or (800) 967-6925.

Melinda Clair of **Your Ride of Casper,** tel. (307) 577-1226, offers customized historical van tours of the area.

CASPER VICINITY

CASPER MOUNTAIN

Scenic mountain country is just a hop, skip, and a jump away from Casper. When the thermometer tops 100° F, Casper folks escape to the cool mountains just a 15-minute drive from town. Snow often lingers until July. Rotary Park, seven miles south of Casper on S. Poplar St. (State Hwy. 252), has a number of official and unofficial trails that climb the steep canyon cut by Garden Creek. The creek drops 50 feet over **Garden Creek Falls,** one of the few waterfalls in this part of Wyoming. A viewpoint is just a short distance up the trail, or you can cross the bridge and follow a second path (actually a maze of routes) to the top of the falls, one mile up. Other trails head out to a ridge offering views of the surrounding country.

The steep, winding drive up Casper Mountain has turnouts offering panoramas that stretch all the way to the Big Horn Mountains 125 miles

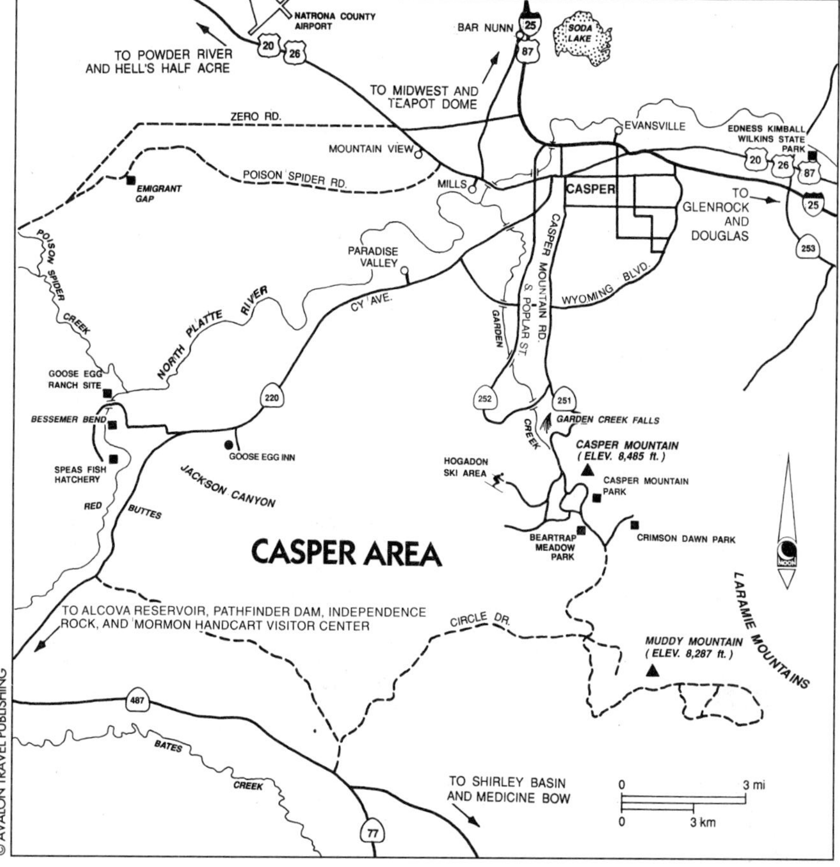

north. Casper Mountain's flattened 8,100-foot summit is carpeted by ponderosa pine trees and pleasant grassy meadows.

Camping

Several county parks—Casper Mountain, Crimson Dawn, Beartrap Meadow, and Ponderosa—are very popular getaways where deer and elk are found. The five **campgrounds** (tel. 307-235-9325) on Casper Mountain cost $5 per night; all are open Memorial Day to mid-October. Water is available only at Beartrap Campground (the nicest) and Casper Mountain Campground. Red Valley separates Casper Mountain from its neighbor five miles to the south, **Muddy Mountain.** The gravel road climbs up Muddy Mountain, where the BLM maintains two campgrounds ($5; open mid-June to late November; tel. 307-261-7500), a self-guided nature trail, and other scenic paths. For more information on the various Casper Mountain parks, call (307) 234-6821. The short **Lee McCune Braille Trail** has plaques describing the natural world in Braille and English. Even sighted people find the trail eye-opening. Nearby is a summer camp for the blind.

Hogadon Ski Area

First opened in 1959, the city-run Hogadon Ski Area is nine miles south of Casper near the top of the mountain. A family area, it includes hills ranging from the easiest bunny slope to black diamonds. Eleven different runs are fed by two chairlifts and a Poma lift, with a vertical rise of 600 feet. Ski and snowboard rentals and lessons are available, and there's a cafeteria. Lift tickets cost $20 for adults, $17 for ages 12-18, $15 for ages 5-11; free for younger kids. Half-day rates are $15 for all age groups, and a Poma-only ticket costs $5. Hogadon is open Wed.-Sun. 9 a.m.-4 p.m. from Thanksgiving to early April. Call (307) 235-8369 for information and snow conditions.

Cross-country Skiing and Snowmobiling

Casper Mountain often has surprisingly good powder conditions. **Natrona County Parks,** tel. (307) 235-9325, maintains 15 miles of groomed cross-country ski trails and a warming hut. Some trails are lit at night. In addition, you'll find extensive undeveloped areas where more adventurous backcountry skiers can practice telemarking. Rent cross-country skis from **Mountain Sports,** 543 S. Center, tel. (307) 266-1136; **Backcountry Mountain Works,** 4120 S. Poplar, tel. (307) 234-5330; or **Dean's Sporting Goods,** 260 S. Center, tel. (307) 234-2788. Casper Mountain also has more than 60 miles of groomed snowmobile trails.

Near Hogadon Ski Area on Casper Mountain, **Snowy Peak Adventures,** tel. (307) 473-2039, rents snowmobiles in the winter.

Crimson Dawn Museum

This is a place best experienced early in the morning, when the crimson light of dawn brushes across the ochre-colored earth and streams into the dark green forests. Come here alone to really feel the magic that captivated Neal Forsling almost 70 years ago. After growing up in Independence, Missouri—and nearly marrying Harry Truman—she headed west to Casper. There Neal married a lawyer, but a bitter divorce sent her fleeing to then-remote Casper Mountain with her two children, looking to start anew as a homesteader. She quickly fell in love with the country and later fell in love with local rancher Jim Forsling. They were married and settled into a fiercely independent life without electricity or running water and with but a few neighbors. The idyll was broken one bitterly cold winter day when Jim was skiing back from town with a backpack filled with supplies. Caught in a blizzard, he froze to death just a few miles from the cabin. He was 38 years old.

Neal adjusted to the loss by turning inward to grasp the spirit of the land, by painting out her emotions, and by opening outward to her own and neighboring children with stories which grew into a complex series of fairy tales detailing the good and evil witches, leprechauns, and trolls inhabiting these woods and fields. Midsummers' Eve was a special time when children and adults could enter this magical world through her storytelling. In 1973, Neal Forsling gave her land and cabin to Natrona County for use as a park. She died a few years later and is buried nearby, but her extraordinary love for the earth is revealed in the small cabin, mystical paintings, fairy tales, and the trails that lead through the woods to shrines celebrating the good witches, magical creatures, and witty forest spirits who haunt this land. Neal's philosophy is summed up by a sign in her cabin:

What I had, I lost
What I saved, I spent
What I gave, I have.

Today, her old log home is a small museum (tel. 307-235-1303) open Sat.-Thurs. 11 a.m.-7 p.m. from mid-June to mid-October.

Inside the cabin are several of Forsling's somewhat crude paintings—seemingly inspired by both Vincent van Gogh and Grandma Moses—which reveal her mystical sensibilities. A framed letter from Missouri childhood friend Bess Truman hangs on one wall. You may want to purchase a copy of *Crimson Dawn,* a collection of Forsling's tales. And be sure to wander along the nearby woodland trails to enjoy the 20 shrines she created—my personal favorite is Sean the leprechaun. Get to the park by heading 12 miles south of Casper along State Hwy. 251 and following the signs to Crimson Dawn.

On **Midsummer's Eve** (June 21), be sure to be in Crimson Dawn for a wonderfully mystical celebration of Casper Mountain's witches and spirits. The celebration has gone on every year since 1929. Visitors get to meet the local denizens in person and are invited to throw handfuls of the dark red earth into the bonfire; if it burns, your wish will come true. Hundreds of Casperites will also be there to celebrate—along with a handful of pompous protesters from Sonlight Ministries.

WYOMING STATE MUSEUM

Joseph M. Carey

BESSEMER BEND

The bucolic Bessemer Bend area—10 miles southwest of Casper along State Hwy. 220—abounds in history, both real and imagined. A lazy curve in the North Platte River, Bessemer Bend was an important 19th-century crossing point for wagon trains. Rock walls from a shelter built in 1812 by the Astorians are still visible on a knoll overlooking the river. Between 1860 and 1861, the Red Butte Pony Express station stood at the river bend, site of the longest of all Pony Express rides, a 320-mile gallop by Buffalo Bill Cody that lasted a grueling 21 hours and 40 minutes. The nearby Red Buttes were also where Custard's Wagon Train Fight took place (described under History in the Casper section). Bessemer City sprang up along the bend in 1888, calling itself "Queen City of the Plains." It lasted only a couple of years, and when Casper was voted the Natrona County seat, Bessemer City quietly faded away. Many of its buildings were moved to Casper, and today Bessemer City is a just field of alfalfa.

Along the east side of the North Platte River at Bessemer Bend is the site of the famed **Goose Egg Ranch,** once one of Wyoming's largest cattle spreads. In *The Virginian,* Owen Wister used Goose Egg Ranch for a memorable scene in which two drunken cowboys switch blankets on a dozen babies while their parents are dancing, creating havoc when the ranch families drive home with the wrong children. Owned for many years by the Carey family—both father Joseph M. Carey and son Robert Carey served as governor and U.S. senator—it was later renamed the CY Ranch. The southern half of Casper is built on what was once CY land—hence CY Ave., one of the city's main thoroughfares. Ironically, the old Goose Egg ranch house died partly because of the fame brought to it in *The Virginian.* The abandoned stone buildings gradually deteriorated as tourists chipped away for momentos. Fearing that the buildings might collapse, the owners finally tore down the ranch in 1951. John Wayne's oilfield firefighter movie, *Hellfighters,* was filmed not far away in 1968.

Today folks come to Bessemer Bend to enjoy a steak at Goose Egg Inn or to watch wintering golden and bald eagles in nearby Jackson Canyon—named for famed Yellowstone photographer William H. Jackson. Another five miles down State Hwy. 220 is **Dan Speas Fish Hatchery,** tel. (307) 473-8890, Wyoming's largest trout-rearing facility. The hatchery produces more than three million rainbow, brown, and cutthroat trout annually. It's open daily 8 a.m.-5 p.m.

THE "LAKE DISTRICT"

The 655-mile-long North Platte River rises in Colorado, heads north into Wyoming, and then curves a long lazy loop to the east, cutting across western Nebraska and finally joining the South Platte River near the city of North Platte. The entire basin covers 32,000 square miles and in Wyoming is fed by the Sweetwater, Medicine Bow, and Laramie Rivers. The name "Platte" is French for "Broad"; Indians called the river "Nebraska," meaning "flat." Both are appropriate titles along much of the river's path. Cottonwood trees line the banks, and the river offers an essential watering hole for wildlife. (Early settlers in Wyoming called the Platte "a mile wide and an inch deep," and "too thick to drink and too thin to plow.")

Once one of the most impressive rivers in the Plains states—at flood stage it ran 150 yards wide and 10-15 feet deep—the North Platte has been reduced to little more than a creek through much of Wyoming. Near Fort Laramie, where wagon trains in the 1850s found a treacherous crossing, the river today sometimes ceases to flow at all, lying in shallow puddles in the late summer sun. A look at the map makes it obvious what has happened to the water: agriculture has siphoned it all away.

RECLAMATION

Without irrigation, farming was difficult or impossible in much of the arid West, and the thousands of homesteaders who tried to survive on 640 acres soon saw their hopes and dreams fizzle in the withering summer heat. Irrigation seemed natural for these desert lands. John Wesley Powell's idea of arid lands reclamation through dams and irrigation canals gradually gained favor, and by the 1890s Wyoming's politicians were claiming that irrigation could turn 12 to 15 million acres of the state into productive farmland. The Carey Act—named for Wyoming's Sen. Joseph M. Carey—tested these claims by having the federal government donate land to the states to be reclaimed by settlers. Wyoming became the first state to try out the new law, but only 10% of the two million acres in the program were finally patented. The costs were simply too high and the return too low; funding for the massive dams and irrigation canals could only come from the federal government. The Reclamation Act of 1902 was designed to do just that.

When Reclamation Act money started flowing, the North Platte was one of the first to be dammed (or damned, depending upon one's perspective). It seemed a potential godsend for farmers who had long used waterwheels to lift water from the river into adjacent irrigation ditches. Today, eight giant dams hold back the river and its tributaries in Wyoming: the Seminoe, Kortes, Pathfinder, Alcova, and Gray Reef above

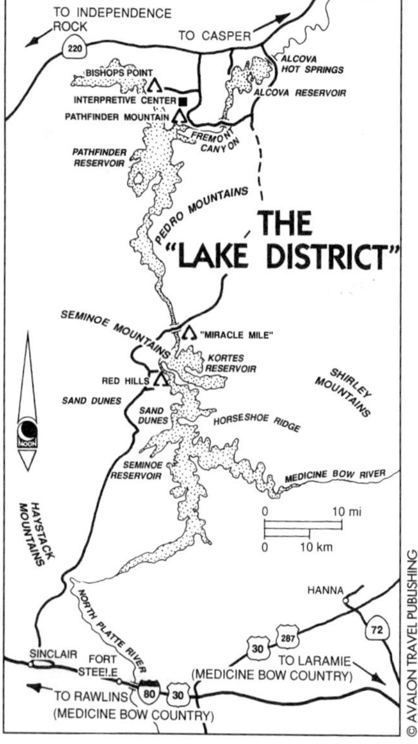

the city of Casper, and the Glendo, Guernsey, and Grayrocks farther downstream. Two long irrigation canals—the Interstate Canal and the Fort Laramie Canal—supply water to farms east of Wheatland. Ironically, nearly 80% of the water behind Wyoming dams on the North Platte goes to fields in neighboring Nebraska. This is also true at most of the other large reclamation projects in Wyoming: Bighorn Canyon water goes to Montana, Keyhole Reservoir water to South Dakota, Jackson Lake water to Idaho, and Flaming Gorge water to Utah. Meanwhile, more than 100,000 acres of once-valuable farming and grazing land in Wyoming lie under these massive reservoirs. Wyoming, one of the driest states in the nation, has become an exporter of huge quantities of water to surrounding states.

SEMINOE RESERVOIR

The 295-foot-high concrete arch Seminoe Dam was completed in 1939 and is the farthest upstream of the North Platte River dams. It holds back more than a million acre-feet of water which drives a power plant that produces 45 megawatts of electricity. The reservoir is bounded by 3,821-acre **Seminoe State Park,** tel. (307) 320-3013, named for the nearby Seminoe Mountains, which in turn were named after the French trapper Basil Cimineau Lajeunesse—folks apparently had a hard time spelling his middle name. Day-use of the park costs $5 for nonresident vehicles, $2 if you're driving a Wyoming vehicle. The reservoir stretches almost 20 miles south of the dam through desolate, rocky mountains and gigantic dunes of white sand. Sandy beaches along the shoreline attract swimmers in late summer. Juniper and ponderosa pine trees dot the hills, while sagebrush, greasewood, yucca, and salt sage grow on the lower slopes. The steep 500-foot knife edge of Horseshoe Ridge is visible on the eastern shore. Golden eagles nest along the southern arm of Seminoe Reservoir, and bighorn sheep and elk have been reintroduced. The area also abounds with sage grouse.

Practicalities

Seminoe has two state park **campgrounds** ($9 for nonresidents or $4 for Wyoming residents, open mid-April to mid-October) along its northwest shore. Water, toilets, and boat ramps are available at each. You can also camp for free on Bureau of Reclamation sand dunes along the lake's southern arm. The reservoir is popular for fishing (rainbow, brown, and cutthroat trout, and walleye) and water-skiing. Gas and limited provisions are available at Seminoe Boat Club. Access from Rawlins and Sinclair to the western shore of Seminoe is relatively easy via a 34-mile-long paved road, but the 70 miles of mixed pavement and gravel from Casper are a bit harder to take. The eastern shore is even less accessible.

An overlook at the dam site provides views into the steep rocky canyon and the dam that spans the chasm. North of this, the road drops steeply into the canyon and then climbs up through Morgan Creek Canyon, where big ponderosa pines, willows, and cottonwoods line the creek. A few miles beyond this, the road descends over a pass and then down through Hamilton Creek Canyon, finally emerging into open sagebrush country near the **Miracle Mile** of the North Platte River. You'll find free camping—among the cottonwoods that line the riverbank—and excellent trout fishing. More free camping is at Sage Creek Rd., a half mile north of the river crossing. The name Miracle Mile—actually three miles of free-flowing river—refers to this popular "blue ribbon" fishery, maintained by regulated flows from the 244-foot-high **Kortes Dam** power plant just upstream. In reality, the miracle is that any stretch of the North Platte still has anything resembling natural flows.

PATHFINDER RESERVOIR

Pathfinder Reservoir is 30 miles southwest of Casper on State Hwy. 220 and then another 10 miles in along County Rd. 409. In 1905, the federal government provided funds for this, the first dam in eastern Wyoming, to be built near the junction of the Sweetwater and North Platte Rivers. Proponents claimed that the reservoir would irrigate more than 700,000 acres, primarily in Wyoming, but, instead, only 130,000 acres were irrigated, nearly all in Nebraska.

Completed in 1909, Pathfinder Dam is considered an engineering marvel for its time and is listed on the National Register of Historic Places.

The 214-foot-high arched structure is made up of large granite blocks quarried from adjacent hills and held together with cement and steel hauled by wagon teams from Casper, 45 miles away. (The trip sometimes took three weeks.)

Pathfinder is named for explorer John C. Frémont, "Pathfinder of the West." In 1842 he ventured down the river and—against the advice of his guides—decided to run the canyon below the present dam site (now Fremont Canyon). He and his men narrowly escaped alive, as Frémont described:

To go back was impossible; the torrent before us was a sheet of foam; and, shut up in the chasm by the rocks, which in some places seemed to almost meet overhead, the roar of the waters was deafening . . . the boat struck a concealed rock immediately at the foot of the fall, which whirled her over in an instant. . . . For a hundred yards below, the current was covered with floating books and boxes, bales of blankets, and scattered articles of clothing. . . . For a moment, I felt somewhat disheartened. All our books—almost every record of the journey—our journals and registers of astronomical and barometrical observations—had been lost in a moment.

Practicalities

Pathfinder Reservoir splits into two arms, following the upstream path of the Sweetwater and North Platte Rivers. **Pathfinder National Wildlife Refuge** covers 16,807 acres of land around scattered parts of the reservoir and is home to many mammals and birds. Canada geese nest along the shore, and white pelicans nest on an island here. **Camping** is available at four campgrounds on the east shore of Pathfinder Reservoir ($5; open Memorial Day to mid-October; tel. 307-235-9325), or you can camp for free along much of the lake's hundred-mile shore (except within the refuge). The deep-blue lake is a popular place for anglers in search of cutthroat, brown, and rainbow trout, or walleye. Sailboarders find some of Wyoming's finest sailing conditions. **Pathfinder Marina** has rental boats, fishing gear, gas, and a snack bar.

Not far from the dam is an old stone building that once housed the dam tender but is today used as the **Pathfinder Interpretive Center.** Summer hours are Saturday 11 a.m.-5 p.m. and Sunday 10 a.m.-4 p.m.; ask at the adjacent frame house for a peek inside at other times. A pleasant 1.5-mile loop trail crosses the dam, follows Fremont Canyon (lined with hundreds of cliff-swallow nests), and then re-crosses the river over an impressive swinging footbridge before returning to the interpretive center. The interpretive center has a brochure describing sights along the path.

The Lynching of Cattle Kate

Deep beneath the waters of Pathfinder Reservoir lies the site of one of the most infamous Wyoming lynchings. In 1889, James Averell and Ella "Cattle Kate" Watson operated a ranch here. Local cattle barons accused Averell of housing rustlers and operating a saloon and gambling house for them, with Cattle Kate running a sideline business in which cattle were exchanged for "personal favors." The charges were apparently a smoke screen put up by A.J. Bothwell and other large landowners who were angry that Averell and Watson had filed homestead claims on land being grazed by Bothwell's cattle. When Averell had the temerity to call the cattle barons "land sharks" in a letter to the Casper newspaper, they responded by sending a party out to eliminate the two. Averell and Watson were found hanging from a tree along the Sweetwater River. Later, the six men who perpetrated the hanging escaped prosecution when the chief witness suddenly disappeared—apparently murdered by one of the lynching party. Bothwell went on to gain title to Averell and Watson's land, despite national newspaper complaints about "the barbaric lynching of a woman in Wyoming Territory."

ALCOVA RESERVOIR

Although much smaller than Pathfinder or Seminoe Reservoirs, Alcova is a favorite recreation spot for the people of Casper. Sailboarding, sailing, water-skiing, and ice fishing are all popular sports on this windy lake 30 miles southwest of Casper. The upper portion of the reservoir reaches into famed **Fremont Canyon,** a mini-Grand Canyon whose red vertical cliffs rise 500 feet above the river. Access is via dirt roads from both sides. The water makes for exciting river-running if you have a kayak and the necessary skills. Golden eagles nest here. It's also very popular with rock climbers. You'll find dozens of climbs here, up to a rating of 5.13. For details, stop by Mountain Sports in Casper for a copy of Steve Petro's *Climber's Guide to Fremont Canyon and Dome Rock.* A good place to watch climbers is the Fremont Canyon bridge. Anglers try their luck with the rainbow and cutthroat trout and walleye.

The name Alcova comes from **Alcova Hot Springs** (129° F water), so named because of its location within a series of coves. At the turn of the 20th century, developers tried to turn the hot springs into a spa, but the propensity of Wyomingites to take baths but once a week made the venture a failure. The springs were covered by the reservoir, but an artesian well below the dam pours forth the naturally heated water. Bring your swimsuit!

Practicalities

The 265-foot-high Alcova Dam, part of the depression-era Kendrick Project, was completed in 1938; a 36-megawatt power plant was added in the 1980s. Facilities here include picnic areas, swimming beaches, five summertime campgrounds ($5) and an RV site ($12 with hookups) near the marina; call (307) 235-9325 for details. At **Alcova Lake Marina,** tel. (307) 472-6666, you can rent boats and buy gas or supplies; open mid-April to mid-September. Water leaves Alcova Dam and flows into small **Gray Reef Reservoir,** used to control the fluctuating discharges from Alcova and to generate more power. From here some of the water is diverted into the 62-mile Casper Canal to irrigate 24,000 acres of alfalfa, barley, oats, and corn west of Casper. A campground ($5; open Memorial Day to mid-October) below Gray Reef Dam is a favorite place to launch canoes for a leisurely float down the river. Rent canoes, flat-bottom boats, and mountain bikes from **Eagle Creek Recreation Rental,** tel. (307) 473-2832, near Alcova Reservoir.

Off a dirt road 20 miles south of Alcova and seven miles from Pathfinder Reservoir, **Sand Creek Ranch,** tel. (307) 234-9597, offers B&B accommodations on a 30,000-acre ranch. The remote location offers grand Wyoming scenery and lodging in either a modern log home or in private cabins. Three rooms (shared bath) are available in the house for $75 s or an overpriced $150 d. A better deal are the two cabins for $75. These can sleep six or more, and one offers the ultimate in seclusion—a location five miles from the ranch house. A full breakfast is served, and kids, pets, and horses are welcome. Open June-November. Budget-Premium.

OREGON TRAIL LANDMARKS

Three of the most famous landmarks along the entire Oregon Trail lie within Natrona County: Independence Rock, Devil's Gate, and Split Rock. Travelers anticipated these landmarks, for they marked the start of a long, gentle approach to the Continental Divide 80 miles west. The route past these landmarks paralleled the Sweetwater River—a ribbon of lush grass in a rugged, desolate landscape. The names applied to adjacent mountains and creeks offer clues to the land's harshness: Rattlesnake Mountains, Poison Spider Creek, Greasewood Creek, Sulfur Creek, and Stinking Creek. Steamboat Lake, just a few miles north of Independence Rock, was a source of bicarbonate of soda used to bake bread. Cattle that drank the lake's putrid water died, while bread made with this baking soda took on a greenish cast. But along the Sweetwater, horses and oxen could find forage, firewood was available, and the clean mountain water offered a relief from the alkaline springs to the east. (The name Sweetwater arose when a mule team carrying sugar lost its load in the river.) Today, State Hwy. 220 crosses the old Oregon Trail several miles east of its junction with US Hwy. 287 at Muddy Gap. The highway parallels the trail for the next 45 miles west.

INDEPENDENCE ROCK

Head southwest from Casper along State Hwy. 220 for 55 miles till the granitic dome of Independence Rock rises above the flat surrounding plain. Though not as spectacular or colorful, the setting seems reminiscent of Australia's Ayers Rock. Independence Rock is 1,950 feet long by 850 feet wide; its smoothly rounded top reaches to 136 feet over the surrounding plain. Travelers could not resist the chance to note their passing on this gigantic billboard; an estimated 50,000 names were carved, chipped, or painted on Independence Rock during the mid-19th century. Father Jean Pierre DeSmet, a famed Jesuit missionary, labeled it "the Great Register of the Desert." His initials, along with the names of Captain Bonneville, John C. Frémont, and many other explorers, were etched into the rock face.

August 16

Moved on up the creek saw the notable rock Independence with the names of its numerious visitors most of which are nearly obliterated by the weather & ravages of time amongst which I observed the names of two of my old friends the notable mountaneers Thos. Fitzpatrick & W. L. Sublette as likewise one of our noblest politicians Henry Clay coupled in division with that of Martin Van Buren a few miles further up the creek pases through the south point of ruged & solid looking granite rock by a verry narrow pass after passing which we entered a valy Surounded by low ruged mountains except to the West whare a defiel Shews itself the lower vally of this creek is well clothed with short grass the upper with sand & sage the mountains with short scattering pines but in many places nothing but the bear rock in large steep Surfaces made 8 miles & encamped for the night on a good plat of grass

—MOUNTAIN MAN JAMES CLYMAN DESCRIBING INDEPENDENCE ROCK IN 1844

Independence Rock apparently received its name from explorer and mountain man William Sublette, who arrived here on July 4, 1830, leading the first wagon train across the overland route. Oregon Trail emigrants tried to reach the rock around July 4 to be on schedule for Oregon. When the rock came into view, it was a source of rejoicing, for it offered a welcome place to rest alongside the Sweetwater River. During the heyday of migration along the Oregon Trail, dozens of wagon trains would find themselves at the rock on Independence Day, and the celebrations included patriotic flag-waving, the firing of guns, big dinners, and other festivities. Many people did not make it beyond Independence Rock; many unmarked graves surround the rock.

Exploring the Rock

Today, the state has a modern rest area next to Independence Rock with signs detailing the area's rich history. Hundreds of the original names carved into Independence Rock are still visible, though weathering and lichen have obliterated thousands more. Unfortunately, more recent travelers have added their names, sometimes covering up names over a hundred years old. Independence Rock can be climbed from a number of points along the perimeter, providing fine views of the surrounding countryside. Some of the oldest and best-preserved names are on top; the oldest known is dated 1824. A path circles the rock, making for an interesting mile-long hike. You can spot names on all sides, and you're bound to see deer and other wildlife along the Sweetwater River. A small footbridge crosses the still-visible Oregon Trail route here. Beware of rattlesnakes around Independence Rock.

DEVIL'S GATE

Visible from Independence Rock and just seven miles to the southwest is another famed Oregon Trail landmark, Devil's Gate. Over the centuries, the Sweetwater River has gradually sliced a giant cleft through the Rattlesnake Mountains, leaving 330-foot cliffs on both sides of a 1,500-foot-long canyon. (An Indian legend offers an alternative origin for Devil's Gate: a gigantic tusked beast had roamed Sweetwater Valley,

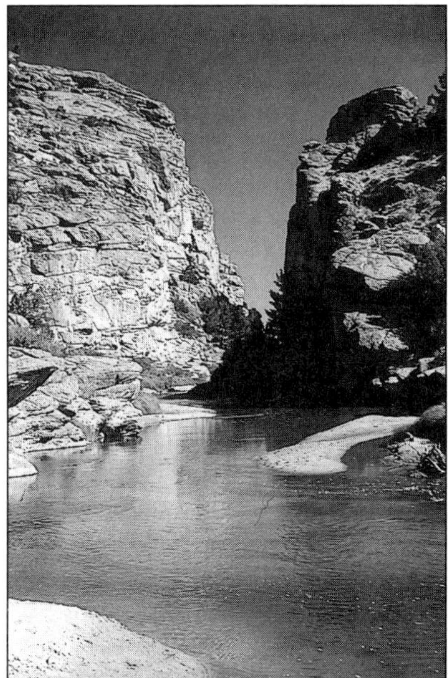

the landmark Devil's Gate

and when the Indians finally managed to mortally wound the animal it gouged out the nearby mountains in its death agony.) Devil's Gate was another favorite emigrant campsite. The cut is hard to miss, especially from the east—the direction of most Oregon Trail travelers. Today, the BLM maintains a historic site along State Hwy. 220 with a short loop trail and signboards. At least 20 emigrant graves are nearby.

MARTIN'S COVE

Disaster on the Plains

Just two miles northwest of Devil's Gate, Martin's Cove is the site of the most disastrous experience along the Oregon and Mormon Trails. In 1856, a group of 1,620 British converts to the Mormon religion sailed from Liverpool for America, intent upon reaching Salt Lake City before winter. The total cost of the trip to Utah, including ship passage from England and Scandinavia, was just $45 per person.

Instead of the usual wagons, many of these destitute emigrants pushed or pulled small handcarts that held their meager possessions. The converts left Iowa in five groups that summer, but the last two were delayed because their handcarts had not been completed in time. Finally, a company led by James G. Willie left Iowa City on July 15, and a group of 576 people under the direction of Edward Martin departed on July 26. The emigrants knew they were taking a big risk by leaving so late, but were anxious to reach "Zion" in Salt Lake City.

Trouble started early. The hurriedly built handcarts had been constructed of unseasoned wood that shrank and cracked as the carts rolled over the hot plains of Nebraska. When some broke down, the load was transferred to others, weakening them as well. Then, near present-day Glenrock, the emigrants decided to lighten their carts by discarding extra food, clothing, and blankets—items they would shortly need. Unable to afford the bridge toll at present-day Casper, they waded across the freezing North Platte River on October 19. Soon a blizzard dumped 18 inches of snow on them and the weather turned bitterly cold, with temperatures dropping to -14° F. The elderly and children died first; eventually even the strongest began to perish. Some bodies were covered with stones to protect them from wolves, but others were simply left on the frozen ground, strewn over 60 miles of trail. When a rescue wagon from Salt Lake City finally arrived on November 1, they found the survivors huddling in Martin's Cove, a protected area near Devil's Gate. Rescuer Daniel W. Jones wrote:

> *There were old men pulling and tugging their carts, sometimes loaded with a sick wife or children, women pulling along sick husbands; little children six to eight years old struggling through the mud and snow. . . . The provisions we took amounted to almost nothing among so many people, many of them now on very short rations, some almost starving.*

The company of foolhardy emigrants finally reached Salt Lake City in late November, but 145 members had died along the way, and many others lost limbs from frostbite. The handcart company led by James G. Willie suffered a similar fate, losing 67 people to the elements at South Pass.

Mormon Handcart Visitor Center

In 1872 the French-Canadian trapper Thomas De Beau Soleil (Thomas Sun) established a ranch in the Martin's Cove area. Many of the Tom Sun Ranch buildings survive, including Soleil's original cabin (now on the National Register of Historic Places). The buildings were purchased by the Mormon church in 1996, and the old ranch house was transformed into the Mormon Handcart Visitor Center, tel. (307) 328-2953. Stop here to learn more about the handcart companies in this excellent free facility, open daily 8 a.m.-7 p.m. June-Aug., and daily 9 a.m.-4 p.m. the rest of the year. A genealogy center provides a way to search your family history, and an old schoolhouse houses artifacts from the Sun family. Visitors can borrow a handcart replica to walk a 4.5-mile portion of the Oregon/Mormon Trail, or to go on an overnight walk to campgrounds located three and six miles from the center. A primitive campground and RV park (running water but no showers) is on the grounds at the Handcart Visitor Center. All of these, and the exhibits, are entirely free. The website is www.handcart.com.

SPLIT ROCK

The final of the three geologic landmarks that lined the Oregon Trail through present-day Natrona County is Split Rock, a bite taken out of a solid granite mountain. The cleft was visible for two days as emigrants trudged along; it seemed to be a gunsight aimed toward the west. In the early 1860s, a Pony Express station, an overland stage station, a telegraph station, and a garrison of troops were located nearby. Today, Split Rock is noted at a turnout 10 miles west of Muddy Gap Junction along US Hwy. 287. Tourists sail past in minutes what took the emigrants many long and treacherous days. See Lander Vicinity in the Wind River Mountains Country chapter for points west of here on US Hwy. 287 including Jeffrey City and Ice Slough. If you're heading south to Rawlins on US Hwy. 287, see Heading North under Rawlins in the Medicine Bow Country chapter.

SALT CREEK OIL FIELD

Forty miles north of Casper is the Salt Creek Oil Field, considered the largest light oil field in the world. The 10-mile-long field covers a land of sage, sand, and rock that has produced over 600 million barrels of oil and 700 million cubic feet of gas. Much more oil has been found nearby. A drive up State Hwy. 259 is a trip through a bizarre alien world of desert land carpeted with giant grasshopper-like electric pumpjacks spaced every couple hundred feet to the horizon. Actually, they look more like the little plastic ostriches sold in tourist shops—the ones that keep tipping down to a bowl of water to "drink." The pumpjacks don't run all the time, allowing the oil to accumulate in the well before pumping resumes. West of the company town of Midwest, things get even stranger, with an incredible grid of pumpjacks, dirt roads, power lines, and storage tanks crisscrossing the harsh land.

HISTORY

This famed oil field occupies a classic anticlinal structure that traps oil—hundred-foot cliffs surround the field. Wyoming's territorial geologist, Samuel Aughey, discovered these unusual structures and brought the first speculators here to file placer claims in 1884. The first well in the area was drilled in 1889 by a Pennsylvania oilman, M.P. Shannon. The oil was hauled by horse-drawn wagon to Casper, 50 miles away. In 1904, Shannon sold his small Casper refinery and 105,000 acres of Salt Creek leases to European speculators for $350,000.

Four years later the real boom came when a Dutch-financed company struck black gold at 1,050 feet in the Salt Creek Field, spouting oil in a massive gusher. When the news hit, battles over land claims quickly escalated to the shouting and shooting stage. The Midwest Oil Company was formed and built the first pipeline to Casper in 1911 to feed the new Midwest refinery there. The Fransco Company added another refinery the following year, and Standard Oil of Indiana built a cracking plant to retrieve more gasoline from the crude.

As WW I steamed over the horizon, the field suddenly gained vital national importance; oil shipped to the allies from Salt Creek was considered an important factor in the defeat of Kaiser Wilhelm. After the war Standard Oil (now Amoco) bought out all of Midwest's Salt Creek properties, but the 14 remaining companies competed with each other for the crude, with oil derricks within spitting distance of each other.

Production declined as the companies attempted to pump the oil too fast, trying to get it before it flowed into neighboring wells. Finally, in 1939, Salt Creek became the first oil field in America to run as a unitized operation with joint management of the various wells for greater efficiency and conservation. Production in Salt Creek reached a peak in 1923 (when it produced five percent of the nation's oil), but the introduction of gas injection in the 1920s and water flooding in the 1950s helped push more oil to the wellheads. Today, more than 100 years after its discovery, workers have recovered just a third of the oil at Salt Creek. Culling the remaining oil will require more sophisticated techniques such as flooding with carbon dioxide. Even still, Salt Creek's current yield of 12,000 barrels a day accounts for two-thirds of Natrona County's oil production. It's Wyoming's third-largest producing field.

MIDWEST AND EDGERTON

The twin oil towns of Midwest (pop. 360) and Edgerton (pop. 160) lie near the center of the Salt Creek Field. A paved road north of Midwest leads to the Shannon Pool oil field, where oil was first discovered. Thousands of drill holes surround the towns, laced together by a grid of dirt roads, power lines, and pipes.

Midwest

The company town of Midwest is named for Midwest Oil Company, now a part of Amoco. Its four straight streets contain rows of identical wooden houses built in the 1920s and now showing their age. The stench of sulfur from a gas-recovery plant south of town permeates the air. Midwest's golf course is dotted with oil pumps, and folks attending Mass at the Catholic church can hear the quiet, rhythmic "ker-thunk" of a pumpjack just a hundred feet away. Midwest was especially hard hit by the slide in oil prices in the '80s; assessed valuation plummeted from $9.2 million in 1987 to $1.5 million in 1989! More than a decade later, the economy is still marginal, peeling paint decorates the small wooden box houses, and the town is peppered with boarded-up buildings, aging cars, and a sense of the doldrums.

Worth a look is the small **Salt Creek Museum,** 531 Peak St., tel. (307) 437-6513. Inside, you'll find a fun collection of memorabilia and junk, with bedpans, historic photos, farm tools, trophies, old high-school lockers, and even dinosaur eggs. The museum is open Mon.-Fri. 8 a.m.-5 p.m.; get a key from the Town Hall out front, or call Pauline Schultz at (307) 437-6633 for tours. The general store sells groceries, booze, and gas. Midwest claims one trivial historical footnote: in 1925 the nation's first interscholastic football game was played under artificial lights here.

Edgerton

The dumpy little settlement of Edgerton has a bit more to offer, with a grocery, a bank, two bars, a library, a gas station, and an old-time hardware store. For meals, try **Edgerton Cafe.**

The only local lodging place is **Tea Pot Motor Lodge** in Edgerton, tel. (307) 437-6541, where rooms cost $30 s or $34 d. Budget. Buses from **Powder River/Coach USA,** tel. (877) 765-2100, stop here, heading both north and south. The big local event—including parades, dancing, food, and a "sand greens" golf tournament—comes in August, when both towns celebrate **Salt Creek Days.** Call (307) 437-6513 for details. Points northwest of Midwest and Edgerton are covered in the Powder River chapter.

BRIAN BARDWELL

TEMPEST IN A TEAPOT

Twenty-five miles north of Casper along US Hwy. 87 is a distinctive butte, Teapot Rock. Until a 1962 windstorm knocked down the "spout" that bent away from one side, the rock resembled a teapot. In the first decades of this century, rapid growth in the oil industry sent prospectors and speculators all over the west in search of black gold. To ensure adequate fuel supplies for the navy's ships after WW I, the government set aside three large oil reserves—Elk Hills and Buena Vista in California, and Wyoming's Teapot Dome Oil Field (named for Teapot Rock).

In 1921 and 1922, Secretary of the Interior Albert B. Fall secretly leased Teapot Dome to Edward Doheny and Harry Sinclair, owners of Mammoth Oil Company—could anyone have ever come up with a more fitting name for a corrupt corporation? Although the action was technically legal, the $100,000 bribe paid by Doheny to President Harding's interior secretary was decidedly not legal, and Fall was forced to resign. The action brought a plethora of charges against the giant oil companies, and political cartoonists had a heyday with Teapot Dome. Interior Secretary Fall was convicted of accepting bribes and spent a year in prison. Harry Sinclair—for whom both the oil company and the Wyoming town are named—hired detectives to spy on a jury investigating Teapot Dome and was sent to jail in 1929 for contempt of court. He also spent three months in jail for refusing to testify before a Senate committee investigating the scandal. Today, the U.S. Navy still owns thousands of acres at Teapot Dome, and there are hundreds of oil wells a few miles east of the highway. A sign points out Naval Petroleum Reserve Number 3, but you won't find any historical signs mentioning this rather sordid piece of Wyoming history. The mailboxes and nearby white buildings of Teapot Dome Ranch mark the site of Teapot Rock.

HEADING WEST

West of Casper, US Hwy. 20/26 passes through the heart of Wyoming, a dry landscape of sage and grass. For a fascinating diversion, follow the BLM's **Big Horn/Red Wall Byway** in a 100-mile loop over country roads with grand vistas and an outlaw past (Butch Cassidy hid out here). The road starts from the intersection of US Hwy. 20/26 and County Rd. 125, 13 miles northwest of Casper; get a route map from the BLM office in Casper, tel. (307) 261-7600. The road is rough in places, and high-clearance vehicles are recommended. No services along the way, so be sure to carry food, water, and extra clothes. Don't attempt this route in rainy weather when the roads become slick.

POWDER RIVER

The tiny settlement of Powder River (pop. 50) lies along US Hwy. 20/26 where it crosses this famous river 35 lonely miles west of Casper. Not much is here today; writer James Conaway called the town "little more than a Texaco station and a bunch of pronghorn antelope looking at it." On the third weekend in July, however, several hundred people flock (pun intended) to town for the annual **Sheepherder's Fair.** It features dog trials, sheep roping and hooking, a lamb cook-off, and sheepherding demonstrations of all sorts. Calcutta wagering goes on for most events, and a band plays country-and-western favorites late into the evening for a happy throng of dancers.

HELL'S HALF ACRE

Forty-five miles west of Casper is one of the freaks of nature, Hell's Half Acre. Actually covering 320 acres, the area includes a strange collection of deeply eroded and colorful badlands surrounded by featureless sage-covered plains. Ancient coal deposits within the badlands caught on fire and burned for many years, and when explorer Captain Bonneville passed by in 1833, he labeled it Devils Kitchen because of these sulfurous fumes. The name Hell's Half Acre was a later title. Indians used these badlands as a buffalo trap, driving herds to their deaths over the canyon walls. In the late 19th century, after whites had slaughtered the bison to the brink of extinction, bone pickers gleaned thousands of these bones from Hell's Half Acre for eastern fertilizer plants. Archaeologists later discovered additional bison bones, along with arrowheads and other artifacts. Hell's Half Acre was the setting for the 1996 sci-fi movie *Starship Trooper*—a space-station "city" was built on the south half of the badlands. Visitors today enjoy wandering through these colorful badlands. Hell's Half Acre is well worth a stop, but be forewarned that a kitschy souvenir shop, cafe, motel (tel. 307-472-0018), and RV park detract from the view. It's a great place to meet busloads of tottering tourists from hell.

MONETA, LYSITE, AND LOST CABIN

Slow-paced **Lysite** is decidedly off the beaten track, eight miles north of another nowheresville place, **Moneta** (pop. 10). At one time the main route into the Bighorn Basin and Yellowstone lay along the Lysite road, but with completion of a highway through Wind River Canyon in 1927, traffic bypassed this area. Lysite has an old-time country store and is the sort of town where horses are still a means of transportation. The Lysite library is housed in a building slightly larger than a shoe box.

Deer Creek Ranch, a 4,000-acre spread in remote country southeast of Moneta, offers a fully equipped house for $65 s or $130 d, including a family-style dinner. For more information, call (307) 457-2451 or see the website: www. wyomingbnb-ranchrec.com/deercreek. Premium.

Lost Cabin

Three miles east of Lysite is the flyspeck of a town called **Lost Cabin,** named for a gold mine in the Big Horn Mountains. Miner Allen Hulburt and two partners discovered a stream filled with gold, but Indians killed his partners and partially burned their cabin. The dazed miner scooped up as much gold as he could carry and fled to Casper, where his tale pricked more than a few ears. Despite repeated efforts by Hulburt and others, the Lost Cabin mine was never again found. (This is only one of many such tales about the fabled mine.)

Lost Cabin is centered around the elaborate mansion of John B. Okie. He came to Wyoming as a cowboy with only the clothes on his back, decided sheep were a better bet, and gradually became a millionaire. Okie once ran 30,000 sheep through the surrounding country, gaining the title of "Sheep King." His mansion—called "The Big Tepee" by local Indians—was built in 1900 for $30,000 and contained carved fireplaces, Asian chandeliers, imported furniture, stained-glass, and Persian prayer rugs. Surrounding it were a greenhouse with flowers tended by Japanese gardeners, a roller rink, a dance hall, and even an aviary housing 140 exotic birds. A power plant was built to supply electricity for Okie's town. In 1930, Okie drowned in a nearby reservoir while hunting ducks. The beautiful old home is not open to the public but is visible from the gate.

Castle Gardens

A remote and little-known archaeological site is Castle Gardens, in desolate country south of Moneta. Head south from Moneta (bear right at the first "Y" in the road, a half mile south of town) for 16 miles on a gravel road, and then turn east on a dirt road that takes you another six miles to the site. The latter road is quite rutted—not recommended for RVs or after rains, when the road turns into a quagmire. Signs at Moneta and at the turnoff keep you from getting lost. At Castle Gardens are all sorts of odd sandstone formations: toadstools, spires, and various creatures seem to appear. It's easy to see how this would be a sacred spot for the Indians who came here centuries ago. Small juniper and limber pines grow amid the gray rocks and sand, creating a garden in the castles of Castle Gardens. There's no camping here, but you will find picnic tables and an outhouse.

Dozens of Indian pictographs (presumably Shoshonean in origin) have been sharply incised into the soft rock walls. They include many in the shield motif, believed to represent the round shields of Indian warriors. While they may be up to 900 years old, these figures are probably more recent than the pecked style of pictographs present in the Dinwoody Creek and Legend Rock areas. Castle Gardens' figures that show horses or tepees are clearly from the period after A.D. 1700. The most elaborate shield found here—the figure of a turtle painted green, yellow, and red—is now in the State Museum in Cheyenne. The remaining pictographs are protected by chainlink fences, but vandals have marred many of these priceless artifacts with graffiti. The site leaves you with mixed emotions: a multitude of questions about what the images represent, a feeling of closeness to the natural world in this remote and fascinating place, and an utter disgust for those who would destroy this cultural heritage.

WEST TO SHOSHONI

The 85 miles of highway (US Hwy. 20/26) that connect Casper with Shoshoni cross an almost featureless plain, a place that seems to define the word "bleak." With no trees in sight, the clouds throw moving shadows across a landscape of sage and grass. This is antelope country. Even the ranches are few and far between out here, and cattle take slow, desultory steps in the summer heat or brace against the bitter winds of winter. For many travelers this is pedal-to-the-metal country, a place to crank up the country tunes and sail on west.

WIND RIVER MOUNTAINS COUNTRY

The Wind River Mountains—Wyoming's highest and longest range—form a dramatic divide between two of the state's most important rivers. The east side drains into the Wind River, eventually reaching the Atlantic Ocean, and the western slopes drop into the Green River and eventually the Pacific. The name Wind River Mountains originated as a Crow Indian reference to the warm Chinook winds that blow down the Wind River Valley.

The Land

This chapter covers Sublette and Fremont Counties, named for two of the state's most famous explorers. Fremont County is a land of sharp contrasts. The eastern end consists of a spacious, arid landscape of sage, grass, and antelope, while to the west you'll find the fluorescent green of irrigated fields along the Wind River and the pastel badlands near Dubois. Along the southern and western borders rise the snow-crested Wind River and Absaroka Mountains. At almost six million acres, this is Wyoming's second-largest county after Sweetwater.

The centerpiece of Fremont County is the Wind River Reservation, home to both the Eastern Shoshone and the Northern Arapaho peoples. Within the reservation itself lie the tiny towns of Fort Washakie, Ethete, and Arapahoe, as well as the larger non-Indian settlement of Riverton. Lander borders it on the south; farther south stand the historic mining towns of South Pass and Atlantic City. West of the reservation, the town of Dubois provides an entry point into the Absarokas, the Tetons, and Yellowstone.

The Wind River Valley is farming and ranching country. Some 150,000 acres of alfalfa hay (considered some of the best in America), feed and malt barley, sugar beets, and oats are under irrigation each year. This is Wyoming's second-biggest agricultural county, and is home to the largest number of horses in the state.

A substantial amount of oil and natural-gas production takes place on the Wind River Reser-

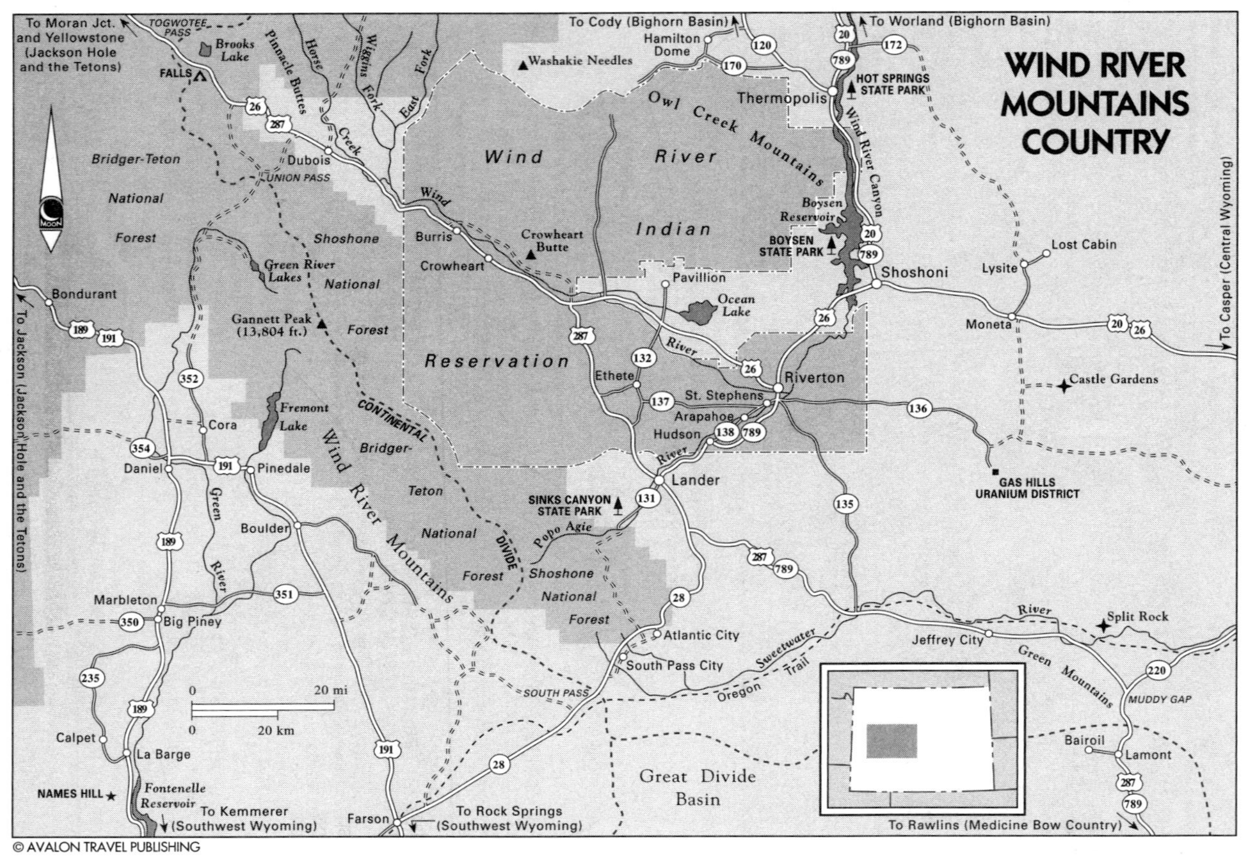

WIND RIVER MOUNTAINS COUNTRY
To Moran Jct. and Yellowstone (Jackson Hole and the Tetons)
TOGWOTEE PASS
Brooks Lake
FALLS
Pinnacle Buttes
Horse Creek
Wiggins Fork
East Fork
To Cody (Bighorn Basin)
Hamilton Dome
Washakie Needles
To Worland (Bighorn Basin)
HOT SPRINGS STATE PARK
Thermopolis
Owl Creek Mountains
Wind River Canyon
Wind River Indian Reservation
Boysen Reservoir
BOYSEN STATE PARK
Shoshoni
Lysite
Lost Cabin
Moneta
To Casper (Central Wyoming)
Castle Gardens
GAS HILLS URANIUM DISTRICT
Bridger-Teton National Forest
Dubois
UNION PASS
Burris
Crowheart
Crowheart Butte
Pavillion
Ocean Lake
Shoshone National Forest
Green River Lakes
Gannett Peak (13,804 ft.)
Bondurant
To Jackson (Jackson Hole and the Tetons)
Ethete
Riverton
St. Stephens
Arapahoe
Hudson
Lander
CONTINENTAL DIVIDE
Fremont Lake
Cora
Daniel
Pinedale
Boulder
Wind River Mountains
Bridger-Teton National Forest
SINKS CANYON STATE PARK
Popo Agie
Shoshone National Forest
Green River
Marbleton
Big Piney
Atlantic City
South Pass City
SOUTH PASS
Sweetwater River
Oregon Trail
Jeffrey City
Split Rock
Green Mountains
MUDDY GAP
Bairoil
Lamont
0 20 mi
0 20 km
Calpet
La Barge
NAMES HILL
Fontenelle Reservoir
To Kemmerer (Southwest Wyoming)
Farson
To Rock Springs (Southwest Wyoming)
Great Divide Basin
To Rawlins (Medicine Bow Country)
MOON
© AVALON TRAVEL PUBLISHING

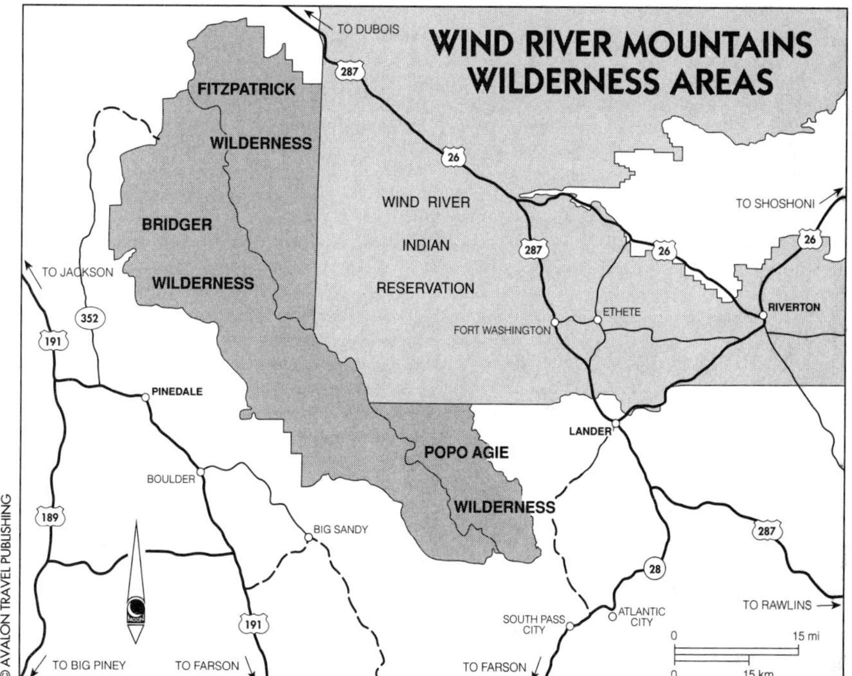

vation, where energy royalties bring in millions of dollars each year. Uranium was discovered in the Gas Hills area east of Riverton during the 1950s and spawned a major industry in the 1960s and '70s before plummeting when the Three-Mile Island accident of 1981 brought the dangers of nuclear power to the forefront.

Sublette County has just 4,500 individuals spread over 10,495 square miles. Cattle exceed people by a 16:1 margin, and you'll find only one town of any size—Pinedale—with a few folks living in the little burgs of Big Piney, Marbleton, Boulder, and Daniel. Not surprisingly, the big industry here is ranching, although the area's scenic beauty draws increasing numbers of tourists. You'll find magnificent vistas of the Winds all along the western front—far more dramatic than from the eastern side. Based in Riverton, the **Wind River Visitors Council,** tel. (800) 645-6233, has brochures with information on the entire area, including events, lodging, outdoor activities, and more.

RIVERTON

Near the confluence of the Big Wind River and Little Wind River, aptly named Riverton (pop. 10,000) is the largest settlement in Fremont County and the eighth-largest city in the state. The Wind River Reservation surrounds Riverton on all sides. It's a mid-American suburbia sort of place where chain stores and fast-food outlets dominate the outskirts. Even Riverton city hall is housed in a strip mall! Cheap gas and low-priced hotels make visiting easier. Modern Central Wyoming College attracts students from throughout the area.

RIVERTON AREA CLIMATE

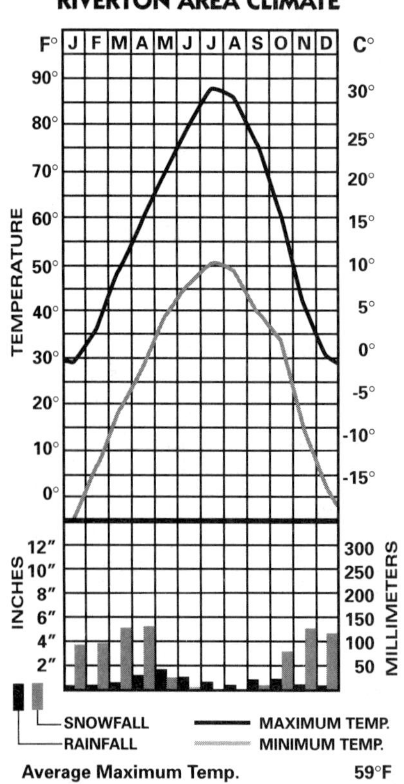

Average Maximum Temp.	**59°F**
Average Minimum Temp.	**26.9°F**
Annual Rainfall	**8.85″**
Annual Snowfall	**33.1″**

HISTORY

The Riverton area was the site of two trapping and trading rendezvous, in 1830 and 1838. The land became part of the Wind River Reservation in 1868, but a portion was ceded by the Shoshone and Arapaho tribes in 1904. Almost overnight, the town of Riverton sprang up as would-be farmers drew lots for prime farmland. It still has the state's largest dairy. Canals were dug and fields planted with crops; more than 100,000 acres of irrigated farmland surround Riverton today.

During the 1960s and '70s, enormous uranium deposits were developed in the nearby Gas Hills area. Hundreds of millions of dollars poured into the local economy created rapid growth, but when nuclear power suddenly lost its luster so did Riverton. After the bust that followed, the town began to diversify and has been slowly rebounding; today businesses include Bonneville Transloaders, a soda-ash hauling company; the Brunton Co., manufacturer of compasses, binoculars, and pocket transits; and various government agencies. The area is becoming increasingly popular with retirees.

SIGHTS

The **Riverton Museum,** 700 E. Park Ave., tel. (307) 856-2665, is open Tues.-Sat. 10 a.m.-4 p.m. year-round; no charge. Local historical exhibits in this rambling, surprisingly large museum include a tepee containing a buffalo robe and powwow drum, an Indian cradleboard with saddle, a model of the Carissa Mine at South Pass, various old farm and mining equipment, and an interesting exhibit on oil drilling. Take a gander at Desert Demon, a stuffed wild mustang that proved untamable—hence his current, more sedate, bullet-tamed condition. While here, also check out the photos of Leslie King, the father of

SIGHTSEEING HIGHLIGHTS FOR WIND RIVER MOUNTAINS COUNTRY

Yellowstone Drug Store in Shoshoni

Hudson steak houses

Eagle Bronze Foundry in Lander

Sinks Canyon and the Loop Road near Lander

Wind River Reservation, including St. Stephens Mission, St. Michael's Mission (Ethete), Chief Washakie Plunge, Shoshone Tribal Cultural Center, and Sacagawea Cemetery (all in Fort Washakie), Crowheart Butte, and Whiskey Basin

Dubois badlands

Togwotee Pass west of Dubois, including Brooks Lake

Green River Lakes and Cirque of the Towers in the Wind River Mountains

South Pass area, including South Pass State Historic Site and Atlantic City

Farson Mercantile

Museum of the Mountain Man and 1840 rendezvous site near Daniel

Granite Hot Springs

Popular events: Labor Day Powwow in Arapahoe (Labor Day weekend), Eastern Shoshone Indian Days Powwow and Rodeo in Fort Washakie (June), Riverton Rendezvous (July), International Climbers' Festival in Lander (July), Green River Rendezvous in Pinedale (July), and The Drift near Pinedale (October)

former president Gerald R. Ford and a prominent Riverton-area rancher. (President Ford's parents were divorced, and his mother later married a Mr. Ford.) Gerald Ford worked as a Yellowstone National Park ranger after graduating from college in Michigan but is not known to have fallen into any geysers.

Riverton Livestock Auction, on Fairgrounds Rd., tel. (307) 856-2209, is Wyoming's second-largest livestock auction barn, after Torrington. Its monthly horse sales are the most enjoyable.

ACCOMMODATIONS AND CAMPING

Motels

Riverton has more than a dozen different places to bed down for the night, all priced quite reasonably. Accommodations are listed below from least to most expensive. Add a seven percent tax to these rates.

Budget: Jackpine Motel, 120 S. Federal, tel. (307) 856-9251, charges $28 s or $32 d, and has microwaves and fridges in the rooms. **Mountain View Motel,** 720 W. Main, tel. (307) 856-2418 or (800) 856-2418, has rooms for $28 s or $32 d, but take a look before staying here.

Inexpensive: Driftwood Inn, 611 W. Main, tel. (307) 856-4811 or (800) 821-2914, offers motel accommodations for $30 s or $36 d, and family rooms for $60 (these sleep four). You may want to see the rooms before committing to a stay here.

A fine older place is **Hi-Lo Motel,** 414 N. Federal, tel. (307) 856-9223. Rates are $31 s or $36-42 d, with fridges and microwaves in all rooms.

Paintbrush Motel, 1550 N. Federal, tel. (307) 856-9238 or (800) 204-9238, has well-kept older units for $35 s or $45 d, including some with fridges and microwaves.

The newly remodeled **Roomers Motel,** 319 N. Federal, tel. (307) 857-1735 or (888) 857-4097, features comfortable and clean theme rooms for $32 s or $35 d. Fridges and microwaves can be found in most of these.

Another well-maintained place—in a quiet location—is **Thunderbird Motel,** 203 E. Fremont, tel. (307) 856-9201 or (888) 498-9200, where rooms go for $36 s or $42-46 d.

Days Inn, 909 W. Main St., tel. (307) 856-9677 or (800) 329-7466, has recently refurbished rooms for $41-51 s or $52-65 d, including a continental breakfast.

Get a comfortable room for $45 s or $50-55 d at **Tomahawk Motor Lodge,** 208 E. Main, tel. (307) 856-9201 or (800) 637-7378.

One of the nicest places to stay is **Sundowner Station Motel,** 1616 N. Federal, tel. (307) 856-6503 or (800) 874-1116, where the rates are $48-50 s or $50-54 d, including access to an exercise room and sauna. Some rooms also include fridges and microwaves.

Find standard motel units at **Super 8 Motel,**

1040 N. Federal, tel. (307) 857-2400 or (800) 800-8000, for $49 s or $54 d, including a continental breakfast.

Expensive: Holiday Inn, 900 E. Sunset, tel. (307) 856-8100 or (800) 465-4329, has rooms for $89 s or d. Amenities include an indoor pool and fitness center, an outdoor courtyard, and a restaurant and lounge.

Bed and Breakfast

For a taste of country living, try **Cottonwood Ranch B&B,** tel. (307) 856-3064, a 250-acre working farm and ranch with three guest rooms (shared baths) in a family homestead. Located 13 miles northwest of Riverton, the ranch serves a full farm breakfast (other meals can be arranged) and welcomes kids. Rates are $50 s or $55 d. Inexpensive.

Camping

The nearest public camping ($9 for nonresidents, $4 for Wyoming residents; open year-round) is 20 miles north in **Boysen State Park,** tel. (307) 876-2796.

Rudy's Camper Court, 622 E. Lincoln Ave., tel. (307) 856-9764, charges $17 for RVs, $11 for tents. Showers for noncampers cost $3. Open year-round.

Owl Creek Kampground, five miles northeast of Riverton on US Hwy. 26, tel. (307) 856-2869, has shady in-the-trees tent and RV sites for $17; showers for noncampers are $3. Open all year.

Wind River RV Park, 1618 E. Park Ave., tel. (307) 857-3000 or (800) 528-3913, has riverside tent sites, teepees, and RV sites with hookups for $22. Showers run $2 for noncampers; open year-round.

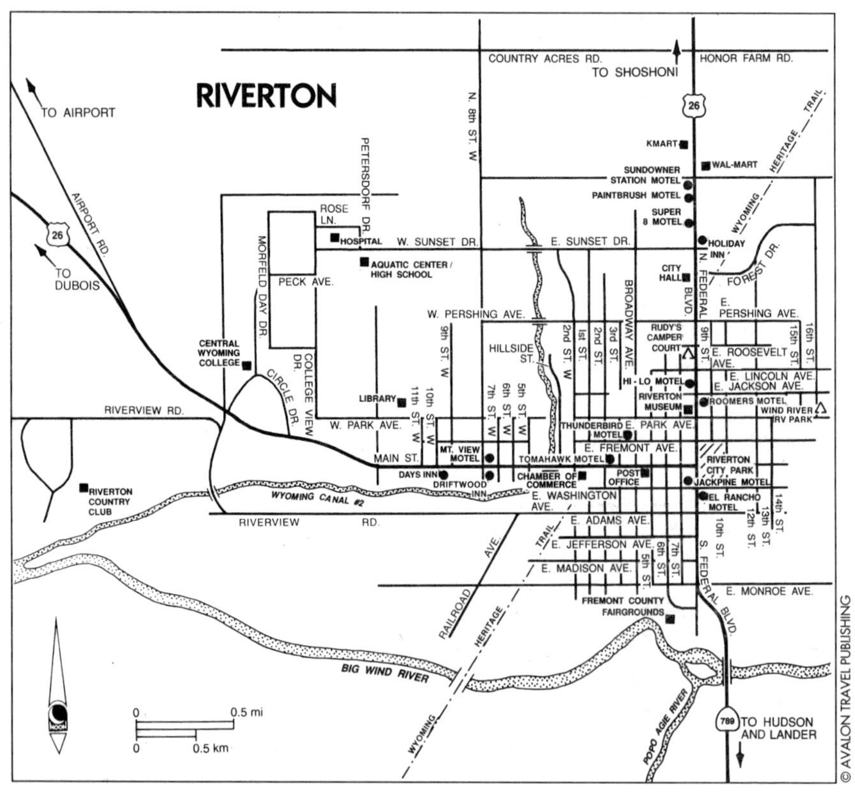

CATHY CARLSON

Fort Rendezvous Campground, tel. (307) 856-1144, has RV sites with hookups for $15; no tents. It's two miles south of Riverton along the Little Wind River and open year-round.

Get groceries from **Woodward's IGA,** 619 N. Federal, tel. (307) 856-9042; **Safeway,** 708 N. Federal Way, tel. (307) 856-6524; or **Smith's,** 1200 W. Main, tel. (307) 856-4931.

FOOD

One of the best local eateries is, surprisingly, **Airport Cafe,** at the airport, tel. (307) 856-2838, where cinnamon rolls and pies are specialties. Fly out here for an inexpensive home-style breakfast. **Country Cove Restaurant,** 301 E. Main, tel. (307) 856-9813, makes dependably good home-style breakfasts and lunches.

Get espresso coffees, fruit smoothes, baked goods, and lunchtime sandwiches and bagels from **Split Rock Coffee & Bakery,** 219 E. Main St., tel. (307) 856-4334.

The Bull Steakhouse, 1100 W. Main, tel. (307) 856-4728, has consistently fine filet mignon, seafood, soup, a salad bar, and daily lunch specials, but save room for the distinctive desserts. The atmosphere is casual, and the service is punctual. Dozens of Indian portraits line the walls. Also extremely popular with locals are two steak houses in nearby Hudson (described below).

Claimsteak, inside Sundowner Station at 1616 N. Federal, tel. (307) 856-6503, is a good family spot with reasonable prices and excellent prime rib. Head to **Golden Corral,** 400 N. Federal Blvd., tel. (307) 856-1152, for stuff-it-in meals from a sprawling salad bar/buffet.

Housed in the same building as the chamber of commerce, **The Depot,** 101 S. 1st St., tel. (307) 856-2221, is a popular lunch and dinner spot with the finest Mexican meals in town. Don't order too much; the enchiladas and chimichangas are big enough for two people.

China Panda, 300 N. Federal Blvd., tel. (307) 856-7666, serves a popular lunchtime Chinese buffet.

You'll find all the fast-food chains on N. Federal Boulevard, or on the west end of Main Street. The cheapest meal deal in town is at Little Caesars in the Kmart store on N. Federal, where you can get pizza by the slice.

OTHER PRACTICALITIES

Entertainment

The bar at Riverton's bowling alley—**StarLite Lanes,** 837 N. Federal, tel. (307) 856-5944—has country music, and **Good Time Charlie's Lounge,** 502 E. Main St., tel. (307) 856-4285, generally has rock bands most weekends.

Watch movies at **Acme Theatre,** 312 E. Main, tel. (307) 856-3415, or **Gem Theatre,** 119 S. 3rd St. E, tel. (307) 856-9589. Central Wyoming College's **Peck Summer Theatre** produces plays both on campus and for dinner entertainment at local restaurants. Call (307) 856-5087 for upcoming productions.

Events

Each February, the **Wild West Winter Carnival** includes an ice-sculpture contest in Riverton and many other events at Boysen Reservoir. Summer kicks off with the **Mountain Man Rendezvous** the last weekend in June on the site of the 1838 rendezvous. Events include shooting matches, basket-making, beading, Indian dancing, a mini-powwow, and other old-time activities.

The **Riverton Rendezvous** covers the second and third weekends of July and takes place at the 1838 rendezvous site. In addition to dozens of mountain men and women, the rendezvous features food and craft booths, an antique car and bike show, a rodeo, demolition derby, cowboy poetry, live music, stock car races, pig wrestling, and a big **Hot Air Balloon Rally** (third weekend), where you're likely to see more than two dozen colorful balloons lifting off at sunrise.

The **Fremont County Fair and Rodeo** comes to the Riverton Fairground the first full week of August, with a carnival, parade, demolition derby, PRCA rodeo, musical entertainment, and fun for all ages. In mid-August, the Riverton Museum sponsors a **Riverton Museum Days,** with demonstrations of pioneer skills and arts such as storytelling, old-fashioned cooking, and folk music. Meet all sorts of people in turn-of-the-20th-century costumes and horse-drawn carriages. You can have more fun at the **Cowboy Poetry Roundup** in mid-October, where the cowpokes spin tales at the largest cowboy poetry event in Wyoming.

Shopping

You'll find distinctive and creative hand-thrown pottery at **The Clay Works,** 519 W. Main, tel. (307) 856-9686. **Wind River Gallery,** 312 E. Main St., tel. (307) 856-1402, displays pieces by local artists.

Books and Briar, 313 E. Main, tel. (307) 856-1797, a surprisingly nice bookshop in downtown Riverton, sells quite a few Wyoming and Indian titles. Also worth a visit is **Book Junction,** 806 N. Federal Blvd., tel. (307) 856-9270. Surf the Net or check your e-mail at **Internet Snack Shack,** 303 E. Main.

Recreation

The 25-mile **Wyoming Heritage Trail** follows an old railroad grade from Riverton to Shoshoni, providing the chance to hike or mountain-bike. The trail cuts diagonally across Riverton along the route of the old Chicago-Northwestern Railroad. It's paved through town and gravel the rest of the way.

Riverton has a fine indoor **Aquatic Center** at the high school on W. Sunset Dr., tel. (307) 856-4230, with a sauna and a whirlpool. The 18-hole **Riverton Country Club** is at 4275 Country Club Dr., tel. (307) 856-4779. **Out Sportin',** 310 E. Main, tel. (307) 856-1373 or (800) 371-1373, sells bikes and supplies.

Information and Services

Find the friendly folks at **Riverton Chamber of Commerce** inside the old railroad depot at 1st and Main, tel. (307) 856-4801 or (800) 325-2732; open Mon.-Fri. 8 a.m.-5 p.m. year-round. Or visit them on the Internet at www.rivertonchamber.org.

The attractive 109-acre campus of **Central Wyoming College,** tel. (307) 855-2000 or (800) 442-1228, is on the west edge of town along US Hwy. 26. Founded in 1966, it offers two-year programs in more than 50 fields for over 1,000 full-time students. An impressive campus **Arts Center** houses a small gallery with changing exhibits. The college also has a good-sized library. Riverton's modern **public library,** tel. (307) 856-3556, is at 1330 W. Park Avenue.

For fast cash, you'll find **ATMs** at most local banks. Wash clothes at **American Dry Cleaning & Laundry,** 515 S. Federal Blvd.; **Driftwood Laundry,** 611 W. Main; or **Riverton Laundromat,** 470 E. Pershing Avenue.

Transportation

Riverton Airport, two miles northwest of town, has daily connections to Denver on **United Express/Great Lakes Aviation,** tel. (800) 241-6522. **JB's Taxi,** tel. (307) 850-5643, provides local service, or rent cars at the airport from **Avis,** tel. (307) 856-5052 or (800) 831-2847, or **Hertz,** tel. (307) 654-3131 or (800) 654-3131.

Powder River/Coach USA, tel. (800) 442-3682, has daily bus service from Riverton throughout northern and eastern Wyoming.

Wind River Transportation Authority (WRTA), tel. (307) 856-7118 or (800) 439-7118, offers scheduled bus service connecting Riverton with other towns in the Wind River Basin, including Lander, Hudson, Ft. Washakie, and Ethete. In addition, they provide on-demand service to other parts of western and southwestern Wyoming. Travelers can call for a ride to Jackson, Salt Lake City, Dubois, Pinedale, Rock Springs, and other places.

RIVERTON VICINITY

SHOSHONI

During the late 1970s Shoshoni (pop. 500) was a booming oil and uranium town, but the bust of the '80s left abandoned streets with tall grass and peeling paint and plywood windows on much of downtown. Tumbleweeds rolled down Main Street, and locals joked that no one wanted to be the last to turn out the lights because they were afraid of getting stuck with the electric bill! People are now moving back to Shoshoni, and things have begun to turn around in the last few years. You still aren't likely to confuse Shoshoni with Jackson, but at least the town isn't as bleak as Jeffrey City.

Practicalities

Shoshoni's main attraction is the **Yellowstone Drug Store,** tel. (307) 876-2539. During the summer months, legions of tourists stop here for ice-cream floats and ultrathick malts at the old-time soda fountain. In a typical year the store makes and scoops 15,000 gallons of ice cream for more than 50,000 malts and shakes! In addition to ice cream, the store sells everything from cowboy hats to teddy bears. Trivial tidbit: former president Ford's grandfather once owned this store.

Also in Shoshoni is the interesting little **CU Rock Shop.** You can still find ancient tepee rings northwest of town, and rock hounds enjoy looking for petrified wood, agate, tourmaline, and other stones in the area. Shoshoni is bordered on the north by Badwater Creek and on the south by Poison Creek. East of Shoshoni is an arid landscape of badlands topography. See Casper Vicinity in the Central Wyoming chapter for points east of Shoshoni, including the minuscule towns of Lysite, Lost Cabin, and Moneta.

Aside from Yellowstone Drug, Shoshoni's primary redeeming qualities are reasonably priced accommodations and gas. **Desert Inn Motel,** 605 W. 2nd St., tel. (307) 876-2273, has rooms for $28 s or $37-45 d; some contain full kitchens. Inexpensive. The smaller **Shoshoni Motel,** 503 W. 2nd, tel. (307) 876-2216, charges $24 s or $27 d. Budget. **Boysen State Park** is just a few miles north of here, with camping facilities costing $9 for nonresidents or $4 for Wyoming residents.

You'll find rodeo action during the summer months at Shoshoni's rodeo arena, along with the **Flywheelers Antique Engine and Tractor Show** in June.

Powder River/Coach USA, tel. (800) 442-3682, has daily buses from Shoshoni to northern and eastern Wyoming.

BOYSEN STATE PARK

Established in 1956, Boysen State Park, tel. (307) 876-2796, surrounds a reservoir named for Asmus Boysen, a Danish emigrant who built the first dam here in 1907-08. When the water from his dam covered tracks of the Burlington Railroad, the railroad sued and had his dam blown up. The dam that now backs up the Wind River is a 230-foot-high earthen structure completed in 1961 and located at the entrance to Wind River Canyon. Boysen Reservoir is a motorboat playground popular with water-skiers and anglers (it's home to the biggest walleye in Wyoming; a 17-pound monster was caught in 1991). Its relatively warm waters attract swimmers to the beach near park headquarters.

Boysen Reservoir lies primarily within the Wind River Indian Reservation and is surrounded by open desert country. A nearly straight highway (US Hwy. 20) rolls north from Shoshoni over the arid hills and rocky buttes, providing a few good vistas across the lake. Southwest of Shoshoni, US Hwy. 26 crosses an arm of the reservoir. **Boysen Lake Marina,** on the north end near the entrance to Wind River Canyon, tel. (307) 876-2772, has a restaurant, grocery store, and RV spaces ($13). The reservoir is surrounded by a dozen state park campgrounds ($9 for nonresidents, or $4 for Wyoming residents; open year-round). Day-use costs $5 for nonresidents, or $2 for cars with Wyoming plates.

The **Wild West Winter Carnival** comes to Boysen (and Riverton) in mid-February, featuring souped-up snowmobile races, ice-fishing contests, chariot races, ice sculptures, mountain-bike races, broomball, bowling on ice, ATV races, and a carnival. In late June, the **Governor's Cup Walleye Tournament** at Boysen hands out a $7,500 grand prize.

GAS HILLS

The paved but almost-untraveled Gas Hills Rd. (State Hwy. 136) leads east from the Riverton area to several now-closed open-pit uranium mines, including the Lucky McMine, discovered in 1953 by Neil and Maxine McNeice and mined for many years. Perhaps a third of the nation's uranium reserves remain in these arid hills. Today signs warn trespassers of the nuclear hazard in the abandoned mines. Dirt roads from the end of the pavement—approximately 45 miles east of Riverton—lead south to Jeffrey City, northwest to tiny Waltman, and east to Casper along Poison Spider Road. This is some of the most remote and desolate country you will ever find, with nary a tree in sight. The antelope love this sage-and-grass landscape. **Castle Gardens** (more in the Central Wyoming chapter) can also be accessed from Gas Hills Road. A sign on the road—easy to miss—points out the turnoff.

HUDSON

You could easily drive through Hudson (pop. 360) without paying any attention to this rather run-down little place, but that would be a mistake. Attractions include a multitude of shuttered shops, Riviera of Hudson Beauty Salon, and an aging Sinclair sign painted on the side of a brick building. Hudson has a distinct sense of decay, but off the main drag lie quiet, cottonwood-lined streets, simple frame homes, and gardens filled with tall yellow sunflowers. This place overflows with character and characters.

Hudson was established in 1905 and became a major coal-mining center in the early part of the 20th century. Most of those who settled here were European emigrants, and the town still maintains a strong ethnic flavor; the old fire truck says "Dago Red" on the front. Nowhere is this ethnic heritage as evident as in the two Slavic steak houses that attract folks from all over the state. **Svilar's,** tel. (307) 332-4516, is the oldest, and its owners are staunchly Republican. Mama Bessie Svilar founded the restaurant in the 1920s to serve the hungry local miners, but it soon began drawing travelers out of their way to tiny Hudson. Restaurant critic Red Fenwick noted that Svilar's "put Hudson on the map in big red letters that dripped with gravy and honey and meat juices." Mama Svilar died in 1981, but the food is still great, and the bar remains a popular place for drinks.

Just across the road is **Club El Toro,** tel. (307) 332-4627, owned by the Vinich family and offering similarly fine steaks and other hearty fare. The homemade ravioli hors d'oeuvres are a specialty, and the Sunday lunch buffet ($8) attracts a loyal following. The Vinich family—well-known Wyoming Democrats—also own **Union Bar,** another very popular Hudson hangout.

After stuffing yourself at Svilar's or Club El Toro, ask about the badlands country east of Hudson. You'll find some fascinating eroded formations just a few miles out. For baked goods, drop by the appropriately named **Down Home Bake Shop,** tel. (307) 335-7700.

Wind River Transportation Authority (WRTA), tel. (307) 856-7118 or (800) 439-7118, offers scheduled bus service connecting Hudson with other towns in the Wind River Basin, including Lander, Riverton, Ft. Washakie, and Ethete.

LANDER

Friendly Lander (pop. 7,500) lies along the banks of the Popo Agie River, with the majestic Wind River Mountains rising just to the west. The town has a state training school for the developmentally disabled, which employs more than 500 people, and there are many jobs in government, ranching, and construction. Smaller and much more homey than nearby Riverton—where Kmart and Wal-Mart reign supreme—Lander seems to epitomize the changing face of Wyoming. It has undergone a rebirth as younger folks move in to raise families, opening shops, restaurants, and small businesses. The town is home to several organizations geared to the outdoors, including the National Outdoor Leadership School, a major local employer. The relatively mild winters and lack of wind here make it an attractive place to retire, and Lander's proximity to the Popo Agie Wilderness makes it a jumping-off place for mountain treks into the high country. Lander is also the southeastern starting point for the 365-mile Continental Divide Snowmobile Trail, which reaches around the Wind Rivers and all the way to Yellowstone. I still can't figure out how it does it, but Lander somehow has managed to rope in some of the most affable locals anywhere. It's a delightful town.

HISTORY

Lander began in 1869 when the army established a small military post, Camp Augur (later Camp Brown), to protect Shoshones from attacks by the Sioux and Arapaho. Two years later the post was moved to Fort Washakie. The rich valley along the Popo Agie River proved easy to irrigate and grew ample crops to feed hungry miners in nearby South Pass. Settlers moved here from the dying gold mines of South Pass in the late 1870s, creating the crossroads settlement of Pushroot (named because the vegetables grew so well here). It was later renamed Lander, after Col. Frederick W. Lander, who had surveyed the Oregon Trail's Lander Cutoff. One of the town's early denizens was the outlaw Butch Cassidy, who bought a ranch near Dubois and was often seen at Lander poker tables and dance halls. The town grew more rapidly once the railroad arrived in 1906, but it took local farmers a while to adjust. When the first train rolled into town, people crowded around, and the engineer jokingly yelled from his cab, "Stand back, I'm gonna turn around." The crowd scattered in fear. During the 1960s and '70s, Lander became a mining boomtown as hundreds of workers commuted to the Columbia-Geneva iron mine and mill near Atlantic City. The mine closed in 1983.

SIGHTS

Lander's primary sights aren't in town, but just a short drive away in Sinks Canyon; see below for details. The city's fine Pioneer Museum closed in 1998 due to structural and funding problems. Hopefully, it will return in the future, but a new building may need to be constructed, so don't hold your breath. In the meantime, the Department of Game & Fish has opened a **Wildlife Education Center** in its building at 260 Buena Vista Dr., tel. (307) 332-2688. The center features wildlife dioramas representing Wyoming's ecosystems, and it also includes interactive displays.

In recent years Lander has gained notoriety for the bronze statutes that line Main St., including a giant bull elk at Pronghorn Lodge (note to the owners: pronghorn are antelope, not elk). These statues are the creations of **Eagle Bronze Foundry,** located in an industrial park at 130 Poppy St., tel. (307) 332-5436. One of the largest foundries in the western U.S., Eagle Bronze employees 60 people. The foundry's pieces can be found in such places as NFL stadiums and outside the headquarters of Cabella's. One piece they completed (it's in Dallas) is the largest bronze monument on the planet. The foundry has a fine art gallery, and interesting tours are offered Mon.-Fri. at 10 a.m.

The **One-Shot Museum,** 545 Main St., tel. (307) 332-8190, has memorabilia from this bizarre organization for antelope hunters. See Events below for details on the One-Shot Antelope Hunt each September.

Getting Jaded

The Jeffrey City area (60 miles east of Lander) is world-famous for its nephrite jade, a mineral found only in Asia, British Columbia, and Wyoming. The jade comes from Crooks Mountain, and much of it was discovered in the 1930s and '40s by Bert Rhoads, who established **Rhoads' Jewelry,** 423 Main, tel. (307) 332-4439. His wife, Verla, discovered the largest piece of jade ever found—a 3,366-pound boulder that required heavy mining equipment to haul out. Wyoming jade varies greatly in value depending upon color and rarity. Some of it sells for around $7.50 a pound, but Wyoming emerald jade can sell for several thousand dollars per carat. Warning: Much of the jewelry sold as "Wyoming jade" actually comes from British Columbia. Buy only from reputable dealers.

NOLS

Established in 1965 by legendary mountaineer Paul Petzoldt—who died in 1999 at the age of 91—the National Outdoor Leadership School (NOLS), is headquartered in an old brick building at 288 Main Street. In the intervening years this nonprofit school has grown to become the na-

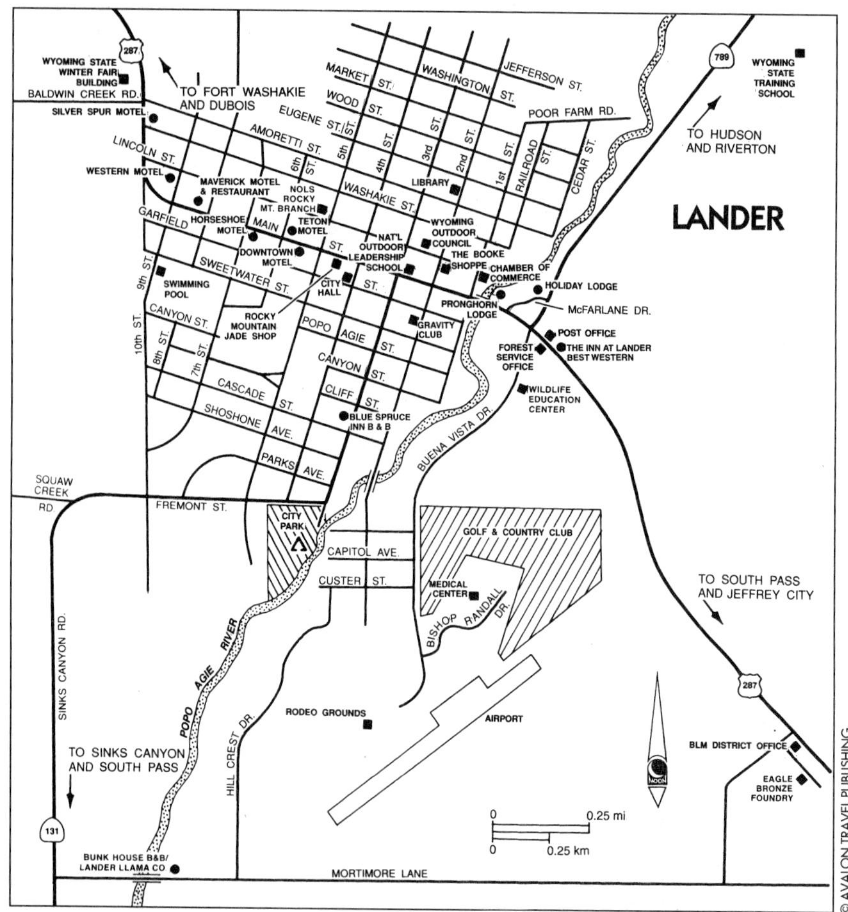

tion's leading source for training in wilderness skills and outdoor leadership. Staff members at NOLS have achieved a reputation as the purists in the field, emphasizing low-impact camping, respect for the land, and safety. The school publishes several excellent books on wilderness mountaineering, backcountry first aid, and minimizing your impacts. The Wilderness Medicine Institute (based in Colorado) is now also owned by NOLS. Trivial facts: NOLS is the fourth-largest purchaser of US Geological Survey maps in the country and the largest outfitting permittee on federal lands anywhere.

Today NOLS offers classes all over the world lasting from two weeks to three months and covering everything from Alaska sea kayaking to a semester in Australia. These are *not,* however, glorified adventure travel; you'll need to carry your own gear, help with cooking and cleanup, and be willing to work hard. You can rent equipment from NOLS for the classes. The school also owns a grand old hotel in downtown Lander which is used to house students and instructors when they aren't in the backcountry. College credit is available for some courses, as is a limited amount of financial aid. Visit the NOLS website, www.nols.edu, for details, or call (307) 332-5300 for a catalog of classes.

In addition to the main headquarters, Lander is also home to the **NOLS Rocky Mountain Branch,** 502 Lincoln St., tel. (307) 332-4784. More than 1,100 students come here each year to take part in backpacking, horsepacking, and mountaineering trips to the Wind River Mountains and Absaroka Range, including a 19-day winter course for hardcore adventurers. The branch office sells new and used gear of all types, and rents tents, backpacks, sleeping bags, clothes, hiking boots, stoves, fishing poles, and other outdoor supplies. Other NOLS regional offices are located in Alaska, Arizona, Idaho, and Washington, and the organization has international bases in Australia, Canada, Chile, Kenya, and Mexico.

Environmental Groups

Because of its proximity to the glorious Wind River Mountains, Lander has become a center for the environmental movement in Wyoming. Lander is home to the **Wyoming Outdoor Council,** an organization founded in 1967 that emphasizes conservation education and environmental lobbying, especially on such issues as wilderness, wildlife, growth impacts, and waste management. Tax-deductible memberships start at $25 a year. The council's office is at 262 Lincoln St., tel. (307) 332-7031.

The Nature Conservancy has its Wyoming state office at 258 Main St., tel. (307) 332-2971. The organization works with landowners to protect important habitat through conservation easements, land donations, and acquisitions. More than 350,000 acres in Wyoming have been protected. Three of these areas are open to the public: the Tensleep Preserve (see the Bighorn Basin chapter), Sweetwater River Project (see Lander Vicinity below), and Red Canyon Ranch Preserve (see South Pass Area later in this chapter).

ACCOMMODATIONS AND CAMPING

Motels

Lander motels are arranged below from least to most expensive. Add a seven percent tax to these rates.

Budget: Western Motel, 151 N. 9th, tel. (307) 332-4270, has some of the least expensive rooms in town: $28 s or $30 d. Kitchenettes are $10 extra.

Inexpensive: Horseshoe Motel, 685 Main St., tel. (307) 332-4915, has rooms for $30 s or $35-38 d, including some with fridges and microwaves. **Teton Motel,** 586 Main St., tel. (307) 332-3582, charges $33-41 s or d and has an outdoor pool. Kitchenettes are $45 s or d.

Stay in clean and comfortable rooms at **Maverick Motel,** 808 Main St., tel. (307) 332-2300 or (877) 622-2300. Rates are $35 s or $39-42 d.

A friendly, easygoing place to stay is **Holiday Lodge (National 9 Inn),** 210 McFarlane Dr., tel. (307) 332-2511 or (800) 624-1974. Rates are $37 s or $42-47 d. Kitchenettes are $5 extra, and a jacuzzi is available for the guests. Some rooms contain microwaves and fridges, and pets are accepted.

Stay at **Silver Spur Motel,** 1240 Main St., tel. (307) 332-5189 or (800) 922-7831, for $39 s or $49 d. Amenities include an outdoor pool and a large deck facing the mountains. Kitchenettes are $5 extra, and family rooms are $75 for six people.

Main St., Lander circa 1883

LANDER PIONEER MUSEUM

At the **Downtown Motel,** 569 Main St., tel. (307) 332-3171, rooms cost $39-49 s or d, including some with microwaves and fridges.

Moderate: The Inn at Lander (Best Western), 260 Grand View Dr., tel. (307) 332-2847 or (800) 528-1234, charges $51-69 s or $69-79 d. It features an outdoor pool, jacuzzi, and exercise room. A continental breakfast is served.

Pronghorn Lodge (Budget Host), 150 E. Main St., tel. (307) 332-3940 or (800) 283-4678, www.wyoming.com/~thepronghorn, has rooms for $53 s or $58-64 d, and suites (these sleep four) for $67. Amenities include a jacuzzi, continental breakfast, and exercise room.

Bed and Breakfasts

In a quiet neighborhood a few blocks from downtown, **Blue Spruce Inn B&B,** 677 S. 3rd St., tel. (307) 332-8253 or (888) 503-3311, is a large brick home built in 1920 and nicely furnished with period pieces. It has four guest rooms with private baths, as well as a rec room housing a dartboard and pool table. Outside are flower gardens, tall spruce trees, and a veranda with a swing. Friendly and helpful owners, too. Rates are $70 s or $80 d, including a full breakfast. Find the inn on the web at www.bluespruceinn.com. Well-behaved kids only. Moderate.

Just two miles from downtown, **Bunk House B&B,** tel. (307) 332-5624 or (800) 582-5262, seems a world away. An old barn has been transformed into a comfortably rustic place to spend the night. Although it isn't spacious and has no phone, this is a perfect spot for families. A branch of the Popo Agie River flows through the property, and llamas are right outside the door. Breakfast is a make-it-yourself affair, but the ingredients—along with a stove and fridge—are provided. The bunkhouse costs $75 per night for up to five people. Owners Scott and Therese Woodruff run **Lander Llama Company,** and the nearby pastures contain 50 llamas used for backcountry trips. Guests will love the chance to feed and pet them. Get more info by visiting the website: www.landerllama.com. Moderate.

Head five miles west of Lander to **Piece of Cake B&B,** 2343 Baldwin Creek Rd., tel. (307) 332-7608, a historic log home with two guest rooms ($80 d) and four cabins ($90 d), all with private baths. The cabins contain microwaves, fridges, and small porches facing the Wind River Mountains. A full breakfast is served, and kids are welcome. Moderate-Expensive.

For privacy with a view of the Wind River Mountains, stay at **Outlaw B&B,** five miles northwest of Lander, tel. (307) 332-9655. This modern log cabin is furnished with handcrafted log beds, and it has a kitchenette and private bath. A full breakfast is served in the nearby ranch house, and kids are welcome. Rates are $90 d. Expensive.

Guest Houses

Horse lovers will enjoy a night at **High Country Arabians Guest House,** tel. (307) 332-2106, www.highcountryarabians.com. This spacious new home is three miles from Lander and sleeps six people. A deck faces the pasture, where you'll see the owner's Arabian horses. The entire house rents for $165 per night, including a complimentary breakfast. Luxury.

Eight miles northwest of Lander along the North Fork of the Popo Agie River, **Black Mountain Ranch Country Guest House,** tel. (307) 332-6442, is a 3,400-square-foot home with four beautifully furnished bedrooms, three baths, a full kitchen, and laundry. It's available for $450 per week, or $90 per night (four night minimum). The owners also run an adjacent gift shop specializing in dried flower arrangements and antiques. Expensive.

Cottage House of Squaw Creek, tel. (307) 332-5003, www.rmisp.com/cottagehouse, is on Squaw Creek Llama Ranch, five miles west of Lander. The modern log cottage has a view of the mountains. Inside, an upstairs bedroom fills the upper level, and the downstairs has a kitchen, living room, bath, and laundry. The cottage sleeps six and can be rented as a guest house for $65 s or $78 d with a minimum stay of three nights. Extra persons are $10 each, and ingredients for a make-it-yourself breakfast are available for an extra $20. Moderate.

Guest Ranches

At an elevation of 9,200 feet on the edge of the Popo Agie Wilderness, **Allen's Diamond Four Ranch,** tel. (307) 332-2995, provides a delightful outdoors adventure. The owners are NOLS instructors, and the ranch emphasizes horseback riding, natural history hikes, wildlife watching, and fishing. Overnight pack trips and cattle roundups are also available. The ranch has basic accommodations with woodstoves and propane lights, but no electricity. Guests bring their own sleeping bags and pillows. No swimming pools or golf courses at *this* ranch! The ranch is open July-Sept. and can accommodate a maximum of 10 guests. All-inclusive weekly rates are $1,590 for two people. Get details on the web at www.wyoming.com/~dmndfour. Luxury.

Three Quarter Circle Ranch, tel. (307) 332-2995, is 25 miles southeast of Lander on the edge of the Red Desert. This 35,000-acre ranch covers a mix of rugged country that includes arid rangeland, lush valleys, and crimson red sandstone bluffs. It's a working cattle ranch where the emphasis is on turning grass into beef without harming the environment. A maximum of eight guests stay in simple mobile homes and are fed hearty cowboy meals. Activity centers around horseback riding, and guests take part in checking or rounding up cattle on the open range, saddling horses, and branding calves. This is a great place to experience a no-frills taste of the West. All-inclusive weekly rates are $1,990 for two people, or $350 for two people per day. For more information, go to the web at www.wyoming.com/~dmndfour. Luxury.

Camping and RV Parks

Camping costs nothing at **Lander City Park,** 405 Fremont St., right along the banks of the Popo Agie River. Pitch tents on the shady grass here or park RVs in the lot. Local high-schoolers often pull in for a bit of extracurricular activity, so don't expect a quiet night. Camping is available May-September. Take showers at the Lander swimming pool, next to the junior high school, or at local RV parks.

Sinks Canyon State Park, 10 miles southwest of Lander on State Hwy. 131, has two campgrounds ($9 for nonresidents, or $4 for Wyoming residents) open May-October. For more information on Sinks Canyon, see Lander Vicinity, below.

Several private campgrounds operate in the Lander area. Riverside tent sites ($5 per person; no RVs) are available at **Holiday Lodge,** 210 McFarlane Dr., tel. (307) 332-2511 or (800) 624-1974. Tenters can use the motel's hot tub for free. Noncampers can use the showers for $3.

Five miles northwest on US Hwy. 287 (inside the Wind River Indian Reservation), **Rocky Acres Campground,** tel. (307) 332-6953, is open May-October. Rates are $10 for tents, $13 for RVs.

Ray Lake Campground, nine miles northwest on US Hwy. 287, tel. (307) 332-9333, charges $7 for tents, $14 for RVs; open May to early September. Showers for noncampers run $2.

On a hill out the east end of town, **Sleeping Bear RV Park and Campground,** 715 E. Main, tel. (307) 332-5159 or (888) 757-2327, www.sleeping-rv-park.com, has tent sites for $13 and RV sites with hookups for $22. Open all year.

Hart Ranch Hideout RV Resort, 10 miles southeast on US Hwy. 287, tel. (307) 332-3836 or (800) 914-9226, has tent sites for $14 and

RV sites with hookups for $19; open May-October. Noncampers can use the showers for $3.

FOOD

Lander is blessed with a number of excellent restaurants. For a light start on the day, head to Lander's standout espresso place, **The Magpie,** 159 N. 2nd, tel. (307) 332-5565. You'll find healthy light breakfasts, and creative salads for lunch. It's a great place to hang out. **Highwayman Cafe,** on the south end of town, tel. (307) 332-4628, serves sourdough pancakes for breakfast. Another favorite breakfast place is **The Maverick,** 808 Main St., tel. (307) 332-2300, where you'll also find excellent prime rib at dinner. On weekends, **The Showboat** at 1st and Main has an all-you-can-eat buffet. Open daily at 6 a.m., it serves breakfast all day.

Wildflour Bagels and Bread, 545 Main, tel. (307) 332-9728, is the best local bakery, specializing in hand-rolled bagels and delicious fresh breads. Lunch specials include homemade soup in a bread bowl. Get deli sandwiches at **The Breadboard,** 1350 W. Main, tel. (307) 332-6090. For ice cream, stop by **Hooligan's,** 351 Main, tel. (307) 332-5050.

Meet the NOLS outdoorsy gang at **Gannett Grill,** 126 Main St., tel. (307) 332-8228. The cafe offers pizzas, sandwiches, half-pound burgers, salads, and bar munchies (including perfect crinkle-cut battered fries), and has a few picnic tables outside for summer afternoons. The historic Lander Bar (connected) pours regional microbrews and has a pool table. Gannett Grill fills most summer evenings with an informal and noisy crowd. Highly recommended.

Tony's Pizza Shack, 637 Main, tel. (307) 332-3900, makes good pizzas using homemade dough; their breadsticks are a local favorite.

The Hitching Rack, half a mile south on US Hwy. 287, tel. (307) 332-4322, has a big salad bar and homemade soups. This is the place locals go out for steak and seafood dinners (it's not open for other meals). Actually, two of the most popular night-out places are 10 miles northeast in Hudson: Svilar's and Club El Toro.

In an 1888 brick building that once housed a Chinese laundry, **The Ranch,** 148 Main, tel. (307) 332-7388 or (800) 714-7388, serves Texas-style barbecued ribs, chicken, sausage, and brisket. In the back, you'll find **Popo Agie Brewing Co.**—the only brewery in Fremont County. It always has several fresh beers on tap.

China Garden, 162 N. 6th St., tel. (307) 332-7666, has Chinese lunch specials, reasonable dinners, and vegetarian dishes. Fairly authentic, too. **Big Noi Restaurant,** 280 N. Hwy. 789, tel. (307) 332-3102, serves authentic Thai food and more standard American fare. This is the only Thai restaurant in Wyoming!

For groceries, head to **Mr. D's Food Center,** 725 Main St., tel. (307) 332-2964, or **Safeway,** 485 Main St., tel. (307) 332-4950.

OUTDOOR RECREATION

Rock Climbing

When most folks think of recreation in Lander, they think of the wonderful mountain country just a few miles away (see Popo Agie Wilderness). **Wild Iris Mountain Sports,** 333 Main St., tel. (307) 332-4541 or (888) 284-5968, sells books detailing local climbing areas, including the **Wild Iris Climbing Area,** 29 miles south of Lander on Limestone Mountain. The Wild Iris area has around 150 different climbs, with pitches from 5.7 to 5.14. The BLM's **Baldwin Creek Rock Climbing Area** is another challenging area with climbs ranging in difficulty from 5.11 to 5.14. Get a map and access details (high-clearance vehicles are recommended) from the BLM office at 1335 Main St., tel. (307) 332-8400. Climbers will want to talk with folks at Wild Iris about other rock faces in Sinks Canyon and at Fossil Hill.

If you can't get out, **The Gravity Club,** 221 S. 2nd St., tel. (307) 332-6339, has a climbing wall, rents climbing shoes and other gear, and offers lessons.

Horseback and Wagon Treks

Several local companies offer horseback or wagon rides along the Oregon Trail and other historic paths. Most treks last a week, and the companies provide horses, food, tents, and equipment; you provide the sleeping bag. Trips include the Oregon Trail, Pony Express rides, Butch Cassidy's Hole-in-the-Wall country, rides across the Great Divide Basin, and horse and cattle drives. The all-inclusive cost ranges from $1,000 to

$1,800 per person, depending upon the trip and the company. The local companies are: **Great Divide Tours,** tel. (307) 332-3123 or (800) 458-1915, www.rmisp.com/greatdivide; **Rocky Mountain Horseback Adventures,** tel. (307) 332-8535 or (800) 408-9149; and **Western Encounters,** tel. (307) 332-5434 or (800) 572-1230, www.horseriders.com. Contact them for details.

Other Recreation

Rent mountain bikes, cross-country and downhill skis, snowboards, or snowshoes from **Freewheel Ski & Cycle,** 258 Main St., tel. (307) 332-6616 or (800) 490-6616.

Lander's Olympic-size **swimming pool,** 450 S. 9th, tel. (307) 332-2272, is open year-round. You'll also find a weight room and hydrotherapy pool here. The 18-hole **Lander Golf Club** is on Capitol Hill, tel. (307) 332-4653. During the winter, skate for free at City Park, where you'll also find a warming hut and skate rentals.

OTHER PRACTICALITIES

Entertainment

Lander Bar, 126 Main, tel. (307) 332-7009, has live music most weekends and an attractive outside deck. Other places to check for music are **Gannett Grill,** 126 Main St., tel. (307) 332-8228; **One Shot Lounge,** 695 Main, tel. (307) 332-2692; **The Hitching Rack,** half a mile south on US Hwy. 287, tel. (307) 332-4322; and Hudson's **Club El Toro.**

Watch flicks at **Grand Theatre,** 250 Main St., tel. (307) 332-3300.

Events

Lander plays host to the **Wyoming State Winter Fair** the first weekend in February, with livestock exhibits, dog weight-pulling contests, horse shows, entertainment, and dancing.

Lander is one of 12 stops in early February's **Rocky Mountain Stage Stop Sled Dog Race,** an event that attracts some of the nation's best mushers with a $100,000 purse. The race begins and ends in Jackson. Call (307) 734-1163 for details, or check the website: www.wyomingstagestop.org.

Lander Valley Powwow takes place in early May, with Indian dancing, a princess contest, food, and crafts. From early July to mid-August, Wednesday evening **Native American Cultural Programs** are offered at Jaycee Park (1st and Main).

On the second weekend of June the **Popo Agie Rendezvous** commemorates the 1829 rendezvous held near here. Activities include a mountain-man encampment, parade, art auction, buffalo barbecue, pack race, and all sorts of historical demonstrations and games.

Pioneer Days, a three-day party around the Fourth of July, is Lander's big event. It features a parade with dozens of floats, marching bands, vintage autos, and performers, along with a buffalo barbecue, Indian dancing, street dances, and evening fireworks. The primary event is the **rodeo,** the oldest paid rodeo on earth, first established in 1893.

An **International Climbers' Festival** attracts rock climbers to Lander the second weekend of July with clinics and competitions, slide shows and films, a trade fair, mountain-bike racing, and more. Call (307) 332-6697 for details, or visit the web at www.climbersfestival.org.

New in 2000 was a series of outdoor folk concerts held in Sinks Canyon during July and August. Contact the chamber of commerce for details, tel. (307) 332-3892 or (800) 433-0662.

The **One-Shot Antelope Hunt** attracts hunters in mid-September; teams of three head out to see how quickly they can bring down an antelope with just one shot. The governors of Wyoming and Colorado are "team captains," and celebrities sometimes participate. All sorts of convoluted rules and ridiculous ceremonies make this akin to a fraternity initiation rite. Old men find strange ways to amuse themselves, including cross-dressing!

Shopping

Lander is a town of book readers and supports three good bookshops. **Main Street Books,** 381 Main St., tel. (307) 332-7661, is the largest, with books in the front, plus espresso and Internet access in the rear. **The Booke Shoppe,** 160 N. 2nd, tel. (307) 332-6221 or (800) 706-4476, has a fine selection of books on Wyoming and a friendly staff, and **Cabin Fever Books,** 163 S. 5th, tel. (307) 332-9580 or (800) 836-9580, offers both new and used titles.

Stop by **Wild Iris Mountain Sports,** 333 Main St., tel. (307) 332-4541 or (888) 284-5968, for outdoor gear and climbing books, including guides to climbing areas in Fremont Canyon, Dome Rock, Sinks Canyon, Baldwin Creek, and Wild Iris. Owner Todd Skinner is a world-renowned rock climber; in 1999 he and six others were the first to free climb a 3,800-foot cliff in Greenland—tallest in the world. The shop is managed by another well-known climber, Amy Whisler. Check the shop's bulletin board for climbing partners or used gear.

Information and Services

The **Lander Chamber of Commerce** is in the old railroad depot at 160 N. 1st St., tel. (307) 332-3892 or (800) 433-0662; open Mon.-Fri. 9 a.m.-5 p.m. all year. Find it on the web at www.landerchamber.org. The chamber rents taped audio tours of the Loop Road, describing sights along the way, for $6 plus a refundable deposit.

The **BLM District Office** is at 1335 Main St., tel. (307) 332-7822, and the Forest Service's **Washakie Ranger District Office** is at 333 E. Main, tel. (307) 332-8400. Stop at the Forest Service office for Shoshone National Forest maps and hiking information, plus lobby exhibits on the forest. The staff can also provide a list of permitted horsepackers, llama outfitters, and even a local company that provides pack goats for use in the backcountry.

Lander's **post office** stands at the junction of US Hwy. 287 and State Hwy. 789, tel. (307) 332-2126. Unfortunately, it rests atop what was previously Wyoming's only in-town prairie-dog town. The **Fremont County Library** can be found at 2nd and Amoretti, tel. (307) 332-5194. Most local banks and the larger stores have **ATMs. Lander Valley Medical Center,** 1320 Bishop Randall Dr., tel. (307) 332-4420, has emergency medical services. Wash clothes at **American Dry Cleaning & Laundry,** 494 Main St. or 550 Lincoln Street.

Transportation and Tours

The nearest airport with scheduled flights is in Riverton, 25 miles from Lander. **Winds Aloft,** tel. (307) 332-9233, provides flightseeing trips over the Wind River Mountains out of the small Lander airport.

Rent cars from **Fremont Motors,** 555 E. Main St., tel. (307) 332-4355, or **Rent-A-Wreck,** 323 N. 2nd St., tel. (307) 332-9965.

Sleeping Bear RV Park Taxi & Tour Service, 715 Main St., tel. (307) 332-5159 or (888) 757-2327, provides transportation throughout the area, including to and from Jackson and Dubois. The company also provides drop-off services to Wind River Mountain trailheads, and it's popular with RVers who don't want to drive their monster vehicles up Sinks Canyon or to other scenic areas. Tours are offered on a daily basis in the summer.

Wind River Transportation Authority (WRTA), tel. (307) 856-7118 or (800) 439-7118, offers on-demand bus service throughout the area, Riverton airport shuttles, and connections all the way to Jackson, Rock Springs, Rawlins, Pinedale, Cody, and Salt Lake City. It also operates a twice-daily scheduled shuttle connecting Lander with Ethete, Hudson, and Riverton.

LANDER VICINITY

EAST ON US HIGHWAY 287

A few miles east of Lander on US Hwy. 287, the highway passes an impressive vermilion sandstone butte. Near here is a beautiful, century-old red-rock barn that once stabled horses used on the stage route through here. In 1884, Wyoming's first oil well was drilled not far away. The site—now called the Dallas oil field—was known to Indians and described in Washington Irving's *Adventures of Captain Bonneville* as the "Great Tar Springs." Nineteenth-century emigrants used the oil to grease wagon axles, in lamps, and as a balm for their aches. Mountain man Osborne Russell described coming across the spring in 1837:

> *This spring produces about one gallon per hour of pure oil of Coal or rather Coal Tar the scent of which is often carried on the wind 5 or 6 mls. The Oil issues from the ground within 30 feet of the stream and runs off slowly into the water Camp stopped here eight days We set fire to the spring when there was 2 or 3 Bbls. of oil on the ground about it, it burnt very quick and clear but produced a dense column of thick black smoke the oil above ground being consumed the fire soon went out.*

As you continue eastward, the Wind River Mountains gradually diminish in magnitude. Stop to look up at them for a while. It is easy to see how the pioneers from the east—where a mountain is anything over 1,000 feet—would watch these mountains grow closer with each day's travel and wonder at their rugged crowns. It's also easy to see why they would choose to go around the southern end of this range—at South Pass—instead of crossing over the top.

Along the Sweetwater

River Campground, tel. (307) 544-9318, sits at the junction of US Hwy. 287 and State Hwy. 135 along the Sweetwater River. Open May-Sept., the campground has tent spaces for $9, bike camping for $4 per person, and RV sites for $12. Showers cost $2 for noncampers.

A mile west of the junction along US Hwy. 287 is the Nature Conservancy's **Sweetwater River Project,** a 3,000-acre natural area that preserves 16 miles of riparian habitat along the Oregon Trail. The preserve is open only to Nature Conservancy members, but camping and rustic cabins are available. For access information, call the Conservancy in Lander at (307) 332-2971.

Ice Slough

Forty miles east of Lander, the highway passes a marker describing Ice Slough, one of many landmarks along this portion of the Oregon Trail. Dense grasses in a small marsh kept ice all through the summer, a real treat for emigrants on a hot summer day. The trail is visible just to the right of the historical sign that describes Ice Slough; it's just north of the wire gate. In *Roughing It,* Mark Twain described Ice Slough as follows:

> *In the night we sailed by a most notable curiosity, and one we had been hearing a good deal about for a day or two, and were suffering to see. This was what might be called a natural ice-house. It was August, now, and sweltering weather in the day-time, yet at one of the stations the men could scrape the soil on the hill-side under the lee of a range of boulders, and at a depth of six inches cut out pure blocks of ice—hard, compactly frozen, and clear as crystal.*

Jeffrey City

The bleak, almost-ghost town of Jeffrey City is a casualty of the bust that followed the uranium-mining boom of the 1970s. First called Home on the Range, the town was renamed for a Rawlins philanthropist, Dr. Charles W. Jeffrey. The town was built on the nuclear industry, and as a company town its survival was tied to the fortunes of Western Nuclear Company. By 1980, the population had swollen to 3,000. Today, weeds grow through the concrete sidewalks around empty bunkhouses with plywood-covered windows. The modern grade school looks rather forlorn in all this desolation. Open still are Split Rock Bar & Cafe, the Sinclair station (with a few groceries), and **J.C. Motel**—also called the Coats Motel—tel. (307) 544-9317, where rooms run $22 s or $25 d. Budget. Ranching, oil, and gas keep Jeffrey City from drying up and blowing away, and a uranium mine in the desert south of town is ready to reopen if prices ever rise. Rock hounds should ask for directions to the famed jade deposits around the city, but make sure you're on public land or have permission from landowners.

East of Jeffrey City lies definitive Wyoming country with rolling sage and grassland, a few weathered old homesteads, and distant mountains on all sides. A sign notes the turnoff to **Cottonwood Campground** ($6; open June-Oct.), a BLM facility six miles east of Jeffrey City and then eight miles south on Green Mountain Loop Road. You aren't likely to meet many folks here. Free campsites can be found at county-run **Green Mountain Park,** on the road to Cottonwood Campground.

See the Central Wyoming chapter for more on the country east and north of Jeffrey City, including the Oregon Trail sites of Independence Rock, Devils Gate, and Split Rock, and the Indian pictographs at Castle Gardens.

SINKS CANYON AND THE LOOP ROAD

State Hwy. 131 climbs south from Lander through fascinating Sinks Canyon and then over the mountains to Atlantic City. A popular loop trip is to follow this road to Atlantic City, returning to Lander via State Hwy. 28, a total distance of 56 miles. Plan to spend at least a full day if you want to savor the many sights along the way. Locally known as the Loop Road, it is very popular with both visitors and residents. **Bighorn sheep** were transplanted into Sinks Canyon in 1987 and a dozen or so survive; look for them along the road. Rock climbers practice their skills on the steep cliffs of the canyon. Of interest to climbers and geologists are the three different types of rock in a five-mile stretch: sandstone, limestone, and granite. You'll find several campgrounds here, lots of lakes, trails, and big mountain country. Get to State Hwy. 131 by heading south on Lander's 5th Street. Sinks Canyon begins seven miles away.

The Sinks

The Popo Agie River (usually pronounced "po-PO-zha," but you'll hear lots of other versions) begins in the snowfields of the Wind River Mountains and drops northeast to its junction with the Wind River near Riverton. **Sinks Canyon State Park** contains one of Wyoming's geological wonders. Here the Middle Fork of the Popo Agie plunges into a cave (the "Sinks"), only to emerge again a half mile down in a gigantic spring (the "Rise"). The river's name—Popo Agie—is a Crow Indian word meaning "Beginning of the Waters." Apparently, the stream originally flowed aboveground—it still does during high spring runoff—but over time a cave formed in the water-soluble Madison Limestone that underlies this region, allowing the water to disappear into enormous underground caverns or convoluted passages from which it slowly drains. In 1983, researchers put dye in the Sinks. The dye did reappear at the rise, but not until two hours later! The water was also a few degrees warmer, and more water appeared than entered the cavern. Lots of fat rainbow and brown trout congregate in the pool at the Rise, waiting for visitors to toss them bits of food. A vending machine sells fish food (fish do not live by bread alone). No fishing allowed. Also keep your eyes open for the muskrat that lives in the spring here.

Sinks Visitor Center, tel. (307) 332-3077, houses displays of fish and animals, along with geological exhibits. Open daily 8 a.m.-7 p.m. during the summer only. The windows face down this steep-walled canyon, offering dramatic vistas. The cave into which the stream disappears is directly behind the visitor center. This area is a fine place to watch birds. Look for dippers—the odd birds that walk underwater—on the rocks above the Sinks.

Three nearby campgrounds operate April-Oct.: state-run **Sawmill Campground** and **Popo Agie Campground** ($9 for nonresidents, or $4 for Wyoming residents) plus, just up the road, the Forest Service's **Sinks Canyon Campground** ($8). Get brochures at the visitor center for the mile-long **nature trail** near Popo Agie Campground. More interesting is the **Popo Agie Falls Trail,** which takes off from Bruce Picnic Ground a mile above Popo Agie Campground. This fairly easy 1.5-mile trail climbs 600 feet in elevation to a series of attractive waterfalls, the largest being 60 feet. Horses and mountain bikes are allowed on the trail, which is passable for some wheelchairs. During the winter, skiers enjoy groomed cross-country trails in the canyon at Popo Agie Campground.

Into the Mountains

Beyond the state park, the road turns to gravel and switchbacks steeply up the canyon's south face. The Owl Creek Mountains—50 miles to the north—are visible from the overlook. The road is usually open mid-June to mid-October and gets washboarded in sections, so be ready for a buckin'-bronc ride and lots of traffic on summer weekends. The rough ride is made worthwhile by excellent vistas and several attractive lakes (enlarged by dams). This is primarily lodgepole and limber pine country, but around Louis Lake you'll discover some huge old Engelmann spruce and subalpine fir trees. (There is talk of paving Loop Road, but many locals want to keep it unpaved.)

The Forest Service maintains five delightful campgrounds along the Loop Road: **Fiddler's Lake** ($6; open July to mid-September), **Louis Lake** ($6; open July to mid-September), **Popo Agie** (free; open July to mid-September), **Sinks Canyon** ($6; open June-Oct.), and **Worthen Meadows** ($6; open July to mid-September). Fiddler's Lake has fully accessible facilities and, at 9,400 feet, is the highest. Louis Lake is easily the most popular, made more scenic by a sharp granite cliff that rises directly behind the lake. There's good fishing for brown and Mackinaw trout, and moose are commonly seen around Louis Lake's margins. Other folks car-camp for free around Frye Lake or off the road. Hiking trails head west from Loop Road to the lake-dotted Popo Agie Wilderness (see Wind River Mountains, below).

CATHY CARLSON

The Resort at Louis Lake, tel. (307) 332-5549 or (888) 422-2246, rents rustic four-person cabins (built in 1937) with oil lanterns, handmade furnishings, and a shared bathhouse for $60 per night. Newer cabins (these sleep up to eight) contain kitchens and private baths and cost $130 per night. Also available are horseback rides, horse and llama pack trips, drop-pack trips, and rentals of fishing boats, sailboats, canoes, mountain bikes, backpacking gear, snowshoes, and cross-country skis. This is a classic Wyoming lodge with a peaceful mountain setting and friendly owners. Book well ahead; it's full all summer long! The cabins are available all year and make a favorite winter base for cross-country skiing and snowmobiling. The web address is www.wyoming.com/~louislake. Budget.

South from Louis Lake the road opens into a high plateau with limber pine trees and wide vistas south to the Oregon Buttes. Antelope are common in the sagebrush country, and moose are seen in the aspen stands along the road and in the marshes around Fiddler's Lake. The Loop Road meets State Hwy. 28 beside the now-abandoned U.S. Steel iron-ore mine. From here you can continue back to Lander on the highway or visit historic South Pass (see South Pass Area later in this chapter).

WIND RIVER INDIAN RESERVATION

At more than 2.2 million acres, the Wind River is one of America's largest Indian reservations. Home to both the Northern Arapaho and the Eastern Shoshone tribes, it reaches some 70 miles from north to south and 55 miles east to west. You'll find some of the most unforgettable vistas in Wyoming here: fabulous badlands on the western edge; the beautiful Wind River, where the cottonwoods glow a brilliant yellow in the cool fall air; deep green irrigated pastures where horses, sheep, and cattle graze; and desolate, wide-open spaces where only cactus, sagebrush, jackrabbits, and rattlesnakes grow. Bright yellow sunflowers add color to the roadsides in late summer, and horses seem to be everywhere. All this is backdropped by the enormous, snowcapped Wind River Mountains. The eminent guide Jim Bridger reportedly attempted to convince Brigham Young that this basin would be a far better home for the Mormons than the deserts around Salt Lake. Young refused to listen. It is just as well, for this was—and still is—Indian country.

The Wind River Reservation was the scene for the classic Zane Grey Western, *War Paint,* a film that featured Tim McCoy and hundreds of Arapaho and Shoshone Indians. Today, hundreds of people, both Indian and nonnative, come to watch a different form of entertainment—the many powwows that occur throughout the summer months on the reservation. The annual sun-dance ceremonies are more intense, spiritual events at which outsiders are only tolerated. The Shoshone and Arapaho peoples maintain separate sun dances and powwows; absolutely no cameras or tape recorders are allowed during the sun dances.

Despite the close proximity of the reservation to Lander and Riverton, very little interaction goes on between Indians and nonnatives except in business situations. After more than 120 years, the various cultures—Arapaho, Shoshone, and Anglo—are still like oil and water. Some whites continue to view the Indians as disorganized, drunken, and lazy, while some Indians regard whites as pushy, materialistic, selfish, and disrespectful. Relations are also somewhat strained between the Shoshones and Arapaho, who still maintain a degree of animosity born of warfare a century ago.

Public Access

Although you can drive through with no problems, access to many parts of the reservation is controlled by Indian authorities, and trespassers may be fined. If you want to explore the reservation, pick up a copy of the fishing regulations from sporting-goods stores in the towns of Lander, Riverton, and Dubois, or from the **Tribal Fish and Game Office** in Fort Washakie, tel. (307) 332-7207. These regulations detail not only fishing, but also hiking, boating, camping, and other recreation options on the reservation. For any of these activities you'll need a reservation fishing permit plus a recreation stamp. Nonresident rates total $25 for one day or $65 for one week. Restrictions apply, and a number of areas, including the entire northern end of the reservation, are closed to the non-Indian public. Hunting by outsiders on the reservation is strictly verboten. The map that comes with the permit lists public camping areas on the reservation.

SHOSHONE HISTORY

Originally peoples of the Great Basin, the Shoshones first entered southwestern Wyoming in the 16th century, then gradually pushed northward until they controlled most of the land now known as Wyoming, as well as territory all the way into Canada. As they moved onto the plains, and with the acquisition of the horse, Shoshone life changed drastically from a simple Stone Age culture of grubbing for roots and eating whatever they could catch by hand to a sophisticated buffalo-centered livelihood. Because Shoshone culture extended far to the south, they came into contact with Spanish traders and were some of the first Indians to have horses. The Shoshone introduced horses to the northern plains region around 1700, forever transforming Plains Indian culture. To the trappers and traders who first encountered them, the Shoshone were known as "the Snakes," because of the serpentine hand signals they used to signify their tribal name. The word *Shoshone* refers to the simple willow-and-sagebrush lodges in which they lived before the great flowering of their culture in the 18th and 19th centuries. The Eastern Shoshone occupied western Wyoming, while their cousins the Western Shoshone lived in Idaho.

In the late 18th century, the expanding Shoshone culture was halted when their ene-

CHIEF WASHAKIE

The history of Wyoming in the 19th century is one that resonates with battles between Indians and the invading white settlers. Only one tribe—the Shoshone—provided an exception to this rule. The reason for this stems from Chief Washakie (pronounced "WASH-a-key"), a man whose life spanned the entire tumultuous century. Washakie was born in 1798 of Shoshone and Flathead parents. His birth name was Pina Quanah, but later in life he gained the name Washakie—literally, "The Rattler"—a reference to a rattle made from the dried scrotum of a buffalo that he used to scare Sioux ponies during his daring raids. Because his father was killed by the Blackfeet tribe, Washakie lived something of an orphan's existence, growing up among both the Lemhi and Bannock tribes. He eventually joined the Eastern Shoshones and quickly proved himself a fearless and extraordinary warrior.

THERMOPOLIS MUSEUM

In the 1830s, Washakie—fluent in sign language—met and became a close friend of famed mountain man Jim Bridger, and one of his daughters became Bridger's third wife. From Bridger and other trappers, Washakie learned English, along with a realization that a union with whites against his enemies was wiser than trying to fight the countless hordes coming across the plains from the east. Around 1843, after the death of the previous chief, Washakie gained control over a band of Shoshones based in the Upper Green River. As their lifelong chief, he was recognized as an extraordinarily charismatic and forceful leader and a skilled orator. Because of his skills, Washakie was sought out by white settlers whenever trouble appeared with other tribes.

Washakie's people had been devastated over the years by smallpox, cholera, and other diseases, and they were no match for the Sioux, Cheyenne, and Arapaho. Because of this, he viewed an allegiance with whites as a way to push back other tribes. When some of his young warriors began to complain that the old man was losing his warrior abilities and becoming a lackey of the whites, Washakie disappeared for a few weeks and returned with seven enemy scalps. The grumbling ended. Those Shoshones who attacked whites became instant outcasts.

In 1876, Washakie's Shoshones joined with General Crook against the Sioux and Cheyenne in the Battle of the Rosebud. The battle was a standoff, but Washakie's sage advice almost certainly prevented Crook's troops from facing what befell General Custer a week later. When Pres. Chester A. Arthur visited Wyoming in 1883, he asked Chief Washakie to meet him at a reception in Fort Washakie. The proud chief demurred, instead insisting that the president come to him. They met in Washakie's tepee.

Chief Washakie died on the Wind River Reservation on Feb. 22, 1900, and was buried with a full military funeral, the only Indian chief ever to be so honored. The procession—escorted by the U.S. cavalry—stretched nearly two miles. He was 102 years old and had led his people for more than 60 years. With Washakie died the tradition of having one man as chief of the Shoshones. Although his name is not nearly as well known today as that of Red Cloud or Crazy Horse, Washakie deserves a place as one of the great warriors and peacemakers of American history. A dozen different Wyoming places are named in his honor, including the Washakie Wilderness and Mt. Washakie.

POWWOWS

The Indian "powwow" (an Algonquian term meaning "medicine man") is a colorful celebration of Native American culture that cuts across tribal boundaries. Nobody knows the exact origin of powwows, but they may have developed from the Grass Dance of the Omaha and Pawnee tribes, who passed the dance on to various Plains tribes. The dance was used as a way of communicating with the Great Spirit, and the rhythmic beat of the drum helped send prayers skyward. Buffalo Bill Cody first introduced Indian dancers to audiences all over America and Europe, and in 1887 the Ponca Tribe began the first Indian fair and powwow. Other tribes joined in, and powwows became increasingly popular with the coming of the 20th century. The creation of "fancy dancing" allowed more personalized costumes and dances. Women were allowed to dance and by the 1940s, Indians began traveling long distances to join other tribal powwows.

Dancers perform to a beat set up by different groups of drummers, who sing a repetitious song as they pound out the rhythm. The chant evokes images of somber ceremonies far out on the plains and of a lost culture. The dances originated from different tribes but have been adapted using the more colorful synthetic fabrics and beads of today. Professional dancers travel a circuit throughout the western states, and even non-Indians take part in powwows. Contestants wear numbers similar to those at track meets or rodeos and compete for cash awards (up to $5,000 at the biggest national powwows).

Traditional and Fancy Dancing

Two main styles of powwow dance exist. In **traditional dancing,** the movements are slow and graceful, and dancers adhere to more authentic costumes and traditional dance steps. Male dancers wear bustles of eagle feathers, representing the birds of prey that once gathered over battlefields to feed on dead warriors. They also wear head roaches made from porcupine guard hairs. **Fancy dancing** is more casual—sort of an anything-goes dance in which the steps are chosen by the individual dancers. It generally involves lots of spins, bows, and head movements. Men's costumes are equally free-form, with all sorts of gaudy additions, particularly colorful bustles added to the shoulders and arms. Women's costumes for both traditional and fancy dancing are not as showy as men's, although they do include bells, elk teeth (or plastic copies), and shell decorations on the dresses, along with shawls and necklaces of hairpipe (originally small hollow bones, now often plastic).

Powwow Activities

The Wind River Reservation has a half dozen powwows throughout the year, most of which are held outdoors in arbor arenas. Tepees are set up and the event becomes a joyful celebration of life and culture. Most of these are three-day-weekend events involving not just singing and dancing, but also traditional games, parades, and a "giveaway ceremony." Activities last all day and late into the evening. Things generally begin with a festive parade that includes a military honor guard and a powwow queen seated atop a car hood. Visitors are welcome at powwows, and photos are not usually a problem, although this is less true at Arapaho powwows. Be sure to stand when the eagle staff is brought in during the grand entry, and those wearing hats should remove them. If an eagle feather drops to the ground, all action must stop until it has been properly returned.

For general information on powwows and other events on the reservation, call the Shoshone Tribal Cultural Center at (307) 332-9106 or the Lander Chamber of Commerce at (307) 332-3892 or (800) 433-0662.

mies—the Sioux, Crow, and Arapaho—forced the Shoshone west of the Laramie Mountains. The Wind River and Fort Bridger vicinities became wintering areas. After a spring sun dance and buffalo hunt, the various tribal members would move into the mountains of northern Utah to hunt, fish, and gather berries and roots. Each fall the entire tribe would gather in the Great Divide Basin and head across the Continental Divide for the fall buffalo hunt in the Wind River and Bighorn basins. Led by Chief Washakie, the Eastern Shoshone—unlike most other Plains Indians—maintained an unbroken friendship with the invading whites.

Onto the Reservation

The Shoshones were not recognized in the great Fort Laramie Treaty of 1851, and the Wind River Basin and Bighorn Basin where they had long lived were assigned to the Crows. The Fort Bridger Treaty of 1863 gave the Shoshones and Bannocks a reservation covering parts of Colorado, Utah, Wyoming, and Idaho. In 1868, this enormous, 45-million-acre spread was whittled down to just the 2.2-million acre Wind River region, and the Bannocks were given a separate Idaho reservation.

Several years later, the government lopped off 600,000 acres around the rich gold region of South Pass City, paying Chief Washakie $500 a year and $5,000 worth of cattle for five years—around four cents an acre. More land—Thermopolis Hot Springs—was ceded to the government in 1897 for $60,000, and in 1905 1.4 million acres were opened to homesteaders north of the Wind River. In exchange for the latter, the Shoshones and Arapaho received per-capita payments, schools, payment for water rights, and an irrigation system on what remained of their reservation. The reservation and adjacent lands are now some of the state's most important agricultural regions.

In 1878, Wyoming's territorial governor asked Chief Washakie if the destitute Arapaho—archenemies of the Shoshone—could be allowed to stay temporarily on the Wind River Reservation. Washakie's sympathetic heart finally gave in:

> *It is plain they can go no further now. Take them down to where Popo Agie walks into Wind River and let them stay until the grass comes again. But when the grass comes again take them off my reservation. I want my words written down on paper with the white man's ink. I want all you to sign as witnesses to what I have said. And I want a copy of that paper. I have spoken.*

Despite this agreement, the "temporary" arrangement became permanent, and urgent pleas by Washakie went unheeded. Once again the government had abused its most loyal friend.

Many years after Chief Washakie's death, the Shoshones sued over this gross injustice. In 1937, the tribe was awarded $6.4 million for the land given to the Arapaho, minus the expenses for every building ever built by the government on the reservation and any services rendered. The cheapskate federal government even deducted $125 for a silver saddle given by President Grant to Chief Washakie as a token of appreciation! What was left amounted to a grand total of $2,350 per capita, distributed almost entirely in various Bureau of Indian Affairs (BIA)-run programs.

ARAPAHO HISTORY

The Arapaho—a Blackfeet Indian term meaning "Tattooed People"—always called themselves simply "Our People." They originally lived a farming life in what is now central Minnesota, but the arrival of whites on the East Coast created a domino effect among eastern Indians, pushing tribes westward on top of each other. Because of this pressure, the Arapaho, along with the Sioux and Crow, migrated onto the Great Plains in the late 18th century. They quickly adopted the nomadic life associated with Plains Indian culture, a life centered on the buffalo and made possible by the horse. Pressure from the Sioux—who numbered perhaps 25,000 individuals, versus 3,000 Arapaho—forced the Arapaho to join with the Cheyenne and move south to the Arkansas and Platte River regions.

Around 1830, the Arapaho split into northern and southern divisions, due in part to the establishment of Fort Laramie on the Laramie River in Wyoming and Bent's Fort on the Arkansas River in Colorado. For many years, the Northern Arapaho wintered in northern Colorado, scattering along the North Platte River with the coming of spring and then gathering again in late summer to hunt buffalo and prepare for winter. In the 1851 Fort Laramie Treaty, the Arapaho and Cheyenne tribes were assigned the area east of the Rockies between the Arkansas and North Platte Rivers, but as gold was discovered in the Rockies whites began to push the Arapaho off this land.

After Cheyenne and Arapaho warriors began raiding white ranches in Colorado during the early 1860s, the governor demanded action. In the Sand Creek Massacre of 1864, a peaceful Cheyenne and Arapaho village was viciously attacked by U.S. cavalry soldiers under Colonel John M. Chivington. The action sparked a massive retaliation—Arapaho, Sioux, and Cheyenne warriors sacked Julesburg, Colorado, tore down miles of telegraph wire, stampeded cattle herds, and burned ranches and stage stations throughout the Rockies.

After this, the Arapaho shifted their living patterns and began spending winters along Wyoming's Powder River and summers in the Medicine Bow country to the south. They continued to attack Shoshones on the Wind River Reservation, emigrant trains along the Overland Trail, and miners around South Pass until the early 1870s, but gradually lessened their raids as the futility of their condition became more apparent.

The end came in the Bates Battle of 1874, when the Shoshones and the U.S. Army attacked the Arapaho, leaving them demoralized and without horses or supplies. In the late 1870s, many Arapaho served as army scouts, and some even joined an Arapaho unit of the army during the 1880s. Best-known of the Arapaho scouts was Friday, an orphan Arapaho boy adopted by mountain man and Indian agent Thomas Fitzpatrick and taught in eastern schools. He returned to his tribe and became their most important translator and a force for peace. It was probably Friday's friendship with Chief Washakie that led Washakie to finally tolerate Arapaho on his reservation.

Onto the Reservation

With the buffalo gone and their way of life under constant pressure from white settlers and the deadly diseases they brought, the Arapaho were in desperate straits, shuttling from one temporary home to another. The government refused to set aside a separate reservation, insisting that they live with the Cheyenne in Oklahoma or the Sioux in South Dakota, far from their Wyoming home.

In 1878, the Northern Arapaho were shoehorned onto the Wind River Reservation with their hated enemies in what was to be a "temporary" stay. Only 913 Arapaho—mostly women and children—remained from the tribe that had once been so powerful. (Interestingly, the Arapaho now outnumber the Shoshones on the reservation.) The two bands of Arapaho that settled on the Wind River Reservation were led by Chief Black Coal, whose people settled in present-day Arapahoe, and Chief Sharp Nose, whose people settled around present-day Ethete. Chief Sharp Nose served with the U.S. Army and later lobbied in Washington for the General Allotment Act of 1887, which issued parcels of land (160 acres to the head of a house, 80 acres to single persons over 18, 40 acres to those under 18) to everyone on the reservation. Sharp Nose even named one of his sons after General Crook, whom he fought alongside during the Sioux wars of the 1870s.

The two tribes continue to jointly occupy the Wind River Reservation, with the Arapaho holding the eastern half (the towns of Ethete and Arapahoe) and the Shoshones the west (the towns of Fort Washakie, Burris, and Crowheart). In 1891, the Arapaho were given equal rights on the reservation, despite Shoshone Chief Washakie's continued attempts to have them removed. Although Chief Washakie's son married an Arapaho woman there is still very little intermarriage between the tribes and little blending of the two cultures, even after more than a century.

RESERVATION LIFE

In the early reservation years every effort was made to break the spirit of the "savages" and make them into red-skinned Europeans (today's derogatory term is "Apples"—red on the outside, white on the inside). Even that most basic attribute—one's name—was taken away in the 1890s by the Commissioner of Indian Affairs. Thus, Yellow Calf became George Caldwell and Night Horse became Henry Lee Tyler. Even William Shakespeare and Cornelius Vanderbilt suddenly became tribal members! The effort was not entirely successful—William Shakespeare was credited with bringing Peyotism—an important Native American religion today—to the Wind River Reservation. Other measures helped weaken the culture, including the repression of native religious practices, indoctrination by Christian missionaries, prohibition of face painting, and the forced cutting of young boys' long black hair. Today, the nation is paying the price for these all-too-successful attempts to destroy Native American culture.

Most of the 4,500 Arapaho and 2,500 Shoshones live in housing built by the tribal council or in the hundreds of mobile homes that dot the reservation. From a non-Indian point of view, they are decidedly untidy, with junk of all sorts piled outside; but the folks who live here really don't care what outsiders think. (I recently saw a bumper sticker on a reservation car that said, "My other car is junk too.") You'll find older log cabins all over the back roads, their sod roofs collapsing and their log walls slowly returning to the earth. A number of missions are scattered throughout this area, marked by attractive log or stucco churches.

Oil and gas revenues from a number of major fields on the reservation provide millions of dollars each year in the form of monthly dividend payments. These royalties—along with various BIA assistance programs, ranching, farming, and tribal-owned businesses and leases—are the main source of income. A Business Council serves as the manager of tribal income. The Arapaho tend to emphasize communal sharing and oppose miscegenation much more than the Shoshones, who are more likely to marry whites and own private land.

Most people on the reservation are poor and many are unemployed, having lost their jobs when the uranium mines closed down and the oil companies left. Pawnshops in Lander and Riverton often acquire valuable cultural items from desperate individuals when the money runs out before the month does. For many on the reservation, sports are the way out. Every kid, it seems, plays basketball; hoops hang outside all the trailer homes and government-built houses. For older folks, bingo is a major source of entertainment—there are games almost every night of the year.

Despair and Hope

The Wind River Reservation has serious problems with drugs and alcohol; nearly a third of the children are born with fetal alcohol syndrome. Many young people—and older folks, too—die in alcohol-related car accidents or fights, and suicide and infant mortality rates are distressingly high. More than half of all Indian residents of the Wind River reservation have incomes that fall below federal poverty guidelines. Despite all the problems, the Arapaho and Shoshone peoples take pride in their cultural history. To attack the problems of alcoholism and the loss of cultural identity, young people learn their native tongue in special classes and take part in powwows, sun dances, and personal vision quests. The warrior tradition is expressed in a high enlistment in the nation's armed forces.

The reservation is a center for fine beaded clothing and moccasins much prized by collectors. Arapaho patterns are geometric in nature, with rectangles and triangles appearing frequently. Arapaho women generally use red, black, blue, yellow, orange, and white as the main colors, with mountains, tepees, and butterflies as common motifs. Eastern Shoshone patterns tend to be more circular, with the rose a popular theme.

ARAPAHOE AND ST. STEPHENS

The town of Arapahoe (known locally as Lower Arapahoe) is a small village on the southeastern edge of the reservation. It arose from animosity between the tribes, as a subagency through which annuities could be distributed to the Arapaho without their having to face the taunts of "beggar" or "dog eater" from the Shoshones at Fort Washakie. The town's prominent white water tower is visible for many miles. The **Northern Arapaho Powwow** (oldest on the reservation) is held here the first weekend of August.

St. Stephens Mission

In 1884, the St. Stephens Mission was established by Father John Jutz, a Jesuit missionary. Chief Black Coal consented to allow a mission to be built and later proved an ardent supporter of the school for Arapaho children. Until 1939, the Catholic Church operated a boarding school here. It was replaced by a day school that ran until the 1970s, when it became increasingly difficult to find priests and nuns to run the mission.

Visitors entering St. Stephens Mission pass a modern grade school built in 1983 and run by a secular corporation with an entirely Indian leadership. The most interesting sight at the mission is **St. Stephens Church,** built in 1928. Its white stucco exterior is covered with brilliant Arapaho geometric symbols. If the doors are unlocked, take a look at the colorful interior painted by local high-school students. Mass takes place on Sunday at 8 a.m., 10 a.m., and 5 p.m.

The **St. Stephens Mission Heritage Center,** tel. (307) 856-4330, contains a small museum and gift shop. Some of the most interesting items for sale are collector dolls dressed in Arapaho costume. They're open Mon.-Wed. and Friday 9 a.m.-noon and 1-3:30 p.m. year-round. While here, pick up a copy of the quarterly magazine ***Wind River Rendezvous,*** published by the mission; subscriptions are just $10 per year. Although this is a religious organization, the magazine deals with a range of historical and social issues. Call (307) 856-6797 for subscription details.

A cemetery near the mission contains the graves of Chief Lone Bear, Francis Setting Eagle, and John Broken Horn, along with that of his wife, Sarah Broken Horn—a white woman (born Lizzie Fletcher) who had been captured as a child and raised as an Indian. (See Arlington in the Medicine Bow Country chapter for more on this story.) The outlaw Butch Cassidy was a frequent visitor to Chief Lone Bear's camp.

ETHETE

Ethete (pronounced "EEE-thuh-tee") is the primary Arapaho settlement on the reservation. People live in trailer homes scattered on small plots around town or in ticky-tacky box houses built by the BIA. (The prefabricated houses are known as the "Easter Egg Village" because of the bright colors.) Tepee poles lean against the barns, and the bright tribal colors and geometric patterns dominate the laundromat/video store. "Downtown" Ethete consists of a stoplight—the only one on the reservation—surrounded by a grocery store, a gas station, a community hall, a high school, and the above-mentioned laundromat. All this is entirely forgettable, but not nearby St. Michael's Mission (described below).

The **Ethete Powwow** is held in mid-July. Also in July, the Ethete powwow grounds come alive with the **Northern Arapaho Sun Dance** ceremony (no cameras allowed).

Wind River Transportation Authority (WRTA), tel. (307) 856-7118 or (800) 439-7118, offers scheduled bus service connecting Ethete with other towns in the Wind River Basin, including Lander, Riverton, Hudson, and Ft. Washakie.

St. Michael's Mission

Established in 1887 by Rev. John Roberts of the Episcopal Church, this mission is the town's reason for existence. When Chief Sharp Nose was asked for his approval to build here, the response was "*Ethete,*" meaning "Good." Constructed between 1910 and 1917, the buildings are arranged in a circle around a grassy lawn. Most are fabricated from cobblestones, with Arapaho designs on the doors, but the **Church of Our Father's House** is of log. Inside this fascinating building built in the shape of a cross are rustic handmade wooden benches and a central Arapaho drum. Altar seats are made of elk antlers, and the back window faces the great Wind River Mountains. Sunday communion starts at 11 a.m.

Across the circle is the **Arapaho Cultural Museum,** tel. (307) 332-4819, housing a small but remarkable collection of artifacts that includes beaded garments, medicine pouches, peace pipes, warbonnets, and photographs. It is open Mon.-Sat. 10 a.m.-4 p.m. mid-April to Labor Day and by appointment the rest of the year. No charge. If nobody is here, knock on the house next to the church to have someone let you in.

FORT WASHAKIE

Fort Washakie is the center of activity on the Wind River Reservation. The BIA compound is here (locals insist the initials stand for Boss Indians Around) and so is the tribal council headquarters. Fort Washakie was the home of Chief Washakie, the longtime leader of the Shoshones. Behind Chief Washakie's town are a series of

"HOOP DANCER"

BY BRUCE COCKBURN

Out of my throat appears this chuckle
A true 20th Century sound
A little crazed and having no tonal centre

The echoes of this laugh fade for a long time
Snaking among those jumbled pedestrians
Following that struggling Cedric taxicab
Sliding over the seeming infinity of white light and neon

With no warning, mind's eye winks like a lifespan
And opens again on memory flash of prairie Indian
Dancers—they're on a stage, all jigging motion
And flare of bright feathers, surrounded by white faces
Floating on a sea of mind
Hoop dancer struts in front—drum and voices blend with endless rain

There's a time line
Something like vertical, like perpendicular
Cutting through figures shuffling on horizontal plane
Cutting through the survival pride of the dancers
Through the guilty, sentimental warmth of the crowd;
Through to some essence common to us, to original man
To perhaps descendants numberless. . . . or few
Where it intersects the space at hand
This shaman with the hoops stands
Aligned like living magnetic needle between deep past and looming future
Butterfly pierced on each drum beat, wing beat, static spark,
storm front, energy circle delineated by leaping limbs

1st man last man dancing man man dancing
Hoops in hand trampled grass circle spreading
Voices flame above crazy coyote heartbeat drum

I see sunrise on the plains big river at dusk
Perpetual pillar of dust on prairie rim and always overhead
those wings—circling, turning

He's the earth he's the egg he's the eagle always circling
Always turning—always comes back to the centre

Hoops whirling, now transparent feet touch down on anaconda
Streets and on the next leap dissolve slowly into the moving lights

Rainbow steps, jerking universe
Goodbye, Man-in-time
And just beyond the clatter and cars the last long notes of wild
voices ring
Like Roland's horn

SACAGAWEA

Fictional books about Sacagawea (pronounced "sak-uh-juh-WEE-uh") describe her as a beautiful Indian maiden, a guide, a peacemaker, a heroine, and a mother—sort of the original Superwoman. Historian James Truslow Adams declared her one of the six most important women in American history. The reality is a bit less romantic but still fascinating. Sacagawea—her name meant "Bird Woman" in Shoshone—was born around 1784 in what is now eastern Idaho. As a child, she was captured by the Minnetaree tribe and later sold to a French-Canadian trapper and interpreter named Toussaint Charbonneau. He eventually made her one of his many wives.

The Lewis and Clark Expedition

In 1803, Pres. Thomas Jefferson negotiated the Louisiana Purchase from the French. For the fire-sale price of $16 million he suddenly doubled the size of the young United States of America. Captains Meriwether Lewis and William Clark were selected to lead a secret exploration of this vast land. They left St. Louis in late 1804 and camped that first winter in North Dakota, where they met Sacagawea and her husband Charbonneau. Lewis and Clark didn't think much of the ill-tempered and untrustworthy Charbonneau, but they realized the value of having with the expedition a Shoshone woman who was fluent in English and French. Charbonneau was hired, with the stipulation that his wife come along.

Over the winter, Sacagawea gave birth to a baby boy (Baptiste), and when the troupe headed out two months later, the child was on her back in a cradle board. Contrary to the romanticized novels, her role was not so much that of guide as interpreter, as one who knew the edible plants along the way, and as a symbol of the expedition's friendly intentions.

When the expedition reached the Continental Divide, they fortuitously happened upon Sacagawea's sister and brother, whom she had not seen since being kidnapped six years before. The Shoshones agreed to provide guides and horses to cross the Rockies.

After an arduous journey, the exploration party reached the Pacific Ocean that fall and established winter quarters near the mouth of the Columbia River. They returned across the mountains the following summer, and Sacagawea, Charbonneau, and their son returned to their old existence in Mandan country. The rest of the expedition party reached St. Louis on Sept. 23, 1806, long after everyone but President Jefferson had given them up for dead. The trip proved a vital step in bringing the Northwest under the U.S. flag.

Later Years

From here, Sacagawea's story becomes murkier. Some researchers claim that she died in 1812 of "putrid fever" at Fort Mandan in North Dakota. This version is generally told by Dakota folks. Wyoming partisans prefer another story: that the woman who died so young was one of Charbonneau's other wives, and that Sacagawea continued to live for many more years. After leaving her abusive husband, she wandered all over the West—gaining the name Wad-ze-Wipe ("Lost Woman")—before finally ending up on the Wind River Reservation with her fellow Shoshones. She served a crucial role as translator for Chief Washakie in negotiations to establish the reservation and was often seen wearing one of the peace medals given out by Lewis and Clark. Sacagawea (or at least the Wyoming version) died on April 9, 1884, and was buried near Fort Washakie in a cemetery overlooking the Wind River. Although the Shoshones had heard her tell of the expedition many times, it wasn't until 25 years later that Anglo historians began to realize who the "Lost Woman" really was. The 13,569-foot Mt. Sacagawea in the Wind River Mountains is named for the remarkable woman who remained unrecognized much of her life. An image representing Sacagawea also appears on America's one-dollar coins.

dramatic escarpments and canyons, and through a gap in the hills you can peer into the mighty Wind River Mountains.

In 1869, the U.S. Army established a fort, Camp Augur (later Camp Brown), along the Popo Agie River to protect the Shoshones from attacks by Arapaho and Sioux warriors. The fort was later moved a dozen miles west and renamed Fort Washakie, making this the only fort ever named for an Indian chief. It remained open until 1909, when the threat of conflict between the Shoshones and Arapaho had diminished. A few buildings still stand, including a **stone guardhouse.** They are now used by the BIA.

Sights

Despite its minuscule size, Fort Washakie has an array of interesting sights. The **Shoshone Tribal Cultural Center** is housed in the historic "White House" on the BIA compound. Built in 1913, it now serves as an information and heritage center. Inside, find Chief Washakie's leather shirt, pipe, and pipe bag, along with other historical items; unfortunately, Washakie's eagle-feather headdress is no longer available for viewing due to its fragility. Upstairs is a library with Native American titles. The cultural center is open Mon.-Fri. 9 a.m.-4 p.m. year-round; admission costs $1. Very informative hour-long walking tours are available (fee charged), but call ahead for reservations; tel. (307) 332-9106. A small gift shop here sells locally made moccasins, belts, jewelry, paintings, and Indian dance regalia.

South Fork Rd. west from Fort Washakie passes the **Washakie Graveyard.** A substantial granite memorial notes that Washakie was "Always loyal to the government and his white brothers. A wise ruler." Washakie was buried here with full military honors, perhaps the only chief of his time to be so honored by the U.S. government. Directly across the road from the cemetery is the **R.V. Greeves Art Gallery,** tel. (307) 332-3557, open by appointment only. Greeves is one of state's better-known sculptors; his *The Unknown* is in the Buffalo Bill Historical Center.

Continue another mile along this road (stay left at the "Y" and turn left again at the Full Gospel Revival Center's log church) to the **Sacagawea Cemetery,** perhaps the most beautiful cemetery in Wyoming. The remote setting offers views of the Wind River Mountains. When I last visited, the sun was playing behind darkly rumbling thunderheads atop the Wind Rivers while horses whinnied in the fields below. Sacagawea's gravesite (the Wyoming version) is marked by an impressive granite headstone, and one of her sons, John Baptiste, is buried alongside. A granddaughter and other descendants are up the hill. The graveyard also contains an old log church and a number of old bed frames over graves, a burial practice that was common for many years on the reservation. See the special topic on Sacagawea for more on this remarkable woman.

The historic **Shoshone Episcopal Mission** is on Trout Creek Rd., 1.5 miles southwest of Fort Washakie (turn east just beyond the Hines General Store), and was founded in 1883 by Rev. John Roberts, a Welsh missionary known as "White Robe." A boarding school for Indian girls was built in 1891. The two-story brick-and-stone building still stands, though the school closed in 1945. A simple log mission chapel is nearby.

Hot Springs

Three miles east of Fort Washakie on the way to Ethete is **Chief Washakie Plunge,** tel. (307) 332-4530, where 110° F sulfur-rich water flows from a hot springs into an outdoor swimming pool complete with a water slide, diving board, and jacuzzi. The springs were a favorite place of Chief Washakie. Maybe these mineral waters are what helped him live for 102 years! The pool is open April-Oct. and costs $5 for adults, $2.50 for seniors and students. Private indoor tub baths are also available, and the facilities are handicap accessible. Open Wed.-Sun. noon-8 p.m.

Arts and Crafts

Wind River Trading Co., tel. (307) 332-3267, next to Hines General Store, has tacky mass-produced beadwork, moccasins, blankets, and baskets. Fortunately, the store also houses **Gallery of the Wind,** tel. (307) 332-4321, containing moccasins, beaded garments, and jewelry from the Wind River Reservation. The Shoshone Tribal Cultural Center, described above, also has locally made pieces, or visit the nursing home, Morning Star Manor. Individuals worth contacting for beadwork or art include Nathaniel Barney, Stan DeVinney, Zella Guina, and Pauley Brooks; check with the cultural center for details.

Practicalities

Just behind Wind River Trading on North Fork Rd. is tiny **Post Diner,** tel. (307) 332-3689, with authentic Indian tacos.

Situated along the Wind River between Crowheart and Dubois, **Early Guest Ranch,** tel. (307) 455-4055 or (800) 532-4055, has dude ranch accommodations on deeded land inside the reservation borders. The ranch has room for 18 guests in nicely refurbished log cabins with private baths. All-inclusive rates are $300 per night for two people, including lodging, horseback riding, three big meals, and river rafting. It also offers lodging and breakfast only for $85 d. The ranch is open mid-June to mid-September. For more information, go to the web at www.earlyranch.com. Expensive-Luxury.

Ray Lake Campground, at the intersection of US Hwy. 287 and State Hwy. 132, tel. (307) 332-9333, charges $10 for tents, $14 for RVs. Tepees ($15) are also available, and the cafe has meals and souvenirs, including Indian jewelry. It's run by friendly folks, and the remote country setting provides classic Wyoming scenery. Open May to early September. There are no other lodging options on the reservation, although many places are available in the surrounding towns of Lander, Riverton, and Dubois.

Events

Powwows fill the calendar on the Wind River Reservation, with events nearly every summer weekend; for details call the Riverton Chamber of Commerce, tel. (307) 856-4801 or (800) 325-2732. The **Arapahoe Community Powwow** takes place the second weekend of June in the town of Arapahoe. On the fourth weekend of June, Fort Washakie is home to the **Treaty Day Celebration,** which includes Indian games, dancing, and a feast. It is immediately followed by the **Eastern Shoshone Indian Days Powwow and Rodeo,** which attracts participants from across the west. The all-Indian rodeo features bull riding, saddle bronc and bareback riding, calf roping, team roping, and the favorite—Indian relay horse racing, in which bareback riders rocket around the track in a chaos of flying dirt and colliding horses. In Ethete, powwows are held the fourth weekend of May, the Fourth of July, and on the fourth weekend of July. But the biggest of them all is the town's **Labor Day Powwow.** The **Northern Arapaho Powwow** (oldest on the reservation) is held in Arapahoe the first weekend of August. In addition to the powwows, **sun dances** take place in July at Ethete and Shoshone.

WEST TO DUBOIS

As you head northwest along US Hwy. 26/287, the Wind River Mountains and Absarokas grow ever closer, and the Wind River Valley begins to narrow. Crowheart Butte dominates the skyline to the north for many miles, and then you drop over a rise to discover a stunning landscape of red-rock badlands accented by the green of cottonwoods along the Wind River. For the next 20 miles, travelers are treated to a constantly changing panorama of gloriously colorful badlands topography, with 11,635-foot Ramshorn Peak rising in the distance. It's a geologist's dreamworld. Several reservoirs provide irrigation and recreation on the Wind River Reservation. Largest is **Bull Lake,** along the western margin. The Shoshones say that it is haunted by a supernatural water buffalo. The aquamarine waters of **Ocean Lake** are well-known for bass and crappie fishing. Other people come to swim, water-ski, windsurf, hunt, or birdwatch. Seven free camping areas are scattered around the lakeshore.

Pavillion

This lilliputian farming settlement lies north of the Wind River approximately 25 miles from Riverton. One place makes it worth the detour: the **'50s Diner,** tel. (307) 856-6118. Step inside for delectable hamburgers and homemade pies to die for, or to plunk quarters in the jukebox filled with hits from a slower era. Photos of Marilyn Monroe and James Dean watch you from the walls. If you're old enough to know all the jukebox songs, you may qualify for the $2.25 lunch specials for seniors. The diner is open three meals a day Mon.-Fri. and for breakfast and lunch on Sunday. Classic Americana!

Crowheart Butte

The tiny settlement of **Crowheart** consists of an old-fashioned country store and gas station surrounded by irrigated fields and grazing cattle. A couple miles northeast of the store—and visible for many miles in any direction—is a regal summit, Crowheart Butte, looking like a pyramid whose top got caught in a giant lawn mower.

The name comes from an 1866 battle in the Wind River Valley. The Shoshones and Bannocks fought the Crows over hunting rights. The Crows had been "given" the valley in the Fort Laramie Treaty of 1851, while the Shoshones and Bannocks were "given" the same land in the 1863 Fort Bridger Treaty. Four days of intense fighting led to a standoff, and to prevent further bloodshed the chiefs declared a winner-takes-all fight near this butte. Charging each other on horseback with lances drawn, both were thrown in the collision, and the fight turned to a hand-to-hand struggle. In the battle, Shoshone Chief Washakie killed Crow Chief Big Robber and then carried his heart around on a lance, a gesture of admiration for a brave fighter. Hence the name, Crowheart Butte. When Chief Washakie was later asked about the story, he replied, "When a man is in battle and his blood runs hot, he sometimes does things that he is sorry for afterwards. I cannot remember everything that happened so long ago." Washakie later took one of the captured Crow girls as one of his wives.

Crowheart Butte is regarded as something of a sacred place by local Indians and is used as a place of spiritual renewal for young men on a vision quest. A small rock shelter stands on the top for this purpose. Non-Indians are legally forbidden to climb Crowheart Butte, and legends claim that those who do so may disappear.

Whiskey Basin

The highway continues its slow and scenic climb to Dubois, crossing the cottonwood-lined Wind River three times en route. Approximately 25 miles west of Crowheart (five miles east of Dubois), a sign points the way to Whiskey Basin. Follow the gravel road two miles to the **Dubois State Fish Hatchery,** where rainbow, cutthroat, golden, brook, and brown trout as well as grayling are raised. Open daily 8 a.m.-5 p.m. The bucolic setting is hard to beat: a tree-lined creek surrounded by sage, mountains, and badlands.

A short distance up the road is a wildlife viewing kiosk for the **Whiskey Basin Wildlife Habitat Area.** During the winter months the valley is home to the largest population of **Rocky Mountain bighorn sheep** anywhere on earth. Some 900 sheep congregate here because of the mild winters and the shallow snow. Although you're likely to find sheep all winter, the best time to photograph them is in the breeding season, from late November through December. During this period you'll see rams charging head-first into each other over the chance to mate. It's enough to give you a headache. The lambs are born in late May and early June high up on rocky slopes. Five-hour **winter wildlife tours** ($30 per person) are offered by the National Bighorn Sheep Interpretive Center in Dubois; call (307) 455-

3429 for reservations. Bighorn sheep are also sometimes seen in the meadows along the highway or in the hills just above Dubois.

Beyond the wildlife viewing kiosk, the road follows Torrey Creek up past a string of three small bodies of water: Torrey, Ring, and Trail Lakes. These were created by retreating glaciers centuries ago, but small dams have enlarged them. State Game and Fish **campsites** (free) are located along Ring and Trail Lakes. **Ring Lake Ranch,** tel. (307) 455-2663, houses an ecumenical religious facility used for a variety of retreats, seminars, and other activities.

A very popular trailhead at the end of the road up Whiskey Basin (12 miles from the turnoff) provides access to the primary route up to Dinwoody Glacier and 13,804-foot Gannett Peak (Wyoming's highest). Keep your eyes open for the osprey nest at mile five. The Audubon Society has a field camp at mile eight.

You'll discover quite a few Indian **pictographs** on large boulders in the Trail Lake vicinity; look for them along the hillside between Trail and Ring Lakes. These figures—some four feet tall—are elaborate otherworldly creations with horns and headdresses, and they are believed to represent shamans performing ceremonies under altered states of consciousness. While their age is unknown, they are probably at least 2,000 years old and of Athapaskan (a Canadian tribe) rather than Shoshonean origin. This is some of the oldest rock art in Wyoming.

DUBOIS

Approaching Dubois (pop. 1,000) from either direction, you drive through the extraordinary red, yellow, and gray badlands that set this country apart. The luxuriant Wind River winds its way down a narrow valley where horses graze in the irrigated pastures and old barns and newer log homes stand against the hills, while the tree-covered Absaroka and Wind River Mountains ring distant views. The town of Dubois consists of a long main street that makes a startlingly abrupt elbow turn and then points due west toward the mountains. The many log buildings and snatches of wooden sidewalks give the place an authentic frontier feel. Locals live in cabins, trailer homes, and simple frame houses. Dubois weather is famously mild; warm Chinook winds often melt any snow that falls. Grand scenery reigns in all directions. Snowmobilers, hunters, and anglers have discovered that Dubois provides a good place to relax in Wyoming's "banana belt" while at the same time remaining close to the more temperamental mountains. The area basks in an average of 300 days of sunshine each year. By the way, Dubois is pronounced "DU-boys"; other pronunciations will reveal your tenderfoot status. Locals sometimes jokingly call it "Dubious."

HISTORY

Dubois began in the 1880s when pioneer ranchers and more than a few rustlers—including

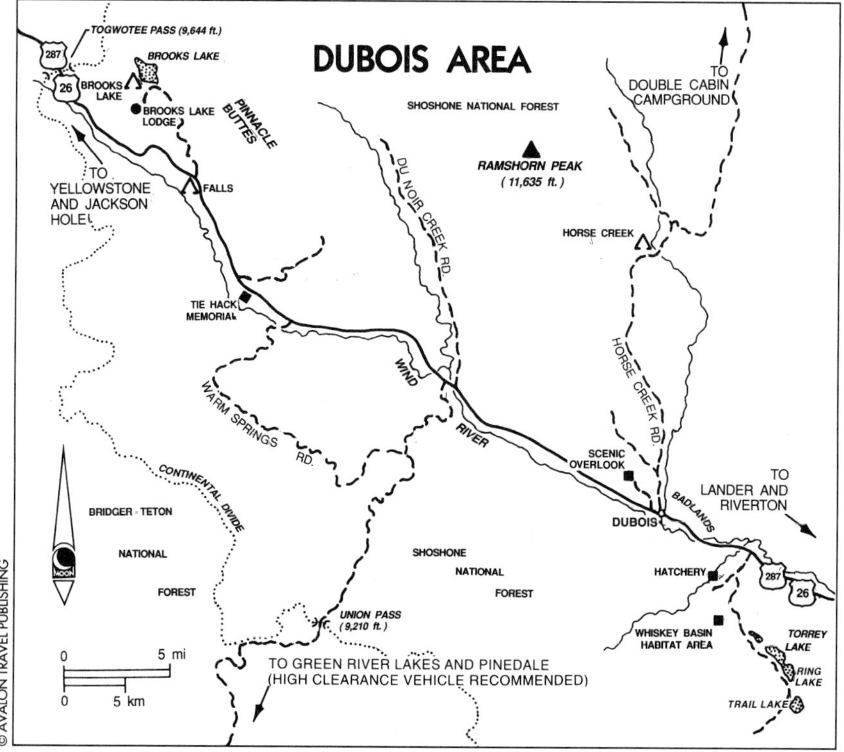

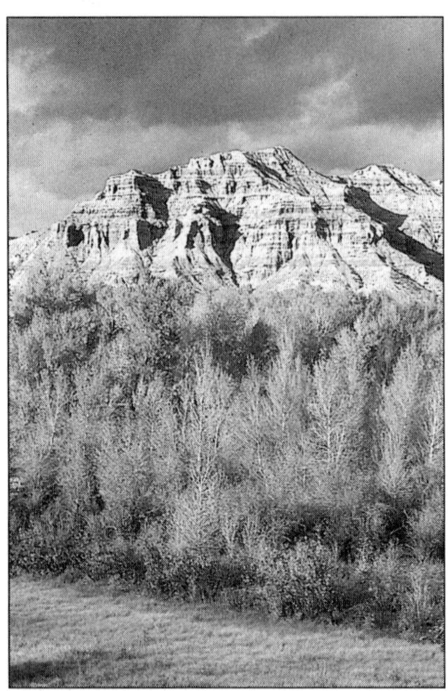

the badlands near Dubois

Butch Cassidy—settled in the area, followed by Scandinavian hand-loggers who cut lodgepole for railroad ties. The town that grew up along the juncture of Horse Creek and the Wind River was first known as Never Sweat, but when citizens applied for a post office the Postal Service refused to allow the name and suggested Dubois instead—the name of an Idaho senator who just happened to be on the Senate committee that provided funding for the post office.

Like many edge-of-the-mountain towns, Dubois is in transition. For most of its existence, it served as a logging and ranching center. In 1987, the Louisiana Pacific sawmill shut down, throwing many loggers and millworkers onto the unemployment rolls. Loggers blamed environmentalists and the Forest Service for sharply reducing the timber available; environmentalists countered that the company was simply using the reductions as an excuse to close an aging mill. After everyone ran out of mud to sling, they decided to look at what Dubois had to offer and discovered that, lo and behold, they just happened to be sitting in an almost-undiscovered recreational and retirement gold mine. In the 1990s the town leapt full-force into the tourism business. The transformation of Dubois to a visitor-oriented economy certainly has its downside—elaborate "trophy" log summer homes are beginning to overrun the lush pastures on both ends of town—but so far this pretty little place has been spared the onslaught of "industrial tourism." Stay tuned.

SIGHTS

National Bighorn Sheep Center

The National Bighorn Sheep Interpretive Center, 907 W. Ramshorn, tel. (307) 455-3429 or (888) 209-2795, www.bighorn.org, houses displays on desert bighorn, Rocky Mountain bighorn, stone sheep, and Dall sheep. The museum details how the population was brought back from the brink of extinction, and it includes fine hands-on exhibits and interactive displays on how bighorns live. Also here is a diorama of a Sheepeater Indian trap and mounted specimens around a 16-foot-high central "mountain." A theater shows videos on bighorn sheep and other topics, and a gift shop sells books and other items. The center is open daily 9 a.m.-8 p.m. Memorial Day to Labor Day, and Thurs.-Mon. 9 a.m.-4 p.m. the rest of the year. Entrance costs $2 for adults, 75 cents for kids under 13, or $5 for families.

In winter months the center offers **wildlife tours** of the Whiskey Basin Habitat Area just west of town (see West to Dubois under Wind River Indian Reservation earlier in this chapter). These five-hour van trips cost $20 per person and include binoculars and spotting scopes to view the animals. They operate on weekends from mid-November through March. Reservations are recommended; call the center for details.

Museum and Gallery

The **Dubois Museum,** 909 W. Ramshorn (right next door to the Bighorn Sheep Center), tel. (307) 455-2284, is open daily 9 a.m.-5 p.m. June-Aug., and daily 10 a.m.-5 p.m. in September; closed the rest of the year. Entrance is $1 for adults, 50 cents for kids under 12, or $3 for the whole family. The museum houses exhibits on the Sheepeater Indians and various cultural artifacts, petrified wood, and displays on ranch life, natural history, and the tie hacks. Be sure to check out the hilarious photo of 1930s' movie star Tim McCoy teaching golf to a rather skeptical group of Shoshone Indians! Out front are five historic log cabins. Upstairs from the museum is the **Headwaters Community Arts and Conference Center,** where a spacious gallery displays the works of local artists.

Other Sights

Just west of Dubois is a signed turnoff to a **scenic overlook.** The gravel road climbs sharply (no RVs) for approximately a mile to the viewpoint, where signs note the surrounding peaks. Enjoy marvelous views of 11,635-foot Ramshorn Peak from here. **Rocky Mountain bighorn sheep** crowd the Dubois area in the winter. Many are visible on the hills just south of town, with hundreds more gathered in the Whiskey Basin Habitat Area, five miles east and described above.

The magnificent badlands on both sides of Dubois—but especially to the east—are well worth exploring. The Bureau of Land Management maintains a fascinating **Badlands Interpretive Trail** up Mason Draw, 2.4 miles northeast of town. Pick up a booklet describing the trail at the visitor center. Depending upon your route, the hike should take an hour or two to complete.

Rock hounds will find all sorts of petrified wood, agates, and other colorful rocks up the Wiggins Fork and Horse Creek drainages; ask at the chamber of commerce for directions.

One thing you certainly would not expect to find in Dubois is a training center for lawyers, but famed Wyoming attorney Gerry Spence has one on his Thunderbird Ranch east of town. His **Trial Lawyers College** puts some 50 lawyers through an intense four-week session each summer, with mock trials and professional actors. Watch your step with all these lawyers around Dubois!

ACCOMMODATIONS

Motels

Dubois makes an excellent stopping point on the way to Yellowstone and Grand Teton National Parks, with lodging prices well below those in Jackson Hole. All places are open year-round unless noted otherwise, and all except Black Bear and Super 8 can be found on the web at www.dteworld.com/wyoming/lodging.htm. Accommodations are listed below from least to most expensive. Add a seven percent sales and lodging tax to these rates.

If you're looking for quietude, head three miles east of town to **Riverside Inn & Campground,** tel. (307) 455-2337 or (877) 489-2337, where the motel rooms are $30 s or $40-44 d. The motel has fishing access to a private stretch of the river. Inexpensive.

Right on the river, **Wind River Motel,** 519 W. Ramshorn, tel. (307) 455-2611 or (877) 455-2621, has a mix of rustic cabins, motel rooms, and suites for $30-75 s or d. Some rooms contain kitchenettes. Open April-November. Budget-Moderate.

Trail's End Motel, 511 Ramshorn, tel. (307) 455-2540 or (888) 455-6660, has recently remodeled rooms for $34-56 s or $42-64 d. Amenities include in-room fridges and microwaves, decks facing the Wind River, an exercise facility, and an outdoor jacuzzi. Inexpensive-Moderate.

A half mile east of Dubois, **Chinook Winds Mountain Lodge,** tel. (307) 455-2987 or (800) 863-0354, has a variety of rooms. Riverside motel units are $40 s or $50-80 d and contain small fridges. Cabins with full kitchens cost $75 d. The Wind River is right out the back door. Inexpensive-Moderate.

Find newly remodeled accommodations at the largest motel in town, **Stagecoach Motor Inn,** 103 Ramshorn, tel. (307) 455-2303 or (800) 455-5090. Rates are $45 s or $55-60 d, including use of an outdoor pool; kitchenettes cost $75 and sleep four. Suites are also available. Inexpensive-Moderate.

For historic rooms, stay at **Twin Pines Lodge & Cabins,** 218 Ramshorn, tel. (307) 455-2600 or (800) 550-6332. Built in 1934 and listed on the National Register of Historic Places, the lodge has modern and rustic cabins for $42 s or $55 d, with fridges in all rooms. Inexpensive.

A fine riverside place is **Black Bear Country Inn,** 505 W. Ramshorn, tel. (307) 455-2344 or (800) 873-2327, where the rooms cost $44-50 s or d, including fridges and microwaves. Kitchenette apartments sleep five people and cost $65. The motel is open mid-May through Thanksgiving. Inexpensive.

Branding Iron Motel, 401 Ramshorn, tel. (307) 455-2893 or (800) 341-8000, has cozy and well-maintained duplex log cabins that were built in the 1940s. Rates are $48-53 s or d; kitchenettes cost $6 extra. Inexpensive.

Two miles west of town is **Super 8 Motel,** tel. (307) 455-3694 or (800) 800-8000, where the rooms are $51 s or $54 d, including access to a jacuzzi. Inexpensive.

A mile west of town is **Bald Mountain Inn,** tel. (307) 455-2844 or (800) 682-9323, where spacious motel rooms with kitchenettes are $54 s or d. Two-story townhouse units with fireplaces and kitchens cost $90 a night and can sleep six. Bring your fishing pole; the Wind River is just out back. Inexpensive.

Bed and Breakfasts

Jakey's Fork Homestead, tel. (307) 455-2769, has B&B accommodations in a delightful century-old homestead four miles east of town. Near the bighorn sheep refuge in Whiskey Basin, Jakey's Fork offers extraordinary views of both the Wind River Mountains and nearby badlands. Birdwatchers will find a host of feathered friends in the trees and marsh. Be sure to ask owner Irene Bridges about Butch Cassidy's encounter with Indians nearby. Guests can stay in the modern home or a rustic sod-covered cabin. A sauna and jacuzzi bathtub are available, and the rooms have shared baths. A full breakfast is served. Rates are $85 d in the house or $110 d ($130 for four people) in the cabin. Weekly rates are also available. Children will enjoy the toy-filled playroom. Get more info at www.cruising-america.com/jakeysfork. Expensive.

Just two blocks from downtown Dubois is **The Stone House B&B,** 207 S. 1st St., tel. (307) 455-2555. Inside this stately stone home are two guest rooms ($45 s or $50 d) with shared baths, along with a basement suite ($70 d) that has a private bath. A full breakfast is served each morning, and the sitting room faces Whiskey Mountain, a good place to watch for bighorn sheep. Inexpensive-Moderate.

Six miles west of Dubois is **Mountain Top B&B at Triple EEE Ranch,** tel. (307) 455-2304 or (800) 353-2555, which offers a modern lodge and duplex cabins on 20 acres. There are fine views of the Wind River Valley. This is primarily a dude ranch (see below for details), but unfilled rooms are offered on a nightly basis for $95 d including a big breakfast. The six guest rooms include private baths and access to a jacuzzi. Horseback rides are available. For more info, call or check the website: www.dudesville.com. Expensive.

Dude Ranches

Fifteen different dude ranches/mountain lodges are found in the Dubois area. Six are described below, and another nine places are described in the Over Togwotee Pass section below.

Ten miles out East Fork Rd., **Lazy L&B Ranch,** tel. (307) 455-2839 or (800) 453-9488, is a century-old ranch offering creekside log cabins, horseback riding, overnight pack trips, cowboy poetry and songs, a swimming pool, hot tub, stocked fishing ponds, kids' programs, volleyball and pool, fly-fishing, and a rifle range. The ranch's horseback-riding program is excellent, and guests can choose trips through the badlands or high into the mountains. Lazy L&B is open late May to September, with all-inclusive weekly rates of $1,950 for two people. Get more details by calling or check the website: www.ranchweb.com/lazyl&b. Luxury.

Sixteen miles north of Dubois in gorgeous Dunoir Valley, **Absaroka Ranch,** tel. (307) 455-2275, has all the typical guest ranch offerings: horseback riding, guided fly-fishing, hiking, cookouts, and pack trips. The ranch accommodates just 18 guests and emphasizes the personal touch. It is surrounded by national forest land and has a comfortable main lodge (built in 1910), attractively restored log cabins, and a redwood sauna. The ranch is open mid-June to mid-September. All-inclusive weekly rates are $2,500 for two people. Luxury.

Bitterroot Ranch, tel. (307) 455-2778 or (800) 545-0019, emphasizes horseback riding for experienced riders; each guest gets use of three horses. The owners breed Arabian horses and offer cross-country jumping courses, pack trips, fly-fishing, and kids' programs. Both French and German are spoken here, attracting an international clientele. The ranch is open June to mid-September and has space for 32 guests in a dozen cabins. The web address is www.ranchweb.com/bitterroot. All-inclusive weekly rates are $2,800 for two people. Luxury.

South of Dubois in beautiful Jakeys Fork Canyon, **CM Ranch,** tel. (307) 455-2331 or (800)

455-0721, is one of Wyoming's oldest dude ranches; it's been here since 1927. The ranch offers dramatic badlands topography and a variety of fossils, making it a favorite of geologists (and the amateur version). Trails lead into the adjacent Fitzpatrick Wilderness, a favorite destination for horseback trips. Fishing is another popular activity, and a fishing guide is available. The immaculate lodge buildings have space for 60 guests, and kids love the big outdoor pool. All-inclusive weekly rates at this delightful old-time ranch are $2,000-2,200 for two people. The web address is www.cmranch.com. Luxury.

Operating as a dude ranch since 1920, **T-Cross Ranch,** tel. (307) 455-2206, is 15 miles north of Dubois near Horse Creek and is open June to mid-September. Surrounded by the Shoshone National Forest, this remote ranch has weekly accommodations for $2,100 for two people, including horseback riding, all meals, activities for kids, trout fishing, and a hot tub. Backcountry pack trips and other activities are also available. Lodging is in comfortable log cabins, and the main lodge has a massive stone fireplace and spacious front porch. Get more information by calling or checking the web address: www.ranchweb.com/tcross. Luxury.

Elk Trails Ranch, tel. (307) 455-3615, is a small adult-oriented riding ranch 25 miles northeast of Dubois off East Fork Road. The modern log cabins are surrounded by beautiful mountain country and have space for a maximum of six people. Day rides and fishing are the primary attractions. Rates are $145 per person/day, with a three night minimum stay required. Get more information at www.elktrails.com. Luxury.

Camping

The closest public camping spot is **Horse Creek Campground** ($8; open June-Oct.), 12 miles north of Dubois on Horse Creek Road.

Circle-Up Camper Court, 225 W. Welty, tel. (307) 455-2238, charges $14 for tents (some shade), $19 for RVs, and $25 for basic cabins. Kids love the tepees for $17. Noncampers may use the showers here for $4. Open year-round, this is one of Wyoming's better private campgrounds. You can also park RVs ($20) or pitch tents ($15) at **Riverside Inn & Campground,** three miles east of town, tel. (307) 455-2337 or (877) 489-2337.

FOOD

Cowboy Cafe, 115 E. Ramshorn, tel. (307) 455-2595, has good home-style breakfasts with big helpings of biscuits and gravy. For a real artery-clogger, try the steak and eggs. The Cowboy is extremely popular with both locals and tourists.

The setting is old-fashioned, but **Ramshorn Inn,** 202 E. Ramshorn, tel. (307) 455-2400, serves surprisingly light fare—bagels, sandwiches, and espresso—for breakfast and lunch.

Village Cafe/Daylight Donut, 515 W. Ramshorn, tel. (307) 455-2122, is an interesting family place offering doughnuts and coffee in the mornings and steak dinners each evening.

Get malts and sundaes from the old-time soda fountain inside the **Dubois Drugstore,** 126 E. Ramshorn, tel. (307) 455-2300.

Anita's Cafe, 106 E. Ramshorn, tel. (307) 455-3828, sits right along Horse Creek and serves gourmet lunches and dinners. Very nice. Open summer only.

Bernie's Cafe, 1408 Warm Springs Dr., tel. (307) 455-2115, opens at 6 a.m. each morning, and it doesn't close till 10 p.m. You'll find down-home cooking, fast service, and all-American meals for reasonable prices. It's a family favorite.

Rustic Pine Steakhouse, 119 E. Ramshorn, tel. (307) 455-2772, is a carnivore's delight, with prime rib on Friday and Saturday nights; open for dinner only.

Cavallo Creek Grille, 112 E. Ramshorn, tel. (307) 455-3979, offers delicious lunches of salads, soup, and panini sandwiches, along with 10-inch pizzas from a wood-fired oven served Mon.-Sat. evenings. On Sunday nights, all-you-can-eat pizza is $9; they pass around a variety of pizzas straight out of the oven.

Get groceries at **Ramshorn Food Farm,** 610 W. Ramshorn, tel. (307) 455-2402. For pastries, breads, and tasty hardtack made from an old Swedish recipe, stop by **Circle-Up Camper Court,** 225 W. Welty, tel. (307) 455-2238.

FUN AND GAMES

Entertainment

Dubois is a hopping place during the summer, especially on weekends. **Ramshorn Inn,** 202

a well-outfitted participant in the Whiskey Mountain Buckskinners Wind River Rendezvous

E. Ramshorn, tel. (307) 455-2400, often has rock bands in the summer, while both and **Rustic Pine,** 119 E. Ramshorn, tel. (307) 455-2430, and **Outlaw Saloon,** 204 W. Ramshorn, tel. (307) 455-2387, offer country-and-western bands. The Rustic Pine is a classic western bar with elk and moose heads, plenty of old wood, and a pool table. Check out the ashtrays, which note, "God spends his vacation here." The famous Tuesday night **square dances** bring in dudes from local ranches in July and August. You may want to avoid this night if you don't want to be overwhelmed with fellow visitors.

Events

Dubois is one of 12 stops in early February's **Rocky Mountain Stage Stop Sled Dog Race,** an event that attracts some of the nation's best mushers with a $100,000 purse. The race begins and ends in Jackson. Call (307) 734-1163 for details, or check the website: www.wyomingstagestop.org.

The Dubois **Fourth of July** weekend is the biggest local event. The town comes alive with an ice-cream social, parade, Western barbecue, fireworks, and rubber-ducky races down the river. A **National Art Show** comes to the arts center on the last week of July, attracting both professionals and amateurs. **Whiskey Mountain Buckskinners Wind River Rendezvous** on the second weekend of August includes some impressive black-powder marksmanship contests. Also don't miss the Dubois firefighter's **buffalo barbecue** during rendezvous weekend. Get details on these and other events from the Dubois Chamber of Commerce, tel. (307) 455-2556.

Summer Recreation

Dubois sits at the confluence of the Wind River and Horse Creek, and both streams provide good trout fishing right in town. Hot springs keep the Wind River flowing all year. See the visitor center for descriptions of local fishing holes and for brochures from local outfitters who offer pack trips and horseback rides.

The nine-hole **Antelope Hills Golf Course,** tel. (307) 455-2888, is on the western end of Dubois. Rent **mountain bikes** from Double Bar J Guest Ranch, 20 miles west of Dubois, tel. (307) 455-2681.

Winter Recreation

Based in Dubois, **Washakie Outfitting,** tel. (307) 733-3602 or (800) 249-0662, www.dogsledwashakie.com, leads a variety of excellent dogsled tours from Cowboy Village Resort at Togwotee (40 miles west of Dubois) and from Brooks Lake Lodge (23 miles west of Dubois). Iditarod veteran Billy Snodgrass offers half-day ($131), full-day ($175), overnight ($325), and extended trips and also runs teams from Teton Village in Jackson Hole. This is the real thing, with Alaskan husky racing dogs pulling sleds through some of the most dramatic country imaginable.

Geyser Creek Dog Sled Adventures, tel. (307) 739-0165 or (800) 531-6874, www.dogsledadv.com, also leads dogsled tours of the Brooks Lake area and longer trips all the way up to a three-day sled trip that includes overnight stops in a tepee and a yurt. All-day rates are $195 for adults, $95 for kids under age 10.

The Absarokas and Wind River Mountains around Dubois are extremely popular with snowmobilers during the winter months, and several places rent "sleds" in town and nearby. Don't expect peace and quiet with all these machines roaring through the backcountry! More than 300 miles of trails head out in all directions. **Cross-country skiers** find trails near Falls Campground and Brooks Lake (both 23 miles west of town) and Cowboy Village Resort at Togwotee (40 miles west), and in backcountry areas off-limits to snowmobiles.

OTHER PRACTICALITIES

Shopping

Sew What, 112 E. Ramshorn, tel. (307) 455-3373, sews authentic Old Western clothing using its own designs. The company also sells Wyoming-made jewelry, baskets, quilts, leather goods, and clothing. Inside the lobby of **Black Bear Country Inn,** 505 W. Ramshorn, tel. (307) 455-2344 or (800) 873-2327, you'll find more then 500 different teddy bears on display (and for sale). It's touted as the largest selection of teddy bears in the West. Don't let your two-year-old know about this place!

Trapline Gallery, 120 E. Ramshorn, tel. (307) 455-2800, sells Indian-crafted beadwork, jewelry, and artwork, as well as furs. **Horse Creek Traders,** 104 E. Ramshorn, tel. (307) 455-3345, has an impressive collection of antique trade beads for sale, along with tacky antler carvings and Indian trinkets. A few doors down is a nice bookshop, **Two Ocean Books,** tel. (307) 455-3554. **Water Wheel Gift Shop,** 113 E. Ramshorn, tel. (307) 455-2112, also carries a selection of Wyoming titles.

Purchase topographic maps at historic **Welty's General Store,** 113 W. Ramshorn, tel. (307) 455-2377, which has haphazard hours, and fishing supplies from **Wind River Fly Shop,** 116 E. Ramshorn, tel. (307) 455-2109, or **Whiskey Mountain Tackle,** 1418 Warm Springs Dr., tel. (307) 455-2587.

Information and Services

The **Dubois Chamber of Commerce,** 616 W. Ramshorn, tel. (307) 455-2556, is open Mon.-Sat. 9 a.m.-7 p.m., Sunday noon-5 p.m. Memorial Day to Labor Day; and Mon.-Fri. 9 a.m.-5 p.m. the rest of the year. Ask for a self-guided tour map of old logging flumes, tie-hack cabins, and other historic structures. The chamber's web address is www.dteworld.com/duboiscc.

Stop by the Forest Service's **Wind River Ranger District** office at 1403 W. Ramshorn (one

TIE HACKS

Many of the trees cut in Wyoming's forests between 1870 and 1940 went to supply railroad ties for an ever-expanding network of rails throughout the Rockies. The men who cut these ties—tie hacks—spent long, hard months in the mountains, working through the winter. Many of the woodsmen were emigrants from Sweden, Norway, Finland, Austria, and Italy. Tie hacks first felled a suitable lodgepole pine using a bucksaw, then limbed the tree and used a broadax to hew the tie into shape, finally peeling the remaining bark from the sides and cutting it to length. Hundreds of thousands of ties—each eight feet long and at least five inches on each side—were produced annually by tie hacks. Horses dragged the ties down to a creek bank or flume to await high spring flows, when thousands of ties could be sent downriver at once. The enormous log jams that resulted sometimes required dynamite to loosen. Downstream booms caught the logs where they could be hauled up and loaded onto railway cars.

Tie hacks found work in many parts of Wyoming, but especially in the Medicine Bow Mountains, Laramie Mountains, Sierra Madre, Big Horn Mountains, and Wind River Mountains, where major streams provided a way for the ties to reach the railheads. In the upper Wind River country, the industry spanned three decades, from 1914 to 1946, and more than 10 million ties were cut and floated downstream to Riverton, where they were used by the Chicago and Northwestern Railroad. A stone monument to the tie hacks stands along US Hwy. 26/287 approximately 18 miles west of Dubois. The visitor center in Dubois has a handout that provides a self-guided tour of historical sights associated with the tie hacks.

mile west of town), tel. (307) 455-2466, for maps of Shoshone and Bridger-Teton National Forests ($4) and info on local trails. They also have a listing of local horsepacking outfitters. See the chapter on Bighorn Basin for more on the Washakie Wilderness. The Fitzpatrick Wilderness is described under Wind River Mountains, below.

Dubois does not have a hospital, but the **Dubois Medical Center,** 706 Meckem, tel. (307) 455-2516, has a nurse practitioner. Wash clothes at the laundromat on W. Ramshorn across from Branding Iron Motel.

Transportation

Wind River Transportation Authority (WRTA), tel. (307) 856-7118 or (800) 439-7118, has on-demand van service to western and southwestern Wyoming. Travelers can call for a ride to Jackson, Salt Lake City, Lander, Riverton, Pinedale, Rock Springs, and other places. **Trail's End Motel,** tel. (307) 455-2540, provides shuttle van service to the airports in Jackson or Riverton.

DUBOIS VICINITY

Anyone who loves the outdoors will discover an abundance of pleasures around Dubois. There's good fishing for rainbow, cutthroat, brown, and brook trout in the Wind River and for rainbow, brook, and Mackinaw trout in the many alpine lakes, plus lots of deer, elk, and bighorn sheep. Hikers and horse-packers will find hundreds of miles of Forest Service trails in the area. Photographers love the brilliantly colored badlands that frame Dubois on both the east and west sides. And each winter, hundreds of 'bilers climb on their sleds and cross-country skiers strap on their boards to enter the world of deep powder in the Absarokas.

Horse Creek Area

Horse Creek Rd. heads north from Dubois and provides scenic views of the Absarokas and nearby badland country. **Horse Creek Campground** ($6; open June-Oct.) is 12 miles north. Forest Rd. 504 continues another five miles, providing access to the Washakie Wilderness via Horse Creek Trail. Forest Rd. 508 splits off near Horse Creek Campground and leads another 17 miles to **Double Cabin Campground** ($6; open June-September). Several trails head into the wilderness from here; most popular are Frontier Creek Trail and the Wiggins Fork Trail. You'll find remnants of a petrified forest six miles up the Frontier Creek Trail, but the site has been rather picked over by illegal collectors. It's unlawful to remove petrified wood from a wilderness area. Please leave pieces where you find them. For other Washakie Wilderness trails info, ask at the Dubois Ranger Station. Several dude ranches are in the area.

Union Pass

The first road across the Absarokas headed through Union Pass southwest of Dubois. The pass forms a divide between the waters of the Columbia, Colorado, and Mississippi Rivers and marks the boundary of the Absaroka, Wind River, and Gros Ventre Mountain Ranges. Near the pass are an interpretive sign and a nature trail through a flower-filled meadow. Union Pass Rd. (gravel) leaves US Hwy. 26/287 approximately nine miles northwest of Dubois and climbs across to connect with State Hwy. 352 north of Pinedale. On the west side of the pass the road becomes rougher and should only be attempted in dry weather. Not for RVs; high-clearance vehicles are recommended.

The Union Pass area is popular with mountain-bikers, cross-country skiers, and far too many wintertime snowmobilers. **Lakes Lodge,** tel. (307) 455-2171 or (888) 655-5253, five miles up Union Pass Rd., has condo-style cabins ($45 d) a bar, restaurant, and winter snowmobile rentals. Closed mid-April through May. Inexpensive.

A beautiful 20-mile side road begins a few miles up Union Pass Rd., heads along Warm Springs Creek, and eventually reconnects with US Hwy. 26/287. Find fantastic views of the Absaroka and Wind River Ranges along this route. The remains of an old tie-hack logging flume are visible, and a warm spring (85° F) flows into the creek.

OVER TOGWOTEE PASS

The enjoyable drive west from Dubois first cuts through the colorful badlands, playing tag with the Wind River as it begins a long ascent to 9,644-foot Togwotee Pass (pronounced "TOE-go-tee"). The pass is named for a subchief under Chief Washakie. Togwotee was one of the last independent Sheepeater Indians—a branch of the Shoshones—and the man who led a U.S. government exploratory expedition over this pass in 1873. He even guided Pres. Chester Arthur on his monthlong visit to Yellowstone in 1883.

Togwotee Pass is one of the most scenic drives imaginable, with Ramshorn Peak peeking down from the north for several miles until the road plunges into dense lodgepole forests (Shoshone National Forest) with lingering glimpses of the Pinnacle Buttes. At the crest it emerges into grass-, willow-, and flower-bedecked meadows with Blackrock Creek winding through. Whitebark pine and Engelmann spruce trees cover the nearby slopes. As the highway drops down the western side into the Bridger-Teton National Forest, another marvelous mountain range—the Tetons—dominates the horizon in dramatic fashion. Snow lies along the roadsides until early July; notice the high posts along the road used by wintertime snowplows. Togwotee Pass is a complete shock after all the miles of sagebrush and grassland that control the heartland of Wyoming. It's like entering another world—a world of cool, forested mountains and lofty peaks instead of the arid land with horizonwide vistas.

Pinnacle Buttes and Brooks Lake

Dominating the view along US Hwy. 26/287 for perhaps 15 miles are the castlelike Pinnacle Buttes. Twenty-three miles west of Dubois, you'll come to the turnoff to Brooks Lake, elevation 9,100 feet. Take it, even if you don't plan on camping here. A five-mile gravel road leads to the cliff-rimmed lake, and a clear creek flows east and south from here. The Forest Service's excellent **Pinnacles** and **Brooks Lake** Campgrounds are along the lakeshore and cost $9 a night; open mid-June to mid-September. Facing the lake is historic Brooks Lake Lodge (see below).

Back on the main highway, you'll want to stop at **Falls Campground** (also $9; open June to mid-September). Here, Brooks Creek tumbles into a deep canyon. Catch very impressive views of **Brooks Creek Falls** along the short trail beginning from the parking lot. In wintertime, cross-country skiers will find an easy but ungroomed ski trail that heads out two miles from here. **Wind River Lake** is another five miles up the hill, just below the pass. It's a gorgeous place for picnics, with deep blue water and the sharp cliffs of Pinnacle Buttes behind.

Mountain Lodges and Dude Ranches

Six miles west of Dubois is **Triple EEE Ranch,** tel. (307) 455-2304 or (800) 353-2555, a recently built guest ranch on a small spread next to Shoshone National Forest. Guests (maximum of 18 people) stay in the lodge or in duplex cabins that afford gorgeous views of Wind River Valley. Horseback riding is a favorite activity, but guests also enjoy fishing, hiking, wildlife watching, cookouts, sing-alongs, or simply relaxing in the hot tub. Special children's programs are also offered. Weekly all-inclusive rates are $1,790 for two people. For details, visit the website: www.dudesville.com. Luxury.

Fourteen miles west of Dubois—and right on the Continental Divide Snowmobile Trail—**Timberline Ranch,** tel. (307) 455-2513, has wintertime lodging in cabins and condo accommodations. Call for rates. The ranch also rents snowmobiles and has a restaurant and bar. It is open to the public mid-September through March. In the summer, the ranch houses a geology field camp run by Ohio's Miami University.

Sixteen miles west of Dubois is **Mackenzie Highland Ranch,** tel. (307) 455-3415, where accommodations are offered in a variety of cabins and other rustic buildings. Lodging starts at $45 d for the simplest cabin with shared bath, up to $210 for a four-bedroom home (it sleeps eight) with two baths and a full kitchen. There's a three-night minimum stay. Trail rides, meals, and guided fishing trips are offered in the summer, and the ranch is a base for snowmobilers, skiers, dog mushers, and hunters at other times of the year. Inexpensive. A portion of Mackenzie Highland Ranch becomes a base for lepidopterology research each summer, with graduate-level classes offered through Sam Houston State University. This unique program is run by professor Karölis Bagdonas, a specialist on moths and butterflies; he discovered the vital importance of moths in the diet of Yellowstone grizzlies.

Crooked Creek Guest Ranch, tel. (307) 455-3035 or (888) 238-2647, is 16 miles from Dubois along Union Pass Road. In the summer, the ranch has horseback rides, hiking, fly-fishing, barbecues, wagon rides, and other activities. In winter it's the haunt of snowmobilers (the Continental Divide Snowmobile Trail is very close). The ranch rents snowmobiles, sells gas, and has a convenience store. Guests stay in modern log cabins and dine in the main lodge. All-inclusive weekly rates are $1,790 for two people in the summer. Get more information by pointing your browser to www.ranchweb.com/crookedcreek. Luxury.

Seventeen miles west of Dubois, **Wapiti Ridge Ranch,** tel. (307) 455-2219, has a dozen motel-type units for $40 s or $70 d, including a continental breakfast in summer or full breakfast in winter. The rooms are comfortable and nicely furnished, but they do not contain televisions or phones. This is a popular spot for hunters in the fall and snowmobilers in winter. No smoking. Moderate.

In the mountains 18 miles west of Dubois, **Triangle C Dude Ranch,** tel. (307) 455-2225 or (800) 661-4928, was established as the first tie-hack camp in the region and now operates as a summertime guest ranch and wintertime snowmobiling and cross-country skiing center. In summer, the main emphasis is horseback riding, but guests will also enjoy fishing, hiking, children's activities, black-powder shoots, archery, mountain-biking, canoeing, and evening entertainment. Weekly rates are $1,800-2,800 for two people, though shorter three-night visits are possible in the shoulder season. The ranch is open Memorial Day to Labor Day. Find it on the web at www.ranchweb.com/trianglec. Luxury.

Twenty miles west of Dubois is **Pinnacle Buttes Lodge and Campground,** tel. (307) 455-2506 or (800) 934-3569, www.pinnaclebuttes.com, where motel rooms are $70 and cabins with kitchenettes (but no TVs) go for $90. The cabins and motel rooms sleep four people each. You'll also find a restaurant with home-cooked meals, an outdoor pool, jacuzzi, and camping spaces ($10 for tents, $19 for RVs). Open year-round. Moderate-Expensive.

Double Bar J Guest Ranch, 20 miles west of Dubois, tel. (307) 455-2681, has log cabin accommodations, horseback rides, mountain-biking, fishing, evening barbecues, and a sauna. Weekly all-inclusive rates in the summer are $1,680 for two people, or stay by the night for $330 d all-inclusive. In the winter the ranch offers cross-country skiing and snowmobiling. Find them on the web at www.doublebarj.com. Luxury.

Brooks Lake Lodge

With a spectacular dual backdrop of Brooks Lake and the Pinnacles, Brooks Lake Lodge is in a class of its own. The enormous great hall (on the National Register of Historic Places) is filled with big-game trophies from all over the world. Built from lodgepole logs in 1922, this classic Western lodge has long served travelers en route to Yellowstone. It was completely restored in the late 1980s and now has six guest rooms in the main lodge and six more private cabins in the trees; all are furnished with handmade lodgepole furniture. Guests can relax in the jacuzzi or explore the magnificent country nearby.

Brooks Lake Lodge is 23 miles west of Dubois—or 33 miles east of Moran Junction—and then five miles in from US Hwy. 26/287 along Brooks Lake Road. It's open July-Sept. and then late December to March. There's a three-night minimum stay in summer, when the rates are $390 d per day in the lodge or $430 d per day in the cabins. This includes all meals, horseback riding, canoeing, and fishing. Weekly rates are also available. Be sure to reserve far ahead. Come winter, Brooks Lake Lodge is a popular skiing and snowmobiling spot. Overnight winter accommodations are $300 d per night in the lodge or $350 d per night in the cabins, including breakfast, dinner, and cross-country skis. Couples can stay here midweek for $525-625 per couple for two nights, including meals. Snowmobile rentals are available. The restaurant is open to nonguests for lunch in the winter months, but reservations are mandatory; call a week ahead to be sure of a table. Get details by calling (307) 455-2121, or look on the web at www.brookslake.com. Luxury.

Both **Washakie Outfitting,** tel. (307) 733-3602, and **Geyser Creek Dogsled Adventures,** tel. (307) 739-0165 or (800) 531-6874, offer dogsled tours of the Brooks Lake area. See the Jackson Hole and the Tetons chapter for info on **Cowboy Village Resort at Togwotee,** a few miles west of Togwotee Pass.

WIND RIVER MOUNTAINS

The Wind River Mountains begin near South Pass and continue 100 miles northwest to Union Pass, forming part of America's Continental Divide backbone. The range is visible for more than a hundred miles across the sagebrush country of central and southwestern Wyoming, its rugged snowcapped peaks gleaming in the light. The Shoshones traversed this range each spring and fall, and Sheepeater Indians hunted in the high country, but to most of the white pioneers whose wagon trains rolled across South Pass the peaks represented a forbidding, mysterious place. In 1868, writer James Chisholm offered a description of the range that still rings true today:

> *I think the best inspired painter that ever drew would fail in attempting to describe these mighty mountains. He may convey correctly enough an impression of their shape, their vast extent and sublime beauty. But there is something always left out which escapes all his colors and all his skill. Their aspects shift and vary continually. Their very shapes seem to undergo a perpetual transformation like the clouds above them. There is a mystery like the mystery of the sea—a silence not of death but of eternity.*

Today, the Wind River Mountains are considered Wyoming's premier backpacking area, offering perhaps 700 miles of trails. Much of the country is well above timberline, featuring glacially carved mountains and countless small lakes. Mountain climbers enjoy practicing moves on thousands of granitic precipices representing all degrees of difficulty. The Wind River Mountains contain Gannett Peak—at 13,804 feet the tallest in Wyoming—and all but one of the state's 15 other highest peaks. The 150 glaciers in the mountains all formed during the Little Ice Age, between A.D. 1400 and 1850. The glaciers that actually carved these mountains were far larger—so massive, in fact, that they covered the mountaintops to great depths and spilled over to create the hanging valleys, cirques, alpine lakes, U-shaped valleys, and steep cliffs of today.

Three different Forest Service wilderness areas cap these mountains; the largest is Bridger Wilderness, on the western side of the Continental Divide (in Bridger-Teton National Forest); the other two are Popo Agie and Fitzpatrick Wilderness Areas east of the crest (in Shoshone National Forest). Add in the BLM's Scab Creek Wilderness Study Area for a total of more than 735,000 roadless acres. The lower elevations of the Wind Rivers are also U.S. Forest Service lands but are managed for other purposes—primarily timber harvesting and grazing. On the northeast border is the Wind River Reservation, which includes some of the high mountain country, but access is restricted. Contact the Tribal Fish and Game Office in Fort Washakie, tel. (307) 332-7207, to purchase a limited hiking, fishing, and camping permit and recreation stamp ($25 for a day or $65 per week for nonresidents).

Wildlife

Most of the streams and larger lakes in the Wind Rivers have been planted with rainbow, cutthroat, California golden, brook, German brown, or Mackinaw trout and grayling and mountain whitefish. Although grizzlies are only infrequently sighted, black bears are still in these mountains—mainly below treeline—and have caused considerable problems in recent years. Always hang food out of their reach; check with local Forest Service offices for current conditions and precautions. Other creatures—mosquitoes and biting flies—are more common annoyances in the mountains. Be sure to bring insect repellent during July and August, when they are at their worst. Other critters you're likely to see include bighorn sheep, moose, elk, mule deer, and coyotes. Pikas and yellow-bellied marmots are common in the high-country boulder fields.

Access

Three highways circle the Wind River Range: US Hwy. 26/287 on the northeast, US Hwy. 191 on the southwest, and State Hwy. 28 on the southeast. The mountains are traversed by only one road, gravel Union Pass Road. Most people cross the relatively gentle southern slopes at

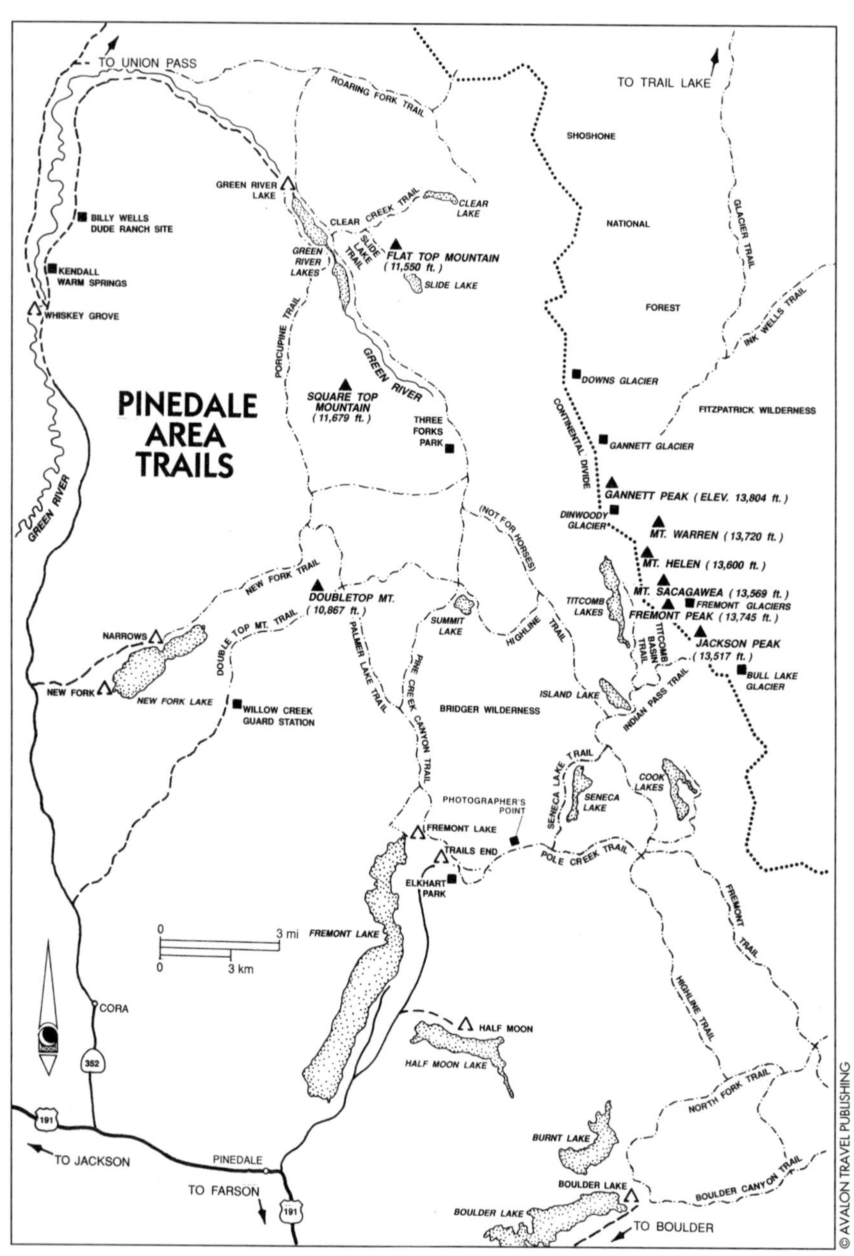
PINEDALE AREA TRAILS
TO UNION PASS
ROARING FORK TRAIL
TO TRAIL LAKE
SHOSHONE
NATIONAL
FOREST
GREEN RIVER LAKE
CLEAR CREEK TRAIL
CLEAR LAKE
BILLY WELLS DUDE RANCH SITE
GREEN RIVER LAKES
SLIDE LAKE TRAIL
FLAT TOP MOUNTAIN (11,550 ft.)
SLIDE LAKE
KENDALL WARM SPRINGS
WHISKEY GROVE
GLACIER TRAIL
INK WELLS TRAIL
PORCUPINE TRAIL
GREEN RIVER
SQUARE TOP MOUNTAIN (11,679 ft.)
DOWNS GLACIER
FITZPATRICK WILDERNESS
THREE FORKS PARK
CONTINENTAL DIVIDE
GANNETT GLACIER
GANNETT PEAK (ELEV. 13,804 ft.)
DINWOODY GLACIER
(NOT FOR HORSES)
MT. WARREN (13,720 ft.)
MT. HELEN (13,600 ft.)
NEW FORK TRAIL
DOUBLETOP MT. (10,867 ft.)
MT. SACAGAWEA (13,569 ft.)
FREMONT GLACIERS
TITCOMB LAKES
FREMONT PEAK (13,745 ft.)
SUMMIT LAKE
HIGHLINE TRAIL
NARROWS
DOUBLE TOP MT. TRAIL
PALMER LAKE TRAIL
PINE CREEK CANYON TRAIL
TITCOMB BASIN TRAIL
JACKSON PEAK (13,517 ft.)
BULL LAKE GLACIER
NEW FORK
NEW FORK LAKE
WILLOW CREEK GUARD STATION
BRIDGER WILDERNESS
ISLAND LAKE
INDIAN PASS TRAIL
SENECA LAKE TRAIL
COOK LAKES
SENECA LAKE
PHOTOGRAPHER'S POINT
FREMONT LAKE
TRAILS END
POLE CREEK TRAIL
ELKHART PARK
FREMONT TRAIL
0
3 mi
0
3 km
FREMONT LAKE
HIGHLINE TRAIL
CORA
HALF MOON
HALF MOON LAKE
352
MOON
NORTH FORK TRAIL
191
TO JACKSON
BURNT LAKE
PINEDALE
TO FARSON
BOULDER LAKE
BOULDER CANYON TRAIL
191
BOULDER LAKE
TO BOULDER
GREEN RIVER

South Pass or over Togwotee Pass to the northeast. You can gain access to the three wilderness areas from either side, but the high passes and long distances keep many hikers on one side or the other. See descriptions of the three different wilderness areas (below) for specific access points.

Most trails in the Wind Rivers are relatively free of snow by early July and remain so until mid-September, but the high passes may not open until late July. Because of the open country in the alpine, off-trail travel is relatively easy here but is advised only for experienced hikers who know how to read topographic maps and can take care of themselves in an emergency. Be prepared for the thunderstorms that often roll in during the afternoon; lightning is a real problem above timberline. It can snow at any time in this mountain country; night temperatures can drop below freezing even in midsummer. You won't find a lot of wood in many parts of the range, so be sure to bring a gas stove to cook on. In addition, wood fires are prohibited at many of the most heavily used sites.

Unlike the mountain country farther north, most of the people who head into the Winds do so on foot rather than atop a horse. Horses are used by a quarter of the people, and "spot-packing," in which horses carry supplies for base camps but everyone hikes in on foot, is a popular way to get into the backcountry without carrying everything on your back. Many outfitters offer these services; stop by local Forest Service offices for a list of outfitters. Most backcountry users do not need permits, but visitor permits (free) are required for groups using stock animals and organized groups like the Boy Scouts and schools.

More Info

Forest Service ranger stations in Lander (Popo Agie Wilderness), Dubois (Fitzpatrick Wilderness), and Pinedale (Bridger Wilderness) can provide information on their respective areas. An area map ($4) of Southern Shoshone National Forest covers the Fitzpatrick and Popo Agie Wilderness Areas, while a Pinedale area map ($4) covers the Bridger Wilderness. Maps, copies of backcountry use regulations, and lists of approved outfitters are available from Forest Service offices.

Below, you'll find brief descriptions of the most popular hikes, but with literally hundreds of treks available in the Winds don't think these are your only options. In fact, to avoid the crowds you should probably pick up a few topo maps and discover your own trails. The late Finis Mitchell's *Wind River Trails* (Salt Lake City: Wasatch Publications) is a folksy, inexpensive guide by a man who hiked this country from 1909 nearly until his death in the 1990s. Mitchell personally planted trout in dozens of high-country lakes during the 1930s and even had a mountain named for him. Pick up this guide if you plan to do any fishing. *Climbing and Hiking in the Wind River Mountains* by Joe Kelsey (San Francisco: Sierra Club Books) has accurate information on most of the hiking trails and describes hundreds of technical climbs. For a guide directed specifically to hiking, not climbing, see *Walking the Winds: A Hiking & Fishing Guide to Wyoming's Wind River Range,* by Rebecca Woods (Jackson, WY: White Willow Publishing). Topographic maps are available from sporting-goods stores in the surrounding towns.

GREEN RIVER LAKES AREA

The long drive to Green River Lakes is one of the most popular getaways in the Wind River Mountains. The road parallels the Green River as it first drifts northward then makes a U-turn to meander across southwestern Wyoming, eventually joining the Colorado River in Utah. Willows line the riverbanks in this open valley, while sagebrush and aspen cover the hills. Cattle and horses graze on the lush grasses.

Get to Green River Lakes by driving seven miles west of Pinedale on US Hwy. 191, and then north up State Hwy. 352. The first 26 miles of the road to Green River Lakes are paved and kept plowed all winter. Approximately 15 miles up, a sign points the way to **New Fork Lake,** four miles away on a gravel road. Camp here at either **New Fork Lake Campground** ($4; open June to mid-September) or the popular **Narrows Campground** ($6; open June to mid-September). Make reservations ($8.65 extra charge) for Narrows Campground by calling (877) 444-6777, or make them on the web at www.reserveusa.com. **New Fork Trail** takes off from the Narrows Campground, providing one of many routes into the Winds.

At the Forest Service border, state maintenance ends and the road becomes gravel and gets rougher and more washboarded as you go the remaining 18 miles. Watch the weather, since this upper portion can become a quagmire after heavy rains. It's especially a problem if you're towing a trailer. Fantastic scenery makes the trip worthwhile despite the road conditions. Look for some enormous "erratic" boulders a couple of miles up the road from here, evidence of the glaciers that once scoured this valley and carried the boulders along with them.

Just inside the Forest Service border, a signboard describes the tie drives that sent several hundred thousand railroad ties down the Green River between 1869 and 1871. They made it all the way to Green River City (130 miles away), where a boom caught them and they were loaded on railcars. The crew boss, Charles Deloney, later became first superintendent of the Yellowstone Preserve and opened the first store in Jackson. The Green River Lumber and Tie Company came here in the 1890s, employing at least 50 men who lived in the town of Kendall. The company only lasted until 1904, but you can still find the tall stumps in the second-growth forests nearby.

Approximately three miles beyond the Bridger-Teton National Forest border, a rough gravel road splits off and heads over **Union Pass** to Dubois. Although this route was used by Indians and mountain men, today it probably sees more use by snowmobiles in the winter than cars in summertime. Although very rough in spots and muddy each spring, the road is passable in midsummer, even for two-wheel-drive cars. Union Pass Rd. is especially popular with elk hunters in the fall. The Forest Service's **Whiskey Grove Campground** ($4; open mid-June to mid-September) is just west across the bridge at the site of the old logging town of Kendall.

Kendall Warm Springs

Back on Green River Lakes Rd., you pass Kendall Warm Springs 1.5 miles above the turnoff to the campground, its 85° F waters issuing from a few hundred feet up the hill. This is the only place in the world where you can find **Kendall dace.** Fully grown, they are just two inches long, or, as the Forest Service notes, shorter than their scientific name, *Rhinichthys osculus thermalis.* The water drops over a 12-foot-high travertine terrace into Green River. The terrace was built up over thousands of years; at the same time the river was cutting into its banks, thus separating these fish and allowing them to survive away from larger predators. To protect them, wading is not allowed in the waters of Kendall Warm Springs.

More Sights

Another two miles up the road are the log and red-sandstone remains of **Gros Ventre Lodge,** one of Wyoming's first dude ranches. Billy Wells built a hunting lodge here in 1897 and operated it until 1906, when stricter enforcement of game laws made it more difficult to attract clients. The lodge drew wealthy big-game hunters from England and the East Coast who enjoyed the chance to slaughter wildlife. (Bannock Indians who hunted out of season in nearby Jackson Hole were shot at, while rich white "sportsmen" could take whatever they wanted for trophies.)

The road ends at the popular **Green River Lakes Campground** ($7; open mid-June to mid-September). Weekends and the July Fourth holiday may fill the campground to overflowing. A number of unofficial campsites are just off the road below the lake. **Square Top Mountain** stares back across the lake, one of the most photographed spots in Wyoming. It is especially beautiful at sunrise, when the water is calm and the first light catches its cliff faces. By the way, when winter comes, ice drapes the front of Square Top, creating the longest single-pitch ice route in the nation. It has never been climbed. Trails in the Green River Lakes area are described below.

BRIDGER WILDERNESS

The 428,169-acre Bridger Wilderness reaches 90 miles along the western side of the Wind River Mountains, encompassing 27 active glaciers, 2,300 alpine lakes, and 600 miles of trails. It's named for famed mountain man and guide Jim Bridger and was first designated a primitive area in 1931, gaining wilderness status with the original Wilderness Act of 1964. Despite this status, a considerable amount of sheep grazing still takes place in the Bridger Wilderness; it was "grandfathered" in with the wilderness legislation. Sheep are allowed to graze on the southern end of the wilderness (south of Raid Lake), while cattle graze north of there. The Forest Service office in Pinedale is now trying to control sheep grazing more and reduce the conflicts between backcountry hikers and the herds.

Regulations and Access

Before heading out, be sure to pick up a copy of Bridger Wilderness regulations from the Pinedale Forest Service office, tel. (307) 367-4326. Call ahead for the latest on trail conditions and snow depths in the high country and for recommendations on avoiding crowded areas. The office also loans out **bear-resistant food storage containers** for a $25 deposit, plus a $1 per night donation. These are available on a first-come, first-served basis, or you can buy your own at The Outdoor Shop in Pinedale. Habituated black bears are becoming a problem in many backcountry camps, and some have even learned how to obtain properly hung food.

To keep from polluting the water, pitch your tent at least 200 feet from lakes or trails in the wilderness and 100 feet from streams. Campfires are only allowed below timberline and only then with dead and down wood; gas stoves are recommended. Organized groups such as scouts or school groups, and groups traveling with horses, mules, llamas, and pack goats must all get a free visitor permit from the Pinedale District office. If you're using an outfitter to pack in your supplies, make sure the Forest Service permits them to operate within the wilderness.

Access to the Bridger Wilderness comes from nine different entrances along the western side of the range. The three most popular points of entry are described below, as are a number of favorite trails. If you're looking for solitude, you may want to avoid these popular paths. Note that the open alpine country means that anyone with topographic maps and a good sense of orientation can strike off in interesting directions and quickly escape the crowds. If you plan to do any fishing, be sure to pick up the Forest Service's guide to fishing lakes in the Bridger Wilderness, with details on which species are where.

Green River Lakes Trails

Easily the most scenic entry into the Winds is from Green River Lakes, located on the end of a paved-then-dirt road that leads north from Cora. The road ends at a campground ($7) facing onto Lower Green River Lake, where the unforgettable 11,679-foot summit of Square Top Mountain dominates the view.

For an easy five-mile day-hike, follow the trails that circle Lower Green River Lake (Highline Trail on the east and Lakeside Trail on the west). You'll have excellent views of Flat Top Mountain (not to be confused with Square Top Mountain) from the Lakeside Trail and of the Clear Creek Falls along the Highline Trail. Keep your eyes open for moose and osprey. An interesting side trip is the short hike to Upper Green River Lake, where Square Top proves even more startling. Another side trip heads up **Clear Creek Trail**—it takes off from the southeastern end of Lower Green River Lake, climbs two miles to a natural bridge, then continues an equal distance to Clear Lake. Some of this country was burned in a 1988 fire. Flat Top is relatively easy to climb; see one of the trail guides for specifics.

Those interested in longer hikes will find several trails in the Green River Lakes area. **Roaring Fork Trail** climbs up to Faler Lake, 14 miles away and 2,200 feet higher. The **Highline Trail** follows the northeast shore of Lower Green River Lake and then continues south to the uppermost headwaters of the Green River. From there, the trail stays in the alpine much of the way to its destination at the Big Sandy Trailhead on the southern end of the Bridger Wilderness. The total distance is 72 miles, but few people actually follow it that far, preferring to branch off to other sights. Another popular trek is up **Porcupine Trail** to Porcupine Pass and then down **New Fork Trail** to New Fork Lake (a total of approximately 17 miles). Porcupine Trail begins at the upper end of Lower Green River Lake, splitting off from Lakeside Trail.

Elkhart Park Trails

A paved road heads northeast from Pinedale along the eastern side of Fremont Lake, ending 15 miles later at Elkhart Park Trailhead (elevation 9,100 feet). The Forest Service generally has someone around to answer questions at the big parking area that fills with cars in July and August. An overlook along the way provides vistas across Fremont Lake and Bridger Wilderness. The **Trails End Campground** at Elkhart Park ($7) is open from late June to mid-September. For a pleasant day-hike that ends with a bang-up vista of Fremont Peak and the Wind River Range, hike four miles out the Pole Creek Trail to **Photographer's Point.**

Backcountry trails head out from Elkhart in two directions. **Pine Creek Canyon Trail** leads north, providing a relatively direct connection with Summit Lake (13 miles) and then down into Green River Lakes (30 miles total). Because of its steepness, it is not recommended for stock use. The main drawback to this trail is that it loses 2,000 feet by dropping into Pine Creek Canyon—elevation that you must regain to reach Summit Lake. You can make a nice loop by heading east from Summit Lake along the Highline Trail to Elbow Lake and Seneca Lake, where you follow the Seneca Lake and Pole Creek Trails back to Elkhart Park. This loop takes you through some of the more scenic areas in the wilderness and covers approximately 31 miles.

The most popular destination from Elkhart is **Titcomb Basin.** Access from Elkhart Park is via a series of connected trails: the Pole Creek, Seneca Lake, Indian Pass, and Titcomb Basin Trails. Many hikers and climbers overnight at Island Lake, making for very crowded conditions much of the summer. It is 15 miles from Elkhart Park to Upper Titcomb Lake, a mountain cirque with abundant wildflowers. A side hike goes up through gorgeous Indian Basin to Indian Pass (three miles). Mountaineers can then descend to the Knife Point and Bull Lake glaciers within the Fitzpatrick Wilderness.

The valley above Titcomb Basin is open, giving climbers access to the west side of a whole row of peaks, including Mt. Helen (13,600 feet), Mt. Sacagawea (13,569 feet), Jackson Peak (13,517 feet), and **Fremont Peak** (13,745 feet). Climbers can tackle the last two without technical expertise, although Fremont does require some rough scrambling in places. It is most easily climbed from the southwest side; see a topographic map to find the route. Those with greater expertise will find many outstanding opportunities to test their skills on the cliff faces here. Warning: A number of folks have died climbing Fremont Peak; use extreme caution when rock scrambling, and never push beyond your skills or ability.

Fremont Peak is named for **John C. Frémont,** the son-in-law of Sen. Thomas Hart Benton, promoter of the Manifest Destiny that would lead Americans all the way to the Pacific. Because of this familial association, Frémont was given the task of exploring and mapping the western territories, work that brought him the nickname the "Great Pathfinder." Some of his ventures—such as floating through the wild waters of Fremont Canyon on the North Platte River, or crossing the Rockies in the dead of winter—were downright stupid, and his guides tried to stop him. Frémont's best asset was his wife, who painted his adventures in such a heroic light that his presidential ambitions were nearly realized.

In 1842, Frémont and his men climbed what appeared to be the highest mountain in the Wind River range, a summit they called Snow Peak (now Fremont Peak). From the west, it is obvious why Frémont and his men would mistake this for the highest: Gannett Peak (59 feet taller) is barely visible from a distance, hidden behind other summits. It was not until years later that the mistake was discovered. Frémont was led on his wilderness treks by men with far more experience—including Kit Carson and Tom Fitzpatrick—and his real role was to transfer their innate knowledge of the land onto maps. (Although most people believe Frémont did climb the peak bearing his name, others say he climbed another peak instead, or none at all. One of his scouts, Basil Lajeunesse, stated bluntly, "Frémont never ascended the peak." Perhaps that would account for the discrepancies between what Frémont described and what is actually there.)

Big Sandy Trails

One of the most popular entry points into the Bridger Wilderness is from Big Sandy Trailhead. Access is from a number of different directions, but all require long stretches of gravel road. Easiest access is from the north. From the town of Boulder, take State Hwy. 353 where it turns west off US Hwy. 191 and follow it till it turns to gravel (16 miles). Bear left at the intersection a half mile up and go another nine miles to another junction (signed), where you again turn left and go seven more miles to the turnoff (left) to the Forest Service's Dutch Joe Guard Station and then on to

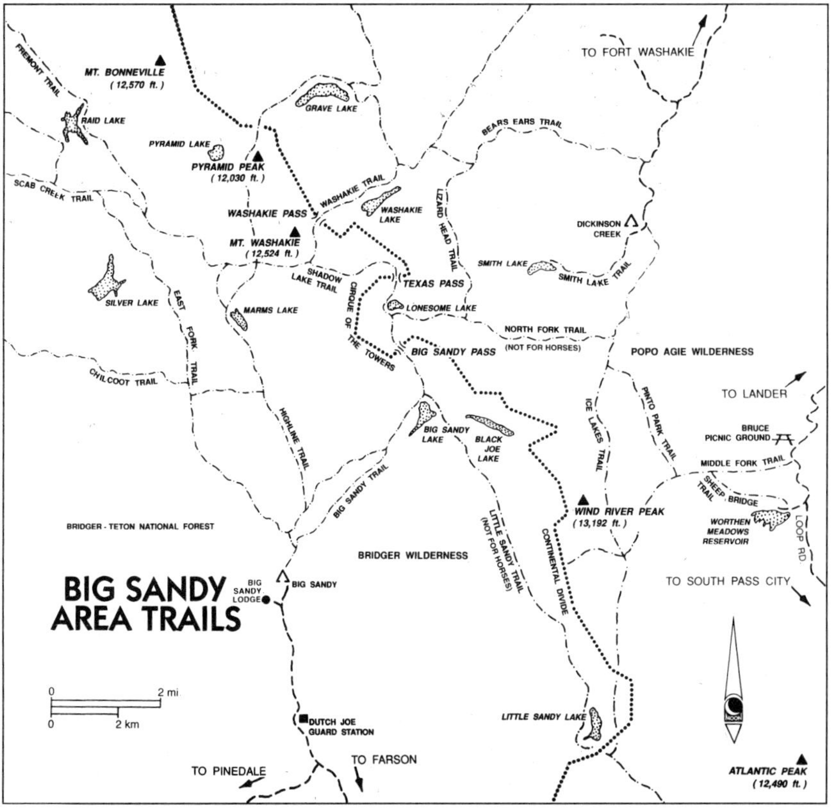

BIG SANDY AREA TRAILS

Big Sandy Opening. The road ends at **Big Sandy Campground** ($4; open mid-June to mid-September), where the trails begin. The Forest Service generally has someone stationed here in the summer. Note that the rough road into Big Sandy becomes slick and hazardous when it rains, so watch the weather reports closely. This is especially a problem if you're towing a trailer.

Big Sandy Lodge is just to the north near the end of Big Sandy Rd. (44 miles from Boulder) and provides guided trail rides and a historic lodge (built in 1929) containing a trophy-filled lounge and two stone fireplaces. Ten rustic log cabins lack electricity or running water. Three meals per day are available for guests; others can eat here by reservation. Spot-pack trips and guided pack trips are also available, or you can stay by the week with everything included. There are no phones here, but you can leave messages at (307) 382-6513. Write the lodge at P.O. Box 223, Boulder, WY 82923, for more info and reservations. Open June-October. Recommended.

A maze of trails departs from Big Sandy Opening. The **Highline Trail** heads north, extending across the Bridger Wilderness to Green River Lakes, and continues from there to Union Pass, 100 miles away. The trail connects with numerous others, including **Shadow Lake Trail,** a 2.5-mile route to this alpine lake. More adventurous types can continue up over Texas Pass and down to Lonesome Lake in the Cirque of the Towers, a distance of 15 miles. (The very popular Cirque of the Towers area is described below under Popo Agie Wilderness.)

Another side route off the Highline Trail is the **Washakie Trail,** a path used by this famous Shoshone chief during his people's biannual migration between the Wind River Valley and the Green River country. This trail goes into the Washakie Lakes area of the Popo Agie Wilderness, where you can connect with the Bears Ears Trail (see below).

The most popular trail out of Big Sandy Opening is **Big Sandy Trail,** a 5.5-mile trek to crowded Big Sandy Lake, where it meets a spider web of trails and cairn-marked paths to other high-country lakes. Beyond the lake, **Big Sandy Pass Trail** climbs steeply up North Creek and over Big Sandy Pass (shown as Jackass Pass on some maps) before dropping into Lonesome Lake and Cirque of the Towers (total distance 8.5 miles). Big Sandy Pass Trail is a long—but beautiful—slog. A strenuous loop trip consists of the Big Sandy Trail-Big Sandy Pass Trail route combined with the Texas Pass-Shadow Lake Trail-Highline Trail route described above. Total distance is 24 miles.

FITZPATRICK WILDERNESS

The 198,838-acre Fitzpatrick Wilderness occupies the northeast side of the Wind River Mountains, sandwiched between the Bridger Wilderness just over the Continental Divide and the Wind River Indian Reservation to the east. The wilderness is a rugged landscape of rock and ice, with dozens of mountain lakes and cascading mountain brooks. Wyoming's highest mountain, Gannett Peak, forms part of the western border, and 44 active glaciers crowd against the summits; the largest covers 1,220 acres. The Fitzpatrick is a favorite of folks with considerable backpacking or mountaineering experience.

Although long maintained as a primitive area, the Fitzpatrick Wilderness was officially established by Congress in 1976 and is named for Tom Fitzpatrick, a respected mountain man, guide, head of the Rocky Mountain Fur Company, army scout, and Indian agent. To the Indians, he was "Broken Hand," a name received after he lost three fingers in a rifle accident while being pursued by Blackfeet Indians; despite this, he still managed to kill two of his attackers. As an Indian agent, Tom Fitzpatrick pushed for a number of important treaties, including the 1851 Fort Laramie Treaty. His untimely death from pneumonia in 1854 was a blow to the peace process, and few of the agents who followed could match Fitzpatrick's diplomatic skills or knowledge of the West. Fitzpatrick's adopted Arapaho son, Friday (named for the day of the week on which Fitzpatrick found him), later became a respected chief and translator for his people.

Access

The primary entrance point into the Fitzpatrick Wilderness is from **Trail Lake.** Head five miles southeast from Dubois on US Hwy. 26/287 and turn right (south) onto a gravel road. The road leads into Whiskey Basin, with a rutted dirt road continuing to the left past a string of small lakes, the last being Trail Lake. The trails begin here, 12 miles off the highway. Note that access to the Cold Springs/Burris Trailhead requires that you cross Wind River Reservation land. You'll need to hire an Indian outfitter to drive you to the trailhead, and you'll have to obtain a reservation fishing/hiking permit and recreation stamp (nonresidents of Wyoming pay $25 for a day or $65 per person for a week). Contact the Tribal Fish and Game Office in Fort Washakie, tel. (307) 332-7207, for details.

Forest Service regulations in the Fitzpatrick prohibit camping within 100 feet of trails or lakes. In addition, no campfires or overnight horse use is allowed above the confluence of Dinwoody and Knoll Lake Creeks. For details, contact the Forest Service's **Wind River Ranger District** office in Dubois, tel. (307) 455-2466.

Trails

Three major trails lead from Trail Lake into the high country. The **Whiskey Mountain Trail** climbs over the peak of the same name and then on to heavily used Simpson Lake, a dozen miles away. From here it's possible for experienced hikers to continue over a pass above Sandra Lake (another 3.5 miles) and then down into the Roaring Fork drainage of the Bridger Wilderness. The **Bomber Basin Trail** leads from Trail Lake Trailhead to Bomber Lake, eight miles away and 2,600 feet higher, crossing the deep canyon created by Torrey Creek on a high bridge. The basin is named for a B-17 bomber that crashed here during WW II when its crew was practicing a strafing run on either a bear or a bighorn sheep. The plane wreckage is still here. The upper portion of this trail (above Bomber Falls) is not maintained but is passable.

A very popular moderately long hike is up **Glacier Trail** all the way to Dinwoody Glacier. It is a sweaty and difficult 23 miles but passes lots of lakes and ruggedly beautiful alpine country. Bighorn sheep are often seen along the way. The first several miles are without water, so be sure to bring plenty with you. The trail ends at the glacier, providing access for mountaineers who want to scale 13,804-foot **Gannett Peak,** highest in Wyoming. (The peak is named for Henry Gannett, chief topographer for the Hayden Survey of the 1870s, and it was first climbed in 1922 by Arthur Tate and Floyd Stahlnaker.) Because it is nearly surrounded by glaciers, most routes require roping up—particularly the popular one across Gooseneck Glacier. Many mountaineers come up this trail to climb Gannett and the cluster of peaks over 13,000 feet just to the south, including Mt. Woodrow Wilson, the Sphinx, Mt. Warren, Doublet Peak, and Turret Peak. See Joe Kelsey's *Climbing and Hiking in the Wind River Mountains* for details. If you want to go with the pros, two first-rate mountaineering operations based in Jackson Hole lead climbs up Gannett Peak: **Exum Mountain Guides,** tel. (307) 733-2297, and **Jackson Hole Mountain Guides,** tel. (307) 733-4979. These aren't cheap; expect to pay $1,500 for a six-day trip.

POPO AGIE WILDERNESS

The Popo Agie Wilderness is a 101,991-acre parcel of magnificent mountain real estate with jagged peaks, deep valleys, and more than 240 lakes. At least 20 peaks rise above 13,000 feet; Wind River Peak is the tallest at 13,225 feet. Popo Agie was first established as a primitive area in 1932 and enlarged and reclassified as wilderness in 1984. The Popo Agie is bounded to the west by the Bridger Wilderness and to the north by the Wind River Indian Reservation. Access to the Popo Agie Wilderness is generally from the east side, in the Lander vicinity, although it is possible to cross the Continental Divide from the Bridger Wilderness via several different passes. Camping is not allowed within 200 feet of trails, lakes, or streams. Anyone bringing in horses, mules, llamas, or pack goats will need to get a free livestock-use permit from the Forest Service. Get this and other Popo Agie Wilderness information from the **Washakie Ranger District Office** in Lander, tel. (307) 332-5460.

Dickinson Park Access

The primary jumping-off point into the Popo Agie Wilderness is the Dickinson Park area, northwest of Lander at an elevation of 9,300 feet. Get here by turning west on Moccasin Lake Rd. (paved) just south of Fort Washakie at the Hines Store. Stay right where the road turns to dirt and continue to Moccasin Lake/Dickinson Park junction, a total of 19 very rough and rutted miles. Turn left here and head another four miles to **Dickinson Creek Campground** (free; open July to mid-September), passing the Dickinson Park Work Center along the way. Note that you'll pass a "No Trespassing without Proper Tribal Travel Permit" sign on Moccasin Lake Rd.; it's okay to ignore this if you're en route to Dickinson Park.

Allen's Diamond Four Ranch, tel. (307) 332-2995, www.wyoming.com/~dmndfour, is near the Dickinson Park Campground and offers very rustic dude-ranch accommodations with three meals a day, horseback riding, fishing, and nature hikes. They also have guided horsepacking trips and spot-pack trips. This is popular with those who want to hike while still enjoying the pleasures of a horse-packed base camp.

The **Bears Ears Trail** takes off from the end of a half-mile dirt road that turns west at the Dickinson Park Work Center and climbs quickly into the alpine before going over Adams Pass. It passes Bears Ears Mountain (look for the "ears") and follows through the alpine before dropping into the lake-filled headwaters of the South Fork of the Little Wind River, 14 miles away. Along the way are all sorts of connections to other trails, including a variety of loops.

From the Dickinson Campground trailhead, the popular **Smith Lake Trail** heads south and then west to Smith and then Cathedral Lakes (eight miles). The **North Fork Trail** splits off the Smith Lake Trail approximately a quarter-mile up. This trail will eventually (15 miles) take you straight to Lonesome Lake at the base of the soaring Cirque of the Towers. Unfortunately, the hike requires four different fordings of the North

Cirque of the Towers rises behind Lonesome Lake.

Fork of the Popo Agie River, a dangerous feat for your feet when the water is high. It's best to wait till late summer.

Loop Road Access

The Loop Road (State Hwy. 131) cuts south from Lander through Sinks Canyon and then over the mountains to South Pass, providing a number of entry points into the Popo Agie Wilderness. **Middle Fork Trail** begins at **Bruce Picnic Ground,** 13 miles south of Lander on the Loop Road, and follows the Middle Fork of the Popo Agie River upstream to Sweetwater Gap (16 miles), where you enter the Bridger Wilderness. Many people use this trail to reach the Cirque of the Towers area via the Pinto Park and North Fork Trails (total one-way distance approximately 23 miles). The **Tayo Creek Trail** splits off from the Middle Fork Trail approximately 13 miles up and continues another four miles to Tayo Lakes. **Sheep Bridge Trail** begins at **Worthen Reservoir,** 20 miles south of Lander on Loop Road, and heads west for three miles to its junction with the Middle Fork Trail. Many people use this to cut distance and elevation off their trek into the Tayo Lake or Cirque of the Towers areas. (It starts 1,200 feet higher than the Middle Fork Trail.)

Cirque of the Towers

This is one of the best-known and most-visited places in the Wind River Mountains, an incredible semicircle of pinnacles at the headwaters of the North Fork of the Popo Agie River. **Lonesome Lake** is in the center, backdropped by peaks with such names as Warbonnet, Pingora, Sharks Nose, Camels Hump, Lizard Head, and Watch Tower. All of these are well-known in the climbing community and attract folks from around the globe. Lonesome Lake is not so lonesome these days; on a typical day in early August you're likely to find a minitown of tents in the vicinity. Campers are required to camp at least a quarter mile from the lake, and no campfires are allowed.

The most popular way to reach Cirque of the Towers is from the Big Sandy Opening Trailhead (see Bridger Wilderness, above), but the longer North Fork Trail (described above) is also commonly used and does not require traversing any passes. The other popularly used route is the Sheep Bridge Trail (described above). Campers often choose to base themselves at Big Sandy Lake and then day-hike into Cirque of the Towers. It makes for a long day, but at least you won't need to carry a heavy pack over challenging Big Sandy Pass.

SOUTH PASS AREA

At the southern end of the Wind River Mountains, a broad, relatively gentle pass provides a corridor across the Continental Divide. This part of Wyoming is packed with history. Today, State Hwy. 28 traverses South Pass, then climbs south and west from Lander, past beautiful **Red Canyon,** where maroon sandstone rocks rise like a backbone out of the sage and grass rangeland. The 35,000-acre **Red Canyon Ranch Preserve** is a working cattle ranch maintained by the Nature Conservancy. It's a center for research on the ecological effects of different grazing techniques; call (307) 332-3388 for access information, classes, and guided walks.

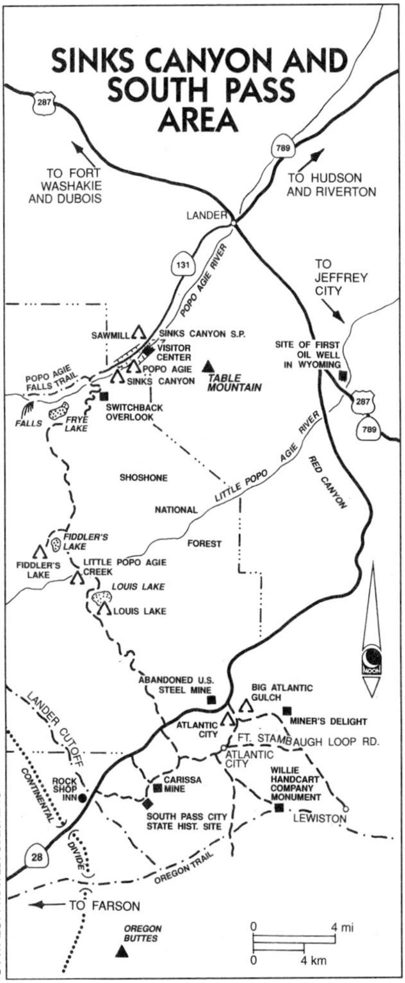

SINKS CANYON AND SOUTH PASS AREA

West of Red Canyon, the highway passes just north of the almost-ghost towns of Atlantic City and South Pass before starting the long descent into the Green River Basin and the junction town of Farson. Winters on the pass are long, cold, and windy; the snow fences stretch for miles along the highway.

Gold was first mined here during the middle 1860s, and a long series of booms and busts followed. For a brief time in 1867-68, the **Sweetwater Mines** attracted national attention, and thousands of men (and a few women) flocked to the area. The land was officially part of the Wind River Reservation at the time, but legalities didn't matter much when gold could be found. South Pass was ceded by the Shoshones in 1878. Prospectors still head out each spring in search of the elusive mother lode, and various schemes to reopen the old mines surface periodically. Today the area is enjoyed by thousands of tourists and others attracted by the rich historical and recreational opportunities.

Over the Pass

We traveled up a long, gradual slope, or plain, free of rocks, trees, or gullies, and came at half past eleven o'clock to the summit of the South Pass of the Rocky Mountains. . . . The ascent was so smooth and gentle, and the level ground at the summit so much like a prairie region, that it was not easy to tell when we had reached the exact line of the divide.

—FROM THE DIARY ENTRY OF OREGON TRAIL EMIGRANT MARGARET A. FRINK, JUNE 24, 1850

South Pass was first discovered by the game animals who traversed this country and the Indian hunters who followed them. The first whites to traipse through were the Astorians, fur traders led by Robert Stuart in 1812. The first wagon wheels rolled over South Pass in 1824, and between 1841 and 1866 more than 350,000 emigrants followed what had become the primary route west. Of all the sights along the Oregon Trail, South Pass was one of the most anticipated. West of here the waters flow to the Pacific Ocean, and the entire country became known as the Oregon Territory (hence the **Oregon Buttes** south of South Pass). Travelers took great pleasure in stopping at Pacific Springs, happy in the knowledge that its waters eventually reached the Pacific. An important stage and Pony Express station stood here; some of the buildings from a later ranch are still standing.

Today, State Hwy. 28 traces a similar route across South Pass. Signboards denote various historic sites along the way. At the signboard that describes the Oregon Trail, a rough dirt road leads a mile back to the clear waters of Pacific Creek, where posts mark the historic route. Don't believe everything you read on the signs, however: the **Parting of the Ways** monument actually marks the South Pass City-Green River stage road where it intersects the Oregon Trail rather than the famous point where the Sublette Cutoff took Oregon- and California-bound travelers west while Mormon voyagers (and others in need of supplies) diverged southwest to Fort Bridger. The true Parting of the Ways lies 10 miles southwest of this marker. The highway west to Farson rolls up and down the sage-carpeted hills, cutting straight as a carpenter's plumb line. The Wind River Mountains dominate the northern horizon, while to the south the distant Killpecker Sand Dunes slide into view.

SOUTH PASS IN 1861

In 1861, Mark Twain rumbled west through Wyoming on a stagecoach, a trip later made famous in his book *Roughing It.* At South Pass, Twain found that the pre-mining-days settlement was not exactly a hubbub of activity:

Toward dawn we got under way again, and presently as we sat with raised curtains enjoying our early-morning smoke and contemplating the first splendor of the rising sun as it swept down the long array of mountain peaks, flushing and gilding crag after crag and summit after summit, as if the invisible Creator reviewed his gray veterans and they saluted with a smile, we hove in sight of South Pass City. The hotelkeeper, the postmaster, the blacksmith, the mayor, the constable, the city marshal and the principal citizen and property holder, all came out and greeted us cheerily, and we gave him good day. . . . South Pass City consisted of four log cabins, one of which was unfinished, and the gentleman with all those offices and titles was the chiefest of the ten citizens of the place. Think of hotelkeeper, postmaster, blacksmith, mayor, constable, city marshal and principal citizen all condensed into one person and crammed into one skin. Bemis said he was "a perfect Allen's revolver of dignities." And he said that if he were to die as postmaster, or as blacksmith, or as postmaster and blacksmith both, the people might stand it; but if he were to die all over, it would be a frightful loss to the community.

SOUTH PASS CITY

At 7,800 feet above sea level, South Pass City is one of Wyoming's highest settlements. Tall snow fences line the roads here in an attempt to halt the snow that blows all winter long. Although commonly called a ghost town, South Pass City never really died out. The town is now a State Historic Site, providing one of the most interesting and authentic historical settings in Wyoming.

Gold in the Hills

During the days of '49, many thousands of would-be miners streamed through South Pass on their way to California, little knowing that gold lay beneath their feet. Gold was first found in 1842, but its discoverer was killed by Indians; other miners faced similar fates. First to file a claim was Henry Reedal, who discovered what became known as the Carissa Lode in 1867. Shortly thereafter, the Miner's Delight Lode was discovered. The finds attracted an onslaught of miners, and by that fall the town of South Pass City had mushroomed into Wyoming's largest settlement, with nearly 3,000 residents.

The discovery of gold at South Pass helped propel the effort to make Wyoming a territory separate from Dakota, a move that took place the following year. At its rip-roaring peak, there was even an effort to make South Pass the Wyoming territorial capital. The town included six general stores, three butcher shops, several restaurants, two breweries, seven blacksmith shops, five hotels, and dozens of saloons and "sporting houses." In 1868, writer James Chisholm described his return to the town after an absence: "Late at night we arrived at Miner's Delight where everything was just as we had left it. The card table in the corner was in full blast. The parties whom we had left on a drunk were now sobering off and those we had left sober were getting on a drunk."

The Carissa Mine's shafts would eventually reach 400 feet down, and the mill would produce gold worth more than six million dollars. But this was primarily hard-rock mining, requiring large capital investments and long hours. The lack of water in this arid country meant that placer mining was possible only in the spring, while summers were spent toiling in the hard-rock mines for $5 a day. The Sweetwater mines were a short-lived bubble that burst almost as quickly as it grew. Instead of the hoped-for mother lode, miners found only small pockets of gold. Within five years most of the miners gave up and moved away. By 1875, fewer than a hundred people remained. But South Pass City refused to die. There were more booms (followed by busts) in the 1880s, 1890s, 1930s, and 1960s. Miners still come to these hills in search of gold.

WYOMING STATE MUSEUM

Esther Hobart Morris

Women's Suffrage

Given the rough mining crowd that jammed the streets of South Pass City, it seems odd to find the town at the center of the effort to gain equal rights for women. In late 1869, the first territorial representative from South Pass City, William Bright, introduced a women's-suffrage bill before the first territorial legislature. It was a measure supported by his wife and a number of other South Pass women but probably opposed by many of the local men. The measure surprised almost everyone by being passed and signed into law by Gov. John Campbell. In anger, the local judge resigned his post as justice of the peace for South Pass City, only to be replaced by a woman, Esther Hobart Morris. She was the first woman judge in America. In her eight and a half months of service, Morris tried 26 cases and gained recognition for her fairness, along with considerable national exposure.

The more exalted claim that Morris was the "Mother of Women's Suffrage" is suspect. In 1869, she is supposed to have held a tea party in which the South Pass City women extracted a promise from then-candidate William Bright to introduce legislation granting women the right to vote. The tea party tale was concocted by her son—a newspaper editor—after her death but gained entry into the history books as fact. A statue of Morris in front of the state capitol credits her with the bill. Morris herself never claimed any such thing, and in fact was not an active suffragist. According to Bright, the reason he introduced the legislation was not because of lobbying by local women but because "if Negroes had the right to vote, women like [his] wife and mother should also."

South Pass State Historic Site

In 1965, South Pass City's buildings risked being carted off to Southern California's Knott's Berry Farm theme park. With the help of Alice "Flaming Mame" Messick, a committee of Wyoming folks outbid the Californians for the buildings and managed to keep them. The following year, the state purchased the site and began the process of restoration. South Pass State Historic Site contains some 25 old buildings and 30,000 authentic artifacts, 90% of which actually came from the area. The buildings are open daily 9 a.m.-6 p.m. May 15 through September; $2 for nonresident adults, $1 for Wyoming residents, and free for kids under age 18. Call (307) 332-3684 for details. The rest of the year, visitors can wander the streets, but many items are in storage and the windows are covered with plywood.

On summertime weekends the old town comes alive with gold-panning and blacksmithing demonstrations by costumed old-timers. Be sure to drop by the Morris cabin for fresh-baked cookies. The **Old-Fashioned Fourth of July** celebration at South Pass is great fun, with country dancing, a barbecue, a pie-baking contest, horseshoe pitching, old-time music, exhibits, and lots of folks in old-time costumes.

Entrance fees are collected at the **visitor center** in what was once an 1890 dance hall. Inside are interpretive displays and a book and gift shop. The small theater shows a 28-minute video on the area's rich history. Pick up a brochure here describing the buildings. A short way up the street is the **Smith Sherlock Co. Store,** where you can check out the old items or buy licorice candy, sarsaparilla, and historical books. Next door is a small museum with historical photos.

Other interesting buildings that have been restored and furnished with original items include a blacksmith shop, a restaurant, butcher shop, hotel, miner's cabin, saloon, newspaper office, bank, school, and a dugout cave used to keep perishables cool. A gold mining exhibit on the hill behind town has a huge stamp mill, carts, and railroad track, along with other mining equipment. Gold panning demonstrations are given periodically throughout the summer. **Sweetwater County Jail,** built in 1870, is the oldest nonmilitary government building in Wyoming, and the **"pest house"** was a place where patients with contagious diseases were left in isolation. Built in 1869, this is the state's oldest hospital, though the level of treatment wasn't always the finest.

The reconstructed **Esther Morris cabin** stands at the eastern end of the row of buildings. Out front is a granite marker from 1939 that credits her with originating women's suffrage. Next to it is a more recent disclaimer. Adding more insult to injury is the fact that the reconstructed cabin is now believed to be in the wrong place; the actual Morris cabin site is not far away, and this was the location of a print shop instead.

Just east of the Morris cabin is a half-mile **nature trail** along Willow Creek offering the chance to explore the Carie Shields Mine (it produced $35,000 worth of gold) and other mines, cabins, and mill sights. Be careful where you walk around these old structures. Along the creek you're likely to see all sorts of animals, from beavers and bighorn sheep to mule deer and moose. Pick up a trail map at the Smith-Sherlock Store. The state also has a 10-km **volksmarch trail** that is popular with the RV crowd.

Practicalities

Outside the State Historic Site is a cluster of old log cabins owned by a handful of locals. **CNL Clothier** makes authentic natural-fiber historic clothing including Old West military clothing, dresses, and cowboy gear. The 1880-style cowboy slicker is especially popular. Everything here is based upon careful research and uses patterns from original garments. The clothes are often used in museums and Hollywood movies. The shop also sells Wyoming history books and has snacks. Call (307) 332-6810 for a copy of their mail-order catalog.

The Rock Shop, tel. (307) 332-7396, on State Hwy. 28 one mile west of the turnoff to South Pass City, has a cafe, bar, fuel, and cabins, but no rocks for sale. The lodge is fairly new and has a full restaurant and eight modern cabins that run $58 for up to four people. Open year-round, this is a popular wintertime stopping point for snowmobilers on the Continental Divide Snowmobile Trail as well as cross-country skiers. Budget. **South Pass Cross-Country Ski Trails**

take off from behind the Rock Shop, with a range of trails covering seven kilometers. The Wind River Nordic Ski Club maintains the trails, but they may not always be groomed.

Oregon Trail Trips

A number of companies offer wagon-train or horseback trips across various parts of Wyoming, including the Oregon Trail. These typically last five to seven days and cost $1,000-1,500 per person. The price includes horses, meals, equipment, and tents, but you'll need to bring a sleeping bag (they can rent you a bag). Contact the following companies for details on the various options: **Western Encounters,** tel. (307) 332-5434 or (800) 572-1230, www.horseriders.com; **Great Divide Tours,** tel. (307) 332-3123 or (800) 458-1915, www.rmisp.com/greatdivide; **Rocky Mountain Horseback Adventures,** tel. (307) 332-8535 or (800) 408-9149; and **Historic Trails West,** tel. (307) 266-4868 or (800) 327-4052, www.historictrailswest.com.

ATLANTIC CITY

The funky, friendly little town of Atlantic City has dirt streets, old log and stone buildings, and a delightfully infectious country atmosphere. It's the sort of town where old-timers plunk themselves atop the Merc's barstools to talk cattle, football, and the old days; where many homes (and the church, too) still have outhouses; and where the big event is the volunteer fire department picnic (late August). Residents pile up huge stacks of firewood to make it through the long, cold winters. The snow can get deep here near the top of the Continental Divide (elevation 7,660 feet). One winter, the drifts topped 27 feet and the snowplows didn't get in for several weeks! Most residents like the quiet beauty that winter brings to Atlantic City and depend upon snowmobiles and skis to get around. This is one of the few places left in Wyoming where the past seems so immediately present.

History

Atlantic City was formed in 1868 when gold mines had attracted thousands of miners to the Sweetwater Mining District. As miners arrived in South Pass, they spread out over the surrounding country in search of other gold deposits, founding the settlements of Atlantic City, Miner's Delight, and Lewiston at promising locations. As with most frontier towns, saloons vastly outnumbered churches in early Atlantic City. The first county sheriff owned a local brothel! **Fort Stambaugh** was established a few miles to the east in 1870 to protect miners from Sioux and Arapaho raids. It lasted only until 1878, and the buildings were auctioned off four years later.

In the 1880s, another miniboom hit as French capitalist Emile Granier built a 25-mile-long ditch from the Wind River Mountains to Atlantic City for hydraulic mining. The effort failed when the money ran out before gold could be found. Another boom hit in the late 1920s and '30s when a dredge worked its way down Rock Creek (leaving behind enormous piles of gravel). By the early 1960s, Atlantic City's population had been reduced to a handful of folks. Development of a U.S. Steel iron-ore (taconite) strip mine nearby brought prosperity after 1962, but the mine closed in 1983 and left behind a gaping pit now filled with water. Today Atlantic City depends upon tourism and summer homes. But as a local brochure notes, "The wind of this old gold town always whispers of another boom on its way."

The Merc

Atlantic City's main attractions are its mining-era buildings, many dating from the turn of the 20th century. The centerpiece is **Atlantic City Mercantile,** built in 1893 from adobe brick. Its false front is covered with old metal siding, and the interior is stuffed with stuffed heads, historic photos, mining artifacts, an old woodstove (usually in use), and a rich sense of the past. Pick up a brochure inside describing the town's many other historic buildings.

The "Merc," tel. (307) 332-5143 or (888) 257-0215, rents A-frame cabins for $55 s or d during the summer (Inexpensive) and allows RV parking June-Oct. for $10. The bar often has live music on Saturday nights, along with a piano where you can display your own musical talents at other times. Maybe someone decided to shoot the piano player and missed, since the mirror behind the bar has a bullet hole. The Merc's dinners are renowned throughout this part of Wyoming. In the front, you can munch on inexpensive but very good burgers all week. Back-

CALAMITY JANE

Calamity Jane—born Martha Jane Canary in 1852—is surely one of the most unusual characters to come out of the 19th-century West. In an era when the few women who found their way west almost invariably fell into one of three categories—housewife, washerwoman, or prostitute—Calamity Jane was all three, plus a lot more. At age 12, Martha Canary's family trekked west from Missouri to Montana. The trip took five months, and by the time they reached Virginia City she noted: "I was considered a remarkable good shot and a fearless rider for a girl of my age." Her mother died shortly after they arrived, and the family had a hard time surviving the harsh winter; Martha and her sisters were forced to beg on the streets. Her father died the following spring, and from that time on, Martha Canary was on her own. She landed in Miners Delight (near South Pass City) in 1870-71; here some claim she "entertained" men at Hyde's Hall Saloon. She certainly occasionally worked in "the sporting profession."

A Man's World

It was around this time that Calamity Jane gained her nickname. She claimed in a brief autobiography to have signed on as a scout for General Custer in Fort Russell, Wyoming, and to have soon thereafter "donned the uniform of a soldier. It was a bit awkward at first but I soon got to be perfectly at home in men's clothes." At other times she even masqueraded as a man and could by all accounts work, shoot, drink, and cuss as hard as the rough-edged men around her. While employed as a scout for General Crook's campaign near Sheridan she supposedly rescued the post commander, Captain Egan, from an Indian raid, helping him to safety. Egan then named her "Calamity Jane, the heroine of the plains." The name stuck for life.

Whether the story is true or not, Calamity Jane *did* live up to the sobriquet many times in later years. She was often found nursing men down with smallpox—she was immune to the disease—buying meals for the destitute, or assisting ill "soiled doves," even if it meant rolling a man for his money to pay the bills. She saved many lives at a time when life was short and cheap. This is not to suggest that Calamity Jane was the Mother Teresa of the Plains; the same woman who could care so much for others could also be loud and obnoxious when drunk—which was often. Her binges were legendary and landed her behind bars on numerous occasions, including a monthlong stint in the Rawlins jail for a drunken brawl with one of her many husbands and an eight-day trip to the Laramie jail for drunkenness. Beer would never do: "Give me a shot of booze and slop her over the brim" was always the bartender's order. As a friend (Deadwood madam Dora DuFran) noted:

YELLOWSTONE NATIONAL PARK

Her many friends—she had no enemies—would buy her drinks until she reached the howling stage. Then someone would steer her to the next saloon. Her time was limited in each one when that howling began. She would finally wind up by howling up and down Main Street. Even the law was paralyzed. Nothing could quell the howling completely, so some friend would escort her home with a quart of whiskey hugged to her breast to act as a night cap and put her to sleep. In the morning she would awaken with a hangover and start all over again. The only way to sober her up was to tell her someone was sick and needed her services. Not another drink would she take. Next day she would be ready for business.

In her autobiography, Calamity Jane said she married Clinton Burk in El Paso and went on to give birth to a girl "the very image of its father . . . but who has the temper of its mother." Nobody knows what became of the girl in later life, but Calamity went on to marry several other men. DuFran noted that "Jane had a very affectionate nature. There were very few preachers around to bother her, so whenever she got tired of one man she soon selected a new one." Calamity also alludes in her autobiography to an affair with famed gambler and gunfighter Wild Bill Hickok, and after her death a woman professed to be their illegitimate child raised by a wealthy East Coast family. Most folks put little stock in Calamity's relationship with Wild Bill, though the two did end up in Deadwood in 1876. A desperado shot Wild Bill in the back while he was seated at a gambling table; Calamity claimed to have helped capture the murderer.

Workin' and Boozin'

In later years, Calamity Jane seemed to spin her way across the West, stopping long enough to make money as a prospector, stagecoach driver, laundress, or some less seemly trade before getting the urge (or urging) to move on. Given the regimented code of behavior under which women lived in her era, it's easy to see how her appearance caused such a stir. Newspapers trumpeted her arrival in town, and saloons attracted crowds as her exploits grew with each telling. Someone was always willing to buy a round of drinks for the chance to hear Calamity's tales. As a young woman she was certainly attractive, but the years of hard drinking and rough living were not especially kind. As author Ellen Mueller put it, however, "perhaps the men standing in a saloon dead broke and hankering for a drink would have found the woman beautiful who would get drinks 'on the house' for everybody."

Though she spent a brief period with Buffalo Bill's Wild West Show, Calamity Jane's biggest moment of glory came in an 1895 return to Deadwood after a 17-year absence. A masquerade ball was held in her honor, and the local newspaper noted that

she was in great demand by the Dancers, many who were anxious to spend 25¢ to dance with her, just to have it to say they had danced with "Calamity Jane." She had a fair sized jag on board, and this, together with a vile cigar which she smoked, made her look anything but the beautiful woman which novelists and story writer have said so much about.

Calamity died in 1904, just 52 years old. Her deathbed plea was to be buried next to Wild Bill Hickok, who she said was the only man she had ever loved. Her funeral was one of the largest ever for Deadwood. Today, they lie next to each other at the Mt. Moriah Cemetery overlooking town. The testimony of fellow tough-living Dora DuFran again sums up Calamity's life best:

It is easy for a woman to be good who has been brought up with every protection from the evils of the world and with good associates. Calamity was a product of the wild and woolly west. She was not immoral; but unmoral. She took more on her shoulders than most women could. She performed many hundreds of deeds of kindness and received very little pay for her work. With her upbringing, how could she be anything but unmoral.

room guests, on the other hand, are treated to an old-timey setting of oil lanterns and pine walls and a menu (entrées $10-33) that includes aspen-grilled meats and seafood Thurs.-Sun. in the summer or Fri.-Sat. in winter. Come here on the fourth Wednesday of the month for a seven-course Basque dinner ($22). Reservations are advised.

More Buildings

The stone structure a block to the east of the Merc housed the **McAuley Store,** later Hyde's Hall. Calamity Jane once provided the entertainment in the saloon here. Up the hill is **St. Andrews Episcopal Church,** a rustic old log church built in 1913 and still used today. The **Gratrix Cabin,** a block east of the church, was built in the late 1860s and was home to Judge Buck Gratrix, a man who noted that he lived in three different counties, two territories, and one state while living in one place!

One of the most attractive structures in Atlantic City is the mint-condition **Miner's Delight Bed and Breakfast,** tel. (307) 332-0248 or (888) 292-0248. Originally known as the Carpenter Hotel, the building was constructed in 1895 and run as a boardinghouse for miners and others until 1961. Today it's a cozy B&B with two Victorian-style rooms with private baths in the main building ($75 s or d), along with four rustic hand-chinked log cabins ($60 s or d) with shared bath facilities. A full country breakfast is included. The owner also cooks up big seven-course dinners Thurs.-Sat. nights for $20 per person. They're served family-style. Call ahead for dinner reservations. Miner's Delight is open all year. Moderate.

Nearby Sights

Rock Creek flows through Atlantic City, and on the west end of town the banks are lined with huge piles of boulders left behind by the gold-dredging operations of the '30s. Fort Stambaugh Rd. heads east from Atlantic City and follows a 12-mile loop past the site of Fort Stambaugh (not marked) and the ghost town of Miner's Delight. A side road leads to **Lewiston,** another abandoned gold-mining town. The loop road is a very scenic drive through open grassland and scattered patches of young aspen and lodgepole. (Miners wiped out previous stands.) Antelope are sure to be seen along the way. The settlement called **Miner's Delight** consists of a dozen log buildings in various states of decay. A small beaver pond and graveyard are also in Miner's Delight, with other old mining buildings visible just west of here.

The road west from Atlantic City to South Pass City passes more old gold mines, notably the **Duncan Mine** (two miles out) and the famous **Carissa Mine,** just before dropping down to South Pass City. Most of the mines and buildings are on private land, and many contain hazardous structures and shafts without covers. Watch your step!

A little over seven miles south of Atlantic City is a monument to the **Willie Handcart Company.** In 1856, a large group of Mormon emigrants led by James G. Willie was caught in a series of early winter storms and camped here awaiting help and provisions from Salt Lake City. Sixty-seven of them died before they could reach the promised land. This and the Mormon handcart monuments at Rocky Ridge and Rock Creek are described in a pamphlet available at South Pass State Historic Site. (See the Central Wyoming chapter for details on another Mormon handcart disaster at Martin's Cove.)

Practicalities

Groceries are not available in either Atlantic City or South Pass, so stock up elsewhere. Atlantic City Mercantile and Miner's Delight B&B both have meals and rooms and are described above.

The BLM maintains two attractive campgrounds ($6; open June-Oct.) in young aspen stands—very pretty in the fall—along the Fort Stambaugh Loop Rd.: **Atlantic City Campground** and **Big Atlantic Gulch Campground.** Big Atlantic Gulch doesn't have water.

Atlantic City is one of 12 stops in early February's **Rocky Mountain Stage Stop Sled Dog Race,** an event that attracts some of the nation's best mushers with a $100,000 purse. The race begins and ends in Jackson. Call (307) 734-1163 for details, or check the website: www.wyomingstagestop.org.

FARSON AREA

Farson (pop. 300) stands at the busy highway junction where State Hwy. 28 and US Hwy. 191 greet each other. Locals live in trailer homes—the modern versions of log cabins—and work at a couple of local businesses. All around are long, straight roads, flat sagebrush desert, a few irrigated pastures, and antelope. It's a long way to anywhere else, so almost everyone stops for a road break at this oasis of sorts. In the simmering summer sun, **Farson Mercantile,** tel. (307) 273-9511, is crowded with people buying ice-cream cones to eat in the shade of the olive trees out front. Join the crowd; these are *huge* cones—"one scoop" is actually two or three scoops. No wonder so many Americans are overweight! The old brick two-story store is a classic country market.

Oregon Trail Cafe, tel. (307) 273-9631, named for the historic trail which passed right through the center of Farson, offers standard road grub, while at **Mitch's Cafe,** tel. (307) 273-9606, you're more likely to find locals atop the burlwood seats.

Sitzman's Motel, tel. (307) 273-9246, charges $35-45 s or d, but is often full in midsummer and during the fall hunting season. Inexpensive.

Park RVs behind Farson Mercantile at **Oregon Trail Campground,** tel. (307) 273-5586; $4 for tents or $12 for RVs. It's open May-September.

HEADING SOUTH

Four miles south of Farson is tiny **Eden,** where irrigated green fields bring the arid landscape alive. Of note here is the old **Oregon Trail Baptist Church,** with its brown log walls, quaint bell tower, and back window facing the Wind River Mountains. The view probably makes it hard to concentrate on the service. Kitty-corner across the road is the Eden Saloon, where the view may not be as great, but after a few beers it really doesn't matter. Bicentennial Park makes a shady place to enjoy a picnic. South of Eden, US Hwy. 191 cruises into the bleak Bad Lands Hills country on its way to Rock Springs. Killpecker Dunes rise on the eastern horizon.

HEADING NORTH

Immediately north of Farson, the highway crosses the Big Sandy River—little more than a creek much of the year, with Big Sandy Reservoir (free camping here) holding back much of its water for irrigation. Flat irrigated fields of hay surround Farson. As you continue north to Pinedale (58 miles), the jagged snow-topped crowns of the Wind River Mountains loom ever larger and the sagebrush grows more abundant on the arid landscape rolling away to the mountains. The highway crosses both the **Sublette Cutoff**—one of the original routes to Oregon Country—and the 1858 **Lander Cutoff,** the first federal road west of the Mississippi. Tune in to KQSW (96.5 FM) for country tunes to speed you on your way.

A gravel road that begins two miles east of Farson and heads north along Little Sandy Creek and then northwest to Boulder is even more dramatic, passing along the foothills of the Winds. It's used for access to the Big Sandy Trailhead into the Bridger Wilderness. This is one of my favorite drives in Wyoming. Clouds often drape the distant mountains, but when they part—like curtains at a Broadway premier—they reveal the 13,000-foot crest of the Wind River Mountains in all its majesty. This is truly one of the classic western vistas, and the interplay of land, light, and sky creates an unforgettable scene.

The land knocks you out: mountains climb above the distant plain, crowning the eastern horizon with slanting patches of enormous rock faces and snow-mantled slopes, reflecting back the light from a westering sun. Antelope glance up as you drive past; a rough-legged hawk hunches down on a fence post; several horses paw the ground. Periodically a narrow set of pickup-truck tracks angles over the horizon to some remote ranch. In places like this, it is hard not to love the wildly beautiful state of Wyoming.

PINEDALE

Located in the upper Green River Valley, with the Wind River Mountains creating a dramatic backdrop, Pinedale (pop. 1,300) is surrounded by hay-filled meadows, grazing horses, and modern ranchettes. In addition to the economic mainstays of ranching and tourism, Pinedale is also a minor governmental center with BLM, Forest Service, Game and Fish, and Sublette County offices.

Pinedale is similar in many ways to its neighbor across the mountains, Dubois. Both towns were long dependent upon ranching and logging but are now starting to appreciate the visitors who come simply to enjoy the country. Pinedale has a solid core of downtown businesses, new log houses sprouting on the outskirts, and its first national chain operation (a Best Western motel). Residents fear that it could become "another Jackson," but the town has kept its Old West flavor without falling (yet) under the complete domination of the almighty tourist dollar. Wealthy people from all over the nation have bought up old ranches around Pinedale, turning them into summer homes; their small jets crowd the tarmac—if it can be called that—at the local airport. Most of these folks are corporate bigwigs, such as the head of PepsiCo, but others include John Barlow (former lyricist for the Grateful Dead) and James Baker III (former secretary of state).

During the Drift each fall, cowboys separate cattle from local ranches.

History

The first inhabitants of the Upper Green River Valley were the Shoshone, Gros Ventre, Sheepeater, and Crow Indians who hunted buffalo, elk, and antelope in this rich country. Whites first came as explorers and fur trappers in the early 1800s, and by the 1830s this was the "capital" of the fur trade in the Rockies. Six different rendezvous were held along the Upper Green River. The first white settler arrived with his cattle in 1878, and within a few years a small trading center sprang up alongside Pine Creek. The town prospered with development of the tie-hack industry in the late 19th century. Pinedale was platted in 1899 and later became the Sublette County seat.

Catching the Drift

The Upper Green River is still very important cattle country; in fact, it's the largest range allotment in the entire national forest system, home to 7,500 cattle. Get here in June to watch cowboys (locals more commonly use the term "riders") pushing the cattle into the mountains. Some are driven as far as 90 miles from the winter range in the desert. Cattle graze in the mountains all summer, watched over by a handful of riders who stay in cabins or trailers. Each fall, the cattle drift back down from their summer home in the mountains when cool mid-October weather hits the high country. Six miles north of Pinedale at the junction of US Hwy. 191 and State Hwy. 352, cowboys from 20 local ranches sort out the 300-700 cattle that pile up against fences in the "Green River Drift."

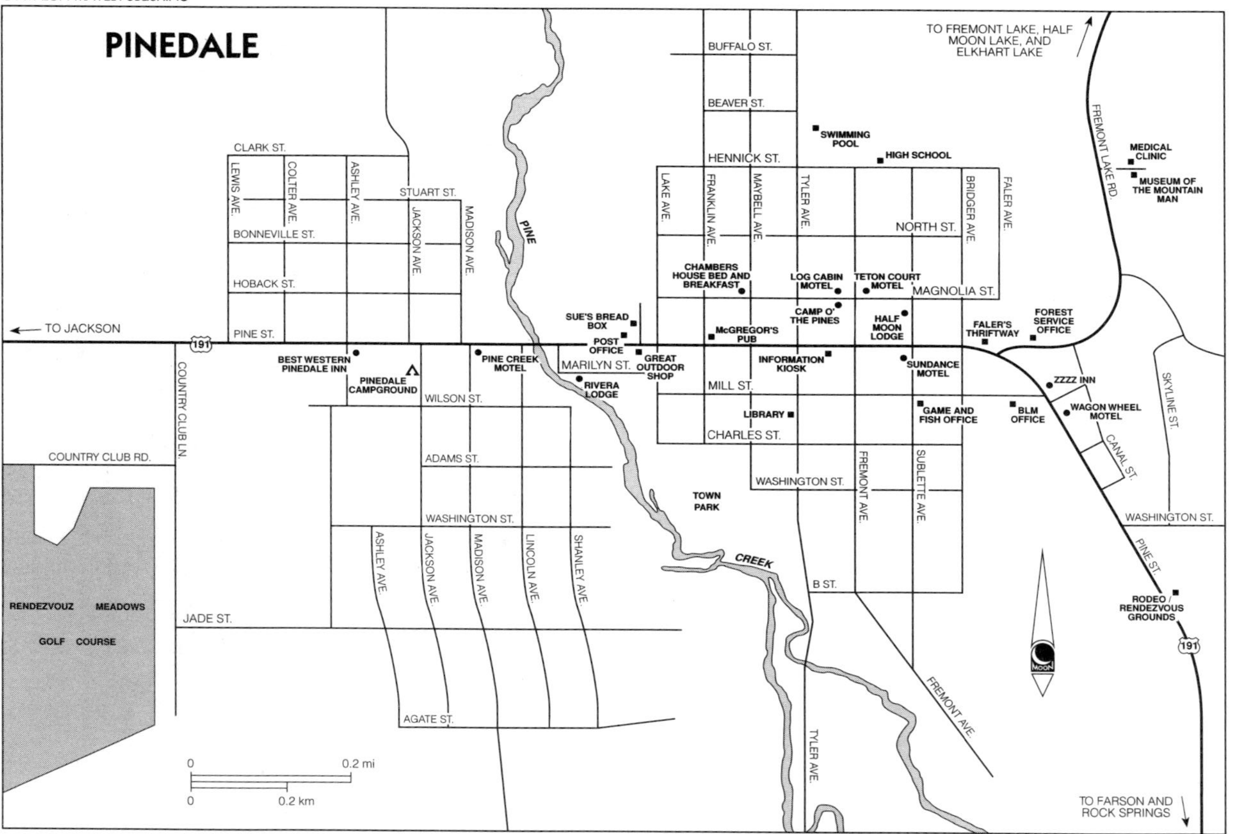
© AVALON TRAVEL PUBLISHING
PINEDALE
TO FREMONT LAKE, HALF MOON LAKE, AND ELKHART LAKE
BUFFALO ST.
BEAVER ST.
SWIMMING POOL
HIGH SCHOOL
HENNICK ST.
FREMONT LAKE RD.
MEDICAL CLINIC
MUSEUM OF THE MOUNTAIN MAN
CLARK ST.
STUART ST.
LEWIS AVE.
COLTER AVE.
ASHLEY AVE.
JACKSON AVE.
MADISON AVE.
BONNEVILLE ST.
HOBACK ST.
PINE ST.
PINE
LAKE AVE.
FRANKLIN AVE.
MAYBELL AVE.
TYLER AVE.
NORTH ST.
BRIDGER AVE.
FALER AVE.
CHAMBERS HOUSE BED AND BREAKFAST
LOG CABIN MOTEL
TETON COURT MOTEL
MAGNOLIA ST.
CAMP O' THE PINES
HALF MOON LODGE
FALER'S THRIFTWAY
FOREST SERVICE OFFICE
SUE'S BREAD BOX
McGREGOR'S PUB
POST OFFICE
TO JACKSON
191
BEST WESTERN PINEDALE INN
PINEDALE CAMPGROUND
PINE CREEK MOTEL
MARILYN ST.
GREAT OUTDOOR SHOP
INFORMATION KIOSK
SUNDANCE MOTEL
ZZZZ INN
SKYLINE ST.
RIVERA LODGE
MILL ST.
WILSON ST.
GAME AND FISH OFFICE
BLM OFFICE
WAGON WHEEL MOTEL
LIBRARY
CHARLES ST.
CANAL ST.
COUNTRY CLUB RD.
COUNTRY CLUB LN.
ADAMS ST.
WASHINGTON ST.
FREMONT AVE.
SUBLETTE AVE.
TOWN PARK
WASHINGTON ST.
WASHINGTON ST.
ASHLEY AVE.
JACKSON AVE.
MADISON AVE.
LINCOLN AVE.
SHANLEY AVE.
CREEK
PINE ST.
B ST.
RENDEZVOUZ MEADOWS
GOLF COURSE
JADE ST.
RODEO / RENDEZVOUS GROUNDS
191
FREMONT AVE.
AGATE ST.
0
0.2 mi
0
0.2 km
TYLER AVE.
TO FARSON AND ROCK SPRINGS

MOUNTAIN MEN

The era of the fur trapper is one of the most colorful slices of American history, a time when a rough and hardy breed of men took to the Rockies in search of furs and adventure. Romanticized in such films as *Jeremiah Johnson,* the trappers actually played but a brief role in history and numbered fewer than 1,000 individuals. Their real importance lay in acting as the opening wedge for the West, a vanguard for the settlers and gold miners who would follow their paths—often led by these same mountain men.

The Fur Business

Fashion sent men into the Rockies in the first place, since the waterproof underfur of a beaver could be used to create the beaver hat, all the rage in the early part of the 19th century. (It cost a month's wages for a man in England to buy a fine beaver hat in the 1820s!) Beavers in the eastern U.S. were soon trapped out, forcing trappers to head farther and farther west. Several companies competed for the lucrative fur market, but John Jacob Astor's American Fur Company proved the most successful. In 1811, Astor sent a party of men across the Rockies to the mouth of the Columbia to build a trading post and then set up a chain of posts across the West. The men—known as the Astorians—were probably the first whites to follow the route that would later become the Oregon Trail.

John Jacob Astor's trappers went head to head against the Rocky Mountain Fur Company, which was owned at various times by some of the most famous mountain men—Jedediah Smith, David Jackson, William and Milton Sublette, Jim Bridger, Thomas Fitzpatrick, and others. Competition for furs became so intense that Astor's men began following Jim Bridger and Tom Fitzpatrick to discover their trapping grounds. After trying unsuccessfully to shake the men tailing them, Bridger and Fitzpatrick deliberately headed into the heart of Blackfeet country, where Indians killed the leader of Astor's party and managed to leave Bridger with an arrowhead in his shoulder that was not removed until three years later.

A large number of Indians (particularly from the Flathead and Nez Percé tribes) were also involved in the fur trade, and a standard Indian trade value was 240 beaver pelts for a riding horse. In the mountains, anything from the world back east had considerable value: guns sold for $100 each, blankets for $40 apiece, tobacco for $3 a pound, and alcohol (often diluted) for up to $64 a gallon. After just two years of such trading, William Ashley retired with an $80,000 profit. Control of the fur market continued to change hands as the Rocky Mountain Fur Company and the American Fur Company competed with each other and with a mysterious company headed by Capt. Benjamin Bonneville,

the Summer Rendezvous

YELLOWSTONE NATIONAL PARK

which some believe was a front for the U.S. Army to explore the West.

Most of the men who trapped in the Rockies were hired and outfitted by the fur companies, but others worked under contract and traded furs for overpriced supplies. Many men found themselves in debt to the company at the end of a season. At the top of the heap were the free trappers, men who worked either alone or with others but who sold their furs to whoever offered the highest prices. Some men—primarily those who brought trade goods to the rendezvous—became rich in the process. Others, such as John Colter, Jim Bridger, James Beckwourth, Jedediah Smith, Thomas Fitzpatrick, and Kit Carson, would achieve fame for their rich knowledge of the land and their ability to survive against insurmountable odds. Many trappers married Indian women, learned sign language and various Indian tongues, and lived in tepees.

Trappers worked through the winter months when the beaver pelts were their finest; most summers were spent hunting and fishing, or hanging out with fellow trappers or friendly Indians. In his *Journal of a Trapper 1834-1843,* Osborne Russell described a campfire scene among fellow mountain men:

> *A large fire was soon blazing encircled with sides of Elk ribs and meat cut in slices supported on sticks down which the grease ran in torrents The repast being over the jovial tale goes round the circle the peals of loud laughter break upon the stillness of the night which after being mimicked in the echo from rock to rock it dies away in the solitary. Every tale puts an auditor in mind of something similar to it but under different circumstances which being told the "laughing part" gives rise to increasing merriment and furnishes more subjects for good jokes and witty sayings such as Swift never dreamed of Thus the evening passed with eating drinking and stories enlivened with witty humor until near Midnight all being wrapped in their blankets lying around the fire gradually falling to sleep one by one until the last tale is "encored" by the snoring of the drowsy audience The Speaker takes the hint breaks off the subject and wrapping his blanket more closely about him soon joins the snoring party—The light of the fire being supersed by that of the Moon just rising from behind the Eastern Mountains a sullen gloom is cast over the remaining fragments of the feast and all is silent except the occasional howling of the solitary wolf on the neighboring mountain whose senses are attracted by the flavors of roasted meat but fearing to approach nearer he sits upon a rock and bewails his calamities in piteous moans which are re-echoed among the Mountains.*

A good trapper could take in upward of 150 beaver in a year, worth $4-6 apiece. It was an arduous job, and the constant threat of attacks by the Blackfeet Indians made it even more difficult. The great letting-go came with the summer rendezvous, an event anticipated for months ahead of time.

The Rendezvous

William H. Ashley, founder of the Rocky Mountain Fur Company, was one of the most important figures in the fur trade. In 1822, he ran an ad in a St. Louis paper that read:

> *To Enterprising Young Men. The subscriber wishes to engage ONE HUNDRED MEN, to ascend the river Missouri to its source, there to be employed for one, two or three years.—For particulars enquire of Major Andrew Henry, near the Lead Mines, in the County of Washington, (who will ascend with, and command the party) or to the subscriber at St. Louis.*
> *—Wm. H. Ashley.*

Ashley's company of men—along with $10,000 in supplies—made it up into the Yellowstone River country, where he left them the following year, promising to resupply them in 1825 on the Henrys

(continued on next page)

MOUNTAIN MEN

(continued)

Fork near its confluence with the Green River, along the present-day Wyoming-Utah border. Thus began the first rendezvous. They would take place every summer until 1840. Ashley failed to bring booze that first summer and the rendezvous only lasted two days. In future years, however, the whiskey flowed freely and the festivities lasted for weeks.

The rendezvous—a French word meaning "appointed place of meeting"—was a time when both white and Indian trappers could sell their furs, trade for needed supplies and Indian squaws (the women had little say in the matter but most took considerable pleasure in the arrangement), meet with old friends, get rip-roaring drunk, and engage in storytelling, gambling, gun duels, and contests of all sorts. Horse racing, wrestling bouts, and shooting contests were favorites—Kit Carson killed Shunar, a big French bully, in a duel during one of the Green River rendezvous. Debauchery reigned supreme in these three-week-long affairs, and by the time they were over, many of the trappers had lost their entire year's earnings.

During the heyday of the fur trade, a common saying was "all trails lead to the Seedskeedee [Green River]." Six rendezvous were held here in the 1830s, others were held in the Wind River/Popo Agie River area, on Ham's Fork of the Green River, and in Idaho and Utah. Sites were chosen where there was space for up to 500 mountain men and 3,000 Indians, plenty of game, ample grazing for the thousands of horses, and good water. Not coincidentally, all were held in Shoshone country rather than farther east or north, where the hostile Sioux, Blackfeet, and Crow held sway. Despite such precautions, over half of Ashley's men were scalped by Indians.

Changing Times

The end of the rendezvous system—and most of the Rocky Mountain fur trapping—came about for a variety of reasons: overtrapping, the financial panic of 1837, and the growing use of other materials—particularly the South American nutria and Chinese silk—for hats. In addition, permanent trading posts such as Fort Laramie drew Indians away from the mountains to trade for buffalo robes instead of beaver furs. By 1840, when the last rendezvous was held on the banks of the Green River near present-day Pinedale, it was obvious there would be no more. One of the longtime trappers, Robert Newell, said to his partner, Joseph Meek:

> *We are done with this life in the mountains—done with wading in beaver dams, and freezing or starving alternately—done with Indian trading and Indian fighting. The fur trade is dead in the Rocky Mountains, and it is no place for us now, if ever it was. We are young yet, and have life before us. We cannot waste it here; we cannot or will not return to the States. Let us go down to the Wallamet and take farms.*

Museum of the Mountain Man

Pinedale's Museum of the Mountain Man, 700 E. Hennick St., tel. (307) 367-4101, is open daily 10 a.m.-6 p.m. May-Sept., and by appointment the rest of the year. Entrance costs $4 for adults, $3 for seniors, $2 for ages 6-12; free for under age six. Located on a hill overlooking town, this modern, spacious museum contains displays, artifacts, and memorabilia from the fur-trapping era. Jim Bridger's rifle is here, as are a covered wagon and a fascinating educational video about the fur trade. You'll learn about the daily lives of the different types of trappers (free vs. company men), how they trapped beaver and processed furs, and how the market for hats helped open the American West. Downstairs are changing displays on the history of Sublette County, including a VD poster from WW II that warns: "Use Prophylaxis. Fool the Axis!" A gift shop sells historical books. The museum puts on special programs, living history demonstrations, and evening lectures on the history of the West during the rendezvous.

ACCOMMODATIONS AND CAMPING

Motels

Pinedale has a number of attractive lodging places offering friendly and clean rooms in pleasant settings. Because of this, more and more folks are choosing to spend time in Pinedale on their way to Yellowstone, thus avoiding the crowds and higher rates in Jackson. It's a good idea to book a month ahead for July and August to be sure of space. Accommodations are listed below from least to most expensive. Add a four percent tax to these rates.

Wagon Wheel Motel, 407 S. US Hwy. 191, tel. (307) 367-2871, has a range of room types, but all are in good condition and spacious. Prices run $40-70 s or $50-85 d. Inexpensive-Moderate.

Teton Court Motel, 123 E. Magnolia, tel. (307) 367-4317, charges $42 s or $48 d. The older rooms are clean, and kitchenettes are available. Open May-October. Inexpensive.

The appropriately named **Log Cabin Motel,** 49 E. Magnolia, tel. (307) 367-4579, features 10 attractive and beautifully maintained cabins. Built in 1929, they are now on the National Register of Historic Places. The smallest cabins go for $45 s or $55 d. Larger two-bedroom units sleep four, have kitchenettes, and cost $70-75 s or $75-90 d. Open mid-May through September. Inexpensive.

Rivera Lodge, 442 W. Marilyn, tel. (307) 367-2424, is right in town, but it's off the main street and quiet. The cozy and well-maintained cabins sit along Pine Creek and are open May to mid-October. Most have kitchenettes. Rates are $49-80 s or d. Friendly owners, too. Inexpensive-Moderate.

Camp O' The Pines, 38 N. Fremont, tel. (307) 367-4536, has older rooms for $50-75 s or d; kitchenettes are $75 and sleep four. Inexpensive-Moderate.

Half Moon Lodge Motel, 46 N. Sublette, tel. (307) 367-2851, has recently remodeled rooms for $56 s or $60-65 d. It's open May-October. Moderate.

Sun Dance Motel, 148 E. Pine, tel. (307) 367-4336 or (800) 833-9178, has clean and quiet rooms for $59-65 s or d. Other options include a suite or cabin with kitchenette (both sleep six) for $89. The web address is www.98.net/sundance. Open May-October. Inexpensive-Expensive.

Pine Creek Ranch, tel. (307) 367-6887, is a gorgeous century-old cabin on the edge of town along Pine Creek. The three-bedroom log cabin is perfect for families (it sleeps eight) and includes a full kitchen, living room with fireplace, and two baths. Rates are $60 s or $85 d. Moderate.

Pine Creek Inn, 650 W. Pine, tel. (307) 367-2191 or (888) 839-7446, charges $62-68 s or d for rooms, including some with kitchenettes. They may be closed during the winter months. Moderate.

ZZZZ Inn, 327 S. US Hwy. 191, tel. (307) 367-2121, has rooms starting at $85; open late May-September. Expensive.

Pinedale's largest motel is the **Best Western Pinedale Inn,** 850 W. Pine St., tel. (307) 367-6869 or (800) 528-1234. Rooms are $89-99 s or d, and amenities include an indoor pool, jacuzzi, fitness center, and continental breakfast. Don't expect the friendliest service here. Expensive.

Bed and Breakfasts

Along US Hwy. 191 a mile west of Pinedale, **Window on the Winds B&B,** tel. (307) 367-2600 or (888) 367-1345, offers a sweeping view of the mountains from the central room, plus a sunroom with jacuzzi. It's a warm and friendly place with four guest rooms (private or shared baths), an outdoor hot tub, and a filling breakfast. Rates are $75 d. Children and pets are welcome. The Internet address is www.cruising-america.com/windowonwinds. Moderate.

Right in town you'll find **Chambers House B&B,** 111 W. Magnolia St., tel. (307) 367-2168 or (800) 567-2168, an elegant two-story log home. Inside are five guest rooms (private or shared baths) and two sitting rooms. Built in 1933, the home was recently renovated. Rates are $50-95 s or $60-105 d, including a full breakfast. Children and dogs are welcome. Moderate-Expensive.

Pole Creek Ranch B&B, three miles southeast of Pinedale, tel. (307) 367-4433, is a modern log home in the country with an outdoor jacuzzi, a barn, and corrals. Three guest rooms share a bath; horse riding and buggy rides are available by arrangement. The view of the Wind River Mountains is impressive, and the friendly owners will be happy to share their Christianity. Horseback and covered-wagon rides are also available. Rates are $45 s or $55 d, including a full breakfast. Kids and pets welcome. The website is www.bbonline.com/wy/polecreek. Inexpensive.

Guest Ranches and Resorts

Half Moon Lake Resort, tel. (307) 367-6373, www.halfmoonlake.com, is a full-service facility overlooking the lake for which it is named. Stay in modern log cabins with fridges and microwaves ($105-170), and enjoy meals in a pleasant restaurant with a redwood deck along the shore. Fishing boats, pontoon boats, and canoes are available for rent, along with horseback riding, pack trips, and fishing. The restaurant serves three meals a day. Expensive-Luxury.

Five miles northeast of Pinedale on the south end of Fremont Lake is **Lakeside Lodge Resort & Marina,** tel. (307) 367-2221, www.lakeside-lodge.com. Accommodations include rustic log cabins with shared baths ($60 s or $65 d), standard motel rooms ($60 s or $65 d), and new log cabins along the shore containing fireplaces, two queen beds, and private baths for $105 s or $115 d. RV hookups are $20. The lodge is open mid-May to mid-October. Moderate-Premium.

Overlooking the Green River 30 miles north of Pinedale, **Elk Ridge Lodge,** tel. (307) 367-2553, has modern guest-ranch accommodations by the night ($70 d) in modern log buildings on the edge of the national forest. Meals, horseback rides, fishing, and float trips are available in summer, and the lodge is a destination for snowmobilers in winter. Moderate.

Fort William Guest Ranch, eight miles east of town, tel. (307) 367-4670, is a rustic lodge with nightly accommodations ($75 d including breakfast), a hot tub, restaurant, lounge, and dance floor, plus an abundance of nearby outdoor activities: horseback riding, guided pack trips, spot-packing, and fly-fishing. Open May-October. Find the ranch on the web at www.fortwilliam.com. Moderate.

Green River Guest Ranch, 25 miles northwest of Pinedale, tel. (307) 367-2314, has horseback rides, overnight cookout trips, pack trips, gear drops, spot-pack trips, and guided fishing and float trips. In the winter it rents snowmobiles and offers guided snowmobile tours. Guest stay by the night in comfortably rustic cabins with baths. Rates are $60 d in remodeled rooms, or $25 per person in the bunkhouse. Also here is The Place Restaurant & Bar. Inexpensive.

Twenty-nine miles north of Pinedale, miles up the Green River Lakes Rd., the secluded and historic **DC Bar Guest Ranch,** tel. (307) 367-2268 or (888) 803-7316, has room for up to 25 guests in seven cabins. Amenities include a hot tub, horseback rides, fishing, and pack trips. A two-night minimum stay is required, but most folks stay at least five nights. The all-inclusive rate is very reasonable: $130 for two people per night. In addition to summertime use, the ranch is popular for wintertime snowmobiling and fall hunting trips. Get details by calling or visiting the website: www.bwo.com. Premium.

Flying A Ranch, tel. (307) 367-2385 (summers) or (800) 678-6543, is for adults only and has space for just 12 guests in a casual Western atmosphere. Horseback rides are the featured attraction, but guests also enjoy wildlife watching, hiking, fishing, mountain-biking, or simply relaxing with a book or luxuriating in the hot tub. The ranch was built in 1929, and both the main lodge and cabins have been carefully restored. Each cabin features handmade furniture, a private bath, kitchenette, and fireplace or woodstove. Some provide extraordinary views of the Wind River Mountains. Weekly rates at Flying A are $2,400 for two people, all-inclusive. Get more information at www.flyinga.com. Luxury.

Lozier's Box R Ranch, near Cora, tel. (307) 367-2291 or (800) 822-8466, is a working cattle ranch with accommodations for 20 guests. Dudes get horseback rides, whitewater float trips, fishing, and the chance to head into the backcountry on pack trips and drop camps. It's open late May to mid-September. All-inclusive weekly rates are $1,790-2,590 for two people. The web address is www.boxr.com. Luxury.

See also Boulder Lake Lodge, described under Boulder below.

Camping

The closest public camping is **Fremont Lake Campground** ($7; open late May to mid-September), seven miles northeast of Pinedale along the lake. Make campsite reservations ($8.65 extra charge) by calling (877) 444-6777, or make them on the web at www.reserveusa.com. Even if you aren't staying here or planning any wilderness hikes from the trailheads, *do* take the 15-mile (paved) drive from Pinedale to road's end, where you'll find the free Upper Fremont Lake Campground. The rugged crest of the Wind River Mountains forms a dramatic vista along the way. **Half Moon Lake Campground** ($4; open June to mid-September) is on the northwest shore of Half Moon Lake, 10 miles northeast of Pinedale. A dozen other Forest Service and BLM campgrounds are dotted all along the western side of the Wind River Mountains. See Pinedale Vicinity for additional BLM campsites northwest of Pinedale.

The private **Pinedale Campground,** 204 S. Jackson Ave, tel. (307) 367-4555, charges $11 for tents, $18 for RVs; open May-October. Showers for noncampers are $4. This is ye olde parking lot masquerading as a "campground."

Lakeside Lodge Resort & Marina at Fremont Lake, five miles northeast of town, tel. (307) 367-2221, charges $10 for tents and $20 for RVs. Open mid-May to mid-October.

FOOD

Reflecting its proximity to Jackson, Pinedale's food prices are higher than in most parts of the state—but so is the quality. Travelers will find a good mix of fare, from traditional steak houses to more yuppified eateries.

Breakfast and Lunch

In existence for more than three decades, **Patio Grill,** 35 W. Pine, tel. (307) 367-4611, serves dependably good family breakfasts, along with lunch and dinners. **Sue's Bread Box,** 423 W. Pine (behind the post office), tel. (307) 367-2150, has earthy breakfasts and deli lunches with homemade soups and sourdough bread. Be sure to get one of the half-pound cinnamon rolls.

For a filling lunchtime pizza buffet, head to **Wind River Rendezvous Pizza,** 4 Country Club Lane, tel. (307) 367-6760. **Grinders,** 807 W. Pine, tel. (307) 367-4769, has decent sub sandwiches and is a hangout for local high school kids.

Dinner

A favorite of both locals and visitors, **McGregor's Pub,** 25 N. Franklin Ave., tel. (307) 367-4443, specializes in prime rib, steak, and seafood but also has good lunches served on an outside deck in the summer. Located next to the Cowboy Bar, **Della Rose Restaurant,** 120 W. Pine, tel. (307) 367-2810, has family meals, fresh-baked pastries, and gourmet coffees.

LaVoie Brewery & Grill, 406 W. Pine St., tel. (307) 367-2337, provides fresh-brewed beers and a light menu that includes nachos, sandwiches, bratwurst, and grilled (!) pizzas. It's a fine place to relax with the locals over a brew.

Elk Country Bar-B-Q, 709 W. Pine St., tel. (307) 367-2252, cranks out delicious Texas-style barbecued brisket and pork ribs grilled over mesquite fires. This isn't a white-linen sort of place; the meals come on paper plates. Open summers only.

Calamity Jane's, in the Corral Bar at 30 W. Pine, tel. (307) 367-2469, is the place to go for burgers and fries, grinders, Mexican food, and pizzas. But it's a bar, so the atmosphere might not be for everyone.

Stockman's Steak Pub, 117 W. Pine, tel. (307) 367-4563, has the finest steaks in Pinedale, plus a good salad bar, veal, seafood, and chicken.

Eight miles east of town on Fall Creek Rd. is **Fort William Guest Ranch,** tel. (307) 367-4670, where the specialties include thick steaks, beans, and other hearty fare served Thurs.-Mon. in the summer. For a meal with a view, drive five miles northeast of Pinedale along Fremont Lake to **Lakeside Lodge Resort and Marina,** tel. (307) 367-2221. Fine food and stunning vistas of the Wind River Mountains.

Groceries

Get groceries at **Faler's Thriftway,** 341 E. Pine, tel. (307) 367-2131. Inside is a deli, plus one of the largest collections of critter heads anywhere. The city park at Washington and Tyler is a peaceful place for picnic lunches.

ENTERTAINMENT AND EVENTS

Entertainment

Both **Cowboy Bar,** 104 W. Pine, tel. (307) 367-4520, and **Stockman's Bar,** 16 N. Maybell Ave., tel. (307) 367-4562, have live country-and-western tunes some summer weekends. Stockman's attracts a younger crowd. **Fort William Guest Ranch,** eight miles east of Pinedale, tel. (307) 367-4670, is a popular place to unwind in a cozy atmosphere; open May-Oct. only. Out at Green River Guest Ranch (25 miles northwest of Pinedale), **The Place Restaurant & Bar,** tel. (307) 367-2314, has a pool table surrounded by mounted animal heads.

Events

Pinedale is one of 12 stops in early February's **Rocky Mountain Stage Stop Sled Dog Race,** an event that attracts some of the nation's best mushers with a $100,000 purse. The race begins and ends in Jackson. Call (307) 734-1163 for details, or check the website: www.wyomingstagestop.org.

Pinedale's main event is the **Green River Rendezvous,** held the second weekend in July. Established in 1936, this is one of the oldest celebrations of the mountain-man rendezvous era and commemorates the raucous activities of the 1830s on nearby Horse Creek. The highlight is the rendezvous pageant, which attracts more than 2,000 visitors. Other activities include a parade, family carnival, fur and bead trading, living-history demonstrations, a shoot-out, rodeos, live music, arts and crafts, and a traditional buffalo barbecue featuring foods similar to those eaten at the original rendezvous.

RECREATION

Summer Recreation

Swim year-round at the high school's **indoor pool,** tel. (307) 367-2832. Golfers will enjoy Pinedale's nine-hole **Rendezvous Meadows Golf Course,** tel. (307) 367-4252.

Horseback rides are available from Fort William Guest Ranch, tel. (307) 367-4670; Elk Ridge Lodge, tel. (307) 367-2553; DC Bar Guest Ranch, tel. (307) 367-2268; Boulder Lake Lodge, tel. (307) 537-5400 or (800) 788-5401; and Pole Creek Ranch B&B, tel. (307) 367-4433.

Stop by the **Pinedale Ranger District office** at 29 E. Fremont Lake Rd., tel. (307) 367-4326, for maps ($4) and hiking info on trails in the nearby Bridger Wilderness. The office can also provide a listing of fishing guides and permitted wilderness outfitters.

The **Great Outdoor Shop,** 332 W. Pine, tel. (307) 367-2440, www.greatoutdoorshop.com, sells quality outdoor gear of all types, along with topo maps. They also offer a **taxi service** to Wind River Mountain trailheads from Pinedale, Jackson, or Rock Springs. Ask about equipment rentals in the summer. Faler's Thriftway has additional outdoor supplies.

The **Wilderness Adventure Center,** tel. (888) 419-9992, www.wildernesscenter.com, provides outdoor education for ages 9-18 at a camp on Burnt Lake east of Pinedale. Established in 1956 by the Skinner family, this was the first youth-oriented wilderness program of its kind in the nation. The family tradition continues, and Todd Skinner—one of the world's best mountaineers—teaches some courses. Kids learn mountaineering, rock climbing, horseback riding, and other skills during two-week summer sessions.

On the Water

The east slope of the Wind River Mountains contains several large lakes created when glaciers retreated after the last major ice age some 10,000 years ago. The terminal moraines they left behind acted as dams, although some have been enlarged with human-created dams in recent years. The lakes are very popular with anglers. **Fremont Lake** is Wyoming's second-largest natural lake, reaching 12 miles in length, a half mile across, and up to 600 feet deep. It's just three miles northeast of Pinedale and is famous for Mackinaw that approach 40 pounds. Fremont has three Forest Service campgrounds along its shore (free to $7; one accessible only by boat). Rent a fishing boat, canoe, kayak, or pontoon boat from **Lakeside Lodge Resort & Marina,** tel. (307) 367-2221, open May through early September. Accommodations and a restaurant are also here.

Other lakes of note are **Half Moon Lake, Willow Lake,** and **Boulder Lake.** (See Wind River Mountains earlier in this chapter for info on the Green River and New Fork Lakes.) All of these lakes have Forest Service campgrounds ($4) and trails that lead into the Bridger Wilderness. In addition, the BLM maintains free camping areas on the west end of Boulder Lake and at Scab Creek (southeast of Boulder Lake).

The lakes and streams near Pinedale offer outstanding fishing for cutthroat, rainbow, brook, Mackinaw, golden, and brown trout, plus grayling and whitefish. A number of local outfitters offer float-fishing trips down the Green River; see the chamber of commerce for a listing. **Two Rivers Emporium,** tel. (307) 367-4131 or (800) 329-4353, www.2rivers.net, is a good place to find fly-fishing supplies and conditions, or to book a drift trip. Canoeists or kayakers will also enjoy floating stretches of the Green. The Forest Service office has details. Swim at Pinedale's Olympic-sized **indoor pool,** tel. (307) 367-2832, at the high school on the corner of Hennick St. and Tyler Avenue.

Winter Recreation

The **White Pine Ski Area** reopened in the winter of 1999 with a new chairlift and day lodge. Call the chamber of commerce at (307) 367-2242 for details. Cross-country skiers should pick up a copy of the **Skyline Drive Nordic Touring Trails** map from the Forest Service or chamber of commerce office in Pinedale. The 60 km of trails are marked but not always groomed. More adventurous skiers will find all sorts of places to explore in the Bridger Wilderness just a few miles east of Pinedale. Rent cross-country skis from the **Great Outdoor Shop,** 332 W. Pine, tel. (307) 367-2440.

The lower elevations of the Wind River Mountains are also extremely popular with snowmobilers; trails head out right from town. See the chamber of commerce for a list of local companies offering snowmobile rentals and tours. The 365-mile **Continental Divide Snowmobile Trail** passes right by Pinedale, continuing north to Yellowstone and around the Wind River Mountains to Lander. **Green River Outfitters,** tel. (307) 367-2416, leads snowmobile tours into the mountains around Pinedale, including overnight trips to a mountain cabin.

INFORMATION AND SERVICES

An **information kiosk** on Pine St. near Fremont Ave., tel. (307) 367-2242, is open daily 9 a.m.-5 p.m. April-Oct., and Mon.-Fri. 10 a.m.-2 p.m. the rest of the year. For Pinedale information on the web—and links to local businesses—visit www.pinedaleonline.com.

The Forest Service's **Pinedale Ranger District Office** is at 29 E. Fremont Lake Rd., tel. (307) 367-4326. Find the **BLM Office** at 431 W. Pine St., tel. (307) 367-4358, and the town **library** at 155 S. Tyler St., tel. (307) 367-4114. Wash clothes at **Highlander Center Laundromat** on Pine St., and get (unlaundered) cash from the **ATMs** at 1st National Bank of Pinedale or inside the Trailside Store.

Shopping

In business since 1947, the **Cowboy Shop,** 137 W. Pine, tel. (307) 367-4300, www.cowboyshop.com, has an outstanding selection of Western clothes, boots, and other necessities of life. Recommended. **Moosley Books,** 7 W. Pine St., tel. (307) 367-6622, sells books on Wyoming and the West.

Transportation

Drivers en route to Jackson should fill up in Pinedale; gas prices only get higher from here north. **Wind River Transportation Authority** (WRTA), tel. (307) 856-7118 or (800) 439-7118, provides on-demand service in western and southwestern Wyoming. You can call them for service to other Wyoming towns, including Dubois, Evanston, Jackson, Lander, Riverton, and Rock Springs.

VICINITY OF PINEDALE

BOULDER

A dozen miles south of Pinedale is Boulder, and on the drive down (about halfway between the two towns) you'll pass two roadside telephone poles topped by active osprey nests.

Boulder (pop. 70) holds a handful of businesses. The classic **Boulder Store** is nearly a century old. Next door is **Basecamp Restaurant,** serving three meals a day, including deli sandwiches for lunch and prime rib at dinner. The modern **Boulder Inn,** tel. (307) 537-5480, has hand-hewn lodgpole-pine furnishings, including two rooms with king beds. Rates are $65-80 s or $68-88 d. Moderate-Expensive.

The BLM's free **Stokes Crossing Campground** is two miles east on State Hwy. 353, then eight miles north on a gravel road. Located along Boulder Creek, this is a relaxing place for anglers.

A mile north of Boulder is **Wind River View Campground,** tel. (307) 537-5453, open mid-May to mid-September. There's no shade on this exposed site, but the mountain views are noteworthy. This is a membership camp, but RVers can stay here for $4 if they're willing to put up with a sales pitch.

Twelve miles up State Hwy. 353, **Boulder Lake Lodge,** tel. (307) 537-5400 or (800) 788-5401, www.boulderlake.com, is a modern ranch with guest rooms for $60 d. In addition to lodging, they serve family-style meals and offer horseback rides, along with pack trips and spot-packing. Also available are all-inclusive one-week stays for $1,385 per person. The ranch is open Memorial Day through October. Moderate-Luxury.

DANIEL

Head 11 miles west of Pinedale and then another mile south on US Hwy. 189 to tiny Daniel, where the country bar makes some of the best Bloody Marys in Wyoming.

West of Daniel, the **David Ranch,** tel. (307) 859-8228, provides a chance to sample the cowboy life in spades. Guests stay in comfortable log cabins and enjoy ranch-style meals in the main house. Days are spent on horseback rides, herding cattle, or participating in cattle drives. The ranch is open mid-May to mid-September, with a maximum of 10 guests. Weekly rates are $2,100-3,600 for two people (no kids). The website is www.davidranch.com. Luxury.

The BLM's **Warren Bridge Campground** ($6; open all year) sits beside the Green River approximately nine miles north of Daniel on US Hwy. 191/189. Another dozen rustic campsites (free) are spread out along 10 miles of the gravel road that parallels the river upstream. These grassy sites are very popular with anglers; ask the attendant at Warren Bridge Campground which ones are available.

A roadside marker north of Daniel notes the site of **Fort Bonneville,** built in 1832 to serve as a fur-trade center run by Capt. Benjamin Bonneville. It lasted only a year but gained the nickname "Fort Nonsense" because of the severely cold and snowy winters that made life difficult for Bonneville's men. The fort consisted of two blockhouses guarding a perimeter of tall log posts.

1840 RENDEZVOUS SITE

Two miles south and then 2.5 miles east of Daniel is the site of the 1840 rendezvous, the last grand gathering of mountain men and Indians. The dirt access road cuts through barren sage and grass country, but the vista changes abruptly as you reach the site. Below you the Green River twists its way through a lush landscape of grass, cattle, and cottonwoods. It's pretty easy to see why the rendezvous was held in this area! Get here for a summer sunrise, when you can imagine a multitude of Indians and mountain men spread out below for the annual festivities. The meadow contains a memorial to missionaries Narcissa Whitman and Eliza Spalding, who in 1836 became the first white women to venture by land across the American continent.

A tiny shrine overlooks the meadow, marking Wyoming's first Mass, performed by Belgian

Jesuit missionary **Father Pierre Jean DeSmet** during the 1840 rendezvous. DeSmet's description of the event is as follows:

> *On Sunday, the 5th of July, I had the consolation of celebrating the holy sacrifice of Mass* sub dio *[under the open sky]. The altar was placed on an elevation and surrounded with boughs and garlands of flowers; I addressed the congregation in French and English, and spoke also by an interpreter to the Flatheads and Snake Indians. It was a spectacle truly moving for the heart of a missionary, to behold an assembly composed of so many different nations, who all assisted at our holy mysteries with great satisfaction. The Canadians sang hymns in French and Latin, and the Indians in their native tongue.*

An idealist of the first order, DeSmet spent more than three decades working with Indians in an attempt to protect them from being subsumed by America's territorial ambitions. His goal was to create communities where Indians could preserve their culture while adopting some of the technological advantages of Western civilization. Although the mission failed miserably, DeSmet was one of the few 19th-century men who maintained lifelong friendships with the Indians. "Blackrobe," as he was known, always traveled unarmed throughout the West and served as a peacemaker during treaty negotiations. The shrine on the site of DeSmet's 1840 service is used during a commemorative mass on the second Sunday of each July.

Pinckney Sublette, one of four brothers from the famous family of fur trappers, is buried not far from the DeSmet monument. Just up the dirt road are the red log barn and white log home of the historic Quarter Circle 5 Ranch, a definitive Wyoming spread.

BIG PINEY

An oil boomtown in the late 1970s, Big Piney (pop. 500) faced hard post-boom times but has been on the rebound of late. It now putters along with a handful of small businesses. The settlement doesn't have a lot to offer, but you may want to look around the **Green River Valley Museum,** tel. (307) 276-5343, which reveals a sampling of the area's oil and gas history. Open Tues.-Sat. noon-4 p.m. June-October. Get local information here or from the town office.

Practicalities

The BLM maintains a handful of free riverside sites at **New Fork River Campground,** 12 miles east of Marbleton on State Hwy. 351. Stay in basic rooms at **Big Piney Motel,** tel. (307) 276-3352, for $32 s or d. Budget. **Lain's Sports Center & Motel,** tel. (307) 276-3303, has dirt-cheap rates but you'll be staying in dumpy old trailers. No standouts on the food scene here, but **Happy Trails Cafe,** tel. (307) 276-5776, is open for lunch and dinner, with pizza, chicken baskets, sandwiches, and ice cream.

The main annual event is the **Big Piney Chuck Wagon Days** on the Fourth of July. Festivities include a rodeo, a parade, fireworks, and a free barbecue. Big Piney is also home to the **Sublette County Fair** held the first weekend of August each year. One of the attractions here is the Little Buckaroo Rodeo for children. Other rodeos take place throughout the summer at the fairgrounds.

The town has a library and the Forest Service's **Big Piney Ranger District Office,** tel. (307) 276-3375, where you can find out about the route west into the Wyoming Range. A public **swimming pool** is at the high school on the west side of town.

MARBLETON

Marbleton (pop. 700) is just a couple hundred yards up US Hwy. 189 from Big Piney. Stop here for a look around the **Made in Wyoming** shop, tel. (307) 276-3317, which features the works of 100 artisans from across the state. You'll find everything from willow furniture and handmade quilts to porcelain dolls and Christmas decorations for sale. Watch flicks at **The Flick Theatre,** tel. (307) 276-5404.

Country Chalet Inn, tel. (307) 276-3391, is a good place to stay, with rooms for $34 s or $40 d. Inexpensive. For a few bucks more ($38 s or $44 d), **Marbleton Inn,** tel. (307) 276-5231, offers the best lodging accommodations in the area (Inexpensive) and serves all-American meals at **Three Pines Restaurant,** tel. (307) 276-3523. Across the street is **Rio Verde Grill,** tel. (307) 276-5353, serving Mexican food. Camp at **Harper's RV Park,** tel. (307) 276-3611; $17 for RVs, $10 for tents. Open year-round.

Backpackers and campers can wash off road grime in hot showers at the **Laundry Basket Laundromat.**

The **Waterhole,** tel. (307) 276-9977, is the center of nightlife in the area and puts on a popular cowboy open golf tournament each summer.

HEADING NORTH

North of Marbleton, the enormous Wind River Mountains become more conspicuous and the highway crosses the **Lander Cutoff,** its ruts now barely discernible across the sagebrush. Built in 1858 by Col. Frederick W. Lander and his soldiers, it served two purposes: it was a shorter route to California and Oregon and a way to bypass the Mormon communities in Utah. The route offered good grazing and water as well as abundant game, and it quickly became the preferred route to California and Oregon. It was also the only portion of the Oregon Trail funded with government money.

TO JACKSON HOLE

US Hwy. 189/191 provides a scenic route to Hoback Junction and Jackson Hole, crossing the Green River and then slowly climbing into the hills. Aspens begin to appear on the hilltops, and willows line the creeks. The 11,000-foot-tall Gros Ventre Mountains are visible to the northwest. Gradually, lodgepole pine and aspen begin to replace the sagebrush. At **the Rim,** the road enters Bridger-Teton National Forest. West of here, the land drains into the Hoback River, which joins the Snake River at Hoback Junction 40 miles away. The road curves gradually down through this mountainous country, crossing the Hoback River again and again. (The crossroads settlement of Hoback Junction is covered in the Jackson Hole and the Tetons chapter.)

Bondurant

The spread-out town of Bondurant (pop. 100) straggles along the road through a gorgeous mountain valley, its pastures dotted with piles of hay, creekside willows, and grazing horses. The Gros Ventre Mountains form a dramatic backdrop, but the developments consist of just a few scattered log homes. Bondurant is named for Sarah Ellen and Benjamin Franklin Bondurant, the first settlers here. Between 1907 and 1927 they ran a popular dude ranch and had as pets all sorts of wild animals: antelope, elk, even young bears.

On the west end of "town," **Elkhorn Bar and Trading Post,** tel. (307) 733-8358, consists of a friendly general store and country watering hole, a gas station, and a laundromat. Six small cabins ($55 d) contain fridges and microwaves; open year-round. Inexpensive. The bar has a menu that includes pizzas, burritos, and sandwiches on weekdays, with steaks on Friday and Saturday nights.

Over the Fourth of July weekend, Bondurant comes alive with a **Horseback Poker Ride,** in which more than a hundred horseback riders compete.

Hoback Canyon

A few miles west of Bondurant, the road clings to the walls of Hoback Canyon as it passes the high face of Battle Mountain, site of one of the few conflicts between Indians and whites in this part of Wyoming. It was here in 1895 that whites from Jackson Hole attacked Bannock Indians who had been hunting "out of season" along the Hoback River. Just before you reach Hoback Junction, a signpost describes John Hoback, the trapper and guide who led the Astorian trappers of Wilson Price Hunt through here in 1811.

Granite Hot Springs

Just west of Battle Mountain on US Hwy. 189/191 is the turnoff to Granite Hot Springs, tel. (307) 734-7400. *Do* take this very scenic side trip! A well-maintained gravel road follows Granite Creek for 10 miles, affording impressive views of the Gros Ventre Range and the 50-foot drop of **Granite Falls.** The road ends at a parking lot just a short walk from the hot springs. The deep pool (93-112° F) was built in 1933 by the CCC and is open 10 a.m. till dusk during the summer, and 10 a.m.-5 p.m. in winter (closed in the fall and spring). No showers or running water at the pool. The cost is $5.50 for adults, $3.50 for ages 3-12; free for infants. Suits and towels can also be rented, and the shop sells candy, pop, and bottled water. Granite Canyon Rd. is not plowed in winter but is groomed for use by both snowmobilers and cross-country skiers. A nearby campground ($12) is open late June to September. The campground rarely fills up, but you can make reservations for the busy Fourth of July holiday weekend by calling (307) 734-7400. Dispersed camping is allowed on the road to Granite Hot Springs, except along the final 1.3 miles before the springs.

JACKSON HOLE AND THE TETONS

Jackson Hole is one of the most-visited slices of wild country in North America, attracting well over three million travelers each year. They come here for a multitude of reasons: to camp under the stars in Grand Teton National Park, to play and shop in the New West town of Jackson, to hike flower-bedecked trails up forested valleys, to ride sleighs among thousands of elk, to raft down the Snake River, to ski or snowboard at one of the local resorts, or to simply stand in wonderment as the sun colors the sky behind the mountains. Many continue on north to Yellowstone National Park, another place on everyone's must-see list. Drive north from Jackson toward Yellowstone and you'll quickly discover the biggest reason so many people are attracted to this place—its beauty. The Tetons act as a magnet, drawing your eyes away from the road and forcing you to stop and absorb some of their majesty. Welcome to one of the world's great wonderlands.

In the lingo of the mountain men, a "hole" was a large valley ringed by mountain ranges, and each was named for the trapper who based himself there. Jackson Hole, on Wyoming's far western border, is justifiably the most famous of all these intermountain valleys. Although Jackson Hole reaches an impressive 40 miles north to south and up to 10 miles across, the magnificent range of mountains to the west is what defines this valley. Shoshone Indians who wandered through this country called the peaks Teewinot ("Many Pinnacles"); later explorers would use such labels as Shark's Teeth or Pilot Knobs. But it was lonely French-Canadian trappers arriving in the early 1800s who provided the name that stuck: les Trois Tetons (literally, "the Three Tits").

Contrary to what you may have been told, Jackson Hole is *not* named for Michael Jackson. The valley, originally called Jackson's Hole, was instead named for likable trapper David E. Jackson, one of the men who helped establish the Rocky Mountain Fur Company. When Jackson and his partners sold out in 1830, they realized a profit of over $50,000. Jackson's presence remains in the names of both Jackson Hole and Jackson Lake. Eventually, more polite

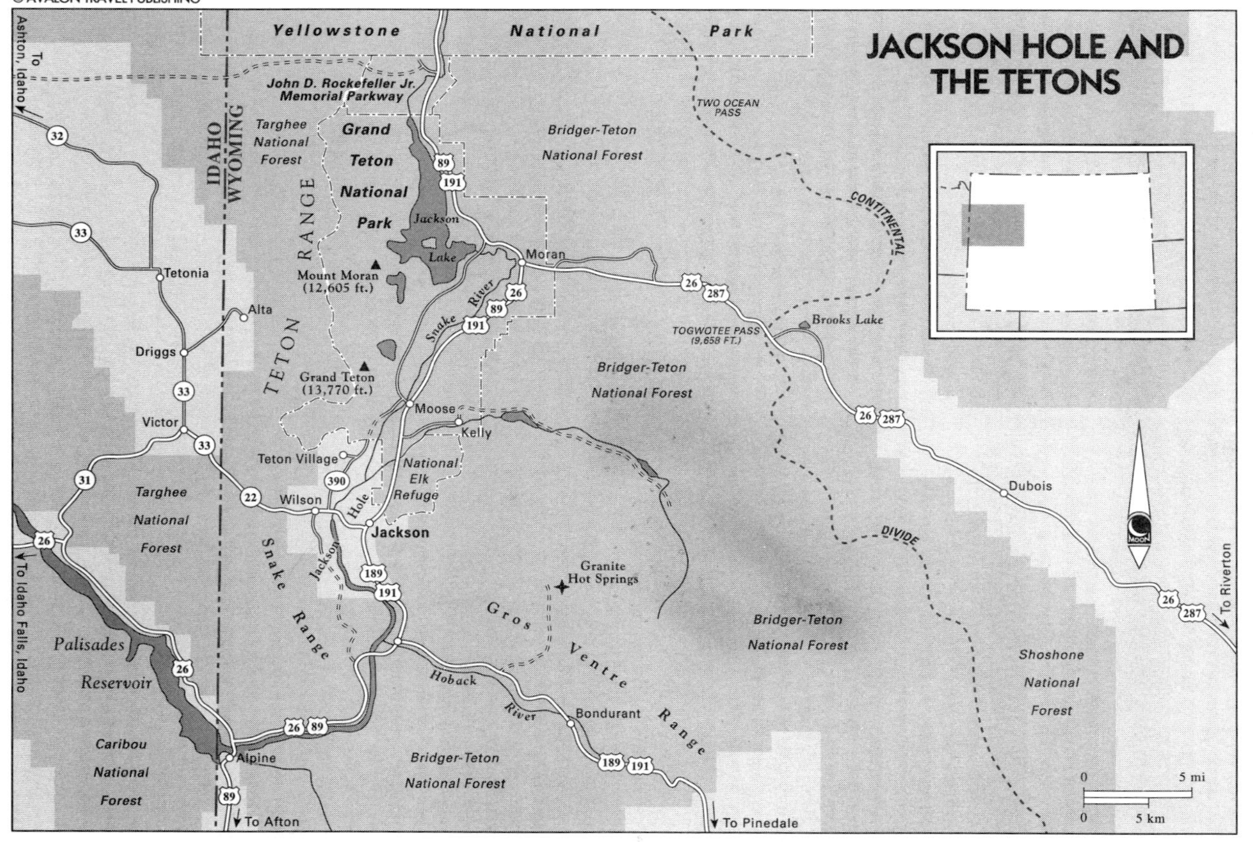
© AVALON TRAVEL PUBLISHING
JACKSON HOLE AND THE TETONS
Yellowstone National Park
John D. Rockefeller Jr. Memorial Parkway
Targhee National Forest
Grand Teton National Park
Bridger-Teton National Forest
TWO OCEAN PASS
CONTINENTAL DIVIDE
IDAHO
WYOMING
To Ashton, Idaho
Tetonia
Alta
Driggs
Victor
TETON RANGE
Mount Moran (12,605 ft.)
Grand Teton (13,770 ft.)
Jackson Lake
Moran
Snake River
TOGWOTEE PASS (9,658 FT.)
Brooks Lake
Moose
Kelly
Teton Village
National Elk Refuge
Wilson
Jackson Hole
Jackson
Dubois
To Riverton
Granite Hot Springs
Gros Ventre Range
Snake Range
Palisades Reservoir
To Idaho Falls, Idaho
Hoback River
Bondurant
Caribou National Forest
Shoshone National Forest
Alpine
To Afton
To Pinedale
0 5 mi
0 5 km

folks began calling the valley Jackson Hole, in an attempt to end the ribald stories associated with the name Jackson's Hole. (It's easy to imagine the jokes with both Jackson's Hole and the Tetons in the same place.) By the way, in 1991, a group calling itself the Committee to Restore Decency to Our National Parks created quite a stir by suggesting that Grand Teton National Park be renamed. A letter sent to the Park Service and various members of Congress noted: "Though a great many Americans may be oblivious to this vulgarity, hundreds of millions of French people around the world are not! How embarrassing that these spectacular, majestic mountains are reduced to a dirty joke overseas." After a flurry of letters in response, the hoax was revealed; it was a prank by staff members of *Spy* magazine.

SIGHTSEEING HIGHLIGHTS FOR JACKSON HOLE AND THE TETONS

Town of Jackson, including Town Square, National Museum of Wildlife Art, art galleries, gourmet restaurants, upscale shops, and luxurious lodging places

National Elk Refuge (primarily in winter)

Snake River whitewater rafting and trout fishing

Horseback rides and chuck wagon cookouts

Grand Targhee Ski Resort, Jackson Hole Mountain Resort, and Snow King Resort (winter skiing and summertime lift rides)

Grand Teton National Park for spectacular mountain vistas, Jenny Lake day-hikes, Signal Mountain, Jackson Lake Lodge, Colter Bay Indian Arts Museum, and Mormon Row

Gros Ventre River Valley

Popular events: International Rocky Mountain Stage Stop Sled Dog Race (February), Pole-Peddle-Paddle Race (April), Elk Antler Auction (May), Grand Teton Music Festival (all summer), Jackson Hole Rodeo (all summer), Jackson Shoot-out (all summer), and Jackson Hole Fall Arts Festival (September)

HISTORY

The first people to cross the mountain passes into Jackson Hole probably arrived while the last massive glaciers were still retreating. Clovis stone arrowheads—a style used at least 11,000 years ago—have been found along the edges of the valley. These early peoples were replaced in the 16th and 17th centuries by the Shoshone, Bannock, Blackfeet, Crow, and Gros Ventre tribes, who hunted bison from horses. When the first fur trappers tramped into Jackson Hole, they found Indian paths throughout the valley.

John Colter

Transport yourself back to the early 19th century, a time when people from the new nation called America saw the world west of the Mississippi River as just a blank spot on the map. In 1803, Thomas Jefferson purchased the Louisiana Territory from France, and to learn more about this gigantic piece of real estate he sent Meriwether Lewis and William Clark on a military expedition to the Pacific coast, a trip that took nearly two and a half years. Although the expedition skirted

the "Colter Stone," with Colter's name inscribed on one face and the date 1808 on the other

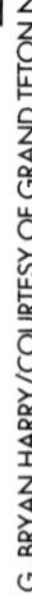

around Wyoming—heading across Montana instead—it proved the opening wedge for the settlement of the West and, indirectly, the discovery of Jackson Hole. On the return trip, the party met two fur trappers en route to the upper Missouri River. One of Lewis and Clark's respected scouts, John Colter, was allowed to join the trappers, "provided no one of the party would ask or expect a Similar permission."

After a winter of trapping with his partners, Colter headed alone down the Platte River, but before he could get back to civilization he met up with a company of trappers led by Manuel Lisa. They were on their way to the Rockies, determined to cash in on the huge demand for beaver furs by trapping the rich beaver streams that Lewis and Clark had described. Wealth beckoned, and John Colter gladly turned around again, guiding Lisa's men up to the mouth of the Big Horn River, where they built a small fort. From there Colter was sent on a mission: contact Indians throughout the region, trading beads and other items for beaver furs.

His wanderings in the winter of 1807-08 were the first white exploration of this region. A map produced by William Clark in 1814 and based upon Colter's recollections shows an incredible midwinter journey around Yellowstone and Jackson Lakes, across the Tetons twice, and up through Jackson Hole. He did not get back to the fort until the following spring, telling tales of huge mountain ranges and a spectacular geothermal area that others quickly laughed off as "Colter's Hell."

Colter went on to become one of the most famous of all mountain men, and his later harrowing escape from the Blackfeet in Montana has become the stuff of legend. After being captured and stripped naked, he was forced to literally run for his life. Somehow he managed to outdistance his pursuers for six miles before hiding in a pile of logs until dark. He walked barefoot the 300 miles back to Manual Lisa's fort, surviving on roots and tree bark. Shortly thereafter, Colter was reported to have thrown his hat on the ground, declaring, "I'll be damned if I ever come into [this country] again." He returned to St. Louis, married, and established a farm near that of fellow explorer Daniel Boone. Colter lived long enough to give William Clark a description of the country he had visited, but he died from jaundice just three years later, in 1813.

Because of the abundance of beavers along tributaries of the Snake River, Jackson Hole became an important crossroads for the Rocky Mountain fur trade. Although no rendezvous was ever held in the valley, many of the most famous mountain men spent time here. They first trapped beavers in Jackson Hole in 1811, but it was not until the 1820s that fur trapping really came into its own as mountain men fanned through the wilderness in search of the "soft gold." This quest continued for the next two decades, finally dying out when overtrapping made beavers harder to find and silk hats replaced fur hats. After the last rendezvous in 1840, most of the old trappers headed on to new adventures, the best becoming guides for those en route to Oregon and California. Because Jackson Hole was not near the Oregon

JACKSON HOLE IN 1835

This Valley is called "Jackson Hole" it is generally from 5 to 15 mls wide: the southern part where the river enters the mountain is hilly and uneven but the Northern portion is wide smooth and comparatively even the whole being covered with wild sage and Surrounded by high and rugged mountains upon whose summits the snow remains during the hottest months in Summer. The alluvial bottoms along the river and streams inter sect it thro. the valley produce a luxuriant groth of vegetation among which wild flax and a species of onion are abundant. The great altitude of this place however connected with the cold descending from the mountains at night I think would be a serious obstruction to growth of most Kinds of cultivated grains. This valley like all other parts of the country abounds with game.

—FROM *JOURNAL OF A TRAPPER 1834-1843,* BY OSBORNE RUSSELL

Trail or other routes west, the area remained virtually deserted until the late 19th century.

Settlers

The first Jackson Hole homesteaders arrived in 1884, followed quickly by others coming to escape the law. The settlers survived by grazing cattle, harvesting hay, and acting as guides for rich hunters from Europe and eastern states. Gradually they filled the richest parts of the valley with homesteads. Conflicts soon arose between the Bannock Indians, who had been hunting in Jackson Hole for more than a hundred years, and the new settlers who made money guiding wealthy sportsmen.

By 1895, Wyoming had enacted game laws prohibiting hunting during 10 months of the year. Claiming that the Indians were taking elk out of season, Constable William Manning and 26 settlers arrested a group of 28 Indians (mostly women and children) who had been hunting in Hoback Canyon. When the Bannocks attempted to flee, an elderly Indian was shot four times in the back and died. Most of the others escaped. Settlers in Jackson Hole feared revenge and called in the cavalry, but the Indians who had been hunting in the area all returned peaceably to their Idaho reservation. Astoundingly, *The New York Times* headlined its report of the incident, "Settlers Massacred—Indians Kill Every One at Jackson's Hole—Courier Brings the News—Red Men Apply the Torch to All the Houses in the Valley." Absolutely none of this was true, but the attack by whites succeeded in forcing the Indians off their traditional hunting grounds, an action eventually upheld in a landmark U.S. Supreme Court case.

THE WHITE SHOSHONE

The little Jackson Hole-area town of Wilson is named for one of Wyoming's most fascinating characters, "Uncle Nick" Wilson. Born in 1842, Wilson grew up in Utah, where he made friends with a fellow sheepherder, an Indian boy, and learned to speak his language. Then Nick's life suddenly took a strange twist. The mother of Chief Washakie (from Wyoming's Wind River Reservation) had recently lost a son, and in a dream she was told that a white boy would come to take his place. Unable to convince her otherwise, Washakie sent his men out to find the new son. They came across Nick and offered him a pinto pony and the chance to fish, hunt, and ride horses all he wanted. It didn't take much persuading, and for the next two years he lived as a Shoshone, learning to hunt buffalo, to use a bow and arrow, and to answer to his new name, Yagaiki. He became a favorite of Chief Washakie, but when word came (falsely) that Nick's father was threatening to attack the Shoshones with an army of men to retrieve his son, the chief reluctantly helped Nick return home.

At age 18, Nick Wilson became one of the first Pony Express riders, a job that nearly killed him when he was struck in the head during a Paiute Indian attack. A doctor managed to remove the arrow point, but Wilson remained in a coma for nearly two weeks. Thereafter, Wilson always wore a hat to cover the scar, even inside buildings. He went on to become an Army scout and a driver for the Overland Stage before returning to a more sedate life as a farmer. Many years later, in 1889, Nick Wilson led a party of five Mormon families over steep Teton Pass and down to the rich grazing lands in Jackson Hole. The town that grew up around them became Wilson. In later years, "Uncle Nick" recounted his adventures in *The White Indian Boy.*

JACKSON HOLE MUSEUM & TETON COUNTY HISTORICAL SOCIETY

Jackson Hole Comes of Age

By the turn of the 20th century, the Jackson Hole settlements of Jackson, Wilson, Kelly, and Moran had all been established. The towns grew slowly; people survived by ranching, guiding, and engaging in the strange new business of tending to wealthy "dudes" from back east. Eventually, tourism would vastly eclipse raising cattle in importance, but even today Teton County has nearly as many cattle as people.

Jackson, the largest town in Jackson Hole, was established in 1897 when Grace Miller (wife of a local banker known derisively as "Old Twelve Percent") bought a large plot of land and planned a townsite. In an event that should come as no surprise in "The Equality State," Jackson later became the first town in America to be entirely governed by women. The year was 1920, and not only was the mayor a woman (Grace Miller), but so were all four council members, the city clerk, the treasurer, and even the town marshal. They remained in office until 1923.

Over the years Jackson has grown, spurred on by the creation of Grand Teton National Park and the development of Jackson Hole Mountain Resort. In the last two decades Jackson Hole has seen almost continuous growth; tourists have flooded the region to play, investors have built golf courses and ostentatious hotels, and wealthy families have snatched up their own parcels of paradise. Although much of the area is public land and will remain undeveloped, rapid growth on private land is transforming Jackson Hole into the Wyoming version of Vail. The standard quip is that the billionaires are buying land so fast that they're driving the millionaires out of Jackson Hole. Even the formerly quiet town of Wilson has not managed to fight off the development onslaught, with a massive new grade school and a collection of modest new homes that locals call Whoville (after those in the Dr. Seuss book). As one who once lived in Wilson, I can appreciate the joke now going the rounds: How many Wilsonites does it take to change a light bulb? Seven. One to screw it in, and the other six to talk about how good the old one used to be.

JACKSON

The town of Jackson (pop. 8,000) lies near the southern end of Jackson Hole, hemmed in on three sides by Snow King Mountain, the Gros Ventre Range, and East Gros Ventre Butte. At 6,200 feet in elevation, Jackson experiences cold snowy winters, wet springs, delightfully warm and sunny summers, and crisp but color-filled falls. Jackson is quite unlike any other place in Wyoming; on a typical summer day more than 35,000 tourists flood the town. Sit on a bench in Town Square on a summer day and you're likely to see cars from every state in the Union. Tourists dart in and out of the many gift shops, art galleries, fine restaurants, Western-style saloons, and trendy boutiques. The cowboy hats all look as if the price tags just came off. This sure isn't Rock Springs!

In other parts of Wyoming, Jackson is viewed with a mixture of awe and disdain—awe over its booming economy, but disdain that Jackson is not a "real" town, just a false front put up to sell things to outsiders. Yes, Jackson is almost wholly dependent upon the almighty tourist dollar, but as a result it enjoys a cultural richness lacking in other parts of the state. Besides, if you don't like all the commercial foolishness, it's easy to escape to a campsite or remote trail in the wonderful countryside of nearby Grand Teton National Park or Bridger-Teton National Forest.

Keep your eyes open around Jackson and you're likely to see famous (or infamous, depending upon your perspective) residents such as actor Harrison Ford, former Secretary of the Interior James Watt (who resigned in disgrace in 1983), attorney Gerald Spence (of Karen Silkwood and Imelda Marcos notoriety), former Wyoming governor Clifford Hansen, Yvon Chouinard (mountaineer and founder of Patagonia), actress Connie Stevens, industrial heir Charles DuPont, and members of the extended Rockefeller family.

SIGHTS

Town Square

In 1932, the local Rotary Club planted trees in the center of Jackson, adding four picturesque arch-

Jackson's elk antler arches are featured attractions at Town Square.

es made from hundreds of elk antlers. Today the trees offer summertime shade, and at any time of day or night you'll find visitors admiring or getting photos taken in front of the arches that mark the corners of Town Square. During the winter, the snow-covered arches and trees are draped with lights, giving the square a festive atmosphere. Surrounded by dozens of boardwalk-fronted galleries, bars, restaurants, factory outlets, and gift shops, the square is the focal point of tourist activity in Jackson. During the summer, stagecoaches wait to transport you on a leisurely ride around town, and each evening "cowboys" put on a free **shoot-out** for throngs of camera-happy tourists. The shoot-out starts every summer night (except Sunday) at 6:30 p.m. They've been killing each other like this since 1955. With stereotypical players and questionable acting, the "mountain law" system seems in dire need of reform. Most folks love the sham; Kodak and Fuji love it even more. Warning: the sound of blanks is surprisingly loud and can be frightening for small children.

National Museum of Wildlife Art

Jackson is home to the magnificent National Museum of Wildlife Art, which lies two miles north of town along US Hwy. 26/89, directly across from the National Elk Refuge. Built from brown Arizona sandstone, the exterior blends in with nearby rock outcroppings. Step inside the doors of this 51,000-square-foot museum to discover a marvelous interior space. As visitors enter the main gallery, a larger-than-life bronze mountain lion crouches above, ready to pounce. Kids will enjoy the hands-on Children's Gallery. Adults will appreciate the artwork spread through a dozen galleries, along with the video theater, Rising Sage Cafe (delicious lunches), 200-seat auditorium, and gift shop.

The museum collection features pieces by Carl Rungius, George Catlin, Albert Bierstadt, Karl Bodmer, Alfred Jacob Miller, N.C. Wyeth, Conrad Schwiering, John Clymer, Charles Russell, Robert Bateman, and many others. Of particular interest are the reconstructed studio of John Clymer and the spacious Carl Rungius Gallery, where you'll find the most complete collection of his paintings in the nation. Also of note is the exhibit on the American bison, which documents these once vastly abundant animals and their slaughter. Six galleries contain changing exhibitions of photography, painting, and other art. Spotting scopes in the lobby and the cozy members' lounge (open to the public) are useful for watching residents of the adjacent National Elk Refuge. Call (307) 733-5771 for details on the museum, or check their website, www.wildlifeart.org.

Admission to the museum costs $6 for adults, $5 for seniors and students, $14 for families; kids under six get in free. It's open daily 8 a.m.-5 p.m. Memorial Day through Labor Day; daily 9 a.m.-5 p.m. December to early April; and Mon.-Sat. 9 a.m.-5 p.m. and Sunday 1-5 p.m. in the fall and spring (Labor Day through November and early April through Memorial Day). Very informative 45-minute free museum tours are given daily at 11 a.m. or by request for groups.

Wildlife films, slide lectures, talks, concerts, kid programs, and other activities take place throughout the year in the auditorium and galleries; pick up a schedule of events at the entrance desk. One of the most popular events is the **Miniature Show and Sale** in mid-September; it attracts more than a hundred of the country's leading artists.

During the winter, come to the museum to purchase tickets for sleigh rides on the refuge. A combination museum entrance and Elk Refuge sleigh ride costs $15 for adults, $11 for ages 6-12, free for kids under six.

Historical Museums

The small **Jackson Hole Museum,** 105 N. Glenwood, tel. (307) 733-2414, has a surprising homespun charm. Inside are displays and collections illustrating the days when Indians, trappers, cattlemen, and dude ranchers made this magnificent valley their home. Check out the Paul Bunyan-size bear trap and the old postcards. Admission costs $3 for adults, $2 for seniors, $1 for students, and $6 for families. Hours are Mon.-Sat. 9:30 a.m.-6 p.m. and Sunday 10 a.m.-5 p.m. from Memorial Day to early October; closed the rest of the year. The museum sponsors hour-long **historical walking tours** of Jackson's downtown on Tuesday, Thursday, Friday, and Saturday at 10 a.m. Memorial Day through Labor Day. These cost $2 for adults, $1 for seniors and students, or $5 for families.

The **Jackson Hole Historical Center,** 105 Mercill Ave., tel. (307) 733-9605, is a small research facility housing photo archives, a library of old books from the area, a fine exhibit on the fur trade, and an impressive collection of Indian trade beads and mountain-man paraphernalia. A replica of the "Colter stone" is also on display, as are rotating exhibits through the year. Hours are Mon.-Fri. 8 a.m.-5 p.m. year-round; free admission.

SAVING JACKSON HOLE

The Jackson Hole economy has been stuck in permanent high gear for the last few decades as expensive homes spread across old ranchlands, retailers such as Kmart moved in, and the town of Jackson grew from a sleepy burg to a national focal point for outdoor fun. Today, development reaches for miles south from Jackson itself. Despite the fact that 97% of the land in Teton County is in the public domain, the 70,000 acres of private land that remain are rapidly being developed, and Jackson Hole is in grave danger of losing the wild beauty that has attracted visitors for more than a century. This is immediately obvious to anyone arriving in Jackson. Instead of the wide open spaces that remain protected by public land ownership, the edges of Jackson are falling under a proliferation of trophy homes, real-estate offices, chain motels, fast-food outlets, megamarts, gas stations, and elaborate banks, all competing beneath a thicket of signs. Summertime traffic jams are becoming all too common in this once-quiet place where more than 35,000 visitors can now be found on a summer afternoon.

In 1994, Jackson voters got fed up with the pace of development and voted to scrap the town's two-percent lodging tax, which had provided over a million dollars per year in funding to promote Jackson Hole around the world. Despite this lack of promotional effort, growth shows no signs of slowing down. A large new Albertson's grocery store went up in 1999, and an even bigger Smith's is expected to open by 2001. Housing costs continue to spiral upward, pushed by the arrival of a wealthy clientele willing to drop $1 million or more for a Jackson Hole home.

The **Jackson Hole Conservation Alliance,** tel. (307) 733-9417, www.jhalliance.com, is a 1,600-member environmental group that works to preserve the remaining natural areas of Jackson Hole. Membership starts at $25 a year and includes a bimonthly newsletter and a chance to help control the many developments that threaten this still-beautiful valley.

Another influential local group is the **Jackson Hole Land Trust,** tel. (307) 733-4707, www.jhlt.org, a nonprofit organization that obtains conservation easements to maintain ranches and other land threatened by development. They have protected more than 10,000 acres in the valley in this way, including the 1,740-acre Walton Ranch, visible along the highway between Jackson and Wilson.

Art in Jackson

Artists have long been attracted by the beauty of Jackson Hole and the Tetons. Mount Moran, the 12,805-foot summit behind Jackson Lake, is named for Thomas Moran, whose watercolors helped persuade Congress to set aside Yellowstone as the first national park. The late Conrad Schwiering's paintings of the Tetons have attained international fame—one was even used on the Postal Service's Wyoming Centennial stamp in 1990. Ansel Adams's photograph of the Tetons remains etched in the American consciousness as one of the archetypal wilderness images. A copy of the image was included in the payload of the *Voyager II* spacecraft currently en route out of our solar system. Today many artists live or work in Jackson Hole, and locals proclaim it "Art Center of the Rockies," ranking it with New York, San Francisco, Santa Fe, and Scottsdale.

More than 30 galleries crowd the center of Jackson, their collections covering the spectrum from Indian art of questionable authenticity to impressive photographic exhibits and shows by nationally acclaimed painters. Unfortunately, many of these galleries offer recycled ideas now manufactured in mass quantity with every possible cliché thrown in. Particularly egregious examples are the Southwestern-style pastel pottery, the glowing country scenes at Thomas Kinkade Gallery, and the prints of sexy Indian maidens with windblown hair and strategically torn garments. See the local free newspapers for a complete rundown of current exhibitions and displays, along with maps showing gallery locations, but don't believe everything the galleries say about themselves in their ads.

Several galleries are worth a visit, most notably the outstanding National Museum of Wildlife Art (described above). The nonprofit **Art Association,** 260 W. Pearl, tel. (307) 733-6379, has art classes of all types throughout the year and displays changing exhibitions by local artists in its **Artwest Gallery,** open Mon.-Fri. 9 a.m.-4:30 p.m. **Fiber & Pulp,** 365 N. Glenwood, tel. (307) 734-2599, has workshops in book and paper arts, including short training sessions on such topics as bookbinding, silk painting, Polaroid dye transfers, and mask making.

Just off Town Square at the corner of Center and Deloney, **Trailside Galleries,** tel. (307) 733-3186, www.trailsidegalleries.com, focuses on Western works, but you'll also find everything from impressionism to wildlife art here. More unusual is the nearby **Center Street Gallery,** 110 Center St., tel. (307) 733-1115 or (888) 733-1115, where the emphasis is on brightly colored contemporary art and jewelry.

See Jackson maps in color map supplement.

Jackson's finest gallery space is **Martin-Harris Gallery,** 60 E. Broadway (upstairs next to Snake River Grill), tel. (307) 733-0350 or (800) 366-7814, specializing in contemporary Western ("New West") paintings and sculptures by nationally known artists. Also of note here are the collectibles and one-of-a-kind pieces of handcrafted furniture. But bring plenty of cash or a big limit on your credit card. Last time I visited they were asking $21,000 for a desk—but it was probably worth every penny.

Also downtown, the **Caswell Gallery & Sculpture Garden,** 145 E. Broadway, tel. (307) 734-2660, is home to Jackson's only outdoor sculpture garden, with wildlife bronzes by Rip Caswell. Not my cup of tea (or espresso for that matter), but you may appreciate the innovative sculptures from other artisans displayed in this gallery. **Jack Dennis' Wyoming Gallery,** 50 E. Broadway, tel. (307) 733-7548, specializes in wildlife and traditional landscape paintings. **Rawson Galleries** features traditional (and a few avant-garde) watercolors, displayed in a crowded space at 50 King St., tel. (307) 733-7306.

The **Joanne Hennes Studio & Gallery,** 5850 N. Larkspur Dr. (off Spring Gulch Rd. near the Jackson Hole Golf and Tennis Club), tel. (307) 733-2593, features oil and watercolor paintings of the Tetons by Joanne Hennes. Two of her commissioned works hang in the Moose Visitor Center and Jenny Lake Lodge.

One of Jackson's largest private exhibition spaces is **Wilcox Gallery,** a mile north of town on US Hwy. 26/89, tel. (307) 733-6450. Inside are traditional oil paintings by Jim Wilcox, along with works by other prominent Western painters and sculptors.

For art from the natural world, head six miles south of town on US Hwy. 89 to **Fossil Works & Ulrich Studio.** Inside are beautifully prepared fish fossils from the Kemmerer area (where the Ulrich's have a fossil quarry), including tabletops, flooring tiles, wall pieces, and other prepared specimens. The gallery is open by appointment only; call (307) 733-1019 or (307) 733-3613.

For a different kind of art, head to **Dancer's Workshop,** downstairs in the Pink Garter Plaza at 49 W. Broadway, tel. (307) 733-6398, which offers country-and-western, modern, ballet, tap, and jazz dance classes throughout the year, with nationally known guest artists in the summer.

Photo Galleries

Many nationally known photographers live or work in Jackson Hole and exhibit their prints in Jackson galleries. Tom Mangelsen displays his outstanding wildlife and landscape photos at **Images of Nature Gallery,** 170 N. Cache Dr., tel. (307) 733-9752. Inside **Light Reflections,** 35 E. Deloney, tel. (307) 733-4016 or (800) 346-5223, are many of Fred Joy's large-format visions of the American West. Also well worth a visit is **Wild by Nature Gallery,** 95 W. Deloney, tel. (307) 733-8877, where photographer Henry H. Holdsworth offers prints of his striking wildlife and nature imagery.

Kitsch

If you're a fan of the *National Enquirer,* check out the weird and wacky collection at **Ripley's Believe It or Not,** 140 N. Cache, tel. (307) 734-0000. Here you'll discover a shrunken head, six-legged buffalo calf, six-foot long cigar, antique bedpan collection, and even art created from dryer lint. Who says art is only for the elite? Entrance costs a steep $8 for adults, $5 for ages 5-12; free for kids under five. The family rate is $30, a bargain price for families of 10 from Salt Lake City. Ripley's is open daily 9 a.m.-10 p.m. May-Oct., and daily 9 a.m.-6 p.m. the rest of the year.

Head a dozen miles south of Jackson to Hoback Junction for more weirdness at **Teton Mystery,** tel. (307) 733-4285. What is it? Pay your money and find out.

NATIONAL ELK REFUGE

Just two miles north of Jackson is the National Elk Refuge, winter home for thousands of these majestic animals. During the summer, the elk range up to 65 miles away to feed on grasses, shrubs, and forbs in alpine meadows. But as the snows descend each fall, the elk move downslope, wintering in Jackson Hole and the surrounding country. The chance to view elk up close from a horse-drawn sleigh makes a trip to the National Elk Refuge one of the most popular wintertime activities for Jackson Hole visitors.

History

When the first ranchers arrived in Jackson Hole in the late 19th century, they moved onto land that had long been an elk migration route and wintering ground. The ranchers soon found elk raiding their haystacks and competing with cattle for forage, particularly during severe winters.

The conflicts reached a peak early in the 20th century when three consecutive severe winters killed thousands of elk, leading one settler to claim that he had "walked for a mile on dead elk lying from one to four deep."

Fortunately, local rancher and hunting guide Stephen N. Leek had been given a camera by one of the sportsmen he had guided, George Eastman (founder of Kodak). Leek's disturbing photos of starving and dead elk found a national audience and helped pressure the state of Wyoming to appropriate $5,000 to buy hay in 1909. Two years later the federal government began purchasing land for a permanent winter elk refuge, a refuge that would eventually cover nearly 25,000 acres. Today it's administered by the U.S. Fish & Wildlife Service. Famed biologist, illustrator, and conservationist Olaus Murie came to Jackson Hole in 1927 to begin his studies of the elk, remaining here until his death in 1963. Murie and his wife, Margaret "Mardie" Murie, chronicled their adventures in *Wapiti Wilderness* (Colorado Associated University Press). Conservationist Mardie Murie—now over 90—still lives in Moose, holding near-sainthood status among conservationists.

Today more than 10,000 elk (two-thirds of the local population) spend November through May on the refuge. Because development has reduced elk habitat in the valley to a quarter of its original size, refuge managers try to improve the remaining land by seeding, irrigation, and prescribed burning. In addition, during the most difficult foraging period, the elk are fed pelleted alfalfa paid for in part by sales of elk antlers collected on the refuge. During this time, each elk eats more than seven pounds of supplemental alfalfa a day, or 30 tons per day for the entire herd. Elk head back into the mountains with the melting of snow each April and May; during the summer months you'll only see a few on the refuge.

Visiting the Refuge

The National Elk Refuge, tel. (307) 733-9212, is primarily a winter attraction, although it's also an excellent place to watch birds and other wildlife in summer. Trumpeter swans nest and winter here. The refuge has staff members on duty year-round in the Wyoming State Information Center. Find them on the web at www.r6.fws.gov/refuges/natlelk.

The main winter attraction here is the chance to see thousands of elk up close from one of the **horse-drawn sleighs** that take visitors on trips through the refuge. The elk are accustomed to these sleighs and pay them little heed, although people on foot would scare them. A tour of the National Elk Refuge is always a highlight for wintertime visitors to Jackson Hole. In December and January the bulls have impressive antlers that they start to shed by the end of February. The months of January and February are good times to see sparring matches. You might also catch a glimpse of a wolf or two since a pack now resides in the area year-round and hunts elk in winter. Morning is the best time to look for wolves.

Begin your wintertime visit to the refuge at the National Museum of Wildlife Art, two miles north of Jackson on Hwy. 26/89. Purchase your sleigh ride tickets here; $12 for adults, $8 for ages 6-12, free for kids under age six. A better deal is the combination ticket that includes museum entrance and an Elk Refuge sleigh ride for $15 adults, $11 ages 6-12, and free for kids under six. For reservations, call Bar-T-Five (they run the sleighs) at (307) 733-5386 or (800) 772-5386. The museum shows an interpretive slide show about the refuge while you're waiting for a shuttle bus to take you downhill to the delightful sleighs. The sleighs run daily 10 a.m.-4 p.m. between mid-December and early April (closed Christmas), heading out as soon as enough folks show up for a ride—generally just long enough for the early-comers to finish watching the slide show. The rides last 45-60 minutes. Be sure to bring along warm clothes, as the wind can get bitterly cold.

Special START (Southern Teton Area Rapid Transit) buses connect Jackson with the Elk Refuge and the Museum of Wildlife Art for just $1 each way; call (307) 733-4521 for details. If you don't want to wait for a bus, call **All Star Taxi,** tel. (307) 733-2888 or (800) 378-2944, or **Buckboard Cab,** tel. (307) 733-1112, both of which offer shuttle service to the museum from Teton Village or downtown Jackson.

Four miles north of town and next to the elk refuge is the **Jackson National Fish Hatchery,** tel. (307) 733-2510, which rears a half million cutthroat and lake trout annually. It's open daily 8 a.m.-4 p.m. year-round.

ACCOMMODATIONS

As one of the premier centers for tourism in Wyoming, Jackson Hole is jam-packed with more than 70 different motels, hotels, and B&Bs, plus many more condominiums and guest ranches. Other lodging can be found just to the north within or near Grand Teton National Park; these are detailed in Grand Teton Practicalities later in this chapter. See Additional Jackson Hole Accommodations in the appendix for a listing of motels and hotels that are not described below.

Because of the town's popularity, lodgings in Jackson command premium prices—a marked contrast to rates in other parts of Wyoming. With a few exceptions, you can expect to pay a minimum of $85 s or d during the peak visitor seasons of July-Aug. and late December to early January. Rates can drop over 50% in the off-season, so if you can visit March-May or late September to mid-December, you'll save a lot of cash. (The same Super 8 Motel rooms that go for $140 in July cost just $52 in April!) In the town of Jackson, the highest rates are usually in July and August, while at Teton Village, skiers send lodging prices to their peak between mid-December and early January.

Reservations are highly recommended. For midsummer, make reservations at least two months ahead—longer if you really want to be certain of a place—and during the Christmas-to-New Year's period you should probably reserve six months in advance to ensure a spot. Summer weekends tend to be the most crowded, with many families driving up from Salt Lake City for a cooling break in the mountains.

Jackson hostels, motels, and hotels are arranged below by price, with the least expensive places first. Add a six percent tax to these rates.

Hostels

Jackson's least-expensive lodging option, the **Bunkhouse,** tel. (307) 733-3668 or (800) 234-4507, www.anvilmotel.com, is in the basement of the Anvil Motel at 215 N. Cache Drive. Right in town, it almost always has space. The hostel costs $22 per person and includes a TV room and a kitchen with a refrigerator and microwave (but no stove or dishes). The big sleeping room contains 30 bunk beds with linen and adjacent storage lockers; bring your own lock. Though men's and women's showers and restrooms are separate, the sleeping space is coed. It can get pretty noisy with all those snoring bodies in one room at night, so earplugs are a smart purchase. Check in after 3 p.m. and be out by 11 a.m. Alcohol is not allowed. Folks who aren't staying here can take showers for $5. Inexpensive.

Out in Teton Village, **Hostel X,** tel. (307) 733-3415, www.hostelx.com, provides a quieter alternative, with four-person dorms for $19 per person (but you need to be an AYH member). They also have private rooms for $47 d. The lounge includes a TV, pay phones, a pool table, ping pong, a children's play area, fireplace, microwave, games, Internet access to check your e-mail, and a ski-waxing room. Inexpensive.

Easiest on the Wallet

The definition of "budget" lodging has to be stretched a bit in Jackson, where even fairly basic rooms with older furnishings go for $60 a night. The following lodgings have at least some of their rooms for under $90.

Hostel X features very small, plain-vanilla rooms (no TV or phones) and a central area for camaraderie. Rates are $47 s or d. Because of its Teton Village location at the foot of Jackson Hole Mountain Resort, it is very popular with skiers on a budget; reserve three months ahead for midwinter rooms. Inexpensive. See Hostels above for details on Hostel X.

In a quiet part of town but just a few blocks from Town Square is **Alpine Motel,** 70 S. Jean St., tel. (307) 739-3200. Most of the rooms contain old-fashioned furnishings (including tiny TVs), but they're clean and cost just $54 s or $58 d. Remodeled rooms with Motel 6-style furnishings are $68 s or $72 d. Add $8 to these rates for four people in a room. A small outdoor pool is on the premises, and some rooms include fridges and microwaves. Moderate.

Despite its name, **The Cottages at Snow King,** 470 King St., tel. (307) 733-3480 or (800) 483-8667, www.townsquareinns.com, doesn't have cottages, but it does rent out modest but comfortable motel rooms in a residential part of town. These range from modest rooms with one queen bed and a fridge for $64 d, up to full-kitchen units that sleep four for $102. Winter rates provide skiers with some of the best deals in Jackson: $125-200 d for seven days! Moderate.

Sagebrush Motel, 550 W. Broadway, tel. (307) 733-0336, has a variety of units. Motel rooms with older furnishings and kitchenettes cost a reasonable $65-84 s or d. Cabin units start at $70 s or d, but those with kitchens ($94 for up to four people) are much nicer. Sagebrush Motel is open May-Oct. only. Moderate.

Kudar's Motel, 260 N. Cache Dr., tel. (307) 733-2823, offers rather plain motel rooms with "antique" furnishings and microscopic televisions for reasonable prices: $65 d. Of more interest are their rustic log cabins that were built in 1938. These go for $75-90 d, and the larger ones can sleep six. Moderate-Expensive.

One of Jackson's better deals for standard motel rooms is—not surprisingly—**Motel 6,** 1370 W. Broadway, tel. (307) 733-1620 or (800) 466-8356, but even here peak summer rates are $70 s or $76 d. You'll find predictable rooms and an outdoor pool, but reserve six months in advance for July and August. The off-season rates ($34 s or $40 d) are a much better bargain. Moderate.

Twelve miles south of Jackson in Hoback Junction, **Hoback River Resort,** tel. (307) 733-5129, www.jacksonholenet.com/hrr, has large motel rooms and cabins for up to six people on attractive grounds facing the Hoback River. The rooms are very clean and well maintained. But the location—away from busy downtown Jackson—is the real draw here. Rates are $70-80 s or d in motel rooms with decks; $95 s or d in cabins with full kitchens (but no maid service). A three-night minimum stay is required in the cabins. Moderate-Expensive.

Another good place is **Anvil Motel,** 215 N. Cache Dr., tel. (307) 733-3668 or (800) 234-4507, www.anvilmotel.com, where the modern rooms are $90 d or $115 for two beds (four people). All rooms here have microwaves and small fridges. An outdoor jacuzzi is available. Expensive. Just around the corner at 240 N. Glenwood is **El Rancho Motel,** with the same owners and phone number as the Anvil. The small rooms here have older furnishings. Rooms with one bed cost $75 d; larger rooms with two beds are $105 for up to four people. Guests can use the Anvil Motel's jacuzzi. Moderate-Expensive.

Log Cabin Motels

Several local motels offer log cabin accommodations for a step back to the Old West while keeping such newer amenities as televisions and private baths.

Hitching Post Lodge, 460 E. Broadway, tel. (307) 733-2606 or (800) 821-8351, www.jacksonholenet.com/htchngp, is in a residential part of Jackson but within walking distance of downtown. The lovingly maintained cabins cluster around a central lodge built in 1931, and guests will appreciate the summertime outdoor pool and wintertime jacuzzi. A light breakfast is served in the lodge in winter. Cabins cost $78-136 s or d, while newer two-bedroom suites have kitchenettes and run $149-199 for up to four people. All units contain lodgepole beds, fridges, and microwaves. Moderate-Luxury.

Set amid tall cottonwood trees, **Wagon Wheel Village,** 435 N. Cache Dr., tel. (307) 733-2357 or (800) 323-9279, www.wagonwheelvillage.com, has a number of well-maintained and cozy log cabins, along with log motel units. Rates are $87 s or $92-119 d, including access to two outside hot tubs. More luxurious are their modern log-style suites ($129 for four people), each with a fireplace, fridge, microwave, and small deck facing Flat Creek. Wagon Wheel Village is closed in April and November. Expensive-Premium.

Near a busy Jackson intersection, **Cowboy Village Log Cabin Resort,** 120 Flat Creek Dr., tel. (307) 733-3121 or (800) 962-4988, www.cowboyvillage.com, has 84 modern and jammed-together cabins with kitchenettes. Rates are $139 for up to three; $169 for up to six in two-bedroom units. Guests have access to two enclosed jacuzzis. Premium-Luxury.

Other places with log units include Sagebrush Motel, Hoback River Resort, and Kudar's Motel (described above), along with Antler Motel and Elk Country Inn (described below).

Costlier but Comfortable

Many Jackson motels fall in the $90-130 range, with pricing factors being location, type of room, quality of furnishings, and presence of amenities such as pools and hot tubs. A number of comfortable midrange motels are described below. These are not the corporate lodging giants, but they offer good value and down-home friendliness.

The rooms are a bit on the crowded side, but guests appreciate the friendly service and extra touches at **Sundance Inn,** 135 W. Broadway, tel.

(307) 733-3444 or (888) 478-6326, www.sundanceinnjackson.com. The motel is close to Town Square and serves a light homemade breakfast plus evening cookies and lemonade. Guests can also use the outdoor jacuzzi (with alleyway ambience, alas). Standard rooms cost $79-99 s or d, while two-room suites are $139 d or $159 for four people. Moderate-Premium.

Rawhide Motel, 75 S. Millward, tel. (307) 733-1216 or (800) 835-2999, www.rawhidemotel.com, is a fine place with large rooms containing handmade lodgepole furniture. Rates are $88-108 s or $93-113 d. Expensive-Premium.

It's quite a distance from Jackson, but **Hatchet Motel,** tel. (307) 543-2413 or (877) 543-2413, www.hatchetmotel.com, has clean and friendly country accommodations in a great setting. The motel is in Buffalo Valley, 39 miles northeast of Jackson (eight miles east of Moran Junction) on US Hwy. 26/287, and is open year-round. Well-maintained rooms go for $90 s or d. A restaurant, general store, and gas station are also on the premises. Expensive.

Anglers Inn, 265 N. Millward St., tel. (307) 733-3682 or (800) 867-4667, www.anglersinn.net, has attractive rooms with Western fixtures, lodgepole beds and chairs, new carpets, and small baths. This cozy motel is right on Flat Creek, but just a couple of blocks from Town Square. Rates are $95-105 s or d, and the rooms contain fridges and microwaves. Expensive.

Antler Motel, 50 W. Pearl Ave., tel. (307) 733-2535 or (800) 522-2406, www.townsquareinns.com, is a large property with 100 recently remodeled rooms. Most contain two queen beds and cost $98 s or d, but also available are a dozen large family rooms/suites ($120 d) with three beds and space for up to 10 people. Some of these contain wood-burning fireplaces or jetted tubs. Rounding out the options here are some attractive Panabode log cabins starting at $88 d. All guests have access to an exercise room, sauna, and large indoor jacuzzi. Expensive-Premium.

One of the nicer moderately priced Jackson motels is **Wolf Moon Inn,** 285 N. Cache Dr., tel. (307) 733-2287 or (800) 964-2387, www.jak-biz.com/wolfmooninn. The clean and spacious rooms contain new furnishings, fridges, and ceiling fans. Rates are $85-95 s or d in standard rooms or $149 for six people in two-room suites. Expensive.

You'll find a quiet escape at **Western Motel,** 225 S. Glenwood, tel. (307) 733-3291 or (800) 845-7999, www.jak-biz.com/westernmotel. Standard rooms cost $99-109 for up to four people, and some have fridges and microwaves. Eight-person suites with two bedrooms, two baths, and a kitchen are $219. Also available is a two-bedroom house containing a fireplace and hot tub for $219. The motel has a seasonal outdoor pool. Expensive.

Buckrail Lodge, 110 E. Karns Ave., tel. (307) 733-2079, www.jacksonwy.com/buckrail, is in a quiet part of town six blocks from Town Square. The immaculate grounds include an outdoor jacuzzi, and the 12 motel rooms are all in faux-log-cabin style. The well-maintained rooms all have two queen beds and are decorated with Western-style furnishings. Rates are $100-110 d or $110-120 for four people. No phones in the rooms, and Buckrail is closed mid-October through April. Premium.

Elk Country Inn, 480 W. Pearl, tel. (307) 733-2364 or (800) 483-8667, www.townsquareinns.com, is popular with families and small groups of travelers. The spacious motel rooms (a bit old fashioned but nicely maintained) all have three beds and cost $112 for up to four people; add $6 for loft units that sleep six and include kitchenettes. Modern log cabins with kitchenettes and lodgepole furnishings go for $136 d. The inn also has a hot tub and ski-waxing room. Premium.

Top-end Accommodations

It should come as no surprise that tony Jackson Hole has a number of elaborate, pricey, and sumptuous places to stay, with rooms starting around $150 and hitting the stratosphere at more than $700 a night.

An excellent in-town choice is **Parkway Inn,** 125 N. Jackson St., tel. (307) 733-3143 or (800) 247-8390, www.parkwayinn.com. This midsize lodge has a delightful Victorian ambience with antique furniture and quilts in every room. The rooms are spacious and immaculate, and guests can also enjoy a small indoor lap pool, two jacuzzis, two saunas, and a big exercise gym. A light breakfast is served in the lobby each morning. Rates are $149 d for standard rooms with two queen beds or a king bed, or $174-184 d for two-room suites; $12 each for additional guests (maximum of four in a room). Premium-Luxury.

An excellent nine-room lodge just a few blocks from Town Square, **Inn on the Creek,** 295 N. Millwood, tel. (307) 739-1565 or (800) 669-9534, www.innonthecreek.com, has a peaceful location beside Flat Creek. Standard rooms ($169 s or d) feature designer furnishings, down comforters, and VCRs. The deluxe rooms ($209 s or d) also include balconies, fireplaces, and in-room jacuzzis. The gorgeous suite ($379) sleeps up to six and has a full kitchen, jacuzzi bath, and private patio. A light breakfast is served in the comfortable lounge, and all guests have access to the outdoor jacuzzi facing the creek. Luxury.

If you're looking for attractive accommodations in Teton Village instead of Jackson, your best bet is **Best Western Resort Hotel at Jackson Hole,** tel. (307) 733-3657 or (800) 445-4655, www.resorthotelatjh.com. The refurbished New West-style lobby is the primary focal point here, and the rooms continue the theme with attractive lamps, pine furniture, and prints. Facilities include a heated outdoor pool (open year-round), indoor and outdoor jacuzzis, a sauna, ski lockers, and concierge service. Be sure to check out the amusing bench out front. Rates are $169-199 s or d. Luxury.

A very attractive downtown lodging is **Davy Jackson Inn,** 85 Perry Ave., tel. (307) 739-2294 or (800) 584-0532, www.davyjackson.com, where the modern rooms come in a variety of styles, including some with old-fashioned claw-foot tubs. Suites include steam showers, gas fireplaces, and king-size canopy beds. All guests are served a full breakfast and can relax in the outdoor hot tub. Rates are $179-229 s or d. Luxury.

Close to Town Square, the **Wort Hotel,** 50 N. Glenwood St., tel. (307) 733-2190 or (800) 322-2727, www.worthotel.com, has been a Jackson favorite since 1941 and is the only downtown hotel earning a four-diamond rating from AAA. A disastrous 1980 fire—started by a bird that built a nest too close to a neon sign—destroyed the roof and upper floor. The hotel was completely restored within a year, and today it's better than ever, with such modern amenities as a fitness center and two jacuzzis. The lobby, with its grand central staircase and stone fireplace with crackling fire, makes a fine place to meet friends. The SilverDollar Bar & Grille serves meals, or sidle up to the famous curving bar—inlaid with 2,032 uncirculated silver dollars from 1921. The hotel's spacious rooms are attractively decorated with a New West motif that includes lodgepole-pine beds, creative fixtures, and barbed-wire-patterned wallpaper. Rates are $194-210 d for standard rooms; junior suites cost $265, and luxury suites will set you back $450 d. Luxury.

Rusty Parrot Lodge, 175 N. Jackson, tel. (307) 733-2000 or (800) 458-2004, www.rustyparrot.com, offers outstanding lodging just two blocks from Town Square. The 31 rooms feature handcrafted furniture, original artwork, oversize tubs, and goose-down comforters; some also contain fireplaces and jacuzzi tubs. A gourmet breakfast (it's never the same) is served each morning in the luxurious dining room, and guests can relax in the jacuzzi on a deck overlooking Jackson, borrow a book from the library, or enjoy a massage, aromatherapy session, or facial from Body Sage Day Spa (extra charge). Rates are $250-275 s or d for standard rooms; $500 d for luxurious suites. No children under age 12. Luxury.

Some of the most dramatic vistas of the Tetons are from the luxurious **Spring Creek Ranch,** tel. (307) 733-8833 or (800) 443-6139, www.springcreekranch.com. Located on a thousand-acre estate, the resort sits high atop Gros Ventre Butte four miles west of Jackson and includes a wide range of lodging options. Hotel rooms are $250 s or d; suites, studios, and one-bedroom condos cost $295-375 s or d; while one- to three-bedroom condos are $475-1,200 and sleep four to six. Also available are executive homes that sleep eight and cost a mere $1,400 per night. All rooms contain fireplaces and lodgepole furnishings. Amenities at Spring Creek Ranch include a private pond, tennis courts, and an outdoor pool and jacuzzi. Luxury.

Teton Pines Resort & Country Club, tel. (307) 733-1005 or (800) 238-2223, www.tetonpines.com, is four miles south of Teton Village and features the amenities you'd expect in a year-round resort, including an 18-hole golf course, tennis center, and classy restaurant. The accommodations are varied, but all include a continental breakfast, access to the outdoor pool and jacuzzi, athletic-club privileges, concierge service, and airport shuttle. One-bedroom units (with separate his and hers baths) are $350 d, while two-bedroom and living-room suites cost $695 for four. Fully furnished three-bedroom townhouses sleep eight people and cost $895. Each townhouse has a kitchen, two decks, a fireplace, washer and dryer, and garage. Luxury.

Atop Gros Ventre Butte near Spring Creek Ranch is stunning **Amangani,** tel. (307) 734-7333 or (877) 734-7333, www.amanresorts.com, the only representative of Amanresorts in America. (Most of the company's other lavish resorts are in Southeast Asia.) Aman groupies and business travelers know to expect the utmost in luxury, and they will certainly not be disappointed here, starting with a knowledgeable DIB (dressed-in-black) staff and spare-no-expenses construction. The three-story sandstone-faced hotel contains 40 suites, each with a patined-metal fireplace, mountain-facing balcony, king-size bed, deep soaking tub (with a window view), minibar, and terrazzo dining table. Amangani's central lobby is particularly impressive, blending sandstone columns, redwood accents, custom furnishings, and soaring two-story windows. Outside, a whirlpool and heated 35-meter pool enjoy a remarkable view of the Tetons. Among other amenities are a complete health center (exercise facility, gym, steam rooms, yoga and meditation classes, and massage), a gourmet restaurant, and a lounge. Amangani's accommodations include suites ($550 d), deluxe suites ($650 d), and three luxury suites with two baths and spacious balconies ($750 d). Luxury.

Bed and Breakfasts

Jackson holds many fine B&Bs, where those who can afford it can relax in comfort at the homes of locals. Be sure to reserve space far ahead during the peak summer season, though you might get lucky at the last minute if someone cancels. **Jackson Hole Bed & Breakfast,** tel. (307) 734-1999 or (800) 542-2632, www.jacksonholebus.com, offers one-stop B&B shopping—call to make reservations at any of a dozen local B&Bs or to obtain the latest information on availability.

On the way to Teton Village, **Teton View B&B,** 2136 Coyote Loop, tel. (307) 733-7954, www.tetonview.com, features three guest rooms with shared or private baths for $99-120 s or d. Guests enjoy a full breakfast and a dramatic view of the Tetons from the outdoor jacuzzi. A five-night minimum stay is required in the winter months. Expensive-Premium.

Moose Meadows B&B, tel. (307) 733-9510, sits on five acres just east of Wilson. A major renovation in 1999 transformed this 4,200-square-foot ranch-style home into an elegant place to stay, with Teton vistas from the dining area, and a jacuzzi on the deck. There are five guest rooms (four with private bath), plus a barn and pasture for those who bring horses. A full breakfast is served each morning. Rates are $100-180 d, with a three-night minimum stay in the summer. Children are welcome. Expensive-Luxury.

You'll find outdoorsy owners at **Alpine House Country Inn,** 285 N. Glenwood, tel. (307) 739-

Built in 1901, the Painted Porch is a popular Jackson Hole B&B.

1570 or (800) 753-1421, www.alpinehouse.com. Both Hans and Nancy Johnstone were skiers for U.S. Olympic teams. The modern timber-frame lodge is just two blocks from Jackson's Town Square. With an addition completed in 2000, Alpine House now has 21 guest rooms in two connected buildings. The buildings are bright and modern, accented by Swedish-style stenciling on the walls. All rooms have private baths and balconies, plus access to the jacuzzi. A healthy full breakfast is served, along with evening wine and cheese. Children are welcome. Rates are $130 s or d in the original rooms, and $160 s or d in the new building, which also features TVs, gas fireplaces, and jacuzzi tubs. Suites cost $265 d. Premium-Luxury.

For quiet close-to-downtown accommodations, another fine option is **The Huff House Inn,** 240 E. Deloney Ave., tel. (307) 733-4164, www.cruising-america.com/huff.html. Built in 1917, this was for many years the home of one of Jackson's first doctors, Charles Huff. Today it is a gracious place with a feminine sense of style. The five guest rooms ($133-174 s or d) are attractive, and all have private baths. Also available are four modern cottages with cathedral ceilings, king-size beds, sleeper-sofas, VCRs, and jacuzzi tubs. These go for $194 d. An outdoor jacuzzi is on the premises, and a creative full breakfast is served family-style each morning. Kids are welcome in the cottages. Premium-Luxury.

On the road to Teton Village, **The Painted Porch,** 3755 N. Moose-Wilson Rd., tel. (307) 733-1981, was built in 1901 in Idaho and moved here many years later. Located on three acres and surrounded by a white picket fence and tall aspen trees, this rambling red farmhouse contains four attractive guest rooms, each with its own personality—from frilly lace to cowboy culture. All also have private baths. Rates are $135-235 s or d, including a full breakfast. Children over age six are welcome, and a two-night minimum stay is required. Find them on the web at www.jacksonholenet.com/paintedporch. Premium-Luxury.

A personal favorite—it gets high marks from all who visit—is **Teton Treehouse B&B,** tel. (307) 733-3233, a gorgeous four-story hillside home in Wilson. This spacious open-beam B&B sits up 95 steps (needless to say, it's not accessible for disabled people) and contains six guest rooms with private baths. It really does offer the feeling of living in a treehouse, and it's a great place for birdwatchers. Decks provide impressive views across the valley below, and you can soak in the outdoor hot tub each evening and enjoy a healthy full breakfast each morning while the owners regale you with stories of Jackson Hole. Lodging costs $145-180 s or d. No young children, but kids age 10 and over are welcome. There's a four-night minimum stay in July and August. Find them on the web at www.cruising-america.com/tetontreehouse. Premium-Luxury.

Near the Aspens along the road to Teton Village, **The Sassy Moose Inn,** tel. (307) 733-1277 or (800) 356-1277, is a modest log house with five guest rooms, each with private bath, TV, and VCR. A full breakfast is served each morning, along with complimentary wine and fruit. An indoor jacuzzi is also available. Lodging rates are $149 s or d. Family rooms provide space for kids, and pets are welcome (a rarity for B&Bs). Get more information on the web at www.bbonline.com/wy/sassymoose. Premium.

Built in 1993, **Nowlin Creek Inn,** 660 E. Broadway, tel. (307) 733-0882 or (800) 533-0882, www.jackson-hole-lodging.com, has five spacious and brightly lit guest rooms for $160-195 d. All of these include private baths, and three also contain fireplaces. A full breakfast is served, and guests can use the jacuzzi in the small backyard. In addition, the inn has a 1920 two-bedroom log cabin with full kitchen and bath ($250 for up to six people; breakfast not included). From the front porch you can look across to the National Elk Refuge, but it's just six blocks to the center of Jackson. The Western decor—including a mix of old and new—reflects the owners' strong artistic sensibilities. A three-night minimum stay is required June-September. Children are welcome. Luxury.

A recommended place is **Wildflower Inn,** tel. (307) 733-4710, www.jacksonholenet.com/wildflower. This spacious log house sits on three acres of country land along Teton Village Rd. and contains five bright guest rooms. Four rooms have their own private decks, and all contain private baths and handcrafted lodgepole log beds. One of the rooms is actually a suite with a separate sitting room, jacuzzi tub, and gas fireplace. Wildflower's hot tub sits inside a plant-filled solarium. The owner/builders are an Exum climbing guide and a former ski instructor. Rates are $200 d ($280 d in the suite) including an earthy breakfast served family-style. Children are welcome. Luxury.

One of the most impressive local lodging options is **Bentwood B&B,** just north of the junction on the road to Teton Village, tel. (307) 739-1411. This 6,000-square-foot log home sits amid tall cottonwood trees and is a favorite place for weddings and receptions. The grand living room is centered around a three-story stone fireplace, and each of the five luxurious guest rooms has its own fireplace, deck or balcony, and jetted tub. The loft room is perfect for families. The interior is filled with Western styling and English antiques, not to mention gracious hosts and two gregarious dogs. Drinks and hors d'oeuvres are served each evening, and morning brings a creative breakfast. Rates are $235-325 s or d. Children are welcome in this very special place. Get the full scoop by visiting the website: www.bentwoodinn.com. Luxury.

Condominium Rentals

Condominiums provide one of the most popular lodging options for families and groups visiting Jackson Hole. These privately owned places are maintained by a number of local property-management companies and range from small studio apartments to spacious five-bedroom houses. All are completely furnished (including dishes) and have fireplaces, cable TV, phones, and midstay maid service. The nicest also include access to pools and jacuzzis and have balconies overlooking the spectacular Tetons. Many of the condominiums are in Teton Village (adjacent to the ski area) or just to the south in Teton Pines or the Aspens; others are scattered around Jackson Hole.

Condo prices vary widely, but during the winter holiday season, expect to pay $150-200 per night for studios (one or two people). Two-bedroom units (up to four people) cost $200-400 per night, and full four-bedroom condos (these sleep eight and also have a private jacuzzi and stone fireplace) are $700-800. The fanciest places at the base of the tram will set you back over $1,400 per night in the peak winter season! Summer and off-peak rates are 40-50% lower, with spring and fall rates 50-75% less than peak-season prices. In fall or spring, condos offer a real bargain for traveling families looking to stay several nights in the area. Minimum stays of between two and seven nights are required throughout the year.

If you have the luxury of time, do a little comparison shopping before renting a condo. Things to ask include whether you have access to a pool and jacuzzi, how close you are to the ski slopes, how frequent the maid service is, and whether the units include such amenities as VCRs and washing machines. Also be sure to find out what beds are in the rooms, since couples might not enjoy sleeping in twin bunk beds.

For condo rental information, including prices and available dates, you can go to www.jacksonholenet.com and click on lodging, which will give you connections to most of the larger condo companies. You can also contact the following rental companies directly:

Black Diamond Vacation Rentals, tel. (307) 733-6170 or (800) 325-8605, www.blackdiamondvrre.com

Ely & Associates, tel. (307) 733-8604 or (800) 735-8310, www.jackson-hole-vacations.com

Jackson Hole Lodge, tel. (307) 733-2992 or (800) 604-9404, www.jacksonholelodge.com

Jackson Hole Resort Lodging, tel. (307) 733-3990 or (800) 443-8613, www.jhresortlodging.com

Jackson Home Management, tel. (307) 739-3000 or (800) 739-3009, www.jhomemgmt.com

Mountain Property Management, tel. (307) 733-1684 or (800) 992-9948, www.jacksonholenet.com/mtnprop

MTA Resorts of Jackson Hole, tel. (307) 733-0613 or (800) 272-8824, www.mtaresorts.com

Rendezvous Mountain Rentals, tel. (307) 739-9050 or (800) 739-2565, www.rmrentals.com

Snow King Resort Condominiums, tel. (307) 733-5200 or (800) 522-5464, www.snowking.com.

The largest of these companies—and a good place to begin your search—is Jackson Hole

Resort Lodging. Owned by Jackson Hole Mountain Resort, it manages 400 units, more than all the other companies combined. Among the largest of the other management companies on the list are Black Diamond Vacation Rentals, Jackson Hole Lodge, and Snow King Resort Condominiums. Additional condos are available at Spring Creek Ranch and at Teton Pines Resort & Country Club; see Top-end Accommodations, above.

Cabins

A number of Jackson Hole places offer log-cabin accommodations for a taste of old-time living. These small places are generally rented for several days or a week at a time and are favorites of families and groups. They may or may not have TVs and phones, and maid service may not be on a daily basis. See Log Cabin Motels above and Grand Teton Practicalities later in this chapter for additional places with cabin-style accommodations in Jackson Hole.

Buffalo Valley Ranch, tel. (307) 543-2026 or (888) 543-2477, has six cabins with fine views of the Buffalo Valley and the Tetons. The cabins range from basic older units that share a bathhouse and cost $45 d, to modern log affairs with two bedrooms and kitchenettes that sleep six for $100. You'll find them next to Heart Six Ranch in Buffalo Valley, 45 miles northeast of Jackson. Buffalo Valley Ranch offers horseback rides in the summer. Inexpensive-Expensive.

Moulton Ranch on Historic Mormon Row, tel. (307) 733-3749, offers several cabins in one of Jackson Hole's most majestic locations. This is the only private property on Mormon Row inside Grand Teton National Park, and the much-photographed Moulton Barn—one of the prototypical Wyoming images—is just a few hundred feet away. The four cabins are cozy but not at all elaborate. Nevertheless, where else might you awake to a spectacular Teton vista with bison grazing outside your window? Rates start at just $50 for a two-person cabin with a separate bathhouse, up to $85 for a cabin that sleeps six and has a fridge and microwave. Inexpensive-Moderate.

Camp Creek Inn, 16 miles south of Jackson in quiet Hoback Canyon, tel. (307) 733-3099 or (877) 338-4868, www.camp-creek-inn.com, has nine A-frame cabins costing $75 for up to four people. No TVs or phones in the rooms, but a bar and restaurant are on the grounds. Camp Creek also offers horseback rides, pack trips, fishing trips, snowmobiling, and mountain-biking. Moderate.

Six miles south of Jackson along busy US Hwy. 89, **Old West Cabins,** tel. (307) 733-0333, has 14 modern log cabins with kitchenettes. The smallest one is $79 d, and the largest is a six-person cabin for $149. Moderate-Premium.

Snowking Inn, 35 Snow King Ave., tel. (307) 733-1007 or (800) 648-2602, www.snowkinginn.com, is a delightful and relaxing little place just six blocks from Town Square and right across from Snow King Resort. The two suites are nicely furnished and contain full kitchens and decks with barbecues. Rates are $95 d, including such amenities as CD players, a basket of fruit, and a fridge stocked with juices. Snowking Inn is open May-September. The proprietor also owns Jackson Hole Whitewater. Expensive.

Out in the quiet town of Kelly (12 miles northeast of Jackson), **Anne Kent Cabins,** tel. (307) 733-4773, offers rustic accommodations with an unbeatable view of the Tetons. These cabins are perfect for those who want a real taste of Wyoming from a family with a long local history. Two rental options are available. Your best bet is to request the very comfortable log house, which has bedrooms in the loft and basement, two baths, a complete kitchen, washer, and dryer. The home could sleep 10 people. Next door are two cabins that rent together. The front one (built in 1939) includes a bedroom and kitchen, while the back cabin contains a second bedroom plus bath. The Anne Kent Cabins feature handmade lodgepole furniture created by co-owner Ron Davler, who creates them next door at Jackson Hole Log & Rawhide Furniture. Rates for either the log house or cabins are $100 d, plus $25 per person for additional guests; kids free. Expensive.

Split Creek Ranch, tel. (307) 733-7522, www.splitcreekranch.com, is seven miles north of Jackson and right along the Snake River. The ranch covers 25 acres of land and is a good place to see elk, moose, and other animals. Nine rooms are available. Eight of these are attractive log motel-type units ($100-110 d; plus $8 for additional people), and one is a separate honeymoon cabin ($180 d) with a fireplace, full kitchen, and private jacuzzi. The other units contain either kitchenettes or microwaves and fridges. The ranch has a new barnlike building that contains a workout facility, jacuzzi, and sitting room with fireplace. Evening campfires are a favorite of guests, and other amenities include a stocked fishing pond, continental breakfasts, and chuck wagon barbecues in the summer. Split Creek Ranch is open all year; this is a good place for cross-country skiers in the winter. There's a two-night minimum stay. Expensive-Luxury.

Mad Dog Ranch Cabins, tel. (307) 733-3729 or (800) 992-2246, www.maddogranch.com, has nine modern duplex cottages along Teton Village Road. All cottages have two bedrooms, sleeping lofts, kitchens, and woodstoves. An outdoor jacuzzi is available year-round. The cabins start at $149 d and range up to $219 for six people. Premium.

You'll discover spectacular views of the Tetons from **Luton's Log Cabins,** 36 miles northeast of Jackson (five miles east of Moran Junction), tel. (307) 543-2489. The modern duplex cabins have full kitchens, private baths, and front porches facing the mountains. One-bedroom units cost $148 d or $158 for four people, and two-bedroom units are $230-260 for six people. They're open May-November. For more information, visit www.tetoncabins.com. Premium.

Budges' Slide Lake Cabins, tel. (307) 733-9061, www.jacksonholecabins.com, consists of four secluded but modern cabins along Slide Lake, six miles east of Kelly. Each has a woodstove, full kitchen, and phone. Rates are $215 d, plus $10 each for additional people. Luxury.

Home Rentals

Jackson Hole home rentals are available from **Absolute Heaven in the Tetons,** tel. (307) 733-4881; **Flying J Vacation Rentals,** tel. (307) 733-4245; **Harley Varley Lodge,** tel. (307) 733-7072 or (800) 342-0833; **Andrei Moskowitz Vacation Home,** tel. (212) 721-2280 or (800) 682-0180; and **Mountain Valley Properties,** tel. (800) 993-0936, www.jacksonholenet.com/mvp.

Don't Fence Me Inn, tel. (307) 733-7979, is a 5,000-square-foot custom log home on six acres along Teton Village Road. The eight big bedrooms provide space for 20 people, but the $1,000-a-night price tag and three-night minimum stay will scare many folks off. The home is set back from the road, with a pond in the back and an active osprey nest nearby. Luxury.

Rancho Alegre Lodge, 3600 S. Park Loop Rd., tel. (307) 733-7988, www.ranchoalegre.com, offers Jackson's most expensive lodging. On a 50-acre spread facing the Tetons, this 10,000-square-foot structure houses seven bedrooms (each with its own TV, phone, feather bed, and fridge) and offers a hunting lodge decor and such amenities as a concierge, private chef (additional fee for meals), seven fireplaces, a jacuzzi, and pool table. Full house rentals are $2,000 per night with a two-night minimum stay. Up to 14 people can stay for this price, or, save money and rent it all month for only $40,000! At these prices, the lodge is primarily used for weddings, corporate retreats, large (and wealthy) families, and ski groups. In the off-season, individual suite rentals are available for $300-550 d per night. Luxury.

Guest Ranches

Jackson Hole is a natural place for dude ranches and is home to several of the best-known and most luxurious ones in the state. These are wonderful places for families looking to rough-it in style. A 15% gratuity is standard for the dude ranch staff and guides. In addition to the local places listed alphabetically below, many more guest ranches are just over Togwotee Pass in the Dubois area and to the south in the Pinedale area; get details on these in the Wind River Mountains Country chapter.

Built in 1927, **Crescent H Ranch,** tel. (307) 733-3674 or (888) 838-6671, www.crescenth.com, covers 1,300 acres south of Wilson. The ranch specializes in fishing packages ($6,200 for two people per week!) that include a fly-fishing school along with guided fishing trips. Also available are traditional ranch vacations with horseback riding, hiking, and fishing. These cost $4,900 for two people per week, all-inclusive. Meals at the Crescent H are a special treat, with gourmet food three times a day. The ranch has room for 25 guests in 10 cabins, and a seven-night minimum stay is required in midsummer.

Twelve miles east of Moran Junction in Buffalo Valley (43 miles northeast of Jackson), **Diamond D Ranch,** tel. (307) 543-2479 or (800) 233-6299, has modern cabins with great views of the Tetons. The ranch offers weekly stays June-Sept., with a variety of Western adventures, including horseback riding, kids' programs, hayrides, cookouts, fishing, overnight pack trips, and wildlife tours. All-inclusive weekly rates are $2,000 for two people. The ranch hosts a maximum of 36 people. In the fall, nightly rates are available at $100 d without meals. Get detailed information on the web at www.diamonddranch.com.

Looking for a wonderfully peaceful place to relax? Twenty miles up a dirt road in undeveloped Gros Ventre Valley (30 miles northeast of Jackson), **Goosewing Ranch,** tel. (307) 733-5251 or (888) 733-5251, is probably the most remote guest ranch in the Jackson Hole area. The well-appointed modern log cabins have fireplaces, private baths, and decks. Guests can use the outdoor jacuzzi all year and the outdoor heated pool in the summer. Popular summertime activities include horseback excursions, riding instruction, fishing, and hiking. All-inclusive weekly summertime rates are $2,960 for two people. There's a three-night minimum stay. When winter arrives, the ranch becomes a favorite destination for snowmobiling, with a variety of packages available. Get details on the ranch at www.goosewingranch.com.

Gros Ventre River Ranch, tel. (307) 733-4138, sits up undiscovered Gros Ventre River Valley, 18 miles northeast of Jackson near Slide Lake. This small ranch has accommodations for up to 34 guests in modern log cabins or a homestead house, and it serves delicious meals. The main activities are horseback riding, world-class fly-fishing, cookouts, canoeing, and mountain-biking. The lodge has a pool table, ping pong, and a large-screen television. A one-week minimum stay is required May-Oct., and weekly all-inclusive rates are $2,400-2,800 for two people. In the winter, the ranch becomes a base for cross-country skiing and snowmobiling, with four-person cabins costing $175 per night with a three-night minimum; no maid service or meals. Get details on the web at www.ranchweb.com/grosventre.

Heart Six Ranch, tel. (307) 543-2477 or (888) 543-2477, www.heartsix.com, is in Buffalo Valley, 12 miles east of Moran Junction (43 miles northeast of Jackson). It's a classic family dude ranch with log cabins, kids' programs, day trips to Yellowstone National Park and the Jackson Hole rodeo, and a range of evening activities including cookouts, nature programs, and country music. All-inclusive weekly rates are $2,500 for two people. The ranch takes in up to 50 guests at a time and is open year-round. Only weekly stays are available June-Aug., but at other times of the year the ranch offers nightly lodging for $50 s or $75 d, plus $25 if you want three meals a day. This is a favorite base for snowmobilers mid-December through March.

Wyoming's most elaborate—and expensive—guest ranch, **Lost Creek Ranch,** is 21 miles north of Jackson, tel. (307) 733-3435. This showplace resort emphasizes fitness, with a spa facility that includes exercise classes, a weight room, steam room, sauna, and jacuzzi, along with massage and facials (extra charge). Guests stay in modern duplex log cabins and enjoy gourmet meals in the main lodge's patio overlooking the Tetons. Amenities include such nontraditional items as a heated swimming pool, tennis courts, and a skeet range, in addition to more standard horseback riding, kids' programs, float trips, hiking, and fly-fishing. It's all a bit too Disneyesque for my tastes, and the prices are too Madison Avenue. Weekly all-inclusive rates are $5,240 for two people in a duplex cabin, or an astounding $12,064 for four people (even if two of these are children!) in a luxurious two-bedroom, two-bath cabin with a living room and fireplace. Some consider this a small price to pay for such pampering. The ranch hosts up to 60 guests at a time and is open late May to mid-October. A one-week minimum stay is required except after Labor Day, when it drops to a three-night minimum. Call for details or visit the place virtually at www.lostcreek.com.

You may get lucky and find a space at historic **Moose Head Ranch,** 13 miles north of Moose, tel. (307) 733-3141 in the summer, or (850) 877-1431 the rest of the year. This family ranch has space for 45 guests, and it receives so many repeat customers that it's almost always booked up. The ranch is entirely surrounded by Grand Teton National Park and features modern log cabins, horseback riding, private trout ponds, fly-fishing lessons, and excellent meals. There's a five-night minimum stay, and all-inclusive rates are $3,300 per week for two people. The ranch is open mid-June through August.

Another historic dude ranch is **R Lazy S Ranch,** 13 miles northeast of Jackson, tel. (307) 733-2655. The ranch has space for 45 guests who enjoy horseback rides, fishing, and other

Western adventures. Tykes under age seven are not allowed, but older kids can take advantage of a special program just for them. A one-week minimum stay is required. All-inclusive rates are $2,114-2,870 for two people per week, and the ranch is open mid-June through September. For additional information, look on the web at www.rlazys.com.

Located along the rolling Gros Ventre River, **Red Rock Ranch,** tel. (307) 733-6288, faces spectacular orange-red badlands. The ranch is 32 miles northeast of Jackson, and the quiet location and drop-dead scenery are reason enough to stay here. Guests settle into comfortable log cabins with woodstoves, and they can take part in horseback riding, cattle drives, cookouts, and other activities. The ranch also features kids' programs, a fishing pond, swimming pool, and jacuzzi. There's space for a maximum of 30 guests, and a six-night minimum stay is required. Open June to mid-October. All-inclusive rates are $2,280 for two people for six nights. For more information, log onto the web at www.redrock-ranch.com.

Spotted Horse Ranch, tel. (307) 733-2097 or (800) 528-2084, lies on the banks of the Hoback River, 16 miles south of Jackson. The ranch exudes a comfortable rusticity; the main lodge and cabins contain lodgepole furniture, and guests stay in log cabins with modern conveniences. Activities include horseback riding (some Appaloosas), fly-fishing, and cookouts, and you can unwind in the jacuzzi or sauna. All-inclusive weekly rates are $2,680 for two people. A three-night minimum stay is required. For more details, stop by the website: www.spottedhorseranch.com.

At the base of the mountains in Wilson, **Trail Creek Ranch,** tel. (307) 733-2610, is an old-time 300-acre dude ranch with space for 25 guests. They specialize in horseback riding (of course), but also offer hiking, fishing, weekly cookouts, and a swimming pool. A one-week minimum stay is standard, and all-inclusive rates are $2,800 for two people per week. The ranch is open mid-June to Labor Day.

Located within Grand Teton National Park, 25 miles north of Jackson, **Triangle X Guest Ranch,** tel. (307) 733-2183, www.trianglex.com, is a classic family-oriented ranch with stunning Teton views. The ranch has been in the Turner family for more than six decades. Activities center around horseback riding, but also include kids' programs and nightly events such as Dutch-oven cookouts, naturalist presentations, square dancing, and campfire sing-alongs. All-inclusive weekly rates are $1,145 for two people. The ranch is open May-Oct. and Jan.-March. In the winter months Triangle X goes upscale, with fewer guests (maximum of 35 versus 80 in the summer), a jacuzzi, and three gourmet meals a day. The nightly winter rate is $200 d, including lodging, meals, and use of cross-country skis and snowshoes. There's a two-night minimum stay in winter and a one-week minimum stay in summer.

A longtime favorite—it began taking guests in the 1920s—is **Turpin Meadows Guest Ranch,** tel. (307) 543-2496 or (800) 743-2496, www.turpinmeadow.com. The ranch's Buffalo Valley location provides impressive Teton vistas, along with all the traditional ranch activities: horseback riding, cookouts, and pack trips. Turpin Meadows also has special kids' activities two days a week, as well as weekly natural history programs by Forest Service naturalists. Guests stay in modern cabins and have access to an indoor jacuzzi. Summertime all-inclusive rates are $252/day for two people, with a three-night minimum stay. The ranch is open year-round and is a favorite snowmobile spot in the winter months.

Mountain Resorts

Two noteworthy mountain resorts are east of Moran Junction off US Hwy. 26/287. At Togwotee Pass (9,658 feet) the highway tops the Continental Divide and then slides eastward towards Dubois and the Wind River Valley. The Togwotee Pass area is famous for luxuriously deep snow all winter and is a destination for snowmobilers, cross-country skiers, and dogsledding enthusiasts. Just north of the pass is Teton Wilderness, a place to discover what solitude means. Facing west from the pass, the Teton Range offers up a jagged horizon line. This entire area provides a delicious escape from hectic Jackson and is home to two attractive high-elevation resorts: Cowboy Village Resort at Togwotee and Brooks Lake Lodge. Additional resorts and dude ranches farther to the east are described in the Wind River Mountains Country chapter.

Forty-eight miles northeast of Jackson and just a few miles west of Togwotee Pass is **Cow-**

JACKSON HOLE/GRAND TETON PUBLIC CAMPGROUNDS

The following public campgrounds are available on a first-come basis with no reservations. They are listed by distance and direction from Jackson. Get details for each by calling Bridger-Teton National Forest (BTNF; tel. 307-739-5400), Grand Teton National Park (GTNP; tel. 307-739-3603), or Targhee National Forest (TNF; tel. 208-354-2312). See the text for private RV campgrounds in the area.

CAMPGROUNDS NORTH OF JACKSON

Curtis Canyon Campground; $10, BTNF; seven miles northeast of Jackson, open early June to mid-Sept., six miles of gravel road with fine view of the Tetons

Gros Ventre Campground; $12, GTNP; 10 miles northeast of Jackson, open May to early Oct., along Gros Ventre River, often fills by evening in mid-summer

Atherton Creek Campground; $10, BTNF; 18 miles northeast of Jackson, open early June-Oct., six miles up Gros Ventre Road near Gros Ventre River

Jenny Lake Campground; $12, GTNP; 20 miles north of Jackson, open mid-May to late Sept., tents only (no RVs), campground fills by 8 a.m. in mid-summer

Red Hills Campground; $8, BTNF; 22 miles northeast of Jackson, open early June-Oct., 12 miles up Gros Ventre Road (partly dirt) along Gros Ventre River

Crystal Creek Campground; $8, BTNF; 23 miles northeast of Jackson, open early June-Oct., five miles up Gros Ventre Road (dirt) along Gros Ventre River

Signal Mountain Campground; $12, GTNP; 32 miles north of Jackson, open early May to mid-Oct., on Jackson Lake, dump station, campground fills by 10 a.m. in mid-summer

Colter Bay Campground; $12, GTNP; 40 miles north of Jackson, open mid-May to late Sept., on Jackson Lake, coin-operated showers, dump station, campground fills by noon in mid-summer

Hatchet Campground; $10, BTNF; 40 miles northeast of Jackson, open late June to mid-Sept., in Buffalo Valley

Blackrock Bicycle Campground; free, BTNF; 40 miles northeast of Jackson, open mid-June to early Sept., bikes only, three miles off Hwy. 26/287 in Buffalo Valley, no potable water

Box Creek Campground; free, BTNF; 46 miles northeast of Jackson, open June-Sept., on Buffalo Valley Road, no potable water

Pacific Creek Campground; free, BTNF; 46 miles north of Jackson, open June to early Sept., 12 miles up Pacific Creek Road (enter through Grand Teton National Park)

Lizard Creek Campground; $12, GTNP; 48 miles north of Jackson, open early June to early Sept., on Jackson Lake, campground fills by 2 p.m. in mid-summer

Turpin Meadow Campground; $10, BTNF; 48 miles northeast of Jackson, open June to early Sept., in Buffalo Valley

Sheffield Creek Campground; free, BTNF; 55 miles north of Jackson, open mid-June to mid-Nov., small site off Hwy. 89/191/287 near Flagg Ranch Resort, poor road access until late summer

CAMPGROUNDS SOUTH OF JACKSON

Cabin Creek Campground; $12, BTNF; 19 miles south of Jackson, open late May to mid-Sept., along Snake River Canyon

Elbow Campground; $15, BTNF; 22 miles south of Jackson, open mid-June to mid-Oct., along Snake River Canyon, may be closed in 2000 due to highway construction

Hoback Campground; $12, BTNF; 22 miles southeast of Jackson, open early June to mid-Sept., along Hoback River eight miles east of Hoback Junction

East Table Creek Campground; $15, BTNF; 24 miles south of Jackson, open early June to mid-Oct., along Snake River, road construction may be nearby

Station Creek Campground; $15, BTNF; 25 miles south of Jackson, open mid-June to mid-Oct., along Snake River Canyon, road construction may be nearby

Kozy Campground; $10, BTNF; 30 miles southeast of Jackson, open early June to mid-Sept., along Hoback River 13 miles east of Hoback Junction

Granite Creek Campground; $12, BTNF; 35 miles southeast of Jackson, open late June to mid-Sept., near Granite Hot Springs, nine miles up Granite Creek Road (gravel), reservable only over 4th of July by calling (307) 734-7400

CAMPGROUNDS WEST OF JACKSON

Trail Creek Campground; $6, TNF; 20 miles west of Jackson, open mid-June to mid-Sept., on the west side of Teton Pass

Mike Harris Campground; $6, TNF; 21 miles west of Jackson, open mid-June to mid-Sept., on the west side of Teton Pass

boy Village Resort at Togwotee, tel. (307) 733-8800 or (800) 543-2847, a pleasantly rustic place to spend a night or a week. The resort is a busy place, offering horseback rides, mountain-bike tours, fly-fishing, and backcountry pack trips in summer, along with snowmobiling (the primary winter activity), dogsledding, and cross-country skiing when the snow flies. Togwotee has a variety of accommodations, and guests will enjoy summertime naturalist programs, plus a sauna and four large jacuzzis. Summer rates are $109 d for rooms in the lodge, $129 d for mini-suites, and $159 d for cabins. The mini-suites and cabins sleep up to six people ($8 per person for more than two). In winter, the resort has package deals that include lodging, breakfast and dinner, snowmobile use, a guide, and free airport shuttle. There's a four-night minimum stay in the winter. The resort also houses a steak house, bar, gas station, and convenience store. Togwotee is closed from early April to early June, and from mid-October to mid-November. Get details on the web at www.cowboyvillage.com.

Brooks Lake Lodge, tel. (307) 455-2121, www.brookslake.com, has what may be the finest location of any lodge in Wyoming, with a placid lake in front and the cliffs of Pinnacle Buttes nearby. Built in 1922, the lodge has long served travelers en route to Yellowstone, and its enormous great hall contains big-game trophies from all over the world. The lodge was completely restored in the late 1980s and is now on the National Register of Historic Places. Six guest rooms are available in the main lodge, and six private cabins are hidden in the trees; all are furnished with handmade lodgepole furniture. Guests can ease into the jacuzzi or put on hiking or cowboy boots to explore the magnificent country nearby. The turnoff for Brooks Lake Lodge is 65 miles northeast of Jackson (34 miles east of Moran Junction or 23 miles west of Dubois) and another five miles off the highway via Brooks Lake Road. The lodge is open July-Sept. and late December to March. There's a three-night minimum stay in summer, when the rates are $390 d per day in the lodge or $430 d per day in the cabins. This includes all meals, horseback riding, canoeing, and fishing. Weekly rates are also available, but be sure to reserve far ahead. In winter Brooks Lake Lodge is a popular cross-country skiing and snowmobiling spot. Overnight winter accommodations are $300 d per night in the lodge or $350 d per night in the cabins, including breakfast, dinner, and use of skis. Couples can stay here midweek for $525-625 for two nights, including meals. Snowmobile rentals are available. The restaurant is open to the public for lunch in the winter months, but reservations are mandatory; call a week ahead to reserve a table.

CAMPING

Public Campgrounds

Both the National Park Service and the U.S. Forest Service maintain campgrounds around Jackson Hole. The Jackson Hole/Grand Teton Public Campgrounds chart shows 24 public campgrounds within 50 miles of Jackson. For more specifics on public sites, contact Bridger-Teton National Forest in Jackson at 340 N. Cache Dr., tel. (307) 739-5500, www.fs.fed.us/btnf, or Grand

Teton National Park in Moose, tel. (307) 739-3603, www.nps.gov/grte. In addition to these sites, many people camp for free on dispersed sites on Forest Service lands; see the Forest Service for locations and restrictions.

RV Parks

Jackson has a number of RV parks scattered around town and in surrounding areas. Additional privately run campgrounds are located at Colter Bay and Flagg Ranch Resort inside Grand Teton National Park. For details on these, see Grand Teton National Park below.

None of the private RV parks in the town of Jackson is really noteworthy; "parking lots" would be a better term. They can also be surprisingly expensive—some places charge more for a tent space than it would cost to stay in a motel room in many Wyoming towns! Even more expensive is a ticket for parking RVs overnight on Jackson city streets. It's illegal to do so, and the ordinance is strictly enforced by local police.

Virginian RV Park, 750 W. Broadway, tel. (307) 733-7189 or (800) 321-6982 (summer) or (800) 262-4999 (winter), is the biggest RV parking lot in the area, with over 100 sites on the south end of town. Full hookups costs $34-42; no tents. Guests at the RV park can use the Virginian Lodge's outdoor pool and jacuzzi. It's open May to mid-October. Find the park and lodge on the web at www.virginianlodge.com.

Elk Country Inn, 480 W. Pearl, tel. (307) 733-2364 or (800) 483-8667, www.townsquareinns.com, has a cluster of graveled RV sites for $35, but tents are not allowed; open all year.

Wagon Wheel RV Park & Campground, 525 N. Cache, tel. (307) 733-4588, www.wagonwheelvillage.com, is along Flat Creek on the north end of town. Located behind the motel of the same name, it has both RV hookups ($32) and grassy tent spaces ($15) and is open May-September.

Teton Village KOA, tel. (307) 733-5354 or (800) 562-9043, www.koa.com, is five miles south of Teton Village and six miles from Jackson. The location is out of the way and quiet, with trees providing shade (lacking in other local RV parks). Full RV hookups cost $36, tent sites are $26, and basic camping cabins run $43 d. Also here are a game room and playground. It's open May to mid-October.

Grand Teton Park RV Park is 37 miles northeast of Jackson (six miles east of Moran Junction) along Hwy. 26/287, tel. (307) 733-1980 or (800) 563-6469, www.yellowstonerv.com. There are good views of the Tetons, and facilities include a hot tub, recreation room, and grocery store. The cost is $36 for RVs, $25 for tents. Simple camping cabins go for $44-48, and tepees run $35-39. Open year-round.

Three private campgrounds are in the Hoback Junction area, 12 miles south of Jackson. **Lazy J Corral,** tel. (307) 733-1554, is right on the highway at Hoback Junction and has RV sites for $20; no tent spaces. Open May-October. **Snake River Park KOA,** tel. (307) 733-7078 or (800) 562-1878, www.koa.com, is a mile north of Hoback Junction and has RV spaces for $36, tent sites for $27, and simple "kamping kabins" for $45 d. Open April to mid-October.

Lone Eagle Resort Campground, four miles southeast of Hoback Junction, tel. (307) 733-1090 or (800) 321-3800, www.loneeagleresort.com, sits on 20 acres of land and has a range of amenities including an outdoor pool, hot tub, playground, and game room, along with river trips (extra charge) and bike rentals. Full-hookup RV sites cost $36, and tent sites are $10; open mid-May through September. They also rent tent cabins for $29 and basic log cabins for $67.

FOOD

Jackson stands out from the rest of Wyoming on the culinary scene: chicken-fried steak may be available, but it certainly isn't the house specialty! You won't need to look far to find good food; in fact, the town seems to overflow with impressive (and even more impressively priced) eateries. If you stood in Town Square and walked in any direction for a block you would find at least one restaurant that would be a standout in any other Wyoming town. More than 70 local restaurants do business here—in a town that contains just 8,000 people. To get an idea of what to expect at local restaurants, pick up a copy of the free ***Jackson Hole Dining Guide*** at the visitor center or local restaurants. You'll find the same info online at www.focusproductions.com/jhdining. The guide includes sample menus and brief descriptions of most local establishments. If you don't find a place to your liking among those listed in the dining guide or below, be assured that all the major fast-food outlets line Jackson's streets, ready to grease your digestive tract. And if you just want to eat in, call **Mountain Express,** tel. (307) 734-0123, which will deliver meals from a dozen local restaurants to your motel room in Jackson or Teton Village.

Breakfast

The best breakfast place in Jackson isn't in Jackson, but in Wilson, where **Nora's Fish Creek Inn,** tel. (307) 733-8288, www.jacksonholenet.com/noras, attracts a full house each morning. The food is great, the atmosphere is authentically rustic, and the waitresses are always friendly and fast. Nora's also serves tried-and-true lunches and dinners at very good prices. Highly recommended, but you may have to contend with a smoky atmosphere at the counter in the morning.

Very popular for breakfast and lunch is **Jedediah's House of Sourdough,** 135 E. Broadway, tel. (307) 733-5671, where, as the name implies, sourdough pancakes are the morning specialty. Housed in a 1910 log cabin, the restaurant gets noisy and crowded in the morning, making it a perfect spot for families with young kids. The lunch menu stars burgers, sandwiches, and salads.

Another longtime breakfast and lunch standout is **The Bunnery,** 130 N. Cache Dr., tel. (307) 733-5474. Good omelets, and delicious lunch sandwiches on freshly baked breads.

The old-time crowd heads to **LeJay's Sportsman's Cafe,** 72 S. Glenwood St., tel. (307) 733-3110, a greasy spoon open 24 hours a day. This is the place to go when no other restaurant is open and your stomach is demanding all-American grub. But be ready for clouds of cigarette smoke. Other local breakfast places are listed below under Espresso and Light Meals.

Lunch

One of the most popular noontime spots in Jackson is **Sweetwater Restaurant,** 85 King St., tel. (307) 733-3553, where the lunch menu includes dependably good salads, homemade soups, and a variety of earthy sandwiches. For dinner, try mesquite-grilled chicken or the spinach-and-feta vegetarian casserole. Dinner entrées $16-20. Recommended.

Pearl Street Bagels, 145 Pearl St., tel. (307) 739-1218, serves home-baked bagels (they're on the small side, however) along with espresso and juices. Open daily till 6 p.m. in the summer. They have a second shop in Wilson, tel. (307) 739-1261. The latter is *the* groovy place to be seen in Wilson (OK, so are Nora's and the 'Coach).

Get delicious sub sandwiches on tangy homemade bread at **New York City Sub Shop,** 25 S. Glenwood St., tel. (307) 733-4414. Fastest sandwich makers in the business and vastly better than Subway.

If you're in search of a substantial vegetarian breakfast or lunch, try the cafe at **Harvest Natural Foods,** 130 W. Broadway, tel. (307) 733-5418. The salad-and-soup bar in the back is a favorite lunch break for locals. Great sandwiches, fruit smoothies, and baked goods, too. You won't go wrong here.

Established in 1912 and in the same place since 1937, **Jackson Drug,** right off Town Square at 15 E. Deloney Ave., tel. (307) 733-2442, has an always-crowded soda fountain that serves homemade ice cream and shakes.

For lunches in the Teton Village area, stop by **Westside Store & Deli,** tel. (307) 733-6202, located in the Aspens. The deli will be glad to pack you a big picnic lunch, and it also sells such dinner entrées as lemon dijon chicken, lasagna, and ribs.

Espresso and Light Meals

The hip crowd heads for breakfast and lunch to two excellent local cafes: Betty Rock and Shades. **Betty Rock Cafe and Coffeehouse,** 325 W. Pearl, tel. (307) 733-0747, is a great and noisy place for lunch, with delectable homemade breads, paninis, salads, soups, and espresso. Highly recommended. You'll find similar food and service at the oft-crowded **Shades Cafe,** 82 S. King St., tel. (307) 733-2015. This tiny log cabin has a shady summer-only patio on the side. Breakfasts feature waffles, egg dishes, fruit, and yogurt, plus lattes, mochas, and other coffee drinks. At lunch, the standouts are salads, quiches, burritos, and paninis. Shades is a relaxing place to hang out with the latte habitués, though it does close early in the fall, winter, and spring.

Out in Teton Village across from the tram, **Village Cafe,** tel. (307) 733-5998, serves very good breakfasts, baked goods, sandwiches, lasagna, burritos, Starbucks espresso, and microbrewed beer. Open summers and winters only.

The National Museum of Wildlife Art, two miles north of Jackson on US Hwy. 26/89, houses a delightfully bright little restaurant with dramatic vistas across the National Elk Refuge. Called **Rising Sage Cafe,** tel. (307) 733-8649, the place has a lunch menu that includes panini, pita and hummus, homemade soups served in a bread bowl, salads, and espresso. It's open the same hours as the museum. **Charlie's Jackson Hole Coffee Company,** 49 W. Broadway (upstairs in Pink Garter Plaza), tel. (307) 733-9192 or (800) 771-9192, has espresso and sweets, along with a computer terminal for Internet access.

American

The most popular locals' eatery is **Bubba's Bar-B-Que Restaurant,** 515 W. Broadway, tel. (307) 733-2288. Each evening the parking lot out front is jammed with folks waiting patiently for a chance to gnaw on barbecued spare ribs, savor the spicy chicken wings, or fill up at the salad bar. Lunch is a real bargain, with specials under $5. They don't serve alcohol, but you can bring in your own beer or wine. Although based in Jackson, Bubba's now has restaurants in five other locations around Wyoming, Colorado, and Idaho.

Get great all-American burgers at the '50s-style **Billy's Burgers,** 55 N. Cache Dr., tel. (307) 733-3279. This is the same location as the more upscale Cadillac Grille. The Billy burger is a half-pound monster. Not on the menu, but recommended if you aren't absolutely famished, is the one-third-pound Betty burger. Ask for it.

Next door to Billy's and the Cadillac is the **Million Dollar Cowboy Steakhouse,** tel. (307) 733-4790, with "casual Western elegance" and great steaks, from porterhouse to filet mignon. In addition, the menu includes salads, rack of lamb, seafood, pasta, and vegetarian specials. The bar features a dozen different single malt scotches. Also popular is **Gun Barrel Steakhouse,** 862 W. Broadway, tel. (307) 733-3287, www.gunbarrel.com, where the mesquite-grilled steaks, elk, and buffalo are served up in a hunting-lodge atmosphere with trophy game mounts; they came from a wildlife museum that previously occupied the site. You'll find lots of historic guns and other Old West paraphernalia around the Gun Barrel too, making this an interesting place to explore even if you aren't hungry. It's a bit on the pricey side, with dinner entrées for $15-25. The bar has a wide choice of beers on tap.

Head three miles south of town on US Hwy. 89 to find some of the finest steaks in Jackson Hole at the **Steak Pub,** tel. (307) 733-6977. Dinners are served in a rustic log-cabin setting. Another recommended place is **Camp Creek Inn,** 16 miles south of Jackson in Hoback Canyon, tel. (307) 733-3099 or (800) 228-8460. The cozy fireplace and rustic setting make this a good place to escape the Jackson Hole crowds. Very good steaks and prime rib, and "no mercy" one-

Billy's Burgers, home of the half-pound Billy burger

pound burgers enough to fill even Rush Limbaugh's lardbelly.

Housed within the classic Wort Hotel at 50 N. Glenwood St., **SilverDollar Bar & Grill,** tel. (307) 733-2190, serves surprising and delicious dinners, including fresh Rocky Mountain trout, buffalo T-bones, and peppercorn-encrusted elk chops. Very good Caesar salads too. The bar next door is a fun place for an after-dinner drink.

Horse Creek Station, 10 miles south of Jackson, tel. (307) 733-0810, serves delicious smokehouse meats including pork chops, baby back ribs, chicken, prime rib, and brisket in a casual Old West atmosphere with stuffed animal heads on the walls. A very popular place with both locals and ski bums is the **Mangy Moose** in Teton Village, tel. (307) 733-4913, where you'll find a big salad bar and fair prices on steak, pasta, chicken, and seafood (dinner entrées $11-23). Downstairs is Rainbow Cafe, offering inexpensive burgers, pizza, sandwiches, corned-beef-hash omelets, and other breakfast and lunch fare.

Get chicken atchaflaya, seafood gumbo, crawfish and shrimp étouffée, fried catfish, and other Cajun specialties at **The Acadian House,** 180 N. Millward, tel. (307) 739-1269. Not everything here is Cajun; they also serve such diverse entrées as mahimahi and Thai curry vegetable sauté.

Wilson's **Stagecoach Bar,** tel. (307) 733-4407, makes delicious nachos, burgers, and other pub grub.

Pasta and Pizza

One of the tried-and-true local eateries is **Anthony's Italian Restaurant,** 62 S. Glenwood St., tel. (307) 733-3717. In business since 1977, Anthony's has a reputation for simple food (a bit heavy for some tastes) and attentive, efficient service. Prices are very reasonable, and vegetarians will find several good menu items. Dinners come with homemade soup, salad, and fresh-baked garlic bread—guaranteed to fill you up and then some.

Hidden away on the north end of town, **Nani's Genuine Pasta House,** 242 N. Glenwood, tel. (307) 733-3888, www.nanis.com, is Jackson's gourmet Italian restaurant. Meals are served in a charming little home with an old-country ambience and friendly service. Prices are surprisingly reasonable, with most entrées for $10-17. Many vegan dishes are also available. Be sure to ask about the nightly specials.

Several pizza places stand out in Jackson. You'll find **Calico Italian Restaurant & Bar,** tel. (307) 733-2460, in a garish red and white building three-quarters of a mile north on Teton Village Road. The menu has gone a bit upscale of late, but prices are still reasonable, with entrées for $8-17. During the summer, be sure to get a side salad, fresh from the big house garden; kids will love the two-and-a-half-acre lawn. The bar at Calico is a very popular locals' watering hole. **Mountain High Pizza Pie,** 120 W. Broadway, tel. (307) 733-3646, is a favorite downtown place offering free delivery in Jackson. From mid-October through April, Mountain High's under-$7 stuff-yourself lunchtime pizza buffet (Mon.-Fri. 11:30 a.m.-2 p.m.) is the best meal deal in Jackson. See Breweries below for two other notable pizza places in Jackson Hole.

Continental/Nouvelle Cuisine

If you want fine continental dining and aren't scared off by entrées costing $20 or more, Jackson has much to offer.

Just off Town Square, **Snake River Grill,** upstairs at 84 E. Broadway, tel. (307) 733-0557, is one of Jackson's finest gourmet restaurants—with prices to match (entrées $16-29). The meals are exquisite, and the seasonal menu typically contains a variety of seafood, free-range beef, and organic vegetables that are artfully presented. A few outside tables face the square. Reservations are a must; reserve a week in advance for prime-time seatings in the summer. Snake River Grill is a good place to watch for Jackson's best-known resident, Harrison Ford. Closed November and April.

The Range, 225 N. Cache Dr., tel. (307) 733-5481, serves acclaimed nouvelle-cuisine dinners, making this a favorite of out-on-the-town locals and visitors. The menu varies seasonally, the sauces are delectable, and there are always nightly fish and game specialties. Entrées are $16-27.

For views so spectacular they make it difficult to concentrate on your meal, don't miss **The Granary,** tel. (307) 733-8833, located atop East Gros Ventre Butte west of Jackson. This is also a very popular place for evening cocktails, and the Sunday brunch here is the best around. Dinner entrées run $15-28.

An excellent in-town continental restaurant is **The Blue Lion,** 160 N. Millward St., tel. (307)

733-3912. The front patio makes for delightful summertime dining. Try the Southwestern tempeh crepes or Sicilian chicken. Jackson's most popular nouvelle-cuisine restaurant is **Cadillac Grille,** 55 N. Cache (on the square), tel. (307) 733-3279. The food is artfully prepared and includes a changing menu of seafood, grilled meats, and game. The art-deco decor of the Cadillac helps make it one of the most crowded tourist hangouts in town. Portions tend toward the small side.

Jenny Lake Lodge, inside Grand Teton National Park, is famous for gourmet American cuisine served in an elegantly cozy log lodge. The Sunday dinner buffet is legendary. Open June-Sept. only; call (307) 733-4647 for reservations (required).

Restaurant Terroir, 45 S. Glenwood, tel. (307) 739-2500, is an exquisite little place with a handful of tables and a classy white-linen setting. The menu blends American, Asian, and French influences to create a memorable meal. Entrées are $18-20. The wine list is one of the best in Jackson, with over 200 choices. This isn't a place to bring the kids, but it's fine for a special romantic meal. Open for dinners only; call for reservations (highly recommended).

Inside the ultraluxurious Amangani Resort atop Gros Ventre Butte, **Amangani Grill,** tel. (307) 734-7333 or (877) 734-7333, is open to the public for three meals a day, with a menu that changes frequently. Reservations are advised, and this is decidedly *not* a place for T-shirts or shorts. Dinner entrées are typically $24-32.

Out in the Aspens on Teton Village Rd., **Stiegler's,** tel. (307) 733-1071, has a menu with names big enough to eat—you could start with leberknödel suppe, before a main course of veal sweetbreads forestiere, followed by a topfen palatschinken. The dense Austrian cuisine is outstanding, but the portions are small.

If you enjoy German cooking, particularly veal, lamb, and game, head to the **Alpenhof,** tel. (307) 733-3462, in Teton Village. The **Alpenhof Bistro** upstairs has a more casual setting and a less-expensive dinner menu. People come to the bistro for balcony dining with a close-up view of Teton Village.

South of the Border

For the fastest Mexican food in town (with the possible exception of Taco Bell), drop by **Sanchez Mexican Food,** 75 S. Glenwood, tel. (307) 732-2326, where burritos, tacos, and enchiladas are all under $7. They also have a few seats inside and picnic tables out front. **The Merry Piglets,** 160 N. Cache Dr., tel. (307) 733-2966, is an unpretentious little spot with very good Mexican meals, including the specialty, the cheese crisp. Excellent margaritas too. The restaurant has been here for over three decades.

Mama Inez, 380 W. Pearl, tel. (307) 739-9166, has fill-you-up servings of authentic Mexican cooking, including chimichangas, fajitas, and enchiladas. The largest and most popular Mexican restaurant is **Vista Grande,** tel. (307) 733-6964, on the road to Teton Village. The biggest drawing cards here are the pitchers of margaritas; the food itself is reasonably priced but nothing special.

Asian Food

Chinatown Restaurant, 850 W. Broadway, tel. (307) 733-8856, makes good Chinese dishes—particularly the mu shu vegetables, lemon chicken, and pot stickers—and offers bargain-priced lunch specials. Busy **Lame Duck Chinese Restaurant,** 600 E. Broadway, tel. (307) 733-4311, serves a mix of Asian specialties, including Chinese, Japanese, and even a few Thai specialties. The food is less traditional than Chinatown's. Service can be slow. Get freshly rolled sushi at **Masa Sushi,** tel. (307) 733-2311, located at the Inn at Jackson Hole in Teton Village. Hint to anyone who knows a Thai restaurant owner anywhere in America (or Thailand for that matter): tell them to move to Jackson where people are dying for good Thai food. It never ceases to amaze me that the town has no Thai restaurants.

Breweries

Before Prohibition in 1920, nearly every town in Wyoming had its own brewery, making such local favorites as Hillcrest, Schoenhofen, and Sweetwater. After repeal of "the noble experiment," breweries again popped up, but competition from industrial giants such as Anheuser-Busch and Coors forced the last Wyoming operation—Sheridan Brewing—out of business in 1954. It was another 34 years before commercial beermaking returned. In 1988, Charlie Otto started a tiny backyard operation in Wilson. His **Otto Brothers Brewing Company,** tel. (307) 733-9000, www.ottobrothers.com, now brews its beer just over Teton Pass in Victor, Idaho, but you can sample

Teton Ale, Old Faithful Ale, Moose Juice Stout, Teton Golden Ale, Teton Huckleberry Wheat, and Teton Pass Porter at the company's old 1932 log cabin in Wilson. Sample the beers ($2 for a taste of all six), get a classy Teton Ale T-shirt, or order up savory pizzas, calzones, and salads. It's open daily 4-9 p.m. winter and summer, but call ahead in the fall and spring. You'll find Otto Brothers beers on tap at many Jackson-area bars and restaurants and for sale in six-pack bottles. Or take some home in a "growler," a half-gallon refillable bottle available from local liquor stores.

Snake River Brewing Co. & Restaurant, 265 S. Millward, tel. (307) 739-2337, is the opposite of low-key Otto Brothers. The brewery and restaurant are housed in a bright and spacious old warehouse that has been beautifully remodeled. It fills with a young and convivial crowd of outdoors enthusiasts most evenings, and it features nearly a dozen Snake River beers on tap. The award-winning Zonker Stout is always among these, along with Snake River Lager, and Snake River Pale Ale. The lunch and dinner cafe menu includes delicious thin-crust wood-fired pizzas and calzones, flavorful appetizers, daily pasta specials, sandwiches, and salads. Great food in a lively atmosphere. It's one of *the* places to be seen in Jackson.

Wine Shops

The most complete local wine and beer shops are **Westside Wine & Spirits,** in the Aspens along Teton Village Rd., tel. (307) 733-5038; **The Liquor Store,** next to Albertson's on W. Broadway, tel. (307) 733-4466; and **Dornan's** in Moose, tel. (307) 733-2415, ext. 202. **Broadway Bottle Company,** 200 W. Broadway, tel. (307) 739-9463, also has a fine selection and offers free Friday afternoon wine tastings all summer long, featuring a different choice of wines each week. It's a great way to learn about various vintages from wine experts. You'll generally find the lowest wine prices from **Jackson's Original Discount Liquor Store at Sidewinders,** 802 W. Broadway, tel. (307) 734-5766.

Bakeries

The Bunnery, 130 N. Cache Dr., tel. (307) 733-5474, bakes a big variety of treats and sweets, but it's best known for its hearty-flavored OSM (oat, sunflower, and millet) bread—on the pricey side at around $4 a loaf. Another place for fresh baked goods is **Harvest Natural Foods,** 130 W. Broadway, tel. (307) 733-5418.

The location is a bit out of the way, but a visit to **Wild Flour Bakery,** 345 N. Glenwood, tel. (307) 734-2455, is a must if you're in search of French baguettes and other breads. You can also find the company's goods in several local grocers, and they bake the house bread for several of Jackson's gourmet restaurants. Wild Flour also bakes cookies and muffins.

Housed in the Stagecoach Bar in Wilson, **Patty-Cake West,** tel. (307) 733-7225, creates wonderful sweets and also serves burgers, sandwiches, Mexican food, and espresso.

Groceries

Get groceries from the new **Albertson's,** on the south end of town at the corner of Buffalo Way and Broadway, tel. (307) 733-5950. Inside you'll find a bakery, pharmacy, deli, one-hour photo lab, bank branch, and coffee bar. Meet the locals at the less ostentatious (and generally cheaper) **Food Town,** in the Powderhorn Mall at 970 W. Broadway, tel. (307) 733-0450. As this was written, a large new Smiths grocery store was in the planning stages for Jackson. It is expected to open in 2001 on the south end of town near the corner of High School Rd. and US Hwy. 89.

The best spot for fresh vegetables and fruit is the little **market stand** next to the Maverik gas station on the south end of town. It's open Thurs.-Sat. only in the summer, and it has better prices and higher quality than local grocers.

In business since 1947, **Jackson Hole Buffalo Meat,** 1655 Berger Lane, tel. (307) 733-8343 or (800) 543-6328, www.jhbuffalomeat.com, sells smoked buffalo salami, jerky, roast, and burgers, along with buffalo meat gift packs and New Zealand elk steaks.

For health foods, head downtown to **Harvest Natural Foods,** 130 W. Broadway, tel. (307) 733-5418, or the smaller **Here & Now Natural Foods,** 1925 Moose-Wilson Rd., tel. (307) 733-2742.

ENTERTAINMENT AND THE ARTS

Nightlife

Barflies will keep buzzing in Jackson, especially during midsummer and midwinter, when visitors pack local saloons every night of the week. At least one nightclub always seems to have live tunes; check Jackson's free newspapers to see what's where. Cover charges are generally $3-5 on the weekends, and most other times you'll get in free.

The famous **Million Dollar Cowboy Bar,** on the west side of Town Square, tel. (307) 733-2207, is a favorite of real cowboys and their wannabe cousins. Inside the Cowboy you'll discover burled lodgepole pine beams, four pool tables (nearly always in use), display cases with stuffed dead bears and other cuddly critters, bars inlaid with old silver dollars, and barstools made from old saddles. Until the 1950s, the Cowboy was Jackson's center for illegal gambling. Bartenders kept a close eye on Teton Pass, where messengers used mirrors to deliver warnings of coming federal revenuers, giving folks at the bar time to hide the gaming tables in a back room. Today the dance floor fills with honky-tonking couples as the bands croon lonesome cowboy tunes six nights a week. Looking to learn swing and two-step dancing? Every Thursday you can join an excellent free beginners' class at 7:30 p.m., then dance up a storm when the band comes on at 9.

Just across the square and up the stairs is **Rancher Spirits & Billiards,** where you'll find a room filled with a half dozen pool tables for billiards aficionados. **SilverDollar Bar & Grill,** in the Wort Hotel at 50 N. Glenwood St., tel. (307) 733-2190, offers a setting that might seem more fitting in Las Vegas: gaudy pink neon lights curve around a bar inlaid with 2,032 (count 'em!) silver dollars. It tends to attract an older crowd, and the music is generally of the piano or acoustic variety.

Right next to the tram in Teton Village is **Mangy Moose Saloon,** tel. (307) 733-4913, Jackson Hole's jumpingest pick-up spot and *the* place to rock out. The Moose attracts a hip skier/outdoorsy crowd with rock, blues, or world beat bands Wed.-Sat. both summer and winter. This is also where you'll hear nationally known acts.

Sidewinders Tavern & Sports Grill, 802 W. Broadway, tel. (307) 734-5766, is filled with big-screen TVs for sports enthusiasts. It also offers bands on Saturday nights and Latino dance tunes on Tuesday. Smokers head to the cigar bar, but there's also a big smoke-free section.

The **Shady Lady Saloon** at Snow King Resort, 400 E. Snow King Ave., tel. (307) 733-5200, typically serves up live rock, jazz, or bluegrass music on Wednesday nights. More popular are the Monday night **hootenannies** held in the lodge room of the Snow King Center, where local musicians get together to jam in an all-acoustic set. Join the onstage fun if you have musical talent, or can pretend.

Over in Wilson, **The Stagecoach Bar,** tel. (307) 733-4407, is *the* place to be on Sunday nights 5:30-10 p.m. (Wyoming bars close their doors at 10 p.m. on Sunday.) In the early '70s, when hippies risked getting their heads shaved by rednecks at Jackson's Cowboy Bar, they found the 'Coach a more tolerant place. Today tobacco-chewing cowpokes show their partners slick moves on the tiny dance floor as the Stagecoach Band runs through the country tunes one more time—the band has performed here every Sunday since February 16, 1969! On Thursday nights the 'Coach turns the clock back with disco fever as DJs spin the retro grooves for a polyester-dressed crowd. For more entertainment, try a game of pool. Or just chow down on a tasty buffalo burger. Outside you'll find picnic tables and a volleyball court for pickup games in the summer.

Other spots with occasional live music are the **Acadian House,** 180 N. Millward, tel. (307) 739-1269; the **Spur Bar,** at Dornan's in Moose, tel. (307) 733-2415, ext. 200; **The Granary,** atop East Gros Ventre Butte, tel. (307) 733-8833; **Leek's Marina Restaurant,** along Jackson Lake, tel. (307) 543-2494; and **Teton Pines,** on Teton Village Rd., tel. (307) 733-1005.

Classical Music

In existence since 1962, the **Grand Teton Music Festival** takes place at Walk Festival Hall in Teton Village, with performances of classical and modern works by a cast of 200 world-renowned symphony musicians. Concerts take place evenings late June to late August each year, with chamber music on Tuesday and Wednesday, small ensembles on Thursday, and festival orchestra concerts on Friday and Saturday. They also perform a free outdoor "Music in the Hole" concert on the Fourth of July, plus special young people's concerts later in July. The three-hour-long Friday morning rehearsals are just $5. Call (307) 733-3050 for a schedule of events and ticket prices, or get details on the web at www.gtmf.org.

Musicals and Movies

In addition to the bar scene, summers bring a number of lighthearted acting ventures to Jackson. For family musicals such as *Paint Your Wagon* or *The Unsinkable Molly Brown,* head to **Jackson Hole Playhouse,** 145 W. Deloney, tel. (307) 733-6994. Shows take place Mon.-Sat. evenings in a campy 1890s-style setting. A family saloon (no alcohol) and restaurant are next door.

Productions of Broadway and Western musical comedies play throughout the summer at **Mainstage Theatre,** in the newly remodeled Pink Garter Plaza at 50 W. Broadway, tel. (307) 733-3670. The rest of the year, the Mainstage puts on more serious plays and attracts national touring productions and comedians. Both Mainstage and Jackson Hole Playhouse are very popular with families, and reservations are strongly recommended.

Watch flicks at **Teton Theatre,** 120 N. Cache Dr., **Jackson Hole Twin Cinema,** 295 W. Pearl St., or **MovieWorks Cinema Four-plex,** 860 S. US Hwy. 89. All three of these have the same ownership and phone number: (307) 733-6744.

Rodeo

On Wednesday and Saturday nights in the summer you can watch bucking broncs, bull riders, rodeo clowns, and hard-riding cowboys at the **Jackson Hole Rodeo,** on the Teton County Fair Grounds. Kids get to join in the amusing calf scramble. The rodeo starts at 8 p.m. and costs $8-10 for adults, $6 for ages 4-12, free for kids under four, $25 for the whole family. Rodeos take place from Memorial Day to Labor Day; call (307) 733-2805 for details.

Chuck Wagon Cookouts

Jackson Hole is home to six different chuck wagon eateries offering all-you-can-eat barbecue cookouts and Western musical performances all summer long. Each has its own advantages such as professional musicians, wagon rides, horseback rides, or a particularly beautiful setting. Reservations are highly recommended at all of these.

Run by the Thomas family since 1973, **Bar-T-Five,** 790 Cache Creek Rd., tel. (307) 733-5386 or (800) 772-5386, www.bartfive.com, is one of the best chuck wagon feeds. Horse-drawn Conestoga-style wagons depart just east of Snow King, carrying visitors along Cache Creek past costumed mountain men, cowboys, and Indians. At the in-the-trees cookout site cowboys serenade your meal, tell stories, and crack corny jokes that aren't entirely politically correct. It's great fun for families and busloads of Japanese tourists. Rates are $28 for adults, $21 for ages 6-12, and free for kids under six. Open mid-May through September, with departures at 5:30 and 6:30 p.m. each evening. Recommended.

A/OK Corral, 10 miles south of Jackson near Hoback Junction, tel. (307) 733-6556, www.horsecreekranch.com, has 45-minute horseback or wagon rides that end at an outdoor cookout. Big ranch breakfasts and steak suppers are on the menu. Breakfasts cost $30 for adults, $12 for kids; dinners are $40 for adults with the horseback ride, $28 with a covered-wagon ride. For kids, a covered-wagon ride and dinner are $16. Western musical entertainment is provided with the evening meals.

In beautiful Buffalo Valley, 40 miles northeast of Jackson, **Box K Ranch,** tel. (307) 543-2407 or (800) 729-1410, has two-hour covered-wagon rides into Bridger-Teton National Forest, with magnificent views of the Tetons along the way. The cowboy cookout features steak, barbecue beans, baked potatoes, dessert, and nonalcoholic drinks, all served amid tall aspen trees. Dinners are $25 for adults, $20 for kids 4-11. Breakfast cookouts cost $15 for adults, $12 for kids. Kids under age four are free. Closed Sunday.

Also in Buffalo Valley is **Diamond Cross Ranch,** tel. (307) 543-2015, where you get to watch a horse whisperer at work, listen to cowboy poetry, and enjoy a seven-course chuck wagon dinner for $25.

Along the Teton Village Rd. near Teton Pines, the **Bar J,** tel. (307) 733-3370 or (800) 905-2275, www.barjchuckwagon.com, seats 750 people and fills up many summer evenings. In existence for more than 40 years, Bar J is known for its first-rate musicians who fiddle, sing, yodel, tell jokes, and offer up cowboy poetry. The menu includes a choice of barbecued beef, chicken and beef, or rib-eye steak—each served with baked potatoes, beans, biscuits, applesauce, spice cake, and lemonade (no alcohol). Dinner and entertainment take place in a cavernous building and cost $14-19 for adults (depending upon your meal), $6 for kids under eight, and free for tots. Open Memorial Day to late September, with dinner at 7:30 each evening; many folks arrive earlier to get front-row seats for the show. The Bar J does not offer wagon or horseback rides.

Certainly the most unusual local offering is the **Pitchfork Fondue** at Lucas Lazy Double A Ranch, 5330 N. Spring Gulch Rd., tel. (307) 734-2541. Sirloin steak is cooked on a pitchfork in a cauldron of hot oil! I'm told it's better than it sounds. The meal also includes salads, potatoes, rolls, lemonade, and dessert. The price is $17 for adults, $9 for kids. Open Memorial Day through September.

Green River Outfitters, tel. (307) 733-1044, offers combination trail rides and cookouts in the Gros Ventre Mountains 35 miles south of Jackson. These cost $120 per person, including guided horseback rides, roundtrip transport from Jackson, and a barbecued-steak lunch. Overnight rides and multiday pack trips are also available.

EVENTS

Jackson Hole is packed with entertaining events almost every day of the year. Some of these are little homegrown affairs such as the county fair, while others attract people from near and far. Of particular note are the International Rocky Mountain Stage Stop Sled Dog Race, the Pole-Peddle-Paddle Race, the Elk Antler Auction, the Grand Teton Music Festival, and the Jackson Hole Fall Arts Festival. (In addition to the events listed below, see Grand Targhee Ski Resort later in this chapter for a year-round calendar of events on the other side of the Tetons.)

Winter

December is a particularly beautiful time in downtown Jackson. Lights decorate the elk-antler arches, and a variety of events take place. Buy arts and crafts during the **Christmas Bazaar** early in the month, or take the kids to visit Saint Nick and his elves on Town Square starting in mid-December; they're there daily 5-7 p.m.

Kick the year off by watching (or participating in) the annual **torchlight ski parades** at all three local ski areas. They take place on Christmas evening and New Year's Eve at both Jackson Hole Mountain Resort and Grand Targhee Ski Resort, and on New Year's Eve at Snow King.

Each February, local Shriners hold horse-drawn **cutter races**—essentially a wild chariot race on a quarter mile of ice—at Melody Ranch, six miles south of Jackson. Call (307) 733-1938 for more info.

In existence since 1996, the **International Rocky Mountain Stage Stop Sled Dog Race** (IRMSSSDR) is the largest sled dog race in the lower 48 states. Unlike the Iditarod and most other mushing events, this one is run in short 30- to 80-mile stages totaling 400 miles, with teams ending in a new town each night. As with the Tour de France, it's the total time that counts in this stage race. The race is the creation of Iditarod musher Frank Teasley and nurse Jayne Ottman, who came up with the idea as a way to raise awareness of the need to immunize children; it's unofficially called "The Race to Immunize." The IRMSSSDR (try saying that fast!) starts in Jackson and travels through Moran, Dubois, Pinedale, Lander, Atlantic City, Mountain View, Lyman, Evanston, Kemmerer, Afton, Box Y Guest Ranch (Greys River area), and Alpine before ending in Jackson. Each town has its own activities associated with the event. The race boasts a $100,000 purse and has attracted some of the top names in dog mushing. It's held over 12 days in late January and early February, and it may be linked to the 2002 Salt Lake City Winter Olympics as an exhibition event. Call (307) 734-1163 for details, or check the website: www.wyomingstagestop.org.

Also in February, the **Cowboy Ski Challenge** provides a different kind of race, with skiers pulled behind a horse and rider at speeds of up to 40 miles an hour. The race takes place at the base of Jackson Hole Mountain Resort.

Ski races take place all winter long, ranging from elegant "Powder Eight" Championships in early March to blazingly fast downhill races. (Volunteer to work one of the gates at a downhill race and you get to ski free the rest of the day.) In mid-March, the **Connie Stevens Celebrity Extravaganza** attracts Hollywood types for a weekend of skiing, indoor tennis, and ice hockey to support people with disabilities.

One of the most popular (and dumbest) Jackson events is the **World Championship Snowmobile Hillclimb,** in which man (or woman) and machine churn up the slopes at Snow King Resort. The event takes place in late March.

The ski season ends the first weekend of April with the **Pole-Pedal-Paddle Race,** combining alpine skiing, cross-country skiing, cycling, and canoeing in a wild, tough competition. It's the largest such event in the West and great fun for spectators and contestants—many of whom dress up in goofy costumes. Call (307) 733-6433 for details.

Spring

Spring in Jackson Hole is the least favorite time of the year for many locals. The snow is going, leaving behind brown grass and trees; biking and hiking trails aren't yet passable; and the river is too cold to enjoy. For many folks, this is the time to load up the car and head to Utah for a desert hike in Canyonlands. Despite this, April and May can be a good time to visit, especially if you want to avoid the crowds, need to save money on lodging, or are planning to stay for the summer and need a job and a place to live. (Housing gets progressively more difficult to find after April.)

On the third Saturday in May, the world's only public **elk antler auction** takes place at Town Square, attracting hundreds of buyers from all over the globe. Local Boy Scouts collect five tons of antlers from the nearby National Elk Refuge each spring, with 80% of the proceeds helping to fund feeding of the elk. This may sound like an odd event, but the take is over $100,000! Prices average $10 per pound and the bidding gets highly competitive; perfectly matched pairs can go for over $2,000. The antlers are used in taxidermy, belt buckles, furniture, and most important, to satisfy the high demand for antlers in the insatiable (pun intended) South Korean and Chinese aphrodisiac markets. There's more than a touch of irony in the Boy Scouts making money from the sale of sexual stimulants! Call (307) 733-5935 for more info.

Summer

Memorial Day weekend brings **Old West Days,** complete with a parade, Indian dancing, street dance, barbecue dinner, blacksmithing demonstrations, children's rodeo, music, and **mountain-man rendezvous.** Call (307) 733-3316 for details. The **Fourth of July** is another big event in Jackson, with a parade, rodeo, barbecue, and an impressive fireworks show from Snow King Mountain. Another very popular Fourth of July event is the free **Music in the Hole** outdoor classical concert by the Grand Teton Music Festival orchestra; call (307) 733-1128.

All summer long, the **Jackson Hole Rodeo** brings spills and thrills to town every Wednesday and Saturday night. See Entertainment and the Arts above for the full scoop on this must-see event. Another ongoing event is the **Grand Teton Music Festival,** providing summertime classical music at Teton Village. See Entertainment and the Arts above for details.

The last week of July brings an always-fun **Teton County Fair,** tel. (307) 733-5289, with 4-H exhibits, pig wrestling in the mud, free pony rides and a petting zoo, live music and comedy acts, a carnival, rodeos, and everyone's favorite: a bang-up demolition derby on the final Sunday night.

In early September, the invitation-only **Jackson Hole One-Fly Contest** attracts anglers from all over, including a number of celebrity competitors. For details, call (307) 733-3270 or (800) 570-3270.

Fall

Jackson Hole is at its most glorious in the fall, as aspens and cottonwoods turn a fire of yellow and orange against the Teton backdrop. Most tourists have fled back home, leaving locals and hardier visitors to savor the cool autumn nights. The peak time for **fall colors** is generally the first week of October—considerably later than most people expect. The primary autumn event is the **Jackson Hole Fall Arts Festival,** featuring exhibits at the National Museum of Wildlife Art and local galleries, a miniature art show, art demonstrations, silent auctions, live music, and other events over a 10-day period from mid- to late September. Also fun is a "quick draw" in which artists paint, draw, and sculpt while you watch; the pieces are then auctioned off. For more info and a schedule of the many events, call (307) 733-3316. The festival's **Arts for the Parks National Art Competition** attracts thousands of paintings representing scenes from America's national parks. This isn't for amateurs; the purse is $50,000. The banquet and silent auction seats fill by mid-August; call (307) 733-

2787 or (800) 553-2787 for reservations. In early October, **Quilting in the Tetons** brings a week of exhibits, classes, workshops, and quilting demonstrations. Call (307) 733-3087 for details, or point your browser to www.quiltthetetons.org.

RIVER RAFTING

Jackson Hole's most popular summertime recreational activity is running Wyoming's largest river, the Snake. Each year more than 150,000 people climb aboard rafts, canoes, and kayaks to float down placid reaches of the Snake or to blast through the boiling rapids of Snake River Canyon. (As an aside, the name "Snake" comes from the Shoshone Indians, who used serpentine hand movements as sign language for their tribal name—a motion trappers misinterpreted as a snake and applied to the river flowing through Shoshone land.)

Almost 20 different rafting companies offer dozens of different raft trips each day of the summer. Although you may be able to walk up

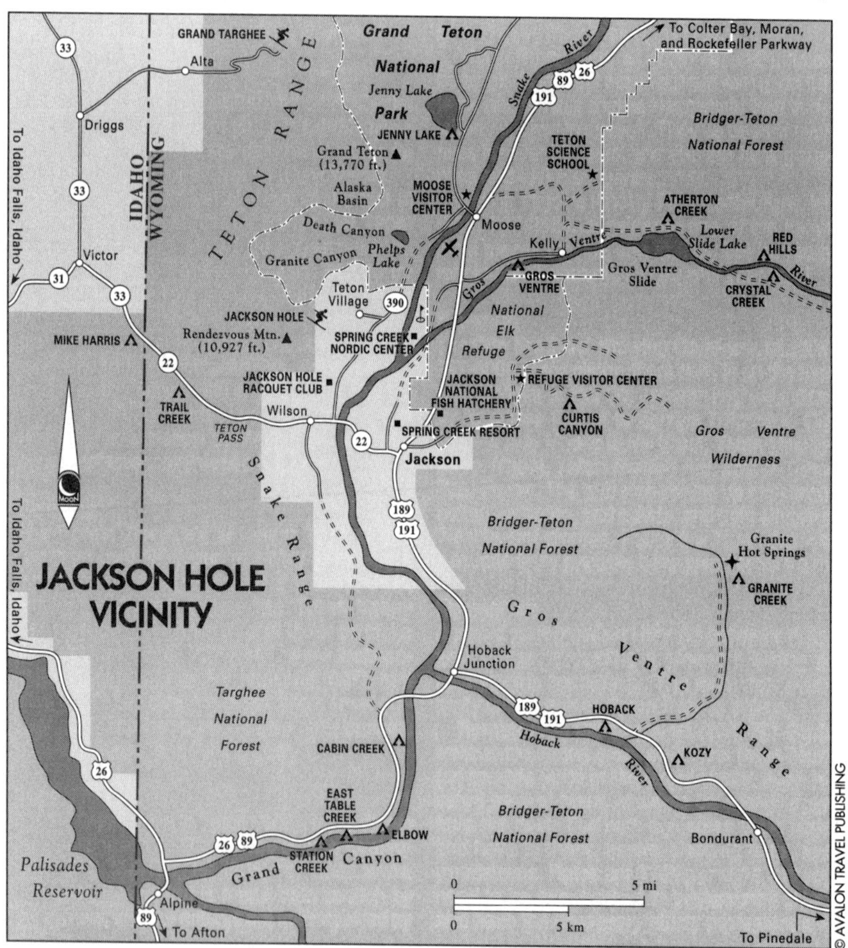

and get a raft trip the same day, it's a good idea to reserve ahead for any river trip in July and August. In general, try to book a trip three or four days in advance if possible, and at least one week ahead if you need a specific time, prefer an overnight float trip, or are traveling with a larger group. One or two people are more likely to get onboard at the last minute.

You may want to ask around to determine the advantages of each company. Some are cheaper but require you to drive a good distance from town; others offer more experienced crews; still others provide various perks such as fancy meals, U-paddle trips, overnight camps along the river, interpretive trips, or boats with fewer (or more) people. A number of operators also lead seven-hour combination trips that include a lazy float followed by a meal break and a wild whitewater run.

The rafting companies generally operate from mid-May to late September, and river conditions change through the season. Highest flows—and the wildest rides—are generally in May and June. Get a complete listing of floating and boating outfits, along with descriptive brochures, from the Wyoming State Information Center in Jackson.

Float Trips

The gentlest way to see the Snake is by taking one of the many commercial float trips. Along the way, you'll be treated to stunning views of the Tetons and glimpses of eagles, ospreys, beavers, and perhaps moose or other wildlife along the riverbanks. A number of companies—Fort Jackson, Grand Teton Lodge Co., Heart Six Ranch, Signal Mountain, Solitude, and Triangle X—offer five- or 10-mile scenic float trips along the quiet stretch within Grand Teton National Park, generally putting in at Deadman's Bar or Schwabacher Landing and taking out in Moose. Flagg Ranch Resort has float and whitewater rafting on the Snake River above Jackson Lake. Several other rafting operations offer 13-mile float trips outside the park (these typically include a lunch), putting in at the bridge near Wilson and taking out above Hoback Junction. These companies include Barker-Ewing, Dave Hansen, Flagg Ranch/O.A.R.S., Lewis & Clark, Lone Eagle, Sands, and Teton Expeditions.

Prices run $32-40 for adults and $22-30 for children. Age limits vary, but kids must generally be at least eight to float the river. Roundtrip transportation from Jackson is included by most (but not all) companies. A wide variety of special voyages are also available, including overnight camping, and fish-and-float trips.

Call one of the following raft companies for details, or pick up their slick brochures at the visitor center or from their offices scattered around town: **Barker-Ewing Float Trips,** tel. (307) 733-1000 or (800) 448-4202, www.barker-ewing.com; **Dave Hansen Whitewater,** tel. (307) 733-6295 or (800) 732-6295, www.davehansenwhitewater.com; **Fort Jackson Scenic Snake River Float Trips,** tel. (307) 733-2583 or (800) 735-8430; **Grand Teton Lodge Float Trips,** tel. (307) 543-2811 or (800) 628-9988, www.gtlc.com; **Heart Six Ranch,** tel. (307) 543-2477 or (888) 543-2477, www.heartsix.com; **Lewis & Clark Expeditions,** tel. (307) 733-4022 or (800) 824-5375, www.lewisandclarkexped.com; **Lone Eagle Whitewater,** tel. (307) 733-1090 or (800) 321-3800, www.loneeagleresort.com; **Mad River Boat Trips,** tel. (307) 733-6203 or (800) 458-7238, www.mad-river.com; **Sands Wild Water,** tel. (307) 733-4410 or (800) 358-8184, www.sandswhitewater.com; **Signal Mountain Lodge & Marina,** tel. (307) 733-5470 or (307) 543-2831, www.signalmtnlodge.com; **Solitude Scenic Float Trips,** tel. (307) 733-2871 or (888) 704-2800, www.jacksonwy.com/solitude; **Teton Expeditions** (the same folks run Jackson Hole Whitewater), tel. (307) 733-1007 or (888) 700-7238, www.tetonexpeditions.com; and **Triangle X Float Trips,** tel. (307) 733-5500, www.trianglex.com. **Flagg Ranch Rafting,** tel. (307) 543-2861 or (800) 443-2311, www.flaggranch.com, leads 10-mile float trips down the upper Snake River, starting at Flagg Ranch Resort and heading downriver to Jackson Lake. These trips are actually run using O.A.R.S. boats and guides. O.A.R.S. also leads one- to five-day sea kayaking trips around Jackson Lake; see Grand Teton National Park for details.

Note that a few of these operators are regarded as "training grounds" for other companies; recommended rafting outfits with good records include Barker-Ewing, Flagg Ranch/O.A.R.S., Solitude, Teton Expeditions, and Triangle X.

Whitewater Trips

Below Jackson, the Snake enters the wild Snake River Canyon, a stretch early explorers labeled "the accursed mad river." The usual put-in point for whitewater "rapid transit" trips is West Table Creek Campground, 26 miles south of Jackson. The take-out point is Sheep Gulch, eight miles downstream. In between the two, the river rocks and rolls through the narrow canyon, pumping past waterfalls and eagle nests and then over the two biggest rapids, Big Kahuna and Lunch Counter, followed by the smaller Rope and Champagne Rapids. For a look at the action from the highway, stop at the paved turnout at milepost 124, where a trail leads down to Lunch Counter. The river changes greatly through the season, with the highest water and wildest rides in June. By August the water has warmed enough for a quick dip. Be sure to ask your river guide about the Jeep that sits in 60 feet of water below Lunch Counter!

Whitewater trips last around three and a half hours (including transportation from Jackson) and cost $30-40 for adults, $29-34 for children (age limits vary). Seven-hour combination trips that include a float trip, meal, and whitewater run are $55-60 for adults or $50 for kids. Overnight trips (same river distance as the combination trips) cost approximately $112 for adults and $85 for kids. You'll find discounted rates early or late in the summer and with operators who use Titanic-size 16-person rafts. The U-paddle versions are more fun than letting the guide do all the work in an oar raft, and the smaller eight-person rafts provide the most challenging (and wettest) runs. Most companies include roundtrip transportation from Jackson.

Expect to get wet, so wear lightweight clothes and bring a jacket for the return ride. Most rafting companies provide wetsuits and booties. Note that this is not exactly a wilderness experience, especially in mid-July, when stretches of the river look like a Los Angeles freeway with traffic jams of rafts, kayaks, inner tubes, and other flotsam and jetsam. The river isn't as crowded on weekdays and early in the morning; take an 8 a.m. run for the fewest people.

Don't take your own camera along unless it's waterproof; bankside float-tographers are positioned along the biggest rapids to shoot both commercial and private rafters. Stop by Float-O-Graphs at 130 W. Broadway, tel. (307) 733-6453 or (888) 478-7427, www.floatographs.com, for a photo from your run. Another company with a similar service is **Whitewater Photos & Video,** 140 N. Cache Dr., tel. (307) 733-7015 or (800) 948-3426.

For details on whitewater raft trips, contact one of the following companies: **Barker-Ewing Whitewater,** tel. (307) 733-1000 or (800) 448-4202, www.barker-ewing.com; **Dave Hansen Whitewater,** tel. (307) 733-6295 or (800) 732-6295, www.davehansenwhitewater.com; **Jackson Hole Whitewater,** tel. (307) 733-1007 or (800) 700-7238, www.jhwhitewater.com; **Lewis & Clark Expeditions,** tel. (307) 733-4022 or (800) 824-5375, www.lewisandclarkexped.com; **Lone Eagle Whitewater,** tel. (307) 733-1090 or (800) 321-3800, www.loneeagleresort.com; **Mad River Boat Trips,** tel. (307) 733-6203 or (800) 458-7238, www.mad-river.com; **Sands Wild Water,** tel. (307) 733-4410 or (800) 358-8184, www.sandswhitewater.com; or **Snake River Park Whitewater,** tel. (307) 733-7078 or (800) 562-1878, www.srpkoa.com.

Recommended companies with good safety records and well-trained staff include Barker-Ewing, Dave Hansen, Jackson Hole Whitewater, and Sands. The largest local rafting company, Mad River, has a reputation as a proving ground for novice guides. It's your choice, but I also would personally not raft with either Lone Eagle Whitewater or Snake River Park Whitewater.

Float It Yourself

Grand Teton National Park in Moose, tel. (307) 739-3602, has useful information on running the park portions of the river; ask for a copy of *Floating the Snake River.* Note that life jackets, boat permits ($5 for a seven-day permit), and registration are required to run the river through the park, and that inner tubes and air mattresses are prohibited. Floating the gentler parts (between Jackson Lake Dam and Pacific Creek) is generally easy for even novice boaters and canoeists, but below that point things get more dicey. The water averages two or three feet deep, but it sometimes exceeds 10 feet and flow rates are often more than 8,000 cubic feet per second, creating logjams, braided channels, strong currents, and dangerous sweepers. Peak flows are between mid-June and early July. Inexperienced rafters or anglers die nearly every year in the river. Flow-rate signs are posted at most river landings, the Moose Visitor Center, and the Buffalo Ranger Station in Moran. If you're planning to raft or kayak on the whitewater parts of the Snake River, be sure to contact the Bridger-Teton National Forest office in Jackson, tel. (307) 739-5500, for additional information.

Excellent waterproof maps of the Grand Canyon of the Snake River are sold at the Forest Service office at 340 N. Cache. In addition to showing the rapids, these maps describe local geology and other features.

Rent rafts from **Riding & Rafts** in Alpine, tel. (307) 654-9900; **Rent-A-Raft** in Hoback Junction, tel. (307) 733-2728 or (800) 321-7328; or **Leisure Sports** in Jackson at 1075 S. US Hwy. 89, tel. (307) 733-3040. Call local taxi companies for rafting shuttle services.

FISHING AND BOATING

Fishing

Jackson Hole has some of the finest angling in Wyoming, with native Snake River cutthroat (a distinct subspecies) and brook trout in the river, along with Mackinaw (lake trout), cutthroat, and brown trout in the lakes. The Snake is a particular favorite of beginning fly-fishing enthusiasts; popular shoreside fishing spots are just below Jackson Lake Dam and near the Wilson Bridge. (I've heard complaints from some readers that they had no luck fishing in Jackson Hole, but others pull in fish every time they go out.) Jackson Lake may provide higher odds for catching a fish, but you'll need to rent a boat from one of the marinas. This is the place parents take kids to increase their odds of catching a fish. Another very popular fishing hole is just below the dam on Jackson Lake. Flat Creek on the National Elk Refuge is an acclaimed spot for fly-fishing. Note that Wyoming fishing licenses are valid within Grand Teton National Park but not in Yellowstone, where you'll need a separate permit.

Many local companies offer guided fly-fishing float trips down the Snake River and other area waterways. Two people (same price for one person) should expect to pay $325-350 a day for a guide, rods and reels, lunch, and boat. Your fishing license and flies are extra. The visitor center has a listing of local fishing guides and outfitters, and its racks are filled with their brochures.

If you'd rather do it yourself, pick up a copy of the free ***Western Fishing Newsletter,*** which offers descriptions of regional fishing areas and advice on which lures to try. Find it at **Jack Dennis' Outdoor Shop,** 50 E. Broadway, tel. (307) 733-3270 or (800) 570-3270, www.jackdennis.com. While there, you may want to buy a regional guide to fishing such as *Flyfisher's Guide to Wyoming* by Ken Retallic (Gallatin Gateway, MT: Wilderness Adventures Press) or *Fishing Wyoming* by Kenneth Lee Graham (Helena, MT: Falcon Publishing Co.).

Jackson has several excellent fly-fishing shops, including the aforementioned Jack Dennis' Outdoor Shop. **Westbank Anglers,** 3670 Teton Village Rd., tel. (307) 733-6483 or (800) 922-3474, www.westbank.com, is a nationally known fly-fishing dealer with a slick mail-order catalog, excellent fishing clinics, and float trips.

> *Somewhere at the eastern base of the Tetons did those hoofprints disappear into a mountain sanctuary where many crooked paths have led. He that took another man's possession, or he that took another man's life, could always run here if the law or popular justice were too hot at his heels. Steep ranges and forests walled him in from the world on all four sides, almost without a break; and every entrance lay through intricate solitudes. Snake River came into the place through canyons and mournful pines and marshes, to the north, and went out at the south between formidable chasms. Every tributary to this stream rose among high peaks and ridges, and descended into the valley by well-nigh impenetrable courses. . . . Down in the bottom was a spread of level land, broad, and beautiful, with the blue and silver Tetons rising from its chain of lakes to the west and other heights residing over its other sides.*
>
> —FROM OWEN WISTER'S *THE VIRGINIAN*

Both **High Country Flies,** 185 N. Center St., tel. (307) 733-7210, www.highcountryflies.com, and **Orvis Jackson Hole,** 485 W. Broadway, tel. (307) 733-5407, offer fly-fishing classes and sell quality gear. Rent fishing rods, fly rods, float tubes, and waders from Jack Dennis, High Country Flies, or **Leisure Sports,** 1075 S. US Hwy. 89, tel. (307) 733-3040.

Kayaking and Canoeing

Snake River Kayak & Canoe School, 155 W. Gill St., tel. (307) 733-3127 or (800) 529-2501, www.snakeriverkayak.com, offers sea kayaking and canoeing classes. Full-day private lessons—including transportation, boats, paddles, wetsuit, rubber booties, and lifejackets—cost $230 per person; with two students they are $130 per person. Beginners may want to start out with one of the three-hour "rubber duckie" inflatable kayak river trips for $45. In addition, the school has sea kayak tours of Yellowstone Lake. **Teton Aquatics,** at the same address and phone, rents practically anything that floats: canoes, sea kayaks, whitewater kayaks, inflatable kayaks, rowboats, and rafts, all with paddles and roof racks included. Also available for rent are scuba equipment, water skis, dry bags, and life jackets.

The folks at **Rendezvous River Sports** (a.k.a. Jackson Hole Kayak School), 1033 W. Broadway, tel. (307) 733-2471 or (800) 733-2471, www.jhkayakschool.com, teach a wide range of kayaking courses from the absolute beginner level to advanced "hairboating" for experts. Classes include kayak roll clinics ($75), river rescue ($120), and special women's and kids' classes. Two-day introductory classes cost $235; four days of instruction is $450. Private lessons are available, and the company rents sea kayaks and whitewater kayaks.

Leisure Sports, 1075 South US Hwy. 89, tel. (307) 733-3040, rents rafts, canoes, kayaks, inflatable kayaks, water skis, wet suits, dry bags, life jackets, and all sorts of other outdoor equipment (including jet skis). They can also provide a shuttle service for rafters. **Adventure Sports** in Moose, tel. (307) 733-3307, also rents canoes and kayaks.

Windsurfing

Jackson Lake is a popular sailboarding place with moderate winds (perfect for beginners) and an impressive Teton backdrop. Advanced windsurfers looking for stronger wind conditions head to Slide Lake east of Kelly or to blow-me-down Yellowstone Lake. Equipment rentals are not available locally.

OTHER SUMMER RECREATION

Horsin' Around

Think of the Wild West and one animal always comes to mind—the horse. A ride on Old Paint gives city slickers a chance to saunter back in time to a simpler era and to simultaneously learn how ornery and opinionated horses can be. If it rains, you'll also learn why cowboys are so enthralled with cowboy hats. In Jackson Hole you can choose from brief half-day trail rides in Grand Teton National Park all the way up to weeklong pack trips into the rugged Teton Wilderness. The visitor center has a brochure listing more than a dozen local outfitters and stables that provide trail rides and pack trips.

For rides by the hour or day (approximately $20 for a one-hour ride or $75 for all day), try **Scott's Jackson Hole Trail Rides** in Teton Village, tel. (307) 733-6992; **Snow King Stables,** behind Snow King Resort, tel. (307) 733-5781, www.snowking.com; **Spring Creek Ranch,** atop Gros Ventre Butte off Spring Gulch Rd., tel. (307) 733-8833 or (800) 443-6139, www.springcreekranch. com; **A/OK Corral,** in Hoback Junction, tel. (307) 733-6556, www.horsecreekranch.com; **Mill Iron Ranch,** 10 miles south of Jackson, tel. (307) 733-6390 or (888) 808-6390, www.jacksonwy.com/millironranch; or **Goosewing Ranch,** 25 miles east of Kelly near the Gros Ventre Wilderness, tel. (307) 733-5251 or (888) 733-5251, www.goosewingranch.com. Of these, Scott's Jackson Hole Trail Rides, Spring Creek Ranch, and Mill Iron Ranch are very well liked, but you probably won't go wrong with any of these companies. Farther afield are a number of companies offering trail rides, including four that operate out of Buffalo Valley (45 miles northeast of Jackson): **Buffalo Valley Ranch,** tel. (307) 543-2026 or (888) 543-2477; **Two Ocean Pass Ranch & Outfitting,** tel. (307) 543-2309 or (800) 726-2409; **Turpin Meadow Ranch,** tel. (307) 543-2496 or (800) 743-2496, www.turpinmeadow.com; and **Yellowstone Outfitters/**

Wagons West, tel. (800) 447-4711. More trail rides are offered at **Cowboy Village Resort at Togwotee,** tel. (307) 733-8800 or (800) 543-2847, www.cowboyvillage.com, 48 miles northeast of Jackson on the way to Togwotee Pass. The minimum age for horseback riding is typically five or six; these young children typically ride while the horse is being led around by a parent. Many of the companies above also offer combination horseback rides and cookouts for an extra fee.

Rides of all sorts are available in Grand Teton National Park at **Jackson Lake Lodge** and **Colter Bay Corral;** call (307) 733-2811 or (800) 628-9988 for specifics. In Alpine (35 miles southwest of Jackson), **Riding & Rafts,** tel. (307) 654-9900, offers unguided horse rentals for $15 for the first hour and $12 for subsequent hours; it's the only place for do-it-yourselfers in the area.

Experienced riders head out Spring Creek Rd. to **Spring Creek Equestrian Center,** tel. (307) 739-9062. The center (not connected with Spring Creek Ranch) emphasizes English riding, with lessons in dressage, cross-country, and jumping. Facilities include a heated indoor arena, three outdoor arenas, a cross-country course, and a small tack store. The equestrian center is open to the public, but is primarily for those looking to enroll in extended lessons, particularly people with their own horses.

Jackson Hole Llamas, tel. (307) 739-9582 or (800) 830-7316, www.jhllamas.com, offers backcountry treks with these fascinating and gentle animals.

Wagon Trains

Two local companies lead overnight wagon-train rides (in wagons with rubber tires) into the country around Jackson Hole. **Wagons West,** tel. (307) 886-9693 or (800) 447-4711, charges $595 for four days (bring your sleeping bag) and also has one-night and five-night packages. **Double H Bar,** tel. (307) 734-6101 or (888) 734-6101, www.jacksonholenet.com/tetonwagon, charges $745 for a three-night package that includes horseback and wagon riding, meals, and camping gear.

Mountain-biking

Jackson Hole offers all sorts of adventures for cyclists, particularly those with mountain bikes. **Teton Cycle Works,** 175 N. Glenwood St., tel. (307) 733-4386; **Hoback Sports,** 40 S. Millward St., tel. (307) 733-5335, www.hobacksports.com; **The Edge Sports,** 490 W. Broadway, tel. (307) 734-3916; **Leisure Sports,** 1075 S. US Hwy. 89, tel. (307) 733-3040; **Wilson Backcountry Sports,** in Teton Village, tel. (307) 733-5228; **Teton Village Sports,** in Teton Village, tel. (307) 733-2181 or (800) 874-4224; and **Adventure Sports** in Moose, tel. (307) 733-3307, all rent mountain bikes and helmets for around $25 per day, $15 per half day. Several of these also rent hybrid bikes, bike trailers, car racks, and kids' bikes, and most sell and repair bikes.

The easiest places to ride are the **Jackson Hole Community Pathways,** a series of several paved paths. A four-mile section starts behind the main post office on Maple Way, crosses US Hwy. 89, and continues past the high school be-

getting ready to hit the trail

fore turning north to meet the road to Wilson (State 22). Another six-mile portion heads south of town, paralleling the highway almost to the Snake River bridge. It provides a connection to the very popular Game Creek Trail, which meets the Cache Creek Trail, circling back to Jackson behind Snow King. In addition, two shorter trails are in the Wilson and Teton Pines areas. Get details from the Friends of Pathways, tel. (307) 733-4534, www.jhpathways.org.

Most bike shops provide maps of local mountain-bike routes, or you can purchase a waterproof Jackson Hole mountain-biking map. Note that mountain bikes are not allowed on hiking trails in Grand Teton National Park or in Forest Service wilderness areas. If you visit Jackson early in the season, check out the Jenny Lake road inside the park; in April it's plowed but closed to cars. Great for an easy and very scenic mountain-bike ride.

Half-day mountain-bike tours are available for $40-50 per day from **Fat Tire Tours/Hoback Sports,** tel. (307) 733-5335, www.hobacksports.com; one of the tours includes a chairlift ride to the top of Snow King. **Teton Mountain Bike Tours,** tel. (307) 733-0712 or (800) 733-0788, www.tetonmtbike.com, offers scenic half- or all-day bike trips through Grand Teton and Yellowstone National Parks as well as Bridger-Teton National Forest and the National Elk Refuge. These are for all levels of ability, with prices starting at $30 for a three-hour ride.

Scenic Rides

Take a fast and very scenic ride to the top of Rendezvous Mountain (10,450 feet) aboard the **aerial tram** at Teton Village. The tram ride takes 10 minutes, gains more than 4,000 feet in elevation, and costs $16 for adults, $13 for seniors, $6 for ages 6-17, free for kids under six. Call (307) 733-2753 or (800) 450-0477 for details. Open daily late May to late September, this is a sensational way to reach the alpine. On top is a small snack shop, but you should bring a lunch since the choices are limited and pricey. Several trails provide enjoyable hikes from the top, and naturalists lead free two-hour walks at 9:30 a.m. and 12:30 p.m. daily. You can rent hiking boots at Nick Wilson's Cafe and Gift Shop, at the base of the mountain. Be sure to pack drinking water and a warm jacket. The summit of Rendezvous Mountain is a favorite place for paragliders to launch. Tandem paragliding flights ($175) are available from **Two Can Fly Paragliding,** tel. (307) 739-2626. No experience is needed for these half-hour flights.

At Snow King Mountain right on the edge of Jackson, the resort's main **chairlift** operates during the summer, taking folks for a 20-minute ride to the summit of the 7,751-foot mountain for $7 ($5 for kids under 13, $6 for seniors). The chairlift runs daily 9 a.m.-6 p.m. On top you'll find a short nature trail and panoramic views of the Tetons. Call (307) 733-5200 for details. Also at Snow King is the 2,500-foot-long **Alpine Slide,** a favorite of kids. For adults and teens, the cost is $8 for one ride or $19 for three rides; for ages 6-12, it's $7 for one ride or $16 for three; and for children under six (riding with an adult) it's $1 per ride. Call (307) 733-7680 for details.

On the other side of the Tetons at **Grand Targhee Ski Resort,** you can ride the chairlift for $8 ($5 for kids) to the 10,200-foot summit of Fred's Mountain, where Grand Teton stands just seven miles away. The lift operates Wednesday, Saturday, and Sunday in June, and Wed.-Sun. in July and August.

Swimming

Jackson is home to the marvelous **Teton County/Jackson Recreation Center,** 155 E. Gill St., tel. (307) 739-9025, which includes an indoor aquatics complex with a lap pool, corkscrew water slide, and hot tub, plus a wading pool featuring a waterfall, slide, and water geyser. After your workout, relax in the sauna and steam room. Nonresident prices are a steep $6 for adults, $4.75 for seniors and ages 13-17, $3.50 for ages 3-12, and $16 for families. The rec center also offers a variety of courses and activities, including yoga, toddler swimming, basketball, volleyball, and aerobics. It's open Mon.-Fri. 6 a.m.-9 p.m., Saturday noon-9 p.m., and Sunday noon-7 p.m.

Out of the way is the wonderful hot mineral pool (93-112° F) at **Granite Hot Springs,** tel. (307) 733-6318. Head south 12 miles to Hoback Junction and then 12 miles east on US Hwy. 189 to the turnoff for Granite. The pool is another 10 miles out a well-maintained gravel road—a total of 35 miles from Jackson. Entrance is $5.50 for adults, $3.50 for ages 3-12, free for infants; open daily 10 a.m. till dusk in the summer.

Golf and Tennis

Jackson Hole Golf & Tennis Club, a mile north of town, tel. (307) 733-3111, has an 18-hole golf course (rated one of the 10 best in America), a private swimming pool, and tennis courts. Also here is The Strutting Grouse Restaurant and Lounge, the perfect place for outdoor dining on the patio.

The **Teton Pines Country Club,** on Teton Village Rd., tel. (307) 733-1773 or (800) 238-2223, www.tetonpines.com, is Jackson Hole's other golf spot. Its Arnold Palmer-designed 18-hole championship course is very challenging; 14 of the holes require over-water shots. The club also features a grand clubhouse, tennis courts, a large (and private) outdoor pool, and fine dining at The Pines restaurant. Both Teton Pines and Jackson Hole Golf & Tennis Club have rentals and lessons for golfers and tennis aficionados. And for the truly serious professional golfer, **Alpine Miniature Golf,** tel. (307) 733-5200, offers a Lilliputian 18-hole course next to the Alpine Slide at Snow King Resort.

More Sports

Teton Rock Gym, 1116 Maple Way, tel. (307) 733-0707, offers large indoor climbing walls, a weight room, climbing instruction, and gear rentals. See Grand Teton National Park for other mountain-climbing options.

If you're feeling flush with cash, call **Rainbow Balloon Flights,** tel. (307) 733-0470 or (800) 378-0470, or **Wyoming Balloon Co.,** tel. (307) 739-0900, both of which offer one-hour hot-air balloon flights for $175 per person. Wyoming Balloon Co. takes off from the Jackson Hole side of the mountains. Rainbow picks people up in Jackson and transports them over the mountains to Teton Valley, Idaho, for the flight.

For something a bit less exciting, there's always the local bowling alley, **Jackson Bowl,** at 1110 Maple Way, tel. (307) 733-2695.

Take exercise classes at **Jackson Hole Athletic Club,** 875 W. Broadway, tel. (307) 733-8830, which has a gymnasium with Nautilus and other equipment.

Hikes, Historical Walks, and Photo Treks

During June, July, and August, the **Teton County Parks and Recreation Department,** inside the Teton County/Jackson Recreation Center at 155 E. Gill St., tel. (307) 739-9025, sponsors various outings, including hikes for adults every Tuesday and Thursday ($7); senior walks on Monday morning (free); and kids outings with swimming, hiking, and more on Wednesday and Friday ($5). The office also rents out volleyballs, horseshoes, and croquet sets.

The Jackson Hole Museum, 105 N. Glenwood, tel. (307) 733-2414, leads hour-long **historical walking tours** of Jackson's downtown at 11 a.m. on Tuesday, Thursday, Friday, and some Saturdays, Memorial Day-September. The cost is $2 for adults, $1 for seniors and students, and $5 for families.

Educational nature walks into the mountains around Jackson are offered by **The Hole Hiking Experience,** tel. (307) 690-4453, www.holehike.com. Rates start at $45 ($32 for kids) for a four-hour hike. For a free version, Grand Teton National Park offers its own guided walks and nature talks throughout the year (see Grand Teton National Park for details). **Great Plains Wildlife Institute,** tel. (307) 733-2623, www.wildlifesafari.com, specializes in wildlife safaris and photography expeditions within Grand Teton and Yellowstone National Parks. The most unusual local tours are the **Movie Tours of Jackson's Hole,** where you'll learn the stories and see the locations for such films as *Shane* and *The Big Trail,* not to mention *Son of Lassie, Rocky IV,* and other forgettable flicks. Call (307) 690-6909 to schedule a tour, or visit www.jhinet.com/astrocowboy.

WINTER RECREATION

For details on the many skiing and snowboarding opportunities in and around Jackson Hole, see the Downhill Skiing and Snowboarding and Cross-country Skiing sections later in this chapter.

Ice Skating

Each winter, the town of Wilson floods a hockey-rink-size part of the town park for skating, hockey, and broomball. A warming hut stands next to the rink. Jackson maintains a smaller ice rink at 155 E. Gill Ave., plus a rink in Snow King Ballpark which is used for hockey and broomball. All three of these are free to the public and are lighted 6-10 p.m. Call (307) 733-5056 for details.

All three local ski resorts have ice skating and skate rentals. You'll find skating ponds in Teton Village at the base of **Jackson Hole Mountain Resort** and over in Alta at **Grand Targhee Ski Resort.** For the out-of-the-elements version, skate over to **Snow King Resort,** tel. (307) 733-3000 or (800) 522-5464, where the indoor ice-skating rink is open in the winter and offers skate rentals and lessons.

Snowshoeing

Snowshoeing began as a way to get around in the winter, and the old-fashioned wood-and-rawhide snowshoes were bulky and heavy. In recent years snowshoeing has become a popular form of recreation, as new technology created lightweight and easily maneuverable snowshoes. Snowshoeing requires no real training—just strap on the 'shoes, grab a pair of poles, and start walking. But be careful where you walk; see the special topic Safety in Avalanche Country for tips.

Grand Teton National Park has excellent naturalist-led **snowshoe hikes** several times each week during the winter months. Snowshoes are provided at no charge, and no experience is necessary. These generally depart at 2 p.m. from the visitor center in Moose, but for specifics call (307) 739-3399. Reservations are required; no kids under eight.

Snowshoe walks into the mountains around Jackson are also offered by **The Hole Hiking Experience,** tel. (307) 690-4453, www.holehike.com, the only company permitted to guide snowshoeing trips in Bridger-Teton and Targhee National Forests. The company's most popular trips go to Shadow Mountain north of Kelly.

All three local ski resorts offer snowshoeing. Guided snowshoe tours at **Snow King Resort** depart from the top of the Summit Lift. These are perfect for those looking for a break from skiing and snowboarding; call (307) 734-8077 for reservations and details. At **Jackson Hole Mountain Resort,** naturalist-led snowshoe hikes are included in the price of your lift ticket; call (307) 739-2753 for details. For information on snowshoe tours at **Grand Targhee Ski Resort,** call (800) 827-4433. Snowshoe trails and tours are also available at **Spring Creek Ranch Nordic Center,** three miles north of State 22 on Spring Gulch Rd., tel. (307) 733-1004 or (800) 443-6139. Spring Creek specializes in moonlight tours that climb East Gros Ventre Butte.

Rent snowshoes from **Skinny Skis,** 65 W. Deloney Ave., tel. (307) 733-6094 or (888) 733-7205, www.skinnyskis.com; **Teton Mountaineering,** 170 N. Cache Dr., tel. (307) 733-3595 or (800) 850-3595, www.tetonmtn.com; **Jack Dennis' Outdoor Shop,** 50 E. Broadway, tel. (307) 733-3270 or (800) 570-3270, www.jackdennis.com; **Gart Sports,** 485 W. Broadway, tel. (307) 733-4449; **Wilson Backcountry Sports,** Wilson, tel. (307) 733-5228; **Leisure Sports,** 1055 S. US Hwy. 89, tel. (307) 733-3040; and **Grand Targhee Ski Resort** in Alta, tel. (307) 353-2300 or (800) 827-4433.

Sleigh Rides

Several companies offer romantic dinner horse-drawn sleigh rides in the Jackson Hole area mid-December through March. Make reservations well in advance for these popular trips. If you don't have the cash for one of these, take a daytime sleigh ride at the National Elk Refuge (described earlier in this chapter).

Jackson Hole Mountain Resort picks up Teton Village guests for a romantic 30-minute ride to a rustic log cabin where they are served a four-course roast prime-rib or broiled salmon dinner. Prices are $50 for adults, $31 for children under 11. Call (307) 739-2603 for reservations (advised).

Spring Creek Ranch, tel. (307) 733-8833 or (800) 443-6139, www.springcreekranch.com, transports guests on an hour-long sleigh ride to the top of Gros Ventre Butte for dinner at the Granary restaurant. The cost is $48 for adults, $30 for kids under 12. They also offer a one-hour afternoon sleigh ride (no dinner) for $12 per person. No sleigh rides on Monday.

Dinner sleigh rides are also offered at **Grand Targhee Ski Resort,** tel. (800) 827-4433, where a horse-drawn sleigh transports you to a remote yurt for a Western-style meal; $30 for adults, $15 for kids.

Tubing

Two local ski areas have sliding parks with customized inner tubes and rope tows. At Snow King Resort it's called **King Tubes,** tel. (307) 734-8823, and is available during ski hours as well as in the evenings. Rates are $6/hour for adults, $5/hour for kids. The **Grand Targhee Ski Resort** tube park is open for après-ski fun only (after 5 p.m.) and costs $5 per hour; call (800) 827-4433 for details.

Dogsledding

Founded by Iditarod musher Frank Teasley, **Jackson Hole Iditarod Sled Dog Tours,** tel. (307) 733-7388 or (800) 554-7388, www.jhsledog.com, offers half-day trips ($135 per person including lunch) and all-day trips ($225 per person including a big dinner) up Shadow Mountain, along the Gros Ventre River, and out to Granite Hot Springs. Overnight trips to remote lodges are also available.

Washakie Outfitting, tel. (307) 733-3602 or (800) 249-0662, www.dogsledwashakie.com, leads a variety of dogsled tours in the Jackson Hole area, including one-and-a-half hour rides out of Teton Village for $60 ($40 for kids). For a more remote experience join their trips from Cowboy Village Resort at Togwotee (48 miles north of Jackson) or Brooks Lake Lodge (65 miles northeast of Jackson). On these, Iditarod veteran Billy Snodgrass offers half-day ($131), full-day ($175), overnight ($325), and extended trips with Alaskan husky racing dogs.

Geyser Creek Dog Sled Adventures, tel. (307) 739-0165 or (800) 531-6874, www.dogsledadv.com, also leads dogsled tours of the Brooks Lake area and offers longer trips as well, including a three-day sled adventure that makes overnight stops at a tepee and a yurt. All-day rates are $195 for adults, $95 for kids under age 10.

Grand Targhee Ski Resort, tel. (800) 827-4433, www.sharplink.com/dogsled, offers dogsled trips on the west side of the Tetons. Half-day rates are $115 for one or $200 for two people on a sled. They also lead moonlight dogsled tours where you can join the dogs in howling at the moon.

Snowmobiling

One of Jackson Hole's most popular—and controversial—wintertime activities is snowmobiling. Hundreds of miles of packed and groomed snowmobile trails head into Bridger-Teton National Forest as well as Yellowstone and Grand Teton National Parks. Some of the most popular places include the Togwotee Pass area 48 miles north of Jackson, Cache Creek Rd. east of town, and Granite Hot Springs Rd. 25 miles southeast. More than a dozen different Jackson companies offer guided all-day snowmobile trips into Yellowstone and elsewhere. Yellowstone tours typically cost $155-180 for one rider or $245-270 for two riders (including breakfast and lunch). Tours to other areas are usually less expensive, and some motels offer package deals. You can also rent machines for self-guided trips for around $120 per day. The visitor center has a complete listing of local snowmobile-rental companies and maps of snowmobile trails.

The controversial 365-mile-long **Continental Divide Snowmobile Trail** passes through the heart of Grand Teton National Park, connecting the Yellowstone road network with snowmobile trails that reach all the way to Atlantic City at the southern end of the Wind River Mountains. Unfortunately, this means that snowmobiles now roar into two of America's great national parks. Don't be a part of this desecration; instead, enjoy these parks in quieter, less hurried ways such as on snowshoes or cross-country skis.

SHOPPING

If you have the money, Jackson is a great place to buy everything from artwork to mountain bikes. Even if you just hitchhiked in and have no cash to spare, it's always fun to wander through the shops and galleries surrounding Town Square. The corporate chains and factory outlets have moved into Jackson, with a number of the standards to choose from: The Gap, Eddie Bauer, Pendleton, Ralph Lauren Polo, Häagen-Dazs, Big Dogs, and Scandia Down.

Outdoor Gear

Outdoor enthusiasts will discover several excellent shops in Jackson. Climbers, backpackers, and cross-country skiers head to **Teton Mountaineering,** 170 N. Cache Dr., tel. (307) 733-3595 or (800) 850-3595, www.tetonmtn.com, for quality equipment, maps, and travel guides. This is America's oldest climbing shop. They also rent tents, sleeping bags, backpacks, cookstoves, climbing shoes, ice axes, cross-country skis, and even climbing and skiing videos. Check the bulletin board for used items.

Jack Dennis' Outdoor Shop, 50 E. Broadway, tel. (307) 733-3270 or (800) 570-3270, www.jackdennis.com, is a large upscale store that sells fly-fishing and camping gear in the summer and skis and warm clothes during the winter. They also rent almost anything: tents, stoves, lanterns, cookware, sleeping bags, fishing poles, fly rods, waders, float tubes, backpacks, skis, snowshoes, and more.

Skinny Skis, 65 W. Deloney Ave., tel. (307) 733-6094 or (888) 733-7205, www.skinnyskis.com, has more in the way of high-quality clothing and supplies, especially cross-country ski gear. Rent sleeping bags, tents, climbing shoes, ice axes, rollerblades, baby carriers, and backpacks here. Another place to rent outdoor gear of all types—including volleyball sets, fishing gear, float tubes, tarps, tents, sleeping bags, backpacks, campstoves, and lanterns—is **Leisure Sports,** 1075 S. US Hwy. 89, tel. (307) 733-3040. **Moosely Seconds,** 150 E. Broadway, tel. (307) 733-7176, has outdoor gear at good prices, including seconds from Patagonia, Grammici, Lowe, and other companies. A second Moosely Seconds out in Moose (tel. 307-739-1801) sells climbing and outdoor gear and rents trekking poles, ice axes, crampons, rock shoes, approach shoes, plastic boots, day packs, and snowshoes. The Moose store is open summers only.

Gart Sports, 485 W. Broadway, tel. (307) 733-4449, is a large store with a variety of outdoor and sports gear. Purchase used outdoor gear of all types from **Gear Revival,** 854 W. Broadway, tel. (307) 739-8699. The least expensive place to buy rugged outdoor wear, cowboy boots, and cowboy hats is **Corral West Ranchwear,** 840 W. Broadway, tel. (307) 733-0247.

Wyoming Wear, an Afton-based local manufacturer of colorful high-quality outdoor clothing, operates a retail shop near the square at 20 W. Broadway, tel. (307) 733-2991. Despite the name, nearly everything here is made from high-tech fabrics such as Polartec fleece. Wyoming Wear also produces a mail-order catalog; call (800) 732-2991 for a copy, or visit them on the web at www.wyomingwear.com. You can purchase many of the company's items (but not their famous fleece socks) online from www.rei.com.

Bargain Shopping

Buy used clothing and other items at **Browse 'N Buy Thrift Shop,** 139 N. Cache Dr., tel. (307) 733-7524, or the more chaotic **Orville's,** 285 W. Pearl, tel. (307) 733-3165. Hint: Browse 'N Buy puts out new items on Wednesday, attracting a queue of discount shoppers for their 1 p.m. opening. Get there early for the real deals! Orville's sometimes sells old Wyoming license plates—a big hit with European tourists. You can also find Wyoming license plates at the little country store in the town of Kelly, 15 miles north of Jackson.

INFORMATION AND SERVICES

Information Sources

Anyone new to Jackson Hole should be sure to visit the spacious **Wyoming State Information Center** on the north end of town at 532 N. Cache Dr., tel. (307) 733-3316, www.jacksonholechamber.com. Hours are daily 8 a.m.-7 p.m. between Memorial Day and Labor Day, and daily 8 a.m.-5 p.m. the rest of the year. (The phone is answered only on weekdays, but on weekends you can leave a message and they will send you an information packet.) The information center is a two-level, sod-roofed wooden building with natural history displays, a blizzard of free leaflets extolling the merits of local businesses, a gift shop selling books and maps, and an upstairs rear deck overlooking the National Elk Refuge. Ducks and trumpeter swans are visible on the marsh in the summer, and elk can be seen in the winter. The information center is staffed by the Jackson Hole Chamber of Commerce, along with Fish & Wildlife Service and Forest Service personnel in the summer. In addition to the main information center, you'll find racks of brochures at the airport, outside the Pink Garter Plaza on the corner of W. Broadway and Glenwood, at the stagecoach stop on Town Square, and at the Mangy Moose in Teton Village.

The **Bridger-Teton National Forest** supervisor's office is at 340 N. Cache Dr., tel. (307) 739-5500, www.fs.fed.us/btnf. It's open Mon.-Fri. 8 a.m.-4:30 p.m. Get information and Forest Service maps from the Wyoming State Information Center.

Find **National Public Radio** on your dial at 90.3 FM. The locals' station is **KMTN** at 96.9 FM. Other Jackson radio stations are KZJH 95.3 FM and KSGT 1340 AM.

Jackson Hole on the Web

I have attempted to incorporate Internet addresses for most Jackson Hole businesses, but these change constantly as more and more businesses go online and get their own domain name. By the time you read this virtually all Jackson Hole businesses may be on the web. If they aren't listed in the text, try one of the Internet search engines. A great place to begin your web tour is the chamber of commerce site: www.jacksonholechamber.com. Also very useful are www.jackson-hole.com, from Circumerro Publishing; and www.jacksonholenet.com, sponsored by *Jackson Hole Magazine.* All three of these contain links to dozens of local businesses of all types. You may also want to check out another local site, www.jacksonnetwork.com, which includes links to other Wyoming communities and even a joke of the day. Federal government websites for the local area include Grand Teton National Park at www.nps.gov/grte, Yellowstone National Park at www.nps.gov/yell, Bridger-Teton National Forest at www.fs.fed.us/btnf, and Targhee National Forest at www.fs.fed.us/tnf.

Trip Planning

A number of local travel agencies offer reservation services for those who prefer to leave the planning to someone else. They can set up airline tickets, rental cars, lodging, horseback riding, fishing trips, whitewater rafting, ski vacations, and all sorts of other packages. The biggest is **Jackson Hole Central Reservations,** tel. (307) 733-4005 or (800) 443-6931. Find them on the web at www.jacksonholeresort.com (primarily summer info) or www.jhsnow.com (geared to winter use). Central Reservations will also send out big glossy brochures describing local ski areas and lodging. Also helpful for trip planning is the smaller **Resort Reservations,** tel. (307) 733-6331 or (800) 329-9205, www.jacksonholeres.com.

Post Offices

Jackson's main post office is at 1070 Maple Way, near Powderhorn Lane, tel. (307) 733-3650; open Mon.-Fri. 8:30 a.m.-5 p.m., Saturday 10 a.m.-1 p.m. Other post offices are downtown at 220 W. Pearl Ave., tel. (307) 739-1740; in Teton Village, tel. (307) 733-3575; in Wilson, tel. (307) 733-3335; and in Kelly, tel. (307) 733-8884.

Recycling

Just because you're on vacation doesn't mean you should just throw everything away. Jackson has a good recycling program and accepts newspaper, aluminum cans, glass, tin cans, plastic milk jugs, magazines, catalogs, cardboard, and white office paper. The recycling center, tel. (307) 733-7678, is the big brown building two miles south of the high school on US Hwy. 89. Bins are accessible 24 hours a day.

Medical Help

Because of the abundance of ski and snowboard accidents, orthopaedic specialists are in high demand in Jackson and are some of the best around. Physicians at Orthopaedics of Jackson Hole also tend to the U.S. and French national ski teams! For emergency medical attention, head to **St. John's Hospital,** 625 E. Broadway, tel. (307) 733-3636. Medical service by appointment or on a walk-in basis is available at several local clinics, including: **InstaCare of Jackson,** 545 W. Broadway, tel. (307) 733-7003; **Emerg-A-Care,** 975 W. Broadway (Powderhorn Mall), tel. (307) 733-8002; and **Jackson Hole Medical Clinic,** 988 S. US Hwy. 89, tel. (307) 739-8999. Unfortunately, none of these will bill your insurance company; you'll have to fork out the $75-80 and hope for a refund later.

Banking

Get fast cash from **ATMs** in more than a dozen locations around town—in banks, Albertson's, downtown in front of Sirk Shirts, at the airport, and in Teton Village and the Aspens. Note that most if not all local ATMs charge an extra $1.50 "service charge." Jackson has four different banks, several with ludicrously ostentatious structures (probably paid for in part by these service charges). You can escape this rip-off by making a purchase with your ATM card at one of the grocery stores and simultaneously withdrawing extra cash.

International travelers will appreciate the **currency exchange** at three Jackson State Bank locations: 112 Center St., 50 Buffalo Way, and in the Aspens on Teton Village Road. Call (307) 733-3737 for details.

Library

The spacious **Teton County Library,** 125 Virginian Lane, tel. (307) 733-2164, is the kind of library every town should have. Inside this new building is a large collection of books about Wyoming and the West, plus a great kids' section (complete with a fenced-in children's garden with a tepee). Computers provide **Internet access** and are available by reservation (call the library a day in advance) or on a walk-up-and-wait basis. Library hours are Mon.-Thurs. 10 a.m.-9 p.m., Friday 10 a.m.-5:30 p.m., Saturday 10 a.m.-5 p.m., and Sunday 1-5 p.m.

If you plan to be in the Jackson area for a week or more, it may be worth your while to get a visitor's library card. For a one-time fee of $5 you can check out up to four books at a time.

Books

Unlike many Wyoming towns where the book selection consists of a few bodice-buster romance novels in the local pharmacy, Jackson is blessed with several fine bookstores. **Teton Bookshop,** 25 S. Glenwood, tel. (307) 733-9220, is a small downtown shop with a knowledgeable staff. The larger **Valley Bookstore,** 125 N. Cache Dr., tel. (307) 733-4533, www.valleybook.com, sometimes has author signings and readings. **Main Event,** in the Powderhorn Mall at 980 W. Broadway, tel. (307) 733-7112, sells new books and CDs and rents a wide choice of videos. A few doors away in the mall is **Jackson Hole Book Traders,** tel. (307) 734-6001, where you'll find a surprising selection of used and rare books. **The Open Door,** 65 E. Pearl Ave., tel. (307) 734-9101, sells New Age titles.

Up in Grand Teton National Park, find natural history books and maps at the **Moose Visitor Center,** tel. (307) 739-3399, and **Colter Bay Indian Arts Museum,** tel. (307) 543-2467.

Newspapers

Jackson has not just one but two thick local newspapers, each produced in tabloid format. The ***Jackson Hole News*** (www.jacksonhole-news.com) and the ***Jackson Hole Guide*** (www.jhguide.com) both publish weekly editions with local news for 50 cents, as well as weekday freebies found in shops in Jackson, Wilson, and Teton Village. The *Guide* typically represents more traditional Wyoming views (i.e., it's basically Republican) while the *News* has more liberal leanings. Despite any leanings, both are excellent sources of information and strive for balanced coverage of news.

Children in Jackson

Those traveling with children will find an abundance of kid-friendly options in Jackson Hole. A few noteworthy examples include: the hands-on Children's Gallery at the National Museum of Wildlife Art; playgrounds at Mike Yokel Jr. Park (Kelly and Hall Sts.) and Miller Park (Powderhorn Lane and Maple Way); the excellent swimming pool and corkscrew water slide at the Teton County Recreation Center; the fine children's section of the library; chuck wagon dinners at Bar-T-Five or Bar J; comedies and melodramas at Jackson Hole Playhouse or Mainstage Theatre; the aerial tram up Rendezvous Mountain at Jackson Hole Resort; the evening shoot-outs at Town Square; horseback or wagon rides; and a boat ride and hike at Jenny Lake inside Grand Teton National Park. During the summer, older kids will also enjoy hiking, mountain-biking, Snake River float and whitewater trips, the Alpine Slide at Snow King Resort, and the putting course at Alpine Miniature Golf. In winter, snowboarding and skiing are favorites of older kids, but sleigh rides, dogsledding, ice skating, and snowshoeing are also fun.

For those traveling with tots, **Baby's Away,** tel. (307) 733-0387, rents all sorts of baby supplies, including car seats, cribs, gates, backpacks, swings, and high chairs. They have a similar operation at Grand Targhee Ski Resort, tel. (307) 787-2182, and will deliver locally. You'll find more stroller and backpack rentals—along with kids' clothing—at **Teton Kids,** 130 E. Broadway, tel. (307) 739-2176. Just down the street is a large toy shop, **Broadway Toys and Togs,** 48 E. Broadway, tel. (307) 733-3918. **Second Helpings,** 141 E. Pearl Ave., tel. (307) 733-9466, has a big selection of quality used baby and children's clothes. Call **Babysitting by the Tetons,** tel. (307) 733-0754, for child care.

Dog Kennels

Thinking of bringing a dog to Jackson but not sure what to do if the hotel won't allow pets?

Several local kennels will keep an eye on Fido for you. Try **Kindness Kennels,** 1225 S. Gregory Lane, tel. (307) 733-2633; **Jackson Hole Veterinary Clinic,** Rafter J Subdivision, tel. (307) 733-4279; or **Spring Creek Kennels,** 1035 W. Broadway, tel. (307) 733-1606.

Other Services

Wash clothes at **Soap Opera Laundry,** 850 W. Broadway, tel. (307) 733-5584, or **Ryan Cleaners,** 545 N. Cache Dr., tel. (307) 733-2938. You'll find public lockers at Jackson Hole Mountain Resort during the winter.

To keep in touch with folks via e-mail, use the free terminals in the library (see above) or go to **Cyber City Grill,** 265 W. Broadway, tel. (307) 734-2582, where Internet access costs $5 for a half hour.

Amy Haggart of **Valley Valet,** tel. (307) 734-4116, offers a variety of services for those who would rather enjoy the scenery than run around on errands. For a fee, she'll shop for your groceries or other items, and she can also provide child care and arrange rental of a cellular phone.

LIVING IN JACKSON HOLE

Jackson Hole is an increasingly popular place to live and work—a fact that angers many longtime residents who themselves came here to escape crowds elsewhere. The surrounding country is grand, with many things to do and places to explore, the weather is delightful, and you're likely to meet others with similar interests. Jobs such as waiting tables, operating ski lifts, driving tour buses, cleaning hotels and condos, and doing construction work are plentiful. The unemployment rate generally hovers around two percent, and housing is so scarce—and jobs so plentiful—that the local rescue mission kicks folks out after a week if they don't find work. Wages are not high, but have improved with the rising demand for workers. Get to Jackson in mid-May and you'll find the papers filled with half a dozen pages of employment ads, and Help Wanted signs at virtually every shop. Even in midsummer, many places are still looking for help.

Finding Work

The best jobs are those that either offer such perks as housing or free ski passes, or give you lots of free time to explore the area. To get an idea of available jobs, check local classified ads or stop by the Wyoming Job Service Center, 545 N. Cache Dr., tel. (307) 733-4091. You can also search for jobs on the state's Job Bank homepage: http://wyjobs.state.wy.us. Another good place to check is www.jacksonholejobs.com.

Navigating the Housing Maze

Unfortunately, because of Jackson Hole's popularity, finding a place to live is extremely difficult, especially during the peak summer and winter tourist seasons. As the moneyed class has moved in, those who work in service jobs find it tougher and tougher to obtain affordable housing. Reports of workers living out of their cars or commuting from Idaho are not uncommon. Land prices (and consequently housing costs) have been rising an average of 15% per year over the past decade. Because of this, the median home price is now twice what the median household income will buy! One-bedroom apartments rent for $700-900 per month, and buying a two-bedroom tract home will probably set you back at least $250,000. The median single-family home costs almost $400,000. More prestigious local homes sell for $1-3 million, and the very finest log mansions ("log cabins on steroids") fetch well over $5 million each. The inflation of real estate has attracted the major players: both Christie's and Sotheby's (the auction folks) have offices in Jackson.

A few Jackson-area businesses include housing as a way to lure workers, but this is the exception; many employees are forced to live under less-than-ideal conditions such as sleeping in tents during the summer or jamming into too-small apartments. The best times to look for a place to live are in April and November. Check the papers as well as local laundromat and grocery-store bulletin boards for apartments or cabins. The "Trash and Treasure" morning program on radio station KMTN (96.9 FM) is another place to try.

TRANSPORTATION

Access to Jackson Hole has become easier in recent years, with several airlines and daily buses now serving the city. Most summer visitors arrive by car, though a few more adventurous souls pedal in on bikes. If you're looking for or offering a ride, KMTN (96.9 FM), tel. (307) 733-4500, has daily ride-finder announcements during its "Trash and Treasure" radio program. Tune in weekdays 9:30-9:50 a.m.

By Air

Jackson Hole Airport is eight miles north of Jackson inside Grand Teton National Park. It's the only commercial airport within any national park. The airport is small and cozy, but has daily jet service to several American cities. The tarmac is often crowded with Lear jets and other transportation symbols of the elite. Those who don't have the bucks for their own private jet can choose **Delta/Delta Skywest,** tel. (800) 221-1212, www.delta-air.com (service through Salt Lake City); **American,** tel. (800) 433-7300, www.aa.com (flights from Dallas in the summer and Chicago in the winter); and **United/United Express,** tel. (800) 241-6522, www.unitedairlines.com (year-round service from Denver and winter service out of Los Angeles). **Jackson Hole Aviation,** tel. (307) 733-4767 or (800) 437-5387, offers scenic flights over the valley and charter air service.

Airport Shuttles

Alltrans/Gray Line, tel. (307) 733-4325 or (800) 443-6133, www.jacksonholenet.com/grayline, provides airport shuttle service to and from motels in Jackson ($12 one-way or $19 roundtrip per person) and Teton Village ($19 one-way or $29 roundtrip per person). The shuttles meet most commercial airline flights in the summer and winter months, but you should make advance reservations to be sure of an airport pick-up. Make outgoing reservations for motel pick-up a day in advance.

Taxicabs

Local taxis provide direct service from the airport to Jackson; $18 for one or two people. To Teton Village you're best off getting a roundtrip ticket for $27 per person. The taxi companies are: **Airport Taxi/Alltrans,** tel. (307) 733-1700 or (800) 443-6133; **All Star Taxi,** tel. (307) 733-2888 or (800) 378-2944; **Buckboard Cab,** tel. (307) 733-1112; **Cowboy Cab,** tel. (307) 734-8188; and **Teton Taxi & Backcountry Shuttle,** tel. (307) 733-1506. **Downhill Express,** tel. (307) 734-9525 or (877) 943-3574, may have lower rates than the other taxis, and it also provides service to Idaho Falls, West Yellowstone, and other destinations.

Car Rentals

Most of the national and regional chains offer rental cars in town or at the airport. Rent cars from **Alamo,** tel. (307) 733-0671 or (800) 327-9633, www.freeways.com; **Aspen Rent-A-Car,** tel. (307) 733-9224 or (877) 222-7736, www.aspenrentacar.com; **Avis,** tel. (307) 733-3422 or (800) 831-2847, www.avis.com; **Budget,** tel. (307) 733-2206 or (800) 527-0700, www.drivebudget.com; **Eagle Rent-A-Car,** tel. (307) 739-9999 or (800) 582-2128; **Hertz,** tel. (307) 733-2272 or (800) 654-3131, www.hertz.com; **Leisure Sports,** 1075 S. US Hwy. 89, tel. (307) 733-3040; **National,** tel. (307) 733-0735 or (800) 227-7368, www.nationalcar.com; **Rent-A-Wreck,** tel. (307) 733-5014 or (800) 637-7147, www.rent--a-wreck.com; **Rent Rite,** tel. (307) 739-9999; and **Thrifty,** tel. (307) 739-9300 or (800) 367-2277, www.thrifty.com. Of these, Alamo, Avis, Budget, and Hertz all have counters at the airport; most others provide a shuttle bus to town. You may be better off getting a car in town where you don't have to pay the additional taxes imposed at the airport.

Most Jackson Hole rental companies also offer 4WD cars and minivans. The best deals (if you don't mind used cars) are generally from Rent-A-Wreck. Note that peak-season car rental rates in Jackson are on the high side; expect to pay around $55 a day for a midsize car. Reserve cars at least a month ahead during the summer and two months ahead for midsummer or Christmas to New Year's.

START Buses

Local buses are operated by Southern Teton Area Rapid Transit and serve Jackson and Teton Village all year. START fares are 50 cents within town and $2 to Teton Village (cheaper for seniors and children). Discount coupons are available for multiple rides in the winter. Hours of operation are generally 7:30 a.m.-10 p.m. During the summer, buses run seven days a week, with in-town service every 15 minutes after 10 a.m. Service to Teton Village is eight times a day in the summer and more often in the winter. Reduced bus service is available in the fall and spring. Get bus schedules and route maps in the visitor center. Buses stop near most Jackson hotels and motels and are equipped to carry skis (in winter) and bikes (in summer) on outside racks. Wintertime service is also offered to the National Museum of Wildlife Art. Unfortunately, START buses do not run to the airport, Kelly, Moose, or Wilson. Call (307) 733-4521 for more information.

Buses and Tours

Greyhound buses don't come even close to Jackson; the nearest stopping places are Evanston, West Yellowstone, Idaho Falls, and the regional hub at Salt Lake City. **Jackson Hole Express,** tel. (307) 733-1719 or (800) 652-9510, www.jacksonholebus.com, provides daily bus or van connections between Salt Lake City ($45 one-way) or Idaho Falls ($20 one-way) and Jackson.

Community and Rural Transportation (CART), tel. (208) 354-2240 or (800) 657-7439, www.cyberhighway.net/~cartbus, has twice-daily bus service between Idaho Falls and Jackson for $19 one-way.

Wind River Transportation Authority (WRTA), tel. (307) 856-7118 or (800) 439-7118, provides on-demand service in western and southwestern Wyoming. You can call them for service between Salt Lake City and Jackson, or to other Wyoming towns, including Pinedale, Dubois, Evanston, Rock Springs, Lander, and Riverton.

Grand Teton Lodge Company, tel. (307) 733-2811 or (800) 628-9988, www.gtlc.com, has twice-daily summer shuttle buses between Jackson and Jackson Lake Lodge for $15 one-way (plus a $10 park entrance fee), and on to Colter Bay Village for an additional $2.75 one-way. Buses depart from the Homewood parking lot on the corner of Gill and Cache. Transportation from the airport to Jackson Lake Lodge is $20 one-way. They also lead narrated bus tours of Grand Teton National Park on Monday, Wednesday, and Friday for $20 ($10 for kids under 12) and of Yellowstone National Park on Tuesday, Thursday, and Saturday for $44 ($26 for kids). Tours depart from Jackson Lake Lodge at 8:30 each summer morning.

Daily summertime bus tours of Grand Teton and Yellowstone National Parks are available from **Gray Line,** tel. (307) 733-4325 or (800) 443-6133, www.jacksonholenet.com/grayline. Yellowstone tours last 11 hours and cost $48 plus park entrance fees. Eight-hour Grand Teton tours are $45 plus the park entrance. Those without vehicles can use these tours for access to the parks; reserve ahead to schedule a pick-up in Jackson, Grand Teton, or Yellowstone. In Yellowstone, travelers can connect with other buses to West Yellowstone (Montana), Gardiner (Montana), or Cody. Gray Line's four-day tours of the Yellowstone and Grand Teton areas start at $654 for one person or $830 for two, including lodging (but only one meal). During the winter, Gray Line has daily bus runs to Flagg Ranch Resort for $35 one-way ($50 roundtrip), arriving in time to meet the snowcoach departures for Yellowstone. Reservations are required. Both **Buckboard Cab,** tel. (307) 733-1112, and **All Star Taxi,** tel. (307) 733-2888 or (800) 378-2944, also offer shuttles to Flagg Ranch Resort in the winter months ($75 for one to three people), as well as guided van tours of Jackson Hole and surrounding areas.

Other companies offering guided van tours of the area include: **Callowishus Park Touring Company,** tel. (307) 733-9521, www.ulster.net/~heberle; **Jackson's Hole Adventure,** tel. (307) 654-7849 or (800) 392-3165; **Rocky Mountain Outdoor Adventures,** tel. (307) 739-1001 or (888) 557-6465; and **Upstream Anglers/Outdoor Adventures,** tel. (307) 739-9443 or (800) 642-8979.

DOWNHILL SKIING AND SNOWBOARDING

Jackson Hole is fast gaining an international reputation as a winter destination. As access has become easier and the facilities more developed, many people have discovered the wonders of a Jackson Hole winter, especially one centered around a week of skiing or snowboarding. Three very different ski resorts attract the crowds: Grand Targhee for down-home, powder-to-the-butt conditions; Snow King for steep, inexpensive, edge-of-town slopes; and Jackson Hole for flashy, world-class skiing. All three places have rental equipment, ski schools, and special programs for kids. Snowboarders and telemarkers are welcome on the slopes. These resorts combine with an incredible abundance of developed and wild places to ski cross-country to make Jackson Hole one of the premier ski destinations in America.

See your travel agent for package trips to any of the Jackson-area resorts. For daily ski reports—including information on both downhill and Nordic areas and the backcountry—listen to KMTN (FM 96.9) in the morning. Hot tip: If you plan to spend more than a couple of days in the area, it is probably worth your while to join the **Jackson Hole Ski Club,** tel. (307) 733-6433. In return for a $30 annual membership, you receive an impressive number of premiums, including discounted rates for lift tickets, lodging, meals, drinks, snowmobile trips, and shopping at dozens of local stores. Join up at any local ski shop.

Ski and Snowboard Rentals

Rent or buy downhill skis and snowboards from: **Hoback Sports,** 40 S. Millward St., tel. (307) 733-5335, www.hobacksports.com; **The Edge Sports,** 490 W. Broadway, tel. (307) 734-3916; **Gart Sports,** 485 W. Broadway, tel. (307) 733-4449; **Jack Dennis' Outdoor Shop,** 50 E. Broadway, tel. (307) 733-3270 or (800) 570-3270, www.jackdennis.com, and in Teton Village, tel. (307) 733-6838; **Pepi Stiegler Sports** in Teton Village, tel. (307) 733-4505; **Wildernest Sports,** Teton Village, tel. (307) 733-4297; **Teton Village Sports,** tel. (307) 733-2181 or (800) 874-4224; or **Leisure Sports,** 1055 S. US Hwy. 89, tel. (307) 733-3040. Rentals are also available at all three ski areas.

Snowboarders will find the latest gear at **Boardroom of Jackson Hole,** 245 W. Pearl, tel. (307) 733-8327; **Hole in the Wall Snowboard Shop,** tel. (307) 739-2689; **Lowrider Board Shop,** at Pepi Stiegler Sports in Teton

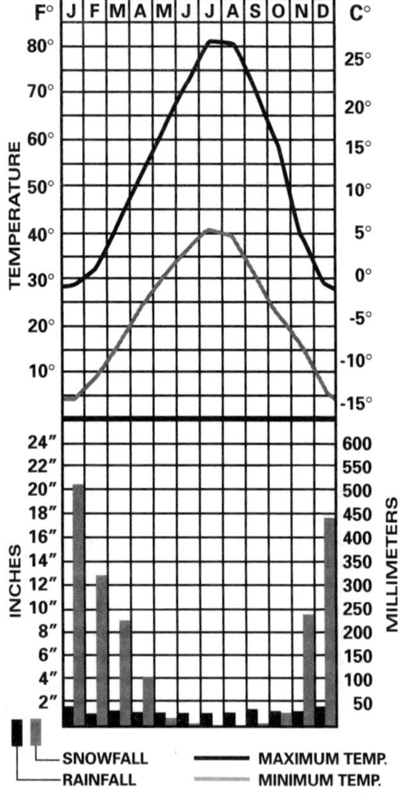

Village, tel. (307) 733-4505; and **Village Board Shop,** at Teton Village Sports, tel. (307) 733-2181 or (800) 874-4224. At Grand Targhee Ski Resort, rent or buy boards from **Phat Fred's,** tel. (307) 353-2300 or (800) 827-4433.

GRAND TARGHEE SKI RESORT

On the west side of the Tetons 44 miles from Jackson, Grand Targhee Ski Resort offers the friendliness of a small resort with the amenities and snow you'd expect at a major one. To get here you'll need to drive into Idaho and turn east at Driggs. The resort sits at the end of the road 12 miles east of Driggs and just six miles inside Wyoming. Their motto says it all: "Snow from heaven, not from hoses." With an annual snowfall topping 500 inches (42 feet!)—most of which is champagne powder—Targhee became the secret spot where powderhounds got all they could ever want. Ski magazines consistently rank it as having North America's best snow. In fact, the resort guarantees its snow: if you find conditions not to your liking, you can turn in your ticket within an hour of purchase and get a "snow check" good for another day of skiing.

Now owned by Booth Creek Resorts—one of the largest ski resort management companies in the nation—Grand Targhee has seen a number of changes in recent years, including remodeled lodging facilities and the addition of a tube park and ice skating rink for après-ski fun. The most significant change is a new quad chairlift that opens in 2000 on adjacent Peaked Mountain, providing access to 500 acres of intermediate skiing terrain. In addition, Grand Targhee is negotiating a land swap with the Forest Service to gain ownership of the public land on which the resort sits. If this happens (and it is very controversial), it may lead to a number of major developments at Targhee. But some things won't change: the beautifully groomed slopes, the uncrowded and relaxed setting, the dramatic Teton backdrop, and the friendly staff, including a number of cowboy-hatted potato farmers who double as lift operators.

The biggest drawback to Grand Targhee Ski Resort is the same thing that makes it so great—the weather. Lots of snow means lots of clouds and storms, and because it snows so much there are many days when the name cynics apply—"Grand Foghee"—seems more appropriate. Many folks who have returned to Targhee year after year have still not seen the magnificent Grand Teton backdrop behind the ski area! Be sure to bring your goggles. The new quad lift up adjacent Peaked Mountain will provide intermediate skiing on slopes that are more protected and suffer less wind and fog.

Skiing and Snowboarding

Call (800) 827-4433 for details on Grand Targhee Ski Resort, or find them on the web at www.grandtarghee.com. As of the 2000-01 winter season, the resort will offer up two quads, one double chairlift, and a surface lift on Fred's Mountain, plus a quad on adjacent Peaked Mountain. The top elevation is 10,200 feet, with the longest run dropping 2,200 feet over almost three miles. Although only 300 acres are groomed, that means you'll always find track-free skiing on the remaining 1,200 acres of ungroomed powder (bring your snorkel). In addition, snowcat skiing ($240 per day including lunch and guide) will continue to be offered on Peaked Mountain.

Lift tickets at Grand Targhee cost $42 a day ($30 a half day) for adults and $25 per day for children ages 14 and under and seniors (free under age six). Discounts are offered for multiday lift tickets or lodging-and-ski packages.

Fully 70% of Targhee's groomed runs are intermediate to advanced-intermediate, but advanced skiers will find an extraordinary number of deep-powder faces to explore. Snowboarders can play at the half-pipe. The ski school offers lessons for all abilities, and children's programs make it possible for parents to leave their kids behind. Cross-country skiers enjoy the Nordic center (see Cross-country Skiing below). Rental skis and snowboards are available at the base of the mountain. The ski area usually opens in mid-November and closes in late April, though some years you may be able to ski even into July. Lifts operate 9:30 a.m.-4 p.m. daily.

Other Winter Activities

Moon Mountain Ranch (www.sharplink.com/dogsled) leads **dogsled tours** from the lodge in the winter months, starting with a half-day trip for $115 per adult for single riders, or $100 per adult with two riders. Lunch trips and moonlight rides are also available. Guided **snowshoe wildlife tours** ($28) will appeal to amateur naturalists, and on the **sleigh ride dinner** ($30 for adults; $15 for kids), you'll ride in a horse-drawn sleigh to a yurt where a Western-style meal is served. Targhee's **tubing park** ($5/hour) is a fun place for kids to slide down a snowy hill, and Targhee also has an outdoor **skating pond** and skate rentals. Child care is available, and a **Kid's Club** at Targhee provides supervised activities.

Summer Activities

Not far from Grand Targhee are several popular summertime hiking trails (see Jedediah Smith Wilderness later in this chapter). The resort itself is a popular place to relax in the summer and offers many activities. The quad chairlift ($8 for adults, $5 for ages 6-14) takes you up the 10,200-foot summit of Fred's Mountain for strikingly close views of the Tetons. The lift operates Wednesday, Saturday, and Sunday in June, and Wed.-Sun. in July and August. A Forest Service naturalist leads mountaintop **guided walks** on weekends, or by request Wed.-Friday. The resort rents mountain bikes and lets you take them up the chairlift for a fast downhill run; guided mountain-bike tours are available.

Horseback rides and lessons are a favorite Targhee summertime activity; one-hour rides are $22. The climbing wall is open to all abilities and is a good place to learn some basic (or advanced) rock-climbing moves. Even more challenging is the adventure ropes course, for those who've always wanted to walk the high wire. Other summer activities/facilities at Targhee include Dutch oven dinners, basketball, an outdoor swimming pool and hot tub, a fitness center, tetherball, paragliding, tennis, and volleyball. The nine-hole **Targhee Village Golf Course** is just down the road. After all this, you'll probably want to relax with a massage, aromatherapy, facial, or steam bath from the on-site spa.

The **Targhee Institute** offers four-day science programs for children in the summer, including a range of fun classes. The institute also directs weeklong elderhostel programs April to early December. Call (307) 353-2233 for details.

Targhee Lodging

Call Targhee at (307) 353-2300 or (800) 827-4433 for details on lodging options at or near the resort, or visit the website: www.grandtarghee.com. The three lodges at the base of the mountain—Targhee Lodge, Teewinot Lodge, and Sioux Lodge (all in the Luxury price category)—offer ski-in, ski-out access, a large heated outdoor pool, hot tub, and workout room. Rates quoted below are for the winter holiday season; they're approximately 40% lower in the summertime. Most lodging places are closed from early September to mid-November, and from mid-April to mid-June.

Get standard motel accommodations at **Targhee Lodge** for $154 d. Deluxe hotel rooms with lodgepole furnishings and access to an indoor hot tub are $200 d at **Teewinot Lodge.** The lobby here is a fine place to relax in front of the fire on winter evenings. **Sioux Lodge** continues the Western theme with lodgepole furnishings, but also has kitchenettes, adobe-style fireplaces, and small balconies. Studio units are $269 d, loft units $364 d, and two-bedroom units $478 d. Rates are higher for more than two people in a room. The two-bedroom units can sleep eight for $557 per night. A wide variety of ski-and-lodging package deals are also available for stays over three nights. A package that provides seven nights lodging and six days of skiing costs $1,560 for two people during the holiday season at Targhee Lodge; rates are considerably higher in Teewinot or Sioux Lodge.

The resort also has off-site condo lodging available approximately 10 miles down the hill at **Teton Creek Resort** and **Powder Valley Condominiums** (also Luxury price category). Choose from one-, two-, and three-bedroom condominiums, each with fireplace, kitchen, private patio, and VCR. Outdoor jacuzzis are also available. Nightly holiday-season rates start at $155 for the one-bedroom units up to $345 for eight people in a three-bedroom unit. Most people rent these condos on a weekly basis; four people can stay in a two-bedroom unit for $657 per week during the winter holiday season.

In addition to the places at the base of the resort, lodging is available just down the hill in Alta, Wyoming, and in the nearby Idaho towns of Driggs, Victor, and Tetonia. For details on these, see Teton Valley, Idaho, below.

Food and Entertainment

At the base of Grand Targhee is a compact cluster of shops and lodging places. You won't have to walk far to find a cafeteria, pizza place, and burger joint. The nicest place is **Skadi's,** serving hearty breakfasts and lunches, along with cozy dinners. Grand Targhee's social center is the **Trap Bar,** with live music on winter weekends, and pub grub on the menu all the time. Guests at Targhee can also take a horse-drawn sleigh on a 15-minute ride to a Mongolian-style yurt for a home-cooked steak or chicken dinner. The price is $30 ($15 for kids ages 14 and under), and reservations are required. Other shops here sell groceries, ski and snowboard gear, clothing, and gifts.

Lost Horizon Dinner Club, tel. (307) 353-8226, is five miles below the resort in the town of Alta and is highly recommended for a relaxing formal dinner. See Alta, Wyoming, at the end of this chapter, for details.

Getting There

Grand Targhee is 42 miles northwest of Jackson on the western side of the Tetons in Alta, Wyoming. Get there by driving over Teton Pass (occasionally closed by winter storms), north through Victor and Driggs, Idaho, and then east back into Wyoming.

The **Targhee Express** bus makes daily wintertime trips (90 minutes each way) to Grand Targhee from Jackson and Teton Village. Buses leave from several Jackson motels around 7:30 a.m. and return from Targhee at 4:30 p.m. for a roundtrip fare of $51, including a full-day lift ticket. (Roundtrip bus fare alone costs $13.) Reservations are required; make them before 9 p.m. on the night before by calling (307) 733-3101 or (307) 734-9754. You can also pick up tickets from the company's Jackson offices at 110 W. Broadway or inside the Mangy Moose Building at Teton Village. Van service is also available year-round to airports in Jackson or Idaho Falls, Idaho. Call the resort for details; tel. (307) 353-2300 or (800) 827-4433.

Downhill Express, tel. (307) 734-9525 or (877) 943-3574, has a similar over-the-Tetons bus service for skiers.

Events

End the year—and start the new one—with **Torchlight Parades** at Grand Targhee on the evenings of December 25 and 31. Also on New Year's Eve is a fireworks display over the mountain. Each March, the resort celebrates telemark skiing with **Nordic Fest.** Ski races of all sorts take place, including the potato race and Elvis jumping contest.

Grand Targhee is home to two very popular outdoor music festivals during the summer. **Rockin' the Tetons Music & Microbrew Festival** comes on the second weekend of July and features well-known rock and blues musicians. It's also a good time to sample some of the region's best microbrews. The equally popular **Targhee Bluegrass Festival** appears in mid-August, again featuring national acts. Bring your dancin' shoes! Both of these attract hundreds of people, so call the resort well ahead of time for camping or lodging reservations.

JACKSON HOLE MOUNTAIN RESORT

Just 12 miles northwest of Jackson is Jackson Hole Mountain Resort, the largest and best-known Wyoming ski area. A true skiers' and snowboarders' mountain, Jackson Hole is considered the most varied and challenging of any American ski area. The powder is usually deep (average snowfall is 38 feet), lift lines are short, the slopes are relatively uncrowded, and the vistas are unbelievable. First opened in 1965, Jackson Hole Mountain Resort has become one of the nation's favorite ski areas.

The resort has invested many millions of dollars over the last several years, upgrading facilities, adding lifts, expanding snowmaking, completing a spacious children's center, and building an ice rink and snowboarding half-pipe. These improvements have helped expand the resort's reputation as an expert's paradise to also include facilities more friendly to families and intermediate skiers. The mountain has one unusual feature that occurs in midwinter: a temperature inversion frequently develops over the valley, meaning that when it's bitterly cold at the base of the mountain, the top is 15-20° F warmer. Skiers often remain on the upper slopes all day to enjoy these warmer temperatures.

Reach Jackson Hole Mountain Resort at tel. (307) 733-2292 or (888) 333-7766, or on the web at www.jacksonhole.com.

Superlatives

With an unsurpassed 4,139-foot vertical drop (longest in the U.S.), 2,500 acres of terrain spread over two adjacent mountains, runs that exceed four miles in length, and 24 miles of groomed trails, Jackson Hole Mountain Resort is truly a place of superlatives. Half the resort's 60 runs are in the advanced category—including several of the notorious double-diamonds—but it is so large that even rank beginners will find plenty of bunny slopes on which to practice.

The only way to the summit of 10,450-foot Rendezvous Mountain is aboard one of the 63-passenger aerial tram cars. Powered by 500-horsepower engines, they climb nearly two and a half miles in 10 minutes, offering jaw-dropping views across Jackson Hole. Rendezvous Mountain is where experts strut their stuff on these steep and fast slopes, and if you're not at least close to the expert status you'll find your blood pressure rising as the tram heads up the mountain. More than a few skiers and boarders have taken the tram back down after seeing what lies below. And yes, those death-defying cliff-jumping shots are real; from the tram, check out infamous Corbet's Couloir, a rocky gully that requires a leap of faith and suicidal urges.

Fortunately, intermediate skiers and boarders are not given short shrift at Jackson Hole Mountain Resort, particularly on the friendlier slopes of 8,481-foot Apres Vous Mountain. Intermediate (and advanced) downhillers could spend all day playing on these slopes, and the 1999/2000-season addition of a high-speed quad here means that riders can blast to the summit of Apres Vous in just five minutes. Because of the speed of this and other new lifts, the wait at the base is now usually just a few minutes.

In addition to these lifts, you can ride a gondola, three other quad chairs, a triple chair, double chair, and poma lift. Snowboarders will appreciate the half-pipe and boarders' terrain trail. The resort's Kids Ranch provides supervised day care, including a spacious play area. Not far away is a special "magic carpet" (a conveyer belt of sorts) for children learning to ski or snowboard.

Rates and Services

Get to Teton Village from the town of Jackson by hopping on the START bus ($2 each way). This is the only inexpensive part of a visit to Jackson Hole Resort, since prices for lift tickets approach the stratosphere. Single-day tickets for all lifts (including the tram) are $54 for adults ($40 per half day) and $27 ($20 per half day) for kids under 14 and seniors. Multiday all-lift tickets—the most common kind bought—are $240 a week (five days of skiing) for adults or $120 a week for kids. Lifts are open 9 a.m.-4 p.m. daily (last tram departs at 3:30 p.m.) from around Thanksgiving till early April.

Skis and snowboards can be rented at shops in Jackson or Teton Village. The ski school offers a special Kinderschule program for children, and beginning snowboarders can learn from the pros. Jackson Hole Resort even has special steep snowboarding and skiing camps, where you learn from extreme downhill fanatics. Tommy Moe—gold and silver medalist at the 1994 Lillehammer Winter Olympics—teaches a four-day ski camp at the resort in January and is a ski ambassador for the resort; he also owns a home in the area. Jackson Hole's director of skiing (he headed the ski school here for 30 years) is Pepi Stiegler, the Austrian winner of a silver medal in the 1960 Olympics and a gold medal in the 1964 Olympics. You can get two hours of instruction from Pepi on weekday mornings; call

(307) 739-2663 for reservations and Olympic-class prices.

Ski hosts are scattered around the mountain, ready to provide information and free hourly tours of the slopes from the top of Rendezvous Mountain. Racers and spectators will enjoy NASTAR events each Sunday, Tuesday, and Thursday, along with various other competitions throughout the winter.

If you're looking for untracked powder, call **Jackson Hole Guide Service,** tel. (307) 739-2663, which leads small groups of folks to parts of the mountain off-limits to mere mortals. Powder-hound skiers with a ton of cash will find unparalleled outback conditions accessed via **High Mountain Heli-Skiing,** tel. (307) 733-3274, www.skitvs.com. Note, however, that the areas where the choppers land are under consideration for wilderness status, and heli-skiing in these backcountry areas is not supported by some local environmental groups.

For more information on Jackson Hole Mountain Resort, call (307) 733-2292 or (888) 333-7766. Get recorded snow conditions by calling (307) 733-2291; the messages are changed each morning before 5 a.m. Find them on the Internet at www.jacksonhole.com.

Teton Village

At the base of the mountain is the Swiss-style Teton Village—alias "the Vill." Everything skiers and boarders need is crowded together here: lodges, a hostel, condominiums, espresso stands, restaurants, après-ski bars, gift shops, groceries, booze, ski and snowboard rentals, storage lockers, car rentals, a skating pond, child care, and even a travel agency for escapes to Hawaii.

On-the-mountain facilities include Casper Restaurant at the bottom of Casper Bowl, and snack bars at the top of the tram, the base of Thunder chairlift, and the top of Apres Vous chairlift. Casper Restaurant serves a barbecue picnic most days and is a popular place to meet up with friends for lunch.

SNOW KING RESORT

Snow King Resort has three things that other local ski areas lack: location, location, and location. The resort sits directly behind town and just seven blocks from Town Square. This is the locals' place, Jackson's "town hill," but it also offers surprisingly challenging runs. It may not be the largest or fanciest place around, but the King's ski runs make up in difficulty what they lack in size. From below, the mountain (7,871 feet tall) looks impossibly steep and narrow. High atop the big chairlift, the vista provides a panoramic tour of Jackson Hole and the Tetons.

Snow King was the first ski area in Wyoming—it opened in 1939—and one of the first in North America. The original chapter of the National Ski Patrol was established here in 1941. The mountain has a 1,571-foot vertical drop. You'll find more than 400 acres of skiable terrain at Snow King, with the longest run stretching nearly a mile. A triple chair, two double chairs, and a Poma lift climb the mountainside. Other features include snowmaking, a tubing park, and a very popular 300-foot half-pipe and terrain park for snowboarders. It's the only local resort with lights for nighttime skiing.

Rates and Services

Prices for lift tickets at Snow King are well below those at other Jackson Hole resorts: $30 a day ($20 per half day) for adults and $20 a day ($12 per half day) for kids under 15 and seniors. Hours of operation are 9:30 a.m.-4:30 p.m., with **night skiing** (Mon.-Sat. 4:30-8:30 p.m.) available on the lower sections of Snow King for an additional $14 for adults or $9 for kids and seniors. In addition, the King has hourly rates for lift tickets ($9/hour for adults, $5/hour for kids and seniors), perfect for skiers and boarders who arrive late in the afternoon and want to hit the slopes for an hour. With some of the best snowmaking in Wyoming, the resort usually opens by Thanksgiving and remains in operation till early April.

At the base of Snow King you'll discover a lodge with reasonable ski-and-stay packages. A plethora of lodging options are scattered around the adjacent town of Jackson. Also at Snow King are two restaurants, the Shady Lady Saloon, ski and snowboard rentals and lessons, plus a variety of other facilities, including an indoor ice rink and mountaintop snack-shack. Guided snowshoe tours are available; call (307) 734-8077 for details. Jackson's START buses offer frequent service to town (50 cents) or Teton Village ($2). For more info on Snow King Resort, call (307) 733-5200 or (800) 522-5464 (outside Wyoming), or find them on the Internet at www.snowking.com.

CROSS-COUNTRY SKIING

For many Jackson Hole residents the word "skiing" means heading across frozen Jenny Lake or telemarking down the bowls of Teton Pass rather than sliding down the slopes of the local resorts. Jackson Hole has become a center for cross-country enthusiasts and offers an impressive range of conditions—from flat-tracking along summertime golf courses where a gourmet restaurant awaits, to remote wilderness settings where a complete knowledge of snowpack structure, avalanche hazards, and winter survival techniques is essential. Beginners will probably want to start out at a Nordic center, progressing to local paths and the more gentle lift-serviced ski runs with experience. More advanced skiers will quickly discover incredible snow in the surrounding mountains.

Ski Rentals

Rent or buy cross-country skis from: **Skinny Skis,** 65 W. Deloney Ave., tel. (307) 733-6094 or (888) 733-7205, www.skinnyskis.com; **Teton Mountaineering,** 170 N. Cache Dr., tel. (307) 733-3595 or (800) 850-3595, www.tetonmtn.com; **Jack Dennis' Outdoor Shop,** 50 E. Broadway, tel. (307) 733-3270 or (800) 570-3270, www.jackdennis.com; **Wilson Backcountry Sports,** Wilson, tel. (307) 733-5228; or **Leisure Sports,** 1055 S. US Hwy. 89, tel. (307) 733-3040. All the local Nordic centers also rent equipment. Most places rent both classical cross-country skis and skate skis (much faster and a better workout), along with telemarking equipment. In addition, randonnée (alpine touring) skis are available from Wilson Backcountry Sports, Teton Mountaineering, and Skinny Skis.

NORDIC CENTERS

Jackson Hole Nordic Center

Nordic skiing enthusiasts will find three different developed facilities near Jackson and others at Grand Targhee and near Togwotee Pass. Largest is Jackson Hole Nordic Center, tel. (307) 739-2629, with 17 km of groomed trails—both set track and skating lanes that cover a wide range of conditions. Call (307) 733-2291 for the snow report. Located in Teton Village, this is the best place to learn cross-country skiing. Daily trail passes are $8 a day for adults or $5 a day for children and seniors. Traditional cross-country skis, skate skis, and telemarking equipment are available for rent, along with lessons. Hours are daily 8:30 a.m.-4:30 p.m. After 12:30 p.m., you can exchange your alpine lift ticket at Jackson Hole Mountain Resort for one at the Nordic center (but, hey, it better be for no extra charge since you already dropped $54!). The center offers a wide spectrum of lessons and tours.

Teton Pines Cross-Country Ski Center

Located along Teton Village Rd., Teton Pines features 14 km of groomed track (both classical and skating) on a summertime golf course. Daily trail passes cost $8 for adults or $5 for children, and ski rentals and lessons are available. Hours are daily 9 a.m.-5 p.m. The clubhouse here has a pricey restaurant for gourmet après-ski lunches and dinners. Get details by calling (307) 733-1005 or (800) 238-2223, or on the web at www.tetonpines.com.

Spring Creek Ranch Nordic Center

Three miles north of State Hwy. 22 on Spring Gulch Rd., Spring Creek, tel. (307) 733-1004 or (800) 443-6139, www.springcreekranch.com, is open 9:30 a.m.-4:30 p.m. daily. If you're staying in town, you can catch the free shuttle bus at the Wort Hotel; call the Nordic center for specifics. Guests of the Spring Creek Ranch ski free here. The center has 15 km of gentle groomed trails with skating lanes, making this perfect for beginners. Trail passes are $8 a day for adults or $5 a day for seniors or kids. Ski rentals and lessons are available. Half-day guid-

ed ski tours cost $45, and guided snowshoe tours are $30 for a half day (including snowshoe rental). There's a two-person minimum on ski and snowshoe tours. The center also has separate snowshoe trails ($5) available if you want to head out on your own.

Brooks Lake Lodge

Considerably farther afield, but worth the drive, is Brooks Lake Lodge, 65 miles northeast of Jackson near Togwotee Pass. The lodge has some of the most incredible scenery and cross-country skiing in the West, and it's five miles off the highway on a machine-packed road, making it a perfect destination for overnight trips. Once there, you'll find another five km of groomed trails plus access to the nearby Teton Wilderness, where skiers can escape the snowmobiles. Get details by calling (307) 455-2121 or visting the website, www.brookslake.com. See Accommodations above for more on Brooks Lake Lodge.

Grand Targhee Nordic Center

On the west side of the Tetons 44 miles out of Jackson, Grand Targhee Nordic Center, tel. (307) 353-2300 or (800) 827-4433, www.grandtarghee.com, has 15 km of groomed cross-country ski trails covering rolling terrain. Trail passes are $8 for adults and $5 for seniors and kids. Lessons, ski rentals, and a variety of tours are also available. Hours are daily 9:30 a.m.-4 p.m. Guests with Targhee lodging packages can ski free on the cross-country tracks.

ON YOUR OWN

Nordic skiers who would rather explore Jackson Hole and the mountains that surround it on their own will discover an extraordinary range of options, from beginner-level treks along old roads to places where only the most advanced skiers dare venture. Because Jackson has so many cross-country fanatics (and visiting enthusiasts), tracks are quickly broken along the more popular routes, making it easier for those who follow. For complete coverage of all these options, pick up a copy of the helpful free winter outdoors guide ***Trailhead*** at Skinny Skis, 65 W. Deloney Ave., tel. (307) 733-6094 or (888) 733-7205, www.skinnyskis.com. The store also rents cross-country, skating, and telemark skis, and snowshoes. If you're heading out on your own, be prepared for deep snow (four feet in the valley) and temperatures that often plummet below zero at night.

The **Teton County Parks and Recreation Department,** inside the recreation center at 155 E. Gill, tel. (307) 739-9025, leads a variety of all-day cross-country ski outings every Tuesday from mid-December to mid-March for $7-10 per person. Bring your own skis and a lunch—they provide the guide and transportation. The department also offers a full-moon ski tour once each winter.

Ski Tours

Jackson Hole Mountain Guides, tel. (307) 733-4979 or (800) 239-7642, www.jhmg.com, runs wintertime ski tours, avalanche courses, and ski mountaineering outings, along with rock- and ice-climbing classes. Longer winter trips, including a six-day Teton Crest tour, are also available.

Over on the western slopes of the Tetons, **Rendezvous Ski Tours** maintains three Mongolian-style yurts in the Jedediah Smith Wilderness, each located several hours of skiing (or hiking) from the next. The huts can sleep up to eight and have kitchens, bunks, sleeping bags, and woodstoves. Rates are $165 per night, but you need to be experienced in backcountry skiing and have the necessary safety equipment and avalanche training. If you don't quite measure up, they can provide guided backcountry ski tours to the huts ($360/day for two people). A good base for these trips is the company's modern three-bedroom guest house at the mouth of Fox Creek Canyon, eight miles north of Victor. The home comes complete with all the amenities, including a hot tub. You can rent the entire place for $300, or $75 d if you're willing to share with other folks, including a make-it-yourself breakfast. For details on the various options, call Rendezvous at (208) 787-2906, or look them up on the web at www.skithetetons.com.

Jackson Area

Even rank beginners will enjoy exploring several local spots. Get to **Moose-Wilson Road** by heading a mile north of Teton Village to where the plowing ends. The nearly level road continues for two scenic miles across a creek and

SAFETY IN AVALANCHE COUNTRY

Backcountry skiing is becoming increasingly popular in the mountains surrounding Jackson Hole. Unfortunately, many skiers fail to take the necessary precautions. Given the enormous snowfalls that occur, the steep slopes the snow piles up on, and the high winds that accompany many storms, it should come as no surprise that avalanches are a real danger.

Nearly all avalanches are triggered by the victims. If you really want to avoid avalanches, ski only on groomed ski trails or "bombproof" slopes, which, because of aspect, shape, and slope angle, never seem to slide. Unfortunately, this isn't always possible, so an understanding of the conditions that lead to avalanches is imperative for backcountry skiers. The Forest Service produces a useful booklet called ***Basic Guidelines for Winter Recreation,*** available in many of its offices around Wyoming. The best way to learn about backcountry safety is through an avalanche class. These are offered in the Jackson area by **American Avalanche Institute,** tel. (307) 733-3315, www.avalanchecourse.com; **Skinny Skis,** tel. (307) 733-6094 or (888) 733-7205, www.skinnyskis.com; **Teton Mountaineering,** tel. (307) 733-3595 or (800) 850-3595, www.tetonmtn.com; and **Jackson Hole Mountain Guides,** tel. (307) 733-4979 or (800) 239-7642, www.jhmg.com. Failing that, you can help protect yourself by following these precautions when you head into the backcountry:

- Before leaving, get up-to-date avalanche information. On the web, you can visit www.avalanche.org for links to avalanche forecasting sites throughout the Western states. For the Jackson Hole area, contact the 24-hour Forest Service's **Backcountry Avalanche Hazard & Weather Forecast,** tel. (307) 733-2664, www.untracked.com/forecast. For areas around Yellowstone—including West Yellowstone and Cooke City on the margins and the Washburn Range inside the park—contact the **Avalanche Advisory Hotline** in Bozeman, tel. (406) 587-6981, www.gomontana.com/avalanche. If they say the avalanche danger is high, ski on the flats instead.
- Be sure to carry extra warm clothes, water, high-energy snacks, a dual-frequency avalanche transceiver (make sure it's turned on and you know how to use it!), a lightweight snow shovel (for digging snow pits or excavating avalanche victims), an emergency snow shelter, first-aid supplies, a Swiss Army or Leatherman knife, topographic map, an extra plastic ski tip, flashlight, matches, and compass. Many skiers also carry that cure-all, duct tape, wrapped around a ski pole. Let a responsible person know exactly where you are going and when you expect to return. It's also a good idea to carry special ski poles that extend into probes in case of an avalanche. Check with local ski shops, or talk to Forest Service or Park Service folks for details on specific areas.
- Check the angle of an area before you ski through it; slopes of 30-45 degrees are the most dangerous; lesser slopes do not slide as frequently.
- Watch the weather; winds over 15 mph can pile snow much more deeply on lee slopes, causing dangerous loading on the snowpack. Especially avoid skiing on or below cornices.
- Avoid the leeward side of ridges, where snow loading can be greatest.
- Be aware of gullies and bowls; they're more likely to slip than flat open slopes or ridgetops. Stay out of gullies at the bottom of wide bowls; these are natural avalanche chutes.
- Look out for cracks in the snow, and listen for hollow snow underfoot. These are strong signs of dangerous conditions.
- Look at the trees. Smaller trees may indicate that avalanches rip through an area frequently, knocking over the larger ones. Avalanches can, however, also run through forested areas.
- Know how much new snow has fallen recently. Heavy new snow over older weak snow layers is a sure sign of extreme danger on potential avalanche slopes. Most avalanches slip during or immediately after a storm.
- Learn how to dig a snow pit and how to read the various snow layers. Particularly important are the very weak layers of depth hoar or surface hoar that have been buried under heavy new snow.

through groves of aspen. For more adventure, turn off at the **Granite Canyon Trailhead** (a mile up the unplowed Moose-Wilson Rd.) and follow the trail along the moraine, which offers a range of skiing conditions. Just don't ski into the canyon, where avalanches are a hazard.

The closest place to Jackson for on-your-own cross-country skiing is **Cache Creek Canyon.** The trailhead is at the east end of Cache Creek Dr., where the plowing ends at a parking lot. Snowmobiles and skiers have packed the route. For a longer trip, take the Rafferty ski lift at Snow King and then ski west through the trees and down to Cache Creek, returning via the road. Ask at Snow King Resort for specifics. Another popular local place is along the **Snake River dikes,** where State Hwy. 22 crosses the river a mile east of Wilson. The dikes extend along both sides of the river for several miles, making for easy skiing. This is also a good place to watch ducks, moose, and other critters or to listen to the river rolling over the rocks.

Grand Teton National Park Area

A bit farther afield, but well worth the detour, are several trails in Grand Teton National Park. Orange markers denote the paths, but these are not machine-groomed, just tracks laid down by other skiers. Park at the Cottonwood Creek bridge (the road isn't plowed beyond this) and head out for **Jenny Lake** (nine miles roundtrip) or **Taggart Lake** (three miles roundtrip). Just three miles south of Moose on Moose-Wilson Rd., you may also want to try the trail to **Phelps Lake** (five miles roundtrip). Or, if you have more ambition and skill (along with avalanche beacons and other gear), longer routes could take you far up into the canyons of the Tetons. Be sure to stop at the Moose Visitor Center for current conditions and a copy of their trail map. Overnight ski tourers must also register here.

For unsurpassed vistas of the Tetons, try skiing to the top of 8,252-foot **Shadow Mountain,** 14 miles northeast of Jackson. From the town of Kelly, drive another five miles north to a parking area—the road isn't plowed beyond this—and then ski up the nearby Forest Service road that snakes up the mountain. It's fairly steep in places and seven miles roundtrip. Snowmobilers also use this road, so be ready to move out of the way quickly.

Granite Hot Springs

One of the most popular ski- and snowmobile-in sites is Granite Hot Springs, tel. (307) 734-7400, a delightful hot-spring-fed pool on Forest Service land. Get there by driving 25 miles southeast of Jackson into Hoback Canyon and then skiing 10 miles in from the signed parking area. The route is not difficult, but due to the distance it isn't recommended for beginners unless they are prepared for a 20-mile roundtrip trek. The pool costs $5.50 for adults, $3.50 for ages 3-12, and free for infants. It's open 10 a.m. to dusk. Bring your swimsuit or rent a suit and towel here. Ask the attendant about places to snow camp nearby.

Teton Pass

Locals head to 8,429-foot Teton Pass when they really want to test their abilities. The summit parking area fills with cars on fresh-snow mornings as everyone from advanced beginners to world-class ski mountaineers heads out for a day in the powder or a week of wilderness trekking in the Tetons. Snow depths of eight feet or more are not uncommon in midwinter. (The snow once became so deep on the pass that it took plows two weeks to clear the road!) The slopes around Teton Pass cover the full spectrum, but be sure you know your own ability and how to avoid avalanches. Check the above-mentioned Skinny Skis *Trailhead Guide* for specifics on Teton Pass, or talk to folks at Skinny Skis or Teton Mountaineering. This is the backcountry, so you won't see any signs at the various bowls; ask other skiers if you aren't sure which is which. Avalanches do occur in some of these bowls, and it's possible to get lost up here during a storm, so come prepared.

Those without backcountry experience should contact **Rendezvous Ski Tours,** tel. (208) 787-2906; **Jackson Hole Mountain Guides,** tel. (307) 733-4979 or (800) 239-7642, www.jhmg.com; or **Jackson Hole Nordic Center,** tel. (307) 739-2629, for guided ski tours at Teton Pass and elsewhere. Expect to pay around $175 for one person or $215 for two people.

BRIDGER-TETON NATIONAL FOREST

Bridger-Teton ("the B-T") National Forest is the second-largest national forest in the Lower 48, stretching southward for 135 miles from the Yellowstone border and covering 3.4 million acres. Portions of the forest are described elsewhere (see Bridger Wilderness in the Wind River Mountains Country chapter and Greys River Area in the Southwest chapter). In Jackson Hole, the two areas of most interest for recreation are the Teton Wilderness and the Gros Ventre Wilderness. Because of its extensive wilderness areas, the B-T has more outfitters than any other national forest in the nation. Much of the remaining nonwilderness land managed by the Forest Service is multiple-use, meaning lots of logging, cattle grazing, and oil and gas leasing.

The Bridger-Teton National Forest **supervisor's office** is at 340 N. Cache Dr. in Jackson, tel. (307) 739-5500, www.fs.fed.us/btnf. It's open Mon.-Fri. 8 a.m.-4:30 p.m. The Wyoming State Information Center, a block or so north on Cache, usually has a Forest Service worker who can provide recreation information. The center also sells Bridger-Teton maps and has a good choice of books. Local ranger stations are the **Jackson Ranger District,** also at 340 N. Cache Dr., tel. (307) 739-5400, and the **Blackrock Ranger Station,** nine miles east of Moran Junction, tel. (307) 543-2386.

TETON WILDERNESS

The Teton Wilderness covers 585,468 acres of mountain country, bordered to the north by Yellowstone National Park, to the west by Grand Teton National Park, and to the east by the Washakie Wilderness. Established as a primitive area in 1934, it was declared one of the nation's first wilderness areas upon passage of the 1964 Wilderness Act. The Teton Wilderness offers a diverse mixture of rolling lands carpeted with lodgepole pine, spacious grassy meadows, roaring rivers, and dramatic mountains. Elevations range from 7,500 feet to the 12,165-foot summit of Younts Peak. The Continental Divide slices across the wilderness, with headwaters of the Yellowstone River draining the eastern half and headwaters of the Buffalo and Snake Rivers flowing down the western side.

One of the most unusual places within Teton Wilderness is **Two Ocean Creek,** where a creek abruptly splits at a rock and the two branches never rejoin. One branch becomes Atlantic Creek, and its waters eventually reach the Atlantic Ocean, while the other becomes Pacific Creek and its waters flow to the Snake River, the Columbia River, and thence into the Pacific Ocean! Mountain man Osborne Russell described this phenomenon in 1835:

> *On the South side about midway of the prairie stands a high snowy peak from whence issues a Stream of water which after entering the plain it divides equally one half running West and other East thus bidding adieu to each other one bound for the Pacific and the other for the Atlantic ocean. Here a trout of 12 inches in length may cross the mountains in safety. Poets have sung of the "meeting of the waters" and fish climbing cataracts but the "parting of the waters and fish crossing mountains" I believe remains unsung yet by all except the solitary Trapper who sits under the shade of a spreading pine whistling blank-verse and beating time to the tune with a whip on his trap sack whilst musing on the parting advice of these waters.*

Two natural events have had a major effect on the Teton Wilderness. On July 21, 1987, a world-record high-elevation tornado created a massive blowdown of trees around the Enos Lake area. The blowdown covered 10,000 acres, and trails are only now being rebuilt through this incredible jackstraw pile (since this is a wilderness area, chainsaws cannot be used). In 1988, extreme drought conditions led to a series of major fires in Yellowstone and surrounding areas. Within the Teton Wilderness, the Huck and Mink Creek Fires burned (in varying degrees of severity) approximately 200,000 acres. Over half of the wilderness remained untouched.

Don't let these incidents dissuade you from visiting; this is still a marvelous and little-used area. Herds of elk graze in alpine areas, and many consider the Thorofare country abutting Yellowstone National Park the most remote place in the Lower 48. This is prime grizzly habitat, so be very cautious at all times. Poles for hanging food have been placed at most campsites, as have bear-resistant boxes or barrels. Local Forest Service offices have brochures showing the locations of these poles. You can rent bear-resistant backpacker food tubes or horse panniers from the Blackrock Ranger District, tel. (307) 543-2386. It's a good idea to make reservations for these before your trip.

Access

Three primary trailheads provide access to the Teton Wilderness: Pacific Creek on the southwestern end, Turpin Meadow on the Buffalo Fork River, and Brooks Lake just east of the Continental Divide. Campgrounds are at each of these trailheads. Teton Wilderness is a favorite of Wyoming people, particularly those with horses, and in the fall elk hunters come here from across the nation. Distances are so great that few backpackers head into this wilderness area. No permits are needed, but it's a good idea to stop in at the **Blackrock Ranger District,** tel. (307) 543-2386, nine miles east of Moran Junction on US Hwy. 26/287, for topographic maps and info on current trail conditions, bear problems, regulations, and a list of permitted outfitters offering horse or llama trips.

For a shorter trip, you could take a guided horseback ride with one of two companies based at the Turpin Meadow Trailhead: **Two Ocean Pass Ranch & Outfitting,** tel. (307) 543-2309 or (800) 726-2409; and **Yellowstone Outfitters,** tel. (307) 543-2418 or (800) 447-4711. Additional rides are available from nearby **Turpin Meadow Ranch,** tel. (307) 543-2496 or (800) 743-2496, www.turpinmeadow.com, and **Buffalo Valley Ranch,** tel. (307) 543-2026 or (888) 543-2477. All four of these have horses available for hourly or all-day rides into the Teton Wilderness. **Teton Horseback Adventures,** tel. (307) 543-9119, www.horsebackadv.com, has horseback rides out of the Pacific Creek Trailhead.

Unfortunately, the USGS maps fail to show the many Teton Wilderness trails built and maintained (or not maintained) by private outfitters. These can make hiking confusing. A few of the many possible hikes are described below.

Whetstone Creek

Whetstone Creek Trail begins at the Pacific Creek Trailhead, on the southwest side of Teton Wilderness. An enjoyable 20-mile roundtrip hike leaves the trailhead and follows Pacific Creek for 1.5 miles before splitting left to follow Whetstone Creek. Bear left when the trail splits again another three miles upstream and continue through a series of small meadows to the junction with Pilgrim Creek Trail. Turn right here and follow this two more miles to Coulter Creek Trail, climbing up Coulter Creek to scenic Coulter Basin and then dropping down along the East Fork of Whetstone

taking a water break in North Fork Meadow within the Teton Wilderness

Creek. This rejoins the Whetstone Creek Trail and returns you to the trailhead, passing many attractive small meadows along the way. The upper half of this loop hike was burned in 1988; some areas were heavily scorched, while others are quite patchy. Flowers are abundant in the burned areas, and this is important elk habitat.

South Fork to Soda Fork

A fine loop hike leaves Turpin Meadow and follows South Buffalo Fork River to South Fork Falls. Just above this, a trail splits off and climbs to Nowlin Meadow (excellent views of Smokehouse Mountain) and then down to Soda Fork River, where it joins the Soda Fork Trail. Follow this trail back downstream to huge Soda Fork Meadow (a good place to see moose and occasionally grizzlies) and then back to Turpin Meadow, a distance of approximately 23 miles roundtrip. For a fascinating side trip from this route, head up the Soda Fork into the alpine at Crater Lake, a six-mile hike above the Nowlin Meadow-Soda Fork Trail junction. The outlet stream at Crater Lake disappears into a gaping hole, emerging as a large creek two miles below at Big Springs. It's an incredible sight.

Cub Creek Area

The Brooks Lake area just east of Togwotee Pass is a very popular summertime camping and fishing place with magnificent views. Brooks Lake Trail follows the western shore of Brooks Lake and continues past Upper Brooks Lakes to Bear Cub Pass. From here, the trail drops down to Cub Creek, where you'll find several good campsites. You can make a long and very scenic loop by following the trail up Cub Creek into the alpine country and then back down along the South Buffalo Fork River to Lower Pendergraft Meadow. From here, take Cub Creek Trail back up along Cub Creek to Bear Cub Pass and back out to Brooks Lake. Get a topographic map before heading into this remote country. Total distance is approximately 33 miles roundtrip.

GROS VENTRE WILDERNESS

The 287,000-acre Gros Ventre Wilderness was established in 1984 and covers the mountain country just east of Jackson Hole. This range trends mainly in a northwest-southeast direction and is probably best known for Sleeping Indian Mountain (maps now call it Sheep Mountain but locals never use that appellation), the distinctive rocky summit visible from Jackson Hole. Although there are densely forested areas at lower elevations, the central portion of the wilderness lies above timberline, and many peaks top 10,000 feet. Tallest is Doubletop Peak at 11,682 feet. The Tetons are visible from almost any high point in the Gros Ventre, and meadows line the lower-elevation streams. Elk, mule deer, bighorn sheep, moose, and black bears are found here, and a few grizzlies have been reported. The Forest Service office in Jackson has more info on the wilderness, including brief trail descriptions and maps.

Access and Trails

A number of roads provide good access to the Gros Ventre Wilderness: Gros Ventre River Rd. on the northern border; Flat Creek, Curtis Canyon, and Cache Creek Rds. on the western margin; and Granite Creek Rd. to the south. Note that hikes beginning or ending in the Granite Creek area have the added advantage of nearby Granite Hot Springs, a great place to soak tired muscles.

An enjoyable two-day trip begins at **Jackpine Creek Trailhead** on Granite Creek Rd., 35 miles southeast of Jackson. Follow Jackpine Creek Trail up to Shoal Lake and then loop back down via the Swift Creek Trail. The distance is approximately 16 miles roundtrip but involves gaining and then losing 4,000 feet of elevation. Another good hike is to follow **Highline Trail** from the Granite Creek area across to Cache Creek, a distance of 16 miles. This route passes just below a row of high and rugged mountains, but since it isn't a loop route, you'll need to hitchhike or arrange a car shuttle back. Plan on three days for this scenic hike. A third hike begins at the **Goosewing Ranger Station,** 12 miles east of Slide Lake on Gros Ventre River Road. Take the trail from here to Two Echo Park (a fine camping spot) and then continue up to Six Lakes. You can return via the same trail or take the Crystal Creek Trail back to Red Rock Ranch and hitch back to Goosewing. The trail distance is approximately 23 miles roundtrip.

TARGHEE NATIONAL FOREST

The 1.8 million-acre Targhee National Forest extends along the western face of the Tetons and then south and west into Idaho. Much of the forest is heavily logged, but two wilderness areas protect most of the Wyoming portion of the Targhee. Also note that cattle and sheep graze many backcountry areas. Check with the Forest Service office in Driggs, Idaho (tel. 208-354-2312), for areas you can go to avoid running into livestock. Get additional details on Targhee National Forest on the web at www.fs.fed.us/tnf.

JEDEDIAH SMITH WILDERNESS

The 123,451-acre Jedediah Smith Wilderness lies on the west side of the Teton Range, facing Idaho but lying entirely within Wyoming. Access is primarily from the Idaho side, although trails breach the mountain passes at various points, making it possible to enter from Grand Teton National Park. This area was not declared a wilderness until 1984. A second wilderness area, the 10,820-acre **Winegar Hole Wilderness** (pronounced "WINE-a-gur"), lies along the southern border of Yellowstone National Park. Grizzlies love this country, but hikers will find it uninteresting and without trails. In contrast, the Jedediah Smith Wilderness contains nearly 300 miles of paths and some incredible high-mountain scenery.

A number of mostly gravel roads lead up from the Driggs and Victor areas into the Tetons. Get a map ($4) showing wilderness trails and access points from the Targhee National Forest ranger station in Driggs, Idaho, tel. (208) 354-2312, or from the Forest Service offices in Jackson. Be sure to camp at least 200 feet from lakes and 100 feet from streams. If you plan to cross into Grand Teton National Park from the west side, you will need to get a camping permit in advance. Both grizzly and black bears are present throughout the Tetons, so all food must be either hung out of their reach or stored in bear-resistant containers. As this was written, the Forest Service was considering instituting backcountry user fees in the Jedediah Smith Wilderness; contact the Driggs office for the latest.

Hidden Corral Basin

At the northern end of the wilderness, Hidden Corral Basin provides a fine loop hike. Locals (primarily those on horseback) crowd this area on late-summer weekends. Get to the trailhead by driving north from Tetonia on Idaho 32 to Lamont, then turn north on a gravel road. Follow it a mile and then turn right (east) onto Coyote Meadows Road. The trailhead is approximately 10 miles up, where the road dead-ends. An eight-mile trail parallels South Bitch Creek (the name Bitch Creek comes from the French word for a female deer, *biche*) to Hidden Corral, where you may see moose. Be sure to bring a fishing pole to try for the cutthroats.

Above Hidden Corral you can make a pleasant loop back by turning north onto the trail to Nord Pass and then dropping down along the Carrot Ridge and Conant Basin Trails to Bitch Creek Trail and then on to Coyote Meadows, a distance of 21 miles roundtrip. Note that this is grizzly and black bear country, and bear resistant containers are required. By the way, Hidden Corral received its name in the outlaw days, when rustlers would steal horses in Idaho, change the brands, and then hold them in this natural corral until the branding wounds healed. The horses were then sold to Wyoming ranchers. Owen Wister's *The Virginian* describes a pursuit of horse thieves through Bitch Creek country.

Alaska Basin

The most popular hiking trail in the Jedediah Smith begins near the **Teton Canyon Campground** ($8; open mid-May to mid-September) and leads through flower-bedecked meadows to mountain-rimmed Alaska Basin. It's great country, but don't expect a true wilderness experience since many other hikers will also be hiking and camping here. Get to the campground by following the Grand Targhee Ski Resort signs east from Driggs, Idaho. A gravel road splits off to the right approximately three miles beyond the little settlement of Alta. Follow it to the campground. (If you miss the turn, you'll end up at the ski area.) For an enjoyable loop, follow Alaska Basin Trail up the canyon to Basin Lakes and then head southwest along the Teton Crest Trail to the Teton Shelf Trail. Follow this back to its junction with the Alaska Basin Trail, dropping down the Devils Stairs—a series of very steep switchbacks. You can then take the Alaska Basin Trail back to Teton Campground, a roundtrip distance of approximately 19 miles. You could also use these trails to access the high peaks of the Tetons or to cross the mountains into Death Canyon within Grand Teton National Park (camping permit required). Campfires and horse camping are not allowed in Alaska Basin.

Moose Meadows

For a somewhat less crowded hiking experience, check out the Moose Meadows area on the southern end of the Jedediah Smith Wilderness. Get to the trailhead by going three miles southeast of Victor on Idaho State Hwy. 33. Turn north (left) on Moose Creek Rd. and follow it to the trailhead. The trail parallels Moose Creek to Moose Meadows, a good place to camp. You'll need to ford the creek twice, so this is best hiked in late summer. At the meadows, the trail deadends into Teton Crest Trail, providing access to Grand Teton National Park through some gorgeous alpine country. A nice loop can be made by heading south along this trail to flower-covered Coal Creek Meadows. A trail leads from here past 10,068-foot Taylor Mountain (an easy side trip with magnificent views), down to Taylor Basin, through lodgepole forests, and then back to your starting point. This loop hike will take you 15 miles roundtrip.

TETON VALLEY, IDAHO

The west side of the Tetons is dramatically different from the Jackson Hole side. As the road descends from Teton Pass into Teton Valley, Idaho (a.k.a. Pierre's Hole), the lush farming country spreads out before you, reaching 30 miles long and 15 miles across. This, the "quiet side" of the Tetons offers a slower pace than bustling Jackson, but the Teton Range vistas are equally dramatic.

In recent years the growth in Jackson Hole has spilled across the mountains. The potato farms, horse pastures, and country towns are now starting to undergo the same transformation that first hit Jackson in the 1970s. As land prices soar and affordable housing becomes more difficult to find in Jackson, more and more people have opted to move over the pass and commute to jobs from the Idaho side. Glossy ads now fill *Teton Valley Magazine,* offering ranchland with a view, luxurious log homes, cozy second homes, balloon flights, espresso coffee, mountain-bike rentals, and handmade lodgepole furniture. Despite these changes, Teton Valley remains a laid-back place, and spud farming is still a part of the local economy. The primary town here—it's the county seat—is Driggs, with tiny Victor nine miles south, and even more insignificant Tetonia eight miles north.

See Don Root's *Idaho Handbook* (Moon Travel Handbooks, www.moon.com) for excellent coverage of eastern Idaho, including the Swan Valley to the south and the Island Park area to the north.

HISTORY

The area now known as Teton Valley was used for centuries by various Indian tribes, including the Bannock, Blackfeet, Crow, Gros Ventre, Shoshone, and Nez Percé. John Colter—a member of the Lewis and Clark expedition—was the first white man to reach this area, wandering through in the winter of 1807-08. In 1931, an Idaho farmer claimed to have plowed up a stone carved into the shape of a human face, with "John Colter 1808" etched into the sides. The rock later turned out to be a hoax created by a man anxious to obtain a horse concession with Grand Teton National Park. He got the concession after donating the rock to the park museum.

Vieux Pierre, an Iroquois fur trapper for the Hudson's Bay Company, made this area his base in the 1820s, but was later killed by Blackfeet Indians in Montana. Many people still call the valley Pierre's Hole. Two fur trapper rendezvous took place in Pierre's Hole, but the 1832 event proved pivotal. Some 1,000 Indians, trappers, and traders gathered for an annual orgy of trading, imbibing, and general partying. When a column of men on horseback appeared, two white trappers headed out for a meeting. The column turned out to be a group of Gros Ventre Indians, and the meeting quickly turned sour. One trapper shot the Gros Ventre chief point-blank, killing him. A battle quickly ensued that left 38 people dead on both sides and forced rendezvous participants to scatter. Later rendezvous were held in valleys where the animosities were not as high. For the next 50 years, virtually the only whites in Pierre's Hole were horse thieves and outlaws. Hiram C. Lapham was the first to try his hand at ranching in the valley, but his cattle were rustled by three outlaws, including Ed Harrington, alias Ed Trafton; see the special topic Lone Highwayman of Yellowstone for more on the area's most notorious scoundrel.

In 1888, a lawyer from Salt Lake City, B.W. Driggs, came to the valley and liked what he found. With his encouragement, a flood of Mormon settlers arrived over the next few years, establishing farms the entire length of Teton Valley. By the 1940s the valley was home to a cheese factory, sawmills, a railroad line, and numerous sprawling ranches. Teton Valley's population plummeted in the 1960s, but in 1969 development began at Grand Targhee Ski Resort, and the economy started to turn around. Recent years have seen the area come into its own as tourism-related businesses began to eclipse farming and ranching. By the late 1990s, the valley was positively booming, and Teton County, Idaho, was one of the fastest-growing counties (on a percentage basis) in the nation.

VICTOR

Twenty-four miles west of Jackson, the town of Victor, Idaho, is little more than the proverbial wide spot in the road. It does, however, have several places that make it worth visiting.

Pierre's Playhouse, on Main St. in Victor, tel. (208) 787-2249, www.pierresplayhouse.com, offers up old-fashioned melodramas twice weekly from mid-June to early September. A Dutch-oven chicken dinner is served before the show. You know you're in for a serious production when the villian is named Gustavo Scumsuckler.

Accommodations

Built in the 1940s, **Timberline Inn,** 38 W. Center St., tel. (208) 787-2772 or (800) 711-4667, has a log-cabin exterior, with standard motel rooms for $50 s or d. Open June-October. Inexpensive.

Four miles southeast of Victor at the foot of Teton Pass, **Moose Creek Ranch,** tel. (208) 787-2784 or (800) 676-0075, has guest ranch accommodations on a weekly basis; $2,190 for two people. The rate includes lodging, meals, horseback lessons and rides, children's programs, whitewater float trips, chuck wagon dinners, and other ranch activities. Accommodations are cozy cabins with private baths, and the ranch also has an outdoor pool and jacuzzi. Get additional information by visiting the website, www.webfactor.com/mooscrk. Luxury.

Camping

The Forest Service's pleasant **Trail Creek Campground** ($6; open mid-May to mid-September) is six miles southeast of Victor and just across the Wyoming state line. **Teton Valley Campground,** one mile west of Victor on Idaho Hwy. 31, tel. (208) 787-2647, www.jacksonholenet.com/tvc, has RV hookups ($27), tent sites ($19), basic cabins ($36), and a small outdoor pool. The campground also rents canoes, mountain bikes, and fishing gear.

Food

For the finest meals in Teton Valley, make dinner reservations at **The Old Dewey House Restaurant,** 37 S. Main St., tel. (208) 787-2092, www.odh.com. Everything is made from scratch by the owners, and the entrées are accompanied by freshly baked breads, salads with homemade dressings, fresh vegetables, and spicy appetizers. Entrées ($14-31) change frequently at this eight-table restaurant, but house favorites include blackened chicken and jalapeño cream sauce, charbroiled rack of lamb, and Mexican-style baked fish. Delectable desserts, too. The menu warns: "undisciplined children will be impounded and sold into slavery, or fed to the Yellowstone wolves!" Closed Tuesday. The same characters also run tiny Grumpy's Goat Shack next door, with wines, beers, and appetizers, including wonderful roasted garlic with homemade goat cheese from their own goats.

Victor Emporium, tel. (208) 787-2221, houses an old-fashioned soda fountain with good fish tacos and famous shakes—especially their huckleberry shakes in season. They've been in business for over 50 years, and also sell fishing supplies and Idaho souvenirs.

Also in Victor is **Knotty Pine Restaurant,** tel. (208) 787-2866, considered one of the better local places for ribs and steaks, but be ready for clouds of cigarette smoke with your meal.

Brewpub

The **Otto Brothers' Brewing Company,** tel. (208) 787-9000, www.ottobrothers.com, is on the east side of Victor at 430 Old Jackson Highway. Drop by for a free tour or to sample Teton Ale, Old Faithful Ale, Moose Juice Stout, Teton Huckleberry Wheat, Teton Golden Ale, and/or Teton Pass Porter. The pub also serves up brick-oven pizzas, calzones, and salads, and sells attractive T-shirts and glasses. Hours are Tues.-Sat. 4-9 p.m., with tours available by request before 6 p.m.

Recreation

A paved path parallels Hwy. 33 between Victor and Driggs, providing a pleasant biking or rollerblading opportunity. The route may eventually continue over Teton Pass to Wilson.

Rendezvous Ski Tours, tel. (208) 787-2906, www.skithetetons.com, maintains three Mongolian-style yurts in the backcountry, each located several hours of skiing (or hiking) apart from the next. The huts can sleep up to eight and have kitchens, bunks, sleeping bags, and woodstoves. Rates are $165 per night, but you need to be experienced in backcountry skiing and have the necessary safety equipment and avalanche training. If you don't quite measure up, they also offer guided backcountry ski tours to the huts ($360/day for two people). A good base for these trips is the company's modern three-bedroom guest house at the mouth of Fox Creek Canyon, eight miles north of Victor. The home comes complete with all the amenities, including a hot tub. You can rent the entire place for $300, or get just a room for $75 d if you're willing to share with other folks. Rates include a make-it-yourself breakfast.

DRIGGS

Driggs (pop. 850) is an odd conglomeration of a town, mixing an old-time farming settlement and newfangled recreation mecca. There isn't much to the town itself, so it's pretty easy to find your way around

Sights

Driggs is perhaps best known as home to the delightfully amusing **Spud Drive-In,** here since 1953. You can't miss the big truck out front with a flatbed-sized "potato" on the back. The drive-in even attracts folks from Jackson, who cross the pass for an evening of fun beneath the stars. Call (208) 354-2727 or (800) 799-7783 for upcoming flicks. For the in-house version, head to **Spud Too Theatre,** 190 N. Main St., tel. (208) 354-2718. Both places are locally famous for their Gladys burger and Spud buds—served by carhops at the drive-in or right to your seat at the theater.

A tiny one-room museum sits behind the American Legion building in Driggs, but it has no set hours; call (208) 354-2282 or (208) 354-2200 for a visit. A new museum building just north of Driggs is expected to open in 2001.

Accommodations

For a town this small, Driggs offers a surprising number of places to stay. In addition to those listed below, you'll find others just east in Alta, Wyoming (described below).

The Pines Motel-Guest Haus, 105 S. Main St., tel. (208) 354-2774 or (800) 354-2778, is a delightful European-style guest house built in 1900. Run by the Nielson family, the home has

LONE HIGHWAYMAN OF YELLOWSTONE

Because of its remote location, Teton Valley became a rendezvous place for rustlers and outlaws in the 1880s. Horses stolen from the soldiers at Fort Hall, along with cattle "liberated" from Wyoming and Montana ranches, made their way through Pierre's Hole to the railroads. Hiram C. Lapham was the first to try his hand at ranching in the valley, but his cattle quickly disappeared. With the help of a posse from Rexburg, Lapham tracked down the culprits, one of whom was killed in the ensuing gunfight. The others surrendered, but they escaped from jail when the wife of bandit Ed Harrington smuggled a gun to him in clothing worn by his baby. Harrington and partner Lum Nickerson were eventually tracked down and sent to jail.

Although Harrington was sentenced to 25 years, the governor pardoned him after just three. Harrington went on to become Teton Valley's first postman, but his criminal activity continued. Using the alias Ed Trafton, Harrington went on to rob stores throughout Teton Valley, and eventually spent another two years behind bars. After getting out, he turned his attention to the tourism business in Yellowstone, but not in the standard way. Though it was never proven, he was suspected of being behind a string of stagecoach robberies in 1908 in which cash and jewelry were taken from tourists at gunpoint. Harrington's most brazen feat came on July 29, 1914, when he single-handedly robbed 15 stages, earning the nickname "the lone highwayman of Yellowstone." The tourists were particularly impressed with his gentlemanly manner as he asked them to "please" hand over all their cash and jewelry. Harrington made off with $915.35 in cash and $130 in jewelry, but he made the mistake of posing for photos in the process. He was caught the following year and spent five years in Leavenworth Prison.

When Harrington died, a letter in his pocket claimed that he had been Owen Wister's model for the Virginian in his famous novel. Others suspected that he was more likely to have been Wister's model for the villain, Trampas.

eight-rooms, each different but all nicely appointed with tasteful touches such as handmade quilts. A jacuzzi is available outside. Rates are very reasonable: $35 d or $40 d, and children are welcome. Breakfasts cost $10 per person. Inexpensive.

Super 8 Motel, on the north side of Driggs at 133 Hwy. 33, tel. (208) 354-8888 or (800) 800-8000, has standard rooms for $40 s or $50 d, including a continental breakfast and jacuzzi. Inexpensive.

Intermountain Lodge, 34 Ski Hill Rd. (a mile east of Driggs), tel. (208) 354-8153, offers modern log cabin lodging with an outdoor jacuzzi. All rooms include kitchenettes. Rates are $49-59 s or d. Inexpensive.

Best Western Teton West, 476 N. Main St., tel. (208) 354-2363 or (800) 252-2363, features a continental breakfast, indoor pool, and jacuzzi. Rates are $46 s or $60 d in standard rooms, or $100 for kitchenettes. It may be closed in the fall. Moderate-Expensive.

Teton Ranch, tel. (208) 456-2010 or (888) 456-2012, www.tetonranch.com, offers three log homes on a working ranch. Each contains two bedrooms, a fireplace, and kitchen and costs $150-225 for four people. The cabins are six miles northeast of Driggs; reserve three to six months ahead for the peak summer season. There's a two-night minimum stay. Moderate-Expensive.

Short-term bookings for townhouses, homes, cabins, and condos in the area are provided by two property management companies: **Grand Valley Lodging,** tel. (208) 354-8890 or (800) 746-5518, www.tetonvalley.net/gvlodge; and **Teton Valley Property Management,** tel. (208) 354-8881 or (888) 354-8881, www.tetonvalley-idaho.com. Rates range from $120 to $400 per night. These are popular with families and ski groups heading to Grand Targhee Ski Resort.

Bed and Breakfasts

On the southern edge of Driggs, **Three Peaks Inn B&B,** tel. (208) 354-8912, boasts Teton Range views and an outdoor hot tub. The five spacious guest rooms have private or shared baths and are furnished with lodgepole pieces. Rates are $65-85 s or d, including a hearty breakfast. Kids are welcome. Moderate.

Locanda di Fiori (The Inn of Flowers), tel. (208) 456-0909, is a modern log cabin seven miles north of Driggs. You'll find masses of wildflowers nearby (hence the name) and stunning views of the Tetons to the east. Two comfortable guest rooms are available, both with private baths and entrances, plus access to an outdoor jacuzzi. A full breakfast is served each morning, along with wine and cheese in the evening. Rates are $95 d. The inn is open June-Oct.; no kids under age 15. Expensive.

Willowpine B&B Guest Home, 136 E. Little Ave., tel. (208) 354-2735, has three guest rooms with shared baths in a refurbished 1940s home. It's right in town. Rates are $65 s or d, including a full breakfast. No kids. Moderate.

Teton Creek B&B, 41 S. Baseline Rd., tel. (208) 354-2584, has four guest rooms and a jacuzzi; $55-65 d. Inexpensive-Moderate.

Teton Sunrise Inn, tel. (208) 456-2777 or (888) 456-2777, www.tetonsunriseinn.com, is a newly built B&B halfway between Driggs and Tetonia (three miles in either direction). The lodge-style home contains five large guest rooms, each with a private bath. An enclosed jacuzzi faces the Tetons, and a full breakfast is served, along with evening snacks. Rates are $80 d, and children are welcome. Moderate.

Camping

The nearest public campsites are at **Teton Canyon Campground** ($8; open mid-May to mid-September), 11 miles east of Driggs in the Tetons. This is a delightful camping spot, and the trailhead into beautiful (and very popular) Alaska Basin is nearby. Park RVs at **Larsen's Mobile Park,** 97 S. Main St., tel. (208) 354-2205, for $15 per night; no showers.

Food

One benefit of Teton Valley's rapid growth is a dramatic improvement in the local restaurant scene. Driggs now has several good dining places. (The best local meals, however, are Dewey's in Victor and Lost Horizon in Alta.)

Start your day at **The Breakfast Shoppe,** 95 S. Main St., tel. (208) 354-8294, where the specialties are delicious eggs Benedict (six types!), huevos rancheros, and Belgian waffles. Everything is made from scratch, but don't ask for a recipe; the sauces are a family secret. They also serve light lunches, including a tasty Cajun club sandwich. Recommended. **Main Street Grill,**

68 N. Main St., tel. (208) 354-3303, is another lunch place with good sandwiches.

Inside Outfitters Mall at 189 N. Main St., **Auntie M's Sweet Shoppe & Coffee,** tel. (208) 354-2010, serves espresso, teas, cookies, homemade pies, and tasty lunches in a bright and classy setting.

For fast eats in a '50s-style diner, try **Mike's Eats,** on Main St., tel. (208) 354-2797. The menu includes Navajo fry bread, buffalo burgers, and smoked rainbow trout, along with malts and homemade pies. Open summers only.

Bunk House Bistro, 285 N. Main St., tel. (208) 354-3770, emphasizes "cowboy" breakfasts and lunches all week, with Friday and Saturday dinners starring pasta, seafood, and prime rib. The kitchen is small, so you may need to wait for your meal, but the servings are substantial. Reservations recommended.

In the evening, stop by the attractive **O'Rourke's Sports Bar & Grille,** 42 E. Little Ave., tel. (208) 354-8115, where you can watch sports on the tube while you munch delicious pizzas, sandwiches, and burgers.

Inside a 1916 home off the main drag, **Royal Wolf,** tel. (208) 354-8365, is another place with a big choice of beers on tap, plus a diverse dinner menu. A pool table, dartboards, and sports on the TVs provide for extraculinary fun.

Tony's Pizza & Pasta, 364 N. Main St., tel. (208) 354-8829, serves hand-tossed New York-style pizzas, plus focaccia, calzone, and Italian meals. Choose from a long list of microbrewed beers, with many on draught. Tony's flavorful "Avalanche" pizza comes with ricotta, mozzarella, and garlic—but no tomato sauce. No smoking here.

Get malts, shakes, and hot fudge sundaes at the old soda fountain inside **Corner Drug,** 10 S. Main St., tel. (208) 354-2334. Lime freezes are their claim to fame. For fruit smoothies and espresso, along with light breakfasts and lunches, squeeze into **Squeeze to Please,** tel. (208) 354-2801, east of town at the Teton Valley Fitness Center, 50 Ski Hill Road. This is also one of the few places in North America where you'll find that Argentinian favorite, *yerba matte.*

The main place for groceries is **Broulim's,** 52 S. Main St., tel. (208) 354-2350. Right next door is tiny **Barrels and Bins,** tel. (208) 354-2307, selling health foods and freeze-dried backcountry meals.

Teton Valley Events

The main summer event comes on **Fourth of July** weekend and is highlighted by the **Teton Valley Balloon Festival,** with sunrise launches, tethered balloon rides for the kids, and live bands in the evening. Also in Driggs that weekend are an arts-and-crafts fair, old-time-fiddle contest, antique-car show, and fireworks. Victor offers up a small-town Independence Day parade and breakfast feed, while Grand Targhee Ski Resort puts on a cross-country bike race that attracts everyone from beginners to pros.

Grand Targhee Ski Resort is home to two very popular outdoor music festivals each summer: **Rockin' the Tetons Music & Microbrew Festival** on the second weekend of July, and the mellower **Targhee Bluegrass Festival** in mid-August. Call the resort for details, tel. (800) 827-4433.

Heritage Days in late July celebrates the area's Mormon settlers; featured attractions are a parade through the center of Driggs, art shows, and a theatrical production. **Taste of the Tetons** arrives in early August, with local restaurants showing off their fare to raise funds for the nonprofit Teton Regional Land Trust. Call (208) 354-8939 for information on the event or this organization.

In mid-August, the **Teton County Fair** brings down-home fun with livestock judging, arts and crafts, quilts, pies, jams, and other fare on display. Call (208) 354-2961 for details.

Teton Valley Recreation

Outdoor enthusiasts will discover an array of activities at all times of the year in the Driggs area. The Teton River runs the entire length of Teton Valley and is renowned among fly-fishing enthusiasts. A plethora of hikes can be found both to the east in the Tetons and to the west in the Big Hole Mountains. See Targhee National Forest earlier in this chapter for details on Alaska Basin; it's one of the most popular day (or multinight) hikes in the area. The Forest Service office in Driggs has details on other hiking options if you're looking for a less crowded experience.

The **National Outdoor Leadership School** (NOLS) has an office off the main road south of Driggs at 166 E. 200 S., tel. (208) 354-8443. This is one of nine regional NOLS offices scattered around the globe; headquarters is in Lander, Wyoming. The Driggs office runs summertime backpacking and whitewater training, plus backcountry skiing classes in the winter. Classes last two weeks to three months. Find NOLS on the web at www.nols.edu.

A paved path parallels Hwy. 33 between Victor and Driggs, providing an easy biking and rollerblading opportunity. The path will eventually continue north all the way to Ashton along an old railroad right-of-way.

One block up the road to Grand Targhee Ski Resort, **Peaked Sports,** 70 E. Little Ave., tel. (208) 354-2354 or (800) 705-2354, rents mountain bikes, bike trailers, and rollerblades. **Big Hole Mountain Sports,** 99 S. Main St., tel. (208) 354-2209 or (877) 574-3377, www.boardsnbikes.com, is for the real biking enthusiast. The store rents high-quality mountain bikes in the summer and snowboards in winter. Ask at Big Hole for their guide to local biking trails. On Thursday afternoons you can join locals for a ride out local trails, but this is for advanced riders only—unless you want to get left in the dust.

Rainbow Balloon Flights, tel. (307) 733-0470 or (800) 378-0470, offers one-hour hot-air balloon flights over Teton Valley, and **Teton Aviation Center,** tel. (208) 354-3100 or (800) 472-6382, www.tetonaviation.com, offers scenic glider and airplane rides during the summer.

In the winter months, **Basin Auto,** 180 N. Main St., tel. (208) 354-2297, has snowmobile rentals and guided tours.

Shopping

For a unique shopping experience at "the cultural hub of the universe," drop by **Mountaineering Outfitters,** 62 N. Main St., tel. (208) 354-2222 or (800) 359-2410. Inside the jam-packed aisles are hiking boots, sleeping bags, Patagonia clothing (good prices), army-surplus wool pants, and maps. Owner Fred Mugler opened his shop in 1971 and has been cramming it with supplies ever since. Stop for a chat and a laugh.

Considerably more organized is **Yöstmark Mountain Equipment,** 12 E. Little Ave., tel. (208) 354-2828, www.yostmark.com, which sells a wide range of outdoor equipment. They also rent fishing gear, drift boats, backpacks, tents, sleeping bags, boots, inflatable kayaks, rafts, rollerblades, and all sorts of other outdoor gear, along with snowshoes, cross-country skis, skate skis, and alpine touring skis in the winter. Open every (!) day of the year 8 a.m.-7 p.m. Ask them about backcountry ski tours.

Find an excellent and eclectic selection of regional books at the friendly **Dark Horse Books,** 76 N. Main St., tel. (208) 354-8882. In the back is Big Hole Music, selling CDs. Kids will love the selection of toys and travel games at **Dragonfly Toys,** 24 E. Little Ave., tel. (208) 354-3458. **Bergmeyer Manufacturing Co.,** 229 N. Hwy. 33, tel. (208) 354-8611 or (800) 348-3356, creates quality log furniture in traditional styles.

Information and Services

The **Teton Valley Chamber of Commerce,** tel. (208) 354-2500, www.tetonvalleychamber.com, has an office inside Aspen Artworks downtown on Main Street. Their hours are officially Mon.-Fri. 10 a.m.-3 p.m., but call first to make sure someone is there. Another source for information—with links to local businesses—is on the web at www.tetonguide.com.

Get Targhee National Forest information from the **Teton Basin Ranger District Office,** just south of town at 525 S. Main St., tel. (208) 354-2312.

Teton Valley Hospital is at 283 N. 1st East, tel. (208) 354-2383. Also here is **Teton Valley Medical Center,** tel. (208) 354-2302, for non-emergency care.

Transportation

Community and Rural Transportation (CART), tel. (208) 354-2240 or (800) 657-7439, www.cyberhighway.net/~cartbus, has bus service between Driggs and Rexburg five days a week.

Downhill Express, tel. (307) 734-9525 or (877) 943-3574, provides a daily shuttle service from Driggs and Victor to Teton Village (Jackson Hole Mountain Resort) and Jackson (Snow King Resort) in the winter.

Rent cars from **Aspen Rent-A-Car,** tel. (208) 354-3386 or (877) 882-7736, at Grand Teton Motors on the north end of Driggs.

TETONIA

Tiny Tetonia is eight miles north of Driggs. The town is surrounded by farming country and grand old barns; it's a good place to see kids riding horseback. The crest of the tourist wave is just starting to lap at the shores of Tetonia, and at last check no local place sold espresso, focaccia, or cell phones.

Accommodations

The newest Teton Valley motel, **Teton Mountain View Lodge,** tel. (208) 456-2741 or (800) 625-2232, www.tetonmountainlodge.com, has large rooms with rustic furnishings; some also have fireplaces. Other amenities include a continental breakfast and enclosed jacuzzi. Rates are $60-110 s or d. Moderate-Expensive.

Occupying a 4,000-acre spread five miles northeast of Tetonia, **Teton Ridge Ranch,** 200 Valley View Rd., tel. (208) 456-2650, provides guest ranch accommodations. The modern 10,000-square-foot log lodge forms a central focal point, but a cottage is also available for guests. Rates are $550 d per day including excellent meals, horseback riding, and fishing in their stocked ponds. A three-night minimum stay is required, and the ranch has space for 14 guests. During the winter months they provide groomed cross-country ski trails. Winter rates are $450 d per day, including lodging, meals, and guided skiing. Open mid-June through October, and mid-December to mid-March. Luxury.

East of Tetonia in the Teton foothills inside Wyoming, **Beard's Mountain Ranch,** tel. (307) 576-2694, has a two-bedroom cabin with kitchenette. Rates are $85 d, and the cabin can sleep up to six. The ranch also offers horseback riding and guided fishing trips. Moderate.

Food

Trail's End Cafe, tel. (208) 456-2202, attracts local farmers and ranchers from all around for home-cooked meals of turkey, gravy, mashed Idaho potatoes, burgers, and other hearty fare. The homemade pies are worth the visit. This is where you'll meet the hardworking good ole boys. Open at 6 a.m. daily.

Recreation

Teton Stage Co. has horseback rides in the Tetonia area; call (208) 465-3075 for reservations (required). **Robson Snowmobile Outfitters,** tel. (208) 456-2805, guides snowmobile tours into nearby mountains.

Shopping

A Tetonia company called **Drawknife** creates one-of-a-kind billiard tables using hand-carved lodgepole bases and top-quality tabletops. Find them at 516 N. Hwy. 33, tel. (800) 320-0527, or on the web at www.drawknife.com.

ALTA, WYOMING

The tiny place called Alta sits right along the Wyoming border and just six miles northeast of Driggs, Idaho. There are no stores in Alta, but the settlement does have a stellar restaurant and several places to stay. East from Alta, the road climbs through heavily timbered country, with periodic views of the Big Hole Mountains to the west and up-close looks at the Teton Range. Also in Alta is the nine-hole **Targhee Village Golf Course,** tel. (208) 354-8577.

Well-known **Grand Targhee Ski Resort,** tel. (800) 827-4433, www.grandtarghee.com, is only five miles above Alta and is the main attraction for the entire Teton Valley area. The resort offers excellent skiing and snowboarding in winter, along with a wide range of summer activities. Get the complete scoop, including details for on-mountain lodging and meals in Downhill Skiing and Snowboarding above.

Accommodations

Alta Lodge B&B, tel. (307) 353-2582 or (800) 707-2582, www.pdt.net/altalodge, is a large modern home with tall picture windows framing the Tetons. Four guest rooms are here (two with private baths), and a jacuzzi is available. Rates are $65-85 d, including a full breakfast. No kids. Moderate.

Teton Teepee Lodge, 470 W. Alta Rd., tel. (307) 353-8176 or (800) 353-8176, contains a spacious common area at the center of a tepee-shaped building. Twenty-one guest rooms (no TV or phones in rooms) surround it, and two large dorm rooms—primarily used by kids—occupy a lower level. The lodge is a favorite of skiers and snowboarders, with a large central stone fireplace, dining area, pool table, game room, TV room, and outdoor jacuzzi. In the winter, the rooms are rented on a package basis only: $816 for three days for two people, including private room, breakfast, dinner, drinks, transportation to Grand Targhee, and lift tickets. For five days, the all-inclusive rate is $1,240 for two people. In summer the lodge is a popular place for family reunions and weddings, but they also rent individual rooms for $60 per night and dorm beds for $25 per person for adults, $20 for ages 15-18, and $15 for ages 6-14. Summertime rates include a full breakfast and drinks. Get the complete story at www.tetonteepee.com. Moderate-Luxury.

Also in Alta is **Wilson Creekside Inn B&B,** 130 Alta North Rd., tel. (307) 353-2409, where you'll find a century-old home on a 200-acre sheep farm. Four guest rooms are available and all contain family heirlooms. One costs $80 d and includes a king-size bed and private bath; the others share a bath and run $70 d. An outdoor jacuzzi is available, and guests are served an ample country breakfast. Kids are welcome, but no credit cards. The owner's son raises some 150 ewes on the ranch. Moderate.

Call **Grand Targhee Vacation Rentals** at (887) 667-4663 for one-, two-, and three-bedroom condo rentals at Teton Creek Resort, 8.5 miles below Grand Targhee Ski Resort, or at Powder Valley Condominiums, 10 miles away. Guests at either place may use the fitness center, outdoor pool, and two jacuzzis at Teton Creek Resort. Rates are $250 per night in the winter holiday season, with a three-night minimum. Luxury.

Food

Lost Horizon Dinner Club, tel. (307) 353-8226, is one of two standout places in the Teton Valley area (the other being the Dewey Restaurant in Victor). The restaurant/home has room for just a dozen guests, who sit down to a memorable 10-course Japanese and Chinese meal ($40) prepared by co-owner and chef Shigako Irwin. This isn't for vegetarians, or for those in a hurry; expect to be here for over three leisurely hours. Dinners are served Fri.-Sun. nights, and reservations are required. Formal dress isn't necessary, but don't come in shorts, sandals, or T-shirts. Recommended.

GRAND TETON NATIONAL PARK

Grand Teton National Park remains one of the preeminent symbols of American wilderness. The Tetons rise abruptly from the valley floor, their bare triangular ridges looking like broken shards of glass from some cosmic accident of creation. With six different summits topping 12,000 feet, plus some of the finest climbing and hiking in Wyoming, the Tetons are a paradise for lovers of the outdoors. They have long been a favorite of photographers and sightseers and once even appeared in an ad promoting Colorado tourism! The Tetons change character with the seasons. In summer the sagebrush flats are a garden of flowers set against the mountain backdrop. When autumn arrives, the cottonwoods and aspens become swaths of yellow and orange. Winter turns everything a glorious, sparkling white, set against the fluorescent blue sky.

GEOLOGY

Building a Mountain Range

The precipitous Teton Range contains perhaps the most complex geologic history in North America. Although the Tetons are ancient by any human scale, they are the youngest mountains in the Rockies, less than 10 million years old (versus 60 million years for the nearby Wind River Mountains). The Tetons are a fault-block range, formed when the earth's crust cracked along an angled fault. Forces within the earth have pushed the western side (the Tetons) up, while the eastern portion (Jackson Hole) dropped down like a trapdoor. Geologists believe the fault could slip up to 10 feet at a time, producing a violent earthquake. All this shifting has created one of the most dramatic and asymmetric mountain faces on earth.

Unlike typical mountain ranges, the highest parts are not at the center of the range but along the eastern edge, where uplifting continues. The western slope, which drops gently into Idaho, is much less dramatic, though the views are still very impressive. This tilting-and-subsidence process is still going on today, pushed by the movement of a plume of magma beneath Yellowstone as the continental plate slides over the top. Because of this subsidence, the town of Wilson in Jackson Hole now lies 10 feet below

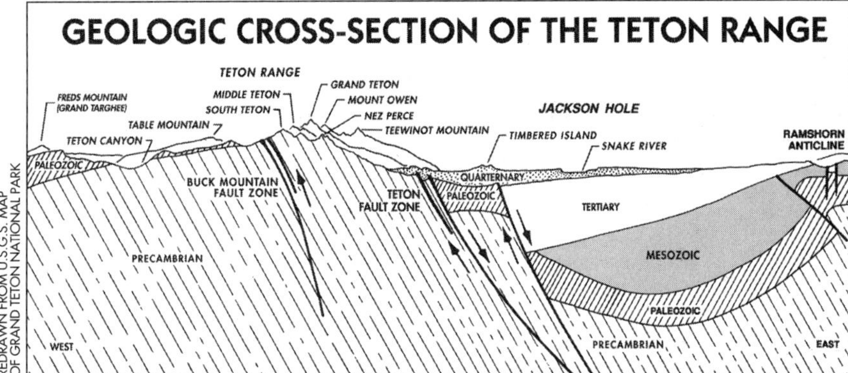

the level of the nearby Snake River; only riverside dikes protect the town from flooding.

As the mountains rose along this fault, millennia of overlying deposits were stripped away by erosion, leaving three-million-year-old Precambrian rock jutting into the air above the more recent sedimentary deposits in the valley. Because of this shifting and erosion, sandstone deposits atop Mt. Moran match those 24,000 feet below Jackson Hole. Although the most recent major earthquake on the Teton Fault was at least 2,000 years ago, geologists are convinced that Jackson Hole could experience a major temblor at any time.

Rivers of Ice

In counterpoint to the uplifting actions that created the general outline of the Tetons, erosional forces have been wearing them down again. Glaciers—created when more snow falls than melts off—have proven one of the most important of these erosional processes. After a period of several years and under the weight of additional snow, the accumulated snow crystals change into ice. Gravity pulls this ice slowly downhill, creating what is essentially a frozen river that grinds against whatever lies in the way, plucking loose rocks and soil and polishing hard bedrock. This debris moves slowly down the glacier as if on a conveyer belt, eventually reaching the glacier's terminus.

When a glacier remains the same size for a long period, large piles of glacial debris accumulate at its end, creating what glaciologists call a terminal moraine. One of these created Jackson Lake, when a huge glacier dumped tons of rock at its snout. After the glacier melted back, this terminal moraine became a natural dam for the waters of the Snake River. Similar mounds of glacial debris dammed the creeks that formed Jenny, Leigh, Bradley, Taggart, and Phelps Lakes within Grand Teton National Park.

The earth has experienced cyclical periods of glaciation for hundreds of thousands of years, probably due to changes in the earth's orbit around the sun. During the colder portions of these cycles, glaciers appear and advance. The entire Yellowstone region has undergone a series of massive glaciations, the last of which is called the Pinedale Glaciation. It began around 70,000 years ago and had essentially disappeared by 15,000 years ago. At its peak, the Pinedale Glaciation covered all of Yellowstone and reached well into Jackson Hole.

Streams flowed from the ends of these glaciers, carrying along gravel, sand, silt, and clay. The cobbles and sands from these streams were dropped on the flat valley below, while the finer silts and clays continued downstream, leaving behind soils too rocky and nutrient-poor to support trees. Only sagebrush grows on this plain today, while the surrounding hills and mountain slopes (which were spared this rocky deposition) are covered with lodgepole and subalpine fir forests. Trees can also be found covering the silty terminal moraines that ring the lakes.

Other reminders of the glacial past are the "potholes" (more accurately termed "kettles") that dot the plain south of Signal Mountain. These

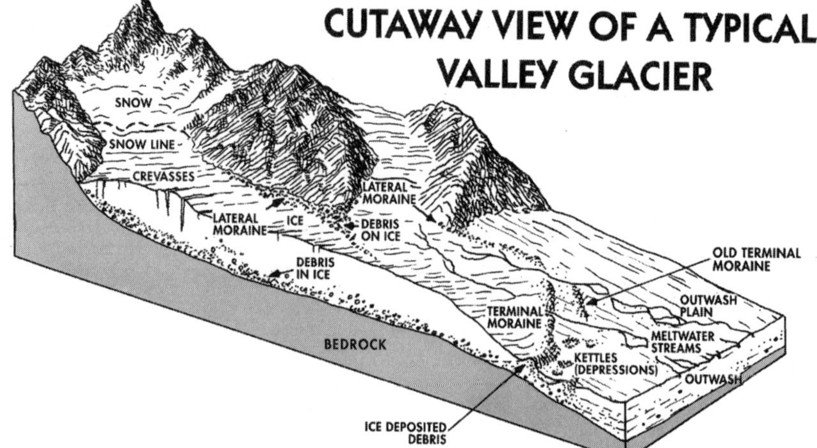

REDRAWN FROM *CREATION OF THE TETON LANDSCAPE* BY J.D. LOVE AND JOHN C. REED, JR.

depressions were created when large blocks of ice were buried under glacial outwash. When the ice melted, it left a kettle-shaped pond surrounded by glacial debris. Only a dozen or so small glaciers remain in the Tetons; the largest is the 3,500-foot-long Teton Glacier, visible on the northeastern face of Grand Teton. For a far more detailed picture of Teton geology, read *Interpreting the Landscape: Recent and Ongoing Geology of Grand Teton & Yellowstone National Parks,* by John Good and Kenneth Pierce (Moose: Grand Teton Natural History Association).

WILDLIFE

Grand Teton National Park is an excellent place to look for wildlife. Moose are often seen in the willow meadows along Jackson Lake, south of the settlement of Moose, and along the Snake River. The best times to see animals are in the early morning or at dusk. Herds of pronghorn antelope are common on the sagebrush flats near Kelly. Elk are frequent sights in fall as they migrate down from the high country to the elk refuge near Jackson, but smaller numbers are in the park during the summer. (Grand Teton is the only national park outside Alaska that allows hunting. The rules are pretty strange, however, requiring elk hunters to become temporarily deputized park rangers before they head out!) Grizzlies are currently found only on the park's northern margins, but black bears are present in wooded canyons and riverbeds, so be sure to use caution when hiking or camping in the park. Moose are often seen along the Snake River, at Oxbow Bend, and at Willow Flats. Other animals to look for are bald eagles and ospreys along the Snake River and trumpeter swans and Canada geese in ponds and lakes. Look for mule deer in meadow areas and at forest edges, such as those near Colter Bay.

Bison

Herds of bison (buffalo) are commonly seen in the Moran Junction area and in the Mormon Row area. They were present historically (hence the name Buffalo River) but had been extinct for perhaps a century when eight bison were released into Grand Teton National Park in 1969. The population grew slowly for the first decade until they discovered the free alfalfa handout at the elk refuge north of Jackson. Partly because of this winter feeding, the population has grown to almost 400 animals—much to the chagrin of the elk-refuge managers. A small number of bison are hunted outside the park to control their numbers.

Wolves

Wolves were reintroduced to Yellowstone National Park starting in 1995, and they continue to spread into new territory. By the winter of 1998-99, they had moved into Grand Teton National

Park and are now denning in the park. They're most easily seen in the winter, particularly on the adjacent National Elk Refuge where they prey on elk, but they may sometimes be seen during the summer inside the park.

PARK HISTORY

Once the wonders of Yellowstone came to widespread public attention, it took only a few months for Congress to declare that area a national park. But the magnificent mountain range to the south proved an entirely different story. Early on, there were suggestions that Yellowstone be expanded to include the Tetons, but it would take decades of wrangling before Jackson Hole would finally be preserved.

"Damning" Jackson Lake

Jackson Lake represents one of the sadder chapters in the history of northwestern Wyoming. Jackson Lake Dam was built in the winter of 1910-11 to supply water for Idaho potato and beet farmers. The town of Moran was built to house construction workers for Jackson Lake Dam and at one time included more than a hundred ramshackle structures. Virtually nothing remains of the town. The 70-foot-tall dam increased the size of the natural lake, flooding out more than 7,200 acres of trees and creating a tangle of floating and submerged trunks and stumps. To some, the dam seemed like the serpent in the Garden of Eden, a symbol of the development that would destroy the valley if not stopped. The trees remained in Jackson Lake for many years, creating an eyesore until the Park Service and the CCC finally launched a massive cleanup project in the 1930s. The dam was completely rebuilt in 1988-89, and while the lake now looks quite attractive, it remains yet another example of how Wyoming provides water for farmers in surrounding states. Late in the fall—especially in dry years—the lake can drop to a large puddle with long stretches of exposed bottom at the upper end. Fortunately, Idaho irrigators did not succeed in their planned dams on Jenny, Leigh, and Taggart Lakes in what is now Grand Teton National Park.

About 400 bison live in Grand Teton National Park.

Dudes and Development

Because of the rocky soils and long winters, Jackson Hole has always been a marginal place for cattle ranching, and only in the southern end of the valley are the soils rich enough to support a decent crop of hay. It was this poor soil and harsh climate that saved Jackson Hole from early development and forced the ranchers to bring in dudes to supplement their income. (One old-timer noted, "Dudes winter better than cattle.")

The first Jackson Hole dude ranch, the JY, was established in 1908 along Phelps Lake by Louis Joy. It was followed a few years later by the Bar BC Ranch of Struthers Burt, an acclaimed East Coast author who had come west as a dude but learned enough to go into the business for himself. The dude ranchers were some of the first to realize the value of Jackson Hole and to support its preservation. Burt proposed that the valley and mountains be saved not as a traditional park but as a "museum on the hoof," where ranching and tourism would join hands to stave off commercial developments. The roads would remain unpaved, all homes would be log, and Jackson would stay a frontier town. Needless to say, that didn't happen.

The movement to save Jackson Hole coalesced in a 1923 meeting at the cabin of Maude Noble. Horace Albright, superintendent of Yellowstone National Park, was there, along with local dude ranchers, businessmen, and cattlemen eager to save the remote valley from exploitation. To accomplish this goal, they proposed finding a wealthy philanthropist who might be willing to invest the two million dollars that would be needed to buy the land. Fortunately, one of Struthers Burt's friends happened to be Kenneth Chorley, an assistant to John D. Rockefeller Jr. Burt used this contact to get Rockefeller interested in the project.

Rocky to the Rescue

In 1926, Rockefeller traveled west for a 12-day trip to Yellowstone. Horace Albright used the chance to take him on a side trip into Jackson Hole and to proselytize for protection of the valley. What they saw portended badly for the future: the Jenny Lake dance hall, roadside tourist camps and hot dog stands, rusting abandoned cars, and a place that billboards proclaimed "Home of the Hollywood Cowboy." Rockefeller was angered by the prospect of crass commercial developments blanketing Jackson Hole and quickly signed on to the idea of purchasing the land and giving it to the Park Service.

To cover his tracks as he bought the land, Rockefeller formed the Snake River Land Company—if ranchers had known that the Rockefeller clan was behind the scheme, they would have either refused to sell or jacked up the price. Only a few residents—mostly supporters—knew of the plan. The local banker, Robert Miller, served as land-purchasing agent, although even he opposed letting the Park Service gain control of the valley. Miller used his position to buy out ranches with delinquent mortgages at his Jackson State Bank and then resigned, claiming the whole thing was part of a sinister plot to run the ranchers out and halt "progress." In 1929, Congress voted to establish a small Grand Teton National Park that would encompass the mountains themselves—which stood little chance of development—but not much else. Conservationists knew that without preservation of the valley below, the wonderful vistas would be lost.

A National Battleground

Rockefeller and Albright finally went public with their land-purchasing scheme in 1930, releasing a tidal wave of outrage. Antipark forces led by Sen. Milward Simpson (father of recently retired Sen. Alan Simpson) spent the next decade fighting the park tooth and nail, charging that it would destroy the economy of Jackson Hole and that ranchers would lose their livelihood. Rockefeller's agents were falsely accused of trying to intimidate holdouts with strong-arm tactics. Congress refused to accept Rockefeller's gift, and local opposition blocked the bill for more than a decade.

Finally, in 1943, President Roosevelt made an end run around the antipark forces; he accepted the 32,000 acres purchased by Rockefeller, added 130,000 acres of Forest Service land, and declared it the Jackson Hole National Monument. The move outraged those in the valley, prompting more hearings and bills to abolish the new national monument. Wyoming's politicians attacked Roosevelt's actions. A bill overturning the decision was pocket-vetoed by the president, but for the next several years, the Wyoming delegation kept reintroducing the measure.

Things came to a head when Wallace Beery—a Reaganesque Hollywood actor—threatened to "shoot to kill" park officials. Beery—who had to use a stepladder to climb on his horse—organized a cattle drive across the monument. Unable to find anyone to fire on in the new monument, his cadres sat on a creek bank and drank a case of beer, cussing out the damn bureaucrats. So much for the Wild West.

By 1947, the tide had turned as increasing postwar tourism revitalized the local economy. Finally, in 1950, a compromise was reached granting ranchers lifetime grazing rights and the right to trail their cattle across the park en route to summer grazing lands. The new-and-improved Grand Teton National Park had finally come to fruition.

Postmortem

Some of the early fears that Rockefeller would use the new park for his own gain seem at least partly justified. His descendants still own the old JY Ranch and use Phelps Lake as something of a semiprivate playground, while most of the other dude ranches have long since been taken over by the Park Service. Rockefeller also built the enormous Grand Teton Lodge along Jackson Lake and facilities at Colter Bay Village and Jenny Lake, leading some to accuse the family of attempting to monopolize services within the park. The company, Rockresorts, was sold in 1986 to CSX Corporation, which now manages Jackson Lake Lodge, Jenny Lake Lodge, and Colter Bay Village, along with Jackson Hole Golf & Tennis Club (near Jackson).

Looking back on the controversial creation of Grand Teton National Park, it's easy to see how wrong park opponents were. Teton County has Wyoming's most vibrant economy, and millions of people arrive each year to enjoy the beauty of the undeveloped Tetons. As writer Nathaniel Burt noted, "The old enemies of the park are riding the profitable bandwagon of unlimited tourism with high hearts and open palms." Park opponents' claims that the Park Service would "lock up" the land ring as hollow as similar antiwilderness claims today by descendants of the same politicians who opposed Grand Teton half a century ago. Without inclusion of the land purchased by Rockefeller, it is easy to imagine the valley covered with all sorts of summer-home developments, RV campgrounds, souvenir shops, motels, billboards, and neon signs. Take a look at the town of Jackson to see what might have been.

TOURING GRAND TETON

Grand Teton National Park has fewer "attractions" than Yellowstone—its big sister to the north—and an easy day's drive takes you past the road-accessible portions of Grand Teton. The real attractions are the mountains and the incomparable views one gets of them from Jackson Hole. This is one backdrop you will never tire of seeing.

Roads

Grand Teton is bisected by the main north-south highway (US Hwy. 26/89/191) and by the road heading east over Togwotee Pass (US Hwy. 26/287). Both of these routes are kept open year-round, although wintertime plowing ends at Flagg Ranch Resort, just south of the Yellowstone boundary. In addition, a paved park road cuts south from Jackson Lake Dam to Jenny Lake and Moose. Only the southern end of this is plowed in winter; the remainder becomes a snowmobile and cross-country ski route. South of Moose, a narrow, winding road connects the park to Teton Village, nine miles away. It is rough dirt in places (no trailers or RVs) and is closed in winter.

The following tour takes you past points of interest along the main roads. The route follows a general clockwise direction beginning at the **Moose Visitor Center,** tel. (307) 739-3399. Before heading out, step inside the center (open daily) for an introduction to the park and a look at the natural history videos, books, and oil paintings. A large three-dimensional map here reveals the lay of the land.

Menor's Ferry Area

Just inside the South Entrance to Grand Teton National Park, a side road leads to **Chapel of the Transfiguration** and Menor's Ferry. The rustic log church (built in 1925) is most notable for its dramatic setting. The back window faces directly toward the Tetons, providing ample distractions for worshippers. The bell out front was cast in 1842. Nearby **Menor's Ferry** is named for William D. Menor, who first homesteaded here in 1894 and later built a cable ferry to make it easier to cross the river. His old whitewashed store still stands. You can cross the river in a reconstructed version of the old ferry when the water level is low enough; check out the ingenious propulsion mechanism that uses the current to pull it across. For many years, Menor's ferry served as the primary means of crossing the river in the central part of Jackson Hole. Wagons were charged 50 cents, while those on horseback paid 25 cents. (William Menor's brother, Holiday, lived on the opposite side of the river, but the two often feuded, yelling insults across the water at each other and refusing to acknowledge one another for years at a time.) Also here is the half-mile **Menor's Ferry Trail;** a brochure describes historic points of interest along the path. Bill Menor's cabin houses a small country store that sells the old-fashioned supplies he stocked at the turn of the 20th century. It is open daily 9 a.m.-4:30 p.m. from Memorial Day to late September; closed the remainder of the year.

Menor sold out to Maude Noble in 1918, and she ran the ferry until 1927, when a bridge was built near the present one in Moose. Her cabin

BEAVER DICK LEIGH

Around 1863, Richard "Beaver Dick" Leigh became the first white man to attempt a permanent life in Jackson Hole. An Englishman by birth, Beaver Dick lived in a log cabin with his Shoshone wife, Jenny, and their four children, scraping out the barest existence by hunting, trapping, and guiding. As guide for the 1872 Hayden Survey of the Jackson Hole area, Beaver Dick gained the respect of the surveyors, who named Leigh Lake for him and Jenny Lake for his wife. Today a local bar denigrates this remarkable man by calling itself Beaver Dick's and using a cartoonish image of him in its ads. The real man was nothing like this, and reading his diaries and letters is a lesson in how difficult life was for early Wyoming settlers. On one terrible Christmas in 1876, Beaver Dick watched his entire family—Jenny, their newborn baby, and the four other children—all slowly die from smallpox. Their deaths left him badly shaken, as he related in a letter to a friend:

> *i got Dick in the house and to bed and Tom went over to get Mr. Anes. Wile Tom and Anes was sounding the ice to see if a horse could cross my wife was struck with Death. she rased up and looked me streaght in the face and then she got excited . . . and she sade she was going to die and all our childron wold die and maby i wold die . . . she was laying very quiet now for about 2 hours when she asked for a drink of water. i was laying downe with one of my daughters on eatch arme keeping them quiet because of the fevor. i told Anes what she wanted and he gave hur a drink and 10 minuts more she was ded . . . i can not wright one hundreth part that pased thrue my mind at this time as i thaught deth was on me. i sade Jinny i will sone be with you and fell asleep. Tom sade i ad beene a sleep a half hour when i woke up everything was wet with presperation i was very weak. i lade for 10 or 15 minuts and saw William and Anne Jane had to be taken up to ease themselves every 5 minuts and Dick Juner very restlas . . . Anne Jane died about 8 o clock about the time every year i used to give them a candy puling and thay menchond about the candy puling many times wile sick . . . William died on the 25 about 9 or 10 o clock in the evening*

YELLOWSTONE NATIONAL PARK

Beaver Dick and Jenny Leigh with their children

. . . on the 26th Dick Juner died . . . Elizabeth was over all danger but this, and she caught cold and sweled up agane and died on the 28 of Dec about 2 o clock in the morning. this was the hardist blow of all . . . i shall improve the place and live and die near my famley but i shall not be able to do enything for a few months for my mind is disturbed at the sights that i see around me and [the] work that my famley as done wile thay were liveing.

But the human spirit is remarkably resilient. Beaver Dick later married a Bannock girl, raised another family, and guided for others, even meeting Theodore Roosevelt on one of his hunting trips. Beaver Dick Leigh died in 1899 and was buried on a ridge overlooking Idaho's Teton Basin.

now houses an excellent collection of historical photos from Jackson Hole. Maude Noble gained a measure of fame in 1923 when she hosted the gathering of residents to save Jackson Hole from development (see above for park history).

Taggart and Bradley Lakes

Heading northwest beyond the Menor's Ferry area, the main road climbs up an old river bench, created by flooding from the rapid melting of the glaciers, and passes the trailhead to the turquoise waters of Taggart Lake. The land around here was burned in the 1,028-acre Beaver Creek lightning fire of 1985, and summers find a riot of wildflowers. A very popular day-hike leads from the parking lot at the trailhead to Taggart Lake and then back via the Beaver Creek Trail, a distance of 4.4 miles roundtrip. A side loop to Bradley Lake adds about two miles to this. These trails provide a fine way to explore the damlike glacial moraines that created these lakes. You can also continue beyond Bradley Lake on a trail that climbs to beautiful Amphitheater Lake, the primary access point for climbs up Grand Teton. (Climbers generally begin from Jenny Lake, however.)

Jenny Lake

The most loved of all Grand Teton lakes is Jenny Lake, nestled at the foot of Cascade Canyon and surrounded by a luxuriant forest of Engelmann spruce, subalpine fir, and lodgepole pine. Jenny Lake is named for Jenny Leigh, the Shoshone wife of Beaver Dick Leigh (see special topic). A one-way loop road leads south past Jenny and String Lakes, providing excellent views of the **Cathedral Group:** Teewinot, Grand Teton, and Mt. Owen. This is the most popular part of the park, and day-hikers will find a plethora of trails to sample, along with crowds of fellow hikers. Paths lead around both Jenny and String Lakes, while another nearly level trail follows the east shore of Leigh Lake to several pleasant sandy beaches. String Lake is narrow but very pretty and makes a fine place for canoeing or swimming. Get supplies from the small store at Jenny Lake, and info or guidebooks from the **Jenny Lake Ranger Station.** Coin-operated storage lockers are next to the store.

Beautiful **Jenny Lake Lodge** sits on the northeast end of the lake and is one of the finest lodging places in Jackson Hole. The gourmet meals—especially the Sunday evening buffet—are legendary, but be sure to make reservations by calling (307) 733-4647.

Inspiration Point and Cascade Canyon

One of the most popular attractions in the area is Inspiration Point, on the west side of Jenny Lake. It's 2.4 miles by trail from the Jenny Lake Ranger Station on the east side, or you can ride one of the summertime shuttle boats that cross the lake every 20 minutes or so for $5 roundtrip. In midsummer, the shuttle boat lines lengthen around 11 a.m., so get here early in the morning to avoid the crush and to better your odds at finding a parking spot. Afternoon thunderstorms frequently build up over the Tetons; another good reason to start your hike early. Boat tickets are not available in advance. Scenic boat cruises and fishing-boat rentals are also available at Jenny Lake; call (307) 733-2703.

From the boat dock on the west side, the trail climbs a half mile to picturesque **Hidden Falls,** then continues steeply another half mile to Inspiration Point, which overlooks Jackson Hole from 400 feet above Jenny Lake. Avoid the crowds on the way down from Inspiration Point by following a second trail back to Jenny Lake. If you miss the last boat at 6 p.m., it's a 2.4-mile hike around the lake to the parking area.

Many day-hikers continue at least part of the way up Cascade Canyon from Inspiration Point. The trail climbs gradually, gaining 640 feet in the next 3.6 miles, and provides a good chance to fish for trout or watch for moose and other animals along Cascade Creek. Those with strong legs can make a *very* long day-hike all the way up to Lake Solitude (18.4 miles roundtrip) or even Hurricane Pass (23.2 miles roundtrip and gaining almost 3,600 feet on the way up). If you're into hiking that far, it probably makes more sense to reserve a backcountry campsite and take things a bit more leisurely. See Backcountry Hiking below for details.

Signal Mountain Area

As the road approaches Jackson Lake, a paved but narrow side road (no RVs or trailers) turns east and leads to the summit of Signal Mountain, 800 feet above Jackson Hole. On top are panoramic views of the Tetons, Jackson Lake, the Snake River, and the long valley below. To the south lies **The Potholes,** a hummocky area created when huge blocks of ice were left behind by retreating glaciers. The melting ice created depressions, some of which are still filled with water. Signal Mountain was burned by a massive 1879 fire and offers a good opportunity to see how Yellowstone may look in a century.

Hugging the southeast shore of Jackson Lake, **Signal Mountain Lodge,** tel. (307) 733-5470 or (307) 543-2831, www.signalmtnlodge.com, includes cabins and campsites, plus a gift shop, convenience store, gas station, marina with boat rentals, restaurant, and bar. Just east of the lodge is **Chapel of the Sacred Heart,** a small Roman Catholic church. The road then crosses **Jackson Lake Dam,** which raises the water level by 39 feet, alters the river's natural flow, and inundates a large area upstream. Many conservationists fought to have Jackson Lake excluded from the park, concerned that it would establish a bad precedent for allowing reservoirs in other parks. Nevertheless, once you get away from the dam, the lake appears relatively natural today.

Along Jackson Lake

A turnout near Jackson Lake Junction provides views over **Willow Flats,** where moose are frequently seen, especially in the morning. Topping a bluff overlooking the flats is **Jackson Lake Lodge,** built in the 1950s with the $5 million financial backing of John D. Rockefeller Jr. Architects are not thrilled about the design (one author termed it "the ugliest building in Western Wyoming"), but the 60-foot-tall back windows frame an unbelievable view of the Tetons and Jackson Lake. Immediately across from the lodge is a trail leading to **Emma Matilda** and **Two Ocean** Lakes. It is 14 miles roundtrip around both lakes, with lots of wildlife along the way, including moose, trumpeter swans, pelicans, and ducks. You may have to contend with large groups on horseback.

Colter Bay

Colter Bay Village is one of the most developed parts of Grand Teton National Park, with a full marina, stores, a gas station, cabins, a campground, restaurants, and acres of parking. The main attraction here is the visitor center, which houses the **Colter Bay Indian Arts Museum,** tel. (307) 739-3594. It's open daily 8 a.m.-5 p.m. mid-May to Memorial Day; daily 8 a.m.-8 p.m. from early June to Labor Day; and daily 8 a.m.-5 p.m. from Labor Day to mid-October. The museum is closed the rest of the year. Admission is free. Inside you will find the extraordinary David T. Vernon collection of Indian pieces, the finest of its kind in any national park and one of the best anywhere in Wyoming. The collection spreads through several rooms on two floors and includes exquisitely beaded buckskin dresses, moccasins, kachina dolls, masks, ceremonial pipes, warbonnets, shields, bows, a blanket that belonged to Chief Sitting Bull, and other decorated items. Indian craft-making demonstrations are given daily Memorial Day to Labor Day. This museum should not be missed! Step out back to join the shoreside fun or to rent a canoe or boat from the nearby marina.

A mostly level trail leads from the marina out to **Hermitage Point** before looping back again, a distance of nine miles roundtrip. Along the way you pass beaver ponds and willow patches where trumpeter swans, moose, and ducks are commonly seen. Get a map of Colter Bay trails from the visitor center. Shorter loop paths include the two-mile **Lakeshore Trail** and the three-mile **Swan Lake-Heron Pond Trail.**

Rockefeller Memorial Parkway

North of Colter Bay, the highway cruises along the shore of Jackson Lake for the next nine miles, providing a number of fine vantage points of the Tetons. The burned area on the opposite shore was ignited by lightning in the 1974 Waterfalls Canyon Fire, which consumed 3,700 acres. By late fall each year, Idaho spud farmers have drawn down water in the lake, leaving a long, barren shoreline at the upper end.

Shortly after the road leaves the upper end of Jackson Lake, a signboard announces your entrance into **John D. Rockefeller Jr. Memorial Parkway.** This 24,000-acre parcel of land was transferred to the National Park Service in 1972 in commemoration of Rockefeller's unstinting work in establishing Grand Teton National Park. The land forms a connection between Grand Teton and Yellowstone and is managed by Grand Teton National Park. Much of this area was severely burned by the 1988 Huck Fire, which began when strong winds blew a tree into power lines. Despite immediate efforts to control the blaze, it consumed 4,000 acres in the first two hours and later grew to cover nearly 200,000 acres, primarily within the Forest Service's Teton Wilderness. Dense young lodgepole pines now carpet much of the land.

On the northern end of Rockefeller Parkway is **Flagg Ranch Resort,** tel. (307) 543-2861 or (800) 443-2311, www.flaggranch.com, where the modern facilities include a store, gas station, cabins, restaurant, and campground. During the winter, this is the jumping-off point for snowcoach and snowmobile trips into Yellowstone, and snowmobiles are available for rent.

Two nearby trails provide easy day-hikes. The nearly level **Polecat Creek Loop Trail** is 2.3 miles roundtrip and follows a ridge overlooking a marsh and through conifer forests. **Flagg Canyon Trail** is five miles roundtrip and provides views of a rocky canyon cut through by the Snake River.

Grassy Lake Road

Grassy Lake Rd. takes off just north of Flagg Ranch Resort and continues 52 miles to Ashton, Idaho. It's a scenic drive, but don't attempt this narrow and rough dirt road with a trailer or an RV. This route provides a shortcut to the Bechler River area of Yellowstone and is a popular wintertime snowmobile route. Huckleberry Hot Springs, a short hike north from the Grassy Lake Rd. bridge over the Snake River, was the site of a public swimming pool until 1983, when the facility was razed by the Park Service. The hot springs are accessible via an unmaintained trail, but you'll need to wade Polecat Creek to reach them. Although they remain popular with hikers and cross-country skiers, it's worth noting that the springs may pose a risk from dangerously high radiation levels.

A few miles east of the Idaho/Wyoming border on Grassy Lake Rd. is **Squirrel Meadows,** where Targhee National Forest has a guard station that is available for rent. It sleeps six and costs $40; call (208) 652-7442 for details. During the winter, access is via snowmobile or skis for the last 12 miles to the cabin from the Idaho side. Lodging is also available just across the Idaho border in cabins at **Squirrel Creek Elk Ranch,** tel. (208) 652-3972.

Jackson Lake to Moran Junction

Heading east and south from Jackson Lake, the road immediately passes **Oxbow Bend,** where the turnout is almost always filled with folks looking for geese, ducks, moose, and other animals. The oxbow was formed when the meandering river cut off an old loop. The calm water here is a delightful place for canoes, though the mosquitoes can be a major annoyance in midsummer. Come fall, photographers line the shoulder of the road for classic shots of flaming aspen trees with Grand Teton and **Mt. Moran** in the background. Mt. Moran is the massive peak with a flattened summit, a skillet-shaped glacier across its front, and a distinctive black vertical diabase dike that looks like a scar from some ancient battle. It rises 12,605 feet above sea level and is named for Thomas Moran, whose beautiful paintings of Yellowstone helped persuade Congress to set aside that area as the world's first national park.

At **Moran Junction** you pass the park's Buffalo Entrance Station and meet the road to Togwotee Pass and Dubois. A post office and school are the only developments remaining here. The epic Western *The Big Trail* was filmed nearby in 1930, starring an actor named John Wayne in his first speaking role. (Wayne had never ridden a horse before this.) An interesting side trip is to head east from Moran on US Hwy. 26/287 for three miles to **Buffalo Valley Road.** This narrow and scenic road leads to Turpin Meadow, a major entryway into the Teton Wilderness (see Bridger-Teton National Forest earlier in this chapter). It is very pretty—especially in early summer when flowers carpet the fields. Buck-and-rail fences line the road, and the pastures are filled with horses and cattle. Beyond Turpin Meadow, the road turns to gravel and climbs sharply uphill, rejoining the main highway a couple of miles below Cowboy Village Resort at Togwotee. The Blackrock Ranger Station of Bridger-Teton National Forest is eight miles east of Moran Junction on US Hwy. 26/287. Nearby is historic **Rosie's Cabin,** built early in the 20th century by Rudolph Rosencrans, an Austrian emigrant who was the first forest ranger in this part of the Tetons.

Moran Junction to Moose

Heading south from Moran, US Hwy. 26/89/191 immediately crosses the Buffalo River (a.k.a. Buffalo Fork of the Snake River), where bison were once abundant. With a little help from humans, bison have been reestablished and are now often seen just south of here along the road. The turnoff to the **Cunningham Cabin** is six miles south of Moran Junction. The structure actually consists of two sod-roofed log cabins connected by a covered walkway called a "dogtrot." Built around 1890, it served first as living quarters and later as a barn and smithy. A park brochure describes the locations of other structures on the property.

Pierce Cunningham came here as a homesteader and with his wife Margaret settled to raise cattle. Although this was some of the better land in this part of the valley, the soil was still so rocky that they had a hard time digging fencepost holes. Instead, they opted to build the buck-and-rail fences that have become a hallmark of Jackson Hole ranches. Cunningham Ranch gained notoriety in 1893 when a posse surrounded two suspected horse thieves who were wintering at Cunningham's place while he was away. Vigilantes shot and killed George Spencer and Mike Burnett in an example of "mountain justice." Later, however, suspicions arose that hired killers working for wealthy cattle barons had led the posse and that the murdered men may have been innocent. **Spread Creek** is just north of the Cunningham cabin; it gained its name by having two mouths, separated by a distance of three miles.

The highway next rolls past **Triangle X Ranch,** one of the most famous dude ranches in Jackson Hole. Although it's on park land, the Turner family has managed Triangle X for over 60 years. (One of the owners, John Turner, was director of the U.S. Fish & Wildlife Service under President Bush.) Stop by just after sunup to watch wranglers driving 120 head of horses to the corrals. It's a scene straight out of an old Marlboro ad.

Southwest from Triangle X, the road climbs along an ancient river terrace and passes **Hedrick Pond,** where the 1963 Henry Fonda movie *Spencer's Mountain* was filmed. Although the book on which it was based was set in Virginia, the producers found the Tetons a considerably more impressive location. Trumpeter swans are often seen on the pond. Hedrick Pond isn't really visible from the road and there are no signs pointing it out, but you can get there by parking near the S-curve road sign 1.4 miles south of Triangle X. The pond is a good example of a kettle pond, created when retreating glaciers left behind a block of ice covered with gravel and other deposits. The ice melted, leaving behind a depression that filled to become Hedrick Pond.

Several turnouts provide very popular photo-opportunity spots, the most famous being **Snake River Overlook.** Ansel Adams's famous shot of the Tetons was taken here and has been repeated with less success by generations of photographers. Throughout the summer, a progression of different flowers blooms in the open sagebrush flats along the road, adding brilliant slashes of color. They're prettiest in late June; in the high country, the peak comes a month or more later than elsewhere.

Just north of Snake River Overlook is the turnoff to **Deadman's Bar.** A steep partially dirt road (not for RVs) drops down to one of the primary river-access points used by river rafters. The river bar received its name from an incident in 1886. Four German prospectors entered the area, but only one—John Tonnar—emerged. Bodies of the other three were found along the

Snake River, and Tonnar was charged with murder. The jury in Evanston believed his claim of self-defense, and he was set free, an act that so angered locals that they vowed to take care of future Jackson Hole criminals with a shotgun. A skull from one of the victims is on display in the Jackson Hole Museum.

Another popular put-in for river runners is **Schwabacher Landing,** at the end of a one-mile gravel road that splits off just north of the Glacier View Turnout. This is a pleasant place for riverside picnics. Some of the most famous Teton Range photos—the ones you see in local galleries—were taken just a few hundred yards upstream from the parking area.

Blacktail Butte and Mormon Row

A mile north of the turnoff to Moose, Antelope Flats Rd. heads east along Ditch Creek. Just south of here lies Blacktail Butte, a timbered knoll rising over the surrounding sagebrush plains. It's a favorite of rock climbers and has a hiking trail up the back (east) side. You will want to stop at the much-photographed old farm buildings known as Mormon Row. The farmland here was homesteaded by predominantly Mormon settlers in the early 1900s but was later purchased by Rockefeller's Snake River Land Company and transferred to the Park Service. Only one set of buildings—an acre of the Moulton Ranch—is still in private hands. The other buildings were allowed to decay until the 1990s when the Park Service recognized their value and stepped in to preserve the structures. Herds of bison often wander past the old farmsteads in the summer months, providing one of the best places to view them. Also keep your eyes open for small groups of pronghorn antelope in the vicinity.

Teton Science School

Hidden away in a valley along upper Ditch Creek is Teton Science School, a fine hands-on school for both young and old. Founded in 1967 as a summer field-biology program for high-school kids, it has grown into a year-round program with classes that run the gamut from elementary-school level all the way up to intensive college courses and a residency program. Summertime visitors will enjoy their one- to four-day adult seminars on such diverse subjects as entomology for fly-fishers, birdwatching, the biology of bugs, wildflower identification, river channels, and grizzly bear biology. These are limited to 12 students and fill up fast, so make reservations in the spring to be sure of a spot. The school's excellent month-long wilderness EMT course in early winter ($2,000 per person) is one of the few programs of its kind in the nation. TSS also offers a fine **winter speaker series** ($5) at the National Museum of Wildlife Art covering a spectrum of scientific, environmental, and social issues.

Based at the old Elbo dude ranch (started in 1932), Teton Science School includes two dormitories, a central kitchen, dining area, and other log structures. Visitors to the school should visit the **Murie Natural History Museum,** which displays thousands of specimens of birds, mammals, and plants. Included are casts of animal tracks used by famed wildlife biologist Olaus Murie in producing his *Peterson's Guide to Animal Tracks.* It's open to the public, but call ahead to arrange an appointment. Get a copy of the course catalog by contacting TSS at (307) 733-4765, or find it on the web at www.tetonscience.org.

Shadow Mountain Area

North from the Teton Science School turnoff, the paved road splits. Turn left (west) on Antelope Flats Rd. to head back to Mormon Row and the main highway, or continue straight ahead to climb up Shadow Mountain (8,252 feet). The name comes from the shadows of the Tetons that fall across the mountain's face each evening. The road is paved for the first mile or so, but turns to gravel as it snakes rather steeply up the mountain. The road is definitely not recommended for RVs or trailers, or for any vehicles after rains when some sections turn to slippery mud. The views from the top of Shadow Mountain are truly amazing, with the Tetons in all their glory. A number of dispersed campsites can be found along this route.

Kelly and Vicinity

The small settlement of Kelly borders on the southeastern end of Grand Teton National Park and has log homes and a cluster of Mongolian-style yurts—certainly the most unusual dwellings in Wyoming. Folks living in the yurts share a common bathhouse and rent the land. The town has a shoebox-size post office and a small store that sells snacks, gifts, and old Wyoming license plates. The Park Service's **Gros Ventre Campground** is three miles west of here.

Gros Ventre Rd. leads east from the Kelly area, passing **Kelly Warm Spring** on the right. Its shallow and warm waters are a favorite place for local kayakers to practice their rolls or for families to swim on a summer afternoon. A short distance up the road and off to the north (left) are the collapsing remains of the ***Shane* cabin,** where a scene from the classic 1951 Western was filmed. Beyond this, the road enters Bridger-Teton National Forest and the Slide Lake area, where there is a Forest Service campground.

Gros Ventre Slide

One of the most extraordinary geologic events in recent Wyoming history took place in the Gros Ventre (pronounced "GROW-vont"—"Big Belly" in French trapper lingo) Canyon, named for the Gros Ventre Indians of this area. Sheep Mountain, on the south side of the canyon, consists of sandstone underlain by a layer of shale that becomes slippery when wet. Melting snow and heavy rains in the spring of 1925 lubricated this layer of shale, and on June 23 the entire north end of the mountain—a section 2,000 feet wide and a mile long—suddenly slid a mile and a half downslope, instantly damming the river below and creating Slide Lake. A rancher in the valley, Guil Huff, watched in amazement as the mountain began to move, but he managed to gallop his horse out of the way as the slide roared within 30 feet. Huff's ranch floated away on the new lake several days later.

For two years folks kept a wary eye on the makeshift dam of rock and mud. Then, on May 18, 1927, the dam suddenly gave way, pushing an enormous wall of water through the downstream town of Kelly. Six people perished in the flood, and when the water reached Snake River Canyon nine hours later it filled the canyon to the rim with boiling water, trees, houses, and debris. Today a smaller Slide Lake still exists, and the massive landslide that created it more than 75 years ago remains an exposed gouge visible for miles around. Geologists say that, under the right conditions, more of Sheep Mountain could slide. Dead trees still stand in the upper end of Slide Lake.

Gros Ventre River Valley

Above Slide Lake (six miles up), the road turns to gravel, becoming quite rutted in places. Surprising scenery makes the sometimes bone-jarring route easier to take. The landscape here is far different from that of the Tetons, with brilliant red-orange badlands hills rising sharply above the Gros Ventre River. Two more Forest Service campgrounds (Red Hills and Crystal Creek) are four miles above Slide Lake, or you can camp in dispersed sites off the road. The road continues another 15 beautiful miles along the river, getting rougher at the upper end. Several remote guest ranches are up here. Beyond Cow Creek Trailhead (29 miles from Kelly) the route is virtually impassable unless you have a high-clearance 4WD and are ready to get stuck. Hard-core mountain-bikers sometimes continue up this road/trail and then drop down into the Green River watershed north of Pinedale. Cow Creek Trail and other paths lead into the Gros Ventre Wilderness, which borders the south side of the road. On the drive back down the Gros Ventre River valley you will discover some fine views across to the Tetons.

Moose-Wilson Road

This narrow and winding road heads south from park headquarters in Moose, continuing nine miles to Teton Village. It is paved most of the way, but a sometimes bone-jarring middle section is dirt. Keep your speed down to reduce the amount of dust in the air. No trailers or RVs are allowed, and the road is not plowed in the winter. It is especially pretty in the fall when the aspens are turning, and it's a good place to watch for moose and other animals in summer or for easy cross-country ski adventures on a sunny winter day. Two backcountry trailheads—Death Canyon Trailhead and Granite Canyon Trailhead—are accessed from the Moose-Wilson Road.

A long loop hike up Death Canyon is described as an overnight hike below. For something less challenging, start from Death Canyon Trailhead (three miles south of Moose) and hike about a mile to **Phelps Lake Overlook,** where you get a view across this beautiful mountain lake 600 feet below. The historic JY Ranch (built in 1908) sits back from Phelps Lake and still belongs to the Rockefeller family; any motorboats you see are probably theirs. This is one of the only remaining private inholdings within Grand Teton National

Park. From Phelps Lake Overlook you can hike steeply down for a lakeside picnic on the sandy beach (four miles roundtrip from the trailhead). An alternative day-hiking option is to continue from the overlook to **Death Canyon Patrol Cabin.** Getting to the cabin requires losing 400 feet in elevation and then climbing 1,000 feet higher. The small log cabin was built by the Civilian Conservation Corps in the 1930s and is still used by trail maintenance crews. Continue a half mile beyond the cabin up the trail to Fox Creek Pass for a dramatic vista into Death Canyon. It's a bit over eight miles roundtrip between this viewpoint and Death Canyon Trailhead.

BACKCOUNTRY HIKING

The precipitous Tetons that look so dramatic from the roads are even more impressive up close and personal. Grand Teton National Park is laced with 200 miles of trails, and hikers can choose anything from simple day-treks to week-long trips along the crest of the range. Unlike nearby Yellowstone, where most of the country is forested, the Tetons contain extensive Alpine scenery. This means, however, that many of the high passes won't be free of snow until late July and may require ice axes before then. Check at the visitor centers or Jenny Lake Ranger Station for current trail conditions. In addition, this high country can be dangerous when the frequent thunderstorms roll through in summer. A number of people have been killed by lightning strikes in the Tetons.

The most popular hiking area centers on the crest of the Tetons and the lakes that lie at its feet, most notably Jenny Lake. **Teton Crest Trail** stretches from Teton Pass north all the way to Cascade Canyon, with numerous connecting paths from both sides of the range. Three relatively short (two- to three-day) loop hikes are described below. For more complete descriptions of park trails, see *Jackson Hole Hikes* by Rebecca Woods (Jackson: White Willow Publishing) or *Teton Trails* by Katy Duffy and Darwin Wile (Moose: Grand Teton Natural History Association). Get topographic maps at the Moose Visitor Center or Teton Mountaineering in Jackson. Best is the waterproof version produced by Trails Illustrated.

Regulations and Permits

The hiking trails of Grand Teton National Park are some of the most heavily used paths in Wyoming, and strict regulations are enforced. Backcountry-use permits are required of all overnight hikers, and you'll need to specify a particular camping zone or site for each night of your trip. Get permits and detailed backcountry brochures from the visitor centers in Moose or Colter Bay or the Jenny Lake Ranger Station. Get there early in the morning during the summer for permits to popular trails. A limited number of backcountry permits can be reserved in advance from January 1 to May 15 by writing the Per-

Grand Teton National Park offers some of the finest hiking in Wyoming.

mits Office, Grand Teton National Park, P.O. Drawer 170, Moose, WY 83012. For faster service, send a fax to (307) 739-3438. You'll need to pick the permit up in person. Get more information on permits and reservations by calling (307) 739-3309 or (307) 739-3397.

Safety in the Backcountry

Grizzlies are only found in the northern end of Grand Teton, but you still need to hang all food, since black bears roam throughout the park, particularly in the forested areas along the lakes. Special boxes are provided for food storage at some backcountry campsites. Campfires are not allowed at higher elevations, so be sure to bring a cooking stove. Bikes are not permitted on trails anywhere in the park.

Backcountry hikers (and day-hikers for that matter) need to be aware of the dangers from summertime thunderstorms in the Tetons. A

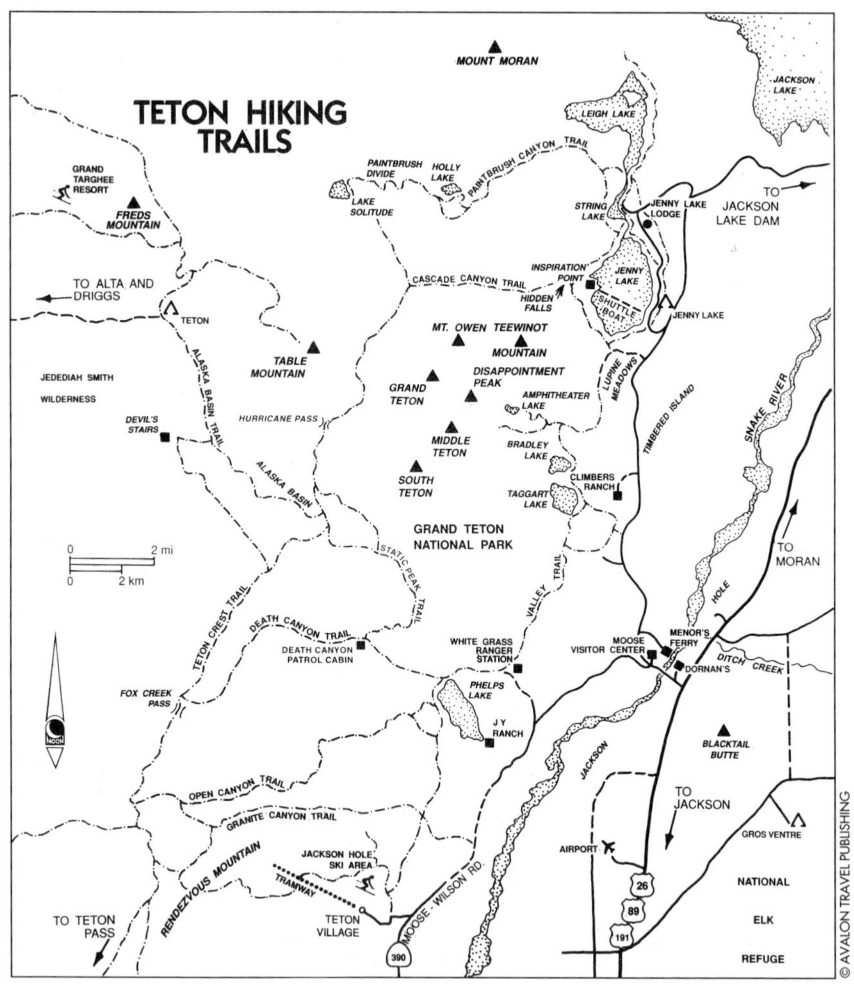

common weather pattern is for clear mornings to build to blustery thunderstorms in late afternoon, followed by gradual clearing as evening arrives. Lightning is a major threat in the park's exposed alpine country, and rain showers can be surprisingly heavy at times. Make sure all your gear is wrapped in plastic (garbage bags work well), and carry a rain poncho or other rainwear.

Cascade Canyon to Paintbrush Canyon
One of the most popular hikes in Grand Teton is this 19-mile loop trip up Cascade Canyon, over Paintbrush Divide, and down Paintbrush Canyon (or vice versa). The trip offers a little of everything: dense forests, alpine lakes, flower-covered meadows, and magnificent views of Grand Teton. This trip is best done in late summer, since a cornice of snow typically blocks Paintbrush Divide until the latter part of July. Most folks do it as an overnight trip, but it's possible to do the entire loop in a single very long day if you're in good shape and have a masochistic streak. Be sure to bring plenty of water along.

Begin at the String Lake Trailhead and head south around Jenny Lake, stopping to enjoy the views (and crowds) at Inspiration Point before heading up along Cascade Creek. The trail splits at the upper end of this canyon; turning left takes you to Hurricane Pass and the Teton Crest Trail where you'll discover wonderful views of the back side of Grand Teton. Instead, turn right (north) and head up to beautiful Lake Solitude. Behind you, Teewinot, Mt. Owen, and Grand Teton are framed by the glacially carved valley walls. Above Lake Solitude, the trail climbs sharply to Paintbrush Divide and then switchbacks even more quickly down into Paintbrush Canyon. The trail eventually leads back to String Lake. Be sure to stop at beautiful Holly Lake on the way down.

Death Canyon Loop
Another fine loop trip departs from the Death Canyon Trailhead, approximately three miles south of park headquarters on the Moose-Wilson Road. Many hiking options are available here, with trails leading to Phelps Lake, up Open Canyon, or into Death Canyon. (The name came about when a survey party was in the area in 1899 and one of the men disappeared. He was never seen again.) Despite the name, Death Canyon provides a wonderful 26-mile loop hike that takes you over three high passes and into spectacular alpine country. From the trailhead, hike to Phelps Lake Overlook before dropping down to a junction where you turn right to hike up Death Canyon. Bear left at a patrol cabin built in the 1930s, and continue climbing all the way to Fox Creek Pass (9,520 feet). After this the going is fairly easy for the next three miles along Death Canyon Shelf to Mt. Meek Pass, where you drop into famous Alaska Basin (described under Targhee National Forest earlier in this chapter). Return to your starting point by climbing east from Alaska Basin over Static Peak Divide (10,800 feet) and then switchbacking downhill to the CCC cabin and the trailhead. This is a late-season trek since snow often blocks the passes till July; get snow conditions at the Jenny Lake Ranger Station.

Amphitheater Lake
A relatively short but very steep hike begins at the Lupine Meadows Trailhead just south of Jenny Lake. Amphitheater Lake is only five miles up the trail but is 3,000 feet higher, making this the quickest climb to the Teton treeline. Many folks day-hike this trail to savor the wonderful vistas across Jackson Hole along the way. Camping is available at Surprise Lake, a half mile below Amphitheater Lake. More adventurous folks may want to climb **Disappointment Peak,** the 11,618-foot summit directly in front of Grand Teton. (It was named by climbers who mistakenly thought they were on the east face of Grand Teton.) If you plan to do so, first talk to the climbing rangers at Jenny Lake—and only attempt it if you're able to handle a few areas of Class 3 moves.

Rendezvous Mountain to Death Canyon
This 23-mile-long loop hike is different in that much of the way is downhill. Begin at the Jackson Hole tram in Teton Village, where a $16 ticket takes you to the top of Rendezvous Mountain. From the summit, the trail leads down to a saddle, across the South Fork of Granite Creek, and up to Teton Crest Trail. Head north on this trail to Marion Lake—a popular camping site—and then over Fox Creek Pass. The trail splits, and the right fork drops sharply down into scenic Death Canyon, named when a member of a survey party disappeared here in 1903. At the lower

end of Death Canyon, cliffs rise nearly 3,000 feet on both sides. The trail forks at Phelps Lake, and from here you can either hike back to Teton Village via the Valley Trail or head to the trailhead at White Grass Ranger Station, 1.5 miles northeast of Phelps Lake. Note: If you reverse the direction of this hike you can save your money, since there is no charge for riding the tram down to Teton Village.

MOUNTAIN CLIMBING

The Tetons are considered some of the premier mountaineering country in the nation, with solid rock, good access, and a wide range of climbing conditions. Hundreds of climbing routes have been described for the main peaks, but the goal of many climbers is Grand Teton, better known as "the Grand." At 13,770 feet, this is Wyoming's second-highest summit, exceeded only by 13,804-foot Gannett Peak in the Wind River Mountains.

First to the Top

In the climbing trade, first ascents always rate highly, but the identity of the first climbers to have scaled Grand Teton has long been a matter of debate. The official record belongs to the party of William Owen (as in nearby Mt. Owen), Bishop Spalding (as in nearby Spalding Peak), John Shive, and Frank Petersen, who reached the summit in 1898. Today, however, it appears that they were preceded by two members of the 1872 Hayden Expedition: Nathaniel P. Langford (first superintendent of Yellowstone National Park) and John Stevenson. In addition, another party made it to the top in 1893. Owen made a big deal out of his climb and spent 30 years trying to work himself into the record books by claiming the Langford party never reached the top. The whole thing got quite nasty, with Owen even accusing Langford of bribing the author of a history book to gain top honors. In 1929, Owen convinced the Wyoming Legislature to declare his group the first on top. Few people believe it today, and the whole thing looks pretty foolish since even seven-year-old kids have made it up the Grand. Several thousand people climb the mountain each summer, many with no previous climbing experience (but with excellent guides and a couple days of training). And just to prove that it could be done, in 1971 one fanatic actually skied the Grand (he's the ski-school director at Snow King Resort), followed in 1989 by a snowboarder. Both lived to tell the tale.

Getting There

Most climbing takes place after the snow has melted back (mid-July) and before conditions again deteriorate (late September). Overnight mountain climbing or off-trail hiking requires a special permit available from the **Jenny Lake Ranger Station** which is staffed daily June to mid-September. There's no need to register if you're climbing or doing off-trail hiking for the day only, just for overnight trips. (Still, it's a good idea to leave a detailed trip itinerary with a responsible person in case of an emergency.) In the winter months, register at the Moose Visitor Center. The climbing rangers—one of the most prestigious and hazardous jobs in the park—are all highly experienced mountaineers and can provide specific route information for the various summits. Call (307) 739-3604 for recorded climbing info, or talk to folks at the Jenny Lake Ranger Station, tel. (307) 739-3343, for weather conditions, route information, and permits.

Many climbers who scale Grand Teton follow the Amphitheater Lake Trail from Lupine Meadows to its junction with the Garnet Canyon Trail. This leads to the **Lower Saddle,** which separates Grand Teton and Middle Teton. Exum and the Park Service have base-camp huts and steel storage boxes here, along with an outhouse. Other folks pitch tents behind boulders in this extraordinarily windy mountain gap. See Park Service handouts for camping restrictions and recommendations in this fragile alpine area where heavy use by 4,000 climbers each year has caused considerable damage. The final assault on the summit of Grand Teton requires technical equipment and expertise. No motorized drills are allowed for the placement of climbing bolts. Mountaineers can stay at **Climbers' Ranch,** near Taggart Lake, for $7 a night including bunk accommodations with showers and covered cooking areas; bring your own sleeping bag and food. The ranch is open mid-June to mid-September only. Call (307) 733-7271 for reservations.

Climbing Schools

Jackson Hole is blessed with two of the finest climbing schools in North America: **Jackson Hole Mountain Guides,** 165 N. Glenwood, tel. (307) 733-4979 or (800) 239-7642, www.jhmg.com; and **Exum Mountain Guides,** tel. (307) 733-2297, www.exumguides.com, with a summertime office at the south end of Jenny Lake near the boat dock. Both are authorized concessions of the National Park Service and the U.S. Forest Service and offer a wide range of classes, snow training, and climbs in the Tetons and elsewhere—even as far away as Alaska and the Himalayas. Exum has been around since 1931, when Glenn Exum pioneered the first solo climb of what has become the most popular route to the top of the Grand, the Exum Route. It's the only company permitted to guide all Teton peaks and routes throughout the year. Exum's base camp is in the busy Lower Saddle area, while Jackson Hole Mountain Guides' base camp is 450 feet lower in elevation in a more secluded location (it takes an extra hour of climbing on the day of your ascent). Exum has some of the most experienced guides in the world, but they take up to four clients in a group, while Jackson Hole limits its Grand Teton ascent parties to three clients.

During midsummer, you'll pay around $330-520 (depending upon the number of people in the group) for an ascent of Grand Teton; this includes two days of basic and intermediate training followed by a two-day climb up the Grand and back. Food, gear, and shelter are also included. If you're planning to climb the Grand during the peak summer season, be sure to make reservations several months in advance to be assured of a spot. For July and August, make Grand Teton climbing reservations before the end of March.

One-day basic and intermediate climbing schools cost $75-110, but reservations are not generally needed for these. Also available are climbs of other faces such as Baxter's Pinnacle, Symmetry Spire, and Cube Point, along with more advanced classes and climbs in the Wind River Mountains and up Devils Tower and other precipices throughout the western states. In addition, both companies offer many winter classes, such as avalanche safety and ski or snowboard mountaineering.

On Your Own

If you already have the experience and want to do your own climbing, the most accessible local spot is **Blacktail Butte,** just north of Moose near Ditch Creek. The parking lot here fills on warm summer afternoons as hang-dogging enthusiasts try their moves on the rock face. Get climbing gear at **Moosely Seconds Mountaineering** in Moose, tel. (307) 739-1801, or in Jackson at **Teton Mountaineering,** 170 N. Cache Dr., tel. (307) 733-3595 or (800) 850-3595, www.tetonmtn.com. Both stores rent climbing shoes and other gear. **Teton Rock Gym,** 1116 Maple Way, tel. (307) 733-0707, has challenging indoor climbing walls where you can practice your moves. They also offer classes for beginners and rent climbing gear.

For complete details on local climbing, see Ortenburger and Jackson's *A Complete Guide to the Teton Range* (Seattle, WA: The Mountaineers Books) or the smaller but well-written *Teton Classics,* by Richard Rossiter (Evergreen, CO: Chockstone Press).

OTHER PARK RECREATION

Boating and Fishing

Canoeists will discover several excellent places to paddle within Grand Teton, particularly the Snake River Oxbow Bend, String Lake, and Leigh Lake. Boaters within Grand Teton will need to purchase a permit; seven-day permits cost $10 for motorboats, $5 for nonmotorized craft. Motorboats are only allowed on Jackson Lake, Jenny Lake (7.5-horsepower max), and Phelps Lake. Sailboarding, water-skiing, and sailing are permitted on Jackson Lake. For info on floating the Snake River through the park, see Jackson earlier in this chapter.

Jackson Lake has three marinas. At **Signal Mountain Lodge Marina,** tel. (307) 733-5470 or (307) 543-2831, www.signalmtnlodge.com, you can rent water-ski boats and skis, life jackets, deck cruisers, fishing boats, pontoon boats, and canoes. **Colter Bay Marina,** tel. (307) 543-2811 or (800) 628-9988, www.gtlc.com, is near a Park Service campground, cabins, and the Colter Bay Indian Arts Museum. It's an exceptionally busy place in the summer, with motorboat, pontoon boat, and canoe rentals, along with guides to take you to the hot fishing spots. Scenic boat cruises ($12 for adults, $6 for kids under 12) are also available from Colter Bay Marina, as are breakfast or evening cruise-and-dine trips ($24 for breakfast; $39 for dinner). A short distance north of Colter Bay is **Leek's Marina,** tel. (307) 543-2494, a simple place with a couple of docks, a pizza restaurant, and gas pumps.

Grand Teton National Park anglers must have a valid Wyoming state fishing license ($6 for one day). Pick up a handout describing fishing creel and size limits from park visitor centers. For more on fishing and river rafting within the park, see the appropriate sections under Jackson.

Sea Kayaking

O.A.R.S., tel. (209) 736-4677 or (800) 346-6277, www.oars.com, offers one- to five-day sea kayaking trips around Jackson Lake—perfect for beginning kayakers and families. You don't need any paddling experience for these trips, which are supported by a motorized skiff. One-night overnight trips cost $205 for adults or $165 for youths; five-day kayak trips will set you back $680 for adults or $585 for kids. O.A.R.S. also has combination trips that include kayaking on the lake and rafting down the Snake River. Their two-day combo trips cost $345 for adults or $285 for youths; four-day trips run $500 for adults or $515 for kids. Tents and sleeping bags are available for rent on O.A.R.S. overnight trips, or bring your own. Reserve ahead for these popular trips.

Trail Rides

Horseback and wagon rides—including popular breakfast and dinner rides—take place at **Jackson Lake Lodge Corral** and **Colter Bay Village Corral.** Get details from Grand Teton Lodge Company, tel. (307) 733-2811 or (800) 628-9988, www.gtlc.com. In the Rockefeller Parkway between Grand Teton and Yellowstone, **Flagg Ranch Resort,** tel. (307) 543-2861 or (800) 443-2311, www.flaggranch.com, offers hour-long horseback trail rides in the summer.

Winter Recreation

The snow-covered landscape of Grand Teton National Park draws cross-country skiers, snowshoers, and snowmobilers throughout the winter. **Cross-country skiing** is possible on a number of trails within the lower reaches of the park, but the high country is dangerous due to extreme avalanche hazards. Park ski trails are not machine-groomed but are generally well packed by other skiers. After a new snowfall you'll need to break trail as you follow the orange markers. See Cross-country Skiing earlier in this chapter for information on Nordic skiing in the park, or pick up a brochure describing ski trails from the Moose Visitor Center. If you're planning to camp overnight in the park, you'll need to get a free permit here as well. Skiers and snowshoers are not allowed on the Continental Divide Snowmobile Trail for safety reasons. Unfortunately, snowmobiles ride on Teton Park Rd., so your peace and solitude may be broken by the roar of distant machines.

Park naturalists lead two-hour **snowshoe hikes** from late December through March and provide snowshoes at no charge. No experience necessary. The hikes generally depart from the Moose Visitor Center at 2 p.m. several times a week. Reservations are required; no kids under age eight. Call (307) 739-3399 for details on these and other winter activities in the park.

The controversial 365-mile-long **Continental Divide Snowmobile Trail** now cuts through 33 miles of Grand Teton National Park, providing a link between the Wind River Mountains and Yellowstone National Park. Within Grand Teton it is generally open from early January to mid-March and essentially parallels US Hwy. 26/287 from the east park boundary to Moran Junction and then along US Hwy. 89 north to Yellowstone. A spur trail connects the trail with other snowmobile routes along the Teton Park Rd. and up Signal Mountain. Snowmobiles are only allowed on designated routes, and specific regulations are enforced within the park. Get a copy of the park snowmobiling handout from the Moose Lake Visitor Center, or call (307) 739-3612 for recorded info on the Continental Divide Snowmobile Trail. For details on snowmobile rentals and tours in the Jackson area, see Jackson earlier in this chapter.

During the winter, **Gray Line,** tel. (307) 733-4325 or (800) 443-6133, www.jacksonholenet.com/grayline, has daily bus runs between Jackson and Flagg Ranch Resort for $35 one-way or $50 roundtrip, arriving in time to meet the snowcoach departures for Yellowstone. Reservations are required. Both **Buckboard Cab,** tel. (307) 733-1112, and **All Star Taxi,** tel. (307)

733-2888 or (800) 378-2944, also offer shuttles to Flagg Ranch Resort in the winter; $75 for one to three people.

PARK CAMPGROUNDS

Grand Teton National Park has five places to camp: Colter Bay Campground, Lizard Creek Campground, Gros Ventre Campground, Signal Mountain Campground, and Jenny Lake Campground. See the Jackson Hole Public Campgrounds chart for details of these and nearby Forest Service campgrounds. Accommodations at all park campgrounds cost $12 and are on a first-come, first-served basis with no reservations. By midafternoon in the peak summer season all park campgrounds may well be full. The largest—and last to fill—is Gros Ventre Campground, near the town of Kelly. The most scenic—and quickest to fill—is Jenny Lake Campground. Showers and a laundromat are available in Colter Bay Village. All Grand Teton National Park campgrounds are closed in the winter, but limited tent camping and RV parking ($5; restrooms and water but no hookups) is available near the Colter Bay Visitor Center. Call (307) 739-3603 for additional park campground information.

In addition to the public campgrounds, park concessioners maintain two seasonal RV parks. **Flagg Ranch Resort** in Rockefeller Parkway, tel. (307) 543-2861 or (800) 443-2311, www.flaggranch.com, has RV sites with full hookups for $31, and tent sites for $20. It's open early to mid-May till early October; reservations are highly recommended. On the south shore of Jackson Lake, **Colter Bay RV Park,** tel. (307) 543-3100 or (800) 628-9988, www.gtlc.com, charges $30-32 for RVs and is open late May to early October. No tent spaces available here. Evening nature programs are offered in the summer.

GRAND TETON LODGING

Several places provide concessioner lodging inside Grand Teton National Park. As in all national parks, none of the lodge rooms contain TVs or radios. See Jackson, above, for dozens of other lodging places south and east of the park.

Jackson Lake Lodge

Built on a grand scale, the 385-room Jackson Lake Lodge, tel. (307) 543-3100 or (800) 628-9988, www.gtlc.com, occupies a bluff above Willow Flats on the southeast side of Jackson Lake. Sixty-foot-high windows look across to the Tetons, and the spacious central hall is flanked by fireplaces. Outside are two large swimming pools, and the building houses restaurants, a cocktail lounge, gift shop, newsstand, clothing shop, and an ATM. All rooms contain two double beds. Cottages are $135-198 d, rooms in the main lodge cost $115-198 d, and the luxury suite will set you back $500 d. The lodge is open mid-May to mid-October. Premium-Luxury.

The Tetons loom over Jackson Lake and the marina at Colter Bay Village.

Jenny Lake Lodge

For four-star accommodations right at the base of the Tetons, stay at Jenny Lake Lodge, tel. (307) 733-4647 or (800) 628-9988, www.gtlc.com, where 37 comfortably appointed cabins surround a cozy Old West main lodge. This is a marvelous honeymoon or big-splurge place, and the $318 s or $398 d price (or go for one of the luxurious suites at $540-560 d) includes horseback rides, bikes, breakfast, and a six-course dinner. (Note, however, that the meals are only served at specific times, so you'll need to adjust your schedule accordingly; some find the regimented schedule too confining.) The big Sunday night buffet is a special treat that attracts folks from Jackson. Jenny Lake Lodge is open early June to early October. Luxury.

Colter Bay Village

Family-oriented Colter Bay Village, tel. (307) 543-3100 or (800) 628-9988, www.gtlc.com, has 166 rustic cabins of varying sizes and types, some of which sleep six people. The most basic are simple canvas-and-log tent cabins with outdoor grills and picnic tables, woodstoves, and bring-your-own-bedding bunks. These cost just $31 d ($3 for each additional person). Restrooms are nearby, and the showers are coin-operated. Guests at the tent cabins can rent sleeping bags and other camping supplies. The experience isn't even remotely like staying at Jenny Lake Lodge! Step up to basic log units that share a bath for $32 d, or get one with a private bath for $66-94 d. Two-room cabins with a connecting bath are $120 for up to four people. Colter Bay Village is open late May to late September. Budget-Expensive.

Dornan's

Near park headquarters in Moose, Dornan's Spur Ranch Cabins, tel. (307) 733-2522, www.dornans.com, has a dozen modern log cabins filled with handcrafted lodgepole pine furniture. One-bedroom cabins are $140 d or $170 for up to four people, and two-bedroom cabins cost $200 and can sleep up to six. There's a three-night minimum stay in the summer. All cabins have full kitchens and are open year-round. Premium.

Signal Mountain Lodge

On the south shore of Jackson Lake, Signal Mountain Lodge, tel. (307) 733-5470 or (307) 543-2831, www.signalmtnlodge.com, has accommodations that range from simple log cabins starting at $80 to two-room lakefront bungalows with kitchenettes for $170. It's open early May to mid-October. Moderate-Luxury.

Flagg Ranch Resort

In Rockefeller Parkway just three miles south of Yellowstone, Flagg Ranch Resort, tel. (307) 543-2861 or (800) 443-2311, www.flaggranch.com, has modern fourplex cabins with patios for $131 d in the summer, or $99 d in winter; kids stay free. It's open mid-May to mid-October and mid-December to mid-March. The main lodge contains a restaurant, gift shop, and large fireplace. Premium.

GRAND TETON PRACTICALITIES

Getting In

Entrance to Grand Teton National Park is $20 per vehicle, or $10 for individuals entering by bicycle, foot, or as a bus passenger. Motorcycles and snowmobiles are $15. The pass covers entrance to both Yellowstone and Grand Teton National Parks and is good for seven days. If you're planning to be here longer or to make additional visits, get an annual pass covering both parks for $40, or the Golden Eagle Passport—good for all national parks—for $50 a year. A Golden Age Passport for all national parks is available to anyone over 62 for a one-time fee of $10, and people with disabilities can get a free Golden Access Passport. Both of these also give the holders 50% reductions in most camping fees. Call (307) 739-3600 for additional park information, or visit the park on the web at www.nps.gov/grte.

At the entrance stations, park visitors receive a copy of ***Teewinot,*** the park newspaper. It lists park facilities and services, along with interpretive programs, nature walks, and other activities. Family favorites for generations are the evening campfire programs held at campground amphitheaters throughout the summer.

Visitor Centers

Grand Teton National Park headquarters is in the settlement of Moose near the southern end of the park. **Moose Visitor Center,** tel. (307) 739-3399, is open daily 8 a.m.-7 p.m. from early June to early September, and daily (except Christmas) 8 a.m.-5 p.m. the rest of the year. **Jenny Lake Visitor Center** is open daily 8 a.m.-7 p.m. from early June to early September, and daily 8 a.m.-5 p.m. the rest of September; closed the remainder of the year.

On the east side of Jackson Lake, **Colter Bay Visitor Center,** tel. (307) 739-3594, is open daily 8 a.m.-8 p.m. from early June to early September, and daily 8 a.m.-5 p.m. from early September to early October; closed in winter.

Just north of Grand Teton inside John D. Rockefeller Jr. Memorial Parkway is **Flagg Ranch Information Station,** open daily 9 a.m.-6 p.m. between early June and early September, and with varying hours from mid-December to mid-March.

Support Organizations

The **Grand Teton Natural History Association** operates bookstores in the visitor centers and the store at Menor's Ferry. The association also provides a mail-order service for books about the park. For a free catalog, call (307) 739-3403, or visit the website: www.grandteton.com/gtnha.

The **Grand Teton National Park Foundation,** tel. (307) 739-3410, provides support for park projects that would not otherwise be funded, and all contributions are tax-deductible.

Restaurants

Summertime restaurants and other eateries are located at Colter Bay Village, Signal Mountain, Flagg Ranch Resort, Jenny Lake, Jackson Lake Lodge, and Leek's Marina (with a pizzeria that has open mike for musicians on Monday nights). At **Jackson Lake Lodge,** the Pool Grill and BBQ features poolside dining on summer nights, and the Mural Room offers 60-foot windows fronting the Tetons (reservations are required in the summertime). Marvelous old **Jenny Lake Lodge** has impeccable service, windows that face the mountains, and a cozy setting. Six-course dinners and sumptuous Sunday night buffets are the featured attractions, and the wine list is extensive. Lunch is à la carte, but breakfast and dinner are fixed price (and pricey). Jenny Lake Lodge is open June to mid-October, and reservations are required; call (307) 733-4647. This is a dress-up place, so a jacket is recommended for dinner.

An old favorite with a more egalitarian setting is **Dornan's Chuck Wagon Restaurant,** tel. (307) 733-2415, www.dornans.com, offering very reasonable meals every summer since 1948. These include all-you-can-eat pancake breakfasts ($6.25), lunchtime sandwiches, and old-fashioned chuck wagon dinners ($12) of barbecued ribs, beef stew, mashed potatoes, and other filling fare. Across the street—and open all year—is Dornan's **Spur Bar/Moose Pizza & Pasta Co.,** tel. (307) 733-2415, offering a wide range of superb homemade pizzas, sandwiches, calzones, and pastas. Dining is available on two outside decks facing the Tetons, and folk music is offered once or twice a month year-round. The bar puts on monthly wine tastings ($5-15) on the first Monday of the month, Oct.-May.

Services

The little settlement of Moose has several businesses in addition to Dornan's Restaurant. **Adventure Sports,** tel. (307) 733-3307, rents mountain bikes, canoes, and kayaks. Next door is **Moosely Seconds,** tel. (307) 739-1801, with good deals on outdoor clothing and climbing gear; open mid-May through September. They also rent ice axes, crampons, rock shoes, trekking poles, approach shoes, plastic boots, day packs, and snowshoes. **Snake River Anglers,** tel. (307) 733-3699, sells and rents fishing supplies and camping equipment.

Across the road are several more Dornan's operations; tel. (307) 733-2415. **The Trading Post** is open all year, selling groceries, tasty deli sandwiches, fresh baked goods, and camping supplies. **Dornan's Wine Shoppe** has the biggest selection of fine wine and beer in Jackson Hole, including over 1,700 different wines. Also at Dornan's are the Spur Bar/Moose Pizza & Pasta (described above), a gift shop, and an **ATM** for cash. The gift shop rents cross-country skis, snowshoes, and pull-behind sleds in the winter months. You'll find additional ATMs at Jackson Lake Lodge and Colter Bay Village.

Colter Bay General Store, tel. (307) 733-2811, has a good choice of groceries and supplies, and in summer, smaller general stores and convenience stores operate at Signal Mountain, Flagg Ranch Resort, and Jenny Lake. The store at Flagg Ranch Resort is open in both summer and winter seasons (mid-May to mid-October, and mid-December to mid-March).

Gas is available year-round at Moose and Flagg Ranch Resort and summers only at Colter Bay Village and Jackson Lake Lodge. You'll find gift shops at Signal Mountain, Flagg Ranch Resort, Jackson Lake Lodge, Moose, and Colter Bay. **Post offices** are located at Colter Bay Village (summer only), and year-round at Moran, Moose Junction, and Kelly. Get emergency medical assistance at the **Grand Teton Medical Clinic,** tel. (307) 543-2514, near the Chevron station at Jackson Lake Lodge. It's open daily 10 a.m.-6 p.m. mid-May to mid-October. The nearest hospital is in Jackson.

Transportation and Tours

Grand Teton Lodge Company, tel. (307) 733-2811 or (800) 628-9988, www.gtlc.com, has three-times-daily summer shuttle buses connecting Jackson with Jackson Lake Lodge for $15 one-way, and on to Colter Bay Village for an additional $2.75 one-way. Transportation to the airport is $20 one-way. In Jackson, the buses depart from the Homewood parking lot on the corner of Gill St. and N. Cache Drive. The company also offers three-hour bus tours of Grand Teton National Park on Monday, Wednesday, and Friday for $20 ($10 for kids under 12) and eight-hour tours of Yellowstone National Park on Tuesday, Thursday, and Saturday for $44 ($26 for kids). Tours depart from Jackson Lake Lodge at 8:30 in the morning.

Daily summertime bus tours of Grand Teton and Yellowstone National Parks are available from **Gray Line,** tel. (307) 733-4325 or (800) 443-6133, www.jacksonholenet.com/grayline. Yellowstone tours last 11 hours and cost $48 plus park entrance fees. Eight-hour Grand Teton tours are $45 plus the park entrance. Those without vehicles can use these tours for access to the parks; reserve ahead to schedule a pick-up in Jackson, Grand Teton, or Yellowstone. In Yellowstone, travelers can connect with other buses to West Yellowstone, Gardiner, or Cody. Gray Line's four-day tours of Yellowstone and Grand Teton start at $654 for one person or $830 for two, including lodging. See Jackson earlier in this chapter for other transportation and tours in the Jackson Hole area.

Based in Jackson, **Great Plains Wildlife Institute,** tel. (307) 733-2623, www.wildlifesafari.com, leads a range of wildlife-viewing safaris in Grand Teton and Yellowstone.

YELLOWSTONE NATIONAL PARK

The words "national park" seem to stimulate an almost Pavlovian response: Yellowstone. The geysers, canyons, and bears of Yellowstone National Park are so intertwined in our collective consciousness that even 1960s' American cartoons used the park as a model—Jellystone Park, where Yogi Bear and Boo Boo were constantly out to thwart the rangers. One source estimated that nearly a third of the U.S. population has visited the park, and each year three million people roll through its gates.

Yellowstone has always been a place of wonder. There is considerable evidence that the Indians who first lived in this area viewed it as a place of great spiritual power and treated it with reverence. Yellowstone was to later become the birthplace for the national-park movement, and Americans today still love the park, though they don't always treat it with reverence.

There is something about Yellowstone National Park that calls people back again and again, something more than simply the chance to see the curiosities of the natural world. Generation after generation of parents have brought their children to see the place that they recall from their own childhood visits. Other cultures have the Ganges River, Rome, or Mecca as places with deep spiritual meaning. In America, our national parks have become places for similar renewal, and as the nation's first national park, Yellowstone remains one of our most valued treasures.

So, into the park we come in our cars with our crying babies in the back—babies who suddenly quiet down at the sight of a bison or elk. I recall bringing relatives to Yellowstone after I had worked in the vicinity all summer and had become a bit jaded. Their emotional reaction surprised me, and more than a decade later they still tell stories of the bison calves, the astounding geysers, the rush of the waterfalls, and the night they spent at Old Faithful Inn. Yellowstone is a collective religious experience that sends us back to our roots in the natural world.

The smell of wood smoke from a campfire, the picnic lunch on the shore of Lake Yellowstone, the backcountry horseback ride, the hike down to the lip of Lower Falls, the quick strike of a trout on the line, the gasp of the crowd as the first spurt of Old Faithful jets upward, the campfire program where a park ranger talks about the lives of grizzlies, the herds of bison wading Firehole River, the evening piano tunes drifting through the air at Lake Hotel, the howl of a distant wolf, and even the infamous rubber tomahawks—all of these things combine to leave an indelible mark on visitors to Yellowstone National Park.

The Setting

On a map, Yellowstone appears as a gigantic box wedged so tightly against the northwest corner of Wyoming that it squeezes over into Montana and Idaho. The park measures 63 by 54 miles and covers 2.2 million acres, making it one of the largest national parks in the Lower 48 (though it is dwarfed by Alaska's Wrangell-St. Elias National Park and Preserve, which covers almost six times as much land). The United Nations has declared Yellowstone both a World Biosphere Reserve and a World Heritage Site.

The park is accessible from all four sides, and a loop road provides easy access to all the best-known sights. Because of its popularity as a destination, tourist towns have grown up on all sides of Yellowstone: Jackson to the south, Cody to the east, Gardiner and Cooke City on the northern margin, and West Yellowstone on the western border. Also because so many people visit the park, there is a well-developed network of facilities inside the park, including campgrounds, hotels, restaurants, gift shops, ATMs, one-hour photo shops, espresso stands, and other supposed necessities of modern life. Although less than two percent of the park is developed, Yellowstone contains more than 2,000 buildings of various types. In some spots (most egregiously around Old Faithful), these developments have grown to the point that the natural world seems simply a backdrop for the human world that pulls visitors in to buy T-shirts or to watch park slide shows on wildlife or geysers while missing the real thing just outside the door.

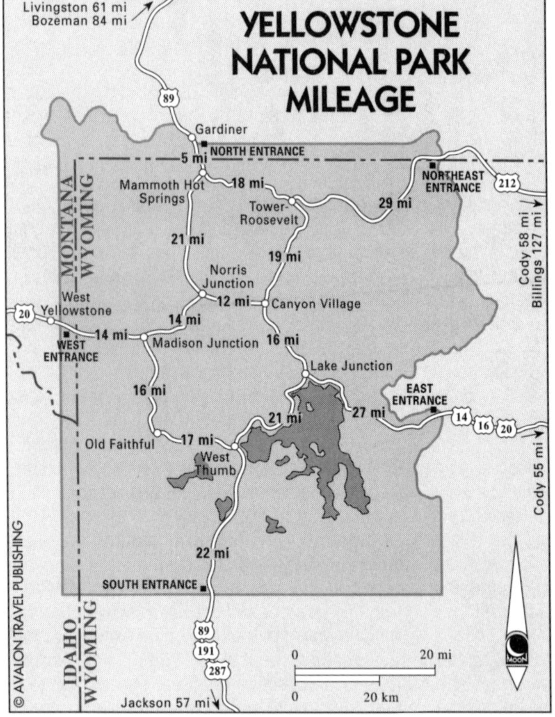

More than any other national park, Yellowstone seems to provide the oddities of nature, creating, as historian Aubrey L. Haines noted, "a false impression that the park is only a colossal, steam-operated freak show." Yellowstone is a mix of the real and the unreal, a place where our fantasies of what nature should be blend with the reality of crowds of fellow travelers and the impact we have on the place we love so much. During midsummer, a trip into Yellowstone can be something less than a natural experience. Long lines of cars back up be-

SIGHTSEEING HIGHLIGHTS FOR YELLOWSTONE NATIONAL PARK

Upper Geyser Basin, including Old Faithful, Old Faithful Inn, Morning Glory Pool, Giant Geyser, and Riverside Geyser

Grand Prismatic Spring in Midway Geyser Basin

Great Fountain Geyser

Fountain Paint Pot

Norris Geyser Basin, including Echinus Geyser

Mammoth Hot Springs and the Albright Visitor Center (Thomas Moran paintings)

Lamar Valley wolf viewing

Tower Fall

Mount Washburn

Grand Canyon of the Yellowstone, including Brink of the Lower Falls, Uncle Tom's Trail, Artist Point, and Inspiration Point

Hayden Valley

Mud Volcano

Yellowstone Lake, Fishing Bridge, and Lake Yellowstone Hotel

Wildlife viewing, particularly bison, elk, wolves, grizzlies, and moose

hind RVs creeping up the too-narrow roads, and throngs of visitors crowd the benches around Old Faithful Geyser waiting for an eruption, while dozens of others cluster around bewildered elk to get photos for their scrapbooks. But despite this—or perhaps because most folks prefer to stay on paved paths—many parts of the park remain virtually uninhabited. In the Yellowstone backcountry, one can still walk for days without seeing more than a handful of other hardy hikers.

A Place of Controversy

Yellowstone National Park evokes a torrent of emotions in anyone with a knowledge of and concern for the natural world. Perhaps more than any other wild place in America, the park seems to be in a perpetual state of controversy, be it over fire policies, geothermal bioprospecting, bison management, winter use, or some other issue—there's always something getting folks stirred up. Perhaps it is because so many Americans have visited the park that we feel a vested interest in what it means to us. Writer Paul Schullery in his wonderful book *Searching for Yellowstone* put it best when he noted, "Caring for Yellowstone National Park brings to mind all the metaphors of growth and change; it is a process more organic than political; a crucible of ideas, ambitions, dreams, and belief systems; a cultural, intellectual, and spiritual crossroads at which we are forever debating which way to turn." As visitation has risen in recent years, more and more folks have begun to suggest some sort of limits on numbers to preserve the experience and protect the park. Don't-tread-on-me Westerners consider the idea of limits an example of environmental extremism for the elite, but as visitation increases, conflicts and controversies are a natural outcome.

GEOLOGY

Yellowstone is, without a doubt, the most geologically fascinating place on this planet. Here the forces that elsewhere lie deep within the earth seem close enough to touch. They're palpable not only in the geysers and hot springs but also in the lake that fills part of an enormous caldera, the earthquakes that shake this land, the evidence of massive glaciations, and the deeply eroded Grand Canyon of the Yellowstone.

FIRE AND ICE

The Yellowstone Hotspot

When geologists began to study the Yellowstone area in depth they found a surprising pattern. Extending far to the southwest was a chain of volcanic fields, the most ancient of which—16 million years old—lay in northern Nevada. In addition, geologic fault lines created a hundred-mile-wide semicircle around the Yellowstone area, as if some deep-seated force were pushing the land outward and upward the way a ripple moves across a pond.

Both the volcanic activity and the wavelike pattern of faults are due to the same source: a plume of superheated material moving up from the core of the planet through a narrow tube, creating a hotspot beneath the earth's crust. As the North American continent has slid to the southwest over the eons, this plume has traced a line of volcanoes across the West, and as the land continues to move, the plume causes massive deformations in the crust that show up as mountain ranges, fault lines, and earthquakes. It's a little like somebody tugging a piece of cloth across a candle. Approximately 40 such hotspots are known to exist around the globe, but most are beneath the seas. Other than Yellowstone, the best-known example is the chain of Hawaiian Islands. The earth has been moving over the Yellowstone hotspot at the rate of 15 miles per million years for the last 10 million years, and on the present track, the spot might eventually end up in around Hudson Bay in a 100 million years or so. Don't hold your breath.

Tambora on Steroids

The volcanic activity revealed by Yellowstone's geysers, hot springs, and fumaroles is not always benign. Within the last two million years there have been three stupendous volcanic eruptions in the area, the most recent taking place 650,000 years ago. The largest of these eruptions took place two million years ago and created an event beyond the realm of imagination: 600 cubic miles of ash were blasted into the atmosphere! This eruption—probably one of the largest to ever occur on earth—ejected 17 times more material than the massive Tambora eruption of 1815, an explosion that was heard 1,600 miles away. And, compared to an explosion that is better known to Americans, the 1980 eruption of Mt. St. Helens, the first Yellowstone event was 2,400 times as large. Ash from this first Yellowstone eruption carried east to Iowa, north to Saskatchewan, south to the Gulf of Mexico, and west to California. This titanic infusion of ash into the atmosphere undoubtedly affected the global climate for years to follow.

The process that creates these explosions starts when molten rock pushes up from the center of the earth, bulging the land upward into an enormous dome. Eventually the pressure becomes too great and fractures develop around the dome's margins, sending hot gases, ash, and rock blasting into the atmosphere. After the most recent eruption (650,000 years ago), the magma chamber collapsed into a gigantic, smoldering pit reaching 28 by 47 miles in surface area and perhaps several thousand feet deep. Over time, additional molten rock pushed up from underneath and flowed as thick lava over the land. The most recent of these lava flows was 70,000 years ago.

Two resurgent domes—one near Old Faithful and the other just north of Yellowstone Lake near LeHardy Rapids—have been discovered by geologists. Measurements at LeHardy Rapids showed that the land rose almost three feet from 1923 to 1985, though it has since been subsiding. This upsurge raised the outlet of Yellowstone Lake, causing the water level to increase and flooding trees along the lake's margins. Obviously, Yellowstone's volcanism is far from dead, and scientists believe another eruption is possible or even likely, though nobody knows when it might occur.

Glaciation

Not everything in Yellowstone is the result of volcanic activity. The entire Yellowstone region has undergone a series of at least eight major glaciations over the last million years, the last of which—the Pinedale Glaciation—began around 70,000 years ago. At its peak, the Pinedale Glaciation covered almost all of Yellowstone and reached southward into Jackson Hole and north much of the way to Livingston, Montana. Over Yellowstone Lake the icefield was 4,000 feet thick and covered 10,000-foot mountains. This period of glaciation ended about 15,000 years ago, but trees did not begin to appear in the Yellowstone area until 11,500 years ago, and it wasn't till around 5,000 years ago that the landscape began to appear as it does today.

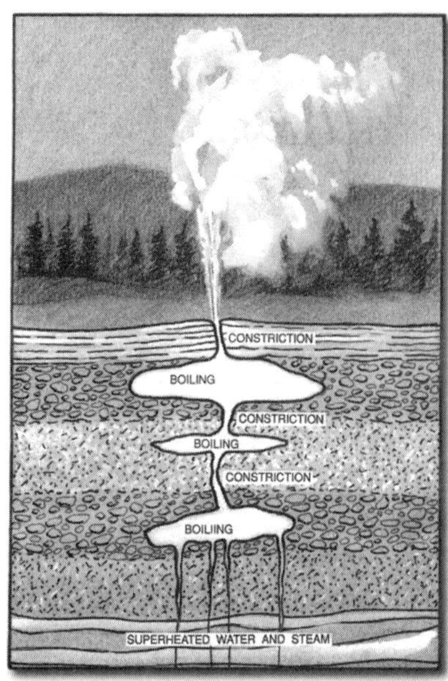

GEYSERS

Yellowstone is famous for geysers, and geyser-gazers will not be disappointed. At least 60% of the world's geysers are in the park, making this easily the largest and most diverse collection in existence. Yellowstone's more than 300 geysers are spread over nine different basins, with half of these in Upper Geyser Basin, the home of Old Faithful.

Geysers need three essentials to exist: water, heat, and fractured rock. The water comes from snow and rain falling on this high plateau, while the heat comes from molten rock close to the earth's surface. Massive pressures from below have created a ring of fractures around the edge of Yellowstone's caldera. This is one of the hottest places on the planet, with heat flows more than 60 times the global average.

How They Work

Geysers operate because cold water is dense and sinks, while hot water is less dense and rises. The periodic eruption of geysers is due to constrictions in the underground channels that prevent an adequate heat exchange with the surface. Precipitation slowly moves into the earth, eventually contacting the molten rock. Because of high pressures at these depths, water can reach extreme temperatures without vaporizing (as in a pressure cooker). As this superheated water rises back toward the surface, it emerges in hot springs, fumaroles, mud pots, and geysers. The most spectacular of these phenomena are geysers. Two general types of geysers exist in Yellowstone. Fountain geysers (such as Great Fountain Geyser) explode from pools of water and tend to spray water more widely, while cone-type geysers (such as Old Faithful) jet out of nozzlelike formations.

In a geyser, steam bubbles upward from the superheated source of water and expands as it rises. These bubbles block the plumbing system, keeping hot water from reaching the surface. Eventually, however, pressure from the bubbles begins to force the cooler water above out of the vent. This initial release triggers a more violent reaction as the sudden lessening of pressure allows the entire column to begin boiling, explosively expelling steam and water to produce a geyser. Once the eruption has emptied the plumbing system, water gradually seeps back into the chambers to begin the process anew. Some of Yellowstone's geysers have enormous underground caverns that fill with water; in its rare eruptions, massive Steamboat Geyser can blast a million gallons of water into the air!

As an aside, the term geyser is one of the few Icelandic terms in the English language; it means to "gush forth." There are probably 30 active geysers in Iceland, many more on Russia's Kamchatka Peninsula, and a few in New Zealand, where geothermal development has greatly lessened geyser activity.

Preserving the Geysers

Unfortunately, some of Yellowstone's geysers have been lost because of human stupidity or vandalism. At one time, it was considered great sport to stuff logs, rocks, and even chairs into the geysers for a little added show. Others poured chemicals into them to make them play. As a result of such actions, some geysers have been severely damaged or destroyed, and a number of hot springs have become collection points for coins, rocks, sticks, and trash. It shouldn't be necessary to point out that such actions ruin these thermal areas for everyone and destroy something that may have been going on for hundreds of years.

OTHER GEOTHERMAL ACTIVITY

Although geysers are Yellowstone's best-known features, they make up only a tiny fraction of perhaps 10,000 thermal features in the park. **Hot springs** appear where water can reach the ground surface relatively easily, allowing for a dissipation of the heat that builds up in the chambers of geysers. When less groundwater is present, you may find **fumaroles,** vents that shoot steam, carbon dioxide, and even hydrogen sulfide gas. **Mud pots** (also called paint pots) are essentially wet fumaroles. Hydrogen sulfide gas comines with water to produce hydrosulfuric acid. This acid breaks down surrounding rocks to form clay, and the clay combines with water to create mud. As gas passes through the mud it creates the bubbling mud pots. Probably the best examples of these different forms are at Fountain Paint Pot in Lower Geyser Basin, where geysers and hot springs are found in the wetter areas below, while mud pots and fumaroles sit atop a small hill.

The colors in Yellowstone's hot springs come from a variety of sources, including algae and bacteria as well as various minerals, particularly sulfur, iron oxides, and arsenic sulfide. The algae and bacteria are highly temperature-specific and help to create the distinct bands of colors around many hot springs. Interestingly, many of these algal species are found only in hot springs, though they exist around the world. The bacteria have proven of considerable interest to science because of their ability to survive such high temperatures. One such organism, *Thermus aquaticus,* was discovered in a Yellowstone hot springs in 1967, and scientists extracted an enzyme that was later used to develop the increasingly important technique of DNA fingerprinting. Above 190° F, even these hot-water bacteria and algae cannot survive, so the hottest springs may appear a deep blue due to the water's ability to absorb all wavelengths of light except blue, which is reflected back into our eyes.

More Terminology

A couple of other terms are worth learning before heading out to see the sights of Yellowstone. **Sinter** (also called "geyserite") is a deposit composed primarily of silica. The silica is dissolved by hot water deep underground and brought to the surface in geysers or hot springs. At the surface the water evaporates, leaving behind the light gray sinter, which can create large mounds (up to 30 feet high) around the older geysers. The rate of accumulation is very slow, and some of the park's geysers have obviously been active for many thousands of years. The other precipitate that is sometimes deposited around Yellowstone's hot springs and geysers is **travertine,** consisting of calcium carbonate that has been dissolved underground. (See Mammoth Hot Springs below for more on this process.)

A Note of Warning

The surface around many of the hot springs and geysers is surprisingly thin, and people have been killed or seriously injured by falling through into the boiling water. Stay on the boardwalks in developed areas, and use extreme caution around backcountry thermal features. If in doubt, stay away!

THE YELLOWSTONE ECOSYSTEM

One of the largest intact temperate-zone ecosystems on the planet, Yellowstone was for decades viewed as an island of nature surrounded by a world of human development. Unfortunately, this attitude has led to a host of problems. Despite its size, Yellowstone alone is not large enough to support a viable population of all the animals that once existed within its borders, and developments outside the park pose threats within. In recent years, there have been increasing calls to treat the park as part of the larger Greater Yellowstone Ecosystem—18 million acres of land at the juncture of Wyoming, Montana, and Idaho covering both public and private lands. With each year that passes it has become more obvious that Yellowstone can never be simply an island. Most of the issues that have made headlines in the last decade or so—from fisheries problems to snowmobile use—have been ones that spread beyond the artificial park boundaries.

Within surrounding lands, conflicts between development and preservation are even more obvious than within the park itself. Logging is one of the most apparent of these, and along the park's western border aerial photos reveal a perfectly straight line, with lodgepole pines on the park side and old clearcuts on the Forest Service side. One of these was the largest timber sale ever made outside of Alaska! Near the park boundaries, housing developments, the massive growth of the tourism industry, oil and gas drilling, mining, a grizzly bear and wolf theme park and other activities all create potential problems within the park and for the Yellowstone ecosystem as a whole.

The way everything is tied together is perhaps best exemplified by two seemingly unrelated issues that have been on the front burner in recent years: bison and snowmobiles. I talk more about both later, but needless to say environmentalists think there are far too many snowmobiles heading into the park, and Montana ranchers think there are far too many bison coming out of the park about the same time of year. As a result, bison are being sent to slaughter, sometimes in large numbers. But these two problems are partially linked; some bison exit the park on roads kept smooth for the snowmobiles. If the roads were not groomed it is possible that more of the bison would remain inside the park in heavy snow years. The point here is not that we should immediately ban all snowmobiles in Yellowstone, but that our actions can have unforeseen ramifications both outside and inside the park.

PLANTS

Yellowstone National Park is primarily a series of high plateaus ranging from 7,500 to 8,500 feet in elevation. Surrounding this gently rolling expanse are the Absaroka Mountains along the east and north sides and the Gallatin Range in the northwestern corner. Elevations are lowest along the northern end of the park, where the Yellowstone River and other streams cut through. Here one

> *At this place there is also large numbers of hot Springs some of which have formed cones of limestone 20 feet high of a Snowy whiteness which make a splendid appearance standing among the ever green pines Some of the lower peaks are very serviceable to the hunter in preparing his dinner when hungry for here his kettle is always ready and boiling his meat being suspended in the water by a string is soon prepared for his meal without further trouble. . . . Standing upon an eminence and superficially viewing these natural monuments one is half inclined to believe himself in the neighborhood of the ruins of some ancients City whose temples had been constructed of the whitest marble.*
>
> —MOUNTAIN MAN OSBORNE RUSSELL, DESCRIBING THE FIREHOLE RIVER AREA IN 1839

finds open country with sagebrush, grasses, and shrubs, along with patches of aspen and Douglas-fir. Farther south on the central plateaus are the extensive lodgepole pine forests that cover more than half the park.

At higher and cooler elevations, lodgepole pine forests give way to groves of Engelmann spruce and subalpine fir, which in turn leave the highest elevations to stands of whitebark pine—an important food source for grizzlies. At timberline (approximately 10,000 feet), even these trees give way and only low-growing forbs, grasses, and shrubs survive. Not all areas follow this simple elevational gradient, however. The park contains extensive wet meadow areas in the Bechler and upper Yellowstone River areas. Other broad openings are found along the Gardner River, in Pelican Valley, and in Hayden Valley.

WILDLIFE

Yellowstone is world-famous for its wildlife and provides a marvelous natural setting in which to view bison, elk, moose, wolves, coyotes, pronghorn antelope, bighorn sheep, and other critters. One of the easiest ways to find wildlife is simply by watching for the brake lights, the cars pulled half off the road, and the cameras all pointed in one direction. Inevitably, you'll find an elk or a bison placidly munching away, trying to remain oblivious to the chaos that surrounds it. Be sure to bring binoculars for your trip to Yellowstone. A spotting scope is also very helpful in searching for distant bears and wolves.

The Park Service has a free brochure showing where you're most likely to see wildlife in Yellowstone. Pick one up at any visitor center. During the summer, the best wildlife-viewing hours are early in the morning and in the late afternoon to early evening. Because of the constant parade of visitors and the lack of hunting, many of Yellowstone's animals appear to almost ignore the presence of people, and it isn't uncommon to see visitors approach an animal without respecting its need for space. Although they may appear tame, Yellowstone's animals really are wild, and attacks are not uncommon. Those quiet bison can suddenly erupt with an enormous ferocity if provoked by photographers who come too close. Between 1983 and 1994, four people were killed by bison in Yellowstone and Grand Teton National Parks. **Stay at least 25 yards away from bison and elk and at least 100 yards away from bears.** (Those with a perverse sense of humor will want to visit the Park Service's website for a short video showing a bison throwing a too-close visitor into a tree; find it under wildlife viewing at www.nps.gov/yell.) Do not under any circumstances feed the park's animals. This creates an unnatural dependency, is unhealthy for the animal, and may even lead to its death.

The park contains some 60 different species of resident mammals, ranging from shrews and bats to bison and grizzlies. Some 309 species of birds have been recorded, along with 18 species of fish (five of which are nonnative), four amphibians, and six reptiles. The only poisonous animal is the prairie rattlesnake, found at low elevations in the northern end of Yellowstone. Oh yes, countless insect species, too. Some Yellowstone critters are more friendly than others, most notably the mosquitoes that show up in large numbers early in the summer. By mid-August they're much less of a hassle, and winter visitors will have no problems at all with mosquitoes!

Trumpeter swans—beautiful white birds with seven-foot wingspans—are a fairly common sight in Yellowstone, particularly on the Madison and Yellowstone Rivers and on Yellowstone Lake. Many trumpeter swans winter in hot spring areas. These are some of the largest birds in America, weighing 20-30 pounds. Another large white bird here is the ungainly-looking and bulbous-billed white pelican, a common sight on Yellowstone Lake and near Fishing Bridge. Upward of 350 pairs of pelicans nest on the Molly Islands in Yellowstone Lake; this is one of the largest white-pelican breeding colonies in the Rockies. Bald eagles—America's national bird—and ospreys have managed comebacks in recent years and are frequently seen along the Yellowstone River and above Yellowstone Lake. Look for golden eagles flying over the open grasslands of Lamar Valley or Hayden Valley.

Killing the Predators

Wildlife has always been one of the big drawing cards at Yellowstone, and early on there were constant charges of mass slaughter by poachers and market hunters. It was not until 1894 that Congress passed the Lacey Act, finally making it illegal to hunt within the park. Unfortunately, predators such as wolves, coyotes, mountain lions, and wolverines were regarded as despoilers of the elk, deer, and moose and became fair targets for poisoning and shooting by early park managers. (This happened throughout the West, not just in the park.) The campaign proved all too successful, devastating the wolf and mountain lion populations. In recent years, wolves have returned in a spectacular way, though mountain lion numbers remain low.

Controversy on the Northern Range

A recurring area of strife in Yellowstone has been the suggestion that elk and bison are overgrazing and destroying the Lamar and Yellowstone River basins, an area known as the northern range. The issue periodically flares up, fed in part by the efforts of Montana ranchers and others who suffer from bison and elk that migrate out of Yellowstone onto their land each winter. They—and some researchers—believe that the Park Service has allowed too many animals to survive and that the land is being damaged by overgrazing. Most research, however, points in the opposite direction—that the land is not overgrazed, and that ecological processes are working fine in a system termed "natural regulation." The populations of elk and bison fluctuate over time; some years numbers are up, and other years they drop due to harsh winters, predation, hunting outside the park, or other factors.

Bears

During Yellowstone's early years, bears were commonly viewed as either pets or nuisances. Cubs were tethered to poles in front of the hotels, and other bears fed on the garbage piles that grew up around the camps and hotels. Older folks still recall the bear-feeding grounds at the garbage dumps, where visitors might see 50 bears pawing through the refuse. These feeding shows continued until 1941, but it wasn't until 1970 that the park's open-pit dumps were finally sealed off and the garbage cans bear-proofed. Closure of the dumps helped create confrontations between "garbage bears" and humans; the bears nearly always lost. Between 1970 and 1972 dozens of grizzlies died in showdowns with humans in the park or surrounding areas. Fortunately, careful management in the intervening years has helped the population to rebound. Today there are believed to be at least 300-350 grizzlies in the Greater Yellowstone Ecosystem, and their numbers have been increasing fairly steadily since the 1980s. (Some scientists believe there are more than 600 grizzlies.)

Both black and grizzly bears are found throughout Yellowstone, but the days of bear jams along the park roads are long past, since rangers actively work to prevent bears from becoming habituated to people. Most bears have returned to their more natural ways of living, although problems still crop up with individuals wandering through campgrounds in search of food. You're more likely to encounter a bear in the backcountry areas, and some places are closed to hiking for extended periods each year for this reason. The best places to watch for grizzlies along the road system are in the Hayden and Lamar Valleys, near Mt. Washburn, and in the Antelope Creek drainage.

One unusual aspect of the Yellowstone grizzlies was just discovered in recent years: the importance of moths as a food source in the grizzly diet. Millions of army cutworm moths congregate on Yellowstone's high alpine slopes during the summer, where they feed on nectar from the abundant flowers. Bears are attracted to this food source because of the insect's abundance and high fat content. Researchers have sometimes seen two dozen bears feeding on a single slope!

Safety in grizzly country is always a concern, but statistically you are considerably more likely to be hurt in a traffic accident than to be mauled by a bear. There were just 22 bear-caused injuries in the park between 1980 and 1997—one injury for every 2.1 million visitors! Most of these injuries took place in backcountry areas and involved female bears with cubs or yearlings, and nearly all attacks took place following a surprise encounter with a bear. Three people were killed by Yellowstone bears in the last three decades of the 20th century, the most recent being a 1986 fatality caused when a photographer approached an adult female grizzly too closely. For details on staying safe around bears, see the special topic Bear Country in the Introduction chapter.

The **Yellowstone Grizzly Foundation,** tel. (307) 734-8643, http://home.wyoming.com/~ygf, is an excellent nonprofit organization dedicated to conserving grizzlies within the Greater Yellowstone Ecosystem. Established by Steve and Marilynn French—who have been studying grizzly bears since 1983—the foundation emphasizes nonintrusive observations. One of their groundbreaking projects collected hair samples as bears crawled under barbed wire. DNA analysis of these hairs led to a new understanding of how grizzly bears in Yellowstone are related to other bears. It turns out that more than 90% of Yellowstone grizzlies originated from the same maternal lineage, a fact that may have important ramifications for management. The research also showed that the grizzlies of Yellowstone differ markedly from Alaskan grizzlies such as those found at the wildlife park in West Yellowstone.

Bighorn Sheep

These stocky mountain dwellers are named for the massive curling horns of the males (rams) and can be seen in several parts of Yellowstone. They have a tan-colored coat with a white rump patch. Bighorns were once abundant throughout the western U.S., and early trappers in the mountains east of Yellowstone reported finding thousands of sheep in and around the present-day park. They were also an important source of food for the Sheepeater Indians who lived in Yellowstone before the arrival of whites. Bighorn sheep were virtually wiped out by hunters in the late 19th century, and domestic sheep overran their lands and brought deadly diseases. Within a few decades, the millions of sheep that had roamed the West were reduced to a few hundred survivors.

Both the rams and ewes (females) have horns that remain for life, but only the rams get the massive curl for which bighorn sheep are known. Rams are 125-275 pounds in size, with ewes 75-150 pounds. During the mating season in November and December you're likely to see the original head-bangers in action as rams clash to establish dominance. The clashes can be surprisingly violent, and to protect the brain, bighorns have a double cranium that absorbs much of the shock. Those with the larger horns are typically the dominant bighorns and the primary breeders. The young lambs are born in May and June. In the summer months the sexes separate, with the ewes and lambs remaining lower while the bachelor herds climb higher into the mountains. Bighorns use their ability to climb steep and rocky terrain as protection from predators such as coyotes, wolves, and mountain lions. Winter often finds bighorns in mixed herds at lower elevations. Around 250 bighorns live within Yellowstone National Park, with much larger populations in the surrounding national forests.

Look for bighorn sheep on cliffs in the Gardner River Canyon between Mammoth Hot Springs and the town of Gardiner. Ewes and lambs are also frequently seen just off the road on Dunraven Pass north of Canyon, and day-hikers commonly encounter rams up-close on the slopes of Mt. Washburn. Another place where bighorns may be seen is along Specimen Ridge.

Bison

Before their virtual annihilation in the 19th century, 60 million bison were spread across America. When Yellowstone was established in 1872, hundreds of mountain bison (also called wood bison) still ranged across this high plateau. Sport and meat hunting—legal until 1894—and later poaching reduced the population so that by 1902 perhaps fewer than 25 remained. That year, 21 plains bison were brought in from private ranches in Montana and Texas to help restore the Yellowstone herd, and today there are approximately 2,500 in the park, making this the largest free-ranging herd of bison anywhere on earth. Unfortunately, interbreeding between the mountain and plains bison means that the animals in Yellowstone today are genetically different from the original inhabitants.

Bison are typically found in open country throughout the park, including Hayden, Lamar, and Pelican Valleys, along with the Firehole River Basin (including Old Faithful). A favorite time to see bison in Yellowstone is late May, just after the new calves have been born. The calves' antics are always good for laughs. Be sure to use caution around bison; many people have been gored when they've come too close. Always stay at least 25 yards away, preferably farther.

Bison are carriers of brucellosis, a disease that causes cows to abort calves and is the source of undulant fever in humans. Brucellosis can be spread when a contaminated fetus or birthing material is licked by other animals, a situation that is unlikely given the timing of bison movements. In 1985, Yellowstone's bison began wandering north into the Gardiner area for the

Yellowstone is home to one of the largest free-ranging herds of bison anywhere.

winter. Montana and Wyoming are certified as "brucellosis-free" states, and although there is absolutely no evidence that wild bison have ever transmitted the disease to cattle, ranchers feared that the bison might threaten Montana's brucellosis-free status. If cattle become infected with brucellosis, ranchers might potentially be prohibited from shipping livestock out of state. (Ironically, the park's far more numerous elk also carry brucellosis. Although they are hunted outside Yellowstone, you won't ever hear Montana authorities talking about slaughtering all elk that wander across Yellowstone's borders.) The state of Wyoming has managed to keep its brucellosis-free status despite the presence of both cattle and bison in Jackson Hole. There, most ranchers vaccinate their cattle and work with the Park Service to keep bison and elk separate from livestock. Why won't it work in Montana? The answer probably has far more to do with Montana politics than biology.

A highly controversial "hunt" during the late 1980s let hunters shoot bison when they wandered outside the park. After a public outcry, the job was turned over to the Montana state Division of Livestock, an agency accustomed to dealing with cattle, not wildlife. Bison that wander out of the park—primarily in the Gardiner and West Yellowstone areas—are hazed in an attempt to push them back in. If this fails, they are typically captured in pens and tested for brucellosis (the blood test is notoriously inaccurate), and those that test positive are usually killed.

Things came to a head in the heavy-snow winter of 1996-97 when nearly 1,100 Yellowstone bison were sent to slaughter, cutting the park bison herd by a third. It was one of the largest killings of bison anywhere since their destruction on the Great Plains in the 1880s. Only a small number of bison were killed in the milder winters of 1997-99, and as this was written the Park Service and Montana were continuing to operate under the controversial bison management plan while putting together a final environmental impact statement on bison management to be released in 2000. You can find out more at the Yellowstone website, www.nps.gov/yell. In the meantime, a number of environmental organizations are pushing for an alternate plan that would put wildlife professionals in charge instead of the Department of Livestock, encourage vaccination of livestock, alter cattle-grazing practices to prevent them from intermingling with bison, and compensate landowners for damage caused to fences and other property.

Coyotes

Although wolves get the media attention, visitors to Yellowstone are probably more likely to see another native of the dog family: the coyote. Keep your eyes open for coyotes anywhere in Yellowstone but especially in open grassy areas where they are more easily spotted. During the summer, they're often seen in small packs or alone as they hunt small mammals such as mice, voles, and pocket gophers. At other times of the year they prey on larger animals, including the calves of elk and pronghorn antelope, and scavenge carrion.

Differentiating coyotes from wolves can be a bit tricky, especially from a distance without binoculars. Coyotes are considerably smaller animals; adult male coyotes weigh around 30 pounds, while wolves are far more massive, with many weighing 100 pounds or more. The wolf has a large head, short and rounded ears, and a broad and blocky muzzle, while the coyote has a small head, large and pointy ears, and a narrow, pointy nose. From a distance coyotes are more delicate in appearance, with smaller feet and thin legs.

The coyotes within Yellowstone generally live in packs containing six or seven animals led by a dominant pair called the alpha male and female. Most packs have a long family lineage and a well-defined territory; some coyote packs have been using the same denning areas for at least 50 years! The average coyote lives around six years. The alphas mate in early February, and pups are born in early April. Other members of the pack guard the den from wolves and other predators and regurgitate food to feed the pups.

Before the reintroduction of wolves, coyotes were the big dogs (so to speak) in northern Yellowstone and the primary predators of elk calves, killing about 1,200 each year. Wolves occupy a similar ecological niche to coyotes, and their return has led to a 50% reduction in coyote numbers in northern Yellowstone. Some of this comes from outright killing of coyotes by the far larger wolves, particularly the killing of alpha coyotes. The ever-resourceful coyotes have responded by banding together in larger packs, denning in rocky areas, becoming more wary, and staying on the margins of wolf territories. Despite the competition, coyotes remain common and are certainly in no danger of being displaced from Yellowstone; after all, both species were here for thousands of years before the extermination of wolves in the 20th century. Good places to look for coyotes are in the Blacktail Plateau area and Lamar Valley, along with the Upper and Lower Geyser Basins near Old Faithful.

Deer

Mule deer (also known as black-tailed deer) are common in many parts of Yellowstone during the summer months, but most migrate to lower elevations when winter comes. They are typically found in open areas containing sagebrush or grass. Mule deer are named for their long, mule-like ears. They also have black-tipped tails and a peculiar way of pogoing away when frightened. Adult males (bucks) grow antlers each summer, and mating season arrives in November and December. Fawns are born in May or June.

The smaller **white-tailed deer** are occasionally seen within Yellowstone but are far less common. You are most likely to find them along rivers or in brushy areas at low elevations, such as around Mammoth Hot Springs or in Lamar Valley. Other places to watch for them are along Yellowstone Lake and in the Upper Geyser Basin.

Elk

One animal virtually every visitor to Yellowstone sees is elk. About 30,000 of these regal animals summer in the park, and approximately 15,000 remain through the winter, primarily on the north end of Yellowstone. In summer, look for elk in Mammoth Hot Springs, Elk Park, and Gibbon Meadows, but you're certain to also see them elsewhere in Yellowstone. Bull elk can top 700 pounds, while the cows (females) weigh around 500-525 pounds, making elk the second-largest members of the deer family after moose. Each summer, adult bulls grow massive antlers that can weigh 30 pounds or more, and these antlers prove useful in the fall mating season as bulls spar with each other. Dominant bulls herd females into harems during the rut and may sometimes control 25 or so cows, mating with those that come into estrus and battling with rivals intent upon taking over their harems. The bugling of bull elk is a common autumn sound in Yellowstone, as anyone who visits Mammoth Hot Springs at that time of year can attest. It's a strange sound that starts out low, followed by a trumpetlike call and then a series of odd grunts. Approximately 90% of the elk cows become pregnant each year.

The mating season ends by mid- to late November, and winter snows push the elk to lower elevations on the north side of Yellowstone or out of the park into surrounding areas. With the arrival of spring, bulls lose their antlers, and elk start moving back toward the high country.

Calves are born in late May or early June (sometimes during the migration) and weigh 25-40 pounds at birth. Elk—particularly young calves—are an important food source for predators in Yellowstone; almost a third of the calves are killed each year by wolves, grizzly and black bears, coyotes, and golden eagles.

Moose

The largest members of the deer family, moose are typically seen eating willow bushes in riparian areas inside Yellowstone National Park. During the winter, these moose migrate into high-elevation forests where the snow isn't as deep (tree branches hold the snow) or as crusty as in the open. In these forests they browse on subalpine fir and Douglas-fir. The fires of 1988 burned through many of these forests, and the loss of cover has hurt the Yellowstone moose population. The best places to look for moose are Hayden Valley, around Yellowstone Lake, the Willow Park area north of Norris, the southwestern corner along the Bechler and Falls Rivers, and along the Gallatin, Lamar, and Lewis River drainages.

Pronghorn Antelope

These speedy and colorful ungulates (hoofed mammals) are common sights on the plains of Wyoming, but most of Yellowstone doesn't provide adequate habitat. Pronghorn antelope are only found in sagebrush and grassy areas on the northern end of the park from Lamar Valley to the Gardiner area. Their populations declined sharply in the 1990s within the park, and as of 1999 pronghorn numbered around 200. Coyotes and other predators take many newborn fawns each spring and may be a significant factor in the decline, combined with a number of other factors such as inbreeding due to the small population; changes in vegetation; loss of habitat to development in their Paradise Valley wintering area north of the park; increasing numbers of fences across their range; and hunting.

Wolves

The wolves are back! One of the most exciting developments for visitors to Yellowstone has been the reintroduction of wolves to the park, making this one of the few places in the Lower 48 where they can be viewed in the wild. Wolves once ranged across nearly all of North America, but white settlers regarded them—along with mountain lions, grizzly bears, and coyotes—as threats to livestock and unwanted predators upon game animals. Even in Yellowstone wolves were hunted and poisoned by both the army and the Park Service. By 1940, the wolf was probably gone from the park, though a few lone animals turned up briefly again in the early 1970s.

In the U.S., until 1995 wolves could only be found in Alaska, in northern Minnesota, and in Isle Royale and Glacier National Parks. With the more enlightened public attitude evident in recent years, ecologists and conservationists began pushing for the reintroduction of wolves to Yellowstone, considered one of the few remaining areas in the Lower 48 that could support a viable wolf population.

The proposal to return wolves to Yellowstone set off a firestorm from ranchers (with the ardent support of Wyoming's Republican senators) who feared that they would wander outside the park to destroy sheep and cattle. Opponents said hundreds of livestock would be killed each year around the park and that the reintroduction cost might reach $1.8 million per wolf, a figure that proved grossly inflated. Despite these dire predictions, the U.S. Fish & Wildlife Service began reintroducing wolves to Yellowstone in 1995, initially releasing 14 gray wolves that had been captured in British Columbia. Additional wolves were set free the following spring. During the next six years things went far better than anyone had predicted. By 1999 biologists estimated that 12 groups of wolves totaling 167 individuals inhabited the Greater Yellowstone Ecosystem from north of Yellowstone to the Jackson area.

The return of the wolf to Yellowstone has created a buzz of excitement as visitors gather to watch for wolves. The best place to look is the open terrain of Lamar Valley, where the **Druid Peak and Rose Creek Packs** have taken up residence and are visible at many times of the year. The best time to go looking is early in the morning or near dusk. And, yes, you may well hear their plaintive cry from your campground late at night. Binoculars or spotting scopes are very helpful for roadside wolf watching; do not follow the wolves around since this may disturb them and affect their survival. Denning activity typically takes place early April to early May, with active denning areas closed to humans; check with the Park Service for currently closed areas.

Wolves are the largest members of the canids (dog family), with males averaging 70-120 pounds and stretching up to six feet long from head to tail. They are much more massive than coyotes, though the two are sometimes confused. Wolves live in packs of two to eight, led by an alpha male and alpha female, and establish territories to exclude other wolf packs. Most pack members are from an extended family, but they may include outside members. The alphas are the only ones that generally mate, and a litter of six or so pups is born in early spring. Once they are weaned, the pack feeds pups regurgitated meat until they are large enough to join the hunt. Wolves hunt primarily in the evening and morning hours when their prey—elk, deer, moose, bison, and pronghorn—are feeding.

PARK HISTORY

Yellowstone National Park has a rich and fascinating history that reaches back through thousands of years of settlement. The most thorough source for history is *The Yellowstone Story* (Boulder: University Press of Colorado), an excellent two-volume set by former park historian Aubrey L. Haines. For an engaging and personal journey through the past, read *Searching for Yellowstone* by Paul Schullery (New York: Houghton Mifflin).

SHEEPEATER INDIANS

The last major glaciation ended around 15,000 years ago, and the first peoples may have reached Yellowstone while the ice was still retreating. There is good evidence that the country was occupied for at least 10,000 years, though the tribes apparently changed over time. By the mid-19th century, the country was surrounded by Blackfeet to the north, Crow to the east, and Shoshone and Bannock to the south and west. These tribes all traveled through and hunted in Yellowstone, building temporary shelters, called wickiups, made of aspen poles covered with pine boughs; a few of these still exist in the park. The primary inhabitants of this high plateau were the Sheepeater Indians, who may have been here for over 2,000 years. Of Shoshone stock, the Sheepeaters hunted bighorn sheep (hence the name) and made bows from the sheep horns, but their diet also included other animals, fish, roots, and berries. Because they did not have horses, the Sheepeaters used dog-pulled travois to carry their few possessions from camp to camp. Summers were spent in high alpine meadows and along passes, where they hunted migrating game animals or gathered roots and berries. They wintered in protected canyons.

The Sheepeaters were smaller than other Indians and have achieved an aura of mystery since so little is known of their way of living. Yellowstone was at the heart of their territory, but with the arrival of whites came devastating diseases, particularly smallpox. The survivors joined their Shoshone brothers on the Wind River Reservation or the Bannock Reservation in Idaho. The last of the tribe left Yellowstone in the 1870s.

YELLOWSTONE NATIONAL PARK

Sheepeater Indian in wickiup

THE NEZ PERCÉ WAR

One of the saddest episodes in the history of Yellowstone took place in 1877 and involved the Nez Percé Indians of Oregon's Wallowa Valley. When the government tried to force the people of Chief White Bird and Chief Joseph onto an Idaho reservation so that white ranchers could have their lands, they stubbornly refused. A few drunken young men killed four whites, and subsequent raids led to the deaths of at least 14 more. The Army retaliated but was turned back by the Nez Percé. Rather than face government reinforcements, more than 1,000 Nez Percé began a 1,800-mile flight in a desperate bid to reach Canada. A series of running battles followed as the Indians managed to confound the inept Army using their geographic knowledge and battle skills. The Nez Percé entered Yellowstone from the west, and a few hotheads immediately attacked vacationing tourists and prospectors. Two whites were killed in the park, others were kidnapped, and another man nearly died from his wounds.

The Nez Percé exited Yellowstone two weeks after they arrived, narrowly missing an encounter with their implacable foe, Gen. William T. Sherman, who just happened to be vacationing in Yellowstone at the time. East of the park, the Indians plotted a masterful escape from two columns of Army forces, feinting a move down the Shoshone River and then heading north along a route that left their pursuers gasping in amazement—straight up the narrow Clarks Fork Canyon, "where rocks on each side came so near together that two horses abreast could hardly pass." Finally, less than 40 miles from the international border with Canada, the Army caught up with the Nez Percé, and after a fierce battle the tribe was forced to surrender (although 300 did make good their escape).

Chief Joseph's haunting words still echo through the years: "Hear me, my chiefs, I am tired; my heart is sick and sad. From where the sun now stands, I will fight no more forever." Despite promises that they would be allowed to return to their traditional home, the Nez Percé were instead hustled onto reservations in Oklahoma and Washington while whites remained on their ancestral lands. Chief Joseph spent the rest of his life on Washington's Colville Reservation and died in 1904, reportedly of a broken heart. Yellowstone's Nez Percé Creek, which feeds the Firehole River, is named for this desperate bid for freedom.

Chief Joseph in October 1887 immediately after his surrender at Bear Paw

YELLOWSTONE NATIONAL PARK

FUR TRAPPERS

The word "Yellowstone" appears to have come from the Minnetaree Indians, who called the river "Mi tse a-da-zi," a word French-Canadian trappers translated into "Rive des Roche Jaunes"—literally, "Yellow Rock River." The Indians apparently called it this because of the yellowish bluffs along the river near Billings, Montana (not because of the colorful Grand Canyon of the Yellowstone). The term "Yellow Stone" was first used on a map made in 1797. When the Lewis and Clark Expedition traveled through the country north of Yellowstone in 1805-06, the Indians told them tales of this mysterious place: "There is frequently heard a loud noise like thunder, which makes the earth tremble, they state that they seldom go there because children Cannot sleep—and Conceive it possessed of spirits, who were adverse that men Should be near them." (This certainly was not the attitude of all the native peoples, for the park had long been inhabited.) The first white man to come through Yellowstone is believed to be John Colter, a former member of the Lewis and Clark Expedition who wandered through the region in the winter of 1807-08. A map based on Colter's recollections shows Yellowstone Lake ("Eustis Lake"), along with an area of "Hot Spring Brimstone."

As fur trappers spread through the Rockies in the 1820s and '30s, many discovered the geysers and hot springs of Yellowstone, and stories quickly spread around the rendezvous fires. The word of the trappers was passed on to later settlers and explorers but not entirely believed. After all, mountain man Jim Bridger described not just petrified trees, but petrified birds singing petrified songs! His tales of a river that "ran so fast that it became hot on the bottom" could well have referred to the Firehole River. When Bridger tried to lead a party of military explorers into Yellowstone, they were stymied by deep snows. Still, the word gradually got out that something very strange could be found in this part of the mountains. Little remains today from the mountain-man era, although in 1880 the letters "J.O.R. Aug. 19, 1819" were found carved in a tree near the Upper Falls of the Yellowstone, and later a cache of iron beaver traps similar to those used by the Hudson's Bay Company was discovered near Obsidian Cliff.

EXPEDITIONS

National attention finally came to Yellowstone with a series of three expeditions to check out the wild claims of local prospectors. In 1869, David E. Folsom, Charles W. Cook, and William Peterson headed south from Bozeman, finding the Grand Canyon, Lake Yellowstone, and the geyser basins. When a friend pressured them to submit a description of their travels for publication, the *New York Tribune* refused to publish it, noting that the paper "had a reputation that they could not risk with such unreliable material."

The adventures of this first expedition led another group of explorers into Yellowstone the following year, but this time money was the motive. Jay Cooke's Northern Pacific Railroad needed investors for a planned route across Montana. A good public-relations campaign was the first step, and it happened to coincide with the visit of a former Montana tax collector named Nathaniel P. Langford, who had heard of the discoveries of Folsom, Cook, and Peterson. The party of 19 soldiers and civilians, including Langford, headed out in August of 1870 under Gen. Henry D. Washburn. They were thrilled by what they discovered and proceeded to give the geysers names—Old Faithful, Castle, Giant, Grotto, Giantess—which became permanently attached to the features. The joy of the trip was marred when one man—Truman Everts—became separated from the others and then lost his horse. He was not found until 37 days later, by which time he weighed just 50 pounds. His rescuer did not even recognize him as human. Amazingly, Everts survived and recovered.

With the return of the Washburn Expedition, national newspapers and magazines finally began to pay attention to Yellowstone, and Langford began lecturing in the East on what they had found. One of those listening was Dr. Ferdinand V. Hayden, director of the U.S. Geological Survey. Hayden asked Congress to fund an official investigation. With the help of Representatives James G. Blaine (coincidentally a supporter of the Northern Pacific Railroad) and conservationist Henry M. Dawes, Congress appropriated $40,000 for an exploration of "the sources of the Missouri and Yellowstone Rivers." Thus began the most famous and influential trip into Yellowstone, the 1871 Hayden Expedition. The troop included 34 men, an escort of cavalry, painter Thomas Moran, and photographer William H. Jackson.

ESTABLISHING THE PARK

When Hayden returned to Washington to prepare his report, he found a letter from railroad promoter Jay Cooke. In the letter, Cooke proposed that "Congress pass a bill reserving the Great Geyser Basin as a public park forever—just as it has reserved that far inferior wonder the Yosemite valley and big trees." (Abraham Lincoln had established Yosemite earlier as a state park.) In an amazingly short time, a bill was introduced to set aside the land, and Hayden rushed to arrange a display in the Capitol rotunda of geological specimens, sketches by Moran, and photos by Jackson. The bill easily passed both houses of Congress and was signed into law on March 1, 1872, by Pres. Ulysses S. Grant. The first national park had come into existence, a culmination not just of the discoveries in Yellowstone but also of a growing appreciation for preserving the wonders of the natural world.

Congress saw no need to set aside money for this new creation, since it seemed to be doing fine already. Besides, it was thought that Jay Cooke's new railroad would soon arrive, making it easy for thousands of vacationers to explore Yellowstone. In turn, concessioners would build roads and hotels and pay the government franchise fees. The park was placed under the control of the secretary of the interior, with Nathaniel P. Langford as its unpaid superintendent. Meanwhile, the planned railroad fizzled when Jay Cooke & Co. declared bankruptcy, precipitating the panic of 1873.

ROADS AND RAILROADS

Because of the difficult access, fewer than 500 people visited in each of Yellowstone's first few years as a park, most to soak in tubs at Mammoth Hot Springs. Not a few decided to take home souvenirs, bringing pickaxes and shovels for that purpose. Meanwhile, hunters—including some working for the Mammoth Hotel—began shooting the park's abundant game. Two brothers who had a ranch just north of the park killed 2,000 elk in a single year. Superintendent Langford did little to stop the slaughter and only bothered to visit the park twice. Finally, in 1877, the secretary of the interior fired him, putting Philetus W. Norris in charge instead. Norris proved a good choice, despite a knack for applying his name to everything in sight. (Most of his attempts at immortality have been replaced by other titles, but Norris Geyser Basin, Norris Road, and even the town of Norris, Michigan, remain.)

Norris oversaw construction of the first major road in Yellowstone, a rough 60-mile route built in just 30 days to connect Upper Geyser Basin with Mammoth and the western entrance. All of this was precipitated by the raids of the Nez Percé Indians earlier that summer and threats that the Bannock Indians would strike next. In addition, Norris began, but never completed, the Queen's Laundry, a bathhouse that is considered the first government building built for the public in any national park. The log walls are still visible in a meadow near Lower Geyser Basin.

By 1882, Norris had managed to alienate the company that helped found the park, the Northern Pacific Railroad. The company announced plans to build a railroad line to the geysers and construct a large hotel, "being assured by the Government of a monopoly therein." Norris's opposition led to his being fired and replaced by railroad man Patrick H. Conger. Soon, however, the scheme began to unravel. The Yellowstone Park Improvement Company—whose vice-president happened to be construction superintendent for the Northern Pacific's branch line into Gardiner—had planned not just a lodging monopoly but also a monopoly on all transportation, timber rights, and ranching privileges in the park. Later it was discovered that the company had contracted for 20,000 pounds of venison (killed in the park) to feed the construction crews. As one newspaper writer commented, "It is a 'Park Improvement Company' doing this, and I suppose they consider it an improvement to rid the park, as far as possible, of game."

Finally, in 1884 Congress acted by limiting the land that could be leased—thus effectively ending the railroad's plans—and adding funding to hire 10 assistants to patrol Yellowstone. Unfortunately, they neglected to include any penalties for the poachers and despoilers other than expulsion, so even the few assistants who did decent work found the culprits quickly returning. The problems were myriad. Cooke City miners were fishing with spears, seine nets, and even dynamite. Guides were throwing rocks into the geysers, squatters had ensconced themselves on prime land in Lamar Valley, and visitors were leaving fires unattended and breaking off specimens from the geysers.

Superintendent Conger was later replaced by Robert E. Carpenter, a man about whom historian Hiram Chittenden noted, "In his opinion, the Park was created to be an instrument of profit to those who were shrewd enough to grasp the opportunity." Carpenter lobbied Congress to remove lands from the park so that the Northern Pacific could construct a railroad along the Yellowstone and Lamar Rivers to Cooke City. In return, friends promised to locate claims in his name along the route so that he too might profit from the venture. The landgrab fell apart when the Senate vetoed the move, and Carpenter was summarily removed from office. Not long thereafter, Congress flatly refused to fund the civilian administration of Yellowstone, and the Secretary of the Interior was forced to request the aid of the military in 1886. It proved a fortuitous step.

THE ARMY YEARS

The U.S. Army finally brought a semblance of order to Yellowstone, eliminating the political appointees who viewed the park as a place to get rich. That first year, a temporary fort—Camp Sheridan—was thrown up and a troop of soldiers arrived, but it wasn't until 1891 that work began on a permanent Fort Yellowstone at Mammoth. By 1904, the fort consisted of some 26 buildings housing 120 men. The soldiers had clear objectives—protecting wildlife (or at least bison and elk) from poachers, fighting fires, stopping vandalism, and generally achieving order out of chaos. These goals were accomplished with a fervor that gained widespread respect, and in a way that would later influence the organization of the National Park Service. One of the major accomplishments of the soldiers was completion of the Grand Loop Road, which passes most of Yellowstone's attractions. The basic pattern was completed by 1905.

Fort Yellowstone was a favorite station for soldiers, and it was considered something of an honor to be sent to such a setting. The life of the soldiers was not always easy, however, and a number died in the bitter winters or in accidents. A series of 16 soldier stations—actually little more than large cabins—was established around the park, and each was manned year-round, usually by four soldiers.

Before the arrival of cars, many visitors to Yellowstone were wealthy people from the East Coast or Europe intent upon doing the grand tour of the West. The railroads (Northern Pacific to the north, Union Pacific to the west, and the Burlington to the east) deposited them near park borders, where they were met by carriages, Tallyhos (26-passenger stagecoaches), and surreys. In 1915, some 3,000 horses were in use within the park! Most "dudes" paid approximately $50 for a six-day tour that included transportation, meals, and lodging at the hotels. They paid another $2.50 for the privilege of sailing across Lake Yellowstone on the steamship *Zillah.* By contrast, another group, the "sagebrushers," came to Yellowstone in smaller numbers, arriving in their own wagons or hiring a coach to transport them between the "Wylie Way" campgrounds. These seasonal tent camps were scattered around the park, providing an inexpensive ($35 for a seven-day tour) way to see the sights. Even as early as 1908, Yellowstone was being seen by 18,000 visitors a year.

The Northern Pacific was still intent upon carving Yellowstone into a moneymaking resort, even going so far as to propose an electric railroad, to be powered by a dam at the falls of the Yellowstone River. Fortunately, equally powerful forces—notably Gen. Philip Sheridan and naturalist Joseph Bird Grinnell—saw through their designs and thwarted each attempt to bring railroads into Yellowstone. Still, the Northern Pacific's interests were represented by its indirect control of many of Yellowstone's hotels, stagecoaches, wagons, and other vehicles used to transport tourists.

All this changed when the first car was allowed through the gate on August 1, 1915. (Entrance fees were a surprisingly stiff $5 for single-seat vehicles and $7.50 for five-passenger cars.) Almost immediately, it became clear that horses and cars could not mix, and motor buses replaced the old coaches. From then on, the park would be increasingly a place for "autoists." Interestingly, within a year the park would come under the jurisdiction of the newly created National Park Service.

THE PARK SERVICE TAKES OVER

After years of army control, supporters of a separate National Park Service finally had their way in 1916. The congressional act created a dual role for the new park system: to "conserve the scenery" and to "provide for the enjoyment of the same," a contradictory mandate that would later lead to all sorts of conflicts. The first couple of years were tenuous, as management flip-flopped between the army and civilians; the final changeover came in 1918 and ended three decades of military supervision. The management of Yellowstone fell on the shoulders of two men, Horace M. Albright and his mentor,

THE YELLOWSTONE FIRES OF 1988

Many will long remember the summer of 1988 as the year that fires seared Yellowstone National Park. TV reporters flocked to the park, pronouncing the destruction of America's most famous national wonder as they stood before trees turned into towering torches and 27,000-foot clouds of black smoke. Newspaper headlines screamed, "Park Sizzles," "Winds Whip Fiery Frenzy Out of Control," and "Firestorms Blacken Yellowstone." Residents of nearby towns complained of lost tourism dollars, choking smoke, and intentionally lit backfires that threatened their homes and businesses. Wyoming politicians berated the Park Service's "Let Burn" policy; President Reagan expressed astonishment that fires were ever allowed to burn in the national parks, though the policy had been in place for 16 years. Perhaps the most enduring image is from a forest that had been blown down by tornado-force winds in 1984 and then burned by the wind-whipped fires of 1988. The media ate it up, with one headline reading, "Total Destruction: Intense Heat and Flames from the Fires in Yellowstone Left Nothing but Powdered Ash and Charcoal Near Norris Junction." Unfortunately, the real story behind the fires of '88 was lost in this media feeding frenzy.

A Century of Change

In reality, these fires were not unprecedented; we were just fortunate enough to witness a spectacle of nature that may not occur for another 300 years. When Yellowstone National Park was established in 1872, most of the land was carpeted with a mixture of variously aged lodgepole-pine stands established after a series of large fires. Fewer large fires, partly due to a fire-suppression policy in effect until 1972, meant that by the 1980s a third of the park's lodgepole stands were more than 200 years old. Yellowstone was ripe to burn.

Since the early 1950s, Smokey the Bear had drummed an incessant message: "Only You Can Prevent Forest Fires." Forest fires were viewed as dangerous, destructive forces that had to be stopped to protect our valuable public lands. Unfortunately, this immensely effective and generally valid ad campaign convinced the public that *all* fires were bad. Ecological research has shown not only that this is wrong, but that putting out all fires can sometimes create conditions far more dangerous than if fires had been allowed to burn in the first place. Fire, like the other processes that have affected Yellowstone—cataclysmic volcanic explosions, geothermal activity, and massive glaciation—is neither good nor evil. It is simply a part of the natural world that national parks are attempting to preserve. Unfortunately, national parks are no longer surrounded by similarly undeveloped land, so when fires burned in Yellowstone and adjacent Forest Service lands they also affected nearby towns and the people who made a living from tourism or logging.

Fire in Lodgepole Forests

Fire has played an important role in lodgepole-pine forests for thousands if not millions of years, and as a result the trees have evolved an unusual adaptation. Some of the cones are sealed with a resin that melts in a fire, thus releasing the seeds. The parent trees are killed, but a new generation is guaranteed by the thousands of pine seeds released to

(continued on next page)

THE YELLOWSTONE FIRES OF 1988

(continued)

the bare, nutrient-rich soil underneath the blackened overstory. Within five years the landscape is dotted with thousands of young pines, competing with a verdant cover of grasses and flowers.

Although some animals are killed in the wildfires (including, in 1988, 269 of Yellowstone's 30,000 elk), and others die from severe winter weather or a lack of food immediately after the fire, the decades immediately following major fires create conditions that are unusually rich for many animals. Wildlife diversity in lodgepole forests reaches a peak within the first 25 years after a fire as woodpeckers, mountain bluebirds, and other birds feed on insects in the dead trees, and elk and bears graze on the lush grasses.

As the forest ages, a dense thicket of trees develops, keeping light from reaching the forest floor and making it difficult for understory plants to survive. These trees are eventually thinned by disease and windthrow, creating openings in the forest, but after 200-300 years without fire, lodgepole forests become a tangle of fallen trees that are difficult to walk through, are of lesser value to many animals, and burn easily. They also become susceptible to attacks by bark beetles, such as those that killed thousands of acres of trees in Yellowstone starting in the 1960s and continuing through the 1980s. These beetle-killed trees added to the fuel available to burn once a fire started.

Yellowstone in 1988

Yellowstone's 1988 fires were due not just to the heavy fuel loading from aging forests but also to weather conditions that were the driest and windiest on record. The winter of 1987-88 had been a mild one, and by spring there was a moderate to severe drought in the park, lessened only by above-normal rainfall in April and May. Since 1972, when Yellowstone Park officials first began allowing certain lightning fires to burn in backcountry areas, the acreage burned had totaled less than two percent of the park. (Mistakenly called a "let burn" policy, the natural fire program actually involved close monitoring of these lightning-ignited fires to determine when and if a fire should be suppressed. All human-caused fires were immediately suppressed, as were any that threatened property or life.)

When the first lightning fires of the 1988 season began in late May, those in the backcountry areas were allowed to burn, as fire management officials anticipated normal summer weather conditions. Many went out on their own, but when June and July came and the rains failed to materialize, the fires began to spread rapidly. Alarmed park officials declared them wildfires and sent crews to put them out. (Ironically, the largest fire, the North Fork/Wolf Lake Complex, was started by a logger outside the park who tossed a lit cigarette to the ground. Although firefighters immediately attacked the blaze, it consumed more than 500,000 acres.) As the summer progressed, more and more firefighters were called in, eventually totaling over 25,000 personnel, at a cost exceeding $120 million. Firefighters managed to protect most park buildings but had little effect on the forest fires themselves. Experts say that conditions in the summer of 1988 were so severe that even if firefighters had immediately responded to all the natural fires, it would likely have made little difference. Yellowstone has experienced these massive fires in the past and will again in the future, no matter what humans do.

Out of Control

August brought worsening conditions with each passing day. Winds blew steadily at 20-40 miles an hour, and gusts to 70 mph threw firebrands two miles in beyond the firefront, across fire lines, roads, and even over the Lewis River Canyon. The amount of moisture in the large logs was less than that in kiln-dried wood. By mid-August, more than 25 fires were burning simultaneously across the park and in surrounding national forests, with many joining together to create massive complexes such as the Clover-Mist Fire, the Snake River Complex, and the North Fork/Wolf Lake Complex. On a single day-September 7-more than 100,000 acres burned. Also torched that day were 20 cabins and outbuildings in the vicinity of Old Faithful (out of the more than 400 structures there). Fortunately, all the major historical buildings were spared. The fires seemed poised to consume the remainder of Yellowstone, but four days later the season's first snow carpeted the park. Within a few days firefighters had the upper hand.

A Transformed Landscape

The fires had burned nearly 800,000 acres—more than a third of the park—plus another 600,000 acres on adjacent Forest Service lands. Of the park total, 41% were canopy fires in which all the trees were killed, and another 35% were a mixture of ground fires and canopy fires. The remainder were lighter burns. Less than a tenth of one percent of the land was burned hot enough to sterilize the soil. The fires killed countless small mammals, along with at least 269 elk, nine bison, six black bears, four deer, and two moose. The drought of 1988 followed by the severe winter of 1988-89 led to a large die-off of elk and bison, but their carcasses provided food for predators. Since then, wildlife populations have rebounded and may even exceed levels before the fires.

It's been over a decade since the last of the massive fires were put out, and much has changed, including the park's natural-fire program. It was replaced by a somewhat more conservative version that requires managers to provide daily certifications that fires are controllable and that they will remain "in prescription" for another 24 hours. Visitors to Yellowstone today will find dense thickets of young lodgepole pines in many areas that burned, and the first seedlings of other evergreen species starting to emerge. In other places, grasses, colorful wildflowers, forbs, and other plants dominate. Not everything burned, of course, so you'll also see many green older forests next to burned stands, creating a complex mosaic of habitats that supports a higher diversity of animal life. Once you grow accustomed to the burned areas and understand that they are a part of the natural process, they actually add interest to the park and help you appreciate Yellowstone as a functioning ecosystem rather than a static collection of plants and animals.

Take a hike through one of the burned areas to discover the wealth of new life within Yellowstone. Vistas that were long blocked by forests are now more open and will gradually become more so; by 2008 most of the standing dead trees will have fallen. The Park Service has placed informative signboards at sites around Yellowstone describing the fires and the changes they brought about. Stop by the Grant Village Visitor Center for an informative exhibit and to watch a film on the fires of 1988 and the transformations they brought about.

Stephen Mather, both of whom had been heavily involved in lobbying to create the new agency. Mather became the Park Service's first director, while Albright served as superintendent at Yellowstone and later stepped into Mather's shoes to head the agency.

Albright quickly upgraded facilities to meet the influx of motorists who demanded more camping facilities but also cabins, lodges, cafeterias, and bathhouses. Forty-six camps of one sort or another were constructed (only 12 survive today), fulfilling Albright's dream of "a motorist's paradise." The focus of the new Park Service was clearly visitation rather than preservation. Albright assembled a first-rate force of park rangers and instituted the environmental-education programs that have been the agency's hallmark ever since.

As the automobile took over Yellowstone, the railroads gradually lost their sway, and the final passenger train to the park's gateway towns stopped in 1960. In the 1950s, the Park Service initiated "Mission 66," a decade-long project to upgrade facilities and add more lodging. By the late '60s, a growing appreciation for the natural world was shifting public opinion away from such developments, and the 1973 master plan scaled back proposed developments. From day one, Yellowstone National Park had been set up for what Edward Abbey called "industrial tourism." The park had come into existence in part because of a railroad promoter who hoped to gain from its development, and it grew to maturity on a diet of roads, hotels, and curio shops. In recent years, Americans have taken a second look at this heritage and have begun to wonder which matters more: providing a public playground or preserving an area that is unique on this planet. The inherent conflict between the need for public facilities and services in Yellowstone and the survival of a functioning ecosystem will continue to create a tug-of-war between various factions.

Certainly the most famous recent event was the series of massive fires that swept across nearly half of Yellowstone in 1988. The land has recovered surprisingly well since then, and in recent years other issues came to the fore: wolf reintroduction, bison being killed on the park boundaries, snowmobile and other winter use, and problems caused by exotic species and fish disease. There's always something stewing in the mud pots of Yellowstone! Some things have been improving in recent years, including efforts to repair aging roads and to replace outdated buildings in the park. Despite any problems and controversies, the park is just as fascinating as ever. The geysers never cease to amaze, the scenery remains majestic, Grand Canyon of the Yellowstone is still just as stunning, and the superb wildlife-viewing continues to make this the Serengeti of America.

TOURING YELLOWSTONE

Yellowstone is perhaps the most accessible national park in America. Nearly all the famous sights are within a couple hundred feet of the Grand Loop Road, a 142-mile figure-eight through the middle of the park. The speed limit on all park roads is a vigilantly enforced 45 mph (or less); exceed the limit and you're likely to get a ticket! Whatever you do, *don't* see Yellowstone at 45 miles an hour; that's like seeing the Louvre from a passing train.

For all too many visitors, Yellowstone becomes a checklist of places to visit, geysers to watch, and animals to see. This tends to inspire an attitude that treats this great national treasure as a drive-through theme park, where the animals come out to perform and the geyser eruptions are predicted so everyone can be there on time. If you're one of this crowd, give yourself a giant kick in the rear and take a walk, even if it is just around Upper Geyser Basin where you see something beyond Old Faithful.

The following loop tour of Yellowstone begins in the south and traces a clockwise path around the Grand Loop with a number of side trips. Although it is possible to follow this sequence (or some variation) the entire distance, a far better way to learn about Yellowstone is to stop for a while in the places that are the most interesting to you and really explore them, rather than trying to see everything in a cursory way. If you have the time, the entire park is well worth visiting, but if you only have a day or two, pick a couple of spots and see them right. And don't just check out the views everyone else sees; find a nearby trail and do a little exploring on your own. If you are planning a trip to the area, try to set aside a bare minimum of three days in Yellowstone.

Most roads in Yellowstone close with the first heavy snows of early November and usually open again by mid-May. The roads connecting Mammoth to West Yellowstone open first, and Dunraven Pass is plowed last. Only the road between Mammoth and Cooke City is kept open all year. If you're planning a trip early or late in the season, call the park for current road conditions; tel. (307) 344-7381, ext. 5, and then ext. 2. The same information can be found on the park webpage: www.nps.gov/yell.

SOUTH ENTRANCE ROAD

The South Entrance Station consists of several log structures right along the Snake River. Just 1.5 miles beyond the entrance is an easily missed turnout where you can walk down to 30-foot-high **Moose Falls.** Beyond this, the road climbs up a long, gentle ramp to Pitchstone Plateau, passing green forests of lodgepole pine. Stop at a turnout to look back at the majestic Tetons. Abruptly, this gentle country is broken by the edge of **Lewis River Canyon,** with rhyolite walls that up to 600 feet. The fires of 1988 burned hot through much of this area, and dead trees line both sides of the canyon in all directions, though young trees are now carpeting many areas.

The road parallels the river for the next seven miles. Nearly everyone stops for a look at 29-foot-high **Lewis Falls.** Camping is available at the south end of **Lewis Lake,** which, like the lake, falls, river, and canyon are all named for the Lewis and Clark expedition's Meriwether Lewis. Lewis Lake is the park's third-largest body of water (after Yellowstone Lake and Shoshone Lake) and is popular with canoeists, kayakers, and anglers. The clear waters contain brown trout and Mackinaw (lake trout). Approximately four miles north of Lewis Lake, the highway tops the Continental Divide, 7,988 feet above sea level. This is one of three such crossings that roads make within Yellowstone.

Day-hikes in the Lewis Lake Area

Two trailheads a mile north of Lewis Lake provide access west to Shoshone Lake and east to Heart Lake. At the Dogshead Trailhead you can choose between two trails to Shoshone Lake, both of which cross land burned in the 1988 fires. The four-mile-long **Dogshead Trail** is more direct, while the seven-mile **Lewis Channel Trail** takes a much more scenic trek via the channel that connects Shoshone and Lewis Lakes. This slow-flowing channel is popular with anglers who come to fish for brown and cutthroat trout during the fall spawning season, and it's also used by canoeists and kayakers heading into Shoshone Lake. Once you reach Shoshone Lake, follow Delacy Creek Trail northward along the shore for fine vistas. The area gets considerable overnight use, and campsites are scattered around the lake.

Heart Lake Trailhead is on the opposite side of the road and south a few hundred feet from Dogshead Trailhead. Heart Lake is a scenic and interesting area that gets considerable day-use, but it's probably best visited on a backpacking trip of several days or longer since it's an eight-mile (one-way) hike to the lake. Be sure to bring water with you. Hardcore hikers may want to attempt a day-trip all the way to the summit of Mt. Sheridan, but this is 22 miles roundtrip, and you gain (and lose) 2,700 feet in elevation along the way. The Heart Lake area is closed to access before July because of grizzly activity. For details on longer hikes in the Heart Lake and Shoshone Lake areas, see Into the Backcountry later in this chapter.

Grant Village

Named for American president Ulysses S. Grant, who established Yellowstone, Grant Village was built in the 1980s to replace facilities at Fishing Bridge, an area of important grizzly habitat. Unfortunately, instead of one bad development, Yellowstone now has two—a number of the buildings at Fishing Bridge still stand. Unlike some of the more historic places in Yellowstone where a natural rusticity prevailed, Grant Village has less charm than most Kmarts. A steak house restaurant juts out along the shore of Yellowstone Lake, and the lodging at Grant Village forms a chintzy condo backdrop. Other facilities include a campground, store, gas station, and post office. Much of the area around here was consumed in the 1988 Snake River Fire; unfortunately, the fire missed this scar on the Yellowstone landscape.

Grant Village Visitor Center, tel. (307) 242-2650, houses an interesting exhibit and film on the fires of 1988. These provide a good background to help understand the changes taking place as the burned areas recover. (See the special topic The Yellowstone Fires of 1988 for an overview.) The visitor center is open daily 8 a.m.-7 p.m. Memorial Day to Labor Day, and daily 9 a.m.-5 p.m. in September. It's closed from early October to Memorial Day. (Hours may vary depending upon park budgets and staffing.)

West Thumb

If you look at a map of Yellowstone Lake, it's possible to imagine the lake as a giant hand with three mangled fingers heading south and a gnarled thumb hitching west. Hence the name West Thumb. This portion of Yellowstone Lake is the deepest (to 390 feet) and is actually a caldera that filled with water after erupting 150,000 years ago. There is still considerable heat just below the surface, as revealed by **West Thumb Geyser Basin.** A short loop trail leads through steaming hot springs and pools. Right on the shore is **Fishing Cone,** where tourists once caught fish and then plopped them in the cone to be cooked; after a number of clowning tourists were injured, the Park Service put a stop to this stunt. The **West Thumb Information Station** is open daily 9 a.m.-5 p.m. from Memorial Day through late September and has a small bookstore. (Hours may vary depending upon park budgets and staffing.) In wintertime the station is used as a warming hut.

WEST THUMB TO UPPER GEYSER BASIN

Heading west from West Thumb, the highway climbs over the Continental Divide twice. Most of these forests escaped the 1988 fires. A few miles beyond the eastern crossing of the divide is a turnout at **Shoshone Point,** where you catch glimpses of Shoshone Lake and the Tetons. In 1914, highwayman Ed Trafton (his real name was Ed Harrington) held up 15 stagecoaches as they passed by this point carrying tourists. He got away with $915.35 in cash and $130 in jewelry but made the rather obvious mistake of posing for photos. He was caught the following year and spent five years in Leavenworth. When he died, a letter in his pocket claimed that he had been Owen Wister's model for the Virginian. Others suspected that he was more likely to have been Wister's model for the villain, Trampas.

DeLacy Creek Trail provides access to Shoshone Lake—Yellowstone's largest backcountry lake—and begins at the picnic area between the two passes. It's three miles to the lake, which is circled by more trails. Keep your eyes open for moose and other animals in the meadows along the way. The western crossing of the Continental Divide is at **Craig Pass,** where a tiny pond (Isa Lake) empties into both the Atlantic and Pacific Oceans through its two outlet streams.

Approximately 14 miles beyond West Thumb, pull off to see the Firehole River as it drops over **Kepler Cascades.** Just to the east, a wide and partly paved trail (actually an old road) leads five miles roundtrip to **Lone Star Geyser.** This is a popular route for bicyclists in the summer and skiers in the winter. Bikes are not allowed beyond the geyser. Lone Star Geyser erupts every three hours from a distinctive nine-foot-high cone, with eruptions generally reaching 45 feet and lasting for 30 minutes. Hikers can also get to Lone Star via the Howard Eaton Trail out of Old Faithful. For a longer hike, you can continue south from Lone Star on **Shoshone Lake Trail** to Shoshone Lake, eight fairly easy miles from the main road. (See Into the Backcountry later in this chapter for other Shoshone Lake hikes.)

OLD FAITHFUL AREA CLIMATE

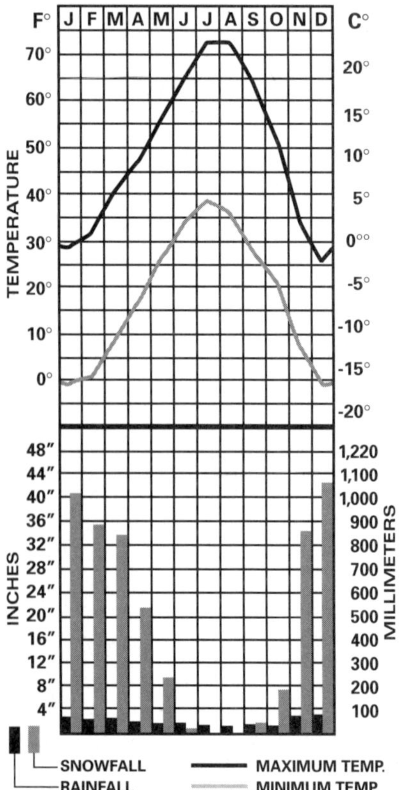

Average Maximum Temp.	**49.4°F**
Average Minimum Temp.	**18.1°F**
Annual Rainfall	**25.38″**
Annual Snowfall	**228.3″**

UPPER GEYSER BASIN

As you approach Old Faithful from either direction, the two-lane road suddenly widens into four, and a cloverleaf exit takes you to Yellowstone's most fabulous sight. Welcome to Upper Geyser Basin, home of Old Faithful, some 400 buildings of all sizes, and a small town's worth of people. For many folks, this is the heart of Yellowstone, and a visit to the park without seeing Old Faithful is like a baseball game without the national anthem. If you came to Yellowstone to see the wonders of nature, you're going to see more than your share here, but you'll probably have to share your share with hundreds of other folks. On busy summer days more than 25,000 visitors come through the Old Faithful area! Fortunately, the Upper Geyser Basin contains the largest concentration of geysers in the world, and the adventurous will even discover places almost nobody ever visits. But be very careful—the crust can be dangerously thin around some of the hot springs and geysers, and people have been badly scalded and even killed by missteps. Stay on the boardwalks and trails.

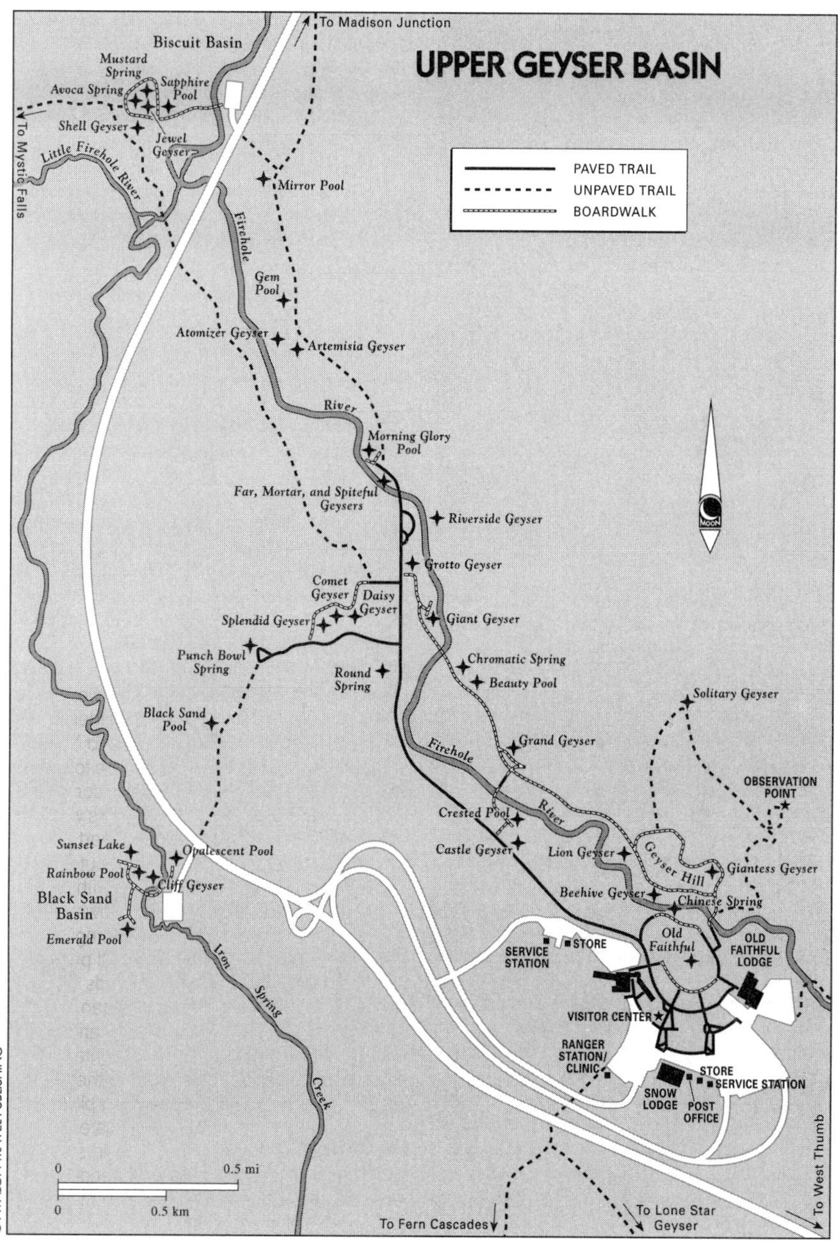
UPPER GEYSER BASIN
PAVED TRAIL
UNPAVED TRAIL
BOARDWALK
To Madison Junction
Biscuit Basin
Mustard Spring
Sapphire Pool
Avoca Spring
Shell Geyser
Jewel Geyser
To Mystic Falls
Little Firehole River
Mirror Pool
Firehole
Gem Pool
Atomizer Geyser
Artemisia Geyser
River
Morning Glory Pool
Far, Mortar, and Spiteful Geysers
Riverside Geyser
Grotto Geyser
Comet Geyser
Daisy Geyser
Splendid Geyser
Giant Geyser
Punch Bowl Spring
Round Spring
Chromatic Spring
Beauty Pool
Solitary Geyser
Black Sand Pool
Grand Geyser
Firehole
OBSERVATION POINT
Crested Pool
River
Castle Geyser
Lion Geyser
Geyser Hill
Giantess Geyser
Sunset Lake
Opalescent Pool
Rainbow Pool
Cliff Geyser
Beehive Geyser
Chinese Spring
Black Sand Basin
Emerald Pool
Old Faithful
OLD FAITHFUL LODGE
SERVICE STATION
STORE
Iron
Spring
Creek
VISITOR CENTER
RANGER STATION/ CLINIC
STORE
SERVICE STATION
SNOW LODGE
POST OFFICE
0
0.5 mi
0
0.5 km
To Fern Cascades
To Lone Star Geyser
To West Thumb
MOON

Yellowstone's most famous geyser—Old Faithful—erupts about once every 80 minutes.

Old Faithful

The one sight seen by virtually everyone who comes to Yellowstone is Old Faithful Geyser, easily the most visited geyser in the world. Old Faithful is neither the tallest nor the most frequently erupting geyser in Yellowstone, but it always provides a good show and is both highly accessible and fairly predictable. Contrary to the rumors, Old Faithful never erupted "every hour on the hour," but for many years its period was a little over an hour. It has slowed down in recent years and is now averaging around 80 minutes per cycle. In general, the longer the length of the eruption, the longer the interval till the next eruption. Check at the visitor center for the latest prognostications on this and other geysers in the basin.

An almost level paved path circles Old Faithful, providing many different angles from which to view the eruptions, although none of these is particularly close to the geyser because of the danger from hot water. Along the north side is **Chinese Spring,** named in 1885 for a short-lived laundry operation. Apparently, the washman had filled the spring with clothes and soap, not knowing that soap can cause geysers to erupt. One newspaper correspondent claimed—though the tale obviously suffered from embellishment and racism—that,

> *The soap awakened the imprisoned giant; with a roar that made the earth tremble, and a shriek of a steam whistle, a cloud of steam and a column of boiling water shot up into the air a hundred feet, carrying soap, raiment, tent and Chinaman along with the rush, and dropping them at various intervals along the way.*

Old Faithful provides a textbook example of geyser activity. The first signs of life are when water begins to splash out of the vent in what is called preplay. This splashing can last up to 20 minutes, but it's generally only a few minutes before the real thing. The water quickly spears into the sky, reaching 100-180 feet for two to five minutes before rapidly dropping down. During a typical eruption, between 3,700 and 8,400 gallons of water are sent skyward.

On any given summer day, the scene at Old Faithful is almost comical. Just before the predicted eruption time, the benches encircling the south and east sides are jammed with hundreds of people waiting expectantly for the geyser to erupt, and with each tentative spray the camera shutters begin to click. Listen closely and you'll hear half the languages of Europe and Asia. Once the action is over, there is a mad rush back into the visitor center, the stores, and Old Faithful Inn, and within a few minutes the benches are virtually empty. A tale is told of two concessioner employees who once decided to have fun at Old Faithful by placing a large crank atop a box and putting the contraption near the geyser. When they knew it was ready to erupt, they ran out and turned the crank just as Old Faithful shot into the air. Their employer failed to find humor in the prank, and both were fired, or so the story claims.

Geyser Hill Area

Upper Geyser Basin is laced with paved trails that lead to dozens of nearby geysers and hot springs. The easiest path loops around Geyser

Hill, just across the Firehole River from Old Faithful. Here are more than 40 different geysers. Check at the visitor center to get an idea of current activity and predicted eruptions, and while there pick up the excellent Upper Geyser Basin map (50 cents), which describes some of them. Several geysers are particularly noteworthy. When it plays, **Beehive Geyser** (it has a tall, beehive-shaped cone) vents water as high as 180 feet into the air. These spectacular eruptions vary in frequency; one time you visit they may be 10 days apart, while the next time you come they may be happening twice every 24 hours or so. **Lion Geyser Group** consists of four different interconnected geysers with varying periods of activity. Listen for the roaring sound when Lion is ready to erupt. **Giantess Geyser** may not be active for years at a time—or may erupt several times a year—but the eruptions are sensationally powerful, sending water 100-200 feet skyward. **Doublet Pool** is a beautiful deep-blue pool that is a favorite of photographers. Not far away is **Sponge Geyser,** which rockets water 2.29 billion angstroms into the air (that's nine inches for the nonscientific crowd). It's considered the smallest named geyser in Yellowstone and gets its title by sending up a spurt of water big enough to be mopped up with a sponge.

From the surface of a rocky plain or table, burst forth columns of water of various dimensions, projected high in the air, accompanied by loud explosions, and sulphurous vapors, which were highly disagreeable to the smell. . . . The largest of these wonderful fountains, projects a column of boiling water several feet in diameter, to the height of more than one hundred and fifty feet. . . . After having witnessed three of them, I ventured near enough to put my hand into the water of its basin, but withdrew it instantly, for the heat of the water in this immense couldron, was altogether to great for comfort, and the agitation of the water, disagreeable effluvium continually exuding, and the hollow unearthly rumbling under the rock on which I stood, so ill accorded with my notions of personal safety, that I retreated back precipitately to a respectful distance.

—YELLOWSTONE'S FIRST "TOURIST,"
ANGUS FERRIS, IN 1833

Observation Point Loop Trail splits off shortly after you cross the bridge on the way to Geyser Hill and climbs to an excellent overlook where you can watch eruptions of Old Faithful. This is also a good place to view the effects of, and recovery from, the 1988 North Fork Fire. It's two miles rountrip to Observatin Point from the visitor center. Another easy trail splits off from this path to **Solitary Geyser**—actually just a pool that periodically burps four-foot splashes of hot water. This is not a natural geyser. In 1915, the hot spring here was tapped to provide water for Old Faithful Geyser Bath, a concession that lasted until 1948. The lowering of the water level in the pool completely changed the plumbing system of the hot springs and turned it into a geyser that at one time shot 25 feet in the air. The system still hasn't recovered, although water levels have been restored for more than 40 years.

More Geyser Gazing

Another easy, paved path follows the Firehole River downstream, looping back along the other side for a total distance of three miles. Other trails head off from this loop to the Fairy Falls Trailhead, Biscuit Basin, and Black Sand Basin. The loop is a very popular wintertime ski path, and portions are open to bikes in the summer. Twelve-foot-high **Castle Geyser** does indeed resemble a ruined old castle. Because of its size and the slow accretion of sinter (silica) to form this cone, it is believed to be somewhere between 5,000 and 50,000 years old. Castle sends up a column of water and steam 90 feet into the air and usually erupts every 10-12 hours. Check at the visitor center for current activity.

Daisy Geyser is farther down the path and off to the left. It is usually one of the most predictable of the geysers, erupting to 75 feet approximately every 90-115 minutes. The water shoots out at a sharp angle and is visible all over the basin, making this a real crowd pleaser. Just east of

Daisy is **Radiator Geyser,** which isn't much to look at—eruptions to two feet—but was named when this area was a parking lot and the sudden eruption under a car led people to think its radiator was overheating. A personal favorite, **Grotto Geyser** is certainly the weirdest of all the geysers, having formed around a tangle of long-petrified tree stumps. It is in eruption a third of the time, but most eruptions only reach 10 feet.

Look for **Riverside Geyser** across the Firehole from the path and not far below Grotto. This picturesque geyser arches spray 75 feet over the river and is one of the most predictable, with 20-minute-long eruptions approximately every six hours. The paved trail crosses the river and ends at **Morning Glory Pool.** For many years, the main road passed this colorful pool, which became something of a wishing well for not just coins but trash, rocks, logs, and other debris. Because of this junk, the pool began to cool, and the beautiful blue color is now tinged by brown and green algae, despite efforts to remove the debris.

Turning back at Morning Glory, recross the bridge and head left where the path splits at Grotto Geyser. **Giant Geyser** is on the left along the river. Years may pass between eruptions of Giant (or it might erupt every week or so), but when it does go, the name rings true, since the water often tops 200 feet. Cross the river again and pass **Beauty Pool** and **Chromatic Pool,** which are connected below the ground so that one declines as the other rises. Very pretty. **Grand Geyser** is a wonderful sight. The water column erupts in a towering burst every 7-15 hours, with a series of bursts lasting 10 minutes or so and sometimes reaching 200 feet. It's the tallest predictable geyser on the planet. When Grand isn't playing, watch for smaller eruptions from nearby **Turban** and **Sawmill** Geysers. Cross the river again just beyond Grand Geyser and pass **Crested Pool** on your way back to Castle Geyser. The pool contains deep-blue water that is constantly boiling, preventing the survival of algae.

Black Sand Basin

Just a mile west of Old Faithful is Black Sand Basin, a small cluster of geysers and hot springs. Most enjoyable is unpredictable **Cliff Geyser,** which often sends a spray of hot water 25-30 feet over Iron Spring Creek. Three colorful pools are quite interesting in the basin: **Emerald Pool, Rainbow Pool,** and **Sunset Lake. Handkerchief Pool** is now just a small spouter but was famous for many years as a place where visitors could drop a handkerchief in one end and then recover it later at another vent. In 1929, vandals jammed logs in the pool, destroying this little game. The pool was covered with gravel in subsequent eruptions of Rainbow Pool.

Biscuit Basin and Mystic Falls

Three miles north of Old Faithful, this basin is named for biscuitlike formations that were found in one of the pools; they were destroyed in an eruption following the 1959 Hebgen Lake earthquake. From the parking lot, the trail leads across the Firehole River to **Sapphire Pool** and then past **Jewel Geyser,** which typically erupts every 10 minutes to a height of 15-20 feet. The boardwalk follows a short loop through the other sights of Biscuit Basin.

From the west end of the boardwalk, a one-mile trail leads to where the Little Firehole River cascades 100 feet over **Mystic Falls.** You can switchback farther up the trail to the top of the falls and then connect with another trail for the loop back to Biscuit Basin (three miles roundtrip). This is a very nice short hike and can be lengthened into a trip to **Little Firehole Meadows** (10 miles roundtrip), where bison are often seen in the summer.

Old Faithful Inn

Matching one of the great sights of the natural world is one of America's grandest hotels, Old Faithful Inn. Said to be the largest log structure of its kind in existence, the inn has delighted generations of visitors and continues to enthrall all who enter. The building was designed by Robert Reamer and built in the winter of 1903-04. Its steeply angled roofline reaches seven stories high, with gables jutting out from the sides and flags flying from the roof. Surprisingly, the hotel does not face the geyser. Instead, it was built facing sideways to allow newly arriving visitors the opportunity to view the geyser as they stepped from carriages. As you open the rustic split-log front doors with their handwrought hardware, you enter a world of the past. The central lobby towers more than 75 feet overhead and is

Historic Old Faithful Inn is one of the most fascinating buildings in any national park.

dominated by a massive four-sided stone fireplace that required 500 tons of stone from a nearby quarry. Four overhanging balconies extend above, each bordered by posts made from gnarled lodgepole burls found within the park. Above the fireplace is an enormous clock designed by Reamer and built on the site by a blacksmith. Reamer also designed the two wings that were added in 1913 and 1928.

On warm summer evenings, visitors stand out on the porch where they can watch Old Faithful erupting or sit inside at the handcrafted tables to write letters as music spills from the grand piano. It's enough to warm the heart of even the most cynical curmudgeon. A good restaurant is on the premises, along with a rustic but comfortable bar, a gift shop, fast-food eatery, ice cream shop, and ATM. Free 45-minute **tours** of Old Faithful Inn are given daily at 9:30 a.m., 11 a.m., 2 p.m., and 3:30 p.m. from mid-May to late September. Meet at the fireplace in the lobby. Old Faithful Inn closes during the winter; it would be hard to imagine trying to heat such a cavern when it's 30° below zero outside!

Another nearby building of interest is **Old Faithful Lodge.** Built in 1928, this is the large stone-and-log building just south of the geyser of the same name. The giant fireplace inside is a joy on frosty evenings, and cafeteria windows face the geyser. Much newer, but an instant classic, is the award-winning **Old Faithful Snow Lodge,** which opened in 1999. This large building offers a sense of rustic elegance, with heavy timbers, a window-lined main entrance, a large stone fireplace, overstuffed couches, and handmade wrought-iron light fixtures and accents. It is one of just two places (the other being Mammoth Hot Springs Hotel) open in the winter months. The new Snow Lodge replaces a dowdy utilitarian structure that was torn down in 1998.

Old Faithful Services

The Park Service's **Old Faithful Visitor Center,** tel. (307) 545-2750, is generally open mid-April to early November and mid-December to mid-March. It's open daily 8 a.m.-7 p.m. from Memorial Day to Labor Day, daily 8 a.m.-6 p.m. the rest of September, and daily 9 a.m.-5 p.m. at other times. (Hours may vary depending upon park budgets and staffing.) Among the films about Yellowstone shown throughout the day here is a fascinating new production (narrated by Walter Cronkite) on the lifeforms that survive in Yellowstone's hot springs. The center has a fine selection of books, maps, and other Yellowstone publications, and it also posts predictions for six of the major geysers (including Old Faithful) during the summer. The rangers can provide you with all sorts of other info, from where to see bighorn sheep to where to find the restrooms. A much-needed new visitor center is in the planning stages for Old Faithful, but don't expect to see it till 2005 or so, since the Park Service needs to raise $15 million for its construction.

Backcountry permits are available from the ranger station; food, supplies, and postcards can be purchased at either of the two Hamilton Stores. Old Faithful Inn has a gift shop, restaurant, snack bar, ice cream parlor, lounge, and ATM. Cafeteria meals, espresso, and baked goods are available at Old Faithful Lodge, and Old Faithful Snow Lodge houses a restaurant and snack bar. Both of these also have gift shops. In addition, the Old Faithful area has two gas stations, a post office, photo shop, and medical clinic. See Yellowstone Camping and Lodging later in this chapter for lodging details. Note that camping is *not* available in the Old Faithful area, and it's illegal to stay overnight in the parking lots. The closest campgrounds are in Madison (16 miles north) and Grant Village (19 miles southeast).

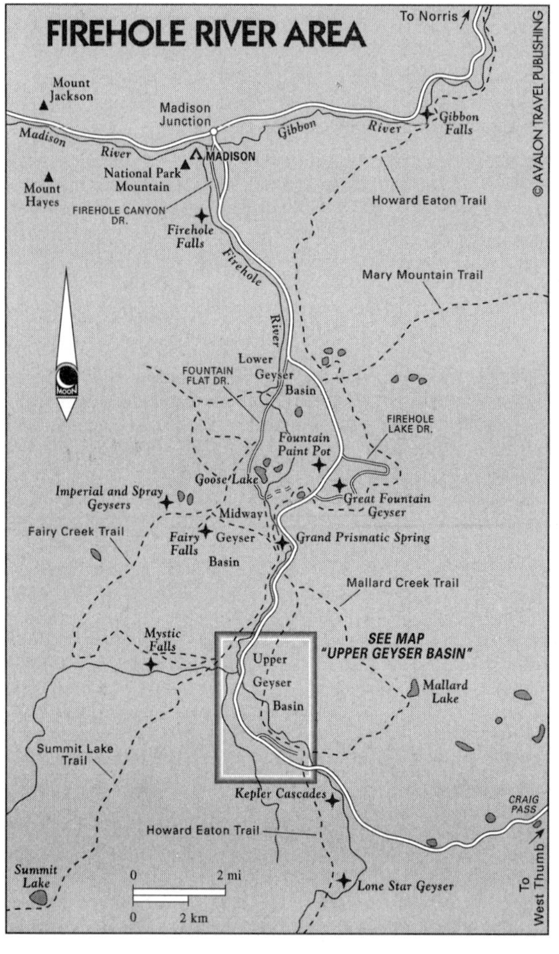

MIDWAY AND LOWER GEYSER BASINS

Heading north from Upper Geyser Basin, the road follows the Firehole River past Midway and Lower Geyser Basins, both of which are quite interesting. This stretch of the river is very popular with fly-fishing enthusiasts, and several side roads provide access to a variety of hot springs and other sights.

Fairy Falls

Just south of Midway Geyser Basin (or 4.5 miles north of the Old Faithful Interchange) is a turnoff that leads to the southern end of Fountain Freight Road. This four-mile-long trail is closed to cars, but it's a great place for mountain-bikers and those out for a relatively level walk. A steel bridge crosses the Firehole River at the trailhead, and the road soon passes the west side of Grand Prismatic Spring; rough trails lead up the hillside for a better view. A mile up from the trailhead you'll come to **Fairy Falls Trail** on your left. It's an easy 1.5-mile walk to the falls, a 200-foot ribbon of water that cascades into a large pool. The hike to Fairy Falls can be combined with longer treks to Little Firehole Meadow and Mystic Falls (both described above) or to a pair of small peaks called Twin Buttes. A half mile beyond Fairy Falls is **Imperial Geyser,** which was active in the 1920s and from 1966-84, but is now just a boiling pool. Nearby **Spray Geyser** erupts frequently, sending water six feet in the air. For a longer version of the hike to Fairy Falls (10 miles roundtrip), start from the north end, where Fountain Flat Drive ends.

Midway Geyser Basin

Midway is a large and readily accessible geyser basin with a loop path leading to most of the sights. **Excelsior Geyser** is actually an enormous hot spring that pours 4,000 gallons per minute of steaming water into the Firehole River. The water is a deep turquoise-blue. During the 1880s, this was a truly stupendous geyser, with explosions that reached 380 feet in the air and were almost as wide. These violent eruptions apparently damaged the plumbing system that fed them, and the geyser was dormant for nearly a century until smaller eruptions took place in 1985. At 370 feet across, **Grand Prismatic Spring** is Yellowstone's largest hot spring. The brilliant reds and yellows around the edges of the blue pool are from algae and bacteria that can tolerate temperatures of 170° F. It's difficult to get a good perspective on this spring from the ground; see aerial photos to really appreciate its pulchritude.

At length we came to a boiling Lake about 300 ft in diameter forming nearly a complete circle as we approached on the south side The steam which arose from it was of three distinct Colors from the west side for one third of the diameter it was white, in the middle it was pale red, and the remaining third on the east light sky blue Whether it was something peculiar in the state of the atmosphere the day being cloudy or whether it was some Chemical properties contained in the water which produced this phenomenon I am unable to say and shall leave the explanation to some scientific tourist who may have the Curiosity to visit this place at some future period—The water was of deep indigo blue boiling like an imense caldron running over the white rock which had formed the edges to the height of 4 or 5 feet from the surface of the earth sloping gradually for 60 or 70 feet. What a field of speculation this presents for chemist and geologist.

—MOUNTAIN MAN
OSBORNE RUSSELL DESCRIBING
GRAND PRISMATIC SPRING IN 1839

Firehole Lake Drive

This road (one-way heading north) goes three miles through Lower Geyser Basin, the park's most extensive geyser basin. **Great Fountain Geyser** is truly one of the most spectacular geysers in Yellowstone. Charles Cook, of the 1869 Cook-Folsom-Peterson Expedition, recalled his impression of the geyser: "We could not contain our enthusiasm; with one accord we all took off our hats and yelled with all our might." Modern-day visitors would not be faulted for reacting similarly.

Great Fountain erupts every 8-12 hours (although it can be irregular) and usually reaches 100 feet, but has been known to blast over 200 feet. Eruptions begin approximately an hour after water starts to overflow from the crater and last for 45-60 minutes in a series of decreasingly active eruptive cycles; but don't leave too early or you may miss the real show! Eruption predictions are posted at the geyser. While you're waiting, watch the periodic eruptions of **White Dome Geyser** just a hundred yards down the road. Because of its massive 30-foot cone, this is believed to be one of the oldest geysers in the park. Eruptions occur every 10 minutes to three hours and spray 30 feet into the air.

Another mile ahead, the road literally cuts into the mound of **Pink Cone Geyser,** which now erupts every 6-15 hours and reaches a height of 25 feet. The pink color comes from manganese oxide. Just up from here at the bend in the road is **Firehole Lake,** which discharges 3,500 gallons of water per minute into Tangled Creek, which in turn drains across the road into **Hot Lake. Steady Geyser** is unusual in that it forms both sinter (silica) and travertine (calcium carbonate) deposits. The geyser is along the edge of Hot Lake and, true to its name, erupts almost continuously, though the height is only five feet.

Firehole Lake Dr. continues another mile to its junction with the main road right across from the parking area for Fountain Paint Pot. (In the winter, Firehole Lake Dr. is popular with skiers but is closed to snowmobiles.)

Fountain Paint Pot

Always a favorite of visitors, Fountain Paint Pot seems to have a playfulness about it that belies the immense power just below the surface. Pick up a trail guide as you head up the walkway. **Silex Spring,** off to the right as you walk up the small hill, is colored by different kinds of algae and bacteria. The spring has been known to erupt as a geyser (to 20 feet) but is currently dormant. The famous Fountain Paint Pot is a few steps up the boardwalk and consists of colorful muds that change in consistency throughout the season depending upon soil moisture. The pressure from steam and gases under the Paint Pot can throw gobs of mud up to 20 feet into the air. Just north of here are fumaroles that spray steam, carbon dioxide, and hydrogen sulfide into the air. Continuing down the boardwalk, you come upon an impressive overlook above a multitude of geysers that change constantly in activity, including **Morning Geyser,** which erupts to over 150 feet. The most active is **Clepsydra Geyser,** in eruption much of the time. **Fountain Geyser** is usually active every 11 hours or so and can occasionally reach 80 feet. Very impressive, particularly at sunset. The rest of the loop trail passes dead lodgepole pines that are being petrified as the silica is absorbed, creating a bobby-socks appearance.

Fountain Flat

Fountain Flat Dr. provides access to meadows along the Firehole River and is a good place to see bison and elk. The paved road ends after a mile at a parking area, but hikers and cyclists (or skiers in winter) can continue another four miles on Old Fountain Freight Road to its junction with the main road again near Midway Geyser Basin. The road ends in a parking area near **Ojo Caliente**—a small hot springs with a big odor—right along the river. Several more hot springs are upstream from here, and the **Fairy Falls Trail** starts three miles south of the parking area. See Midway Geyser Basin above for details on this very scenic and popular day-hike.

Firehole Canyon Drive

This one-way road (south only) curves for two miles through Firehole Canyon, where dark rhyolite cliffs rise hundreds of feet above the river. The road begins just south of Madison Junction and was intensely burned in the 1988 North Fork Fire, giving the canyon's name a dual meaning. **Firehole Falls,** a 40-foot drop, is worth stopping to see, as is **Firehole Cascades** a bit farther up. Kids of all ages enjoy the very popular hot-springs-warmed swimming hole a short distance up the road. It's one of the few places along the Yellowstone road system where swimming is openly allowed (albeit not encouraged). No lifeguard, of course.

MADISON JUNCTION TO WEST YELLOWSTONE

At Madison Junction, the Gibbon and Firehole Rivers join to form the Madison River, a major tributary of the Missouri River. The 14-mile drive from Madison Junction to the West Entrance closely parallels this scenic river, in which geese, ducks, and trumpeter swans are commonly seen. Bison and elk are other critters to watch for in the open meadows. The 406,359-acre North Fork Fire of 1988 ripped through most of the Madison River country, so be ready for many blackened trees, but also expect to see many flowers in midsummer. The river is open only to fly-fishing and is considered one of the finest places in the nation to catch trout (though they can be a real challenge to fool). On warm summer evenings, you're likely to see dozens of anglers casting for wily rainbow and brown trout and mountain whitefish. **West Entrance** is the busiest of all the park entry stations, handling more than a third of the more than 3 million people who enter Yellowstone each year. The tourist town of West Yellowstone, Montana (see Gateway Towns later in this chapter), is right outside the boundary.

Madison Canyon is flanked by mountains named for two photographers who had a marked influence on Yellowstone. To the north is 8,257-foot **Mt. Jackson** (as in William H. Jackson, whose photos helped bring the area to national attention), and to the south is distinctive, 8,235-foot **Mt. Haynes,** named for the man who held the park photo concession for nearly four decades. These mountains and the surrounding slopes were created by rhyolite lava flows.

THE NORTHWEST CORNER

Highway 191 heads north from West Yellowstone, Montana, to Bozeman, passing through a small corner of Yellowstone National Park en route. There are no entrance stations or developed facilities here, but the area provides backcountry access for hikers and horsepackers from several trailheads. The drive itself is quite scenic, and the road is wide and smooth. The road enters the park approximately 10 miles north of West Yellowstone and gradually climbs through stretches that were burned in the fires of 1988 before emerging into unburned alpine meadows near tiny Divide Lake. North of here, US Hwy. 191 follows the growing Gallatin River downhill through a pretty mix of meadows, sagebrush, rocky outcrops, and forested hillsides with grassy carpets beneath. Approximately 31 miles north of West Yellowstone, the road exits Yellowstone and enters Gallatin National Forest. It's another 17 miles from here to the turnoff for Big Sky Resort or 60 miles from the park boundary to Bozeman.

Bighorn Peak Hike

If you're up for a long and challenging day-hike, climb Bighorn Peak on the northern boundary of Yellowstone. Start from the Black Butte Creek Trailhead just south of milepost 29 on US Hwy. 191. The hike is steep, rising 3,100 feet in just seven miles and providing spectacular views. Look for pieces of petrified wood along the way, but leave them in place; it's illegal to take them from the park. As an added bonus, this country was untouched by the 1988 fires. Be sure to bring plenty of water since it is nonexistent on the upper portion of this hike. It is possible to do an overnight loop trip (21 miles roundtrip) by continuing north from Bighorn Peak along the beautiful **Sky Rim Trail** and dropping back down Dailey Creek Trail to Black Butte Cutoff Trail. (A backcountry permit is required for this, however.) This connects to Black Butte Trail and your starting point. See one of the Yellowstone hiking guides for details on this hike.

MADISON JUNCTION TO NORRIS

The **Madison Information Station,** near Madison Junction, is open daily 8 a.m.-7 p.m. Memorial Day to Labor Day and daily 9 a.m.-5 p.m. from Labor Day to mid-October. Closed in winter. (Hours may vary depending upon park budgets and staffing.) A small bookstore is also here. Directly behind Madison Junction Campground is 7,500-foot **National Park Mountain,** named in honor of a fabled incident in 1870. Three explorers were gathered around the campfire, discussing the wonders that they had found in this area, when one suggested that rather than letting all these wonders pass into private hands, they should be set aside as a national park. Thus was born the concept that led to the world's first national park. The tale was passed on as the gospel truth for so long that the mountain was named in honor of this evening. Unfortunately, the story was a complete fabrication. Cynics may read something into the fact that National Park Mountain was torched by the fires of 1988.

North of Madison Junction, the road (in very poor condition when this was written) follows the Gibbon River nearly all of the 14 miles to Norris. It crosses the river five times and hangs right on the edge through Gibbon Canyon. The pretty, 84-foot-high **Gibbon Falls** is approximately five miles up the road and situated right at the edge of the enormous caldera that fills the center of Yellowstone. The 1988 fires consumed most of the trees around the falls. Another five miles beyond this, the road emerges from the canyon into grassy **Gibbon Meadows,** where elk and bison are commonly seen. The prominent peak visible to the north is 10,336-foot Mt. Holmes. On the west end of Gibbon Meadows is a barren area that contains **Sylvan Springs Geyser Basin.** No maintained trail leads to this small collection of pools and springs, but hikers sometimes head across the north end of the meadows at the Gibbon River Picnic Area. The path is wet most of the summer.

An easy half-mile trail leads to **Artist Paint Pots,** filled with colorful plopping and steaming mud pots and hot springs. Although it's a short hike, the paint pots see far fewer visitors than roadside sites, making it a nice place to escape the crowds. The forest was burned in the North

Fork Fire, so it's also a good place to see how the lodgepole pines are regenerating. Just south of the parking area for Artist Paint Pots is a trail to **Monument Geyser Basin,** where there isn't much activity, but the tall sinter cones form all sorts of bizarre shapes, including Thermos Bottle Geyser. The mile-long hike climbs 500 feet and provides views of the surrounding country. Another attraction is **Chocolate Pots,** found along the highway just north of Gibbon Meadows. The reddish-brown color comes from iron, aluminum, and manganese oxides. Just before you reach Norris, the road crosses through the appropriately named **Elk Park.**

NORRIS GEYSER BASIN

Although Old Faithful and the Upper Geyser Basin are more famous, many visitors to Yellowstone find Norris Geyser Basin equally interesting. Norris sits atop the junction of several major fault lines, providing conduits for heat from the molten lava below. Because of this, it is apparently the hottest geyser basin in North America, if not the world; a scientific team found temperatures of 459° F at 1,087 feet underground and was forced to quit drilling when the pressure threatened to destroy the drilling rig! Because of considerable sulfur (and hence sulfuric acid) in the springs and geysers, the water at Norris is quite acidic; a majority of the world's acid geysers are here. The acidic water kills lodgepole trees in the basin, creating an open, nearly barren place. Norris Basin has been around at least 115,000 years, making it the oldest of any of Yellowstone's active geyser basins. It is a constantly changing place, with small geysers seeming to come and go on an almost daily basis.

The paved trail from the oft-crowded parking area leads to **Norris Museum,** tel. (307) 344-2812, built of stone in 1929-30. The small museum houses exhibit panels on hot springs and geothermal activity and is generally open daily 8 a.m.-7 p.m. from Memorial Day to Labor Day, and daily 9 a.m.-5 p.m. from Labor Day to mid-October. (Hours may vary due to park budgets and staffing.) Pick up a detailed brochure describing the various features at Norris. Ranger-led walks are given several times a day in the summer. From the museum, the Norris Basin spreads both north and south, with two rather different trails to hike. Take the time to walk along both. The Norris Campground is only a quarter mile from the geyser basin.

Porcelain Basin

Just behind the museum is an overlook that provides an impressive view across Porcelain Basin. The path descends into the basin, along the way passing hissing steam vents, bubbling hot pools, and small geysers, including **Dark Cavern Geyser,** which erupts several times an hour to 20 feet. **Whirligig Geyser** is another one that is often active, spraying a fan of water. (Watch your glasses and camera lenses in the steam; silica deposits can be very hard to remove.) For an enjoyable short walk, follow the boardwalk around the mile-long loop. Stop to admire the bright colors in the steaming water, indicators of iron, arsenic, and other elements, along with algae and cyanobacteria.

Back Basin

A mile-long loop trail takes you to the sights within the Back Basin south of the museum. Before heading out, check at the museum for the latest on geyser activity. Most people follow the path in a clockwise direction, coming first to **Emerald Spring,** a beautiful green pool with acidic water just below boiling. A little ways farther down the path is **Steamboat Geyser.** Wait a few minutes and you're likely to see one of its minor eruptions, which may reach 40 feet. On rare occasions, Steamboat erupts with a fury that is hard to believe, blasting over 300 feet into the air—more than twice the height of Old Faithful—making this the world's tallest geyser. Eruptions can last up to 20 minutes, enough time to pour out a million gallons of water, and the explosions have been heard up to 14 miles away. Steamboat's unforgettable eruptions cannot be predicted; a 50-year span once passed between eruptions, while at other times several eruptions may occur in one year.

The path splits just below Steamboat; on the right is **Cistern Spring,** whose deep blue waters are constantly building deposits of sinter and have flooded the nearby lodgepole-pine forests, killing the trees. If you turn left where the trail splits, you come to **Echinus Geyser,** a personal favorite. (The name—Greek for "spiny"—comes from the pebbles that lie around the geyser; resembling sea urchins, they are a result of sinter accumulation.) In the recent past Echinus erupted every hour or so and was one of the most dependable and enjoyable geysers in the park. At last check it was far less regular, and you may have to wait several hours for an eruption. When it does erupt, the geyser sends explosions of acidic steam and water (pH 3.5) 40-60 feet. These generally last 6-14 minutes but sometimes continue for up to an hour or more. Unlike Old Faithful, this is one geyser where you can get up close and personal. Bench-sitters may get splashed, although the water is not hot enough to burn.

Continue along this trail beyond Echinus to see many more hot springs and steam vents. **Porkchop Geyser** was in continuous eruption for several years, but in 1989 it self-destructed in an explosion that threw rocks more than 200 feet, leaving behind a bubbling hot spring.

NORRIS JUNCTION TO CANYON

From Norris Geyser Basin to Canyon, the road cuts across the center of the park on the high Solfatara Plateau. This dozen-mile stretch of road is best known for what looks like a scene from an atomic blast, with the blackened remains of a forest seemingly blown down by the ferocity of the 1988 North Fork Fire. This is the place the news media focused on after the fires, making it appear as if it were typical of the park as a whole. In reality, the lodgepole pines were all uprooted in a wild 1984 windstorm that flattened many miles of forest both here and farther south in the Teton Wilderness. The dead trees dried out over the next four years, and when the wind-whipped fires arrived, the trees went up in a holocaust. In 50 years, this may well be a meadow. **Virginia Cascades Road** is a 2.5-mile-long, one-way road that circles around this blow-down area and provides a view of the 60-foot-tall Virginia Cascade of the Gibbon River. Back on the main highway heading east, keep your eyes open for elk and bison as the road approaches Canyon. Also note the thick young forest of lodgepole pines that was established after a fire burned through in 1955.

NORRIS JUNCTION TO MAMMOTH

The park road between Norris and Mammoth Hot Springs provides a number of interesting sights, although much of this country burned in the 1988 North Fork Fire. Just beyond the highway junction is the **Norris Soldier Station.** Built by the army in 1897 and modified in 1908, it is one of just three still standing in the park. The attractive log building now houses the small **Museum of the National Park Ranger,** tel. (307) 344-7353, with displays and a video on the history of park rangers. It is open daily 9 a.m.-6 p.m. from Memorial Day to Labor Day, and daily 9 a.m.-5 p.m. the rest of September. (Hours may vary depending upon park budgets and staffing.) Closed in winter.

Just up the road is **Frying Pan Spring** (named for its shape), where the water is actually not that hot. The bubbles are from pungent-smelling hydrogen-sulfide gas. **Roaring Mountain** is a bleak, steaming mountainside four miles north of Norris. In 1902, the mountain erupted into activity with fumaroles that made a roar audible at great distances. It is far less active today and is best seen in winter, when the temperature difference results in much more steam.

Obsidian Cliff

Stop at Obsidian Cliff to see the black glassy rocks formed when lava cooled very rapidly. One mountain man (not, as many sources claim, Jim Bridger) told tall tales of "Glass Mountain," where his shots at an elk kept missing. When he got closer, he found he had actually been firing at a clear mountain of glass. The elk was 25 miles away, but the mountain acted as a telescope to make the animal appear close. Obsidian Cliff was an important source of rock Indians used in making arrowheads and other tools. The obsidian from here was of such value that Indians traded it extensively; obsidian points made from this rock have even been found in Ohio and Ontario. (It is illegal to remove obsidian; leave it for future generations to enjoy.) North of here the countryside opens up along Obsidian Creek at **Willow Park,** one of the best places to see moose, especially in the fall.

Sheepeater Cliff and Golden Gate

Approximately 13 miles north of Norris, the road passes Indian Creek Campground and the basalt columns of Sheepeater Cliff, named for the Indian inhabitants of these mountains. North of this, the country opens into Swan Lake Flats, where you get a fine gander at 10,992-foot Electric Peak nine miles to the northwest.

At Golden Gate the road suddenly enters a narrow defile, through which flows Glen Creek. Stop to look over the edge of **Rustic Falls** and to note how the road is cantilevered over the cliff edge. Acrophobics should *not* stop here. Instead, have someone else drive, close your eyes, and say three Hail Marys.

Bunsen Peak

Just south of Mammoth is Bunsen Peak, an 8,564-foot inactive volcanic cone. Any chemistry student will recognize the name, for Robert Wilhelm Eberhard von Bunsen not only first explained the action of geysers but also invented the Bunsen burner. Parts of Bunsen Peak look like a chemistry experiment run amok. The North Fork Fire of 1988 swept through this area in a patchy mosaic, leaving long strips of unburned trees next to those that are now just blackened telephone poles.

Bunsen Peak Road is a dirt track open to hikers and mountain-bikers but closed to cars. Starting approximately five miles south of Mammoth and just beyond the Golden Gate, it circles the east side of the mountain, connecting with the main road six miles later. Approximately four miles in on the road is a side trail to **Osprey Falls.** This steep trail drops 800 feet in less than a mile to the base of a stunning 150-foot waterfall, but you'll need to climb back out the same way, so don't get too late of a start. Trails also lead to the summit of Bunsen Peak from both the east and west sides. Most folks choose the west trail (four miles roundtrip with an elevation difference of 1,300 feet), which begins a short way up the road from the Golden Gate entrance. From the mountaintop you can drop down the east side and hike back along the road, making a total of nine miles roundtrip.

The Hoodoos

North of Golden Gate, the main road soon passes the Hoodoos, a fascinating jumble of travertine boulders leaning in all directions. The rocks were created by hot springs thousands of years ago and toppled from the east face of Terrace Mountain. Just before Mammoth, turn left onto Upper Terrace Dr., a half-mile loop road providing access to the upper end of Mammoth Hot Springs. (No trailers or large RVs.)

MAMMOTH HOT SPRINGS VICINITY

Mammoth Hot Springs lies at an elevation of 6,239 feet near the northern border of Yellowstone, just five miles from the town of Gardiner, Montana. Here you'll find park headquarters, a variety of other facilities, and delightfully colorful hot springs. The Mammoth area is an important wintering spot for elk, pronghorn antelope, deer, and bison. During the fall, at least one bull elk and his harem can be seen wandering across the green lawns, while lesser males bugle challenges from behind the buildings or over the hill. The bugling may even keep you awake at night if you're staying in the Mammoth Hotel.

Origins

Mammoth Hot Springs consists of a series of multihued terraces down which hot, mineral-laden water trickles. This water originates as snow and rain that falls on the surrounding country, although some is believed to come from the Norris area, 20 miles to the south. As it passes through the earth, the water comes into contact with volcanic magma containing massive amounts of carbon dioxide, creating carbonic acid. The now-acidic water passes through and dissolves the region's sedimentary limestone, and the calcium carbonate remains in solution until it reaches the surface at Mammoth. Once at the surface, the carbon dioxide begins to escape into the atmosphere, reducing the acidity and causing the lime to precipitate out, forming the travertine terraces that are so prominent here. As the water flows over small obstructions, more carbon dioxide is released, causing accumulations that eventually grow into the lips that surround the terrace pools. The rate of accumulation of travertine (calcium carbonate) is astounding: more than two tons a day at Mammoth Hot Springs. Some terraces grow by eight inches a year. The first explorers were fascinated by these terraces; mountain man Jim Bridger noted that they made for delightful baths. A later operation—long since ended—coated knickknacks by dipping them in the hot springs!

The springs are constantly changing as underground passages are blocked by limestone deposits, forcing the water in new directions. As a result, old dried-out terraces stand on all sides, while new ones grow each day. Areas that were active just a few years ago may now be simply gray masses of crumbling travertine rock, and new areas may appear and spread in a matter of days. Mammoth is guaranteed to be different every time you visit. One of the most interesting aspects of the hot springs here is the variety of colors, results of the many different species of algae and bacteria that live in the water. Various factors, including temperature and acidity, affect the survival of different species; bright yellow algae live in the hottest areas, while cooler waters are colored orange and brown by other algae.

Visiting the Springs

Mammoth Hot Springs covers a steep hillside and consists of a series of colorful springs in various stages of accretion or decay. The area is accessible by road from below or above (Upper Terrace Dr.), and a boardwalk/staircase connects the two. At the bottom of Mammoth Hot Springs and off to the right is a 37-foot-tall mass of travertine known as **Liberty Cap** for its faint similarity to the caps worn in the French Revolution. The spring that created this no longer flows. (You may well find the Liberty Cap shows a more striking similarity to a certain anatomical feature found only on males.)

Because of their continuously changing nature, I won't attempt to describe the springs at Mammoth, but do pick up the Park Service's very informative brochure from the box at the parking area. Across the road is **Opal Terrace,** one of the more active springs. It began flow-

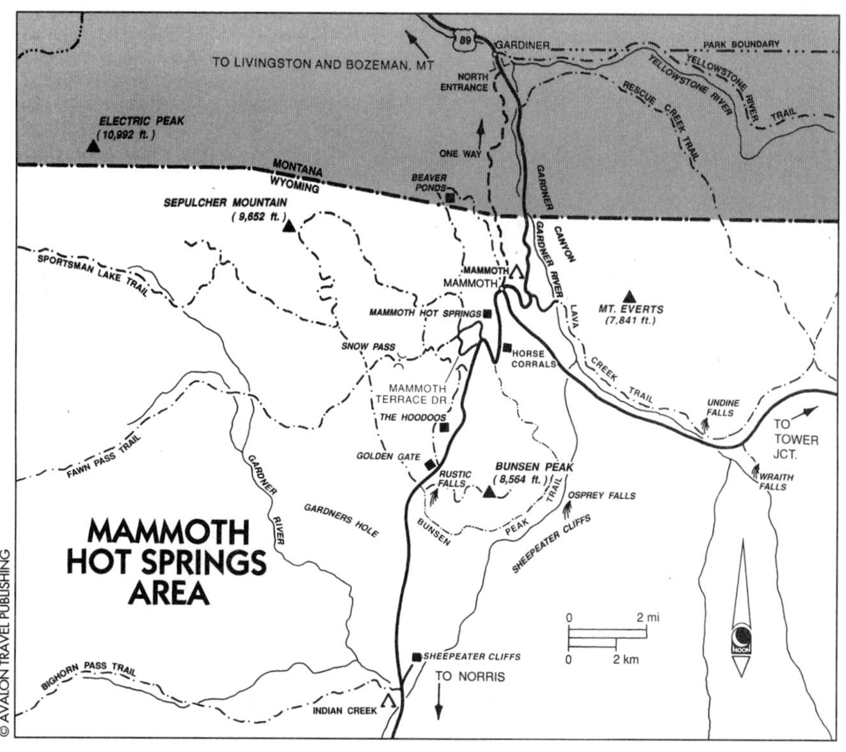

travertine terraces at Mammoth Hot Springs

ing in 1926 and has continued to expand over the years; it now is heading toward a house built in 1907 and designed by Robert Reamer (the architect of Old Faithful Inn).

All the water flowing out of Mammoth terraces quickly disappears into underground caverns. In front of the Mammoth Hotel are two sinkholes from which steam often rises. Caverns above the terraces were once open to the public but later were closed when it became apparent that they contained poisonous gases. Dead birds are sometimes found around one of the small pools in this area appropriately named Poison Spring.

Buildings

Albright Visitor Center, tel. (307) 344-2263, is named for Horace Albright, the first National Park Service superintendent at Yellowstone. The center is housed in the army's old bachelor officers' quarters and is open daily 8 a.m.-7 p.m. from Memorial Day to Labor Day, daily 9 a.m.-5 p.m. the rest of the year. Spread over the two floors are exhibits on park wildlife and history, but the real treats are the works of two artists who helped bring Yellowstone's magnificent scenery to public attention. Twenty-three of painter Thomas Moran's famous Yellowstone watercolors line the walls, and his studio has been re-created in one corner. Equally impressive are 26 classic photographs—including one of Thomas Moran at Mammoth Hot Springs—taken by William H. Jackson during the 1871 Hayden Survey. The paintings and photos are must-sees for anyone with an artistic bent. (By the way, you can check out a gallery of paintings by Moran and photos by Jackson on the web at www.cr.nps.gov/csd/exhibits/moran.) The center also has an information desk, racks of books, and films about the park and Moran. Check at the information desk for schedules of wildlife talks and frequent ranger-led walks to surrounding sights in the summer.

Mammoth contains a number of other historic structures built during the army's tenure at Fort Yellowstone. The most distinctive are the six buildings (all in a row) constructed between 1891 and 1909 as quarters for the officers and captains. Most of the grunt soldiers lived just behind here in barracks, one of which is now the park administration building. The U.S. Engineers Department was housed in an odd stone building with obvious Asian influences; it's right across from the visitor center.

Although one wing survives from a hotel built in 1911, most of the **Mammoth Hot Springs Hotel** was constructed in 1937. Step inside to view the large map of the United States built from 15 different types of wood. Mammoth also features a Hamilton Store, post office, gas station, restaurant, fast-food eatery, medical clinic, and horseback rides. Mammoth Campground is just down the road.

North to Montana

The main road north from Mammoth Hot Springs follows the Gardner River, dropping nearly 1,000 feet in elevation before reaching the town of Gardiner, Montana. (Both the river and the misspelled town are named for Johnson Gardner, a ruthless trapper from the 1820s.) The river is a favorite of fly-fishing enthusiasts. A turnout near the Wyoming/Montana border notes the "boiling river" section of the Gardner River; it's well worth a stop. Sometimes during the winter you can spot bighorn sheep on the mountain slopes just north of the river as you head down to Gardiner.

The "back way" to Gardiner is the Old Gardiner Rd., a five-mile gravel road (great for mountain bikes, but not for RVs or trailers) that starts behind Mammoth Hot Springs Hotel. Traffic is downhill only, so you'll need to take the main road for your return into the park; mountain bikes can go in both directions. This is one of the best places to spot pronghorn antelope in the park, and it also provides a fine escape from the crowds at Mammoth.

Day-hikes

For a relatively easy loop hike, try the five-mile (roundtrip) **Beaver Ponds Trail,** which begins between Liberty Cap and the stone house. It gains 500 feet in elevation, passing through spruce and fir forests along the way and ending at several small beaver ponds. The path then drops down to join Old Gardiner Rd., which you can follow back to Mammoth. This trail provides a good opportunity to see mule deer, elk, pronghorn antelope, and moose, but is best hiked in the spring or fall when temperatures are cooler. Black bears are sometimes seen along the way, so be sure to make noise while you walk.

A longer (12 miles roundtrip) hike is the **Sepulcher Mountain Trail,** which climbs to the top of this 9,652-foot peak just northwest of Mammoth. There are several possible routes to the top, and any of them can be combined into a very nice loop hike. One begins at the same place as the Beaver Ponds Trail. You'll find many flowers in the expansive meadows on the south side of Sepulcher Mountain (named for several strange rocks at its summit). From Mammoth, it is a 3,400-foot elevation gain, so be ready to sweat. Before heading out, check at the visitor center to see if there are any major bear problems in the area and to get a topographic map and hiking tips.

MAMMOTH TO TOWER JUNCTION

The 18-mile drive from Mammoth to Tower Junction takes visitors through some of the driest and most open country in Yellowstone. Two waterfalls provide stopping places along the way. Beautiful **Undine Falls** is a 60-foot-high double falls immediately north of the road. Just up the road is a gentle half-mile path to the base of **Wraith Falls,** where Lupine Creek cascades 90 feet. Look for ducks and trumpeter swans in **Blacktail Pond,** a couple of miles farther east.

Blacktail Plateau Drive, approximately nine miles east of Mammoth, turns off from the main road. The rough seven-mile dirt road is a one-way route that loosely follows the Bannock Trail, a path used by the Bannock tribe on their way to buffalo-hunting grounds east of here. Their travois trails are still visible. The Bannocks used this route from 1838 to 1878, but it had probably been used for hundreds or thousands of years by various tribes crossing the high plateau. Much of Blacktail Plateau Dr. is through open sagebrush, grass, and aspen country, where you're likely to see deer and pronghorn antelope. The trees are very pretty in the fall. On the east end, the road drops back into a forest burned by a severe crown fire in 1988 but now containing young aspen and lodgepole trees and abundant summertime flowers.

The Park Service has developed a two-thirds-mile boardwalk **Forces of the Northern Range Self-Guiding Trail** approximately six miles east of Mammoth Hot Springs. Trailside exhibits describe the natural world. A half mile beyond where Blacktail Plateau Dr. rejoins the main road is the turnoff to the **petrified tree.** The 20-foot-tall stump of an ancient redwood tree (50 million years old) stands behind iron bars; a second petrified tree that used to stand nearby was stolen piece by piece over the years by thoughtless tourists. The **Tower Ranger Station,** originally occupied by the U.S. Army, is just before Tower Junction where the road splits, leading to either Northeast Entrance Rd. or Canyon.

NORTHEAST ENTRANCE ROAD

Of the five primary entryways into Yellowstone, Northeast Entrance is the least traveled, making this a great place to escape the hordes in midsummer. It is also one of the best places to see tall mountains in Yellowstone. The road heads east from Tower Junction and immediately enters **Lamar Valley,** an area of grass and sage along the sinuous Lamar River. Osborne Russell, who trapped this country in the 1830s, described it with affection:

We descended the stream about 15 mls thro. the dense forest and at length came to a beautiful valley about 8 Mls. long and 3 or 4 wide surrounded by dark and lofty mountains. The stream after running thro. the center in a NW direction rushed down a tremendous canyon of basaltic rock apparently just wide enough to admit its waters. The banks of the stream in the valley were low and skirted in many places with beautiful Cotton wood groves. Here we found a few Snake indians comprising 6 men 7 women and 8 or 10 children who were the only Inhabitants of this lonely and secluded spot. They were all neatly clothed in dressed deer and Sheep skins of the best quality and seemed to be perfectly contented and happy. . . . We stopped at this place and for my own part I almost wished I could spend the remainder of my days in a place like this where happiness and contentment seemed to rein in wild romantic splendor surrounded by majestic battlements which seemed to support the heavens and shut out all hostile intruders. . . . There is something in the wild romantic scenery of this valley which I cannot . . . describe; but the impressions made upon my mind while gazing from a high eminence on the surrounding landscape one evening as the sun was gently gliding behind the western mountain and casting its gigantic shadows across the vale were such as time can never efface from my memory.

This is still one of the best places in Yellowstone to view bison. Elk and mule deer are also commonly seen, and the reintroduction of wolves has added another dimension to wildlife viewing. The valley contains a number of small ponds created when the retreating glaciers left large blocks of ice that formed "kettles." Erratic glacial boulders are scattered along the way. There are campgrounds at Slough Creek and Pebble Creek, and very good fishing in Slough Creek, too.

Yellowstone River Picnic Area

Picnic areas don't generally merit a mention, but this one—1.5 miles east of Tower Junction on the Northeast Entrance Rd.—is an exception because of its proximity to a grand view. A two-mile trail takes off from here for Grand Canyon of the Yellowstone River. The hike is easy and provides a good chance to see bighorn sheep, but be careful to stay away from the canyon rim. For a loop hike (four miles roundtrip), continue to the Specimen Ridge Trail where you turn left and follow it back to your starting point.

Slough Creek Area

Slough Creek Campground is a favorite of fly-fishers who come here for the area's acclaimed cutthroat trout. The **Slough Creek Trail** starts at the campground and is one of the more distinctive in the park. The trail—actually a wagon road—makes for a delightfully gentle day-hike through Douglas-fir forests and open meadows all the way to the park boundary, 11 miles north of the campground, and is used for access to Silver Tip Ranch. This is the only way into the ranch, and because no motor vehicles are allowed you may meet folks on a horse-drawn wagon during your hike. Day-hikers often go up the road as far as the first meadow, a distance of eight miles roundtrip.

Yellowstone Association Institute

The nonprofit Yellowstone Association Institute (see the special topic Yellowstone Association) teaches many classes out of Lamar Valley's historic Buffalo Ranch, approximately 10 miles east of Tower Junction. To augment the park's small wild herd, bison were brought here in 1902 from private ranches. The bison stayed in pens at night and were herded during the day. After 1915, they were allowed to roam freely in summer, although all the park's bison were rounded up and driven here for the winter months. After 1938, the roundups ended, but the bison were fed hay every winter in Lamar Valley. Finally in 1952, even this was halted and the bison were allowed to roam throughout the park. The historic buildings are worth a look, or better still, take one of the institute's excellent classes.

Specimen Ridge

Just east of the historic Buffalo Ranch is a turnout across from Specimen Ridge, where explorers discovered the standing trunks of petrified trees that had been buried in volcanic ash and mudflows some 50 million years ago. Over the centuries, the trunks literally turned to stone as silica entered the wood. The process was repeated again and again over the centuries as new forests gradually developed atop the volcanic deposits, only to be buried by later flows. Scientists have found 27 different forests on top of each other, containing walnut, magnolia, oak, redwood, and maple—evidence that the climate was once more like that of today's midwestern states. Erosion eventually revealed the trees, many of which are still standing. This is one of the largest areas of petrified trees known to exist.

There is no trail to the petrified forest, but during the summer rangers lead hikes into the area. Check at the Mammoth Visitor Center for upcoming treks. Mark Marschall's *Yellowstone Trails* provides a description of the 1.5-mile route if you want to try it on your own. A lesser-known petrified forest in the northwest corner of Yellowstone is accessible via US Hwy. 191.

Wolf Watching

Between the Slough Creek and Pebble Creek Campgrounds, wolf aficionados fill roadside turnouts each morning and evening, waiting patiently for members of the Druid Peak or Rose Creek Packs to appear. Bring your binoculars or spotting scope! During the wolf denning season, the Park Service prohibits parking or walking along certain stretches of the road, but two turnouts are available.

Northeast Entrance

At the east end of Lamar Valley, the road continues northeast up Soda Butte Creek and between the steep rocky cliffs of Barronette Peak (10,404 feet) and Abiathar Peak (10,928 feet). Stop at **Soda Butte,** where you'll find a small travertine mound similar to those at Mammoth. Although the springs are no longer very active, the air still reeks of hydrogen sulfide, the "rotten egg" gas. South of Soda Butte and several miles up a backcountry trail is **Wahb Springs,** found within Death Gulch. Here poisonous gases are emitted from the ground, killing animals in the vicinity. Early explorers reported finding dead bears that had been overcome by the fumes.

North of Pebble Creek Campground, the road squeezes through chilly **Icebox Canyon** and into the lodgepole pine forests. It follows the creek all the way to the edge of the park, crossing into Montana two miles before the park border. The **Northeast Entrance Station** is a classic log building built in 1935 and now designated a National Historic Landmark. The twin towns of Silver Gate and Cooke City (see Gateway Towns later in this chapter) are just up the road.

A fine day-hike starts from the Warm Creek Picnic Area, 1.5 miles west of the entrance station. The trail climbs 1,100 feet in 1.5 miles before dropping into flower-filled mountain meadows along Pebble Creek. If you continue more than two miles you'll need to ford the creek, which can be deep before late summer. Backpackers use this trail for longer trips into the area; see Into the Backcountry below for details.

TOWER JUNCTION TO CANYON

Roosevelt Lodge

Lying at the junction of the roads to Canyon, Mammoth, and Lamar Valley, Roosevelt Lodge was built in 1920 and named for Pres. Theodore Roosevelt, who camped a few miles to the south during his 1903 visit. Roosevelt, a lifelong supporter of Yellowstone, helped push through legislation that clamped down upon the rampant destruction of park wildlife early in the 20th century.

The Roosevelt area is a favorite of families, many of whom return year after year. The lodge building has the rough-edged flavor of a hunting lodge and a peacefulness that you won't find at Old Faithful, Canyon, or Mammoth. Inside the lodge are two giant stone fireplaces, and the porch out front has comfortable rocking chairs. Rustic cabins, a restaurant, and gift shop are here, along with horseback and wagon rides. The location is a great base for wolf-watchers and anglers.

Stop at the overlook to **Calcite Springs,** two miles southeast of the junction, where a walkway provides dramatic views into the canyon of the Yellowstone River, with steaming geothermal activity far below. The cliff faces contain a wide strip of columnar basalt, some of which overhangs the highway just to the south.

> *Here is your country. Cherish these natural wonders, cherish the natural resources, cherish the History and Romance as a sacred heritage, for your children and your children's children. Do not let selfish men or greedy interests skin your country of its beauty, its riches or its romance.*
>
> —THEODORE ROOSEVELT IN 1903

Tower Fall

On summer afternoons the parking lot at Tower Fall fills with cars as folks stop to see Tower Creek plummeting 132 feet before joining the Yellowstone River. The towerlike black rocks of the area are made of volcanic basalt. Nearby are a campground and a Hamilton Store. Tower Fall overlook is just a couple hundred paved feet from the parking area, or you can follow the path a half mile down the switchbacks to the canyon bottom, where the vista is far more impressive and a rainbow is sometimes visible. Be prepared to get wet in the spray! A ford of the Yellowstone River—used by Bannock Indians in the 19th century—is just a quarter mile away. For more than a hundred years, a huge boulder stood atop Tower Fall; the water and gravity finally won in 1986.

Dunraven Pass and Mt. Washburn

Continuing southward, the road climbs along Antelope Creek and eventually switchbacks up the aptly named Mae West Curve. The North Fork Fire swept through this country in 1988, but the area is now verdant with new trees, grasses, and flowers. **Dunraven Pass** (8,859 feet) is named for the Earl of Dunraven, who visited the park in 1874 and whose widely read book *The Great Divide* brought Yellowstone to the attention of wealthy European travelers. This is the highest point along any park road, even higher than the three other places where the road crosses the Continental Divide! Look for whitebark pines near the road, and be sure to stop just south of here for a view across to the distant Grand Canyon of the Yellowstone.

For an outstanding day-hike, climb **Mt. Washburn,** a 10,243-foot peak with commanding vistas in all directions. The two trails up the mountain both gain about the same elevation (1,400 feet) and are around six miles roundtrip. The most popular route begins from the often-full parking lot at Dunraven Pass and heads up from the south side. A few miles north of the pass, the old Chittenden Rd. turns off and leads to another access point; drive the first mile up this road to a large parking area and then hike—or mountain-bike—to the summit of Washburn from the north side. Many wildflowers bloom in midsummer, and bighorn sheep may be seen right along the trail. Bring warm clothes and rain gear, since conditions on top may be much cooler and windier than below.

GRAND CANYON OF THE YELLOWSTONE

Yellowstone is best known for its geysers and animals, but for many visitors the Grand Canyon is its most memorable feature. This 20-mile-long canyon ranges from 1,500 to 4,000 feet across and has colorful yellow, pink, orange, and buff cliffs that drop as much as 1,200 feet on either side. The river itself tumbles abruptly over two massive waterfalls, sending up a roar audible for miles along the rims. Grand Canyon is accessible by road from both the north and south sides, with equally amazing views. The lodgepole pine forests around here escaped the fires of 1988.

Carving a Canyon

After the massive volcanic eruptions some 650,000 years ago, rhyolite lava flows came through what is now the Grand Canyon. The flows eventually cooled, but geothermal activity within the rhyolite weakened the rock with hot steam and gasses, making it susceptible to erosion. Over the centuries, a series of glaciers blocked water upstream, each time creating a lake. As each glacier retreated it undammed the stream, allowing the water in the lake to empty suddenly. The weakened rhyolite was easily eroded by these periodic floods of water and glacial debris, thus revealing pastel yellow and red canyon walls colored by the thermal activities. The **Lower Falls** are at the edge of the thermal basin, above rock that was not weakened by geothermal activity. The **Upper Falls** are at a con-

Lower Falls of the Yellowstone River plummet more than 300 feet.

tact point between hard rhyolite that does not erode easily and a band of rhyolite that contains more easily eroded volcanic glass. Today, the canyon is eroding more slowly, having increased in depth just 50 feet over the last 10,000 years.

Canyon Village

Canyon Village on the north rim is a forgettable shopping mall in the wilderness, complete with various stores and eating places, a post office, gas station, cabins, lodges, and a campground. It's a good place to come on a rainy summer afternoon when the kids are starting to scream for ice cream. Horseback rides are available less than a mile south of here. Step into **Canyon Visitor Center,** tel. (307) 242-2550, for park information or to see the natural history exhibits. Hours are daily 8 a.m.-7 p.m. Memorial Day to mid-September, and daily 9 a.m.-6 p.m. till mid-October. (Hours may vary depending upon park budgets and staffing.) Closed in winter. A new and much improved visitor center is in the works and should open by 2004.

North Rim Vistas

A one-way road takes visitors to a series of extremely popular overlooks along the north rim of Grand Canyon of the Yellowstone. Farthest east is **Inspiration Point,** where the views of the canyon and Lower Falls are, well, inspirational. **North Rim Trail** leads along the rim from Inspiration Point up to Chittenden Bridge, three miles away. Some sections of this scenic and nearly level path are paved. Just a couple hundred feet up from Inspiration Point, be sure to look for a 500-ton boulder deposited by a glacier during the glaciation that ended 15,000 years ago. It originated in the Beartooth Mountains at least 30 miles north of here and was carried south atop a moving river of ice.

The five-mile-long **Seven Mile Hole Trail** takes off near this boulder, providing fantastic views for the first mile or so, minus the crowds at Inspiration Point. Look for **Silver Cord Cascade,** a thin ribbon of water dropping over the opposite wall of the canyon, but be careful not to go too close to the very loose edge. It's a very long way down! The trail switchbacks steeply to the Yellowstone River, passing odoriferous thermal areas en route. Many anglers come to Seven Mile Hole (it's seven miles downriver from Lower Falls) while other folks come to relax along the river. Save your energy for the strenuous 1,400-foot climb back up. Three campsites are available near the base of the trail for those who want to make this an overnight hike (permit required).

The one-way road continues westward to overlooks at **Grandview** and **Lookout Point.** From Lookout Point, a half-mile trail drops several hundred feet to **Red Rock Point** for a closer view of Lower Falls. Farthest west along the one-way North Rim Rd. is the trail to the **Brink of the Lower Falls.** The trail is half a mile long and paved, descending 600 feet to a viewing area where you can peer over the edge as the water plummets in a thunderous roar over the 308-foot precipice (twice the height of Niagara Falls). This is probably the most breathtaking sight in Yellowstone, but if you suffer from vertigo don't even think about looking over the brink! Just south of where the one-way road rejoins the main highway is a turnoff to the **Brink of the Upper Falls,** where a short walk takes you to a less dramatic but still beautiful view of the 109-foot-high Upper Falls.

A party of prospectors wandered north into this country in 1867, following the Yellowstone River downstream without suspecting the canyon below. A. Bart Henderson wrote in his diary of strolling down the river and being

> *very much surprised to see the water disappear from my sight. I walked out on a rock & made two steps at the same time, one forward, the other backward, for I had unawares as it were, looked down into the depth or bowels of the earth, into which the Yellow plunged as if to cool the infernal region that lay under all this wonderful country of lava and boiling springs.*

South Rim Vistas

The south rim is lined with additional dramatic views into Grand Canyon. Cross the Chittenden Bridge over the Yellowstone River (otters are sometimes seen playing in the river below) and continue a half mile to Uncle Tom's parking area, where a short trail leads to views of the Upper Falls and Crystal Falls. More unusual is **Uncle Tom's Trail,** which descends 500 feet to Lower Falls. The trail is partly paved, but it's steep and includes 328 metal steps before you get to the bottom. Good exercise if you're in shape. It was named for "Uncle" Tom Richardson who, with the help of wooden ladders and ropes, led paying tourists to the base of the falls around the turn of the 20th century. Because there was no bridge, Uncle Tom also rowed his guests across the river near the present Chittenden Bridge. After his permit was revoked in 1903, visitors had to make do on their own.

A mile beyond Uncle Tom's parking area, the road ends at the parking area for **Artist Point,** the most famous of all Grand Canyon viewpoints. A short paved path leads to an astoundingly beautiful point where one can look upriver to the Lower Falls or down the opposite direction into the canyon. Look for thermal activity far below. The point is apparently where artist Thomas Moran painted a number of his famous watercolors. **South Rim Trail** begins at the Chittenden Bridge and follows along the rim to Artist Point (two

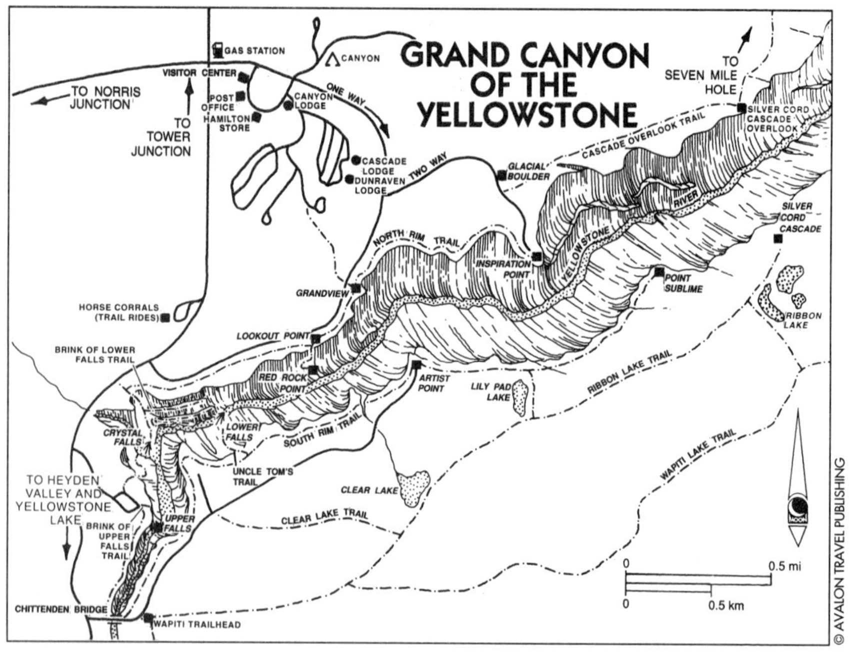

miles), providing more viewpoints along the way. The least-traveled part of this trail continues eastward from Artist Point another 1.5 miles to **Point Sublime,** with many fine looks into and across the canyon. This path provides an escape from the throngs at Artist Point, as well as a chance to see the kaleidoscopically colored canyon, hear the roar of the river from far below, and watch for squirrels and birds. But be careful to stay away from the edge where the rocks are loose—I doubt that anyone could survive such a fall.

For a longer day-hike, take **Ribbon Lake Trail,** which branches off the South Rim Trail a half mile east of Artist Point. This path takes you to a pair of lakes, and a spur trail leads to a hill that provides a wonderful view of the canyon and Silver Cord Cascade. With a drop of 1,200 feet, Silver Cord is the highest falls in Yellowstone. Also nearby are two campsites for those wanting to spend a night on the rim of the canyon; see Into the Backcountry below for camping details. From Artist Point parking area to Ribbon Lake, it's four miles roundtrip. A variety of other trails on the South Rim provide alternate starting points and possible loop hikes to the Ribbon Lake area.

CANYON TO LAKE JUNCTION

Hayden Valley

Just a few miles south of Canyon, the country abruptly opens into beautiful Hayden Valley, named for Ferdinand V. Hayden, leader of the 1871 expedition into Yellowstone. Reaching eight miles across, this relatively level part of the park was once occupied by an arm of Yellowstone Lake. The sediments left behind by the lake, along with glacial till, do not hold sufficient water to support trees. As a result, the area is occupied primarily by grasses, forbs, and sage. This is one of the best areas in the park to see wildlife, especially bison and elk. The Yellowstone River wanders across Hayden Valley, and streams enter from various sides. The waterways are excellent places to look for Canada geese, trumpeter swans, pelicans, and many kinds of ducks. Although they are less common, grizzly bears sometimes can be found feeding in the eastern end of the valley. Because of the bears, hikers need to be especially cautious when tramping through the grasses and shrubs, where it is easy to surprise a bear or to be likewise surprised. On the north end of Hayden Valley, the road crosses **Alum Creek,** named for its highly alkaline water, which could make anything shrink. In the horse-and-buggy days, Yellowstone wags claimed that a man had forded the creek with a team of horses and a wagon, but came out the other side with four Shetland ponies pulling a basket!

Mud Volcano Area

Shortly after the road climbs south out of Hayden Valley, it passes one of the most interesting of Yellowstone's many thermal basins. On the east side of the road, a turnout overlooks **Sulphur Caldron,** where a highly acidic pool is filled with sulfur-tinted waters and the air is filled with the odor of hydrogen-sulfide gas. Directly across the road is the Mud Volcano area, where a two-thirds-mile loop trail provides what could be a tour through a very bad case of heartburn. Pick up a Park Service brochure from the box for descriptions of all the bizarre features. The area is in a constant state of flux as springs dry up or begin overflowing, killing trees in their path. One of the most interesting features is **Black Dragons Caldron,** where an explosive spring blasts constantly through a mass of boiling black mud. The wildest place at Mud Volcano is **Dragon's Mouth,** which the Park Service notes is named for "the rhythmic belching of steam and the flashing tongue of water shooting out from the cavernous opening." It's easy to imagine the fires of hell not far below this. The waters are 180° F. During the winter months, the Mud Volcano area is a good place to see elk or bison.

Along the Yellowstone

South of Mud Volcano, the road parallels the Yellowstone River. At **LeHardy Rapids** a boardwalk provides an overlook where early summer visitors see blush-red spawning cutthroats. In late summer, this part of the Yellowstone River is a very popular fly-fishing spot—some call it the finest stream cutthroat fishing in the world—and a good place to view ducks and swans. Earlier in the year, it's open only to the bears that gorge on the cutthroats. By the way, the Yellowstone River, which begins at Yellowstone Lake, is the longest free-flowing (undammed) river in the Lower 48.

YELLOWSTONE LAKE

When first-time visitors see Yellowstone Lake, they are stunned by its magnitude. The statistics are impressive: 110 miles of shoreline, 20 miles north to south and 14 miles east to west, with an average depth of 139 feet and a maximum depth of 390 feet. Yellowstone Lake can seem a sheet of glass laid to the horizon at one moment and just a half hour later be a roiling ocean of whitecaps and wind-whipped waves. These changeable waters can be dangerous to those in canoes or small boats; a number of people have drowned, including experienced park rangers. The water is covered by ice at least half of the year, and breakup does not come until late May or early June. Even in summer, water temperatures are often only in the 40s. David Folsom, who was part of an exploration party traveling through the area in 1869, described Yellowstone Lake as an

> *inland sea, its crystal waves dancing and sparkling in the sunlight as if laughing with joy for their wild freedom. It is a scene of transcendent beauty which has been viewed by few white men, and we felt glad to have looked upon it before its primeval solitude should be broken by the crowds of pleasure seekers which at no distant day will throng its shores.*

Fishing Bridge

The area around famous Fishing Bridge (built in 1937) was for many years a favorite place to catch cutthroat trout. Unfortunately, these same fish are a major food source for grizzlies, and this area is considered some of the most important bear habitat in Yellowstone. Conflicts between bears and humans led to the death of 16 grizzlies here. To help restore trout populations and to proved food for the grizzlies, the Park Service banned fishing from Fishing Bridge in 1973 and tried to move the developments to the Grant Village area. Lobbying by folks from Cody (worried lest they lose some of the tourist traffic) kept some of the facilities at Fishing Bridge from closing. Remaining facilities include an RV park, Hamilton Store, and gas station. **Fishing Bridge Visitor Center,** tel. (307) 242-2450, houses exhibits of birds, animals, and geology. It's open daily 8 a.m.-7 p.m. Memorial Day to mid-September, and daily 9 a.m.-6 p.m. from mid-September to mid-October. (Hours may vary depending upon park budgets and staffing.) Closed the remainder of the year. The bridge itself is still a very popular stopping point and a good place to see large cutthroat trout in the shallows. For a nice loop hike, take **Elephant Back Mountain Trail,** which begins a mile south of Fishing Bridge Junction. This three-mile (roundtrip) trail climbs 800 feet in elevation through dense lodgepole forests to panoramic views across Yellowstone Lake and into Pelican Valley.

Lake Yellowstone Hotel

Lake Yellowstone Hotel, the oldest extant park hostelry, was built in 1889-91 by the Northern Pacific Railroad and originally consisted of a simple boxlike structure facing Yellowstone Lake. The hotel was sold to Harry Child in 1901, and two years later Robert Reamer—the architect who designed Old Faithful Inn—was given free rein to transform this into a more attractive place. Hard to believe that the same architect could create a grand log masterpiece and a sprawling Southern colonial mansion with distinctive Ionic columns in the same park! Lake Yellowstone Hotel is the second-largest wood-framed building in North America and requires 500 gallons of paint each year to keep it in shape. During the 1960s and '70s the hotel fell into disrepair under the management of General Host Corporation, and in disgust, the Park Service bought out the concession and leased it to another company. Major renovations in the 1980s transformed the dowdy old structure into a luxurious grand hotel with much of the charm it had when Pres. Calvin Coolidge stayed here in the 1920s. Today, Lake Yellowstone Hotel is one of the nicest lodging places in the park, with fine vistas out over the lake and comfortable quarters. Relax with a drink in the sunlit Sun Room; string quartets play here many summer evenings. Free 45-minute **tours** of historic Lake Yellowstone Hotel are given each evening at 6:15 p.m. from early June to late September. The hotel also houses a gift shop and snack bar.

Be sure to take a walk along the lakeshore out front of the hotel, where the Absaroka Range forms a backdrop far to the east. The highest mountain is Avalanche Peak (10,566 feet). Al-

The rambling Lake Yellowstone Hotel is the second-largest wood-framed building in North America.

most due south is the 10,308-foot summit of Mt. Sheridan, named for Gen. Philip Sheridan, a longtime supporter of expanding the park to include the Tetons. Watch for the big white pelicans catching fish on the lake. Just east of Lake Yellowstone Hotel is the **Lake Ranger Station,** built in 1922-23 and now on the National Register of Historic Places. Inside the octagonal main room you will find a massive central fireplace, exposed log rafters, and rustic light fixtures. Not far away is **Lake Lodge,** another rustic log structure that houses a reasonably priced cafeteria fronting the lake. A Hamilton Store stands nearby, and dozens of very plain cabins are behind.

To West Thumb

The highway south from Lake Junction to West Thumb follows the lakeshore nearly the entire distance. A campground and boat harbor are at **Bridge Bay,** along with a ranger station, marina, and store. Stop here for hour-long boat tours of Yellowstone Lake, offered several times a day throughout the summer, or for guided fishing trips and boat rentals.

For an enjoyable day-hike, visit **Natural Bridge,** a 51-foot-high span of rock that was carved by the waters of Bridge Creek. The three-mile (roundtrip) trail starts from the marina parking lot. The last part of the way into Natural Bridge is along a paved road that was until recently open to cars. Cyclists can ride bikes to Natural Bridge on a separate trail that starts south of the marina.

Back on the main road, keep your eyes open for Canada geese and trumpeter swans as you drive south. **Gull Point Dr.,** a two-mile-long side road, offers views of **Stevenson Island** just offshore; farther south, **Frank Island** and tiny **Dot Island** become visible. The small **Potts Hot Springs Basin,** just north of West Thumb, is named for fur trapper Daniel T. Potts, one of the first white men to explore the Yellowstone country. His travels here in 1826 were described the following year in a Philadelphia newspaper article. It was perhaps the first published mention of Yellowstone Lake and the hot springs.

EAST ENTRANCE ROAD

Heading east from Fishing Bridge, the road follows the shore of Yellowstone Lake past country that escaped the fires of 1988. Three miles east of the bridge are Indian Pond—popular with birders—and the trailhead for **Storm Point Trail.** This pleasant three-mile (roundtrip) loop trail is essentially level and goes past a large colony of yellow-bellied marmots before reaching Storm Point, where waves often pound against the rocks. The trail is often closed in spring and early summer because of grizzlies, and mosquitoes may make a June or July trip less enjoyable. North of here, Pelican Valley is considered important grizzly habitat and is closed to all overnight camping year-round. Even daytime use is not allowed until July 4, and then only between 9 a.m. and 7 p.m. Before venturing out on the Storm Point Trail or into Pelican Valley, check at the Lake Ranger Station for current bear info. The half-mile-long **Pelican Creek Nature Trail** starts a mile east of Fishing Bridge and provides an easy hike to a beach along Yellowstone Lake. Much of the way is on boardwalk over a marshy area.

At **Steamboat Point** the road swings out along the shore, providing excellent views across the lake and of a noisy fumarole. For an even better view (don't miss this one!), take the **Lake Butte Overlook** road, which continues one mile to a small parking area a thousand feet above the lake. This is a fine place to watch sunsets and to get a feeling for the enormity of Yellowstone Lake. Back on the main highway and heading east, Yellowstone Lake is soon behind you and visible in only a few spots as the road climbs gradually, passing scenic **Sylvan Lake,** a nice place for picnics. Just up the road is tiny Eleanor Lake (little more than a puddle) and the trail to 10,566-foot **Avalanche Peak.** This two-mile-long unmarked trail begins across the road on the east side of the creek and climbs steeply. It emerges from the forest halfway up, with the top gained via a scree slope. At the summit, you can see most of the peaks in the Absarokas and in the Tetons 70 miles away, but snow is present on top till mid-July.

Immediately east of Eleanor Lake, the main road climbs to 8,530-foot **Sylvan Pass,** flanked by Hoyt Peak on the north and Top Notch Peak to the south. Steep scree slopes drop down both sides. East of Sylvan Pass, the road descends quickly along Middle Creek (a tributary of the Shoshone River), providing good views to the south of Mt. Langford and Mt. Doane. **East Entrance Ranger Station** was built by the army in 1904. For many years, the road leading up to Sylvan Pass from the east took drivers across Corkscrew Bridge, a bridge that literally looped over itself as the road climbed steeply up the narrow valley. The road continues eastward to Cody through beautiful Wapiti Valley; see the Bighorn Basin chapter for details.

YELLOWSTONE CAMPING AND LODGING

PARK CAMPGROUNDS

Tent camping in Yellowstone's early days left a bit to be desired. One 1884 tourist noted that during the height of the summer season, "the principle upon which the beds are populated is said to be the addition of visitors so long as they may arrive, or until the occupants 'go for their guns.' The plan is simple, and relieves the authorities of responsibility." It's still crowded in the park, but at least guns are prohibited in the park today!

Camping is available at a dozen sites scattered along the road network; see the Yellowstone National Park Campgrounds chart for specifics, or call the Park Service at (307) 344-2114 for recorded campground information. Reservations are available for five concessioner-managed campgrounds: Bridge Bay Campground, Canyon Campground, Grant Village Campground, Madison Campground, and Fishing Bridge RV Park. Call Amfac Parks & Resorts at (307) 344-7311 for reservations (no extra charge), or find them on the web at www.travelyellowstone.com. The other seven (Park Service-managed) campgrounds inside Yellowstone are available on a first-come, first-camped basis with no reservations. You can pay with cash, checks, or credit cards. Only Mammoth Campground remains open year-round. Roadside or parking-lot camping is not allowed, and rangers *do* enforce this prohibition.

During July and August, virtually all campsites in Yellowstone fill *before noon,* so get there early! The busiest weekends are—not surprisingly—around July 4 and Labor Day. Yellowstone's most popular campgrounds fill up even in late fall and early summer.

Other Camping Options

When everything else is packed, folks head to campgrounds on surrounding Forest Service lands or to motels in the gateway towns. See Shoshone National Forest in the Big Horn Basin chapter for areas east of Yellowstone, and see Jackson Hole/Grand Teton Public Campgrounds for areas to the south. Other campgrounds, both public and private, are described under the various park gateways—Cody, Jackson, Dubois, West Yellowstone, Gardiner, Cooke City, and Silver Gate. The farther you get from Yellowstone, the more likely you are to find space. If you reach Nebraska, you should have no trouble at all. Campers can take showers (fee charged) at Old Faithful Lodge, Grant Village, Fishing Bridge RV Park, and Canyon Village Campground.

PARK ACCOMMODATIONS

Yellowstone accommodations range from extremely basic cabins with four thin walls starting at $34 d, up to luxury suites that cost more than $400. Following a fine old Park Service tradition, none of the rooms has TVs or radios and only a few contain phones. What they do offer is the chance to relax in comfortable accommodations and explore the magical world outside. Most are open early June to mid-September. During the winter months, only Mammoth Hot Springs Hotel and the Old Faithful Snow Lodge remain open inside the park. Several hundred more motels and other lodging places operate outside park boundaries in the towns of Jackson, Cody, West Yellowstone, Gardiner, Cooke City, and elsewhere. See appropriate sections of this book for details.

Amfac Parks & Resorts is Yellowstone's official lodging concessioner. For reservations, call (307) 344-7311, or visit the website: www.travelyellowstone.com. **Make Yellowstone lodging reservations six months ahead** for the park's prime hotels, or you may find that the only rooms available are in Grant Village, the laughing stock of park lodges. Those traveling with small children should also request cribs when making reservations.

Hotels and Cabins

At the turn of the 20th century, most visitors to Yellowstone stayed in park hotels rather than roughing it on the ground. Three of these wonderful old lodging places remain: Old Faithful Inn, Lake Yellowstone Hotel, and Mammoth Hot

YELLOWSTONE NATIONAL PARK CAMPGROUNDS

Bridge Bay Campground; $15; fills early, flush toilets, dump station, generators permitted, open mid-May to late September, call (303) 297-2757 for reservations

Canyon Campground; $15; fills early, laundry facilities, showers for $3 extra per person, flush toilets, dump station, generators permitted, open early June to mid-September, call (303) 297-2757 for reservations

Fishing Bridge RV Park; $27; fills early, hard-sided RVs only, full hookups, laundry facilities, showers $3 extra per person, flush toilets, sewer system, generators permitted, open mid-May to mid-September; call (303) 297-2757 for reservations

Grant Village Campground; $15; fills early, showers nearby for $3 per person, flush toilets, dump station, generators permitted, open late June to early October, call (303) 297-2757 for reservations

Indian Creek Campground; $10; vault toilets, open mid-June to mid-September

Lewis Lake Campground; $10; vault toilets, fills early, open mid-June to early November

Madison Campground; $15; fills early; flush toilets, dump station, generators permitted, open May to early November; call (303) 297-2757 for reservations

Mammoth Campground; $12; near a residential area and along the park road, flush toilets, generators permitted, open year-round

Norris Campground; $12; fills early, flush toilets, generators permitted, open mid-May to late September

Pebble Creek Campground; $10; vault toilets, open early June to late September

Slough Creek Campground; $10; vault toilets, open late May through October

Tower Fall Campground; $10; fills early, vault toilets, open mid-May to late September

Springs Hotel. In addition, the new Old Faithful Snow Lodge joins the list as a modern classic. Not all lodging options inside the park are nearly as pleasant, however. Hundreds of simple boxes are clustered in the Lake, Mammoth, Old Faithful, and Roosevelt areas. Most of these cabins offer basic accommodations, a roof over your head, and communal showers, but the more expensive cabins are considerably nicer. A few of these even include private jacuzzis. Fortunately, prices are fairly reasonable for all of the cabins. In addition, two attractive and modern lodges are available at Canyon, along with standard motel rooms at Grant Village. All told, more than 2,200 rooms and cabins provide overnight accommodations in Yellowstone.

Lodging rates are listed below for two people; children under age 12 stay free. Add an extra $10 per person for additional older kids or adults in the hotel rooms or cabins. Prices may be lower in May when snow still covers much of the park. Call Amfac Parks & Resorts at (307) 344-7311 for reservations at any of these, or find them on the web at www.travelyellowstone.com. Rates listed below are without tax, which is six percent on the south half of the park (inside Teton County—including Old Faithful, Grant Village, and Lake Village) and eight percent on the north half (inside Park County—including Roosevelt, Mammoth Hot Springs, and Canyon Village).

Canyon Village

The centrally located **Canyon Lodge** is just a half mile from Grand Canyon of the Yellowstone, one of the park's premier attractions. The main lodge is part of a late-1950s' complex of ugly structures built around a large parking lot. The area has all the charm of an aging shopping mall from an era when bigger meant better. The lodge itself covers the space of a football field and houses a dining room, cafeteria, lounge, and snack shop, but no guest rooms. Behind the lodge in the trees (at least the setting is peaceful), the road circles past three sprawling clusters of cabins, all with private baths. You'll find 540 cabins here. The most basic "pioneer" units start at $54 d and aren't much to look at outside but are actually fairly roomy and comfortable inside. Two newer types of cabins are available at Canyon: the "frontier" units for $82 d and the "western" cabins for $107 d. Providing far better accommodations are two 1990s additions: **Dunraven Lodge** and **Cascade Lodge.** Rooms at both of these attractive log- and rock-trimmed structures are furnished with rustic lodgepole pieces and have two double beds and private baths. Rooms in the lodges cost $111 d. The cabins and lodges at Canyon are open from early June to mid-September. Inexpensive-Expensive.

Grant Village

The southernmost lodging in Yellowstone, **Grant Village** offers accommodations in cramped condo-type units from the 1980s, with exceptional parking-lot views from the rooms. The buildings would be completely out of place in *any* national park, especially Yellowstone. Six lodge buildings contain motel-type units for $88 d, and recently redecorated rooms are $102 d. All rooms have two double beds and private baths. Nearby concessioner facilities include a restaurant, lounge, snack shop, and gift shop. Grant Village is open from late May through September. Expensive.

Lake Village

The Lake Village area has a variety of lodging options for travelers. **Lake Yellowstone Hotel** is a fascinating classic building with a magnificent view across Yellowstone Lake. Begun in 1889, the building expanded and changed over the decades to yield its current configuration of 158 guest rooms. The hotel has been lovingly restored and exudes a grandeur and charm rarely found today. It's the sort of place where Fred Astaire and Ginger Rogers would feel comfortable dancing—if they were still alive. The inviting hotel rooms all contain updated furnishings and range from standard units ($140 d on the backside or $152 d facing the lake) to spacious suites ($401 d). Out back (no view and modest furnishings) is an annex where rooms cost $102 d. Downstairs is a good restaurant (reservations required for dinner), along with a fast-food eatery; the cafeteria at Lake Lodge is only a short walk away. Free tours of the hotel are given each evening from early June to late September. The real treat at Lake Yellowstone Hotel is the Sun Room, where rows of windows front the lake. The room's ambience is further enhanced by period wicker furnishings and evening chamber music or classical piano. It's a great place to sip a martini or write a postcard. The hotel is open mid-May through September. Expensive-Luxury.

Behind Lake Yellowstone Hotel more than a hundred rather dingy old boxes have been jammed together in row after identical row to create the **Lake Yellowstone Hotel Cabins.** Fortunately, they're fairly reasonable ($82 d), and cabin guests can pretend they're traveling on a more ample budget by spending time in the hotel dining room and the Sun Room. Lake Yellowstone Hotel Cabins all contain two double beds and private baths, and they're open mid-May through September. Moderate.

A short distance east of Lake Yellowstone Hotel is **Lake Lodge.** Built in the 1920s, this archetypal log building has a gracious lobby containing two stone fireplaces, rustic furnishings, and an open ceiling where the supporting log trusses and beams are visible. One end of the building houses a large and reasonably priced cafeteria with picture windows framing Lake Yellowstone, and the other end contains a recreation hall for employees. Lodging options here are not nearly as gracious, consisting of plain-vanilla "pioneer" cabins from the 1920s and '30s, each with a double bed and private bath for $51 d, and a bit more comfortable "western" cabins built in the 1950s and '60s that include two double beds and private baths with showers for $107 d. The 186 cabins at Lake Lodge are open mid-June to mid-September. Guests here often walk over to the nearby Lake Yellowstone Hotel for fine dining and the chance to relax in the Sun Room. Inexpensive-Expensive.

Mammoth Hot Springs

The rambling **Mammoth Hot Springs Hotel** sits in the northwest corner of Yellowstone near park headquarters in the settlement of Mammoth. Built in 1937 (okay, one wing was constructed in 1911 and the original hotel was built even earlier), the hotel has 222 rooms in a variety of configurations. Elk are common sights on the hotel grounds, and in the fall the bulls' bugling may well wake you in the morning. There's live piano music downstairs in the map room most summer evenings as a counterpoint to the elk songs. Also just off the lobby is a gift shop. Just steps away are Park Service headquarters, the fine Albright Visitor Center and other historical buildings, along with places to eat, buy groceries, gas, and trinkets. Hotel rooms are comfortable but modest at Mammoth. Several rooms on each floor provide low-cost accommodations ($54 d) with communal baths, but most have two beds and private baths ($88 d); ask for a corner room with windows if available. The hotel also houses two luxury suites ($267 d). Behind the hotel are 116 cabins, including budget units without bath ($51 d) and very attractive duplex "frontier" cottages (from $82 d). Four units also have private outdoor jacuzzis and are the nicest cabins in the park ($122 d). The hotel and cabins are open from early May to mid-October. In addition, this hotel is one of two in the park (the other being Old Faithful Snow Lodge) that opens when the snow flies; the winter season runs mid-December to early March. In winter, the hot tubs are available on an hourly basis, offering a great way to relax after a day of cross-country skiing. Inexpensive-Luxury.

Old Faithful

The Old Faithful area contains a plethora of lodging options, including two large hotels—Old Faithful Inn and Old Faithful Snow Lodge—and several dozen cabins.

Built in 1903-04, the timeless **Old Faithful Inn** (described in Touring Yellowstone above) is easily the most delightful place to stay inside Yellowstone—if not in all of America. I wouldn't trade it for a thousand Hiltons. If you're able to get a room here during your visit to the park, do so; you certainly won't regret it! The hotel contains 327 guest rooms to suit all budgets. Even those staying in the most basic rooms here will enjoy the five-star lobby with its towering stone fireplace that always has a fire going, the old-fashioned writing tables, cushy overstuffed chairs, classy bar and restaurant, and evening piano music. Most rooms in the original section of the hotel are cramped spaces with in-room sinks, bare bulb lighting, old carpets, log walls, and communal baths down the hall; these go for $55 d. Of the cheap rooms, the best ones (these are often reserved a year ahead) are the dormer rooms on the second floor, but those who stay there must walk past folks in the lobby to take a shower! Many other types of rooms are available throughout this sprawling hotel. The nicely appointed midrange rooms ($89 d) are very comfortable and contain two double beds and tub baths. Premium rooms vary in price from $111 to $151 d depending upon whether or not they face the geyser, but personally I don't think they are much better than the midrange units. If you have the money, rent a suite ($345 d); suites 176 and 177 have the finest views of Old Faithful. Old Faithful Inn is open early May to mid-October. Inexpensive-Luxury.

Although it is an attractively rustic building that would be a major focal point almost anywhere else, **Old Faithful Lodge** is overshadowed by its grand neighbor, Old Faithful Inn. The lodge does not contain guest rooms but houses a large cafeteria (open for lunch and dinner only), recreation hall, gift shop, bake shop, ice cream stand, espresso cart, and showers. Unlike the inn, Old Faithful Lodge has enormous windows that face the geyser, providing those eating in the cafeteria with dramatic views of the eruptions. The lodge was built from massive fir logs, and stone pillars add to a feeling of permanence. Behind and beside Old Faithful Lodge are approximately 130 moderately priced duplex cabins. The simplest share communal bathhouses and start for just $34 d; these are the cheapest rooms in Yellowstone. Somewhat nicer cabins have one or two beds and private baths. The older ones ("pioneers") cost $45 d, while newer units run $61 d. The cabins at Old Faithful Lodge open around mid-May and close in mid-September. Inexpensive-Moderate.

The 100-room **Old Faithful Snow Lodge** opened in 1999 to widespread acclaim, providing accommodations in both summer and winter (Mammoth Hot Springs Hotel is Yellowstone's only other wintertime hotel). Both inside and out, Snow Lodge evokes the spirit of "parkitecture" from the early 1900s. The building blends the past and present, with timbers (recycled from old buildings), hardwood floors, a central stone fireplace, custom-designed overstuffed couches, and wrought-iron accents, along with all the modern conveniences you expect from a fine hotel (unless you're expecting TVs or radios, which no park hotels contain). Rooms are beautifully appointed and comfortable, and all have private baths. The hotel also houses a restaurant, snack shop, lounge, and gift shop, along with a ski shop and snowmobile rentals in winter. Lodging costs $128 d. In addition, 34 fourplex Snow Lodge Cabins are available behind the building, costing $107 d. These are relatively new (built in 1990) but are quite plain. Each contains two beds and a bath. The Snow Lodge and Cabins are open early May to mid-October, and mid-December to early March. Expensive-Premium.

Roosevelt

Roosevelt Lodge is decidedly off the beaten path to the major Yellowstone sights, and that suits folks who stay here just fine. Located at the junction of the roads to Canyon, Mammoth, and Lamar Valley, this is the place to escape the crowds and return to a quieter and simpler era. Named for Pres. Theodore Roosevelt—perhaps the most conservation-minded president ever—the lodge has the well-worn feeling of an old dude ranch, and many families treat it as such. More than a few folks book cabins for several weeks at a stretch, enjoying the wolf-watching, fly-fishing, horseback and wagon rides, and barbecue cookout dinners. The main lodge features two large stone fireplaces, a family-style restaurant, lounge, gift shop, and big front porch with rocking chairs. Surrounding it are 82 utilitarian cabins. Most basic—and just a step up from camping—are the "Roughrider" cabins, each with two beds, a writing table, and woodstove (the only ones in any Yellowstone lodging places). These cabins share a communal bathhouse, cost $42 d, and fill very quickly. Call far ahead to reserve one of these classics! A bit nicer (but still no private bath) are the economy cabins for $54 d, and you'll also find "frontier" cabins with showers for $82 d. The Roosevelt Lodge and cabins are open mid-June to mid-September. Inexpensive-Moderate.

INTO THE BACKCOUNTRY

The vast majority of Yellowstone visitors act as though they were chained to their cars with a hundred-yard tether—as if by getting away from their vehicles they might miss some other sight down the road. For the two percent or so who *do* abandon their cars, Yellowstone has much to offer beyond the spectacular geysers and canyons for which it is famous. Although many parts of the Yellowstone backcountry are heavily visited, regulations keep the sense of wildness intact by separating campsites and limiting the number of hikers. And if you head out early or late in the season, you'll discover solitude just a few miles from the traffic jams.

Much of Yellowstone consists of rolling lodgepole (or burned lodgepole) forests. With a few exceptions, anyone looking for dramatic alpine scenery would probably be better off heading to Grand Teton National Park, the Beartooth Mountains, or the Wind River Mountains. Despite this, the Yellowstone backcountry is enjoyable to walk through, and many trails lead past waterfalls, geysers, and hot springs. Besides, this is one of the finest places in America to view wildlife—including bison, elk, grizzlies, and wolves—in a setting other than a zoo.

Before August, when they start to die down, you should also be ready for the ubiquitous mosquitoes. Ticks are a nuisance from mid-March to mid-July in lower elevation parts of Yellowstone. The fires of 1988 created some problems for backcountry hikers, but trails have all been cleared and hikers will get a good chance to see how the land is recovering.

Rules and Regulations

The Park Service maintains more than 300 campsites in the Yellowstone backcountry, most of which have pit toilets, fire rings, and storage poles to keep food from bears. Hikers may stay only at designated campsites. Wood fires are not allowed in many areas and are discouraged elsewhere, so be sure to have a gas stove for cooking. Bear-management areas have special regulations; they may be for day-use only, include seasonal restrictions, or specify minimum group sizes. Pets are not allowed on the trails within Yellowstone, and special rules apply for those coming in with horses, mules, burros, and llamas. Because of wet conditions and the lack of forage, no stock animals are permitted before July.

A free backcountry-use permit is required of each overnight party and is available in person from various Yellowstone ranger stations and visitor centers within 48 hours of your hike. Because of the popularity of backcountry trips, it is a very good idea to make reservations before your arrival in the park. Unfortunately, the Park

Service has taken a lesson from the IRS and makes the process as complex as bureaucratically possible. Try to follow me here. Reservations cost $15 per trip, and the reservation forms are available from the Backcountry Office, P.O. Box 168, Yellowstone National Park, WY 82190, tel. (307) 344-2160. Campsite reservation requests must be mailed in, using these forms; reservations are not accepted by phone, fax, or over the web (though this might possibly change). You'll receive a confirmation notice by return mail and will exchange the notice for a permit when you get there; the permit must be obtained in person at a ranger station within 48 hours of your first camping date. Before receiving your permit, you will be given a lengthy rundown on what to expect and what precautions to take, and you'll be shown a bear-safety video. The ranger stations are open seven days a week June-Aug., generally from 8 a.m. to 4:30 p.m.

For a description of backcountry rules, bear safety, and suggestions for hiking and horsepacking, pick up (or request to have it sent to you) Yellowstone's *Backcountry Trip Planner,* which shows locations of campsites throughout the park and provides detailed information on wilderness access and precautions. You may want to also pick up or request the free park pamphlet *Beyond Road's End.*

Those interested in horsepacking or llama trips should call the park at (307) 344-7381 and ask for a list of outfitters authorized to operate in Yellowstone. The outfitters offer everything from daytrips to weeklong adventures deep into the backcountry. You can also find a list of outfitters on the Park Service website, www.nps.gov/yell.

More Info

I have described below a few two- to four-day backcountry hikes covering various parts of Yellowstone. The park has more than 1,000 miles of trails, so this is obviously a tiny sampling of the various hiking options. In addition, quite a few day-hikes are described above in the Touring Yellowstone section.

Before you head out you will probably want to look over your hiking options. Two excellent source books are *Yellowstone Trails,* by Mark Marschall (Mammoth, WY: Yellowstone Association), and *Hiking Yellowstone National Park,* by Bill Schneider (Helena, MT: Falcon Publishing). Get them from park gift shops or visitor centers, which also sell topographic park maps. The best maps are those produced by Trails Illustrated; these feature all the major trails and show the severity of burn from the 1988 fires—a considerable help when planning hiking trips.

NORTH YELLOWSTONE TRAILS

Sportsman Lake Trail and Electric Peak

The land west of Mammoth is some of the most rugged in Yellowstone, with a number of peaks topping 10,000 feet. Several trails cut westward across this country, one of the most interesting being the 24-mile-long Sportsman Lake Trail. The route begins at Glen Creek Trailhead five miles south of Mammoth and follows Glen Creek (a good place to see elk in autumn) for four miles before crossing into the Gardner River drainage. Along the way, a short spur trail leads to pretty Cache Lake. Considerably more challenging is a second side trip, the climb up 10,992-foot **Electric Peak,** tallest mountain in this corner of Yellowstone. Many folks camp near Electric Peak and spend a day climbing. It's eight miles roundtrip and you gain 3,000 feet on the way up, but the trail becomes harder to follow the higher you climb. See a park trail guidebook for details and precautions on this hike. It is possible to day-hike to the top of Electric Peak from the Glen Creek Trailhead, but it's not recommended unless you have a masochistic streak, have done a lot of hiking, and are in great shape.

Beyond the side trail to Electric Peak, Sportsman Lake Trail crosses the Gardner River twice, and there are no bridges. The water can be dangerously deep early in the summer, so this hike is generally done in August or September. After the river fords, the trail climbs to Electric Divide (watch for bighorn sheep) and then drops steeply to Sportsman Lake and down along pretty Fan Creek to the Fawn Pass Trailhead on US Hwy. 191. Because this is a one-way hike you will need to set up some sort of vehicle shuttle. Another problem is bears. This country overflows with grizzly activity, and a party size of four or more is recommended for travel here. Off-trail travel is prohibited in some areas; see the Park Service for details.

Black Canyon of the Yellowstone

For an early-summer backpacking trip, it's hard to beat this 19-mile trek along the northern edge of Yellowstone. Start at the Hellroaring Trailhead, 3.5 miles west of Tower, and follow the Yellowstone River Trail in a steep descent to the river, 600 feet below. A suspension bridge crosses the river and from here on you remain on the north side all the way to Gardiner. One ford at Hellroaring Creek can be dangerous before August, but it can be avoided if you hike a mile or so upstream to a stock bridge crossing. After this, the hike alternates between high ridges overlooking Black Canyon of the Yellowstone and quieter stretches where the trail drops down along the edge of the water. Dramatic Knowles Falls is a highlight. The trail is in good condition, but you may find it very hot and dry in midsummer.

Pebble Creek and Bliss Pass Trails

Pebble Creek Trail cuts through a section of Yellowstone that is far away from the geysers and canyons for which the park is famous. The crowds don't come here, but the country is some of the nicest mountain scenery to be found. The trail connects with the Northeast Entrance road at both ends, making access easy. You can start from either end, but if you begin at Warm Creek Picnic Area (1.5 miles west of the entrance station) you get to the high meadows quicker. From the picnic area the trail climbs 1,100 feet in the first mile and a half, but beyond this it's all downhill. Best time to hike this trail is in late summer, when the water levels are lower (there are four fords) and the mosquitoes have abated. Hikers are treated to abundant alpine flowers and grand mountain scenery along the way, with the chance to see moose or elk in the meadows.

For a longer alternative hike, follow Pebble Creek Trail 5.5 miles from the picnic area and then turn west onto **Bliss Pass Trail.** The path crosses Pebble Creek (quite deep till late summer) before climbing 1,400 feet over Bliss Pass and then dropping down 2,700 feet to Slough Creek Trail. From here it is an easy walk to Slough Creek Campground. Total distance from the Warm Creek Picnic Area to Slough Creek Campground is 20 miles. The easy Slough Creek Trail is described as a day-hike in the Northeast Entrance Road section above.

SOUTH YELLOWSTONE TRAILS

Shoshone Lake

The largest lake in the Lower 48 without direct road access, Shoshone Lake is probably the most visited part of Yellowstone's backcountry. Its shoreline is dotted with more than two dozen campsites, but most of these fill on midsummer nights with hikers, canoeists, and kayakers. Because of the lake's popularity, reserve well ahead for a summertime campsite. On-water access is via Lewis Lake and the Lewis River Channel. Anglers come to fish in the channel or lakes; Shoshone Lake has good numbers of brown, lake, and brook trout, all of which were planted here. Hikers access Shoshone Lake primarily from the DeLacy Creek Trailhead on the north side between West Thumb and Old Faithful, or from the east side via Dogshead Trailhead. A 22-mile trail circles Shoshone Lake, although it is away from the shoreline much of the distance. You may see moose or elk and are certain to meet clouds of mosquitoes before August. The finest lake vistas come from the east side, where the trail follows the lakeshore for four miles. On the west end of the lake, hikers will find **Shoshone Geyser Basin,** an area filled with small geysers, beautiful pools, and bubbling mud pots. Most of the lake escaped the 1988 fires, but trails from the east side (via Dogshead Trailhead) traverse burned stands of lodgepole.

Heart Lake

The Heart Lake area is another extremely popular backcountry and day-hiking area, offering easy access, a pretty lake, hot springs, and impressive mountain vistas. **Heart Lake Trail** begins just north of Lewis Lake (six miles south of Grant Village). The trail is fairly easy, climbing slowly through unburned forests for the first five miles and then following Witch Creek down past burned forests to Heart Lake, eight miles from the trailhead. Witch Creek is fed almost entirely by the hot springs and geysers scattered along it.

Near the Heart Lake patrol cabin the trail splits. Continue straight ahead another 26 miles to eventually reach the isolated and challenging Thorofare Trail on the southeast end of Yellowstone Lake; getting there requires fording the Yellowstone River, which may be waist deep even in late summer. For something a bit less remote, turn right and hike a half mile to the **Mt. Sheridan Trail,** which heads west and climbs 2,800 vertical feet in three miles. Reaching the 10,308-foot summit will certainly leave you winded. A fire lookout at the top provides views across Yellowstone Lake and south to the Tetons.

At the base of Mt. Sheridan and just to the north is a small thermal area that contains **Rustic Geyser** (eruptions to 50 feet, but irregular) and **Columbia Pool,** among other attractions. Be very careful when walking here due to the overhanging rim at the pool edge.

Although many people simply hike to Heart Lake for an overnight trip, there are many longer hikes one could take out of here, including into the remote Thorofare (described below). A complete loop around the lake is approximately 34 miles roundtrip but requires two Snake River fords that are at least to your knees in late July; check with the rangers for flow levels. The Heart Lake area is prime grizzly habitat and is closed until the first of July. Do not take chances in this country!

Bechler River

The southwest portion of Yellowstone is known as Cascade Corner, a reference to its many tall waterfalls; more than half of the park's falls are here. This scenic and wild country escaped the fires of 1988 and is popular with anglers. Primary access is from either the Bechler Ranger Station (pronounced "BECK-ler") or the Cave Falls Trailhead, both of which are well off the beaten path and must be reached via Cave Falls Rd. from the Idaho side. It's 22 miles in from Ashton, Idaho, the last 10 on a gravel road. As an alternative, **Grassy Lake Road** provides a narrow and rough gravel connection to Cave Falls Road. Grassy Lake Rd. begins at Flagg Ranch Resort near Yellowstone's South Entrance; see a good map for the exact route.

All hikers must register at the Bechler Ranger Station, even if they are heading out from Cave Falls Trailhead, three miles farther down the road. Cave Falls itself is a very wide but not particularly tall drop along the Falls River. It's named for a cave on the west end of the waterfall. The Forest Service's **Cave Falls Campground** ($8) is open mid-May through August.

A spiderweb of trails cuts across the Bechler country, leading to many waterfalls and past a number of hot springs. One very popular hike goes from Bechler Ranger Station to the Old Faithful area, a distance of 30 miles; its downhill much of the way if you do this in reverse by starting at Old Faithful. From Bechler Ranger Station the trail cuts across expansive Bechler Meadows and then up narrow Bechler Canyon, passing Colonnade, Ouzel, and Iris Falls along the way. Many people stop overnight at Three River Junction to enjoy the hot springs-warmed water. Beyond this, the trail punches over the Continental Divide and then runs west of Shoshone Lake to Lone Star Geyser and the trailhead at Kepler Cascades. It's best to hike this route in August or September after the Bechler River drops enough to be more safely forded. This also allows time for the meadows to dry out a bit (watch out for leeches) and for the mosquitoes to quiet to a dull roar. For the long trek between Bechler Ranger Station and Old Faithful you will need to set up some sort of vehicle shuttle, but shorter in-and-out loop trips could be created by reading the various Yellowstone hiking guides and studying topographic maps.

The Thorofare

If any part of Yellowstone deserves the title untamed wilderness, it has to be the Thorofare. Situated along Two Ocean Plateau and cut through by the upper Yellowstone River, this broad expanse of unroaded country reaches from Yellowstone Lake into the Teton Wilderness south of the park. This is *the* most remote country anywhere in the Lower 48; at its heart you'd need to hike 30 miles in any direction to reach a road. Because of the distances involved, many people choose to traverse the Thorofare via horseback. There is considerable grizzly activity in this area, so various restrictions are in place. In addition, a number of major river crossings are impassable until late summer. Access to the Thorofare is via Heart Lake Trail (described above), the Thorofare Trail, or through Teton Wilderness within Bridger-Teton National Forest.

The **Thorofare Trail** begins at Nine Mile Trailhead on the East Entrance Rd. and hugs the shore of Yellowstone Lake for the first 17 miles. This stretch was spared from the fires of 1988 and provides some incredible opportunities to watch sunsets over the lake, particularly from campsites near Park Point. The trail continues along Southeast Arm and then follows the broad Thorofare Valley upstream beside the Yellowstone River (great fishing). There are several difficult creek and river crossings before you reach the Thorofare Ranger Station at mile 32. But this is not even the halfway point! Civilization is another 36 miles away. To get there, the often muddy South Boundary Trail heads west over the Continental Divide, through four difficult creek or river fords, through forests burned in the 1988 fires, and past Snake Hot Springs before finally ending at the South Entrance Station.

Needless to say, trips into the Thorofare are only for those with a lot of stamina and extensive backcountry experience. Shorter variations are possible, of course, but most involve hiking in and out the same way. Check at the Lake Ranger Station for conditions in the Thorofare and study Yellowstone hiking guides before even considering a big trip here. It's spectacular and remote country, but that means you're on your own much of the time.

One way to cut nine miles off your hike into the Thorofare is by a boat ride across Yellowstone Lake. The Amfac folks at Bridge Bay Marina (tel. 307-344-7311) can drop you off at a few campsites on the east side, but the cost is over $100 each way. They can carry up to six people for this price. Contact the Park Service's Backcountry Office (tel. 307-344-2160) to find out which campsites are accessible by motorboat. These sites tend to fill up fast so you'll need to reserve well ahead.

OTHER SUMMER RECREATION

FISHING AND BOATING

Catching the Big Ones

In the early years of the park, fish from Yellowstone Lake were a specialty at the various hotels, and because there was no limit on the take, up to 7,500 pounds of fish were caught each year. After commercial fishing was halted, park policy shifted to planting nonnative species. But by the 1970s, Yellowstone Lake had been devastated by overfishing, and new regulations were needed. Beginning in 1973, bait fishing was banned, Fishing Bridge was closed to anglers, and catch-and-release rules were put into place. Increased fish populations have been a boon for wildlife, especially grizzlies, bald eagles, and osprey. Because of these regulations, Yellowstone National Park has achieved an almost mythical status when it comes to fishing. Each year some half a million visitors spend time fishing in the park. The most commonly caught fish in Yellowstone are cutthroat, rainbow, brown, lake, and brook trout, along with mountain whitefish. Grayling are catch-and-release only and are found at only a few small lakes within the park, most notably Grebe Lake. Fishing regulations are quite complex and are described in a pamphlet available at park visitor centers or on the web at www.nps.gov/yell/fishing.htm.

The Yellowstone River is still considered one of the best places in the world to catch cutthroat trout, and the Madison River is a justifiably famous fly-fishing river with a wide range of conditions. Yellowstone Lake is where the lure anglers go to catch cutthroats and lake trout. Beginners may have luck in the Gallatin River, but they're less likely to do well in the Firehole River, where the fish are smart and wary. Peaceful Slough Creek in the northeast corner of Yellowstone is filled with fat rainbows and cutthroats, attracting fly-fishers from around the globe.

Several good books—available in local stores and visitor centers—provide tips on fishing Yellowstone waters. Try one of the following: *Yellowstone Fishes; Ecology, History, and Angling in the Park,* by John Varley and Paul Schullery (Mechanicsburg, PA: Stackpole Books); *Yellowstone Fishing Guide,* by Robert E. Charlton (Ketchum, ID: Lost River Press); or *Fishing Yellowstone,* by Richard Parks (Helena, MT: Falcon Publishing).

Trouble in Paradise

The 1990s were not at all kind to aquatic ecosystems in Yellowstone as a series of diseases and nonnative threats appeared. Per-

Fly-fishing for trout is a favorite activity in Yellowstone.

haps the greatest threat comes from lake trout (Mackinaw), a species that had been illegally planted either accidentally or intentionally in the 1980s or earlier. Lake trout were first discovered in Lake Yellowstone in 1994, and studies have since revealed that many thousands of them now inhabit the lake. A highly aggressive and long-lived species, lake trout feed upon and compete with the prized native cutthroat, threatening to devastate the population. (The average lake trout eats 80-90 cutthroat trout per year in Yellowstone.) Cutthroat spawn in the shallow waters of the lake's tributary streams, where they are caught by grizzly bears, bald eagles, and other animals. Lake trout spawn in deeper waters inaccessible to predators, and because of this, fewer cutthroat and more lake trout could have an impact on grizzlies and eagles. Eradication of the lake trout is virtually impossible, but the Park Service has used gill nets to catch thousands of them. There are no size or possession limits on lake trout caught in Yellowstone Lake or Heart Lake, but any lake trout you catch in these lakes must be kept and shown to rangers to help in determining the population size.

Another problem is threatening trout, especially rainbow trout, throughout the Rockies. Whirling disease, a devastating parasite-caused disease, has seriously hurt populations of rainbow trout in parts of the Madison River outside Yellowstone. The disease was discovered in Yellowstone Lake cutthroats in 1998, and there are fears that it could spread to other lakes and rivers in the park. It is spread in part when mud or water is brought in from contaminated areas on waders, boats, and boots. Be sure to clean up thoroughly before entering or leaving an area. Get details on whirling disease on the web at http://whirlingdisease.org.

As if the other problems weren't enough, the New Zealand mud snail was discovered in park waters in 1995. These miniscule snails (natives of New Zealand) are now in the Firehole, Gibbon, Madison, and Snake Rivers, where they can form dense colonies on aquatic plants and streambed rocks, crowding out native aquatic insects that are a food source for fish.

Fishing Regulations

In most parts of Yellowstone, the fishing season extends from Memorial Day weekend to the first Sunday of November, but check the regulations for specifics. Hayden Valley and certain other waters are entirely closed to fishing. Only artificial lures are allowed, lead is not allowed, and a catch-and-release policy (with exceptions) is in effect for cutthroat and rainbow trout and grayling. Some rivers, including the Madison River, the Firehole River, and the Gibbon River (downstream from Gibbon Falls) are open only to fly-fishing. Barbless hooks are preferable for catch-and-release fishing since they cause less damage and are easier to remove. Anglers don't need a state fishing license but must obtain a special Yellowstone National Park permit, available from visitor centers, ranger stations, and Hamilton Stores, plus fishing shops in surrounding towns. The adult fishing fee is $10 for a 10-day permit or $20 for a season permit. Kids ages 12-15 get permits for free, and younger children do not need a permit. Park visitor centers and ranger stations have copies of current fishing regulations.

Boating
Bridge Bay Marina runs hour-long scenic **boat tours** of Yellowstone Lake ($8.75 for adults, $4.75 for ages 2-11) several times a day in the summer, providing a fine introduction to the area. Also available at the marina are **guided fishing trips** ($52 an hour for up to six people) and **boat rentals** ($6 an hour for a 16-foot rowboat; $29 an hour for a motorboat).

The best Yellowstone Lake fishing is from boats rather than from the shoreline. If you're bringing your own boat or canoe to Yellowstone, pick up a park permit at the Lake Ranger Station or Grant Village Visitor Center. Boat slips are available at Bridge Bay Marina for $9 a night. All streams are closed to watercraft with the exception of the Lewis River Channel between Shoshone and Lewis Lakes. Motorboats are allowed only on Lewis Lake and parts of Yellowstone Lake.

Sea Kayaking
Several companies offer guided sea kayak trips on Yellowstone lakes. **Snake River Kayak & Canoe School,** tel. (307) 733-3127 or (800) 529-2501, www.snakeriverkayak.com, charges $145 per person/day for multiday sea kayak tours around Yellowstone Lake. **Jackson Hole Kayak School,** tel. (307) 733-2471 or (800) 733-2471, www.jhkayakschool.com, has day-tours of Lewis Lake for $130 per person. They also offer three-day tours of Yellowstone Lake for $605 per person, and three-day tours of Lewis and Shoshone Lakes for $550 per person. The overnight trip prices include transportation from Jackson, kayaking and camping gear, supplies, and all meals.

Each September, **O.A.R.S.,** tel. (209) 736-4677 or (800) 346-6277, www.oars.com, offers sea kayaking trips to the quiet south and southeast arms of Yellowstone Lake. Rates are $495 for three days, or $730 for five days. Tents and sleeping bags are available for rent, or bring your own.

BICYCLING

Cycling provides a unique way to see Yellowstone up close. Unfortunately, park roads tend to be narrow and have little or no shoulders, and some are filled with potholes, making for dangerous conditions. These problems are exacerbated early in the year by high snowbanks, so bikes are not allowed on certain roads. Call (307) 344-7381 for current road conditions. If you're planning a cycling trip through Yellowstone, be sure to wear a helmet and high-visibility clothing. A bike mirror also helps. If you want to avoid some of the hassles and don't mind spring conditions, visit the park between late March and the third Friday in April, when motorized vehicles are usually prohibited from entering the park (except for park administrative vehicles). During this period, cyclists are allowed to ride only on the stretch between the West Entrance and Mammoth Hot Springs; other roads are closed to cycling (they're being plowed). Fall is also a good time to ride, since traffic is much lighter than in the summer months. In the summer, the best times to ride are in the morning before traffic thickens or late in the afternoon before the light begins to fade and you become less visible to motorists.

Where to Ride
The best main park roads to ride (less traffic or better visibility and shoulders) are the following sections: Mammoth to Tower, Tower to Cooke City, Canyon to Lake, and Lake to Grant Village. Bikes are not allowed on backcountry trails or boardwalks inside Yellowstone. A number of relatively short but fun mountain-bike rides are available around the park, including the paved trail from Old Faithful to Morning Glory Pool (two miles), the partly paved trail to Lone Star Geyser in the Old Faithful area (two miles), Fountain Flat Dr. (six miles) to the vicinity of Midway Geyser Basin, the old Chittenden Rd. up Mt. Washburn (three miles each way, but gaining 1,400 feet on the way up), Bunsen Peak Rd. near Mammoth (six miles and steep in places), the Old Gardiner Rd. from Mammoth to Gardiner (five miles), and Blacktail Plateau Dr. (seven miles) east of Mammoth. Of these routes, cars are allowed only on the Old Gardiner Rd. and Blacktail Plateau Dr., but traffic is light on these two.

Bike Rentals and Tours
Unfortunately, there are no bike rentals inside Yellowstone or Gardiner, but they are available in the towns of West Yellowstone, Jackson, and Cody. **Backroads** has six-day cycling tours of Yellowstone during the summer. These are of-

fered as either camping trips ($1,198 per person including meals) or trips where you stay at local inns ($1,898 per person including meals). A sag wagon carries your gear, bike rentals are available, and you can choose your own pace. For details call (800) 462-2848 or visit the company's website at www.backroads.com. Contact the Park Service for a list of other permitted bicycle-tour operators.

OTHER RECREATION

Trail Rides and Cookouts

Horseback trail rides are available at Mammoth Hot Springs, Canyon Village, and Roosevelt Lodge and cost $20 for one hour, or $32 for a two-hour ride. Roosevelt also has **stagecoach rides** ($6 for adults or $5.25 for kids) several times a day in the summer, along with **Old West dinner cookouts.** Access to the latter is by either horseback ($50 for a two-hour ride and dinner) or in a wagon ($32 with dinner). Advance reservations are required for the cookouts; get tickets from any hotel or lodge in the park, or contact Amfac Parks & Resorts, tel. (307) 344-7311, www.travelyellowstone.com. A number of outfitters provide backcountry pack trips inside Yellowstone; get a list from Park Service visitor centers or on the web at www.nps.gov/yell, or call the park at (307) 344-7381.

Hot Springs Bathing

Many people are disappointed to discover that there are no places in Yellowstone where you can soak in the hot springs. Not only is it illegal, but it can also be dangerous, since temperatures often approach boiling and bathers can cause severe damage to these surprisingly fragile natural wonders. Legal bathing pools are found in cold-water streams that have hot springs feeding into them. You're not allowed to enter the source pool or stream itself. Families often stop for a swim in the Firehole River along Firehole Canyon Dr. near Madison. The Park Service doesn't encourage this, and there are no lifeguards, so parents need to watch children closely.

Thirty miles north of Yellowstone in the little burg of Pray, Montana, is **Chico Hot Springs.** If you're staying in the Mammoth Hot Springs area of Yellowstone, a side trip to Chico may be worthwhile. The large outdoor pool is a great place to relax, the gourmet restaurant serves some of the best dinners anywhere around, and the classic old hotel is a favorite. For more information, call (406) 333-4933 or (800) 468-9232, or visit the website: www.chicohotsprings.com.

WINTER IN YELLOWSTONE

Winter transforms Yellowstone into an extraordinarily beautiful place where the fires and brimstone of hell meet the bitter cold and snow of winter. The snow often averages four feet in depth but can exceed 10 feet on mountain passes. The snow is usually quite dry, although late in the season conditions deteriorate as temperatures rise. Early in the winter or after major storms, backcountry skiing can be very difficult due to the deep powder. Temperatures are generally in the 10-25° F range during the day, while nights frequently dip below zero. (The record is -66° F, recorded on Feb. 9, 1933.) Winds can make these temperatures feel even colder, so visitors should come prepared for extreme conditions.

The thermal basins are a real wintertime treat. Hot springs that are simply colorful pools in summer send up billows of steam in the winter, coating nearby trees with thick layers of ice and turning them into "ghost trees." The geysers put on astounding displays as boiling water meets frigid air; steam from Old Faithful can tower 1,000 feet into the air! Bison and elk gather around the hot springs, soaking up the heat and searching for dried grasses, and bald eagles are often seen flying over the heated waters of Firehole River. The bison are perhaps the most interesting to watch as they swing their enormous heads from side to side to shovel snow off the grass. Grand Canyon of the Yellowstone is another place transformed by the snow and cold. Although the water still flows, the falls are surrounded by tall cones of ice, and the canyon walls lie under deep snow. A good resource on winter access to Yellowstone is *Yellowstone Winter Guide* by Jeff Henry (Boulder, CO: Roberts Rinehart Publishers).

HISTORICAL WINTER USE

During Yellowstone's first 75 years as a park, winter visitation was almost unknown. The only people in the park were caretakers who spent months at a time with no contact with the world outside. This began to change in 1949, when snow-plane tours were first offered from the West Entrance. The planes skimmed over the surface and could only hold two people—the driver and a passenger—so visitation barely topped 30 people that winter. In 1955, snowcoaches were permitted to come into Yellowstone, and more than 500 people visited, though few stayed overnight.

Snowmobiling Changes Everything

The first snowmobilers arrived in 1963, when the machines were still a novelty. As snowmobiling became increasingly more popular, communities around Yellowstone benefited economically and began promoting the park as a winter wonderland. In the winter of 1971-72 the Park Service began encouraging the use by grooming the roads and opening Old Faithful Snow Lodge (it has since been replaced by a much nicer building of the same name). By the end of that winter, more than 25,000 people had visited. Since then, winter use has rocketed; today, upwards of 140,000 people visit Yellowstone each winter, and the park admits more snowmobiles than all other national parks combined. On a typical day 1,000 snowmobiles roar through the West Yellowstone gate, spewing choking blue smoke that sometimes creates localized pollution that sickens park employees working at entrance stations. (The two-cycle engines used in snowmobiles emit up to a third of their fuel as exhaust, and the haze comes from unburned lube oils.) While these numbers pale in comparison to summer visitation, some worry that snowmobilers and skiers could adversely affect the park's wildlife at a time when the animals are already under great stress.

In the heavy snow winter of 1996-97 large numbers of bison moved out of Yellowstone, some of them along the groomed snowmobile road out the west side of the park. Nearly 1,100 bison were killed that year as part of Montana's effort to protect cattle from brucellosis. The slaughter precipitated a lawsuit by the Fund for Animals that forced the Park Service to rethink its winter use policies. To address the effects of snowmobiles and other uses, in 1999 Yellowstone released a draft environmental impact statement in which the preferred alternative was to plow the road from West Yellowstone to Old Faithful all winter, allowing bus and shuttle van traffic only. Snowmobile use would still be allowed on most other road corridors in the park. The proposal has met with little support. A number of environmental groups are pushing for a complete closure to snowmobiling, while the snowmobile lobby is striving to keep the status quo. The verdict is far from in, but even if the Park Service's preferred option actually goes into effect it won't happen till the winter of 2001-02 at the earliest. In the meantime, snowmobiling will continue to reign supreme, particularly out of West Yellowstone. Get details from the Yellowstone National Park website, www.nps.gov/yell. For the environmentalists' take on winter use issues visit www.saveyellowstone.org; for the snowmobilers' version, head to www.mtsnow.org.

WINTER ROADS

Most of Yellowstone's roads officially close to cars on the Monday after the first Sunday in November and remain shut down all over except for the 56 miles between Mammoth and Cooke City. Roads don't open for cars again until sometime between mid-May and early June. The roads are groomed for snowmobiles and snowcoaches from mid-December to mid-March. The rest of the winter you'll only find skiers and park personnel on the roads. During the winter, the most popular (and crowded) times to visit Yellowstone are around Christmas and New Year's and over the Presidents' Day weekend in February. If you plan to arrive at these times, make lodging reservations six months to a year in advance. The rest of the winter, you should probably reserve at least three months ahead.

WINTER ACCOMMODATIONS

During the winter only two places offer lodging inside the park. **Mammoth Hot Springs Hotel,** on the north end of the park, is the only one accessible by road and has ski and snowshoe trails nearby, but the newly built **Old Faithful Snow Lodge and Cabins** puts you close to the geysers and many miles of ski trails. Each has a restaurant, lounge, gift shop, and rentals of skis and snowshoes. For a fee, Mammoth also offers Sunday breakfast buffets and special dinners and dancing, along with ice-skate and hot-tub rentals. In the winter months, both of these places have two-night discount packages that include lodging, a snowcoach trip, ski rentals, and other specials. For more information on winter lodging options in the park, contact Amfac, tel. (307) 344-7311, www.travelyellowstone.com.

Just south of Yellowstone in the Rockefeller Parkway is **Flagg Ranch Resort,** tel. (307) 543-2861 or (800) 443-2311, www.flaggranch.com, where you'll find newly built cabins that are open in the winter months. See the Jackson Hole and the Tetons chapter for specifics on Flagg Ranch. It's another 55 miles from Flagg Ranch to Jackson, a wintertime base for many Yellowstone visitors. On the east side of Yellowstone, lodging is available just outside the park at Pahaska Teepee and other lodges in the Wapiti Valley/North Fork area; see the Bighorn Basin chapter for details. Other lodging places (described below) can be found just outside the park in the towns of West Yellowstone, Gardiner, Cooke City, and Silver Gate.

The only wintertime camping place is Mammoth Campground, where temperatures are milder and the snow lighter.

WINTER SERVICES

Only the Mammoth and Old Faithful visitor centers are open during the winter season. Free ranger-led activities include evening programs at Mammoth and Old Faithful. Check the winter edition of *Yellowstone Today* for details, or find it on the web at www.nps.gov/yell.

Amfac Parks & Resorts, tel. (307) 344-7311, www.travelyellowstone.com, offers a variety of guided ski and snowmobile tours and provides wildlife bus or van tours; call for details. In addition, the Yellowstone Association Institute (see the special topic on Yellowstone Association) has a number of outstanding winter classes.

The Mammoth Clinic, tel. (307) 344-7965, is open weekdays (except Wednesday afternoons) in the winter for medical emergencies.

Supplies and Warming Huts

The Mammoth general store is open for groceries and supplies year-round, but only meals and gas are available at Old Faithful. Warming huts are located at Old Faithful, Madison Junction, Canyon, West Thumb, Fishing Bridge, and Indian Creek (south of Mammoth Hot Springs). All contain restrooms and snack machines (except Indian Creek and West Thumb), and all are open 24 hours (except for Old Faithful, where other facilities are available). The huts at Madison and Canyon also have snack bars selling hot chili or soup. Park rangers are often at the warming huts during the middle of the day.

SNOWCOACHES

The easiest and most enjoyable way to get into Yellowstone in the winter is on the ungainly snowcoaches—machines that look like something the Norwegian Army might have used during WW II. Most were actually built by a Canadian company, Bombidier. They can be noisy, and the windows fog up (hence the spray bottles of antifreeze). But despite their ancient condition and spartan interiors, these beasts still work well and can carry 10 passengers, gear (two suitcases per person), and skis. You will also see (or ride in) a number of other over-snow vehicles, including vans on tracks.

Snowcoach Tours

A variety of snowcoach tours are provided by Amfac Parks & Resorts, tel. (307) 344-7311, www.travelyellowstone.com. Rates to Old Faithful are $88 roundtrip from Flagg Ranch (where the plowing ends just south of Yellowstone), $79 roundtrip from West Yellowstone, and $84 roundtrip from Mammoth. They also provide tours from Mammoth to Canyon for $79 roundtrip, and Old Faithful to Canyon for $84 roundtrip. Snowcoach tours depart twice a week from Old Faithful for the Firehole River/Fountain Flats area (two and a half hours; $18 roundtrip) and West Thumb Geyser Basin (two and a half hours; $18). All snowcoach tours and transportation are half price for kids ages 2-11 and free for toddlers. Three-hour winter wildlife bus tours to the Lamar Valley ($17-19) depart from Mammoth, providing a good opportunity to see wolves. See below for combination snowcoach and cross-country skiing trips. For any of these trips, be sure to make reservations well in advance.

During the winter, **Gray Line,** tel. (307) 733-4325 or (800) 443-6133, www.jacksonholenet.com/grayline, has daily bus runs from Jackson to Flagg Ranch for $35 one-way, arriving in time to meet the snowcoach departures for Yellowstone.

Based in West Yellowstone, **Yellowstone Alpen Guides,** 555 Yellowstone Ave., tel. (406) 646-9591 or (800) 858-3502, leads skiing tours inside the park, with access via one of their snowcoaches. All-day trips are $99 per person, and they also offer skier drop-offs and multinight trips. Their three-night trip includes two nights in West Yellowstone, a night at Old Faithful Snow Lodge, and two days of wildlife tours for $425 per person. Call for details, or visit them on the web at www.yellowstoneguides.com.

Also based in West Yellowstone, **Yellowstone Expeditions,** tel. (406) 646-9333 or (800) 728-9333, www.yellowstoneexpeditions.com, runs converted vans jacked up above tracks and skis. They offer day-tours from West Yellowstone to Old Faithful ($65 for adults or $45 for kids), as well as to the Canyon area ($75 for adults or $50 for kids) throughout the winter. Skiers can get dropped at Biscuit Basin and ski to Old Faithful where they meet the rest of the group for the return trip. In addition to day-trips, Yellowstone Expeditions has a remote base camp near Canyon that is perfect for those who want to really explore Yellowstone in winter. Guests stay in eight heated tent cabins, with two yurts providing a central kitchen and dining/social area. These overnight trips start at $1,220 for two people for three nights and four days, up to $2,000 for two people for seven nights and eight days. The price includes lodging, food, bedding, roundtrip transportation from West Yellowstone to the base camp near Canyon, and backcountry ski guides. Ski and snowshoe rentals are extra. Days are spent skiing or snowshoeing in the Canyon area or along trails around Hayden Valley, Norris, or Mt. Washburn. The camp sauna is perfect after a long day in the backcountry. This is the only overnight accommodation at the Canyon area in the winter. Recommended.

SKIING AND SNOWSHOEING

Cross-country skis and snowshoes provide the finest ways to see Yellowstone in the winter. Rent them from Old Faithful Snow Lodge or Mammoth Hot Springs Hotel. Both places also provide lessons and guided tours for groups or individuals. The towns surrounding Yellowstone also have shops that rent skis and snowshoes. The Old Faithful area is the center for skiing within Yellowstone, with trails circling the Upper Geyser Basin and leading to nearby sights. You'll find similar ski trails (marked but not groomed) in the

Tower Fall, Canyon, Northeast, and Mammoth areas. Get free ski-trail maps at the visitor centers. Old Faithful Snow Lodge is open in the winter, providing an excellent base for day-trips into nearby areas or for a snowcoach tour of the park.

Skiers and snowshoers sometimes assume that they can't possibly cause problems for Yellowstone's wildlife, but studies show that elk and bison often move away from skiers, which forces the animals to expend energy they need to survive through the bitterly cold winters. It's best to stay on the trails and to keep from skiing into areas where elk or bison may be disturbed by your presence. For more on skiing and winter visitation in the park, see Jeff Henry's *Yellowstone Winter Guide* (Boulder, CO: Roberts Rinehart Publishers), or *Winter Tales and Trails: Skiing, Snowshoeing and Snowboarding in Idaho, the Grand Tetons and Yellowstone National Park* by Ron Watters (Pocatello, ID: Great Rift Press).

Skier and Snowshoe Shuttles

Amfac Parks & Resorts, tel. (307) 344-7311, www.travelyellowstone.com, operates **skier shuttles** ($10.50-11.50 roundtrip) from Mammoth eastward by van to Blacktail Plateau and Tower Junction, or southward by snowcoach to Golden Gate and Indian Creek. From these last two many folks choose to ski back to Mammoth, since it's mostly downhill. A similar snowcoach shuttle is available from Old Faithful to Fairy Falls Trailhead or the Continental Divide area for $9.50. In these last two trips you ski back to the Snow Lodge on your own; the Continental Divide run is eight miles long and primarily downhill.

Skiers will also appreciate the van service offered between Mammoth and Cooke City ($53 roundtrip) where you're given all day to ski into the beautiful Absaroka Mountains. In addition, Amfac has all-day Grand Canyon snowcoach-and-guided-ski tours that depart from Mammoth ($89 roundtrip) or Old Faithful ($92 roundtrip). Guided snowshoe tours (around $27 with snowshoes provided) are offered from Old Faithful and Mammoth twice a week; they last three hours and are a great way to explore the country. Besides these concessioner-run tours, park naturalists sometimes lead ski trips from Old Faithful to nearby sights. Stop by the visitor center for details.

Safety on Skis

Yellowstone's roads are heavily traveled by snowmobiles and snowcoaches, making for all sorts of potential conflicts. Be sure to keep to the right while skiing. Most trails are identified by orange metal markers on the trees. If you're planning a backcountry trip, pick up a use permit from one of the ranger stations. A thorough understanding of winter camping and survival is imperative before you head out on any overnight trip, and avalanche safety classes are a wise investment of your time.

Before heading into backcountry areas you should get avalanche-safety information from the **Avalanche Advisory Hotline** in Bozeman, tel. (406) 587-6981, or on the web from www.gomontana.com/avalanche. The recording does not cover all of the park, but does include the Washburn Range and areas near Cooke City and West Yellowstone.

SNOWMOBILES

Winter snowmobile use in Yellowstone has risen rapidly in recent years, with almost three-quarters of winter visitors aboard them. It's not uncommon to meet long lines of machines ripping down the roads at any time of the day, disrupting Yellowstone's pristine winter silence with their noise and choking blue smoke. Despite the fact that the five national forests surrounding Yellowstone have many hundreds of miles of groomed trails and thousands of square miles of terrain open to the machines, Yellowstone's 180 miles of roads have become the focus of this mechanized winter onslaught.

Practicalities

If you really *must* come into Yellowstone by snowmobile, please show a few courtesies and precautions. In particular, stay on the roads and stay well away from the bison and elk commonly found along or on the roads. This is a highly stressful time of the year for them already, without being harassed by a steady stream of machines. If they stop in the middle of the road, wait for them to move, don't try to make them move. Also, if skiers are on the road, slow down and give them a wide berth as you pass. The speed limit (45 mph) is enforced, and one of the most bizarre Yellowstone sights is a park ranger waiting in a speed trap with his radar gun, ready to catch speeding sleds. Snowmobilers can cut down on pollution from their machines by tuning their engines for high altitudes and using low smoke or biodegradable lubricants along with oxygenated fuels such as gasohol. If you're renting a machine, call around to find a company that uses these lubricants and fuel.

Snowmobiles are available for rent from all four sides of the park, with the majority of 'bilers coming in from West Yellowstone where prices are usually a bit lower. Expect to pay around $120 per day including clothing and helmet for a machine, or $130-180 for a guided tour. The machines can also be rented at Mammoth and Old Faithful inside the park. You'll need a valid driver's license to drive snowmobiles into Yellowstone. Contact chamber of commerce offices in West Yellowstone, Jackson, or Cody for a listing of snowmobile rental companies. You can purchase gas inside the park at Mammoth Hot Springs, Canyon, Fishing Bridge, and Old Faithful.

YELLOWSTONE PRACTICALITIES

THE BASICS

Entrance to Yellowstone costs $20 per vehicle, or $10 for individuals entering by bicycle, foot, or as a bus passenger. Motorcycles and snowmobiles are $15. The pass covers both Yellowstone and Grand Teton National Parks and is good for seven days. If you're planning to be here longer or to make additional visits, get an annual pass covering both parks for $40, or the Golden Eagle Passport—good for all national parks—for $50 a year. A Golden Age Passport for all national parks is available to anyone over 62 for a one-time fee of $10, and people with disabilities can get a free Golden Access Passport. Both of these also give you 50% reductions in most camping fees.

Upon entering the park, you'll receive a Yellowstone map and a copy of ***Yellowstone Today,*** a quarterly newspaper that describes facilities and services and provides camping, fishing, and backcountry information. This is the best source for up-to-date park information. It's also packed with enough warnings to scare off a platoon of Marines. Examples include cautions against falling trees, bathing in thermal pools (infections and/or amoebic meningitis), unpredictable wildlife, improper food storage, health problems from the altitude, steep roads, overexertion, and scalding water. And, oh yes, "swim at your own risk."

Planning a Yellowstone Vacation

If you're planning a trip to Yellowstone, call the park at (307) 344-7381 to request a copy of another free publication, ***Yellowstone Guide.*** It provides detailed up-to-date information on hiking and camping, fishing, services, road construction, safety issues, park highlights, and lots more.

Several print and online sources provide unofficial information on Yellowstone. One of the best private sources is the Lander-based ***Yellowstone Journal,*** tel. (307) 332-2323 or (800) 656-8762, www.yellowstonepark.com. The publication comes out five times a year and is sold in stores inside and around the park.

Visitor Centers

The Park Service maintains visitor centers in six different places: Mammoth Hot Springs, Norris, Old Faithful, Canyon, Fishing Bridge, and Grant Village. All of these sell maps and natural-history books covering the park and surrounding areas. You'll also find smaller information stations at Madison and West Thumb; hours and seasons are listed in Touring Yellowstone above. Get additional information from the Park Service website: www.nps.gov/yell.

Ranger-Naturalist Programs

Park naturalists offer slide shows, films, guided walks, kids' programs, campfire talks, and other activities at the campgrounds and visitor centers. These are always favorites of visitors, and on summer days you can choose from more than two dozen different Yellowstone activities. Get a complete listing in the *Yellowstone Today* paper you receive upon entering the park. Evening slide programs are also offered in the winter months at Mammoth and Old Faithful.

Children in Yellowstone

Yellowstone is a major family destination in the summer months, and visiting the park has become something of a rite of passage for middle-class American families (along with thousands of European and Japanese families). Families will especially appreciate the woodsy campgrounds, the inexpensive but simple cabins, and the reasonable cafeteria meals that are available around the park. Most lodges and hotels have cribs for those traveling with infants. Of special interest to kids ages 5-12 is the **Junior Ranger Program,** in which children attend a nature program, hike a trail, and complete other activities. They're rewarded with an official Junior Ranger patch and are sworn in. It's always a big hit, but your kids may later try to arrest you if you get too close to an elk.

YELLOWSTONE ASSOCIATION

Founded in 1933, the nonprofit Yellowstone Association assists in educational, historical, and scientific programs. It publishes a number of natural history publications and provides funds to the Park Service to produce trail leaflets and park newspapers, along with the excellent *Yellowstone Science* magazine. The association also manages book sales at visitor centers, funds park exhibits and research, and otherwise assists the park in educating the public. It is probably best known for the **Yellowstone Association Institute,** which teaches many of its classes out of the historic Buffalo Ranch in Lamar Valley.

Instructors at the institute lead more than 100 different natural history and humanities classes in the summer months along with a number of others in the winter. Most of these last two to five days and typically cost $50-60 per day. Courses cover the spectrum from fly-fishing to horsepacking, and they provide a great way to learn about this wonderful wild place. Class size is small; most classes contain 10-15 students. Class participants typically stay at the Buffalo Ranch in comfortable log cabins ($15 per person per night) and cook meals in the shared kitchen.

Membership in the Yellowstone Association starts at $25 per year and is tax-deductible. Members get discounts on classes taught by the Yellowstone Association Institute and can sign up earlier than the general populace. Members also receive discounts on purchases of items sold by the Association and quarterly newsletters. For details, and a listing of books on the park, call the Yellowstone Association Institute at (307) 344-2294, or find it on the web at www.yellowstoneassociation.org.

Accessible Yellowstone

Disabled visitors to Yellowstone will find that the park is making a concerted effort to provide accessible facilities, though they also have a long way to go. Most of the major tourist areas have at least some paths that are paved (including at Old Faithful), and accessible accommodations can be found at Canyon, Grant Village, Old Faithful, and Lake. For details, call (307) 344-2018 to request a copy of the *Visitors Guide to Accessible Features in Yellowstone National Park,* or find the same information on the web at www.nps.gov/yell.

Supporting the Park

The **Yellowstone Association** is a nonprofit organization that assists with education, research, publishing, and book sales inside the park. The organization also teaches classes through the Yellowstone Association Institute; see the special topic on Yellowstone Association for details.

The **Yellowstone Park Foundation,** tel. (406) 586-6303, www.ypf.org, is another nonprofit group that works with the National Park Service by providing funds for projects and programs that would not be otherwise supported. All funding comes from individuals and corporations, not from the government. Contact the foundation for more details.

GETTING AROUND

By Car

Yellowstone's roads have long been a source of irritation to travelers. Much of the roadbed was built at the turn of the 20th century, when horses and carriages were the primary means of travel. Increasing traffic and larger vehicles contributed to the rapid deterioration of park roads, as did stretched-thin park maintenance budgets.

By the early 1990s many miles of park roads were pockmarked with bone-jarring potholes. Yellowstone is now in the midst of a massive 20-year road reconstruction program, and each summer you'll find a different section undergoing rebuilding, so be ready for delays somewhere during your journey. Despite the ongoing work, you are certain to find several long stretches of bad—and sometimes unbelievably bad—roads. Check with the park for the latest on the road situation and this year's construction delays.

The speed limit on all park roads is a strictly enforced 45 mph, although during the summer you're not likely to approach this speed, since long lines of traffic form behind monstrous RVs. Gas stations are located at Old Faithful, Canyon Village, Mammoth Hot Springs, Fishing Bridge, Grant Village, and Tower Junction, while repair services are available at all of these except Mammoth Hot Springs and Tower Junction.

Most roads in Yellowstone close on the Monday after the first Sunday in November and usually open again by mid-May. Plowing begins in early March and the roads reopen in sections. The roads connecting Mammoth to West Yellowstone open first, and Dunraven Pass is plowed last. Note that spring storms may cause closures or restrictions on some park roads; get the latest from entrance stations or visitor centers. Only the road between Mammoth and Cooke City is kept plowed all winter long. The roads are groomed for snowmobiles (snow conditions permitting) by mid-December. If you're planning a trip early or late in the season, call the park for current road conditions; tel. (307) 344-7381 ext. 5, and then ext. 2.

Bus Tours

During the summer, most people come into Yellowstone in private cars or RVs, but there *are* other ways of getting around. For many people, a bus tour provides a quick overview of the park while leaving the driving to an expert. This is especially true for RVers who can park at Fishing Bridge RV Park and don't need to worry about driving on narrow park roads.

From mid-May to late September, **Amfac Parks & Resorts,** tel. (307) 344-7311, www.travelyellowstone.com, offers full-day bus tours from Canyon Lodge, Lake Hotel, Old Faithful Inn, Fishing Bridge RV Park, and Grant Village. Tours of either the upper or lower loops are $23-28 for adults or $12-15 for kids (free for children under age 12). A longer Grand Loop tour (not recommended unless you're into sensory overload and more than 10 hours of riding around) costs $33 for adults or $17 for kids. The Grand Loop tour is only available from Mammoth or Gardiner. Amfac also offers **Lamar Valley wildlife excursions** that originate from Canyon Lodge, Bridge Bay, Lake Yellowstone Hotel, or Fishing Bridge RV Park and cost $18-22 for adults or $9-11 for kids. These last three or four hours and provide a great opportunity to catch a glimpse of wolves. In addition, amateur photographers may want to join a professionally taught **Photo Safari** provided several times a week out of Old Faithful Inn and Lake Hotel; $32 for four hours.

Upper or lower loop tours ($35-38) are available out of West Yellowstone from **Buffalo Bus Lines,** tel. (406) 646-9564 or (800) 426-7669, www.yellowstonevacations.com, and **Gray Line,** tel. (406) 646-9374 or (800) 523-3102, www.grayline.com. Additional Yellowstone tours leave out of Cody ($50) aboard **Powder River Coach USA/Grub Steak Expeditions,** tel. (307) 527-6316 or (800) 527-6316, and from Jackson ($48) aboard **Gray Line,** tel. (307) 733-4325 or (800) 443-6133, www.jacksonholenet.com/grayline. Those without vehicles can use Gray Line tours for access to the parks; the bus can pick you up at many places along the road system, but you'll need to schedule this in advance. This is not a separate service from the Gray Line tours; instead the regular tour bus stops, meaning that you get a portion of the tour at the same time.

Based in Bozeman, **4x4 Stage,** tel. (406) 848-2224 or (800) 517-8243, offers by-request connections around the park and to surrounding communities. Call 24 hours ahead for reservations.

For a listing of licensed tour operators offering wildlife, natural history, and photography tours in the park, call the Park Service at (307) 344-7381 or check the official Yellowstone website: www.nps.gov/yell.

FOOD

You'll find restaurants at Mammoth Hot Springs, Lake Yellowstone Hotel, Old Faithful Inn, Old Faithful Snow Lodge, Grant Village, Roosevelt Lodge, and Canyon Lodge. The enormous dining room at Old Faithful Inn is easily the best of these, and also here is a fine lounge backdropped by etched glass windows. Meals throughout the park are reasonably priced and quite good. Typical menus include steak, burgers, seafood, pasta, chicken, and vegetarian dishes. The chocolate pecan pie at Mammoth Hot Springs is noteworthy, as are the breakfast buffet and lunchtime soup-and-salad bar at Old Faithful Inn.

Dinner reservations are *required* in the summer at Old Faithful Inn (tel. 307-545-4999), Lake Yellowstone Hotel (tel. 307-242-3899), and Grant Village (tel. 307-242-3499), and they should be made before your arrival. For a dinner table at Old Faithful Inn, reserve a week ahead if you want a choice of seating times. Alternative dining options exist at all of these locations, but they generally aren't nearly as good. Run-of-the-mill cafeterias can be found at Lake Lodge, Old Faithful Lodge, and Canyon Lodge, and they'll provide box lunches. Not so bland are the Old West cookouts at Roosevelt Lodge, but you'll need to make advance reservations. In addition to these, you'll find smaller places selling burgers, sandwiches, espresso, and ice cream in Mammoth, Old Faithful, Lake, and Canyon. General stores carrying groceries (the choice may be limited) are available at Mammoth, Canyon, Old Faithful, Grant Village, and Lake; the biggest selection is at Canyon.

FACILITIES AND SERVICES

Shopping and Gifts

Nearly every road junction in Yellowstone has some sort of general store, gas station, gift shop, or other facility. **Hamilton Stores** are the most interesting, since they tend to be in rustic old log structures and staffed by friendly retired folks and fresh college kids. Here you'll find all the standard tourist supplies and paraphernalia, groceries, camping equipment, books, and fishing supplies. Old Faithful Lodge usually has an artist in residence working on a new piece (for sale, of course).

Money

You'll discover **ATMs** inside Old Faithful Inn, Lake Yellowstone Hotel, and Canyon Lodge. Both Cirrus- and Plus-system cards are accepted in these machines. Park lodges and hotels are able to provide **currency exchange** (US$50 max) for international travelers Mon.-Fri. 8 a.m.-5 p.m.

Medical Services

For medical emergencies, the park manages **Lake Hospital,** tel. (307) 242-7241, open late May to mid-September; also here are a clinic and pharmacy. The two other medical facilities in the park are: **Old Faithful Clinic,** tel. (307) 545-7325, open May through mid-October; and **Mammoth Hot Springs Clinic,** tel. (307) 344-7965, open year-round. Call 911 for emergencies.

Laundry and Showers

In the summer, find coin-operated washers and dryers at Fishing Bridge RV Park, Canyon Village Campground, and Grant Village Campground. Public showers are at Fishing Bridge RV Park, Lake Lodge, Old Faithful Lodge, Grant Village, and Canyon Village Campground.

Other Services

For a complete directory of the many other Yellowstone visitor services, see *Yellowstone Today,* which you receive upon entering the park. You can also download a copy off the web from the Yellowstone site, www.nps.gov/yell. **Post offices** are at Old Faithful, Lake Village,

Canyon Village, and Grant Village. Check at any visitor center for a schedule of **church services.** Process film (prints only) at **film labs** at Old Faithful, Canyon, and Mammoth. At Mammoth and Old Faithful they will process your film in an hour or less. Trail rides, boat rentals, bus tours, and other services are detailed below.

WORKING IN YELLOWSTONE

During the summer months, both the National Park Service and private concessioners provide several thousand jobs in Yellowstone. These positions rarely last more than six months. You can find much more about Yellowstone jobs—both public and private—by heading to www.nps.gov/yell/technical/jobs on the web.

GREATER YELLOWSTONE COALITION

The primary environmental group involved with protecting Yellowstone and the surrounding public lands is the Greater Yellowstone Coalition, based in Bozeman, Montana. This private nonprofit organization is involved in all sorts of environmental issues within the 10-million-acre Greater Yellowstone Ecosystem, including such hot-button issues as logging, mining, winter use, and bison management. It represents some 8,000 members and publishes a quarterly newsletter detailing various issues. Annual membership costs $25; contact the organization by calling (406) 586-1593, or find it on the web at www.greateryellowstone.org.

Park Service Jobs

Yellowstone National Park hires approximately 400 seasonal employees each year, but many more people apply, so the competition is stiff for new hires. Most seasonals start out as a park ranger (leading naturalist walks, working in entrance stations, etc.) or laborer (building trails, cleaning campgrounds and restrooms, etc.), but more specialized positions are available in the fields of natural resources or law enforcement. Seasonals typically make $6-11 per hour, with housing taken out of this. You must be a U.S. citizen to be employed by the Park Service. Although there is a national register for seasonal rangers, specific vacancy announcements come out when jobs are available, and you will need to apply within the specified time frame and meet all qualifications. For details and application forms, call Yellowstone's personnel office at (307) 344-2052, or head to www.usajobs.opm.gov for a listing of every federal job in the nation, or visit the Department of Interior's site: www.doi.gov/hrm/jobs.html. Get information on law enforcement or interpretive positions at www.sep.nps.gov.

Volunteer Positions

Unpaid volunteers do many jobs in Yellowstone and other national parks, and it isn't necessary to be a U.S. citizen to do volunteer work. The Park Service operates a **Volunteers in Parks** (VIP) program at Yellowstone that includes over 300 people each year. To join the ranks of the employed but unpaid, call the park's VIP coordinator at (307) 344-2039, or visit the volunteer website: www.nps.gov/volunteer.

A national nonprofit organization, the New Hampshire-based **Student Conservation Association** (SCA), tel. (603) 543-1700, www.sca-inc.org, provides workers for Yellowstone who do a wide range of activities, from trail maintenance to answering visitors' questions. Volunteers get most expenses paid. Contact SCA for details.

Concessioner Jobs

The park has two primary concessioners, Amfac Parks & Resorts and Hamilton Stores, along with the smaller Yellowstone Park Service Stations. Most employees of these companies are college students (who live in dorm-style accommodations), retired folks (who live in their RVs), or young people from other countries (including quite a few Eastern Europeans). Don't expect high pay; entry positions start at a little over $5 an hour, with meals and lodging deducted from this. A good overall website for concessioner jobs inside Yellowstone is www.coolworks.com/yell.htm.

Amfac Parks & Resorts is in charge of lodging, restaurants, bus tours, boat rentals, horse rides, and similar services within the park. They are also the largest park and resort management company in the nation, with concessioners in such diverse spots as Everglades National Park and Grand Canyon National Park. The company hires more than 3,000 people each summer in Yellowstone. For more info and an application, call (307) 344-5324, or head to their website: www.ynpjobs.com. It's best to apply early in the year (December and January) for summer jobs. The more competitive winter positions often go to those with previous work experience in the park.

Hamilton Stores is the oldest privately owned concession in the entire national park system, having been around since 1915. The company employs 1,000 folks annually. If you can start in April or May you're considerably more likely to be hired. To receive an application form, call (800) 385-4979, or find details on the Internet at www.hamiltonstores.com/employment. You can contact the Hamilton Stores personnel department directly in the winter months (Nov.-March) at tel. (406) 587-2208, or in summer at tel. (406) 646-7325.

The third concessioner is **Yellowstone Park Service Stations,** the folks who pump Conoco gas and wash your windshield. Get hiring info by calling (406) 848-7333, or on the web at www.coolworks.com/ypss.

YELLOWSTONE GATEWAY TOWNS

Yellowstone National Park is most commonly entered via one of several Wyoming or Montana towns. The Wyoming entry points—Cody, Dubois, and Jackson—are described in other chapters. Described below are four Montana towns that act as park gateways: West Yellowstone, which predictably enough is immediately west of Yellowstone; Gardiner, at the northwest gate just a few miles from Mammoth Hot Springs; and the twin towns of Cooke City and Silver Gate just beyond the Northeast Entrance to Yellowstone. Nearby towns in Montana, including Red Lodge and Livingston, are fully covered in *Montana Handbook,* by W.C. McRae and Judy Jewell. See Don Root's *Idaho Handbook* for coverage of Island Park and the full scoop on the tater state. Both of these books are published by Avalon Travel Publishing (Emeryville, CA, www.moon.com).

WEST YELLOWSTONE

West Yellowstone, Montana, is the definitive Western tourist town. With a year-round population of only 1,000 (three times that in the summer) but more than 50 motels, it's pretty easy to see what makes the cash registers ring. The West Entrance gate—most popular of all Yellowstone entrances—lies just a couple hundred feet away. "West," as the town is known locally, isn't particularly attractive, and in the 1990s a major development added several corporate hotels and other ugly additions to an already crowded mix of restaurants, motels, T-shirt stores, and gift shops.

West Yellowstone may be decidedly middlebrow, but the surrounding land is anything but, with Gallatin (GAL-a-tin) National Forest lying north and west, Targhee National Forest just a few miles to the south, and Yellowstone National Park just a few feet to the east. It's just a couple of miles east from West Yellowstone to the Wyoming border, and the Idaho border lies only nine miles west. Hamilton Stores—one of the primary Yellowstone concessioners—has its summer offices in West Yellowstone.

History

In 1907, the Union Pacific Railroad completed laying tracks for its Oregon Short Line to the western border of Yellowstone. The following summer, Yellowstone Special trains began rolling in from Salt Lake City, dropping tourists for their stagecoach tours of the park. A small town—West Yellowstone—quickly developed on the margins of the park, providing lodging, meals, and tourist trinkets. After WW II, interest in rail travel declined and more and more people came to Yellowstone by automobile. Although the last passengers stepped off the train in 1960, the Union Pacific's historic stone depot and neighboring buildings still stand; they now house a museum, library, police station, jail, medical clinic, and other offices.

The West Yellowstone area was rocked by a devastating magnitude-7.5 earthquake on Aug. 17, 1959. One of the most powerful temblors ever recorded in the Lower 48 states, the quake cracked Hebgen Dam and caused a massive landslide (estimated at over 80 million tons of debris!) that generated a 20-foot-high tsunami and created Earthquake Lake. Twenty-eight people died, and the geysers and hot springs of Yellowstone were dramatically affected for years.

Sights

Museum of the Yellowstone, 124 Yellowstone Ave., tel. (406) 646-7814 or (800) 500-6923, is a stone-and-log structure from the railroad days. It's right along the main highway into the park. Entrance is $6 for adults; $5 for seniors, students, and kids; and $18 for families. Kids under eight get in free. The museum is open daily 8 a.m.-6 p.m. (till 10 p.m. in midsummer) from mid-May to mid-October; closed at other times of the year. Inside are exhibits on the railroads (and their role in helping establish Yellowstone National Park), the 1959 Hebgen Lake earthquake, the Yellowstone fires of 1988, "Old Snaggletooth" the grizzly (and other wildlife), mountain men, and the U.S. cavalry. Videos and movies about Yellowstone are shown in the theater. The Plains Indian collection includes artifacts rarely seen in museums today, including a Blackfeet medicine bundle and other sacred items. The museum also has a good collection of regional books for sale. Out front is a grand old park bus last used in 1959.

Right next door is another wonderful stone structure (built in 1925) that served until the late 1950s as an elegant Union Pacific Dining Lodge. The building has a spacious dining hall containing an enormous fireplace, a 45-foot-tall vaulted ceiling, and handmade light fixtures. Also worth a look-see is an **Oregon Short Line Railroad car** housed at the Holiday Inn Sunspree Resort, 315 Yellowstone Avenue. Built in 1903, the railroad car has been beautifully restored with antiques.

Family-run **Eagle's Store,** on the corner of Canyon and Yellowstone, tel. (406) 646-9300, is definitely worth a stop. Built in the 1920s, this historic log building contains all the standard tourist knickknacks, along with quality Western clothing, jewelry, fishing tackle, and a delightful old-fashioned soda fountain in the summer months.

In the early 1990s, a massive $50 million project covering 67 acres transformed (some might use the term decimated) the town of West Yellowstone. Included are a grizzly and wolf theme park, an IMAX theater, three major hotels, cabins, a restaurant, fast-food joints, an RV park, and post office. The centerpiece is the **Grizzly Discovery Center,** 201 S. Canyon St., home to eight Alaskan and Canadian grizzlies and 10 captive-born gray wolves. Not all the bears are visible at any given time, but visitors are bound to see at least one in the pseudo-natural habitat. The center is open daily all year 8:30 a.m.-8:30 p.m., with wildlife viewing till dusk. Entrance costs $7.50 for adults, $6.50 for seniors, $3 for ages 5-16, free for kids under five. This for-profit center attracts throngs of visitors and photographers who might otherwise never see a grizzly or wolf, and there's always a staff member out to answer any questions. It remains controversial, however. Scientists note that the bears here are genetically quite distinct from those in Yellowstone, and anyone who has spent time around grizzlies in the wild will be dismayed to see them in captivity, even in a facility less oppressive than traditional zoos. The folks at Grizzly Discovery Center counter that all these bears were either raised in captivity or "problem" bears that would almost certainly have been killed had they not been moved here. In addition to the bears and wolves, the center has wildlife exhibits (including a walk-in bear den), bear safety tips (I recommend not entering bear dens), a 40-minute video on bears, plus the obligatory gift shop. Get more info about the center by calling (406) 646-7001 or (800) 257-2570, or visiting them on the web at www.grizzlydiscoveryctr.com.

Directly in front of Grizzly Discovery Center is **Yellowstone IMAX Theatre,** tel. (406) 646-4100 or (888) 854-5862, where you can watch the big-budget production of *Yellowstone* on the 60- by 80-foot screen; other movies typically are on wolves and Alaska. The theater is open daily 9 a.m.-9 p.m. May to mid-October, with reduced hours the rest of the year. Admission costs $7.50 for adults, $5.50 for ages 3-11; free for younger children. The featured attraction is a 35-minute movie that presents Yellowstone history and geology complete with stirring music and a cast of dozens. If you haven't seen IMAX flicks before, hold onto your seat—lots of jaw-dropping scenes here. The movie packs in the crowds on summer days, but the film seems like a Disneylandish version of reality, ignoring many of the things you're likely to see in the park—such as burned forests, crowds of visitors, and potholed roads—and putting history into a pretty little box. Reality wasn't—and isn't—quite like this. Even more disconcerting is that this glorification of the park stands right next to the park. To me it symbolizes the make-a-buck attitude that holds Yellowstone up as an attraction while developing a massive complex on its very margin.

Evidence of the powerful 1959 earthquake is still visible north of West Yellowstone along Hebgen Lake. The Forest Service has an **Earthquake Visitor Center;** get there by heading eight miles north on US Hwy. 191 and turning left on US Hwy. 287. Continue another 17 miles west to the center; open daily 8:30 a.m.-6 p.m. from Memorial Day to late September only.

Hostels

Budget travelers will be happy to discover the West Yellowstone International Hostel (not affiliated with AYH) in the historic **Madison Hotel,** 139 Yellowstone Ave., tel. (406) 646-7745 or (800) 838-7745, http://wyellowstone.com/madisonhotel. Now on the National Register of Historic Places, the hotel has friendly owners and a delightfully rustic lobby crowded with deer and moose heads. Presidents Harding and Hoover stayed here (though it wasn't a hostel at the time). Travelers stay in comfortable bedrooms (three or four beds in each) that have been furnished with handmade lodgepole furniture. The classic hotel rooms are a delightful mix of old and new, providing the ambience of a place that has been here since 1912. No televisions or phones in the rooms, but they do have a small fridge for hostelers in the back. Rates are $18 per person in dorm rooms (three or four beds), or $27-52 d for a private hotel room. They also have standard motel accommodations behind the hotel for $49-79 d. Make hostel reservations a few days ahead in midsummer or get here before evening to be sure of a space in the dorms. It's open Memorial Day to early October only. Budget-Moderate.

The **Madison Winter Hostel,** tel. (406) 646-7100, may or may not be in business when you read this. Housed in the log cabin directly behind the Madison Hotel, this is a low-cost option for single folks in the winter months; beds are $20 per person. The facilities are rustic, but include a full kitchen, washer, and dryer. Call for details. Inexpensive.

Motels

The proximity to Yellowstone makes the town of West Yellowstone an extremely popular stopping place for vacationers in both summer and winter, and more than 2,000 rooms are available. It is also a pricey place to stay; only a few places have rooms for less than $65 during the peak seasons. The streets are lined with more than three dozen motels, so I won't try to list all of them. If you're a member of AAA, check its *TourBook,* which includes 20 of the better places. (Rates are usually lower for AAA members, too.) Be aware that during the summertime, everything in West Yellowstone fills up by early afternoon, so get there early or make advance bookings. Motels can even be full on weekends in late September. Reserve a room in March or April for the peak summer season. Add a four percent lodging tax to the rates listed below.

West Yellowstone Central Reservations, tel. (406) 646-7077 or (888) 646-7077, www.yellowstone.reservations.net, makes reservations for a dozen local motels and RV parks and can also set up wintertime snowcoach tours and snowmobile rentals.

Two recommended economy-end places (no phones in the rooms, however) are **Al's Westward Ho Motel,** 16 Boundary St., tel. (406) 646-7331 or (888) 646-7331, where rooms are $40-48 s or d (kitchenettes $3 more); and **Alpine Motel,** 120 Madison Ave., tel. (406) 646-7544, where rooms go for $45-53 s or d. Both of these are open May-Oct. only. Inexpensive.

For similarly priced lodging available all year, stay at **Lazy G Motel,** 123 Hayden, tel. (406) 646-7586, where the clean and cozy rooms cost $43-53 s or d. All contain fridges and phones; kitchenettes are $10 extra. Inexpensive.

Pony Express Motel, 4 Firehole Ave., tel. (406) 646-7644 or (800) 323-9708, www.yellowstonevacations.com, has a quiet location; $49 for one bed or $64 for two beds. A kitchenette is $75 for up to four people. Inexpensive-Moderate. **Golden West Motel,** 429 Madison Ave., tel. (406) 646-7778, www.wyellowstone.com/goldenwest, is a small motel with a dozen remodeled rooms costing $50 s or d. Open May to mid-October and January to mid-March. Inexpensive.

Three Bear Lodge, 217 Yellowstone Ave., tel. (406) 646-7353 or (800) 646-7353, is probably best known for its popular restaurant of the same name. The 74-room motel features contemporary-styled rooms, plus four indoor jacuzzis and an outdoor pool. Rates start at $73 s or d, up to $108 d for rooms with jetted tubs and $148 for full suites. Get more information by visiting the website: www.three-bear-lodge.com. Moderate-Premium.

Wagon Wheel Cabins and Campground, 408 Gibbon, tel. (406) 646-7872, www.w-yellowstone.com/wagonwheel, has a collection of 10 very attractive cabins, most containing full kitchens. The cabins are on large lots surrounded by trees, and each has a barbecue grill and picnic table. A one-bedroom unit starts at $75 d; the largest unit has three bedrooms and a fireplace, and sleeps six for $174. There's a three-night summertime minimum on the larger cabins, and a five-night minimum in winter. The cabins at Wagon Wheel fill early, so book well ahead. Moderate.

Hibernation Station, 212 Gray Wolf Ave., tel. (406) 646-4200 or (800) 580-3557, www.hibernationstation.com, is quite different from the more homey Wagon Wheel. Here you'll find 35 modern cabins—each a bit different inside—with handmade log furniture and down comforters. Some also contain kitchenettes. Rates start at $99 d for a cabin with a queen bed, or $169 for one that sleeps four and contains a queen-size bunk bed, fireplace, and kitchenette. Families will appreciate the large condo unit with room for eight, a full kitchen and dining area, fireplace and jetted tubs for $269. A big indoor jacuzzi is available for all guests. Moderate-Expensive.

You'll find very good accommodations at **Brandin' Iron Motel,** 201 Canyon St., tel. (406) 646-9411 or (800) 217-4613, www.brandiniron.com. Rooms cost $80 s or $90 d, including fridges, a continental breakfast, and two jacuzzis. Expensive.

One of the nicer lodging places in West Yellowstone is **Stage Coach Inn,** filling an entire block at 209 Madison Ave., tel. (406) 646-7381 or (800) 842-2882, www.yellowstoneinn.com. Rooms go for $109-139 s or d and include access to a sauna and two jacuzzis. The hotel features an impressive Western-style lobby with fireplace, plus a restaurant, coffee shop, and heated underground parking. Premium.

Seven miles west of town, **Lionshead Super 8 Lodge,** tel. (406) 646-9584 or (800) 843-1991, has quality rooms, a country setting, plus a sauna and hot tub. Rooms are $90 s or d. It's very popular with the retirement crowd, who park RVs in the adjacent "campground." Expensive.

The motel chains have moved into West Yellowstone in a big way. One of the nicest of these new motels is **Comfort Inn,** 638 Madison Ave., tel. (406) 646-4212 or (888) 264-2466, www.w-yellowstone.com/comfortinn. The featured attraction here is the biggest indoor pool in town, but the motel also has a small exercise room, jacuzzi, and continental breakfast. Rates are $129 s or d in standard rooms, or $189 for six-person suites. Moderate-Premium.

Days Inn, 118 Electric St., tel. (406) 646-7656 or (800) 548-9551, www.wyellowstone.com/loomis, is another large and modern motel with standard rooms ($110 s or d), along with deluxe suites containing king beds and in-room jacuzzis ($155 d). The motel also has a hot tub, saunas, and a small indoor pool that features the star attraction: a 90-foot water slide. Premium-Luxury.

Best Western Desert Inn, 133 Canyon St., tel. (406) 646-7376 or (800) 528-1234, has an indoor pool and jacuzzi, and serves continental breakfast each morning. Prices fluctuate through the summer and may be higher on weekends and lower on weekdays, but expect to pay around $149 s or d. Premium-Luxury.

Several block-long lodging monstrosities have recently opened on the south side of town. Best of these is probably **Gray Wolf Inn & Suites,** 250 S. Canyon, tel. (406) 646-0000 or (800) 852-8602, www.graywolf-inn.com. The motel features a jacuzzi, sauna, and small indoor pool, plus a breakfast buffet. An added attraction—especially in the winter—is the heated underground parking garage. Rates are $139 s or d in standard rooms, or $189-289 for six-person suites that contain a living room and full kitchen. Premium-Luxury.

The most elaborate place in town is the ludicrously named **West Yellowstone Conference Hotel Holiday Inn Sunspree Resort,** 315 Yellowstone Ave., tel. (406) 646-7365 or (800) 646-7365, with spacious rooms, an indoor pool, exercise room, sauna, and jacuzzi. Standard rooms cost $125 d, two-room family suites are $179 and sleep six, and luxurious executive suites (king bed, jetted tub, and wet bar) run $200. Moderate-Premium.

Guest Houses

There are no B&Bs in West Yellowstone; the last one was driven out of business in 1999 after all the new chain motels flooded the local lodging market. Out in the country eight miles west of town, **Sportsman's High Vacation Rentals,** tel. (406) 646-7865, has six vacation homes and cabins for rent. These range from a luxurious carriage house (perfect for a romantic getaway) that sleeps four for $175 per night, up to a spacious two-story home with five bedrooms and five baths that sleeps eight for $310. All of these contain knotty pine interiors, country-style appointments, and full kitchens. A three-night minimum stay is required in the summer. Moderate-Expensive.

Local companies renting condos include: **Yellowstone Townhouses,** tel. (406) 646-9331; **Yellowstone Village Rental Condos** (near Hebgen Lake), tel. (406) 646-7335 or (800) 276-7335; and **Lodgepole Townhouse,** tel. (406)

646-9253. A three-night minimum stay is required for all of these.

Public Campgrounds

The nearest Park Service camping place is inside Yellowstone at **Madison Campground,** 14 miles east of West Yellowstone. The cost is $15, and it's open May to early November. Get here early since Madison fills quickly and doesn't take reservations. Gallatin National Forest has a number of campgrounds in the West Yellowstone area. Closest is **Baker's Hole Campground** ($10; open Memorial Day to mid-September), three miles north of West Yellowstone. It's open for RVs and other hard-sided vehicles only because of bear problems. Tent campers will need to go north of town to **Hebgen Lake,** where five different tenting areas are strung westward along the lake; closest is the **Lonesomehurst Campground** ($10; open Memorial Day to mid-September), located 12 miles from West Yellowstone. No reservations are taken at any of these Forest Service sites.

The Forest Service maintains four public-use cabins ($25 a night for four people) in the country around West Yellowstone. Three of these are open year-round. The closest is **Basin Station Cabin,** approximately nine miles west of town. Get details on all four cabins by calling (406) 823-6961 or checking the web at www.fs.fed.us/r1/gallatin/recreation.

RV Parks

West Yellowstone has six private campgrounds right in town, and six more are west or north of town. Most of the in-town places are just RV parking lots. Far nicer are two places with shady trees and quiet sites: **Rustic RV Campground,** 634 US Hwy. 20, tel. (406) 646-7387, www.w-yellowstone.com/rusticwagon, ($22 for tents or $32-34 for RVs); and **Wagon Wheel Cabins and Campground,** 408 Gibbon Ave., tel. (406) 646-7872, www.w-yellowstone.com/wagonwheel, ($20 for tents or $30-32 for RVs). Noncampers can shower at either of these for $5. Rustic is open mid-April to mid-October, and Wagon Wheel is open Memorial Day-September. **Canyon Street Laundromat,** 312 Canyon, tel. (406) 646-9733, also has hot showers.

The other in-town RV parks are **Brandin' Iron Inn,** 201 Canyon, tel. (406) 646-9411 or (800) 217-4613 (no tents, but it has a hot tub); **Hideaway RV Campground,** 310 Electric St., tel. (406) 646-9049; **Yellowstone Cabins & RV Park,** 504 US Hwy. 20 West, tel. (406) 646-9350; and **Yellowstone Grizzly RV Park,** 210 S. Electric, tel. (406) 646-4466. Two places are west of town on US Hwy. 20: **Yellowstone Park KOA,** tel. (406) 646-7606 or (800) 562-7591; and **Lionshead Resort/Super 8 Motel,** tel. (406) 646-9584 or (800) 800-8000. The KOA has an outdoor pool. **Campfire Lodge Resort,** tel. (406) 646-7258, and **Yellowstone Holiday Resort,** tel. (406) 646-4242 or (800) 643-4227, both have RV campgrounds along Hebgen Lake north of West Yellowstone.

Food

West Yellowstone has quite a number of good eateries, but prices are generally higher than in Wyoming towns and the menu is plebeian. Expect to pay $10-20 for dinner entrées. For breakfast, run on over to **Running Bear Pancake House,** 538 Madison Ave., tel. (406) 646-7703, but be ready for a long wait in midsummer. Good for lunch too; open 7 a.m.-2 p.m. only.

Get espressos and fresh baked goods—including monster cinnamon rolls—at **Nancy P's,** 29 Canyon St., tel. (406) 646-9737. Open summers only. Stop by **Freeheel & Wheel,** 40 Yellowstone Ave., tel. (406) 646-7744, for a latte or a light lunch and pizza by the slice. Another good espresso destination is **The Book Peddler,** 106 Canyon St., tel. (406) 646-9358 or (800) 253-2855, where you'll find several tables in the back for bagels and coffee. It's a good place to hang out on a cold winter day.

Ernie's Bighorn Deli, 406 Highway Ave., tel. (406) 646-9467, is the local doughnut shop in the morning, and it makes unbeatable sandwiches for lunch. They'll put together a big box lunch if you're heading into the park and want to leave the sandwiches to the experts.

If you're searching for a down-home greasy spoon serving three meals a day, your hunt will end at **Old Town Cafe,** 18 Madison, tel. (406) 646-9633. Chicken fried steaks, biscuits and gravy, buffalo burgers, and hot open-faced sandwiches grace the menu, and pine paneling decorates the walls. Those who love '50s' diners will appreciate the simple and filling meals here.

Pig out cheaply at tiny **Mountain Mike's Cafe,**

38 Canyon, tel. (406) 646-9462, which serves all-American faves: burgers, sandwiches, barbecued ribs, steak, and chicken, plus freshly baked cream pies for dessert.

Justifiably popular for both lunch and dinner, **Bullwinkles,** 19 Madison Ave. W, tel. (406) 646-7974, cranks out steaks, burgers, pork chops, salads, and homemade pastries. Big portions too.

Pete's Rocky Mountain Pizza, 104 Canyon St., tel. (406) 646-7820, has the most creative local pizzas, plus Italian and even Mexican specialties. Free delivery if you just want to eat a pizza in your motel room. **Gusher Pizza and Sandwich Shoppe,** Madison and Dunraven, tel. (406) 646-9050, is a family place with fast service, the best Reubens in these parts, and tolerable pizzas (frozen crust, alas). Wednesday is all-you-can-eat spaghetti night. **Wild West Pizza,** 20 Madison Ave., tel. (406) 646-4400, has pizza by the slice or pie. **Chinatown,** 100 Madison Ave., tel. (406) 646-7088, serves surprisingly authentic Chinese meals.

Three Bear Restaurant, 205 Yellowstone Ave., tel. (406) 646-7811, is a friendly place with an upmarket dinner menu of shrimp, halibut, trout, chicken, and steaks. They have the best salad-and-soup bar in town, and desserts are a specialty, particularly their famous apple brown Betty. Open three meals a day and entirely no-smoking.

Coachman Restaurant, downstairs in the Stage Coach Inn, 209 Madison Ave., tel. (406) 646-7381, serves three meals a day, including big traditional breakfasts (great omelets), along with steak, seafood, and pasta for dinner. They also feature a salad bar and a substantial wine list.

If gourmet meals are your goal, you're probably out of luck in pedestrian West Yellowstone. Best bet? Drive to Big Sky (57 miles north) for the acclaimed **Lone Mountain Ranch,** tel. (406) 995-4644 or (800) 514-4644, www.lmranch.com.

The most unusual local eatery is **Eino's Bar,** tel. (406) 646-9344, nine miles north of town on US Hwy. 191. It's a fun cook-your-own steak, burger, and chicken place with a big indoor grill. Other accoutrements include fresh baked breads, a delicious potato dish, and salads. Open for lunch and dinner year-round. The patio features a view across Hebgen Lake, and the bar has a big-screen TV and pool tables.

Market Place, 22 Madison Ave., tel. (406) 646-9600, and **Food Roundup Supermarket,** on the corner of Madison and Dunraven, tel. (406) 646-7501, are the local grocery stores. Market Place also contains a deli and bakery. For sweet treats, head to **Arrowleaf Ice Cream Parlor,** 29 Canyon St., tel. (406) 646-9776. In addition to shakes, banana splits, and waffle cones, Arrowleaf serves burgers, chili dogs, and surprisingly good homemade soups.

Entertainment

During the summer, you can attend lighthearted comedies and musicals for the whole family at **Playmill Theatre,** 124 Madison Ave., tel. (406) 646-7757, www.playmill.com. Watch flicks at **Bears Den Cinema,** 15 Electric St., tel. (406) 646-7777. In addition to the IMAX films described above, **Yellowstone IMAX Theatre,** tel. (406) 646-4100 or (888) 854-5862, shows Hollywood's latest efforts most evenings.

For live bands try **Stage Coach Inn,** 209 Madison Ave., tel. (406) 646-7381, or **Iron Horse Saloon,** inside the West Yellowstone Conference Hotel at 315 Yellowstone Ave., tel. (406) 646-7365. **Lionshead Super 8 Lodge,** seven miles west of town, tel. (406) 646-9584, has square dancing in the summer.

Events

On the second weekend of March, the **Rendezvous Ski Race,** a nationally known Nordic ski race, attracts hundreds of participants. The following weekend brings a very different event, the **World Snowmobile Expo,** with races, demos, and other activities. A fun parade, live music, and fireworks highlight the town's **Fourth of July** festivities, and the **Yellowstone Rod Run** takes place on the first full weekend of August, bringing vintage cars of all types to the oldest such event in the Pacific Northwest. The **Burnt Hole Mountain Man Rendezvous** on the third weekend of August includes arts and crafts, traditional games, tall-tale competitions, and other old-time events.

Summer Recreation

Horseback trail rides and Western cookouts are available from **Parade Rest Guest Ranch,** seven miles north of town, tel. (406) 646-7217, and **Diamond P Ranch,** seven miles to the west, tel. (406) 646-7246. Several other ranches farther afield also offer horseback rides; contact the chamber of commerce for details.

The 30-km Rendezvous Trail System becomes mountain-bike central when summer rolls around. It starts from the southern edge of town; get a map at the chamber of commerce. A small trail fee is charged. Rent mountain bikes from **Yellowstone Bicycles,** 132 Madison Ave., tel. (406) 646-7815, or **Freeheel & Wheel,** 40 Yellowstone Ave., tel. (406) 646-7744. Freeheel also rents bike trailers and baby joggers; ask about their free daily rides. Both shops have full repair facilities.

Yellowstone Rental & Sports, tel. (406) 646-9377 or (888) 646-9377, rents a wide range of outdoor gear, including tents, sleeping bags, cookstoves, fishing boats, canoes, mountain bikes, baby strollers and car seats, snowshoes, and even backhoes for those who want to dig things up a bit. It's eight miles west of West Yellowstone along US Hwy. 20.

You'll find five different **fly-fishing shops** in town, a reflection of the sport's importance in the Yellowstone area. The shops are: **Arrick's Fishing Flies,** 125 Madison Ave., tel. (406) 646-7290; **Bud Lilly's Trout Shop,** 39 Madison Ave., tel. (406) 646-7801 or (800) 854-9559; **Eagle's Tackle Shop,** 3 Canyon St., tel. (406) 646-7521; **Jacklin's Fly Shop,** 105 Yellowstone Ave., tel. (406) 646-7336; and **Madison River Outfitters,** 117 Canyon St., tel. (406) 646-9644. All of these offer guided fishing and equipment.

Three rafting companies run all-day and half-day whitewater trips down the Gallatin River approximately 50 miles north of West Yellowstone (near Big Sky). The rafting season generally runs from late May to September, and youcan expect to pay around $80 for all day or $40 for a half-day trip. The companies are: **Geyser Whitewater Expeditions,** tel. (406) 995-4989 or (800) 914-9031, www.raftmontana.com; **Montana Whitewater,** tel. (307) 763-4465 or (800) 799-4465, www.montanawhitewater.com; and **Yellowstone Raft Company,** tel. (406) 995-4613 or (800) 348-4376, www.yellowstoneraft.com. Yellowstone Raft Company also leads trips down the challenging Madison River northwest of West Yellowstone, and Geyser Whitewater has scenic float trips for those who'd rather relax.

Winter Recreation

West Yellowstone is infamous for its bitterly cold winters, when the thermometer can drop to -50º F. Fortunately, it doesn't always stay there, and by March the days have often warmed to a balmy 20º F. In November, West becomes a national center for cross-country skiers, with the U.S. Nordic and biathlon ski teams training here.

Two trail systems provide a wide variety of Nordic skiing conditions. The 30-km Rendezvous Trail system takes off from the southern edge of town and is groomed with both classical and skating tracks from early November through April. The nine-km Riverside Trail begins on the east side of town and leads to the Madison River within Yellowstone National Park. This trail is partially groomed and provides a good opportunity to see bison, elk, and possibly moose; it's closed to skate skiing. You can also ski the snowpacked streets in winter. Find many more places for flat tracking or telemarking in adjacent Yellowstone National Park and the Gallatin and Targhee National Forests. Before heading out, get recorded avalanche-safety information from the **Avalanche Advisory Hotline,** tel. (406) 587-6981, or on the web at www.gomontana.com/avalanche.

Rent skinny skis from **Bud Lilly's Trout Shop,** 39 Madison Ave., tel. (406) 646-7801 or (800) 854-9559, or **Freeheel & Wheel,** 40 Yellowstone Ave., tel. (406) 646-7744. Freeheel also rents snowshoes, as does **Yellowstone Rental & Sports,** eight miles west of town on US Hwy. 20, tel. (406) 646-9377 or (888) 646-9377.

Yellowstone Alpen Guides, 555 Yellowstone Ave., tel. (406) 646-9591 or (800) 858-3502, www.yellowstoneguides.com, leads skiing tours inside Yellowstone, with access via one of the company's snowcoaches. All-day trips are $99 per person, and skier drop-offs and multinight trips into the park are available.

The closest downhill ski and snowboard area is the world-class **Big Sky Resort,** 57 miles north of West Yellowstone, tel. (800) 548-4486, www.bigskyresort.com. The resort features 15 lifts and more than 3,500 acres of terrain. You will find excellent cross-country trails at Lone Mountain Ranch near Big Sky.

The chamber of commerce trumpets West as the "snowmobile capital of the world," and each day between November and late March hundreds (and sometimes thousands) of 'bilers show up to roar through Yellowstone's West Entrance or across thousands of acres of adjacent Forest Service lands. On busy days long lines of snowmobiles belch blue smoke into the air while waiting to enter the park.

Nearly 20 different snowmobile tour and rental companies operate out of West Yellowstone. Rentals run around $85-150 per day depending upon the type of machine; guided Yellowstone tours are more expensive—up to around $180 per person per day. Hundreds more folks bring in their own "crotch rockets" to ride on park roads or national forest lands, and many local motels offer snowmobile/lodging packages. The West Yellowstone Chamber of Commerce, tel. (406) 646-7701, can provide current snow and trail conditions, a detailed map of local trails, and a listing of companies that rent snowmobiles.

A less polluting and quieter option is to take a snowcoach tour of Yellowstone from **Yellowstone Alpen Guides,** 555 Yellowstone Ave., tel. (406) 646-9591 or (800) 858-3502, www.yellowstoneguides.com; or **Yellowstone Expeditions,** tel. (406) 646-9333 or (800) 728-9333. Tours cost $65-99 per day, and both companies also have multinight trips.

Information and Services

The **West Yellowstone Chamber of Commerce,** 30 Yellowstone Ave., tel. (406) 646-7701, is open daily 8 a.m.-8 p.m. Memorial Day to Labor Day, and Mon.-Fri. 8 a.m.-5 p.m. the rest of the year. The office is staffed during the summer and winter months by Forest Service and Park Service employees who can provide info on the great outdoors. Find the chamber on the web at www.westyellowstonechamber.com. Another useful site is www.westyellowstone.com, maintained by Circumerro Publishing. Check your e-mail at **West Yellowstone Web Works,** 27 Geyser St., tel. (406) 646-7006, www.wyellowstone.com.

The **Hebgen Lake Ranger District Office** is just north of town on US Hwy. 191/287, tel. (406) 646-7369. Pick up maps of Gallatin National Forest (www.fs.fed.us/r1/gallatin) here, along with an interesting brochure on the Madison River Canyon Earthquake Area.

West Yellowstone's **post office** is at 209 Grizzly Ave., tel. (406) 646-7704. You'll find **ATMs** in several local banks, hotels, and other businesses.

Wash clothes at **Canyon Street Laundromat,** 312 Canyon St., tel. (406) 646-9733; **Econo-Mart Laundromat,** 307 Firehole Ave., tel. (406) 646-7887; or **Swan Cleaners & Laundromat,** 520 Madison Ave., tel. (406) 646-7892. Canyon Street also has shower facilities.

Books

The Book Peddler, 106 Canyon St., tel. (406) 646-9358 or (800) 253-2855, is a large and attractive bookstore with many Montana, Wyoming, and Yellowstone titles. In back is a pleasant cafe selling espresso, bagels, and pastries. This is a great place to hang with the locals. **Bookworm Books,** 14 Canyon, tel. (406) 646-9736, is another good shop with both new and used titles including many first editions; it's open nightly till midnight all summer! The small local **library** is housed in the railroad's old stone dining lodge at 200 Yellowstone Ave., tel. (406) 646-9017.

Transportation

Community Bus Service, tel. (406) 646-7600, provides bus service between West Yellowstone and Bozeman on Tuesday and Thursday in the summer, and Thursday only the rest of the year. There is no charge for this community-sponsored service (!) but a $10 donation is requested. The bus stops in the chamber of commerce parking lot. **Greyhound Bus,** tel. (800) 231-2222, www.greyhound.com, has daily summer-only runs between Bozeman and Salt Lake City, with a stop in West Yellowstone in front of West Yellowstone Office Services at 132 Electric Street.

Sky West/Delta, tel. (406) 646-7351 or (800) 453-9417, has service to West Yellowstone airport (just north of town) from Salt Lake City June-September; the rest of the year the closest air service is in Bozeman or Jackson Hole. In the winter months, **4x4 Stage,** tel. (406) 848-2224 or (800) 517-8243, provides shuttle vans between West Yellowstone and Bozeman airport for $57, with a minimum of four people. Although the company is based in Bozeman, it provides taxi service throughout the area, including into West Yellowstone year-round. Call 24 hours ahead for taxi reservations.

West Yellowstone has some of the highest gas prices anywhere around; fill up before you get here! Rental cars are available through **Budget** (at the airport), tel. (406) 646-7882 or (800)

527-0700; **Big Sky Car Rentals,** tel. (406) 646-9564 or (800) 426-7669, www.yellowstonevacations.com; and **Travelers Station Car Rentals** (summer only), tel. (406) 646-9332 or (800) 548-9551. Big Sky has the cheapest rates, starting around $35 a day for a compact car.

Park Tours

Several companies offer all-day tours of Yellowstone from June through September. **Gray Line,** 633 Madison Ave., tel. (406) 646-9374 or (800) 523-3102, www.grayline.com, offers "lower loop" park tours daily and "upper loop" tours three times a week for $38 plus park entrance fees. They also offer Quake Lake ($38) and Jackson Hole ($49) tours from West Yellowstone, as well as several other regional tours. **Buffalo Bus Lines,** 429 Yellowstone, tel. (406) 646-9564 or (800) 426-7669, www.yellowstonevacations.com, has narrated loop tours of Yellowstone for $35 per person (plus the park entrance fee). On odd days they circle the park's upper loop; on even days they take you to sights along the lower loop road. 4X4 Stage (described above) leads all-day park tours in the summer for $50 per person.

Yellowstone Alpen Guides, 555 Yellowstone Ave., tel. (406) 646-9591 or (800) 858-3502, www.yellowstoneguides.com, leads more personalized tours, from day-trips to multiday excursions. The company provides the naturalist guide, and you travel around the park in the company van or your own car.

GARDINER

The little tourist town of Gardiner, Montana (pop. 800), lies barely outside the northwest entrance to Yellowstone, just three miles from the Wyoming line. The Yellowstone River slices right through town. Park headquarters at Mammoth Hot Springs is just five miles away, and the large warehouses of park concessioner Amfac Parks & Resorts dominate the vicinity. Gardiner is the only year-round entrance to Yellowstone, and the Absaroka-Beartooth Wilderness lies just north of here. The town sits at an elevation of 5,300 feet—some 900 feet lower than Mammoth—and has warm, dry summers and relatively mild winters.

Gardiner was founded in 1883 when the Northern Pacific Railroad extended a line to the edge of Yellowstone, making the town the first major entryway into the park. A reporter of that era described Gardiner as having "200 hardy souls, with 6 restaurants, 1 billiard hall, 2 dance halls, 4 houses of ill-fame, 1 milk man and 21 saloons." Today, the most distinctive structure in town is the monumental stone park entryway—similar to France's Arc de Triomphe—which was for many years the primary entry point into Yellowstone. Built in 1903, **Roosevelt Arch** was dedicated by Pres. Theodore Roosevelt, a man regarded by many as Yellowstone's patron saint. A tablet above the keystone is inscribed, "For the Benefit and Enjoyment of the People." (The

Roosevelt Arch in Gardiner, Montana, marks the northwest entrance to Yellowstone.

arch was actually built to offset the park visitors' initial disappointment at finding the rather ordinary country in this part of Yellowstone!)

Motels and Cabins

Gardiner has many lodging places, but be sure to reserve ahead in the summer; rooms may be hard to find even in mid-September. Rates plummet after (and before) the gold rush of seasonal tourists; $75 summertime rooms suddenly go for $30! Accommodations are listed below from least to most expensive. Add a four percent tax to these rates.

Inexpensive-Moderate: Yellowstone River Motel, tel. (406) 848-7303 or (888) 797-4837, is open May-October. Economy rooms in the older building are $55 s or d, while rooms in the new addition run $75 s or d. A garden patio overlooks the river, and a family unit with kitchenette is also available.

Moderate: Jim Bridger Court, tel. (406) 848-7371 or (888) 858-7508, is a classic Western place with clean and well-kept log cabins built in 1937. Rates are $60 d to $75 for four people; open mid-May to mid-October.

Originally built in the 1950s but updated with newer furnishings, **Hillcrest Cottages,** 200 Scott St., tel. (406) 848-7353 or (800) 970-7353, has 15 units, all with kitchenettes. Most have showers, but a few contain tubs. No phones. Rates are $60 s or $82 d; open May-November.

Riverside Cottages, tel. (406) 848-7719 or (877) 774-2836, www.riversidecottages.com, is a small place with four motel units ($69 s or d) and four cottages ($89 d or $99 for four people) with full kitchens. Everything here has been recently refurbished, and guests will enjoy the deck out back that contains a hot tub overlooking the Yellowstone River.

Yellowstone Village Inn, tel. (406) 848-7417 or (800) 228-8158, has modern rooms for $69-79 s or d. Amenities include an indoor pool, sauna, and light breakfast. The three-story **Motel 6,** tel. (406) 848-7520 or (800) 466-8356, has predictable rooms and a view of the parking lot. Summer rates are $70 s or $78 d. **Westernaire Motel,** tel. (406) 848-7397 or (888) 273-0358, has clean rooms for $70 s or $75 d, but the furnishings are somewhat dated.

Expensive-Luxury: The modern **Best Western by Mammoth Hot Springs,** tel. (406) 848-7311 or (800) 829-9080, has an indoor pool, saunas, and a jacuzzi. Room rates are $84-94 s or d. **Super 8 Motel,** tel. (406) 848-7401 or (800) 800-8000, charges $89 s or d, including an indoor pool and continental breakfast.

Absaroka Lodge, tel. (406) 848-7414 or (800) 755-7414, is a modern motel with immaculate rooms for $90 s or d, and suites with kitchenettes that cost $100 s or d, or $110 for four people. All rooms have balconies overlooking the Yellowstone River.

Out in the country five miles northwest of Gardiner, **Maiden Basin Inn,** tel. (406) 848-7080 or (800) 624-3364, is a modern eight-room lodge with a variety of accommodations. Built by the owner/architect, the inn exudes country charm. Rooms start at $95 for two queens or a king bed. A two-bedroom townhouse with a full kitchen, living room, and loft rents for $185. The latter sleeps seven people. All rooms have private decks where you can sit on a rocking chair with a view of Electric Peak inside Yellowstone. An outdoor hot tub is available, and a continental breakfast is served in the lobby. Maiden Basin Inn is open mid-May to mid-October. Get details at www.maidenbasininn.com.

Comfort Inn, tel. (406) 848-7536 or (800) 228-5150, charges $129 s or d in contemporary rooms; suites and jacuzzi rooms are $169. A light breakfast is available in the lobby, and the motel has three indoor jacuzzis.

The most basic local accommodations are at **Gardiner Town Motel;** call (406) 848-7322 for rates.

Bed and Breakfasts

One of the nicest local lodging places is **Yellowstone Inn B&B,** tel. (406) 848-7000, consisting of a beautifully restored stone house (built in 1903) that has been furnished in a New West style. The four guest rooms cost $74-94 d and have shared or private baths. Out back is a private cottage for $124 d. A full breakfast is served, and guests will enjoy the outdoor jacuzzi. Well-behaved kids are welcome. Find them on the web at www.westerntravel.com/ye. Moderate-Premium.

Also of note is **Yellowstone Suites B&B,** 506 4th St., tel. (406) 848-7937 or (800) 948-7937, www.gomontana.com/ys.html, another stone house that's nearly a century old. Features include Victorian antique furnishings, hardwood floors, a veranda, jacuzzi, and full breakfasts. The four guest rooms have shared or private baths and cost $59-98 s or d; one contains a kitchenette. Kids are welcome. Moderate-Expensive.

Guest Houses

Arch House, tel. (406) 848-2205, is another historic rock home just two blocks from the arch entryway into Yellowstone. The two-bedroom guest house sleeps up to six and includes a full kitchen, bath, living room with stone fireplace, and dining room. The house rents for $125 d, plus $10 each for additional guests. The owners run Electric Peak Espresso next door, a good place to start your morning with a jolt of caffeine. Moderate-Premium.

Above the Rest Lodge, tel. (406) 848-7747 or (800) 406-7748, www.ablodge.qpg.com, has four modern and well-appointed cabins less than two miles north of Gardiner up Jardine Road. Smallest is a one-bedroom unit with a spiral staircase and full kitchen; $125 for four people. Largest is a spacious three-bedroom home that sleeps 10 people for $250 per night. All of these have full kitchens and decks facing Yellowstone. Inexpensive-Moderate.

Out of Town Lodging

Mountain Retreat, tel. (406) 848-7272 or (800) 727-0798, has a fully equipped two-bedroom house ($140 for up to five people) and a two-bedroom cabin ($110 for four people). Both are out in the country 10 miles north of Gardiner; no TV or phones. Inexpensive-Moderate.

Slip and Slide Ranch, tel. (406) 848-7648, sits in the country 12 miles north of Gardiner. Bed and breakfast accommodations are available in the contemporary home, which has three guest rooms, two baths, and a private entrance. Rates are $65 d, including a full breakfast. The B&B rooms are available from mid-May to mid-September. If you really want to escape, the ranch also offers a spacious and modern log lodge two and a half miles in the hills (4WD required). The lodge sleeps five for $150 or up to 12 for $200. A three-night minimum is required, and it is open mid-February to mid-October. The owners are outfitters, and use this lodge for hunters in the fall and winter. Inexpensive-Moderate.

Besides lodging in Gardiner, a number of places are available in Paradise Valley, 20 miles to the north. A good one is **Dome Mountain Cabins and Guest Houses,** tel. (406) 333-4361 or (800) 313-4868, www.domemountain-ranch.com, which has B&B cabin accommodations for $75 d and full-house rentals for $300-700 per night (the largest sleeps 12). Moderate-Premium.

Farther afield but worth a visit if you're heading north is Chico Hot Springs, 30 miles north of Gardiner in Pray, Montana. This classic old hotel sits adjacent to a hot springs-fed pool ($4.75), and the restaurant is an attraction in its own right. Dinner reservations are required. Rooms in the main and lower lodge cost $45-107. A variety of cabins and houses are also available, all the way up to a five-bedroom log home that sleeps 20 for $315 per night. Call (406) 333-4933 or (800) 468-9232 for more information, or visit www.chicohotsprings.com. Horseback rides and fly-fishing are available in the summer, and the saloon swings to country tunes on Friday and Saturday nights year-round. Inexpensive-Expensive.

Camping

Yellowstone National Park's **Mammoth Campground** is five miles up the hill at Mammoth Hot Springs and costs $12. The campground is open year-round, but sits close to a busy road. No reservations. Closer—and more peaceful—is the small **Eagle Creek Campground** ($6; open mid-June through October), less than two miles northeast of Gardiner up the gravel road on the way to Jardine. This Gallatin National Forest campground is approximately 500 feet higher than Gardiner, and you will need to bring water from town or treat water from the creek here. Two other Forest Service campgrounds (free; open mid-June through October) are a few miles up Jardine Road.

Park RVs at **Rocky Mountain Campground,** tel. (406) 848-7251, for $23 ($18 for tents); open mid-May to mid-October. Showers for noncampers cost $4, and a public laundromat is on the site. Campsites are also available in crowded, along-the-river sites at **Yellowstone RV Park,** tel. (406) 848-7496, open May-Oct. on the northwest end of town. Rates are $22-28 for RVs, $17 for tents.

Food

Bear Country Restaurant, tel. (406) 848-7188, has a popular breakfast buffet. **K Bar Club,** tel. (406) 848-9995, doesn't look like much either outside or inside, but the from-scratch pizzas are very good in this locals' hangout (not for kids since this is a bar). Families head to **Outlaw's Pizza,** in the Outpost Mall on the northwest end of town, tel. (406) 848-7733, for standard pizzas, pasta, and calzone, and a small salad bar.

Town Cafe, tel. (406) 848-7322, has sandwiches, burgers, and a big salad bar. Better food is upstairs in the Town Loft (summer only), where you can enjoy the vistas while you eat. Also downtown is **Sawtooth Deli,** tel. (406) 848-7600, with cold and hot subs, grilled sandwiches, soups, salads, and espresso. The covered deck is a favorite local hangout. Closed Nov.-April.

Yellowstone Mine Restaurant, inside the Best Western on the northwest side of town, tel. (406) 848-7336, offers very good but overpriced meals served in an old-timey mine atmosphere. Best steaks around. At **Corral Drive Inn,** tel. (406) 848-7627, Helen and her sons serve up the biggest, juiciest, and messiest (get a handful of napkins) hamburgers anywhere around.

Park Street Grill & Café, tel. (406) 848-7989, seems out of place in down-home Gardiner. Most of the menu isn't your standard Old West fare, though they do serve steaks and prime rib. Instead, it's Italian food with flare, including such delights as shrimp fra diavolo (large shrimp sautéed with garlic, peppers, and tomatoes served over linguine), or penne arribiata (fiery peppers, macaroni, red pepper, garlic, and plum tomato sauce). Meals come with a big house salad, and the atmosphere is rustic elegance. Park Street Grill is open for dinners only ($8-14 entrées), but also has a lunchtime pizza-by-the-slice cafe next door. Open all year.

Shop for groceries, fresh baked goods, and deli items at **Food Farm,** tel. (406) 848-7524, on the northwest end of town.

Events and Entertainment

The big annual event in town is the **Gardiner Rodeo,** which comes around the third weekend of June. An **Art in the Park** craft bazaar takes place in Arch Park on the first weekend of August. End summer with a blast at **Buffalo Days,** held the Friday before Labor Day and featuring an arts and crafts fair, live music and dancing, and plenty of barbecued buffalo, beef, and pork.

Look for live bands on some weekends at the **Two Bit Saloon,** tel. (406) 848-7743.

River Rafting

During the summer, three rafting companies offer whitewater trips from Gardiner down the Yellowstone River. **Yellowstone Raft Company,** tel. (406) 848-7777 or (800) 858-7781, www.yellowstoneraft.com, has been running trips since 1978. Other good companies are **Montana Whitewater,** tel. (307) 763-4465 or (800) 799-4465, www.montanawhitewater.com; and **Wild West Rafting,** tel. (406) 848-2252 or (800) 862-0557, www.wildwestrafting.com.

The rapids in this stretch of the Yellowstone River are relatively gentle, in the Class II-III range, and the featured attractions are half-day eight-mile trips or all-day 17-mile trips. Expect to pay around $30 for adults, $20 for kids for three-hour trips, or $68 for adults, $48 for kids for a full-day voyage. Yellowstone Raft Company also has sit-on-top kayaks and guided fly-fishing trips, and Wild West offers scenic float trips in Paradise Valley north of Gardiner (same prices). In addition to the legit companies listed above, a number of two-bit operators also run whitewater trips each summer, but ask around to get an idea of their reputation before signing up.

Other Recreation

Wilderness Connection, tel. (406) 848-7287, has horseback trips into Yellowstone. In winter, rent cross-country skis from **Park's Fly Shop,** tel. (406) 848-7314. No local companies rent mountain bikes, but if you bring your own there are a pair of fine biking options. The Old Gardiner Rd. to Mammoth gains 900 feet in a distance of five miles and makes for a fun ride back down. Also worth a ride is the old road to Livingston, a gravel road that follows the west side of the Yellowstone River out of Gardiner. It starts near the arch and a few miles up passes an interesting old cemetery with century-old graves.

Shopping

High Country Books and Gifts, on Park St. next to Cecil's Restaurant, tel. (406) 848-7707, has a choice of Western books, along with espresso coffee. **Yellowstone Gallery & Frame-**

works, tel. (406) 848-7306, is an excellent place for quality pottery, jewelry, paintings, and photography. Also worth a look downtown is **Off the Wall Gallery,** tel. (406) 848-7775. **Flying Pig Pawn Shop,** tel. (406) 848-7510, has a variety of used outdoor gear for sale. Stop here for Internet access too; open daily.

Information and Services

The **Gardiner Chamber of Commerce,** on Park at 3rd (near Bear Country Restaurant), tel. (406) 848-7971, has local info and is open Mon.-Sat. 9 a.m.-7 p.m. May-Sept., and Tues.-Thurs. 10 a.m.-4 p.m. the rest of the year. Find them on the web at www.gardinerchamber.com. If the office is closed, check the bulletin board in the center of town.

The **Gardiner District Office** of Gallatin National Forest, tel. (406) 848-7375, www.fs.fed.us/r1/gallatin, has maps and info on the 930,584-acre **Absaroka-Beartooth Wilderness.** The portion around Gardiner is lower in elevation and covered with forests, while farther east are the alpine peaks of the Beartooth Mountains.

The **post office** is on the north end of town along U.S. Hwy. 89, tel. (406) 848-7579. Get fast cash at the **ATM** inside the Exxon station just north of the river, or from the First Interstate Bank on the northwest end of town. Wash clothes at **Arch Laundrette,** just downhill from Cecil's Restaurant on Park Street.

Transportation and Tours

Based in Bozeman, **4x4 Stage,** tel. (406) 848-2224 or (800) 517-8243, offers taxi service throughout the Yellowstone area, including into Gardiner. Call 24 hours ahead for reservations.

From mid-May through September, **Amfac Parks & Resorts,** tel. (307) 344-7311, www.travelyellowstone.com, operates full-day bus tours of Yellowstone out of Gardiner. Rates are $33 for adults, $17 for ages 12-16, and free for kids under 12 (park entrance fees are extra). These are a bit grueling, since you leave at 8:30 a.m. and don't get back till 6:15 p.m.

COOKE CITY AND SILVER GATE

Shortly after you exit Yellowstone's northeast corner along US Hwy. 212, the road widens slightly as it passes through two settlements: Silver Gate and the larger Cooke City, Montana. The towns are just three miles apart and almost within spitting distance of the Wyoming line. The area code—406—is larger than the combined population of both settlements! Although they depend upon tourism, these quiet, homespun places lack the hustle and bustle of West Yellowstone and have a more authentic feel. No leash laws here, you're likely to see dogs sleeping on the sidewalks or wandering lazily down the middle of the road. Most establishments are built of log, befitting the mining heritage of this area. Silver Gate even has a building code that requires all structures to be of log or rustic architecture—it's the only municipality in the country with such a code. Pilot and Index Peaks are the prominent rocky spires visible along the highway east of Cooke City. Dramatic Amphitheater Peak juts out just south of Silver Gate.

During the winter, the road is plowed all the way from Gardiner, through the northern part of Yellowstone, and into Cooke City, making this a popular staging area for snowmobilers and skiers heading into the Beartooth Mountains. East of Cooke City, the Beartooth Highway across 10,947-foot Beartooth Pass is closed by the first of November (often earlier) and doesn't open again until late May.

History

The town of Cooke City was first called Shoo-Fly, but the name was changed in honor of Jay Cooke Jr., a promoter of the Northern Pacific Railroad. The promised railroad never materialized, but the name stuck. Cooke City had its start in 1882 when the boundaries of the Crow Reservation were shifted to the east, opening this area to mining. A small gold rush ensued, and by the following summer, Cooke City had grown to hold several hundred miners, along with two smelters, two sawmills, and a cluster of businesses. At its peak, the town was also home to 13 saloons. As with many 19th-century mining towns, the population of Cooke City had wild swings, with up to 1,000 people at one time, but just 20 souls a few years later. The isolation, modest gold and silver strikes, and high transportation costs (no railroad was ever built into the settlement) kept mining from ever really booming. Today less than a hundred people live in Cooke

City year-round, but the population triples with the arrival of summer residents.

The town of Silver Gate has a briefer history. The land here was first homesteaded in the 1890s, but the town didn't appear until 1932 when John Taylor and J.J. White founded it as a haven for summer residents looking for a home close to Yellowstone. Only a handful of folks live here in the winter, but that swells to 100 or so when the long days of summer return.

The country around Silver Gate and Cooke City was torched in the Storm Creek Fire of 1988, leaving charred hills just a couple hundred feet to the north and prompting alterations in the road signs to read "Cooked City." Today, tourism is the ticket to ride for both Cooke City and Silver Gate. In summer the towns are crowded with folks en route to (or from) Yellowstone. Both Soda Butte Lodge and Miners Saloon in Cooke City have one-armed bandits with slot-machine poker and keno gambling. In the fall, hunters head into the surrounding mountains, and when the snow flies, the snowmobiles come out of hibernation.

Sights

It's hard to miss the red **Cooke City General Store,** tel. (406) 838-2234, one of the oldest buildings in the area. Built in 1886, this classic country market sells groceries, quality T-shirts, and gifts that include Indian jewelry and imported items from all over the globe. Open summers only. Across the street is another summertime place that is well worth a look, **Blain Gallery,** tel. (406) 939-2474. The gallery features original watercolors by Mary Blain, along with pottery, baskets, and beautiful photographs taken in the northeast corner of Yellowstone.

Cooke City Accommodations

Cooke City and Silver Gate have quite a few old-fashioned cabins that provide a delightful Old West feeling. As with other towns surrounding Yellowstone, advance reservations are always a good idea in midsummer. Add a four percent lodging tax to the rates below.

Budget: The least-expensive and funkiest local lodging option is **Yellowstone Yurt Hostel,** tel. (406) 838-2349, where you'll pay just $12 per person. Nothing at all fancy here, just six bunk beds in a cozy Tibetan-style yurt heated by a woodstove. It's a few steps to the shower, toilet, and full kitchen. You should bring a sleeping bag, though a couple of old cotton ones are here. Reservations are always a good idea, and they're necessary in the winter months. No hot water in winter either. The yurt is available mid-May through September and mid-November through March.

Inexpensive-Moderate: Three miles east of Cooke City, **Big Moose Resort,** tel. (406) 838-2393, has simple cabins, gas pumps, and a small store, all open June-October. The seven cabins contain older furnishings and private baths; two include kitchenettes. Rates start at $45 d, up to $65 for a four-person cabin with kitchenette.

Right across the road, **Big Bear Lodge,** tel. (406) 838-2267, www.sandersbigbearlodge.com, is primarily a fishing lodge, but offers nightly accommodations throughout the year. Guests stay in six older but well-kept log cabins, each of which has two double beds. Rates are $55-65 d, and breakfasts are available in the main lodge ($6 per person). The lodge is a popular destination for fly-fishing enthusiasts, who come here on three- to six-night package trips that include lodging, meals, and guided horseback rides and fishing. Anglers head into backcountry areas inside Yellowstone, returning each evening to the lodge. In the winter months, Big Bear is a popular overnight rest for skiers and snowmobilers.

You'll find spacious, clean, and comfortable rooms and cabins at **High Country Motel,** tel. (406) 838-2272. Rates are $45-57 s or d. Cabins with kitchenettes are $10 extra. Open all year, and recommended.

Antler's Log Cabins, tel. (406) 838-2432, www.yellowstonenationalpark.com, charges $45-70 for a range of cabins, some that include kitchens and lofts. It's open late May to October, and Christmas-March.

Alpine Motel, tel. (406) 838-2262, is open all year and has rooms for $55-65 s or d. Inexpensive-Moderate. **Bearclaw Cabins,** tel. (406) 838-2336, has cabin rentals (these sleep four) for $58. No kitchenettes, but open year-round.

Moderate: Hoosier's Motel, tel. (406) 838-2241, has good rooms for $60 s or d; open mid-May to mid-October.

Edelweiss Cabins, tel. (406) 838-2304, charges $60 d or $70 for four people for their six cabins, three of which are new. Most of these contain kitchenettes, and one is handicap-accessible; open year-round.

With 32 guest rooms on two floors, **Soda Butte Lodge,** tel. (406) 838-2251 or (800) 527-6462, is the largest lodging place in the area. The hotel contains one of the best restaurants in these parts (Prospector), and guests are welcome to use the small indoor pool and jacuzzi. Rooms with king beds cost $65, those with two queens are $70, and suites (these sleep six) are $100. Open year-round.

Owned by Beartooth Plateau Outfitters (next door), **Beartooth Plateau Lodge,** tel. (406) 445-2293 or (800) 253-8545, is a comfortable log home with space for six people. It has a full kitchen and bath with clawfoot tub; open June-September. The house rents for $85 d, plus $10 for each additional person.

Elk Horn Lodge, tel. (406) 838-2332, has reasonably priced motel rooms and two cabins. Open all year; call for rates.

Silver Gate Accommodations

Range Riders Lodge, tel. (406) 838-2359, is a classic two-story log building with a bar downstairs and rooms upstairs. Rates are reasonable, $36 d or $46 for four people, but no phones or TVs, and the bath is a few steps down the hall. The original 1930s' furniture is still here. Range Riders is open Memorial Day to Labor Day. Budget-Inexpensive.

Silver Gate Cabins features eight attractive log cabins from the 1930s that contain kitchenettes and cost $55 s or d. Also here are five motel units for $39-45 s or d. Outside, you'll find barbecue grills, volleyball and horseshoes, and a playground for kids. It's open May 15-Sept.; call (406) 838-2371 in the summer or (307) 733-3774 in winter. Inexpensive.

Whispering Pines Lodge, tel. (406) 838-2228 or (888) 777-7554, is one of the nicest and quietest places in the area, and it has a clientele that returns year after year. The nine log cabins are off the main road and along a pretty creek. They're rustic outside, but modern within; some have kitchenettes. Rates are $45-50 for up to four people. Open Memorial Day through September. Budget-Inexpensive.

Grizzly Lodge, tel. (406) 838-2219, www.yellowstonenationalpark.com, is a century-old log building right on the river and close to the Yellowstone border. Guests stay in a variety of rooms (including kitchenettes, two-bedroom units, and rooms with lofts) inside the lodge for $45-75. Also here are a sauna and hot tub. Open Memorial Day through October, and Christmas-New Year's. Inexpensive-Moderate.

Pine Edge Cabins, tel. (406) 838-2222, has 11 attractive cabins that were originally built in the 1930s. All contain kitchenettes and cost $55 d or $65 for four people. The **Yellowstone Ecosystems Studies Science Center** (www.yellowstone.org) is based here, and the cabins are also used by researchers studying coyotes and water quality in the region. Lectures and educational programs are offered. Because of the researchers, not all the cabins may be available to the public. Open year-round. Budget-Inexpensive.

Camping and Public Cabins

Heading east from Cooke City, you'll find five national forest campgrounds ($8; open June-Sept.) within 10 miles of town. Closest is **Soda Butte Campground,** just a half mile from town; another mile to the east is **Colter Campground.** Two Forest Service cabins are also in the area. The four-person **Round Lake Cabin** ($20; open July to mid-September and mid-December through April) is 4.5 miles north of Cooke City up a jeep/hiking trail. The **Kersey Lake Cabin** ($30; open July to mid-September and mid-December to mid-April) is four miles east of Cooke City. This lakeside cabin has a rowboat and sleeps 10 people, but access requires a 1.5-mile hike. For details on Gallatin National Forest campgrounds and cabins, call (406) 848-7375, or visit the website: www.fs.fed.us/r1/gallatin/recreation.

Park RVs ($15) in Silver Gate at **Whispering Pines Lodge,** tel. (406) 838-2228, or in Cooke City at **Wilson's RV Ranch,** tel. (406) 838-2322. Both are open only in the summer months. Showers are available from Soda Butte Inn for $5.

Food

Inside Cooke City's Soda Butte Lodge, **Prospector Restaurant,** tel. (406) 838-2251, is well known for prime rib cooked to perfection, but it's also open for breakfast and lunch. Also here is the **Ore House Saloon,** with sports on the TV and video poker and keno machines to take your money. Everything at Soda Butte is open year-round.

The Bistro, in Cooke City, tel. (406) 838-2160, is open three meals a day, serving standard American fare the first two of these. Dinner is when this authentically French bistro shines, with quality steaks, veal, lamb, and fish.

Beartooth Cafe, in Cooke City, tel. (406) 838-2475, has good sandwiches for lunch, all-American dinners (outstanding free-range Angus beef steaks), and more than 100 kinds of beer. Open summers only. Also in Cooke City, **Pine Tree Cafe,** tel. (406) 838-2213, has reasonable prices, three meals a day, and locally famous milk shakes. This is the best breakfast place in town.

In peaceful Silver Gate, **Log Cabin Cafe,** tel. (406) 838-2367, is a consistent favorite, with well-prepared trout, pasta, barbecued beef, steaks, and homemade soups. Open in the summer and fall only.

Cooke City's **Miner's Saloon,** tel. (406) 838-2214, is a classic Old West bar where the stools are filled with locals and tourists. Pull the handles on the one-armed bandits, or try a game of pool, fooseball, or air hockey. The menu includes surprisingly good pizzas and burgers.

Cooke City Bike Shack, tel. (406) 838-2412, cranks out espresso coffees and is a good place to meet locals. For groceries and supplies, head to Cooke City General Store (described under Sights above) or **Summit Provisions** in Silver Gate, tel. (406) 838-2248.

Entertainment and Events

Drinking is the most popular recreational activity in these parts, but **Range Riders Lodge** in Silver Gate, tel. (406) 838-2359, also has live country music on Friday and Saturday nights all summer long. Find a small-town parade and chili cook-off during **Pig Daze** in mid-June. The twin towns have a fun **fireman's picnic and Fourth of July fireworks,** and Silver Gate is home to **Shakespeare in the Parks** in the middle of summer.

Recreation

Yellowstone is less than four miles away, and it's the obvious site for recreation in the Cooke City-Silver Gate area during the summer months. The **Absaroka-Beartooth Wilderness** is accessible from Cooke City or various other points to the east along the gorgeous Beartooth Highway. One of the more unusual sights is **Grasshopper Glacier,** eight miles north of Cooke City and 4,000 feet higher. The glacier contains the remains of a swarm of locusts that was apparently caught in a snowstorm while flying over the mountains. (See Shoshone National Forest in the Bighorn Basin chapter for more on this wilderness.)

Summertime horseback rides, pack trips into the Absaroka-Beartooth Wilderness, and guided fly-fishing expeditions are provided by three local outfitters: **Beartooth Plateau Outfitters,** tel. (406) 445-2328 or (800) 253-8545; **Castle Creek Outfitters,** tel. (406) 838-2301; and **Skyline Guide Service,** tel. (406) 838-2380. **Greater Yellowstone Flyfishers,** tel. (406) 838-2468, is a full-service fly shop, with lures and other supplies, guided fishing trips, and equipment rentals.

Cooke City Bike Shack, tel. (406) 838-2412, is a hub for the outdoor adventure crowd. Owner Bill Blackford is a jack of all trades, running the espresso machine one minute, and fixing a bike or selling outdoor gear the next. In the winter he guides telemarking and cross-country ski trips; $125 per person for an all-day trek. Backcountry skiers and snowboarders who want to head out on their own can catch a five-mile snowmobile ride ($15 per person) into the high country at Daisy Pass, gaining 2,100 feet of elevation along the way. This makes for a great day of skiing and a fun downhill run back to town.

Reminders of the mining era abound in the surrounding country, but not all of it is benign. Reclamation ponds catch toxic runoff from some of these old mines. The visitor center has a brochure showing Jeep/ATV/mountain-biking trails through the mining country just north of Cooke City.

Cooke City has become a hub for winter sports. Pick up a map of groomed cross-country ski trails and snowmobile routes at the visitor center. Snowmobile rentals are available from **Cooke City Exxon,** tel. (406) 838-2244, and **Yamaha Shop,** tel. (406) 838-2231 or (800) 527-6462. The local snowmobile club grooms approximately 60 miles of trails in the surrounding mountains; call (406) 838-2272 for information. Be sure to also call the **Avalanche Advisory Hotline** at (406) 838-2341 for the latest on backcountry conditions before heading out, or check the website: www.gomontana.com/avalanche.

Information and Services

The **Cooke City-Silver Gate Chamber of Commerce,** tel. (406) 838-2495 (summer) or (406) 838-2272 (winter), has a small summertime visitor center in Cooke City. It's generally open daily 10 a.m.-5 p.m. from June through mid-September. When the visitor center is closed, drop by High Country Motel for local information.

Despite its remoteness, you'll discover three (count 'em) **ATMs** in Cooke City. The town also has a laundromat.

Based in Bozeman, **4x4 Stage,** tel. (406) 848-2224 or (800) 517-8243, offers by-request connections around the park and to surrounding communities, including to Cooke City and Silver Gate. Call 24 hours in advance for reservations.

BIGHORN BASIN

Bighorn Basin is an enormous intermountain desertscape reaching almost 100 miles north to south and 50 miles east to west. Mountain ranges rim the basin—the Absarokas (pronounced "ab-SOR-kas") rise as a western border, the Owl Creek Mountains line the southern horizon, and the snowcapped Big Horns gleam in the east. The basin's rolling desert hills are topped with oil pumpjacks, and the wind blows incessantly. Cactus and sagebrush struggle up through a hardened surface of small rocks, and rugged badlands buttes rise above dry creekbeds. The countryside looks like southern Nevada.

Much of the basin gets less than 10 inches of precipitation per year—in some places just half that, and even in midwinter there isn't much snow on the ground. Three lazy rivers—Big Horn, Greybull, and Shoshone—create long green corridors through this desolation, offering an oasis in the dry desert country. Because of the lack of water, this was one of the last parts of Wyoming to be settled, and most of the towns did not spring up until the 1890s, when passage of the Carey Act brought a flood of irrigation speculators, investors, and farmers. The Carey Act, named for Wyoming Senator Joseph M. Carey, allowed the federal government to donate land to the states for reclamation by settlers. Canals have created wide swatches of irrigated green around the towns and along the rivers. Much of this water comes from the Buffalo Bill Reservoir just west of Cody and a series of canals supplying water to sugar beet and barley farms along the Big Horn and Greybull Rivers.

In the early part of this century boomtimes came to the basin with discoveries of oil and natural gas at Grass Creek and Byron. Along with cattle and sheep ranching (important since the 1880s), these industries still dominate the economy of Bighorn Basin. To most tourists, the basin (with the exception of Cody) is a place to get through on the way to Yellowstone or the Black Hills. Locals, however, call it a retirement haven and offer as proof the dry, sunny climate (more than 300 days of sun per year), relatively mild winters, cheap housing, low crime rate, and proximity to the recreational wonderlands of Yellowstone and the Absaroka and Big Horn Mountains. (In case you're confused, the word "Bighorn" is used for the national forest, canyon, river, lake, and basin, while "Big Horn" is the correct spelling for the mountain range, town, and county. Even Wyoming state maps get these spellings wrong!)

SHOSHONE NATIONAL FOREST

Shoshone National Forest encompasses over 2.4 million acres and extends along a 180-mile strip from the Montana border to the Wind River Mountains. Sagebrush dominates at the lowest elevations, but as you climb, lodgepole, Douglas-fir, Engelmann spruce, and subalpine fir cover the slopes. Above 10,000 feet, the land opens into alpine vegetation and barren rocky peaks. The **Shoshone National Forest Supervisor's Office** is in Cody at 808 Meadowlark Ave., tel. (307) 527-6241, www.fs.fed.us/r2/shoshone. Get information and forest maps ($4) from the supervisor's office or from ranger stations in Cody, Dubois, and Lander.

History

Shoshone is America's oldest national forest. On March 30, 1891, Pres. Benjamin Harrison signed a proclamation creating Yellowstone Park Timberland Reserve adjacent to Yellowstone National Park. At first this title meant very little, but in 1902 Pres. Theodore Roosevelt appointed rancher and artist A.A. Anderson to control grazing and logging and catch poachers. His strong management almost got him lynched. Three years later under Gifford Pinchot, the forest reserves were transferred to the Department of Agriculture and renamed national forests. The land was renamed Shoshone National Forest in 1908.

Recreation

More than half of Shoshone National Forest lies inside wilderness boundaries; the Absaroka-Beartooth, North Absaroka, and Washakie Wilderness Areas cover much of the country east of Yellowstone National Park, while the Wind River Mountains contain the Fitzpatrick and Popo Agie Wildernesses (see the Wind River Mountains Country chapter for more on these areas). Part of the credit for the surprising expanse of wilderness areas on the national forest goes to Buffalo Bill. By bringing people into the area to hunt, fish, and explore, he helped create what one author called a "dude's forest." In addition, the Buffalo Bill Dam (which he vociferously supported) prevented logs from being sent down the North Fork of the Shoshone River and thus made logging less important.

Over 1,500 miles of trails offer hiking and horseback access to much of this country. Shoshone has more than 50 campgrounds, most costing $9 per night during the summer. Once the water has been shut off for the winter months (generally Oct.-April), you can camp for free but will have to haul out your own trash. Space is generally

SIGHTSEEING HIGHLIGHTS FOR BIGHORN BASIN

- Wapiti Valley, Sunlight Basin, and Beartooth Pass within Shoshone National Forest
- Buffalo Bill Historical Center and Trail Town in Cody
- Homesteader Museum in Powell
- Devil Canyon in Bighorn Canyon National Recreation Area
- Aerial Firefighting Museum near Greybull
- Red Gulch Dinosaur Tracksite near Shell
- Medicine Lodge State Park near Hyattville
- Washakie Museum and Cultural Center in Worland
- Hot Springs State Park, Hot Springs Historical Museum, and Wyoming Dinosaur Center in Thermopolis
- Legend Rock Petroglyph Site between Thermopolis and Meeteetse
- Wind River Canyon
- Popular events: Cody Stampede (early July), Cody Nite Rodeo (all summer), Cody Gunslingers Shootout (all summer), and Gift of the Waters Pageant in Thermopolis (August)

available even at the busiest times of year. In addition, free dispersed camping is possible at undeveloped sites throughout the forest, with the exception of heavily traveled US Hwy. 14/16/20, where you must be a half mile off the road.

Though they are uncommon, black bears roam throughout the forest, and grizzlies are found within the northern portions, including the North Absaroka and Washakie Wilderness Areas. Be sure to take the necessary bear precautions anywhere in the backcountry. Bears also sometimes wander into campgrounds along US Hwy. 14/16/20 near Yellowstone National Park. Actually, you are more likely to encounter mosquitoes, deer flies, and horse flies in midsummer, so be sure to bring insect repellent.

WAPITI VALLEY/NORTH FORK

Wapiti Valley provides one of the most popular and scenic routes into or out of Yellowstone National Park, connecting Cody with the park's East Entrance. President Theodore Roosevelt

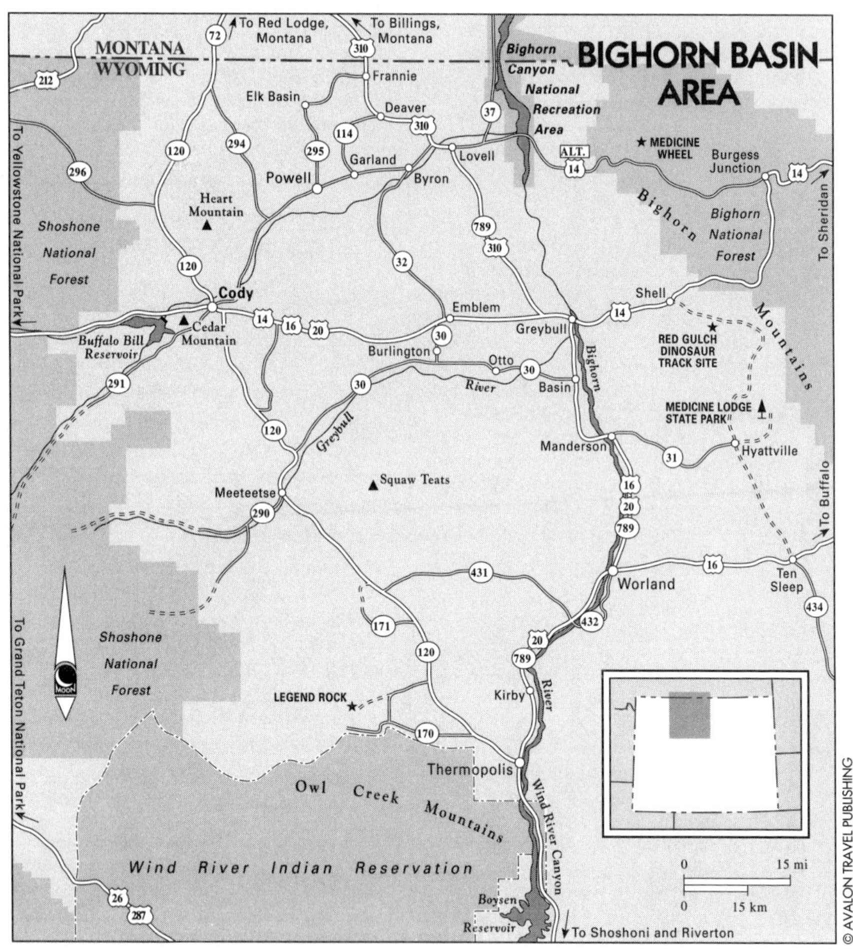

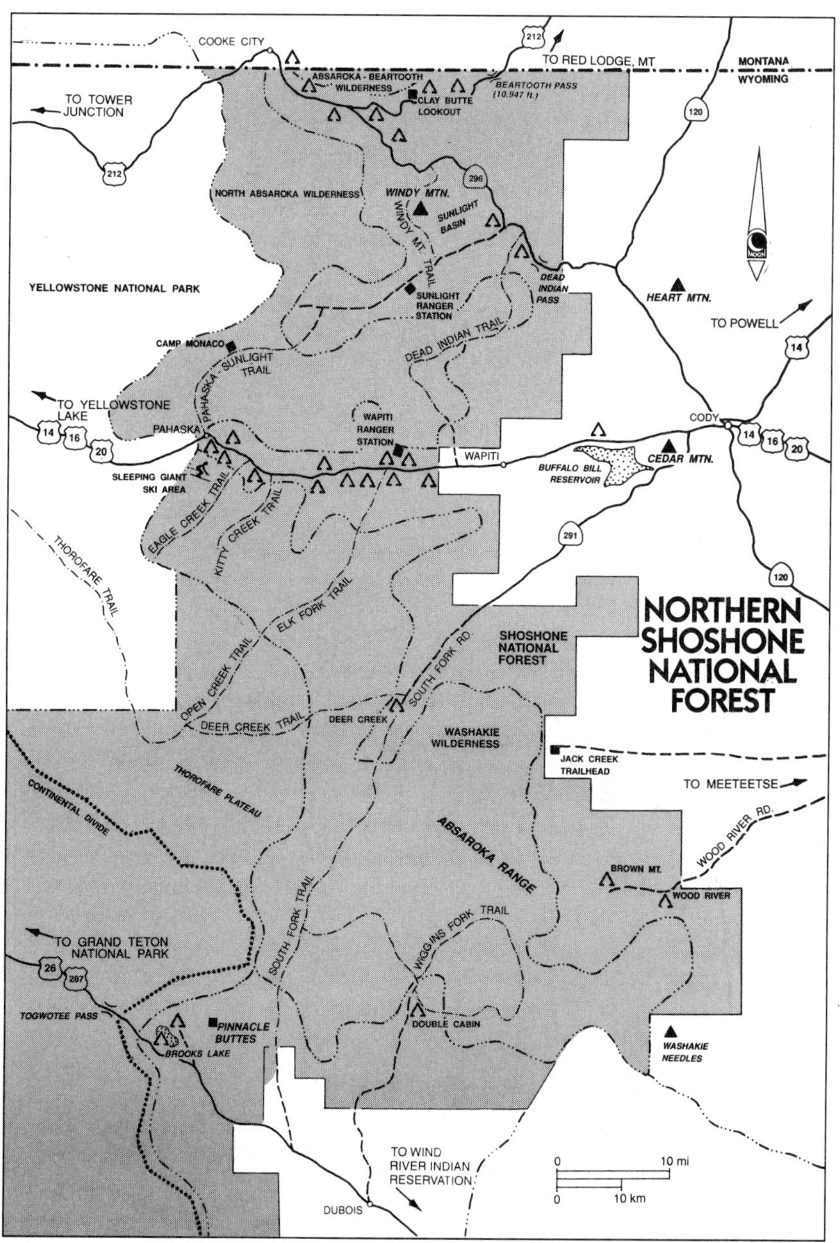

NORTHERN SHOSHONE NATIONAL FOREST
COOKE CITY
212
TO RED LODGE, MT
MONTANA
WYOMING
ABSAROKA - BEARTOOTH WILDERNESS
CLAY BUTTE LOOKOUT
BEARTOOTH PASS (10,947 ft.)
TO TOWER JUNCTION
120
296
NORTH ABSAROKA WILDERNESS
WINDY MTN.
WINDY MT. TRAIL
SUNLIGHT BASIN
YELLOWSTONE NATIONAL PARK
SUNLIGHT RANGER STATION
DEAD INDIAN PASS
HEART MTN.
TO POWELL
CAMP MONACO
PAHASKA - SUNLIGHT TRAIL
DEAD INDIAN TRAIL
14
TO YELLOWSTONE LAKE
PAHASKA
WAPITI RANGER STATION
CODY
16
20
WAPITI
BUFFALO BILL RESERVOIR
CEDAR MTN.
SLEEPING GIANT SKI AREA
EAGLE CREEK TRAIL
KITTY CREEK TRAIL
THOROFARE TRAIL
291
ELK FORK TRAIL
SHOSHONE NATIONAL FOREST
SOUTH FORK RD.
OPEN CREEK TRAIL
DEER CREEK TRAIL
DEER CREEK
WASHAKIE WILDERNESS
JACK CREEK TRAILHEAD
THOROFARE PLATEAU
CONTINENTAL DIVIDE
TO MEETEETSE
WOOD RIVER RD.
ABSAROKA RANGE
BROWN MT.
WOOD RIVER
WIGGINS FORK TRAIL
SOUTH FORK TRAIL
TO GRAND TETON NATIONAL PARK
26
287
TOGWOTEE PASS
PINNACLE BUTTES
BROOKS LAKE
DOUBLE CABIN
WASHAKIE NEEDLES
TO WIND RIVER INDIAN RESERVATION
0
10 mi
10 km
DUBOIS
MOON

came here often and called it "the most scenic 50 miles in the U.S."

Along the way are numerous lodges, dude ranches, and resorts, many of which offer family-style meals, barbecue cookouts, horseback rides, pack trips, fishing, hiking, river rafting, and other outdoor recreation. If you aren't staying on an all-inclusive plan, most of these perks will cost extra, and some—such as horseback rides and meals—are often available to both guests and nonguests alike. The lodgings generally do not have TVs or phones in the rooms, but most will provide transportation from Cody upon request. Those Wapiti lodges and guest ranches that are open in the winter months are favorite bases for snowmobiling and cross-country skiing. For more information on Wapiti Valley businesses, call (307) 587-9595 or look on the web at www.yellowstone-lodging.com.

Also in the valley are Forest Service campgrounds, RV parks, hiking trails, and private summer homes. The fishing is great in the North Fork of the Shoshone River, which US Hwy. 14/16/20 parallels for the entire 50 miles from Yellowstone to Cody.

From East Entrance the highway drops through high forests past an array of volcanic pinnacles and cliffs as the country becomes drier and more open. Cottonwoods line the gradually widening river, and Douglas-firs intermix with sage, grass, and rock at lower elevations. Trailheads provide access to two backcountry areas that border the highway: North Absaroka Wilderness and Washakie Wilderness. A major reconstruction project that ended in 1999 has left the road in excellent condition the entire distance from Cody to Yellowstone.

Pahaska Tepee

Less than three miles from Yellowstone's East Entrance (48 miles west of Cody), Pahaska Tepee was built in 1904 to house Buffalo Bill's guests and others on their way to the park. Pahaska (pronounced "pa-HAZ-ka") was Buffalo Bill's nickname, a Crow Indian word meaning "Long Hair."

The original Pahaska Tepee is a two-story log building that contains a few of Buffalo Bill's original items, including an old buffalo skull over the stone fireplace and several flags that were given to him. Although it is no longer used and in need of major repairs, the lodge is open for fascinating free tours on weekdays during the summer. The bar at Pahaska Tepee is small, but contains a stunning Thomas Molesworth chandelier that was formerly in the Smithsonian; it's said to be worth $2 million. Look around for other furnishings from Molesworth and a beautiful stained-glass window.

On one of Buffalo Bill's many hunting treks with European royalty, he led the Prince of Monaco into the North Fork country. **Camp Monaco,** 15 miles up the Pahaska-Sunlight Trail from Pahaska Tepee, was named in his honor. Unfortunately, the old aspen tree inscribed with the words "Camp Monaco" was killed when the Clover-Mist Fire burned through here in 1988.

Pahaska Tepee Resort has a mix of old and new cabins and small A -frame motel rooms; rates are $96-105 for up to four people. Wintertime guests can use the outdoor jacuzzi. Also here are a restaurant, gift shop, gas pumps, and limited supplies. Pahaska is open May-Oct. and Dec.-March. Expensive. In winter the road is not plowed beyond Pahaska, and the lodge becomes a very popular place to rent snowmobiles and cross-country skis for trips into Yellowstone. Call (307) 527-7701 or (800) 628-7791 for more information on Pahaska, or visit www.pahaska.com.

Skiing and Snowboarding

Just four miles from Yellowstone's East Gate, **Sleeping Giant Ski Area** is a small family skiing and snowboarding hill with a chairlift and T-bar providing a 500-foot vertical rise. Lifts operate mid-December to early April, and tickets cost $20 for adults, $10 for kids. Nordic skis, alpine skis, and snowboards are available for rent. For details, call (307) 587-4044 (Shoshone Lodge), or go to the web at http://skisleepinggiant.com.

Also based here is **North Fork Nordic Trails,** with 40 km of groomed cross-country ski trails over widely varied terrain. The trails lead right to the edge of Yellowstone National Park. Call Pahaska Tepee at (307) 527-7701 for specifics.

Down the Road

Below Sleeping Giant Ski Area the road passes a whole series of delightfully weird volcanic rock formations. Signs point out several of the most obvious. Stop at the **Firefighters' Memorial,** which honors 15 firefighters who were killed nearby in the Blackwater Fire of 1937. The picnic area here has a special pond for anglers with disabilities.

Eight miles farther east is the historic **Wapiti Ranger Station.** Built in 1903, it was the nation's first Forest Service ranger station. Just a few hundred feet away and right along the highway is **Wapiti Wayside Visitor Center,** tel. (307) 587-3925, open Mon.-Fri. 8 a.m.-8 p.m. and Sat.-Sun. 8:30 a.m.-5 p.m. between Memorial Day and Labor Day; closed the rest of the year. Pull in for details on local camping and recreation opportunities, and watch the informative video on safety in bear country. Check the board for recent bear sightings. A few miles to the west (not marked) is Mummy Cave, where a 10,000-year-old mummified body was discovered in 1957.

Next up is a parking area at **Holy City,** an impressive group of dark red volcanic rocks with the Shoshone River cutting away at their base. Try to pick out Anvil Rock, Goose Rock, and Slipper Rock here. The highway leaves Shoshone National Forest and then passes the scattered settlement called **Wapiti**—an Indian word meaning "elk"—20 miles east of Cody. As you might guess, a large elk herd winters in this valley. An unusual volcanic rock ridge near here is locally called Chinese Wall. The eastern half of the road between Cody and Yellowstone passes through this broad and fertile valley; it's quite a change from the rock-lined route to the west. On the east end, the road borders Buffalo Bill Reservoir (see Buffalo Bill State Park below) before plunging through three tunnels on the descent into Cody.

Camping

Nine different Shoshone National Forest campgrounds provide rustic accommodations along the North Fork of the Shoshone River. Most of these are open mid-May through September (some remain open through October) and cost $9 per site; no reservations. All sites have picnic tables, fire rings, potable water, and outhouses. In areas where bears are a problem, the campgrounds also contain bearproof food-storage boxes. All of these Forest Service campgrounds are on the west half of the 50-mile stretch of highway between Cody and Yellowstone. Of these, **Big Game Campground** is closest to Cody at 25 miles to the west, and **Three Mile Campground** is closest to the park, just three miles from Yellowstone's East Gate. Get details on public campgrounds from the Forest Service's Wapiti Wayside Visitor Center (described above). Dispersed camping outside designated campsites is not allowed anywhere between Cody and Yellowstone along US Hwy. 14/16/20.

Two campgrounds are within Buffalo Bill State Park, described below. Also mentioned below are three Wapiti Valley lodges that have RV campgrounds: Elk Valley Inn, Wise Choice Motel, and Yellowstone Valley Inn.

Upper North Fork Accommodations

More than 20 lodges, motels, and guest ranches line the road between Yellowstone and Cody. Lodging places west of the midpoint between Cody and Yellowstone are in the more secluded and wooded canyon country of the upper North Fork of the Shoshone River. These places are listed below, arranged by their distance from downtown Cody on US Hwy. 14/16/20, starting with those nearest the East Entrance to Yellowstone. Places east of the midpoint between Cody and Yellowstone are situated in the broad and beautiful Wapiti Valley and are typically visible from the highway (see Lower Wapiti Valley Accommodations, following).

Pahaska Tepee—the closest lodge to Yellowstone—is described separately, above. **Shoshone Lodge,** tel. (307) 587-4044, 46 miles west of Cody (four miles east of Yellowstone), is a classic mountain lodge with rustic log cabins. Home-cooked meals are served in the main lodge. The cabins have been nicely updated with Western furnishings, and they range in size from one to three rooms; some contain kitchens. Nightly rates are $60-90 s or $70-100 d. Various horseback rides are offered, including breakfast and dinner rides. Shoshone Lodge is open mid-May through October, and you can find them on the web at www.shoshonelodge.com. Moderate-Expensive. The owners of Shoshone Lodge also run Sleeping Giant Ski Area, directly across the road; see above for details.

Established in 1898, **Crossed Sabres Ranch,** tel. (307) 587-3750, 42 miles west of Cody (eight miles east of Yellowstone), has a beautiful century-old lodge. There's space for 40 guests in modernized cabins with log furniture and Western decor. After a day of horseback riding, hiking, river rafting, square dancing, or exploring Yellowstone, guests can relax with an evening cookout or soak in the jacuzzi. All-inclusive weekly packages are $2,000 for two people; open June to mid-September. The website is www.ranchweb.com/csabres. Luxury.

Stay in deluxe log cabins at **Goff Creek Lodge,** tel. (307) 587-3753 or (800) 859-3985, 40 miles west of Cody (10 miles east of Yellowstone). Cabins are offered on either a nightly basis ($95-105 d) or by the week; open May-November. A variety of outdoor adventures fill the bill here, including horseback rides, pack trips, fly-fishing, and chuck wagon cookouts. For details, point your mouse to www.goffcreek.com. Expensive.

Elephant Head Lodge, tel. (307) 587-3980, 40 miles west of Cody (10 miles east of Yellowstone), is a no-frills dude ranch with a gracious main lodge built in 1910. Guests stay in a dozen modernized cabins, all with private baths and most with decks. Filling meals are served in the restaurant, and horseback rides are offered each day. Because of its proximity to the park, Elephant Head makes a good base for exploring Yellowstone. Peak season lodging-only rates start at $85 d per day; the largest cabin sleeps eight people for $150 per day, and has a kitchenette. All-inclusive packages are $240 for two people per day. The ranch is open June-September. For details, visit the website: www.elephantheadlodge.com. Expensive-Luxury.

Absaroka Mountain Lodge, tel. (307) 587-3963, 38 miles west of Cody (12 miles east of Yellowstone), offers old-time hospitality and adventure. Guests stay in comfortable log cabins with private baths and dine in the historic main lodge, built in 1910. Nightly rates are $76-116 d. Horseback rides, breakfast, and lunch are extra. The lodge also has a two-night rate of $250 d that includes meals and rides. Open May-September. Get more info by visiting the website: www.absarokamtlodge.com. Moderate-Premium.

Blackwater Creek Ranch, tel. (307) 587-5201, 35 miles west of Cody (15 miles east of Yellowstone), is a fine place to relax amid the natural beauty of the area. Featured attractions include horseback rides, trout fishing, hiking, games, barbecues, and cowboy sing-alongs. The gracious log cabins contain fireplaces, and meals are served in the modern Old West-style lodge. Also here are an outdoor pool, a large jacuzzi, and a game room with pool and ping-pong tables. Weekly all-inclusive rates run $2,200 for two people. Open May-September. Find the ranch on the web at www.wavecom.net/~bwcranch. Luxury.

A classic Western dude ranch, **UXU Ranch,** tel. (307) 587-2143 or (800) 373-9027, www.uxuranch.com, is 33 miles west of Cody (17 miles east of Yellowstone). It offers horseback riding, hiking, fly-fishing, mountain-biking, and day-trips to Yellowstone and Cody. Guests stay in comfortable cabins containing private baths and porches; some also have fireplaces or gas stoves. After a day of trail riding, you can relax in the big jacuzzi or visit with new friends in the main lodge. Special children's programs and Forest Service talks are available, and the food is memorable. All-inclusive weekly stays cost $2,450 for two people; open June-September. Luxury.

Bill Cody Ranch, tel. (307) 587-6271, 25 miles west of Cody (25 miles east of Yellowstone), has graceful log cabins, a comfortable lodge, horseback and wagon rides, creekside cookouts, trout fishing, a jacuzzi, and more. All-inclusive stays are $270 for two people per night; lodging-only rates are $105 d. The guest ranch is open May-September. Get more information on the web at www.billcodyranch.com. Expensive-Luxury.

Rimrock Dude Ranch, tel. (307) 587-3970, 25 miles west of Cody (25 miles east of Yellowstone), is a classic place with creekside log cabins, horseback riding, backcountry pack trips, a large swimming pool, river rafting, hearty family-style meals, and grand mountain country. Pack trips into the mountains are a special favorite. In the winter, this is a popular destination for snowmobilers; the ranch rents snowmobiles and leads tours into Yellowstone. Summertime weekly rates are $2,400 for two people, all-inclusive. Rimrock is open late May-Sept. and Dec.-March. Find it on the web at www.rimrockranch.com. Luxury.

One of the most distinctive Wapiti Valley places is the nonprofit **Breteche Creek Ranch,** tel. (307) 587-3844, a 7,000-acre working cattle ranch 25 miles west of Cody (25 miles east of Yellowstone). Horseback riding is a staple activity here, but guests also learn about the natural world through workshops in photography, nature writing, and poetry. The ranch lacks electricity. A maximum of

20 people stay in canvas-sided tent cabins set amid the aspen trees; guests share a central bathhouse. Meals are served family-style in a central lodge. All-inclusive rates are $2,200 for two people per week, or $350 for two people per night. Open June-September. The website is www.guestranches.com/breteche. Luxury.

Lower Wapiti Valley Accommodations

Lodging places listed below are east of the midpoint between Yellowstone and Cody, in the broad and open portion of Wapiti Valley; those listed above under Upper North Fork Accommodations are west of the midpoint, in the more secluded and wooded canyon country of the upper river valley.

Trail Inn, tel. (307) 587-3741, 23 miles west of Cody (27 miles east of Yellowstone), sits off the road and along the North Fork Shoshone River. Rustic cabins with private baths are $60 s or d. Open May-September. Inexpensive.

Wise Choice Motel, tel. (307) 587-5004 or (877) 587-5004, 22 miles west of Cody (28 miles east of Yellowstone), has roadside motel rooms for $55-60 s or d, and RV sites for $15. Open mid-April to mid-November. Inexpensive.

Kinkade Guest Kabin B&B, tel. (307) 587-5905, 21 miles west of Cody (29 miles east of Yellowstone), is a two-bedroom log home with a dining room/living area and private baths. Rates are $65-85 s or d. Also available are bunk beds in the barn for $20 per person or in a sheepherder wagon for $10 per person. No showers or running water for the wagon, just an outhouse. All of these options include a filling country breakfast served in the cabin. Open year-round. The website is www.bbonline.com/wy/guestkabin. Budget-Moderate.

Stay in modern log cabins at **Rand Creek Ranch and Guest Lodge,** tel. (307) 527-7176 or (888) 412-7335, 19 miles west of Cody (31 miles east of Yellowstone). The cabins cost $85 s or d; all-inclusive one-week stays are $2,300 for two people, including horseback rides, fishing, lodging, and three meals per day. Rand Creek's main lodge was built in 1905 and is the oldest building in the area. Open May-December. The website is www.randcreekranch.com. Expensive-Luxury.

Elk Valley Inn, tel. (307) 587-4149, 18 miles west of Cody (32 miles east of Yellowstone), has standard motel rooms for $39-59 s or d, and a couple of cabins (one with a kitchenette) for $69 d. Pitch tents ($12) or park RVs ($12-15) in the campground. A private pond has paddleboats for rent, and children will appreciate the fun playground. Open May-September. Inexpensive-Moderate.

At **Yellowstone Valley Inn,** tel. (307) 587-3961 or (888) 705-7703, 18 miles west of Cody (32 miles east of Yellowstone), motel rooms cost $75 s or d, tent spaces are $10, and RV sites with hookups run $20. The inn sits right on the North Fork Shoshone River and has a coffee shop and lounge, plus summertime horseback rides. Open May-November. Moderate.

Streamside Inn, tel. (307) 587-8242 or (800) 285-1282, is 15 miles west of Cody (35 miles east of Yellowstone) near the east end of Buffalo Bill Reservoir. Modern motel rooms go for $56 s or $60-64 d, including a continental breakfast and access to the large outdoor pool and stocked fishing pond. Kitchenettes are available for $10 extra. Horseback rides are also offered, and the inn is open year-round. Get details on the web at www.wtp.net/streamside. Moderate.

Red Pole Ranch, tel. (307) 587-5929 or (800) 326-5928, 11 miles west of Cody (39 miles east of Yellowstone), has motel units for $60-85 s or d, and four-person log cabins with kitchenettes for $100-125. Open May-September. Moderate.

BUFFALO BILL STATE PARK

Six miles west of Cody on US Hwy. 14/16/20, **Buffalo Bill Reservoir** is a very popular place for local boaters and fishermen. Buffalo Bill State Park, tel. (307) 587-9227, encompasses the reservoir and includes two campgrounds ($9 for nonresidents or $4 for Wyoming residents; open May-Sept.) on the north shore. Day-use of the park is $5 for nonresident vehicles or $2 for those with Wyoming plates.

Atop the dam, the impressive **Buffalo Bill Dam visitor center,** tel. (307) 527-6076, has historical displays and jaw-dropping views into the canyon, which plummets 350 feet below you. The center is open daily 8 a.m.-8 p.m. May-Sept.; closed the rest of the year. Even if it's closed, stop for the view over the dam. For more information, check the website: www.bbdvc.org.

Fishing is good for rainbow, cutthroat, brown, and Mackinaw trout in Buffalo Bill Reservoir. The lake also offers some of the finest windsurfing conditions anywhere, with nearly constant 30 mph winds; *Outside* magazine once rated it among the country's 10 best spots. The water's cold—you'll need a wetsuit till mid-June.

History

In 1899, Buffalo Bill Cody acquired the rights to build canals and irrigate some 60,000 acres of land near the new town of Cody. With passage of the Reclamation Act of 1902, the project was taken over by the Reclamation Service and an enormous concrete-arch dam was added to provide water. The 328-foot-high dam was begun in 1904 and required five long years to finish. It cost nearly $1 million and when finally completed was the tallest dam in the world. Seven men died along the way—including a chief engineer—and the first two contractors were forced into bankruptcy as a result of bad weather, floods, engineering difficulties, and labor strife. A lack of sand and crushed gravel forced them to manufacture it from granite, and 200-pound boulders were hand-placed into the concrete to save having to crush more gravel.

Originally named Shoshone Dam, the impoundment was renamed in honor of Buffalo Bill in 1946. A hydroelectric plant and a 25-foot addition to the top were completed in 1993, bringing the total dam height to 353 feet and increasing water storage by 50%. The dam irrigates more than 93,000 downstream acres through the Shoshone Reclamation Project, making it one of the only Wyoming irrigation schemes that actually benefits the state's farmers to a large extent.

The bridge spanning Sunlight Creek is the highest in Wyoming—300 feet above the water.

SUNLIGHT BASIN

The **Chief Joseph Scenic Highway** (State Hwy. 296) is a 46-mile route through a magnificent Wyoming landscape. Popularly known as Sunlight Basin Rd., it is paved and most of it remains open year-round, providing access for backcountry skiers and snowmobilers to the beautiful Beartooth Pass area. (An eight-mile portion between Cooke City, Montana, and Pilot Creek, Wyoming, is not plowed in the winter. It typically opens by early May.) Chief Joseph Highway begins 17 miles north of Cody off State Hwy. 120, with Heart Mountain prominent to the southeast, and climbs sharply up from the dry east side, passing a brilliant red butte en route to **Dead Indian Pass,** named for an incident during an 1878 fight between Bannocks and the U.S. Army. After the battle, Crow scouts found a wounded old Bannock warrior here. They killed and scalped him, burying the body under a pile of rocks. Other tales claim that the name came from the body of an Indian propped up as a ruse to trick the army during Chief Joseph's attempted escape to Canada in 1877. Chief Joseph *did* lead the Nez Percé through this country, avoiding the cavalry by heading up Clarks Fork Canyon, a route the army had considered impassable. An overlook on top of Dead Indian Pass provides a panoramic vista of the rugged mountains and valleys below. The river forms a boundary between the volcanic Absarokas to the south and the granitic Beartooth Mountains to the north.

Indians weren't the only ones killed in this era. In 1870, two miners, Marvin Crandall and T. Dougherty, headed into the Upper Clarks Fork following reports of gold in the area. When they failed to meet up with other miners, a search party was sent out. The searchers were themselves attacked by Indians, but they later found the bodies of Crandall and Dougherty—scalped and decapitated, with their heads atop mining picks. In a perverse bit of humor, tin cups sat in front of each skull and the right hand of each man held a spoon. The men had apparently been killed while eating and the bodies were left as a warning against further white exploration of the area.

West of the overlook, the road switchbacks down hairpin turns into remote and beautiful Sunlight Basin. The name came about in the 1840s. Fur trappers worked this area for beaver and discovered a place flooded with light, but it was so remote that "the only thing that can get into this valley most of the year is sunlight." Today it is considerably more accessible, but still just as beautiful. A gravel side road leads seven miles up the valley to **Sunlight Ranger Station,** built in 1936 by the CCC. It's open summers only. This is some of the finest elk winter range anywhere and the home of a number of scenic old guest ranches (described below).

Back on the main road, a bridge—highest in Wyoming at 300 feet above Sunlight Creek—spans deep, cliff-walled **Sunlight Gorge.** Sorry, no bungee jumping allowed. The highway then continues northwest past Cathedral Cliffs and through a scenic ranching and timbering valley, offering views into the deep gorge that belongs to the Clarks Fork of the Yellowstone River. In some sections, sheer cliffs tower 1,200 feet above the water. Part of the area burned by the 1988 Clover-Mist Fire is visible near **Crandall Ranger Station.** This area also contains the only large herd of mountain goats in Wyoming. Eventually you reach the junction with US Hwy. 212, the Beartooth Highway (see Beartooth Mountains below for a description of this beautiful route).

> *Winter looks like a fictional place, an elaborate simplicity, a Nabokovian invention of rarefied detail. Winds howl all night and day, pushing litters of storm fronts from the Beartooth to the Big Horn Mountains. When it lets up, the mountains disappear. The hayfield that runs east from my house ends in a curl of clouds that have fallen like sails luffing from sky to ground. Snow returns across the field to me, and the cows, dusted with white, look like snowcapped continents drifting.*
>
> —GRETEL EHRLICH IN
> *THE SOLACE OF OPEN SPACES*

Camping and Hiking

The Forest Service's Lake Creek, Hunter Peak, and Dead Indian Campgrounds ($7-9; open mid-May through September) are found along Chief Joseph Scenic Highway. **Dead Indian Trail** (just uphill from Dead Indian Campground) goes two miles to a fine overlook into Clarks Fork Canyon. Also of interest is **Windy Mountain Trail** which climbs 10,262-foot Windy Mountain. It starts from a trailhead four miles east of the Crandall Ranger Station (interesting old log buildings here), is approximately seven miles one-way, and gains 3,700 feet in elevation. Windy Mountain can also be climbed from the other side near the Sunlight Ranger Station. Trailheads into the North Absaroka Wilderness are at the Crandall Ranger Station and beyond the Little Sunlight Campground (free; open year-round) on Forest Rd. 101.

River Running

Clarks Fork of the Yellowstone River (named for William Clark, of the Lewis and Clark expedition) is Wyoming's only designated Wild and Scenic River. Experienced kayakers will find a couple of great stretches of class IV-V whitewater in the upper Clarks Fork. However, use considerable caution—there are several big drops. Be sure to pull out before dangerous Box Canyon, which is considered unrunnable. Find more class IV waters farther down the river. Check with the Forest Service for specifics. Below the rapids are quieter stretches. Based in Cody, **Red Canyon River Trips,** 1374 Sheridan Ave., tel. (307) 587-6988 or (800) 293-0148, leads gentle float trips down a scenic 12-mile section of the Clarks Fork. The half-day trip costs $45 per person and is offered from late May to early August.

Guest Ranches

In the heart of beautiful Sunlight Basin, **Seven D Ranch,** tel. (307) 587-9885, is a family-oriented guest ranch offering horseback rides, cookouts, fly-fishing, hiking, and pack trips. The setting is spectacular—it's where some of the Marlboro ads were shot—and the cabins are comfortable and cozy. Weekly all-inclusive rates are $2,870 for two people. The ranch has space for a maximum of 32 guests. Open mid-June to mid-September; adults only in September. Get details on the web at www.7dranch.com. Luxury.

K Bar Z Guest Ranch, tel. (307) 587-4410, is off the Chief Joseph Scenic Highway in the Crandall Creek area. Nightly log cabin accommodations are available for $75 d, or guests can stay by the week for $1,400 for two people, all-inclusive. Horseback rides, Yellowstone sightseeing, backcountry pack trips, cookouts, and guided fishing trips are also offered, along with wintertime snowmobile rentals. In addition to the usual horse adventures, the ranch has a sauna and hot tub and is open year-round. A maximum of 30 guests can stay here. For more information, find the ranch on the web at www.agonline.com/kbarz. Moderate-Luxury.

Hunter Peak Ranch, 4027 Crandall Rd., tel. (307) 587-3711, is on the banks of the upper Clarks Fork River and offers lodging in rustic log cabins or motel-type rooms. Rates are $80 s or d per night or $400 d per week, with extra charges for meals, horseback rides, and pack trips. The main lodge was built from hand-hewn logs in 1917. Open year-round. Moderate.

Also in Sunlight Basin, **Elk Creek Ranch,** tel. (307) 587-3902 (summers) or (207) 384-5361 (winters), provides a unique opportunity for teenagers to gain a wide range of ranching and wilderness skills. Ranch stays ($2,700 per person all-inclusive for a four-week session) include lots of time on horseback and the opportunity to train horses, build cabins, cut hay, or learn other ranch work. The backpacking adventures ($2,600 per person all-inclusive for a four-week session) give kids plenty of time in the backcountry, where they learn a range of outdoor and mountain-climbing skills. Two month-long sessions are offered each summer with a maximum of 30 kids at a time. For more on these adventures, see the webpage: www.elkcreekranch.com.

Other Services

The little settlement called **Painter** is 21 miles southeast of Cooke City on Chief Joseph Hwy., right along the Clarks Fork River. Here you'll find a general store and gas pumps, along with year-round RV hookups ($20) at **Painter Estates RV Resort,** tel. (307) 527-5248. Not far away is **Cary Inn Restaurant,** tel. (307) 527-5510, serving three meals a day.

SOUTH FORK AREA

South Fork Rd. heads southwest from Cody and follows the South Fork of the Shoshone River for 42 miles to the edge of the Washakie Wilderness (described below). It's a beautiful drive through definitive Western country with tree-covered mountains and the rich valley below.

Lodging

Two dude ranches operate along the South Fork River. **Castle Rock Ranch,** tel. (307) 587-2076 or (800) 356-9965, 17 miles southwest of Cody, has an attractive central lodge with magnificent vistas from the tall windows. Guests stay in log cabins containing handmade furniture and woodstoves or fireplaces; other facilities include an outdoor pool and a sauna. The ranch emphasizes not only horseback riding and fly-fishing but also less-traditional ranch activities such as windsurfing, mountain-biking, and even rock climbing. Special kids' programs are offered. The guest ranch is open June-September.

The **Double Diamond X Ranch,** tel. (307) 527-6276 or (800) 833-7262, is an excellent family-oriented dude ranch near the South Fork River, 34 miles southwest of Cody. The ranch itself only covers 200 acres, but it is surrounded by Shoshone National Forest land. Guests take part in horseback rides, cookouts, square dances, cowboy poetry, and day-trips to Cody. The kid's program is one of the best around, with entertaining and educational activities every day, and the ranch brings in professional entertainers several times a week. There's space for up to 32 guests. Facilities include remodeled log cabins—some dating to 1914—and lodge accommodations, plus an indoor pool and jacuzzi. Meals are noteworthy. All-inclusive rates are $2,920 for two people for six nights; open May-October. Get more info from the website: www.ddxranch.com. Luxury.

BEARTOOTH MOUNTAINS

Spectacular Beartooth Highway (US Hwy. 212) connects Cooke City and Yellowstone National Park with the historic mining town of Red Lodge, Montana. Along the way, it passes through the Beartooth Mountains on a road built by the CCC in the 1930s. Some have called this the most scenic route in America. If you like alpine country, towering rocky spires, and a landscaped dotted with small lakes and scraggly trees, you're going to love this drive. A small corner (23,750 acres out of a total of 945,334 acres) of the **Absaroka-Beartooth Wilderness** lies in Wyoming just north of the highway—the rest is right across the Montana border.

Over the Top

A national scenic byway, Beartooth Highway sails across a high plateau and then over the twin summits of **Beartooth Pass**—the east summit is 10,936 feet, and a short distance farther is the west summit at 10,947 feet. A scenic overlook at west summit provides views of the Absarokas to the south and west, the Beartooths to the north, and Bighorn Basin to the east. Majestic rock faces rise in all directions, the most obvious being Beartooth Mountain (its sharp point resembles the tooth of a bear), Pilot Peak, and Index Peak. This is the highest highway pass in Wyoming and one of the highest in North America.

As the road enters Montana, it passes Beartooth Mountain and begins a rapid elevator ride down folded ribbon curves into the resort town of Red Lodge. On top, keep your eyes open for moose, mule deer, mountain goats, bighorn sheep, marmots, and pikas. Be ready for strange weather at this elevation, including snow at any time of year. The highway is closed with the first heavy snowfall (generally in September) and doesn't open till June. The flowers don't really get going till mid-July.

Twin Lakes Ski Area sits near the Wyoming-Montana border and provides Olympic ski training for teens in June and July. South of the summit is the appropriately named Top-of-the-World Store (see below), and another mile or so farther south is the turnoff to an old fire lookout tower at **Clay Butte,** where you'll discover horizon-to-horizon views of the surrounding countryside. A narrow gravel road climbs three miles to the tower, perched at an elevation of 9,811 feet. The small visitor center here is staffed July to mid-September.

Camping and Supplies

There are four developed campgrounds (all $9; open July-Labor Day) along this stretch of US

Sitting atop Wyoming's highest mountain pass, Top of the World Store is a popular stop for supplies.

Hwy. 212, and more once you drop into Montana. **Beartooth Lake** and **Island Lake** Campgrounds border alpine lakes. In addition, dispersed camping is allowed for free once you get off the main roads. Grizzlies inhabit this country, so be sure to store your food safely.

Top of the World Store, tel. (307) 899-2482 or (307) 587-9043, sits along the highway between the two Forest Service campgrounds. It's a popular stopping point for cyclists and other travelers over the pass. The general store has a limited selection of food and gifts, plus gas pumps, three motel rooms ($30 d; Budget), and a handful of RV spaces ($10). The store and motel generally open in July (when the snow is mostly gone) and close in mid-October.

Hiking

The open country at this elevation is dotted with whitebark pines and Engelmann spruce, and it delivers marvelous cross-country hiking opportunities. Anglers should bring a fishing pole to take a few casts for the brook, cutthroat, and rainbow trout in the alpine lakes. Two major trail systems are found in the High Lakes area.

The **Beartooth High Lakes Trail**—actually a series of trails—connects Island Lake, Beartooth Lake, Beauty Lake, and many smaller alpine ponds and puddles. A good place to start is from the boat ramp at Island Lake; see topographic maps for specific routes. This is a very popular late-summer area for day-hiking or for access to the Beartooth Wilderness. Be sure to bring a compass, topo map, and warm clothes before heading out on a day-hike—the weather can close in very quickly at this elevation, and afternoon thunderstorms are frequent. Always be aware of lightning activity when hiking in this exposed country.

Beartooth Loop National Recreation Trail is just two miles east of Beartooth Pass. This 15-mile loop traverses alpine tundra and passes several lakes and a century-old log stockade of unknown origins.

NORTH ABSAROKA WILDERNESS

The 350,488-acre North Absaroka Wilderness is one of the lesser-known wild places in Wyoming. It abuts Yellowstone National Park to the west and is bordered by the Sunlight Basin and Beartooth Highways to the north and US Hwy. 14/16/20 to the south. North Absaroka Wilderness is primarily used by hunters who arrive on horseback. The few hikers here tend to be quite experienced with backcountry travel and willing to tolerate the lack of trail signs and the steep and frequently washed-out paths. Much of the wilderness is relatively inaccessible, and snow may be present on passes until mid-July. Ask at the ranger stations for current trail conditions, and be sure to get topographic maps before heading out. Large populations of grizzly and black bears, bighorn sheep, moose, and elk are found in the Absaroka Mountains, and golden eagles are a common sight. The tough landscape is of volcanic origin, and the topsoil erodes easily, turning mountain creeks into churning rivers of mud after heavy summer rainstorms.

Hikes

The enormous 1988 Clover-Mist Fire that began in Yellowstone burned through a large portion of the North Absaroka Wilderness, but the land is recovering as young trees and other plants become established. Some areas were also replanted following the fire. Many hikers begin from trailheads near the Crandall Ranger Station along the Chief Joseph Scenic Highway. The **North Crandall Trail** is the most popular, a 16-mile hike up the North Fork of Crandall Creek. It is primarily used by horsepackers and offers great views of Hurricane Mesa along the way. Another popular wilderness path is **Pahaska-Sunlight Trail,** an 18-mile trek that begins at Pahaska Campground on US Hwy. 14/16/20 and heads north through historic Camp Monaco to Sunlight Basin.

WASHAKIE WILDERNESS

Covering 704,529 acres, Washakie Wilderness is one of the largest chunks of wild land in Wyoming. Named for Shoshone Chief Washakie, it lies between US Hwy. 14/16/20 (the road connecting Yellowstone and Cody) and US Hwy. 26/287 (Dubois area). To the west are Yellowstone National Park and Teton Wilderness. The Washakie is a land of deep narrow valleys, mountains of highly erodible volcanic material, and steplike buttes. The mountains—a few top 13,000 feet—are part of the Absaroka Range. About half of the land is forested. One of the unique features of Washakie Wilderness is a petrified forest, a reminder of the region's volcanic past.

Hikes

There are numerous trails through the Washakie Wilderness, but most require that you either return the same way or end at a location far from your starting point. Several trails stretch into Yellowstone National Park and are popular with extended horsepacking trips. The most popular Washakie Wilderness hikes are from US Hwy. 14/16/20 in Wapiti Valley. Most folks use them for short day-hikes or horseback rides rather than attempting longer backcountry treks.

Kitty Creek Trail leaves from the Kitty Creek summer home area, nine miles east of Yellowstone. Low-clearance vehicles will need to park along the highway. The trail follows the creek past two large scenic meadows to Flora Lake, 6.5 miles and 2,500 feet higher. This is the shortest hike in the area and one of the most popular.

The 21-mile-long **Elk Fork Trail** starts at Elk Fork Campground and crosses Elk Creek several times en route to remote Rampart Pass at nearly 11,000 feet. It is steep and rocky in the higher elevations. West of the Continental Divide you enter the Teton Wilderness. For the really ambitious, the Open Creek and Thorofare Trails continue on into Yellowstone National Park.

Deer Creek Trail departs from the free Deer Creek Campground, 42 miles southwest of Cody on State Hwy. 291 (South Fork Rd.). The trail switchbacks very steeply uphill at first and after two miles reaches an attractive waterfall. Continue another eight miles from here to the Continental Divide and the Thorofare portion of the Teton Wilderness. This is probably the quickest route into this remote country and is popular with both horsepackers and hikers.

South Fork Trail takes off from the South Fork Guard Station across the creek from Deer Creek Campground. (Take a signed spur road to get there.) It climbs up along South Fork Creek to Shoshone Pass on the Continental Divide (9,858 feet). From here you can continue on a number of trails to the south, rambling over three more passes to eventually reach Double Cabin Campground, 27 miles north of Dubois. Another long hike into Washakie Wilderness leaves from this campground and follows the **Wiggins Fork Trail** up into a connecting series of paths: Absaroka, Nine Mile, East Fork, and Bug Creek Trails. It ends back at Double Cabin Campground. Total length is 60 miles. Along the way you're likely to see hundreds of elk in the high country as well as bighorn sheep. You won't see many other hikers.

CODY

The city of Cody (pop. 8,800) marks the transition point between the forested mountains of northwest Wyoming and the sage-covered plains of Bighorn Basin. It's a favorite stopping place for Yellowstone tourists. The park is just 54 miles due west of downtown, and other magnificent country spreads in all directions—the Beartooth Mountains and Sunlight Basin to the north, the Absaroka Range and Wapiti Valley to the west and south. Established as an agricultural and tourism center, Cody retains both roles today, though tourism seems to be gaining in importance with each passing year. The town is one of the few places in Wyoming that continued to grow through the 1990s; only Jackson Hole exceeds Cody as a tourism center. Not surprisingly, both are gateways to the national parks that dominate northwest Wyoming. Cody is also home to a number of midsize companies, including oil, mining, and logging operations.

Cody itself has a number of attractions, including the justly famous Buffalo Bill Historical Center, along with Trail Town and other local sights. The Shoshone River flows right through

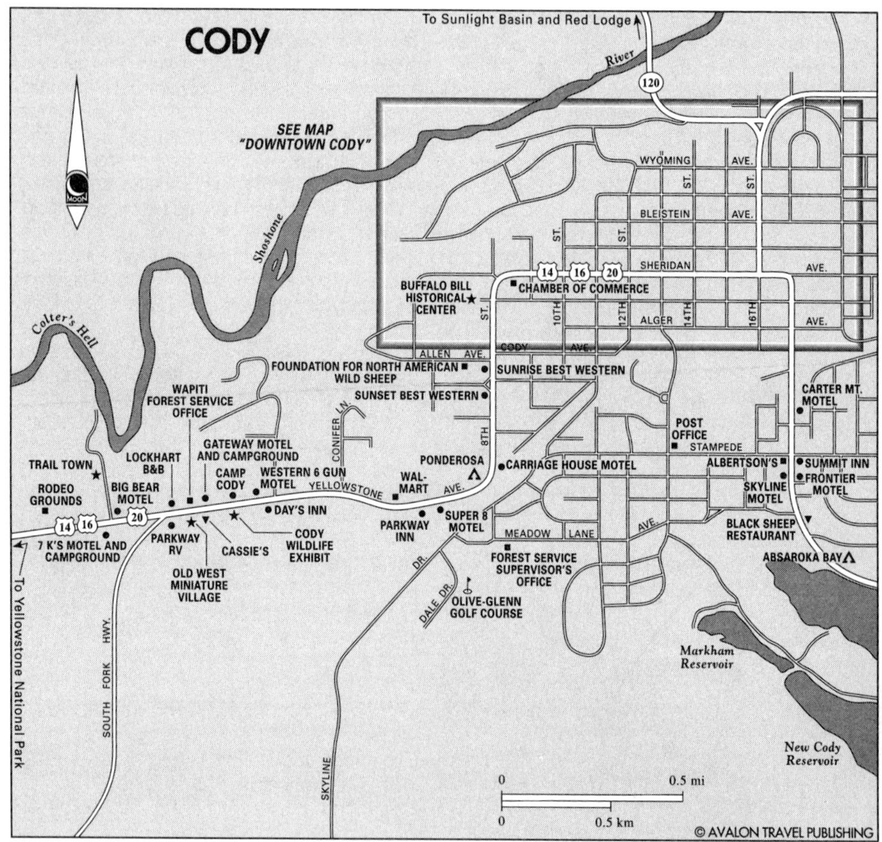

town, providing the opportunity for scenic float trips. Lots of events crowd the summer calendar, from nightly rodeos and shoot-outs, to parades and powwows; biggest of all is the annual Cody Stampede in July. The town also takes pride in a long list of artists that includes Charles Cary Rumsey and Harry Jackson. Famed abstract expressionist Jackson Pollock was born here, but achieved his reputation in New York and never returned to his birthplace.

History

Just west of Cody—past the Wal-Mart, RV parks, fireworks stands, and gas stations—are the Absaroka Mountains, named for the Native Americans who first lived here. They called themselves the Absaroka, or "Children of the Large Beaked Bird." Whites interpreted this as crow, and the natives have been called Crow Indians ever since. Explorer John Colter passed through this region in 1808 while recruiting Indians to supply beaver furs. When Colter returned to the semblance of civilization called Fort Manual Lisa, everyone laughed at his tales of a spectacular geothermal area along the "Stinkingwater River." Soon everyone was calling it "Colter's Hell." But the geysers were real; they still steam along the Shoshone (formerly the Stinkingwater) just west of present-day Cody. Other mountain men came later, followed by miners who found copper and sulfur in Sunlight Basin. The first real settler in the area was a Prussian, Otto Franc, who developed a large cattle spread at the famous Pitchfork Ranch. (Franc is said to have helped finance the Wyoming Stock Growers during the Johnson County War. He was later murdered, and some blamed men affiliated with the homesteaders.)

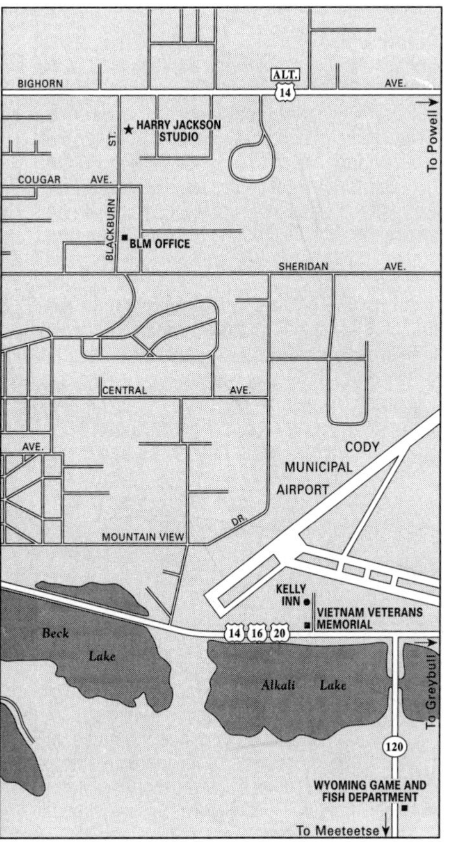

In 1895, William F. "Buffalo Bill" Cody and two partners began plans for the Shoshone Land and Irrigation Company, with headquarters along the Shoshone River just west of the present city of Cody. Cody had spent much time in the Bighorn Basin, guiding parties of wealthy sportsmen, and was convinced that a combination of tourism and irrigated farming could transform this desert land. Officially founded in 1896, the name Cody was a natural choice for this new settlement. At the urging of Buffalo Bill, the Chicago, Burlington, & Quincy Railroad arrived in 1901, bringing in thousands of tourists who continued west up Shoshone Canyon to Yellowstone by stagecoach. Oil was first discovered near Cody in 1904, and Park County is now the second-largest oil producer in the state. Marathon Oil Company has its Rocky Mountain headquarters in Cody and is one of the town's largest employers. Also important are a wallboard manufacturing plant, a lumber mill, and a producer of ranch products.

BUFFALO BILL HISTORICAL CENTER

Each year, more than 300,000 people visit Cody's main attraction, the Buffalo Bill Historical Center. Nowhere else in America is such a major museum in a town with so few people. This is the largest and most impressive museum in Wyoming and the finest Western museum in the world. The late author James Michener once labeled it "the Smithsonian of the West," and his term is even more true today. It's a place where visitors quickly run out of superlatives. The collection focuses—not surprisingly—on the Western frontier and includes thousands of artifacts and works of art spread through more than 237,000 square feet of space. The center actually houses four separate museums, a research library, the boyhood home of Buffalo Bill, and two sculpture gardens.

The original Buffalo Bill Museum opened in 1927 in what is now the chamber of commerce log cabin. Opening in 1959, the Whitney Gallery of Western Art formed a nucleus for the current museum location; later additions included the Buffalo Bill Museum, the Plains Indian Museum, and the Cody Firearms Museum. A new natural history museum is under development and should open early in the 21st century. Other facilities at the Buffalo Bill Historical Center include an outstanding gift shop and bookstore, plus a cafe for light meals. Head to the sculpture garden for a lunchtime buffalo burger beneath the aspen trees.

Events take place all summer long, ranging from powwows to historical talks to cowboy singing. Of note is the **Larom Summer Institute in Western American Studies,** an in-depth two-week history course offered each June. See Events below for other museum activities.

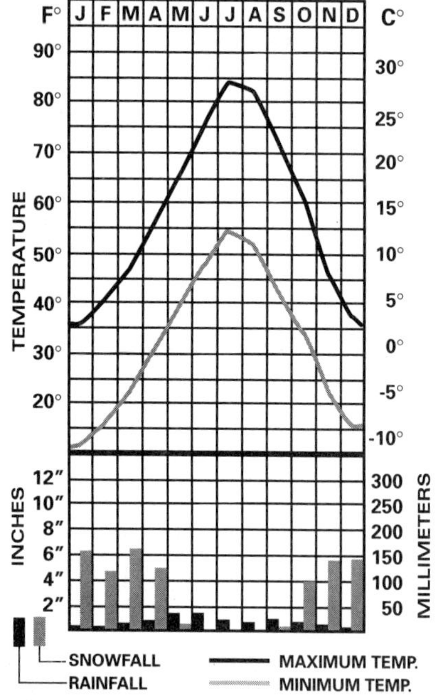

Practicalities

Buffalo Bill Historical Center, tel. (307) 587-4771 or (800) 227-8483, is open year-round. In the busy summer season from June through mid-September, it's open daily 7 a.m.-8 p.m. At other times, hours are reduced: daily 8 a.m.-5 p.m. mid-September through October and during April; daily 8 a.m.-8 p.m. in May. From November through March the museum is open Tues.-Sun. 10 a.m.-3 p.m. Closed Thanksgiving, Christmas, and New Year's Day.

Admission costs $10 for adults, $6 for students 18 and over, and $4 for ages 6-17. Children under six get in free. The admission is good for two days, and it may well take you two days to explore this massive collection! Tours are generally offered only for school groups and VIPs, but the Historical Center often has summertime demonstrations, and the helpful docents can provide additional info. For more on the museum, visit the website: www.bbhc.org.

Outside

Before heading inside, stop to view Buffalo Bill's **boyhood home,** a tiny yellow building built in 1841 by Isaac Cody. The house stood in LeClarie, Iowa, for almost a century. In 1933 it was sawed in half, loaded on two railcars, and hauled to Cody to be reassembled and refurbished. The house is on your left as you face the museum. Flanking the museum on the opposite side is ***The Scout,*** a dramatic, larger-than-life statue of larger-than-life Buffalo Bill. This huge bronze piece was created by New York sculptress Gertrude Vanderbilt Whitney and was unveiled in 1924. Her family later donated 40 acres of surrounding land to the Buffalo Bill Museum. Directly in front of the historical center are three colorfully painted **tepees,** a treat for kids. Once you enter the museum, ask for directions to the **Visitor's Lounge,** where a 10-minute orientation video provides a good introduction. Just inside the entrance on the left is a magnificent feathered cape made in 1839 by a Mesquakie woman from the Great Lakes area; don't miss it.

Buffalo Bill Museum

The Buffalo Bill Museum is a real joy. In it, the life of Buffalo Bill Cody is briefly sketched with all sorts of memorabilia from his Wild West Show including the famous Deadwood Stage, silver-laden saddles, enormous posters, furniture, guns, wagons, and clothing. Be sure to look for "Lucretia Borgia," the Springfield rifle that helped William Cody gain his nickname. Also here are some of the gifts given to Buffalo Bill by European heads of state—including a fur carriage robe from Czar Alexander II—and by Wild Bill Hickok and Sitting Bull. Original film footage from the Wild West Show runs continuously, offering a fascinating and sometimes unintentionally comical glimpse into the past. Amazingly choreographed marching soldiers, fake Indian battles, sign-language conversations, and bucking broncos make it easy to see how the Wild West Show helped inspire Western movies.

Downstairs from the Buffalo Bill Museum is a spacious gallery used for special exhibitions (always worth a look), along with the **Harold McCracken Research Library,** open Mon.-Fri. 8 a.m.-noon and 1-5 p.m. May-October. The library houses thousands of historical photos and books, including more than 300 volumes about Buffalo Bill—mostly dime novels and comic books.

Whitney Gallery of Western Art

The Whitney Gallery contains a stunning collection of masterworks by such Western artists and sculptors as Charles Russell, Frederic Remington, Carl Bodmer, George Catlin, Thomas Moran, Albert Bierstadt, Alfred Jacob Miller, Edgar Paxson, N.C. Wyeth, and others. The studios of Frederic Remington and W.H.D. Koerner have been re-created, and Gertrude Vanderbilt Whitney's *The Scout* is visible from a large window on the north end. The collections of both "cowboy artist" Charles Russell and Frederic Remington—best known for his paintings of battles during the Indian wars—are the most complete here; the museum has more than a hundred of each man's paintings. Next to the Whitney Gallery is **Joseph Henry Sharp Garden,** where you'll find his "Absarokee Hut" filled with the painter's paraphernalia.

The **Kriendler Gallery of Contemporary Western Art** is upstairs from the entrance to the Whitney Gallery, and contains a diverse collection of pieces, including several with a delightfully whimsical twist. Well worth the detour.

Cody Firearms Museum

The Cody Firearms Museum houses one of the most comprehensive collections of American firearms in the world, including everything from 16th-century matchlocks to self-loading semiautomatic pistols. This is one museum where the men outnumber the women. Start your visit by viewing "Lock, Stock, & Barrel," a 10-minute video that describes the history of guns and how they work; it's interesting even for those of us who consider the proliferation of guns a national menace. In fact, the entire firearms collection is remarkably informative and well worth taking time to view.

The museum now contains more than 5,000 weapons, but these aren't just rows of guns in glass cases. Some of the more unusual include a 10-shot repeating flintlock rifle made for the New York Militia around 1825 and a 17th-century windlass crossbow. There are all sorts of displays to explore, including a colonial gun shop, a western stage station, a turn-of-the-20th-century firearms factory, and a truly extraordinary collection of embellished arms. One of the most lavish is an intricately carved flintlock sporting carbine presented by Empress Elizabeth I of Russia to King Louis XV of France. The Boone and Crockett Club's collection of trophy animal heads is here, including an elephant-sized moose housed in a re-created hunting lodge. All told, more implements of destruction and mayhem than you're likely to see at a gathering of Idaho neo-Nazis. Take the elevator to the basement for even more gun displays.

Plains Indian Museum

The largest exhibition space in the historical center encloses the Plains Indian Museum, with items from the Sioux, Cheyenne, Blackfeet, Crow, Arapaho, Shoshone, and Gros Ventre tribes. At first it may seem incongruous that a museum featuring the man once called the "youngest Indian slayer of the plains" should include so much about the culture of Indians, but Cody's later maturity forced him to the realization that Indians had been severely mistreated and that their culture was of great value. His Wild West Shows re-created some semblance of that lost society, if only for show. Some of the more important items here were given to Buffalo Bill by various Indian performers over the years, and the collection of artifacts is now one of the finest in America. Included are an extraordinary painted buffalo robe from 1890 which depicts the Battle of Little Big Horn, elaborately decorated baby carriers, ghost-dance dresses, leather garments, war bonnets, medicine pipes, and even a Pawnee grizzly claw necklace. One of the more unusual items is Lone Dog's Winter Count, with figures representing a 71-year sequence of events affecting the Sioux; it was created in 1877. The moccasin collection fills an entire wall, and one room holds a Sioux camp as it might have appeared in the 1880s. Be sure to check out the exhibit on 10,000-year-old Mummy Cave, discovered in 1957 west of Cody.

OTHER SIGHTS

Trail Town

Point your horses toward the mountains and head 'em two miles west of Cody to a unique collection of historic buildings at Trail Town, tel. (307) 587-5302. The site is open daily 8 a.m.-7 p.m. mid-May to mid-September only; $3 entrance (free for kids under 12). This was the original location of "Cody City" in 1895. Trail Town is the creation of Bob and Terry Edgar. (In 1957 Bob Edgar discovered Mummy Cave—one of the most important archaeological finds in the West.) The Edgars bought the old Arland and Corbett trading post that had stood here since the 1880s and began dragging in other historic Wyoming cabins. Some were transported whole, others were disassembled and then put back together at Trail Town. Currently the site holds 22 buildings dating from 1879 to 1901, plus 100 wagons.

For those who love history, Trail Town is an incredible treasure trove without the fancy gift shops and commercial junk that tag along with most such endeavors. This is the real thing, low-key and genuine. Probably the most famous building here is a cabin from the Hole-in-the-Wall country that Butch Cassidy and the Sundance Kid used as a rendezvous spot. Also at Trail Town is the oldest saloon from this part of Wyoming, complete with bullet holes in the door, and a cabin where Jim White—one of the most famous buffalo hunters—was murdered in 1879. The log home of Crow Indian scout Curley stands along main street too. (Curley was the only one of General Custer's command who escaped alive from the Battle of the Little Big Horn.) Inside the old Burlington Store are a black hearse, arrowheads, a cradleboard, and items from fur traders.

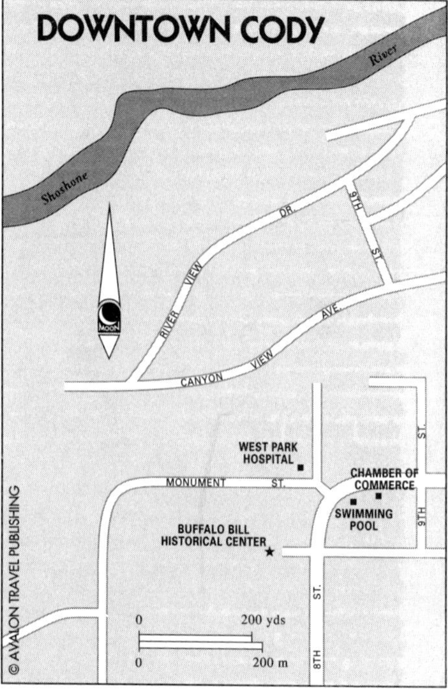

The bodies of buffalo hunter Jim White and several other historic figures have been reinterred in a small graveyard at Trail Town. One of the most interesting of these is Belle Drewry, a prostitute known as "The Woman in Blue." After bouncing around a number of 19th-century mining towns, she ended up in the lawless and now-abandoned town of Arlund, located northwest of Meeteetse. One night in 1897 she shot a cowboy to death during a dance. The following night his outlaw friends took retribution by murdering her. Belle was buried in the blue dress that she always wore. Also buried in the cemetery is **John "Liver Eating" Johnson,** the mountain man portrayed by Robert Redford in the movie *Jeremiah Johnson.* Those who have seen the film will be surprised to learn that Johnson died in 1900 at the Old Soldiers' Home in Los Angeles! Friends sent him there by train from Montana when his health deteriorated, but he only spent a month in California before his death at the age of 76. After the movie came out, schoolchildren in Los Angeles helped promote the moving of Johnson's body closer to his mountain home. Nearly 2,000 people showed up for the reburial in 1974, including Robert Redford. A memorial to explorers John Colter and Jim Bridger also stands near the graveyard. The historic buildings, artifacts, and graves at Trail Town provide a fine counterpoint to the glitzier Buffalo Bill Historical Center.

Irma Hotel

Pick up a copy of the ***Cody Historic Walking Tour*** brochure ($2) at the visitor center for an informative introduction to local buildings and their history. One of the most engaging stories is about the Irma Hotel, named for Buffalo Bill Cody's daughter. It was built in 1902 to house tourists arriving by train and was one of three way stations to Yellowstone built by Cody. The luxurious saloon has a French-made $100,000 cherry wood bar given to Buffalo Bill by Queen Victoria. Many famous people have gathered here over the years.

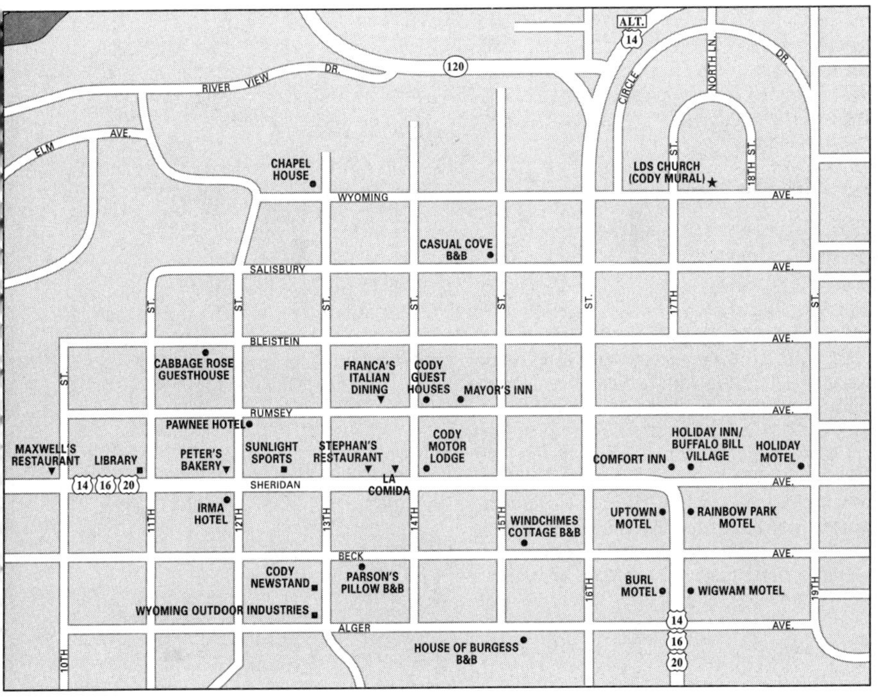

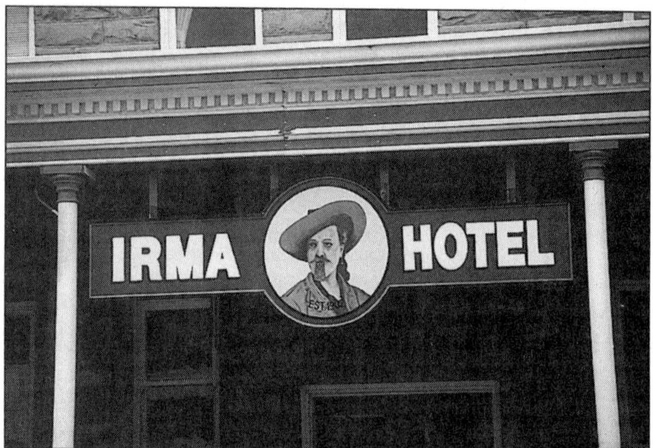

The Irma Hotel is named after Buffalo Bill Cody's daughter.

The **Cody Gunslingers** perform in front of the Irma Mon.-Fri. between Memorial Day and Labor Day. Cody was established long after the era of gunfights in the streets, so this isn't particularly authentic, but it does attract a crowd each evening. The gunfight officially starts at 6 p.m., but the first 15 minutes or so are typically wasted on ads for local businesses. You know you're in America when the advertising even delays a gunfight! Call (307) 587-4221 for details on the gunslingers.

Harry Jackson Studio

Cody's best-known living artist, Harry Jackson, has a large gallery at 602 Blackburn Avenue. His works cover the palette from abstract expressionist paintings, collages, and cubist studies to his more recent sculptures of traditional Old West figures—cowboys and Indians. Many of his sculptures contain distinctively painted surfaces. The sculptures are his best-known works, including the monumental *Sacajawea* at the Buffalo Bill Historical Center and *Horseman* in Beverly Hills. Jackson's pieces have been exhibited throughout the U.S. and in Italy (where his works are cast). Jackson himself divides his time between Cody and Italy. All bronzes (but not his paintings) displayed here are for sale, but they're only for serious art patrons willing to spend thousands of dollars. The gallery is typically open Mon.-Fri. 8 a.m.-5 p.m., but call (307) 587-5508 for the latest.

Art Galleries

The **Buffalo Bill Historical Center** (described above) houses an excellent gift shop with art prints, Indian jewelry, and reproductions of bronze sculptures. Next to the chamber of commerce office at 836 Sheridan Ave. is the **Cody Country Art League,** tel. (307) 587-3597, displaying paintings, sculptures, photos, and crafts for sale. They also offer workshops and juried art shows.

Simpson Gallagher Gallery, 1115 13th St., tel. (307) 587-4022, is one of the finest in Cody, with works that go well beyond the standard Western clichés. **Two Bears at the Irma,** 1192 Sheridan Ave., tel. (307) 587-9400, has a huge selection of silver and turquoise Indian jewelry. Most comes from New Mexico, but a few pieces are from the Wind River Reservation in Wyoming.

Of less interest but possibly worth a peek are two shops with predictable artworks: **Big Horn Gallery,** 1167 Sheridan Ave., tel. (307) 587-6762, and **Kilian Gallery,** 1361 Sheridan Ave., tel. (307) 527-5380.

Old West Miniature Village

Cody has an abundance of offbeat attractions, from talking sheep to sanctified ceilings. The most unusual—and actually worth a visit—is **Old West Miniature Village and Museum** (a.k.a. Tecumseh's Trading Post), 142 W. Yellowstone Ave., tel. (307) 587-5362. Owner Jerry Fick has spent decades creating an enormous diorama that offers a truncated version of Wyoming and Montana history. The term "kitsch" quickly enters your head when you step inside, but you've got to appreciate the effort that went into creating thousands of hand-carved figures and an array of miniature villages. Of considerably more interest is his collection of artifacts that includes a knife from the Battle of Little Bighorn, old-time cowboy garb, the bow and arrows that belonged to Geronimo, and many Plains Indian artifacts. Entrance is $5 for adults, $1 for children; open daily 8 a.m.-8 p.m. May-Sept.; call for winter hours.

Wildlife Exhibits

The **Foundation for North American Wild Sheep** has its national headquarters at 720 Allen Ave., tel. (307) 527-6261 (just south of Buffalo Bill Historical Center). A favorite of wealthy trophy hunters, this nonprofit group funds wild sheep research and conservation. The place is a bit bizarre, with oversized bronze rams and a recording that plays out front even when nobody's around. The building is open Mon.-Fri. 8 a.m.-5 p.m.

The **Cody Wildlife Exhibit,** 433 Yellowstone Hwy., tel. (307) 587-2804, has a rather nice display of more than 400 mounted American and African wildlife—all sorts of record-sized critters, from a 17-foot-tall giraffe to a 2,800-pound buffalo. Admission costs $4 (free for kids under age seven); open daily 9 a.m.-8 p.m. June-September.

More Sights

Cedar Mountain, the 7,889-foot-tall summit overlooking Cody from the west, is where Buffalo Bill had wanted to be buried. A winding 4WD trail climbs to the top, but there's no public access at present. Also here is **Spirit Mountain Cave,** one of the first national monuments ever designated (1909). A lack of interest caused the designation to be withdrawn, but the caverns are still on public land. Spelunkers can get permission to enter from the BLM office in Cody.

Southeast of Cody near Beck Lake is the **Wyoming Vietnam Veterans Memorial,** a black granite memorial modeled after the one in Washington. It contains the names of 137 Wyoming men who were killed or declared missing in action.

If you're really desperate for something to do, visit the **Cody Murals** on the domed ceiling of the LDS church at 1719 Wyoming Avenue. Tours are available daily during the summer; call (307) 587-3290. No, it isn't the Sistine Chapel. The mural (painted in 1951) offers a rosy-tinted version of Mormon Church history and the Bighorn Basin pioneers.

ACCOMMODATIONS

Motels and Hotels

The tourist town of Cody is jam-packed with lodging facilities, but be ready to pay more than anyplace in Wyoming except Jackson Hole. Budget accommodations are nonexistent during the summer, though rates plummet with the first cold nights of fall. The town doesn't have a hostel, but one is definitely needed! Most of the year, lodging in Cody is not a problem as long as you check in before 4 p.m., but during July and August you should reserve a week ahead—and longer for the Cody Stampede in early July.

Cody Area Central Reservations, tel. (307) 587-0200 or (888) 468-6996, makes reservations for many local motels, mountain lodges, and B&Bs at no additional charge, and it's a good one-stop place to plan your trip to the Cody and Yellowstone area. Find the organization on the web at www.wtp.net/codyres.

A number of local places are described below; see Additional Cody Motels in the appendix for other local lodging places. In addition, you will find many dude ranches and lodges in the mountain country around Cody; these are described above in the Wapiti Valley/North Fork, Sunlight Basin, and South Fork Area sections.

Cody's least expensive lodging is also its oldest: the **Pawnee Hotel,** 1032 12th St., tel. (307) 587-2239. Built in 1900, the hotel contains 22 refurbished rooms, including four with clawfoot bathtubs. The least expensive accommodations are $22-25 s or $28-32 d and share a bath down the hall. Rooms with private baths are $32 s or $38 d, and a four-person suite is $48. Budget-Inexpensive.

Uptown Motel, 1562 Sheridan Ave., tel. (307) 587-4245, is a small motel with well-maintained rooms for $50 s or $54-62 d. Some rooms contain microwaves and fridges. Inexpensive-Moderate.

Stay in very attractive log cabins from the 1920s at **Carriage House Motel,** 1816 8th St.,

BUFFALO BILL CODY

For many people today, the name "Buffalo Bill" brings to mind a man who helped slaughter the vast herds of wild bison that once filled the west. But William F. Cody cannot be so easily pigeonholed, for here was one of the most remarkable men of his or any other era—a man who almost single-handedly established the aura of the "Wild West." More than 800 books—many of them the dime-store novels that thrilled generations of youngsters—have been written about Cody. In many of these, the truth was stretched far beyond any semblance of reality, but the real life of William Cody contains so many adventures and plot twists that it seems hard to believe one person could have done so much.

Young Cody

Born to an Iowa farm family in 1846, William Cody started life as had many others of his era. His parents moved to Kansas when he was six, but his abolitionist father, Isaac Cody, soon became embroiled in arguments with the many slaveholders. While defending his views at a public meeting, Isaac Cody was stabbed in the back and fled for his life. When a mob learned of his father's whereabouts, eight-year-old Will Cody rode on his first venture through enemy lines, galloping 35 miles to warn of the impending attack. Three years later, when Isaac Cody died of complications from the stabbing, 11-year-old Will Cody became the family's breadwinner. There were four other children to feed. Will quickly joined the company of Alexander Majors, running dispatches between his Army supply wagons and giving his $40 monthly wages to his mother. In Cody's autobiography he claimed to have killed his first Indian on this trip, an action that gave him the then-enviable title "youngest Indian slayer of the plains."

On his first long wagon trek west, the Army supply wagons were attacked by Mormon zealots who took all the weapons and horses, forcing Cody to walk much of the thousand miles back to his Kansas home. It was apparently on this walk that Cody met Wild Bill Hickok. At Wyoming's Fort Laramie, young Will sat in awe as famed scouts Jim Bridger and Kit Carson reminisced about their adventures. The experience was a turning point in Cody's life; he resolved to one day become a scout. Cody's next job offered excellent training: he became a rider for the Pony Express. At just 15 years of age he already was one of the finest riders in the West and a crack shot with a rifle. On one of his Pony Express rides Cody covered a total of 320 miles in just 21 hours and 40 minutes—the longest Pony Express ride ever. The Civil War had begun, and at age 18 Cody joined the Seventh Kansas Regiment, serving as a scout and spy for the Union Army.

After the Civil War, Will Cody tried his hand at the hotel business and then briefly joined Gen.

BUFFALO BILL HISTORICAL CENTER

Buffalo Bill with Indian children, 1913—this photo was probably taken during the filming of The Indian Wars.

George Custer as a scout before returning to Kansas to do a little land speculating along the route of the newly built railroad. Cody and a partner bought land and laid out a town that they named Rome. For a short while it boomed. One day a man appeared in Rome, offering to take over the town while leaving Cody with only a small portion of the place he had founded. Thinking it was only intimidation from a shady operator, Cody laughed at the man, not knowing that he was president of the railroad's townsite company. The railroad quickly chose another townsite, and three days later all the inhabitants of Rome moved east to the new site, taking their buildings with them. Cody was left with a worthless patch of land.

Buffalo Hunter and Scout

In 1867, Cody found work hunting buffalo to supply fresh meat for the railroad construction crews, a job that soon made him famous as "Buffalo Bill" and paid a hefty $500 a month. With 75 million bison spread from northern Canada to Mexico, and herds so vast that they took many days to pass one point, it seemed impossible that they could ever be killed off. Cody was one of the best hunters in the West; in just eight months, he slaughtered 4,280 buffalo, often saving transportation by driving the herd toward the camp and dropping them within sight of the workers. Cody's name lives on in the jingle: "Buffalo Bill, Buffalo Bill; never missed and never will; always aims and shoots to kill; and the company pays his buffalo bill . . ."

After this stint, Cody finally got the job he wanted—chief scout for the U.S. Army in the West, a job packed with excitement and danger. Conflicts with Indians had reached a fever pitch as more and more whites moved into the last Indian strongholds. Cody worked as scout for Gen. Philip Sheridan, providing information on the Indians' movements, leading troops in pursuit of the warriors, and joining in the battles, including one in which he supposedly killed Chief Tall Bull. His men considered Buffalo Bill good luck, because he managed to keep them out of ambushes.

During the Indian campaigns, the writer/preacher/scoundrel Ned Buntline began writing of Cody's exploits for various New York papers, giving Buffalo Bill his first taste of national acclaim. Soon Buntline had cranked out several romantic novels loosely based on Cody's adventures. America had a new national hero. European and Eastern gentry began asking Cody to guide them on buffalo hunts. On the trips, Cody referred to them as "dudes" and to his camps as "dude ranches"—perhaps the first time anyone had used the terms for such hunters. One of Wyoming's most unusual businesses had begun. Cody's incredible knowledge of the land and hunting impressed the men, but they were stunned to also discover in him a natural showman. In 1872, the Grand Duke Alexis of Russia came to the U.S., and Cody guided him on a hunt that made national headlines and brought even more fame to the 26-year-old. On a trip to New York in 1872, Cody met Buntline again and watched a wildly distorted theater production called *Buffalo Bill.* Amazingly, Cody adjusted quickly to the new surroundings. Dressed in the finest silk clothes but with his long scout's hair under a Western hat, Cody suddenly entered the world of high society.

In a short while, Cody was on the stage himself, performing with Ned Buntline and fellow scout Texas Jack in a play called *Scouts of the Plains.* Although the play was meant to be serious, the acting of all three proved so atrocious that the play had audiences rolling in the aisles with laughter. A New York reviewer called the play "so wonderfully bad it was almost good. The whole performance was so far aside of human experience, so wonderful in its daring feebleness, that no ordinary intellect is capable of comprehending it." Audiences packed the theaters for weeks on end. But Cody was suddenly called back west, for the Sioux were again on the warpath.

Shortly after Cody had returned to guide Gen. Eugene Carr's forces, they learned of the massacre of Custer's men at the Battle of Little Bighorn. In revenge, Carr's men set out to pursue Indians along the border between Nebraska and Wyoming. Under Cody's guidance, they surprised a group of warriors at War Bonnet Creek. Cody shot the chief, Yellow Hand, and immediately scalped him, raising the scalp above his head with the cry "first scalp for Custer!" (Cody later claimed that he scalped the chief because he was wearing an American flag as a loincloth and had a lock of yellow hair from a white woman's scalp pinned to his clothing.) The Sioux immediately fled. If Cody had been famous before, this event propelled him to even more acclaim. It became the grist for countless dime-store novels and was embellished in so many ways over the years that the true story will never be known.

The Wild West Show

Buffalo Bill's days in the real Wild West were over, and he returned to staging shows, eventually starting his famed Wild West extravaganza. This was un-

(continued on next page)

BUFFALO BILL CODY

(continued)

like anything ever done before—an outdoor circus that seemed to transport all who watched to the frontier. One newspaper remarked that Cody had "out-Barnumed Barnum." There were buffalo stampedes, cowboy bronc riding, Indian camps, a Deadwood stage and outlaws, crack shooting by Annie Oakley, and, of course, Buffalo Bill. At its peak in the late 1890s, the show made Cody more than a million dollars in profit each year.

Amazingly, Sitting Bull and Buffalo Bill became good friends. Cody, who had earlier bragged of his many Indian killings, changed his attitude, eventually saying, "In nine cases out of 10 when there is trouble between white men and Indians, it will be found that the white man is responsible." Cody's other attitudes also continued to evolve. He criticized the buffalo hidehunters of the 1870s and 1880s for their reckless slaughter and later became an ardent supporter of game preserves and limitations on hunting seasons.

The Wild West Show became one of the most popular events anywhere in America and Europe, attracting crowds of up to 40,000 people. Queen Victoria was a special fan (although rumors of an affair are probably false). At the peak of his fame around the turn of the century, Buffalo Bill was arguably the world's best-known man. Cody, however, continued to drink heavily. One day, an obviously drunken Buffalo Bill insisted that his cowboys ride Monarch, a massive and dangerous bison in the entourage. When they refused in front of thousands of spectators, Cody himself climbed on top and was immediately thrown to the ground. He spent the next two weeks in a hospital. For the next decade the show continued to tour but gradually lost its novelty as other forms of entertainment, especially movies, came along. Cody used his money to buy the 40,000-acre TE Ranch in northwestern Wyoming near Yellowstone National Park. For him the Bighorn Basin was paradise. The town that he helped establish here was named Cody in his honor, and he backed the massive Shoshone irrigation project.

A Sad Farewell

Unfortunately, Buffalo Bill seemed to have no comprehension of how to save his wealth. He was a notoriously soft touch and would give money to almost anyone who asked. As his fortune slipped away and his show became more dated, Cody was finally forced to join up with H.H. Tammen, the crooked owner of the *Denver Post.* Tammen used the aging Cody's fame to attract people to his own circus. He forced Cody's Wild West Show into bankruptcy in 1913, sold off all the incredible collection of historical artifacts that had been amassed over the years, and left workers to find their own way home. Buffalo Bill was heartbroken, but, still trusting Tammen (or in desperation), he agreed to join his circus almost as a sideshow act.

Three years later, Cody died while visiting his sister in Denver and was buried on Lookout Mountain near Denver. Cody had wanted to be buried on Cedar Mountain above the town of Cody, but even this wish was denied by Tammen, who apparently paid Cody's widow Louisa $10,000 for the privilege of choosing the burial site (and to use the funeral parade to the burial site as an advertisement for his circus troop). When rumors came that folks from Wyoming intended to dig up Cody's body and take it back to its rightful burial place, Tammen had tons of concrete dumped on top of the grave. Louisa Cody went on to outlive not only her husband, but also all four of her children. She ended up caring for her four grandchildren.

Despite the unhappy ending to Buffalo Bill's life, there are few individuals who lived such a diverse and adventure-filled life and who could count so many people as their friends, from the lowliest beggar to the richest king. Cody's life spanned one of the most remarkable eras in American history, and his impact on American culture is still felt today, not just in the image of the West that he created, which lives on in hundreds of Western movies, but also in the Boy Scouts (an organization inspired partly by his exploits), in the city of Cody, and even in the dude ranches that dot Wyoming.

Late in life, Cody was asked how he wanted to be remembered. He replied: "I don't want to die and have people say 'Oh, there goes another old showman.' When I die I want the people of Wyoming who are living on the land that has been made fertile by my work and expenditure to remember me. I would like people to say, 'This is the man who opened up Wyoming to the best of civilization.'"

tel. (307) 587-2572 or (800) 531-2572. The cabins are small and don't have phones, but they've been lovingly remodeled. Rates are $50-65 s or d; two-room suites (these sleep up to six) cost $85-135. Open May-October. Inexpensive.

Buffalo Bill Cody's historic **Irma Hotel,** 1192 Sheridan Ave., tel. (307) 587-4221 or (800) 745-4762, has a great downtown location and all the ambience you could want. It's the real thing—a classic Old West hotel. The eight suites ($87 s or $94 d) provide updated rooms, or stay in the far less noteworthy motel rooms for $62 s or $69 d. Moderate-Expensive.

Parkway Inn, 720 W. Yellowstone Ave., tel. (307) 587-4208, is a nice place with newly remodeled rooms costing $78-88 s or d. Amenities include an outdoor pool and continental breakfast. Open June-September. Moderate-Expensive.

One of the nicest chain motels in town, **Kelly Inn,** tel. (307) 527-5505 or (800) 635-3559, is a mile east of Cody. Standard (but spacious) rooms are $89 s or $99 d; six-person family rooms with fridges and microwaves go for $135, and rooms with jacuzzi tubs cost $135 d. Also here are a sauna, jacuzzi, and exercise room. A light breakfast is available in the lobby. Expensive-Premium.

You'll find best-in-town motel accommodations at **Best Western Sunset,** 1601 8th St., tel. (307) 587-4265 or (800) 624-2727, where the rooms are $109-139 s or d. Amenities include indoor and outdoor pools, a jacuzzi, playground, and fitness facility. Expensive-Premium.

Guest Houses

Families may want to stay in one of the seven nicely furnished homes, cottages, and apartments managed by **Cody Guest Houses,** 1401 Rumsey Ave., tel. (307) 587-6000 or (800) 587-6560, www.wtp.net/cghouses. Most luxurious is a beautiful three-bedroom Victorian home ($450 for six people in the entire house, or $120-199 d for individual rooms). Other places include a remodeled 1930s church (Chapel House) that sleeps four for $175, three cottages starting at $110 d up to $150 for four people, and an efficiency apartment for $80 d. In addition, Cody Guest Houses manages Mayor's Inn B&B, described below.

Cabbage Rose Guest House, 1126 Bleistein Ave., tel. (307) 587-4984, is a century-old home with three bedrooms, one bath, and a full kitchen. Eight people can sleep here comfortably. Rates are $120, and children are welcome. Open May-September. Premium.

Cozy Cody Cottages, tel. (307) 587-9253, has two cottages located at 1403 and 1405 Rumsey Avenue. Rates are $80-110 d, and both places contain private baths, full kitchens, and laundry facilities. Moderate-Expensive.

Bed and Breakfasts

Several historic buildings are now part of the Cody B&B scene, offering a taste of the genteel past. **Parson's Pillow B&B,** 1202 14th St., tel. (307) 587-2382 or (800) 377-2348, is probably the most interesting and enjoys a good central location. Completed in 1902, the building served for many years as a Methodist-Episcopal Church. Today it's a cozy and well-maintained B&B with antique furnishings, four guest rooms, private baths, and full breakfasts. Kids are accepted (but ask first), and the owners are exceptionally hospitable. Rooms cost $65-85 s or d. The web address is www.cruising-america.com/parsonspillow. Moderate.

Another friendly place is **Windchimes Cottage B&B,** 1501 Beck Ave., tel. (307) 527-5310 or (800) 241-5310, with three guest rooms in the large main house (built in the 1920s as a farmhouse), plus a cottage for families. All rooms have private baths. This is a nice place to stay, with filling country-style breakfasts and attractive rooms containing period decor. Rates are $80 s or d. Groups of five can stay in the cottage for $140. Kids are welcome. Moderate.

Also recommended is **House of Burgess B&B,** 1508 Alger Ave., tel. (307) 527-7208, www.cruising-america.com/burgess. On a quiet street just a few blocks from the heart of town, this 1928 brick and frame home features a relaxing and shady backyard, a large living room, and three guest rooms with private baths. Nicest is the treehouse suite ($80 s or $85 d), situated on an upstairs porch; the other rooms are $70 s or $75 d. A light and healthy breakfast is served each morning, and kids are accepted (but call first). A two-night minimum stay is required. Moderate.

For lodging in a classic Cody home, stay at **Mayor's Inn,** 1413 Rumsey Ave., built in 1909 by the town's first mayor and restored to its original opulence. The three guest rooms include private baths with jetted tubs, down comforters, terry cloth robes, and heated floors. A full breakfast is served each morning, and children are welcome. Rates are $105-155 d, or $205 d for the suite with a jetted tub. For details, contact Cody Guest Houses, tel. (307) 587-6000 or (800) 587-6560, www.wtp.net/cghouses. Expensive-Luxury.

Casual Cove B&B, 1431 Salisbury, tel. (307) 587-3622, is a renovated 1908 home with three guest rooms, all with private baths. Room rates are $56-66 s or d, including a full breakfast. No kids under 10. Inexpensive-Moderate.

Lockhart B&B Inn, 109 Yellowstone, tel. (307) 587-6074 or (800) 377-7255, has seven guest rooms with private baths. A full breakfast is served. Rates are $89-98 d including a full breakfast, and kids are welcome. The home once belonged to the writer Caroline Lockhart; see the special topic about her life later in this chapter. It is furnished with antiques, and the baths contain clawfoot tubs and ceiling fans. Family rooms are also available. The B&B went through a series of managers in recent years and the quality suffered greatly. The owner promises improvements, but take a look for yourself before staying here. It's open April to mid-November. Expensive.

Campgrounds and RV Parks

The closest public campground ($9 for nonresidents, or $4 for Wyoming residents) is 11 miles west in Buffalo Bill State Park. Find many more campgrounds (most cost $9) in Shoshone National Forest, but the nearest is 28 miles west of town in Wapiti Valley.

You'll find eight private RV park/campgrounds in Cody. Rates range widely: $14-27 for RVs, or $10-19 for tents. The two best ones are **Ponderosa Campground,** 1815 8th St., tel. (307) 587-9203, open mid-April to mid-October; and **7 K's RV Park,** 232 W. Yellowstone Ave., tel. (307) 587-5890 or (800) 223-9204, open April-October. Both of these have shade trees. **Cody KOA,** two miles east on US Hwy. 14/16/20, tel. (307) 587-2369 or (800) 562-8507, opened in 1964 as the first franchised KOA. Rates are $21 for tents and $29 for RVs. Open May-Sept., with an outdoor pool, free pancake breakfasts, and "kamping kabins" ($39 d). **Camp Cody,** 415 W. Yellowstone Ave., tel. (307) 587-9730 or (888) 231-2267, has RV hookups but no tent spaces. It's open year-round and includes an outdoor pool.

Other park-it spots include **Gateway Campground,** 203 W. Yellowstone Ave., tel. (307) 587-2561; **Parkway RV Campground** 132 W. Yellowstone Ave., tel. (307) 527-5927 or (800) 484-2365, ext. 3881; and **Absaroka Bay RV Park,** US Hwy. 14/16/20 South, tel. (307) 527-7440 or (800) 557-7440. Absaroka's notable for a complete lack of shade; it's located on a windy hill to add to the fun. You can also park RVs at several of the Wapiti Valley lodges (described above), including **Elk Valley Inn, Wise Choice Inn,** and **Yellowstone Valley Inn.** Noncampers can take showers (for a fee) at Gateway Campground, 7 K's RV Park, or Ponderosa Campground.

FOOD

Because Cody is a tourist town, it's no surprise to find many fine places to eat, covering the spectrum from buffalo burgers to Chinese won tons. Of course, Cody also has all the faves—Arby's, Taco John's, Subway, McDonald's, Taco Bell, and more.

Breakfast and Lunch

Hang out with the farmers over breakfast or lunch at **Our Place,** 148 W. Yellowstone, tel. (307) 527-4420. **Cody Coffee Company & Eatery,** 1702 Sheridan Ave., tel. (307) 527-7879, has espresso, pastries, soups, and Italian subs. **Granny's,** 1550 Sheridan Ave., tel. (307) 587-4829, isn't particularly noteworthy, but it stays open 24 hours a day and serves breakfast anytime.

The ever-popular **Maxwell's Fine Food & Spirits,** 937 Sheridan Ave., tel. (307) 527-7749, dishes up homemade lunches that include sandwiches, pasta, and salads. It's a bright and friendly setting, with a patio for sunny days, and a small bakery/coffeeshop. The dinner menu (entrées $10-18) features pasta, seafood, chicken, beef, and vegetarian dishes. Closed Sunday.

Peter's Bakery, 1191 Sheridan Ave., tel. (307) 527-5040, bakes breads, cookies, bagels, and turnovers. It's a great place for sub sandwiches and soups. You won't want to go back to Subway after this; the bread they use is made from scratch, not pulled from the freezer.

Patsy Ann's Pastry & Ladle, 1243 Beck Ave., tel. (307) 527-6297, creates fine sandwiches, homemade soups, and pastries (including great sticky buns).

Sunset House Restaurant, 1651 8th St., tel. (307) 587-2257, is a casual family spot for lunch, and it also features breakfast and dinner buffets.

Silver Dollar Bar & Grill, 1313 Sheridan Ave., tel. (307) 587-3554, makes the best hamburgers and other cowboy grub in town, served in a Western atmosphere. Guaranteed to fill you up.

Dinner

Proud Cut Saloon, 1227 Sheridan Ave., tel. (307) 587-7343, is a fine old-time Wyoming bar and restaurant offering unusual sandwiches at lunchtime and outstanding steak and prime rib for dinner. It's the real thing, with rustic Old West decor. **Irma Hotel,** 1192 Sheridan Ave., tel. (307) 587-4221, is a long-time favorite of locals for lunch and dinner, but the food is nothing special.

In existence since 1922, **Cassie's Supper Club,** 214 Yellowstone Ave., tel. (307) 527-5500, is famous locally for its steaks, prime rib, and shrimp. The Wednesday lunchtime Mexican specials bring out the crowds.

Stefan's Restaurant, 1367 Sheridan Ave., tel. (307) 587-8511, is an enjoyable place with a diverse menu available three meals a day. Dinner entrées ($10-23) are unconventional takes on such favorites as steaks, baby back ribs, Kung Pao chicken, and shrimp scampi. The atmosphere is a bit upscale, but not stuffy. Be sure to save room for the luscious desserts.

International Eats

You'll find outstanding Northern Italian cuisine at **Franca's Italian Dining,** 1374 Rumsey Ave., tel. (307) 587-5354 or (888) 806-5354. The menu changes throughout the week, with a different fixed-price dinner each evening ($17-26). Completely authentic, right down to the Italian chef. Reservations are essential for this quaint little restaurant; call several days ahead to be assured of a table. Franca's doesn't take credit cards.

In the heart of town, **La Comida,** 1385 Sheridan Ave., tel. (307) 587-9556, serves very good Mexican food for reasonable prices. Take in the local scene from the outside patio. On the west side of town, **Zapata's,** 325 W. Yellowstone Ave., tel. (307) 527-7181, offers food with a New Mexican flavor and tasty margaritas. For Chinese food, visit **Hong Kong Restaurant,** 1201 17th St., tel. (307) 587-6420.

Black Sheep Restaurant, on the east end of town at 1901 Mountain View Rd., tel. (307) 527-5895, serves Greek specialties, along with lamb chops, pork loin, steak, seafood, pasta, and hickory-smoked ribs. Dinner entrées cost $10-18.

Pizza Hut, 736 Yellowstone Ave., tel. (307) 527-7819, has predictable pizzas and all-you-can-eat lunch buffets.

Grocers and Specialty Foods

Cody's grocers include a **Smith's** at 1526 Rumsey, tel. (307) 587-6289, and a huge **Albertson's,** 1825 17th St., tel. (307) 527-7007. For natural foods and Wyoming-made gifts, head to **Whole Foods Trading Co.,** 1243 Rumsey, tel. (307) 587-3213. **Wyoming Buffalo Company,** 1276 Sheridan Ave., tel. (307) 587-8708 or (800) 453-0636, specializes in buffalo jerky, salami, sausage, and fresh meat, with a variety of gift packages. Stop in for a free sample.

EVENTS AND ENTERTAINMENT

Summer is a busy time in Cody, with special events nearly every weekend. Cody calls itself "Rodeo Capital of the World," and it packs the calendar with nightly summertime rodeos, plus the famous Cody Stampede. The rodeo grounds are a mile west of town on US Hwy. 14/16/20.

Cody Nite Rodeo

After more than 60 years of operation, the Cody Nite Rodeo is still one of the best in a state filled with rodeos. Shows begin at 8:30 p.m. nightly June-Aug. and always attract a big crowd. The best performances take place Friday and Saturday nights, when you'll see events sanctioned by the Professional Rodeo Cowboys Association (PRCA). A crowd favorite is the calf scramble starring kids from the stands. Tickets cost $10-12 for adults and $4-6 for children. Call (307) 587-5155 or (800) 207-0744 for details, or find the rodeo on the web at www.westwyoming.com/cody-stampede.

Cody Stampede

Independence Day sets the stage for Cody's main event, the Cody Stampede, held July 1-4. Estab-

the Cody Stampede parade

lished in 1922, it attracts thousands of visitors from all over the nation. Parade fans are treated to one each morning (including a kiddie parade), with dozens of marching bands, mountain men, vintage autos, floats, cowboys, and tons of free candy. Special PRCA rodeo performances, a street dance, art shows, running events, fireworks, and a carnival complete the schedule. For more info, call (307) 587-5155 or (800) 207-0744, or visit www.westwyoming.com/cody-stampede.

More Events

At 6 p.m. each evening of the summer, the **Cody Gunslingers** perform downtown at the Irma Hotel. The mock gunfights are entertainment, Western-style. Worth a look if you haven't seen it before, but they do a more professional job at the Jackson shoot-out.

Cowboy Songs and Range Ballads is a unique Western musical festival held the second weekend of April at the Buffalo Bill Historical Center. You'll hear true cowboy music (not country-and-western), along with poetry and stories from cowboys, ranchers, musicians, and folklorists.

Held in the Robbie Powwow Garden in front of the Buffalo Bill Historical Center in late June, the **Plains Indian Powwow** attracts several hundred participants from all over the Rockies and Canada vying for $10,000 in prize money. It includes daylong singing and dancing in tribal regalia and various dance competitions. Visitors can purchase Indian arts and crafts and taste Indian tacos and fry bread.

The **Old West Show & Auction** in mid-June offers the chance for collectors to purchase quality old cowboy gear. It's considered the finest such event in the nation and attracts a wealthy crowd.

Frontier Festival, held in mid-July at the Buffalo Bill Historical Center, is a celebration of the many turn-of-the-20th-century skills that were needed to survive on the frontier. Included are demonstrations of horsepacking, hide tanning, gunsmithing, rawhide braiding, weaving, and other homegrown talents. Various contests, musical performances, and booths make this an enjoyable and popular event.

The **Yellowstone Jazz Festival** in mid-July brings both regional and national jazz groups.

The **Buffalo Bill Art Show & Sale** in mid-September is the biggest art event of the year. It features exhibitions, a symposium, receptions, and an auction.

Music and Entertainment

The downtown **City Park band shell** is the place to be on Friday evenings during the summer; free musical performances start at 6 p.m. **Cassie's,** 214 Yellowstone Ave., tel. (307) 527-5500, has Wednesday night country swing dance lessons, along with country-and-western and mellow rock tunes nightly throughout the summer. Hang around the bar long enough and you can join in that old Cassie's favorite, barroom brawling. **Angie's,** at the Silver Dollar Bar, 1313 Sheridan Ave., tel. (307) 587-3554, sometimes has rock bands. The big dance floor fills up on weekends. **Gibb's Sports Pub,** 1901 Mountain View Rd. (inside the Black Sheep Restaurant), tel. (307) 527-5895, has a big-screen TV for ESPN fanatics, plus a pool table and darts.

Park Drive In, on the east end of Big Horn Dr., tel. (307) 587-2712, is one of the few drive-in theaters left in Wyoming. Open Thurs.-Sun. only. For the indoor version, head to **Cody Theatre,** 1171 Sheridan Ave., tel. (307) 587-2712, or the fourplex version: **Big Horn Cinemas,** 2525 Big Horn Ave., tel. (307) 587-8009.

RECREATION

River Rafting

One of the most popular summertime activities in Cody is floating the class I and II Shoshone River. Beware, however, that even with these mild conditions, you should plan on getting soaked in the rapids. Expect to pay around $20 for adults ($18 for kids) for a six-mile run that lasts 90 minutes, or $26 for adults ($24 for kids) for a 13-mile (three-hour) float. For details, contact **Wyoming River Trips,** 233 Yellowstone Hwy., tel. (307) 587-6661 or (800) 586-6661; **River Runners,** 1491 Sheridan Ave., tel. (307) 527-7238 or (800) 535-7238; or **Red Canyon River Trips,** 1374 Sheridan Ave., tel. (307) 587-6988 or (800) 293-0148.

Founded in 1978, Wyoming River Trips is the most experienced company in Cody. Red Canyon River Trips is newer, but the guides are very experienced and use smaller rafts for a more personalized trip. Both Wyoming River and Red Canyon offer inflatable kayak trips for those who want to run the rapids on their own power. In addition, Red Canyon leads scenic float trips down the Clarks Fork; see Sunlight Basin above for details.

If you want to try rafting or kayaking on your own, you'll find several miles of very technical class IV water with some class V drops below the dam and above DeMaris Springs. Above the dam are stretches of class I and II water with good access from the main highway. Ask locally for flow conditions before heading out since snowmelt and dam releases can dramatically affect water levels. The rafting companies offer half-day whitewater trips down the North Fork above the reservoir for $50 per person including lunch. These trips only run late May through July, when the water level is high.

Most rafters put in three miles west of Cody off Demaris Street. Just upstream from the put-in point is DeMaris Springs, a part of **"Colter's Hell"** that is on private property and not open to the public. The area was once far more active, with hot springs bubbling out of the river and sulfurous smoke rising all around. People actually died from the poisonous gas. Today the geothermal activity has lessened, but the air still smells of sulfur and small hot springs color the cliff faces. Miners worked over nearby hillsides in search of sulfur; the diggings are still apparent. It's also pretty obvious why they first called this the Stinkingwater River.

Horse and Wagon Rides

Horseback rides are available from **Cedar Mountain Trail Rides,** tel. (307) 527-4966, located a mile west of the rodeo grounds; **Gateway Motel and Campground,** 203 Yellowstone, tel. (307) 587-6507; and **Buffalo Bill's Trail Rides,** at the Cody KOA a mile east of the airport, tel. (307) 587-2369. Many of the lodges in Wapiti Valley (see Shoshone National Forest, above) also offer horseback rides as well as longer backcountry pack trips. Get a complete listing of Cody area outfitters and guides from the chamber of commerce, and a list of permitted outfitters from local Forest Service offices.

At the Holiday Inn, **Heart 3 Carriage Service,** tel. (307) 899-1484, has downtown carriage rides all summer long; $35 per carriage.

Each August, horse enthusiasts join in a week-long trip called **High Country Trail Ride.** Most folks bring their own horse, but rentals are also available. The route takes participants through Sunlight Basin, with overnight camping, a support staff, veterinarians, catered meals, and entertainment beneath the circus tent. Call (307) 527-7468 for details.

More Recreation

A spacious new recreation center opens on the south side of Cody in 2000, with a large indoor pool and other facilities; call (307) 587-2550 for details. Other swimming options include an **outdoor pool** across from the Buffalo Bill Historical Center at 1240 Beck Ave., tel. (307) 527-7511, and the **Stock Natatorium** at 9th St. and Beck Ave., tel. (307) 587-2550.

Cody Rock Gym, 1310 Shoshone, tel. (307) 587-5222, has an indoor climbing wall. **Foote's Mountaineering,** 1280 Sheridan Ave., tel. (307) 527-9937, has a 32-foot-high climbing wall outside in the back and also sells a variety of climbing gear, maps, and other supplies.

Rent mountain bikes from **Olde Faithful Bicycle,** 1231 16th St., tel. (307) 527-5110 or (800) 775-6023. The shop also offers mountain-bike tours of the area.

The 18-hole **Olive-Glenn Golf and Country Club,** 802 Meadow Lane, tel. (307) 587-5688, is a PGA championship course with a complete golf shop and upscale restaurant. Families enjoy playing **miniature golf** at the downtown city park, tel. (307) 587-3685. It's open summers only.

Outdoor Gear

For quality backcountry equipment—especially if you travel by horse—be sure to drop by **Wyoming Outdoor Industries,** 1231 13th St., tel. (307) 527-6449 or (800) 725-6853. You won't find Goretex jogbras here, just tough equipment for backcountry use (especially horsepacking), including folding woodstoves, pack saddles, bear-resistant panniers, and wall tents. They also have a mail-order catalog.

Sunlight Sports, 1251 Sheridan Ave., tel. (307) 587-9517, is the largest outdoors shop in town, with tents, climbing equipment, clothes, topographic maps, and more. It also rents cross-country and downhill skis, snowboards, and snowshoes during the winter, and it's the place to go for details on ice climbing in the South Fork area.

Get topographic maps from **Cody Newsstand,** 1121 13th St., tel. (307) 587-2843.

North Fork Anglers, 1438 Sheridan Ave., tel. (307) 527-7274, has anything you might need for fly-fishing, including a full-service retail shop, professional fishing guides, and fly-tying clinics.

INFORMATION AND SERVICES

Get local info from the **Cody Country Chamber of Commerce,** 836 Sheridan Ave., tel. (307) 587-2297 or (800) 393-2639, www.codychamber.org. Hours are Mon.-Sat. 8 a.m.-7 p.m. and Sunday 10 a.m.-3 p.m. Memorial Day to Labor Day, and Mon.-Fri. 8 a.m.-5 p.m. the rest of the year. This log building housed the original Buffalo Bill Museum from 1927 to 1969 and was built as a replica of Cody's TE Ranch. It's on the National Register of Historic Places.

The BLM's **Cody Resources Office** is at 1002 Blackburn Ave., tel. (307) 587-2216. The Forest Service has two local offices: the **Shoshone National Forest Supervisor's Office,** 808 Meadowlark Ave., tel. (307) 527-6241, and the smaller **Wapiti Ranger District Office,** 203 W. Yellowstone, tel. (307) 527-6921. The Shoshone National Forest website is www.fs.fed.us/r2/shoshone.

Cody's **West Park Hospital,** 707 Sheridan Ave., tel. (307) 527-7501 or (800) 654-9447, is the largest in Bighorn Basin and one of the best in the state. The hospital's **Urgent Care Clinic,** 702 Yellowstone Ave., tel. (307) 587-7207, is open daily and doesn't require an appointment.

Get fast cash at **ATMs** scattered throughout Cody, including one inside the Buffalo Bill Historical Center and another in the Wal-Mart store.

Wash clothes at **Skippy's Laundromat,** 728 Yellowstone Ave., tel. (307) 527-6001; **Eastgate Laundry,** 1813 17th St., tel. (307) 587-5355; and **Quick Coin-Op Laundromat,** 930 12th St., tel. (307) 587-6519.

OTHER PRACTICALITIES

Shopping

As you might expect from a tourist town, Cody has more than its share of shops dealing in clunky jewelry, crass T-shirts, and fake Indian trinkets. Fortunately, it's also home to a number of places with a bit more class.

Corral West Ranchwear, 1202 Sheridan Ave., tel. (307) 587-2122, has a large collection of big game heads and a couple of stuffed nine-foot-tall bears. Oh, yes, they also sell inexpensive Western wear. Get fancy Western duds at **Custom Cowboy Shop,** 1286 Sheridan Ave., tel. (307) 527-7300.

Cody Rodeo Company, 1291 Sheridan Ave., tel. (307) 587-5913, sells cowboy gear and rodeo memorabilia in a fun atmosphere. Decorations include a turn-of-the-20th-century back bar from Hardin, Montana, and a **stuffed bull** that stood in front of the Irma Hotel for many years. Get your picture taken atop the bull for $7. Another fun place is **Crafty Quilter,** 1262 Sheridan Ave., tel. (307) 527-6305, which sells handmade quilts.

Traditions West Antique Mall, 1131 Sheridan Ave., tel. (307) 587-7434, is a good place to look for Western antiques. A block away, **Old West Antiques,** 1215 Sheridan Ave., tel. (307) 587-9014, even serves espresso in the back, where you can sit on old barber chairs.

Books

The **Park County Library,** 1057 Sheridan Ave., tel. (307) 587-6204, has regional titles and computers providing Internet access. New books are available from **Cody Newsstand,** 1121 13th St., tel. (307) 587-2843, and **The Thistle,** 1243 Rumsey, tel. (307) 587-6635. Cody Newsstand also has one of the best magazine selections in Bighorn Basin. **Wyoming Well Book Exchange and Oilfield Supply,** 1902 E. Sheridan Ave., tel. (307) 587-4249, has the oddest combination in town: bodice-buster novels and oil-drilling equipment!

Transportation

Yellowstone Regional Airport is just east of town on US Hwy. 14/16/20. **Sky West/Delta,** tel. (307) 587-9740 or (800) 221-1212, has daily flights to Salt Lake City, while **United Express/Great Lakes Aviation,** tel. (307) 527-6443 or (800) 241-6522, connects to Denver. **Spirit Mountain Aviation,** tel. (307) 587-6732, offers scenic flights and charter service. **Phidippides Shuttle Service,** tel. (307) 527-6789, provides shuttle vans to the airport in Billings, Montana.

Rent cars at the airport from **Avis,** tel. (307) 587-5792 or (800) 331-1212; **Budget,** tel. (307) 587-6066 or (800) 527-0700; **Hertz,** tel. (307) 587-2914 or (800) 654-3131; or **Thrifty,** tel. (307) 587-8855 or (888) 794-1025.

Buses from **Powder River/Coach USA,** tel. (800) 442-3682, stop at Daylight Donuts, 1452 Sheridan Ave., providing service to Billings, Montana, along with towns in to northern and eastern Wyoming.

Tours

During the summer, daily lower-loop tours of Yellowstone National Park—$60 for adults, $30 for kids—are available through **Powder River/Coach USA,** tel. (307) 527-3677. You can stay overnight in Yellowstone and return on a later van for no extra charge (on a space-available basis), transfer to Gray Line buses (tel. 307-733-4325 or 800-443-6133) to reach Jackson or West Yellowstone, or catch the vans of 4x4 Stage (tel. 406-388-6404 or 800-517-8243) for Gardiner, West Yellowstone, Cooke City, or Bozeman.

For a more personalized trip, call **Grub Steak Expeditions,** tel. (307) 527-6316 or (800) 527-6316. It leads 12-hour auto tours of the park, along with visits to Sunlight Basin, Wapiti Valley, and the South Fork. Multiday trips are also available. One-day tours cost $300 for two people, plus $75 per person for additional people. These are very popular with families looking for a unique perspective on the park, and some are led by the co-owner, a retired Yellowstone park ranger. Both **Wyoming Touring Adventures,** tel. (307) 587-5136, and **Yellowstone Expedition Services,** tel. 9307) 587-5452 or (888) 808-7990, also offer customized auto tours into Yellowstone with a maximum of six people per group.

CODY VICINITY

See earlier in this chapter for Wapiti Valley, Buffalo Bill Reservoir, Sunlight Basin, and the wonderful mountain country west of Cody. For details on sights to the north, see *Montana Handbook,* by W.C. McRae and Judy Jewell (Moon Travel Handbooks, www.moon.com).

Heart Mountain

Halfway between Cody and Powell is Heart Mountain, so named because its twin summits faintly resemble the traditional valentine. The mountain is visible for many miles in all directions. Geologists scratch their heads over this seemingly upside-down mountain. The Heart Mountain detachment fault stretches for over a hundred miles, cutting southwest from near Cooke City, Montana. To the east are enormous blocks of land that have slid onto the top of more recent deposits, reversing the normal situation in which older rocks lie beneath more recent ones. Scientists know that these limestone and dolomite blocks moved around 45 to 50 million years ago, but none have been able to adequately explain how entire mountains, including Heart, could have slid for dozens of miles.

HEART MOUNTAIN RELOCATION CENTER

For Americans of Japanese ancestry, Heart Mountain might as well have been called Broken Heart Mountain. After the Japanese attack on Pearl Harbor in 1941, Japanese-Americans found their patriotism under increasing suspicion, and the following spring President Roosevelt signed an executive order establishing the War Relocation Authority to move them away from the coasts. The authority built 10 remote "relocation centers" to imprison anyone of Japanese ancestry; one such center went up just east of Heart Mountain and housed 10,767 Japanese-Americans (two-thirds of them born in America). The camp became Wyoming's third-largest settlement. It took just 62 days to complete the 468 barracks, 40 laundry-toilet buildings, Buddhist and Christian churches, high school, fire station, recreation hall, power station, mess hall, hospital, sewage plant, administrative offices, and numerous other structures. (No environmental impact reports on this baby!) Barbed wire surrounded the perimeter, and military police manned nine guard towers with high-beam searchlights and machine guns.

Camp Life

Most of the Japanese-Americans took the forced relocation with remarkable aplomb, realizing the futility of any escape attempt. It almost seemed the patriotic thing to do; "shikata-ga-nai" ("I guess it cannot be helped") became the accepted phrase. Although life in the camp maintained a sense of normalcy—some kids came to enjoy their peaceful high-school years and the picnics in Yellowstone—the camp was far from idyllic. Three or four people were jammed into each room, furniture was minimal, people had to share communal bathhouses, and the winter winds blew through the uninsulated tar paper buildings. Local folks resented the Japanese-Americans but appreciated the cheap farm labor that they provided while Wyoming's sons were off fighting the Germans and Japanese.

After the War

With the war's end in 1945, the camp was closed and the internees were given $25 and a one-way bus ticket home (or rather, to what remained; many found their homes ransacked or sold to others). Over the next four years the 740 acres of land was opened to homesteading, and the barracks were sold at two for $1. Most of the buildings ended up as temporary homes for the new settlers. None of the Japanese-American internees remained in the area, and most of the survivors have little desire to even visit what seemed such a desolate, godforsaken place. They would rather try to forget. See Gretel Ehrlich's *Heart Mountain* for a fictional treatment of life inside the camp.

The Camp Today

Today the only reminders of the Heart Mountain Relocation Center are three buildings, the largest

AMERICAN HERITAGE CENTER, LARAMIE, WY

Heart Mountain Japanese relocation camp, circa 1940s

of which is the old hospital heating plant with its tall brick chimney. Several plaques also mark the camp's site, one noting the more than 600 men who left Heart Mountain facility to join the U.S. Army in Europe. Twenty-one internees and a camp teacher died while fighting in Europe.

The site is 11 miles east of Cody on US Hwy. 14A. Barley fields now surround the former internment camp, while Heart Mountain stands guard over the western flank. Efforts are underway to preserve the remaining buildings and to eventually open a visitor center and museum. The nonprofit **Heart Mountain Wyoming Association** works to preserve the memory of this painful era; call (307) 754-2272 for more information.

EAST TO POWELL

The historic **Eagles Nest Stage Station** stands east of the relocation camp as you head toward Powell. The log cabins and barns were built a century ago by the Lanchbury family, which homesteaded here. Their ranch served as a stage station midway between Meeteetse (then the largest town in Bighorn Basin) and Red Lodge, Montana. Today, a fifth generation of the Lanchburys lives in the restored buildings of historic Eagles Nest. If you're looking for trivia, stop in the tiny settlement of **Ralston** to see the railroad bridge over a highway bridge, atop a creek. This odd collection made it into *Ripley's Believe It or Not!*

MEETEETSE

Along the western edge of Bighorn Basin is a charming little ranching center called Meeteetse (pop. 400). The name is a Shoshone Indian word meaning "Meeting Place of the Chiefs." The Absaroka Mountains rise gently to the south and west, and the Greybull River flows right through town, cottonwood trees on either side. To the north, the highway crosses a rolling land of sage and greasewood, while to the south are rugged badlands. Meeteetse has wooden sidewalks and hitching rails, occasional cattle drives right down Main Street, and a pair of museums.

History

One of the oldest towns in Bighorn Basin, Meeteetse was first settled in the late 1870s by homesteaders and wealthy European cattle barons. By 1890 it was the largest community in the basin. Several original buildings are still standing, including the impressively large **Meeteetse Mercantile,** built in 1899. Inside are locally made collectibles and crafts, a deli and soda fountain (espresso even), and groceries. A few doors away is the **Cowboy Bar,** with more than a century of rough-and-tumble history. The saloon opened in 1893, and it still has the original rosewood and cherry wood back bar. Historical artifacts and local brands fill the walls. More than a few guns have gone off here over the years; at last count the bar contained 56 bullet holes and a shotgun blast! Many well-known people have spent time in this bar, including Buffalo Bill Cody, Tom Horn, Butch Cassidy, and Amelia Earhart.

The last wild black-footed ferrets (see the special topic Black-footed Ferrets in the Southeast Wyoming chapter) were discovered just a dozen miles to the west at the famed Pitchfork Ranch. They were captured in 1987 after an outbreak of canine distemper threatened to kill all the remaining wild ferrets. Bronze ferret statues guard Riverside Park in town, but it may be quite a while (if ever) before living ferrets return.

Museums

Town Hall Museum, tel. (307) 868-2423, built in 1900, is filled with cowboy paraphernalia of all sorts and has a nice collection of old china dolls and historic photographs. It's open Mon.-Sat. 10 a.m.-4 p.m. and Sunday 1-4 p.m. from Memorial Day-September, and by appointment at other times. The museum is the place to go for local information. Find more historical items at **Meeteetse Bank Museum and Archives,** housed in the old Hogg, Cheeseman, and MacDonald's Bank (built in 1901). It's open Tues.-Sat. 9 a.m.-5 p.m. Memorial Day-Sept., with reduced hours the rest of the year. A few doors away is a collection of classic cowboy photographs taken in the 1930s by Charles Beldon. Unfortunately, you'll have to view them through the windows since the small museum that was here has closed.

Accommodations

Oasis Motel, 1702 State St., tel. (307) 868-2551 or (888) 868-5270, has motel rooms for $26 s or $36 d; cabins with kitchenettes for $36 s, $46 d; campsites for $11; and RV spots for $16. **Vision Quest Motel,** 2207 State St., tel. (307) 868-2512, charges $36 s or $41-46 d, and all rooms contain kitchenettes. RV parking costs $12. Vision Quest is closed in the winter. Both Inexpensive.

Broken Spoke B&B, 1947 State St., tel. (307) 868-2362, isn't a traditional B&B, but it does have two simple rooms over the cafe of the same name for just $25 s or $35 d. Guests are served a full breakfast downstairs. Budget.

Grub and Booze

Elkhorn Bar & Grill has the best local burgers and is a meeting spot for local folks, especially on weekend evenings, when country bands sometimes play. **Outlaw Parlor Cafe** at the Cowboy Bar also has good pizzas and steaks, along with old photos from early-day Meeteetse. Be sure to ask the bartender at the Cowboy for the "true" origins of the word Meeteetse. More food can be found at **Lucille's Cafe,** tel. (307) 868-9909.

Other Practicalities

Get local information from the town museums. An indoor **swimming pool** is at the high school.

Visit Meeteetse over **Labor Day weekend** for a small-town parade, street games, a country rodeo, barbecue, arts and crafts, live music, and dancing. Great fun.

MEETEETSE AREA

Wood River Valley

Southwest of Meeteetse, beautiful Wood River Valley is an enjoyable drive or bike ride at any time of the year. It's a great place to watch for moose and elk in the bottomlands, along with a variety of smaller animals. Two free Forest Service **campgrounds** (open June-Nov.) are available near the end of the road. From here you can hike into the **Washakie Wilderness** along any of several different trails; see Shoshone National Forest earlier in this chapter for details.

Wood River Valley Ski Touring Park (free) is 22 miles southwest of town on Wood River Road. The Meeteetse Recreation District runs the park and provides ski rentals in town. The cross-country ski area includes 25 km of groomed trails, wonderful mountain scenery, a warming hut, and a custom-made tent with a woodstove for overnight stays ($15). For more info, call (307) 868-2603, or point your browser to www.meetrecdist.com. **Wood River Lodge,** tel. (307) 868-9211 or (800) 228-9211, has year-round accommodations just two miles away and also runs pack trips into the backcountry.

Kirwin

The abandoned mining town of Kirwin is accessible from the Brown Creek Campground at the end of Wood River Road. You'll need a 4WD (or at least a high-clearance vehicle) to continue the 11 miles past the campground to Kirwin, at an elevation of 9,200 feet. Mountain-bikers in good shape will also enjoy this challenging road. The road is typically accessible late June to early October.

Gold was discovered in the Kirwin area in 1885, and within a few years more than 200 miners were living in this remote, high-elevation site. A 1907 avalanche killed three people and proved the last straw for miners who had been struggling for years with little of no profit. Most of them abandoned their cabins and claims with what they could carry on their backs, never to return. Now within Shoshone National Forest, the old mining town is a fascinating place to explore, with the decaying remains of a hotel and cabins, along with rusting farm and mining machinery. On the drive into Kirwin you pass what remains of Double D Dude Ranch, established in 1931. Famed aviatrix **Amelia Earhart** was having a summer cabin built near here shortly before her 1934 disappearance during an around-the-world flight. The cabin was never finished and only a few rotting logs remain. A monument to Amelia Earhart stands in Meeteetse, and the flight jacket she wore when she became the first woman to cross the Atlantic alone is in the Buffalo Bill Historical Center.

More Nearby Sights

Another historic place—**Palatte Ranch**—is at the end of Pitchfork Rd., a gravel road paralleling the Greybull River. The road ends 30 miles west of Meeteetse at Jack Creek Campground (free). A seven-mile hike from the campground takes you to **Anderson Lodge,** an archetypal log home that was restored by the Forest Service. Palatte Ranch was once owned by A.A. Anderson, first superintendent of the Yellowstone Park Timberland Reserve (now Shoshone National Forest). Check with the Forest Service office in Cody for more information on this area.

Northwest of Meeteetse is an important archaeological site, the **Great Arrow,** a 58-foot-long arrow made from rocks and placed atop a long hogback ridge. Of unknown age, the arrow points toward the Medicine Wheel in the Big Horn Mountains 70 miles to the northeast. The Great Arrow is on private land and not accessible to the public. (See Big Horn Mountains in the Powder River Country chapter for more on Medicine Wheel.)

The turnoff to impressive **Legend Rock Petroglyph Site** is 32 miles southeast of Meeteetse along State Hwy. 120. For details, see Thermopolis later in this chapter.

POWELL

One of the most pleasant settlements in Bighorn Basin, Powell (pop. 5,700) is a clean and prosperous farming, oil, and college town halfway between Cody and Lovell. Declared an All-America City in 1994, it sits at the center of a rich farming region where sugar beets, dry beans, and malting barley (grown for Coors and Anheuser-Busch) are raised. Because these crops are harvested at different times of the year, many farmers grow all three. The big elevators of Powell Bean Growers Association and Baker Bean & Feed border the railroad tracks on the south edge of town. A dozen miles to the north is the giant Elk Basin oil field. First discovered in 1915, it had 150 wells pumping more than 4,200 barrels a day within five years. The field has proven a major factor in the growth of the northern Bighorn Basin, though production is declining as the supply is exhausted.

HISTORY

Powell was named for Maj. John Wesley Powell (1834-1902), the famed one-armed explorer of the Colorado River and an early director of the U.S. Geological Survey. His 1889 report on the agricultural potential of Western desert lands had asserted the value of irrigation in "reclaiming" these areas and proposed a system of dams and canals funded by the government. One of the earliest of these was the mammoth Shoshone Project, involving Buffalo Bill Dam and a series of canals to feed water to the fields along the Shoshone River.

Powell is right at the center of all this irrigation, and homesteaders flocked here in the first two decades of this century. The town sprang up at a campsite used by workers on the Shoshone Project. With the arrival of the Chicago, Burlington and Quincy Railroad (now Burlington Northern), Powell became an agricultural shipping point.

Earl Durand

Folks still talk about "Tarzan of the Tetons," a local kid gone bad. Earl Durand was a crack shot and a mountain man of sorts. He had once traveled by horse and foot to Mexico, and bragged that he could survive on practically anything, even raw bobcat meat. Durand hated being cooped up inside buildings, so when he was arrested for poaching in 1939, he escaped the Cody jail. Five people died in the shooting rampage that followed, and the murders attracted intense national attention. The climax came when Durand robbed a Powell bank and suddenly found himself surrounded. A 17-year-old kid shot—but didn't kill—Durand as he came out of the bank with a screen of hostages. Sensing the futility of the situation, Durand went back inside and committed suicide. Powell's Homesteader Museum has lots of old newspaper clippings on this sad story, and the incident inspired *The Legend of Earl Durand,* a minor 1974 movie starring Slim Pickens, Peter Haskell, and Martin Sheen.

SIGHTS

The **Homesteader Museum,** on the corner of 1st and Clark Sts., tel. (307) 754-9481, is open Tues.-Fri. noon-5 p.m. and Saturday 10 a.m.-2 p.m. May-Sept., or by appointment the rest of the year. The museum captures the hardscrabble life of turn-of-the-20th-century homesteaders in the northern Bighorn Basin. You'll find interesting old photographs, a beautiful collection of dryhead agate, some Indian artifacts, a century-old porcelain doll, and a German grandfather

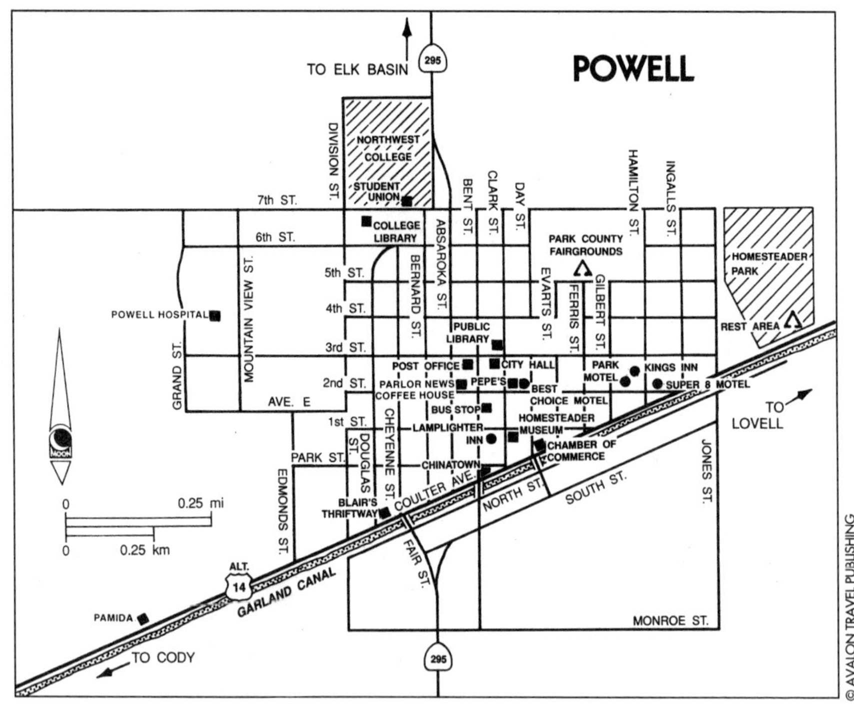

clock, chairs, and bench covered with carved bears. There's lots more junk to check out, but take the time to watch the videotape detailing the history of the nearby Heart Mountain Relocation Center. An adjacent building is filled with horse-drawn machines and old tractors, while outside are a caboose and various pieces of old farm equipment. Museum entrance is free.

The chamber of commerce offers individualized **agricultural tours** of the farms and ranches around Powell, providing a good way to learn about irrigation systems, dairy farms, feed lots, sheep and cattle breeding, irrigation, and crop production. These reasonably priced trips include transportation, a guide, and lunch. Call (307) 754-3483 or (800) 325-4278 for reservations.

Founded in 1946, **Northwest College** is one of the state's top junior colleges, with nearly 2,000 students. The 124-acre campus is quite attractive, with modern brick buildings and fluorescent green lawns (at least in the summer). Two-thirds of the students live on campus, but the school does offer evening classes in the surrounding towns. Northwest is a cultural and social center for Powell and the surrounding area, bringing a variety of theater productions and entertainment, plus art exhibits at the **Northwest Gallery** (open Mon.-Fri. 9 a.m.-4:30 p.m. Sept.-May). For information on Northwest, call (307) 754-6111 or (800) 442-2946, or visit the school on the web at www.nwc.whecn.edu.

PRACTICALITIES

Accommodations

Although it is just 24 miles from Cody, travelers will find distinctly less-expensive accommodations in Powell. **Best Choice Motel,** 337 E. 2nd St., tel. (307) 754-2243 or (800) 308-8447, has rooms for $40-50 s or d. Microwaves and fridges are available. **Lamplighter Inn,** 234 1st St., tel. (307) 754-2226, has standard rooms for $49-59 s or d. Both Inexpensive.

Park Motel, 737 E. 2nd St., tel. (307) 754-2233 or (800) 506-7378, offers comfortable rooms for $49-65 s or d; half of them contain fridges and microwaves. Inexpensive-Moderate.

Super 8 Motel, 845 E. Coulter, tel. (307) 754-7231 or (800) 800-8000, has standard motel rooms for $56 s or d. Inexpensive.

Nicest in town is **Best Western King's Inn,** 777 E. 2nd St., tel. (307) 754-5117 or (800) 441-7778, where rooms cost $64-72 s or d, including use of an outdoor pool. Moderate.

Camping

Park County Fairgrounds, tel. (307) 754-5421, has RV sites ($12) and shower facilities. Open April-September. RVers park for free (no hookups) at the highway rest area in the 57-acre **Homesteader Park** on the east end of town. You can also pitch a tent on the grass here, but the sprinklers come on at night. Open all year.

Food

Start your day with an espresso from **Parlor News Coffeehouse,** 135 E. 2nd St., tel. (307) 754-0717. It's a cozy spot to relax; stop by for ice cream on a warm summer afternoon. Meet the locals for breakfast at **Skyline Family Dining,** 141 E. Coulter, tel. (307) 754-2772, where you'll also find a mean chicken-fried steak for dinner.

Two places have tasty south-of-the-border fare in Powell. **Pepe's Mexican Restaurant,** 333 E. 2nd, tel. (307) 754-4665, and **El Tapatio,** 112 N. Bent, tel. (307) 754-8085.

Powell Drug, 140 N. Bent, tel. (307) 754-2031, has an old-fashioned soda fountain where the root beer floats and malts still attract kids. **Hansel & Gretel's,** 113 S. Bent, tel. (307) 754-2191, serves spaghetti, soups, sandwiches, and delicious homemade pies.

The **Lamplighter Inn,** at the corner of 1st and Clark, tel. (307) 754-2226, is the fanciest place in town, with sandwiches, burgers, and daily specials for lunch, along with steaks, chicken, and seafood for dinner.

Get pizzas from **Pizza on the Run,** 215 E. 1st, tel. (307) 754-5720, or **Pizza Hut,** 855 E. Coulter Ave., tel. (307) 754-9588. **Chinatown Restaurant,** 151 E. Coulter, tel. (307) 754-7924, has Chinese food to eat in or take out, and a buffet lunch.

For sweets, head to **Powell Bakery,** 242 N. Bent St., tel. (307) 754-2971, or **Linda's Sandwich and Ice Cream Shoppe,** 121 N. Bent St., tel. (307) 754-9553.

Pick up groceries at **Blair's Market,** 311 W. Coulter Ave., tel. (307) 754-3122, or **Food Basket IGA,** 421 E. 1st, tel. (307) 754-3602. Blair's contains a good deli and bakery.

Entertainment

Time Out Lounge has live country-and-western music some nights and sports on the TVs the rest of the time. Good bar food, too, including Rocky Mountain oysters. **La Vina's,** 238 S. Douglas, tel. (307) 754-4713, occasionally has live music.

For movies, drop by **Vali Cinema,** 204 N. Bent St., tel. (307) 754-4211, or, for the outdoor version (a rare treat these days), **Vali Drive-In Theatre,** 1070 Rd. 9, tel. (307) 754-5133.

Events

The popular **Foxtrotter Horse Show and Sale** takes place on Father's Day weekend in June. The last full week of July brings the **Park County Fair,** with parades, horseshoe pitching contests, 4-H shows, a demolition derby, tractor pulls, a horse pull, dancing, headline acts, and a carnival. All summer long, **stock car races** take place every Saturday at the fairgrounds and always attract a big crowd; call (307) 754-5421. The second weekend of September brings the grandiosely named **All America Quilt Show** to downtown Powell. **Sheepman's Holiday** in mid-October features sheep events of all sorts, including sheepdog trials. If you happen to be in the area on the first weekend of December, stop by for **Country Christmas,** a three-day festivity with activities and craft exhibits as well as a torchlight parade and a parade with lighted floats.

Recreation

Attractive **Homesteader Park** has a number of modern recreation facilities, including a kids'll-love-it green frog slide at the wading pool. In winter, there is a free ice arena here with skate rentals and a warming hut. The public **swimming pool** is in the high school. The 18-hole **Powell Country Club** is five miles east of Powell, tel. (307) 754-3039. **Classic Lanes,** 162 N. Clark, tel. (307) 754-2422, is the local bowling alley.

Shopping

Mountain Man Moccasin Co., 265 N. Bent, tel. (307) 754-9779 or (800) 734-9779, makes high-quality leather moccasins from deerskin or elk leather. **Powell Office Supply** is at the same address and sells books and topographic maps. More books are sold at the **Northwest College Bookstore,** tel. (307) 754-6308.

Get camping and hiking supplies at **War Surplus,** 130 N. Bent, tel. (307) 754-2694; there always seems to be a surplus of wars, so you might as well buy a couple while you're in town.

Information and Services

The **Powell Valley Chamber of Commerce,** 111 S. Day, tel. (307) 754-3494 or (800) 325-4278, is open Mon.-Fri. 8 a.m.-5 p.m. Relax with a book at the modern **Powell Public Library,** 217 E. 3rd, tel. (307) 754-2261, or the **John Hinkley Memorial Library** on the Northwest College campus, tel. (307) 754-6207. (No, it isn't named for the man who shot President Reagan.) **ATMs** are located in banks and grocery stores around Powell.

Powder River/Coach USA, tel. (307) 754-3914 or (800) 442-3682, stops at Darlin's, 127 N. Bent St., with daily service throughout northern and eastern Wyoming, and connections to other parts of America.

EAST TO LOVELL

A tangle of roads wanders through the country between Lovell and Powell, tying together a cluster of agriculture and oil settlements established by Mormon emigrants. **Cowley** (pop. 500) has a number of impressive old sandstone buildings, plus **Cowtown Cafe** serving homemade pies. Ask for directions to ancient Indian petroglyphs north of town in Blue Wash. The local event is **Pioneer Day** in late July.

Byron (pop. 500) has quite a few old log buildings and is surrounded by dairy farms. Check out the "roadkill" burger (with three patties) at **Half Fast Diner.**

Just two miles south of the Montana border on US Hwy. 310, **Frannie** (pop. 150) straddles the line between Park and Big Horn Counties. Residents say it's "The Biggest Little Town in Wyoming because it takes two counties to hold the people." Stop by **Frannie Tack Shop,** tel. (307) 548-2344 or (800) 552-8836, to see the saddles or get repairs on canvas or leather items. The local ice cream shop is also quite popular.

Deaver has a population of 180 folks but no attractions of note, unless you count the gazebo in the town park. The dot of a place called **Gar-**

land (pop. 50) is home to a boxy old schoolhouse (now occupied by a Church of God) that was built in the early 1900s.

Just east of Lovell, the pungent odors of sulfur and oil hang in the air, and the dry badlands are punctuated by oil pumpjacks in the large Byron Oil Field, discovered in 1918. The other business here is farming. Much of this desert land is now under irrigation, and the lush green farmlands are filled with sugar beets, beans, malting barley, alfalfa, and corn. A sign along US Hwy. 14A notes the **Sidon Canal,** built in 1900 by Mormon settlers of the Bighorn Basin. The 37-mile-long canal was entirely self-financed with land donated by the government, and transports water from the Shoshone River to 20,000 acres of farmland. Mormons claim that Prayer Rock, a large impediment to the canal's construction, was miraculously split as a result of their supplications.

LOVELL

The sleepy little burg of Lovell (pop. 2,200; pronounced "LOVE-ul") calls itself the "City of Roses," a title that comes from Dr. William Horsley, who lived here from 1924 till his death in 1971. Horsley loved roses and in the course of a lifetime of cultivating them became one of the nation's foremost authorities. The "Rose Doctor's" enthusiasm rubbed off on others, and today gardens around town are packed with roses. Oil fields crowd around Lovell, and a Georgia Pacific wallboard plant and two bentonite plants are substantial local employers, but farming is king. The Western Sugar factory stands on the edge of town, providing jobs for workers and a market for local farmers who contract with the plant to grow sugar beets. In late fall, huge mounds of straw-covered beets pile up beside the factory and the rancid/sweet odor of cooking beets fills the air. Stray beets, spilled from overloaded farm trucks, lie along the highway for miles.

Downtown Lovell seems to specialize in empty storefronts, and the settlement doesn't offer much for tourists. It's one of the few towns in Wyoming without a museum, and it's known for an insular attitude toward outsiders, but the surrounding country includes fascinating Bighorn Canyon National Recreation Area and the majestic Big Horn Mountains. A state-run fish rearing station at Tillett Springs, 17 miles north of Lovell, raises cutthroat and rainbow trout.

Like most towns in the northern Bighorn Basin, Lovell is dominated by Mormons. An enormous brick LDS church fills an entire block along the main drag and is often mistaken for an imposing office building. Lovell has wide, clean streets crowded with summertime flower boxes.

HISTORY

The town of Lovell has its roots in the enormous ML Ranch, founded in 1880 by Anthony L. Mason and Henry Clay Lovell (see below for more on the ranch). In 1900, Mormon settlers moved to the remote Bighorn Basin (partly to escape prosecution for polygamy) and working on the Burlington Railroad and developing irrigation projects. The area boomed with the discovery of natural gas and the opening of various factories. A few years later, German emigrants provided labor for the farm fields and then settled down to acquire their own land. Yellowtail Dam on the Bighorn River was built in 1965, and the surrounding land became a national recreation area the following year.

Lovell is said to have the lowest crime rate in Wyoming, but nowhere in the tourist brochures does the city mention the history of two of its most prominent doctors. A few years before his 1971 death, Dr. William Horsley, the famed "Rose Doctor," was forced to resign from the local hospital following a series of homosexual incidents with boys. (You *definitely* won't read this in the glowing stories about Horsley's life in the local press.) But another respected physician, Dr. John Story, gained considerably more notoriety for his actions. Story arrived in 1958 to practice general medicine, joined the local Baptist church, and became a strong conservative community leader. Unfortunately, over the next 25 years he also raped or molested dozens (some say hundreds) of women and girls in his office. A combination of strict Mormon upbringing, sexual ignorance, shame, and fear prevented the victims from talking, and the few who did speak up were called liars. Finally, in 1983, the charges began to surface. The trial turned Lovell inside out. Despite intense pressure from local and state politicians (then-Governor Herschler called the victims' testimony "hogwash"), Story was convicted in April 1985 on several rape charges and is currently serving a 20-year sentence in the Wyoming State Penitentiary. Jack Olson's harrowing book, *Doc,* describes this sorry chapter in recent Wyoming history.

PRACTICALITIES

Motels

Stay at one of four places in Lovell. Cheapest and most basic is **Western Motel,** 180 W. Main St., tel. (307) 548-2781, where rooms are $28 s or $32-38 d, and kitchenettes $60 for up to six people. Open May-October. Budget-Inexpensive. **Horseshoe Bend Motel,** 375 E. Main St., tel. (307) 548-2221 or (800) 548-2850, has comfortable rooms (some with microwaves and fridges) for $36 s or $39-45 d, including access to an outdoor pool. Inexpensive. **Super 8 Motel,** 595 E. Main St., tel. (307) 548-2725 or (800) 800-8000, charges $35 s or $39 d, and **Cattleman Motel,** 470 Montana Ave., tel. (307) 548-2296, has rooms for $38 s or $41-44 d. Both Inexpensive.

Guest Ranches

A 16,000-acre cattle ranch, the **TX Ranch,** tel. (406) 484-2583, offers a unique chance to take part in the cowboy life. It isn't a dude ranch, and visitors end up joining in during spring or fall cattle drives, branding calves and doing roundups. You'll be riding 6-10 hours per day here, and you'll stay in wall tents at the cow camps. No phones, fax machines, or other modern conveniences to interfere with a real Old West adventure. The ranch is primarily in Montana, but some of the operation is in Wyoming. All-inclusive weekly rates are $1,500 for two people. There's a seven-day minimum stay, for a maximum of 18 guests. Open mid-April to mid-October. Get details by visiting the website: www.ranchweb.com/tx. Luxury.

The **Schively Ranch,** tel. (307) 548-6688 or (406) 259-8866, consists of two ranches that cover 45,000 acres on the eastern side of the Pryor Mountains and just across the border inside Montana. Guests can take part in a 55-mile cattle drive each spring or fall, or help in a variety of ranch chores at other times. It's a great way to learn about the real West. One-week rates are $1,500 for two people all-inclusive or $1,990 for two people during the cattle drives, with a maximum of 16 guests. Lodging is in rustic cabins with a central bathhouse. The guest ranch is open mid-April to mid-November. Find it on the web at www.shivelyranch.com. Luxury.

Camping

The best campsites in the Lovell area lie within nearby Bighorn Canyon National Recreation Area ($5; see below for details); closest is Horseshoe Bend Campground, 14 miles from Lovell. In town, camp for free (including showers) at **Lovell Camper Park** on Quebec Ave. north of Main Street. It's a quiet place surrounded by cottonwoods. RVers can pay to stay at **Camp Big Horn RV Park,** 595 E. Main St. (behind the Super 8 Motel), tel. (307) 548-2725. The price is $7 for tents, $12 for RVs; open year-round.

Food

Rose Bowl Cafe, 483 Shoshone Ave., tel. (307) 548-7121, is popular for breakfast and lunch; try one of the huge cinnamon rolls. For pizzas, run over to **Pizza on the Run,** 214 Main St., tel. (307) 548-2206. The nicest local eatery is **Big Horn Restaurant,** next to the Super 8 at 605 E. Main St., tel. (307) 548-6811. This is where folks go for a dinner out or to enjoy a leisurely breakfast. Get groceries and deli food at **Red Apple Supermarket,** 9 E. Main St., tel. (307) 548-9907, which also houses a War Memorial.

Information and Services

For local info, visit the **Lovell Information Center** 287 E. Main, tel. (307) 548-7552. Hours are Mon.-Fri. 8:30 a.m.-12:15 p.m. and 1-5 p.m. from Memorial Day to Labor Day and Mon.-Fri. 8:30 a.m.-12:15 p.m. the rest of the year. The Bighorn National Forest's **Medicine Wheel Ranger District Office,** 604 E. Main, tel. (307) 548-6541, has information on the Medicine Wheel and Bighorn National Forest.

The town **library** is at 3rd St. and Oregon Ave., tel. (307) 548-7228, and the **post office** is at 167 W. 3rd, tel. (307) 548-7605. Find an **ATM** at First National Bank & Trust of Powell, 284 E. Main Street. Wash clothes at **Mustang Laundry,** 340 E. Montana Avenue.

You'll find an Olympic-size indoor **swimming pool** and other recreation facilities on the southwest end of town. **Foster Gulch Golf Course,** tel. (307) 548-2445, is a nine-hole course in the same area.

The big annual event in Lovell is **Mustang Days,** held the last full week in June. Activities include parades, fireworks, barbecues, a follies show, rodeo, and crowning of the Rose Queen.

Powder River/Coach USA, tel. (800) 442-3682, has daily bus service from Lovell to Billings, Montana, and to points throughout northern and eastern Wyoming.

BIGHORN CANYON NATIONAL RECREATION AREA

Just east of Lovell is one of America's lesser-known but most stunning sights, Bighorn Canyon. Over the eons, the Bighorn River has slowly carved out a 2,200-foot-deep chasm through the desert country. Since 1967, when water backed up behind the 525-foot-tall Yellowtail Dam, the canyon has lain under a deep blanket of water—water that provides 250,000 kilowatts of electricity for the western U.S. and irrigates thousands of acres of Montana farmland. The dam itself is—as the raven flies—more than 20 miles north of the Wyoming-Montana border, but its impact reaches 70 river miles upstream, creating Bighorn Lake.

The Setting

The 120,000-acre Bighorn Canyon National Recreation Area is managed by the National Park Service. A $5 per vehicle daily use fee is charged, and it's good for 24 hours from the time of purchase. The fee covers camping, boat launching, hiking, and other activities in the recreation area.

Separate facilities on both ends of the recreation area are linked by a circuitous 180-mile route that takes you through Billings, Montana. (A shorter route includes 18 miles of gravel road.) Because of the distances, most road-bound visitors come to either the Montana side or the Wyoming side but not both. Boaters can traverse the entire reach of the canyon.

Attractions accessible only from Montana include the dam itself (daily tours available through the summer), tel. (406) 666-2412, a short nature trail, and the site of two Bozeman Trail features: Fort C. F. Smith and the Hayfield Fight (both on private land). For details on sights north of the Wyoming border, see *Montana Handbook,* by W.C. McRae and Judy Jewell (Moon Travel Handbooks, www.moon.com).

From the Wyoming side, things are considerably more interesting, even though some of the sights actually lie across the Montana border. A paved road extends 27 miles along the western side of the recreation area, with a rough dirt road continuing 15 more miles to the Crow Indi-

stunning Devil Canyon within Bighorn Canyon National Recreation Area

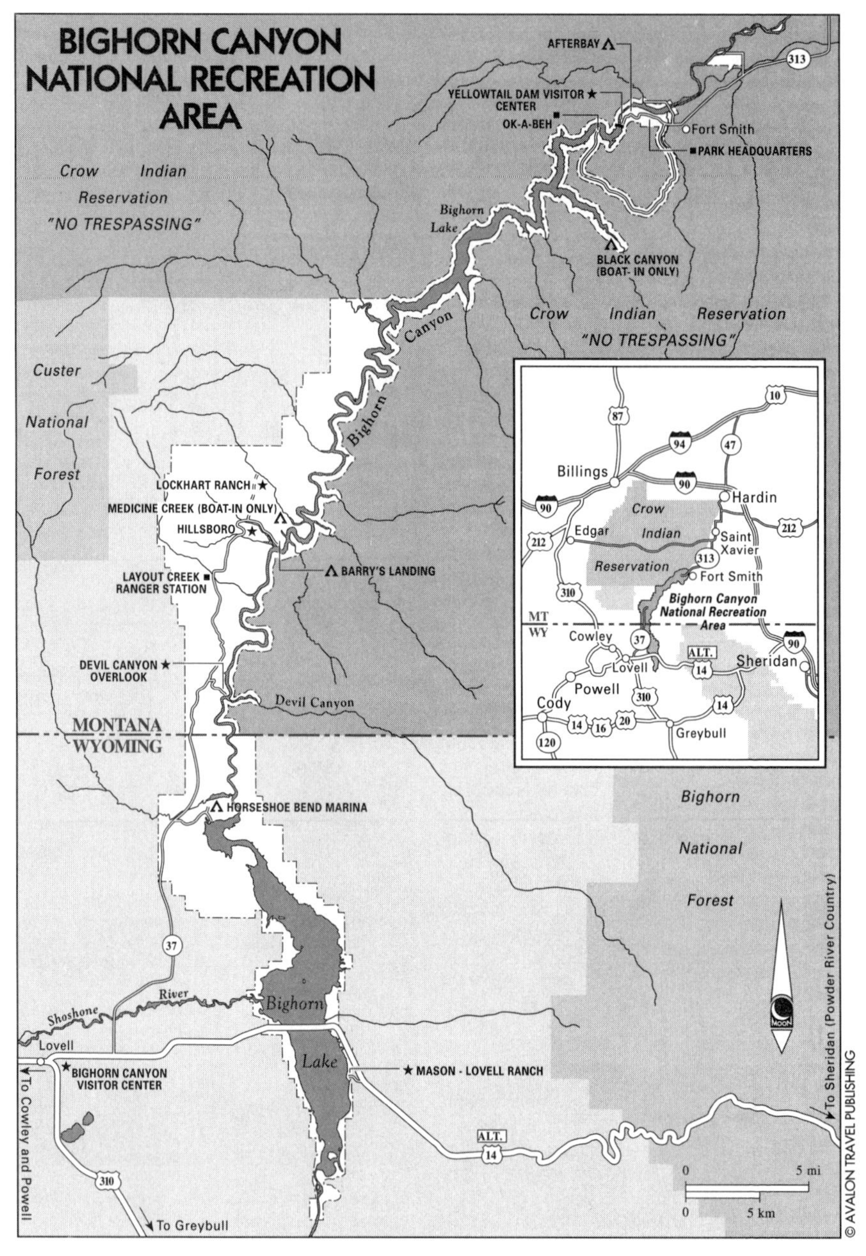
BIGHORN CANYON NATIONAL RECREATION AREA
AFTERBAY
YELLOWTAIL DAM VISITOR CENTER
OK-A-BEH
Fort Smith
PARK HEADQUARTERS
313
Crow Indian Reservation
"NO TRESPASSING"
Bighorn Lake
BLACK CANYON (BOAT- IN ONLY)
Crow Indian Reservation
"NO TRESPASSING"
Bighorn Canyon
Custer National Forest
LOCKHART RANCH
MEDICINE CREEK (BOAT-IN ONLY)
HILLSBORO
BARRY'S LANDING
LAYOUT CREEK RANGER STATION
DEVIL CANYON OVERLOOK
Devil Canyon
MONTANA
WYOMING
HORSESHOE BEND MARINA
37
Shoshone River
Bighorn Lake
Lovell
BIGHORN CANYON VISITOR CENTER
MASON - LOVELL RANCH
To Cowley and Powell
310
To Greybull
ALT. 14
Bighorn National Forest
To Sheridan (Powder River Country)
0 5 mi
0 5 km
Billings
Hardin
Edgar
Crow Indian Reservation
Saint Xavier
Fort Smith
Bighorn Canyon National Recreation Area
MT
WY
Cowley
Lovell
Sheridan
Powell
Cody
Greybull
10
87
94
47
90
212
313
310
37
ALT. 14
120
16
20

an Reservation. Along the way are a couple of campgrounds, the historic Bad Pass Trail, two old ranches, magnificent Bighorn Canyon, and a good chance to see bighorn sheep and wild horses. The road cuts through impressive red and gray badlands carpeted by juniper, sagebrush, and mountain mahogany.

SIGHTS

Devil Canyon Area

The pièce de résistance of Bighorn Canyon National Recreation Area is **Devil Canyon Overlook,** where Devil Canyon joins Bighorn Canyon. From the overlook, the earth drops suddenly away. More than a thousand feet below, motorboats look like miniature toys in a bathtub. A real treat in the canyon is the chance to see **bighorn sheep** up close; more than 100 of these majestic animals live in the national recreation area. Although the more impressive rams tend to hang out in remote parts of the Pryor Mountains in the summer, you can spot ewes and lambs along the road between the state line and Layout Creek. The rams are more likely to be seen during the Nov.-Dec. rutting season, but some will probably be visible until late May.

Precipitous Bighorn Canyon was known as **Bad Pass** by the Indians. The trail they used to reach the buffalo herds followed the canyon rim for many miles and was marked by rock cairns. Some of these cairns are still visible between Devil Canyon Overlook and Barry's Landing, as are some of the caves where they wintered near the canyon bottoms.

Before it was dammed, the river offered a torrent of rushing rapids and falls, with jagged rocks waiting to punch holes in any boat and a canyon so deep that the sun only reached the bottom for a few hours each day. In 1825, the famed mountain man and guide Jim Bridger decided to take a wooden raft down the canyon to see if it could provide a way to ship furs back east. It was a feat that was not matched for many decades, when a motorboat finally ran the wild currents.

Hillsboro

The ghost settlement of Hillsboro is about a mile above Barry's Landing and is accessible only by foot. Established around the turn of the 20th century by a self-proclaimed physician, Grosverner William Barry, the site was originally a gold-mining center. When that didn't pan out, he turned to dude ranching and promoted his ranch as a place where guests could cruise through Bighorn Canyon in motorboats or ride the English Hackney horses. The dude ranch flourished until the 1930s, but the collection of antique furniture and paintings was destroyed by a fire in the winter of 1947-48. Still standing are the old post office and various cabins.

ML Ranch

The great ML Ranch was founded in 1883 by Anthony L. Mason and Henry Clay Lovell. Lovell

More than 100 bighorn sheep live in the national recreation area.

trailed herds of cattle up from Kansas to this newly opened country, building his main headquarters along the Bighorn River just east of the community that was later named for him. The vast unfenced ranch became known as the "Big Outfit" and employed hundreds of cowhands. Grazed by 25,000 cattle, it stretched from Thermopolis all the way to the Crow Reservation in Montana, 90 miles away.

Most of the buildings from the old ML Ranch are now gone, but you can still visit the restored bunkhouse, the blacksmith shop, and two cabins. Most interesting is the bunkhouse—actually three cabins connected by dogtrots (covered breezeways). The end cabins acted as sleeping quarters, the middle one as a cook shack and mess hall. Get here by heading east from Lovell across the bridge over Bighorn Lake. A sign points out the ranch.

Lockhart Ranch

The Lockhart Ranch was where the writer Caroline Lockhart lived off and on from 1926 until her death in 1962. Located north of the Barry's Landing area, it's accessible via a rutted two-mile dirt road—very muddy after a rain. The road is passable in high-clearance cars but not RVs. A quarter-mile path leads down to the ranch, where you'll find more than a dozen log buildings set among the cottonwoods and box elder trees along Davis Creek (a.k.a. Medicine Creek). It's a fascinating and bucolic place to explore.

Other Sights

Adjacent to the Bighorn Canyon National Recreation Area is the 19,424-acre **Yellowtail Wildlife Habitat Management Unit,** a popular place for hunters and birdwatchers. Many dirt roads and trails crisscross the area, and wildlife of all types abounds. During fall migration, the wetlands here are jammed with up to 10,000 ducks. Get a map of the roads and trails of Yellowtail at the Bighorn Canyon Visitor Center.

Caves create a latticework under portions of the recreation area. On the east side of Bighorn Lake is **Bighorn Caverns.** Access is limited to experienced spelunkers and requires 4WD vehicles; get the gate key and directions at the Bighorn Canyon Visitor Center. Not far away is **Horsethief Cave.** Although closed to the public,

CAROLINE LOCKHART

The West overflows with famous men, but women sometimes get unjustly shunted aside in the accolades. One of the most interesting was Caroline Lockhart (1871-1962), a woman who began her career as an actress but turned quickly to journalism as a writer for a Boston newspaper. Using the pen name "Suzette," she became one of the country's first female newspaper reporters. The job led her into all sorts of adventures, from entering a circus cage with a lion that had killed his trainer the previous day, to testing the Boston Fire Department's new fire nets by jumping out a fourth-story hotel window. When she heard of a "Home for Intemperate Women" where the women were being severely mistreated, Caroline decided to investigate by posing as a derelict. She got her story all right, but it took considerable convincing from her editor to get her out. "Release!" shouted the matron running the house. "We can't! She's not cured yet." One of Lockhart's most lasting impacts was the creation of Mother's Day. Although Anna Jarvis came up with the concept, Caroline Lockhart made it a reality by tirelessly promoting the idea in the newspapers.

In 1904, Lockhart took a bold step. After an interview with Buffalo Bill Cody in the town named for him, she decided to move to Wyoming. She purchased the local newspaper, the *Cody Enterprise,* and quickly made a name for herself as a crusader against prohibition and "game hogs" (hunters who killed everything in sight). She also founded the Cody Stampede, the big annual event in Bighorn Basin. Lockhart authored seven novels, including *The Lady Doc,* a book that managed to ruffle local feathers with its too-close-to-the-truth descriptions of real-life Cody people. Despite this, her witty, humorous, and insightful writing gained a national reputation.

In 1925, she sold the *Cody Enterprise* and acquired a ranch that eventually included 7,000 acres of land along the Bighorn River north of Lovell, dividing her time between her Cody home (now the Lockhart Bed and Breakfast) and her ranch. She died at the age of 92. Today her old ranch lies within Bighorn Canyon National Recreation Area.

Natural Trap Cave is of paleontological value. Thirty-five miles northeast of Lovell, a 12- by 15-foot opening drops into the 80-foot-deep cavern. Over the centuries many animals—from prehistoric horses to rabbits—have fallen in.

PRACTICALITIES

Camping

There are three campgrounds in the southern half of Bighorn Canyon and two in the north half. No extra charge to camp; it's included in your $5 entrance fee. Folks in RVs park at **Horseshoe Bend,** which has water, toilets, picnic tables, and shade shelters. The rocky surface and windy conditions make this a challenging place for anyone in a tent. The drive in to Horseshoe Bend passes lovely red sandstone badlands. Campfire programs are generally offered at Horseshoe Bend amphitheater on Saturday evenings in the summer.

Barry's Landing Campground has fewer sites but is a much nicer place to stay. Bring your own water. RVers can park overnight above the boat ramp. Firewood is usually available at both Horseshoe Bend and Barry's Landing. In addition, you can pitch a tent at **Medicine Creek Campground,** though you'll need to hike in along a two-mile dirt road or float in by boat.

Backcountry camping is available throughout the southern end of the recreation area; check at the visitor center for current restrictions and access information. Also be sure to avoid trespassing on the nearby Crow Indian Reservation.

Hiking

Although there are only a few trails in Bighorn Canyon, the open badlands country makes hiking relatively easy. Some trails lead to spectacular canyon rim overviews. Best times are in the fall or in February and March, when temperatures are milder and you're less likely to meet a rattler. Prairie rattlesnakes and black widow spiders are both common in this desert country, so be aware, especially when exploring old buildings.

Crooked Creek Nature Trail, a short path with self-guiding brochures, takes off from the Horseshoe Bend campground. In addition to this, a two-mile trail (actually an old prospecting road) follows the canyon rim from Barry's Landing to the Medicine Creek Campground. You can also hike the mile-long dirt path to the ghost town Hillsboro, described above. Ask at the visitor center for other interesting places to hike in Bighorn Canyon.

On the Water

Most visitors come to Bighorn Canyon to play on the water. You'll see lots of people tooling around in powerful boats, towing water-skiers, trolling for fish, or windsurfing. Fishing is the biggest attraction; walleye, rainbow, and brown trout, yellow perch, ling, crappie, and catfish are commonly caught. Note that because the lake straddles the state line, you'll need to purchase fishing licenses for both Wyoming and Montana if you plan on fishing across the border. Launch ramps are at Barry's Landing and Horseshoe Bend, plus Ok-A-Beh Marina at the north end of the lake. Swimmers hang out at the Horseshoe Bend beach, the only place with a lifeguard; check with the visitors center to see when they're on duty.

Horseshoe Bend Marina, tel. (307) 548-7230, is open Thurs.-Sat. 8 a.m.-10 p.m., and 8 a.m. till a half hour past sunset on other days. The marina rents inner tubes, canoes, fishing boats, paddle boats, and pontoon boats, and sells boat gas, food, and beer. The cafe sells burgers and snacks. Open mid-May to Labor Day.

Ok-A-Beh Marina, tel. (406) 665-2349, on the Montana side, has limited fishing supplies, plus food, boat gas, and boat rentals. Hours are Mon.-Fri. 10 a.m.-7 p.m. and Sat.-Sun. 8 a.m.-8 p.m. Memorial Day to Labor Day.

Information

For a good orientation to the area, stop by **Bighorn Canyon Visitor Center,** tel. (307) 548-2251, just east of Lovell along US Hwy. 14A. It's open daily 8 a.m.-6 p.m. Memorial Day to Labor Day, and daily 8:30 a.m.-5 p.m. the rest of the year (closed Thanksgiving, Christmas, and New Year's Day). The solar-heated center is an attraction in itself; 70% of its heat comes directly from the sun. Inside are a three-dimensional relief map of the canyon, displays on local animals, books and topo maps for sale, and movies on Bighorn Canyon, Pryor Mountain Wild Horse Range, and Medicine Wheel. Check the notice board for other talks or hikes in the recreation area, including the weekend **campfire programs** at Horseshoe Bend Campground (summer only). Summertime canoe tours of the canyon may be available, but call a week ahead for specifics. Be sure to pick up a copy of ***Canyon Echoes,*** the free visitor guide with current information. Ranger stations are found at Horseshoe Bend and Layout Creek. The **Ewing-Snell Historical Site** at Layout Creek contains a restored one-room schoolhouse.

PRYOR MOUNTAIN WILD HORSE RANGE

Pryor Mountain Wild Horse Range covers 47,000 acres on the western side of Bighorn Canyon. Established in 1968 as the nation's first wild horse preserve, it is managed by the Bureau of Land Management. (Two other wild horse ranges now exist, in Nevada and Colorado, and there are another 3,000 wild horses in the Red Desert of southwestern Wyoming.) Pryor Mountain's desert country supports three herds, and periodic roundups keep the population near the carrying capacity of 120 horses. Many of the horses remain out of sight in remote box canyons, but you're likely to see some relatively tame ones along the road between Horseshoe Bend and Layout Creek Ranger Station.

Most "wild horses" of the West are of mixed origin. Some are primarily domestic horses that were released into the wild by local ranchers, others can trace at least some of the bloodlines to Spanish mustangs brought to the New World in the 16th century. Recent studies of wild horses found that the mustangs at Pryor Mountain are the most strongly Spanish of any feral horse herd in America, with little intermixing from more recent breeds. This purity is exhibited in the distinctive colors that include dun, blue roan, grulla, and sabino. Most have dark manes and tails. Other common characteristics are dark leg bandings and a dark line running down the back.

Before protection of the wild horses, many were rounded up for use on ranches or for the glue factory. After 1971, when it became illegal to harass or kill wild horses, their numbers began to grow rapidly. Each year's colt crop increases the herd by 20%, creating competition with native deer and bighorn sheep. Today, the BLM controls numbers through its adopt-a-horse program, removing 25-30 horses every other year from Pryor Mountain and offering them to the public. For details on acquiring a wild horse, call the BLM at (406) 657-6262, or check the web at www.adoptahorse.blm.gov.

GREYBULL

For travelers en route to Yellowstone, the crossroads town of Greybull (pop. 1,800) is a splotch of irrigated green surrounded by desert country. Greybull lies near the junction of Shell Creek and the Bighorn River and at the intersection of US Hwys. 14 and 16-20. As such, it is both an agricultural center and a commercial center. Most of the town lies along the western shore of the river behind a long levee; barren rocky bluffs line the opposite bank. There are bentonite processing plants just north of town, oil pumpjacks farther afield, and irrigated farms along the river. Tip: if you're heading west to Cody and Yellowstone, fill up your tank here. Gas prices usually get more expensive as you approach the mountains.

History

The land around Greybull was first settled in the 1880s by stockmen, with several hundred Mormon homesteaders moving in a decade later to dig irrigation ditches and establish the minuscule farming settlements of **Burlington** (pop. 190) and **Otto** along the Greybull River. Nearby **Emblem** was established by 600 German farmers in the late 1890s. A diversion of the Greybull River was begun in 1895, the first reclamation project under the Carey Act. Originally called Germania, the name was changed to Emblem (a reference to the American flag) during the anti-German hysteria of WW I.

The word Greybull comes from a huge albino buffalo that once roamed this country. The animal was sacred to the Indians, who noted it in pictographs still visible on sandstone bluffs north of town along the river. The town is primarily a creation of the Burlington Railroad in 1909-10, but much of its growth has been fueled by oil and gas developments in the surrounding country.

Completion of US Hwy. 14 across the Big Horn Mountains in the 1930s brought tourists and led to Greybull's development as a way station for folks heading east to the Black Hills or west to Yellowstone. Beginning in 1934, scientists excavated a dozen complete skeletons of dinosaurs near Greybull, and in 1991 Swiss paleontologists excavated one of the largest allosauruses ever found. The railroad is still a major employer in Greybull, as are two bentonite plants, along with Hawkins and Powers Aviation.

SIGHTS

Greybull Museum

The local museum is in the same building as the library (325 Greybull Ave., tel. 307-765-2444). It's open Mon.-Fri. 10 a.m.-8 p.m. and Saturday 10 a.m.-6 p.m. June-Sept., Mon.-Fri. 1-5 p.m. in the spring and fall, and Monday, Wednesday, and Friday 1-4 p.m. in the winter. No charge. Inside are agate collections and polished petrified wood pieces, a fine fossil collection that includes one of the largest fossil ammonites ever found, fossil turtles, and dinosaur bones. Also here are various Indian arrowheads and other historical artifacts, including a New England church made from royal icing! Ask here for directions to the Indian pictograph of the albino bison for which Greybull is named.

Aerial Firefighting Museum

Big Horn County Airport, atop a hill just north of town, is the home of Hawkins & Powers Aviation, a major source of planes used to drop fire retardant on forest fires throughout the West. During the summer fire season it's often a center of intense activity, with 11 air tankers and seven helicopters based here. Included are five of the six PB4Y-2s still flying—in WW II, these planes played an important role in routing the Japanese from the South Pacific. Hawkins & Powers planes have appeared in a number of movies, including the Steven Spielberg firefighting film *Always*. Take a look through the fence at any time, or pay to walk around for a close-up view; $3 for adults, $1.50 for seniors and kids, and free for children under age six. Open Mon.-Fri. 8 a.m.-6 p.m. and Sat.-Sun. 10 a.m.-6 p.m. in the summer, and Mon.-Fri. 8 a.m.-5 p.m. the rest of the year.

Other Sights

Five miles northeast of Greybull is **Devil's Kitchen,** a fascinating arroyo filled with brilliantly colored badlands and many fossils. Get a map from the chamber of commerce and follow it closely; the last turnoff is easy to miss. **Sheep Mountain,** a 15-mile-long hogback of eroded land just north of Greybull, is a favorite of geologists, who marvel at this fossil-packed anticline. Photographers love the vivid reds, browns, and yellows of this desert landscape. A bit farther afield is the Red Gulch Dinosaur Tracksite; see Shell Valley below for details on this important discovery.

Find an attractive flower garden in the shape of the Wyoming state flag at the west end of Greybull Avenue. And if you are really bored, head to the city park to find picnic tables, a jogging track, and the chimney of the first house built in Greybull.

Two other places may merit a visit: **Greybull Wildlife Museum,** 420 Greybull Ave., has a small collection of stuffed critters, and the old-fashioned **Probst Western Store,** 547 Greybull Ave., tel. (307) 765-2171, contains a great selection of cowboy hats, boots, and Western clothes.

PRACTICALITIES

Accommodations

Motels are arranged from least to most expensive. Add a seven percent tax to these rates. See Shell Valley below for nearby dude ranches.

Inexpensive: Sage Motel, 1135 N. 6th Ave., tel. (307) 765-4443, charges $34 s, $42-48 d, or $60 for six people. All rooms contain small fridges. **Antler Motel,** 1116 N. 6th Ave., tel. (307) 765-4404 or (800) 246-1814, is a quiet place with rooms for $35 s or $37 d. All rooms have fridges and microwaves, and five contain kitchenettes. **Three Chief Motel,** 625 N. 6th Ave., tel. (307) 765-4626, has standard rooms for $35 s or $45 d; open April-October. **K-Bar Motel,** 300 Greybull Ave., tel. (307) 765-4426, charges $40-48 s or $45-53 d.

Inexpensive-Moderate: The comfortable **Greybull Motel,** 300 N. 6th Ave., tel. (307) 765-2628, charges $48-66 s or d and has microwaves and fridges in half the rooms.

Moderate: Yellowstone Motel, 247 Greybull Ave., tel. (307) 765-4456, offers recently renovated rooms for $50 s or $66-70 d, including use of an outdoor pool.

The newly built **Wheels Motel,** 1324 N. 6th Ave., tel. (307) 765-2105 or (800) 676-2973, is the nicest motel in town and costs $52 s or $62-65 d. Some rooms contain fridges and recliners.

Camping

Green Oasis RV Park, 540 N. 12th Ave., tel. (307) 765-2856, has tent sites for $12; RV sites for $20. Showers for noncampers cost $3. Open mid-May to September.

Greybull KOA, 333 N. 2nd Ave., tel. (307) 765-2555 or (800) 562-7508, charges $18 for tent sites, $23 for RVs. Showers cost $3 for noncampers. Open March-Nov., with trees and an outdoor pool. It also has basic cabins for $30 d.

Restaurants and Bars

MJ's Cafe at the Greybull KOA, 333 N. 2nd Ave., tel. (307) 765-2555, is easily the most popular local eatery. Good food at a good price and in quantity. Locals drop by for breakfast, for the lunch-time salad bar, and to enjoy prime rib specials on the weekend. For a lighter meal, visit **Bistro & Books,** 510 Greybull Ave., tel. (307) 765-9509. This unpretentious cafe serves espresso, teas, muffins, salads, sandwiches, and soups, and it also has a selection of books for sale.

Lisa's Restaurant, 200 Greybull Ave., tel. (307) 765-4765, serves both Mexican and American fare and fills up most evenings.

Open 24 hours a day, **Wheels Inn Restaurant,** 1336 N. 6th Ave., tel. (307) 765-2456, serves up standard American fare. **Uptown Cafe,** 536 Greybull Ave., tel. (307) 765-2152, is another local favorite with working-class meals. **CC's Pizza,** 427 Greybull Ave., tel. (307) 765-4510, is the local pizza joint. Also in Greybull are a Subway and an A&W drive-in for quick eats. **Ron's Food Farm,** 909 N. 6th, tel. (307) 765-2890, is the place for groceries in Greybull.

Entertainment and Events

For live music, try **Hanging Tree Lounge,** 1040 N 6th Ave., tel. (307) 765-2021, **Smokehouse Saloon** 562 Greybull Ave., tel. (307) 765-2232, or **Silver Spur,** 445 Greybull Ave., tel. (307) 765-2300. The Smokehouse has a 19th-century back bar, plus pool tables and darts. Greybull's big annual event is **Days of '49** (1949 that is), held the second weekend in June; there's a top-notch rodeo, a parade, a barbecue, dancing, and a demolition derby.

Recreation

A marvelous old log building built in the 1920s houses the **Greybull Roller Rink,** 527 S. 1st Ave., tel. (307) 765-2761. Visitors can swim and take showers at the **pool** across from the high school on 6th Ave.; tel. (307) 765-9575. Five miles south of Greybull, **Midway Golf Club,** tel. (307) 568-2255, is a nine-hole course open to the public.

Information and Services

The **Greybull Chamber of Commerce** has a small kiosk next to the library at 325 Greybull Avenue. It's open year-round, Mon.-Fri. 9 a.m.-noon and 2-4 p.m., Saturday 10 a.m.-noon and 2-4 p.m. Get details by calling (307) 765-2100 or (877) 765-2100, or visit the chamber on the web at www.greybull.com.

The **Greybull Public Library** is at 325 Greybull Ave., tel. (307) 765-2551. Find the local **post office** at 119 N. 7th Ave., tel. (307) 347-3321, and **ATMs** at 1st Interstate Bank, 601 Greybull Ave., and inside Ron's Food Farm at 909 N. 6th Avenue. Wash clothes at **Coin-Op Laundromat,** across the street from the A&W on N. 6th Avenue.

Powder River/Coach USA, tel. (800) 442-3682, has daily bus service from Greybull to Billings, Montana, and eastern Wyoming. Buses stop in front of the chamber of commerce office on Greybull Ave.; get tickets inside.

GREYBULL VICINITY

BASIN

South of Greybull, the highway parallels the Bighorn River. Sharp bluffs rise along the eastern side of the river, and cottonwoods and willows crowd the banks. As you head away from the broad river valley, the endless hills are covered with dry grass, sage, and greasewood. It's a plain-Jane, arid landscape. Eight miles away lies the pleasant town of Basin (pop. 1,200). After a stretch of rough going in which the town seemed on its way to extinction, Basin has bounced back a bit. The town putters along on its status as Big Horn County seat and the presence of an impressive state retirement center and a couple of publishing-related businesses, including Wyoming's largest book wholesaler, Wolverine Distributing.

Basin is a relaxing place to retire after a long day of driving. Established in 1896, the town has always been an agricultural center, with both farming and ranching in the surrounding land. In 1897, a bitter custody battle for the county seat split voters between Basin City, as it was then known, and the older town of Otto. Basin City won by 38 votes.

State Hwy. 789 heads south from Basin to dinky **Manderson** (pop. 90), where the only business is a Quick Stop market. South of here the road splits and continues on both sides of Bighorn River to Worland. The main road (on the east side of the river) plays tag with the irrigation ditch much of the way, passing eroded desert bluffs to the east and flat farm country closer to the river. A thin strip of trees runs right down the middle; in fall they look like skeletons against the skyline. Lots of barley, sugar beet, and hayfields.

Lodging and Camping

The **Lilac Motel,** 710 W. C St., tel. (307) 568-3355, has a quiet location and kind owner. Rates are just $31 s or $39 d, and the rooms have microwaves and fridges. Inexpensive. **Camping** is free in the town park, but you'll have to pitch tents on the dirt. Park RVs ($15) at **Rose Garden RV Park,** tel. (307) 568-2943, on the south end of town.

Other Practicalities

Start your day with a dependably fine breakfast (blueberry pancakes recommended) at **RJ's Cafe,** 602 S. 4th St., tel. (307) 568-2246. Cheap coffee too. Get steak and seafood dinners at **Outpost Supper Club,** 151 N. 4th St., tel. (307) 568-2134, and groceries from **Wheeler's Market,** 114 S. 4th St., tel. (307) 568-2325. The latter also houses an **ATM.**

For books, stop by **Big Horn County Library,** 103 W. C St., tel. (307) 568-2388. Wash clothes at the laundromat on D and 4th Streets. There's an outdoor **swimming pool** at the high school.

Stockman's Bar, 105 S. 4th St., tel. (307) 568-9942, has live country music a couple of times a month. Each August, Basin hosts the **Big Horn County Fair,** with livestock judging, a rodeo, barbecue, and more small-town fun.

Powder River/Coach USA, tel. (800) 442-3682, has bus service from Basin to northern and eastern Wyoming.

SHELL VALLEY

Shell Valley is farming and ranching country, its lush irrigated hayfields contrasting sharply with the arid landscape to the west. The tiny town called Shell has a country store/bar and several places to stay. Get burgers and ice cream at **Dirty Annie's,** tel. (307) 765-2304, and prime rib from **Wagonwheel Restaurant and Lounge,** tel. (307) 765-2561. The latter has an outdoor patio.

One mile east of Shell is **Art Shelter Studio Gallery,** where Earl Miller and Karyne Dunbar display their unusual pieces. Call (307) 765-9605 to make sure they're in when you visit. A distinctive old stone school west of Shell, built in 1903, was used as a one-room school until the early 1950s. Several old log buildings are in Shell, including the Community Church, built in 1903.

Red Gulch and Dinosaur Tracks

The Bureau of Land Management's **Red Gulch Scenic Byway** is a 32-mile dirt road through remote and striking country. The northern access point starts on the south side of US Hwy. 14

four miles west of Shell (10 miles east of Greybull) and is well-marked. The first 10 miles of the byway are the most interesting, with spectacular red badlands of the Chugwater Formation on both sides of the road. The road gets very slick and muddy when wet, so don't venture out after a day of rain. When it is dry, it is usually passable in a two-wheel-drive vehicle. This is some of the most remote country in Wyoming; even ranches are few and far between. No phones, gas, or other services are available till Hyattville, 32 miles from your starting point. The area is rich in Indian history; tepee rings and pictographs are scattered over the countryside.

Approximately five miles south of the turnoff from US Hwy. 14 is a parking area for **Red Gulch Dinosaur Tracksite.** In 1997, geologist Erik Kvale was looking over this area when a relative asked him if dinosaur tracks might be found in this formation. "No," he responded. But when he looked at the rocks at his feet, he corrected himself, "but here is one right in front of me." Dr. Kvale's discovery attracted national attention, and the site has become a major attraction for both paleontologists and anyone interested in dinosaurs. Hundreds of three-toed tracks crisscross more than 40 acres; the tracks were apparently made when theropods (meat-eating) dinosaurs walked in mud along a lakeshore. Most are 2-10 inches in length and are fairly shallow, so it may take you some time to find them. They are easiest to see in the low-angled light of morning or dusk. Volunteer guides are here 6-8 p.m. Wed.-Sat. in the summer to talk about the site.

The discovery of these tracks has changed the way paleontologists view the geologic history of Bighorn Basin. Previously it was believed that this entire area had been underwater during the middle Jurassic period (165 million years ago), but these tracks are from land-dwelling dinosaurs. For more information on the tracks and Red Gulch, contact the BLM's Worland office at (307) 347-5100, or see the informative website, accessed through www.wy.blm.gov.

Accommodations

On three acres just south of Shell, **HAP's Trapper Creek B&B,** tel. (307) 765-9685, is a hilltop home facing the magnificent Big Horn Mountains. Two guest rooms are inside the house ($55 d), and the old bunkhouse has been transformed into a spacious third guest room ($65 d). The rooms are eclectically furnished with Western pieces and original artwork, and a light breakfast is served on the big deck. Kids are welcome. Inexpensive-Moderate.

For something completely different, stay at **Trapper's Rest B&B,** tel. (307) 765-9239 or (877) 765-5233, three miles southeast of Shell. The B&B has a rustic two-bedroom cabin (no running water) and a large tepee. A full breakfast is cooked outdoors. The setting is peaceful and quiet, with a tree-lined trout stream nearby. Open July-Sept.; kids welcome.

At the foot of the Big Horns, **The Hideout at Flintner Ranch,** tel. (307) 765-2080 or (800) 354-8637, is a working cattle ranch that has been in operation since 1906. Popular with European tourists, the ranch has 250,000 acres of leased or deeded land, so you'll find plenty of country to explore. Guests stay in modern log cabins with all the amenities, including private baths, phones, televisions, and a hot tub. Activities center around horseback riding and fly-fishing. All-inclusive rates are a stiff $520/night for two people, with a three-night minimum stay in the peak season. The ranch provides space for a maximum of 20 guests. Its website is www.thehideout.com. Open mid-April to mid-November. Luxury.

Kedesh Guest Ranch, four miles east of Shell along US Hwy. 14, tel. (307) 765-2791 or (800) 845-3320, www.kedesh.com, offers log cabin accommodations in grand mountain country. Ranch activity centers around horseback riding, fishing, cookouts, and hayrides, but guests can also join organized trips to Cody or out to explore nearby petroglyphs and dinosaur digs. The hot tub awaits after a long day. All-inclusive weekly rates are $2,100 for two people, and the ranch books a maximum of 25 guests at a time. Open June-September. Luxury.

Two miles west of town, **Shell Creek Guest Ranch,** tel. (307) 765-2420, has modern dude-ranch accommodations including a central ranch house and hot tub. Guests can take part in horseback rides, campfires, barbecues, fossil hunts, fishing trips, and excursions to Cody. Lodging-only rates are $59 per day for two adults. All-inclusive one-week stays are $1,900 for two people. The dude ranch is open year-round. Inexpensive-Luxury.

Park RVs ($14) or pitch tents ($10) at **Shell Campground,** tel. (307) 765-2342; open April to mid-November. Showers are $2 for those not camping here.

HYATTVILLE AREA

Twenty-one miles east of Manderson on State Hwy. 31 is the tiny ranching center of Hyattville. Built in 1905, **Paintrock Grill,** has meals and alcohol downstairs and old-fashioned rooms over the bar. Meals are also available at **Hyattville Cafe,** tel. (307) 469-2242. **Paintrock Adventures,** tel. (307) 469-2274, leads fishing trips and trail rides.

Medicine Lodge State Park

One of Wyoming's most famous archaeological sites, Medicine Lodge State Park is well worth the detour. Get here by heading north from Hyattville and turning right onto Cold Springs Road. After four miles, turn left again at the "Medicine Lodge" sign and follow the dirt road 1.5 miles to the park (the road gets quite slippery when it rains).

The main attraction at Medicine Lodge is a 750-foot-long low cliff that served as a backdrop to 10,000 years of Indian settlements. The cliff is covered with dozens of petroglyphs and pictographs. A small log **visitor center,** tel. (307) 469-2234—built almost a century ago as a cowboy bunkhouse—is open Mon.-Fri. 8 a.m.-5 p.m. and Sat.-Sun. 9 a.m.-8 p.m. May-Labor Day. Inside are displays on the area's incredibly rich archaeological history. Beginning in 1969, researchers uncovered some 60 cultural levels and thousands of artifacts and bones here. It's considered one of the most significant archaeological sites in the West.

A delightful creekside **campground** ($9 for nonresidents, or $4 for Wyoming residents) is just a short distance from the petroglyphs and has restrooms, water, and good fishing for brown trout in the creek. Wheelchair fishing access is also provided. Ask at the visitor center to pick fruit from the old apple trees next to the cabin.

A three-quarter-mile **nature trail** begins near the visitor center, or you can hike up the trail/4WD road along Dry Medicine Lodge Creek. This route passes a natural arch approximately three miles up and goes through a BLM wilderness study area. It's a great place for mountain-biking or a peaceful evening walk.

Staying on Cold Springs Rd.—instead of turning off to Medicine Lodge State Park—takes you 15 miles to Paint Rocks Lakes, a jumping-off point for Cloud Peak Wilderness (described under Big Horn Mountains in the Powder River Country chapter).

Trapper Canyon

North of Hyattville, another interesting place awaits folks willing to do a lot of adventuring. **Trapper Canyon,** located on public land, has colorful walls rising 1,200 feet above Trapper Creek. No trails, and tough access requires serious 4WD vehicles; check with the BLM office in Worland for details.

WORLAND

The prosperous community of Worland (pop. 6,000) depends upon a mixture of agriculture (primarily malt barley and sugar beets), sheep and cattle ranching, oil production, and manufacturing. Sheep glean plowed fields near town, and the Holly Sugar Company's plant on the southwest edge of Worland provides economic stability, keeping more than 20,000 acres in beets. Also important is a major aluminum can factory, which produces three million cans a day, and a Pepsi bottling plant that fills many of these. The town itself has a pleasant Midwestern feel with nightly baseball games through the summer, tree-bordered streets and simple homes in the center, and suburban ranch-style homes spreading across the surrounding countryside. The slow Bighorn River twists its way along the edge of Worland, but just a few miles farther west is desert country with dry rocky buttes, sagebrush, and sheep.

HISTORY

Worland is named for Charlie "Dad" Worland, one of the first homesteaders in this part of the Bighorn Basin and the manager of a stage station and saloon built along the old Bridger Trail in

1900. It wasn't much to look at—a cave dug into the riverbank, with log walls out front. His bar quickly acquired the nickname "The Hole-in-the-Wall." A cigar box just behind the bar served as the local bank, and anyone needing money could borrow it and leave behind an IOU. Other folks settled around Dad Worland, and A.G. Rupp added a general store nearby, also built into the side of the bank to save precious timber. Ray Pendergraft in *Washakie: A Wyoming County History,* relates the following story about early Worland:

> *Once a compactly-built man rode into the settlement, refreshed himself at Worland's saloon, then went on to Rupps for some supplies. On one wall of the store was a poster, complete with a picture. It read, "$5,000 Reward, Dead or Alive Robert Leroy Parker, alias Butch Cassidy." The visitor examined it. "It's not a very good likeness," he told Rupp. Rupp examined the poster, looked at the man, and readily agreed. "You don't want it up there do you, Mr. Rupp?" the man politely asked. "No, I don't," replied Mr. Rupp. "I'll take it down for you," the man said, did so and went on about his selection of supplies.*

Originally located on the western side of the Bighorn River, Worland moved to the other side after the Chicago, Burlington, and Quincy Railroad announced plans to build along the east bank. The nucleus of Worland, 10 buildings, was slid across the river on the ice during the winter of 1905-06. The following year, construction was finished on the 54-mile-long Big Horn irrigation canal, opening some 30,000 acres to agricul-

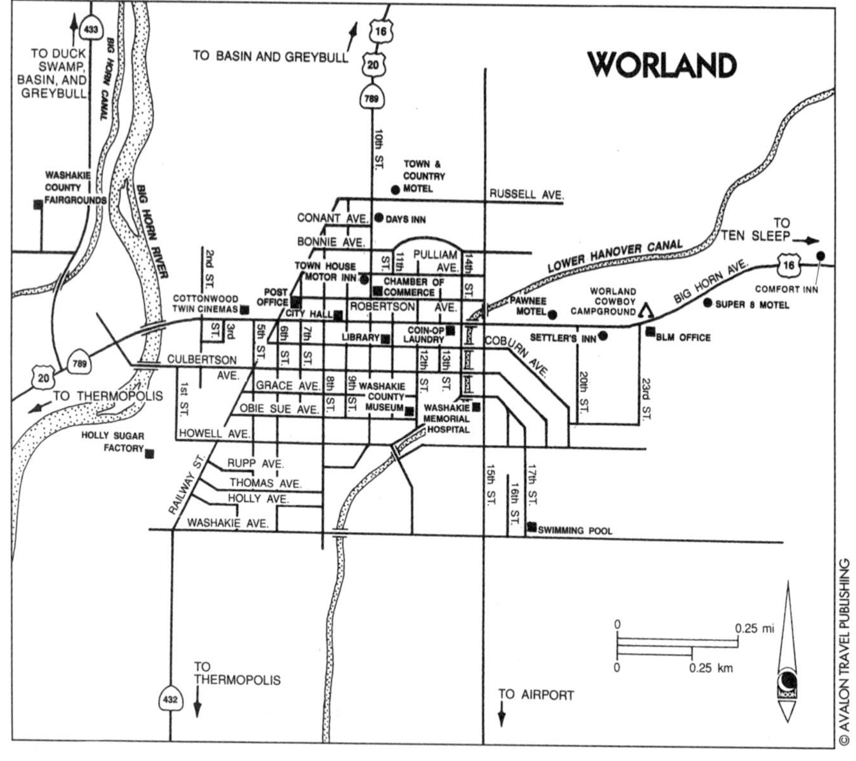

ture. It had been begun almost 20 years earlier. A new sugar beet processing plant in 1917 attracted more farmers and workers from the Midwest and many Germans and Ukrainians. The discovery of oil in the Hidden Dome field in that same year brought boom times as speculators flooded the area. Oil and agriculture, especially sugar beets, have remained important ever since, although oil production has declined as the fields have been pumped out.

SIGHTS

Housed in an old Mormon church, the **Washakie Museum and Cultural Center,** 1115 Obie Sue Ave., tel. (307) 347-4102, is open Tues.-Sat. 9 a.m.-5 p.m. in summer, and Tues.-Fri. 10 a.m.-4 p.m. the rest of the year. Inside this spacious multiroom museum are Indian artifacts from cave sites near Ten Sleep, a re-creation of the A.G. Rupp Store, numerous old photos, an array of cowboy and ranch equipment, and a fine geology and fossil collection. The museum's highlight is a Sheepeater Indian lodge constructed in the 1860s from 130 poles. It was moved here from its original location near Soapy Peak. Also here are mammoth bones from the 11,000-year-old Colby Site, four miles east of Worland. This was one of the largest and oldest known mammoth kills in North America. Kids will enjoy the hands-on exhibits such as the corn sheller and grinder. Local art shows and traveling exhibits can also be found here.

Next to the County Court House at the corner of Big Horn Ave. and 10th St. is a fountain fed by a 4,330-foot-deep **artesian well** 23 miles north of Worland. The well flows at an impressive 14,000 gallons per minute and with sufficient pressure to push water all the way to Worland. The fountain is a good place to fill water jugs for your desert travels. Also on the courthouse grounds is a grotesque 15-foot-tall **Indian statue** carved out of wood by Peter Toth and placed here in 1980. **Pioneer Square,** just across the road, has unusual metal sculptures depicting pioneer settlers.

Head two miles north on State Hwy. 433 to **Duck Swamp,** which includes picnic tables, a paved interpretive trail, and an overlook. A sign describes the Bridger Trail that passed through here.

West of Worland in the Painted Desert, you'll find some of the most interesting badlands country in Wyoming. Of particular note are the **Gooseberry Badlands** on Bureau of Land Management property near Squaw Teats and just off State Hwy. 431. The BLM has developed a fascinating 1.5-mile nature trail through the hoodoo formations here; pick up a descriptive handout from their office in Worland. There's plenty of eroded country to explore, including arches and a variety of bizarrely carved shapes. The bones of a prehistoric horse, *Eohippus,* have been found here.

PRACTICALITIES

Accommodations

Accommodations are listed from least to most expensive. Add a six percent tax to these rates.

Inexpensive: The cheapest place is **Town House Motor Inn,** 119 N. 10th St., tel. (307) 347-2426, where rooms cost $35 s or $40-45 d. Also reasonably priced is **Econo Inn (also called Town & Country Motel),** 1021 Russell St., tel. (307) 347-3249, where rooms go for $38 s or $48 d.

Super 8 Motel, 2500 Big Horn, tel. (307) 347-9236 or (800) 800-8000, charges $43 s or $46 d.

One of the nicest places in town is **Days Inn,** 500 N. 10th St., tel. (307) 347-4251 or (800) 329-7466, where the rooms cost $42-52 s or $50-60 d, including a continental breakfast. Also recommended is **Best Western Settler's Inn,** 2200 Big Horn, tel. (307) 347-8201 or (800) 528-1234, which charges $48-54 s or $54-58 d, including a continental breakfast.

Moderate-Expensive: Worland's newest motel is **Comfort Inn,** 100 N. Rd. 11, tel. (307) 347-9898 or (800) 228-5150. Rates are $59-79 s or $69-89 d, and amenities include an indoor pool, jacuzzi, and continental breakfast.

Camping

No public campgrounds are near Worland (although you can pitch a tent on nearby BLM lands), but the private **Worland Cowboy Campground,** 2311 Big Horn Ave., tel. (307) 347-2329, has shady tent sites for $16, RV spaces for $20. Showers for noncampers cost $5. Open May-October.

Food

Maggie's Cafe, 541 Big Horn Ave., tel. (307) 347-3354, has very reasonable breakfasts and lunches, including homemade soups and breads. Things can get pretty chaotic here at times. Get good breakfasts and lunchtime sandwiches (homemade bread) at **The Office,** 1515 Big Horn Ave., tel. (307) 347-8171; drop by on Friday night for the prime rib special.

Antone's Supper Club, three miles east of town on US Hwy. 16, tel. (307) 347-2301, has a Wednesday night smorgasbord and great deals on sirloin steaks. **Tom and Jerry's Steakhouse,** 1620 Big Horn Ave., tel. (307) 347-9261, is the fanciest place in town and grills the best steaks around.

Ranchito Mexican Food, 544 Big Horn Ave., tel. (307) 347-8501, serves authentic south-of-the-border fare, and **China Garden,** 616 Big Horn Ave., tel. (307) 347-6168, has surprisingly fine Chinese meals.

Pizza Hut, 1927 Big Horn Ave., tel. (307) 347-2434, and **Pizza on the Run,** 1214 Big Horn Ave., tel. (307) 347-2453, are the local pizza joints.

Stop by **Rolling Pin Bakery,** 105 N. 15th St., tel. (307) 347-2763, for fresh breads, cookies, and doughnuts. A good selection of groceries can be found at **Jon's IGA Foodliner,** 221 N. 10th St., tel. (307) 347-3628, or the new **Blair's Market,** on the east end of town.

Events

Military Appreciation Weekend in late June features a parade, picnic, and military jet fly-bys. Worland's big annual event is the **Washakie County Fair** on the first week of August. It includes a parade, country music, and other country-fair fun. In early September, the **Harvest Festival** has hot-air balloons, classic cars, food booths, arts and crafts, contests, and even a sugar-beet-carving contest.

Entertainment

The Office Lounge, 1515 Big Horn Ave., tel. (307) 347-8171, has rock or country bands most weekends, or try **RJ's Saloon** 607 Big Horn Ave., tel. (307) 347-8891. **Cottonwood Twin Cinemas,** 401 Robertson, tel. (307) 347-8414, is the local movie palace.

Recreation

During the summer months, many people float and fish the **Bighorn River** north from Worland. The river is gentle in many stretches, but get detailed info and a map of access sites from the Worland BLM office before putting in. Upstream from Worland to Thermopolis the river has many hazards, and this stretch is not recommended for novices.

There's a community **swimming pool** at the high school, 1706 Washakie Ave., tel. (307) 347-4113, and an 18-hole **Municipal Golf Course,** tel. (307) 347-2695, next to the airport. Roller skate at **Wheels Skate Palace,** 1115 Big Horn Ave., tel. (307) 347-8808, or roll black balls toward white pins at **Hurricane Lanes,** 612 S. 12th, tel. (307) 347-4044.

Information and Services

The **Worland Area Chamber of Commerce** office, tel. (307) 347-3226, sits in front of the county courthouse at 120 N. 10th St. and stays open Mon.-Fri. 8 a.m.-noon and 1-5 p.m. Get info on the web at www.worlandchamber.com.

The **Washakie County Library,** 1019 Coburn Ave., tel. (307) 347-2231, has Internet access. Drop by the **BLM Worland District Office** at 101 S. 23rd St., tel. (307) 347-9871, for information on scenic back roads and nearby places to hike or mountain-bike.

Wash clothes at **Coin-Op Laundry,** 1401 Big Horn Avenue. You'll find **ATMs** at the Conoco Station at 944 Big Horn Ave. and at Key Bank, 120 N. 7th Street. For emergency medical treatment, head to **Washakie Memorial Hospital,** 400 S. 15th St., tel. (307) 347-3221.

Transportation

The Worland Airport is two miles south of town and is served by **United Express/Great Lakes Aviation,** tel. (800) 241-6522, with daily flights to Denver. Rent cars from **Big Horn Chevrolet,** 545 N. 10th Ave., tel. (307) 347-4229, or **Worland Ford,** 500 Big Horn Ave., tel. (307) 347-4236.

Powder River/Coach USA, tel. (800) 442-3682, has daily bus service from Worland to Billings, Montana, and throughout northern and eastern Wyoming. It stops at Daylight Donuts, 400 N. 10th Street.

TEN SLEEP

Ten Sleep (pop. 320) has one of the most picturesque settings in all Wyoming. The drive in from Worland offers a traipse across dry desert badlands crowded with oil pumpjacks and then up into rolling grass and sagebrush country with the tree-covered Big Horn Mountains marking the distant horizon. Great views from atop the long hills before the road descends sharply into a lush green valley cut through by Nowood and Tensleep Creeks. Because of its mountain valley location, the town of Ten Sleep offers an escape from the oppressive summer heat of Bighorn Basin. This verdant valley is one of the few places in Wyoming where apple, peach, and pear trees grow. Rustic log buildings fill this tiny ranching and tourism center. Take away the cars and the asphalt and it's easy to imagine Ten Sleep as the location for some Hollywood film about the Green Valley.

The name Ten Sleep comes from the Sioux Indians who frequently stopped in this valley during their travels between a permanent camp along the Clarks Fork River in Montana and another one along the Platte River. Halfway between the two was Ten Sleeps, so named because they measured distances in the number of nights it took to get to a place. The town of Ten Sleep was established as a trading center for the Scottish and Irish sheepmen who came here in the 1890s.

Sights

The main sights in Ten Sleep are the comfortable, slow-paced town itself and its pretty setting. **Pioneer Museum** behind the Flagstaff Cafe has local artifacts and is open daily 9 a.m.-4 p.m. in the summer. An old sheriff wagon sits on main street ready to haul off the bad guys. Ask at the museum for directions to the Indian pictographs on the Walt Patch Ranch. Lions Club Park has an artesian well that is a favorite place to fill jugs with cold water.

Drop into the **Ten Sleep Saloon,** tel. (307) 366-9208, or the **Big Horn Bar,** tel. (307) 366-9222, for a cold one with local ranchers and cowboys. Ten Sleep Saloon has a bar inlaid with 5,052 pennies and 233 nickels; the bartender claims that they started out with inlaid silver dollars but this is all they had left after the taxes!

Nearby Sights

Just west of Ten Sleep is the turnoff to **Castle Gardens,** a scenic area of wind-carved sandstone badlands in all sizes and shapes. It's a 12-mile drive via a dirt road that may become impassable when wet. Castle Gardens has pic-

the sleepy town of Ten Sleep

THE TEN SLEEP RAID

Cattlemen have always viewed sheep with disdain, regarding them as despoilers of the range, "locusts with hooves" or "range maggots." Cattle reached Wyoming's grazing lands first, and when sheep began to arrive in large numbers around the turn of the 20th century, the cattle owners fought back with intimidation and violence. In many places, the cattlemen declared a "dead line," and any sheep or sheepherder that came into that area risked being killed. (One such line existed in Jackson Hole; even today the county has just 300 sheep as opposed to 12,000 cattle.) Despite these threats, sheep ranching was simply too lucrative to pass up; by 1889, Bighorn Basin was overrun with more than 387,000 sheep—and boasted fewer than 22,000 cattle.

Perhaps 10,000 sheep throughout the state were killed by cattlemen; some flocks were driven over cliffs, others were dynamited or attacked by dogs, and thousands more died from gunshots. Many of Wyoming's sheepherders were viciously attacked, and at least 16 were murdered. The most notorious of all these incidents took place along Spring Creek near Ten Sleep in 1909. Joe Emge, a hotheaded cattleman turned sheepman, announced plans to trail his sheep across the dead line set up in the Nowater Creek area. One April night just after the sheep had reached the grazing grounds, at least half a dozen masked men burst into the camp and murdered Emge, his partner, and a herder. The killers set the wagons afire and shot many sheep before disappearing into the night, leaving a grisly scene to be discovered the next morning.

The investigation pointed directly at a local cattleman, and after testifying before a grand jury one of the suspected raiders was found dead. Officials judged it a suicide, but many suspected that the cattleman had been waylaid by others seeking to silence anyone who might tell the truth. Eventually, two men broke the silence and fingered five others, including several prominent ranchers. All five were convicted and spent from three years to life in prison for the murders. Like the Johnson County War two decades earlier, this incident helped turn many people against the cattlemen. Sheep continued to grow in importance for a while—Wyoming became the largest wool producer in the country—but overgrazing, the severe winter of 1911-12, and the removal of a wool tariff the next year led to a long decline. Even today, though, Wyoming is America's second-largest producer of wool.

nic tables, an outhouse, and two free campsites. A few miles south of Castle Gardens are the **Honeycombs,** where the landscape is pockmarked with holes. Not far away, **Big Cedar Ridge** contains an abundance of fossilized leaves and flowers on BLM land. You can dig in existing pits, but don't start new holes.

Another great drive connects Ten Sleep with tiny Lysite, approximately 60 miles to the south. The first 21 miles are paved to a spot on the map called Big Trails. South of here, the road turns to gravel and takes you along lazy Nowood River through dramatic canyons and past grand old ranches. As you approach Lysite the landscape turns desertlike, with cactus mixing with sage and sand. It's a classic Wyoming drive, and passable in two-wheel-drive vehicles.

The **Salt Lick Trail** is an enjoyable short hike (1.25 miles) into an open forest of ponderosa pine and juniper, with fine views across Bighorn Basin. The trailhead is 5.5 miles east of Ten Sleep.

Tensleep Canyon

Six miles east of town, US Hwy. 16 passes the unmarked entrance to the 8,500-acre **Tensleep Preserve,** managed by The Nature Conservancy. The preserve follows a 12-mile stretch of Canyon Creek and is a great place for day-hikes and to watch for peregrine falcons and Cooper's hawks. Workshops and natural history programs take place here throughout the summer, and camping (in wall tents) and delicious meals are available. The preserve is open to visitors from late May to mid-October. Some parts of the preserve are open only by reservation; get details by calling (307) 366-2671.

Shortly beyond the turnoff to the Tensleep Preserve, the highway climbs up spectacular Tensleep Canyon toward 9,666-foot Powder River Pass in the Big Horn Mountains. **Wigwam Fish Rearing Station,** run by the Wyoming Game and Fish Dept., is five miles east of town. Another six miles up is the turnoff to the old log buildings that house **Ten Sleep Fish Hatchery.** Both of these are open daily for tours. (See the Powder River Country chapter for sights east of here as US Hwy. 16 climbs over the majestic Big Horns.)

Accommodations and Camping

Log Cabin Motel, tel. (307) 366-2320, has rooms for $42 s or d (some with microwaves and fridges) and RV parking for $12. If you're camping elsewhere, take showers at the laundromat here for $3. The nicest local lodging place is **Valley Motel,** tel. (307) 366-2321, where rooms cost $30 s or $38 d. It also has a kitchenette; $48 for four people. Both Inexpensive.

Pitch your tent in town at **Ten Broek RV Park,** tel. (307) 366-2250, for $11 ($12 for RVs); open April-October.

The closest public camping is eight miles east of Ten Sleep inside Bighorn National Forest at **Tensleep Creek Campground.** Only five sites are available ($9; open mid-May through October) at this peaceful riverside spot surrounded by tall cottonwoods. You can also stay at a dozen other Forest Service campgrounds farther east for $7-9. Reserve a place at the Forest Service's Boulder Park, Lakeview, Middle Fork, Sitting Bull, South Fork, and West Tensleep Lake Campgrounds by calling (877) 444-6777 ($8.65 reservation fee). You can also make campsite reservations on the web at www.reserveusa.com.

Food

Flagstaff Cafe, tel. (307) 366-2330, has great breakfasts, burgers, and steaks. Housed in a building that dates from 1914, **Mountain Man Cafe,** tel. (307) 366-2660, still has the original tin ceiling. All-American meals include a salad bar and homemade pies; closed winters.

A classic country store, **Ten Sleep Mercantile** sells groceries and supplies. Quite a lot of fruit grows in the country around town; ask here to see who might have fruit for sale.

Events and Recreation

Come to Ten Sleep on the **Fourth of July** for a very popular rodeo, parade, outdoor dances, and a kids' sheep ride. **Ten Sleep Celebration Days** (second weekend in July) brings a junior rodeo, an ice cream social, races, and family events of all types.

Horseback rides are available locally from **Canyon Creek Adventures,** tel. (307) 374-6666, and **Renegade Rides,** tel. (307) 366-2604 or (888) 447-2604.

THERMOPOLIS

The town of Thermopolis (pop. 3,400) lies on the southern edge of the Bighorn Basin surrounded by the Owl Creek Mountains. It's one of two Wyoming towns established because of a hot springs; the other is Saratoga. Thermopolis comes from the words *thermae* (Latin for "hot springs") and *polis* (Greek for "city"). It is a fitting title, since the world's largest hot springs are the centerpiece of Thermopolis. Hot Springs State Park is right in town, encompassing both a wonderful public bathhouse and several commercial endeavors. The economy of Thermopolis was for a long while dependent upon oil and ranching, but tourism has become increasingly important.

Thermopolis came into existence with the 1896 purchase of Big Springs from the Shoshone and Arapahoes. Streets were laid out wide enough for a 16-mule team to turn around in the middle of the block—something still obvious today, though you don't often see mule teams on the streets. Because of their medicinal value, the hot springs attracted many people, and the town became a health center, particularly for those suffering from arthritis and polio. There wasn't much timber around here, so the first lodging place, the Sage Brush Hotel, was made from a wooden frame laced with sagebrush and covered with a thatched roof of more sage.

HOT SPRINGS STATE PARK

History

Shoshone legend tells of a young warrior and his lover who were standing in the Wind River Canyon when an eagle feather—earned in battles with the enemy—blew out of his hair and wafted down the canyon. They raced after it and found it floating in an enormous hot spring with steam gushing from its mouth. The springs were a gift from the Great Spirit.

Originally part of the Wind River Reservation, Big Springs and 10 square miles of surrounding land were sold to the United States government in 1896 for the bargain price of $60,000. The treaty was signed by Shoshone Chief Washakie and Arapaho Chief Sharp Nose. In it, Washakie stipulated that some of the water must remain free to all people and that a campground be set aside for Indians: "I, Washakie, chief of Shoshones, freely give to the great white father these waters, belov'd by my people; that all may receive that great blessing of bodily health in the bathing." Thus was established Wyoming's first state park.

Today the park is the third-most-popular attraction in Wyoming; only Yellowstone and Grand Teton National Parks bring in more visitors. The park includes a variety of facilities: a state-run bathhouse, two commercial establishments, a

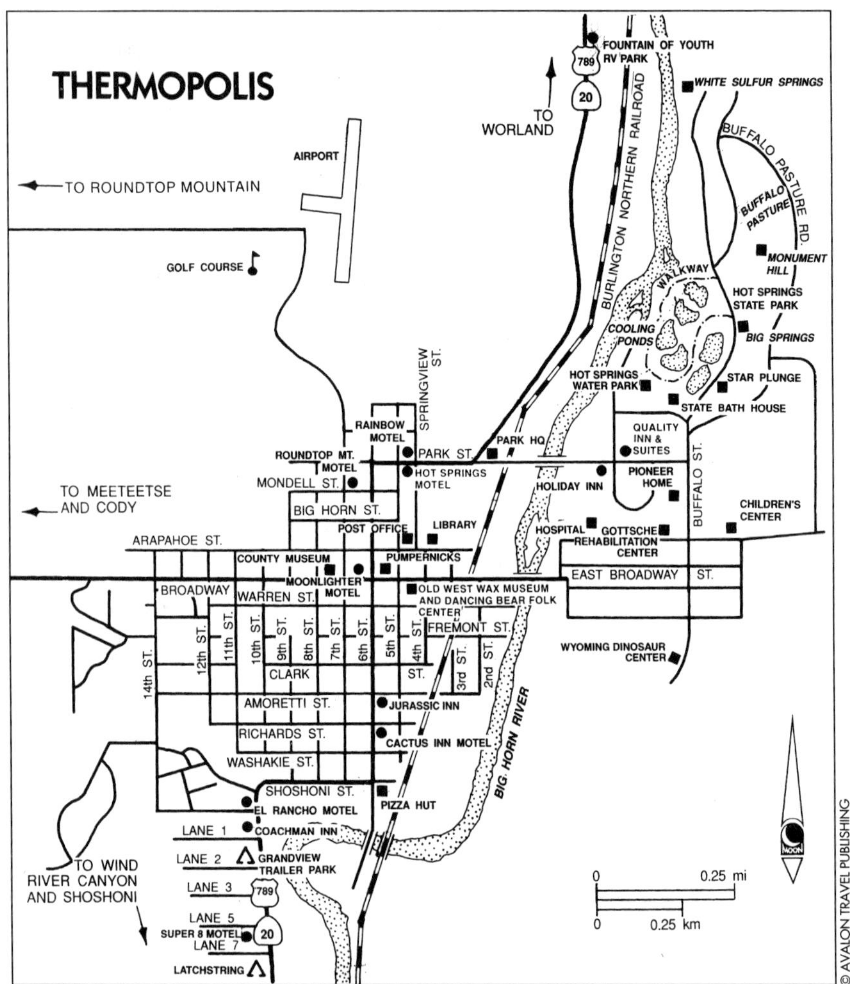

senior center, a rehabilitation center, and even a small herd of buffalo. Adjacent is the Holiday Inn spa facility. Park headquarters is the A-frame structure at the corner of Park St. and US Hwy. 789. Just behind here is an impressive travertine cone created when workers put in a vent pipe.

Big Springs

Big Springs flows at a rate of approximately 2,575 gallons per minute at 135° F and is considered the largest hot springs in the world. The springs are at the base of a small butte; just in case there might be some confusion, someone has placed white rocks along the hillside spelling out "World's Largest Mineral Hot Spring." A number of cooling ponds spread out in front of the springs, dropping water over terraces of lime and gypsum to the Bighorn River. (Because of the hot water, this stretch of the Bighorn River remains open through the winter, attracting ducks and other birds.) The cooling ponds are very colorful, with algae and minerals (particularly calcium carbonate, bicarbonate, sulfate, and sodium) adding splashes of reds, greens, browns, and yellows. A concrete path winds around the terraces and along the river, leading to a scenic **swinging bridge.** Many people who drink the mineral-rich water claim an array of medicinal benefits.

State Bath House

For an incredibly relaxing soak, be sure to visit the very nice State Bath House, tel. (307) 864-3765, open Mon.-Sat. 8 a.m.-5:30 p.m. and Sunday and holidays noon-5:30 p.m. No entry charge. The facilities are always exceptionally clean, and there are lockers to store your clothes. Rent towels and swimsuits here if you didn't bring your own. There are private tubs in the locker rooms (where you can temper the 104° F mineral water with cooler water), or you can head to the central indoor pool or an outdoor soaking pool (open May-Sept. only). The pools are fully handicapped accessible. Attendants make sure folks don't stay in the hot water for more than 20 minutes, since the heat can be weakening. This is not a place to clean up, and no soap is allowed—even in the showers.

More Park Attractions

Hellie's Tepee Spa, tel. (307) 864-9250, in the white domed building next to the state bathhouse, has indoor and outdoor pools, two spiraling water slides, four hot tubs, a steam room, a sauna, a mineral spa, weight room, and snack bar. Adults pay $7, seniors $5, and kids $3. Open daily 9 a.m.-9 p.m. all year. Massages are also available.

Even bigger is **Star Plunge,** tel. (307) 864-3771, also inside the state park, with indoor and outdoor pools, three slippery water slides, a high dive, steam room, vapor cave, three hot tubs, and tanning booths ($5 extra). The 500-foot-long outdoor slide is one of the longest in the nation. Admission to Star Plunge costs $7 adults, $5 seniors, and $2 kids under five. Towels, swimsuits, and inner tubes can also be rented. It's open daily 9 a.m.-9 p.m. year-round. (The state's largest outdoor mineral swimming pool, at Fountain of Youth RV Park, is described below under Campgrounds.)

Also on the grounds of the state park are **Gottsche Rehabilitation Center,** an outpatient treatment facility established in 1959 to make use of the medicinal properties of the hot springs, **Big Horn Basin Children's Center** for children with disabilities, and a **Wyoming Pioneer Home** for the elderly. A small **museum** in the basement of the Pioneer Home features arrowheads, baskets, and other Indian artifacts, as well as antiques from nearby ranches. A statue commemorating Chief Washakie's "gift of the smoking waters" stands in front of the home. Washakie would be proud of all the good his gift has done.

In addition to facilities associated with the hot springs, the park includes shady picnic tables and playgrounds. A rough trail cuts to the top of **Monument Hill** right behind Big Springs. The northeast portion of Hot Springs State Park includes a pasture where a herd of 20 or so **buffalo** roam. A loop road through the pasture gives you a chance to drive by. They are fed daily at 8:30 a.m.

OTHER SIGHTS

Museum

The Hot Springs Historical Museum, 700 Broadway, tel. (307) 864-5183, calls itself "one of the best small museums in the country" and lives up to this billing with an impressive collection of ranching and cowboy gear, historical photos, wagons,

Indian artifacts, and much more. The museum is open Mon.-Sat. 8 a.m.-5 p.m. and Sunday noon-4 p.m. June-Aug., and Mon.-Sat. 9 a.m.-4 p.m. the rest of the year. Entrance costs $3 for adults, $2 seniors and youths. Kids under five get in free. Find it on the web at www.trib.com/~museum.

The museum sprawls through two floors of the main building and lurches across the street to include an agriculture building, an old schoolhouse, a petroleum building, and a caboose. The main museum houses various displays of frontier life: a newspaper shop, dentist's office (complete with frightening tools), blacksmith shop, and general store. The cherry wood bar from the Hole-in-the-Wall Saloon is a particularly popular stopping point; here members of the famous outlaw gang tipped their glasses with sympathetic locals.

The Indian artifact collection downstairs is very impressive, not just because of the thousands of arrowheads but also because it includes an elk hide painted by Shoshone Chief Washakie. Outside, the 1920 Middleton Schoolhouse comes complete with old desks; check out the amusing letters from present-day schoolchildren. Kids of all ages love traipsing through the old Burlington Northern caboose and trying to figure out how the agriculture building's amazing 1926 Case threshing machine worked. The petroleum building houses exhibits on drilling for and refining oil, including old gusher photos and a gigantic power unit once used to pump oil before the arrival of electric pumps.

Wyoming Dinosaur Center

In 1992, three Germans formed a prospecting company to search for fossils in the Bighorn Basin. With the help of an American fossil expert they located a promising site just out of Thermopolis and the following year discovered a sauropod (a plant-eating dinosaur from the Jurassic Period). Realizing that many more dinosaurs lay below the surface, they purchased the land and began digging, later unearthing the most complete skeleton of a brachiosaur ever found, along with many more species. The discoveries led to the creation of the Wyoming Dinosaur Center, housed in a warehouse-type metal building on the eastern edge of town. The facility contains skeletons and casts from dinosaurs found not only nearby but also in Russia, Germany, and China. These include *Tyrannosaurus rex,* dinosaur eggs, and marine reptiles. Although this is a for-profit venture with a gift shop selling educational dinosaur toys, it's not just a gee-whiz exhibit to wow the kids—the emphasis is heavily on science. Excellent displays reveal the evolution of life on the planet (despite what they think in Kansas). Visitors can watch workers prepare specimens in the lab or take a tour of the Warm Springs Ranch dig site two miles away where excavations continue every summer. There's no chance of running out of specimens; the deposit contains an estimated 100,000 bones. The hour-long tours include a bus ride from the Dinosaur Center and a presentation on digging techniques and local geology. These tours cost $10 for adults and $7 for kids and seniors and are free for children under five. Entrance to the Dinosaur Center is $6 for adults, $3.50 for kids and seniors, and free for children under five. Special Kids' Digs take place several times each summer and include classes, geology lessons, and fossil digging. The museum is open daily 8 a.m.-8 p.m. mid-May to mid-September, and daily 10 a.m.-5 p.m. the rest of the year. For more information call (307) 864-2997 or (800) 455-3466, or find the center on the web at www.wyodino.org.

Legend Rock Petroglyph Site

One of the finest sites for Indian rock art in Wyoming lies in the foothills of the Owl Creek Mountains. Get there by driving 21 miles northwest from Thermopolis on State Hwy. 120. Turn left at the *second* Hamilton Dome turnoff (marked with a High Island Ranch sign) and after 5.6 miles, turn right onto the gravel Cottonwood Creek Road. Continue two miles, and just past the second cattle guard take the road on your left. Follow it a short distance to a parking area in front of a green gate marked "Legend Rock." The petroglyphs are a half-mile walk down from here. (If you want to drive down the hill, borrow the key for the gate from the Hot Springs State Park office in Thermopolis, tel. 307-864-2176.) The total distance from State Hwy. 120 to the petroglyph site is eight miles.

Hundreds of petroglyphs covering several time periods and styles have been found on the nearby sandstone cliffs. There are deer, bison, elk, and various human figures, but most unusual is a rabbit, the only one known in Wyoming rock art. The rabbit is similar to ones on Mimbres ceramic items from A.D. 1000; the Mimbres are from New Mexico. The rock art at Legend Rock may have been associated with shamanism and ritual healing, and some sections have been dated to 2,000 years old. Please do your part to protect this sacred site by not touching the petroglyphs. Owl Creek flows not far away, and oil pumpjacks dot the nearby hills (Hamilton Dome is one of the most important oil fields in Bighorn Basin).

West of Legend Rock is **Anchor Dam,** a major engineering blunder. Shortly after the dam was completed in 1960, a 300-foot-wide sinkhole developed in the porous limestone underlaying the reservoir. The hole was filled with dirt and rock, but it collapsed again. The second time the repair held, but new sinkholes appear each year. After decades of this—and millions of dollars down the proverbial sinkhole—the reservoir still only fills halfway in the best years.

Other Sights

Thermopolis seems to attract an unusual mix of attractions, the strangest being the **Old West Wax Museum and Dancing Bear Folk Center,** 119 S. 6th, tel. (307) 864-9396. The 250 teddy bears hang out downstairs, and some are arranged in "historical" settings—including teddy bears on the Titanic. Also here is a textile studio, plus classes and demonstrations. Upstairs is a wax museum that was housed in Jackson for many years. It includes a number of Old West figures such as Butch Cassidy, Chief Washakie, and General Custer. This odd combination of wax figures and stuffed bears is open daily 9 a.m.-7 p.m. in the summer, and daily 10 a.m.-5 p.m. the rest of the year. Entrance costs $3.50 for adults, or $2.50 for seniors and kids; free for children under eight. It's on the web at www.dancingbear.org.

ACCOMMODATIONS AND CAMPING

Motels

Because of the popularity of Thermopolis during the summer, it's a good idea to reserve ahead (or check in early) to be assured of a place. Accommodations are listed below from least to most expensive. Add a seven percent tax to the rates.

Hot Springs Motel, 401 Park St., tel. (307) 864-2303, wins the prize for cheapest rooms in town: $30 s or $40 d, including some with kitchenettes. No phones in the rooms. Inexpensive. **Cactus Inn,** US Hwy. 20 South, tel. (307) 864-3155, charges $35 s or $45 d for standard rooms, and $85 for a two-room suite. All rooms have fridges and microwaves, and kitchenettes are available. Inexpensive-Moderate.

Named for the many dinosaur bones in the area, **Jurassic Inn,** 501 S. 6th, tel. (307) 864-2325 or (888) 710-3466, charges $35-45 s or d, including in-room fridges. The similarly priced **Coachman Inn,** 112 US Hwy. 20 South, tel. (307) 864-3141 or (888) 864-3854, has recently remodeled rooms, some with small fridges, for $38 s or $48 d. Stay at **El Rancho Motel,** 924 Shoshoni Rd., tel. (307) 864-2341 or (800) 283-2777, for $45 s or $50-55 d. All Inexpensive.

Rainbow Motel, 408 Park St., tel. (307) 864-2129 or (800) 554-8815, has a wide range of remodeled rooms. Standard rooms are $40-55 s or d, kitchenettes are $55 d; six-person suites and family rooms (some with kitchenettes) run $65-99. Inexpensive.

Roundtop Mountain Motel, 412 N. 6th, tel. (307) 864-3126 or (800) 584-9126, charges $59 s or $65 d for motel rooms, or $69 s or d for modern log cabins with full kitchenettes. Recommended. Moderate.

Best Western Moonlighter Motel, 600 Broadway, tel. (307) 864-2321 or (800) 528-1234, is one of the nicer local motels, with rooms for $58-60 s or $61-82 d, including use of an outdoor pool. Moderate.

Rooms go for $70 s or $75 d at the modern **Super 8 Motel,** Lane 5, Hwy. 20 S, tel. (307) 864-5515 or (800) 800-8000. Amenities include an indoor pool, jacuzzi, and continental breakfast. Moderate.

Inside Hot Springs State Park, **Quality Inn & Suites,** tel. (307) 864-2939 or (888) 919-9009, www.wyomingvacations.com, was known for many years as the Plaza Hotel. The historic brick walls remain, but that's where the similarity ends following a $2 million refurbishing. Bright and spacious rooms feature custom-made lodgepole furniture. Rates are $70-90 s or d, including a continental breakfast; suites (some with fireplaces) cost $105 s or d. The courtyard contains a small swimming pool and hot mineral spa. Moderate-Expensive.

Also within Hot Springs State Park, **Holiday Inn of the Waters,** tel. (307) 864-3131 or (800) 465-4329, is extremely popular with the over-65 set. Facilities include an outdoor pool, racquetball courts, an exercise room, mineral spa, soaking tubs, a steam room, massage, and more. Most of these cost extra. Summertime room rates are $98 s or d, but the rest of the year the motel offers reasonable two-night packages ($130-140 d) that include a complimentary dinner and bottle of champagne. Expensive.

Other Lodging Options

Faye's B&B, 1020 Arapahoe St., tel. (307) 864-5166, or (307) 864-3733 after 10 p.m., is a contemporary home that has four large guest rooms with king-size beds and shared baths. Rates are $70 s or $75 d, including a big ranch-style breakfast. Kids are accepted. Moderate.

The 45,000-acre **High Island Ranch & Cattle Co.,** tel. (307) 867-2374, is a working ranch with a gorgeously remote setting at Hamilton Dome north of Thermopolis. Guests can take part in cattle drives each spring and fall, May brandings, roundups, trout fishing, and other cowpoke adventures. Especially popular are the authentic 1800s cattle drives (no vehicles used). No hot tubs here—this is the real thing, with guests staying in canvas tents along the trail (bring your sleeping bag) and rustic cabins or bunkhouses at the ranch. Visits are by the week only and cost $1,990-3,100 for two people, all-inclusive. There's room for a maximum of 25 guests, and ranch activities take place late May to mid-September. Find the ranch on the web at www.gorp.com/highisland. Luxury.

Campgrounds

The closest public camping is 17 miles south in Wind River Canyon (see below). **Fountain of Youth RV Park,** two miles north of Thermopolis on US Hwy. 20, tel. (307) 864-3265, boasts Wyoming's largest mineral swimming pool, fed by what was intended to be an oil well. In 1918, C.F. Cross began drilling, but instead of hitting oil he struck hot mineral water, blowing the pipe casing out of the ground. Eventually a small travertine cone formed around the old casing. The "Sacajawea" well still flows at a rate of 1.3 million gallons per day. Not surprisingly, this is a very popular place with the "snowbird" RV crowd. The Labor Day breakfast in the pool is a favorite event. Open March-Oct., it costs $19 for RVs—same rate for tent spaces.

Grandview RV Park, 122 US Hwy. 20 S, tel. (307) 864-3463, has tent spaces for $13, RV hookups for $16. Showers for noncampers cost $3. Open mid-March to mid-November.

Eagle RV Park, on the south edge of town, tel. (307) 864-5262, charges $13 for tents, $18 for RVs. Basic cabins cost $18, and showers for noncampers are $3. Open mid-April through October.

Country Campin', tel. (307) 864-2416 or (800) 609-2244, lives up to its name with a country location five miles northeast of Thermopolis along the Bighorn River. Tent spaces are $14, and RV hookups cost $18; tepee rentals ($25) are a fun family option. Open mid-April through October.

FOOD

Some of the best lunches and dinners in Thermopolis can be found at **Pumpernick's,** 512 Broadway, tel. (307) 864-5151. Try the pita-pocket sandwiches for lunch, or the homemade desserts. Pumpernick's outside patio is a pleasant place for summertime dining. The unpretentious **Feed Bag,** 530 Arapahoe, tel. (307) 864-5177, serves all-American meals at a reasonable price. Very good home-baked sourdough bread. **Manhattan Inn Restaurant,** 526 Broadway, tel. (307) 864-2501, has spicy barbecued beef rib and excellent malts.

Legion Supper Club, at the golf course on Airport Hill, tel. (307) 864-3918, is the local steak and seafood spot. Pricey, but good. The Sunday brunch buffet is especially popular.

The Safari Club, at the Holiday Inn within Hot Springs State Park, tel. (307) 864-3131, has reasonably priced buffet breakfasts and a diverse dinner menu (entrées $7-22) that includes blackened prime rib, Alaskan king crab, and buffalo burgers. The walls are lined with dozens of big-game trophy mounts and pictures of great white hunters standing over their deceased quarry. Owner Jim Mills killed most of the animals hanging around here, creating what might be called a low-maintenance zoo. It's either appealing or appalling, depending upon your perspective. Bands sometimes play in the adjacent bar, where you can join the locals watching a game on the big-screen TV or at the pool table.

Get groceries from **Consumers' Thriftway,** 600 S. 6th, tel. (307) 864-3112, or **Don's IGA,** 225 S. 4th, tel. (307) 864-5576. Don's also has a small deli and bakery. Espresso and books are available at **The Storyteller,** 528 Broadway, tel. (307) 864-3272. Thermopolis has several fast-food places, including Pizza Hut, McDonald's, Taco John's, Blimpie's, and Subway.

OTHER PRACTICALITIES

Events and Entertainment

Held the first weekend in August at Hot Springs State Park, the **Gift of the Waters Pageant** commemorates the transfer of Big Springs to the federal government in 1896. The pageant has been presented every summer since 1950, with a cast that includes both local residents and Shoshone from the Wind River Indian Reservation in full regalia. A tepee camp is set up near the hot springs for the festivities. Other events during Gift of the Waters include Indian dancing, a parade, and an arts-and-crafts fair. **Hot Springs County Fair** is held that same weekend, with all the standard agricultural and ranching exhibits. In mid-August, **Ranch Days Rodeo** is a competition in which local ranches compete with one another.

Catch the latest flicks at **The Ritz,** 309 Arapahoe, tel. (307) 864-3118.

Recreation

Most of the recreation in Thermopolis takes place around the hot springs pools, but there are other things to do as well. **Roundtop Mountain,** the distinctive butte that dominates the area, is an enjoyable but fairly steep hike. Take 7th St. to Airport Hill and turn on the first left. After the cemetery, turn right onto a gravel road that takes you to the trailhead.

Rent clunker **bikes** from the Holiday Inn, tel. (307) 864-3131. The nine-hole **Legion Golf Course,** tel. (307) 864-5294, is on Airport Hill north of town. Miniature golfers may prefer **Sweet Spot Mini Golf,** 510 Park Street. The local bowling alley is also the A&W stand; find **A&W Bowling Center** at 942 Shoshoni.

A unique way to discover the Old West is the **Outlaw Trail Ride** in mid-August. This week-long, 100-mile trip follows the "Outlaw Trail" from the Hole-in-the-Wall country of Butch Cassidy and the Sundance Kid to Thermopolis. This isn't for dudes—you'll need to bring your own horse, bedroll, and gear—but excellent meals are provided. A trail ride fee covers food, horse feed, nightly entertainment, and more. Call (307) 864-2287 for information on this authentic not-for-profit adventure.

Shopping

The **Wild Bunch Gallery,** 426 S. 6th St., tel. (307) 864-2208 or (800) 637-5340, sells limited-edition prints and original paintings. Note the swastikas embedded in the bricks above the Andreen Consignment Shop at 509 Broadway; they're actually Indian symbols from a pre-Nazi era.

Information and Services

The **Thermopolis Chamber of Commerce,** tel. (307) 864-3192 or (800) 786-6772, has its office in the museum at 700 Broadway. Open Mon.-Fri. 8 a.m.-6 p.m. and Saturday 10 a.m.-4 p.m. in the summer, and Mon.-Fri. 9 a.m.-4 p.m. the rest of the year. Find the chamber on the web at www.thermopolis.com.

Hot Springs County Library is at 344 Arapahoe St., tel. (307) 864-3104. Wash your clothes at **Wishy Washy Laundromat,** 630 Shoshoni; open 24 hours a day in the summer. Get cash from **ATMs** at Don's IGA on 4th and Warren or the Texaco station on the south end of town.

Powder River/Coach USA, tel. (800) 442-3682, stops at Larry's Small Engine, 437 Warren, with scheduled bus service from Thermopolis to northern and eastern Wyoming.

WIND RIVER CANYON

South of Thermopolis, the highway cuts across lush irrigated farm fields. Turn around and you'll see the steep slopes of Roundtop Mountain dominating the vistas. The highway bridges the Bighorn River and then, four miles south of town, abruptly enters magnificent Wind River Canyon. At this point the river's name changes just as abruptly. Lewis and Clark had named the Bighorn River, Crow Indians the Wind River. Early explorers somehow concluded that they were two separate waterways and in the confusion Wind River Canyon became the "Wedding of the Waters." Above this point the river is called the Wind, below it the Big Horn. A bit confusing.

Floating and Fishing

Many people float the Bighorn River, putting in at the Wedding of the Waters and taking out in Thermopolis. It's an enjoyable and leisurely drift with nice scenery and excellent fishing for rainbow trout (average size 15 inches). A special permit is required to fish in the canyon above Wedding of the Waters since it is part of the Wind River Indian Reservation. **Canyon Sporting Goods,** 903 Shoshoni in Thermopolis, tel. (307) 864-2815, sells permits, along with fishing, boating, and camping gear.

Wind River Canyon Whitewater, tel. (307) 864-9343, leads exciting raft trips through the canyon during the summer, with the biggest water generally in June and July. Trips range from a quick two-hour drenching ($31 per person) to full dinner trips ($77 per person). In addition, this Indian-owned company offers overnight rafting trips and guided fishing. Find it on the web at www.wyoming.com/~whitewater. See the chamber of commerce in Thermopolis for a listing of other fishing outfitters.

Geologic History Lesson

The drive through Wind River Canyon is one of the most dramatic in Wyoming; US Hwy. 20 clings to the eastern bank of the river, and canyon walls rise up to 2,500 feet overhead. Tracks of the Burlington Northern Railroad (built in 1913) parallel the river on the other side, threading in and out through several tunnels. This place is a geologist's dream, slicing through rocks that grow progressively older as you continue south, with the oldest dating back to the Precambrian era, 2.7 billion years ago. A succession of roadside signs notes the various rock formations, and the Thermopolis Chamber of Commerce can provide you with a descriptive log of the canyon's complex geology.

At the upper end of the canyon, the road quickly climbs past Boysen Dam and into the open country of Boysen State Park (see Riverton Vicinity in the Wind River Mountains Country chapter). Within the canyon you'll find two attractive **campgrounds,** Upper and Lower Wind River State Park ($9 for nonresidents, or $4 for Wyoming residents). The river flows right alongside, and there are many big old cottonwoods, but highway noise may keep you awake at night. Free tours of **Boysen Powerplant,** tel. (307) 864-3772, are available Mon.-Fri. 8 a.m.-4 p.m., but call ahead to set one up.

DOVER PUBLICATIONS, INC.

POWDER RIVER COUNTRY

Powder River country is the most historically interesting part of a state overflowing with history. For the Indians who made this region their home, the basin was paradise, a place of massive bison herds and abundant forage for horses. Because of this richness, the area became a confrontation point between various Indian tribes and later between Indians and the invading whites who came in along the Bozeman Trail. As history progressed, the clashes were between the whites: cattlemen versus homesteaders, outlaws against lawmen. Today, the clashes have faded into memory, but the rich country remains. Coal, cattle, and sheep rule.

The Powder River Basin stretches from the crest of the Big Horn Mountains to the Black Hills and then south to Casper. The three largest settlements—Gillette, Sheridan, and Buffalo—dominate the region's economy. Sheridan and Buffalo provide gateways to the magnificent Big Horn Mountains, a recreation paradise capped by barren alpine peaks. Rolling grassland predominates across the Powder River Basin, accented by steep-sided buttes and lush riversides. The land is grazed extensively by cattle and sheep, though alfalfa and wheat are grown in many places. Coal, oil, and gas resources are vital to the economy of the area, especially around Gillette, making this the most important energy region in Wyoming. Despite the many large coal mines, the land remains relatively untouched. Nearly everyone chooses to live in the cities and smaller settlements, leaving enormous open expanses of land.

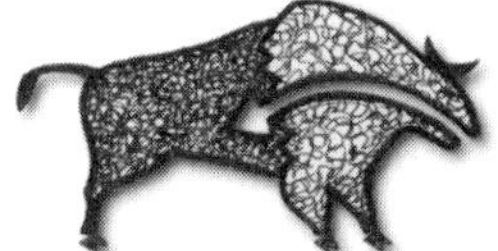
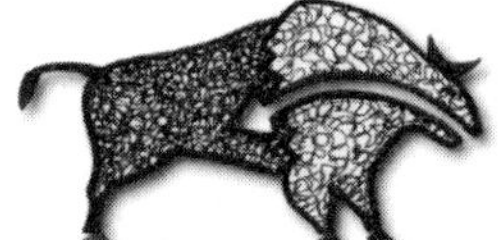
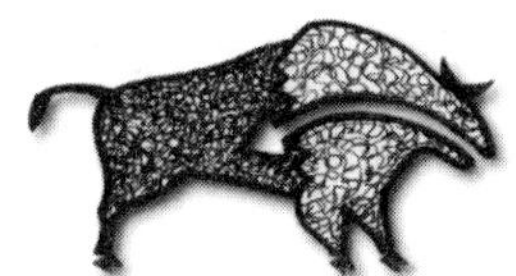

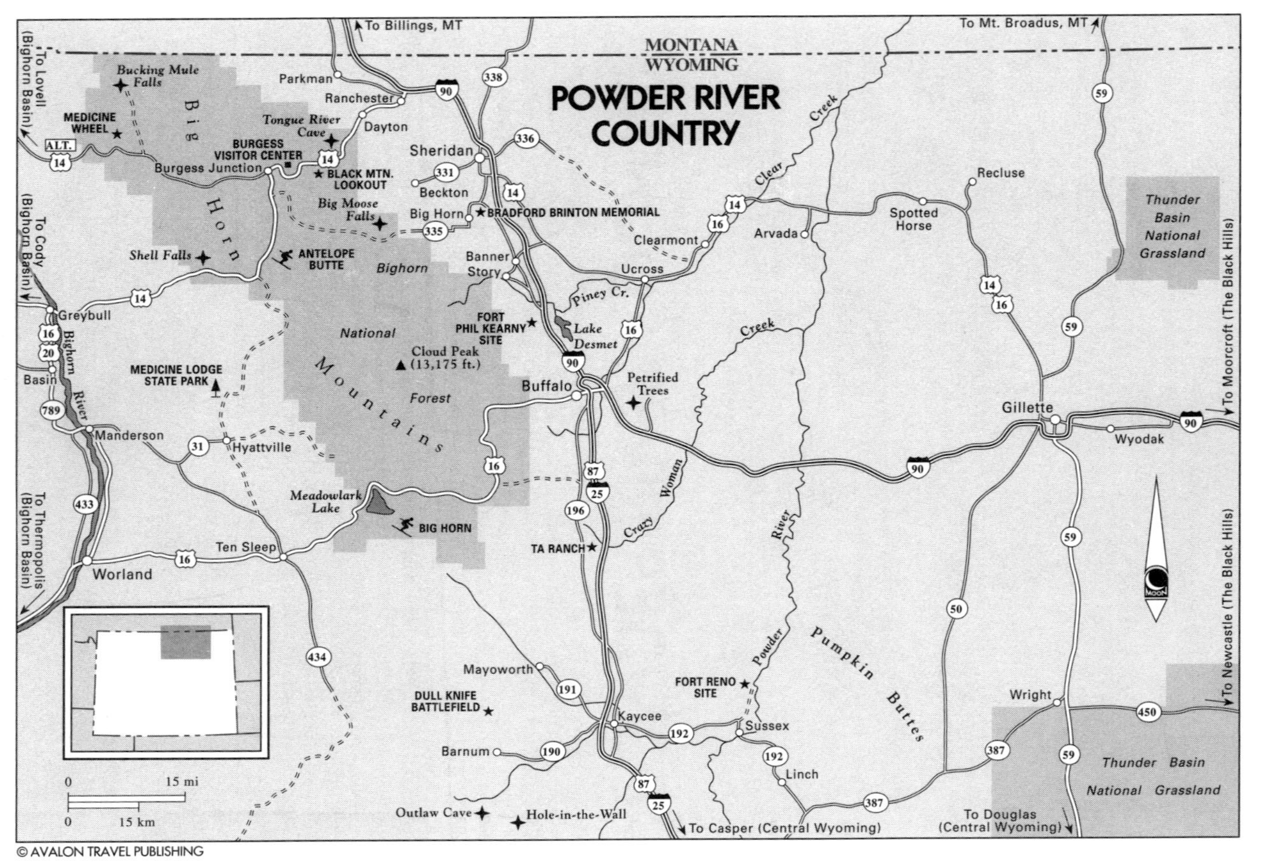
To Billings, MT
To Mt. Broadus, MT
MONTANA
WYOMING
POWDER RIVER
COUNTRY
Bucking Mule Falls
Parkman
Ranchester
Dayton
MEDICINE WHEEL
Big
Tongue River Cave
BURGESS VISITOR CENTER
Burgess Junction
BLACK MTN. LOOKOUT
Sheridan
Beckton
Recluse
Big Moose Falls
Big Horn
BRADFORD BRINTON MEMORIAL
Spotted Horse
Arvada
Clearmont
Clear Creek
Thunder Basin National Grassland
Shell Falls
Horn
ANTELOPE BUTTE
Banner
Story
Ucross
Bighorn
Piney Cr.
FORT PHIL KEARNY SITE
Lake Desmet
Creek
To Lovell (Bighorn Basin)
To Cody (Bighorn Basin)
Greybull
Bighorn River
Basin
MEDICINE LODGE STATE PARK
National
Cloud Peak (13,175 ft.)
Mountains
Forest
Buffalo
Petrified Trees
Gillette
Wyodak
To Moorcroft (The Black Hills)
Manderson
Hyattville
Meadowlark Lake
BIG HORN
Crazy Woman
River
To Thermopolis (Bighorn Basin)
Ten Sleep
Worland
TA RANCH
To Newcastle (The Black Hills)
Mayoworth
DULL KNIFE BATTLEFIELD
FORT RENO SITE
Powder
Pumpkin Buttes
Wright
Kaycee
Sussex
Barnum
Linch
Thunder Basin National Grassland
Outlaw Cave
Hole-in-the-Wall
To Casper (Central Wyoming)
To Douglas (Central Wyoming)
0 15 mi
0 15 km

BIG HORN MOUNTAINS

Sandwiched between two broad basins—Bighorn to the west and Powder River to the east—are the majestic Big Horn Mountains. To the early explorers, this 70-mile-long range was the Shining Mountains, a name inspired by its snowcapped peaks, some topping 13,000 feet. The Indians called it "Ahsahta," meaning "The Big Horns," after the Rocky Mountain bighorn sheep found here. Eventually, whites applied the name to all sorts of places in the region. The mountain country here is carpeted primarily with lodgepole and ponderosa pine, and Engelmann spruce and subalpine fir at higher elevations. While much of the country here is not as rugged as the mountains on the western border of Wyoming, the Big Horns do contain many rocky peaks above 9,000 feet, with 13,175-foot Cloud Peak crowning the skyline. Hundreds of small lakes reflect this dramatic scenery within the Cloud Peak Wilderness.

Nearly the entire range lies within **Bighorn National Forest,** a 1.1 million-acre chunk of public land set aside by Pres. Grover Cleveland in 1897. Forest headquarters is in Sheridan at 1969 S. Sheridan Ave., tel. (307) 672-0751, with district offices in Lovell, tel. (307) 548-6514, and Buffalo, tel. (307) 684-1100. Any of these can provide detailed forest maps ($4) and listings of permitted local outfitters. The **Big Horn Mountain Coalition** is a regionwide group that promotes recreation and development in the area and has links to local chambers of commerce; find the coalition on the web at www.bighorns.com.

This is multiple-use country, with logging, grazing, and recreation the primary attractions. Commercial logging has gone on within the forest for almost a century, and old tie flumes are still visible near Dayton. At one time, vast numbers of sheep grazed the Big Horns, totaling perhaps half a million. Thousands of sheep and cattle still graze in these mountains, and sheepherder camps are common sights in the high meadows.

Most visitors simply drive through the Big Horns on one of the three scenic highways, but the country is well worth stopping to savor, especially if you're a fan of waterfalls. There are many campgrounds, more than 850 miles of hiking trails, and good fishing for rainbow, cutthroat, brook, and brown trout. Come winter, the mountains become a popular destination for cross-country skiers, snowboarders, downhill skiers, and snowmobilers. More than 350 miles of groomed trails help make the Big Horns one of the top 10 snowmobiling destinations in America. A number of mountain lodges rent the beasts.

There's quite a bit of wildlife to see here, too. Bighorn sheep have been reintroduced to the

A sheepherder savors the new day in the Big Horn Mountains.

area and may be seen on the west slope of the mountains. No grizzlies here, but quite a few black bears live in the mountains, especially on the northeastern slopes. Also look for mule and white-tailed deer, elk, and moose. (The moose are not native; they were transplanted from Jackson Hole beginning in 1948.)

CRUISIN' THROUGH

Three paved highways cut across the Big Horn Mountains, providing popular connections between Yellowstone and the Black Hills. US Hwys. 14 and 16 are both kept plowed through the winter, while US Hwy. 14A generally closes November through May. All three have National Scenic Byway status, something that becomes more obvious with each mile you travel.

Highway 16

US Hwy. 16 climbs across the southern end of the range from Ten Sleep to Buffalo and is the easiest way across the Big Horns. More than a dozen Forest Service campgrounds line the route. This was the original "Black and Yellow Trail," first proposed in 1912 as a link between Chicago, the Black Hills, and Yellowstone. The first caravan of automobiles made it over the old sheepwagon track the following year, reaching Yellowstone after 18 hard days on the road. By the 1920s, the highway was marked by poles with alternating black and yellow bands. For many years, this was the main route to Yellowstone.

East from Ten Sleep, US Hwy. 16 parallels cottonwood-lined Tensleep Creek, climbing past impressive red and yellow cliffs. A cross and marker commemorate Gilbert Leigh, an Irish nobleman who fell to his death while hunting here in 1884 (he was caught in an October snowstorm and, unable to see his way, slipped over the cliff). Eventually the switchbacks take you up to **Meadowlark Lake,** a popular winter destination for both cross-country skiers and 'bilers. The dirt road to **High Park Lookout Tower** is two miles east of here. Look for flower-bedecked **St. Christopher's Chapel of the Big Horns** as this side road climbs to the fire tower (not in use). Great views from the top. East of here, the road winds over Powder River Pass, providing breathtaking views into Cloud Peak Wilderness.

SIGHTSEEING HIGHLIGHTS FOR POWDER RIVER COUNTRY

- Big Horn Mountains, including Medicine Wheel and Cloud Peak Wilderness
- Trail End State Historic Site, Sheridan Inn, and King's Saddlery in Sheridan
- Bradford Brinton Memorial Museum near Big Horn
- Fort Phil Kearny
- Jim Gatchell Memorial Museum and Occidental Hotel in Buffalo
- Hole-in-the-Wall Country near Kaycee
- Rockpile Museum and Einstein's Adventurarium in Gillette
- Gillette and Wright area coal mines
- Popular events: Sheridan Wyo Rodeo (July), PRCA Rodeo in Gillette (July), and Deke Latham Memorial PRCA Rodeo in Kaycee (September)

Highway 14

Open all year, US Hwy. 14 offers an equally impressive passage over the Big Horns between Greybull and Dayton. Above the dot of a town called Shell the road passes a remarkably phallic rocky butte, then catches Shell Creek and winds with it through the deep red rocks of dramatic **Shell Canyon,** past Shell Falls and the Antelope Butte Ski Area, before topping out at Granite Pass. (The name "Shell" appears repeatedly throughout the local topography thanks to the fossil invertebrate shells commonly found in the rocks.) At 120-foot-high **Shell Falls,** approximately eight miles east of Shell on US Hwy. 14, you'll find a visitor center with books and maps. It's open daily mid-May to mid-September. Nearby are several short walking trails with interpretive signs. Keep your eyes open for water ouzels, the water-loving gray birds that often nest beneath waterfalls. After joining US Hwy. 14A at Burgess Junction, the road continues to Twin Buttes, Sibley Lake, and the amusing jumble of rocks called Fallen City, before zigzagging sharply down to Tongue River Canyon and

> *The Crow country is a good country; the Great Spirit has put it in exactly the right place. It is good for horses—and what is a country without horses? On the Columbia, the people are poor and dirty; they paddle about in canoes and eat fish. On the Missouri the water is muddy and bad. To the north of the Crow country it is too cold, and to the south it is too hot. The Crow country is just right. The water is clear and sweet. There are plenty of buffalo, elk, deer, antelope, and mountain sheep. It is the best wintering place in the world and has plenty of game. Is it any wonder that the Crows have fought long and hard to defend this country, which we love so much?*
>
> —Crow Chief Arapooish, describing Powder River Basin

the town of Dayton. A Forest Service **visitor center** located a mile and a half east of Burgess Junction near Twin Buttes is open daily 9 a.m.-5 p.m. from mid-May to mid-September.

Highway 14A

US Hwy. 14A (officially this is Alternate US Hwy. 14) is generally cleared of snow by Memorial Day, remaining open till mid-October. Engineers like this road, modeled after similar routes in the Alps. At the time it was built, it was said to be the most expensive stretch of road in America. Locals claim the "A" in "US Hwy. 14A" stands for adventure, and with three different runaway truck ramps and 10% grades on some stretches it's easy to see why. The climb to the top is *very* long and steep, but the views make the tough climb worthwhile. US Hwy. 14A rises over the Big Horns from Lovell to Burgess Junction, where it meets US Hwy. 14. Along the way you're treated to miles of open sage-and-grass country with timbered islands on Bald and Little Bald Mountains, spectacular Bucking Mule Falls, and the famous Medicine Wheel. Watch for moose and deer in the meadows near Burgess Junction.

An enjoyable side loop is **Burgess Road** (Forest Rd. 15). The gravel road starts at Burgess Junction and continues approximately 20 miles to a junction with US Hwy. 14A near Bald Mountain. This side loop provides fine opportunities to view deer and elk, and it provides a grand vista from Burgess Rd. Overlook.

CAMPING

With 32 different Forest Service campgrounds ($8-10) in the area, you should have no trouble finding places to commune with nature. Most are above 5,000 feet in elevation, making for welcome escapes from summertime heat. During weekends in July and August, campgrounds along the main roads are frequently filled (get there before 2 p.m.), but harder-to-reach campgrounds usually have space. Reservations ($8.65 extra) are available for seven popular campgrounds by calling (877) 444-6777, or reserve via the web at www.reserveusa.com. Forest Service offices in Sheridan, Buffalo, and Lovell can all provide details on dates, cost, and access to these camping places, or find the same info on the web at www.fs.fed.us/r2/bighorn. In addition to the official campgrounds, you can camp anywhere in Bighorn National Forest for free, as long as you are a half mile off the main highways.

The BLM's **Five Springs Campground** ($6; open May-Sept.) is just off US Hwy. 14A on the western border of the national forest. Scenic **Five Springs Falls** is nearby.

ACCOMMODATIONS AND FOOD

Scattered throughout the Big Horns are seven mountain lodges and a guest ranch, most of which have bars and restaurants. Several of these are open year-round, providing a good base for snowmobiling and skiing adventures.

Lodges Along US Highway 14

You'll find year-round accommodations at **Bear Lodge Resort,** located at Burgess Junction (8,300 feet in elevation), tel. (307) 655-2444. Standard motel rooms are $69 s or d. Rustic cabins cost $30 (some of these can sleep nine people), but you'll need to bring your own linen and take showers in the lodge. Guests will enjoy the two outdoor hot tubs and the indoor swimming pool. Pitch a tent for $8, park RVs for $19. If you're staying elsewhere, take a shower for $2. Bear Lodge rents mountain bikes in the summer, and in winter you can rent snowmobiles or cross-country skis. The lounge is a great place to shoot a game of pool or tip a brew, and it occasionally has live music. Also here are a full-service restaurant, gas pumps, and a gift shop with a few groceries and supplies. Budget-Moderate.

Arrowhead Lodge, tel. (307) 655-2388 or (307) 672-4111, four miles east of Burgess Junction on US Hwy. 14, offers very basic cabins with kitchenettes for $30-51 s or d, and motel rooms for $44-71 s or d. Park RVs for $15 a night. If you aren't staying here you can use the showers for $3. Arrowhead is open year-round. Budget-Moderate.

Snowshoe Lodge is six miles south of Burgess Junction on US Hwy. 14, just southwest of Antelope Butte Ski Area. Because of its mountain location, the lodge is particularly popular with snowmobilers and skiers in the winter and hunters each fall. It's also a favorite spot for summertime weddings and family reunions. Stay in the lodge for $75 s or $150 d, including a filling dinner and never-leave-hungry breakfast; folks come back just for the meals. Snowshoe Lodge also features an outdoor hot tub, lounge, and double-deck porches. More-rustic accommodations include eight-person cabins for $50/night, and sheepwagons for $35 d. Neither of these have linen, but both provide cooking facilities and outhouses. Also available is a two-bedroom trailer with bath and kitchen; $65 for six people. Winter is the busy season here, and you'll need to book a year ahead for weekends in February and March. Call the lodge at (307) 765-2669, or by radio phone at (307) 568-2960, unit 7113. Inexpensive-Premium.

Spend a delightful week in the Big Horn Mountains at **Ranger Creek Guest Ranch,** tel. (888) 817-7787, www.netset.com/~billc. The lodge is approximately 16 miles east of Shell on Forest Service land near Antelope Butte Ski Area. Guests (maximum 30 people) stay in rustic log cabins around a central bathhouse and enjoy horseback rides, trout fishing, children's programs, day-trips to Cody, evening barbecues, nature talks, and cowboy singing. The ranch is open year-round, with fall hunting trips and winter snowmobiling. A jacuzzi is available to soak those tired bones at day's end. All-inclusive weekly rates are $1,890 for two people, or visit in the off-season for $130 d including breakfast and dinner. Luxury.

Lodges Along US Highway 16

Ol' Wyoming Lodge (formerly called Deer Haven Lodge), 18 miles east of Ten Sleep on US Hwy. 16, tel. (888) 244-4676, charges $28 d for small cabins, or $45 for larger four-person cabins. All are plain-Jane units with woodstoves and a separate bathhouse; bring your own towels. The lodge also has older motel rooms that sleep four for $65. A restaurant, lounge, and gas pumps are on the premises. Budget-Moderate.

Lake Resort, 22 miles east of Ten Sleep (42 miles west of Buffalo) along US Hwy. 16, tel. (307) 366-2424 or (888) 244-4676, has recently undergone a major transformation into the finest resort in the Big Horns. Lodging includes rustic cabins with a central bathhouse ($55 d or $65 for four), motel rooms with private baths ($75 d or $95 for four people), and comfortable cottages with kitchenettes ($90-105 for one-bedroom units). The resort also rents rowboats, canoes, and paddle boats for the lake, as well as mountain bikes to explore surrounding country. It has a restaurant serving three meals a day, plus a lounge and gift shop; open year-round. Horseback rides are available in the summer at nearby Willow Park. Inexpensive-Expensive.

The Pines Lodge, 14 miles west of Buffalo on US Hwy. 16, tel. (307) 351-1010 or (307) 684-5204, has older cabins that sleep four. Rates start at $35 for the most basic units with a separate bathhouse, up to $95 for those with private baths, kitchens, and fireplaces. Kids can throw in a line at the private fishing pond. The cabins are open May-Oct., and the restaurant and lounge are also open on winter weekends. Budget-Expensive.

Open year-round, **South Fork Inn,** 16 miles west of Buffalo on US Hwy. 16, tel. (307) 267-2609, has a wide variety of cabins, from basic units with a shared bathhouse ($45 d) up to six-person units with private bath for $85. Also here is a restaurant and small bar. The corrals at South Fork runs horseback rides and drop-camp trips. Inexpensive.

The Forest Service's historic **Muddy Guard Station** was constructed by the Civilian Conservation Corps in the 1930s and is now available for rent to the public. The log building has propane lights and a woodstove but no running water or electricity. It sleeps up to five and rents for $40 per day. Located 25 miles west of Buffalo on US Hwy. 16, this unique cabin is open year-round; call (307) 684-1100 for reservations. Budget.

WINTER SPORTS

Cross-country Skiing

The Big Horns provide some of the finest snow in Wyoming, with groomed cross-country ski trails at several locations. **Sibley Lake** has 15 miles of trails and a warming hut off US Hwy. 14; **Willow Park** has 23 miles of trails near Meadowlark Lake; and **Pole Creek** has 13 miles of trails and a warming hut off US Hwy. 16. Trail descriptions are available from local Forest Service offices. The rest of the forest makes for outstanding skiing most of the winter, but you'll need to break your own trail.

Downhill Skiing and Snowboarding

Big Horn Ski Resort is next to Lake Resort along US Hwy. 16 (22 miles east of Ten Sleep and 42 miles west of Buffalo) and was formerly called Powder Pass Ski Area. New owners have greatly transformed this small area with an 800-foot vertical rise, and it now has a double and a triple chairlift, lights on all runs, and extensive snowboard facilities that include three half-pipes and a terrain park. Snowmaking equipment will lengthen the ski season, and ice skating is also available. Other improvements include a new ski lodge and professional snowboarding and skiing instruction. The resort opens around Thanksgiving and closes in April. Lifts operate daily through the winter, and tickets cost $30 for adults, or $10 for skiing and boarding under the lights. Get food, drinks, and rentals at the base lodge. Call (888) 244-4676 for more information.

Antelope Butte Ski Area, tel. (307) 655-9530, is a small family ski area 60 miles west of Sheridan and 35 miles east of Greybull on US Hwy. 16. It has two chairlifts and a platter lift; the vertical rise is 1,000 feet from a base elevation of 8,400 feet. Antelope Butte is open Wed.-Sun. and holidays 9:30 a.m.-4 p.m. mid-December through March. Lift tickets cost $25 for adults, $14 for ages 7-15; free for young-uns. Rent skis and snowboards, or take lessons from the ski school. The lodge serves light meals.

Snowmobiling

Snowmobilers will find 300 miles of groomed trails throughout the national forest; get a route map from chamber of commerce offices or the Forest Service. Rent snowmobiles at **Lake Resort,** tel. (307) 366-2424 or (888) 244-4676; **Ol' Wyoming Lodge,** tel. (888) 244-4676; **Bear Lodge Resort,** tel. (307) 655-2444; **Arrowhead Lodge,** tel. (307) 655-2388 or (307) 672-4111; or **South Fork Inn,** tel. (307) 267-2609.

HIKES AND SIGHTS

You'll find plenty to see and do in the Big Horns, including Medicine Wheel and the Cloud Peak Wilderness (see below). Stop by the Forest Service office in Sheridan, Buffalo, or Lovell for descriptions of other hiking trails.

Sheep Mountain Area Trails

Several trails take off from Sheep Mountain Rd. on US Hwy. 14A approximately 30 miles east of Lovell and three miles east of the turnoff to Medicine Wheel. **Littlehorn Trail** parallels the Little Bighorn River for 18 miles. Along the way you'll see 1,600-foot canyon faces and water fountaining off the limestone cliffs of Leaky Mountain. The trailhead is two miles up Sheep Mountain Rd. (Forest Rd. 14). A half mile farther up the road is the trailhead for **Porcupine Falls,** a 200-foot-tall cascade accessible via a very steep half-mile path. Along the way the trail passes a 1930s-era gold mine. Much of the area here was burned in a 1988 forest fire.

One of the not-to-be-missed places in the Big Horns is spectacular **Bucking Mule Falls,** a 600-foot cascade dropping into Devil Canyon. The trailhead for Bucking Mule Falls lies 11 miles off US Hwy. 14A via Sheep Mountain Rd. and Devil Canyon Rd., and the waterfall is a three-mile roundtrip hike. You can also do an 11-mile hike by following the trail to the falls and then continuing south to Porcupine Campground.

More Hikes and Caves

Black Mountain Lookout, west of Dayton on US Hwy. 14, offers surprisingly dramatic vistas from the top of a 9,300-foot peak. This old Forest Service fire lookout is open to the public and sits at the end of a one-mile trail. Get there by turning south on Forest Rd. 16 when it leaves US Hwy. 14 two miles west of the Fallen City area and follow it four miles to the trailhead.

The trailhead for **Tongue River Canyon** is 3.5 miles southwest of Dayton to the end of Tongue Canyon Road. This trail climbs up the canyon for a total of 11.5 miles, offering glimpses of the old McShane brothers' tie flume—built in 1894 and stretching for 26 miles—the fast-flowing blue-ribbon fishing stream (cutthroat, rainbow, brook, and German brown trout), and canyon walls reaching a thousand feet into the air. Ambitious hikers may want to continue all the way to Burgess Junction. Locals float down parts of the river during the spring, when water levels are high.

Tongue River Cave is near the Tongue River Canyon trailhead and stays open all year. With well over a mile of passages, it's one of Wyoming's most popular caves but has been considerably vandalized with broken formations, trash, and graffiti. Because of its size, inexperienced spelunkers can become lost, so ask locally for someone willing to act as a guide. More than 100 other caves honeycomb this country; see the Forest Service for locations and precautions.

Another trail worth exploring if you want an out-of-the-way adventure is the **Little Bighorn River Canyon Trail** starting west of Ranchester along the Wyoming-Montana border. Contact the Forest Service in Sheridan for directions and details on this multiday trek.

An enjoyable waterfall is **Big Goose Falls.** Follow Forest Rd. 26 (it starts approximately five miles south of Burgess Junction on US Hwy. 14) to Big Goose Ranger Station, then continue on via Forest Rd. 296 to the end. The falls are about five miles below the ranger station along the East Fork of Big Goose Creek. They include plunge pools and water-sculpted rocks.

Crazy Woman Canyon

One of the most interesting drives in the Big Horns slices through Crazy Woman Canyon. Several stories exist for the origin of the canyon's name. One claims it's named for an Indian squaw who went insane while living alone in her tepee here. Another version says it came from a white settler who was pushed to insanity when Indians murdered and scalped her husband. Soldiers from Fort Laramie reportedly found her wandering the area. Either way, it wasn't exactly a soothing name for migrants on the old Bozeman Trail! Nevertheless, the canyon cut by cascading Crazy Woman Creek is a stunning one with steep cliffs on both sides. A rough gravel road (high-clearance vehicles are recommended; this isn't for trailers or RVs) heads down from US Hwy. 16 and continues all the way to the mouth of the canyon and then out to State Hwy. 196. The drive is actually more interesting (and easier on your brakes) if you do it from Buffalo westward, but be ready for a long and difficult trip in either direction. **Crazy Woman Canyon Tours,** tel. (307) 684-5609, offers 4WD treks into this country.

MEDICINE WHEEL

High atop a windswept mountain plateau sits one of the best-known and least-understood archaeological sites in America, the Medicine Wheel. Measuring 80 feet across, this uneven "wagon wheel" of stones seems ready to roll over the nearby slopes. Twenty-eight rock spokes radiate out from a central hub, with six smaller rock cairns scattered around the rim. A variety of lesser-known rock structures surround the Medicine Wheel on nearby slopes, including an arrow that supposedly points southwest to another "wheel" near Meeteetse 70 miles away, a large rectangle of stones, and more than 50 tepee rings. An ancient cairn-marked travois trail continues northwest from Medicine Wheel over the Big Horn Mountains.

Origins

Medicine Wheel's origins are shrouded in the depths of time. White prospectors from the nearby gold-mining camp of Bald Mountain City (now entirely gone) discovered the Medicine Wheel around 1885. Carbon-14 dating of wood fragments found in one of the cairns yielded the date A.D. 1760, and scientists now believe the wheel was constructed some time between A.D. 1200 and 1700.

Prevailing theories about the purpose behind the Medicine Wheel fall into two schools: it was either an astronomical observatory or a site for sacred ceremonies. One of the most interesting theories was suggested by astronomer John Eddy in a 1977 *National Geographic* article. He noted that the 28 spokes are equal to the number of days in the lunar month and that two of the cairns served as horizon markers for sunrise and sunset, with the other four cairns marking the rising of three of the brightest stars. These could have signaled the summer solstice. Interestingly, similar alignments occur on a stone wheel in Saskatchewan, Canada.

Other scientists counter that the Indians would have little reason to care exactly when summer solstice occurred—since they were not farmers—and that the rocks probably served some religious function. These researchers point out the striking similarities between the wheel and medicine lodges used during Cheyenne and Sioux sun-dance ceremonies—both have 28 spokes. The first published report (1885) described the Medicine Wheel as consisting of a central hub with spokes leading to stone huts: "It is said that these smaller huts were, during religious ceremonies, occupied by medicine men of different tribes, while the larger hut in the center was supposed to be the abode of Manitour." Various later reports attributed it to the Crow, Sheepeater, Arapaho, and Cheyenne tribes. University of Montana anthropologist Gregory Campbell considers the wheel a source of religious power to Native Americans and notes that it is a place where "powerful events come to the fore" for those who search for strength.

Regardless of its origins or earliest uses, the Medicine Wheel *was* used in historical times—and is still used today—as a place for prayer, meditation, renewal, and vision quests. Chief Joseph of the Nez Percé fasted here, and Shoshone Chief Washakie was said to have gained his "medicine" here. Because of the Medicine Wheel's location and the importance of ceremony in Native American life, it certainly remains a sacred site, whether or not it served any astronomical function.

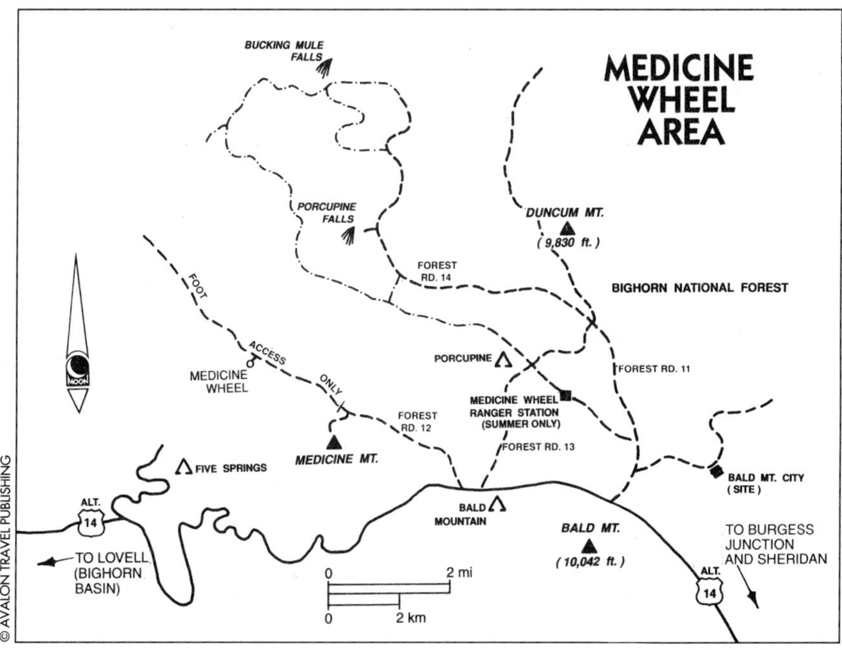

Visiting Medicine Wheel

The signed gravel road into the Medicine Wheel parking area turns off US Hwy. 14A approximately 27 miles east of Lovell. You'll need to walk the last mile and a half to the site, though exceptions are made for people with disabilities and the elderly. Be sure to carry water with you, and take your time; at 9,800 feet in elevation you may get winded easily. The road passes an FAA radar dome on nearby Medicine Mountain; it's used to monitor air traffic in a three-state area and is a disturbing structure to find near such a significant Native American site. Medicine Wheel is open to the public all the time (except during Native American ceremonies), and interpreters are available at the trailhead and at the wheel daily 8 a.m.-6 p.m. from late June through October. The road to Medicine Wheel is usually covered with snow from mid-October to mid-July. For more information, call the Forest Service office in Lovell, tel. (307) 548-6541.

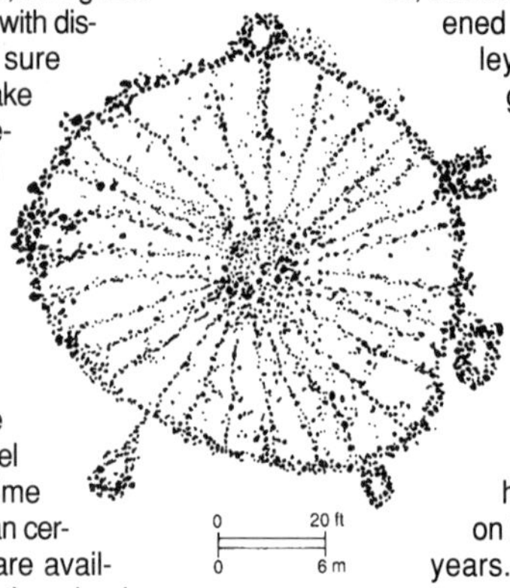

0 20 ft
0 6 m

medicine wheel

A wire fence surrounding the wheel is frequently festooned with strips of cloth, feathers, bells, herbs, flowers, sacred bundles, and other offerings left behind by Indians who come here on personal vision quests and other ceremonies. Such articles are particularly evident following solstices and equinoxes. Respect the importance of this religious site by not disturbing these items.

It is obvious why this mountain was chosen for the Medicine Wheel. The surrounding open country has scattered pine, juniper, and spruce, and the ridge drops off a 150-foot precipice just 50 feet away. From its 9,956-foot elevation, a vast panorama stretches to include the Bighorn Basin, the Wind River, the Absaroka Range, and the Pryor Mountains. Medicine Wheel is also a good place to look for hawks wheeling through the sky, especially red-tailed hawks and kestrels.

CLOUD PEAK WILDERNESS

Although maintained as a primitive area since 1932, the 189,000-acre Cloud Peak Wilderness did not receive official wilderness status until 1984. It's named for 13,175-foot **Cloud Peak,** a rocky mountain visible for a hundred miles in all directions. At one time this entire range was glaciated, and reminders abound in the sharpened peaks, broad U-shaped valleys, and multitude of lakes in glacial tarns. There are even a few small patches of glacial ice. The Big Horns still get plenty of snow, leaving many hiking trails in the high country blocked until July. One oddly named mountain in the wilderness is **Bomber Mountain,** just south of Cloud Peak. An Air Force B-17 bomber crashed here in 1943, killing all 10 men on board. It was not found for two years. For the sad but fascinating story, see *The Bomber Mountain Crash: A Wyoming Mystery* by R. Scott Madsen (Buffalo, WY: Mountain Man Publishing).

With more than 140 miles of trails and thousands of acres stretching above the timberline, hiking and horsepacking opportunities abound throughout Cloud Peak. Bears are not usually a problem in the Cloud Peak Wilderness. Backcountry users must fill out registration cards, available at the trailheads or local Forest Service offices. Be sure to set up camp at least 100 feet from water sources and trails and hang all food out of reach of black bears. Use existing campsites whenever possible to lessen your impact. The Forest Service produces a free map/guide to the wilderness area, which lists additional precautions.

For complete trail and historical info on the wilderness, get *Hiking Wyoming's Cloud Peak Wilderness* by Erik Molvar (Helena, MT: Falcon Press). Be sure to purchase topographic maps before heading out. Local bookstores sell a waterproof Trails Illustrated/National Geographic **wilderness map** for $9. It's worth getting. Check with the Forest Service office in Sheridan, Buffalo, or Lovell for a list of permitted outfitters and wilderness regulations. Always practice "no trace" camping; if you don't know what this means, pick up a handout from any of the Forest Service offices.

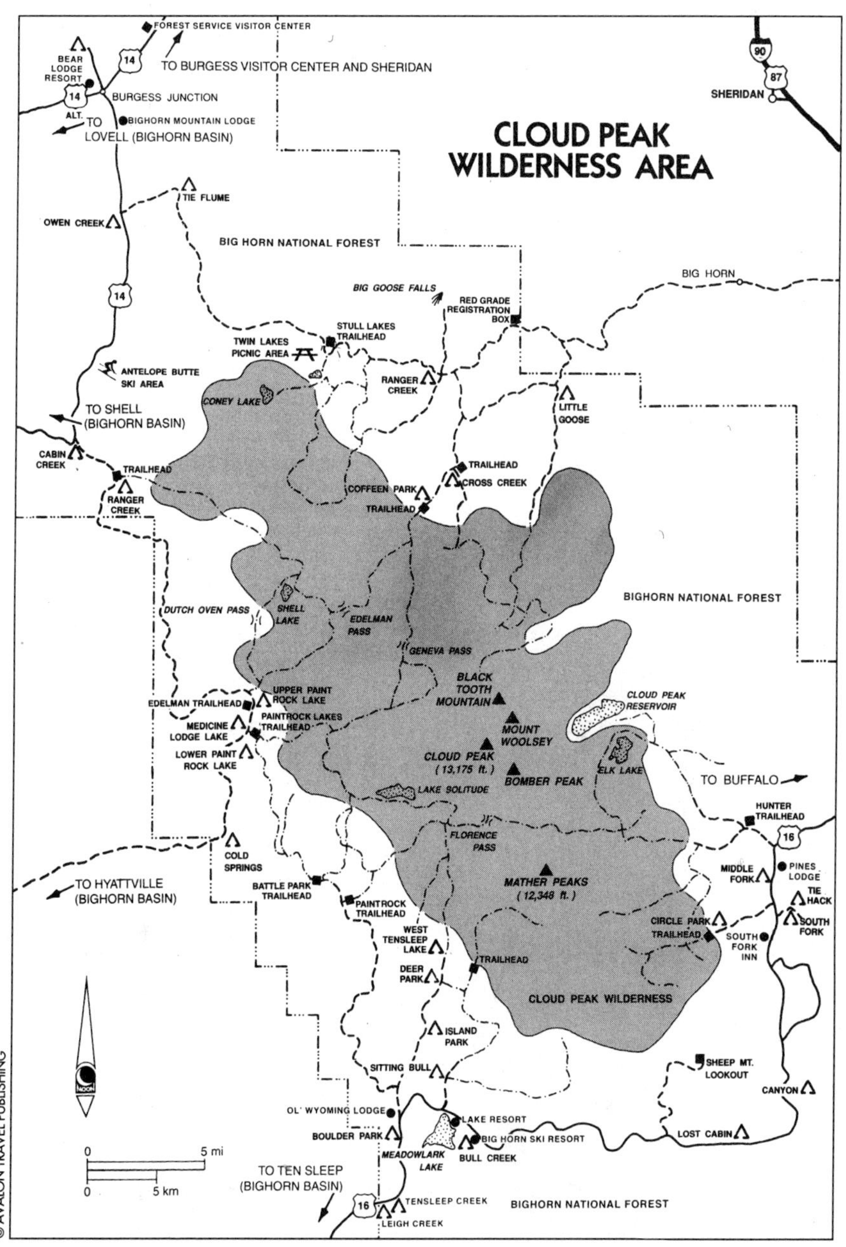
CLOUD PEAK WILDERNESS AREA
FOREST SERVICE VISITOR CENTER
TO BURGESS VISITOR CENTER AND SHERIDAN
BEAR LODGE RESORT
BURGESS JUNCTION
BIGHORN MOUNTAIN LODGE
TO LOVELL (BIGHORN BASIN)
SHERIDAN
TIE FLUME
OWEN CREEK
BIG HORN NATIONAL FOREST
BIG HORN
BIG GOOSE FALLS
RED GRADE REGISTRATION BOX
STULL LAKES TRAILHEAD
TWIN LAKES PICNIC AREA
ANTELOPE BUTTE SKI AREA
RANGER CREEK
CONEY LAKE
LITTLE GOOSE
TO SHELL (BIGHORN BASIN)
CABIN CREEK
TRAILHEAD
RANGER CREEK
TRAILHEAD
CROSS CREEK
COFFEEN PARK
TRAILHEAD
BIGHORN NATIONAL FOREST
DUTCH OVEN PASS
SHELL LAKE
EDELMAN PASS
GENEVA PASS
BLACK TOOTH MOUNTAIN
CLOUD PEAK RESERVOIR
UPPER PAINT ROCK LAKE
EDELMAN TRAILHEAD
MEDICINE LODGE LAKE
PAINTROCK LAKES TRAILHEAD
MOUNT WOOLSEY
LOWER PAINT ROCK LAKE
CLOUD PEAK (13,175 ft.)
BOMBER PEAK
ELK LAKE
TO BUFFALO
LAKE SOLITUDE
HUNTER TRAILHEAD
FLORENCE PASS
COLD SPRINGS
MIDDLE FORK
PINES LODGE
TO HYATTVILLE (BIGHORN BASIN)
BATTLE PARK TRAILHEAD
MATHER PEAKS (12,348 ft.)
TIE HACK
PAINTROCK TRAILHEAD
SOUTH FORK
CIRCLE PARK TRAILHEAD
WEST TENSLEEP LAKE
SOUTH FORK INN
DEER PARK
TRAILHEAD
CLOUD PEAK WILDERNESS
ISLAND PARK
SITTING BULL
SHEEP MT. LOOKOUT
CANYON
OL' WYOMING LODGE
LAKE RESORT
BOULDER PARK
BIG HORN SKI RESORT
LOST CABIN
MEADOWLARK LAKE
BULL CREEK
0 5 mi
0 5 km
TO TEN SLEEP (BIGHORN BASIN)
TENSLEEP CREEK
BIGHORN NATIONAL FOREST
LEIGH CREEK
MOON

Access into Cloud Peak Wilderness is via several entry roads along US Hwy. 16 on the southern border—most of the use comes from this side—and from the north (US Hwy. 14) at Cross Creek and Ranger Creek Campgrounds and near Twin Lakes Picnic Ground. Other entrance points surround Cloud Peak, but many require long hikes up 4WD roads to get to the wilderness boundary.

Trails

The **Stull Lakes-Coney Lake Trail** is one of the shortest hikes into the lake country of Cloud Peak. It climbs three miles from the trailhead (located a quarter mile west of the Twin Lakes picnic area), passes Stull Lake, and ends in the alpine country surrounding Coney Lake. Watch for elk and deer in late summer.

An excellent 21-mile loop hike begins at **Paintrock Lakes Trailhead** on the west side of the wilderness. This route traverses a wide variety of country, from dense timber to rocky mountain passes and small glaciers. The path climbs to a trail junction 1.5 miles west of Cliff Lake. From here, turn left and follow the trail to Geneva Pass (10,300 feet). The trail drops down to Lake Geneva and then follows East Fork Creek to the junction with the Edelman Trail. This path leads over Edelman Pass, around Emerald Lake, and then back down to the Edelman Trailhead, just 1.5 miles by road from your starting point. You'll find all sorts of other hikes and side trips in this area.

Another loop trip takes you to **Lake Solitude.** Begin at the Battle Park Trailhead approximately 15 miles north of Meadowlark Lake. Take the road to Tyrell Ranger Station and turn left after a mile, continuing up the rough gravel road to the trailhead. The trail climbs up Paint Rock Creek past Grace Lake and Lake Solitude to Mistymoon Lake. Beyond this you can either return on the same route or follow the trail down a steep valley to the water-lily-filled Lily Lake. From here, continue downhill to the Paintrock Trailhead on Forest Rd. 17, and turn right (northwest), following the road a mile back to your starting point. The loop is approximately 17 miles roundtrip.

The easiest—and probably busiest—route to the top of **Cloud Peak** takes off from West Tensleep Trailhead on Forest Rd. 27. Plan on a strenuous 10 hours for the 11-mile climb up and back. This is not a developed trail and will require considerable rock hopping, but the spectacularly desolate scenery makes it worthwhile. Be prepared for sudden weather changes, and carry an ice ax into August. For detailed route instructions up Cloud Peak, get a topographic map and a copy of Erik Molvar's trail guide.

The **Elk Lake Loop** (19 miles roundtrip) begins at Hunter Trailhead on the southeast side of the wilderness and involves lots of climbing. Follow the old jeep trail to Soldier Park, a scenic grassy meadow. Turn north at the trail junction and follow the path to Elk Lake. Along the way are some outstanding views across the alpine terrain to Cloud Peak. Turn left at Elk Lake, head up over a pass, and then south to North Clear Creek Trail. Follow it downhill to Soldier Park and back to the trailhead.

SHERIDAN

The attractive and vibrant small city of Sheridan (pop. 15,000) has plenty to see, several fine restaurants and art galleries, great country in the nearby Big Horn Mountains, and a genuine sense of history. At just 3,745 feet above sea level, it claims the lowest elevation of any Wyoming town, making for hot summers. It's only 25 miles from Sheridan to the Montana border via I-90.

The country around Sheridan was settled by a broad mixture of Europeans—everyone from British lords to Polish coal miners. Their heritage carries on in such events as an annual polka festival and weekly polo matches at Big Horn Equestrian Center, the oldest polo club in the nation. Locals brag that Sheridan has a wealth of things to do and a surprising cultural richness without the crowds of Yellowstone and Jackson Hole. The town is, however, losing some of the hard-edged cowboy feel from the past and gaining more yuppified Western wear boutiques, gift shops, galleries, antique stores, and eateries all the time.

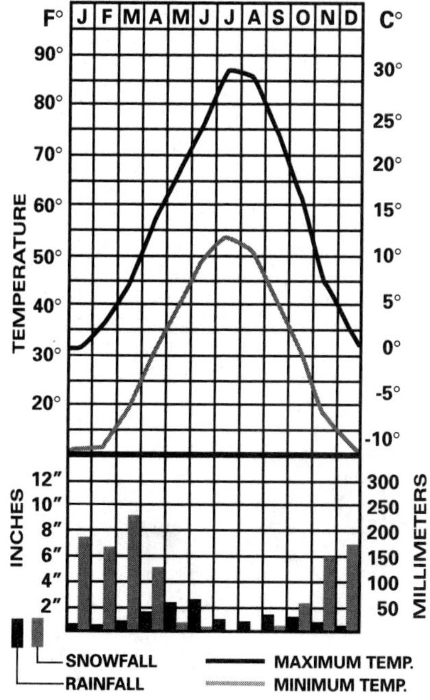

Average Maximum Temp.	**58.7°F**
Average Minimum Temp.	**29.9°F**
Annual Rainfall	**15.29"**
Annual Snowfall	**45"**

HISTORY

Sheridan, like other towns in the Powder River Basin, was built on coal, cattle, farming, and the railroad. In 1882, John D. Loucks took a liking to the country here and decided to establish a town, drawing up a plat on a piece of brown wrapping paper. He named the new place for his commanding officer during the Civil War, Gen. Philip Sheridan, and immediately set about getting others to come. For several years Sheridan competed with nearby Big Horn City for the county seat, a title that ensured survival. Finally, in 1885, Sheridan promoters offered cowboys at the fall roundup free lots in the town. When most accepted, Sheridan finally had enough folks to incorporate. Almost overnight (literally, in some cases), businesses in Big Horn City moved to Sheridan, sometimes bringing their buildings along with them.

When the Burlington and Missouri Railroad reached Sheridan in 1892, the town suddenly changed. Now ranchers could get their cattle to market more easily and visitors could stay in the sumptuous Sheridan Inn. Farming became more profitable as investors built large grain mills and a sugar-processing plant. The first underground coal mines opened in 1883, but it was not until 1903 that the Burlington Railroad began using the coal in its engines. For the next several decades these "black diamonds" were mainstays of the local economy. Sheridan soon had 1,500 people, wooden sidewalks, 30 saloons, six churches, and two opera houses. Small mining towns—Dietz, Acme, Kooi, Model, Riverside, and Carneyville—opened in the surround-

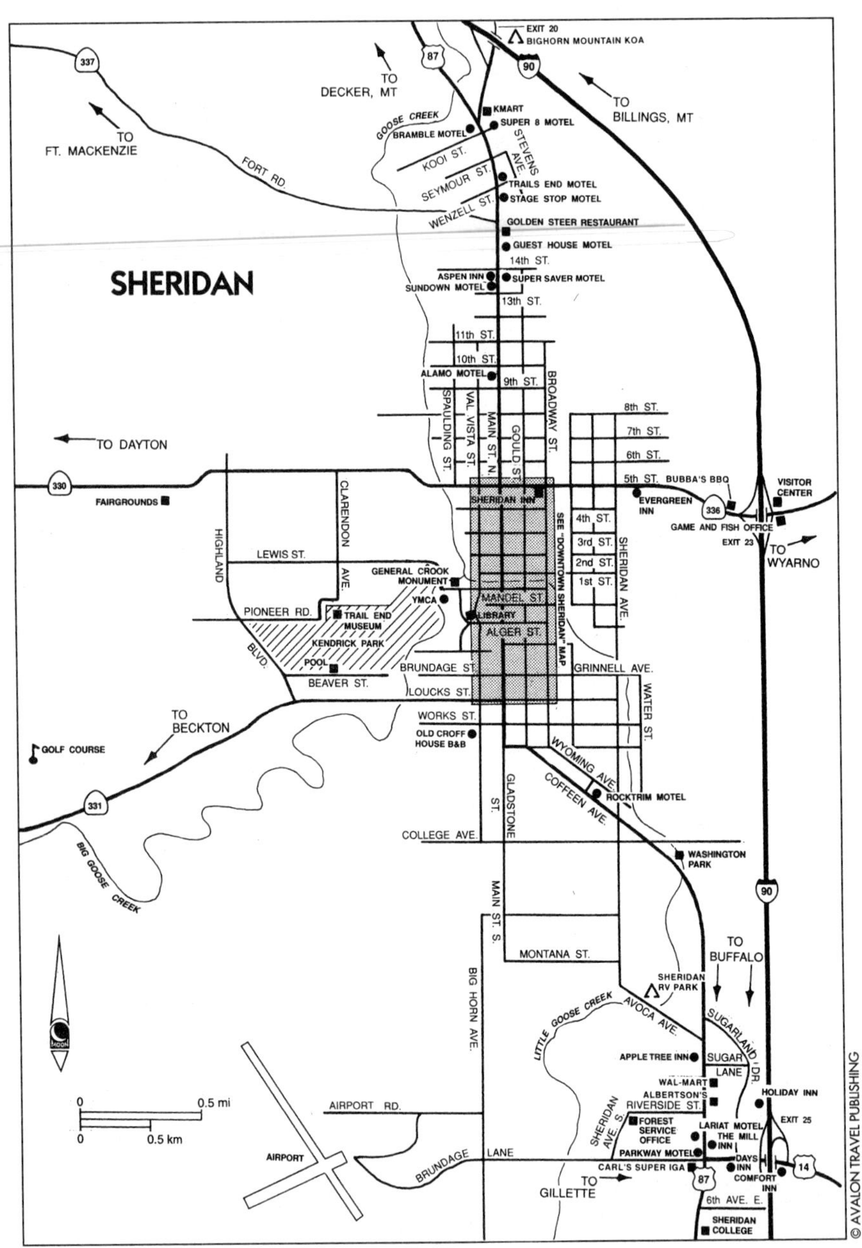
SHERIDAN
EXIT 20
BIGHORN MOUNTAIN KOA
TO DECKER, MT
TO BILLINGS, MT
TO FT. MACKENZIE
FORT RD.
GOOSE CREEK
KMART
SUPER 8 MOTEL
BRAMBLE MOTEL
KOOI ST.
STEVENS AVE.
SEYMOUR ST.
TRAILS END MOTEL
WENZELL ST.
STAGE STOP MOTEL
GOLDEN STEER RESTAURANT
GUEST HOUSE MOTEL
14th ST.
ASPEN INN
SUPER SAVER MOTEL
SUNDOWN MOTEL
13th ST.
11th ST.
10th ST.
ALAMO MOTEL
9th ST.
SPAULDING ST.
VAL VISTA ST.
MAIN ST. N.
GOULD ST.
BROADWAY ST.
8th ST.
7th ST.
6th ST.
5th ST.
BUBBA'S BBQ
VISITOR CENTER
TO DAYTON
FAIRGROUNDS
CLARENDON AVE.
SHERIDAN INN
EVERGREEN INN
GAME AND FISH OFFICE
EXIT 23
TO WYARNO
HIGHLAND BLVD.
LEWIS ST.
SEE "DOWNTOWN SHERIDAN" MAP
4th ST.
3rd ST.
2nd ST.
1st ST.
SHERIDAN AVE.
GENERAL CROOK MONUMENT
YMCA
MANDEL ST.
PIONEER RD.
TRAIL END MUSEUM
LIBRARY
ALGER ST.
KENDRICK PARK
POOL
BRUNDAGE ST.
GRINNELL AVE.
BEAVER ST.
LOUCKS ST.
WATER ST.
TO BECKTON
WORKS ST.
OLD CROFF HOUSE B&B
GOLF COURSE
WYOMING AVE.
COFFEEN AVE.
ROCKTRIM MOTEL
GLADSTONE ST.
BIG GOOSE CREEK
COLLEGE AVE.
WASHINGTON PARK
MAIN ST. S.
MONTANA ST.
TO BUFFALO
BIG HORN AVE.
SHERIDAN RV PARK
LITTLE GOOSE CREEK
AVOCA AVE.
SUGARLAND DR.
APPLE TREE INN
SUGAR LANE
WAL-MART
ALBERTSON'S
RIVERSIDE ST.
HOLIDAY INN
0 0.5 mi
0 0.5 km
AIRPORT RD.
SHERIDAN AVE. S.
FOREST SERVICE OFFICE
LARIAT MOTEL
EXIT 25
THE MILL INN
PARKWAY MOTEL
AIRPORT
BRUNDAGE LANE
CARL'S SUPER IGA
DAYS INN
COMFORT INN
TO GILLETTE
6th AVE. E.
SHERIDAN COLLEGE
MOON
© AVALON TRAVEL PUBLISHING

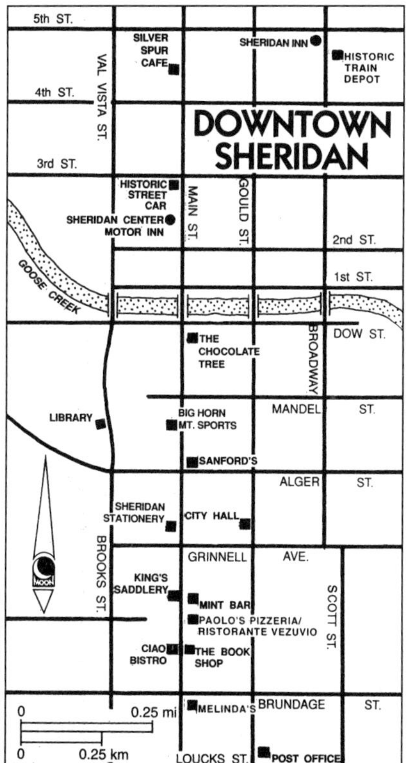

ing countryside, inhabited by thousands of European emigrants; newspapers often featured ads in both Polish and English. Electric streetcars were added in 1911, with frequent interurban service to the surrounding coal mines.

World War II brought prosperity as local mines operated at full tilt and new technology allowed construction of the first open-pit mine. After the war, however, trains shifted to diesel and homes began burning less-polluting natural gas, so that by 1953 the last of the old coal towns had died. With increasing demand for western coal in the 1970s, Sheridan's population boomed again. Sheridan's economy now depends upon a mixture of mining, the railroad, ranching, government jobs, and tourism. Many locals cross into Montana for jobs at the Decker and Spring Creek coal mines, while others work at the local veterans' hospital or the Burlington Northern switching yard. Coal-bed methane gas production promises to become much more important in the future.

SIGHTS

Trail End State Historic Site

On spacious grounds overlooking Sheridan, Trail End Historic Center is the city's best-known attraction. This was the home of John B. Kendrick, a wealthy rancher and a powerful Democratic politician. Born in Texas in 1857, Kendrick was raised as an orphan. He became a ranch hand by age 15 and, after trailing cattle north to Wyoming, fell in love with the country and took a job as a ranch foreman. At age 34, he married the 17-year-old Eula Wulfgen, and they lived on a ranch in southeastern Montana for the next 18 years.

Over the years Kendrick acquired more than 200,000 acres of land in Wyoming and Montana, grazing tens of thousands of his cattle. He personally financed local homesteaders, friends, former employees, and relatives. Politics beckoned once Kendrick was established as a rancher and businessman, and he served first as governor, then as a U.S. senator until his death in 1933. One paper called him "the craftiest politician the state has ever produced." Kendrick helped expose the Teapot Dome Scandal and gained funding for the massive Kendrick Project, a series of dams and irrigation canals on the North Platte River.

Shortly before entering politics, Kendrick selected the site for his end-of-the-trail mansion high atop a hill overlooking Sheridan. Beginning construction in 1908, Trail End took five years to complete and served primarily as a summer home since politics kept Kendrick away the rest of the year. The mansion is in the Flemish Revival style, with curvilinear gables on the third-floor windows, a red-tile roof, hardwood floors, mahogany walls, and exposed-beam ceilings. Many of the sumptuous original furnishings (including a 25-foot-long Kurdistan rug) are still inside. Look for photos of several of Kendrick's ranches upstairs.

The house cost $165,000 in an era when typical homes went for less than $1,000. Its 18 rooms include a third-floor ballroom with a loft where musicians could play without interfering with the dancers below. The built-in central vacuum system still works. Heating Trail End sometimes required up to a ton of coal each day. Out back is a sod-roofed **log cabin** that was moved onto the grounds. Built in 1878, this historic structure served as Sheridan's first post office, and later it was used as a school, store, law office, and bank.

Find Trail End at 400 Clarendon Ave., tel. (307) 674-4589. It is open daily 9 a.m.-6 p.m. June-Aug., and daily 1-4 p.m. in the fall and spring; closed mid-December through March. Entrance costs $2 for nonresidents or $1 for Wyoming residents.

Sheridan Inn

Built in 1893, Sheridan Inn was considered by many to be the premier hotel between Chicago and San Francisco. Visitors included Presidents Theodore Roosevelt, Taft, and Hoover, along with such celebrities as Will Rogers and Ernest Hemingway. Architect Thomas Kimball modeled the Inn after a Scottish hunting lodge, with dormer windows on all 62 rooms; *Ripley's Believe it or Not!* labeled it "The House of 69 Gables," a name that has stuck through the years. Inside, carpenters added hand-hewn ponderosa pine beams, three large cobblestone fireplaces, the Buffalo Bill Bar (imported from England), elegant oak furnishings, and the first electric lights in Sheridan. Col. William F. (Buffalo Bill) Cody was later a co-owner of the hotel and used the veranda to audition performers for his Wild West Show. It was operated as a hotel until 1965 and later as a restaurant and bar.

On the corner of 5th and Broadway, the inn is a registered National Historic Landmark. Tall, 100-year-old cottonwoods guard the front, and the huge porch wraps around the sides. Try to see if you can find all 69 gables. Step inside to explore this gracious place or enjoy a pleasant lunch or dinner. The gift shop sells an interesting booklet about Kate Arnold, who lived here for 65 years and whose ashes are buried in an upstairs wall. Her ghost still shows up periodically to make sure the inn is well managed. Tours are available for groups, but advance notification is required.

A local nonprofit group is restoring the Sheridan to its original status as a classy lodging, eating, and drinking establishment. The project will probably not be completed till 2003, when the upstairs rooms will be restored as part of a luxurious bed and breakfast. Call (307) 674-5440 for details.

King's Saddlery

Well worth a stop is King's Saddlery, 184 N. Main St., tel. (307) 672-2702 or (800) 443-8919, a

Host of presidents and other luminaries, historic Sheridan Inn is called the "House of 69 Gables."

Sheridan-area fixture since the 1940s. When you step inside the doors the smell of leather is almost overwhelming. The long, narrow shop has handmade saddles, leatherwork, ropes, spurs, chaps, belt buckles, cowboy hats, and various other tack for horses and their riders. Be sure to check out the many miles of ropes filling racks in the back room. Many top rodeo cowboys come in to purchase their lariats, and King's sells 40,000 high-quality ropes a year.

The free **King's Western Museum** in the back houses literally hundreds of gorgeous saddles—including a 17th-century Japanese saddle and American saddles dating from before the Civil War—along with rifles, spurs, chaps, tools, old wagons, and carriages. It's one of the finest collections of cowboy memorabilia anywhere. Also here is an impressive display of Indian artifacts including a beaded pottery vase and bridles made a century ago. King's Saddlery is fittingly named: both Queen Elizabeth and the king of Saudi Arabia have visited, and Presidents Clinton and Reagan were both given King's leather belts. King's Saddlery is open Mon.-Sat. 8 a.m.-5 p.m. The store also has a mail-order catalog.

Fort Mackenzie

Built in 1902, Fort Mackenzie never really served much of a military function. Pushed through Congress by Wyoming's powerful senator Francis E. Warren, the fort was ostensibly built as a base to put down Indian uprising on nearby reservations, but the last major Indian battles had occurred 20 years earlier. It was named for Gen. Ranald S. Mackenzie, a veteran of the Civil War and various Indian battles. Over the decades, the size of the fort shrank from 6,280 to 342 acres, and the last troops departed during WW I. In 1922, it became a 339-bed hospital for mentally ill vets. You're welcome to walk around the grounds and admire the old brick buildings, but check in at the administration building first.

Sheridan County Library

Sheridan's excellent library at 320 N. Brooks, tel. (307) 674-8585, encloses a small collection of Indian artifacts and items from early settlers. The Wyoming Room has an extensive collection of old books, maps, and paintings, including a mural of the Wagon Box Fight; upstairs you'll find more historical exhibits and current artwork and a model of the Medicine Wheel. On the library walls are 11 paintings by Bill Gollings (1878-1932), a self-taught, but accomplished, cowboy artist.

Other Sights

A historical marker on the corner of W. Dow and Alger commemorates **General Crook's campsite.** In 1876 the general camped here at the junction of Big and Little Goose Creeks with 1,325 men and 1,900 pack animals after being forced to a stalemate by Sioux and Crow warriors on the Rosebud River. The fight took place just eight days before Custer would die at nearby Little Big Horn.

Directly across from the Sheridan Inn is the old red Sheridan **train depot,** built in 1892 and now housing a bar. Nearby is a huge Chicago, Burlington, and Quincy Railroad **locomotive.** Downtown on 3rd and Gould Sts. is a Sheridan **streetcar** from the early 1900s. History and architecture buffs should pick up a copy of the guide to Sheridan's **Main Street Historic District** at the visitor center. One of the buildings included—the **Mint Bar,** 151 N. Main St., tel. (307) 674-9696—offers a genuine taste of the West. Cartoonist Linda Barry's description of the Mint says it all: "Stuffed animal heads galore. Taxidermied fish galore. Burlwood carpentry galore."

Across the road from the state rest area/information center on 5th St., the **Wyoming Game & Fish Department Visitor Center** contains a number of professionally produced and informative wildlife and fish displays. Although small, this collection is well worth a visit. Hours are Mon.-Fri. 8 a.m.-5 p.m. year-round; call (307) 672-2790 for details.

ACCOMMODATIONS

Motels

Most of Sheridan's motels lie along Coffeen Ave. and Main Street. During the off-season—through early May—you're likely to find lower prices, down to $20 a night at the budget motels. Accommodations are arranged below from least to most expensive. Add an eight percent tax to these rates.

Budget: Super Saver Motel, 1789 N. Main St., tel. (307) 672-0471, has the lowest prices in town ($22 s or $26 d), but you may want to see the rooms first. Additional basic accommodations at **Alamo Motel,** 1326 N. Main St., tel. (307) 672-2455, where the rooms cost $25 s or $29 d.

Budget-Inexpensive: Stage Stop Motel, 2167 N. Main St., tel. (307) 672-3459, is a small, older place with rooms for $28 s or $32-38 d. **Parkway Motel,** 2112 Coffeen Ave., tel. (307) 674-7259, charges $26 s or $30-40 d and has kitchenettes.

Inexpensive: Rock Trim Motel, 449 Coffeen Ave., tel. (307) 672-2464, is a fine economy place with standard rooms for $36-48 s or d and kitchenettes for $52 s or d.

Stay at **Apple Tree Inn,** 1552 Coffeen Ave., tel. (307) 672-2428 or (800) 670-2428, for a reasonable $40 s or $50 d. Amenities include a jacuzzi, sauna, and playground. **Bramble Motel & RV Park,** 2366 N. Main St., tel. (307) 674-4902, has motel rooms for $40 s or $45-50 d. A few kitchenettes are available.

Find spacious and clean motel rooms for $40 s or $50 d at **Guest House Motel,** 2007 N. Main St., tel. (307) 674-7496 or (800) 226-9405.

The units aren't new, but they're clean and well-maintained at **Aspen Inn,** 1744 N. Main St., tel. (307) 672-9064. Rates are $42 s or $48 d. The same owners run the adjacent **Sundown Motel,** 1704 N. Main St., tel. (307) 672-2439, where newly remodeled rooms are available for the same price. A small outdoor pool is on the premises at Sundown Motel.

Trails End Motel, 2125 N. Main St., tel. (307) 672-2477 or (800) 445-4921, has a mix of old and new rooms for $44-60 s or d. Family units are $65 for six people, and log cabins cost $44 d. An indoor pool is on the premises. **Lariat Motel,** 2068 Coffeen Ave., tel. (307) 672-6475, charges $45 s or d.

Moderate: Evergreen Inn, 580 E. 5th St., tel. (307) 672-9757 or (800) 771-4761, is a nice place with an outdoor jacuzzi and fridges in half the rooms. Rates are $56 s or $64 d.

Occupying a historic flour mill, the **Mill Inn,** 2161 Coffeen Ave., tel. (307) 672-6401 or (888) 357-6455, lends a new meaning to the term "hitting the sack." Rates are $57-64 s or $59-68 d, and amenities include an exercise facility, an Old West lobby, and a continental breakfast.

Super 8 Motel, 2435 N. Main St., tel. (307) 672-9725 or (800) 800-8000, charges $66 s or d.

Moderate-Expensive: Best Western Sheridan Center Motor Inn, 609 N. Main St., tel. (307) 674-7421 or (800) 528-1234, is one of the better lodging places in town, with indoor and outdoor pools, a sauna, jacuzzi, and continental breakfast. Rates are $70-80 s or $80-90 d.

At **Days Inn,** 1104 E. Brundage Lane, tel. (307) 672-2888 or (800) 329-7466, amenities include an indoor pool, jacuzzi, and light breakfast. Rates are $75-95 s or $80-110 d.

Expensive: Holiday Inn, 1809 Sugarland Dr., tel. (307) 672-8931 or (800) 465-4329, is the largest and most elaborate lodging place in Sheridan. The hotel features an atrium with a waterfall and two restaurants, plus a small indoor pool, sauna, jacuzzi, exercise room, and racquetball court. Rates are $99-104 s or d.

Expensive-Premium: One of the best local places to stay is **Comfort Inn,** 1450 E. Brundage Lane, tel. (307) 672-5098 or (800) 228-5150, where rooms cost $85-120 s or d, including a continental breakfast and access to the jacuzzi.

Bed and Breakfasts and Guest Houses

Several excellent bed and breakfasts are out in the country south of Sheridan; see South of Sheridan, below, for details. **Old Croff House B&B,** 508 W. Works St., tel. (307) 672-0898, is a pleasant in-town home built in 1917. The home contains three guest rooms (with private or shared baths) and a front porch with an old-fashioned wicker swing. Rates are $65-75 s or d ($90 d for two rooms used as a suite), including a continental breakfast. Kids are welcome. Open June-September. Moderate-Expensive.

Five miles east of Sheridan on Hwy. 14 is **Ranch Willow B&B,** tel. (307) 674-1510 or (800) 354-2830, a gorgeous turn-of-the-20th-century ranch home on 550 acres. The four guest rooms (private or shared baths) are well appointed with handmade furniture, and breakfast includes fresh ranch eggs and organically grown ingredients. Bring your own horse to ride in the indoor arena. Rates are $80-90 s or d. Kids over five are welcome. Moderate-Expensive.

For simple accommodations that can sleep up to six, stay at **Little Goose Coop Guest House,** 637 Val Vista, tel. (307) 672-0886. Rates are $65 s or d, plus $15 per person for additional guests. The house contains a full kitchen, washer, and dryer. Moderate.

King's Main St. B&B, tel. (307) 674-6159, is a nicely decorated "country cottage" in the heart of town at 924 N. Main Street. It's the sort of embellished place that some women tend to love, but it's not for children. The four guest rooms (shared or private baths) are $65-85 s or d, including a light breakfast. Moderate.

Homestead at the Powder Horn Golf Course, tel. (307) 674-1519 or (800) 986-6095, has three guest rooms in a home built in the 1940s. Rates are $99-159, including a full breakfast. Kids are welcome. Get more info at www.thepowderhorn.com. Expensive-Luxury.

Dude Ranches

The Sheridan area is home to several classic dude ranches. The first in the region was run by the Hilman family, who took in their first paying dudes in 1889. It operated until the 1930s. Famous **Eaton's Ranch,** 18 miles west of Sheridan, tel. (307) 655-9285 or (800) 210-1049, is one of the oldest, largest, and best-known dude ranches in America. The three Eaton brothers—Howard, Alden, and Willis—began ranching in North Dakota in 1879 but soon found themselves overwhelmed by visiting friends from the east. Eventually one offered to pay, and thus was born the first dude ranch. Initially these "dudes" (a term that both Buffalo Bill and Howard Eaton took credit for using first in this context) stayed wherever they could find space, eating the cowboy's grub and joining in on chores. In 1904, the brothers bought a ranch along Wyoming's Wolf Creek that would eventually grow to 7,000 acres. Fourth- and fifth-generation members of the Eaton family still run the ranch. The ranch is a big one, accommodating up to 120 dudes in modernized guest cabins. Many families return year after year to the Eaton's. The emphasis—not surprisingly—is on horseback rides; this is one of the few dude ranches where experienced riders can head out on their own (with permission from the ranch). Other facilities include an outdoor pool, trout fishing, and a nearby nine-hole golf course. The ranch is open June-Sept. with a three-night minimum stay. All-inclusive rates are $300 per day for two people. Find the ranch on the web at www.eatonsranch.com. Luxury.

High in the Big Horn Mountains 30 miles southwest of Sheridan, **Spear-O-Wigwam Dude Ranch** has been in operation since 1923. This classic dude ranch—Ernest Hemingway wrote *A Farewell to Arms* while staying here—has comfy log cabins, a large lodge with a stone fireplace, a hot tub, pool tables, and horseback rides or overnight trips into the nearby Cloud Peak Wilderness. A fishing guide is available to teach fly-fishing. There's a three-night minimum stay, and all-inclusive rates are $320 for two people per night, or $2,100 for two people per week. The ranch plays host to a maximum of just 30 guests and is open mid-June to mid-September. For reservations or more information, call toll-free at (888) 818-3833, or call direct at (307) 674-4496 in summer or (307) 655-3217 in winter. Find the ranch on the web at www.spear-o-wigwam.com. Luxury.

Camping

Many campgrounds ($8-10) operate within nearby Bighorn National Forest; they're described in the Big Horn Mountains section above. **Bighorn Mountain KOA,** 63 Decker Rd., tel. (307) 674-8766 or (800) 562-7621, has quiet tent sites for $15 and RV sites for $22. Non-campers may shower for $4 (before 4 p.m. only). Basic "kamping kabins" are $28 d. It's open May to early October and has a pool, jacuzzi, and mini-golf.

Bramble Motel & RV Park, 2366 N. Main, tel. (307) 674-4902, charges $20 for RV sites with hookups; no tents.

On the south end of town along Little Goose Creek, **Sheridan RV Park,** 807 Avoca Ave., tel. (307) 674-0722, has RV sites with hookups for $15 and tent sites for $12; open April to mid-October.

FOOD

Sheridan has a broad choice of eateries, including a remarkable number of truly notable restaurants. You'll find cowboy breakfasts, gourmet lunches, brewpub favorites, and an Italian bistro all within a few blocks of each other.

Breakfast

Tiny **Silver Spur Cafe,** 832 N. Main St., tel. (307) 672-2749, only serves breakfast and lunch, but this is the best down-home cowboy food in town—reasonable prices, too. **Sheridan Palace Cafe,** 138 N. Main St., (307) 672-2391, is an old-time downtown establishment that opens at 6 a.m. for the breakfast early birds.

Lunch and Dinner

Sheridan's finest lunches and dinners are found at **Ciao Bistro,** 120 N. Main St., tel. (307) 672-2838. Wonderful sandwiches, salads, pastas, desserts, and fresh-baked breads. Get here early for lunch to avoid the lines, and make reservations for dinner. Open for lunch Mon.-Fri. and dinner Wed.-Saturday. Dinner entrées are $11-18.

Another place that gets crowded for lunch is **The Chocolate Tree,** 423 N. Main St., tel. (307) 672-6160, where the menu includes gourmet sandwiches, burgers, shrimp scampi, salads, daily specials, and decadent chocolates. It's also open for breakfast and dinner. **Melinda's,** 57 N. Main St., tel. (307) 674-9188, has sandwiches, soups, fresh baked goods, and espresso. Be ready for a wait during the lunchtime rush. Closed Monday.

On the corner of 5th and Broadway, the historic **Sheridan Inn** (described in Sights above) is a favorite of the business-lunch crowd. It's also open for dinners that center around prime rib, steaks, chicken, and seafood; entrées are $10-21. The restaurant is open Tues.-Sat. for lunch and dinner and has a popular Sunday brunch buffet ($11). Call (307) 674-5440 for reservations.

The best local burgers are—surprisingly enough—at **Dairy Queen,** 544 N. Main St., tel. (307) 674-9379. **Golden Steer Restaurant,** 2071 N. Main St., tel. (307) 674-9334, is a family dining place with good steaks. Fill up on barbecued buffalo, chicken, and ribs during the summer evening chuck wagons at **Bighorn Mountain KOA,** 63 Decker Rd., tel. (307) 674-8766.

Little Big Men Pizza, 1424 Coffeen Ave., tel. (307) 672-9877, has reasonable pizza, burger, and salad meal deals, including all-you-can-eat lunch and dinner smorgasbords.

The very popular **Bubba's BBQ,** 850 Sibley Circle. (at I-90 exit 23), tel. (307) 673-5002, is part of a small chain based in Jackson Hole. It serves three meals a day, and while the menu includes pasta, steak, chicken, and prime rib, Bubba's is best known for its finger-lickin' ribs. The salad bar is one of the better ones in town, and you won't go wrong with the buffet lunches or dinners.

Ethnic Eats

For authentic Italian meals, don't miss **Paolo's Pizzeria Ristorante Vezuvio,** downtown at 123 N. Main St., tel. (307) 672-3853. Chef Paolo Formisano moved here from Italy and creates delicious pizzas and salads in an attractive bistro setting.

Get reasonably authentic Chinese cookery at **Golden China Restaurant** in the T&C Shopping Center at Brundage and Coffeen, tel. (307) 674-7181. **Dragon Wall Restaurant,** 425 N. Brooks, tel. (307) 673-6888, has a big Chinese buffet for lunch ($5.50) or dinner ($7.75), including a not-so-Chinese salad and dessert bar. **Kim's Family Restaurant,** 2004 N. Main St., tel. (307) 672-0357, is one of the only Korean restaurants in Wyoming.

Pablo's, 1274 N. Main, tel. (307) 672-0737, serves reasonably priced Mexican food and has a full bar. **Las Margaritas,** 922 Coffeen Ave., tel. (307) 674-0900, is part of a Seattle-based chain of Mexican eateries. Not surprisingly, margaritas are a house specialty.

Brewpub

Sanford's Grub, Pub & Brewery, 1 E. Alger St., tel. (307) 674-1722, is a trendy pub with garage-sale flotsam and jetsam dangling from the ceiling, TVs in all directions, and rock tunes blasting over the speakers. The bar claims one of the largest beer selections in Wyoming with more than 125 brews, including 37 on draught. Several of these are made in the brewpub on the premises. The diverse menu makes this a very popular (and noisy) place to hang out with friends. It's part of a small chain of pubs—others are in Cheyenne, Gillette, and Casper, along with Spearfish, South Dakota.

Grocers

Sheridan has several large grocers, including Albertson's, Safeway, and Decker's Food Center, but your best bet is **Carl's Corner IGA,** on the south side of town at 2254 Coffeen Ave., tel. (307) 674-7945.

OTHER PRACTICALITIES

Entertainment

During the summer, **WYO Theater,** 42 N. Main St., tel. (307) 672-9084, has live plays and musical events. **Carriage House Theater** at Trail End, tel. (307) 672-9886, presents plays Oct.-May and sometimes has children's theater in the summer. Drop by the Kendrick Park band shell for free

Tuesday night **concerts in the park** all summer. Music ranges from polka to jazz.

Enjoy live rock 'n' roll on weekends at **Little Big Men Pizza,** 1424 Coffeen Ave., tel. (307) 672-9877, or watch sports on its big-screen TV. Check **Scooter's,** at the Holiday Inn, 1809 Sugarland Dr., tel. (307) 672-8931, and **Sutton's Tavern,** 1402 N. Main St., tel. (307) 672-5213, for DJ tunes on weekends. Pool, snooker, and darts are featured attractions at the **Caboose Bar,** in the old depot across from the Sheridan Inn. For all-around fun and drinking with your friends, it's hard to beat the classic **Mint Bar,** 151 N. Main St., tel. (307) 674-9696.

Watch movies inside **Centennial Theatres,** 36 E. Alger St., tel. (307) 672-5797, or visit one of Wyoming's few surviving drive-ins: **Skyline Drive In,** 1739 E. Brundage Lane, tel. (307) 674-4532.

Events

Early July attracts chefs and chili connoisseurs to Sheridan for the **Wyoming Chili Cook-off.** The **Sheridan Wyo Rodeo** comes around in mid-July each year, bringing with it not just professional rodeo cowboys at the "world's largest one go-round rodeo" but also a parade down Main Street, a pancake breakfast, country-and-western bands, and street dances. Call (307) 672-2485 or (800) 453-3650 for specifics. Also in mid-July is the **Prairie Rose Arts Festival,** held at the historic Sheridan Inn. This juried event attracts a wide range of artists, woodworkers, potters, and jewelers. Another July event is the delightful free production of **Shakespeare in the Park,** held on the lawn of the Trail End mansion; call (307) 672-9886 for details.

In early August, visit the **Sheridan County Fair,** followed by the **Sheridan County Rodeo** later in the month. The rodeo even includes stick-horse races for those under age four! **Big Horn Mountain Polka Days** is a fun Labor Day weekend event which attracts hundreds of polka enthusiasts to the Holiday Inn Convention Center. Oom-pa-pa!

Recreation

Kendrick City Park has a small game preserve where bison and elk are visible, plus a great playground for kids. Swim at the summer-only **outdoor swimming pool** in the park, and feel like a kid again on the 90-foot-long water slide. There's another pool at the **YMCA,** 417 N. Jefferson, tel. (307) 674-7488, plus racquetball and tennis courts and weight machines.

Golfers will want to try out two 18-hole courses: **Kendrick Golf Course,** three miles west of town, tel. (307) 674-8148, and the championship **Powder Horn Golf Club,** 14 Clubhouse Rd., tel. (307) 672-5323.

Nelson Outfitters, tel. (307) 672-6996, has horseback rides from its base nine miles west of Sheridan.

Big Horn Mountain Sports, 334 N. Main St., tel. (307) 672-6866, has a big choice of outdoor gear and topographic maps. Much of this gear can also be rented, including cross-country skis, snowboards, snowshoes, tents, sleeping bags, backpacks, rollerblades, fly rods, and float tubes. The staff teaches classes in skiing, kayaking, fly-tying, fly-fishing, and rock climbing. **Back Country Bikes,** tel. (307) 672-2453, inside Big Horn Mountain Sports, rents mountain bikes and has helpful maps of nearby cycling trails.

Fly Shop of the Big Horns, 227 N. Main St., tel. (307) 672-5866 or (800) 253-5866, www.troutangler.com, has Orvis gear, classes in fly-casting and fly-tying, and guided fishing trips on the Big Horn and Platte Rivers. Rent float tubes and fins here.

Shopping

You'll find a fine selection of Wyoming titles at **The Book Shop,** 117 N. Main St., tel. (307) 672-6505, and **Sheridan Stationery,** 206 N. Main St., tel. (307) 672-8080. The Book Shop also has occasional poetry readings and other literary events.

Custom Cowboy Shop, 350 N. Main St., tel. (307) 672-7733, has quality boots, hats, saddles, and tack.

Several Sheridan art galleries are worth a peek, including **Medicine Wheel Gallery,** 45 N. Main St., tel. (307) 672-0124; **Bozeman Trail Gallery,** next to King's Saddlery at 190 N. Main St., tel. (307) 672-3928; and **Bucking Buffalo Supply Co.,** 317 N. Main St., tel. (307) 674-4999. The last of these is a fun place packed with quality Western wear, home furnishings, and Indian-made items.

Information and Services

The **Sheridan Visitor Center/State Information Center,** tel. (307) 672-2485 or (800) 453-

3650, is in the rest area at the 5th St. exit off I-90. Inside are various historical displays, a 3-D map, and a panoramic view of the Big Horns from the windows. The center is open daily 8 a.m.-7 p.m. mid-May to mid-October, and Mon.-Fri. 8 a.m.-5 p.m. the rest of the year. Visit on the web at www.visitsheridan.com.

The **Bighorn National Forest Supervisor's Office** is at 1969 S. Sheridan Ave., tel. (307) 672-0751.

For details on sights to the north, see *Montana Handbook,* by W.C. McRae and Judy Jewell (Moon Travel Handbooks, www.moon.com).

With 1,500 students, **Sheridan College,** tel. (307) 674-6446, www.sc.whecn.edu, is one of the largest two-year schools in the state. Founded in 1948, it offers degrees in both academic and technical fields. The **Wyoming Room** of the college library (tel. 307-674-6446) has a variety of Indian artifacts, including vests, moccasins, pipes, and weapons.

ATMs are in many places around Sheridan, including most banks. Wash clothes at **Econ-O-Wash Laundry,** 19 E. 5th St., tel. (307) 672-7899, **Super Saver Laundromat,** 1789 N. Main St., tel. (307) 672-0471, or **Sugarland Laundromat,** in Sugarland Village, tel. (307) 672-5736. If you're heading west over the mountains or south to Buffalo, fill up with gas in Sheridan; prices are usually lower here.

Transportation

Sheridan airport is just southwest of town. **United Express/Great Lakes Aviation,** tel. (800) 631-1500, has daily flights between Sheridan and Denver.

Rent cars at the airport from **Avis,** tel. (307) 672-2226 or (800) 331-1212, or **Enterprise,** tel. (307) 672-6910 or (800) 325-8007. Get them in town from **Truck Corral Auto Rental,** 1320 Coffeen Ave., tel. (307) 672-7955.

Powder River/Coach USA, tel. (307) 674-6188 or (800) 442-3682, has daily bus service to Billings, Montana, and most towns in eastern Wyoming. Buses stop next to Evergreen Inn at 580 E. 5th Street.

NORTHWEST OF SHERIDAN

RANCHESTER

Fifteen miles north of Sheridan, the little village of Ranchester (pop. 700) has a couple of interesting historical sites. **Connor Battlefield State Historic Site** is right in Ranchester's city park. It's a very pleasant place with picnic tables, camping ($9 for nonresidents, $4 for Wyoming residents), and tall cottonwood trees along the Tongue River (so named because of a tonguelike rock along a tributary). Good fishing for brown trout. A cable footbridge leads across the river.

Despite its bucolic setting, the park has a gruesome history representing one of the worst atrocities in the Powder River Basin. The massacre took place in 1865, during a time of hit-and-run battles throughout the plains set off by the mass killing of the Cheyenne at Sand Creek in Colorado and continued in dozens of Indian attacks upon settlers and emigrants. Red Cloud had just struck against Platte Bridge Station (see Casper in the Central Wyoming chapter) a few weeks before, killing 28 men, and the army was eager to avenge that raid as well as attacks along the Bozeman Trail.

General Patrick E. Connor—a proponent of the shoot-first, ask-questions-later school of military diplomacy—attacked Indian villages throughout the West, killing 200 Shoshone in an 1863 Utah attack and then rampaging through Nevada and Idaho. Connor's 1865 expedition to the Powder River included nearly a thousand soldiers and 179 Pawnee and Winnebago scouts. Most of the effort was a failure as Indians kept ahead of the ponderous military wagons, but on August 29 Connor's men came upon Chief Bear's Arapaho village along the Tongue River. Connor ordered his men, "You will not receive overtures of peace or submission from the Indians, but will attack and kill every male Indian over 12 years of age." In a pell-mell rush, Connor's men slaughtered 63 men, women, and children, destroyed 250 lodges along with much of their winter supplies, and captured more than 1,100 ponies. Eight troopers died. No one ever determined whether the Arapaho they encountered were the same ones who had been attacking along the Bozeman Trail. The expedition ended when the government realized it was costing over a million dollars a month for transportation alone. A chastened Connor stashed his supplies at Fort Connor (later renamed Fort Reno) and returned to Fort Laramie.

Four miles west of here on US Hwy. 14, another monument marks the **Sawyer Fight.** Here, two days after Connor attacked the Arapaho along the Tongue River, Arapahoes retaliated against a 100-man roadbuilding expedition led by Col. James Sawyer. Three of his men were killed and the rest were pinned down for nearly two weeks before finally being rescued by Connor's troops.

Ranchester's oddest sight is the **T-Rex Museum,** 1116 Bighorn Dr., tel. (307) 655-3359. Inside are a couple of dinosaur models, a mineral collection, and the featured attraction, a life-size cast of a *Tyrannosaurus rex* skull. Entrance is $3 for adults, $2 for kids, or $8 for a family, but I personally wouldn't pay money for such a minor exhibit.

Lodging

Stay at the clean and friendly **Western Ranchester Motel,** tel. (307) 655-2212 or (800) 341-8000, for $45 s or $47-55 d. Inexpensive. **Lazy R RV Park & Campground,** tel. (307) 655-9284, has RV sites for $12-14.

Built in 1899 by cattle baron Samuel H. Hardin, the **Historic Old Stone House B&B,** 135 Wolf Creek Rd., tel. (307) 655-9239, occupies a hilltop south of Ranchester. The stone house (hence the name) has one room in the main house ($68 s or $78 d) and three spacious rooms in adjacent guest houses ($88 s, or $98 s or d). All rooms have private baths and are furnished with arts and crafts pieces, including some antiques. A full breakfast and evening wine are served, and kids are welcome. The webpage is www.cruising-america.com/oldstone.html. Moderate-Expensive.

Other Practicalities

Ranch House Restaurant, tel. (307) 655-9527, serves up family fare, and **Kelly's Kitchen,** tel. (307) 655-9016, has ice cream and fast food. Get groceries at **Buckhorn Groceries,** tel. (307) 655-9766, and cash from the **ATM** at Ranchester State Bank. The local mini-mall has a laundromat. Children will enjoy the kid-designed **wooden playground** of forts and slides at the elementary school.

Ranchester Days in June or July features a horseshoe tournament, a horse-drawn parade, arts-and-crafts booths, and a street dance.

DAYTON

The village of Dayton (pop. 600) contains the little log-cabin studio of water-colorist **Hans Kleiber** (1887-1966). The studio is now used as a combination museum and visitor center. Kleiber was known as "Artist of the Big Horns," and his works are internationally collected today. Inside are his press, art books, and several etchings. The museum is open daily in the summer and closed the rest of the year. Dayton's old **bell tower,** built in 1910 to warn of fires, is now in the city park.

Accommodations and Food

Foothills Campground and Motel, tel. (307) 655-2547, has cabins for $24 s or d, along with kitchenettes that cost $38 for four people. Budget-Inexpensive. Camp along the river here for $11, or park RVs for $16. Noncampers can shower for $2. Both campground and cabins are open May-Oct. only.

Built in 1892, **Dayton Mercantile,** tel. (307) 655-3100, is now run as a restaurant and gift shop. An upscale deli serves lunches, dinners, and Sunday brunches, and the soda fountain offers sweets. Be sure to head upstairs to the restored dance hall, used for line dancing on some Sunday nights. The Merc is open mid-May through mid-January. While here, ask about **Fun-Da-Mental-U,** with five-day lectures on regional history. Call (307) 672-6715 or (877) 996-3863 for more information. Meals, including a weekend breakfast buffet, are also available at **The Branding Iron,** tel. (307) 655-2334.

Other Practicalities

Dayton Days, held the last weekend in July, has the usual country favorites, including a parade, food and craft booths, a firefighters' water fight, Indian dancing, and a street dance. Anglers will find blue-ribbon trout fishing along the Tongue River. Dayton also has an outdoor **swimming pool** next to the Kleiber cabin; open June-August. The nine-hole **Horseshoe Moun-**

tain Golf Course, tel. (307) 655-9525, includes some unique hazards: horse-hoof-sized potholes from the thoroughbred ranch here.

Summerhouse Books, tel. (307) 655-2367, sells both new and used books. An **ATM** is inside the Sinclair station.

EAST OF SHERIDAN

Some of the prettiest plains country in Wyoming lies along US Hwy. 14, a quiet and scenic road that curls through mile after mile of ranchland and winter wheat. The road heads southeast from Sheridan, gradually narrowing as it climbs through rugged hills and down a long green valley filled with fine ranches and modern homes.

UCROSS

At the crossroads called Ucross, a huge red barn ("Big Red") dominates the view. The 22,000-acre Ucross Ranch is headquarters for the nonprofit Ucross Foundation, tel. (307) 737-2291, which operates an important retreat for writers, painters, poets, composers, sculptors, playwrights, photographers, and other artists. Each year some 60 selected artists enjoy a two- to eight-week residency program that includes individual work spaces, a printmaking studio, gallery, and comfortable living accommodations. It's all to give time for artists to focus on ideas, theories, and works. Author E. Annie Proulx wrote both *Postcards* and *The Shipping News* while staying here; the latter won her a Pulitzer Prize in 1992. Drop in for a tour of the immaculate buildings or to check out gallery exhibitions.

The **Big Red Art Gallery** at Ucross is open Mon.-Fri. 9 a.m.-noon and 1-4:30 p.m. all year, plus Sat.-Sun. 11 a.m.-3 p.m. in the summer months. Big Red was headquarters for the enormous Pratt and Ferris Cattle Co., a spread that extended 35 miles along Clear Creek. At one time, more than 35,000 calves were branded each fall, and the huge barn could hold 30 teams of horses. The "U Cross" was their brand. If you're in the area around the **Fourth of July,** stick around for food, games, live music, and a spectacular fireworks display.

Ucross is also home to **The Ranch at Ucross,** tel. (307) 737-2281 or (800) 447-0194, a luxurious guest ranch that fills with Tauck Tour buses during the summer. The ranch typically has a few rooms available for other travelers, but don't expect to have the place to yourself. Guests stay in condo-type rooms or modern cabins for $130 s or d, including a full breakfast in the restaurant. Also here is an outdoor pool and tennis court. Horseback rides are $15 per hour. The Ranch at Ucross is open May-Oct. only. Premium.

CLEARMONT AND LEITER AREA

The 20 miles east from Ucross are some of the most distinctive in Wyoming. The road parallels cottonwood-bordered Clear Creek, winding its way down the grassy hillsides. The Big Horn Mountains form a dramatic western backdrop, and large ranches dot the countryside with stone buildings and spreading old trees. It's easy to see why the Sioux fought so hard to keep this country out of white hands!

The largest settlement between Gillette and Sheridan, **Clearmont** is a pleasant place with a bit over 100 folks and tall deciduous trees lining the handful of streets. Get mediocre meals or a beer at **Red Arrow Cafe & Bar,** tel. (307) 758-4455. Park RVs here for $12, or pitch a tent for $5. Stop by the small **Pay & Save Groceries** to find food, crafts, and homemade quilts. Clearmont also has a combination library/community center and a pretty little town park with an old concrete jail.

East from Clearmont is minuscule **Leiter,** with a motel and a bar. Get very good steaks at **Leiterville Country Club,** tel. (307) 758-4343. Halfway between Clearmont and Leiter is the **RBL Bison Ranch,** tel. (307) 758-4387 or (800) 597-0109, home to 300 or more bison on a 3,500-acre spread. Daily tours are available May-Sept. for $6 per person. This is a great chance to see buffalo up close—and even feed them. Afterward you can feed *on* them at the restaurant, which serves buffalo burgers and steaks and is open three meals a day. The ranch has three basic cabins with a communal bathhouse for $48 d. Inexpensive. Park RVs for $20; pitch a tent for $5. Accommodations and the restaurant at RBL are open April-October.

The highway crosses the Powder River at the little settlement called **Arvada** and then heads east to Spotted Horse. **Powder River Experience,** tel. (307) 758-4381 or (888) 736-2402, offers ranch vacations on a 24,000-acre spread three miles south of Arvada. Guests ride horseback and join in short cattle drives or other ranch activities. You can stay by the night or the week in the two comfortable guest houses with shared or private baths; meals and lodging included. Rates are $240 for two people per night, all-inclusive. The ranch is open year-round and accepts a maximum of 10 guests at a time. Find it on the web at www.buffalowyoming.com/prexp. Luxury.

SPOTTED HORSE

At Spotted Horse—named for a minor Cheyenne chief—the combination country store/gas station/saloon/cafe is worth a stop, if only to hang out with locals in the bar. Hard times show in the faces of local ranchers. The bar has a jukebox, a few fast-food items on the menu, and cold beer. Its walls are carpeted with an amusing collection of old junk, historic photos, and cheesecake biker shots.

The 1811 overland expedition of the Astorians passed through the Spotted Horse area. During the 1930s, tourists en route to Yellowstone posed on a stuffed bucking bronc in the back paddock, but once I-90 was completed business plummeted and the local economy suffered a long decline.

Twenty miles north of the town of Recluse, **Buffalo Creek Ranch** sprawls over 35,000 acres on the Wyoming-Montana border. A guest house (actually a very comfortable trailer home) can sleep up to six people, and the ranch offers horseback riding, cattle drives, roping lessons, cowboy poetry, cookouts, and other Wild West activities. Guests come here to relax or to explore on foot or mountain bike. All-inclusive rates are $1,700 for two people for a six-night stay. The guest ranch is open mid-April through October; call (406) 427-5112 for details. Luxury.

Southeast from Spotted Horse, the highway curves toward the coal mines of Gillette. The red scoria rock of the highway points through summer-green grass. (Also called clinker, this rock was created when coal burned underground, baking adjacent shale and sandstone to a bright red. Similar red roads exist all over Powder River Basin.) Old windmills pump water for cattle and sheep. From atop the hills a landscape of fences, phone lines, plowed fields, bales of hay, and horses spreads out in all directions. The sun darts between cotton ball clouds as a lone cyclist pumps up the road, swerving around the smashed jackrabbits and

rancher Tooter Rogers in Spotted Horse, Wyoming

May your horse never stumble
Your spurs never rust
Your guts never grumble
Your cinch never bust
May your boots never pinch
Your crops never fail
While you eat lots of beans
And stay out of jail

—FROM A SIGN IN SPOTTED HORSE

passed by pickup trucks with gun racks and drivers with tipped-back cowboy hats. This is the true West, not the region cutesified for the tourists. Red-sided buttes rise above the rolling plains. The new ranch houses—trailer homes—stand next to aging farmsteads and collapsed log cabins; imported pickups sit in the driveways and satellite dishes guard the front yards. If you like grass and sky, brilliant starry nights, antelope, haystacks, and oil wells, you'll love this place. Stop for a while and listen to the silence broken only by the meadowlarks and the wind. God's country.

SOUTH OF SHERIDAN

Although I-90 cuts south of Sheridan toward Buffalo, US Hwy. 87 offers a much more interesting route, taking you through rolling ranch country and past cottonwood-lined draws. Along the way are the little settlements of Big Horn and Story and the historically rich country around old Fort Phil Kearny and the Bozeman Trail. The area's beauty has long attracted wealthy corporate executives and politicians, who come here to relax as gentlemen ranchers in ostentatious homes.

BIG HORN

History

Tiny Big Horn was founded in 1879 by O.P. Hanna (local Indians called him "Big Spit" because of his tobacco chewing), a ceaseless promoter who sent glowing accounts of "Big Horn City" to various newspapers. A reporter decided to investigate and found the town consisted primarily of a few outlaws, including "Big Nose" George Parrott and Jesse James' outlaw brother, Frank. A few homesteaders and settlers did take the bait, however: by 1884 Big Horn City had a hotel, three stores, two blacksmith shops, three saloons, a newspaper, a school, a church, and even a college of sorts.

Sights

Over the years, most of Big Horn's businesses moved to Sheridan, but still here is **Big Horn Mercantile,** built in 1882 and considered the oldest business in northern Wyoming. Take a look inside for the photo of Queen Elizabeth, who visited this historically British area in 1984. From the same era is **Bozeman Trail Inn,** tel. (307) 672-9288, where you'll find one of the oldest bars in Wyoming. A restaurant here is open daily.

A historic 1881 blacksmith shop houses the **Bozeman Trail Museum.** Open Sat.-Sun. 11 a.m.-6 p.m. June-Aug. and by appointment at other times, the museum displays various local memorabilia, historical photos, and a small gift shop. The ceiling is "branded" with local cattle brands. No admission charge. The town park next door makes a pleasant picnic spot.

The **State Bird Farm,** tel. (307) 674-7701, on Bird Farm Rd., raises more than 13,000 pheasants each year. These birds are released around Wyoming shortly before the fall hunting season, just in time to get shot as "wild game." The farm also has show birds including over a dozen species of pheasants, along with peacocks, turkey, chukkar, and guinea hens. Come here in early May to see the cute pheasant chicks.

Polo

Certainly the last thing one might expect to find in Big Horn is a polo field, but the English tradition lives on at **Big Horn Equestrian Center** south of town on Bird Farm Road. Polo games are held on Sundays in the summer and are informal events with changing teams and players of varying abilities. Polo games began on the **Polo Ranch,** a couple miles west of Big Horn, before moving to the present equestrian center in the

1980s. The Polo Ranch itself is hard to miss, with an enormous white barn and immaculate white picket fences. It positively reeks of money. The current owner is an executive with American Standard, the toilet-fixture company, and a financial backer to conservative Christian radio stations around Wyoming. The ranch was formerly owned by ex-U.S. senator Malcolm Wallop, the grandson of Sir Oliver H. Wallop, seventh earl of Portsmouth (who served in the Wyoming Legislature before returning to England to sit in the House of Lords). Oliver Wallop and the two Moncrieffe brothers (see below) bought Western horses for the British Army during the Boer War, shipping 20,000 of them overseas. To test the ponies, the British purchasing officer would ride them the length of a polo field. Malcolm Moncrieffe trained a team on this field and later competed with them in England. Thus began what is believed to be the oldest polo club in America.

Accommodations

At **Bozeman Trail B&B,** tel. (307) 672-2381 or (877) 672-2381, a graceful blue barn (built in 1919) has been transformed into a country bed and breakfast. Owners Toby and Marie Johnson welcome guests, providing four rooms and three baths, a tasty full breakfast, and a relaxing jacuzzi on their 30-acre farm. Sheep, longhorn cattle, and a horse graze in the adjacent pasture. Toby Johnson is a hunting guide, so animal heads fill the interior of the B&B. Room rates are $75-95 d; the loft is perfect for families and friends ($125 for four people). For more information, head to www.thebluebarn.com. Moderate-Expensive.

Two miles southwest of Big Horn and right on Little Goose Creek, **Spear Ranch B&B,** tel. (307) 673-0079, is an impressive mansion with immaculate lawns and a white picket fence out front. Inside are five guest rooms (shared or private baths), ranging from a small bachelor's space ($70 s) to a spacious room with a mahogany bed, creek views, and gas fireplace ($90 d). Two rooms can be joined to create a suite for $150. Not far from the home is a private carriage house containing two bedrooms, a kitchen, and living room; $150 for three people or $175 for five. A full breakfast is included in the rates, and children are welcome. Expensive-Premium.

In the cool pine forests seven miles west of Big Horn, **Spahn's Big Horn Mountain Bed & Breakfast,** tel. (307) 674-8150, is one of the finest B&Bs in Wyoming. The beautiful three-story log home was built by Ron Spahn, a former geologist and lawyer who runs the place with his wife Bobbie, a former nurse. Enjoy a full breakfast on the porch, where the view extends all the way to Montana, a hundred miles across Powder River Basin. It's a great place to watch distant lightning storms. Guests stay in three rooms inside the main house ($95-135 d) or in one of two cabins ($110-125 d) just a short walk away. The cabins are perfect for families or honeymooners. Plan on spending several days here; there's lots to do nearby, and the country is grand. The website is www.bighorn--wyoming.com. Expensive-Premium.

Events

The big annual event in Big Horn is Don King's Labor Day weekend **Steer Roping and Bronc Riding** at the equestrian center. Call (800) 453-3650 for more information. The **Fourth of July** fireworks show in Big Horn is the biggest in the Sheridan area.

BRADFORD BRINTON MEMORIAL MUSEUM

In 1892, two Scottish brothers, William and Malcolm Moncrieffe, built a spacious two-story ranch house along Little Goose Creek. It became headquarters for their Quarter Circle A Ranch. A businessman and lover of the West, Bradford Brinton purchased the ranch in 1923 and enlarged the home to 20 rooms, filled it with elegant furniture, and lined the walls with his art collection. Bradford's sister Helen owned the house after his death in 1936, and upon her own passing in 1960 the building became a museum honoring her brother. The museum, tel. (307) 672-3173, is open daily 9:30 a.m.-5 p.m. from May 15 to early September (closed the rest of the year), with guided tours of the home and a creekside cabin. A donation is requested.

Step inside to taste the genteel life and to view works by some of the West's best-known artists, many of whom were friends of Bradford Brinton. The collection includes over 600 pieces by such artists as John James Audubon, Hans Kleiber, Charles M. Russell, Frederic Remington, and Will Gollings. Also here are impressive Indian handicrafts, a Jefferson peace medal given to an Indian chief, books, and historic documents. A small gallery in the museum sells high-quality gifts. The log lodge of Bradford Brinton sits along Little Goose Creek and is filled with big game trophies. Horses are still raised on the 600-acre ranch, and the rural setting is most enjoyable: mountains rise on two sides and big old cottonwoods border the drive. Get to the Quarter Circle A by heading five miles west on State Hwy. 335 from the junction with US Hwy. 87. Signs point the way.

Red Grade

For a panoramic view of the surrounding country, follow State Hwy. 335 west from the Bradford Brinton Memorial Museum. The road turns to gravel after three miles and then continues into the Big Horn Mountains as Red Grade Rd. (Forest Rd. 26). The route's a bit rough and too steep for RVs but it provides outstanding vistas after just a couple of miles. The road eventually connects with US Hwy. 14, but bring along a Forest Service map.

STORY

The town of Story (pop. 650) is surprisingly different from nearby Sheridan and Buffalo. The road into Story winds more than a thousand feet above the valley floor to the pine-covered slopes of the Big Horns. Locals and visitors come up to escape the hot summer air, to enjoy the restaurants, and to look for deer, elk, moose, and wild turkeys. Story is the site of "Piney Island," a stand of timber used to build nearby Fort Phil Kearny in 1866. The town was named for Nelson Story, the first man to trail cattle north across the Powder River Basin. **Story Fish Hatchery,** established in 1907, raises trout for Wyoming lakes and streams. The visitor center has interpretive exhibits and is open daily 8 a.m.-5 p.m. from mid-April to mid-September; tel. (307) 683-2234.

Accommodations

Several places provide relaxing lodging in the Story area. Set on five wooded acres, **Piney Creek Inn B&B,** tel. (307) 683-2911, is a quiet place providing a variety of accommodations, all with private baths. The rambling log house contains a guest room ($65 d) and two-bedroom suite ($110 for four people). Two cabins are also available. The larger one ($150 for four) has two bedrooms, a kitchen, and spiral staircase, while the newer cabin ($125 d) is a favorite of honeymooners and contains a fireplace, kitchenette, and jacuzzi bathtub. A hearty full breakfast is included, and guests will enjoy the hot tub off the main lodge and the large porch out front. Children are welcome. The friendly owners at Piney Creek also set up tours of the area, trail rides, and a variety of ranch activities. Find them on the web at www.pineycreekinn.com. Inexpensive-Moderate.

Wagonbox Inn, tel. (307) 683-2444 or (800) 308-2444, has cozy cabins starting for $55 d, up to a secluded six-person cabin with a kitchen for $95. Also available are shared-bath bunkhouse accommodations for $40 s or d. All guests can use the sauna and jacuzzi. Reserve a month ahead for midsummer visits here. Inexpensive.

Little Piney Ranch, tel. (307) 683-2806, has two modern cabins for rent by the night or week. A one-bedroom unit is $80, and the two-bedroom one costs $120. Both have living rooms, dining areas, and full kitchens. The cabins are a mile west of old Fort Kearny. Moderate.

Story Pines Motel, tel. (307) 683-2120 or (800) 596-6297, has newly built accommodations for $65 s or d, including access to a hot tub and picnic area. The town laundromat is also here. Moderate.

Occupying a 1,000-acre spread south of Story, **Rafter Y Ranch,** tel. (307) 683-2258, has space for just 20 guests in comfortable log cabins with fireplaces, porches, and private baths. It's a fine place to ride horses or just relax in the foothills of the Big Horns. All-inclusive rates are $280 per day for two people. No minimum stay, but most guests stay at least four days. Open July-August. Luxury.

Food

Wagonbox Inn, tel. (307) 683-2444 or (800) 308-2444, serves some of the best and most innovative food in the area, with prime rib, steaks, chicken, fish, and a substantial wine list. On weekend nights, folks come here for live music.

Piney Creek General Store, tel. (307) 683-2400, is an old-fashioned country store with crowded aisles and a surprisingly good selection. A tiny cafe (Waldorf A' Story) here cranks out three meals a day, including homemade soups, creative sandwiches, and other treats. A few tables are inside, with more outside on the deck. Gourmet Saturday-night dinners have $7-19 entrées. Well worth a stop!

Lodore's Supper Club and Lounge, tel. (307) 683-2355, opened in 1919 and remains a popular dinner destination but the food is forgettable. You're better off coming here for the live C&W bands in the summer.

Other Practicalities

Piney Creek Pottery, tel. (307) 683-2181, sells pottery and other artwork.

For an enjoyable hike along Piney Creek, contact **Cloud Peak Llamas,** tel. (307) 683-2548. The llama carries your lunch and gear; $15 for adults or $7 for kids.

THE BLOODY BOZEMAN

The discovery of gold in Montana during the 1860s triggered an avalanche of miners and businessmen. The fastest route to the Virginia City goldfields headed northwest from Bridger's Ferry (near present-day Douglas) through the Powder River Basin, and then west across Montana. One of the pioneers who scouted and constantly promoted the "Montana Road" was John M. Bozeman (as in Bozeman, Montana). Before being killed by Indians on the Yellowstone River in 1867, he led several groups up the Bozeman Trail, as the route became known. Hundreds of others would die along Bozeman's route to the goldfields. Guide Jim Bridger knew that the Sioux would never stand for whites in their Powder River country—a place they had recently wrested from the Crows, the Shoshone, and the Ara-

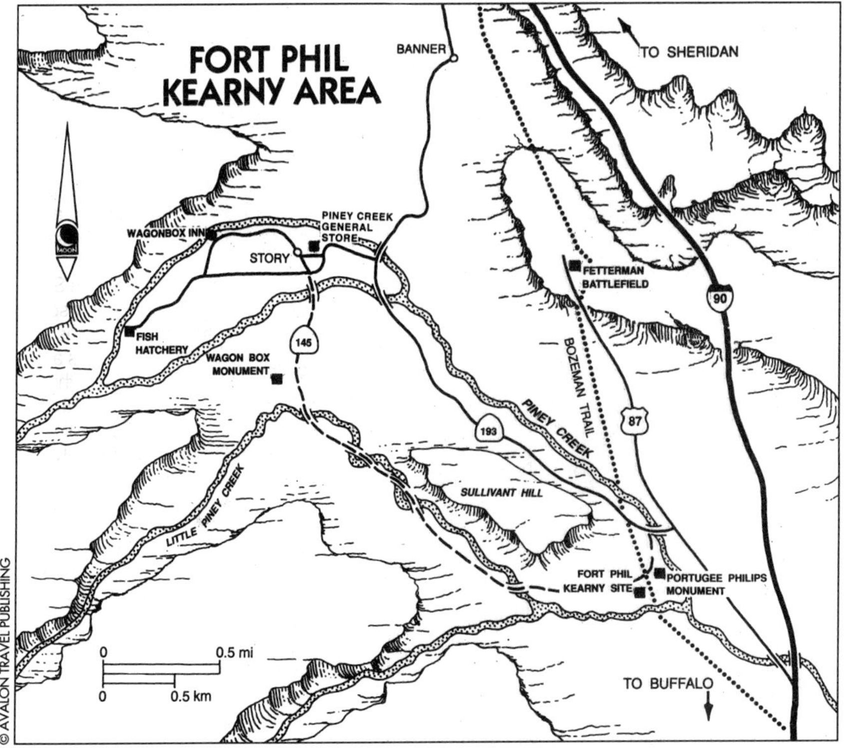

pahoes. Instead, he recommended a different route that would cut west of the Big Horn Mountains. Unfortunately, Bridger's advice went unheeded, and as attacks on emigrant wagon trains increased in 1864, so did pressure to protect them from the Sioux. Appeals to Washington brought military assistance in the form of forts filled with soldiers and cavalry. Parallels between the events that followed and America's experience in Vietnam—from the guerrilla warfare to the hurried exit of U.S. troops at the end of the conflict—are disconcerting.

Red Cloud's War

The first salvo by the army came in General Connor's savage wanderings through the Powder River in 1865 (see Ranchester above). The following year, while treaty negotiations were being held at Fort Laramie, Col. Henry B. Carrington and a battalion of infantry marched in, heading for the Bozeman Trail, where they planned to construct new forts. Red Cloud, a fiery military leader of the Oglala Sioux, grew more and more angry, shouting,

> *Great Father sends us presents and wants new road, but White Chief goes with soldier, to steal road before Indian says yes or no. . . . White man lies and steals. My lodges were many, but now they are few. The white man wants all. The white man must fight, and the Indian will die where his fathers died.*

The treaty was signed by older chiefs and the "Laramie Loafers," who hung around the fort, but not by Red Cloud. He and his warriors stormed out, arriving at Powder River ahead of Colonel Carrington.

Carrington was a strange man to direct this massive undertaking. A political appointee with no battlefield experience—let alone experience with guerrilla warfare—he approached the task of building forts and protecting travelers along the Bozeman Trail with a take-no-chances attitude that rankled his trigger-happy men. The troupe left Nebraska with a 30-piece brass band, carriages, and comfortable furnishings, earning the name "Carrington's Overland Circus."

Once finally in the Powder River country, Carrington split his men into three groups, stationing some at Fort Reno near present-day Buffalo (begun the previous year by General Connor) and sending others to build Fort C.F. Smith in Montana. These way stations were to provide military escorts for travelers and havens from Indian attacks. Instead, they themselves came under attack, and Carrington's men nearly became prisoners inside them.

Fort Phil Kearny

In the heart of the Powder River country, Carrington found what seemed a perfect site for a fort along Little Piney Creek: there was good water, grass so thick that horses could barely walk through it, and timber close at hand. His guide, the famed Jim Bridger, pushed instead for a site farther north, away from the center of Sioux country. To Bridger, these "damn paper collar soldiers" seemed bound and determined to get killed. The new garrison—named Fort Phil Kearny for a Civil War general—measured 600 by 800 feet and was entirely enclosed by a heavy log stockade. Big enough for 1,000 men, it never housed anything close to that many. Both Indian attackers and white defenders came to view this as the West's most-hated fort. From the very first day, Carrington found himself harassed by the Sioux; by mid-December, more than 50 raids on the troops and civilians had left 17 military men and 58 civilians dead. Many of the horses and mules were stolen in the raids, and more than 700 cattle were lost when the Indians created a stampede by driving a herd of buffalo into them. With winter setting in, food and ammunition shortages made conditions worse, and even the nightly band concerts could not maintain morale. Jim Bridger revealed something of even greater concern after one of his scouting trips:

> *Crow chiefs report that it took a half a day's ride to go through the villages of the war parties on Tongue River. The Sioux chiefs said they would not touch the new fort on Powder River [Fort Reno] but would destroy the two new forts, in their hunting grounds, meaning Phil Kearny and C. F. Smith.*

Fetterman Fight

Again and again, the Sioux tempted soldiers into traps, drawing them away with attacks on the vital wood wagons (more than 4,000 logs were used in the stockade) and workers cutting hay, or by stealing horses and then attacking the pursuers. Carrington's caution caused dissension in the ranks, and when a new company of cavalry arrived, led by Capt. William J. Fetterman, the dissension edged on open revolt. Fetterman, like Gen. George A. Custer, had achieved fame for his bravery during the Civil War and, like Custer, would meet an early death. Fetterman viewed the Sioux with reckless disdain, claiming, "I can take 80 men and go to Tongue River through all the Sioux forces." Jim Bridger responded to this boast by telling him, "Your men who fought down South are crazy! They don't know anything about fighting Indians."

On the morning of Dec. 21, 1866, Indians attacked a wood train, and a force of cavalry and infantrymen under Captain Fetterman was sent out. Disobeying orders from Colonel Carrington, Fetterman responded to taunts by Sioux decoys (including young Crazy Horse) by following them into an ambush. Perhaps 2,000 warriors of Red Cloud, High Back Bone, Red Leaf, and Little Wolf suddenly appeared in the tall grass. Within a half hour, all 81 soldiers had been killed. It was, until Custer's last stand a decade later, the worst annihilation of any American force. Carrington had lost his most experienced fighters. Perhaps 30 Sioux died in the raid. Troops sent out to investigate what had happened found the frozen bodies horribly mutilated. They buried the men in a mass grave.

After the Fetterman Fight, just 119 soldiers remained to guard against several thousand Sioux. Fearing further attacks, Carrington put the fort on full alert and sent messengers to Fort Laramie in a desperate bid for help. John "Portugee" Phillips made the 236-mile ride in four nights of hard riding, struggling through subzero temperatures and blinding blizzards and traveling at night to avoid Indian attacks. In a scene straight out of a Hollywood movie, Phillips staggered into a gala Christmas-night ball with the stunning news. His exhausted horse collapsed and died from pneumonia two weeks later. Because of bad weather, help did not reach Fort Phil Kearny for another two weeks, but the feared Indian attacks never came. Colonel Carrington was reassigned to Fort McPherson in Nebraska—accidentally shooting himself in the foot on the way out—and it took many years to clear his name of the Fetterman disaster.

Wagon Box Fight

The tables were turned in the Wagon Box Fight. Woodcutters took the running gear off their wagons to haul logs back to the fort and arranged the wagon boxes in a makeshift fortress filled with ammunition and supplies in case of attack. The attack came on Aug. 2, 1867, when Red Cloud's 3,000 warriors suddenly surrounded 32 woodchoppers and soldiers led by Capt. James Powell. Unbeknownst to Red Cloud, the soldiers were armed with new Springfield rifles that could fire up to 20 rounds a minute. Expecting the soldiers to take time to reload, Red Cloud sent waves of men, only to meet withering gunfire each time. Finally, after six hours of this, soldiers from Fort Phil Kearny arrived with their howitzer and sent the Sioux fleeing. Four soldiers died in the Wagon Box Fight, while estimates of Indian casualties range from six to over a thousand—Sioux warriors removed their dead after a battle, making it impossible to know how many had been killed.

The Fighting Ends

By late 1867, public sentiment had turned against the army's invasion of Sioux country, and the Bozeman Trail had become an anachronism, with miners heading to Montana via steamboat up the Missouri River. Besides, the Union Pacific Railroad was well on its way across Wyoming, and the diversion was no longer needed. (Some historians believe this was the primary reason for the forts being built in the first place.) In 1868, the three Bozeman Trail forts were all abandoned. As the soldiers left Fort Phil Kearny, they turned back to see smoke on the horizon. The Sioux were burning it to the ground. Thus ended, at least temporarily, one of the most senseless conflicts in American history. Red Cloud finally returned to Fort Laramie to sign the treaty, having (he thought) forced the government to leave Powder River to the Sioux. Actually the treaty was ambiguous and contradictory, giving them rights to hunt buffalo on the Powder River but saying they would have to live on reservations in Dakota Territory. Six years later, the country would again boil over when another gold rush—this time in the Black Hills—brought General Custer north to fight the Sioux.

Exploring the Bozeman Trail

The site of **Fort Phil Kearny** is now a National Historic Landmark and is managed by the Wyoming Department of Parks and Cultural Resources. The fort is 17 miles north of Buffalo and 21 miles south of Sheridan off I-90 (take exit 44). Day-use at the fort costs $2 for nonresidents, $1 for Wyoming residents; free for youths under 18. The fort itself is long gone—it was, after all, burned to the ground by the Indians—but a reconstruction project completed in 2000 includes two corner walls and blockhouses on the original site. Signs note former building locations, the cemetery, and the Bozeman Trail.

A fine small **museum** is open daily 8 a.m.-6 p.m. from mid-May through September, and Wed.-Sun. noon-4 p.m. Oct.-Nov. and April to mid-May. Inside, find an excellent model of the fort, videos about the Bozeman Trail and Fort Phil Kearny, and displays on Indian life. For more on the fort, call (307) 684-7687 or (307) 684-7629.

The third weekend of June brings **Bozeman Trail Days** to Fort Phil Kearny, with archaeological tours of the fort and nearby battlegrounds, a living history encampment, fife and drum concerts, Indian dancing, chuck wagon meals, gold panning, and more.

Other Bozeman Trail Sights

Ruts from the Bozeman Trail are still visible along much of its path, and the battle sites are all marked with monuments of various sorts. Portugee Phillips's ride is noted by a pyramid-shaped memorial not far from Fort Phil Kearny. Get to the site of the **Wagon Box Fight** by heading a mile south from Story (good road) or driving northwest from Fort Phil Kearny on a narrow and winding gravel road.

The **Fetterman Fight** is marked by a stone obelisk atop the hill where the final stand was made. Informative plaques provide a full description of events leading up to the battle and its consequences, and a one-mile interpretive trail crosses the battlefield. Access is only from the south; the north section of the road is blocked by a landslide.

BUFFALO

At the base of the Big Horn Mountains, Buffalo (pop. 3,700) is one of those delightful small towns that seem to define rural America. Tourists and locals relax on summer mornings along Clear Creek, while dogs sit in the back of pickup trucks parked on Main Street. Despite the fact that Buffalo's Main Street curves along an old bison trail, the town got its name from Buffalo, New York—the name was picked out of a hat.

Buffalo—the Johnson County seat—is primarily a ranching, oil, and tourism center for the area. The county constitutes the heart of sheep ranching in Wyoming; thousands of sheep roam across the sage-covered land here. Many of these are still tended by Basque shepherds, and longtime residents of Basque heritage are now pillars of the local community.

Not sure it's of any real significance, but the last time I visited Buffalo I noticed two bumper stickers: the one on the pickup truck said "Real men love Jesus," while the one on the import warned "Clear the road. I'm 16."

HISTORY

During Gen. George Crook's 1876 campaign against the Sioux, he had Capt. Edwin Pollock build a supply center along the Powder River. Originally called Cantonment Reno, it was later renamed **Fort McKinney,** after Lt. John A. McKinney, who had been killed in the Dull Knife Battle. In 1878, Fort McKinney was moved 40 miles north to where the Bozeman Trail crossed Clear Creek. Gradually the new fort took shape, not as one of the stockade-walled structures generally thought of, but rather as a collection of barracks, mess halls, and two-story houses with board-and-batten exteriors. Soldiers marched from here to South Dakota's Pine Ridge Reservation to put down the Ghost Dance uprising in 1890. More than 150 Sioux and 25 soldiers died at Wounded Knee, the last major battle between Indians and whites in North America.

The establishment of Fort McKinney created an immediate market for all sorts of businesses. Carpenters, blacksmiths, farmers, loggers, merchants, bartenders, and prostitutes arrived and quickly established the town of Buffalo two miles downstream. By 1883, a Cheyenne newspaper noted a dozen saloons and no churches. "Houses of dissipation" seemed more numerous than any other establishment. Much of the barley harvested locally went to supply two breweries. Buffalo had become the largest town in the northern part of Wyoming. This boom suddenly ended in 1894, when the army declared Fort McKinney excess property and abandoned it. The buildings became the Wyoming Soldiers' and Sailors' Home in 1903 and now house the Veterans' Home of Wyoming. It is still one of the county's largest employers.

After WW II, oil and gas exploration and development of the region's vast coal deposits turned Buffalo into an energy center. Today the coal resources of Johnson County remain essentially undeveloped, but substantial amounts of oil and gas are still produced. Downtown Buffalo has undergone a facelift in recent years as new tourist-oriented businesses move in selling gifts, artwork, antiques, espresso, fly-fishing gear, upscale kids' clothing, and health food.

SIGHTS

Jim Gatchell Memorial Museum

The Powder River Basin's rich history comes to life in this impressive collection, one of the finest small museums in the American West. The focus is upon life in the late 19th century, when a rugged mix of Indians, soldiers, miners, homesteaders, wealthy cattlemen, and outlaws brought turmoil to this land. Historic artifacts gathered by druggist Theodore James Gatchell form the core of a collection of some 15,000 articles. An addition in 1999 doubled the museum's size and made it entirely wheelchair accessible. It now fills two downtown buildings, along with an attached carriage house.

Displayed in the carriage house are several historic wagons, including the de rigueur sheepherder's wagon and chuck wagon. The front building contains historic photos, a model of Fort Phil Kearny, two videos about Bomber Moun-

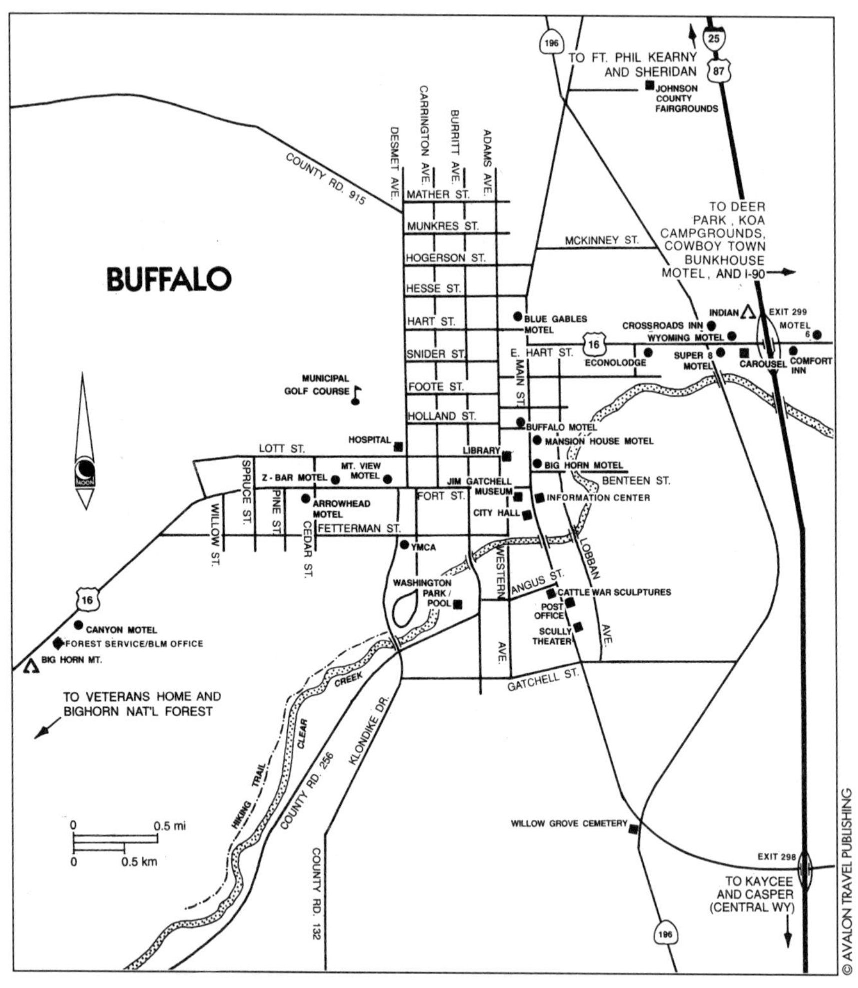

tain, and traveling exhibits. Inside the main building are two floors; downstairs is the standard collection of old junk (including—inexplicably—a piece of coral from Maui!), along with newer walk-through re-creations of the past. Upstairs is a treasure trove of unusual items, including one of the largest collections of Indian artifacts in Wyoming. Featured are detailed dioramas and displays of items found at the sites of various local battles including the Wagon Box Fight, the Johnson County War, and the Fetterman Fight. Most touching is the flattened horn of bugler Adolph Metzger, the last to die at the Fetterman Fight. The note here says his body was the only one the Indians did not mutilate after the massacre but instead covered it with a buffalo robe out of respect for his valor. Other stories say that after trying to fight off the warriors with his hands and bugle, he was taken captive and tortured to death at the Sioux camp.

The Jim Gatchell Memorial Museum is one of the finest small museums in Wyoming.

Scattered around the room are other surprises: an extensive photographic exhibit on the Powder River, a pair of Cheyenne medicine rattles used in the Dance of Victory after Custer's defeat at Little Big Horn, an arrowhead that belonged to Red Cloud, a cartridge belt made by mountain man Jim Bridger, along with the hired gunman Tom Horn's spurs and a bridle he braided while awaiting execution. Ask the folks at the museum to point out a rifle probably used by the cavalry at Little Big Horn and a shell from Custer's handgun. Look around and you'll find even more surprises at this most impressive small museum.

The Jim Gatchell Museum is downtown on the corner of Main and Fort Sts., tel. (307) 684-9331, and has a $2 admission charge (free for kids under age 15). Get more information on the web at www.jimgatchell.com. A small gift shop sells historical books and old Wyoming license plates. The museum is open daily 8 a.m.-8 p.m. from Memorial Day to Labor Day (closed July 4) and has reduced hours in the spring and fall. It's closed Jan.-March, but you can call for an appointment or ask across the street at the chamber of commerce.

BILL NYE ON RUSTLING

Three years ago a guileless tenderfoot came into Wyoming, leading a single Texas steer and carrying a branding iron; now he is the opulent possessor of six hundred head of fine cattle—the ostensible progeny of that one steer. . . . A poor boy can in a few years, with an ordinary Texas steer and a branding iron, get together a band of cattle that would surprise those who figure simply on the ordinary rate of increase. Men soon learn that it is possible and even frequent for a cow wearing a "Z" brand to be the fond and loving mother of a calf wearing the "X" brand, and vice versa. Sometimes a calf will develop a brand that has never been in the family before.

—19TH-CENTURY HUMORIST BILL NYE

Occidental Hotel

Completed in 1910, the Occidental Hotel at 10 N. Main St. was the place where Owen Wister's Virginian "got his man." Over the years many famous people walked through these doors, including Teddy Roosevelt, Herbert Hoover, Calvin Coolidge, Buffalo Bill Cody, Butch Cassidy, and Calamity Jane. In later years it was a residential hotel before closing in 1985. The owners of Zoobooks (a children's series) bought the dilapidated building in the late 1990s and proceeded to lovingly return the building to its glory days. Many of the original fixtures and other items were returned, including the billiard table, stained glass, tin ceilings, light fixtures, piano, and back bar. Today the hotel is operated as a combination publishing business and museum. Brochures provide self-guided tours, and dozens of historical photos line the upstairs walls. Several of the old rooms have been furnished as they appeared in the 1920s, and the saloon now serves as a marvelous community space. The hotel is open Mon.-Sat. 10 a.m.-4 p.m. June to mid-September or by appointment at other times. Entrance costs $2 for adults, free for kids. Call (307) 684-0451 for details.

A number of other interesting structures line Main St.; pick up a walking tour of Buffalo's other historic buildings from the chamber of commerce.

Petrified Forest

One of the more unusual local sights is a petrified forest on BLM land seven miles south of Buffalo. Take the Red Hills exit from I-90 and follow the road another seven miles to Dry Creek Petrified Forest. An easy three-quarter-mile trail loops through the hot sagebrush country, and markers along the way describe the geological history. Some 60 million years ago, this was a swampy plain dominated by towering metasequoia trees. You can still count the growth rings on the petrified stumps, some of which are over four feet in diameter and 60 million years old.

Other Sights

Two bronze sculptures occupy a small park across the street from First National Bank on S. Main Street. Created by local sculptor D. Michael Thomas, they represent combatants in the Johnson County War of 1892. The Johnson County War helped dissuade the Chicago, Burlington, and Quincy Railroad from coming through Buffalo, and for many years Buffalo remained America's largest inland city without a railway. Eventually a spur line was built, connecting Buffalo to Clearmont. Locals called it BC&BM (Buffalo-Clearmont and Back, Maybe) but even it was

THE JOHNSON COUNTY WAR

Wyoming's history is a story of constant conflict—between emigrants and Indians, Chinese and white miners, big ranchers and homesteaders, sheepherders and cattlemen. The Powder River has seen more than its share of confrontations; one of the most notorious was the so-called Johnson County War of 1892, the setting for the 1980 box-office megaflop *Heaven's Gate.*

Barons and Grangers

The first white settlers in the Powder River Basin were the "cattle barons," men who owned enormous herds of cattle but who generally resided on the land only part of the year. During the 1880s, more and more homesteaders ("grangers") began to settle here, fencing their spreads and gradually forcing the large cow outfits onto less and less land. The barons tried to force homesteaders off the land, and several Johnson County grangers were found facedown in gullies, shot in the back. Homesteaders retaliated by appropriating cattle that wandered onto their land—and outlaws made off with other stock.

As rustling increased along the Powder River, the big ranchers found little sympathy in nearby Buffalo, the largest town north of the Platte River. Local juries, either sympathetic with or intimidated by cattle rustlers, failed to convict men who were caught, and even the Buffalo sheriff, "Red" Angus, was accused of being in cahoots with rustlers. The cattle barons feared for their lives. The small ranchers and homesteaders in Buffalo were soon openly at odds with the absentee cattle barons based in the largest town south of the Platte—Cheyenne.

The Invasion

In 1892, the small Johnson County ranchers organized their own roundup, an action that proved too much for the powerful Wyoming Stock Growers Association. In a secret meeting, the association proposed a military coup d'état. On April 6, two days after the association's annual meeting in Cheyenne, a train headed for Douglas with 25 hired Texas gunmen (mostly ex-sheriffs and ex-U.S. marshals) and an equal number of Wyoming men. With them they carried a hit list of 70 suspected rustlers. Cutting the telegraph lines to keep advance word from reaching folks in Johnson County, and traveling in darkened railway cars, the "Invaders" headed north, stopping the train near Casper and continuing on horseback.

abandoned in 1946 due to competition from trucking companies. Wyoming Railroad's **Engine 105** now rusts in the city park.

Children (and those who never really grew up) will love the antique **Carousel Park,** tel. (307) 684-7033, on the east end of town behind Col. Bozeman's Restaurant. This is the only carousel in Wyoming and is open daily Memorial Day to Labor Day for just $1.25 per ride. It includes a dozen custom-carved Wyoming bucking horses. Also here is a 1936 Ferris wheel and a mini-golf course.

Willow Grove Cemetery, on the south end of town, is an interesting place to explore. Here you will find the graves of rustlers Nate Champion and Nick Ray, Sheriff "Red" Angus, homesteader John Tisdale, and others involved in the Johnson County War.

Injured or aged veterans live on the grounds of the **Wyoming Veterans' Home** (old Fort McKinney), two miles west of Buffalo on US Hwy. 16. Of the original fort, only an old cavalry stable and the post hospital building are still standing. Check in at the office (tel. 307-684-5511) before sightseeing.

ACCOMMODATIONS AND CAMPING

Motels

You'll discover plenty of comfortable, exceptionally clean, and friendly motels to choose from in Buffalo, but it's a good idea to reserve well ahead for accommodations in the middle of summer, when tourists flood the area. Be forewarned that motel prices may rise precipitously during the peak summer season, and you may have to pay up to $80 a night. Accommodations are arranged below from least to most expensive. Add a seven percent tax to these rates.

Canyon Motel, 997 Fort St., tel. (307) 684-2957 or (800) 231-0742, has the least expensive local rooms: $36 s or $38-52 d, with kitchenettes for $44-52 s or d, and two-bedroom units

They first came to the KC Ranch—actually just a couple of cabins—and discovered two of the most notorious rustlers, Nate Champion and Nick Ray, holed up inside. In the daylong shoot-out that followed, Ray died quickly, but Champion managed to hold off the Invaders until dusk, when they finally torched the cabin and shot him as he ran for safety. A bloodstained diary found on Champion described his last hours. It ended: "Shooting again. I think they will fire the house this time. It's not night yet. The house is all fired. Goodbye, boys, if I never see you again. Nathan D. Champion."

After this initial success, the Invaders headed on to the friendly TA Ranch, 30 miles north, to rest up for their planned siege of Buffalo. But word got out, and the Invaders suddenly found themselves under attack by a mob of 200 well-armed grangers and rustlers led by Sheriff Red Angus (who was on the hit list). In the shoot-out that followed, two Texans died. The tables had been turned, and the desperate Invaders faced almost certain annihilation. Meanwhile, word had gotten out to acting governor Amos W. Barber (a supporter of the Invaders), who cabled President Harrison for help. Troops from nearby Fort McKinney arrived before the townsfolk could attack with their tanklike wagon and dynamite bombs. Newspapers around the nation castigated the cattle barons for their effrontery; the *Laramie Sentinel* noted, "of all the fool things the stock association ever did this takes the cake."

Justice Denied

The events that followed made a mockery of the legal system. After being rescued by army troops, the Invaders were taken to Cheyenne to stand trial. Not surprisingly, two trappers who had happened upon the raid at the KC Ranch mysteriously disappeared until the trial was over, leaving no witnesses for the prosecution. Everyone pleaded not guilty, but when the judge discovered that Johnson County was unable to pay for the prisoners' room and board, he ordered them all released on their own recognizance.

After being paid by the cattle barons, the hired Texas gunmen immediately skipped town, never to be seen again. The Wyoming men involved in the raid were released when Johnson County had no more money to prosecute. Many of Wyoming's most prominent citizens—including Governor Barber and Senators Carey and Warren—would later be implicated as supporters of the raid. Johnson County would take years to settle down after the battles of 1892, and for a while the big cattlemen lived in fear for their lives.

(these sleep four) with a full kitchen for $52. Inexpensive.

It's hard not to use the word cute for the clean and well-maintained log cabins at **Blue Gables Motel,** on the north side of town at 662 N. Main St., tel. (307) 684-2574 or (800) 684-2574. Rates are $39 s or $59 d, and some cabins contain fridges and microwaves. No phones in the rooms, but the motel does have an outdoor pool. Open April-October. Inexpensive.

You'll also find cozy modern cabins at the clean and friendly **Mountain View Motel and Campground,** 585 Fort St., tel. (307) 684-2881. Cabins go for $40-74 s or d. Inexpensive-Moderate.

Z-Bar Motel, 626 Fort St., tel. (307) 684-5535 or (888) 313-1227, also features very nice log cabins for $43 s or $48-52 d, with fridges in all; cabins with kitchenettes are $6 extra. Inexpensive.

Arrowhead Motel, 749 Fort St., tel. (307) 684-9453 or (800) 824-1719, has rooms for $40-60 s or d; kitchenettes are $5 extra. Inexpensive.

A mile east of town, **Cowboy Town Bunkhouse Motel,** tel. (307) 684-0603 or (888) 323-2865, has newly built cabins for $45-52 s or d. A continental breakfast is served in the summer months, and guests will appreciate the outdoor jacuzzi and barbecue area. Inexpensive.

Guests at **Historic Mansion House Inn,** 313 N. Main St., tel. (307) 684-2218 or (888) 455-9202, can stay in either a century-old home or newer motel units (some with fridges). Rates are $45 s or $65-70 d, including an indoor jacuzzi and continental breakfast. Moderate.

Stay at **Buffalo Motel,** 370 N. Main St., tel. (307) 684-0753 or (888) 684-0753, where the spacious rooms are $45-69 s or d; some contain microwaves and fridges. Inexpensive-Moderate. **Big Horn Motel,** 209 N. Main St., tel. (307) 684-7822 or (800) 936-7822, has recently renovated rooms for $58 s or $58-70 d. Inexpensive-Moderate.

Buffalo's newest lodging place is **Motel 6,** 100 Flat Iron Dr., tel. (307) 684-7000 or (800) 466-8356, where rooms are a surprisingly steep $59 s or $64 d. Moderate.

Comfort Inn, 65 US Hwy. 16 East, tel. (307) 684-9564 or (800) 228-5150, charges $60-120 s or $65-120 d; amenities include an indoor jacuzzi and continental breakfast. Moderate-Premium.

Wyoming Motel, US Hwy. 16 at I-25, tel. (307) 684-5505 or (800) 666-5505, is a comfortable and modern place with an outdoor pool and indoor hot tub. Rates are $62-88 s or d in standard rooms (some containing fridges and microwaves) or $129 for up to eight in the three-bed family units with kitchens. Moderate.

Super 8 Motel, US Hwy. 16 at I-25, tel. (307) 684-2531 or (800) 800-8000, has standard rooms for $65 s or d. Moderate.

The recently renovated **Crossroads Inn,** US Hwy. 16 West, tel. (307) 684-2256 or (800) 852-2302, charges $79 s or $89 d and features an outdoor pool and jacuzzi. Some rooms contain fridges and microwaves. Expensive.

Other Lodging Options

Cloud Peak Inn B&B, 590 N. Burritt, tel. (307) 684-5794 or (800) 715-5794, is a cozy turn-of-the-20th-century home with period antiques and friendly owners. The five spacious guest rooms have shared or private baths. Relax on the front porch or in the jacuzzi. Room rates are $60-80 s or $65-85 d, including a full breakfast. Well-behaved kids are welcome. Find it on the web at www.cpibandb.com. Moderate.

Dry Creek Guest House, tel. (307) 684-7433, is a spacious and modern log cabin ($130 d) just east of town. There's a fine view of the Big Horn Mountains from the deck, and the interior contains a kitchen and private bath. Get more info by visiting the website: www.drycreekguesthouse.com. Premium.

Triple Three Ranch, 333 French Creek Rd. (three miles northwest of town), tel. (307) 684-2832, has two cabins with private baths for $75 d, including a full breakfast. Moderate. Triple Three is also the place where trigger-happy folks go to hunt prairie dogs; the ads claim "250-350 SHOTS PER DAY!!!" Note to the owners: biologists are appalled that prairie dogs are being slaughtered for fun at a time when their population is in rapid decline in many parts of the West. They also note that the endangered black-footed ferrets depend upon prairie dogs for food, and without large and healthy prairie-dog colonies ferrets could never survive in the wild.

Dude Ranches

Thirteen miles west of Buffalo on Hwy. 16, **Paradise Guest Ranch,** tel. (307) 684-7876, is a long-time dude ranch with luxurious log cabins, an outdoor pool, and an indoor jacuzzi. In addition to the main attraction—horseback riding—the ranch has fly-fishing instruction and trips, chuck wagon cookouts and special children's camp-outs. All-inclusive weekly rates are $2,900 for two people. The guest ranch is open late May to mid-October. Find it on the web at www.paradiseranch.com. Luxury.

Another popular dude ranch is **Klondike Guest Ranch,** tel. (307) 684-2390, located 15 miles southwest of Buffalo along Crazy Woman Creek. Horseback riding and fishing keep folks busy, or you can join in the ranch work and help move cattle. Guests stay in log cabins with private baths and eat in the main lodge. All-inclusive weekly rates are $1,850 for two people. Find it on the web at www.klondikeranch.com. Luxury.

HF Bar Ranch, tel. (307) 684-2487, has 25 comfortably restored cabins—mostly from the 1920s and '30s—on a historic ranch 15 miles northwest of Buffalo. Guests get two horseback rides per day, access to the outdoor pool, plus all three meals. The ranch also offers guided fly-fishing, skeet shooting, children's cookouts, weekly swing dancing, pack trips, and game-bird hunting (extra fee). All-inclusive rates are $350 for two people per day; no minimum stay, but most guests stay at least a week. There's space for 100 guests at this big ranch. The dude ranch is open late June to mid-September. Luxury.

Twenty-five miles east of Buffalo, **V Bar F Ranch** has a six-person cabin available for guests, who take part in ranch activities in the summer. The cabin is available on either an all-inclusive basis or as a B&B; call (307) 758-4393 for rates.

Camping

There's camping ($5) at **Lake DeSmet,** eight miles north of Buffalo, but the sites can get steaming hot in midsummer. It is mostly for the RV crowd but has no water or hookups. Other nearby public campgrounds ($8-10) are in Bighorn National Forest approximately 15 miles west of Buffalo on US Hwy. 16.

Big Horn Mountains Campground, two miles west on US Hwy. 16, tel. (307) 684-2307, has tent spaces for $14, RV sites for $17. Showers for noncampers cost $3; open year-round. **Mountain View Motel and Campground,** 585 Fort St., tel. (307) 684-2881, has RV campsites for $18 and tent sites for $15; open all year.

The friendly folks at **Indian Campground,** 660 E. Hart St. (off US Hwy. 16 east of town), tel. (307) 684-9601, charge $16 for tents or $21 for RVs in shady spots. Showers for noncampers run $4. It's open early April through October.

Farther out on US Hwy. 16 is **Deer Park Campground,** tel. (307) 684-5722 or (800) 222-9960, www.deerparkrv.com, where sites cost $15 for tents or $21 for RVs. They also serve meals and have an outdoor pool and jacuzzi, plus a pleasant creekside trail. The evening ice-cream socials are a summertime favorite. Open May to mid-October.

Also along US Hwy. 16 east of town, the **Buffalo KOA,** tel. (307) 684-5423 or (800) 562-5403, has tent sites for $15, RV spaces for $21, and basic "kamping kabins" for $37 d. Open mid-April to mid-October, it boasts an outdoor pool, a jacuzzi, and free pancake breakfasts.

FOOD

For breakfast, buzz on over to the homey **Busy Bee,** 2 N. Main, tel. (307) 684-7544, here since 1928. It's right along Clear Creek, and on summer mornings the benches out front are often crowded with folks waiting to get in. Inside, the seating isn't exactly formal—just 21 stools lining the counter. The pies are locally famous. **Tom's Main Street Diner,** 41 N. Main St., tel. (307) 684-7444, is another very good place for breakfast.

Artworks Too and Cowgirl Coffee Cafe, 94 S. Main St., tel. (307) 684-1299, mixes art on the walls with espresso, bagels, and sinful sweets. It's pleasant enough inside, and it also features a small back patio. This is the sort of place where you could sit for an hour reading a novel.

Several of the chains-including McD's, Hardee's, Pizza Hut, Subway, and Taco John's—are out E. Hart St., but a better choice is **The Breadboard,** 107 E. Hart St., tel. (307) 684-2318, with decent subs on homemade bread, plus soups and spicy chili for lunch. Another good place for fast food, including excellent hickory-smoked fried chicken and ribs, is **Dash Inn,** 620 E. Hart, tel. (307) 684-7930. Downtown, **Seney's Rexall Drug,** 38 S. Main, tel. (307) 684-7182, has an old-fashioned soda fountain offering thick shakes and malts.

A favorite of families and retirees, **Col. Bozeman's,** 675 E. Hart, tel. (307) 684-5555, serves buffalo steaks, burgers, and Mexican dishes.

When folks are looking for an enjoyable evening away from town, they drive to **Pines Lodge,** 14 miles west, tel. (307) 680-8545 or (307) 684-5204, or **South Fork Inn,** 17 miles west, tel. (307) 684-9609. Each place has a bar and lounge, along with the standard supper-club menu.

Get groceries from two markets on the west end of town: **Rocky Mountain Fresh Food IGA,** 440 Fort St., tel. (307) 684-2239, and **DJ's Thriftway,** 895 Fort St., tel. (307) 684-2518.

OTHER PRACTICALITIES

Entertainment

Buffalo has two places to go for live country-and-western tunes some weekends: **Crossroads Inn,** tel. (307) 684-2256, and the **Century Club,** 14 S. Main, tel. (307) 684-2821. **Scully Theater,** 235 S. Main, tel. (307) 684-9311, is the local movie house. Roll balls down the lanes at **Buffalo Bowl,** 90 S. Cedar St., tel. (307) 684-2613.

Events

Powder River Roundup Days in June features a unique rodeo in which teams rather than individuals compete. Come to Buffalo in late June for a **Horseshoe Tournament.** The Jim Gatchell Museum's **Living History Day** in July includes mountain men, horse-drawn wagons, quilting, saddlemaking, Basque dancing, old-time cooking, and more.

All Girls Rodeos take place all summer long at the county fairgrounds. End the summer with a Labor Day weekend country-and-western music **Invitational Jam Session** at the fairgrounds. Buffalo's biggest annual event is the **Johnson County Fair and Rodeo,** held in early August; call (307) 684-7357 for details. A **Christmas Parade** comes to town the first Saturday of December.

Recreation

The free **outdoor swimming pool** in Washington Park is one of the largest in the Rocky Mountains, stretching 120 meters by 80 meters. It has swimming lanes, two diving boards, a slide, and a wading pool for tots. Open daily 11 a.m.-6 p.m. during the summer, this is a great place to play on a hot day. Inside the modern **YMCA,** 101 Klondike Dr., tel. (307) 684-9558, you'll find a pool, jacuzzi, and weight room, along with racquetball and handball courts.

Buffalo's popular **Clear Creek Trail System** makes for a delightful afternoon stroll or bike ride. It follows the creek for 11 miles and is paved to the edge of town. The trail will eventually reach all the way to the foot of the Big Horn Mountains.

Rent bikes from **Indian Campground,** on US Hwy. 16 east of town, tel. (307) 684-9601. Three miles out of town, **Triple Three Ranch,** tel. (307) 684-2832, offers horseback rides.

The 18-hole **Buffalo Municipal Golf Course,** northwest of town, tel. (307) 684-5266, is one of the finest in Wyoming. One hole features a 90-foot vertical drop over 140 yards.

Angler's West, tel. (307) 684-5857, leads boat trips and fishing to Lake DeSmet and other regional lakes.

Shopping

Get books on Wyoming from **The Office,** 33 N. Main, tel. (307) 684-2215. Buffalo has two good fishing shops: **Just Gone Fishing,** 777 Fort St., tel. (307) 684-2755, and **The Sports Lure,** 66 S. Main, tel. (307) 684-7682 or (800) 684-7682. The latter also sells hiking, skiing, and backpacking gear, as well as topo maps. If you think you're starting to see spots, you may be at **Alabam's Polka Dot Spot,** 421 Fort St., tel. (307) 684-7452, a shop geared to hunters and anglers. Pretty strange.

Several local art galleries sell standard Western art prints, but more distinctive is **Margo's Pottery,** 26 N. Main St., tel. (307) 684-9406, where you'll find all sorts of playful earthenware.

Information and Services

The **Buffalo Chamber of Commerce** office, 55 N. Main St., tel. (307) 684-5544 or (800) 227-5122, is open Mon.-Fri. 8 a.m.-6 p.m. and Sat.-Sun. 10 a.m.-4 p.m. in summer, and Mon.-Fri. 8 a.m.-5 p.m. the rest of the year. Good Internet destinations are www.buffalowyoming.org and www.buffalowyoming.com.

The **Johnson County Public Library** is at the intersection of Adams and Lott Sts., tel. (307) 684-5546. Get info on Bighorn National Forest from the **Powder River Ranger District,** 1425 Fort St., tel. (307) 684-1100. The BLM's **Buffa-**

lo Resource Area Office is in the same building and has the same phone number.

ATMs are in local banks and gas stations. Wash clothes at **Tanner's Coin Laundry,** 334 N. Main St., tel. (307) 684-2205.

Transportation

Powder River/Coach USA, tel. (800) 442-3682, connects Buffalo with the rest of northern and eastern Wyoming. Buses stop at Just Gone Fishing, 777 Fort Street.

Rent cars from **Northside Car Sales** (Avis), north of Buffalo, tel. (307) 684-5136. The airport in Buffalo does not have scheduled service, so it came as quite a surprise one day in 1979 when a Western Airlines 737 carrying 94 passengers mistakenly landed in Buffalo instead of Sheridan. Mistakes were made.

BUFFALO VICINITY

LAKE DESMET

Eight miles north of Buffalo is Lake DeSmet, a deep natural lake surrounded by open range country. A stone **monument** to the Belgian Jesuit missionary Father Pierre Jean DeSmet (1801-73) stands along the western shore. DeSmet was one of the few 19th-century men who maintained lifelong friendships with both Indians and whites. The Plains Indians called him "Blackrobe" and trusted him with various peacemaking roles at Fort Laramie. But the Indians viewed the lake named for DeSmet with suspicion, as did early settlers, who told of "Smetty the sea monster" who emerged at night from the seemingly bottomless body of water. When first found by DeSmet in 1851, it was a salt lake—the second-largest in the West (after Great Salt Lake)—but dams and dikes have increased its size and decreased its salinity.

Today, Lake DeSmet is a popular place for local boaters and windsurfers. Try your luck at catching one of the mermaids, but you're more likely to pull in a big rainbow trout. Also here are brown trout, crappie, yellow perch, and rock bass. **Lake DeSmet Fishing Derby** is held each Memorial Day weekend and awards over $50,000 in prizes and cash. Just north of the lake is a bed of coal that, in some places, is more than 200 feet thick—second in thickness only to one in Manchuria. No wonder Texaco owns most of the land around Lake DeSmet!

Practicalities

You'll find **camping** ($5) just south of the Father DeSmet monument. The area has volleyball nets, picnic tables, and outhouses but no shade or drinking water. **Lake Stop Resort,** tel. (307) 684-9051, rents fishing boats, ski boats, and jet skis. Also here are modern four-person cabins with bath for $28 (Budget), along with RV hookups, a cafe, grocery store, and bait shop.

KAYCEE

The town of Kaycee (pop. 290) is named for the nearby KC Ranch and serves as a bentonite, oil, and ranching center. Drive the side roads in spring or fall and you're likely to find yourself behind huge flocks of sheep being herded into or out of the Big Horn Mountains.

Frewen Castle

When the Powder River country was opened to white settlers in the late 1870s, it quickly attracted ranchers and farmers of all types, from homesteaders trying to prove up their 160 acres to wealthy international investors. Two of the most interesting were the English brothers Moreton and Richard Frewen, relatives of Sir Winston Churchill. Coming originally to hunt buffalo, the two saw the lush Powder River area and decided to invest in cattle. Near present-day Kaycee, they erected an elaborate two-story log house, filled it with furniture and fixtures from England, even added an incredible luxury, a telephone. Frewen Castle, as it was soon called, became the center of an enormous spread with at least 60,000 cattle.

Their kingdom attracted English hunting parties and became something of an unofficial dude ranch. (To keep their ladies in the proper spirit, the Frewens set up relay stations to bring hothouse flowers from Denver on galloping horses.)

THE WILD BUNCH

Glorified in the 1969 Oscar-winning film *Butch Cassidy and the Sundance Kid,* the Wild Bunch is one of the most famous of all Western outlaw gangs. The Wild Bunch consisted of a constantly changing membership held together by two friends, Robert Parker ("Butch Cassidy") and Harry Longabaugh (the "Sundance Kid"). In 1884, Parker, then a teenager, met up with a local ranch hand and part-time cattle rustler named Mike Cassidy. Rebelling against a strict Mormon upbringing, Parker picked up a few of the master's tricks before getting caught by the law and told to move on. But when he left Utah for Colorado and Wyoming, he took with him his mentor's name, Cassidy. (The "Butch" apparently came later, when he worked in several Rock Springs butcher shops.) Linking up with other outlaws, Cassidy held up the San Miguel Valley Bank of Telluride and then drifted back to horse stealing in Wyoming. Several years later, those horses landed him in the Wyoming State Prison in Laramie. Cassidy was pardoned by the governor after 18 months, reportedly after agreeing not to pursue that line of work in Wyoming anymore. Other places, however, were fair game.

The Gang

If anything, prison made Cassidy more determined than ever to outwit the lawmen. Joining up with Longabaugh (who picked up his Sundance Kid sobriquet while serving time in the Sundance, Wyoming, jail for horse thievery) and Harvey Logan, alias Kid Curry (a deadly and fearless Montana fugitive), Cassidy assembled a rogues' gallery of rustlers, drifters, killers, and wanted men soon known as the Wild Bunch. They operated from remote hidden canyons in the West, especially Brown's Park in western Colorado, Bighorn Canyon in Montana, Wyoming's Wind River Valley, and the famous Hole-in-the-Wall southwest of Buffalo, Wyoming—places where entire herds of stolen cattle could be hidden and where the finest horses could be trained for quick getaways.

The Wild Bunch achieved a measure of respect from local ranchers who bought horses and cattle at low prices and found ready workers when the outlaws needed to rest up awhile. For many, Cassidy seemed a modern-day Robin Hood, taking from the rich railroads, banks, mines, and cattle barons while leaving the small folks alone. To this day, locals in Kaycee, Wyoming, still talk fondly of the affable Butch Cassidy.

The gang's activities reached a peak in the late 1890s, with bank robberies in Utah, South Dakota, and Idaho (the latter to pay for a lawyer to clear a gang member on a murder charge). Cassidy—breaking his promise to Wyoming's governor—also

The Wild Bunch: Harry Longabaugh (Sundance Kid), Bill Carver, Ben Kilpatrick, Harvey Logan (Kid Curry), and George Parker (Butch Cassidy)

BUFFALO BILL HISTORICAL CENTER

led a train robbery in Wilcox, Wyoming, which netted $50,000, but only after he'd blown up the safe with 10 pounds of dynamite, sending money and banknotes in all directions. Within hours, a sheriff's posse was in hot pursuit, and in a gun battle near Casper the sheriff was killed. Somehow, the Wild Bunch managed to slip through the posse's lines for a clean getaway.

In 1900, they struck another Union Pacific train near Tipton, Wyoming (just east of Rock Springs). Amazingly, the same express messenger was present for both robberies; the first time he had refused to open the railcar door and was literally blown out with explosives. The second time the conductor persuaded him to open the door. Perhaps he knew that the safe held only $54; the train carrying $100,000 worth of gold had passed just a few hours before. Then the Wild Bunch was off to Winnemucca, Nevada, where a bank holdup netted them a cool $32,000. After a fling at Fanny Porter's Sporting House in San Antonio, the gang members bought some new hats at a Fort Worth haberdasher and, dressed as dudes, posed for the famous group portrait later used by Pinkerton detectives. Cassidy and two other gang members tried their hands once more at train robbery in 1901, taking at least $40,000 from a dynamited safe in Montana. The law was closing in, however. Of the gang members who stayed behind, all but one died a violent death. For Butch Cassidy and the Sundance Kid, the future lay in South America.

Gringos

In 1901, Butch and Sundance headed for Argentina. Accompanying them on the journey was Etta Place—a strikingly beautiful woman whom Sundance apparently met in Fanny Porter's Sporting House. (Butch later called her "a fine housekeeper, but a whore at heart.") There they settled with their ill-gotten wealth to a quiet life of ranching, traveling occasionally to Buenos Aires where they stayed in the finest hotels and dressed in formal clothes befitting their new role as bourgeois American settlers. But even in South America, Pinkerton detectives managed to pick up their trail, and, sensing this, the three decided to try their skills in virgin territory. They robbed three banks in Argentina and a train in Bolivia before Etta Place came down with acute appendicitis. A hurried trip took the trio back to the States, but in Denver, where the operation was performed, the Sundance Kid got in trouble for shooting up his hotel room while drunk. Rather than face the law, he fled to New York, where he and Cassidy again boarded a steamer bound for Argentina. Etta remained behind.

The two outlaws now worked part-time at a Peruvian gold mine, using the work as a cover for their periodic forays into banks, trains, and stores in search of money. For many years, most believed that Butch Cassidy and the Sundance Kid died in a blaze of gunfire at a remote village on the Bolivian-Argentine border in 1909. Today, however, it appears that Cassidy escaped (and perhaps the Kid as well), using his reported death as a convenient opportunity to change his ways. According to Larry Pointer's *In Search of Butch Cassidy,* Cassidy later fought with Pancho Villa in the Mexican Revolution, met Wyatt Earp in Alaska, and settled down to running a Spokane machine shop, living under the name of William T. Phillips until his death from cancer in 1937. Several Wyoming residents, old friends of the famous outlaw, met him in Lander and Riverton on a number of occasions before his death. Cassidy reportedly spent considerable time in a fruitless effort to recover buried loot that he had stashed near Mary's Lake in the Wind River Mountains. Today, the Butch and Sundance legends refuse to die. Stop by the towns of Rock Springs, Lander, Laramie, Worland, Dubois, Baggs, or Kaycee and you'll be regaled with more tales of their exploits.

The Frewens' Powder River Cattle Company, Ltd., attracted investments from the British royal family and various lords before reality struck. The cattle did not do as well as expected, competition from surrounding ranchers and rustlers cut into profits, and the disastrous winter of 1886-87 forced the company to the brink of bankruptcy. The Frewens and many other "cattle barons" never really recovered. Today almost nothing remains of Frewen Castle.

Sights

Kaycee's free **Hoofprints of the Past Museum,** tel. (307) 738-2381, is open Mon.-Sat. 9 a.m.-5 p.m. and Sunday 1-5 p.m. Memorial Day to Labor Day, and Mon.-Sat. 2-5 p.m. and Sunday 1-5 p.m. from Labor Day through October. It's closed November to Memorial Day. Inside is a nice collection of items from early settlers, outlaws, and the cattle wars. Look for the wooden potato planter. The museum offers historical tours of the region on the third Saturday of June.

Just south of Kaycee, a marker describes the killing of rustlers Nate Champion and Nick Ray in the Johnson County War of 1892 (see the special topic). The old **KC Ranch house,** where the two were killed by the Invaders, stood here. See Accommodations below for the TA Ranch, where the Invaders holed up after raiding the KC Ranch.

Ten miles east of Kaycee on State Hwy. 192 is a marker noting the first buildings in northern Wyoming, constructed in 1834 by Portuguese trapper Antonio Montero. The log stockade and trading post (known as the **Portuguese Houses**) were abandoned around 1839, and nothing remains on the site. The site of old **Fort Reno** (1865-68) is in the same general vicinity; ask in Kaycee for directions. A monument marks the place, and various remains are still present from this little-known fort.

Fans of country music will know that singer Chris LeDoux has a sheep ranch in the vicinity of Kaycee. LeDoux was a rodeo cowboy for many years, winning the 1976 PRCA world championship in bareback riding. He used his musical abilities to pay for his rodeo travels, and today he sings cowboy songs with a measure of authenticity lacking in other musicians. He still plays the rodeo circuit with his band, but he's also gained a national following.

Accommodations

Cassidy Inn Motel, tel. (307) 738-2250, has basic older rooms (no phones) for $28 s or $35 d. Budget. A bit nicer is **Siesta Motel,** tel. (307) 738-2291, where the rooms are $24 s or $30 d. Budget. The newest place to stay is just west of town at the **Bunk House Motel,** tel. (307) 738-2213, next to the Sinclair station. The seven-unit motel offers lodging for $35 s or $45 for up to four people. Inexpensive. The station also contains an ATM and showers ($6). Just across the road is **KC RV Park,** tel. (307) 738-2233, offering RV sites with hookups for $15; there's a second location on the south end of Kaycee. You'll find **free camping** at the Kaycee town park.

Famous **TA Ranch,** tel. (307) 684-5833 or (800) 368-7398, is approximately 30 miles north of Kaycee along State Hwy. 87. Bullet holes are still visible in many of the wonderful old ranch buildings, which are being preserved for posterity. Still a working cattle ranch covering 8,200 acres, the TA takes in guests April-Oct. and has a capacity of 24 people. The ranch specializes in horseback rides, cattle drives, and fly-fishing, but also offers tours to the Hole-in-the-Wall area and other historic sites. All-inclusive weekly rates are $2,010 for two people. For more information, find the ranch on the web at www.taranch.com. Luxury.

Willow Creek Ranch at Hole-in-the-Wall, tel. (307) 738-2294, is 35 miles southwest of Kaycee and offers one of the most authentic ranch experiences in Wyoming. The ranch covers 57,000 beautiful and remote acres in the Red Wall country made famous by the Hole-in-the-Wall gang. Guests take part in ranch activities, including branding and cattle drives. Photography, bird watching, fishing, and hunting are other popular activities, along with the all-time favorite, kicking back and relaxing. Established in 1882, this working cattle and sheep ranch has space for a maximum of 12 guests, who stay in the renovated 1890 bunkhouse. In addition, two very private cabins eight miles away offer the ultimate in solitude. The ranch is a great place to explore, with lots of outlaw history, plus Indian petroglyphs and tepee rings. All-inclusive weekly rates are $2,820 for two people. Open May to mid-October. Get details by visiting the website: www.willowcreekranch.com. Luxury.

Greenhorn Ranch B&B, tel. (307) 738-2548, is a furnished homestead house 21 miles west of Kaycee out Barnum Road. Located on a working cattle ranch near the Red Wall, the house enjoys a grand setting. The home contains three bedrooms, a full bathroom, large kitchen, laundry room, screened sun room and living room with a piano and woodstove. Rates are $120 per night for four people, including a full breakfast. For details, visit www.cruising-america.com/greenhorn. Reservations required. Moderate.

Other Practicalities

Kaycee has two bars and three restaurants serving all-American meals. You won't go wrong at **Invasion Bar Restaurant,** tel. (307) 738-2211. **Kaycee Country Market** is a delightful old-fashioned place for supplies.

Events in Kaycee include the **Sheepherders Rodeo and Dog Trials** in the first weekend after the Fourth of July, and the very popular **Deke Latham Memorial PRCA Rodeo** on the second weekend of September. Kaycee is the smallest town in America with its own PRCA rodeo, and visitors will be most impressed—the rodeo is one of Wyoming's best.

HOLE-IN-THE-WALL COUNTRY

Outlaw Heaven

The remote country used by the Wild Bunch and other outlaws lies some 30 miles west of Kaycee. Get here by following State Hwy. 190 for 16 miles to where the pavement ends. At the road junction—maps call this Barnum, but there is no town here—a side road leads to Blue Creek Ranch (private), land once homesteaded by Butch Cassidy and the Sundance Kid. Surrounding you are gorgeous red-walled canyons rising above the Middle Fork of the Powder River. Its waters provide a fine place to fish for rainbow, brook, and brown trout.

Turning right (north) leads you to the **Dull Knife Battlefield,** named for an 1876 incident. General Crook's soldiers surprised Dull Knife's band of Northern Cheyenne in this remote valley. The attack killed at least 40 Cheyenne and ended what whites viewed as a campaign of terror and which the Indians viewed as retaliation for the invasion of their last stronghold.

To reach other area sites, turn left (south) on the graded gravel road that parallels the river. Follow the road five miles, past the Bar C Ranch, and bear right at the signed 4WD side road for Outlaw Cave. Beyond the intersection, the road is really only passable in high-clearance vehicles, so you may want to walk the last two miles to the cave. The road crosses a three-quarter-mile long stretch of prehistoric **rock cairns** and then tops a knoll where you'll find **Outlaw Cave Campground** (free but no water). Stop here for impressive views of the Hole-in-the-Wall area.

From the campground, a very steep half-mile path drops 660 feet down to **Outlaw Cave,** actually two small caves used as hideouts by the Wild Bunch and other outlaws. One of the caves is little more than a depression in the rocks but the other is room-sized. Take your fishing pole down to try for trout.

On the opposite side of the road from the campground and up another third of a mile is **Indian Rock Art Cave.** The cave (actually just a rock overhang) contains distinctive but faint Indian rock art, including a large warrior figure, bear claws, and shield designs. A major buffalo jump site (where Indians hunted buffalo by driving them over a cliff) is nearby, along with many tepee rings. The BLM office in Buffalo (tel. 307-684-5586) can provide more detailed access information for the Outlaw Caves/Hole-in-the-Wall country.

Hole-in-the-Wall

The wealthy Frewen brothers who ranched here in the 19th century named this country after London's Hole-in-the-Wall Tavern. The "Hole" lies at the end of a steep "V" in the red cliffs bordering Buffalo Creek. It was accessible via a trail that cuts up the talus slope and into a narrow, funnel-shaped opening. The setting was perfect for rustling and as a hideout from the law, especially for gunmen such as Jesse James, the Logan brothers, and George "Flat Nose" Currie. Some 30 to 40 bandits hung out here in six log cabins, including the most famous inhabitants, the Wild Bunch of Butch Cassidy and the Sundance Kid. The cabins have collapsed over the years, and today a few chunks of foundation are the only remaining evidence of the 19th-century rustlers who were based here. The cliff was easy to defend and offered a vantage point where sentries could warn of approaching lawmen.

Hole-in-the-Wall itself is on public (BLM) land, but much of the surrounding land belongs to ranchers who guard their privacy closely. In addition, the unmaintained roads can turn into a quagmire when it rains and a rutted mess when the mud dries out. High-clearance vehicles are required. After more than a century, horses are still the most dependable way to reach Hole-in-the-Wall! The Bureau of Land Management has signed the route into Hole-in-the-Wall, and a 1.5-mile primitive trail crosses public land to the site. For access information, check with the BLM in Buffalo, tel. (307) 684-1100. One of the best ways to see this area is by staying at the historic Willow Creek Ranch (described above), where the owners will take guests in on horseback.

A number of companies offer horseback trips across various parts of Wyoming, including the "Outlaw Trail" through Hole-in-the-Wall. These typically last a week and include horses, meals, equipment, and tents. Contact the following companies for details on the various options: **West-**

ern Encounters, tel. (307) 332-5434 or (800) 572-1230, www.horseriders.com; **Great Divide Tours,** tel. (307) 332-3123 or (800) 458-1915, www.rmisp.com/greatdivide; **Rocky Mountain Horseback Adventures,** tel. (307) 332-8535 or (800) 408-9149; and **Historic Trails West,** tel. (307) 266-4868 or (800) 327-4052, www.historictrailswest.com.

GILLETTE

Campbell County proclaims itself the "Energy Capital of the Nation," a title gained by producing more coal and oil than any other county in Wyoming. Although oil production is in decline, coal mining continues to increase every year, and local mines shovel up an eighth of the total U.S. production of coal. At the center of all this is Gillette (pop. 21,000), Wyoming's fourth-largest city.

Gillette is a base for tours of nearby coal mines, but it isn't otherwise known as a tourist destination; its prosperous neighborhoods and busy shopping malls are indistinguishable from those of a thousand other homogenized American cities. Gillette is a young town; the median age in 1998 was 29. Interpret this your own way: Gillette actually has an E-Z Street! Despite the lack of any connection to the shaving company, Gillette is jokingly called "Razor City."

HISTORY

When you drive into Gillette, the sense of history permeating much of Wyoming quickly gives way to the raucous present. History is decidedly not Gillette's strong suit, even though the town is nearly a century old. When the Burlington and Missouri route to Sheridan was being planned, it was originally set to go south of the present location, but astute surveyor Edward Gillette discovered a route farther north that saved construction of 30 bridges. Initially, the new company-platted town was to be called "Donkey Town" for its proximity to Donkey Creek, but instead it was named for Gillette. (Edward Gillette later served a term in Washington as a congressman from Wyoming; however, he preferred to live in the more scenic town of Sheridan than in his namesake.) The railroad reached Gillette in 1891, and the town was incorporated the following year. It became a shipping point for local ranchers and homesteaders and grew slowly over the decades.

The Present

Since the late 1960s, Gillette has ridden an enormous growth rocket, powered first by oil and then by coal. Gillette's oil boom really began in the fall of 1967, when a drilling company hit an oil gusher that ignited an enormous fire. Firefighter Red Adair was called in to extinguish the flames, attracting worldwide attention. Hollywood soon followed—John Wayne's *Hellfighters* was based on these events. Other oil companies flooded the area with exploratory rigs, and almost overnight Gillette grew from a sleepy cow town to a major energy center. A frantic scramble for the almighty dollar ensued, with real-estate values quadrupling between 1966 and 1970.

Unlike the rest of Wyoming, where the oil boom of the '70s was quickly followed by the bust of the '80s and '90s, Gillette caught the coal wave just as the oil tide was heading back out to sea. With enormous reserves of low-sulfur coal throughout the surrounding countryside, Campbell County quickly became a major player on the energy scene and is now the most prosperous county in Wyoming. The city's population continues to grow as coal mining, methane gas production, and the Wyodak power plant expand. Today Gillette is the modern version of middle America—shopping malls, spreading suburbia, used-car lots, and fast-food joints. Author Wallace Stegner's description of a California town could fit just as well here: "But mostly it is Main Street, Anywhere, a set used over and over in a hundred B movies, a stroboscopic image pulsing to reassure us by subliminal tricks that though we are nowhere, we are at home."

SIGHTS

The fine **Rockpile Museum,** on US Hwy. 14/16, tel. (307) 682-5723, is open Mon.-Sat. 9 a.m.-8 p.m. and Sunday 12:30-6:30 p.m. June-Aug., and Mon.-Sat. 9 a.m.-5 p.m. the rest of the year. No charge. Out front is a minor local landmark for which the museum was named, along with a Burlington Northern caboose. This spacious museum contains sheep wagons, a horse-drawn hearse—originally from Montana, its first eight customers died from gunshots—a blacksmith shop, an impressive arrowhead collection, and dozens of elaborate spurs and old rifles. A big board contains a directory of several hundred brands. Be sure to check out the floating rocks from Lake DeSmet. Out front is a tiny one-room schoolhouse that could have served double duty as a doghouse. The metal building next door has some very strange sandstone rocks.

The **Campbell County Public Library,** 2101 4-J Rd., tel. (307) 682-3223, is one of the finest in the state. Besides a large collection of books about Wyoming, it houses a remarkable collection of art including paintings by Hans Kleiber, Gene Kloss, and Conrad Schwiering. Out front are lifesize bronze statues of cowboys and horses.

Kids of all ages will have a blast (pun intended) at **Einstein's Adventurarium,** housed in the Lakeway Learning Center at 525 W. Lakeway

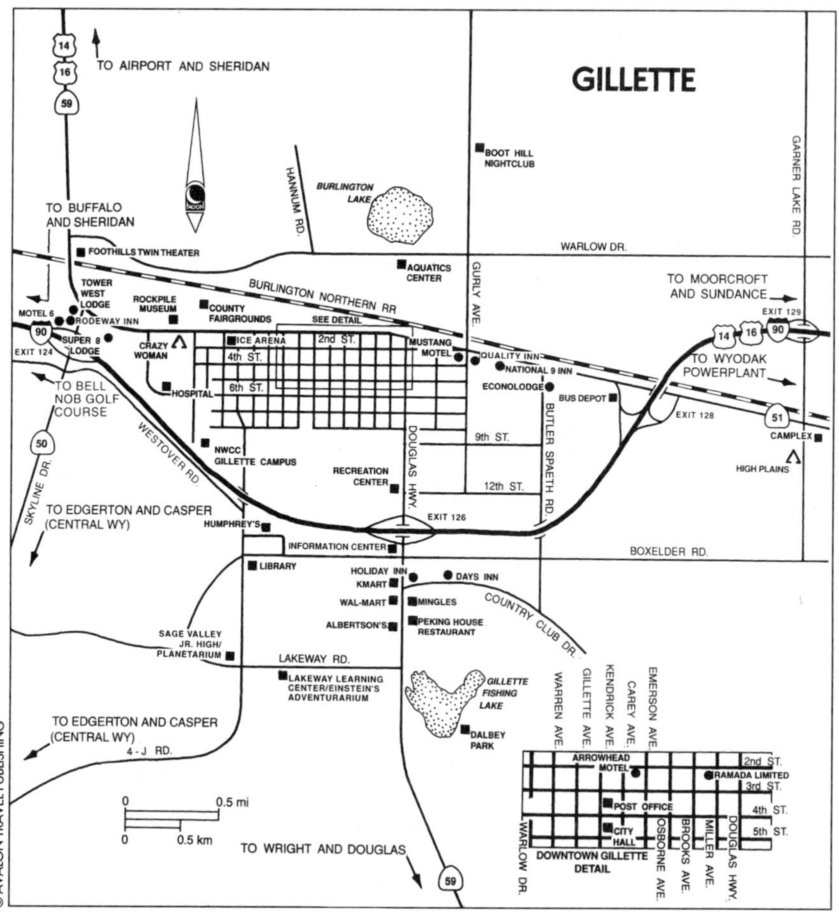

STRIP MINING

Coal mining has been an important part of the Campbell County economy for many years. The first mines were underground, but once the technology developed to remove the overlying soil, strip mining became feasible. Today, 14 Campbell County surface mines (the preferred term in the industry) are scattered along an enormous coal seam five miles wide, over 70 miles long, and 70 feet thick—enough to last hundreds of years. Together, the mines produce a quarter of the nation's coal, and if Campbell County were a nation it would rank fourth in the world in coal reserves, behind the U.S., Russia, and China! Most of the mines are owned by giant multinational corporations including the Lehman Merchant Banking Partners(!), Kennecott Energy, RAG Coal West, and Arch Coal.

Coal production in these mines has risen rapidly in recent years and now tops a staggering 330 million tons annually. Black Thunder Mine, just east of Wright, is the largest mine in America, producing over 40 million tons of coal per year. The Wyodak Mine is the oldest in the Powder River Basin—it opened in 1922—and feeds one of the world's largest air-cooled power plants (also on the site).

Digging the Coal

Powder River Basin mines are heavily mechanized and highly efficient operations with relatively few employees; despite massive increases in production, the number of employees continues to drop. Mining coal here is a relatively simple process, made easier through the use of machinery and blasting equipment that are something beyond gargantuan; all the vehicles seem to be on steroids. Imagine a truck that carries 240 tons of coal—two and a half railroad coal cars' worth—and is powered by a 2,200-horsepower engine. Try changing a flat on it—the tire stands 11 feet tall and weighs four tons! Even this behemoth is dwarfed by the dragline used at the Black Thunder Coal Mine. Its 300-foot boom pulls in a 90-cubic-yard bucket (a typical dump truck holds 12 cubic yards). Powered by electricity, the 3,600-ton machine waddles along like a duck, dragging its power line behind. Blasting loosens the overburden, which is then stripped away and dumped into waiting trucks. (Topsoil is stored for use in later reclamation.) Below this overburden lies the deep black coal seam that must be drilled and blasted. Electric shovels scoop up the loosened coal and dump it into the trucks for delivery to crushing and storage facilities.

The entire scale of the operation comes into focus by watching as mile-long, 110-car trains move constantly through the loading facility, loading a car every minute. Workers can fill up to a dozen trains in a day—over 130,000 tons.

WYOMING COAL PRODUCTION

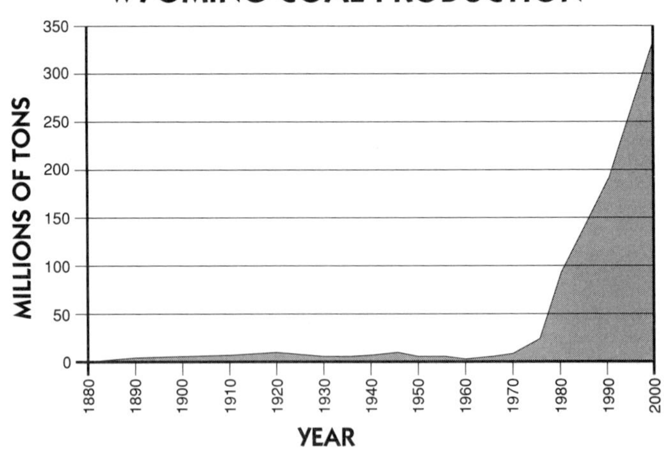

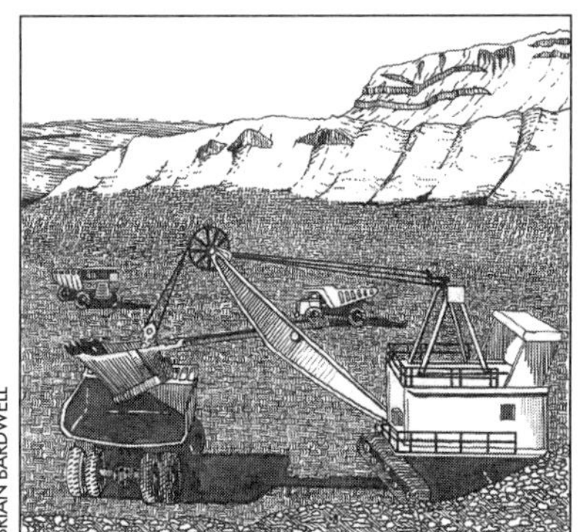

Environmental Impacts

The strip mining of coal has always been a controversial subject, with environmentalists concerned over the impacts from burning coal in an era of acid rain (97% of Wyoming coal is burned for electricity), global warming, and escalating atmospheric carbon dioxide. They also question whether reclamation will really work on Wyoming's arid lands. The other impacts from mining are equally important: access roads divide up antelope and deer habitat, subdivisions for the workers spread out over the countryside, and wells draw down the water table. Mining companies, however, point with pride to herds of antelope grazing near the coal mines and believe that the land can be restored after the coal is gone. Besides, the low-sulfur coal found here is some of the cleanest-burning coal in America.

A visit to the coal mines is an eye-opening odyssey into the Super Bowl of strip mining. No matter what you think about the procedure, a tour of the mines is well worth taking, if only to see the enormous equipment and ponder what burning all this coal will do to the environment. For tour information, contact the Gillette Information Center at (307) 686-0040 or (800) 544-6136.

Rd., tel. (307) 686-3821. The best science museum/kids' center in Wyoming, it is packed with an array of ingenious science exhibits that make learning fun. You can play in the bubble room, learn about light and sound, or meet a parrot, chinchilla, lizard, and ferret. Einstein's is open Mon.-Thurs. 8 a.m.-5 p.m. and Friday 8 a.m.-4 p.m. in the school year, but it's only open for groups or by reservation in the summer.

Just up the road is another enjoyable family venue: the **Planetarium** at Sage Valley Junior High, 1000 W. Lakeway Road. This sophisticated star chamber is one of the finest in any school district in America and includes a laser light system. Special programs are given every Monday evening; call (307) 682-2225 for details.

Cam-Plex, a large and modern multi-events center east of town on Garner Lake Rd., contains an art gallery with changing exhibits, as well as a beautiful 960-seat theater for concerts. Out front of Cam-Plex is an odd collection of items from the past and present. You'll discover turn-of-the-20th-century log cabins and an old locomotive just a few feet from a drilling rig and an enormous coal-hauling dump truck. Kids are guaranteed to have fun in the gargantuan tires. Call (307) 682-0552 for details on Friday evening melodramas at Cam-Plex.

Coal Mine Tours

During the summer, free one-hour tours of a local coal operation (typically Eagle Butte Mine) are offered through the Gillette Information Center. These take place twice daily on weekdays from Memorial Day to Labor Day only. For reservations, call (307) 686-0040 or (800) 544-6136. **Flightline Aviation,** tel. (307) 686-7000, has one-hour aerial tours of the coal mines and surrounding country; $120 for up to four people.

Five miles east of Gillette on I-90 is the **Wyodak Mine,** where tours are available by appointment; call (307) 682-3410. In existence since 1922, the mine feeds the adjacent Wyodak Power Plant, which offers tours Tues.-Thurs.; tel. (307) 687-4280. If tours aren't an option, you may want to peer into the **Eagle Butte Mine** from an overlook five miles north of Gillette on US Hwy. 14/16.

ACCOMMODATIONS AND CAMPING

Motels

Gillette is dominated by the chain motels, and the prices are surprisingly high. Rates tend to drop rather sharply in the winter months, when you'll find a few places for around $25, but they escalate during the Sturgis Rally Week in early August, when everything fills up. Accommodations are listed below from least to most expensive. Add a seven percent tax to these rates.

Get dependable economy accommodations from **Motel 6,** 2105 Rodgers Dr., tel. (307) 686-8600 or (800) 440-6000, where the rooms go for $40 s or $46 d, including access to a jacuzzi. Inexpensive.

Days Inn, 910 E. Boxelder Rd., tel. (307) 682-3999 or (800) 329-7466, charges $50-70 s or $60-80 d, including a continental breakfast. Moderate. Stay at **Super 8 Motel,** 208 S. Decker Ct., tel. (307) 682-8078 or (800) 800-8000, for $55-60 s or d, including a continental breakfast. Inexpensive.

Rodeway Inn, 2011 Rodgers Dr., tel. (307) 686-1989 or (800) 709-6123, charges $55 s or $65 d and features an indoor pool, sauna, jacuzzi, and continental breakfast. Moderate.

Econo Lodge, 409 Butler Spaeth Rd., tel. (307) 682-4757 or (800) 553-2666, has rooms for $60 s or $65 d. Moderate. **National 9 Inn,** 1020 E. US Hwy. 14/16, tel. (307) 682-5111 or (800) 524-9999, charges $70 s or d and has an outdoor pool. Some rooms have fridges and microwaves. Moderate.

Ramada Limited, 608 E. 2nd St., tel. (307) 682-9341 or (800) 272-6232, has an outdoor pool and jacuzzi, along with in-room fridges, microwaves, and a light breakfast. Rooms cost $70-120 s or d. Moderate-Premium. **Quality Inn,** 1002 E. 2nd St., tel. (307) 682-2616 or (800) 228-5151, charges $75 s or $85 d, including a light breakfast. Moderate.

One of the nicest places in town is **Best Western Tower West Lodge,** 109 N. US Hwy. 14/16, tel. (307) 686-2210 or (800) 762-7375. The rooms here go for $85-91 s or $91-97 d; amenities include an indoor pool, jacuzzi, sauna, and weight room. Expensive.

Holiday Inn, 2009 S. Douglas Hwy., tel. (307) 686-3000 or (800) 686-3368, offers standard rooms for $94 s or d, suites for $125 d. Amenities include an indoor pool, sauna, fitness center, and recreation area (pool table, ping pong, and games). Expensive-Premium.

Alternative Accommodations

Gillette's only B&B, **Jost House Inn,** 2708 Ridgecrest Dr., tel. (307) 687-1240 or (877) 685-2707, is a modern home with two spacious guest rooms and two friendly owners. The rooms are elegantly decorated and one contains a king bed, private bath, and private sitting room. The expansive yard, gardens, and columned front porch add to the appeal. A big full breakfast is served each morning, and children over three are welcome. Rates for up to four people are $75-100. Find Jost House in cyberspace at www.newwaveis.com/users/josthousebb. Moderate-Expensive.

Skybow Castle Ranch, tel. (307) 682-3228 or (800) 682-3229, is a 3,000-acre working cattle ranch in the pine forests 15 miles northeast of Gillette. Lodging is available on a nightly or weekly basis; $120 per night for two people including three meals, or $800 per week for two people. Guests stay in rustic cabins with a common bathhouse, and they can join in daily horseback rides (extra fee). There's room for up to 24 guests at Skybow. Premium.

Camping

Campers and RVers will enjoy **Crazy Woman Campground,** 1001 W. 2nd St., tel. (307) 682-3665; open year-round. It's a pleasant place with genuine shade trees, a rarity in Wyoming's private campgrounds. Also here are a jacuzzi, an outdoor pool, and bike rentals. Rates are a stiff $19-30 for RVs or $16-25 for tents. The rather bleak **High Plains Campground,** tel. (307) 687-7339, has more RV sites next to Cam-Plex on the east side of town. Open year-round.

FOOD

The Gillette restaurant scene tends toward middle-brow fare, but a number of places are a vast improvement over the rows of fast-food joints that line the main drags.

A cozy little eatery in the heart of downtown, **Lula Belle,** 101 N. Gillette Ave., tel. (307) 682-9798, is best known for its tasty and filling breakfasts. Another place for breakfasts—served all day—is **Packard's Grill,** 408 S. Douglas Hwy., tel. (307) 686-5149, a no-smoking restaurant. Daily lunch specials and inexpensive all-American dinner choices make this a popular family place. Most dinner entrées are under $9. Get cappuccinos, lattes, light breakfasts, earthy lunches, and sweet treats at **Coffee Friends,** 320 S. Gillette Ave., tel. (307) 686-6119.

Ethnic Eateries

Gillette is blessed with an excellent—and authentic—Chinese eatery: **Hong Kong Restaurant,** 1612 W. 2nd St., tel. (307) 682-5829. Also of note is **Peking House Restaurant,** 2701 S. Douglas Hwy., tel. (307) 682-7868, with a popular lunchtime buffet. Get pizza and pasta at **Ole's Pizza Parlor,** 114 N. US Hwy. 14/16, tel. (307) 682-8484. For authentic Mexican food and great margaritas, try **Las Margaritas,** 2107 S. Douglas Hwy., tel. (307) 682-6545.

Lunch and Dinner

Humphrey's Bar & Grill, 408 W. Juniper Lane, tel. (307) 682-0100, is a favorite lunch place for the business crowd with a diverse pub grub menu and Wednesday night ribs. Humphrey's has more than 50 beers on tap, and the small brewery here makes five of them. The feeling is a bit formulaic: walls crowded with sporting photos and memorabilia, and TVs tuned to all-sports channels.

The big salad bar/dessert bar at **Golden Corral,** 2700 S. Douglas Hwy., tel. (307) 682-9130, makes for a bargain meal. **Bailey's Bar & Grill,** 301 S. Gillette Ave., tel. (307) 686-7667, is a fine place for such homemade lunch and dinner specialties as chicken-fried steak, burgers, and Mexican fare. Great finger food, too. The award-winning **Prime Rib Restaurant,** 1205 S. Douglas Hwy., tel. (307) 682-2944, is another very good place for prime rib, and also has a diverse menu of steak, pasta, chicken, and seafood. The wine and champagne list is extensive.

Get groceries from any of the big chains: Albertson's, Buttery, Decker's, and IGA. **Breanna's Bakery,** 208 S. Gillette Ave., tel. (307) 686-0570, has doughnuts, sweets, pastries, and freshly baked breads.

OTHER PRACTICALITIES

Entertainment

Head to Gillette City Park on Thursday nights at 7 p.m. during June and July for the **Concerts in the Park** series. Music ranges from bluegrass to classical. The **Powder River Symphony Orchestra,** tel. (307) 686-5767, performs at Cam-Plex in March, May, October, and December. You'll find community drama at its corniest during the **melodrama shows** held at Cam-Plex on Friday evenings June-August. Call (307) 686-3025 for details.

Top 40 and oldies bands play most nights at **Partners Saloon** inside the Tower West Lodge at 109 N. US Hwy. 14/16, tel. (307) 686-2210. **Kicks Lounge** in the Holiday Inn at 2009 S. Douglas Hwy., tel. (307) 686-3000, is the place to go for rock and pop tunes six nights a week and a happy-hour buffet Mon.-Fri. evenings. **Prime Rib Restaurant,** 1205 S. Douglas Hwy., tel. (307) 682-2944, also has occasional live entertainment, as does **Jake's Tavern,** 5201 S. Douglas Hwy., tel. (307) 686-3781. Jake's features happy-hour prices 5-7 p.m. seven days a week. **Mingles,** 2209 S. Douglas Hwy., tel. (307) 686-1222, has half a dozen pool tables and a big-screen TV. **Good Times Lounge,** 2701 S. Douglas Hwy., tel. (307) 682-0808, has live country-and-western music some nights.

For movies, head to **Foothills Twin Theatre,** 650 N. US Hwy. 14/16, tel. (307) 682-6766; **Sky-Hi Theatres,** on S. Douglas Hwy., tel. (307) 682-7628; or **Skyline Drive In Theatre,** 2201 S. Douglas Hwy., tel. (307) 674-4532.

Events

All summer long you'll find **stock car racing** on Saturday nights at Thunder Basin Stock Car Track, on Garner Lake Road. Gillette's **Fourth of July** celebration is the biggest in northeastern Wyoming. In addition to an impressive fireworks show, you'll find a pancake breakfast, a parade, mud volleyball, firehose water fights, and even a Ping-Pong drop (a Ping-Pong drop?). **Parkfest** brings a full day of musical entertainment at Cam-Plex Park the second Saturday of August. The **Campbell County Fair** in mid-August includes livestock judging, arts-and-crafts exhibits, and other old-time favorites.

Cam-Plex, a large and modern multi-events center east of town on Garner Lake Rd., frequently has concerts, cattle shows, rodeos, conventions, and other events. During the summertime, rodeos take place almost every weekend, the biggest being the **PRCA Rodeo** in late July and early August. The highlight of the PRCA

Rodeo is the camel (!) race. In late November and early December, Gillette plays host to a series of **Christmas crafts fairs**—call the visitor center at (307) 686-0040 or (800) 544-6136 for details.

Recreation

Gillette has some of the finest recreation facilities in Wyoming, a reflection of the prospering local economy. **Campbell County Recreation Center,** 1000 S. Douglas Hwy., tel. (307) 682-5470, houses an indoor pool with a diving well, a 383-foot water slide (summer only), weight rooms, racquetball and squash courts, a gym, and a sauna. Enjoy fabulous *free* summertime swimming at the **Gillette Water Park,** tel. (307) 682-1962. Located outdoors at Gillette and 10th, the park has a main pool with geysers and waterfalls, a wading pool with a slide for kids, a deep diving pool, and a sand play area. There's also an indoor **Aquatics Center** in town for competitive swimming events.

Bird-watchers should head to **McManamen Park** on W. Warlow Dr., where viewing blinds let you look for ducks and other birds.

Campbell County's modern **ice arena,** 121 S. 4-J Rd., tel. (307) 687-1555, is open mid-October to mid-March. Roller skaters will enjoy **Razor City Skateland,** 885 Hannum Rd., tel. (307) 682-3529, and bowlers can roll their own at **Camelanes Bowling Center,** 1005 W. 2nd St., tel. (307) 682-4811, or **Frontier Lanes,** 5700 S. Douglas Hwy., tel. (307) 687-0261. Golfers hobnob at **Bell Nob Golf Links,** 1316 Overdale Dr., tel. (307) 686-7069, or **Gillette Golf Club,** 1800 Country Club Rd., tel. (307) 686-4774.

Information and Services

The **Gillette Visitors Center,** tel. (307) 686-0040 or (800) 544-6136, is at 1810 S. Douglas Hwy. (next to the Flying J Truckstop at exit 126) and is open daily 8 a.m.-5 p.m. Memorial Day to Labor Day, and Mon.-Fri. 8 a.m.-5 p.m. the rest of the year. Visit www.gillettewyoming.com for more on the area.

Get books at **Daniels Books,** 320 S. Gillette Ave., tel. (307) 682-8266, and pick up Wyoming-made gifts two blocks away at **The Appetizer,** 118 S. Gillette Ave., tel. (307) 686-0793.

Gillette is home to the state's fastest-growing junior college (over 900 students), the **Gillette Campus** of Northern Wyoming Community College. Located at 720 W. 8th St., tel. (307) 686-0254, the campus offers a range of classes and degree programs from business to mining.

Transportation

The Gillette airport is five miles north of town. **United Express/Great Lakes Aviation,** tel. (307) 685-2280 or (800) 241-6522, has service to Denver.

Rent cars from **A & A Auto & RV Rental,** tel. (307) 686-8250; **Avis,** tel. (307) 682-8588 or (800) 831-2847; **Enterprise,** tel. (307) 686-5655 or (800) 325-8007; **Hertz,** tel. (307) 686-0550 or (800) 654-3131; or **U-Save Auto Rental,** tel. (307) 682-2815. Avis and Hertz have cars at the airport.

Powder River/Coach USA, 1700 E. US Hwy. 14/16, tel. (307) 682-0960 or (800) 442-3682, has daily bus service throughout northern and eastern Wyoming. (Look for the big Petrolane propane tank to find this easy-to-miss bus station.)

The two local taxi companies are **City Cab,** tel. (307) 685-1000, and **Gillette Taxi Cab & Courier,** tel. (307) 686-4090.

HEADING SOUTH

Two roads point south from Gillette; more remote State Hwy. 50 makes a fine bike route. This distinctive red highway was built from scoria. The alternative route, State Hwy. 59, takes you into the heart of the mixed-grass prairie, with oil pumpjacks, windmills, enormous bales of hay, and thousands of cattle and sheep. Tumbleweeds are plastered against the barbed-wire fences and abandoned farm equipment rusts on hilltops. The Belle Ayr mine stands on the eastern horizon a dozen miles south of town, with flat-topped mesas and nipple-shaped buttes adding a little spice to the scenery. Far to the west, the Big Horn Mountains rise from the plains. Be sure to pause for a look at the grasses—blue grama is especially pretty when seen up close.

Durham Buffalo Ranch

Approximately 30 miles south of Gillette is Durham Buffalo Ranch, home of the largest private buffalo herd in existence. The Flocchini family owns a 55,000-acre spread here and is dedicated to returning the land to its original state, when bison and other native animals dominated the prairie landscape. Watch for some of the 3,500 head of buffalo along the highway. Herds more than 1,000 times this size once roamed across the land, and this is a rare opportunity to see bison today in a relatively natural setting. Call (307) 939-1271 for tour information (groups only).

Wright

Wright sits right in the center of America's largest low-sulfur coal deposit. Established in 1976, the town quickly grew to some 1,200 residents. Modern schools, a small shopping mall, and six churches popped up, along with trailer courts and suburban split-level homes on curving streets. Funded partly by Arco, Wright was built to house workers for nearby coal mines. It's a pretty weird place. Imagine an enclave of middle-class America plunked down in a setting straight out of *High Plains Drifter.*

On the east end of town off State Hwy. 387, the small **Wright Centennial Museum,** tel. (307) 464-1222, houses local homestead-era items. Out front is a 70-ton truck that was retired from hauling coal when it was replaced with much larger versions. The museum is open Mon.-Fri. 10 a.m.-5 p.m. from mid-May to mid-October.

The **Latigo Hills Mall** is Wright's focal point, and includes a grocery store, cafe, bar, pizza shop, hardware store/gift shop, library, bank (with ATM), post office, bowling alley ("Rolling Thunder Lanes"), dentist, laundromat, and hair salon. There's even a massage therapist.

Wright Area Chamber of Commerce, tel. (307) 464-1312, is also in the mall and is open Mon.-Fri. 8 a.m.-noon and 1-5 p.m. Get buffalo burgers at **Reno Junction Cafe,** tel. (307) 939-1298, at the junction of State Hwys. 387 and 59. The town also has a fine **recreation center,** tel. (307) 464-0198, with an indoor pool, racquetball courts, a weight room, and a gym.

Stay at **National 9 Inn,** tel. (307) 464-1510 or (800) 524-9999, where rooms go for $48 s or $53 d; kitchenettes $5 extra. Inexpensive. Park RVs ($15) or pitch a tent ($9) at **Sagebluff RV Park,** a mile west of town on State Hwy. 387, tel. (307) 464-1305; open all year.

The annual event here is **Wright Days,** held the third week of June with games, parades, and the obligatory rodeo—including a kids' rodeo. Gigantic coal strip mines surround Wright; all of them use Paul Bunyan-scale equipment and skeleton crews of employees. Much of this is public land belonging to Thunder Basin National Grassland, meaning enormous revenues for the federal government and severance taxes for the state of Wyoming. The coal trains seem to never end. Stop on the railroad overpass near the dot of a settlement called Bill and you'll see a hundred cars of coal pass every couple of minutes, with empty trains waiting on the sidings. Most of this coal is on its way to electric-generating plants in Texas and the Midwest.

THE BLACK HILLS

In Wyoming's Northeast corner, the Black Hills of South Dakota roll across an arbitrary line, bringing a quiet beauty that differs greatly from other parts of the state. Here, the Belle Fourche River (pronounced "bell-FOOSH," French for "Beautiful Fork") cuts northeast past rich pastures before taking a sudden right angle to the southeast as it heads to the Missouri River. Tiny towns nestle in the forested hills, and cattle graze on the riverbanks. Nearby, one of the most stunning of all sights—Devils Tower—seems almost alive in its abrupt rise from the pastoral landscape. South of the Black Hills in Weston County, the hill country quickly opens into the mixed-grass prairie of the plains. This out-of-the-way part of Wyoming is truly a special place. It's no wonder that the Sioux considered the Black Hills the home of the Great Spirit.

Only 13,000 people live in Crook and Weston Counties, scattered on rural ranches or in the small settlements of Sundance and Hulett in the midst of Wyoming's Black Hills, along with Newcastle, Moorcroft, and Upton along the southern edge. Cattle grazing, bentonite mining, oil wells, logging, and tourism provide the jobs.

The Land

The Black Hills stretch in a long ellipse, 125 miles north to south and 65 miles across, rising 3,000 to 4,000 feet above the surrounding plains. South Dakota's Harney Peak, at 7,242 feet, is the tallest mountain in the Black Hills; in fact, it's the tallest peak between the South Dakota-Wyoming line and the Atlantic Ocean. The most famous geological attraction in this part of Wyoming is the imposing Devils Tower, but the Black Hills north of Sundance are also captivating, especially in the spring and fall. Most visitors who come to northeast Wyoming do so as part of a trip that includes Yellowstone and various South Dakota sights: Mt. Rushmore, Deadwood, the Crazy Horse Memorial, and Jewel Cave.

From a distance, the dusky green carpet of ponderosa pine darkens the hills—hence the Sioux name Paha Sapa, meaning "Hills that are Black." The Black Hills are a blend of rocky hills crowded with pine and aspen forests, open meadows, and valleys lined with bur oak. This is one of the few places you're likely to see native oak trees in Wyoming.

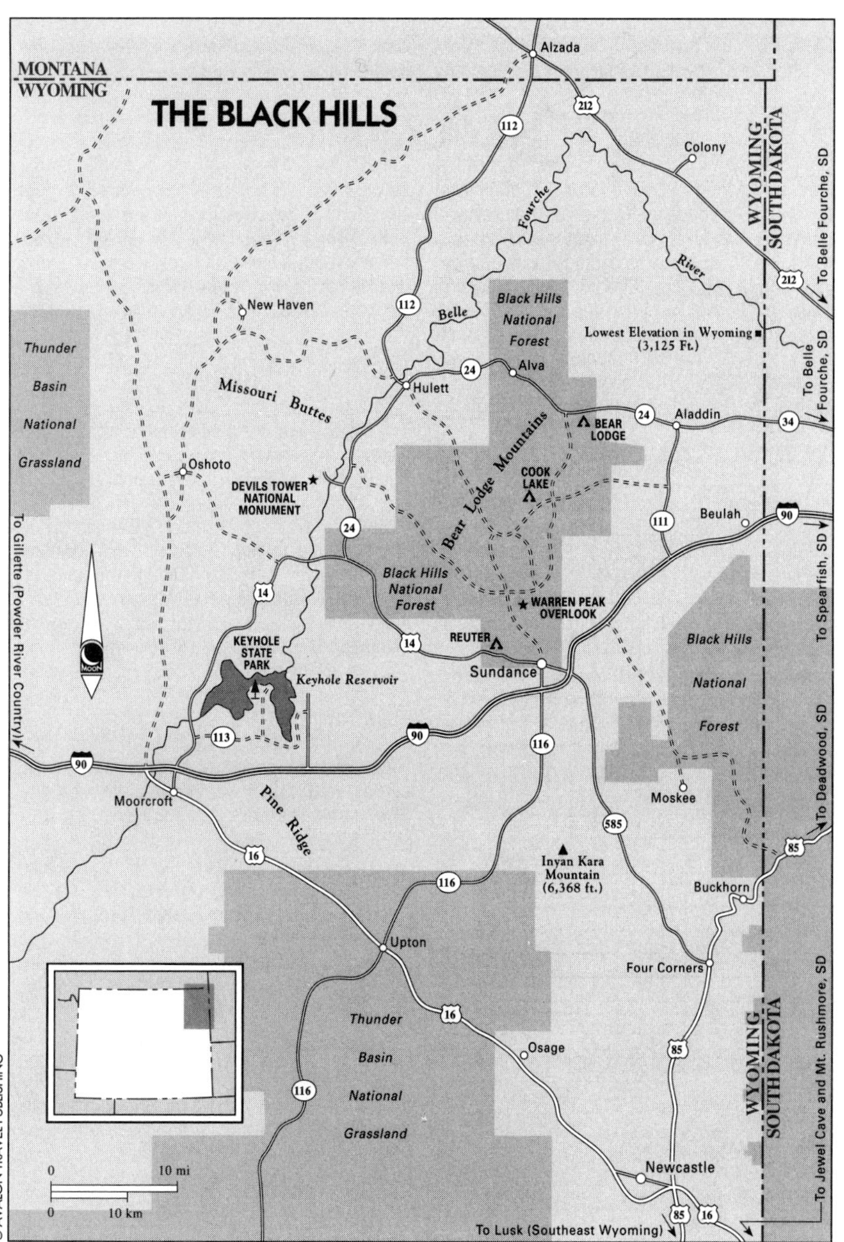
THE BLACK HILLS
MONTANA
WYOMING
Alzada
Colony
Fourche
River
Belle
WYOMING
SOUTH DAKOTA
To Belle Fourche, SD
New Haven
Black Hills National Forest
Lowest Elevation in Wyoming
(3,125 Ft.)
To Belle Fourche, SD
Thunder Basin National Grassland
Alva
Hulett
Missouri Buttes
Bear Lodge Mountains
BEAR LODGE
Aladdin
Oshoto
DEVILS TOWER NATIONAL MONUMENT
COOK LAKE
Beulah
To Gillette (Powder River Country)
To Spearfish, SD
Black Hills National Forest
WARREN PEAK OVERLOOK
KEYHOLE STATE PARK
REUTER
Sundance
Black Hills National Forest
Keyhole Reservoir
Moorcroft
Pine Ridge
Moskee
To Deadwood, SD
Inyan Kara Mountain
(6,368 ft.)
Buckhorn
Upton
Four Corners
Thunder Basin National Grassland
Osage
To Jewel Cave and Mt. Rushmore, SD
WYOMING
SOUTH DAKOTA
0
10 mi
0
10 km
Newcastle
To Lusk (Southeast Wyoming)
MOON

White-tailed deer are abundant throughout the Black Hills, and herds of elk are found southeast of Sundance. Merriam's turkeys are a common sight all through this country. Introduced from New Mexico in 1948, they are now the most widespread game-bird species in northeast Wyoming.

NEWCASTLE

Newcastle (pop. 3,300) sits at the junction of several major roads and serves as a gateway to the Black Hills. Like much of northeast Wyoming, the town's economy is a mixture of energy, ranching, and logging. Every half hour, day and night, traffic backs up on the railroad tracks across Main Street to wait as a hundred soot-black coal cars rumble past bound for midwestern power plants. A Newcastle refinery produces jet fuel for South Dakota's giant Ellsworth Air Force Base, and a natural-gas processing plant sits 25 miles south of town in the midst of the Finn-Shurley fields. Large ranches encompass the town, dotted with oil pumpjacks, windmills, and Herefords. Piles of fresh-cut ponderosa pine surround Newcastle's big sawmill.

NEWCASTLE AREA CLIMATE

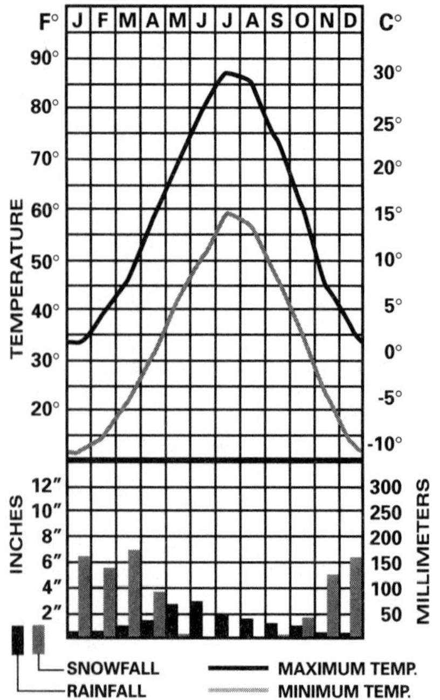

Average Maximum Temp.	**59.2°F**
Average Minimum Temp.	**34.1°F**
Annual Rainfall	**15.12″**
Annual Snowfall	**36.1″**

HISTORY

The first white settlement of the Newcastle area came in 1875, when Professor Walter P. Jenney and Lt. Col. R.I. Dodge led 432 soldiers and an army of mining engineers, scientists, and mapmakers to a base camp along Beaver Creek. They built the Jenney Stockade, which became a stage station and distribution point along the Cheyenne-Deadwood Trail. Many of the West's most famous characters stopped by en route to Deadwood, including Wild Bill Hickok, Calamity Jane, and Wyatt Earp.

Tubb Town

In 1888, the Chicago, Burlington, and Quincy Railroad announced plans to construct tracks across northeast Wyoming and into Montana. Speculators established Tubb Town, a ram-

SIGHTSEEING HIGHLIGHTS FOR THE BLACK HILLS

Anna Miller Museum in Newcastle

Crook County Museum in Sundance

Black Hills National Forest north of Sundance

Aladdin Store

Devils Tower National Monument

Popular events: All Girl Rodeo in Newcastle (May), Weston County Fair in Newcastle (August), and Crook County Fair and Rodeo in Sundance (August)

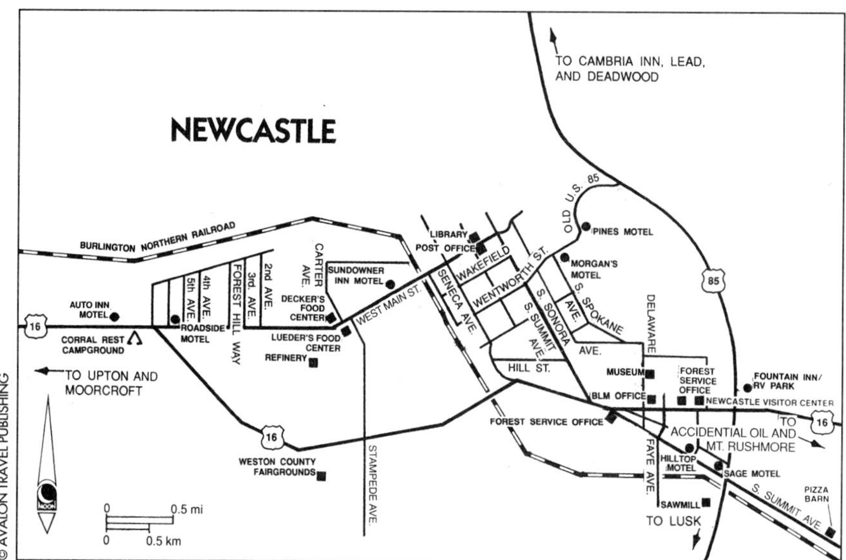

shackle collection of saloons, hotels, and "sporting houses" along the proposed railroad route. All visitors were required to pay a toll (of sorts) upon entrance: "set 'em up for the bunch." The party didn't last long—when the Burlington Railroad decided instead to build a town a few miles west at present-day Newcastle, Tubb Town faded into history. At Whoopup Canyon (so named because the spring floods came "a-whoopin' through"), a railroad worker attempted to pry the cap off a 25-pound can of black powder. After struggling without success, he decided to try a more forceful approach—using a pickax to punch a hole in the lid. His coworkers found little left to bury.

The Cambria Mines

Coal was discovered in Cambria Canyon in the 1880s, and the coal-mining town of Cambria popped up almost overnight. It became a model community, with a water system, modern homes, three churches, electric lights, and some of the safest underground mines in the nation. Alcohol was banned, along with bawdy entertainment. At its peak more than 1,500 people lived in Cambria, but when the coal ran out in 1928 the mines were forced to close.

The discovery of coal at Cambria led the Burlington Railroad to establish a townsite as near the mouth of Cambria Canyon as possible, with a spur to the four mines. The town was called Newcastle, after the English coal port of Newcastle-upon-Tyne. At first, the wide-open frontier sensibility of Newcastle contrasted sharply with that of quiet, sedate Cambria. When the new mayor, Frank Mondell (who had established the Cambria mines), decided to get rid of 20 of Newcastle's undesirables, a local hotel owner—fearing that he would lose most of his business—shot the mayor. Mondell (who later served for 26 years as Wyoming's lone congressional representative) carried the bullet in his spine the rest of his life.

After the Cambria mines closed, the town of Newcastle faded, but with the discovery of huge oil deposits nearby in the 1950s it boomed again. By the mid-'50s more than 25,000 people crowded the surrounding countryside. A bust soon followed, only to lead to a similar cycle in the 1970s. Now Newcastle perks along on an economy equal parts oil, coal, logging, and ranching. Folks from Nebraska or Kansas would feel right at home among the quiet streets, staid older homes, pickup trucks, and freight trains.

The coal-mining town of Cambria was considered a model community in its time.

SIGHTS

Anna Miller Museum

The Newcastle museum at Delaware St. and US Hwy. 16, tel. (307) 746-4188, is open Mon.-Fri. 9 a.m.-5 p.m. all year, plus Saturday 9 a.m.-noon June-August. It's housed in the old National Guard Cavalry Barn, a stone structure built in the 1930s by the Work Projects Administration. Inside is the typical collection of local paraphernalia: items from the Cambria mines, a horse-drawn hearse, a noose (not, however, the one vigilantes used to hang murderer Diamond Slim Clifton from the Newcastle railroad trestle), dinosaur bones, and a scale model of the giant KB&C ranch. Be sure to try a couple of cranks on the old noisemaker—it was used to disrupt newlyweds on their first night. Anna Miller, for whom the museum was named, was a local school superintendent whose husband, Sheriff Billy Miller, was the last white man to die in a battle with the Indians. He was killed in 1903.

Outside the museum you'll find a furnished one-room schoolhouse built in 1890, a homesteader cabin, and the **Jenney Stockade cabin** (built in 1875), the oldest building in the Black Hills. Ask at the museum for directions to the Cheyenne-Deadwood Trail ruts.

Accidental Oil Company

Certainly the most amusing sight around Newcastle is the kitschy Accidental Oil Company. In 1966 (around the time Jed Clampett of television's *Beverly Hillbillies* was "shootin' at some food, and up from the ground came a bubbling crude—oil that is, black gold, Texas tea . . ."), Newcastle rancher Al Smith decided to dig a hole to see how far down it was to oil. Using a pick and shovel, and later dynamite, he actually struck oil at a depth of 21 feet. The "world's only hand-dug oil well" is now a small run-down tourist trap along US Hwy. 16 four miles east of Newcastle. Outside are steam-powered oil rigs and antique pumps. An old oil-storage tank encloses a gift shop, and you can walk down to view the oil-bearing rock under black light. Accidental Oil, tel. (307) 746-2042, is open Mon.-Sat. 9 a.m.-6 p.m. and Sunday 11 a.m.-5 p.m. June-Aug.; closed the rest of the year. The gift shop is open all year. The attraction offers thirty-minute tours of the well—with a discussion on petroleum geology—cost $5 for adults, $3 for kids, or $15 for families. Pure Americana.

ACCOMMODATIONS AND CAMPING

Motels

You'll find a good variety of lodging options in Newcastle. During Sturgis Rally Week (the first week of August) rates at many local motels rise sharply, and the rooms are often booked up almost a year in advance. See Newcastle Vicinity, below, for three other lodging options in the Four Corners area. Add a six percent tax to motel rates listed below.

Several places provide older rooms for economy prices. **Hilltop Motel,** 1121 S. Summit, tel. (307) 746-4494, charges $30 s or $36-42 d, and has kitchenettes for $5 extra. Inexpensive. **Sage Motel,** 1227 S. Summit, tel. (307) 746-2724, may be a better bet, with comfortable and cozy rooms for $28-30 s or $32-34 d. Budget.

Sundowner Inn Motel, 451 W. Main, tel. (307) 746-2796, charges $30-40 s or d for older rooms, all containing fridges. Talk about wearing your beliefs on your sleeve—when I last visited, the Sundowner sign proclaimed: "Under Christian management. Verse of the week: Proverbs 15: 1-5." Budget-Inexpensive.

Roadside Motel, 1605 W. Main St., tel. (307) 746-9640, charges $32-38 s or d; two rooms contain kitchenettes. The rooms are spotlessly clean. Budget-Inexpensive. At **Auto Inn Motel,** 2503 W. Main, tel. (307) 746-2734, rates are $36 s or $38-48 d, the rooms have fridges, and a continental breakfast is served. Inexpensive.

Two attractive, clean, and friendly motels—Morgan's and Pines—have quiet out-of-the-way locations just a few blocks off the main drag. Open April-Nov., **Morgan's Motel,** 205 S. Spokane, tel. (307) 746-2715, charges $35 s or d. Inexpensive. Just up the hill is **Pines Motel,** 248 E. Wentworth, tel. (307) 746-4334, where rooms with fridges cost $42 s or $50 d; kitchenettes for $66 s or d. Inexpensive-Moderate. Both places are recommended.

On the east end of town, **Fountain Inn,** tel. (307) 746-4426 or (800) 882-8858, is the largest Newcastle motel and the only one with an outdoor pool. Rates here are $59 s or $64-69 d. Moderate.

Bed and Breakfasts

Set amid majestic Black Hills country eight miles north of Newcastle, the **Flying V Cambria Inn,** tel. (307) 746-2096, offers country accommodations in a historic stone building. Built in the 1920s, the inn has an excellent restaurant and 10 guest rooms with a mix of antique and modern furnishings. Room rates are $46 s or $69 d, including a full breakfast. Some rooms have shared baths, and suites are also available. The Cambria is open June-December. For more info, check the website: www.trib.com/~flyingv. Moderate.

In the Black Hills 17 miles northeast of Newcastle, **EVA—Great Spirit Ranch B&B,** tel. (307) 746-2537, is a spacious modern log home on 1,000 acres of ranch land. Owner Irene Spillane cooks up big country breakfasts and will fill you with details on the area's rich human and natural history. The four guest rooms have shared or private baths and cost $74 s or d ($100 d with three meals a day). Kids are welcome. This is a wonderful place to relax in a remote and beautiful setting. Moderate.

Camping and Cabins

You can pitch a tent for free anywhere on nearby public lands within both Thunder Basin National Grassland (see Douglas Vicinity in the Central Wyoming chapter) and Black Hills National Forest. For access to Black Hills National Forest, head nine miles east on US Hwy. 16 and then turn north up Forest Rd. 117 (just a few hundred feet before the South Dakota border). **Beaver Creek Campground** ($8; open all year) is right on the Wyoming-South Dakota border 23 miles northeast of Newcastle near the place called Mallo. The Park Service's **Jewel Cave National Monument,** tel. (605) 673-2288, has camping inside South Dakota, 25 miles east of Newcastle.

For something completely different, stay at the Forest Service's **Summit Ridge Lookout** on the South Dakota/Wyoming border northeast of Newcastle. You don't actually stay in the fire tower itself (it's still in use), but in the log cabin at the base. Rates are $20 per day, with space for four people; call (307) 746-2782 for reservations.

Back in Newcastle, **Corral Rest RV Camp,** 2206 W. Main, tel. (307) 746-2007, has tent sites for $10 and RV sites for $15; open mid-April to mid-November. Showers for noncampers cost $2, and the RV park has an indoor pool.

Crystal Park Campground in front of Fountain Inn, 3 Seminoe Ave., tel. (307) 746-4426 or (800) 882-8858, is open year-round with tent sites for $9, RV sites for $13. Showers for noncampers are $2.

FOOD

For excellent breakfasts, a good salad bar, and all-American dinners, head to **Old Mill Inn,** 500 W. Main, tel. (307) 746-4608. The building itself is worth a look; they don't build places like this anymore. Completed in 1905, the mill produced Toomey's Flapjack Flour and Toomey's Biscuit Mix until going out of business in 1965. It was later transformed into a restaurant.

On the southeast end of town, **Pizza Barn,** 66 Old US Hwy. 85, tel. (307) 746-4686, is one of the best steak establishments in this part of Wyoming. You'll also find reasonable all-you-can-eat barbecued ribs on Wednesday evening and pizzas nightly.

Historic **Flying V Cambria Inn,** eight miles north of town on US Hwy. 85, tel. (307) 746-2096, offers delicious prime rib, steaks, seafood, and Italian meals. Big portions and great food in a nostalgic setting; open June-Dec. only.

For fast food and sit-down meals in a friendly diner setting, head to **Hi-16 Drive In,** 2951 W. Main, tel. (307) 746-4055. Newcastle's fast-food choices include Subway, Taco John's, and Pizza Hut (the lunch buffet here is a good deal).

The best meal deals (and entertainment) in the area are across the South Dakota line. Deadwood's gambling casinos serve a big variety of food, including inexpensive steak dinners. This is where Newcastle folks go for an evening out. Two recommended Deadwood restaurants are Biff Malibu's (pasta) and Kitty's Chinatown (Chinese). The meals may be reasonable, but be forewarned that lodging in Deadwood is on the pricey side.

Get groceries in Newcastle at **Decker's Food Center,** 709 W. Main, tel. (307) 746-2779, or **Lueder's Food Center,** 622 W. Main, tel. (307) 746-3511. Decker's has a good bakery.

OTHER PRACTICALITIES

Entertainment

The **Dogie** (as in "Git along, little dogie"), 111 W. Main St., tel. (307) 746-2187, is the local movie house. The bar at **Old Mill Inn,** 500 W. Main, tel. (307) 746-4608, has over 100 beers, including many microbrews. Newcastle's live music scene is almost nonexistent; to party, locals head to happenin' Deadwood, South Dakota (50 miles away).

Events

The biggest local event isn't in Newcastle. It's South Dakota's **Sturgis Bike Rally,** the second week of August. Not a good time to come through town on a Honda motorcycle! A number of events actually take place in Newcastle, including the **All Girl Rodeo** in late May. This unique professional event is the largest female rodeo in Wyoming. You're likely to find other rodeos going on at the fairgrounds most summer weekends. Also in May are **Living History Days,** when visitors will learn about the lives of pioneers.

The annual **Perino Horse Sale** in June brings people from all over the nation and is a great opportunity to see these beautiful animals. Also popular is **Sagebrush Days** in late June, featuring a parade, carnival, watermelon feed, street dance, and other events. Newcastle's main local event is the **Weston County Fair,** held the first week of August.

Information and Services

Just west of the intersection of US Hwys. 16 and 85, the **Newcastle Visitor Center,** tel. (307) 746-2739 or (800) 835-0157, is open Mon.-Fri. 9 a.m.-5 p.m. all year, plus Saturday 9 a.m.-1 p.m. and Sunday noon-4 p.m. May-September. Find them on the web at www.trib.com/newcastle. While here, be sure to pick up "Beaver Creek: A Trip Through Time," a brochure describing a loop tour of sites in the area; it's filled with delightful descriptions of historical events.

The **Bureau of Land Management** office is at 1101 Washington, tel. (307) 746-4453, and the Forest Service's **Custer/Elk Mountain Ranger Station** is at 1225 Washington Blvd., tel. (307) 746-2782. Nearly all the land they manage is across the border in South Dakota.

The **Weston County Library** is at 23 W. Main, tel. (307) 746-2206. Swim at the high school's **indoor pool,** 15 Stampede, tel. (307) 746-2713.

Play a few rounds of golf at **Newcastle Country Club,** 2302 W. Main, tel. (307) 746-2639.

Newcastle does not have bus or plane service. Both local banks have **ATMs,** and others can be found in the Pamida store and at Coffee Cup Fuel Stop.

NEWCASTLE VICINITY

Heading North

North of Newcastle, US Hwy. 85 climbs quickly into the pine-covered Black Hills, providing wide vistas over the town and across the open plains to the south. Eight miles north of Newcastle is **Flying V Cambria Inn,** constructed in 1928 as a resort for and memorial to the Cambria miners. It was completed just a few months before the mines closed down for good. Now listed on the National Register of Historic Places, the inn is open for meals and lodging, tel. (307) 746-2096. The ghost town of Cambria slowly crumbles on private land nearby.

Another nine miles north is **Red Butte,** a steep-sided sandstone peak rising right along the road like a miniature Devils Tower. A local landmark, it was said to have been used by both Indians and early whites as a lookout. Not far away is the site of the 1878 Canyon Springs robbery on the old Cheyenne-Deadwood Stage Route. A passenger and an outlaw died in the shoot-out, and at least $20,000 (some accounts claim up to $140,000) in gold was taken and buried nearby. Many years later, a local farmer digging potatoes near Red Butte apparently found some of the loot. Packing up his family, he split town without a word.

Four Corners Area

North of Red Butte, the land begins to open up into an undulating grassy terrain with rich red-black soil. Just a couple more miles up the road is a combination general store, cafe, and post office at **Four Corners.** The owners also run the adjacent **Four Corners Country Inn,** tel. (307) 746-4776, with nicely furnished rooms (shared or private baths) for $25 s or $35 d. Inexpensive. RV sites with hookups are $15, and tent sites cost $10; showers available.

Mallo Rd. (gravel) heads east from Four Corners into South Dakota, offering a colorful fall drive as the aspens turn a brilliant yellow. The Forest Service's **Beaver Creek Campground** ($8; open all year) is six miles east of Four Corners and right across the state line inside South Dakota. Just a mile inside Wyoming is spacious **Mallo Camp & Resort,** tel. (307) 746-4094, where modern motel rooms are $40-45 d, including access to two large communal kitchens. Inexpensive. RV camping is $15 (no showers) and primitive tent spaces are $5. Mallo Resort is a very popular snowmobile destination in the winter months.

Soldier Creek Lodge, 25135 Hwy. 85, tel. (307) 746-4797 or (800) 251-9165, http://w3.trib-com/ ~echoswe, is a rambling structure that is popular with groups, who come here for weddings, snowmobiling, and hunting. The 60-person lodge does, however, rent out rooms for $45-55 s or $90-110 d, including breakfast. Expensive.

Heading South

South of Newcastle, US Hwy. 85 is an arrow aimed at the horizon, pointing across the almost-flat landscape of grass, wind, and antelope. A few bottomland trees line the creeks, and the Cheyenne River etches a narrow line through the land, nearly dry in the late-summer heat. This is the heart of the great mixed-grass prairie that borders eastern Wyoming and reaches into adjacent Nebraska and south into Colorado.

UPTON AREA

On the edge of Upton (pop. 1,000), a sign makes no bones about where you are: the "Best Town on Earth!" Who am I to argue? Like its neighbors—Osage and Newcastle—Upton lies right along the edge of the Black Hills, with ponderosa pines topping the ridge to the north (appropriately named Pine Ridge) and open-range country spreading to the south. The Chicago, Burlington, and Quincy Railroad established a depot here in 1892, and railroad tracks now form Upton's southern border. Beyond this, State Hwy. 116 climbs over gentle grassy hills through the heart of Thunder Basin National Grassland. It's a high-plains landscape filled with windmills and scattered ranches and grazed by sheep, cattle, antelope, and mule deer. The sky completely dominates the landscape, sending giant white thunderheads over the plains. Upton's limited economy is dependent upon American Colloid's bentonite mine, local ranchers, oil pumping, and coal mining in nearby Campbell County.

Upton's tiny **Red Onion Museum** houses local items, including the featured attraction: a two-headed Hereford calf born on a local ranch. The museum is open Mon.-Fri. 10 a.m.-noon and 1-4:30 p.m. On the west side of Upton are reconstructed cabins (one built of sod) near the original townsite.

Osage

Halfway between Newcastle and Upton, tiny Osage (pop. 300) has a bar but not much else to show for having once been the center of the oil industry in northeast Wyoming. In 1920, a huge gusher turned the surrounding country into a madhouse of oil prospectors and turned Osage into a tent city of 1,500 people. When the boom inevitably turned to bust, only a core of folks remained in what is now a railroad way station. The only surviving business is a bar.

Upton Practicalities

Stay at the basic **Upton Motel,** tel. (307) 468-9282, for $30 s or $35 d; or the much nicer **Weston Inn Motel,** tel. (307) 468-2401, for $36 s or $40-51 d. Both Inexpensive. Microwaves and fridges are available at the Weston.

If you don't mind in-town, no-shade camping in a parking lot, pitch a tent next to the **Country Market Conoco,** tel. (307) 468-2551. The cost is $4 a night, $10 for RVs.

The Drug Store, tel. (307) 468-2770, claims the "best malts in Wyoming." Drop by to see for yourself. The **Stagecoach Inn** is a popular eating spot, or get groceries at **Joe's Food Center,** tel. (307) 468-2372. You can hang out at the public **library** on Pine and 4th Sts., tel. (307) 468-2324.

MOORCROFT

Moorcroft (pop. 800) is a nondescript ranching and oil field town perched within a few miles of popular Keyhole Reservoir. It isn't particularly attractive, but it will do as a stop on the way to somewhere else. Because the famed Texas Trail passed through it, Moorcroft became an important cattle town. Up until the end of WW II, it served as the largest cattle shipping point along the entire Chicago, Burlington, and Quincy Railroad. The local historical stopping place is **Helen Robinson Zimmerschied Western-Texas Trail Museum,** at 200 S. Bighorn, tel. (307) 756-9300. Open Mon.-Fri. noon-4 p.m. summers only; no charge. The name is almost bigger than the museum's collection of local items.

Practicalities

Lodging is available at tiny **Wyoming Motel,** 111 W. Converse, tel. (307) 756-3452, for $38 s or $40 d (Inexpensive), and at the considerably better **Moorcroft Motel,** 214 Yellowstone Ave., tel. (307) 756-3411. Nicest place in town is **Cozy Motel,** 219 W. Converse, tel. (307) 756-3486, where rooms are $35-69 s or d. Inexpensive-Moderate.

Get meals at **Donna's Diner,** 203 W. Converse, tel. (307) 756-3422, and groceries from **Diehl's Super Market** on N. Bighorn Ave., tel. (307) 756-3491. For quick sandwiches, drop by the **Subway** on the east end of Moorcroft.

The main summertime event is **Moorcroft Jubilee Days** in early July, featuring a parade, games, barbecue, street dance, and bed races.

No local visitor center; drop by **Town Hall,** 104 N. Big Horn, tel. (307) 756-3526, for more about the moors and mores of Moorcroft. Moorcroft's **library** is at 105 E. Converse, tel. (307) 756-3232. Wash clothes at the **Laundry Basket Laundromat** on the west side of town.

Powder River/Coach USA, tel. (800) 442-3682, has daily bus service from Moorcroft throughout northern and eastern Wyoming.

KEYHOLE STATE PARK

Keyhole State Park, tel. (307) 756-3596, surrounds Keyhole Reservoir, a 14,720-acre warm-water lake that backs up water from the Belle Fourche River. (The name comes from the "keyhole" brand, used by a local ranch.) The dam was built in 1952 by the Bureau of Reclamation and supplies irrigation water for South Dakota farmers. Most of the visitors are locals, but it's an okay place to camp. Pine trees crowd hills to the east while grass and sage grow around the reservoir's western shore. Anglers angle for the biggest walleye and northern pike in the state, bird watchers watch for Merriam's turkeys and white pelicans, and snowmobilers 'bile around in winter.

Practicalities

Day-use of the park is $5 for nonresident vehicles, $2 for Wyoming vehicles. **Camping** costs $9 for nonresidents, or $4 for Wyoming residents, at eight different state campgrounds along the lake's east and south shores. Nicest are Pats Point and Pronghorn Campgrounds.

Get to Keyhole State Park from I-90 by taking the Pine Ridge exit and continuing eight miles north. You'll find a swimming beach here, and the little settlement of **Pine Haven** (pop. 150) contains **Keyhole Marina,** tel. (307) 756-9529, with supplies and boat rentals, a cafe, and RV hookups. Get supplies, booze, and grub from **Pine Haven Bar & Grill,** tel. (307) 756-9707. **Keyhole Golf Club,** tel. (307) 756-3775, has a nine-hole golf course. Every **Fourth of July,** the town of Pine Haven launches a grand display of fireworks over Keyhole Reservoir.

SUNDANCE

The quiet hamlet of Sundance (pop. 1,200) nestles at the foot of Sundance Mountain. The mountain—"Temple of the Sioux"—rises a thousand feet above town and was an important sacred spot to the various tribes who claimed this land. Sun dances were performed at its base each year. Sundance got its start in 1879, when rancher Albert Hoge set up a trading post here. The town grew slowly until the 1950s, when Sundance Air Base arrived. Since its closing, the town of Sundance has settled into middle age with the old standbys of ranching and logging its economic mainstays, though tourism is increasingly important.

SIGHTS

Crook County Museum

The local museum, tel. (307) 283-3666, is housed in the basement of the Crook County Courthouse on Cleveland Street. Hours are Mon.-Fri. 8 a.m.-8 p.m. June-Aug., and Mon.-Fri. 8 a.m.-5 p.m. the rest of the year. Inside you'll find the usual collection of local paraphernalia such as arrowheads, wooden wheelchairs, bison skulls, a Civil War battle flag, and cowboy gear, plus more interesting displays on the Vore buffalo jump site, along with dioramas of an Indian buffalo trap and of Custer's 1874 camp at Inyan Kara Creek. The real attractions are the momentos from Harry Longabaugh's visit to the town. Better known as the "Sundance Kid," (see the special topic The Wild Bunch), Longabaugh spent 18 months in Sundance's Crook County Jail for horse stealing before being pardoned by the governor in 1889. The museum has his indictment and wanted poster, along with the criminal bar docket signed by Longabaugh during his trial and furnishings from the original courthouse. A replica (built in 1983) of the jail that once housed the Sundance Kid stands beside the old stone high school.

Around Sundance

Access to 5,829-foot **Sundance Mountain** is via a dirt road that heads east from State Hwy. 116 about a half mile south of town. An enjoyable trail leads to the top, gaining 800 feet in elevation along the way. From the summit, you're treated with views of the nearby Black Hills and, on clear days, even the Big Horn Mountains 180 miles west. Call landowner Cecil Cundy at (307) 283-2193 for permission to hike this trail.

Three miles west of the small settlement of **Beulah** (on the South Dakota border, 18 miles east of Sundance) is the **Vore Buffalo Jump,** where Indians drove thousands of bison into a pit between A.D. 1500-1800. The 200-foot-deep sinkhole is visible from I-90, and visitors are welcome to watch the ongoing archaeological excavations in July and August each summer. Scientists believe 20,000 bison may have been killed here over the centuries. A nonprofit foundation has plans to eventually cover the site and develop educational exhibits and a museum. For details, contact the University of Wyoming, tel. (307) 766-2208 or (307) 766-5136.

The drive south from Beulah to Buckhorn provides a good taste of the Black Hills canyon country. Follow Sand Creek Rd. south from the freeway at Beulah, and you can drive for about

SUN DANCES

The most spectacular religious ceremony of the Plains Indians was the sun dance. An annual event, it frequently attracted hundreds or even thousands of tribal onlookers, serving not simply as an important religious service but also as a social and political rally. Native American legends say that it originated centuries ago when a hunter was approached by a buffalo who suddenly spoke to him, offering a cure for sickness. Much later, an eagle came to another young man in a dream, prescribing the complete ceremony. The name is something of a misnomer, since the dance was not a worship of the sun but a highly involved ceremony representing the creation of life and the triumph of good over evil. The specifics varied somewhat between the tribes. A common Native American term for it is "Thirsting Dance," referring to the long periods of dancing without water.

The sun dance was always held in late spring or early summer and led by a young man who spent considerable time learning the complex ceremonial steps from a priest. If he passed the test, the pledger gained immense status in the village as a fearless leader. The festivities lasted up to two weeks, with the main ceremony an intense four-day event. Central to the sun dance were an eagle representation (air), a buffalo head (earth), and a pole connecting the two to signify the sacred Tree of Life. The ceremony took place in a lodge, generally built around a central pole that forked at the top. After the sacred cottonwood tree had been selected by a scouting party, warriors attacked the tree in a furious charge. If it withstood this symbolic assault, the tree was cut down by a respected tribal woman and carried to the sun-dance site, where it was carefully erected. A bundle of brush (to represent an eagle or thunderbird nest) and a buffalo-skull altar were placed in the fork of the pole. Twelve other poles (the number varied with different tribes) were erected around the central one, with cross beams to the center. (Missionaries would later claim that the 12 poles around the central one were ritualistic representations of Jesus and the 12 apostles.) Brush was then laced around the outside to provide partial shade.

Supplicants spent four days without food or water, dancing, praying, blowing on eagle-bone whistles, and staring at the buffalo head, the sun, or a sacred doll as they waited for a vision of power. In most tribes, the sun dance also involved self-mutilation. Assistants commonly cut small pieces of skin from the candidates' arms and shoulders as a blood sacrifice to the Great Spirit. (According to several accounts, before the battle at Little Big Horn, Sitting Bull sacrificed 100 pieces of flesh in a sun-dance ceremony, after which a vision told him of the coming destruction of General Custer and his men.) Torture commonly went even further, as assistants cut slices into the back or chest of the dancers and

30 miles through canyons, the deserted mining town of Moskee, and on to Buckhorn along US Hwy. 85. In the spring and fall a 4WD may be needed for the muddy conditions, and the route is closed in winter. The Sand Hill Country Club and state fish hatchery at Ranch A are favorites of deer, especially in fall and early winter, when hundreds of deer are visible from the road. There's no hunting here, so you're likely to see a number of trophy-sized animals.

Eleven miles south of Sundance on State Hwy. 116 is **Inyan Kara Mountain** (an Indian name meaning "Stone-Made Peak"), a 6,368-foot summit that dominates the surrounding country. In 1874, Gen. George A. Custer led a large scientific expedition through this region en route to the Black Hills. Among others, Custer climbed the mountain, carving "G. Custer '74" on a rock near the summit. The inscribed rock is still here, but call landowner Marshall Nussbaum (tel. 307-283-2851) for permission to cross his land on the way up the mountain.

PRACTICALITIES

Accommodations

Visitors will find five places to stay in the Sundance area. Be sure to book up to a year ahead if you plan to visit during the Sturgis Rally Week the first week of August. (Some local motels jack the rates 50% for this event.)

Find very nice accommodations at **Bear Lodge Motel,** 218 Cleveland, tel. (307) 283-1611 or (800) 341-8000, which has a jacuzzi and rooms for $56-64 s or d. Inexpensive-Moderate. **Arrowhead**

DOVER PUBLICATIONS, INC.

slid bone skewers into the muscle. Thongs would be attached between the skewers and the central pole, while other skewers held heavy buffalo skulls to be dragged behind. Candidates would lean back until the ropes were taut, jerking as they danced. Eventually the skin and muscle ripped loose and the dancers collapsed on the ground. In some tribes, the dancers were actually lifted off the ground by these tethers.

Whites found the sun dance's torture difficult to understand and thought even less of such sexual aspects of the ceremony as the parading of a giant phallus. When the Indians were forced onto reservations, the sun dance was outlawed, although some tribes continued to practice it secretly. Finally, in the late 1920s, the government relented, and a more sedate version of the dance was resurrected. The traditional blood sacrifice still exists among some tribes but not in Wyoming. Today, the sun dance is performed in separate ceremonies by both the Shoshone and the Arapahoes on the Wind River Reservation. Visitors may watch but cannot take photos or videos.

The sun dance is now performed primarily as a thanksgiving ceremony, to cure disease, and to pray for the coming year. After several days of preparation, the main ceremony lasts for four days. Without food or water, the dancers move into a trance state that brings visions and power. One authority describes dancers seeing the buffalo head shaking and steam coming out of its nostrils as the power is imparted. On the fourth day, a bucket of water is passed around to signal the end of the sun dance, and that evening more dancing and feasting complete the ceremony.

Motel, right next door at 214 Cleveland, tel. (307) 283-3307 or (800) 456-6016, has comfortable rooms for $50-60 s or d. Inexpensive.

Deane's Pine View Motel, 117 N. 8th St., tel. (307) 283-2262, has cabins for $43 s or d and units with kitchenettes for $55 (sleep four). It's open April-November. Inexpensive.

Sundance Mountain Inn, 26 Hwy. 585, tel. (307) 283-3737 or (888) 347—2794, offers recently renovated rooms for $79-89 s or d. Amenities include an indoor pool and jacuzzi. Open mid-May to mid-October. Moderate-Expensive.

The town's fanciest and newest lodging is the **Best Western Inn at Sundance,** on the east edge of town at 121 S. 6th, tel. (307) 283-2800 or (800) 238-0965. Rates are $59-89 s or $64-99 d, including a light breakfast and access to an indoor pool and jacuzzi. Moderate-Expensive.

Camping

You can reserve a spot at the Forest Service's fine **Reuter Campground** ($8), just four miles northwest of Sundance, by calling (877) 444-6777 ($8.65 reservation fee). Make reservations on the web at www.reserveusa.com. See Black Hills National Forest and Devils Tower National Forest below for other public campgrounds. The private **Mountain View Campground,** tel. (307) 283-2270, 1.5 miles east of town, has tent sites for $13, RV spaces for $18. An outdoor pool and jacuzzi are on site.

Food

Higbee's Cafe, 101 N. 3rd, tel. (307) 283-2165, is open Mon.-Fri. only, cranking out dependably good all-American breakfasts and lunches. For three meals a day with daily specials, head to

Log Cabin Cafe, 1620 Cleveland, tel. (307) 283-3393. **Aro Restaurant,** 307 Cleveland, tel. (307) 283-2000, has homemade soups and Friday-night prime rib; it's probably the best place in town.

Country Cottage, downtown on Cleveland, tel. (307) 283-2450, has frozen yogurt cones, locally made gifts, and a Subway shop for quick lunches. Get groceries from **Decker's Food Center,** 106 N. 7th, tel. (307) 283-3155.

Recreation and Events

Swim in the large **outdoor pool** at the grade school, tel. (307) 283-2133; open June-September. Golfers will enjoy the nine-hole **Sundance Country Club,** tel. (307) 283-1191, on the east end of town.

The main event in Sundance is the **Crook County Fair and Rodeo,** which comes to town in early August.

Information and Services

The small **Sundance Information Center,** in the rest area at exit 189 off I-90, tel. (307) 283-2440, is open daily 8 a.m.-7 p.m. from mid-May through August, then daily 8 a.m.-5 p.m. until mid-October; it's closed the rest of the year. On the web, get Sundance info at www.sundancewyoming.com.

The Forest Service's **Bearlodge Ranger District** is a mile east of town, tel. (307) 283-1361. The **post office** is at 2nd and Main Sts., tel. (307) 283-3939, and the **Crook County Library** is at 414 Main St., tel. (307) 283-1006. Get fast cash from **ATMs** inside the Texaco and Conoco gas stations.

Powder River/Coach USA, tel. (800) 442-3682, has daily service to other parts of eastern and northern Wyoming, plus eastward runs to Spearfish, Sturgis, and Rapid City, South Dakota.

BLACK HILLS NATIONAL FOREST

Black Hills National Forest lies primarily within South Dakota but reaches across the state line near Sundance. It was established in 1897 by Pres. Grover Cleveland after a series of large forest fires focused attention on the need to protect the timber resource. The Forest Service's very first commercial timber sale was held within the Black Hills, and the area is still a supplier for lumber mills in Hulett and Newcastle. Nearby, South Dakota's Black Hills contain a wide range of justifiably famous sites: the Homestake Gold Mine at Lead, historic Deadwood—now a gambler's mecca—Jewel and Wind Caves, Mt. Rushmore, Crazy Horse Memorial, and an enormous bison herd inside Custer State Park. Black Hills National Forest offices inside Wyoming can be found at Sundance, tel. (307) 283-1361, and Newcastle, tel. (307) 746-2782. Stop by for a forest map ($4) and information on camping and local sights.

Scenic Drives

Many gravel roads wind up through the forested hills, and fall colors are brilliant along the aspen-lined stretches of the road just south of Cook Lake. A considerable amount of logging goes on within the ponderosa pine forests here, but it is selective logging, not clearcutting, and hence not as visible. Be sure to stop at **Warren Peak Lookout** eight miles north of Sundance. The road is paved to this point, and you can climb the tower for a magnificent vista and a chance to visit folks at one of the few active fire lookouts remaining in Wyoming. **Grand Canyon Creek,** southwest of Sundance along County Rd. 141, offers a long, scenic route into the hills of South Dakota, but be ready for 25 miles of gravel road.

Hiking

Dozens of miles of hiking, biking, horseback riding, and cross-country ski trails twist through the hills just north of Sundance. For details, pick up a "Sundance and Carson Draw Trails" map from the Forest Service office in Sundance or Newcastle. Good starting points for day-hikes are the Cook Lake, Reuter, and Sundance Campgrounds mentioned below.

Camping

Four campgrounds lie within the Wyoming portion of the national forest. **Sundance Campground** ($10; open May-Nov.) has campsites and horse corrals less than three miles north of Sundance. **Reuter Campground** ($8; open all year) is five miles northwest of Sundance, and **Cook Lake Campground** ($11; open all year) is 16 miles north of Sundance on a tiny forest pond. You can make advance reservations for all three of these ($8.65 fee) by calling (877) 444-6777, or make reservations on the web at www.reserveusa.com. Free camping is also available at small **Bearlodge Campground** (open all year), seven miles west of Aladdin on State Hwy. 24. In addition, free dispersed camping is allowed on Forest Service land throughout the Black Hills. Over on the South Dakota side of the line, you'll find more than two dozen additional Forest Service campgrounds.

THE NORTHERN BLACK HILLS

ALADDIN AND VICINITY

Aladdin (pop. 10) was established in the 1870s to supply coal for gold smelters in Lead and Deadwood, South Dakota. During Prohibition, these mines housed moonshine stills. At 3,740 feet, it's the lowest settlement in Wyoming. Don't blink or you'll miss it, but if you do blink turn around and stop for a visit. Aladdin is dominated by the fluorescent red **Aladdin Store,** tel. (307) 896-2226, built in 1896 and operating continuously ever since. Out front is a "liar's bench" for local storytellers; inside is a potbelly stove and an ancient post office with the original boxes. It's worth a visit for a taste of unspoiled Americana. A small antique shop is upstairs with interesting collectibles from the area, and RVs can park in the lot beside the store.

Next to the Aladdin Store is **Hard Buck Cafe and Motel,** with all-American grub and basic budget accommodations ($20 s or $25 d). More surprising is the naturopathic doctor's office; he's regarded as one of the best in the region. Across the street is a shady town park. The Aladdin Arena is home to an annual **Bronc Match and Horseshow** in late August.

Ten miles northeast of Aladdin is the **lowest point in Wyoming.** From here, the Belle Fourche River drops only another 3,125 feet on its several-thousand-mile descent to the sea via the Missouri and Mississippi Rivers. Just east of Aladdin is the **Tipple Mine Historical Site,** with restored coal-loading chutes and other facilities. Approximately two miles east of Aladdin is a historical marker noting the still-visible tracks left by the party of 110 wagons, 2,000 animals, and 1,000 men led by Gen. George A. Custer in the summer of 1874. Despite the Treaty of 1868 that reaffirmed this as Sioux Indian land, Custer's geologists, scouts, miners, and engineers had come to explore the Black Hills and investigate the rumors of gold. Gold was indeed found by Custer's miners, and when word got out the rush was on. Custer's own rush to judgment at Montana's Little Big Horn had also begun. He and all 268 of his men would die there just two years later.

On the other side of Aladdin, State Hwy. 24 follows Beaver Creek past 150-foot-tall sandstone cliffs, ridge-top pines, and valley-bottom oaks. Old farmsteads appear, surrounded by fields filled with huge pyramid-like hay piles. The dot of a place called **Alva** (pop. 50) has a few old homes in the midst of the Bear Lodge Mountains but nothing in the way of services. West of Alva the road climbs up into rolling grassy hills with trees in the draws and cattle grazing along the Belle Fourche River.

HULETT AND VICINITY

The tiny logging and ranching town of Hulett (pop. 500) lies right along the Belle Fourche and is just 10 miles north of Devils Tower National Monument. Two lumber mills saw up timber from the adjacent Black Hills National Forest. The side of **Hulett National Bank** has burned-in brands from local cattle ranchers. A couple of miles west of Hulett you'll see bison grazing at a private ranch while magnificent Devils Tower looms on the horizon.

Food and Accommodations

For food in Hulett, try **Ponderosa Cafe** or **Pizza Plus.** The town also has a country grocery store, a bank, a hardware store, and a medical clinic. Get espresso at **Hulett Motel,** tel. (307) 467-5220, where standard rooms are $50 s or d, and suites run $60 for up to five people. Open May-

November. Inexpensive. **Pioneer Motel,** tel. (307) 467-5656, has rooms for $45 s or d. Most contain fridges, and kitchenettes are also available. Inexpensive. Park RVs at **S-A RV Camp,** a not-so-glorified parking lot, for $12; open May-November. Showers cost $1 extra.

Ten miles southeast of Hulett, **Diamond L Guest Ranch,** tel. (307) 467-5236 or (800) 851-5909, houses a dozen or so guests at a time. The main activity is horseback riding, but you can also join in the chores and pretend to be a real ranch hand or just soak in the hot tub. There's a three-night minimum stay in the summer, but most guests book by the week. All-inclusive weekly rates are $1,850 for two people. During the winter months, the ranch is popular with snowmobilers; nightly winter rates are $250 d including three meals. Find the ranch on the web at www.diamondlranch.com. Luxury.

Tumbling T Guest Ranch, tel. (307) 467-5625, is an 8,000-acre ranch just four miles from Devils Tower. The ranch accommodates up to 38 guests in a newly built lodge and bunkhouse, and meals are a culinary treat. It's open all year, with horseback riding and fly-fishing the primary activities in summer, followed by hunting in the fall and cross-country skiing all winter. Lodging is available on a nightly basis for $30 s or $60 d including a full breakfast, or on an all-inclusive weekly rate of $1,000 for two people. Inexpensive-Premium.

Just three miles west of Devils Tower, **Lake Guest Ranch,** tel. (307) 467-5908, is a working ranch with 2,000 head of cattle. Guests stay in the lodge or separate cabins and enjoy the chance to ride the range and learn to work cattle. Lodging is on a weekly basis; call for details.

Entertainment and Events

For entertainment, most evenings you'll find folks at the horseshoe pit next to the hardware store, or you can head to **Rodeo Saloon** or **Ponderosa Bar** for a beer with the locals.

Hulett Rodeo takes place on the second weekend of June each year and is a great local event. Actually, the biggest local event isn't actually in Hulett, but in nearby Sturgis, South Dakota. Sturgis Rally Week (first week of August) attracts thousands of motorcyclists to the Black Hills, filling every hotel and bar for a hundred miles in all directions. Hulett's **Ham and Jam**—a hog roast on Wednesday of Rally Week—is a big local draw.

Other Practicalities

Get Hulett info on the web at www.hulett.org. Hulett's **library** is in the high school. **The Stockman,** tel. (307) 467-5953, sells antiques and the paintings of local artists Bob Coronato and Tom Waugh; open summers only.

Golfers will appreciate **Devils Tower Country Club,** tel. (307) 467-5773, which has an 18-hole course.

Oshoto

West and then south from Hulett is the tiny town of Oshoto (a Native American word meaning "Bad Weather"), accessible only via gravel roads. No services; all that's here is a post office. The Brislawn Cayuse Ranch near Oshoto is one of the last places in America to have pure-blooded Spanish Mustangs—tough, small horses that were the pride of the Wild West.

Alzada and Colony

North from Hulett, State Hwy. 112 heads to the Montana border settlement of Alzada, cutting across land not unlike the foothills of California's Sierra Nevada. Cottonwoods and oaks fill the draws, and grassy meadows alternate with tree-topped hills. Very scenic, with an abundance of white-tailed deer all the way. The road doesn't really go anywhere most tourists are heading; because of this, it is perfect for cyclists and anyone with an explorer's streak. From Alzada, US Hwy. 212 cuts southeast across Wyoming and to the South Dakota town of Belle Fourche. Along the way it passes a couple of bentonite mines in the grass-and-sage country around the nothing settlement called Colony. Antelope and cattle abound. Talk about confusion: since there's no post office in Colony, Wyoming, locals have South Dakota addresses on a Montana delivery route! For details on sights to the north, see *Montana Handbook,* by W.C. McRae and Judy Jewell (Moon Travel Handbooks, www.moon.com).

DEVILS TOWER NATIONAL MONUMENT

In the 1977 film *Close Encounters of the Third Kind,* Devils Tower was used as the contact point for aliens and humans. It was an appropriate choice. Rising 1,267 feet above the surrounding plain, this otherworldly apparition seems an appropriate metaphor for the mystery of life and our attempts to understand the universe. The flat-topped column of rock seems to push out of the earth like an enormous sawed-off stump from Paul Bunyan's forest. From a distance, Devils Tower looks as if it had been scratched by some giant beast, with parallel gouges running up the sides. Up closer, the gouges turn into enormous columns of rock molded into hexagonal columns (some have four, five, or seven sides). In the setting sun, Devils Tower glows a golden red long after the surrounding hills no longer reflect the sun's rays, and as night comes on, the stars and moon outline its bold shape against the horizon.

Devils Tower is surrounded by ponderosa pine and bur-oak forests, and the winding Belle Fourche River flows less than a mile away. A large colony of **black-tailed prairie dogs** prospers along the river just inside the park with hundreds of the little critters running around, much to the delight of tourists. You're also likely to see white-tailed deer feeding in the meadows. On top, Devils Tower is a fairly flat oval approximately 300 feet by 180 feet.

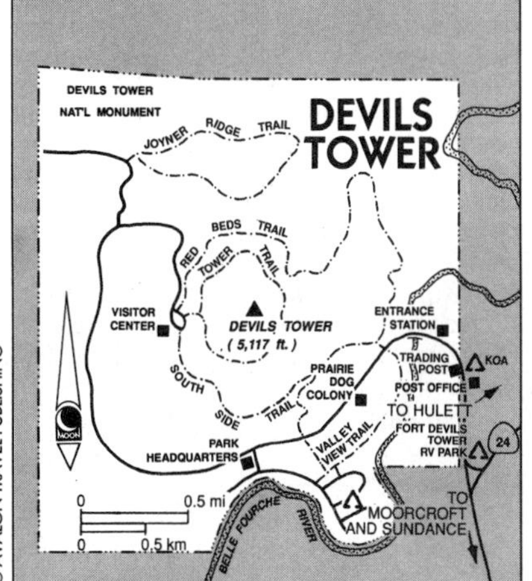

Geology

Geologists still dispute the precise way that Devils Tower formed, but they agree that the process began some 65 million years ago when a mass of molten magma was forced up through the overlying sedimentary rocks. As the igneous material cooled and contracted, vertical fractures formed in the magma, creating long columnar joints—the "scratches" up the side of Devils Tower today. (Some of these columns are as big as 14 feet in diameter!) Eventually, rain and snow eroded away the surrounding sedimentary rock and the Belle Fourche River carried it away, leaving behind the harder core of Devils Tower. Surrounding the 1,000-foot-wide base of the Tower is a mass of talus from fallen pieces of columns, but erosion of this very hard igneous rock is very slow. The four prominent peaks of the **Missouri Buttes,** four miles northwest of Devils Tower, were formed in a similar manner. At 500 to 800 feet in height, they are not as dramatic and lie outside the national monument's boundaries.

HISTORY

Devils Tower was known to Native Americans by a variety of names, most commonly Bear Lodge, Tree Lodge, or Bear's Tepee. Fur trappers and early explorers certainly knew of the existence of Bear Lodge, but it wasn't until 1857 that any note of it was made—an exploration party led by Lt. G.K. Warren saw the rock from a distance. In 1875, Col. Richard I. Dodge finally led a U.S. Geological Survey party to the formation. Dodge somehow came up with the name Devils Tower, claiming that the Native Americans called it "Bad God's Tower." Despite protests that "Bear Lodge" had long been the aboriginal name, the label Devils Tower stuck. Indians in the area regard the name Devils Tower an affront, since they consider this a sacred place.

the otherworldly Devils Tower

Establishing the Monument

After the Indians had been driven from their traditional homeland in the 1870s, northeast Wyoming was opened to settlement by whites. Most lands were available to the homesteaders, but the General Land Office prevented developers from gaining this freak of geology. Wyoming already had America's first national park in Yellowstone, and support soon grew to make the Tower a second one. After years of effort, Pres. Theodore Roosevelt proclaimed Devils Tower the country's first national monument in 1906. Unfortunately, the final monument was only 1,153 acres in size and excludes the Missouri Buttes.

The First Climb

In the early years of Devils Tower National Monument, the area served as a popular spot for picnics and camping, especially on the Fourth of July, when Independence Day celebrations attracted settlers from the entire region. The most famous of all these came in 1893. Handbills announced that the "unclimbable" summit would be scaled and "On July 4th, 1893, Old Glory will be flung to the breeze from the top of the Tower, 800 feet from the ground by Wm. Rogers." The stunt was well planned. Several days before, two local ranchers, William Rogers and Willard Ripley, drove wooden pegs into a long crack that led to the top and tied the pegs together with strips of wood to make a ladder. They hauled a 12-foot flagpole to the top and returned on July 4 to scale the ladder in front of 800 people. Once on top (it took an hour to climb), Rogers unfurled a flag but a gust of wind blew it off. Wives of the promoters tore it up and sold the pieces as souvenirs (stripes cost 25 cents, stars 50). The climb had been a smashing success.

On July 4, 1895, Mrs. Rogers became the first woman to climb the ladder to the top of Devils Tower, and many other adventurous folks followed over the next several decades. The ladder was last climbed in 1927, but pieces of it are still visible today along the southeast side of the Tower. An iron stairway to the top, proposed by Wyoming's Congressman Mondell as a tourist attraction, was never built.

Developing the Tower

For many years, Devils Tower remained undeveloped, and it was not until 1928 that a bridge was built across the Belle Fourche River to the site. During the Depression, the CCC constructed a log visitor center, new roads, trails, picnic areas, and a campground. Visitation increased as access became easier and more families acquired automobiles. One of the strangest events came in 1941, when George Hopkins—one of the top skydivers in the world—parachuted out of a plane to the top of Devils Tower as a publicity stunt. He had planned to descend on a 1,000 foot rope, but the rope landed on the side of the Devils Tower, leaving him stranded on top. Newspapers all over the country headlined his plight. Food and blankets were dropped to him, and for the next six days he spent a lonely vigil on top waiting to be rescued. Finally, Jack Durrance, a mountain climber who had scaled Devils Tower three years before, arrived to lead seven other climbers to the top and help Hopkins down. Many years later, in 1976, *Close Encounters of the Third Kind* was filmed here. Several hundred locals appeared in the crowd scenes. When the movie was released the following year, tourism here hit the stars.

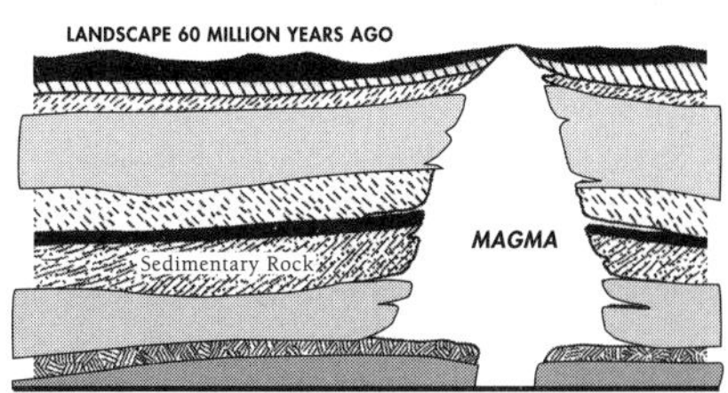

CLIMBING THE TOWER

Although Devils Tower was first climbed in 1893 on a wooden ladder, the first ascent using modern rock-climbing techniques was not until 1937. Led by Fritz Wiessner, three New York City climbers made it to the top in a little under five hours. Over the years, as climbing technology has improved and as more people have been attracted to the sport, Devils Tower has become one of the favorite climbing spots in the nation. During the summer you're bound to meet several dozen climbers heading for the base of Devils Tower each morning. More than 40,000 people have reached the top, and the figure grows by 5,000 each year.

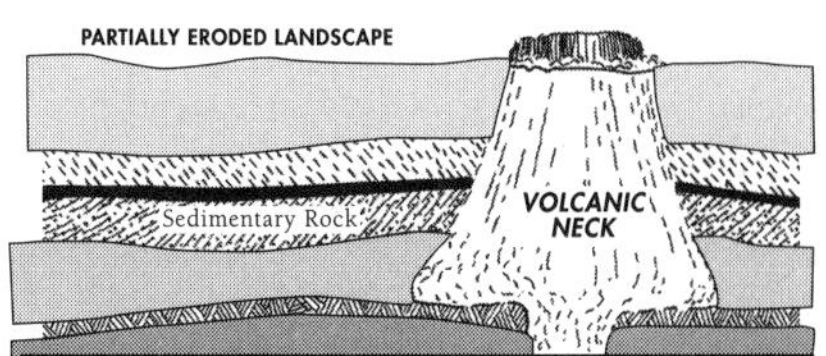

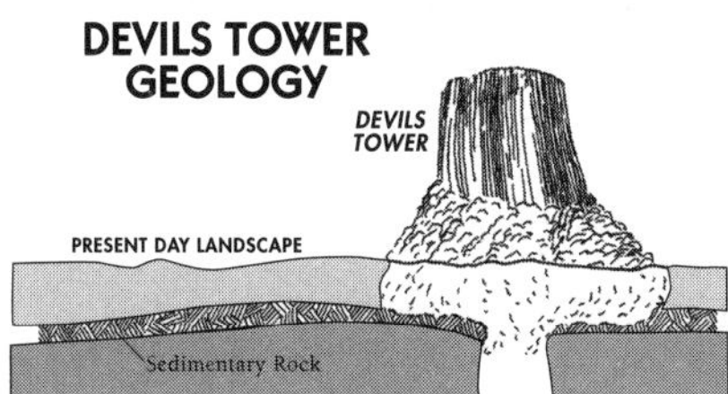

Thousands of climbers ascend the cliffs of Devils Tower each year.

Climbing has not been without controversy. Some Indian leaders have called climbing the rock a sacrilege and demanded it be closed, while climbers have trumpeted it as one of the premier crack-climbing areas in the nation. The Park Service came up with a compromise plan that includes a voluntary climbing closure for the month of June. Additional regulations were put into place emphasizing clean climbing techniques and restricting access to falcon nesting areas during the breeding season. Be sure to contact the monument for specifics and safety information before you climb.

For information on the various routes (at least 220 have been climbed), pick up one of the technical guidebooks in the visitor center: *Devils Tower National Monument—A Climber's Guide* by Steve Gardiner and Dick Guilmette (Devils Tower Natural History Association), or *Free Climbs of Devils Tower* by Dingus McGee and

KIOWA DEVILS TOWER LEGEND

The place we call Devils Tower was known to the Kiowa Indians as T'sou'a'e, meaning "Aloft on a Rock." Many tales are told about the origins of this mystical place, but the best known is that of the Kiowa. Once upon a time, the people camped along a stream that had many bears. Seven sisters and their brother were playing nearby when the boy suddenly turned into a ferocious bear and began chasing the girls. In desperation, the girls climbed on a small rock and prayed, "Rock, take pity on us—rock, save us!" The rock started to grow, pushing them higher and higher as the bear clawed at the sides, trying to get them. Eventually the seven girls were pushed upward into the sky, forming the points of the Big Dipper. The gouges from the bear remain today on the sides of Devils Tower.

The Last Pioneer Woman (I somehow suspect that these are pseudonyms). Displays in the visitor center and at a kiosk out front describe climbing routes and techniques. Climbing demonstrations are given here each day during the summer. If you're planning to climb Devils Tower, be sure to register at the visitor center.

Climbing Guides

Those who want to climb Devils Tower but lack the skills or equipment have several options. Andy Petefish, owner of **Tower Guides,** leads climbs throughout summer and has a fine reputation. Rates here may be a bit higher than the other companies, but you're getting the most experienced Devils Tower guide around. Expect to pay around $250 for a private one-day ascent, or $100 per day for climbing instruction (maximum of four students). For details, stop by his office next to the KOA at the entrance, or call (307) 467-5589 or (888) 345-9061. The website is www.towerguides.com.

Other companies permitted by the Park Service to lead climbs include: **Jackson Hole Mountain Guides** in Jackson, tel. (307) 733-4979 or (800) 239-7642, www.jhmg.com; **Exum Mountain Guides,** tel. (307) 733-2297, www.exumguides.com; **National Outdoors Leadership School (NOLS)** in Lander, tel. (307) 332-4784; and **Sylvan Rocks Climbing School** in Hill City, South Dakota, tel. (605) 574-2425. Contact the Park Service for additional permitted commercial guide companies.

HIKING TRAILS

Four different trails loop through this small national monument, providing fine views of Devils Tower and the surrounding country. Most popular is the 1.3-mile **Tower Trail,** which circles the Tower. It's an easy paved path with periodic openings offering impressive views of the summit, along with side paths to see the nearby Missouri Buttes and the Belle Fourche River. Look through the peep sight to find the old wooden ladder that once went all the way to the top of Devils Tower.

Red Beds/South Side Trail is a three-mile dirt path that also takes off near the visitor center but makes a longer, less-crowded loop around Devils Tower. Along the way you get nice views of the Belle Fourche River and the Red Beds, iron-stained bluffs near the river. A 30-minute side loop, the 1.5-mile **Valley View Trail,** takes you to the prairie dog town and the Belle Fourche River.

You'll catch the finest views of Devils Tower from the **Joyner Ridge Trail,** a 1.5-mile path. Views from this hilltop trail are unforgettable, especially at sunrise and sunset. It's a delightful secret escape from crowds elsewhere.

PRACTICALITIES

Access and Information

For general park information, call the **Devils Tower National Monument office** at (307) 467-5283, or visit the web at www.nps.gov/deto. The monument is 33 miles northeast of Moorcroft. Access is from State Hwy. 24, seven miles north of its junction with US Hwy. 14. Entrance costs $8 for vehicles, $3 for hikers or cyclists, and the passes are good for seven days. Annual passes to the monument cost $20, or you can purchase a Golden Eagle Pass ($50), which lets you into all national parks and monuments. Seniors get in free with a Golden Age Pass (for a one-time fee of $10). The monument is open year-round 24 hours a day, although most of the over 300,000 annual visitors arrive during the summer.

Beyond the entrance station, it is approximately three miles along a paved road to the base of Devils Tower, where you'll find a pleasant old log **visitor center,** tel. (307) 467-5283, and a parking lot that overflows on sunny summer days with rock climbers, day-hikers, and gawkers. The visitor center is open daily 8 a.m.-8 p.m. from Memorial Day to Labor Day, and daily 9 a.m.-4 p.m. from mid-March to Memorial Day and from Labor Day to mid-November (but these hours could change). Inside the visitor center, you can watch a video on the history of Devils Tower, look at ecological displays and photos showing the dozens of climbing routes, and buy books on local lore. The center is closed from mid-November to mid-March, but you can get information on winter weekdays from park headquarters.

Campfire programs are held several times a week during the summer at the campground amphitheater, with the standard Park Service fare of talks, tunes, and transparencies. Ranger walks and talks take place throughout the summer; ask at the visitor center for upcoming events.

Camping, Food, and More

The Park Service maintains a fine **campground** ($12; open May-Oct.) a half mile inside the entrance. In midsummer, get a space at the campground in the morning to be sure of having a spot. There's an eight-person limit at the campsites.

Just outside the monument are two private campgrounds. At **Devils Tower KOA,** tel. (307) 467-5395 or (800) 562-5785, sites cost $18 for tents, $24 for RVs, and $35 d for simple cabins. The KOA has an outdoor pool and is open mid-May to late September. Horseback rides are available here, and if you haven't seen it before, you can watch *Close Encounters* on the TV. Most folks stock up on food in nearby towns, but the cafe here serves meals, ice cream, and espresso, and a general store sells limited supplies and gifts.

Devils Tower Trading Post is directly across the road from the KOA and stocks a few food items, gifts, and trinkets, and has a fast-food eatery. Just up the road is the other nearby private campground: **Fort Devils Tower RV Park,** tel. (307) 467-5655. Rates are $12 for tents or $15 for RVs. It's open mid-April through October, with a saloon and restaurant for meals.

A **post office,** tel. (307) 467-5937, stands just outside the park entrance gate. Each Fourth of July folks come from miles around to watch a big **fireworks** show put on by the KOA near Devils Tower.

> *If the reader thinks he is done, now, and that this book has no moral to it, he is in error. The moral of it is this: If you are of any account, stay at home and make your way by faithful diligence; but if you are "no account," go away from home, and then you will* have *to work, whether you want to or not. Thus you become a blessing to your friends by ceasing to be a nuisance to them—if the people you go among suffer by the operation.*
>
> —MARK TWAIN
> IN *ROUGHING IT*

APPENDIX

ADDITIONAL CHEYENNE MOTELS

The Southeast Wyoming chapter contains descriptions of selected Cheyenne lodging places. Listed below from least to most expensive are motels not described elsewhere. Rates may be considerably lower in the off-season, and higher during Frontier Days. Add a seven percent tax to these rates.

Ranger Motel, 909 W. Lincolnway, tel. (307) 634-7995; $26 s or $33 d; older accommodations, see rooms first. Budget.

Home Ranch Motel, 2414 E. Lincolnway, tel. (307) 634-3575; $28 s or $30 d; in-room fridges. Budget.

Lariat Motel, 600 Central Ave., tel. (307) 635-8439; $28 s or $32 d; kitchenettes available, see rooms first. Budget.

Sands Motel, 1000 W. Lincolnway, tel. (307) 634-7771; $28 s or $35 d. Budget.

Guest Ranch Motel, 1100 W. Lincolnway, tel. (307) 634-2137; $30-40 s or d. Budget-Inexpensive.

Firebird Motel, 1905 E. Lincolnway, tel. (307) 632-5505; $31-35 s or d; older but clean rooms, outdoor pool. Budget.

Sapp Brothers Big C Motel, six miles east on I-80 (exit 370), tel. (307) 632-6600; $35 s or $38 d; truck stop. Inexpensive.

Round-Up Motel, 403 S. Greeley Hwy., tel. (307) 634-7741; $35 s or $39 d; kitchenettes available by the week. Inexpensive.

Stage Coach Motel, 1515 W. Lincolnway, tel. (307) 634-4495; $35-40 s or $45-50 d; AAA approved. Inexpensive.

EconoLodge, 2512 W. Lincolnway, tel. (307) 632-7556 or (800) 553-2666; $35-45 s or $41-51 d; soaking tubs, indoor pool, jacuzzi, exercise equipment, continental breakfast, AAA approved. Inexpensive.

Atlas Motel, 1524 W. Lincolnway, tel. (307) 632-9214; $36 s or $40 d; older units, some with kitchenettes. Inexpensive.

Frontier Motel, 1400 W. Lincolnway, tel. (307) 634-7961; $40-50 s or d; older motel but well maintained. Inexpensive.

Days Inn, 2360 W. Lincolnway, tel. (307) 778-8877 or (800) 329-7466; $44-77 s or $54-82 d ($120 s or d during Frontier Days); jacuzzi, sauna, limited exercise facility, continental breakfast, AAA approved. Inexpensive-Moderate.

Motel 6, 1735 Westland Rd., tel. (307) 635-6806 or (800) 466-8356, www.motel6.com; $46 s or $52 d ($5 less Sun.-Thurs. nights); outdoor pool. Inexpensive.

Super 8 Motel, 1900 W. Lincolnway, tel. (307) 635-8741 or (800) 800-8000; $47 s or $52 d ($100 s or d during Frontier Days); fridges and microwaves in some rooms. Inexpensive.

Lincoln Court Motel, 1720 W. Lincolnway, tel. (307) 638-3302; $51-63 s or d; outdoor pool, playground, fitness room, continental breakfast, privileges at jacuzzi and sauna next door, AAA approved. Inexpensive-Moderate.

Fairfield Inn (Marriott), 1415 Stillwater Ave., tel. (307) 637-4070 or (800) 228-2800; $52-62 s or $58-79 d; indoor pool, jacuzzi, game room, continental breakfast, some rooms with microwaves and fridges, AAA approved. Inexpensive-Moderate.

Quality Inn, 5401 Walker Rd., tel. (307) 632-8901 or (800) 876-8901, www.qualityinn.com; $58 s or $68 d ($175 s or d during Frontier Days); outdoor pool, microwaves and fridges in all rooms, continental breakfast. Moderate.

La Quinta Inn, 2410 W. Lincolnway, tel. (307) 632-7117 or (800) 531-5900, www.laquinta.com; $65-80 s or $75-90 d; recently renovated rooms, outdoor pool, some rooms with fridges and microwaves, AAA approved. Moderate-Expensive.

Comfort Inn, 2245 Etchepare Dr., tel. (307) 638-7202 or (800) 777-7218, www.comfortinn.com; $69-79 s or d ($125 s or d in Frontier Days); outdoor pool, continental breakfast, in-room VCRs, AAA approved. Moderate.

Holiday Inn, 204 W. Fox Farm Rd., tel. (307) 638-4466 or (800) 465-4329, www.holiday-inn.com/cheyennewy; $89 s or d; newly renovated rooms with Wyoming decor, indoor pool, jacuzzi, sauna, airport shuttle, exercise room. Expensive.

ADDITIONAL CASPER MOTELS

The Central Wyoming chapter contains descriptions of selected Casper lodging places. Listed below from least to most expensive are motels not described elsewhere. Rates may be lower in the off-season. Add a seven percent tax to these rates.

Bel Air Motel, 5400 W. Yellowstone, tel. (307) 472-1930; $18 s or $22 d; weekly rates available, see rooms first. Budget.

Sand & Sage Motel, 901 W. Yellowstone, tel. (307) 237-2088; $23 s or $28 d; kitchenettes available on a weekly basis. Budget.

Virginian Motel, 830 E. A St., tel. (307) 266-3959; $25 s or $29 d; see rooms first, fridges and microwaves available, no phones. Budget.

Ranch House Motel, 1130 E. F St., tel. (307) 266-4044; $25-29 s or d; fridges in rooms, weekly rates available. Budget.

Yellowstone Motel, 1610 E. Yellowstone, tel. (307) 234-9174; $25-35 s or $28-40 d; all rooms with fridges and some with microwaves; kitchenettes (sleep up to six) for $50-65. Budget-Moderate.

All American Inn, 5755 CY Ave., tel. (307) 235-6688; $29 s or $32-35 d. Budget.

First Interstate Inn, Wyoming Blvd. at I-25, tel. (307) 234-9125; $40 s or $50 d. Inexpensive.

Super 8 Motel, 3838 CY Ave., tel. (307) 266-3480 or (888) 266-0497; $43 s or $50 d; continental breakfast, AAA approved. Inexpensive.

Kelly Inn, 821 N. Poplar, tel. (307) 266-2400 or (800) 635-3559, $46 s or $52 d, jacuzzi, sauna, continental breakfast, AAA approved. Inexpensive.

Shilo Inn, 739 Luker Lane, Evansville, tel. (307) 237-1335 or (800) 222-2244; $55-65 s or d; indoor pool, jacuzzi, sauna, steam room, breakfast buffet, evening drinks, airport shuttle. Inexpensive-Moderate.

Parkway Plaza Hotel, 123 W. E St., tel. (307) 235-1777 or (800) 270-7829; $60 s or $65 d; suites for $75-250; large hotel with outdoor pool, jacuzzi, sauna, fitness center, airport shuttle, AAA approved. Moderate-Luxury.

Comfort Inn, 480 Lathrop Rd., Evansville, tel. (307) 235-3038 or (800) 228-5150; $70-85 s or $75-90 d; indoor pool, jacuzzi, continental breakfast. Moderate-Expensive.

ADDITIONAL JACKSON HOLE ACCOMMODATIONS

See the text for descriptions of many Jackson Hole lodging places, including condos, cabins, bed and breakfasts, hotels, motels, guest ranches, and hostels. This appendix provides brief descriptions of places not included in the text, but that offer good alternatives. Accommodations are listed from least to most expensive, and rates may be considerably lower in the off-season. Add a six percent tax to these rates.

Teton Gables Motel, 1140 W. Broadway, tel. (307) 733-3723; $75-85 s or d; older motel, but will be renovated in late 2000 (prices will probably rise). Moderate.

Four Winds Motel, 150 N. Millward St., tel. (307) 733-2474 or (800) 228-6461; $82-102 s or d; AAA approved. Moderate-Expensive.

Pony Express Motel, 50 S. Millward St., tel. (307) 733-2658 or (800) 526-2658; $85-92 s or d; outdoor jacuzzi and heated pool open all year, AAA approved. Expensive.

Pioneer Motel, 325 N. Cache Dr., tel. (307) 733-3673 or (800) 550-0330, www.pioneermotel.com; $85-115 s or d; microwaves and refrigerators, homemade quilts, AAA approved. Expensive-Premium.

Crystal Springs Inn, in Teton Village, tel. (307) 733-4423 or (800) 735-8342; $86-98 s or d; fridges in rooms. Expensive.

Teton Inn, 165 W. Gill St., tel. (307) 733-3883 or (800) 851-0700; $90 s or d; small and friendly, to be renovated in 2000 (prices will probably rise), AAA approved. Expensive.

Prospector Motel, 155 N. Jackson, tel. (307) 733-4858 or (800) 851-0070, www.jacksonprospector.com; $90-110 s or d; small and friendly motel, outdoor jacuzzi; to be renovated in 2000 (prices will probably rise), AAA approved. Expensive.

Flat Creek Motel, one mile north of town on U.S. Hwy. 89, tel. (307) 733-5276 or (800) 438-9338, www.flatcreekmotel.com; $92-109 s or d for rooms with fridges and microwaves; fully equipped kitchens cost $125 for up to four people; large motel facing Elk Refuge with jacuzzi, sauna, ski waxing room. Expensive.

Village Center Inn, Teton Village, tel. (307) 733-3155 or (800) 735-8342; $92-105 s or d for studio or loft units (sleep five); $134 for two-bedroom units (sleep six); all units with full kitchens. Expensive.

Elk Refuge Inn, one mile north of town on U.S. Hwy. 89, tel. (307) 733-3582 or (800) 544-3582, www.elkrefugeinn.com; $95 s or $98 d; kitchenettes $115 for up to four people; overlooks the National Elk Refuge, horse corrals available, AAA approved. Expensive.

Stagecoach Motel, 291 N. Glenwood, tel. (307) 733-3451 or (800) 421-1447, www.blissnet.com/~stagecoach; $95-110 s or d, kitchen suites for $150 d; older motel but in good condition, fairly small rooms, open June-September. Expensive-Premium.

Ranch Inn, 45 E. Pearl St., tel. (307) 733-6363 or (800) 348-5599, www.ranchinn.com; standard rooms $98 s or $110 d with fridges and microwaves; tower rooms $145 for four; half-suites $165 d; suites with kitchenettes, fireplaces, and balconies $175 d; luxury suites with jacuzzi tubs $180 d; indoor and outdoor jacuzzis, continental breakfast. Expensive-Luxury.

Trapper Inn, 235 N. Cache Dr., tel. (307) 733-2648 or (800) 341-8000, www.trapperinn.com; $98-129 s or d for standard rooms; suites $160-217 for four people (some have jacuzzi tubs and king-size beds); indoor and outdoor jacuzzis, fridges and microwaves in many rooms, AAA approved. Expensive-Premium.

Virginian Lodge, 750 W. Broadway, tel. (307) 733-2792 or (800) 262-4999, www.virginianlodge.com; $99-109 s or d; kitchenette suites for $135 (sleep four); jacuzzi suites $165 (sleep four); two-bedroom suites $185 (sleep six); big motel with large outdoor pool and jacuzzi, AAA approved. Expensive.

Cache Creek Motel, 390 N. Glenwood, tel. (307) 733-7781 or (800) 843-4788, www.cachecreekmotel.com; $100-110 s or d; suites for $175-200 for up to six; full kitchens in all rooms, outdoor jacuzzi, ski lockers, AAA approved. Expensive.

49'er Inn & Suites (Quality Inn), 330 W. Pearl, tel. (307) 733-7550 or (800) 483-8667, www.townsquareinns.com; $104-172 s, $108-172 d;

fireplace and jacuzzi suites with kitchenettes for $172 d; large indoor jacuzzi, sauna, continental breakfast, exercise room, AAA approved. Expensive-Luxury.

Alpenhof Lodge, Teton Village, tel. (307) 733-3242 or (800) 732-3244, www.jacksonhole. com/alpenhof; summer rates: $114-388 d; ski season rates: $138-428 d; wide range of rooms available, along with four-person suites; some rooms with Bavarian furnishings, original artwork, and fireplaces; heated year-round outdoor pool, jacuzzi, sauna, ski lockers, game room. Premium-Luxury.

Golden Eagle Inn, 325 E. Broadway, tel. (307) 733-2042; $115 s or d for standard rooms; two-bedroom house with full kitchen for $235 d ($255 for six); quiet location, outdoor seasonal pool, AAA approved. Premium-Luxury.

Painted Buffalo Inn, 400 W. Broadway, tel. (307) 733-4340 or (800) 288-3866, www.paintedbuffalo.com; $120 s, $125-130 d in standard rooms, $170 d in family units; AAA approved. Premium.

Super 8 Motel, 750 S. US Hwy. 89, tel. (307) 733-6833 or (800) 800-8000, www.super8. com; $130-140 s or d. Premium.

Jackson Hole Lodge, 420 W. Broadway, tel. (307) 733-2992 or (800) 604-9404, www.jacksonholelodge.com; $134 for up to four people in motel rooms; condos, all with kitchens, include studios ($184 for three people), one-bedroom units ($219 for four people), and two-bedroom units ($304 for up to eight people); large indoor pool, wading pool, two jacuzzis, sauna, AAA approved. Premium-Luxury.

Days Inn of Jackson Hole, 1280 W. Broadway, tel. (307) 739-9010 or (800) 329-7466, www.daysinnjacksonhole.com; $159-199 s or d for standard rooms; $219-239 for suites with fireplaces and jacuzzi tubs; expanded continental breakfast, large jacuzzi, sauna, in-room safes, microwaves and fridges in some rooms, AAA approved. Luxury.

The Inn at Jackson Hole (Best Western), Teton Village, tel. (307) 733-2311 or (800) 842-7666, www.innatjh.com; $179-279 s or d; outdoor pool, three outdoor jacuzzis, sauna, ski lockers, some rooms with loft and kitchenette. Luxury.

Wyoming Inn (Red Lion), 930 W. Broadway, tel. (307) 734-0035 or (800) 844-0035, www. wyoming-inn.com; $189-249 s or d; corporate-style motel with ostentatious lobby, large rooms, jacuzzi, light breakfast, some rooms with fireplaces and jacuzzis, free access to health club (across the street), free airport shuttle, AAA approved. Luxury.

Snow King Resort, 400 E. Snow King, tel. (307) 733-5200 or (800) 522-5464, www.snowking. com; $200 s or $210 d for motel rooms; $280 for two-bedroom condos with kitchen, up to $410-430 for four-bedroom condos; heated outdoor pool (open year-round), three outdoor jacuzzis, game room, indoor ice rink, sauna, fitness room, concierge, free airport shuttle, AAA approved. Luxury.

The Lodge at Jackson Hole (Best Western), 80 S. Scott Lane, tel. (307) 739-9703 or (800) 458-3866, www.lodgeatjh.com; $209 s or d for mini-suites; three-story lodge on south end of town, indoor and outdoor heated year-round pools, indoor and outdoor jacuzzis, sauna, continental breakfast, fridges and microwaves, three phones per room, in-room safes, ski lockers, AAA approved. Luxury.

ADDITIONAL CODY MOTELS

The Bighorn Basin chapter contains descriptions of selected Cody lodging places. Listed below from least to most expensive are motels not described elsewhere. Rates may be lower in the off-season. Add an eight percent tax to these rates.

Frontier Motel, U.S. Hwy. 14/16/20 E, tel. (307) 527-7119; $40 s, $44-52 d, kitchenettes for $73 d. Inexpensive-Moderate.

Rainbow Park Motel, 1136 17th St., tel. (307) 587-6251 or (800) 341-8000; $44 s, $47-60 d, kitchenettes $5 extra, AAA approved. Inexpensive-Moderate.

Skyline Motor Inn, 1919 17th St., tel. (307) 587-4201 or (800) 843-8809; $48 s, $56-62 d, $68 for four; outdoor pool, AAA approved. Inexpensive-Moderate.

Wigwam Motel, 1701 Alger Ave., tel. (307) 587-3861; $48-55 s or d; older motel. Inexpensive.

Holiday Motel, 1807 Sheridan Ave., tel. (307) 587-4258 or (800) 341-8000; $51 s, $54-65 d; recently refurbished, AAA approved. Inexpensive-Moderate.

7 K's Motel, 232 W. Yellowstone Ave., tel. (307) 587-5890 or (800) 223-9204; $55-65 s or d; outdoor pool, no phones in rooms, open April-September. Inexpensive-Moderate.

Big Bear Motel, 139 W. Yellowstone Ave., tel. (307) 587-3117 or (800) 325-7163; $55-65 s or d; outdoor pool, no phones in rooms, open April-Oct., AAA approved. Inexpensive-Moderate.

Gateway Motel and RV Park, 203 Yellowstone, tel. (307) 587-2561; motel rooms for $55-70, rustic cabins from 1946 with kitchenettes for $45; no phones in rooms, open April-September. Inexpensive-Moderate.

Carter Mountain Motel, 1701 Central Ave., tel. (307) 587-4295; standard rooms (some with fridges) for $69-79 s or d; suites with full kitchens (largest ones sleep up to nine people) for $89-125; all rooms new or recently remodeled. Moderate.

Western 6 Gun Motel, 433 W. Yellowstone Ave., tel. (307) 587-4835; $69-79 s or d; suites with fridges $92 for four people; open May-September. Moderate.

River's View Motel, 109 W. Yellowstone Ave., tel. (307) 587-6074 or (800) 377-7255; standard rooms $75-95 s or d with microwaves and fridges; cabin $85 d or $120 for six; see rooms first; open April to mid-November. Moderate-Expensive.

Buffalo Bill Village Resort, 1701 Sheridan Ave., tel. (307) 587-5544 or (800) 527-5544; $79-89 s, $89-99 d; refurbished 1920s-era log cabins equipped with modern amenities, small outdoor pool, airport transport, open May-Sept., AAA approved. Expensive.

Comfort Inn at Buffalo Bill Village Resort, 1601 Sheridan Ave., tel. (307) 587-5556 or (800) 329-7466; $79-129 s or d; outdoor pool, continental breakfast, airport transport, AAA approved. Moderate-Premium.

Burl Inn, 1213 17th St., tel. (307) 587-2084 or (800) 388-2084; $80 s or $85 d; honeymoon suite with king bed and jacuzzi tub for $105; handcrafted burled wood beds and lamps, closed January, AAA approved. Expensive.

Super 8 Motel, 730 W. Yellowstone Ave., tel. (307) 527-6214 or (800) 800-8000; $80-115 s or $90-115 d. Expensive-Premium.

Cody Motor Lodge, 1455 Sheridan Ave., tel. (307) 527-6291 or (800) 340-2639; $85-88 s or d; spacious rooms, six-person kitchenettes for $130. Expensive-Premium.

Best Western Sunrise, 1407 8th St., tel. (307) 587-5566 or (800) 528-1234; $85-99 s or d; outdoor pool, continental breakfast, AAA approved. Expensive.

Days Inn, 524 W. Yellowstone Ave., tel. (307) 527-6604 or (800) 325-2525; $85-115 s, $95-125 d; indoor pool, jacuzzi, continental breakfast, AAA approved. Expensive-Premium.

Holiday Inn at Buffalo Bill Village Resort, 1701 Sheridan Ave., tel. (307) 587-5555 or (800) 527-5544; $99-129 s or d; large motel, outdoor pool, airport transport, AAA approved. Expensive-Premium.

BOOKLIST

Note: A number of the books listed below are now out of print. You can find many of them in Wyoming libraries, or check the web for special orders or rare-book auctions. Amazon.com, barnesandnoble.com, and other online sites will also search used bookstores for out of print titles.

DESCRIPTION AND TRAVEL

Anderson, Susan. *Living in Wyoming: Settling for More.* Oakland, CA: Rockridge Press, 1990. A witty and insightful book about the people of Wyoming. Outstanding photos by Zbigniew Bzdak.

Burt, Nathaniel. *Wyoming.* Oakland, CA: Compass American Guides, 1998. Provides a tour of Wyoming and its historical attractions. Photography by Don Pitcher.

Cook, Jeannie (ed.) *Buffalo Bill's Town in the Rockies: A Pictorial History of Cody, Wyoming.* Cody, WY: Park County Historical Society, 1996. A photographic visit to Cody's interesting past.

Ehrlich, Gretel. *The Solace of Open Spaces.* New York, NY: Viking Penguin Inc., 1985. A stunningly beautiful collection of observations and stories about ranch life in Wyoming from one of America's finest writers.

Ehrlich, Gretel. *A Match to the Heart.* New York: Pantheon Books, 1994. The harrowing story of Gretel Ehrlich's long recovery after being struck by lightning while working on the Wyoming range.

Kilgore, Gene. *Gene Kilgore's Ranch Vacations.* Santa Fe: John Muir Publications, 1999. The definitive guide to dude and guest ranches in Wyoming and the rest of North America. Includes detailed, up-to-date descriptions of the best places to be a city-slicker cowboy.

Lewis, Dan. *8,000 Miles of Dirt: A Backroad Travel Guide to Wyoming.* Casper, WY: Hawks Book Co., 1992. Describes dozens of the state's most enjoyable back roads in a folksy but not always informative manner. (Example: The chapter on the Outlaw Cave drive doesn't bother to mention the cave's most famous inhabitant, Butch Cassidy!)

McClure, Michael. *Camping Wyoming.* Atlantic City, WY: WigRaf Publishing, 1999. An amazingly detailed guide to virtually every possible Wyoming camping spot.

McWilliams, Esther. *The Beauty of the Big Horns.* Woodburn, OR: America Publishing Co., 1998. A fine coffee-table photographic book on the Big Horn Mountains.

Mealey, Catherine E. *The Best of Wyoming.* Laramie, WY: Meadowlark Press, 1990. Contains brief county-by-county descriptions of the state's attractions.

Munn, Debra D. *Ghosts on the Range: Eerie True Tales of Wyoming.* Boulder, CO: Pruett Publishing, 1991. A very popular book with ghost stories from across the state.

Parent, Laurence. *Scenic Driving Wyoming.* Missoula, MT: Falcon Publishing, 1997. The best and most complete guide to scenic roads in Wyoming.

Roberts, Steven L., David L. Roberts, and Phil Roberts. *Wyoming Almanac.* Laramie, WY: Skyline West Press, 1997. Packed with almost 500 pages of Wyoming trivia, including such things as the average market price for Wyoming low-sulfur coal and the number of cabooses now used for other purposes. Hard to plow through it all, but there are some real gems buried in this avalanche of facts.

Skinner, Holly L. *Only the River Runs Easy: A Historical Portrait of the Upper Green River Valley.* Boulder, CO: Pruett Publishing Co., 1985. An attractive and lovingly written history of the Upper Green River. Out of print.

Urbanek, Mae. *Wyoming Place Names.* Missoula, MT: Mountain Press Publishing Co., 1988. An excellent sourcebook for the names of everything from Abiathar Peak to the town of Zenith.

Williamson, Chilton, Jr. *Roughnecking It.* New York, NY: Simon and Schuster, 1982. A funny, insightful, and disturbing portrait of Wyoming during the oil-boom years of the the early 1980s. Gonzo journalism at its best. Out of print.

Work Projects Administration. *Wyoming: A Guide to its History, Highways, and People.* Lincoln, NE: University of Nebraska Press, 1981. Reprint of a depression-era guide to Wyoming originally printed in 1940, this classic guide still makes fascinating reading. Out of print.

ONWARD TRAVEL

The following is a shameless promotion for other Moon Travel Handbooks covering the region. All of these are authoritative guides for their respective states or regions. Find them on the web at www.moon.com.

McRae, W.C., and Judy Jewell. *Montana Handbook.* Emeryville, CA: Avalon Travel Publishing, 1999.

Metzger, Stephen. *Colorado Handbook.* Emeryville, CA: Avalon Travel Publishing, 1999.

Pitcher, Don. *Yellowstone-Grand Teton Handbook.* Emeryville, CA: Avalon Travel Publishing, 2000.

Root, Don. *Idaho Handbook.* Emeryville, CA: Avalon Travel Publishing, 1997.

Weir, Bill, and W.C. McRae. *Utah Handbook.* Emeryville, CA: Avalon Travel Publishing, 1997.

GEOLOGY AND GEOGRAPHY

Blackstone, D.L., Jr. *Traveler's Guide to the Geology of Wyoming.* Laramie, WY: Geological Survey of Wyoming, 1988. An excellent overview of Wyoming's geological history and how to see it in today's landscapes.

Largeson, David R., and Darwin R. Spearing. *Roadside Geology of Wyoming.* Missoula, MT: Mountain Press Publishing Co., 1988. Wyoming is perhaps the most geologically interesting of all the states. This is an invaluable road guide for anyone wanting to know more about geology without resorting to dense textbooks.

McPhee, John. *Rising from the Plains.* New York, NY: The Noonday Press, 1986. A delightful intertwining of the story of Wyoming's complex geology and the life of its preeminent geologist, David Love.

McPhee, John. *Basin and Range.* New York: Farrar, Straus & Giroux, 1980. The book details how the landscape of Wyoming was created. Only this Pulitzer Prize-winning author could turn the complex story of plate tectonics into such an easy-to-read volume.

Robinson, Charles. *Geology of Devils Tower.* Devils Tower, WY: Devils Tower Natural History Association, 1995. The definitive geologic story of this famous national monument.

FICTION

Ehrlich, Gretel. *Heart Mountain.* New York, NY: Viking Penguin Inc., 1988. A touching novel about life in the Heart Mountain Relocation Camp near Cody, the forced home for hundreds of Japanese-Americans during WW II.

Nye, Bill. *Bill Nye's Western Humor.* Lincoln, NE: University of Nebraska Press, 1968. A collection of delightfully wry essays by one of America's best-known 19th-century humorists. Out of print.

Wister, Owen. *The Virginian.* Originally published in 1902 and now available from various publishers. The classic Western novel that established the cowboy hero and the lure of Wyoming.

Proulx, Annie. *Close Range: Wyoming Stories.* Scribner: New York, NY, 1999. Pulitzer prize-winning novelist Annie Proulx now lives in Wyoming, and this book takes on the characters in her home state. Wyomingites may take umbrage at her unflattering portrayals, but take these stories for what they are, fiction. A good read.

BIOGRAPHY

Alter, Cecil. J. *Jim Bridger.* Norman, OK: University of Oklahoma Press, 1979. The incredible story of the most famous of all mountain men.

Anonymous. *The Sweet Smell of Sagebrush: A Prisoner's Diary 1903-1912.* Rawlins, WY: Friends of the Old Penitentiary, 1990. This wonderful small volume contains the writings of an "anonymous" criminal (John Kirby) who served four terms in the Rawlins penitentiary for horse stealing and other crimes. It not only provides descriptions of his many escapades outside the law but also opens a window on the criminal mind.

Killoren, John J. *Come Blackrobe, DeSmet and the Indian Tragedy.* Norman, OK: University of Oklahoma Press, 1995. The story of Jesuit missionary Pierre Jean DeSmet, who spent his life in a futile attempt to protect the Plains Indians from the Manifest Destiny of American culture.

Olsen, Jack. *Doc: The Rape of the Town of Lovell.* New York, NY: Dell, 1990. The true but hard-to-believe story of a respected physician who raped dozens of women in this small, religious town.

Pointer, Larry. *In Search of Butch Cassidy.* Norman, OK: University of Oklahoma Press, 1989. A thoroughly researched book that seems to show that Butch Cassidy's death in South America was a ruse and that he died much later in Seattle.

Rosa, Joseph G. and Robin May. *Buffalo Bill and His Wild West.* Lawrence, KS: University Press of Kansas, 1989. One of the newer books on Buffalo Bill, with a somewhat revisionist take on his life and times. Rich in detail on Cody's Wild West show.

Russell, Don. *The Lives and Legends of Buffalo Bill.* Norman, OK: University of Oklahoma Press, 1979. The most complete biography on the life of Buffalo Bill Cody.

Woods, L. Milton. *Moreton Frewen's Western Adventures.* Boulder, CO: Roberts Rinehart, Inc., 1986. The strange tale of a wealthy British adventurer who made and lost his (and other folks') fortunes in Wyoming. Out of print.

OUTDOOR RECREATION

Note: See also **Jackson Hole and Grand Teton National Park** and **Yellowstone National Park,** below.

Graham, Kenneth Lee. *Fishing Wyoming.* Helena, MT: Falcon Publishing Co., 1998. A 300-page tome that goes far beyond the standard coverage of Yellowstone and Jackson Hole.

Guillmette, Richard, Renée Carrier, and Steve Gardiner. *Devils Tower National Monument: A Climber's Guide.* Devils Tower, WY: Devils Tower Natural History Association, 1995. A detailed guide to one of the most varied and enjoyable rock faces in Wyoming.

Harper, Skip, and Rob Kelman. *The Climbs of Greater Vedauwoo.* Fort Collins, CO: Heel and Toe Publishers, 1994. A detailed guide to rock climbing in the Vedauwoos east of Laramie.

Herrero, Stephen. *Bear Attacks: Their Causes and Avoidance.* New York, NY: Lyons Press, 1998. An authoritative volume on the lives of bears and staying safe in their country.

Hunger, Bill. *The Hiker's Guide to Wyoming.* Helena, MT: Falcon Publishing, 1992. A fine, detailed book that describes 75 different hikes in all parts of the state.

Mitchell, Finis. *Wind River Trails.* Salt Lake City, UT: University of Utah Press, 1999. A folksy, inexpensive guide by a man who hiked this country for 80 years.

Molvar, Erik. *Hiking Wyoming's Cloud Peak Wilderness.* Helena, MT: Falcon Publishing Co., 1999. A complete and up-to-date guide to the Big Horn's dramatic wilderness country.

Retallic, Ken. *Flyfisher's Guide to Wyoming.* Gallatin Gateway, MT: Wilderness Adventures Press, 1998. An excellent guide; particularly helpful for anglers headed to Yellowstone.

Schneider, Bill. *Bear Aware: Hiking and Camping in Bear Country.* Helena, MT: Falcon Publishing Co., 1998. A handy pocket-size book that is easy to read and up to date.

Woods, Rebecca. *Walking the Winds: A Hiking & Fishing Guide to Wyoming's Wind River Range.* Jackson, WY: White Willow Publishing, 1994. A useful and up-to-date guide to hiking trails in the Winds.

HISTORY

Baber, D.F. *The Longest Rope.* Caldwell, ID: The Caxton Printers, Ltd., 1953. The fascinating story of the Johnson County War as told by William Walker, the only surviving "rustler" witness of the siege at KC Ranch. Out of print.

Bille, Ed. *Early Days at Salt Creek and Teapot Dome.* Casper, WY: Mountain States Lithographing Co., 1978. The story of oil boom times in Wyoming's most famous oil fields. Many fine old photos. Out of print.

Brown, Larry K. *The Hog Ranches of Wyoming: Liquor, Lust, and Lies Under Sagebrush Skies.* Glendo, WY: High Plains Press, 1995. A playful book about the saloon/dance hall/brothels that sprang up around Wyoming's frontier forts.

Bryans, Bill. *Deer Creek: Frontiers Crossroad in Pre-Territorial Wyoming.* Casper, WY: Mountain States Lithographing Co., 1990. A surprisingly engaging history of the Glenrock area, an important way station on the Oregon/Mormon/California Trail.

Burt, Struthers. *Powder River: Let 'er Buck.* New York, NY: Rinehart, 1938. A classic book on this famous part of Wyoming by one of the finest writers to come out of the state. Out of print.

Carlisle, Bill. *Lone Bandit. An Autobiography.* Pasadena, CA: Trails End Publishing Co., 1946. The story of the last of the old Wyoming outlaws, the "gentleman train robber" who later opened a popular Laramie motel. Out of print.

Cheyenne Centennial Committee. *The Magic City on the Plains: Cheyenne 1867-1967.* Cheyenne, WY: Cheyenne Centennial Committee, 1967. A comprehensive history of Cheyenne. Out of print.

Coffman, Lloyd W. *Blazing a Wagon Trail to Oregon.* Springfield, OR: Echo Books, 1993. The experience and drama—much told in the participants' own words—of the "great migration," with details on Fort Bridger, Fort Laramie, Independence Rock, and other Wyoming stopping places.

Combs, Barry B. *Westward to Promontory: Building the Union Pacific Across the Plains and Mountains.* New York, NY: Crown Publishers, 1986. How the West was really won. Includes a wonderful collection of historic photos by Andrew J. Russell. Out of print.

DeVoto, Bernard. *Across the Wide Missouri.* New York, NY: Houghton Mifflin Co., 1990. Reissue of a 1947 book on the Rocky Mountain fur trade and how it shaped American culture. A classic.

Edgar, Bob, and Jack Turnell. *Brand of a Legend.* Greybull, WY: Wolverine Gallery, 1978. The story of the Pitchfork, one of Wyoming's most famous ranches. Includes many of Charles Belden's wonderful old photographs. Out of print.

Gowans, Fred R., and Eugene E. Campbell. *Fort Bridger, Island in the Wilderness.* Provo, UT: Brigham Young University Press, 1975. An excellent book about the first way station specifically built to serve emigrants on the Oregon Trail. Out of print.

Gowans, Fred R. *Rocky Mountain Rendezvous: A History of the Fur Trade Rendezvous 1825-1840.* Layton, UT: Gibbs Smith Publisher, 1989. Describes each of the rendezvous in detail.

Gunderson, Mary Alice. *Devils Tower: Stories in Stone.* Glendo, WY: High Plains Press, 1988. A small book on the history of Devils Tower National Monument.

Haines, Aubrey L., ed. *Journal of a Trapper: Osborne Russell.* Lincoln, NE: University of Nebraska Press, 1965 (reprinted from the 19th-century original volume). The fascinating first-person account of a fur trapper from 1834-43. A classic and surprisingly well-written book.

Haines, Aubrey L. *Historic Sites Along the Oregon Trail.* St. Louis, MO: The Patrice Press,

1994. Details many of the interesting places on this historic route.

Hanesworth, Robert D. *Daddy of 'Em All; The Story of Cheyenne Frontier Days.* Cheyenne, WY: Flintlock Publishing Co., 1967. Stories and photos from the early days of Cheyenne's Frontier Days celebration. Out of print.

Hedgpeth, Don. *Spurs Were A-Jinglin'.* Cody, WY: Northland Press, 1975. Brief text follows the excellent photos by Charles J. Belden of cowboys and ranching in the early parts of the 20th century. Out of print.

Hill, William E. *The California Trail: Yesterday and Today.* Boulder, CO: Pruett Publishing Company, 1986. Filled with historic photos and drawings of the Oregon and California Trail along with more recent photos from the same places. Out of print.

Homsher, Lola M., ed. *South Pass, 1868; James Chisholm's Journal of the Wyoming Gold Rush.* Lincoln, NE: University of Nebraska Press, 1960. Tales of life in the gold-mining town of South Pass shortly after the first wave of boomers had left. Very interesting.

Jost, Loren. *Fremont County Wyoming.* Virginia Beach, VA: The Donning Co. Publishers, 1996. An attractive volume containing hundreds of historical images and a description of Fremont County history.

Junge, Mark. *Wyoming: A Pictorial History.* Virginia Beach, VA: The Donning Co. Publishers, 1989. A gorgeous coffee-table book filled with historic black-and-white photos from throughout Wyoming. Out of print.

Kahin, Sharon, and Laurie Rufe. *In the Shadows of the Rockies: A Photographic History of the Pioneer Experience in Wyoming's Bighorn Basin.* Powell, WY: Northwest Community College, 1983. Outstanding photos and interesting historical quotes on the Bighorn Basin. Out of print.

Larson, T.A. *History of Wyoming.* Lincoln, NE: University of Nebraska Press, 1990. The definitive tome (663 pages worth) on Wyoming's history, with an emphasis on politics and development rather than on outlaws and Indian wars.

Lavender, David. *Fort Laramie and the Changing Frontier.* Washington, D.C.: U.S. Department of the Interior, National Park Service, 1984. An interesting little book filled with the history of the people who made Fort Laramie a primary center of trade and war in the West. Excellent illustrations, too.

Lindmier, Tom, and Steve Mount. *I See by Your Outfit: Historic Cowboy Gear of the Northern Plains.* Glendo, WY: High Plains Press, 1996. An authoritative guide to what *real* cowboys wore. Filled with interesting historical photos.

Madsen, R. Scott. *The Bomber Mountain Crash: A Wyoming Mystery.* Buffalo, WY: Mountain Man Publishing, 1995. A local author untangles the sad tale of the WW II crash of a B-17F Flying Fortress in the Big Horn Mountains. Based upon exhaustive research. Out of print.

Marcy, Randolph B. *The Prairie Traveler.* New York, NY: Perigee Books, 1859, reprinted in 1994. A telling portrait of life on the frontier as told by a U.S. Army captain. It was considered the essential handbook for travelers.

Mead, Jean. *Casper Country.* Boulder, CO: Pruett Publishing Co., 1987. A profusely illustrated history of Casper. Out of print.

Mercer, Asa Shinn. *Banditti of the Plains* or *The Cattlemen's Invasion of Wyoming in 1892: the Crowning Infamy of the Ages.* Norman, OK: University of Oklahoma Press, 1976. A reprint of a classic book about the Johnson County War.

Morgan, Dale, ed. *Overland in 1846: Diaries and Letters of the California-Oregon Trail.* Lincoln, NE: University of Nebraska Press, 1994. A two-volume collection of diaries offering many fascinating insights into the lives of the emigrants.

Mothershead, Harmon Ross. *The Swan Land and Cattle Company, Ltd.* Norman, OK: University of Oklahoma Press, 1971. The story of the most famous of all Wyoming ranches, the million-acre spread begun by Alexander Swan in 1883. Out of print.

Munkres, Robert L. *Saleratus and Sagebrush: The Oregon Trail Through Wyoming.* Cheyenne, WY: Wyoming State Archives and Historical Department, 1974. This interesting small book offers eyewitness accounts from many travelers along the Oregon Trail. Out of print.

Murray, Robert A. *The Bozeman Trail: Highway of History*. Boulder, CO: Pruett Publishing Company, 1988. An attractively illustrated history of the West's most violent trail.

Osgood, Ernest Staples. *The Day of the Cattleman.* Chicago, IL: University of Chicago Press, 1929. An authoritative history of the 50 years when cowboys and cattle barons ruled Wyoming and Montana. Out of print.

Parkman, Francis. *The Oregon Trail.* New York, NY: Viking Penguin, 1886. A classic first-person account of the great westward migration. Reprinted in 1989.

Pinkerton, Joan Tregs. *Knights of the Broadax.* Caldwell, ID: The Caxton Printers, Inc., 1981. An account of the life of tie hacks in the upper Wind River country.

Rhode, Robert B. *Booms & Busts on Bitter Creek: A History of Rock Springs, Wyoming.* Boulder, CO: Pruett Publishing Co., 1999. A fine history of one of Wyoming's most turbulent cities.

Sandoval, Judith Hancock. *Historic Ranches of Wyoming.* Casper, WY: Mountain States Lithographing, 1986. Details nearly a hundred of the state's classic old ranches. Out of print.

Spring, Agnes Wright. *The Cheyenne and Black Hills Stage and Express Routes.* Lincoln, NE: University of Nebraska Press, 1948. Tales from the early days of eastern Wyoming. Out of print.

Thompson, George A. *Throw Down the Box!* Salt Lake City, UT: Dream Garden Press, 1989. A book about the Gilmer and Salisbury stagecoaches, including the famous Cheyenne and Black Hills branch line. Out of print.

Thybony, Scott, Robert G. Rosenberg, and Elizabeth Mullett Rosenberg. *The Medicine Bows: Wyoming's Mountain Country.* Caldwell, ID: The Caxton Printers, Inc., 1985. An outstanding historical account of the Indians, explorers, miners, and tie hacks who called this scenic part of Wyoming home. Out of print.

Twain, Mark. *Roughing It.* New York, NY: New American Library,1994. First published in 1872, this is one of the classics of American literature. Samuel Clemens' witty descriptions of the Old West seem ageless.

NATIVE AMERICANS

Clark, Ella E., and Margot Edmonds. *Sacagawea of the Lewis and Clark Expedition.* Berkeley, CA: University of California Press, 1984. A fascinating investigation into the true stories behind one of the best-known women in American history. Bursts a few bubbles.

Frison, George C. *Prehistoric Hunters of the High Plains.* New York, NY: Academic Press, 1991. The authoritative source on the earliest inhabitants of Wyoming.

Hendry, Mary Helen. *Indian Rock Art in Wyoming.* Lincoln, NE: Augstams Printing, 1983. Detailed descriptions of rock-art sites in the state. The author's listed ages for the rock art are probably too recent, and she intentionally omits locations.

Lowie, Robert. *Indians of the Plains.* Lincoln, NE: University of Nebraska Press, 1982. Famed anthropologist Robert Lowie presents a detailed picture of life on the plains before the arrival of whites.

Nadeau, Remi. *Fort Laramie and the Sioux Indians.* New York, NY: Crest Publishers: 1997. A thorough historical account of the impact of Fort Laramie on the high-plains Indians.

Trenholm, Virginia Cole, and Maurine Carley. *The Shoshonis: Sentinels of the Rockies.* Norman, OK: University of Oklahoma Press, 1964. The history of Chief Washakie and the Shoshone tribe.

Trenholm, Virginia Cole. *The Arapahoes, Our People.* Norman, OK: University of Oklahoma Press, 1986. The story of this important Wyoming tribe from prehistory to the tribe's forced relocation to the Wind River Reservation.

Urbanek, Mae. *Chief Washakie.* Boulder, CO: Johnson Publishing Co., 1971. The fascinating story of the chief who led the Shoshone people for 60 years while always remaining a friend of whites. Out of print.

Utley, Robert M. *The Indian Frontier of the American West 1846-1890.* Albuquerque, NM: University of New Mexico Press, 1984. An even-handed portrayal of a half century of conflict between Indians and whites.

NATURAL HISTORY

Note: See also **Jackson Hole and Grand Teton National Park** and **Yellowstone National Park,** below.

Baxter, George T., and Michael D. Stone. *Amphibians and Reptiles of Wyoming.* Cheyenne, WY: Wyoming Game and Fish Department, 1985. Everything you wanted to know about the state's snakes, frogs, toads, salamanders, and other cold-blooded critters.

Blair, Neal. *The History of Wildlife Management in Wyoming.* Cheyenne, WY: Wyoming Game and Fish Department, 1987. A large, detailed book covering the time from when the bison blackened the plains to the present.

Clark, Tim W., and Mark R. Stromberg. *Mammals in Wyoming.* Lawrence, KS: University of Kansas Museum of Natural History, 1987. The definitive guide to 117 native or naturalized Wyoming mammals: their identification, distribution, biology, and ecology.

Crowe, Douglas M. *Furbearers of Wyoming.* Cheyenne, WY: Wyoming Department of Game and Fish, 1986. A small book describing the state's fur-coated critters, with distribution maps.

Dorn, Robert D. *Manual of the Vascular Plants of Wyoming.* Cheyenne, WY: Mountain West Publishing Company, 1988. The authoritative key to Wyoming plants; a dense book with few illustrations. For botanists. Out of print.

Knight, Dennis H. *Mountains and Plains: the Ecology of Wyoming Landscapes.* New Haven, CT: Yale University Press, 1994. The definitive textbook on the ecology of Wyoming. Thorough and well written, but the $50 price may scare you away.

Petersen, David. *Among the Elk.* Flagstaff, AZ: Northland Publishing, 1988. The story of wapiti, with outstanding photos by Alan D. Carey. Out of print.

JACKSON HOLE AND GRAND TETON NATIONAL PARK

Note: A number of natural history and geology books encompass both Yellowstone and Grand Teton National Parks. See Yellowstone National Park below for additional titles with overlapping coverage.

History

Betts, Robert B. *Along the Ramparts of the Tetons: the Saga of Jackson Hole, Wyoming.* Boulder, CO: Colorado Associated University Press, 1978. A substantial, detailed, and beautifully written book about the history of Jackson Hole.

Burt, Nathaniel. *Jackson Hole Journal.* Norman, OK: University of Oklahoma Press, 1983. Tales of growing up as a dude in Jackson Hole. Contains some very amusing stories.

Hayden, Elizabeth Wied, and Cynthia Nielsen. *Origins, A Guide to the Place Names of Grand Teton National Park and the Surrounding Area.* Moose, WY: Grand Teton Natural History Association, 1988. A guide to the obscure sources for place names in Grand Teton.

Huidekoper, Virginia. *The Early Days in Jackson Hole.* Boulder, CO: Colorado Associated University Press, 1978. Filled with over 100 photos from old-time Jackson Hole. Out of print.

Righter, Robert W. *Crucible for Conservation: The Creation of Grand Teton National Park.* Boulder, CO: Colorado Associated University Press, 1982. The story of how the Tetons were spared through a half-century battle.

Ringholz, Raye C. *Little Town Blues: Voices from the Changing West.* Salt Lake City, UT: Gibbs-Smith Publisher, 1992. A cautionary note on the consequences of unbridled growth, this important small book visits several small towns in the West—including Jackson—where the rural qualities and beauty that attract visitors are being inundated by tourism and development.

Thompson, Edith M., and William Leigh Thompson. *Beaver Dick: The Honor and the Heartbreak.* Laramie, WY: Jelm Mountain Press,

1982. A touching historical biography of Beaver Dick Leigh, one of the first white men to settle in Jackson Hole. Out of print.

Natural History

Carrighar, Sally. *One Day at Teton Marsh.* Lincoln, NE: University of Nebraska Press, 1979. A classic natural history of life in a Jackson Hole marsh. Made into a movie by Walt Disney. Out of print.

Clark, Tim W. *Ecology of Jackson Hole, Wyoming: A Primer.* Salt Lake City, UT: Paragon Press, 1981. An excellent scientific introduction to ecological interrelationships within Jackson Hole. Out of print.

Murie, Margaret, and Olaus Murie. *Wapiti Wilderness.* Boulder, CO: Colorado Associated University Press, 1986. The lives of two of America's most-loved conservationists in Jackson Hole and their work with elk.

Raynes, Bert. *Birds of Grand Teton National Park and the Surrounding Area.* Moose, WY: Grand Teton Natural History Association, 1984. A guide to local birds. Out of print.

Shaw, Richard J. *Plants of Grand Teton and Yellowstone National Parks.* Salt Lake City, UT: Wheelwright Press, 1981. Photos and descriptions of the most commonly found plants in the parks.

Hiking, Climbing, and Skiing

Carter, Tom. *Day Hiking Grand Teton National Park.* Garland, TX: Dayhiking Press, 1993. A pocket-size guide to 15 day-treks in the park.

Dufy, Katy and Darwin Wile. *Teton Trails.* Moose, WY: Grand Teton Natural History Association, 1995. A useful guide to more than 200 miles of trails in the park.

Ortenburger, Leigh N., and Reynold G. Jackson. *A Complete Guide to the Teton Range.* Seattle, WA: Mountaineers Books, 1996. The definitive (415 pages!) climbing guide for the Tetons.

Rossiter, Richard. *Teton Classics: 50 Selected Climbs in Grand Teton National Park.* Evergreen, CO: Chockstone Press, 1997. A small and nicely illustrated guide to 50 climbing routes in the Tetons.

Watters, Ron. *Winter Tales and Trails: Skiing, Snowshoeing and Snowboarding in Idaho, the Grand Tetons and Yellowstone National Park.* Pocatello, ID: Great Rift Press, 1997. A book that combines lucid writing on the area's rich history with guides to winter trails. More than 350 pages of details from an expert in the field.

Woods, Rebecca. *Jackson Hole Hikes.* Jackson, WY: White Willow Publishing, 1999. An excellent guide that includes trails in Grand Teton National Park and surrounding national forest areas. Easy to use and informative.

Geology

Good, John M. and Kenneth L. Pierce. *Interpreting the Landscape: Recent and Ongoing Geology of Grand Teton and Yellowstone National Parks.* Moose, WY: Grand Teton Natural History Association, 1996. This attractive book has the latest geologic research on the parks and presents it in an understandable format with excellent illustrations.

Love, J.D., and John C. Reed Jr. *Creation of the Teton Landscape: the Geologic Story of Grand Teton National Park.* Moose, WY: Grand Teton Natural History Association, 1995. A small but authoritatively detailed guide to the geology of Jackson Hole and the Tetons.

YELLOWSTONE NATIONAL PARK

Note: A number of natural history and geology books encompass both Yellowstone and Grand Teton National Parks. See Grand Teton National Park above for additional titles with overlapping coverage.

Fishing

Charlton, Robert E. *Yellowstone Fishing Guide.* Ketchum, ID: Lost River Press, 1990. A detailed guide to fishing in the park. Leaves no trickle unfished.

Parks, Richard. *Fishing Yellowstone.* Helena, MT: Falcon Publishing, 1998. One of several authoritative guides, this one provides details on fly- and lure fishing, along with descriptions of more than 100 sites.

Varley, John D. and Paul D. Schullery. *Yellowstone Fishes: Ecology, History, and Angling in the Park.* Mechanicsburg, PA: Stackpole Books, 1998. The comprehensive guide to the fish of Yellowstone, written by two authorities in the field.

Geology

Bryan, Scott. T. *The Geysers of Yellowstone.* Boulder, CO: University Press of Colorado, 1995. The definitive guide to more than 400 geysers and other geothermal features in Yellowstone.

Fritz, William J. *Roadside Geology of the Yellowstone Country.* Missoula, MT: Mountain Press Publishing Co., 1986. All the park roads are covered in this easy-to-follow Yellowstone geology primer.

Schreier, Carl. *Yellowstone's Geysers, Hot Springs and Fumaroles.* Moose, WY: Homestead Publishing, 1987. An attractive small book filled with color photos and brief descriptions.

Hiking

Bach, Orville E., Jr. *Hiking the Yellowstone Backcountry.* San Francisco, CA: Sierra Club Books, 1998. A pocket-size guide to hiking, canoeing, biking, and skiing in the park.

Carter, Tom. *Day Hiking Yellowstone.* Garland, TX: Dayhiking Press, 1991. A pocket-size guide to 20 day-treks, coordinated with the Trails Illustrated topographic maps.

Marschall, Mark C. *Yellowstone Trails: A Hiking Guide.* Yellowstone National Park, WY: The Yellowstone Association, 1999. An excellent, up-to-date, and detailed guidebook to the park's 1,000 miles of hiking trails.

Schneider, Bill. *Hiking Yellowstone National Park.* Helena, MT: Falcon Publishing, 1997. Clear maps and helpful trail profiles make this the most useful book for anyone heading out on Yellowstone hiking routes. Contains descriptions of more than 100 trails.

History

Bartlett, Richard A. *Yellowstone: A Wilderness Besieged.* Tucson, AZ: University of Arizona Press, 1989. The history of Yellowstone and the fight to prevent its destruction by railroad magnates, concessioners, and others.

Haines, Aubrey L. *The Yellowstone Story: A History of Our First National Park.* Boulder, CO: University Press of Colorado, 1996. A definitive two-volume history of the park. Volume one (history up to the park's establishment) is the most interesting.

Haines, Aubrey L. *Yellowstone Place Names: Mirrors of History.* Boulder, CO: University Press of Colorado, 1996. For the Trivial Pursuit enthusiast; 318 pages of detailed descriptions with every possible name from every obscure corner of Yellowstone.

Janetski, Joel C. *Indians of Yellowstone Park.* Salt Lake City, UT: University of Utah Press, 1987. A general overview of the earliest settlers in Yellowstone and later conflicts with incoming whites.

Milstein, Michael. *Yellowstone Album: 125 Years of America's Best Idea.* Billings, MT: The Billings Gazette, 1996. A delightful book filled with historical photographs, along with photos of postcards, souvenirs, and other tourist artifacts.

Schreier, Carl, ed. *Yellowstone: Selected Photographs 1870-1960.* Moose, WY: Homestead Publishing, 1989. An outstanding collection of historical photographs from the park.

Natural History

Craighead, Frank J. *Track of the Grizzly.* San Francisco, CA: Sierra Club Books, 1982. The life of grizzlies in Yellowstone, by one of the most famous bear researchers.

Krakell, Dean, II. *Downriver: A Yellowstone Journey.* San Francisco, CA: Sierra Club Books, 1987. A extraordinarily moving journey down the magnificent Yellowstone River.

McEneaney, Terry. *Birds of Yellowstone.* Boulder, CO: Roberts Rinehart, 1988. A guide to Yellowstone birds and where to find them.

Schullery, Paul, ed. *Yellowstone Bear Tales.* Boulder, CO: Roberts Rinehart Publishers, 1991. First-person stories of bear encounters from a range of travelers—including Pres. Theodore Roosevelt—between 1880 and 1950.

Scott, Douglas M., and Suvi A. Scott. *Wildlife of Yellowstone and Grand Teton National Parks.* Salt Lake City, UT: Wheelwright Press, 1990. A brief descriptive guide to Yellowstone and Grand Teton critters.

Shaw, Richard J. *Wildflowers of Yellowstone and Grand Teton National Parks.* Salt Lake City, UT: Wheelwright Press, 1992. Color photos and short descriptions of more than 100 wildflowers in the Greater Yellowstone Ecosystem.

Wuerthner, George. *Yellowstone: A Visitor's Companion.* Mechanicsburg, PA: Stackpole Books, 1992. A detailed guide to the natural history of Yellowstone.

Other Yellowstone Books

Henry, Jeff. *Yellowstone Winter Guide.* Boulder, CO: Roberts Rinehart Publishers, 1998. A detailed guide to visiting Yellowstone in the winter; especially good for cross-country skiers.

Olsen, Ken, Dena Olsen, and Steve and Hazel Scharosch. *Cross-Country Skiing Yellowstone Country.* Helena, MT: Falcon Publishing, 1994. Detailed descriptions of 200 miles of ski trails in and near the park, including helpful trail profiles.

Reese, Rick and Terry Tempest Williams. *Greater Yellowstone: The National Park and Adjacent Wildlands.* Helena, MT: American Geographic Publishing, 1991. An attractive book with considerable information on ecological conditions in one of the Lower 48's largest intact ecosystems.

Schmidt, Jeremy, and Steven Fuller. *Yellowstone Grand Teton Road Guide: The Essential Guide for Motorists.* Jackson, WY: Free Wheeling Travel Guides, 1998. A nicely done pocket-size guide to the roads of the two parks, with accurate, up-to-date information.

Schullery, Paul. *Searching for Yellowstone.* New York, NY: Houghton Mifflin Co., 1997. An eloquently written book by a longtime park ranger whose knowledge of the park goes far beyond the hype. Must-reading for anyone who cares about Yellowstone.

INDEX

ART MUSEUMS/EXHIBITS

B

BACKCOUNTRY SPORTS/ RECREATION

C

CAMPGROUNDS/RV PARKS

CLIMBING

CROSS-COUNTRY SKIING

DINOSAURS/FOSSILS

DOWNHILL SKIING/ SNOWBOARDING

E

FAIRS/CARNIVALS

FISH/FISHING

FRONTIER MUSEUMS/EXHIBITS

G

GEYSERS

GRAND TETON NATIONAL PARK

GUEST RANCHES

H

HIKING/BACKPACKING

HISTORIC SITES/STRUCTURES

HORSEBACK RIDING/TRAIL RIDES

K

KID STUFF

L

M

MOUNTAIN MEN/RENDEZVOUS

MOVIE LOCALES/TRIVIA

MUSIC VENUES

N

NATIVE AMERICANS

OUTLAWS/RUSTLERS

QR

RODEOS

SCENIC DRIVES

SNOWMOBILING

STATE PARKS/ RECREATION AREAS/HISTORIC SITES

T

UNUSUAL CLAIMS TO FAME

WALKING TOURS/NATURE TRAILS

WATERFALLS

WILDERNESS AREAS/WILDLIFE REFUGES

XYZ

YELLOWSTONE NATIONAL PARK

ABOUT THE AUTHOR

Born in Atlanta, Georgia, Don Pitcher grew up all over the East Coast—from Florida to Maine. He moved west to attend college and immediately fell in love with its wide open spaces. After receiving a master's degree in fire ecology from the University of California at Berkeley, he worked seasonally for a variety of state and federal agencies. Over the years Don did all sorts of outdoor work: calling spotted owls in northern California, mapping grizzly habitat in Wyoming's Teton Wilderness, and doing a wide range of work in Alaska: building backcountry trails, running salmon weirs, conducting forest fire research, and working with brown bears.

Although trained as an ecologist, Don Pitcher's love of travel led him into the field of writing and photography. In addition to this book, he is author of **Wyoming Handbook,** *Washington Handbook, Alaska-Yukon Handbook,* and *Berkeley Inside/Out.* He has photographed books on Wyoming and Alaska for Compass American Guides, and his photographs have also appeared in numerous books, calendars, magazines, and advertisements. Don bases his travels out of Homer, Alaska, where he lives with his wife, Karen Shemet, and daughter, Aziza Bali. You can contact him at www.donpitcher.com.

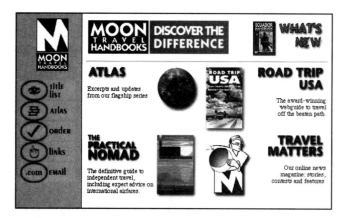

LOSE YOURSELF IN THE EXPERIENCE, NOT THE CROWD

For more than 25 years, Moon Travel Handbooks have been the guidebooks of choice for adventurous travelers. Our award-winning Handbook series provides focused, comprehensive coverage of distinct destinations all over the world. Each Handbook is like an entire bookcase of cultural insight and introductory information in one portable volume. Our goal at Moon is to give travelers all the background and practical information they'll need for an extraordinary travel experience.

The following pages include a complete list of Handbooks, covering North America and Hawaii, Mexico, Latin America and the Caribbean, and Asia and the Pacific.To purchase Moon Travel Handbooks, check your local bookstore or check our Web site at **www.moon.com** for current prices and editions.

"An in-depth dunk into the land, the people and their history, arts, and politics."

—Student Travels

"I consider these books to be superior to Lonely Planet. When Moon produces a book it is more humorous, incisive, and off-beat."

—Toronto Sun

"Outdoor enthusiasts gravitate to the well-written Moon Travel Handbooks. In addition to politically correct historic and cultural features, the series focuses on flora, fauna and outdoor recreation. Maps and meticulous directions also are a trademark of Moon guides."

—Houston Chronicle

"Moon [Travel Handbooks] . . . bring a healthy respect to the places they investigate. Best of all, they provide a host of odd nuggets that give a place texture and prod the wary traveler from the beaten path. The finest are written with such care and insight they deserve listing as literature."

—American Geographical Society

"Moon Travel Handbooks offer in-depth historical essays and useful maps, enhanced by a sense of humor and a neat, compact format."

—Swing

"Perfect for the more adventurous, these are long on history, sightseeing and nitty-gritty information and very price-specific."

—Columbus Dispatch

"Moon guides manage to be comprehensive and countercultural at the same time . . . Handbooks are packed with maps, photographs, drawings, and sidebars that constitute a college-level introduction to each country's history, culture, people, and crafts."

—National Geographic Traveler

"Few travel guides do a better job helping travelers create their own itineraries than the Moon Travel Handbook series. The authors have a knack for homing in on the essentials."

—Colorado Springs *Gazette Telegraph*

MEXICO

"These books will delight the armchair traveler, aid the undecided person in selecting a destination, and guide the seasoned road warrior looking for lesser-known hideaways."

—*Mexican Meanderings* Newsletter

"From tourist traps to off-the-beaten track hideaways, these guides offer consistent, accurate details without pretension."

—Foreign Service Journal

Archaeological Mexico Andrew Coe	**$19.95** 420 pages, 27 maps
Baja Handbook Joe Cummings	**$16.95** 540 pages, 46 maps
Cabo Handbook Joe Cummings	**$14.95** 270 pages, 17 maps
Cancún Handbook Chicki Mallan	**$14.95** 240 pages, 25 maps
Colonial Mexico Chicki Mallan	**$18.95** 400 pages, 38 maps
Mexico Handbook Joe Cummings and Chicki Mallan	**$21.95** 1,200 pages, 201 maps
Northern Mexico Handbook Joe Cummings	**$17.95** 610 pages, 69 maps
Pacific Mexico Handbook Bruce Whipperman	**$17.95** 580 pages, 68 maps
Puerto Vallarta Handbook Bruce Whipperman	**$14.95** 330 pages, 36 maps
Yucatán Handbook Chicki Mallan	**$16.95** 400 pages, 52 maps

"Beyond question, the most comprehensive Mexican resources available for those who prefer deep travel to shallow tourism. But don't worry, the fiesta-fun stuff's all here too."

—New York Daily News

LATIN AMERICA AND THE CARIBBEAN

"Solidly packed with practical information and full of significant cultural asides that will enlighten you on the whys and wherefores of things you might easily see but not easily grasp."

—Boston Globe

Belize Handbook	**$15.95**
Chicki Mallan and Patti Lange	390 pages, 45 maps
Caribbean Vacations	**$18.95**
Karl Luntta	910 pages, 64 maps
Costa Rica Handbook	**$19.95**
Christopher P. Baker	780 pages, 73 maps
Cuba Handbook	**$19.95**
Christopher P. Baker	740 pages, 70 maps
Dominican Republic Handbook	**$15.95**
Gaylord Dold	420 pages, 24 maps
Ecuador Handbook	**$16.95**
Julian Smith	450 pages, 43 maps
Honduras Handbook	**$15.95**
Chris Humphrey	330 pages, 40 maps
Jamaica Handbook	**$15.95**
Karl Luntta	330 pages, 17 maps
Virgin Islands Handbook	**$13.95**
Karl Luntta	220 pages, 19 maps

NORTH AMERICA AND HAWAII

"These domestic guides convey the same sense of exoticism that their foreign counterparts do, making home-country travel seem like far-flung adventure."

—Sierra Magazine

Alaska-Yukon Handbook	**$17.95**
Deke Castleman and Don Pitcher	530 pages, 92 maps
Alberta and the Northwest Territories Handbook	**$18.95**
Andrew Hempstead	520 pages, 79 maps
Arizona Handbook	**$18.95**
Bill Weir	600 pages, 36 maps
Atlantic Canada Handbook	**$18.95**
Mark Morris	490 pages, 60 maps
Big Island of Hawaii Handbook	**$15.95**
J.D. Bisignani	390 pages, 25 maps
Boston Handbook	**$13.95**
Jeff Perk	200 pages, 20 maps
British Columbia Handbook	**$16.95**
Jane King and Andrew Hempstead	430 pages, 69 maps

Canadian Rockies Handbook Andrew Hempstead	**$14.95** 220 pages, 22 maps
Colorado Handbook Stephen Metzger	**$17.95** 480 pages, 46 maps
Georgia Handbook Kap Stann	**$17.95** 380 pages, 44 maps
Grand Canyon Handbook Bill Weir	**$14.95** 220 pages, 10 maps
Hawaii Handbook J.D. Bisignani	**$19.95** 1,030 pages, 88 maps
Honolulu-Waikiki Handbook J.D. Bisignani	**$14.95** 360 pages, 20 maps
Idaho Handbook Don Root	**$18.95** 610 pages, 42 maps
Kauai Handbook J.D. Bisignani	**$15.95** 320 pages, 23 maps
Los Angeles Handbook Kim Weir	**$16.95** 370 pages, 15 maps
Maine Handbook Kathleen M. Brandes	**$18.95** 660 pages, 27 maps
Massachusetts Handbook Jeff Perk	**$18.95** 600 pages, 23 maps
Maui Handbook J.D. Bisignani	**$15.95** 450 pages, 37 maps
Michigan Handbook Tina Lassen	**$15.95** 360 pages, 32 maps
Montana Handbook Judy Jewell and W.C. McRae	**$17.95** 490 pages, 52 maps
Nevada Handbook Deke Castleman	**$18.95** 530 pages, 40 maps
New Hampshire Handbook Steve Lantos	**$18.95** 500 pages, 18 maps
New Mexico Handbook Stephen Metzger	**$15.95** 360 pages, 47 maps
New York Handbook Christiane Bird	**$19.95** 780 pages, 95 maps
New York City Handbook Christiane Bird	**$13.95** 300 pages, 20 maps
North Carolina Handbook Rob Hirtz and Jenny Daughtry Hirtz	**$14.95** 320 pages, 27 maps
Northern California Handbook Kim Weir	**$19.95** 800 pages, 50 maps
Ohio Handbook David K. Wright	**$15.95** 340 pages, 18 maps
Oregon Handbook Stuart Warren and Ted Long Ishikawa	**$17.95** 590 pages, 34 maps

Pennsylvania Handbook	**$18.95**
Joanne Miller	448 pages, 40 maps
Road Trip USA	**$24.00**
Jamie Jensen	940 pages, 175 maps
Road Trip USA Getaways: Chicago	**$9.95**
	60 pages, 1 map
Road Trip USA Getaways: Seattle	**$9.95**
	60 pages, 1 map
Santa Fe-Taos Handbook	**$13.95**
Stephen Metzger	160 pages, 13 maps
South Carolina Handbook	**$16.95**
Mike Sigalas	400 pages, 20 maps
Southern California Handbook	**$19.95**
Kim Weir	720 pages, 26 maps
Tennessee Handbook	**$17.95**
Jeff Bradley	530 pages, 42 maps
Texas Handbook	**$18.95**
Joe Cummings	690 pages, 70 maps
Utah Handbook	**$17.95**
Bill Weir and W.C. McRae	490 pages, 40 maps
Virginia Handbook	**$15.95**
Julian Smith	410 pages, 37 maps
Washington Handbook	**$19.95**
Don Pitcher	840 pages, 111 maps
Wisconsin Handbook	**$18.95**
Thomas Huhti	590 pages, 69 maps
Wyoming Handbook	**$17.95**
Don Pitcher	610 pages, 80 maps

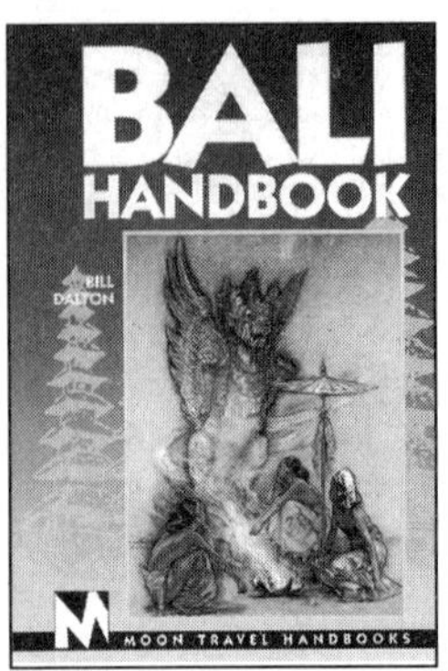

ASIA AND THE PACIFIC

"Scores of maps, detailed practical info down to business hours of small-town libraries. You can't beat the Asian titles for sheer heft. (The) series is sort of an American Lonely Planet, with better writing but fewer titles. (The) individual voice of researchers comes through."

—Travel & Leisure

Australia Handbook	**$21.95**
Marael Johnson, Andrew Hempstead, and Nadina Purdon	940 pages, 141 maps
Bali Handbook	**$19.95**
Bill Dalton	750 pages, 54 maps
Fiji Islands Handbook	**$14.95**
David Stanley	350 pages, 42 maps
Hong Kong Handbook	**$16.95**
Kerry Moran	378 pages, 49 maps

Indonesia Handbook **$25.00**
Bill Dalton 1,380 pages, 249 maps

Micronesia Handbook **$16.95**
Neil M. Levy 340 pages, 70 maps

Nepal Handbook **$18.95**
Kerry Moran 490 pages, 51 maps

New Zealand Handbook **$19.95**
Jane King 620 pages, 81 maps

Outback Australia Handbook **$18.95**
Marael Johnson 450 pages, 57 maps

Philippines Handbook **$17.95**
Peter Harper and Laurie Fullerton 670 pages, 116 maps

Singapore Handbook **$15.95**
Carl Parkes 350 pages, 29 maps

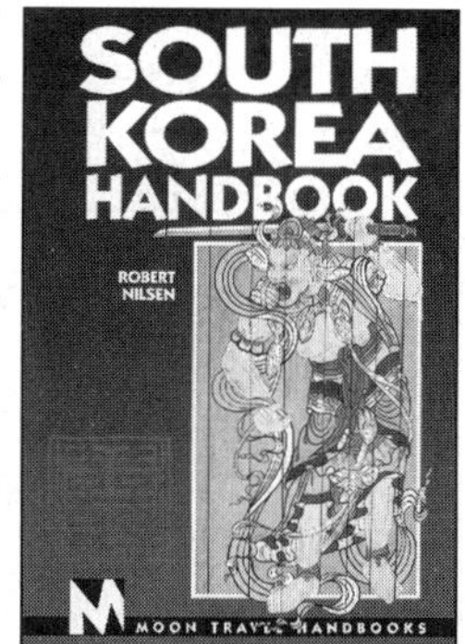

South Korea Handbook **$19.95**
Robert Nilsen 820 pages, 141 maps

South Pacific Handbook **$24.00**
David Stanley 920 pages, 147 maps

Southeast Asia Handbook **$21.95**
Carl Parkes 1,080 pages, 204 maps

Tahiti Handbook **$15.95**
David Stanley 450 pages, 51 maps

Thailand Handbook **$19.95**
Carl Parkes 860 pages, 142 maps

Vietnam, Cambodia & Laos Handbook **$18.95**
Michael Buckley 760 pages, 116 maps

OTHER GREAT TITLES FROM MOON

"For hardy wanderers, few guides come more highly recommended than the Handbooks. They include good maps, steer clear of fluff and flackery, and offer plenty of money-saving tips. They also give you the kind of information that visitors to strange lands—on any budget—need to survive."

—US News & World Report

Moon Handbook **$10.00**
Carl Koppeschaar 150 pages, 8 maps

The Practical Nomad: How to Travel Around the World **$17.95**
Edward Hasbrouck 580 pages

Staying Healthy in Asia, Africa, and Latin America **$11.95**
Dirk Schroeder 230 pages, 4 maps

THE PRACTICAL NOMAD

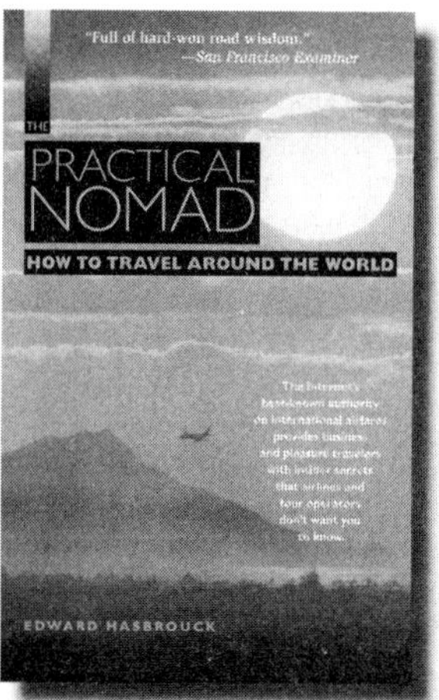

$17.95 580 pages

✈ TAKE THE PLUNGE

"The greatest barriers to long-term travel by Americans are the disempowered feelings that leave them afraid to ask for the time off. Just do it."

✈ TAKE NOTHING FOR GRANTED

"Even 'What time is it?' is a highly politicized question in some areas, and the answer may depend on your informant's ethnicity and political allegiance as well as the proximity of the secret police."

✈ TAKE THIS BOOK

With experience helping thousands of his globetrotting clients plan their trips around the world, travel industry insider Edward Hasbrouck provides the secrets that can save readers money and valuable travel time.
An indispensable complement to destination-specific travel guides, *The Practical Nomad* includes:

airfare strategies
ticket discounts
long-term travel considerations
travel documents
border crossings
entry requirements
government offices
travel publications
Internet information resources

"One of the best travel advice books ever published. . . .
A fantastic resource."
—Big World

U.S.~METRIC CONVERSION

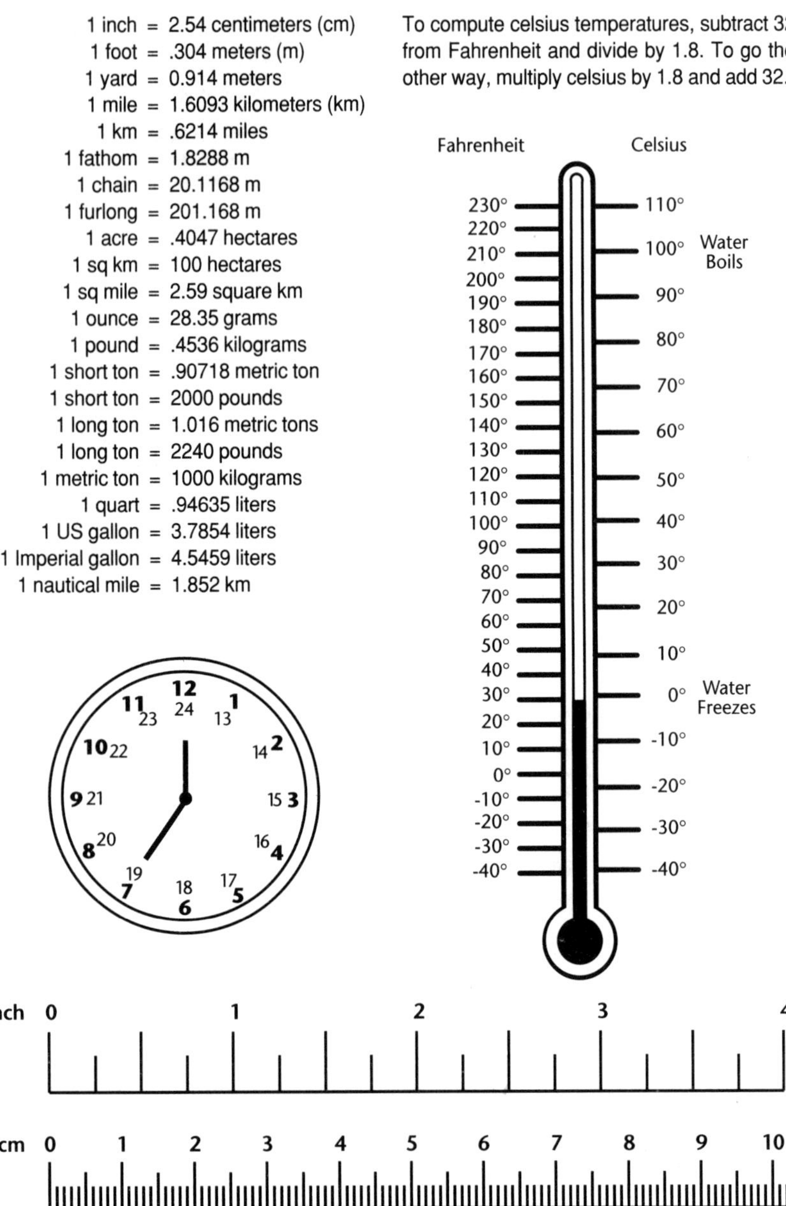

1 inch	=	2.54 centimeters (cm)
1 foot	=	.304 meters (m)
1 yard	=	0.914 meters
1 mile	=	1.6093 kilometers (km)
1 km	=	.6214 miles
1 fathom	=	1.8288 m
1 chain	=	20.1168 m
1 furlong	=	201.168 m
1 acre	=	.4047 hectares
1 sq km	=	100 hectares
1 sq mile	=	2.59 square km
1 ounce	=	28.35 grams
1 pound	=	.4536 kilograms
1 short ton	=	.90718 metric ton
1 short ton	=	2000 pounds
1 long ton	=	1.016 metric tons
1 long ton	=	2240 pounds
1 metric ton	=	1000 kilograms
1 quart	=	.94635 liters
1 US gallon	=	3.7854 liters
1 Imperial gallon	=	4.5459 liters
1 nautical mile	=	1.852 km

To compute celsius temperatures, subtract 32 from Fahrenheit and divide by 1.8. To go the other way, multiply celsius by 1.8 and add 32.

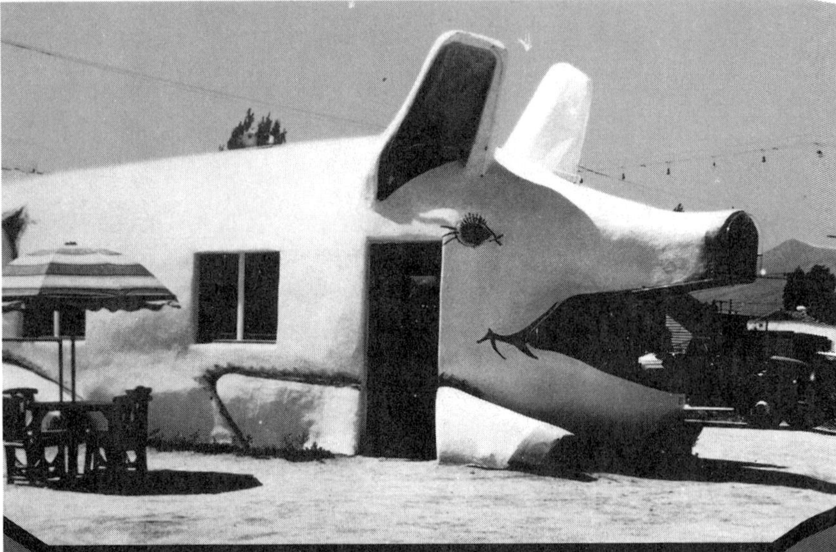

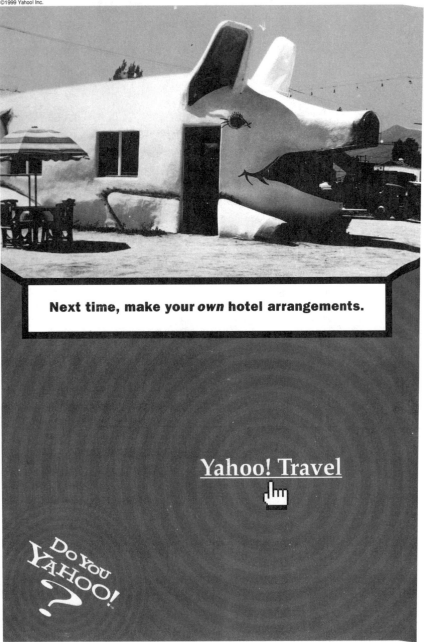